CENTRES OF PLANT DIVERSITY

A Guide and Strategy for their Conservation

WWF

The World Wide Fund For Nature (WWF) – founded in 1961 – is the largest international, private nature conservation organization in the world. Based in Switzerland, WWF has national affiliates and associate organizations on five continents. WWF works to conserve the natural environment and ecological processes essential to life on Earth.

WWF aims to create awareness of threats to the natural environment, to generate and attract on a worldwide basis the strongest moral and financial support for safeguarding the living world and to convert such support into action based on scientific priorities. Since 1961, WWF has channelled over US$130 million into more than 5000 projects in some 130 countries which have saved animals and plants from extinction and helped to conserve natural areas all over the world. It has served as a catalyst for conservation action, and has brought its influence to bear on critical conservation needs by working with and influencing governments, non-governmental organizations, scientists, industry and the general public.

IUCN – THE WORLD CONSERVATION UNION

IUCN – The World Conservation Union – founded in 1948, is a membership organization comprising governments, non-governmental organizations, research institutions and conservation agencies in 120 countries. The Union promotes the protection and utilization of living resources.

Several thousand scientists and experts from all continents form part of a network supporting the work of its six Commissions: threatened species, protected areas, ecology, sustainable development, environmental law and environmental education and training. Its thematic programmes include tropical forests, wetlands, marine ecosystems, plants, the Sahel, Antarctica, population and natural resources, and women in conservation. These activities enable IUCN to develop sound policies and programmes for the conservation of biological diversity and sustainable development of natural resources.

Availability of further information from WCMC

Background data and more general information on the sites documented in this volume have been donated by WWF and IUCN to the World Conservation Monitoring Centre (WCMC), 219 Huntingdon Road, Cambridge CB3 0DL, U.K., where they form part of WCMC's Biodiversity Information Service and where they are available for consultation. Both map and text information are also available from WCMC in electronic format. Readers may be interested to note that the maps (or modified versions of the maps) of Centres of Plant Diversity in this volume can be overlain with other geographic information, such as protected area boundaries and vegetation cover, through the Geographical Information System (Biodiversity Map Library) at WCMC.

CENTRES OF PLANT DIVERSITY

A Guide and Strategy for their Conservation

Project Director: V.H. HEYWOOD
Project Coordinator: S.D. DAVIS

VOLUME 2
ASIA, AUSTRALASIA and THE PACIFIC

edited by

S.D. DAVIS, V.H. HEYWOOD AND A.C. HAMILTON

published by
The World Wide Fund For Nature (WWF)
and IUCN – The World Conservation Union

with financial support from the
European Commission (EC) and the
U.K. Overseas Development Administration (ODA)

1995

Citation: WWF and IUCN (1994–1995). Centres of plant diversity. A guide and strategy for their conservation. 3 volumes. IUCN Publications Unit, Cambridge, U.K.

British Library Cataloguing-in-Publication Data
A catalogue record for this book is available from the British Library.
ISBN 2-8317-0198-8

Designed and produced by the Nature Conservation Bureau Limited, Newbury, Berkshire, U.K.

Printed by Information Press, Oxford, U.K.

TABLE OF CONTENTS: VOLUME 2

CONTENTS OF VOLUMES 1 AND 3

PREFACE

The balance between people and their environment is being upset. Escalating human numbers and increasing demands for material resources are leading to the transformation and degradation of ecosystems worldwide, with consequent loss of genetic diversity and an inevitable rise in the extinction of species. More and more land is being converted to intensive production of food, timber and other plant products, much of the world's pasture land is overgrazed, and soil erosion and salinization are reducing the fertility of farmlands, especially in semi-arid regions. Wild species are being displaced or overcropped, and wild ecosystems can no longer be taken for granted as reservoirs of genetic diversity and regulators of the cycles of the elements.

Plants are a central component of this threatened nature. The loss of plants is very significant, for they stand at the base of food webs and provide habitats for other organisms. Although people in some modern societies may be mentally distanced from the reality of nature and are unaware of the services it provides, even city inhabitants are part of wider ecosystems, based on wild plants and natural vegetation. For example, genes from the wild can play major roles in the breeding of new varieties of food crops and other cultivated plants. New medicines continue to be derived from wild species. In many countries, natural and semi-natural ecosystems provide many plant products essential for human welfare, including fuelwood, timber, fibre, medicinal plants, fruits and nuts. Forests protect catchments and thus help regulate the flow of water for drinking, hydropower and irrigation. And wild nature – not the least wild plants – contribute to the natural beauty of the world that we rightly cherish.

In Rio de Janeiro in June 1992 over a hundred Heads of States and Governments signed a new International Convention on the Conservation of Biological Diversity – that is, of the world's rich variety of genes, species and ecosystems. They did so not out of altruism, but because they recognized that these resources were economically valuable and important to the future of humanity. Under the Convention – which entered into legal force at the end of 1993 – each country accepts a responsibility to safeguard its own natural diversity and to cooperate internationally, especially to help poorer countries enjoy the benefits of their living resources.

All ecosystems contribute to the biological wealth of the planet, but some have a much higher diversity than others. Tropical forest contains a much richer flora than tundra, and some areas of tropical forest have many more plant species than others. Even agricultural land varies in the diversity it supports, from the richness of traditional agriculture with its many local varieties of crops, to the ecological deserts of industrial farming with high-yielding monocultures. To be effective, conservation of biodiversity must depend in part on surveys to identify how species and ecosystems are distributed and to identify key sites where diversity is greatest.

The three volumes comprising *Centres of Plant Diversity* are the product of information received from hundreds of botanists from many countries. They have worked together to identify some of the most important sites for plants worldwide. These are priority areas for conservation. These volumes are offered to national conservation authorities and to global conservation organizations as an aid in their work, especially in implementing the obligations of States under the Convention.

A publication like this can only be a beginning. Strategies to conserve plant diversity are needed at all geographical levels – global, national and local – and should form an integral part of all land development plans. And strategies have to be turned into action. Many of the sites described in these volumes are subject to threats and pressures and solutions will depend on finding a balance between different interests, site by site. The solutions are likely to be almost as diverse as the sites, since the environmental features of the latter and the nature of the threats to them vary so widely.

People are at the heart of conservation as well as the source of many threats. Virtually all terrestrial ecosystems, even those that appear to be more pristine, have long included people as components. For example, there are very few, if any, areas of tropical forest which do not provide local people with products for their use, and which have not been altered as a result of interaction with the users over the centuries. And, although local people have been components of natural ecosystems, sometimes for tens of thousands of years, their present day interactions with their environment are not necessarily harmonious.

The conservation aim is to conserve the diversity of nature: clearly this must be achieved within the context of cultural diversity. Conservationists must work with local communities, understanding how they use and manage nature, examining whether current practices are sustainable (both for particular species and in terms of wider impacts) and, if necessary, searching for alternative approaches. Moreover, cultures, whether of local people or professionals, including botanists, land managers and legislators, are not static. The search for appropriate practices, which will conserve plant diversity, perhaps while using it and other environmental resources sustainably, will be a continuing process.

It is our hope that these volumes will stimulate such activities throughout the world, not only at the key localities identified here. Without urgent, informed, practical action, the marvellous plant wealth of our planet will not be conserved, and future generations will be the poorer.

Claude Martin, Director General, WWF International (World Wide Fund For Nature).

Martin Holdgate, former Director General, IUCN – The World Conservation Union.

ACKNOWLEDGEMENTS

The *Centres of Plant Diversity (CPD)* project, a major international collaborative exercise, has involved over 400 botanists, conservationists and resource managers worldwide, together with over 100 collaborating institutions and organizations. Without this enormous amount of help and support, the project would not have been possible. We wish to thank all those who contributed to the text.

A full list of contributors and collaborating organizations is given below, and authors and contributors to individual Data Sheets are given at the end of each sheet. Here, we would like in particular to acknowledge the major contributions to the project provided by Dr Dennis Adams, Dr John R. Akeroyd, Professor Peter S. Ashton, Dr Henk J. Beentje, Dr Robert W. Boden, Professor Loutfy Boulos, Dr David R. Given, Dr Alan C. Hamilton, Professor K. Iwatsuki, Professor R.J. Johns, Dr Ruth Kiew, Professor Valentin A. Krassilov, Dr Domingo Madulid, Dr Robert R. Mill, Dr Tony Miller, Professor P. van Royen, Dr B.D. Sharma, Dr Sy Sohmer, Dr Peter F. Stevens, Dr Wendy Strahm, Professor Wang Xianpu and Professor Yang Zhouhuai, who undertook the preparation of regional texts and/or contributed a number of site Data Sheets, and (with others) helped in the selection of sites for inclusion in the project.

The CPD project has been co-ordinated by the IUCN Plant Conservation Office at Kew, U.K. Throughout this period, the project benefited enormously from the valuable help, advice and information provided by colleagues and staff of the Herbarium of the Royal Botanic Gardens, Kew, as well as from use of Kew's extensive library facilities. We thank all those members of Kew's staff who contributed to individual Data Sheets, in particular Professor Robert J. Johns, who provided extensive help with writing the section on New Guinea, and to Dr John Dransfield for checking sheets for Malaysia and Indonesia. Special thanks are also extended to Milan Svanderlik and colleagues in Media Resources for their help in producing a set of posters on the project which were used throughout the world at CPD Workshops. Particular thanks are extended to the Director, Professor Ghillean Prance, and to the Keeper of the Herbarium, Professor Gren Ll. Lucas, for their support. Indeed, the initial concept of identifying centres of plant diversity and endemism owes much to Gren Lucas and Hugh Synge (then of the IUCN Threatened Plants Unit). Acknowledgement must also be made of the role played by the IUCN/WWF Plant Advisory Group, initially under the chairmanship of Dr Peter Raven, and subsequently Professor Arturo Gómez-Pompa, in planning and developing the CPD project.

Much of the co-ordinating work for the Americas was undertaken by colleagues at the Department of Botany at the National Museum of Natural History, Smithsonian Institution, Washington, D.C., U.S.A. In particular, we would like to thank Olga Herrera-MacBryde for her dedication in compiling and writing many of the accounts for South and Central America, and for her part in editing the volume on the Americas (Volume 3 in the series). Additional editors for the Americas volume were Dr Bruce MacBryde, Jane Villa-Lobos, Jane MacKnight and Dr Wayt Thomas.

Sadly, during the latter stages of the project, Dr Alwyn Gentry, who had substantially prepared the Regional Overview for South America, died in a plane crash whilst carrying out a forest survey in Ecuador. The text on South America owes much to the extensive knowledge on the botany of the region which he had accumulated. We acknowledge the help of Dr Carlos B. Villamil and Dr Otto Huber in completing the South American overview, and of Jane Villa-Lobos for help with Central America. Shirley L. Maina and Dr Robert A. DeFilipps are thanked for their contributions for North America.

We are indebted to colleagues at the Royal Botanic Garden, Edinburgh, who undertook (with Professor Loutfy Boulos) much of the co-ordinating work for South West Asia and the Middle East. We particularly thank the Deputy Regius Keeper, Dr David G. Mann, and make special mention of the valuable contributions to the project provided by Dr Tony Miller and Dr Robert Mill.

Grateful thanks are also extended to the members of the IUCN Australasian Plant Specialist Group (co-ordinated by Dr Robert W. Boden): John Benson, Stephen Harris, Frank Ingwersen, Dr John Leigh, Dr Ian Lunt, Dr Bob Parsons and Neville Scarlett. Drs Garry Werren, Geoff Tracey, Stephen Goosem and Peter Stanton also provided much valuable advice and contributions for the Australian section. Similarly, we would like to thank the Secretary for the Environment (Government of India), the Botanical Survey of India and the IUCN Plant Specialist Groups for China and Lower Plants.

For Africa, we would particularly like to thank members of AETFAT (the Association pour l'Etude Taxonomique de la Flore d'Afrique Tropicale) for much helpful advice and valuable contributions.

At the World Conservation Monitoring Centre (WCMC), Cambridge, U.K., the following are thanked for their help: Dr Kerry Walter (Threatened Plants Unit) for providing country plant biodiversity tables; Dr Mark Collins, Dr Richard Luxmoore, Mary Edwards and Clare Billington (Habitats Data Unit) for advice on mapwork and for producing regional maps which formed the basis for those used in all three volumes; and to Jerry Harrison, James Paine, Michael Green and Harriet Gillett (Protected Areas Data Unit) for checking protected areas information. Andrew McCarthy provided much valuable assistance with information on Indonesian protected areas. Dr Tim Johnson is thanked for co-ordinating WCMC's input to the project.

CPD benefited from close collaboration with BirdLife International (formerly known as the International Council for Bird Preservation). We would like to make special mention of contributions of bird data provided by Alison Stattersfield, Mike Crosby, Adrian Long and David Wege. The data on birds will be published more fully by BirdLife International in the *Global directory of Endemic Bird Areas* (Stattersfield *et al.*, in prep.), in which the distributions of all restricted-range bird species will be analysed.

Thanks are expressed to colleagues at Botanic Gardens Conservation International (BGCI), with whom the CPD project shared office space and equipment, and benefited from computer and secretarial support. In particular, we would like to thank Diane Wyse Jackson for technical computer support and Nicky Powell, Erika Keiss and Christine Allen for secretarial help and typing manuscripts. Ros Coles, at WWF, is also thanked for her secretarial support. Kevin McPaul (Computer Unit, Royal Botanic Gardens, Kew) provided valuable assistance in converting several incoming computer diskettes into a readable form. For translations, we thank Sally Horan, Doreen Abeledo, Jennifer Moog and Barbara Windisch, and for map drawing Cecilia Andrade-Herrera, Raúl Puente-Martínez, Alice Tangerini, Carlos Bazán, Jeff Edwards and Martin Walters.

Finally, we give particular thanks to the organizations who provided financial support for the CPD project and without which none of this work would have been possible, namely the Commission of the European Communities (EC), the U.K. Overseas Development Administration (ODA), the World Wide Fund For Nature (WWF), IUCN – The World Conservation Union and, in the U.S.A., Conservation International, the Smithsonian Institution and the Wildcat Foundation. We are most grateful for their support and encouragement throughout the project.

Stephen D. Davis.   Vernon H. Heywood.

The successful completion of this major project has in no small measure been due to the outstanding efforts and commitment of Stephen Davis who has worked unflaggingly and consistently over the whole period of its preparation.

V.H.H.

The opportunity has been taken with production of this volume to make corrections and additions to the introductory material which precedes the regional and data sheet accounts.

This work has proved much more difficult to produce than originally envisaged. Credit for formulating the project is due to Professor Vernon Heywood, formerly of IUCN, and Hugh Synge, formerly of WWF. WWF wishes to acknowledge the efforts of the many contributors and especially the dedication of Stephen Davis and Olga Herrera-MacBryde. The assistance of Botanic Gardens Conservation International (BGCI) (Peter Wyse Jackson) and of the Department of Botany, National Museum of Natural History, Smithsonian Institution for accommodating some of those working on the project is gratefully acknowledged. Here at WWF, Ros Coles has put in monumental efforts, incorporating editorial changes to many of the manuscripts. Also at WWF, I would like to show my appreciation to Clive Wicks, Peter Newborne, Peter Ramshaw and Michael Pimbert for their encouragement and support. The present volume has benefited from careful editing by John Akeroyd.

Special thanks are due to the patience, creativity and understanding of the staff of the Nature Conservation Bureau for their task of laying-out and overseeing the printing of the books. Special contributions have been made by Peter Creed, Charlotte Matthews and Joe Little.

Alan Hamilton
Plants Conservation Officer
WWF International.

LIST OF CONTRIBUTORS

Regional co-ordinators

Volume One:
Europe, Africa, South West Asia and the Middle East

Europe:
    Dr John R. Akeroyd and
    Professor Vernon H. Heywood
Atlantic Ocean Islands:
    Dr Alan C. Hamilton
Africa:
    Dr Henk J. Beentje and
    Stephen D. Davis
Indian Ocean Islands:
    Wendy Strahm
South West Asia and the Middle East:
    Professor Loutfy Boulos,
    Dr Tony Miller and
    Dr Robert R. Mill

Volume Two:
Asia, Australasia and the Pacific

Central and Northern Asia:
    Professor Valentin A. Krassilov
Indian Subcontinent:
    Dr B.D. Sharma,
    Mr A.K. Narayanan and
    Dr Robert R. Mill
China and East Asia:
    Professors Wang Xianpu and Yang Zhouhuai (China),
    Professor Kunio Iwatsuki (Japan) and
    Dr Vu Van Dung (Vietnam)
South East Asia (Malesia):
    Stephen D. Davis
Australia and New Zealand:
    Dr Robert W. Boden and
    Dr David R. Given
Pacific Ocean Islands:
    Professor P. van Royen, Dr Sy Sohmer and
    Stephen D. Davis

Volume Three:
The Americas

North America:
    Dr Robert DeFilipps and
    Shirley L. Maina
Middle America:
    Olga Herrera-MacBryde
South America:
    Olga Herrera-MacBryde
Caribbean Islands:
    Dr Dennis Adams

Major collaborating organizations and institutions

Africa

Association pour l'Etude Taxonomique de la Flore d'Afrique
    Tropicale (AETFAT)

Argentina

Universidad Nacional de Córdoba, Centro de Ecología y
    Recursos Naturales Renovables
Universidad Nacional del Sur, Departamento de Biología,
    Bahia Blanca

Australia

A.C.T. Parks and Conservation Service
Australian National Parks and Wildlife Service, New South
    Wales
Conservation Commission of the Northern Territory
Queensland Herbarium

Belgium

Nationale Plantentuin van België, Meise

Bolivia

Centro de Investigaciones de la Capacidad de Uso Mayor
    de la Tierra (CUMAT), La Paz
Universidad Mayor de San Andrés, La Paz, Centro de Datos
    para la Conservación, Herbario Nacional de Bolivia,
    Instituto de Ecología

Brazil

Centro Nacional de Pesquisas de Recursos Genéticos e
    Biotecnologia (CENARGEN), Brasilia
Centro de Pesquisas de Cacau (CEPEC), Bahia
Fundação Estadual de Engenharia do Meio Ambiente
    (FEEMA), Centro de Botânica do Rio de Janeiro
Instituto Brasileiro de Geografia Estatística (IBGE), Brasilia
Instituto Nacional de Pesquisas da Amazônica (INPA), Manaus
Jardim Botânico do Rio de Janeiro
Museu Paraense Emilio Goeldi, Departamento de Ecologia,
    Belem
Secretaria de Estado do Meio Ambiente, Instituto de Botânica,
    São Paulo
Universidade Estadual de Campinas, Departamento de Botânica
Universidade Estadual Paulista, Departamento de Botânica,
    Rio Claro
Universidade Federal Rural do Rio de Janeiro, Seropédica
Universidade de São Paulo, Instituto de Biociências,
    Departamento de Botânica

Chile

Comité Nacional Pro Defensa de la Fauna y Flora (CODEFF), Santiago
Corporación Nacional Forestal (CONAF), Santiago
Fundación Claudio Gay, Santiago
Pontificia Universidad Católica de Chile, Departamento de Biología Ambiental y de Poblaciones, Santiago
Universidad de Chile, Departamento de Biología, Santiago

China

Commission for Integrated Survey of Natural Resources

Colombia

Corporación Colombiana para la Amazonia (COA), Santafé de Bogotá
Fundación Pro-Sierra Nevada de Santa Marta, Santafé de Bogotá
Fundación Tropenbos-Colombia, Santafé de Bogotá
Instituto Nacional de los Recursos Naturales y del Ambiente (INDERENA), Santafé de Bogotá
Universidad Nacional de Colombia, Instituto de Ciencias Naturales, Santafé de Bogotá

Costa Rica

Fundación Neotrópica, San José
Instituto Nacional de Biodiversidad de Costa Rica (INBio), Heredia
Las Cruces Botanical Garden, Coto Brus
Organization for Tropical Studies, Moravia
Universidad Nacional, Escuela de Ciencias Ambientales, Heredia

Cuba

Jardin Botánico Nacional, La Habana

Denmark

University of Aarhus, Botanical Institute
University of Copenhagen, Botanical Museum and Herbarium

Ecuador

Fundación Ecuatoriana de Estudios Ecológicos (ECOCIENCIA), Quito
Ministerio de Agricultura y Ganadería, Dirección de Desarrollo Forestal, Quito
Museo Nacional de Ciencias Naturales, Herbario Nacional, Quito
Pontificia Universidad Católica del Ecuador, Instituto de Ciencias Naturales, Quito
Río Palenque Science Center, Santo Domingo de los Colorados, Quito
Universidad de Guayaquil, Facultad de Ciencias Naturales, Quito

France

Centre ORSTOM, Nouméa, New Caledonia

Laboratoire de Phanérogamie, Muséum National d'Histoire Naturelle, Paris

French Guiana

Centre ORSTOM, Cayenne

Germany

Universität Hamburg, Institut für Allgemeine Botanik
University of Kassel

Guatemala

Fundación Defensores de la Naturaleza, Guatemala City
Universidad de San Carlos, Centro de Estudios Conservacionistas (CECON), Guatemala City
Universidad del Valle de Guatemala, Departamento de Biología

Honduras

Mosquitia Pawisa (MOPAWI), Tegucigalpa
Universidad Nacional Autónoma de Honduras, Departamento de Biología, Tegucigalpa

Hungary

Eszterhazy Teachers' College

India

Botanical Survey of India
Government of India, Department of Forests

Indonesia

Southeast Asian Regional Centre for Tropical Biology (BIOTROP)
WWF Representation in Indonesia

Italy

International Plant Genetic Resources Institute (IPGRI), formerly International Board for Plant Genetic Resources (IBPGR)

Japan

Botanical Gardens, University of Tokyo

Kuwait

University of Kuwait

Malaysia

Malaysian Nature Society
Sabah Parks
WWF Malaysia

Mexico

Centro Interdisciplinario de Investigación para el Desarrollo Integral Regional, Instituto Politécnico Nacional (CIIDIR-IPN), Durango

Centro de Investigaciones Biológicas de Baja California Sur, La Paz
Instituto de Ecología, Centro Regional del Bajío Pátzcuaro
Instituto de Ecologia, Xalapa, Veracruz
Subsecretaría de Ecología (SEDUE), Dirección de Flora y Fauna Silvestres, Mexico City
Universidad Autónoma Agraria Antonio Narro, Saltillo
Universidad de Guadalajara, Instituto Manantlán de Ecología y Conservación de la Biodiversidad
Universidad Nacional Autónoma de México (UNAM), Mexico City, Centro de Ecología, Instituto de Biología, Departamento de Botánica

Netherlands

Rijksherbarium, Leiden
University of Amsterdam, Hugo de Vries Laboratorium
Wageningen Agricultural University

New Zealand

Invermay Agricultural Centre, Crop and Food Research, Mosgiel

Oman

Office for Conservation of the Environment

Panama

Asociación Nacional para la Conservación de la Naturaleza (ANCON), Panama City
Universidad de Panamá, Departamento de Botánica

Paraguay

Centro de Estudios y Colecciones Biológicas para la Conservación, Asunción
Museo Nacional de Historia Natural del Paraguay, Asunción

Peru

Fundación Peruana para la Conservación de la Naturaleza, Lima
Universidad Mayor de San Marcos, Museo de Historia Natural, Lima
Universidad Nacional Agraria, Centro de Datos para la Conservación, Lima
Universidad Nacional de la Amazonia Peruana, Iquitos

Portugal

Universidade dos Açores, Depart. Ciencias Agrárias

Russia

Institute of Nature Conservation and Reserves
Research Institute of Nature Protection

Saudi Arabia

National Herbarium, Riyadh

South Africa

National Botanical Institute, Kirstenbosch
Rhodes University, Department of Botany
University of Cape Town
University of Pretoria

Spain

Instituto Pirenaico de Ecología, Jaca
Jardín Botánico, Universidad de Valencia
Jardín Botánico "Viera y Clavijo", Las Palmas de Gran Canaria
Real Jardín Botánico, Consejo Superior de Investigaciones Científicas, Madrid
Universidad de Granada

Sri Lanka

University of Peradeniya, Department of Botany

Sweden

University of Uppsala, Department of Systematic Botany

Switzerland

Conservatoire et Jardin botaniques de la Ville de Genève, Geneva

Taiwan

National Taiwan University, Department of Forestry

Turkey

Istanbul Üniversitesi Eczacilik Fakültesi
Society for the Protection of Nature (DHKD)

U.K.

BirdLife International
Botanic Gardens Conservation International
Royal Botanic Garden, Edinburgh
Royal Botanic Gardens, Kew
The Natural History Museum
World Conservation Monitoring Centre
WWF U.K.

U.S.A.

Arizona State University, Department of Botany, Tempe
California Native Plant Society, Sacramento
Conservation International, Washington, D.C.
Drylands Institute, Tuscon
Field Museum of Natural History, Chicago
Harvard University Herbaria, Cambridge
Louisiana State University, Department of Botany, Baton Rouge
Missouri Botanical Garden, St Louis
New York Botanical Garden, Bronx, New York
Smithsonian Institution, Museum of Natural History, Department of Botany, Washington, D.C.

The Nature Conservancy – Latin America Program, Arlington
University of California at Riverside, Department of Botany and Plant Sciences
University of Colorado, Department of Geography, Boulder
University of Florida, Department of Wildlife and Range Sciences, Gainesville
University of Hawaii at Manoa, Honolulu
University of Maryland of Baltimore County, Baltimore
University of Oregon, Department of Biology, Eugene
University of South Florida, Department of Biology, Tampa
U.S. Agency for International Development, Washington, D.C.
U.S. Fish and Wildlife Service, Washington, D.C.
U.S. National Park Service, Washington, D.C.
USDA Agricultural Research Service, Beltsville
WWF U.S., Washington, D.C.

Vietnam

Forest Inventory and Planning Institute, Ministry of Forestry

Zaïre

Association des Botanistes du Zaïre (ASBOZA)

Individual contributors

The following kindly contributed information to the CPD project:

B. Adams, C.D. Adams, D. Aeschimann, M. Aguilar, J. Aguirre, M. Ahmedullah, L. Aké Assi, J.R. Akeroyd, R. Alfaro, K. Alpinar, J. Aranda, D.S.D. Araújo, A. Arévalo, G. Argent, H. Arnal, P.S. Ashton, A. de Avila, M.M.J. van Balgooy, J. Balmer, P. Bamps, J. Beaman, J.S. Beard, S. Beck, H.J. Beentje, D. Benson, J. Benson, B.F. Benz, R. Berazaín, J.B. Besong, M. Bingham, J. Black-Maldonado, R.W. Boden, Bo-Myeong Woo, J. Bosser, L. Boulos, D. Bramwell, F.J. Breteler, D. Brummitt, D. Brunner, T.M. Butynski, R. Bye, A. Byfield, A. Cano, J. Cardiel, L.G. Carrasquilla, A.M.V. de Carvalho, H. Centeno, P. Chai, D. Chamberlain, J.D. Chapman, J. Charles, Shankat Chaudhary, A.S. Chauhan, A. Chaverri, J. Chávez-Salas, M. Cheek, Chin See Chung, M. Cifuentes, A. Cleef, S. Collenette, A. Contreras, M. Costa, I. Cordeiro, M. Correa, I. Cowie, R. Cowling, The Earl of Cranbrook, P.J. Cribb, M. Crosby, H. Cuadros, D. Cuartas, R. Cuevas-Guzmán, A. Cunningham, J. Cunningham, R. Daly, P. Dávila, S.D. Davis, G.W.H. Davison, R.A. DeFilipps, C. Dendaletche, L.V. Denisova, E. Dias, N. Diego, M.O. Dillon, M.A. Dix, C. Dodson, C. Doumenge, F. Dowsett-Lemaire, J. Dransfield, S.J.M. Droop, G.R.F. Drucker, O.A. Druzhinina, J.F. Duivenvoorden, B. Eastwood, D.S. Edwards, I. Edwards, S. Elliott, J.L. Ellis, J. Estrada, T. Ju. Fedorovskaya, R. Felger, R. Ferreyra, T.S. Filgueiras, P. Fisher, R.M. Fonseca, A. Forbes, E. Forero, F.R. Fosberg, R. Foster, J.E.D. Fox, H. Freitag, F. Friedmann, I. Friis, J. Fuertes, F.M. Galera, S.M. Gan III, C. García-Kirkbride, S. Gartlan, A. Garzón, L. Gautier, A.H. Gentry, A.M. Giulietti, D.R. Given, D. Glick, C. Godoy, L.D. Gómez, A. Gómez-Pompa, J.A. González, S. González-Elizondo, R.B. Good, S. Goosem, R. Gopalan, J.-J. de Granville, G. Green, M.J.B. Green, P.S. Green, P. Gregerson, L. Guarino, R. Guedes-Bruni, N. Gunatilleke, R. Guzmán,

P.K. Hajra, T. Hallingbäck, S. Halloy, O. Hamann, A.C. Hamilton, B. Hammel, D. Harder, R.M. Harley, S. Harris, He Shan-an, I. Hedberg, O. Hedberg, I. Hedge, A.N. Henry, F.N. Hepper, P. Herlihy, A. Hernández, J. Hernández-Camacho, B. Herrera, O. Herrera-MacBryde, H. Hewson, V.H. Heywood, C. Hilton-Taylor, R. Hnatiuk, A. Hoffmann, Horng Jye-Su, V.B. Hosagoudar, R.A. Howard, Huang Shiman, O. Huber, B.J. Huntley, K. Hurlbert, Indraneil Das, F. Ingwersen, S. Iremonger, S. Iversen, K. Iwatsuki, N. Jacobsen, T. Jaffré, D. Janzen, J. Jaramillo, E.J. Jardel-Peláez, C. Jeffrey, J. Jérémie, C. Jermy, V. Jiménez, R.J. Johns, M.C. Johnston, M. Jorgensen, W.S. Judd, N. Jürgens, C. Kabuye, M.T. Kalin Arroyo, M. Kappelle, S. Keel, R. Kiew, T. Killeen, D.J.B. Killick, Kim Yong Shik, J. Kirkbride Jr., K. Kitayama, C. Kofron, J. Kokwaro, V.A. Krassilov, A.N. Kuliev, A. Lamb, M. Lamotte, A. Lara, R. Lara, P.K. Latz, Y. Laumonier, A. Lehnhoff, J. Leigh, H.F. Leitão Filho, A. Leiva, J. Lejoly, D. Lellinger, B. León, J.L. León de la Luz, J. Léonard, H.C. de Lima, Li Zhiji, E. Lleras, M. Lock, G.A. Lomakina, A. Long, F. Lorea, E. Lott, J. Lovett, P.P. Lowry II, P. Lowy, L. Lozada, C.A. Lubini, I. Lunt, J. Luteyn, K. MacKinnon, L. Madrigal, D.A. Madulid, G. Maggs, S.L. Maina, B. Makinson, F. Malaisse, T. Maldonado, M.C.H. Mamede, M.A. Mandango, S. Manktelow, M. Marconi, G. Martin, J.F. Maxwell, N.F. McCarten, A.J. McCarthy, W.J.F. McDonald, I. McLeish, J.A. McNeely, R.A. Medellín, W. Meijer, P. Mena, T. Messick, R.R. Mill, A.G. Miller, L.P. de Molas, J. Molero-Mesa, E. Moll, L. Monroy, J. Moore, M. Moraes, Ph. Morat, L.P.C. Morellato, J. Morello, S. Mori, H. Moss, M. Mössmer, C. Muñoz, G.P. Nabhan, J. Nais, J.C. Navarro, D. Neill, B.W. Nelson, C. Nelson, Ngui Siew Kong, S.V. Nikitina, H.P. Nooteboom, P. Núñez, H. Ohashi, J.C. Okafor, B. Ollgaard, C. Ormazábal, C.I. Orozco, B. Orr, A. Ortega, R. Ortiz, R. Ortiz-Quijano, G. Palacios, W. Palacios, Pan Borong, B. Parsons, A.L. Peixoto, R. Petocz, Phan Ke Loc, A. Phillipps, P.B. Phillipson, D.J. Pinkava, M.J. Pires-O'Brien, B. Pitts, M. Plotkin, T. Pócs, R. Polhill, D. Poore, G.T. Prance, J.R. Press, J. Proctor, Qiu Xuezhong, N. Quansah, T.P. Ramamoorthy, L. Ramella, O. Rangel-Ch., T. Ravisankar, A. Rebelo, C. Reynel, M. Ríos, D. Roguet, I. Rojas, M. Roos, P. Rosales, L. Rossi, R. Rowe, P. van Royen, J. Russell-Smith, J. Rzedowski, C. Sáenz, N. Salazar, J.G. Saldarriaga, K.A. Salim, Samhan Nyawa, H. Sánchez, M. Sánchez S., M.J.S. Sands, T. Santisuk, N. Scarlett, C. Schnell, B.D. Sharma, C. Sharpe, D. Sheil, T. Shimizu, P. Silverstone-Sopkin, D.K. Singh, M.W. Skinner, D. Smith, S.H. Sohmer, J. Solomon, V.J. Sosa, J.P. Stanton, A. Stattersfield, P.F. Stevens, B. Stewart-Cox, J. Steyermark, W. Strahm, T.F. Stuessy, Su Zhixian, W.R Sykes, H. Synge, M. Syphan Ouk, Tae Wook Kim, A. Telesca, D. Thomas, W. Thomas, K. Thomsen, M. Thulin, J. Timberlake, V. Toledo, L. Torres, R. Torres, A. Touw, J.G. Tracey, C. Ulloa, L.E. Urrego, E. Vajravelu, J. Valdés-Reyna, O. Valdéz-Rodas, F.M. Valverde, T. Veblen, J.-M. Veillon, J. Vermuelen, H. Verscheure, J. Vidal, J. Villa-Lobos, L.M. Villarreal de Puga, J.A. Villarreal-Quintanilla, C.B. Villamil, L. Villar, J.-F. Villiers, W. Vink, K. Vollesen, L.I. Vorontsova, Vu Van Dung, D.H. Wagner, W.L. Wagner, K. Walter, Wang Xianpu, D. Wege, T. Wendt, M.J.A. Werger, G.L. Werren, J. Whinam, W.A. Whistler, A. Whitten, J.J.F.E. de Wilde, B. Wilson, P. Windisch, B. Woodley, R.P. Wunderlin, J. Wurdack, A.E. van Wyk, G. Yeoman, Yang Zhouhuai, K.R. Young, D. Yuck Beld, T.A. Zanoni, E. Zardini and Zhou Yilian.

INTRODUCTION

Vernon H. Heywood and Stephen D. Davis

The primary tactic in conservation must be to locate the world's hot spots and to protect the entire environment they contain.
Edward O. Wilson, *The Diversity of Life* (1992).

The importance of plant diversity

The diversity of plant life is an essential underpinning of most of our terrestrial ecosystems. Humans and most other animals are almost totally dependent on plants, directly or indirectly, as a source of energy through their ability to convert the sun's energy through photosynthesis. Worldwide tens of thousands of species of higher plants, and several hundred lower plants, are currently used by humans for a wide diversity of purposes – as food, fuel, fibre, oil, herbs, spices, industrial crops and as forage and fodder for domesticated animals. In the tropics alone it has been estimated that 25,000–30,000 species are in use (Heywood 1992) and up to 25,000 species have been used in traditional medicines. In addition, many thousands of species are grown as ornamentals in parks, public and private gardens, as street trees and for shade and shelter.

Very few of these species enter into world trade and only 20–30 of them are staple crops that supply most of human nutrition. A recent study by Prescott-Allen and Prescott-Allen (1990) indicates that 103 species contribute 90% of the national per capita supplies of food plants. The vast majority of the species used by humans do not form part of recorded trade and, therefore, do not appear in official trade statistics. They form a significant part of what is called the hidden economy.

Another important role of plant life is the provision of ecosystem services – the protection of watersheds, stabilization of slopes, improvement of soils, moderation of climate and the provision of a habitat for much of our wild fauna. It is impossible to attach a precise value to such ecosystem services except by counting the costs of failing to maintain them, and of repairing the consequent damage, such as soil erosion and deforestation.

While it is generally accepted today that the conservation of all biodiversity should be our goal, especially through the preservation and sustainable use of natural habitats, this is an ideal that is unlikely to be achieved and there are convincing scientific, economic and sociological reasons for giving priority to the conservation of the major centres of plant diversity throughout the world, especially as this will very often also lead to the conservation of much animal and micro-organism diversity as well.

Recently, BirdLife International (formerly the International Council for Bird Preservation) has published a survey of Endemic Bird Areas (EBAs) as hotspots for biodiversity (ICBP 1992; Stattersfield *et al.*, in prep.) and has suggested that birds can make a unique contribution to determining priorities for the conservation of global biodiversity because (1) they have dispersed to, and diversified in, all regions of the world and (2) they occur in virtually all habitat types and altitudinal zones. These features apply equally well, or with even more force, to plants. However, a third factor, namely that avian taxonomy and geographical distribution of individual bird species are sufficiently well known to permit a comprehensive and rigorous global review and analysis, cannot be claimed for plants. On the other hand, the bird survey covers only 2609 species of birds – those that have had in historical times a global breeding range below 50,000 km² – while there are an estimated 250,000 species of higher plants, the taxonomy and detailed distribution of most of which are poorly known. On the other hand, as we have noted, plants contribute the background habitat for vast numbers of other species, provide many of them with a food source and interact with many of them in pollination and fruit and seed dispersal, so that their significance as determinants of conservation priorities is unrivalled.

Historical background to the Centres of Plant Diversity project

The idea of preparing a world survey of the centres of plant diversity had its origins in an informal meeting convened by G.Ll. Lucas of botanists from the Threatened Plants Unit of the IUCN Conservation Monitoring Centre and staff from the Herbarium of the Royal Botanic Gardens, Kew in 1982, inspired in part by the work of Haffer (1969) on South American bird species. The suggestion was incorporated into the Plants Programme which was being developed by IUCN and WWF in 1984 and, in the first published draft of this Programme (IUCN/WWF 1984), one of the key themes was "Promoting plant conservation in selected countries". The choice of countries was based on an options paper prepared in 1982 by Hugh Synge based on data from the Threatened Plants Unit of the Conservation Monitoring Centre. The countries were:

Africa and Madagascar
Côte d'Ivoire, Liberia, Madagascar, Mauritius, Morocco, Niger, Tanzania;
Asia
India, Indonesia, Malaysia, Nepal, New Caledonia, Sri Lanka;
Central and South America
Brazil, Chile: Juan Fernández, Costa Rica, Ecuador: Galápagos, Honduras, Peru;
Europe
Atlantic Islands, Greece.

Within each country, project sites for conservation action were proposed, based on biological, operational, political and socio-economic considerations.

As part of the process of plant conservation in selected countries, the Threatened Plants Unit of CMC decided to prepare a "Plant Sites Directory" (Davis 1986), later known as "The Plant Sites Red Data Book" (IUCN 1986), that would include accounts of about 150 areas around the world which botanists consider to be of top priority for plant conservation, building on the areas previously selected as noted above. At a meeting in 1987 the Joint IUCN-WWF Plant Advisory Group (PAG) which had been established in 1984 by the Directors General of IUCN and WWF to advise on the overall content and direction of the Plants Programme gave approval to the preparation of a Plant Sites Red Data Book and agreed the concepts and criteria for site selection.

Subsequently, the PAG made a thorough review of the Plant Sites Red Data Book concept and decided to broaden the concept by not just paying attention to sites whose conservation would ensure the survival of most species, but by aiming at a listing of all the major botanical sites and vegetation types considered to be of international importance for the conservation of plant diversity. It was also envisaged that the work would document the many benefits, economic and scientific, that conservation of those areas would bring, outline the potential of each for sustainable development in line with the principles of the World Conservation Strategy (IUCN 1980) and provide an outline strategy for the effective conservation of each centre. The project was renamed *Centres of Plant Diversity: A Guide and Strategy for their Conservation*. Details were given in a brochure published in 1988 (IUCN 1988).

Although work started on the preparation of the project in 1987 and some sample Data Sheets were prepared, major finance for the project was not received until 1989 when WWF International provided a grant and negotiated an arrangement with the UK Overseas Development Administration (ODA) for matching funding and, subsequently, obtained a grant from the European Commission (EC) to fund the project over a three-year period. WWF contracted IUCN to arrange for the implementation of the project and Professor Vernon Heywood, then IUCN's Chief Scientist, Plant Conservation, was nominated to organize and supervise the work. Stephen Davis, then a member of the Threatened Plants Unit of the World Conservation Monitoring Centre, and who had been closely involved in the development of the project concept, was appointed full-time Project Co-ordinator. Olga Herrera-MacBryde, Smithsonian Institution, Washington, D.C., worked full-time on the Latin American section of the project from 1989 under the IUCN-SI Latin American Plants Project. Networks of regional contributors and advisers were subsequently established.

The concept of identifying centres of diversity and endemism

The idea of seeking out high concentrations of diversity among plants, animals or both has a long history in biogeography in one form or another. Attention has frequently been paid to the floristic or faunistic richness of certain areas, such as the tropics of Asia, Africa and the Americas, the Mediterranean climatic regions, such as the Cape of Good Hope, and the concentrations of species on islands, such as Madagascar, Cuba and the islands of Indonesia. Particular emphasis has been given to the large numbers of species that are endemic to such areas, most often with an emphasis on animals, particularly large vertebrates. Another focus has been on particular areas that have been identified as the centres of origin and diversity of crop plants – the so-called Vavilov Centres of Crop Genetic Diversity (Hawkes 1983).

More recently, the concept of sites or centres of high diversity has attracted the attention of conservationists, both as a tool for helping determine which areas should receive priority attention, and also as a challenge as to how to undertake the conservation action necessary, especially as the areas of high diversity are most often found in developing countries which usually have limited human and financial resources available for this purpose.

Much attention has also been directed during the past two or three decades at the large numbers of species that are threatened with extinction at some time in the coming decades (Myers 1986, 1988b; Simberloff 1986; Raven 1987, 1990; Wilson 1988, 1992); the World Conservation Strategy (IUCN 1980) suggested giving conservation priority to those areas where a number of threatened species occur together so as to maximize the benefit from conservation efforts and to reduce the risk of losing large numbers of species if particular areas are not conserved.

Such efforts to seek out areas of high priority for conservation have acquired increased urgency in the light of the accelerating losses throughout the world of natural habitats and the biodiversity they contain, as a result of human action and the growth of the world's population. In particular, attention has been directed at the plight of the world's tropical rain forests which are believed to contain the majority of living organisms but which are being destroyed at an alarmingly high rate (FAO 1990a, b; Whitmore and Sayer 1992).

Determining priority areas for plants

The problem of determining priority areas can be approached at different geographical scales – global, regional, national or local. At a global level, Raven (1987) developed an approach based on analysis of the size of floras that are threatened, and highlighted the fact that about 170,000 of the world's estimated total of 250,000 species of angiosperms grow in tropical regions of the world, with an estimated 85,000 in Latin America, 35,000 in tropical and subtropical Africa (excluding the Cape), and at least 50,000 in tropical and subtropical Asia. He drew attention to the remarkable fact that more than 40,000 plant species – about a quarter of total tropical diversity – occur in Colombia, Ecuador and Peru. Also, the flora of Brazil should be highlighted since it has been estimated to contain between 40,000 and 80,000 species.

Some of these regional figures have been modified subsequently: for example, the count for tropical Africa has been reduced from 35,000 to 21,000 in the light of more accurate assessments (A.L. Stork, pers. comm. to P. Raven 1991) and the figure for tropical Asia appears to have been under-estimated. The total number of single country endemics (excluding Brazil, Paraguay and Papua New Guinea), recorded by the World Conservation Monitoring Centre (see Table 1), and updated by information arising from the present study, is a remarkable 175,976 species, an estimate which casts doubt on the generally accepted global total of about 250,000 species (see also below, p. 7). What is remarkable too is the fact that for many countries of the tropics it is still not possible to provide more than a very rough estimate of the number of species of plants (or of most other groups of organisms) and, for the majority of these countries, the inventory is neither accurate nor complete.

Raven (1987) also singled out areas such as Madagascar, lowland Western Ecuador and the Atlantic forests of Brazil as deserving of critical attention. Each of these areas houses about 10,000 higher plant species and, in each, forest has been reduced to less than 10% of the area which it occupied 50 years ago.

This analysis was developed further by Myers (1988a) who identified 10 tropical forest "hotspots" (defined as areas that feature exceptional concentrations of species with high levels of endemism and face exceptional threats of destruction). Two further hotspots are in the developed world (Hawai'i and Queensland, Australia). Together, these hotspots total about 3.5% of the remaining primary tropical forest, occupy only 0.2% of the land surface of the planet, but contain around 13.8% of the world's plant species. He later extended this analysis by adding another eight areas, four of them in tropical forests and four in Mediterranean type vegetation zones (Myers 1990).

The five areas of Mediterranean-type vegetation – around the Mediterranean itself, in south-western Western Australia, California, central Chile and the Cape region of South Africa – house some 45,000–80,000 higher plant species, depending on how narrowly or widely "Mediterranean" is defined (Heywood 1994b). Of these, an estimated 27,000–35,000 are estimated to be endemic to the areas concerned (data from various sources including Quézel 1985; Cowling et al. 1989; Myers 1990; Greuter 1991; Heywood 1991, 1994b). Southern Africa with some 21,000 species of plants (Cowling et al. 1989), of which 80% are endemic, presents a special case and has the highest species/area ratio in the world (Huntley 1988). All these areas are subjected to a high degree of human disturbance; consequently, the flora and vegetation are significantly threatened.

The selection of sites

The analyses of floristic richness and endemism described above, while providing useful general indications as to which areas might be considered for priority action, have severe limitations in that they are based essentially on species richness and endemism in selected areas, irrespective of the nature, relationships and values of the species concerned, the ecological diversity of the areas and socio-economic factors. Nonetheless they give useful pointers.

In the last 10 years, much effort has been put into considering how habitats of conservation importance should be chosen and which of them should be given priority. These problems have been addressed on many occasions, such as the IVth World Congress on National Parks and Protected Areas (McNeely 1993) and they are reviewed in the WRI-IUCN-UNEP *Global Biodiversity Strategy* (WRI, IUCN and UNEP 1992). The Convention on Biological Diversity, which was agreed at the UNCED at Rio de Janeiro in June 1992, and which came into effect in December 1993, also stresses (in Annex I) the importance of identifying ecosystems and habitats containing high diversity, large numbers of endemic or threatened species and those of social, economic, cultural or scientific importance.

Some authors believe that less time should be spent worrying about the persistence of particular species and more time spent on maintaining the nature and diversity of ecosystem processes. Yet it is species that take part in ecosystem processes

and the fact is that species conservation cannot be separated from that of the habitats in which they occur (Heywood 1994a).

A further criticism of the use of ecological or taxonomic hotspots or mega-diversity regions or countries (Mittermeier and Werner 1988; Myers 1988a) to establish priorities to determine the most important areas to conserve comes from authors such as Dinerstein and Wikramanayake (1993), Pressey et al. (1993) and Williams, Vane-Wright and Humphries (1993). They regard such methods as arbitrary, unsystematic and lacking a paradigm. Pressey et al. (1993) propose three principles for selecting priority regions and regional reserves for the conservation of biodiversity: complementarity, flexibility and irreplaceability and suggest that they can be applied in practice at different scales. At the global level they advocate the use of the WORLDMAP computer program (Vane-Wright, Humphries and Williams 1991) which identifies key regions for conserving the biodiversity of one or more groups at global and national scales. Biodiversity is measured in this case as a combination of the number of species or higher taxa in a region and the taxonomic differences between them, although measures of endemism are also supported. They note that a critical aspect of the system is the implementation of the principle of complementarity which is used to find a priority sequence of regions to represent all taxa by identifying the maximum increment of unrepresented biodiversity possible at each step.

Once a priority region has been identified, there remains the problem of identifying a network of reserves that is able to represent all the features considered as requiring protection. Pressey et al. (1993) give examples of the application of the principles of complementarity and flexibility such as the CODA (Conservation Options and Decisions Analysis) procedure (Bedward, Pressey and Keith 1992) which has been applied to the south-eastern forests of New South Wales to find a network of sites which represent a minimum percentage area of all environments as well as occurrences of rare species and other important features.

Dinerstein and Wikramanayake (1993) present a new approach to conservation planning which they call a Conservation Potential/Threat Index. This index forecasts "how deforestation during the coming decade will affect conservation or establishment of forest reserves." It compares biological richness with reserve size, size of protected area, size of remaining forest cover and deforestation rate and is used to identify conservation potentials, threats and strategies for the 23 Indo-Pacific countries.

The above, and other approaches that will undoubtedly be developed, are to be welcomed. They reflect a growing concern that current approaches to biodiversity conservation worldwide are largely serendipitous, poorly co-ordinated, often ineffective and leave many major problems unsolved. What none of them addresses adequately is the great range of perceptions of biodiversity and priorities from a broad array of different interest groups, be they land use planners, conservation biologists, taxonomists, sociologists, economists, genetic resource agencies or politicians. Any top-down approach, no matter how sophisticated the science, is liable to fail unless full cognizance is taken of the detailed needs, perceptions, aspirations and political realities of the countries and regions concerned. As noted below, in the preparation of this book we adopted from the beginning a principle of involving local experts and, wherever possible, national governmental and non-governmental conservation bodies.

TABLE 1. SPECIES RICHNESS AND ENDEMISM

The following table provides a world list of vascular plant floras arranged alphabetically by region. The data are based on those provided by the World Conservation Monitoring Centre (WCMC) and updated with statistics arising from the CPD project. It should be emphasized that many of the figures are estimates. The reader is referred to the Regional Overviews which provide, in many cases, more detailed flora statistics and information sources. Note that the figures given below for the number of vascular plants have been rounded to the nearest 50–100 species for some regions. A note has been added where this is the case.

	Native vascular plant species	Endemic species	% Species endemism		Native vascular plant species	Endemic species	% Species endemism
AFRICA				Aruba, Bonaire and Curaçao	460	25	5.4
Algeria	3164	250	7.9	Bahamas	1129	118	10.5
Angola	5185	1260	24.3	Barbados	572	3	0.5
Benin	2201	0	0	Bermuda	166	15	9.0
Botswana	2015	17	0.8	Cayman Islands	539	19	3.6
Burkina Faso	>1100	0	0	Cuba	6505	3224	49.6
Burundi	>2500	?	?	Dominica	1227	12	1.0
Cameroon	8260	156	1.9	Grenada	875	4	0.5
Central African Republic	>3600	100	2.8	Grenadines	473	0	0
Chad	>1600	?	?	Guadeloupe	1672	23	1.4
Congo	6000	1200	20.0	Hispaniola	5135	1445	28.1
Côte d'Ivoire	3660	62	1.7	Jamaica	3304	923	27.9
Djibouti	641	2	0.3	Martinique	1505	24	1.6
Egypt	2076	70	3.4	Montserrat	670	2	0.3
Equatorial Guinea	3250	66	2.0	Nevis	260	1	0.4
Ethiopia	>6100	>600	>9.8	Puerto Rico	2492	236	9.5
Gabon	7151	1573	22.0	Saint Kitts	659	1	0.2
Gambia	974	0	0	Saint Lucia	1028	11	1.1
Ghana	3725	43	1.2	Saint Vincent	1134	20	1.8
Guinea	>3000	88	2.9	Trinidad and Tobago	2259	236	10.5
Guinea-Bissau	>1000	12	1.2	Turks and Caicos	448	9	2.0
Kenya	6506	265	4.1				
Lesotho	1591	2	0.1	**CENTRAL AND NORTHERN ASIA**			
Liberia	>2200	103	4.7	Estimate for whole region,			
Libya	1825	134	7.3	comprising Asiatic part of			
Malawi	3765	49	1.3	the former U.S.S.R.	17,500	2500	14.3
Mali	>1741	11	0.6				
Mauritania	1100	?	?	**CHINA AND EAST ASIA**			
Morocco	3675	625	17.0	Cambodia/Laos/Vietnam	>12,800	?	10.0
Mozambique	5692	219	3.8	China	27,100	10,000	36.9
Namibia	3174	?	?	Hong Kong	1984	25	1.3
Niger	1178	0	0	Japan (main islands)	5565	>222	>4.0
Nigeria	4715	205	4.3	Korean Peninsula	2898	407	14.0
Rwanda	>2288	26	1.1	Mongolia	2272	229	10.1
São Tomé and Príncipe	895	134[1]	15.0	Taiwan	3577	1075	30.1
Senegal	2086	26	1.2	Thailand	12,000	?	10.0
Sierra Leone	>1700	74	3.5	Vietnam	8000	>800	>10.0
Somalia	3028	500	16.5	(Note that the statistics for China and Indochina are very			
South Africa	23,420	>16,500	>70.0	approximate.)			
Sudan	>3132	50	1.6				
Swaziland	2715	4	0.2	**EUROPE**			
Tanzania	>10,000	1122	11.2	Albania	3000	24	0.8
Togo	2501	0	0	Austria	3100	35	1.1
Tunisia	2196	?	?	Belgium	1550	1	0.1
Uganda	5406	30	0.6	Bulgaria	3600	320	8.8
Western Sahara	>330	?	?	Cyprus	1650	88	5.3
Zaïre	11,000	1100	10.0	Czech Republic and Slovakia	2600	62	2.4
Zambia	4747	211	4.4	Denmark	1450	1	0.1
Zimbabwe	4440	95	2.1	Faroes	250	1	0.4
				Finland	1045	?	?
ATLANTIC OCEAN ISLANDS				France	4650	133	2.9
Ascension	25	11	44.0	Germany	2700	6	0.2
Azores	300	81	27.0	Greece	5000	742	14.9
Cape Verde	740	92	12.4	Hungary	2200	38	1.7
Canary Islands	1200	500	41.6	Ireland	950	?	?
Iceland	378	1	0.3	Italy	5600	712	12.7
Madeira	1119	106	9.7	Liechtenstein	1400	?	?
Saint Helena	60	50	83.3	Luxembourg	1200	0	0
Tristan da Cunha	40	?	?	Malta	914	5	0.5
				Netherlands	1200	?	?
AUSTRALIA AND NEW ZEALAND				Norway	1600	1	0.1
Australia (mainland)[2]	15,638	14,290	95.4	Poland	2450	3	0.1
Chatham Islands[3]	320	40	12.5	Portugal (mainland)	2600	3	0.1
Lord Howe Island	228	93	40.8	Romania	3400	41	1.4
New Zealand	2400	1942	80.9	Spain (mainland)	5050	941	18.6
Norfolk Island	165	50	30.3	Sweden	1750	1	0.1
Subantarctic Islands	?	35	?	Switzerland	3000	1	0.03
				United Kingdom	1550	16	1.0
CARIBBEAN ISLANDS				Yugoslavia (former territory of)	5350	137	2.6
Anguilla	321	1	3.1	(The figures for vascular plants are rounded to the nearest			
Antigua	845	0	0	50 species.)			

TABLE 1. SPECIES RICHNESS AND ENDEMISM ...continued

	Native vascular plant species	Endemic species	% Species endemism		Native vascular plant species	Endemic species	% Species endemism
INDIAN OCEAN ISLANDS				Tuvalu	44	0	0
British Indian Ocean Territory				Vanuatu	870	150	17.2
(Chagos Archipelago)	100	0	0	Wallis and Futuna	475	7	1.5
Comoros	416	136	33.0	Western Samoa	894	134	15.0
Madagascar	10,000	8000	80.0				
Maldives	277	5	1.8	**SOUTH AMERICA**			
Mauritius[4]	685	311	45.4	Argentina	9370	1100	11.7
Réunion[4]	546	189	34.6	Bolivia	17,350	4000	23.0
Rodrigues[4]	134	47	35.1	Brazil	56,000	?	?
Seychelles	250	87	34.8	Chile	4900–5650	2698	47.8–55.0
				Colombia	51,000	1500	2.9
INDIAN SUBCONTINENT				Ecuador	17,600–21,100	4000	19.0–22.7
Andaman and Nicobar Islands	2270	225	9.9	French Guiana	5625	144	2.6
Bangladesh	5000	?	?	Guyana	6400	?	?
Bhutan	5500	100	1.8	Paraguay	7000–8000	?	?
India	17,000	6800–7650	40.0–45.0	Peru	18,245	5356	29.4
Lakshadweep	348	0	0	Suriname	5000	?	?
Maldives	277	5	1.8	Uruguay	2270	40	1.8
Myanmā (Burma)	14,000	1700	12.1	Venezuela	21,070	8000	38.0
Nepal	7000	350	5.0	(The figures for total number of vascular plants are rounded to the			
Pakistan	5100	400	7.8	nearest 50 species and may vary slightly from those given in the			
Sri Lanka	3370	902	24.5	Regional Overview.)			
MIDDLE AMERICA				**SOUTH EAST ASIA (MALESIA)**			
Belize	2600–3100	150	4.8–5.8	Borneo	20,000–25,000	6000–7000	30.0
Costa Rica	11,100–13,100	600	4.6–5.4	Brunei	6000	?	?
El Salvador	2900	17	0.6	D'Entrecasteaux	>2500	?	?
Guatemala	8650	1171	13.5	Indonesia (available estimates):			
Honduras	5650	148	2.6	Java	4598	230	5.0
Mexico	>20,000	>10,000	?	Sulawesi	5000	?	?
Nicaragua	7600	30–50	0.4–0.7	Sumatra	>10,000	>1200	>10.0
Panama	9900	1222	12.3	Louisiade Archipelago	>3000	?	?
(The figures for total number of vascular plants are rounded to the				Malaysia (available estimates):			
nearest 50 species and may vary slightly from those given in the				Peninsular Malaysia	>9000	2700–4500	30.0–50.0
Regional Overview.)				Sabah and Sarawak	>10,000	?	?
				New Guinea	15,000–20,000	10,500–16,000	70.0–80.0
NORTH AMERICA				Philippines	8931	3500	39.2
Canada	3270	147	4.5	Singapore[6]	1293	2	0.2
Greenland	497	15	3.0	Solomon Islands	3172	30	0.9
U.S.A. (continental)[5]	20,000	4036	20.2				
				SOUTH WEST ASIA AND THE MIDDLE EAST			
PACIFIC OCEAN ISLANDS				Afghanistan	4000	800	20.0
American Samoa	471	15	3.2	Bahrain	248	0	0
Bonin (Ogasawara) Islands	400	150	37.5	Iran	8000	1400	17.5
Cook Islands	284	33	11.6	Iraq	3000	190	6.3
Fed. Micronesia	1194	293	24.5	Israel	2225	165	7.4
Fiji	1628	812	49.9	Jordan	2100	145	7.3
French Polynesia				Kuwait	282	0	0
(incl. Marquesas)	959	560	58.3	Lebanon	2600	311	12.0
Galápagos	541	224	41.4	Oman	1200	73	6.1
Guam	330	69	20.9	Qatar	306	0	0
Hawaiian Islands	1200	1000	83.3	Saudi Arabia	2028	34	1.7
Juan Fernández	210	127	60.4	Syria	3100	395	13.0
Kiribati	22	2	9.1	Turkey	8650	2675	30.9
Marquesas	318	132	41.5	United Arab Emirates	340	0	0
Marshall Islands	100	5	5.0	Yemen[7] (N)	1650	58	3.5
Nauru	54	1	1.9	Yemen[7] (S)	1180	77	6.5
New Caledonia	3322	2551	76.8	Socotra (Yemen)	815	>230	>28.2
Niue	178	1	0.6				
North Marianas	221	81	36.7	**[ANTARCTIC, SOUTH ATLANTIC AND SOUTHERN OCEAN]**			
Palau	175	?	?	Antarctic continent	2	0	0
Pitcairn Islands	76	14	18.4	Falkland Islands (Malvinas)	165	14	8.5
Tokelau Islands	32	0	0	French Southern Territories	50	11	22.0
Tonga	463	25	5.4	(The above region is included here for completeness.)			

Notes:

[1] Refers to single-island endemics.
[2] Latest count for Australia, but an estimated 3000–5000 vascular plant taxa yet to be named.
[3] Figures refer to vascular plant taxa (i.e. species, subspecies and varieties).
[4] Figures refer to flowering plant taxa (i.e. species, subspecies and varieties).
[5] Figures refer to flowering plant species.
[6] Figures for gymnosperms and dicots only.
[7] Yemen was unified in 1991; figures for North Yemen (Yemen Arab Republic), South Yemen (People's Democratic Republic of Yemen) and Socotra are kept separate for convenience.

The objectives of the *Centres of Plant Diversity (CPD)* project are:

❖ to identify which areas around the world, if conserved, would safeguard the greatest number of plant species;
❖ to document the many benefits, economic and scientific, that conservation of those areas would bring to society and to outline the potential value of each for sustainable development;
❖ to outline a strategy for the conservation of the areas selected.

These objectives are fully consonant with the *Convention on Biological Diversity*.

As a consequence of the very extensive involvement of local specialists, and well over 100 government and non-governmental agencies and other conservation bodies in the preparation of the project, including the holding of workshops in several parts of the world, we believe that the resultant three volumes comprising *Centres of Plant Diversity* will provide a unique global and regional review of the nature and distribution of the main concentrations of plant diversity in the world, and a guide to the most practical and cost-effective ways of conserving as much of this diversity as possible, together with its sustainable use. It is our aspiration that CPD will provide not only its sponsors, IUCN, WWF, ODA and the EC, but also governments, aid agencies, development banks and conservation organizations, with a considered overview of the status of plant diversity worldwide and clear guidance on which areas are global and regional priorities for its conservation.

Although the original intention was to select between 150 and 200 sites of global priority, the total number finally chosen greatly exceeds these figures. In addition to the 234 priority sites selected for Data Sheet treatment, many more sites are treated in summary paragraphs in the Regional Overviews. By extending the Regional Overviews in this way, we overcame the problem of making an arbitrary selection of a single site where several potential sites occur in a particular area. In some cases, the Regional Overviews also contain a selection of important botanical areas which do not meet the criteria for selection as CPD sites but which are, nonetheless, areas of important conservation concern because, for example, they may contain the best surviving examples of certain vegetation types.

The criteria and methodology used for selecting sites

The criteria adopted for the selection of sites and vegetation types was based principally on a requirement that each must have one or both of the following two characteristics:

❖ the area is evidently species-rich, even though the number of species present may not be accurately known;
❖ the area is known to contain a large number of species endemic to it.

The following characteristics were also considered in the selection:

❖ the site contains an important genepool of plants of value to humans or that are potentially useful;
❖ the site contains a diverse range of habitat types;

❖ the site contains a significant proportion of species adapted to special edaphic conditions;
❖ the site is threatened or under imminent threat of large-scale devastation.

It has to be stressed that *Centres of Plant Diversity* is concerned with "first order" sites that are of *global* botanical importance. As a consequence some countries have had a number of sites selected, while others have none that qualify for inclusion when viewed on a world basis. If viewed from a national perspective, the selection of sites would have been different. We hope, however, that the publication of these volumes will serve as a stimulus for national programmes aimed at identifying plant sites that are important at a more local level.

The selection process has involved extensive consultations with experts in all the major regions of the world. Networks of individuals and collaborating institutions were established and their advice sought on the listing of sites for the Regional Overviews and for selecting those sites which merit Data Sheet treatment. In Africa, China, India, North America and South America, this involved the holding of workshops within these regions at which data on proposed CPD sites were reviewed and the final selection of Data Sheet sites made. Sometimes this led to some sites being rejected and replaced by others. This is especially true for South America, where the Regional Workshop held in Quito, Ecuador, in 1991 to review the site selection led to a total revision of the phytogeographical divisions of South America and to the major revision of the list of sites previously chosen.

To qualify for Data Sheet treatment, most mainland sites have (or are believed to have) in excess of 1000 vascular plant species, of which at least 100 (i.e. 10%) are endemic either to the site (strictly endemic) or to the phytogeographical region in which the site occurs. In many cases, the number of regional endemics is very much higher than 10% of the flora. In all cases the sites have at least some strict endemics.

The criteria for the selection of islands treated as Data Sheets were somewhat different from those used for mainland sites. Many islands have depauperate floras compared with continental areas, but the level of endemism is often very high. For example, Saint Helena has a flora of only 60 vascular plant species but 50 of these are endemic. Clearly, the high concentration of endemics is of considerable conservation importance, and to restrict the selection of sites to those with floras of, or in excess of, 1000 species would lead to the omission of such important areas.

To qualify for Data Sheet treatment, an island flora must contain at least 50 endemic species or at least 10% of the flora must be endemic. Even so, data were not available for some islands that perhaps warranted inclusion. Comoros, in the Indian Ocean, is a good example of such a situation: the only available figures (416 vascular plant species, of which 136 are endemic) are based on an assessment of the flora made in 1917 which is almost certainly incomplete.

For some islands, the Data Sheet covers the whole island (e.g. Socotra) or an archipelago (e.g. the Canary Islands). South East Asia presented a somewhat different problem: practically the whole region is insular and floristically very rich with high levels of endemism on many of the larger islands. In this case, a number of sites and vegetation types were selected throughout the archipelago, with some islands being represented by more than one Data Sheet to cover a range of vegetation and community types.

There was, in some cases, an element of subjectivity involved in the selection process, and other criteria were used (such as degree of threat, diversity of habitats or soil types, presence of scientifically or economically important species) in deciding which out of a number of similar sites, would be chosen as Data Sheets. But the main criteria and principles outlined above were used to make the initial selection, and always with the help and advice of regional and local expertise.

Content of the Regional Overviews and Data Sheets

Within the constraints imposed by the enormous diversity of the areas covered, a standard format has been adopted for each of the Regional Overviews and Data Sheets. A summary table is provided in each case. There is a certain amount of variation in the headings adopted in the Regional Overviews, but for nearly all the site Data Sheets the following sections are included: Geography, Vegetation, Flora, Useful Plants, Social and Environmental Values, Threats, Conservation and References. An Economic Assessment section is included where data are available.

Analysis of the information on the sites

(i) Regional distribution of Data Sheets

A total of 234 sites are selected for Data Sheet treatment. Their general location is shown in the map on page 11. The distribution of the sites in the different regions is given in Table 2.

TABLE 2. DISTRIBUTION OF DATA SHEETS BY REGION

EUROPE, AFRICA, SOUTH WEST ASIA AND THE MIDDLE EAST

Europe	9
Atlantic Ocean Islands	4
Africa	30
Indian Ocean Islands	3
South West Asia and the Middle East	11
Total	**57**

ASIA, AUSTRALASIA AND THE PACIFIC

Central and Northern Asia	5
Indian Subcontinent	13
China and East Asia	21
South East Asia (Malesia)	41
Australia and New Zealand	14
Pacific Ocean Islands	8
Total	**102**

THE AMERICAS

North America	6
Middle America	20
South America	46
Caribbean Islands	3
Total	**75**
Grand Total	**234**

When considering the figures in Table 2, it must be remembered that the sites vary enormously in size, from extensive mountain systems, such as the Alps, to island complexes, such as the Hawaiian Islands, and to much smaller areas, such as the Sinharaja forest of Sri Lanka. This makes direct comparisons between sites impossible. Attention should also be drawn to the Regional Overviews which place the sites selected in a much wider context and provide a comparative assessment of the biodiversity and conservation status of the different areas within the regions.

(ii) Floristic diversity

It has proved difficult to obtain accurate data on the number of species in some of the sites and even for some areas. Even estimates for individual countries are imprecise in some instances, such as Bolivia, Indonesia and Thailand. The global figures for species richness and endemism can, however, be summarized as follows:

TABLE 3. FLORISTIC DIVERSITY AND ENDEMISM BY REGION

	Species	Endemics	% Endemism
EUROPE, AFRICA, SOUTH WEST ASIA AND THE MIDDLE EAST			
Europe	12,500	3500	28
Atlantic Ocean Islands	2650	785	29.5
Africa	40–45,000	35,000	77–87.5
Indian Ocean Islands	11,000	9000	82
South West Asia and the Middle East	23,000	7100	31
Totals	**89–94,150**	**55,385**	
ASIA, AUSTRALASIA AND THE PACIFIC			
Central and Northern Asia	17,500	2500	14
Indian Subcontinent	25,000	12,000 *	48
China and East Asia	45,000 *	18,650 *	41.5*
South East Asia (Malesia)	42–50,000	29–40,000	70–80
Australia and New Zealand	17,580	16,202	81–90
Pacific Ocean Islands	11–12,000	7000	58–63
Totals	**156–167,080**	**81–96,352**	
THE AMERICAS			
North America	20,000	4198	21
Middle America	30–35,000	14–19,000	46–54
South America	70,000 *	55,000 *	78.5
Caribbean Islands	13,000	6555	50
Totals	**133–138,000**	**80–84,753**	
Grand Totals	**380–399,000**	**216–236,490**	

* very approximate estimate based on available data.

Considerable caution needs to be used in interpreting the figures in this table. It has been exceedingly difficult to obtain accurate figures for many countries. This reflects the relatively poor state of our floristic knowledge, especially in the tropics and subtropics, as has been repeatedly pointed out elsewhere. Effective conservation of biodiversity in the face of such ignorance will be difficult and this is a problem which has to be faced as a matter of urgency. It is notable too that in several regions, such as Africa, Asia, Australia and Latin America, tens of thousands of species are believed still to be undescribed.

The numbers of endemic species given in Table 3 can be totalled meaningfully but the totals of all species in each of the regions, and the sum total of these, are only indicative, as no account is made of the species that are shared between two or more regions. The remarkable total of 236,490 endemic species recorded from the information given in the regional reviews, which themselves reflect the data given in the individual Data Sheets, is surprisingly high when one considers that the *total* number of flowering plants and ferns known today is generally accepted as being around 250,000. It is also substantially higher than the figure of 175,976 endemic species derived from WCMC data (Table 1). The implications are that, if these data can be confirmed, the total number of flowering plant and fern species must be at least of the order of 300,000–350,000 if allowance is made for those species that occur in two or more regions, in more than one continent or are even more widespread.

It is notable too that the total numbers of endemic species (and therefore by implication the total flora) recorded for Asia, Australasia and the Pacific are appreciably higher than those of Latin America and the Caribbean combined. If one takes into account the probability that narrower species concepts are applied in Latin America than in parts, at least, of Asia and the Pacific, as several authors have suggested (e.g. Gentry 1990), the difference will be even greater. This would suggest that conservation agencies might take a closer look at the comparative richness of Latin America/Caribbean and Asia/Pacific in assessing priorities and balance of investment.

If the numbers of Data Sheets for each of the three volumes are compared (Table 4), it will be seen that there is a very broad consistency of treatment.

TABLE 4. COMPARISON OF FLORISTIC RICHNESS (AS MEASURED BY ENDEMICS) AND NUMBERS OF DATA SHEETS FOR REGIONS IN EACH VOLUME OF CPD

Region	Total endemics	Number of Data Sheets
EUROPE, AFRICA, SOUTH WEST ASIA AND THE MIDDLE EAST	55,385	57
ASIA, AUSTRALASIA AND THE PACIFIC	93,352	102
THE AMERICAS	79,086	75

(iii) Conservation status

As one reads through the paragraphs in the Data Sheets on the conservation status of the sites, two worrying trends may be discerned. On the one hand, many sites are not legally protected, or are only protected in part. On the other hand, a considerable proportion of those sites that are officially protected are not effectively managed, being subject to various forms of degradation, ranging from logging to gathering of fuelwood. This emphasizes the need for extending and strengthening the protected area systems of the countries concerned, if the strategy of protecting biodiversity through setting aside and protecting areas of high floristic and ecological richness is to succeed.

Table 5 gives a breakdown by region of the number of sites included partly or fully within legally designated protected areas. From Table 5 and the information presented in the Summary Table (see final section in Introduction), it is encouraging that many CPD sites are represented (at least in part) in existing protected areas, or are proposed for inclusion. Australia is perhaps the best illustration of this. Here, most CPD sites are well-represented within the National Park system, and some areas have additional protection as World Heritage Sites. Of particular note is the Wet Tropics World Heritage Area which includes virtually all of the remaining tropical rain forest in Australia (see the Data Sheet on the Wet Tropics of Queensland – CPD Site Au10, in Volume 2). In other cases, such as Kakadu-Alligator Rivers region and the Western Tasmanian Wilderness (CPD Sites Au4 and Au9, respectively, also covered in Data Sheets in Volume 2), there are important areas outside the existing reserve boundaries which need to be brought into protection to conserve significant elements of the flora.

Closer examination of the current protection of the CPD sites, reveals that the present coverage of legally protected areas is often inadequate to "capture" the full range of vegetation types and areas of greatest floristic richness within a region. Worldwide, less than one in four of the Data Sheet sites (21%) are legally protected in full, and only about one-third of the selected sites (35%) have more than 50% of their areas occurring within existing protected areas.

The largest number of totally unprotected sites occurs in Africa (8 sites) and South East Asia (6 sites); many more sites (17) in South East Asia have less than 50% of their areas occurring within legally designated protected areas. Also of significance is the large number of South American sites (32) which have only a relatively small part of their areas covered by any form of legal protection. A priority must be to extend the coverage of the existing network of protected areas in these regions, and particularly to safeguard remaining plant-rich lowland forests.

Better protection of the lowlands is also a priority for areas with Mediterranean-type climates. In the South-West Botanical Province of Western Australia (CPD Site Au7, see Data Sheet in Volume 2), for example, over a third of the state's Rare and Endangered plants are not protected within the existing reserve system. In the California Floristic Province of U.S.A. (CPD Site NA16, see Data Sheet in Volume 3), the lowlands are particularly under-protected. The lowland flora is also under-represented in the present reserve system in the Cape Floristic Province of South Africa (CPD Site Af53, see Data Sheet in Volume 1), which in terms of the number of species per unit area is probably the richest plant area in the world.

In Central and Northern Asia, the Indian Subcontinent, and South West Asia and the Middle East, few CPD sites have more than 50% of their areas protected within existing reserves. In the case of Central and Northern Asia, none of the CPD sites have more than 50% of their areas protected and, of those which are protected in part, the proportion of the area protected is relatively small. Some of the sites in this region are, however, very large. Again, a priority should be to extend the coverage of the reserve system.

In Europe, Australia and New Zealand, and North America, virtually all CPD sites selected for Data Sheet treatment are included (at least in part) within the existing reserve systems of the regions concerned. Mention has already been made of the protection afforded to CPD sites in Australia; in New Zealand the situation is rather different in that all the sites selected for Data Sheet treatment, whilst being partly included within existing reserves, are nevertheless under threat in at least part of their range. One site in Europe (the Massifs of Gudar and Javalambre in Spain – CPD Site Eu7, see Data Sheet in Volume 1) has no current legal protection.

Even when areas are designated for protection, many are nevertheless threatened, some severely so. This can be seen by comparing figures in Table 5 with those in Table 6, which provides a summary of the degree of threat to CPD sites in each region.

Only 33 sites (15% of the total number of Data Sheet sites) are considered to be safe, or reasonably safe, whereas 119 sites (c. 50% of the total) are either threatened or severely threatened. A further 41 sites worldwide are considered to be vulnerable or at risk, and the remainder (40 sites) are partly threatened (for example where encroachment is occurring in part of an area or around its perimeter).

Of particular note is the degree of threat to many sites in the tropics. For example, none of the sites in Middle America are assessed as "safe" or "reasonably safe". Over half the sites in the region are threatened or severely threatened, irrespective of their designation, in whole or in part, as protected areas.

Some of the most seriously threatened floras are those on islands. For example, all of the CPD Data Sheet sites for the Indian Ocean and the Pacific Ocean are assessed as either at risk or threatened. Of the 8 CPD sites selected for Data Sheet treatment for the Pacific, 5 are classified as severely threatened, including the Hawaiian Islands, which include some of the most endangered floras in the world.

In the moist tropics, the main threats to sites are from encroaching agriculture, including slash and burn agriculture, logging and road building. Road building is often followed by unplanned colonization. In Middle and South America, cattle ranching is also a serious threat to a number of sites. An additional threat in some cases is the quest for oil and gas, together with the associated problems of pollution. In South East Asia, many CPD sites are already National Parks, but their protection status is still not secure; most suffer from encroachment from slash and burn cultivators, and from logging or conversion to oil palm plantations. In some cases in the moist tropics, forest clearance has occurred up to the park boundaries.

Almost all the tropical sites which are already protected (at least on paper) suffer from a lack of adequate funding and trained manpower. This affects the security of the areas. Boundaries may not be properly marked or policed, resulting in valuable resources, such as rattans and timber trees, being illegally exploited in an uncontrolled manner, perhaps not sustainable in the long-term. For some areas there are no effective management plans to protect or utilize important genetic resources, and there is mostly no out-reach programme to involve local people in the management and protection of the forests, and to ensure that utilization of plant resources is undertaken on a sustainable basis. In many cases, land zonation within the protected area and its vicinity is needed to ensure that conservation of biodiversity is balanced against other demands on natural resources.

Effective conservation of the CPD sites depends, therefore, on adequate funding and the political will to establish more protected areas where this is necessary and to ensure that all protected areas are effectively managed.

While it is encouraging to note that there are still many opportunities available for protecting and conserving a large proportion of the Earth's wild plant resources *in situ* (supplemented by *ex situ* procedures as necessary), it is alarming that very few of the areas identified as global priorities are assessed as "safe". With the ever-increasing threats to many sites, the opportunities for conservation are disappearing rapidly and the need for emergency action becomes more frequent. There is therefore an urgent need for action from governments, aid agencies and conservation organizations to achieve the conservation of the areas selected as CPD sites before it is too late.

(iv) Useful plants, social, economic and environmental values

A remarkable diversity of uses of plants is noted in the Regional Overviews, Data Sheets and Summary Tables which follow. Almost all the sites contain important timber trees, fruit trees or medicinal plants. Even in Europe, the native flora contains over 200 crop relatives which represent important genetic resources. For most of the tropical sites detailed information on the uses of plants is not available and a vast amount of research still needs to be undertaken.

TABLE 5. ANALYSIS OF THE CONSERVATION STATUS OF CPD SITES

Region	% area of CPD site within protected area(s)				Total no. of sites	% of sites with >50% or 100% protection	
	0	>0–50	>50–<100	100		>50	100
Africa	8	7	8	7	30	50	23
Atlantic Ocean Islands	-	3	1	-	4	25	0
Australia/New Zealand	-	8	4	2	14	43	14
Caribbean Islands	1	-	1	1	3	67	33
Central and Northern Asia	1	4	-	-	5	0	0
China and East Asia	1	7	4	9	21	62	43
Europe	1	8	-	-	9	0	0
Indian Ocean Islands	-	3	-	-	3	0	0
Indian Subcontinent	2	9	-	2	13	15	15
Middle America	3	8	5	4	20	45	20
North America	-	6	-	-	6	0	0
Pacific	-	5	1	2	8	38	25
South America **	2	32	6	5	45	24	11
South East Asia	6	17	2	16	41	44	39
South West Asia and the Middle East	2	8	-	1	11	9	9
Totals	**27**	**125**	**32**	**49**	**233**	**35**	**21**

Notes:

** The figures for South America exclude one Data Sheet (SA34), for which data are not available.

For CPD sites having Forest Reserve status, a judgement had to be made whether such a designation confers any degree of protection on the flora. If it is clear from the text of the Data Sheet that no protection is afforded, and especially if the area is under imminent threat of large-scale logging, the percentage area of the CPD site protected has been adjusted accordingly.

TABLE 6. DEGREE OF THREAT TO CPD SITES

The table shows the number of CPD Data Sheet sites classified under broad categories of threat. For details on each site, see the Summary Table on page 12, and the individual site Data Sheets.

Region	Safe or reasonably safe	Partly safe but some areas threatened	Vulnerable or at risk	Threatened	Severely threatened
Africa	7	5	7	8	3
Atlantic Ocean Islands	1	-	-	1	2
Australia/ New Zealand	9	2	1	2	-
Caribbean Islands	-	1	1	-	1
Central and Northern Asia	-	-	4	1	-
China and East Asia	2	5	5	5	4
Europe	2	2	-	5	
Indian Ocean Islands	-	-	1	1	1
Indian Subcontinent	2	6	-	3	2
Middle America	-	5	2	10	3
North America	-	2	-	3	1
Pacific	-	-	1	2	5
South America **	7	5	3	14	16
South East Asia	3	7	12	15	4
South West Asia and the Middle East	-	-	4	4	3
Totals	**33**	**40**	**41**	**74**	**45**

Notes:

** The figures for South America exclude one Data Sheet (SA34), for which data are not available.

9

Many of the areas attract large numbers of tourists. Often, it is intact natural vegetation which provides the scenic backdrop, or is the actual focus, for tourism in the areas concerned. If properly planned and controlled to prevent visitor pressure and tourist developments becoming threats to the sites, such visitation could provide substantial long-term financial and employment benefits to the immediate area, as well as to national economies. In a few cases, a partial and preliminary economic assessment of the value of plant resources is given in the Regional Overviews and Data Sheets. This is usually based upon the number of visitors to a protected area, or the amount of wild plant resources gathered from a site.

Mention must also be made of the valuable environmental services provided by the sites, such as the prevention of soil erosion and flooding of downslope agricultural and settled areas, as well as safeguarding watersheds and contributing to climatic stability. It has been impossible to place monetary values on these services within the context of this present work.

The information presented in the Data Sheets and Regional Overviews demonstrates all too clearly the enormous value to humanity of the vast range of riches and economic potential of plant resources. This poses a dramatic challenge to the nations of the world and to the international agencies that are called upon to provide the necessary aid, support, and strategic and practical advice to ensure the survival into the future of this treasure house for humanity.

Summary information on sites selected for Data Sheet treatment

The Summary Table below includes a world list of the 234 sites which have been selected for detailed treatment as Data Sheets in the three volumes comprising *Centres of Plant Diversity*. Any updates to the information given in the Summary Table will be noted in subsequent volumes.

The following notes indicate the sorts of data presented under each column in the table:

(i) Type

A letter code categorizing each of the areas selected for Data Sheet treatment. The following codes are used:

S   Site; where the area is a discrete geographical unit, and where the whole area needs to be conserved.
F   Floristic province, often covering a very wide area, or CPD site covering a whole region. Effective conservation of the flora of such areas often requires a network of reserves to be established, as in many cases it would be impractical to protect the entire province or region.
V   Vegetation type. As in "F", effective conservation often requires representative samples to be protected.

(ii) Area

From information given in the Data Sheets; usually to nearest 1 km² for individual sites, sometimes an estimate to nearest 100 km² or 1000 km² for large regions.

(iii) Altitude

Altitude range in metres.

(iv) Flora

Unless otherwise stated, numbers refer to indigenous vascular plant species, or an estimate based on current botanical knowledge of that (or similar) sites, usually to the nearest 100 species, or to nearest 1000 species for some large tropical sites. An asterisk (*) denotes the exact number of plant species present or so far recorded for a site.

taxa – refers to the number of species, subspecies and varieties.
angiosp. – angiosperms.

(v) Examples of Useful Plants

Important plants or major groups are listed, including names of some commodity groups.

(vi) Vegetation

The major vegetation formations are listed. Information has been summarized from the Data Sheets. The use of some local names for vegetation types has been retained.

(vii) Protected Areas

Categories of protected areas are given where a CPD site is fully or partially protected. In most cases, the area of the protected site is given after the category, or a percentage figure is given for that part of the site which is protected. If a site is fully protected, the entry will just show the category of protection.

Abbreviations used:

BG	Botanic Garden	PFA	Protected Forest Area
BR	Biosphere Reserve	RF	Reserved Forest
FoR	Forest Reserve	SF	State Forest
GR	Game Reserve	SFoRP	State Forest Park
GS	Game Sanctuary	SP	State Park
NM	Nature Monument	SpNR	Special Nature Reserve
NP	National Park	VJR	Virgin Jungle Reserve
NR	Nature/Natural Reserve	WA	Wilderness Area
NS	Nature Sanctuary	WHS	World Heritage Site
NatM	National Monument	WMA	Wilderness Management Area
NatP	Natural Park		
NatS	National Sanctuary	WR	Wildlife Reserve
PA	Protected Area	WS	Wildlife Sanctuary
PF	Protection/Protected Forest		

In many cases, the IUCN Management Category of each protected area is given in the Data Sheet. The definitions of the IUCN Management Categories are given in a separate Appendix.

(viii) Threats

Only the main threats, with the most important ones first, are listed.

(ix) Assessment

A summary of the conservation status of the area, including whether the area is safe, reasonably safe, at risk, threatened or severely threatened. An analysis of the threats and conservation status of the CPD sites is given in the Introduction to this volume.

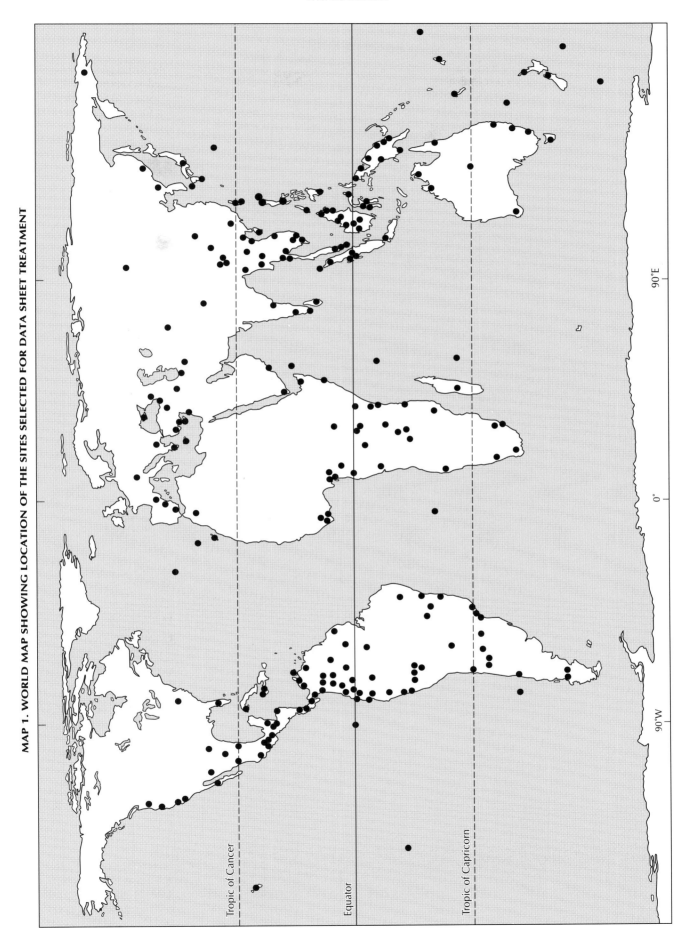

MAP 1. WORLD MAP SHOWING LOCATION OF THE SITES SELECTED FOR DATA SHEET TREATMENT

Tropic of Cancer

Equator

Tropic of Capricorn

90°W

0°

90°E

CENTRES OF PLANT DIVERSITY: SUMMARY INFORMATION ON SITES SELECTED FOR DATA SHEET TREATMENT

Code	Site	Type	Size (km²)	Altitude	Flora	Examples of Useful Plants	Vegetation	Protected Areas	Threats	Assessment
AFRICA										
Af81	Afroalpine region	F	3500	3500–5890 m	350	Grazing, browsing, fuel	Moist tree composite woodland, scrub, tussock grassland, bogs	Considerable areas fall within existing NPs and reserves	Overgrazing, fuelwood collection, fire, tourism	Some areas safe, but others severely threatened; management plans needed
	Cameroon									
Af11	Forest zone, River Dja region	S	8100	200–500 m	2000	Timber trees, essential oils, medicinal plants	Tropical evergreen rain forest, semi-deciduous forest, swamps, secondary forests	FoR and Fauna Reserve, BR, and proposed NP (5000 km²)	Some encroachment on boundaries from cocoa, coffee and subsistence plots	Reasonably safe; threats not as serious as elsewhere
Af12	Korup NP	S	1259	100–1075 m	3500	Medicinal plants, palm canes, chewing sticks, fruit trees	Lowland tropical evergreen rain forest	NP	Over-collecting of bush mango and palm canes, some encroachment	Reasonably secure
Af13	Mount Cameroon	S	1100	0–4095 m	3500	Timber trees (especially African mahogany), medicinal plants	Lowland evergreen rain forest to Afromontane forest, scrub, subalpine and montane grasslands, coastal mangroves	6 FoRs (700 km²), mostly in foothills; proposed Etinde Reserve (360 km²) and Mabeta-Moliwe Reserve (36 km²); Limbe BG.	Agricultural encroachment, fire, logging; potentially grazing	Threatened; most seriously on lower slopes of east and north; montane forest at risk from fire
	Congo/Cabinda/Zaïre									
Af16	Mayombe	S	2500	150–350 m	>1100	Timber trees, medicinal plants, food plants, plants of cultural value	Tropical lowland semi-evergreen forest, Zambezian savanna, wetlands	Proposed BR	Logging, charcoal production, clearance for agriculture	Threatened
	Côte d'Ivoire									
Af2	Taï NP	S	3500	80–623 m	1300	Timber trees, many plants used locally for a variety of purposes	Tropical evergreen rain forest	NP, WHS (all of area), BR (3300 km²)	Logging, agricultural encroachment, gold mining, population pressure	Threatened around perimeter
	Gabon									
Af18	Cristal Mountains	S	9000	0–911 m	>3000	Timber trees (e.g. okoumé), semi-wild oil palms, raphia, medicinal plants	Mainly tropical lowland and hill rain forest	None	No serious threats at present; logging is a potential threat	Not protected; at risk
	Guinea/Côte d'Ivoire/Liberia									
Af4	Mont Nimba	S	480	450–1752 m	>2000	Timber trees, oil palm	Lowland and transitional rain forest, grasslands	Strict NR & WHS (Guinea: 130 km², Côte d'Ivoire: 50 km²; BR (Guinea: 171 km²), proposed NR (Liberian part)	Mining of iron ore (Liberia/Guinea), some clearance for agriculture	Liberian and Guinean part greatly damaged by mining and severely threatened
	Kenya									
Af62	Mount Kenya	S	1500	1600–5199 m	800	Timber trees, fruit trees, medicinal plants	Montane moist and dry forest, bamboo, woodland, giant heaths, moorland	Above 3100 m, NP (715 km²); BR (718 km²); FoR covers 1421 km² of lower slopes	Logging, monocultures on the lower slopes, visitor pressure at higher altitudes	Lower slopes severely threatened

Code	Site	Type	Size (km²)	Altitude	Flora	Examples of Useful Plants	Vegetation	Protected Areas	Threats	Assessment
Liberia										
Af7	Sapo NP	S	1307	100–400 m		Timber trees, medicinal plants, wide range of plants used for making artefacts, tools	Lowland tropical rain forest	NP	Potential logging, illegal hunting	At risk
Malawi										
Af64	Mount Mulanje	S	500	750–3002 m	>800	Mulanje cedar, *Brachystegia*, bamboos, fruit trees	Woodland, evergreen forest, montane grassland, high-altitude scrub, rupicolous communities	FoR	Deforestation, illegal logging of cedars, uncontrolled collection of fuelwood, invasive pines	Severely threatened; action urgently needed
Morocco										
Af84	High Atlas	F	7000	1000–4165 m	1000	Timber trees (e.g. walnut, pine, juniper, relict stands of Atlantic cedar), fodder plants	Cedar, juniper, pine and holm oak forests, scrub, alpine meadows, pseudo-steppe, alpine scree communities	2 NPs (860 km², incl. 1 WS of 8 km²), 1 NR (12 km²); c. 12% of total area	Population pressure leading to clearance for cultivation, overgrazing, fuelwood cutting, timber cutting	Protected area reasonably secure but management needs strengthening; areas outside threatened
Namibia/Angola										
Af50	Kaokoveld	F	70,000	0–2000 m	952*	Medicinal plants, plants of cultural value, fodder plants	Desert/escarpment vegetation, mopane savanna	Angola: most in Iona NP (15,150 km²) and a Partial Reserve; Namibia: small area in NP, rest as Game Conservation Area	Timber cutting, overgrazing, over-collecting of food and medicinal plants	Protection needs strengthening; some parts threatened
Nigeria										
Af24	Cross River NP	S	4227	150–1700 m	>400 trees*	Timber trees, rattans, edible fruits, medicinal plants	Tropical lowland rain forest, freshwater swamp forest, montane forest, grassland	NP	Potential logging, agricultural encroachment	Reasonably secure
Somalia										
Af42	Cal Madow	S	9600	0–2400 m	1000	Frankincense, myrrh, carob relative, timber trees	Dry montane forest, evergreen to deciduous woodland, bushland, semi-desert	Daalo FoR is proposed as NP	Logging, grazing	No protection in practice, but threats to flora probably not severe
Af44	Hobyo	S	3000	0–440 m	<1000	Medicinal plants, plants used for construction	Deciduous bushland and woodland, dune vegetation	None; proposed GR for part of area	Overgrazing, fuelwood collection	No protection, but threats to flora probably not severe
South Africa										
Af53	Cape Floristic Region	F	90,000	0–2325 m	8600	Ornamentals (e.g. bulbs, succulents, proteas, ericas)	Fynbos, shrubland, Afromontane forest	Montane areas well protected in many reserves; <3% of lowlands protected	Agriculture, urbanization, fire, invasive species, high population growth rate	Most mountain fynbos effectively protected; lowlands much less so; 44% of remaining fynbos area protected
South Africa/Lesotho										
Af82	Drakensberg Alpine Region	F	40,000	1800–3482 m	>1750	Forage grasses, grasses and sedges for thatching, rope, hats, fuelwood	Subalpine and alpine grassland and shrubland, scrub, savanna, wetlands	NPs, NRs, WAs cover 2194 km²; Drakensberg/Maluti Ecosystem Conservation Area is a proposed WHS	Overgrazing, soil erosion, arable agriculture, invasive plants	Severely threatened in places; protected areas safe, but coverage inadequate

Code	Site	Type	Size (km²)	Altitude	Flora	Examples of Useful Plants	Vegetation	Protected Areas	Threats	Assessment
South Africa/Swaziland/Mozambique										
Af59	Maputaland-Pondoland Region	F	201,640	0–1800 m	6000–7000	Ornamental plants (e.g. *Agapanthus*, *Gladiolus*), cowpea relatives, 900 medicinal plant species	Grassland, Afromontane forest, coastal, sand and swamp forests, valley bushveld, semi-evergreen bushland/thicket, palmveld, aquatic communities	7.5% in conservation areas, but 93% of conserved area is in northern savanna zone which is not rich in plant endemics	Rapid population growth, slash and burn agriculture, plantation crops, afforestation, urbanization, invasive species, mining	Existing reserve system inadequate to protect plant-rich vegetation types, which remain threatened
South Africa/Namibia										
Af51	Western Cape Domain (Succulent Karoo)	F	111,212	0–1907 m	5000	Ornamentals (e.g. bulbs, succulents), food and medicinal plants	Succulent shrubland (veld) with associated annuals	NP (270 km²) and a few other reserves covering >2% of the region in total	Overgrazing, agriculture, mining, plant collecting, invasive species, urban development	Inadequate coverage of protected areas; threatened
Tanzania										
Af71	East Usambara Mountains	S	280	150–1506 m	1921 taxa*	Ornamental plants (incl. African violet, *Streptocarpus*), timber and pole species	Lowland semi-deciduous and evergreen submontane forests	25 Catchment FoRs, proposed NRs	Logging, pole-cutting, clearance of forest for agriculture, invasive species	Reserves intact; more extensive forest outside threatened and declining
Af33	Mahale-Karobwa Hills	F	24,000	773–2496 m	>2000	Timber trees, plants used for honey and wax collection	Miombo woodland, riverine, lowland, submontane and montane forests, dambos	Mahale Mountain NP (1613 km²)	Shifting cultivation, influx of refugees, proposed road	Threatened
Af57	Rondo Plateau	F	250	300–700 m	800	Timber trees	Dry semi-deciduous lowland forest, woodland and thicket	All remaining forests protected in Rondo FoR	Logging, pole cutting, clearance for farming, burning, inadequate staffing	Threatened
Uganda										
Af25	Bwindi (Impenetrable) Forest	S	321	1160–2607 m	1000	Timber trees, bamboos, medicinal plants	Moist evergreen submontane and montane forests	NP	Logging, over-collection of forest products (e.g. removal of timber and fuelwood)	Isolated forest very threatened despite protection status and conservation projects
Zaïre										
Af49	Garamba NP and surrounding Domaines de Chasses	S	56,727	710–1061 m	1000	Timber trees, papyrus, medicinal plants	Sudanian woodland, savanna, papyrus swamps, riverine forests	NP and WHS (49,200 km²), 3 Domaines de Chasses (7527 km²)	Uncontrolled fires	NP/WHS area safe
Af35	Kundelungu	S	9000	1500–2000 m		Medicinal plants, timber trees, plants of cultural importance	Miombo woodland, grassland, gallery forest	NP (7600 km²)	Fires, charcoal production, hunting	At risk
Af29	Maiko NP	S	10,830	1000–1200 m		Timber trees	Tropical evergreen rain forest, Afromontane forest	NP	Minor threats from conversion to savanna, gold mining	Reasonably safe due to difficulties of access, but more management resources needed
Af30	Salonga NP	S	36,560	350–700 m	1500–2000	Timber trees, medicinal plants	Tropical evergreen rain forest, swamp and riverine forests, grasslands	NP (whole area), WHS (36,000 km²)	Local population pressure, timber cutting, fuelwood cutting, fire, over-collection of medicinal plants	At risk; inadequate trained staff, infrastructure and management planning

Code	Site	Type	Size (km²)	Altitude	Flora	Examples of Useful Plants	Vegetation	Protected Areas	Threats	Assessment
Af37	Upemba NP	S	11,730	350–1100 m	>2400	Fruit trees, fibres, some timber species	Miombo woodland, dry evergreen forest, wooded grassland, swamps	NP	Illegal commercial logging, fire	At risk; inadequate management resources
	Zambia									
Af39	Zambezi Source Area	F	1700	1200–1490 m	>1000	Timber trees, melliferous plants	Riverine, swamp and dry evergreen forest; miombo woodland, bushland, savanna	9% gazetted as PFA	Clearance for agriculture, refugees	At risk from inappropriate land management practices
ATLANTIC OCEAN ISLANDS										
AO1	Azores	F	2304	0–1351 m	300	Timber trees (logged out), fodder plants, fruits, dyes, medicinal plants	Evergreen (laurisilva) forest, montane cloud forest, grasslands, seral communities on volcanic rocks	12 NRs, but only 3 over 10 km²	Clearance for pastures, exotic forestry plantations, invasive plants	Inadequate coverage of protected areas and poor management; threatened
AO2	Canary Islands	F	7542	0–3717 m	1200	Ornamental plants, medicinal plants, timber trees, dry zone pasture grasses	Evergreen (laurisilva and pine) forests, montane and coastal scrub, woodland	4 NPs (273.5 km²), WHS (39.9 km²), BR (5.1 km²), 98 other protected landscapes and parks	Tourist and residential developments, overgrazing, off-road vehicles, invasive plants, fire	Lowlands inadequately protected; seriously threatened
AO3	Madeira/Salvage Islands	F	728 (M) 3 (S)	0–1861 m 0–153 m	1191	Timber trees (now depleted), medicinal plants, Madeiran bilberry, potential ornamental plants	Dry & humid evergreen forests (incl. laurel forest), coastal herb and shrub communities, cliff vegetation	Madeira: NatP (567 km², incl. 6 fully protected areas), Natural Reserve (14 km², land area); Salvage Is: Natural Reserve (whole area)	Introduced plants, tourism, rats, former clearance for agriculture, fire	Reasonably well protected, but control on tourism and eradication of invasive plants needed
AO4	St Helena	F	122	0–823 m	60	Threatened timber trees, incl. endemic ebony, redwood, gumwood	Tree fern thicket, semi-desert, scrub, woodland, severely degraded	c. 10% protected as forest, whole island proposed as BR & WHS	Invasive plants, overgrazing by domestic and feral animals	Rescue and rehabilitation programme underway, but remaining native vegetation still severely threatened
AUSTRALIA/NEW ZEALAND										
	Australia									
Au1	Australian Alps	F	30,000	200–2228 m	780	Timber trees (especially eucalypts)	Grassland, woodland, shrubland, forest, alpine vegetation	NPs and SPs cover 17,000 km²	Tourism, grazing, hydroelectric facilities, fire, feral animals, exotic plants	Generally well protected; reasonably secure
Au2	Border Ranges	F	600	0–1360 m	>1200	Timber trees (e.g. red cedar, rose mahogany), macadamia nuts, ornamental plants	Various types of rain forest, eucalypt forest, woodland, shrubland, heath	NP (majority of area), SF, WHS (NSW part)	Clearance for grazing, rural development, visitor pressure, fire, invasive plants	Generally well protected; proposal to add Queensland part to WHS will improve protection
Au3	Central Australian Mountain Ranges	F	168,000	500–1531 m	1300	Food plants (140 spp. previously used), medicinal plants (70 spp.), timber for artefacts	Hummock grasslands, shrublands, woodlands, open rock and cliff vegetation	23 NPs and reserves cover 2.2% of area	Increasing tourist pressure, exotic weeds, grazing, mining, fire	More or less intact, but Petermann Ranges degraded by grazing. No reserves in Petermann and Musgrave areas

Code	Site	Type	Size (km²)	Altitude	Flora	Examples of Useful Plants	Vegetation	Protected Areas	Threats	Assessment
Au4	Kakadu–Alligator Rivers Region	F	30,000	0–370 m	1400	Many plants used by aborigines	Tropical sclerophyll forest, woodland, rain forest, swamp forest, mangrove, saltmarsh, grassland, sedgeland	NP and WHS covers 19,804 km² (c. 66% of region)	Tourism, invasive weeds	WHS area well protected
Au5	Norfolk and Lord Howe Islands	F	39 (NI) 15 (LH)	0–319 m 0–875 m	392*	Ornamental plants (e.g. Kentia palms, Norfolk Island pine, also a timber tree)	Evergreen rain forest, palm forest, "mossy" forest, pine and hardwood forests	WHS covers all Lord Howe; NP of 4.6 km² on Norfolk Island	Tourism, cattle grazing, introduced plants on Norfolk Island; no major threats on Lord Howe	Lord Howe well protected; both areas secure
Au6	North Kimberley Region	F	99,100	0–854 m	1476*	Pasture grasses, wild fruits and roots formerly eaten by aborigines, medicinal plants	Mostly high-grass savanna woodland, some eucalypt woodland, rain forest patches, mangroves	13,855 km² as NP and NRs, much of rest is virtual wilderness	Grazing pressure in parts, feral animals including cattle, donkeys	Safe due to remoteness, terrain and small permanent population
Au7	South-west Botanical Province	F	309,840	0–400 m	5500	Timber trees, ornamental plants	Eucalypt forest, woodland, mallee, scrub	NPs & NRs cover 25,969 km² (8.4% of area); SForPs cover 17,459 km² (5.6% of area)	Root rot fungus, wild fires	Reserves well protected, but coverage inadequate in agricultural belt
Au8	Sydney Sandstone Region	F	24,000	0–1300 m	2200	Australian red cedar and other hardwoods, ornamental plants	Forest, woodland, shrubland, grassland, coastal dune and swamp, mangrove	NPs and reserves cover 11,709 km² (c. 49% of region)	Urban and industrial development, tourism	Generally well protected
Au9	Western Tasmanian Wilderness	F	14,050	0–1617 m	800	Timbers, especially Huon pine, King Billy pine, ornamental plants	Cool temperate rain and eucalypt forests, alpine vegetation, sub–alpine scrub, moorland, grassland	WHS (13,800 km²) incl. NPs, BR; most of WHS has NP status	Tourism, fire, *Phytophthora* root fungus	WHS well protected. North-west forests unprotected and at risk, but recommended as reserve
Au10	Wet Tropics of Queensland	F	11,000	0–1622 m	>3400	Timber trees, ornamental plants, native food plants, potential medicinal plants	Various types of rain forest, woodlands, shrublands, mangroves	WHS (8990 km²), c. 50 NPs (2073 km²), remainder mainly Crown Land	Tourism, lowland forest clearance, hydro-electric scheme, telecommunication facilities, feral animals, local grazing and logging	Well protected now as WHS, but some areas still at risk, particularly from increasing tourism and illegal clearance
Australia/New Zealand										
Au17	Subantarctic Islands	F	949	0–668 m	35 endemic taxa	Macquarie island cabbage, ornamental plants	Grasslands, fellfields and herbaceous communities, wetlands, forests, coastal vegetation	NRs cover all islands, Macquarie Island has BR status	Introduced plants; introduced cats, rabbits and wekas a threat on Macquarie Island	High level of protection; reasonably safe
New Zealand										
Au16	Chatham Islands	F	965	0–300 m	320	Many species used in Maori culture, ornamental plants	Evergreen cool-temperate forest, peatlands, lagoons, coastal communities	Network of reserves, mostly small in size, more recommended	Clearance for agriculture, feral animals, invasive plants, fire	Threatened; degradation persists with many important sites unprotected
Au14	Northland	F	14,000	0–776 m	620	Timber trees, ornamental plants, many species used in traditional culture	Moist temperate evergreen lowland forest, swamps, coastal communities	>200 protected areas, incl. Waipoua State Forest Sanctuary (91 km²)	Clearance for agriculture, feral animals, weeds, tourism, plantations	Despite many protected areas, many endemics insufficiently protected and at risk

Code	Site	Type	Size (km²)	Altitude	Flora	Examples of Useful Plants	Vegetation	Protected Areas	Threats	Assessment
Au15	North-west Nelson	F	9500	0–1875 m	1200* angiosp.	Timber trees, ornamental plants, plants used in traditional culture	Moist temperate to montane forest, wetlands, alpine vegetation, grassland	NP (225 km²), >40 reserves, proposed NP for much of Crown Land	Logging, mining, agriculture, introduced plants and animals	Threatened
CARIBBEAN ISLANDS										
Cuba										
Cb3	Cajálbana Tableland/Preluda Mountain region	S	100	0–464 m	330	Pines (especially *Pinus caribaea*) used as sources of timber and resins, palms used for roofing	Pine forest, xerophytic thorn scrub, riverine forests	Partly in Mil Cumbres Integrated Management Area (166 km²); whole area traditionally managed as "Forestry Patrimony"	Fire, clearance for agriculture, logging, invasive species, tourism	At risk
Jamaica										
Cb10	Blue and John Crow Mountains	S	782	380–2256 m	>600	Timber trees, medicinal plants, ornamental plants	Montane rain forests, scrub, savanna, cliff vegetation	NP	Clearance for subsistence farming and commercial crops, fire, invasive species, plant collecting	Southern slopes of Blue Mountains severely threatened; rest of area at risk, regulations need to be enforced
Cb11	Cockpit Country	F	430	300–746 m	1500	Few remaining timber trees, potential ornamental plants, yam relatives, several medicinal plants	Evergreen seasonal subtropical forest, mesic limestone forest, scrub thicket	None, although much has FoR status	Clearance for agriculture, fire, road building, illegal timber cutting, fuelwood collection	Severely threatened
CENTRAL AND NORTHERN ASIA										
Armenia/Azerbaijan/Georgia/Russia										
CA2	Caucasus	F	440,000	0–5642 m	6000	c. 300 food plants, 300 medicinal plants, timber trees, ornamental plants	Broadleaved and coniferous forests, montane steppe, subalpine meadows, semi-desert	37 NRs cover 8982 km² (c. 2% of region)	Logging, overgrazing, plant collecting, visitor pressure	Inadequate coverage of protected areas; threatened
Kazakhstan/Kirghizia/Tadzhikistan/Turkmenistan/Uzbekistan										
CA3	Mountains of Middle Asia	F	550,000	100–7495 m	5500	c. 1000 species of useful plants, incl. timbers, medicinal plants, fruit and nut trees, ornamentals	Semi-desert, steppes, broadleaved and coniferous forests, juniper and pistachio woodlands, meadows	18 reserves cover 5720 km² (c. 1% of region)	Industrial/agricultural development in lowlands, overgrazing, tourism, over-collection of medicinal plants	Inadequate coverage of reserves; at risk
Russia										
CA4	Chukotskiy Peninsula	F	117,000	0–2300 m	939*	c. 40 species of food and medicinal plants, c. 400 fodder species	Tundra, steppe, shrub communities, rare hot spring communities	Proposed International Ethno-ecological Park to cover c. 50,000 km²	Mining, overgrazing, waste disposal, visitor pressure	Not protected at present; vulnerable
CA5	Primorye	F	165,900	0–1933 m	1850	Medicinal plants, honey and food plants, timbers, ornamentals	Mixed coniferous forest, oak-pine broadleaved montane woodlands, wetlands	6.5% of region protected in 5 NRs (5299 km²), 8 Refuges (2032 km²), BR (3402 km²)	Logging, pollution, fire, visitor pressure, over-collecting	Some vegetation types and threatened species not included in existing reserves; vulnerable
Russia/Kazakhstan										
CA1	Altai-Sayan	F	1,100,000	300–4506 m	2500	Timber trees, medicinal plants, food plants, ornamentals	Coniferous forests, steppe, subalpine and alpine vegetation, tundra	1.5% protected in 5 NRs (15,595 km²), c. 300 NMs, small floristic refuges	Forest clearance, fire, overgrazing, plant collecting	Coverage of existing reserves inadequate, more being planned

Code	Site	Type	Size (km²)	Altitude	Flora	Examples of Useful Plants	Vegetation	Protected Areas	Threats	Assessment
CHINA AND EAST ASIA										
China										
EA1	Changbai Mts region, Jilin	F	30,000	300–2691 m	2000–2500	>80 medicinal spp.; timber trees, fruits, fodder plants	Coniferous and broadleaved forests, meadows, tundra, alpine vegetation	NR/BR (1906 km²)	Logging, tourism, over-collection of medicinal plants	Area lacks effective management; at risk
EA26	Gaoligong Mts, Nu Jiang River and Biluo Snow Mts, Yunnan	F	10,000	1090–5128 m	2000	Timber trees, medicinal plants, ornamental plants	Evergreen broadleaved and sub-alpine coniferous forests, alpine vegetation	2 NRs (4994 km²)	Clearance for cultivation	Part safe; part severely threatened
EA27	Tropical forests of Hainan Island	V	33,920	0–1867 m	4200–4500	>2900 species used locally; timber trees, medicinal plants, rattans, wild litchi	Tropical lowland seasonal rain and monsoon forests, montane seasonal rain forest, mangroves, savanna	51 NRs cover c. 1500 km² (including marine reserves)	Clearance for cultivation, illegal logging, over-collection of medicinal plants	Severely threatened; reserve coverage adequate, but lack of funds and trained personnel
EA40	High Mountain and Deep Gorge region, Hengduan Mts and Min Jiang River basin, Sichuan	F	4000	600–6250 m	>4000	Medicinal plants, timber trees, oil and starch plants, bamboos	Evergreen and semi-deciduous broadleaved forests, coniferous forests, alpine scrub and meadows, savanna	BR (2072 km²) including NR (2000 km²)	Logging, visitor pressure, road building, over-collection of medicinal plants	Area lacks effective management; at risk
EA31	Limestone region, Zhuang Autonomous Region	F	20,000	100–1300 m	2500–3000	>1000 species used locally; timbers, medicines, bamboo, rattan, ornamentals	Seasonal rain forest, montane evergreen broadleaved and limestone forests	11 NRs (4000 km²)	Illegal timber cutting, lack of conservation awareness by local people	Protected areas need effective management; severely threatened
EA13	Nanling Mt Range	F	30,000	200–2142 m	>3000	>800 spp. used locally; medicinal plants, timber trees, fruits, oil, fibres, dyes, wild vegetables	Evergreen broadleaved forest, montane semi-deciduous broadleaved mixed forests	17 NRs (c. 5000 km²)	Clearance for cultivation, over-collection of medicinal plants	Part safe; part severely threatened
EA6	Taibai Mt region of Qinling Mts, Shaanxi	F	2779	500–3767 m	1900	Medicinal plants, oils, fibres, tannins, fodder plants	Broadleaved deciduous and mixed deciduous evergreen forests, sub-alpine coniferous forests, alpine vegetation	NR (540 km²)	Logging, illegal collection of medicinal plants, tourist pressure	Part safe; part severely threatened
EA29	Xishuangbanna region, Yunnan	F	19,690	500–2429 m	4000–4500	>800 medicinal species, 128 timber trees, bamboos, rattans, fruits	Tropical lowland and montane seasonal rain forests, evergreen dipterocarp forest, monsoon forest, montane evergreen broadleaved forest	5 NRs (2416 km²)	Slash and burn agriculture, clearance for plantation crops, illegal logging, colonization	Severely threatened; reserves cover major plant-rich sites, but threats continue and management inadequate
Japan										
EA49	Mount Hakusan	S	480	1700–2702 m	1300	Timber trees, ornamental plants	Montane deciduous forests, subalpine coniferous forests, alpine vegetation	BR (whole area), NP (477 km²)	Tourism, plant collecting, introduced plants	Management needs strengthening; at risk

Code	Site	Type	Size (km²)	Altitude	Flora	Examples of Useful Plants	Vegetation	Protected Areas	Threats	Assessment
EA50	Yakushima	S	503	0–1935 m	1343*	Genetic resources of the timber tree Cryptomeria japonica	Evergreen broadleaved and laurel forests, Cryptomeria forest, montane scrub	NP covers almost all of island, BR (190 km²)	Tourism	Urgent conservation measures needed; threatened
Korea										
EA44	Mount Halla (Cheju Do)	S	151	800–1950 m	1453	Medicinal plants, fibres, timber trees, ornamental plants	Deciduous broadleaved forest, coniferous forest, scrub, secondary grassland	NP (151 km²), mostly including NR (91 km²)	Visitor pressure, over-collection of medicinal and ornamental plants	Reasonably safe, but summit vegetation at risk from trampling and measures to protect rare species need to be implemented
Taiwan										
EA41	Kenting NP	S	177 (land)	0–526 m	1350	Timber trees, medicinal plants, legumes, ornamental plants	Evergreen broadleaved rain forest, semi-deciduous and littoral forests, grassland, scrub	NP	Tourism, grazing, plant collecting, military facilities	Generally well protected, some parts under threat
Thailand										
EA53	Doi Chiang Dao WS	S	521	<800–2175 m	1200	Teak (logged out) edible fruits	Lowland mixed evergreen-deciduous and dipterocarp-oak forests, montane forest	WS	Fire	Vulnerable
EA55	Doi Suthep-pui NP	S	261	360–1685 m	2063* taxa	Timber trees, bamboos, fruit trees, medicinal and ornamental plants, mushrooms	Monsoon forests, incl. lowland dipterocarp-oak and mixed evergreen-deciduous forests, pine forests	NP, BR (whole area)	Encroachment, tourism, road building, tree cutting, fire, over-collecting of ornamental plants	Lack of resources for conservation measures to be implemented fully; threatened
EA57	Khao Yai NP	S	2168	100–1351 m	2000–2500	Medicinal plants, rattans	Moist evergreen forest, dry evergreen and mixed deciduous forests, grassland	NP	Encroachment of agriculture, illegal logging, over-collection of forest products, dam construction	Threatened around perimeter; conservation and development programme underway
EA59	Thung Yai-Huai Kha Khaeng WHS	S	6427	200–1811 m	>2500	Crop relatives, ornamental plants	Lowland evergreen and deciduous forests, evergreen montane forest	WS/WHS	Encroachment of agriculture, logging, fire, potential dam construction	Management under-resourced; threatened
Vietnam										
EA62	Bach Ma-Hai Van	S	600	0–1450 m	2500	200 timber trees, 108 medicinals, ornamentals, fibres, rattans, edible fruits	Lowland evergreen forest, tropical montane evergreen forest	NP (220 km²), 2 Environment Protection Forests	High local population density, felling of timber trees, fuelwood cutting	Threatened
EA63	Cat Tien BR	S	1372	60–754 m	2500	200 timber trees, 120 medicinals, rattans, bamboos, orchids	Lowland evergreen and semi-deciduous forests, freshwater swamps, bamboos	BR includes NP (379 km²), Rhino Sanctuary (360 km²)	Illegal logging, over-exploitation of rattans and resins	Reasonably secure
EA64	Cuc Phuong NP	S	300	200–636 m	1980*	Timber trees, medicinal plants, bamboos, ornamental plants	Lowland evergreen forest, incl. limestone forest, semi-deciduous forest	NP (222 km²)	Illegal felling of timber trees, fuelwood cutting	Reasonably secure

Code	Site	Type	Size (km²)	Altitude	Flora	Examples of Useful Plants	Vegetation	Protected Areas	Threats	Assessment
EA65	Langbian-Dalat Highland	S	4000	1400–2289 m	2000	100 medicinal plants, ornamental plants (especially orchids), resin trees, rattans	Pine forest, tropical montane evergreen forest, subtropical montane forest	3 NRs (535 km²)	Logging, slash and burn cultivation, fire	Severely threatened
EA66	Yok Don NP	S	650	200–482 m	1500	150 timber trees, tannins, resin trees, edible fruits, ornamental plants	Dry dipterocarp forest, lowland semi-evergreen forest, riverine forest	NP (580 km²)	Illegal logging, hunting, forest fires	Threatened
EUROPE										
Bulgaria/Greece/Serbia										
Eu14	Balkan and Rhodope Massifs	F	10,000	400–2900 m	3000	Medicinal plants, timber trees, ornamental plants	Oak and mixed deciduous forests, fir/spruce forests, shiblyak, grasslands, montane and alpine vegetation	Several NPs; 4 BRs (140 km²)	Tourism, agriculture, overgrazing, fire, political conflicts, changes in land tenure	Extensive and expanding areas under protection; some threats arising from new political order
Cyprus										
Eu18	Troodos Mts	S	1800	1000–1960 m	1650	Timber trees, medicinal herbs, ornamentals	Evergreen scrub, some evergreen oak and coniferous forests, rock and cliff communities	Some areas of forest protected	Tourism and skiing development, road building, fire	Conflict between tourism and conservation, but forests well protected
France/Spain/Andorra										
Eu10	Pyrenees	F	30,000	0–3404 m	3500	c. 20 timber spp., 600 medicinal plant spp., honey and food plants, ornamentals	Evergreen forests, semi-deciduous and deciduous forests, montane and subalpine vegetation, coniferous forests	c. 50 protected areas, including 3 NPs, 7 NatPs, numerous NRs	Tourism, fires, overgrazing leading to soil erosion	Some areas well protected; others threatened
Germany/Austria/France/Italy/Liechtenstein/Slovenia/Switzerland										
Eu11	Alps	F	200,000	100–4800 m	5500	Medicinal plants, food plants, timber trees; 0–20% of the flora is traditionally used	Broadleaved and coniferous forests, meadows, marshes, alpine grasslands, scree/rock vegetation	9 NPs, many NRs; national and regional legislation	Tourism and associated development, intensive land management, hydroelectric schemes, possibly global warming	Threatened; conflict between tourism and conservation. Legislation needs to be enforced
Greece										
Eu17	Crete	F	8700	0–2456 m	1600	Crop relatives, culinary herbs, ornamentals	Evergreen scrub, fragments of evergreen oak, pine and cypress forest, rock and cliff vegetation	1 NP (48.5 km²), a few other small reserves	Tourism, agricultural and industrial developments, plant collecting	Protected area coverage inadequate, but threats less acute than in many other areas
Eu16	Mountains of Southern and Central Greece	F	18,000	1000–2495 m	4000	Timber trees, culinary herbs, chickpea relative	Coniferous and deciduous forests; rock, cliff and scree vegetation	4 NPs (173 km²)	Fire, overgrazing, tourism, mining, plant collecting	Threatened
Spain										
Eu4	Baetic and Sub-Baetic Mts	F	18,000	0–3481 m	>3000	Lavender, thyme and other perfumes, medicinal plants, pines, cork oak, wild olives, ornamentals	Evergreen oak forest, deciduous/coniferous woodlands, pine-juniper scrub, pastures, scree vegetation	13 NatPs (7700 km²)	Overgrazing, urbanisation, tourism, fires, agriculture, plant collecting	Threatened: coastal regions particularly by tourism, montane areas by overgrazing

Code	Site	Type	Size (km²)	Altitude	Flora	Examples of Useful Plants	Vegetation	Protected Areas	Threats	Assessment
Eu7	Massifs of Gudar and Javalambre	F	445	1200–2020 m	>1500	Timber trees (especially pines), medicinal plants	Juniper and pine woodlands, grassland, rock communities	None; until recently traditional land management conserved area well	Tourist developments (e.g. ski resorts)	Until recently well conserved; now threatened
Ukraine/Russia										
Eu21	South Crimean Mountains and Novorossia	F	80,500	0–1200 m	2200	Fruits, medicinal plants, aromatic plants, ornamentals	Maquis, shiblyak; oak, pine, pine-beech woodland, grassland	Crimea: 3 Reserves (160.8 km²), Game Preserve (150 km²); 5 Refuges; Novorossia: 15 Refuges for selected biotopes	Forest clearance, pollution, over-collection of ornamental and medicinal plants	Inadequate reserve coverage; threatened
INDIAN OCEAN ISLANDS										
IO1	Madagascar	F	587,000	0–2876 m	9345	Medicinal plants, fibres, timber trees, edible plants, crop relatives, ornamentals	Rain forest, dry deciduous forest, montane forests, tapia forest, bushland, thicket, mangroves	38 protected areas covering c. 0.7% of land area, 2 BRs, 1 WHS (1520 km²); protected forests cover 4.6% of land area	Clearance for agriculture, fire, overgrazing, mining, tree felling, plant collecting, invasive species	Many important plant sites included in existing protected areas but level of protection inadequate; threatened
Mauritius/Reunion										
IO2	Mascarene Islands	F	4481	0–3069 m	>955 angiosp. taxa	Timber trees (e.g. black ebony) virtually exhausted, palm hearts, coffee relatives, ornamentals	Tropical/subtropical coastal and dry lowland forests to moist montane forests, high-altitude heath	Mauritius: NP & numerous NRs cover 2.4% of land area, BR (36 km²); Rodrigues: 3 NRs (58 ha); Réunion: 1 NR (68 ha), more proposed	Invasive plants, introduced animals, development pressure, population pressure	Réunion: inadequate reserve system; Mauritius and Rodrigues: good reserve network but flora severely threatened
IO3	Seychelles (granitic islands)	F	230	0–905 m	200 angiosp.	Timber trees (over-exploited in past), medicinal plants	Lowland rain forest, hygrophile peak forest, coastal forest, mangroves	2 NPs (37 km²), 8 NRs, 2 SpNRs (351 km²), 2 PAs, 2 WHS	Invasive plants, tourist pressure	Good reserve coverage, but some important areas not covered, management needed; at risk
INDIAN SUBCONTINENT										
India										
IS7	Agastyamalai Hills	F	2000	67–1868 m	2000	Medicinal herbs, timber trees, bamboos, rattans, crop relatives	Tropical dry to wet forests	3 Sanctuaries and a number of RFs protect c. 919 km²; proposed BR	Clearance for hydro-electric projects, plantations, tourism, fire, grazing	Some areas threatened
IS17	Andaman and Nicobar Islands	F	8249	0–726 m	2270	Rice and pepper relatives, timber trees, rattans	Tropical evergreen, semi-evergreen and moist deciduous forests, beach forest, bamboo scrub, mangroves	c. 500 km² land protected in 6 parks, 94 Sanctuaries (mostly small islets); part of Great Nicobar proposed as BR, proposed North Andaman BR	Population pressure, logging, hydroelectric schemes, clearance for agriculture	Some areas severely threatened; some areas reasonably safe at present; protected area coverage inadequate
IS9	Nallamalai Hills	F	7640	300–939 m	758*	Medicinal plants, rice and pepper relatives, bamboos, timbers	Dry and moist deciduous forests, dry evergreen forest, scrub	WS covers 357 km²	Forest clearance, bamboo cutting for paper, fire, fuelwood cutting	Severely threatened

Code	Site	Type	Size (km²)	Altitude	Flora	Examples of Useful Plants	Vegetation	Protected Areas	Threats	Assessment
IS4	Namdapha	S	7000	200–4578 m	5000	Wild relatives of banana, citrus, pepper; timber trees, ornamental plants	Tropical evergreen and semi-evergreen rain forests, alpine vegetation	NP (1985 km²); whole area proposed as BR with core of c. 2500 km²	Shifting cultivation, refugees and other settlers, illegal timber felling	Core area not threatened; perimeter areas under threat
IS2	Nanda Devi	S	2000	1000–7817 m	900* angiosp.	Medicinal plants, ornamental plants, edible plants	Coniferous, birch and rhododendron forests, alpine vegetation	NP and WHS (630 km²), proposed as BR	No major threats; potential dam construction	Effectively secure
IS8	Nilgiri Hills	F	5520	250–2500 m	3240	Medicinal plants, timber trees, fruit tree relatives	Tropical evergreen rain forest to tropical dry thorn forest, montane shola forest and grassland	Several NPs (incl. Silent Valley NP – 89.5 km²), Sanctuaries and RFs; proposed BR	Forest clearance for timber, plantations, roads, development projects	Some areas threatened
Myanmā (Burma)										
IS14	Bago (Pegu) Yomas	F	40,000	100–821 m	2000	Timber trees (especially teak)	Wet evergreen dipterocarp forest, moist and dry teak forests, bamboo scrub	Proposed NP (146 km²), some RFs	Slash and burn cultivation, road building, dam construction	Protection needs strengthening; threatened
IS5	Natma Taung (Mt Victoria) and Rongklang Range (Chin Hills)	F	25,000	500–3053 m	2500	Gingers, peppers, ornamental plants (e.g. orchids)	Tropical and temperate semi-evergreen forests, subtropical evergreen forests, savanna, alpine vegetation	Proposed NP (364 km²)	Slash and burn agriculture	Threatened
IS6	North Myanmā	F	115,712	150–5881 m	6000	Medicinal plants, bamboos, rice	Lowland tropical evergreen rain forest to cool temperate rain forest, pine-oak forest, subalpine scrub	GS (705 km²), WS (215 km²); important plant sites not protected	Slash and burn agriculture	Threatened; inadequate coverage of protected areas
IS16	Taninthayi (Tenasserim)	F	73,845	0–2275 m	3000	Timber trees (especially teak, rosewood), dyes, vegetables, fibres, medicinal plants	Wet evergreen dipterocarp forests to montane rain forest, bamboo scrub, mangroves	WS (49 km²), GS (139 km²), proposed NR (259 km²)	Logging, resin tapping, fuelwood cutting	Severely threatened in north, inadequate coverage of protected areas
Sri Lanka										
IS11	Knuckles	S	182	1068–1906 m	>1000	Timbers, medicinal plants, bamboos, fruit tree relatives, spices, ornamental plants	Lowland dry semi-evergreen to montane evergreen forests, grasslands	No legal protection	Clearance for cardamom, settlements and agriculture, mining, fuelwood cutting	Area below 1200 m under threat
IS12	Peak Wilderness and Horton Plains	S	224/32	700–2238 m/ 1800–2389 m	>1000	Timbers, medicinal plants, bamboos, fruit tree relatives, spices, ornamental plants	Lowland, submontane and montane wet evergreen forests, montane grassland	Sanctuary (Peak Wilderness), NP (Horton Plains)	Religious tourism, fuelwood and timber cutting, mining, fire, invasive grasses	Reasonably secure, but management plan required; some rich forests in upper regions should also be included in protected areas
IS13	Sinharaja	S	112	210–1170 m	700 angiosp.	Timber trees, rattans, fruit tree relatives, medicinal plants, ornamentals	Lowland and submontane wet tropical evergreen rain forests, grasslands	National Heritage Wilderness Area and WHS	Population pressure, encroachment of agriculture, over-collection of medicinal plants, potential hydroelectric scheme	Southern part still under threat, otherwise threats declining and reasonably secure

Code	Site	Type	Size (km²)	Altitude	Flora	Examples of Useful Plants	Vegetation	Protected Areas	Threats	Assessment
MIDDLE AMERICA										
Costa Rica										
MA16	Braulio Carrillo–La Selva region	S	500	35–2906 m	4000–6000	Timber trees, ornamental plants (incl. *Monstera*), vanilla, edible palms	Tropical wet forest to montane rain forests	NP, Biological Station, BR	Ecological isolation, local population pressure, illegal logging, agriculture, grazing	Reasonably secure, but at risk
MA18	Osa Peninsula and Corcovado NP	F	2330	0–745 m	4000–5000	Timber trees, medicinal plants, fruit trees, fibres	Mostly tropical wet forest; also premontane and cloud forests, swamp forest, mangroves	NP (572 km²), FoR (819 km²), small Amerindian reserve, regional Conservation Areas	Mining, logging, road building, colonization	Threatened
Costa Rica/Panama										
MA17	La Amistad BR	S	>10,000	0–3819 m	10,000	Timber trees, medicinal plants, dyes, ornamental plants	Lowland humid forest to subalpine rain páramo	Costa Rica: BR and WHS (6126 km²); Panama: 3 NPs (2345 km²), FoR (200 km²), PF (1250 km²), planned BR	Colonization, agriculture, cattle ranching, fire, oil pipelines, potential mining, road building	Threatened
Guatemala										
MA13	Petén region and Maya BR	F	36,000	10–800 m	3000	Mahogany, edible palms, parlour palms, medicinal plants	Subtropical semi-deciduous moist forest, savanna, wetlands	Maya BR (c. 15,000 km²)	Logging, road building, colonization, grazing, slash and burn agriculture, oil exploration	Region under threat
MA14	Sierra de las Minas region and BR	F	4374	150–3015 m	>2000	Timber trees (e.g. pines), tree ferns, bamboos, medicinal and edible plants	Tropical dry forest and thorn scrub, tropical wet forest to premontane dry forest	BR (2363 km²)	Clearance for agriculture, colonization, logging, road building	BR reasonably safe, other areas threatened
Honduras										
MA15	N.E. Honduras and Río Plátano BR	S	5250	0–1500 m	>2000	Timber trees (especially mahogany and tropical cedar), many plants used locally	Mostly humid tropical and subtropical forests; also mangroves, savanna	BR and WHS (whole area)	Logging, shifting agriculture, cattle grazing, road building, colonization, mining	Threatened
Mexico										
MA5	Cañon of the Zopilote region	F	4383	600–3100 m	>2000	Softwood and hardwood timber trees, medicinal plants, plants of cultural value	Deciduous tropical forest, oak and coniferous forests, montane forests	Ecological SP (36 km²)	Logging, agricultural encroachment, coffee plantations, colonization, potential road building	Inadequate coverage of protected areas; threatened
MA12	Central region of Baja California Peninsula	F	36,000	0–1985 m	>500	Food and fodder plants, medicinal plants, ornamental plants, fuelwood species	Desert vegetation, lagoon communities	BR covers 15,000 km² (c. 42%) of region	Overgrazing, expansion of agriculture, salinization, road building, mining, oil and gas exploration	Severely threatened
MA10	Cuetro Ciénegas region	F	2000	740–3000 m	860*	Timber trees, forage plants, medicinal plants	Grasslands, dune communities, desert scrub, oak-pine woodlands, montane coniferous forests	None	Mining, clearance for agriculture, overgrazing, plant collecting (especially of cacti)	Threatened

Code	Site	Type	Size (km²)	Altitude	Flora	Examples of Useful Plants	Vegetation	Protected Areas	Threats	Assessment
MA9	Gómez Farías region and El Cielo BR	F	2400	200–2200 m	>1000	Temperate and tropical timber trees, fibres, medicinal plants, ornamental plants	Tropical dry forest, tropical semi-deciduous forest, cloud forest, oak and pine forests, scrub	El Cielo BR (1445 km²)	Logging, grazing, agriculture (incl. shifting cultivation), fire, expanding settlements	Regulations to protect BR need to be enforced; threatened, although some areas remote and safe
MA1	Lacandon Rain Forest region	F	6000	80–1750 m	4000	Timber, fruit and spice trees, chicle gum, ornamental palms	Tropical lowland to montane rain forests, semi-deciduous forest, cloud forest, savanna, seasonally-inundated forest, wetlands	2 BRs (3931 km²), 2 NMs (70 km²), Flora & Fauna Reserve (122 km²)	Road building, logging, colonization, clearance for agriculture, cattle grazing, oil drilling	>50% of forest lost, much of rest going at an accelerating rate; severely threatened
MA7	Pacific lowlands, Jalisco: Chamela Biological Station and Cumbres de Cuixmala Reserve	F	350	0–500 m	1120*	Valuable timber trees (e.g. rosewood, lignum vitae), potential ornamentals	Tropical deciduous and semi-deciduous forests	1 Biological Station (1.6 km²), 1 Reserve (7 km²)	Clearance for agriculture, resort development, logging	Reserves reasonably safe, but inadequate coverage; no protection of coastal palm forest; threatened
MA3	Sierra de Juárez	F	1700	500–3250 m	2000	Medicinal plants, timber trees, ornamental plants	Mainly montane cloud forest; also tropical evergreen forest, pine and pine-oak forests	None	Logging, grazing, colonization, fire, clearance for agriculture, plant collecting, potential dam construction	Severely threatened
MA6	Sierra de Manantlán region and BR	S	1396	400–2860 m	2800	>500 spp. have been used traditionally; wild perennial maize, wild beans, oaks, pines	Tropical deciduous and semi-deciduous forests to cloud forest, fir and pine-oak forests	BR	Logging, fire, agriculture, cattle ranching, fuelwood cutting	About 30% in good condition; threatened, although some areas safe
MA4	Tehuacán-Cuicatlán region	F	9000	600–2200 m	2700	Cacti and other ornamental plants, medicinal plants, fibres	Sclerophyll scrub, thorn scrub, early-deciduous forest	BG (1 km²)	Agriculture, overgrazing by goats, salinization, plant collecting (especially of cacti)	Threatened
MA8	Upper Mezquital River region, Sierra Madre Occidental	F	4600	800–3350 m	2900	>450 species used by local people, including food and medicinal plants; timber trees	Conifer, pine-oak and oak forests, some tropical semi-deciduous forest	BR (700 km²)	Logging, overgrazing, road building	Threatened
MA2	Uxpanapa-Chimalapa region	F	7700	100–2250 m	3500	Timber trees (including mahogany), ornamental palms, fruit trees	Evergreen and semi-evergreen rain forest, montane rain forest	None	Logging, colonization, agriculture, grazing, construction of dams and roads	Threatened
Mexico/U.S.A.										
MA11	Apachian/Madrean region	F	180,000	500–3500 m	4000	180 wild relatives of crop plants, >300 food plants, >450 medicinal plants	Coniferous, oak-coniferous and tropical deciduous forests, savanna, chapparal, thorn scrub	<10% of region protected in Mexico; most of region in U.S.A. has some form of protection	Logging, erosion, agricultural encroachment, overgrazing	Part safe, but majority of region not formally protected; areas in northern Mexico severely threatened
Panama										
MA19	Cerro Azul-Cerro Jefe region	S	53	300–1007 m	934*	Timber trees, ornamental plants, potential medicinal plants	Tropical premontane wet and rain forests, tropical wet forest	Whole area within Chagres NP	Grazing, agricultural encroachment, fire	At risk

Code	Site	Type	Size (km²)	Altitude	Flora	Examples of Useful Plants	Vegetation	Protected Areas	Threats	Assessment
MA20	Darién Province and Darién NP	F	16,671	0–1875 m	2440*	Cativo and other valuable timbers, medicinal plants	Tropical lowland dry, moist and wet forests, swamps, premontane and montane forests, cloud forest	NP (also a WHS and BR) covers 5790 km²	Logging, mining, agriculture, colonization, proposed Pan-American Highway	Threatened
NORTH AMERICA										
U.S.A.										
NA16	California Floristic Province	F	324,000	0–4400 m	3500	Timber trees and other forest products, wild grape, ornamental plants, medicinal plants	Coniferous and mixed evergreen forests, oak woodlands, chaparral, coastal scrub, grassland	Parks and reserves protect c. 11% of land area, mostly montane	Population pressure, urban and agricultural development, mining, dams, overgrazing, exotic weeds, off-road vehicle recreation	Highlands reasonably well protected; lowland habitats threatened and inadequately protected
NA29	Central Highlands, Florida	F	10,000	20–94 m	3500	Few timber trees, food plants, potential insecticides	Xerophytic pine and oak scrub, palmetto flatwoods, wetlands	State, federal and private reserves, state and local parks	Citrus plantations, urban, tourist and recreational developments	Inadequate protected area coverage; threatened
NA32	Edwards Plateau, Texas	F	100,000	100–1000 m	2300	Forage species, juniper oil, few timber trees	Semi-arid temperate semi-evergreen forest, grassland, semi-desert scrub	State and municipal parks, several reserves cover <0.05% of region	Clearance for agriculture, grazing, dams, urbanization, introduced species	Protected area coverage very inadequate; threatened
NA16c	Klamath-Siskiyou region	F	55,000	0–2750 m	3500	Timber trees, beargrass, medicinal plants, including *Taxus brevifolia* for cancer drug	Coniferous and mixed evergreen forests, prairies, savanna, subalpine meadows	WAs, NatMs, federal, state and private reserves	Logging, agriculture, urbanization, mining, dams, tourism	Most is relatively safe due to remoteness, but logging and mining are considerable threats
U.S.A./Canada										
NA25	Serpentine flora	V	4550	0–2200 m		Flax and sunflower relatives adapted to low nutrient soils	Grasslands, chaparral, montane woodland	Frenzel Creek Research Natural Area (2.7 km²), TNC Ring Mountain Preserve (25 ha)	Mining, logging, off-road vehicle recreation, urbanization	Inadequate protected area coverage; threatened
U.S.A./Mexico										
NA16g	Vernal pools (California and Baja California)	V	20,000	0–600 m (–2500 m)	>200	*Limnanthes* is potential sperm whale oil substitute, ornamental plants	Annual herbs, wet grassland, aquatics, oak and pine forests	Numerous small pools protected, but more reserves needed	Agriculture, grazing, urban development, mining	Inadequate protected area coverage; severely threatened
PACIFIC OCEAN ISLANDS*										
Chile										
PO8*	Juan Fernández	F	100	0–1319 m	210*	Some potential horticultural species	Mainly forested	NP	Feral animals, invasive plants	Flora acutely threatened; WWF-sponsored rescue programme underway
Ecuador										
PO7*	Galápagos Islands	F	7900	0–1707 m	541*	Tomato and cotton relatives, native timber trees	Wide range of generally arid vegetation types, *Scalesia* forests (much reduced on higher islands)	NP: 7278 km² (96.7% of land area); WHS and BR (7665 km²)	Feral animals, invasive plants, over-exploitation of native woody species, increasing human population, fire	Many plants still at risk despite conservation measures

*Please note that the Data Sheet site codes for the Pacific Ocean Islands have been revised since Volume 1 was published; the codes in Volume 2 are the correct ones.

Code	Site	Type	Size (km²)	Altitude	Flora	Examples of Useful Plants	Vegetation	Protected Areas	Threats	Assessment
PO3*	**Fiji**	F	18,270	0–1324 m	1628	Timber trees, medicinal plants, culturally important plants	Tropical rain, dry and montane forests, grassland, scrub, coastal vegetation	16 protected areas (65 km²) incl. 8 NRs (62 km², mainly rain forest), 1 NP (2.4 km², coastal), several other small forest parks	Logging, clearance for agriculture, feral animals, invasive plants, population pressure, tourism, mining	Threatened; reserves and funding inadequate, numerous proposals never implemented. Need involvement of local population
	French Polynesia									
PO5*	Marquesas	F	1275	0–1260 m	318*	Ornamental species, food plants	Lowland forest, remnants of dry forest, grasslands, xerophytic scrub	4 reserves, but inadequate coverage	Overgrazing, introduced species, fire, many species reduced to small populations	Severely threatened
	New Caledonia									
PO2*	Grande Terre	F	16,890	0–1628 m	3322	Timber trees, ornamental plants, medicinal plants, aromatic plants	Humid evergreen and sclerophyll forests, maquis, mangroves, marshes	9% covered by protected areas, incl. 13 Special Botanical Reserves (155 km²), 1 of which has Strict Nature Reserve status, and 4 Provincial Parks (105 km²)	Fire, mining, clearance for agriculture and grazing, urbanization, invasive plants	Coverage of protected areas inadequate. Sclerophyll and calcareous forests particularly threatened, along with many point endemics
	Japan									
PO1*	Bonin (Ogasawara) Islands	F	73	0–462 m	456*	Ornamental plants (orchids)	Broadleaved evergreen forest, but mostly destroyed	NP (61 km²)	Population pressure, grazing, introduced plants	NP, but much degraded and highly endangered
	U.S.A.									
PO6*	Hawaiian Islands	F	16,641	0–4205 m	1200	Native plants used by indigenous people for all their needs; ornamentals, hardwood trees	Wide range of vegetation types: dry to mesic lowland to subalpine forests, shrublands, grasslands, herblands	2029 km² (12% of land area) protected in many state, federal and private reserves, but not all plant-rich communities covered	Development, introduced plants and animals, fire	Possibly the most endangered island flora in the world; severely threatened
	Western Samoa/American Samoa									
PO4*	Samoan Islands	F	3114	0–1857 m	775	Timber trees, >100 medicinal plants, incl. possible cancer & AIDS treatments	Coastal, lowland and montane rain forests, cloud forest, upland and volcanic scrub, mangroves, marshes	Proposed NPs on Tutuila and Ta'u, American Samoa; 2 village-level reserves on Western Samoa	Increasing population pressure, shifting cultivation, cash crops, logging, invasive plants, hydroelectric scheme	Severely threatened; lowland forests almost eliminated, montane forests increasingly threatened
SOUTH AMERICA										
	Argentina									
SA35	Anconquija region	F	6000	400–5550 m	2000	Timber trees, crop relatives (e.g. tomato relatives), medicinal and ornamental plants	Amazonian winter-dry rain forest to temperate cloud forest, Andean páramo grassland, spiny shrubland	Several protected areas covering c. 370 km², proposed NP of 3000 km²	Logging, clearance for agriculture, grazing, plant collecting, road building, dams, potential mining	Varying degrees of threat; some protected areas reasonably secure, remote areas self-protected; other areas severely threatened
	Argentina/Chile									
SA34	Altoandina					(Information not available)				
SA46	Patagonia	F	500,000	0–2000 m	1200	Forage plants, many species used traditionally for food and medicine	Steppe shrublands and grasslands	Lower portions of 3 NPs/NRs, all of 1 NP/NR (112 km²), 1 NatM (100 km²)	Overgrazing, desertification	Inadequate coverage of protected areas, some areas threatened

*Please note that the Data Sheet site codes for the Pacific Ocean Islands have been revised since Volume 1 was published; the codes in Volume 2 are the correct ones.

Code	Site	Type	Size (km²)	Altitude	Flora	Examples of Useful Plants	Vegetation	Protected Areas	Threats	Assessment
Argentina/Paraguay/Bolivia/Brazil										
SA22	Gran Chaco	F	1,010,000	100–2795 m	1200	Timber trees, medicinal plants, ornamentals, fibres	Xerophytic deciduous to semi-evergreen forests, palm woodlands, savanna, steppes, wetlands	6 NPs and 1 National NR cover 12,720 km² (c. 1%) of region	Logging, agricultural development, oil and gas exploration, road building, colonization, fire	Inadequate protected area coverage, none at all in Bolivian part; some areas threatened
Bolivia										
SA24	Llanos de Mojos region	F	270,000	130–235 m	5000	Forage grasses, legumes, rubber, Brazil nut, palm hearts, pineapple relatives	Mosaic of savanna and various evergreen forest types, wetlands	BR (1350 km²), FoRs, Biological Station, Amerindian territories, regional park, private reserves	Overgrazing, fire, road building, logging	Inadequate protected area coverage; key forest areas severely threatened
SA36	Madidi-Apolo region	F	30,000	250–2000 m	>5000	Timber trees (e.g. mahogany), quinine, medicinal plants, ornamental plants, palm oils	Mainly humid evergreen tropical montane forest, dry forest, cloud forest, grasslands	Proposed NP (18,000 km²)	Logging, road building, colonization, oil exploration	Mostly intact, but without protection; threatened
SA23	South-eastern Santa Cruz	F	70,000	350–1157 m	2000–2500	Timber trees, forage grasses, *Copernicia* palms for telephone poles, forage plants	Dry forest, savanna (cerrado and campo rupestre), wetlands, thorn scrub	National Historical Park (c. 170 km²), 2 proposed NPs (39,000 km²), proposed FoRs, proposed Biological Reserve (6000 km²)	Cattle ranching, agriculture, mining, gas pipeline, road building	Inadequate coverage of protected areas; severely threatened
Brazil										
SA12	Atlantic moist forest of southern Bahia	V	3500	0–1000 m	1500–2200	Brazil-wood, rosewood, and other valuable timbers	Tropical Atlantic rain forest, semi- and dry deciduous forests, littoral forest	<300 km² or <0.1% of original wet forests protected in 6 reserves	Logging, clearance for cattle grazing, cash crops and subsistence agriculture, pulpwood plantations	Inadequate coverage of protected areas, even existing reserves inadequately protected; severely threatened
SA14	Cabo Frio region	F	1500	0–500 m	1500–2200	Brazil-wood, medicinal plants	Coastal evergreen scrub, xeromorphic forest, mangroves, submontane rain forest	Protected areas cover c. 10% of region	Land development, tourism, clearance for cattle grazing, sugar cane plantations	Inadequate coverage of protected areas, even existing reserves inadequately protected; severely threatened
SA19	Caatinga of north-eastern Brazil	V	1,000,000	0–1000 m		Forage plants, fruits, timber trees, palms	Xerophytic deciduous forest to sparse scrub, savanna, gallery and montane forests, cerrado, grassland	3 NPs (1048 km²), 5 Biological Reserves (132 km²), 5 Ecological Stations (13,602 km²), 1 National Forest (383 km²), 2 Environmental Protection Zones	Overgrazing, timber and fuelwood extraction, agriculture, salinization, plant collecting	Inadequate coverage of protected areas; severely threatened
SA21	Distrito Federal	F	5814	750–1336 m	>3000	Timbers, fruit trees, medicinal plants, ornamental plants	Gallery, mesophytic and cerrado forests, wetlands, savannas	Protected areas cover only 3.2% of region and do not protect full range of vegetation types	Population pressure, fires, invasive species, potential dam construction	Inadequate funding and coverage of existing reserves; threatened
SA20	Espinhaço Range region	F	7000	1000–2107 m	>4000	Fruit trees, ornamental plants, medicinal plants	Mainly campo rupestre, with cerrado, marshes, montane to dry deciduous forests	2 NPs (1858 km²), 2 SPs (430 km²), Ecological Station, 3 Environmental Protection Zones	Grazing, erosion, fire, charcoal production, plant collecting, hydroelectric schemes, road building, mining	Inadequate coverage of protected areas; threatened

Code	Site	Type	Size (km²)	Altitude	Flora	Examples of Useful Plants	Vegetation	Protected Areas	Threats	Assessment
SA17	Juréia-Itatins Ecological Station	S	792	0–800 m	>500	Timber trees, edible palms, medicinal plants, ornamental plants	Tropical Atlantic rain forest, restinga forest and scrub, littoral forest, mangroves, grassland	Ecological Station	Illegal logging, over-collection of palm hearts	Isolated and relatively secure
SA5	Manaus region	F	71,000	16–130 m	>1000 tree spp.	Timber trees, rosewood, Brazil nut, fruit trees, edible palms	Terra firme rain forest, permanently and seasonally inundated forests, caatinga forest, scrub, grasslands	Numerous protected areas	Clearance for cattle ranching, oil palm plantations, urban expansion, road building	Inadequate reserve coverage, no várzea (inundated) forests protected nearby
SA15	Mountain ranges of Rio de Janeiro	F	7000	60–2800 m	5000–6000	Timber trees (e.g. Brazil-wood), palmito palm hearts, medicinal plants, ornamental plants	Tropical Atlantic rain forests, high-altitude fields	20 conservation areas cover c. 3220 km² (46%) of region	Clearance for agriculture, settlements, over-collecting of palms and ornamentals, logging	Protected areas lack management plans; forests outside protected areas severely threatened
SA16	Serra do Japi	S	354	800–1300 m	300* tree spp.	Timber trees, fruit trees, medicinal and ornamental plants	Semi-deciduous forests, semi-arid vegetation on rock outcrops	"Historical patrimony" (191 km²), Environmental Protection Zone, small municipal reserve	Population pressure leading to clearance for settlements, industrial developments, logging, air pollution, fire, mining, tourism	Protection status needs strengthening; severely threatened
SA13	Tabuleiro forests, N. Espirito Santo	V	484	28–90 m	637* tree spp.	Timber trees, resins, oils, medicinal plants	Tropical Atlantic rain forest, várzea forest, savanna	FoR (220 km²), 2 Biological Reserves (264 km²)	Fire, logging	Protected areas reasonably secure and protect almost all the remaining forests
SA4	Transverse Dry Belt	F	50,000	5–600 m		Timber trees, Brazil nut, rubber and cocoa relatives, vanilla, curare, rosewood	Lowland (terra firme) semi-deciduous and deciduous forests, permanently and seasonally inundated swamp forests, various savannas	1 Biological Reserve (38,500 km²), 1 National Forest (3150 km²), 2 Ecological Stations (5771 km²), Amerindian reserves	Mining, pollution, logging	Relatively inaccessible but development beginning; protection status needs strengthening
Brazil/Colombia/Venezuela										
SA6	Upper Rio Negro region	F	>250,000	<100–1000 m	>15,000	Centre of diversity for many useful plants, incl. rubber, rosewood, Brazil nut	Amazon caatinga forest and scrub, flood forest (igapó), submontane forest	Well protected in 7 NPs and reserves (c. 34% of region), Amerindian reserves	None; potential threats: gold mining, coca plantations, logging	Relatively safe; further areas proposed as NPs and reserves
Chile										
SA43	Lomas formations of the Atacama Desert	V	>5000	0–1100 m	550	Ornamental plants, potential genetic resources	Desert vegetation of annual, short-lived perennials and woody scrub	NP (438 km²), Nature Reserve (30 km²)	Urbanization, mining, fuelwood cutting, grazing	Inadequate coverage of protected areas; threatened
SA44	Mediterranean region and La Campana NP	F	5000	300–2222 m	2000	Timber trees (e.g. Nothofagus), fruit trees, Chilean honey palm, dyes, medicinal plants, ornamentals	Nothofagus forest, submontane to alpine vegetation, palm forest, bamboo thickets, matorral	2 NPs, 5 National Reserves (840 km²), 1 NS (116 km²), proposed reserve (c. 5000 km²)	Agriculture, cattle ranching, urbanization, road building, mining, fire, fuelwood cutting	Partially protected, but areas outside protected areas are severely threatened
SA45	Temperate rain forest	V	110,000	0–2000 m	450	Timber trees (e.g. Araucaria, Fitzroya)	Evergreen and deciduous temperate rain forests	25 NPs, 14 NRs, 1 NatM	Logging, agriculture, grazing, fire, plantation forestry	Coverage and staffing of existing reserves inadequate; severely threatened

Code	Site	Type	Size (km²)	Altitude	Flora	Examples of Useful Plants	Vegetation	Protected Areas	Threats	Assessment
Colombia										
SA7	Chiribiquete-Araracuara-Cahuinarí region	F	50,000	150–700 m	12,000	Timber trees, rubber, cocoa and hot pepper relatives, fruit trees, medicinal plants	Tropical lowland rain forest, evergreen sclerophyllous scrub, grassland	2 NPs (18,550 km²), 3 Amerindian reserves (3470 km²)	Potential unplanned colonization, burning, road building, mining	Reasonably safe at present due to remoteness; management plan for protected areas yet to be developed
SA39	Colombian Pacific Coast region	F/V	130,000	0–1000 m	8000–9000	Timber trees, fruit trees, medicinal plants, ornamentals	Lowland and premontane tropical pluvial to moist forests, mangroves	4 NPs (2013 km²) and lower portions of 2 NPs	Logging, colonization, agriculture, grazing, mining	Present reserve system inadequate; large areas of forest under threat
SA29	Colombian Central Massif	F	2000	1000–4500 m	1200	Medicinal plants, fodder plants, fuelwood	Páramo, montane and mid-altitude forests, tropical deciduous forest	NP (830 km²), private reserve, Amerindian reserves	Mining, road building, cattle ranching, fire, tree felling, draining of wetlands	Inadequate coverage of protected areas; threatened
SA28	Los Nevados National Natural Park region	S	12,200	300–4600 m	1250	Medicinal plants, dyes, timbers, edible species	Lowland dry forests, oak and laurel forests, páramo, super-páramo	NP (583 km²), 3 other protected areas (115 km²)	Logging, fire, volcanic eruptions, cattle grazing	Region at mid-altitudes severely threatened
SA27	Páramo de Sumapaz	F	15,000	300–4250 m		Plants used for medicine, agriculture, construction	Lowland to montane forests, dry forests, páramo	1 NP (1540 km²)	Road construction, colonization, cattle ranching, logging, mining	Increasingly at risk from population growth and needs; more reserves needed
SA25	Sierra Nevada de Santa Marta	F	12,232	0–5776 m	>1800	Medicinal plants, dyes, cultural species, edible species, timber trees	Humid tropical forest, montane tropical rain forest, cloud forest, páramo	2 National Natural Parks (3980 km²), Amerindian reserves	Colonization, erosion, agriculture, cattle ranching	Severely threatened
SA26	Sierra Nevada del Cocuy-Guantiva	F	4260	500–5493 m		Medicinal plants, spices, plants for construction	Dry xerophytic scrub, Andean forests, páramo	1 NP (3060 km²), including Amerindian reserve (216 km²)	Excessive sheep grazing, agricultural spread, tourism	Improved regulation; an additional reserve and management plans needed
Colombia/Ecuador										
SA30	Volcanoes of Nariñense Plateau	F	1400	3000–4500 m	450	Medicinal plants, edible plants, ornamental plants	Páramo grassland and peat bogs, scrub, forests with *Miconia*	Fauna and Flora Sanctuary (176 km²)	Volcanic eruptions, agriculture, cattle ranching, plantation forestry using exotics	Inadequate protection; severely threatened
Ecuador										
SA40	Ecuadorian Pacific Coast mesic forests	V	3700	0–900 m	5300	Timber trees, ivory-nut palm, ornamental plants	Lowland tropical moist, wet and pluvial forests	FoR (1300 km²), Ecological Reserve (2040 km²), several other small reserves (c. 5 km²)	Logging, colonization, agriculture, grazing	Threatened; some areas severely threatened
SA38	Gran Sumaco and Upper Napo River region	F	9000	300–3732 m	6000	Medicinal plants, crop relatives, culturally important plants	Lowland tropical forest to wet páramo	Biological Station (7 km²); whole area proposed as BR; 2 proposed NPs (1910 km²)	Road building, subsistence agriculture, colonization, cattle ranching, potential mining	Inadequately protected, especially lowlands; threatened
SA31	Páramo and Andean forests of Sangay NP	V/S	5717	1000–5319 m	>3000	Food, fodder and medicinal plants, fibres, ornamental plants	Páramo, Andean and sub-Andean forests	Included within NP and WHS	Road building, logging, colonization, mining, fire, overgrazing, tourism	Reasonably safe, but management plan needs revision and implementation

Code	Site	Type	Size (km²)	Altitude	Flora	Examples of Useful Plants	Vegetation	Protected Areas	Threats	Assessment
SA8	Yasuní NP and Waorani Ethnic Reserve	S	15,920	200–350 m	4000	Wild rubber, vegetable ivory palm, valuable hardwoods, medicinal plants	Tropical moist forest	BR: NP (9820 km²), Ethnic Reserve (6100 km²)	Oil extraction, logging, road building, colonization	Severely threatened
Ecuador/Peru										
SA32	Huancabamba region	F	29,000	1000–4000 m	2000–2500	Timber trees, medicinal plants, ornamental plants	Montane cloud forest, dry forest, páramo	NatS (295 km²)	Logging, agriculture; 75% of original humid forest destroyed	Inadequate protection; severely threatened
French Guiana										
SA3	Saül region	S	>1340	200–762 m	2000	Timber trees, edible palms, rosewood oil, medicinal plants	Mostly lowland moist forest, swamp forest, submontane forest	2 potential NRs (790 km²)	Slash and burn agriculture, fuelwood cutting, gold mining, potential road	Seriously threatened at present; repeated efforts to protect area since 1975
Paraguay										
SA18	Mbaracayú Reserve	S	600	140–450 m		Valuable timbers, fruit trees, edible palms, Paraguayan tea, medicinal plants	Semi-evergreen subtropical moist forest, savanna, lowland bogs	Private reserve	Agriculture, logging, cultivation of narcotic plants	Inadequately protected; region threatened
Peru										
SA41	Cerros de Amotape NP region	S	2314	100–1618 m	>500	Timber trees, forage plants, medicinal plants, ornamental plants, craft plants	Dry forest, matorral	NP (913 km²) forming core area of a BR of 2314 km²	Fuelwood and timber cutting, fire, overgrazing, soil erosion, desertification	At risk
SA37	Eastern slopes of Peruvian Andes	F	250,000	400–3500 m	7000–10,000	Timber trees, ornamental plants	Dry, wet and pluvial tropical and subtropical lowland, premontane and montane forests	3 NPs protect c. 20,000 km²; 2 NatSs, 2 Reserved Zones, 1 PF, 1 National Forest cover 6000 km²	Deforestation from colonization, roads, agriculture, logging, cultivation of narcotics	NPs reasonably safe due to inaccessibility; protection of other reserves inadequate; severe threats in places
SA42	Lomas formations	V	>2000	0–1000 m	600	Potential genetic resources of crop plants (e.g. tomato)	Desert vegetation of annual, short-lived perennial and woody scrub	2 National Reserves, 1 NatS (1228 km²)	Urbanization, grazing, mining, fuelwood cutting	Coastal areas severely threatened, more protected areas and conservation measures needed
SA11	Lowlands of Manú NP: Cocha Cashu Biological Station	S	7500	300–400 m	1900	Spanish cedar, mahogany, cocoa relatives, edible palms and fruits	Mostly evergreen tropical forest	Biological Station (10 km²) within NP of 15,328 km², forming part of a BR of 18,812 km²	Potential road building, oil exploration and mining	Inadequate funding resulting in lack of trained staff; threatened
SA33	Peruvian puna	V	230,000	3300–5000 m	1000–1500	Potato relatives, many traditional Andean crops and medicinal plants, spices	Grasslands, scrub, wetlands, tropical alpine vegetation	9500 km² (4% of area) within 3 NPs, 5 National Reserves, 3 NatSs, 3 Historical Sanctuaries	Overgrazing, fire, soil erosion, mining, fuelwood cutting	Inadequate funding resulting in lack of trained staff; inadequate coverage of protected areas; threatened
SA10	Tambopata region	F	15,000	250–3000 m	2500–3000	Timber trees, Brazil nut, rubber, fruit trees	Subtropical premontane/ montane wet forests, tropical moist forest, swamp forest, savanna	NS (1021 km²), Reserved Zone (14,000 km²), Tambopata Reserve (5.5 km²)	Cattle ranching, subsistence agriculture, gold mining, local population pressure	Conservation measures need implementing in Reserved Zone; threatened

Code	Site	Type	Size (km²)	Altitude	Flora	Examples of Useful Plants	Vegetation	Protected Areas	Threats	Assessment
	Peru/Colombia									
SA9	Iquitos region	F	80,000	105–140 m	>2265	Timber trees, medicinal plants (incl. curare), fibres, >120 spp. of edible fruits	Evergreen Amazonian moist forests, swamps	Peru: National Reserve (in part), Communal Reserve (3225 km²); Colombia: National Natural Park (1700 km²)	Clearance for settlements and agriculture	Inadequate coverage of protected areas; some habitats threatened
	Venezuela									
SA1	Coastal Cordillera	F	45,000	0–2765 m	5000	Quinine and other medicinal plants, quality hardwoods	Montane/submontane semi-deciduous and evergreen forests, hill savanna, cloud forest, coastal and upper montane scrub, mangroves	11 NPs (6640 km²) and 5 NMs	Population pressure, deforestation, colonization, fire, agriculture, roads	Protected areas reasonably secure, but coverage inadequate
SA2	Pantepui region	S/F	7000	1300–3015 m	3000	Ornamentals (e.g. bromeliads, orchids, carnivorous plants), undoubtedly rich in potentially useful species	Montane forests, tepui scrub, pioneer communities on cliffs and rocky areas	NPs and NMs cover entire region	No serious threats, but potential threats from increased tourism and over-collecting	Safe at present but potentially at risk without more effective controls
SOUTH EAST ASIA (MALESIA)										
	Brunei Darussalam									
SEA13	Batu Apoi FoR, Ulu Temburong	S	488	50–1850 m	3000	Timber trees (especially dipterocarps, *Agathis*), medicinal plants, ornamentals	Lowland dipterocarp rain forest, lower and upper montane forests	FoR, planned NP	Logging, potential dam construction	At risk
	Indonesia (Irian Jaya)									
SEA68	Arfak Mountains	F	2200	100–3100 m	3000–4000	Timber trees, rattans, fruit tree relatives, ornamental plants (especially rhododendrons)	Lowland, hill and lower montane rain forests, grassland/heath communities, lake vegetation	NR (450 km²); proposal to extend to 653 km² as Nature Conservation Area	Population pressure, resettlement schemes, agriculture and logging, road building	Lowlands threatened in particular
SEA69	Gunung Lorentz	S	21,500	0–4884 m	3000–4000	Fruits, vegetables, fibres, building materials	Lowland to montane rain forests, mangroves, bogs, swamps, heaths, grasslands, alpine vegetation	NR; proposals for NP, BR & WHS status	Mining, logging, petroleum exploitation, road building, tourism, colonization	Threatened; high-altitude vegetation vulnerable to trampling
SEA70	Mamberamo-Pegunungan Jayawijaya	F	23,244	0–4680 m	2000–3000	Timber trees, especially southern beech, podocarps, conifers	Lowland to montane rain forest, lowland swamp forest, mangroves	Proposed NP/WHS (14,425 km²), GR (8000 km²), proposed GR (819 km²)	Petroleum exploitation, logging at lower altitudes	Lowlands particularly at risk
SEA71	Waigeo	S	14,784	0–999 m		Timber trees, wild sugar cane	Lowland to lower montane rain forest, riverine forest, mangroves, limestone and ultramafic vegetation	NR (1530 km²), marine reserve covers offshore islets and reefs	Potential nickel mining	At risk if mining goes ahead

Code	Site	Type	Size (km²)	Altitude	Flora	Examples of Useful Plants	Vegetation	Protected Areas	Threats	Assessment
Indonesia (Java)										
SEA64	Gunung Gede-Pangrango NP	S	150	1000–3019 m	>1000	Timber trees, medicinal plants, ornamental plants	Mostly montane and submontane rain forests, grass plains	NP (whole areae), BR (140 km²)	Timber and fuelwood cutting, agricultural encroachment, visitor pressure, plant collecting	Encroachment around boundaries; at risk
Indonesia (Kalimantan)										
SEA15	Bukit Raya and Bukit Baka	S	7705	100–2278 m	2000–4000	Timber trees (especially dipterocarps), fruit trees, illipe nuts, rattans	Lowland tropical rain forest, swamp forest, lower and upper montane forests, ericaceous scrub	NP (1811 km²)	Logging, road construction, shifting cultivation	Encroachment in west; at risk
SEA17	Gunung Palung	S	900	0–1160 m		Timber trees, fruit trees, ornamental plants	Dipterocarp rain forests, montane forests, swamp forests, beach forest, mangroves	NP	Logging, shifting cultivation	Buffer zones needed; most of area safe, but some parts at risk
SEA19	Sungai Kayan-Sungai Mentarang NR	S	29,000	100–2556 m	2000	Timber trees, fruit trees, gingers, rattans	Lowland and hill dipterocarp rain forests, montane forests, riverine, swamp and heath forests	NR (16,000 km²); proposed extensions (13,000 km²)	Logging, mining, shifting cultivation	Boundaries at risk
Indonesia (Sulawesi)										
SEA46	Dumoga-Bone NP	S	3000	200–1968 m		Timber trees, rattans	Tropical lowland semi-evergreen rain forest, riverine forest, montane forest, some limestone forest	NP	Over-collection of forest products, shifting cultivation, potential mining, road building	Boundaries threatened but demarcation and zoning being implemented
SEA47	Limestone flora of Sulawesi	V		150–1000 m		Sugar palm, fruit tree relatives, plants for degraded land	Forest over limestone, scrub, lithophytic vegetation	c. 70% of all outcrops unprotected	Quarrying, firewood cutting, clearance for agriculture, fire	Threatened
SEA50	Pegunungan Latimojong	S	580	1000–3455 m		Ornamental plants	Lower and upper montane forests, hill forest, montane grassland, subalpine vegetation	PF; proposed NR	Clearance of lower slopes for agriculture	Lowlands threatened, but most of area not threatened
SEA48	Ultramafic flora of Sulawesi	V	12,000			Plants of potential value for rehabilitating degraded areas	Ultramafic facies of lowland forest, scrub, some montane vegetation	Mostly unprotected	Mostly intact, but agricultural development planned	Threatened
Indonesia (Sumatra)										
SEA41	Gunung Leuser	S	>9000	0–3466 m	2000–3000	Timber trees (especially dipterocarps), fruit trees, medicinal plants, ornamentals	Lowland dipterocarp rain forest, montane and subalpine forests, freshwater swamp forest, marshes	NP (7927 km²), BR (9464 km²)	Encroachment of settlements, agriculture, illegal logging, over-collection of rattans	Threatened, especially in the lowlands; inadequate funding
SEA42	Kerinci-Seblat NP	S	1485	200–3805 m	2000–3000	Fruit trees, timbers (e.g. dipterocarps, *Agathis*), medicinal plants, rattans	Lowland and hill dipterocarp rain forests, montane forests, montane swamp forest	NP	Encroachment of settlements, agriculture, illegal logging, over-collection of rattans	Threatened, especially in the lowlands

Code	Site	Type	Size (km²)	Altitude	Flora	Examples of Useful Plants	Vegetation	Protected Areas	Threats	Assessment
SEA43	Limestone flora of Sumatra	V	5000	150–1500 m	1500–2000	Ornamental plants, fruit tree relatives	Forest over limestone, scrub, lithophytic vegetation	Very few outcrops protected	Quarrying	Threatened
SEA45	Tigapuluh Mountains	S	2000	150–800 m	2000–3000	Timber trees	Tropical lowland evergreen and hill dipterocarp rain forests	None	Logging, conversion to forestry and rubber plantations, shifting cultivation	Eastern lowlands severely threatened
Indonesia/Malaysia										
SEA16	Lanjak-Entimau WS, Batang Ai NP, Gunung Bentuang dan Karimun	S	10,112	500–1284 m		Timber trees, especially dipterocarps, illipe nuts, rattans, fruit tree relatives	Lowland and hill evergreen rain forests, heath, swamp and montane forests	WS (1688 km²), proposed extensions (184 km²), NP (240 km²), NR (8000 km²)	Agricultural encroachment, logging	Boundaries and lower slopes at risk
SEA18	Limestone flora of Borneo	V		0–1710 m		Ornamental plants (especially orchids, gesneriads, begonias, balsams, ferns)	Lowland to upper montane forest on limestone, lithophytic vegetation	Some major areas in Sarawak in NP, few in Sabah in FoRs, proposed NPs in Kalimantan, other sites unprotected	Quarrying, fire, clearance of surrounding forests for agriculture, tourism	Some major areas safe, some relatively safe but unprotected, most others threatened
Malaysia (Peninsular Malaysia)										
SEA2	Endau-Rompin State Parks	S	500	100–1000 m		Timber trees (including dipterocarps), rattans, fruit trees, wild banana relative, medicinal herbs	Mainly tropical lowland rain and hill dipterocarp forest, hill swamp forest, riparian communities	FoR; proposed State Parks	Logging, clearance for development schemes, tourist facilities, commercial collection of ornamental plants	Protection needs strengthening; at risk
SEA3	Limestone flora of Peninsular Malaysia	V	260	0–713 m	>1300	Ornamental plants, especially orchids, begonias, palms, gesneriads	Limestone forest, scrub, lithophytic vegetation	A few outcrops protected in Taman Negara (NP); some occur on FoRs; some are Temple Reserves (no protection to flora)	Quarrying, mining, encroachment from agriculture, fire, tourism, plant collecting	Many outcrops severely threatened, some at risk, a few safe
SEA4	Montane flora of Peninsular Malaysia	V	2180	810–2188 m	>3000	Ornamental plants (especially orchids, pitcher plants, rhododendrons)	Lower and upper montane forests	Most peaks fall within FoRs, G. Tahan is in NP, Cameron Highlands is in WS, G. Kajang is in WR	Large-scale resort development, agriculture/horticulture, road building, plant collecting	Most areas outside NP severely threatened
SEA5	Pulau Tioman	S	72	0–1038 m	1500	Ornamental plants, especially slipper orchids, Rafflesia used medicinally	Coastal forest, hill and upper montane forests, some mangroves	WR	Large-scale resort development, airstrip construction, over-collecting of orchids and Rafflesia	Threatened; protected status not enforced
SEA8	Taman Negara	S	4343	75–2188 m	>3000	Timber and fruit trees, rattans, ornamental plants (e.g. orchids), potential medicinal plants	Lowland, hill and montane rain forests, "padang" vegetation, limestone and quartzite vegetation, riparian communities	NP	Logging, hydroelectric dams, lack of buffer zone, some tourist developments	Safe at present, but frequently threatened

Code	Site	Type	Size (km²)	Altitude	Flora	Examples of Useful Plants	Vegetation	Protected Areas	Threats	Assessment
SEA10	Trengganu Hills	S	150	60–920 m	1500	Timber trees, rattans, ornamental plants	Lowland and hill rain forest	FoR, 3 small VJRs	Logging, land clearance for cultivation	At risk
Malaysia (Sabah)										
SEA22	East Sabah lowland/hill dipterocarp forests	V	20,000	0–1298 m	5000–6000	Timber trees (seraya, keruing, kapur), rattans, fruit trees, ornamentals	Tropical evergreen lowland and hill dipterocarp rain forests	4077 km² protected in conservation areas	Conversion to agriculture, human settlement, tree plantations, unsustainable logging	Threatened, some areas seriously threatened; protection of reserves needs strengthening
SEA24	Kinabalu Park	S	754	150–4101 m	4500	Timber trees, ornamental plants (e.g. pitcher plants, orchids)	Mostly montane rain forest, some tropical lowland rain forest, ultramafic forest, alpine vegetation	SP	Clearance for cultivation, illegal logging, mining, tourism	Boundaries threatened
SEA27	North-east Borneo ultramafic flora	V	3500	0–3000 m	1500	Timber trees, potential ornamental plants, nickel- and manganese-tolerant species	Ultramafic facies of tropical lowland evergreen rain forest, lower and upper montane forests	Kinabalu SP only area of formal protection; small areas in Danum Valley Conservation Area; Mt Silam is a protected watershed	Clearance for cultivation and golf course, logging, fire, dam construction, road building	Inadequate coverage of protected areas; threatened
Malaysia (Sarawak)										
SEA34	Lambir Hills	S	69	30–457 m	1500	Timber trees (incl. 69 dipterocarp spp.), mango and durian relatives, rattans	Lowland mixed dipterocarp forest, heath forest, scrub	NP	Logging, clearance for agriculture	Encroachment around boundaries; threatened
Malaysia/Brunei										
SEA33	Gunung Mulu NP/ Medalam PF/ Labi Hills/Bukit Teraja/Ulu Ingei/ Sungei Ingei	S	1521	30–2376 m	3500	Timber trees, especially dipterocarps, fruit and nut trees, sago palm, rattans, medicinal plants	Lowland mixed dipterocarp to montane forests on sandstones, limestones and shales, heath forests, peat swamp forest	Malaysia: NP, PF; Brunei: PF and Conservation Area within FoR	Logging around perimeter of Mulu NP, shifting cultivation along some rivers, potential threat from road construction	Mostly safe at present, but would be at risk if proposed road went ahead; buffer zones to Mulu NP need to be implemented
Papua New Guinea										
SEA89	Bismarck Falls–Mt Wilhelm–Mt Otto–Schrader Range–Mt Hellwig-Gahavisuka	S	9754	250–4499 m	5000–6000	Traditional food and medicinal plants, timbers, fibres, plants of cultural value	Lowland swamp and rain forest, montane forests, alpine vegetation	Proposed NP (Mt Wilhelm), small Provincial Park (Gahavisuka); region proposed as WHS	Population pressure, logging, agriculture, coffee and cardamom plantations	Protected area coverage inadequate; at risk
SEA91	Huon Peninsula (Mt Bangeta-Rawlinson Range; Cromwell Ranges-Sialum Terraces)	S	3415	0–4120 m	4000–5000	Fruit trees, vegetables, fibres, potential timber species	Lowland tropical rain forest to subalpine forest, grasslands, mangroves	No formal protection	Logging, road building	At risk
SEA98	Menyamya-Aseki-Amungwiwa-Bowutu Mts-Lasanga Island	F	6695	0–3278 m	1500–3000	Fruits, vegetables, fibres, building materials, potential timber species	Lowland rain forests to upper montane forests, ultramafic vegetation	NP (21 km²), local support for conservation area in Bowutu Mts, several reserves throughout region needed	Logging, road building, local population pressure	Severely threatened in places, protected area coverage inadequate

Code	Site	Type	Size (km²)	Altitude	Flora	Examples of Useful Plants	Vegetation	Protected Areas	Threats	Assessment
SEA86	Mt Giluwe-Tari Gap-Doma Peaks	S	3346	1000–4368 m	>3000	Traditional food and medicinal plants, fibres, ornamental plants	Montane and subalpine forests, grasslands, alpine communities	Local reserves in Tari Gap area	Logging, road building, clearance for agricultural plantations, dieback of *Nothofagus*	Protected area coverage inadequate; at risk
SEA92	Southern Fly Platform	F	18,644	0–30 m	>2000	Edible palms, traditional food and medicinal plants	Monsoon and savanna vegetation, mangroves, lowland swamps,	Wildlife Management Area (5900 km²)	No major threats, some grazing pressure from introduced deer, potential threat from mining	Reasonably safe, but protected area coverage inadequate
Philippines										
SEA51	Batan Islands	S	209	0–1008 m	>500	Timbers, fibres, medicinal plants, food plants	Lowland evergreen to mid-montane rain forest, grassland, secondary vegetation	Proposed as Protected Landscape and 2 "critical watersheds" under National Integrated Protected Area System	Typhoons, clearance for grazing, crops, shifting cultivation, over-collection of forest products	Vulnerable, but growing conservation awareness among local people
SEA52	Mt Apo	S	769	500–2954 m	>800	Ornamental plants (e.g. orchids, aroids, begonias), timber trees	Lowland rain forest (mostly cleared), montane forests, "elfin woodland", scrub, grassland	NP	Construction of geothermal plant, clearance for agriculture, illegal logging, shifting cultivation	Severely threatened
SEA57	Mt Pulog	S	115	1000–2929 m	800	Timber tree provenances (especially pines), ornamental plants	Montane forest, pine forest, grassland	NP	Conversion of forest to vegetable and cut-flower gardens, fire	Threatened
SEA59	Palanan Wilderness Area	S	2168	0–1672 m	1500	Timber trees, rattans	Lowland and hill dipterocarp forest, lower montane forest, ultramafic and limestone forests	Wilderness Area; proposed as NP	Illegal logging, shifting cultivation, over-collection of forest products, potential large-scale logging	Mostly safe at present, but could become severely threatened
SEA60	Palawan	F	14,896	0–2085 m	>2000	Timber trees, rattans, almaciga resin, fruit trees, orchids, nipa palm	Lowland evergreen dipterocarp and semi-deciduous forests, ultramafic and limestone forests, mangroves	BR (11,508 km²), NP (39 km²), various other protected areas covering 3.4% of land area	Logging, mining, shifting cultivation, tourism, over-collection of forest products	Inadequately protected; threatened
SEA61	Sibuyan Island	S	445	0–2052 m	700	Timber trees, almaciga resin, ornamental plants	Lowland dipterocarp forest, montane forest, grassland, mangroves	Proposed NR	Logging, slash and burn agriculture, fire, over-exploitation of rattan	Threatened
SOUTH WEST ASIA AND THE MIDDLE EAST										
Iran										
SWA10	Touran Protected Area BR	S	18,604	690–2281 m	1000	Medicinal herbs, food and fodder plants	Semi-desert, psammophytic and halophytic vegetation	Protected Area divided into WR (5650 km²) and Protected Area (12,954 km²); BR covers 10,000 km²	Overgrazing, fuelwood cutting	At risk; protection measures need to be enforced
Iran/Azerbaijan										
SWA18	Hyrcanian forests	V	50,000	0–2500 m		Timber trees, ornamental plants	Broadleaved deciduous forest, shrubland	Several protected areas; no information available on current status	Clearance for agriculture, logging, invasive plants in some coastal areas	Threatened

Code	Site	Type	Size (km²)	Altitude	Flora	Examples of Useful Plants	Vegetation	Protected Areas	Threats	Assessment
Oman/Yemen										
SWA1	Dhofar Fog Oasis	F	30,000	0–2100 m	900	Frankincense, traditional food, fibre and medicinal plants	Mainly dry deciduous shrubland, montane evergreen shrubland, semi-desert grassland	1 small Bird Sanctuary, otherwise none	Population pressure, overgrazing, cutting of wood for fuel and timber	Severely threatened; IUCN proposals for reserves in Oman not yet implemented
Saudi Arabia/Yemen										
SWA5	Highlands of South-western Arabia	F	70,000	200–3760 m	2000	Qat (stimulant), coffee, barley, wheat and sorghum relatives, myrrh	Deciduous and evergreen bushland and thicket, juniper woodland	Asir NP (4150 km²) in Saudi Arabia, proposed areas in Yemen	Uncontrolled cutting of wood for fuel, timber and charcoal; overgrazing, erosion	No effective protection over most of area, remaining woodland severely threatened
Turkey										
SWA12	Anti-Taurus Mts/ Upper Euphrates	F	60,000	700–3734 m	3200	Walnut, medicinal plants, dyes, cereal crop relatives	Oak forest, steppe, montane steppe	NP (428 km²)	Dam construction, re-afforestation projects, rock climbing leading to erosion	Urgent action needed to protect more of the region; threatened
SWA15	Isaurian, Lycaonian and Cilician Taurus	F	45,120	0–3524 m	>2500	Fig, pomegranate, nuts, dune stabilizers	Cilician fir and cedar forests, scrub, thorn-cushion plants, scree vegetation, dune communities	NP (very small), Bird Sanctuary, GR (30 km²)	Road building, export of wild bulbs, overgrazing, tourism, clearance for agriculture	Many important ecosystems unprotected; threatened
SWA19	N.E. Anatolia	F	33,200	0–3932 m	>2460	Cherries, hazelnuts, timber trees	Coastal humid subtropical forest to fir forest, rhododendron scrub, scree vegetation	1 NP	Illegal logging, clearance for agriculture, export of wild bulbs	None of the Little Caucasus is protected; at risk but not as seriously threatened as other areas
SWA16	S.W. Anatolia	F	75,680	0–3070 m	>3365	Cypress, cedar, oriental sweet gum, medicinal herbs	Mediterranean forest and scrub, cedar forest	Several NPs and Protected Zones, 5 Biogenetic Reserves (264.5 km²)	Tourism, overgrazing by goats, export of wild bulbs	Coastal areas severely threatened
Turkey/Iran/Iraq										
SWA14	Mountains of S.E. Turkey, N.W. Iran, N. Iraq	F	147,332	1400–4168 m	2500	Pears, almonds, hawthorns, gum tragacanth	Oak forest, alpine thorn cushion scrub, montane steppe, alpine grassland, scree vegetation	Iran: NP (4636 km²); Turkey: 1 Forest Recreation Area, 1 GR	Influx of refugees, re-afforestation projects, potential dam and irrigation schemes	Inadequate coverage of reserve system, but threats to flora less severe than elsewhere
Turkey/Syria/Lebanon/Israel/Jordan										
SWA17	Levantine Uplands	F	96,675	0–3083 m	4160	Timber trees (e.g. Cilician fir, cedar of Lebanon), fodder plants, spices, edible oils, root vegetables	Oak, pine, cypress, fir and cedar of Lebanon forests, juniper scrub, maquis, garigue, geophytic communities, alpine vegetation	Israel: 7 small reserves; Syria: 2 Protected Areas (6320 km²)	Logging of remaining forests, clearance for agriculture, tourism, urbanization, over-exploitation of essential oils	Threatened; inadequate coverage of protected areas
Yemen										
SWA4	Socotra	F	3625	0–1519 m	815*	Dragon's blood, other resins, gums, aloes	Semi-desert, dry deciduous shrubland, montane semi-evergreen thicket, secondary grassland	None	Overgrazing by goats, fuelwood cutting, potential new development projects	No protection but traditional practices have prevented serious exploitation so far

References

Bedward, M., Pressey, R.L. and Keith, D.A. (1992). A new approach for selecting fully representative reserve networks: addressing efficiency, reserve design and land suitability with an iterative analysis. *Biological Conservation* 62: 115–125.

Cowling, R.M., Gibbs Russell, G.E., Hoffman, M.T and Hilton-Taylor, C. (1989). Patterns of species diversity in Southern Africa. In Huntley, B.J. (ed.), *Biotic diversity in Southern Africa: concepts and conservation*. Oxford University Press, Cape Town. Pp. 19–50.

Davis, S. (1986). Plant Sites Directory. *Threatened Plants Newsletter* No. 16: 17.

Dinerstein, E. and Wikramanayake, E.D. (1993). Beyond "hotspots": how to prioritize investments to conserve biodiversity in the Indo-Pacific region. *Conservation Biology* 7: 530–565.

FAO (1990a). *TFAP Independent Review Report 1990. Appendix 3, section 3.3*. FAO, Rome.

FAO (1990b). *Interim report on Forest Resources Assessment 1990 Project*. Committee on Forestry 10th Session. COFO–90/8(a).

Gentry, A.H. (1990). Herbarium taxonomy versus field knowledge. *Flora Malesiana Bulletin Special Volume* 1: 31–35.

Greuter, W. (1991). Botanical diversity, endemism, rarity, and extinction in the Mediterranean area: an analysis based on the published volumes of Med-Checklist. *Bot. Chron*. 10: 63–79.

Haffer, J. (1969). Speciation in Amazonian forest birds. *Science* 165: 131–137.

Hawkes, J.G. (1983). *The diversity of crop plants*. Harvard University Press, Cambridge, Massachusetts.

Heywood, V.H. (1991). Assessment of the state of the flora of the west Mediterranean basin. In Rejdali, M. and Heywood, V.H. (eds), *Conservation des Ressources Végétales*. Actes Editions, Institut Agronomique et Vétérinaire Hassan II, Rabat. Pp. 9–17.

Heywood, V.H. (1992). Conservation of germplasm of wild species. In Sandlund, O.T., Hindar, K. and Brown, A.H.D. (eds), *Conservation of biodiversity for sustainable development*. Scandinavian University Press, Oslo. Pp. 189–203.

Heywood, V.H. (1994a). The measurement of biodiversity and the politics of implementation. In Forey, P.L., Humphries, C.J. and Vane-Wright, R.I. (eds), *Systematics and conservation evaluation*. Oxford University Press. Pp. 15–22.

Heywood, V.H. (1994b). The Mediterranean flora in the context of world biodiversity. In Olivier, L. and Muracciole, M. (eds), *Connaissance et Conservation de la Flore des Iles de la Méditerranée*. (In press.)

Huntley, B. J. (1988). Conserving and monitoring biotic diversity. Some South African examples. In Wilson, E.O. (ed.), *Biodiversity*. National Academy Press, Washington, D.C. Pp. 248–260.

ICBP (1992). *Putting biodiversity on the map: priority areas for global conservation*. International Council for Bird Preservation, Cambridge, U.K. 90 pp.

IUCN (1980). *World Conservation Strategy: living resource conservation for sustainable development*. IUCN, UNEP and WWF, Gland, Switzerland.

IUCN (1986). *The Plant Sites Red Data Book: a botanists' view of the places that matter*. IUCN, Richmond, U.K. 48 pp.

IUCN (1988). *Centres of Plant Diversity. A guide and strategy for their conservation*. IUCN, Richmond, U.K. 40 pp.

IUCN (1990). *Centres of Plant Diversity. An introduction to the project with guidelines for collaborators*. IUCN, Richmond, U.K. 31 pp.

IUCN/WWF (1984). *The IUCN/WWF Plants Conservation Programme 1984–85*. IUCN/WWF, Gland, Switzerland. 29 pp.

McNeely, J.A. (ed.) (1993). *Parks for life*. Report of the IVth World Congress on National Parks and Protected Areas. IUCN, Gland, Switzerland.

Miller, K.R. (1984). Selecting terrestrial habitats for conservation. In Hall, A.V. (ed.), *Conservation of threatened natural habitats*. South African National Scientific Programmes Report No. 92, Pretoria. Pp. 95–108.

Mittermeier, R.A. and Werner, T.B. (1988). Wealth of plants and animals unites "megadiversity" countries. *Tropicus* 4: 1, 4–5.

Myers, N. (1986). Tackling mass extinctions of species: a great creative challenge. The Horace M. Albright Lectureship in Conservation. University of California, Berkeley.

Myers, N. (1988a). Threatened biotas: "hot-spots" in tropical forests. *Environmentalist* 8: 187–208.

Myers, N. (1988b). Tropical forest and their species. Going, going...? In Wilson, E.O. (ed.), *Biodiversity*. National Academy Press, Washington, D.C. Pp. 28–35.

Myers, N. (1990). The biological challenge extended: extended hot-spots analysis. *Environmentalist* 10: 243–256.

Prescott-Allen, R. and Prescott-Allen, C. (1990). How many plants feed the world? *Conservation Biology* 4: 365–374.

Pressey, R.L., Humphries, C.J., Margules, C.R., Vane-Wright, R.I. and Williams, P.H. (1993). Beyond opportunism: key principles for systematic reserve selection. *Trends in Ecology and Evolution* 8: 124–128.

Quézel, P. (1985). Definition of the Mediterranean region and the origin of its flora. In Gómez Campo, C. (ed.), *Plant conservation in the Mediterranean area*. Junk, Dordrecht.

Raven, P.H. (1987). The scope of the plant conservation problem world-wide. In Bramwell, D., Hamann, O., Heywood, V. and Synge, H. (eds), *Botanic gardens and the World Conservation Strategy*. Academic Press, London. Pp. 10–19.

Raven, P.H. (1990). The politics of preserving biodiversity. *BioScience* 40: 769.

Simberloff, D. (1986). Are we on the verge of a mass extinction in tropical rain forests? In Elliott, D.K. (ed.), *Dynamics of extinction*. Wiley, New York. Pp. 165–180.

Stattersfield, A.J., Crosby, M.J., Long, A.J. and Wege, D.C. (in prep.). *Global directory of Endemic Bird Areas*. BirdLife International, Cambridge, U.K.

Vane-Wright, R.I., Humphries, C.J. and Williams, P.H. (1991). What to protect and the agony of choice. *Biological Conservation* 55: 235–254.

Whitmore, T.C. and Sayer, J.A. (eds) (1992). *Tropical deforestation and species extinction*. IUCN, Gland, Switzerland and Cambridge, U.K., and Chapman and Hall, London. 153 pp.

Williams, P.H., Vane-Wright, R.I. and Humphries, C.J. (1993). Measuring biodiversity for choosing conservation areas. In LaSalle, J. and Gauls, I.D. (eds), *Hymenoptera and biodiversity*. CABI. Pp. 309–328.

Wilson, E.O. (1988). The current state of biodiversity. In Wilson, E.O. (ed.), *Biodiversity*. National Academy Press, Washington, D.C. Pp. 3–18.

Wilson, E.O. (1992). *The diversity of life*. Belknap Press, Harvard University Press, Cambridge, Massachusetts.

WRI, IUCN and UNEP (1992). *Global biodiversity strategy. Guidelines for action to save, study and use the Earth's biotic wealth sustainably and equitably*. WRI, IUCN and UNEP. 244 pp.

REGIONAL OVERVIEW: CENTRAL AND NORTHERN ASIA

VALENTIN A. KRASSILOV

Total land area: c. 16,794,400 km².

Population (1986): 47,668,400[a].

Altitude: -132 m (Mangyshlak Peninsula, Kazakhstan) to 7495 m (summit of Pik Kommunizma).

Natural vegetation: Closed forests cover c. 7,399,000 km² (c. 33% of the region), including extensive coniferous (taiga) forests and montane taiga, together with areas of broadleaved forests in the south-west and Far East; tundra in the north, extensive *Sphagnum* bogs in West Siberia, forest-steppe and steppe across the centre, semi-desert and desert vegetation in the south, montane and alpine vegetation, particularly in the south and Far East.

Number of vascular plants: c. 17,500 species.

Number of regional endemics: c. 2500 species.

Number of vascular plant families: 159.

Number of genera: 1675.

Number of endemic genera: 72.

Important plant families: Apiaceae, Asteraceae, Brassicaceae, Fabaceae, Lamiaceae, Poaceae, Rosaceae.

Source: [a] Europa Publications (1987).

Introduction

For the purposes of this treatment, the region is considered to form most of the territory of the Commonwealth of Independent States (C.I.S.), from the Ural Mountains (Ural'skiy Khrebet) eastwards to the Pacific coast, and southwards to the Caucasus and the Middle Asian mountains, which form the boundaries with South West Asia and the Middle East, and the Indian Subcontinent and East Asian regions, respectively. The Carpathian Mountains (CPD Site Eu20) and the Crimea and Novorossia (CPD Site Eu21) are treated in the Regional Overview for Europe (in Volume 1), while the Far Eastern regions of Chukotskiy (CPD Site CA4) and Primorye (CPD Site CA5) are included in the present treatment.

Geography and geology

The region covers c. 16,794,400 km². In the west are the Ural Mountains, a system of mountains which extend for over 2000 km from north to south, while in the south an almost continuous mountain range stretches from the Caucasus and Kopetdag in the south-west, to the Tien Shan, Altai-Sayan, Yablonovyy Khrebet and Stanovoy Khrebet along the borders of the Indian Subcontinent, China and Mongolia. In the Far East, the region includes the coastal mountain ranges of the Chukotskiy Peninsula, the Khrebet Dzhugdzhur, Kamchatka and the Sikhote-Alin, before finally reaching the Bering Sea and North Pacific Ocean.

Central Asia includes the world's largest plains, which stretch across Siberia (an area of approximately 12.8 million km²), bordering the Turanian Plains in the south and the Arctic in the north, as well as the world's largest lake – Lake Baikal (Ozero Baykal) – which covers an area of 30,500 km² within a tectonic depression. Baikal's waters are 1741 m deep at their deepest, and are well known for containing an endemic-rich biota. Other biologically diverse lakes are Khanka Lake (Ozero Khanka) in the Far East (see Data Sheet on Primorye, CPD Site CA5), Teletskoye Lake in Altai, and Tajmyr Lake in northern Siberia.

Central Asia is underlain by two stable areas of continental crust – the East European (or Russian) and Siberian platforms – comprising crystalline Archaean basement rocks. Mountain ranges to the east of the Siberian platform form concentric arcs of geologically younger rocks towards the periphery of the region. Rocks of the Pacific coastline are Mesozoic and Cenozoic volcanics succeeded by younger geosynclinal rocks. The Far East of Russia is volcanically active.

Quaternary glaciation was more extensive further west (in the European region), while in Siberia and the Far East it was restricted to the highlands. However, permafrost extended as far south as the Vitim Highlands (Vitimskoye Ploskogor'ye) to the east of Lake Baikal.

Climate

Much of the region has a harsh, cold climate, which is particularly severe in the Arctic and sub-Arctic zones in the north. The Arctic belt extends from the Chukotskiy Peninsula in the east to Novoya Zemlya, north of latitude 70°N. The sub-Arctic belt includes the northern margins of the Kola Peninsula, southern Novoya Zemlya and the Nenetski region along the Barents Sea coast, extending to northern Kamchatka. Typically, in the western Arctic, temperatures may stay above freezing for 5 months per year, whereas in the eastern Arctic the temperature may be above freezing for only 2–3 months. Temperatures in the winter may fall to as low as -50°C.

Much of the region to the south of the Arctic and sub-Arctic zones has a temperate climate. Western Siberia and the north-east experience a continental climate. Monthly average temperatures can vary throughout the year by as much as 65°C. The mean July temperature at Yakutsk is 19°C, whereas winters are extremely cold. The coldest place on Earth outside Antarctica – Verkhoyansk – in the centre of eastern Siberia, experiences January temperatures of -68°C. Lake Baikal moderates the climate in the south-west of Siberia.

Towards the south, the mountains of Middle Asia have a continental climate with severe winters but very hot summers. The plains of Central Asia and Kazakhstan have an arid climate with c. 200–300 mm of rainfall per year, most of the rain occurring in the spring.

The subtropical belt includes south-western Central Asia, the Trans-Caucasus, and southern Far Eastern Primorye.

Annual precipitation ranges from 250–500 mm over most of the region; however, in areas influenced strongly by Atlantic air streams and monsoonal climates, as well as areas in the Middle Asian mountains, rainfall can exceed 1000 mm p.a., and reaches 2000 mm on the western slopes of the Altai-Sayan. Semi-desert areas in Kazakhstan and northern Siberia receive less than 200 mm p.a.

Population

The population of the former Soviet Union, west of the Urals, was 47,668,400 in 1986 (Europa Publications 1987). According to the United Nations Population Division, the population of the whole of the former Soviet Union was 288,600,000 in 1990 (World Resources Institute 1992) and projected to rise by 0.64% annually between 1995–2000. Thus, the C.I.S. has approximately 6% of the world's population, and before its division into independent states, the U.S.S.R. had the third largest population of any world state, after China and India. However, the average population density of the whole of C.I.S. is only c. 11 people/km² with many of the largest population centres occurring west of the Urals. Vast areas of the region have very low population densities or are uninhabited. This applies to large areas of Siberia (where the overall population density averages just over two persons/km²), the north-eastern region and the high mountain regions bordering on China and Mongolia. However, population increased by 22.4% between 1968 and 1986 in the Siberian and Far East regions.

During recent decades, the region has experienced rapid urbanization and industrialization. The proportion of people living in towns and cities has risen in 60 years from 18% to 75% as a result of migration from rural areas and natural population growth in the towns. Large population centres occur in the area to the north of the Middle Asian mountains and in some inter-montane depressions, as well as along the Pacific coast of Far Eastern Russia.

Vegetation

The main types of vegetation are arranged in latitudinal belts. Superimposed on this arrangement are the influences of maritime conditions near the coast, altitudinal variations within each of the main zones, and the influence of such factors as grazing animals. It is convenient to discuss the main zones of vegetation from north to south.

Polar desert and tundra

The High Arctic zone includes the Arctic islands and the northernmost parts of the region. Plant cover is mostly restricted to mosses, lichens and algae, although a few flowering plants manage to survive in sheltered places among rocks. Various types of tundra, including dwarf grassland/shrub/moss communities, coincide approximately with the Arctic climatic belt north of latitude 70°N. Southern shrub tundras, in which there is a well-developed tier of *Betula nana* (dwarf birch), are best developed in the sub-Arctic climatic belt north of the Polar Circle. There are also enclaves of southern tundras in the Chukotskiy Peninsula (CPD Site CA4, see Data Sheet).

Forests

Forests in the U.S.S.R. were estimated to cover 7,920,000 km² in 1978 (c. 36% of the land area) (figures quoted in Knystautas 1987). According to the World Resources Institute (1992), closed natural forests cover 7,399,000 km² with a further 1,897,000 km² classed as "other wooded area". "Managed closed forest" in 1980 amounted to 7,399,000 km² (the same figure as that quoted for natural closed forest), while "protected closed forest" in 1980 covered 200,000 km².

In the north, **coniferous (taiga) forest** stretches from northern Europe across Siberia to the Far East of Russia, between the Polar Circle and approximately 56°N in West Siberia and about 55°N in Primorye in the Far East. The main genera are *Larix*, *Pinus*, *Picea* and *Abies*. In West Siberia and as far south as the Altai-Sayan Mountains, the forests consist mainly of species of *Picea* and *Abies* (spruce-fir forests), together with *Pinus sibirica*, while east of the Yenesei River they are replaced by the world's largest extent of larch forest, up to about 70°N. Raised *Sphagnum* bogs, and bogs occurring within taiga, occupy large areas of West Siberia.

Montane taiga occurs throughout large areas of the lower Amur River region and Sikhote-Alin in the Far East (see Data Sheet on Primorye, CPD Site CA5), the Altai-Sayan (CPD Site CA1, see Data Sheet), the Ural Mountains and the Caucasus (CPD Site CA2, see Data Sheet). Montane *Larix* (larch) forests and tundra cover the mid-Siberian and trans-Baikalian Highlands, as well as the mountain ranges of north-east Russia.

A narrow zone of **broadleaved forest** occurs to the south of the taiga in the west and in the Far East. Much of the western forest occurs in the Carpathian Mountains and Crimea (outside the limits of Central Asia), but some also occurs in the Caucasus, where abundant rainfall on the western slopes produces luxuriant mixed broadleaved forests containing *Castanea*, *Fagus* and *Quercus*, with evergreen trees and shrubs in the understorey. In the Far East, the broadleaved forests are northern extensions of those found in China and Korea (see Regional Overview on China and East Asia). In southern Primorye they are subtropical in character.

Forest-steppe and Steppe

Forest-steppe occurs between latitudes 50° and 53°N in areas which are transitional between summer-wet and summer-dry climates. The Eurasian steppe zone occurs to the south of forest-steppe, approximately to 45°N. Steppe is dominated by drought-resistant perennial grasses, such as *Stipa* spp. (feather grass) and *Avena* spp. (oat grass), together with *Carex* spp. In Kazakhstan, the warm and relatively humid climate provides suitable conditions for ephemeral species, and for such bulbous genera as *Tulipa*, which produce a colourful display in spring. In the steppes of Middle Asia, which have a cold dry spring, there are very few ephemeral species.

Semi-deserts and deserts occur around the Aral Sea region, in Kazakhstan and the northern Caspian lowlands and across Middle Asia to the Chinese border. This zone is dominated by semi-shrubs, shrubs, saltbushes (*Atriplex*) and needle grasses (*Stipa* spp.). Within the zone are the great mountain systems of Middle Asia which contain a third to a half of the vascular plant flora of the whole of the Central Asian region (see Data Sheets on Altai-Sayan and the Mountains of Middle Asia, CPD Sites CA1 and CA3, respectively).

Flora

The flora of the former U.S.S.R. includes about 22,000 vascular plant species. This is for territory included partly in the CPD Europe region and (for the most part) Central Asia. It is estimated that the Central Asian region contains about 17,500 vascular species, belonging to 1675 genera and 159 families. Approximately 2500 vascular plant species and 72 genera are endemic to the region.

There are three major floristic regions (Takhtajan 1986). The Circumboreal Region, the largest floristic region in the world, covers the northern part of the area under consideration, including Siberia, the Urals, Caucasus, Sakhalin and Kamchatka. The Irano-Turanian Region includes the vast area of arid lands bordering the Caspian Sea (including Kazakhstan, Turkmeniya and Uzbekistan), the Hindu Kush and spurs of the western Himalayas. In the Far East, the Eastern Asiatic Region covers the southern Kurile Islands, Sakhalin and Primorye.

The flora of Central Asia has been derived from temperate and subtropical floras of the mid-Tertiary. Comparatively little-modified variants of the temperate flora are found in southern Primorye (Manchurian Province of the Far East), the Altai mountain ranges and the main ranges of the Caucasus and the eastern Carpathians (the last named being treated in the Regional Overview for Europe). Relicts of Tethyan subtropical vegetation survive in the Colchis and Talysh Mountains of the Trans-Caucasian ranges.

Xerophytic grasslands (steppes) and shrublands, rich in neo-endemics, evolved since the Miocene and belong to the Mediterranean and Turanian derivatives of the Tethyan flora. They are found in the Middle Asian mountains (CPD Site CA3, see Data Sheet) and in the Crimean Mountains (see Data Sheet on Crimea and Novorossia, CPD Site Eu21, included in the section on Europe).

Tundras of the Siberian north evolved during the Pleistocene glaciation. Remnants of the original Beringian flora (centred in Beringia, between Asia and North America) can be found in eastern Chukotka (see Data Sheet on Chukotskiy Peninsula, CPD Site CA4).

Patterns of species diversity and endemism

Species diversity is concentrated in Asteraceae (which contains 20% of all the region's vascular species), Fabaceae (10%), Poaceae (5%) and Lamiaceae (5%).

Middle Asia is a centre of diversity for Plumbaginaceae, Chenopodiaceae, Polygonaceae, Boraginaceae, Fabaceae and Apiaceae. Poaceae, Cyperaceae, Brassicaceae and Caryophyllaceae are all centred in the arid zone, in Novoya Zemlya and, for the last three families, in eastern Chukotka. The Caucasus is a centre of diversity for Rosaceae, Caryophyllaceae, Dipsacaceae, Valerianaceae, Campanulaceae and Primulaceae, among others, while Far Eastern Russia is rich in Polypodiaceae, Potamogetonaceae, Salicaceae, Saxifragaceae, Betulaceae, Violaceae and Caprifoliaceae (Bobrov 1934–1960; Takhtajan 1981; Borodin *et al.* 1984).

Montane areas are generally richer in species than the surrounding plains. They support both palaeo- and neo-endemics. The Caucasus, Middle Asian mountains and the Manchurian Province of the Far East each contain 5–6 endemic genera. The Altai-Sayan, mid-Siberian, Trans-Baikalian, North-Eastern and Sakhalin-Kuril Provinces each have one endemic genus (*Microstigma, Redowskia, Borodinia, Gorodkovia* and *Miyakea*, respectively).

At the species level, the Altai-Sayan is very rich, with 120 strictly endemic species, while the Trans-Baikalian, North-Eastern and Sakhalin-Kuril regions are much less diverse with only a few endemics. Eastern Chukotka contains an important assemblage of Arctic endemics, although its flora as a whole is relatively poor.

Useful plants

Timber trees

The total reserves of standing timber amount to almost 84,000 million m³, about 80% of which is conifer wood (Knystautas 1987). The most important genera are *Larix* spp. (larch) (covering c. 2,650,000 km²), *Pinus* spp. (pine) (1,204,450 km²) and *Picea* spp. (spruce) (770,000 km²). (Note that these figures refer to forested areas of the former U.S.S.R.)

The forests are being logged on an increasingly large scale, many accessible areas already having been deforested. No figures are available for the rate of deforestation. According to the World Resources Institute (1992), 45,400 km² were reforested each year in the former U.S.S.R. between 1981–1985.

Compared with tropical forests, the northern ("boreal") forests accumulate less carbon in their standing biomass, and more carbon in the soil and leaf litter. Along with extensive areas of bogland in West Siberia, they serve as major carbon sinks. Thus, the northern forests play an important role in the global cycling of carbon and in climate regulation. Tundra vegetation is also important in controlling the amount of carbon dioxide and methane emitted from permafrost areas.

Medicinal plants

About 1000 wild plant species in the region are used in medicines, including the celebrated *Panax ginseng*

(ginseng) and related araliaceous plants. Many uses of plants are known only by native people. One of the most widely used plants is *Hippophaë rhamnoides*, which provides a source of healing oil.

Food and fodder plants

Both taiga and tundra support traditional hunting lifestyles, plant gathering, and reindeer herding communities, while semi-desert formations are used as pastures in traditional sheep and camel herding. Forests throughout the region are widely used as sources of food by local people. Even in urban areas, people will go into the forest to gather flowers, fruits, nuts and fungi for decorative and culinary purposes. *Corylus* (hazel), *Juglans* (walnuts), *Pinus sibirica* and *P. koraiensis* (cedar pines), and numerous species of shrubs and lianas (e.g. *Schizandra chinensis*) are still important food reserves.

Crop plant relatives

All the areas selected as CPD sites are centres of useful and under-utilized plants. The Caucasus (CPD Site CA2) and Middle Asian mountains (CPD Site CA3), in particular, are centres of diversity of wild relatives of cultivated crop plants. These areas could therefore be extremely valuable in providing important genetic resources for agriculture in the future.

Factors causing loss of biodiversity

A total of 444 plant species with limited distributions or small populations are included in the Red Data Book of the U.S.S.R. (Borodin *et al.* 1984). Lists of species in need of active conservation have been drawn up by the Botanical Institute of the former Academy of Sciences of the U.S.S.R. and by the former All-Union Research Institute for Nature Reserves and Nature Conservation. A decree was passed by the Council of Ministers of the former U.S.S.R. by which each of the republics must conserve the rare plants of their territories. The major threats to the native flora and vegetation are summarized below.

Deforestation

Although 80% of the former European U.S.S.R. forest zone has been cleared for agriculture, urban and industrial development, or modified to various extents by logging and other land use practices, considerable timber reserves remain, particularly in the north-east (Komi Province) of European Russia, East Siberia and the northern Far East. Many of the valuable montane forests, notably in Sikhote-Alin and Altai, have been cleared or severely modified by logging or affected by fire. Whereas some areas of the Caucasian and Middle Asian montane forests are now protected, deforestation still continues in Siberia and the Far East.

Agriculture

Much of the original steppe has been ploughed and only 50% of the rich chernozem soil remains in some places, the rest having been lost to erosion. In the 1960s large areas of pasture, formerly used by nomadic herders, were ploughed and have subsequently been degraded to virtual wastelands.

Overgrazing

Overgrazing is a serious threat in such semi-arid regions as Kalmykia, where most of the pasture has been degraded and lost to erosion, as well as in some reindeer-breeding tundra areas, notably on Sibiryakov Island (Ostrov Sibiryakova).

Mining and industrial developments

Rapid industrial expansion has taken place since the end of the Second World War, and this has had both direct and indirect effects on natural habitats. Areas have been cleared for new developments, and pollution of air and water has affected wetlands and large areas of forest. Oil and gas exploration and mining are serious threats to the Siberian tundras where mine spoil has devastated large areas.

Over-collecting

Many species of medicinal and ornamental plants are threatened by over-collecting. The best known example is *Panax ginseng*, which is now Endangered in the wild as a result of over-harvesting for its medicinal properties. Examples of other species under threat from over-collecting are given in the site Data Sheets.

Conservation

There are approximately 60 different categories of protected area which provide for nature conservation to varying extents. About 1.5% of the land area of the C.I.S. is protected in approximately 172 Strict Nature Reserves (Zapovedniki) and 24 National Parks (Natsional'nye parky) (IUCN 1992). The inclusion of 1958 Nature Sanctuaries or Partial Reserves (Zakazniki) brings the coverage of protected areas to 4.1% of the land area. Other less strict or temporary forms of protection include National Hunting Reserves, Refuges, Natural Monuments and Protective Zones in watersheds. 16 areas in the C.I.S. are designated as Biosphere Reserves covering a total area of 91,345 km².

The distribution of these areas is uneven. The northern third of the region includes only 6 reserves covering an area of 57,728 km². Even when more areas are protected, for example in the Caucasus and Lake Baikal region, the existing reserves do not adequately protect all the major vegetation types and many rare plant habitats remain outside the reserve network.

It is estimated that about 30% of the flora of the former U.S.S.R. is protected in reserves and sanctuaries (Knystautas 1987). Preliminary assessments suggest that protected area coverage needs to be at least doubled in areas of high plant diversity, such as the Caucasus and in Primorye in the Far East, while a three-fold expansion (from the present 1.5% to 4.5 %) is urgently needed in the Altai-Sayan region. Protected areas are totally lacking in the Chukotskiy Peninsula, where the Russian part of the International Beringian Park has yet to be established.

There are plans to establish between 40–50 National Parks over the next 10 years, mainly in the Far East, as well as 110 State Nature Reserves to cover at least 6% of the land area by 2005 (IUCN 1992). Much of this expanded system would extend protection of the Arctic islands, northern taiga, mountain and forest-steppe (Nikol'skii *et al.* 1991).

An overview of the protected areas system and conservation legislation throughout the territories of the former U.S.S.R. is given in IUCN (1992).

Alongside the expansion of the protected area system to cover areas of high plant diversity, regional development programmes must also take into account sites of major plant diversity within their respective areas.

Centres of plant diversity and endemism

The following areas are selected for treatment in Data Sheets:

Russia, Kazakhstan

CA1. Altai-Sayan

– see Data Sheet.

Armenia, Azerbaijain, Georgia, Russia

CA2. Caucasus

– see Data Sheet.

Kazakhstan, Kirghizia, Tadzhikistan, Turkmenistan, Uzbekistan

CA3. Mountains of Middle Asia (including the mountain ranges of Kopetdag, Tien Shan, Pamiro-Alai, Pamir and Dzhungarian Alatau)

– see Data Sheet.

Russia

CA4. Chukotskiy Peninsula

– see Data Sheet.

CA5. Primorye

– see Data Sheet.

Other important botanical areas are:

CA6. Baikal region

This area surrounds Lake Baikal in South Siberia, covering c. 500,000 km². The most botanically-rich areas are: the southern, south-eastern and south-western shores of the lake, including eastern spurs of East Sayany, Tunkin Valley and Khamar-Daban ridge, the northern, north-western and

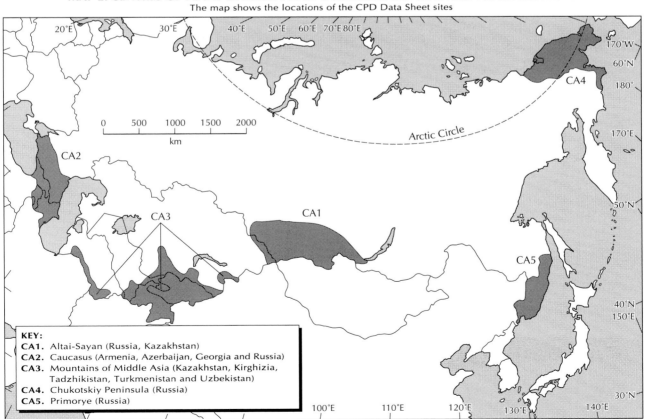

MAP 2. CENTRES OF PLANT DIVERSITY AND ENDEMISM: CENTRAL AND NORTHERN ASIA
The map shows the locations of the CPD Data Sheet sites

KEY:
CA1. Altai-Sayan (Russia, Kazakhstan)
CA2. Caucasus (Armenia, Azerbaijan, Georgia and Russia)
CA3. Mountains of Middle Asia (Kazakhstan, Kirghizia, Tadzhikistan, Turkmenistan and Uzbekistan)
CA4. Chukotskiy Peninsula (Russia)
CA5. Primorye (Russia)

north-eastern shores of the lake, and the Stanovoy highlands. Altitude: 500–2500 m.

- ❖ Vegetation: Coniferous forests, scrub, alpine meadows, steppe, swamps and swamp meadows, thermal spring communities.
- ❖ Flora: 2300 vascular plant taxa, of which c. 15% are endemic.
- ❖ Threats: Timber cutting, overgrazing, industrial development, tourism, over-collection of medicinal herbs and ornamental plants.
- ❖ Conservation: Two Nature Reserves: Baikal Reserve (1657 km²) and Barguzinskiy (2632 km²). Baikal National Park is in the process of being established.

Tadzhikistan, Uzbekistan

CA7. Zeravshan River basin and the Samarkand Mountains

Situated to the west of the Pamir mountain system. Area: c. 20,000 km². Altitude: up to 5000 m.

- ❖ Vegetation: Various types of steppe with ephemeral species and *Artemisia* scrub; alpine meadows above 3000 m.
- ❖ Flora: 1900 vascular plant taxa, of which 90 (5%) are endemic. About 200 species are used as sources of food, medicines, for industrial uses and for their ornamental value.
- ❖ Threats: Overgrazing, timber cutting, clearance for agriculture in the lower areas, fire.
- ❖ Conservation: 3 Nature Reserves in the Zeravshan River basin: Zeravshanskiy (50 km²), ornithological reserve; Iskanderkulsk (300 km²); Cay-Vota botanical reserve (42 km²).

References (Russian titles have been translated.)

Bobrov, E.G. (ed.) (1934-1960). *Flora of the U.S.S.R.*, vols I–XXX. Acad. Sci. U.S.S.R., Leningrad. (In Russian.)

Borodin, A.M. et al. (eds) (1984). *Red Data Book of the USSR. Rare and endangered species of animals and plants*, 2nd Ed. Lesnaya Promyshlennost, Moscow. 478 pp. (In Russian.)

Europa Publications (1987). *The Far East and Australasia 1988*. 19th edition. Europa, London. 1015 pp.

Gibrova, S.A., Isachenko, T.I. and Laurenko, E.M. (ed.) (1980). *Vegetation of the European U.S.S.R.* Nauka, Leningrad. 430 pp. (In Russian.)

Gulisashvili, V.Z., Makhatadze, L.P. and Prilipko, L.I. (1972). *Vegetation of the Caucasus*. Nauka, Moscow. 233 pp. (In Russian.)

IUCN (1992). *Protected areas of the world: a review of national systems. Volume 2: Palaearctic*. IUCN, Gland, Switzerland and Cambridge, U.K. xxviii, 556 pp.

Jurtsev, B.A. (1966). *Hypoarctic botanical-geographical belt and the origin of its flora*. Nauka, Moscow and Leningrad. 94 pp. (In Russian.)

Knystautas, A. (1987). *The natural history of the U.S.S.R.* Century, London. 224 pp.

Lavrenko, E.M. (1960). *On the Sakharo-Gobian desert botanical-geographical province and its divisions*. Doklady Acad. Sci. U.S.S.R. 134 pp. (In Russian.)

Malyshev, L.I. (1972). Floristic perspectives of the Soviet Union. In Vasilchenko, I.T. (ed.), *History of flora and vegetation of Eurasia*. Nauka, Leningrad. Pp. 17–40. (In Russian.)

Nikol'skii, A., Bolshova, L.I. and Karaseva, S.E. (1991). Palaearctic-U.S.S.R. Regional protected areas review. Paper prepared for IV World Parks Congress, Caracas, February 1992. U.S.S.R. Ministry of Natural Resources Management and Environmental Protection, Moscow.

Shumilova, L.V. (1962). *Botanical geography of Siberia*. Tomsk University Press, Tomsk. 439 pp. (In Russian.)

Sochava, V.B. (1960). *Geographical aspects of the Siberian taiga*. Nauka, Novosibirsk. 256 pp. (In Russian.)

Takhtajan, A.L. (ed.) (1981). *Rare and endangered species of the U.S.S.R. flora in need of protection*. Nauka, Leningrad. 264 pp. (In Russian.)

Takhtajan, A.L. (1986). *Floristic regions of the world*. University of California Press, Berkeley. 522 pp.

Voroshilov, V.N. (1966). *Flora of the Soviet Far East*. Nauka, Moscow. 476 pp. (In Russian.)

World Resources Institute (1992). *World resources 1992–93: a guide to the global environment*. Oxford University Press, New York. 385 pp.

ALTAI-SAYAN
Russia, Kazakhstan

Location: Southern Siberia between latitudes 49°00'–56°00'N and longitudes 83°00'–108°00'E.

Area: c. 1,100,000 km².

Altitude: c. 300–4506 m (summit of Gora Belukha).

Vegetation: Mixed coniferous forests, steppe and forest-steppe, subalpine and alpine vegetation, tundra.

Flora: c. 2500 vascular plant species, of which 120 endemic; 1 monotypic endemic genus. c. 200 rare or threatened species.

Useful plants: Timber trees, medicinal plants, food plants, ornamental plants.

Other values: Ecotourism, rich fauna, watershed protection.

Threats: Forest clearance, fire, overgrazing in alpine and subalpine areas, plant collecting.

Conservation: c. 1.5% of the region is protected in 5 Nature Reserves (Zapovedniki) covering c. 15,595 km², c. 300 Natural Monuments and small floristic refuges.

This sheet covers the mountain range within Russia and Kazakhstan. The continuation of the Altai-Sayan in China and Mongolia is discussed in the Regional Overview on China and East Asia. That part of the range in China is designated as CPD Site EA36.

Geography

The Altai-Sayan region covers c. 1,100,000 km² between latitudes 49°00'–56°00'N and longitudes 83°00'–108°00'E, and includes several mountain ranges which form the division between humid boreal forests in the north and the drier steppes of Central Asia. The major ranges are the Altai, Salair, Kuznetskiy Alatau, Sayan and the Khamar-Daban along the border with Mongolia and extending north-east to Lake Baikal (Ozero Baykal). The Altai is the highest system, rising to 4506 m altitude at Gora Belukha in the south-east of the region, and extending some 750 km (outside of the region under consideration) along the border between China and Mongolia (see Regional Overview on China and East Asia). The other massifs are mostly below 3000 m, with the Alatau reaching 2178 m. The Salair is much lower, between 300–500 m, and consists of a plateau sloping to the north. There are three large intermontane depressions – Kuznetskaya, Minusinskaya and Tuvinskaya – occupying about 7% of the total land area.

The main rivers draining the Altai are the Biya, Bukhtarma, Chuya and Katun'. There are about 3500 lakes, mostly of glacial age, but the largest – Teletskoye and Markakol' – occur in tectonic depressions. Most of the rocks are of Precambrian and Palaeozoic origin, including metamorphic shales, granites, marine clastic and carbonate deposits, as well as volcanic rocks. During Proterozoic and lower Palaeozoic times there was massive tectonic activity causing immense upheavals and block-faulting of the orogenic system.

The climate is continental, with permafrost increasing towards the east. Temperatures in the South Altai average 13.8°C in July but drop dramatically to an average of -32.1°C in January. The prevailing winds are from mid-continental dry areas to the south and south-west in winter, and from the north-west in summer. The latter bring moisture to the western Altai, Salair and Alatau slopes which receive, on average, annual precipitation of 2000 mm and snow cover to a depth of 1.5–2 m. The South Altai and Sayan have a much drier climate (110 mm annual precipitation), while the northern slopes of Khamar-Daban, facing Lake Baikal, are comparatively humid (precipitation about 1000 mm per year).

Soils are predominantly black (chernozem) and brown soils of various types, with saline soils occasionally found in intermontane depressions and on slopes up to 1500 m (or even 2200 m in south-eastern Altai). There are also grey soils and dark grey podzolic soils in the forest belt at mid-elevations. At higher elevations, montane meadow and tundra soils occur, including podzolic-gley soils in wet areas.

About 7 million people live in the Altai-Sayan region. Indigenous people – the Altajans, Khakasians, Shorians, Tuvins, Buryats and Kazakhs – comprise about 10% of the population. Before colonization in the late 17th–19th centuries, nomadic cattle farming, hunting and fishing were the main forms of subsistence. Immigrants from outside the region brought agriculture, forestry and mining to the region, the latter developing extensively since the 1930s. Most of the population is concentrated in the western, ore-bearing regions of the Altai, Salair, Alatau and Kuznetsk Basin. Areas of steppe in the intermontane depressions and on lower slopes have been almost entirely converted to agriculture, while sheep and goat herding, cattle breeding, occasionally deer and yak breeding, apiculture and hunting are predominant among the scattered montane population.

Vegetation

The present-day vegetation evolved from the Arcto-Tertiary (turgai) mixed broadleaved formations which were replaced by taiga (northern coniferous forests) and xerophytic communities as the climate cooled during the Pleistocene. The vegetation forms distinct altitudinal zones. The following sequence occurs on the Altai slopes (Kuminov 1960; Ogureeva 1983):

Steppe

Steppe grassland and shrubby steppe typically occur up to 300–400 m altitude, but can extend up to higher altitudes along the larger valleys and on drier slopes. In south-eastern Altai, steppe can occasionally reach the alpine tundra belt. In the west, grassy, wormwood and shrubby steppes are found, the latter with species of *Caragana*, *Lonicera* and *Spiraea*. Mongolian elements increase further to the east and at higher altitudes.

Forest-steppe

Forest-steppe occurs in a belt at 300–700 m above sea-level on more humid slopes, and consists of areas of steppe vegetation inter-mixed with larch (*Larix*) woodlands.

Mixed forest

The forest belt, at 700–1800 m above sea-level, includes several formations, notable among which are the relict mixed coniferous forests of Arcto-Tertiary origin, with *Populus tremula* and *Tilia sibirica* typically occurring in the lower canopy. These forests have a rich herbaceous flora. *Tilia* (lime) dominates in a few refugia in Kuznetskiy Alatau and on Mount Shoria to the south.

Far more extensive are the mixed fir-spruce-cedar pine forests dominated by *Abies sibirica*, *Picea obovata* and *Pinus sibirica*, and containing boreal species in the understorey and herb layers. On the drier eastern and southern slopes, these forests are sometimes replaced by larch-cedar pine woodlands, typical of the Mongolian Altai. At higher altitudes, *Abies* gives way to low spruce woodlands with *Larix sibirica* and *Pinus sibirica*, bordering subalpine meadows. Secondary birch forests, with *Betula pendula* and *B. pubescens*, occur in clearings in the mixed conifer forests. Primary aspen-birch (*Populus-Betula*) forests occur on the Salair Ranges and around the Kuznetsk Depression.

Subalpine vegetation occurs above the tree-line and includes tall grass meadows and low shrubland in more humid sites.

Alpine vegetation consists of herb-rich meadows with species of *Anemone*, *Aquilegia*, *Carex*, *Saxifraga* and *Trollius*. Moss-lichen communities and *Dryas* tundras occur on rocky slopes and on the southern ranges, which have a more continental climate.

Flora

The Altai-Sayan flora contains approximately 2500 vascular plant species, including one endemic monotypic genus (*Microstigma*) and 120 endemic species, mostly subalpine and xerophytic herbs. At high altitudes, especially in the eastern Altai ranges, about 17% of the flora is endemic. Genera with the highest number of endemics are *Astragalus* and *Oxytropis* (Malyshev 1965; Revushkin 1988).

TABLE 7. FLORISTIC DIVERSITY OF THE ALTAI-SAYAN MOUNTAIN RANGES

Range	Species	Relict species	Genera	Families
Altai	974	31	315	73
West Sayan	601	22	227	61
East Sayan	592	16	221	64
Khamar-Daban	453	13	210	55
Alatau	332	31	171	51

Most of the endemics seem to have evolved during the Pleistocene in response to aridity, isolation of montane habitats and occasional hybridization. Palaeo-endemics are much fewer in number, about 7% of all relict species, most having disjunct ranges and restricted to a few refugia (Polozhiy and Krapivkina 1985). About 60 narrow endemics are found in Altai, 10 in West Sayan and 21 in East Sayan high mountain tundras, alpine meadows, and in rocky, carbonate-rich sites. Many near-endemics have the main parts of their ranges in the Altai-Sayan area.

The evolution of the Altai-Sayan flora has been influenced by the orogenic and climatic events of the Late Neogene and Pleistocene epochs. It is a major centre of origin of montane floristic assemblages of northern Asia, which have subsequently spread into East Siberia, Kazakhstan, Central Asia, Mongolia and northern China.

Useful plants

The total timber reserves of the Altai-Sayan region amount to approximately 4500 million m³ and include the largest reserves of cedar pine (*Pinus sibirica*) in Russia, together with other important timber trees such as *P. sylvestris*, *Abies sibirica* and *Larix sibirica*. The latter species produces valuable water-resistant timber used in underwater construction.

Conifers also provide valuable oils, resins and edible nuts. For example, turpentine oil and camphor are produced from resin and oil obtained from *Abies* spp., and local people derive a vitamin-rich oil from species of *Abies*. About 250 kg of edible cedar pine nuts are gathered annually from the forests of west Altai.

Approximately 300 species are used medicinally, including *Hippophaë rhamnoides*, a source of oil used in the treatment of wounds and burns. About 400 tonnes of the oil are produced annually. *Hypericum perforatum*, *Rhodiola rosea* and *Leuzea (Rhaponticum) carthamoides* are other important sources of medicines. About 78,000 tonnes of dried plant material are harvested annually from the wild each year for the production of medicines.

Some 100 native plant species are used as sources of food, including *Allium altaica*, *Asparagus* spp. and *Rheum altaicum*. Sources of starch used by native people include *Fritillaria dagana*, *Lilium martagon* and *Polygonum viviparum*. Spices and aromatic plants include *Anthoxanthum odoratum*, *Hierochloë alpina*, *Rhododendron aureum* and *Thymus serpyllum*. An annual crop of about 300–700 kg/ha of fruit is gathered from wild species of *Ribes*, *Rubus*, *Sorbus* and *Vaccinium*.

More than 100 species of honey-producing plants occur in montane steppes, and subalpine and alpine meadows. These communities also contain a large number of useful fodder plants, including species of *Astragalus*, *Hedysarum*, *Medicago*, *Oxytropis* and *Trifolium*.

About 50 ornamental species are of value, or potential value, in horticulture. These include *Lilium martagon*, *Paeonia anomala*, *Trollius altaicus* and *Viola altaica*.

Social and environmental values

Forests still cover 70% of the northern part of the Altai-Sayan mountain system and 45% of the south. Forests maintain the hydrological regime and stabilize slopes, thereby preventing soil erosion, landslips and catastrophic floods.

The rich fauna includes brown bear, wolf, fox, elk, sable, musk and sika deer, bighorn sheep and snow leopard. *Pinus sibirica* forests are particularly rich, with 44 mammal and 33 bird species having been recorded. The Altai snowcock (*Tetraogallus altaicus*) is a restricted-range species which is endemic to subalpine and alpine habitats above approximately 2000 m in the Altai Mountains.

The forests are important recreation areas. Open landscapes of great natural beauty and floristic diversity are attractive for eco-tourism. However, tourist infrastructure is poorly developed, except at a few famous places, such as to the north of Teletskoye Lake.

Threats

Forest clearance, especially along the banks of the larger rivers, and extensive forest fires are the major threats. Natural recovery of the cedar pine forests takes several hundred years, while reforestation compensates for no more than 1% of the area felled or damaged. As a result of disturbance, primary conifer forests are replaced by secondary birch woodlands.

Subalpine and alpine vegetation suffer from overgrazing, which results in soil erosion on steep slopes. As a result, the natural tree-line is artificially lowered in places.

Plant collecting has reduced the size of populations of many valuable herbs, such as *Adonis vernalis*, *Rhodiola rosea* and *Trollius altaicus*, while the number of visitors in the more densely populated Kuznetsk Basin, Salair, Alatau Kuznetsk and south-western Altai, far exceeds the carrying capacity of the natural ecosystems.

Of 200 rare or threatened species (8% of the total Altai-Sayan flora), 2% are almost Extinct (e.g. *Megadenia bardunovii*), 8% are Endangered and 60% Threatened (e.g. *Aconitum decipiens*, *Iris ludwigii* and *Viola incisa*). Most of the threatened species are relict herbs occurring in fir, aspen-fir and fir-cedar pine forests. *Tilia sibirica* is also under threat. Rare relict associations of *Listera ovata* and *Ophioglossum vulgatum* are found around hot springs in the East Sayan highlands.

Conservation

Existing protected areas cover about 1.5% of the Altai-Sayan region and include five Nature Reserves (Zapovedniki) covering a total area of c. 15,595 km², together with about 300 Natural Monuments and small floristic refuges, ranging from 10 to 50 ha each. Of the existing reserves, four belong to the Russian Federation and one (Markakol'skiy Nature Reserve) to Kazakhstan.

Altaiskiy Nature Reserve (8812 km²), in the north-eastern Altai, contains 1400 vascular plant species, about 70% of the Altai flora. Some 20 rare species are confined to the fir-cedar pine forests, subalpine and alpine meadows and tundras.

Sayano-Shushenskiy Nature Reserve (3904 km²), at 1500–2000 m altitude in the West Sayan Mountains, lies mostly within the coniferous forest belt and includes numerous relict herbs and narrow endemics.

Stolby Nature Reserve (471 km²), in the East Sayan Mountains, contains 550 vascular plant species, including the rare variant of spruce, *Picea obovata* f. *caerulea*.

Baikal'skiy Nature Reserve (1657 km²), in the Khamar-Daban Range, descends to the shores of Lake Baikal and includes taiga and steppe formations. It contains 795 vascular plant species.

Markakol'skiy Nature Reserve (750 km²), in the south-western Altai, includes all the altitudinal zones and contains numerous South Altai endemics.

All the above reserves (Zapovedniki) carry out botanical research and are classified in the IUCN Management Category I (Strict Nature Reserve). However, the present reserve system is inadequate to protect the full range of vegetation in the region; at least 4% coverage is thought to be necessary to provide adequate protection for all the endangered taxa and communities. New reserves are planned, for example in central and south-east Altai, together with a possible Russian-Mongolian trans-frontier reserve.

References (All titles translated from Russian.)

Kuminov, A.V. (1960). *Vegetation cover of Altai*. Acad. Sci. U.S.S.R. Siberian Branch, Novosibirsk. 450 pp.

Malyshev, L.I. (1965). *Montane flora of eastern Sayan*. Nauka, Moskow-Leningrad. 367 pp.

Ogureeva, G.N. (1983). Altitudinal belt structure of the South Siberian montane vegetation. *Moscow Soc. Explor. Natur. Bull. Biol.* 88(1): 66–77.

Polozhiy, A.V. and Krapivkina, E.D. (1985). *Relics of the Tertiary broadleaf forest in the flora of Siberia*. Tomsk University Press, Tomsk. 156 pp.

Revushkin, A.S. (1988). *Montane flora of Altai*. Tomsk University Press, Tomsk. 318 pp.

Sedelnikov, V.N. (1979). *Flora and vegetation of the Kuznetskiy Alatai highlands*. Naika, Novosibirsk. 168 pp.

Acknowledgements

This Data Sheet was prepared by Dr L.I. Vorontsova (Institute of Nature Conservation and Reserves, Moscow).

CAUCASUS
Armenia, Azerbaijan, Georgia and Russia

Location: Between the Azov, Black and Caspian Seas, between latitudes 38°21'–47°15'N and longitudes 36°30'–50°20'E.

Area: c. 440,000 km².

Altitude: 0–5642 m (summit of El'brus).

Vegetation: Lowland broadleaved forests, montane broadleaved and coniferous forests, montane steppe and woodlands, subalpine meadows, semi-desert vegetation.

Flora: c. 6000 vascular plant species, of which 1200 (20%) are endemic. Many Tertiary relict species; c. 340 rare and threatened species.

Useful plants: c. 300 species of food plants, c. 300 medicinal plant species, timber trees, ornamental plants, melliferous plants.

Other values: Rich fauna, tourist attraction, genetic resources of cultivated crops.

Threats: Logging, overgrazing, plant collecting, visitor pressure.

Conservation: c. 2% of the region is protected in 37 Nature Reserves (Zapovedniki) covering c. 8982 km². The Vavilov Institute of Plant Industry stores a large collection of seeds of the region's crop plant relatives.

Geography

The Caucasus Mountains (Bol'shoy Kavkaz) cover an area of c. 440,000 km² in the Russian Federation, Georgia, Armenia and Azerbaijan between the Azov, Black and Caspian Seas. The mountains form part of the boundary between Central Asia and the CPD regions of Europe and Middle East and South West Asia (treated in Volume 1).

The Greater Caucasus consist of several mountain ranges about 180 km wide and extending for 1500 km from north-west to south-east. The central part reaches more than 5000 m above sea-level. The highest peaks are El'brus (5642 m) and Kazbek (5043 m). The northern foothills (known as the Cis-Caucasus) include the Stavropol'skaya and Tersko-Sunjenskian Highlands, as well as the Kubanskian and Tersko-Kumskian Plains.

The Lesser Caucasus lie to the south of the main ranges and extend from the Black Sea coast to the Karabakh and Talysh Mountains. The highest points are about 3700 m above sea-level. To the south are the Armenian Highlands, with individual peaks rising above 4000 m (e.g. Aragats, 4090 m). The Armenian Highlands extend to eastern Anatolia (Turkey) (see Data Sheet on North-east Anatolia, CPD Site SWA19, treated in the South West Asia and Middle East region).

There are large depressions south of the main ranges in the Rioni and Colchis lowlands in the west, and in the Kura-Araksian and Lenkoranian lowlands in the east and south-east. Some of these depressions contain large lakes, the largest of which is Ozero Sevan (Lake Sevan). The principal river systems are those of the Terek, Kuma and Kura, which drain into the Caspian Sea, and the Rioni which drains into the Black Sea.

Geologically, the Caucasus are a series of thrust sheets, or nappes, of geosynclinal deposits of the Palaeozoic and Mesozoic Tethys belts. Ophiolite associations of ultramafic and siliceous rocks, Jurassic volcanic arcs and Cretaceous to Palaeocene flysh deposits are widespread, particularly in the Lesser Caucasus.

The main ranges of the Caucasus lie along the boundary of the temperate and subtropical climatic zones, shielding the latter from cold northerly winds. The Cis-Caucasian plains have a temperate continental climate and are drier to the east. Temperatures during the coldest month (January) are on average -2° to -5°C. In the Colchis lowlands the climate is humid subtropical with mild winters (average January temperatures about 4–6°C) and annual rainfall of about 2500 mm. The eastern Kura-Araksian lowlands have a much drier climate, with a rainfall of no more than 400 mm p.a. and average January temperatures around 1–3.8°C.

Average annual temperatures fall 0.5–0.6°C per 100 m rise in altitude in the Greater Caucasus. Monthly temperatures at 2000 m above sea-level range from -8°C in January to 13°C in August. Westerly winds bring over 2000 mm of rain annually to the Greater Caucasus from the Atlantic Ocean and Mediterranean Sea. The highest rainfalls, up to 4000 mm p.a., occur on the southern and south-western slopes of the Western and Central Greater Caucasus. The eastern slopes are drier, receiving 900–1000 mm p.a. The Armenian Highlands have a more continental climate, the average annual precipitation being 450–550 mm, with most rain falling in spring.

Soil types are extremely diverse, ranging from black soils (chernozem) in the western Cis-Caucasus, and locally in the Armenian Highlands, to brown, podzolic and podzolic-carbonate soils on slopes. Red soils occur in the wetter Colchis depressions and saline soils occur in the eastern lowlands.

The population of the region is about 30 million.

Vegetation

The Caucasus contain a diverse range of vegetation types and several phytogeographical provinces, each of which varies according to altitude (Grossheim 1948). For example, the Euxine Province encompasses the western Trans-Caucasus and is an extension of the Euxine Province of Northeast Anatolia (see CPD Site SWA19, included in the South West Asia and the Middle East region). Lowland swamp forests are replaced by an altitudinal succession of broadleaved and conifer forests, and subalpine and alpine meadows. In the east there are semi-xerophytic shrublands and dry woodlands in the lowland belt succeeded by broadleaved forests with *Quercus iberica*, montane woodlands of *Q. imeretina*, and subalpine and alpine meadows.

Lowland forests are mainly dominated (in wetter sites) by *Alnus barbata*, *Pterocarya pterocarpa* (and other species of Juglandaceae), *Quercus pedunculifera*, *Populus alba* and *P. hybridica*. *Quercus pubescens*, *Ulmus carpinifolia* and *Fraxinus excelsior* occur in drier sites on the lower slopes.

Typical altitudinal succession of montane forest includes the following types: (1) mixed broadleaved *Castanea-Fagus-Zelkova* associations, with *Quercus virgiliana*, *Pterocarya*, *Carpinus caucasica* and an evergreen undergrowth of *Rhododendron*, *Ruscus* and *Ilex*; (2) mixed broadleaved *Quercus castaneifolia-Zelkova-Carpinus* associations, with *Parrotia persica*, *Diospyros lotus* and *Ficus hyrcana* occurring, for example, in the Talysh Mountains at 400–600 m above sea-level; (3) oak forest, with *Quercus macranthera*, typically at 1200–2700 m in the southern Trans-Caucasian region, and floristically richer in the eastern Greater Caucasus, Lesser Caucasus and Talysh Mountains; (4) beech forests, with *Fagus orientalis* dominant in the middle and upper forest belts at 1400–2200 m above sea-level, sometimes descending to 700 m (in the Talysh Mountains) or even down to the lowlands (as at Colchis); (5) coniferous forests at 1100–2300 m, and even as low as 300–400 m in some wet valleys, with *Abies nordmanniana* and *Picea orientalis*, together with *Fagus*, *Acer* and other broadleaved trees at the lower altitudes; and (6) pine forests on northern slopes, mostly of *Pinus kochiana*, with some forests of *P. pityusa* or *P. eldarica* at lower altitudes and locally on the Black Sea coast.

Extensive *Pistacia* woodland occurs in the montane steppe belt and on steep, rocky slopes of the Alasan-Iora watershed, while juniper woodland occurs in northern Caucasus and in the eastern Trans-Caucasus. *Celtis-Acer-Juniperus* woodlands, along with *Cotinus*, *Berberis*, *Ephedra* and *Astragalus* spp., occur in the lower layers. Woodlands near the tree-line include *Acer trautvetteri*, *Quercus macranthera*, *Betula* spp., *Fagus orientalis* and *Rhododendron ponticum*, and alternate with subalpine meadows.

Subalpine meadows occur at 2400–3100 m altitude and are dominated by festucoid grasses and sedges, with *Ranunculus caucasicus* and other herbs. Montane steppe or meadow-steppe associations contain *Festuca valesiaca*, *Stipa* spp., *Paeonia tenuifolia*, and species of *Potentilla*, *Vinca* and *Tanacetum*. The drier Dagestan steppes are unusual in having endemic dominants, e.g. *Stipa*

daghestanica, in association with montane xerophytic species of *Bromopsis*, *Astragalus* and *Scutellaria*. Xerophytic communities are found in Dagestan, South Armenia and Azerbaijan (Nakhichevan Province) on calcareous substrates at 300–1600 m above sea-level. They are floristically rich, with many endemic species.

Semi-desert vegetation occurs in the southern and eastern Trans-Caucasus between the Greater and Lesser Caucasus. Distinct types of halophytic vegetation, with *Halocnemum strobilaceum*, *Suaeda microphylla* and *Salsola ericoides*, occur on saline soils surrounding some lakes, such as Ozero Sevan.

Flora

The Caucasian flora includes an estimated 6000 vascular plant species, representing 1300 genera and 150 families. The most diverse families are, in descending order: Asteraceae (770 species), Fabaceae (510), Poaceae (420), Brassicaceae (320), Apiaceae (300), Caryophyllaceae (280), Rosaceae (240), Lamiaceae (230), Scrophulariaceae (210), Liliaceae *sensu lato* (200), Ranunculaceae (150) and Cyperaceae (150).

There are 1200 endemic species (20% of the total flora), some representing endemic genera, e.g. *Agasyllis* and *Chymsydia* (Apiaceae), *Callicephalus* (Asteraceae) and *Sredinskya* (Primulaceae). There are also many Tertiary relicts, such as *Nelumbo nucifera*, *Parrotia persica* and *Zelkova* spp., as well as elements from the Mediterranean Krymo-Novorossian Province, Asiatic Irano-Turanian Province and a large autochthonous Caucasian component.

Local centres of plant diversity and endemism include the following outstanding areas:

Colchis lowlands

These cover 12,500 km² between latitudes 41°00'–43°30'N and longitudes 40°00'–42°00'E. The climate is subtropical-humid (annual precipitation about 2500 mm). The broadleaved forests are dominated by *Castanea sativa*, *Fagus orientalis*, *Zelkova carpinifolia* and the endemic Colchian oak (*Quercus imeretina*) and include Caucasian, European, Colchian and Asiatic (Hyrcanian, Himalayan and Far Eastern) elements.

The flora include 1500 vascular species, of which 200 are strict endemics. Notable among them are Tertiary relicts. Many endemics, such as *Campanula suanetica*, *Daphne woronowii*, *Gentiana paradoxa* and *Allium circassicum*, occur in woodland communities or on rocky slopes. Wetlands and aquatic communities are also exceptionally rich, with a flora of about 240 vascular plant species.

Talysh subtropical forests

These occur on the eastern slopes of the Talysh Mountains facing the Caspian Sea, and on the adjacent Lenkoran Plains, covering about 370 km² between latitudes 38°20'–39°08'N and longitudes 66°15'–66°25'E. The forests form an ecological "island" surrounded by xerophytic woodlands and represent a north-western outlier of the Hyrcanian Floristic Province extending to the Turanian and South Caspian plains (see Data Sheet on the Hyrcanian Forests, CPD Site SWA18, included in the South West Asia and Middle East region, in Volume 1).

The Talysh flora includes 1167 vascular plant species, 36 of which are Hyrcanian endemics (Karadze 1966; Lvov 1966). Moreover, the most prominent palaeo-endemics, such as *Parrotia persica* and *Quercus castaneifolia*, dominate forest formations that cover foothills, lower slopes and highland plateaux.

Central Greater Caucasus

This includes the richest areas of the Caucasian Floristic Province, especially Balkaria, Digoria and Dagestan. The area rises to over 5000 m and has a temperate, continental climate with average annual precipitation ranging from 500–2000 mm. Glaciers occur at the highest elevations.

There are five endemic genera: *Pseudovesicaria* (Brassicaceae), *Symphyoloma* (Apiaceae), *Pseudobetckea* (Valerianaceae), *Trigonocaryum* (Boraginaceae) and *Cladochaeta* (Asteraceae). Species endemism amounts to 20% of the total flora, with most of the endemics occurring on the upper Central Caucasus slopes. Examples of endemic species include *Corydalis pallidiflora*, *Gentiana grossheimii* and *Papaver oreophyllum*. Takhtajan (1986) lists many endemics.

Armenian Highlands

These represent the Armeno-Iranian Floristic Province, which extends into Turkey, Iran, Afganistan and northern Pakistan. Their floristics have been discussed in detail by Gabrielian and Fajvush (1989). The vegetation includes montane steppes at 1000–3000 m, semi-desert vegetation in the Ararat Depression at 1300–1500 m, patches of Mediterranean forests with *Fagus orientalis*, *Quercus imeretina* and *Carpinus caucasica*, and *Pistacia-Celtis* and *Juniperus* woodlands. Most forests have been cleared or replaced by scrub thickets.

The flora of the Armenian Highlands includes about 1800 vascular plant species. If the extension of the Armenian Highlands into Turkey and Iran is also taken into account, the vascular flora increases to 3200–3500 species (Gabrielian and Fajvush 1989). There are many strict endemics, such as *Centaurea vavilovii*, *Pyrus daralghezica* and *P. sosnovskii*. The rare endemic cereals *Secale vavilovii*, *Triticum boeoticum* and *T. urartu* also occur here, together with other wild relatives of major crops.

Useful plants

The Caucasus are exceptionally rich in useful and potentially useful plant species, including wild relatives of some major crops. It was one of the areas intensively explored by Vavilov in search of wild relatives of cereals and other crops (see Vavilov 1992). The occurrence of the endemic cereals *Secale vavilovii*, *Triticum boeoticum* and *T. urartu* in the Armenian Highlands has already been noted above. The region is also a centre of diversity for such genera as *Pyrus* (pears), *Malus* (apples), *Cerasus* (cherries) and *Corylus* (hazelnuts). *Pyrus* spp. alone yield an annual crop of about 600,000 tonnes.

Many plants are used in traditional medicine, including *Atropa caucasica* and *Datura stramonium*. Volatile oils are derived from species in such genera as *Artemisia*, *Mentha*, *Thymus* and *Ziziphora*. About 200 species are used for honey production, and about 200 species are sources of tannins and dyes.

Ornamental plants of value in horticulture number about 1000 species, and include conifers such as *Taxus baccata* and *Juniperus* spp., ornamental broadleaved trees and shrubs such as *Parrotia persica* and *Rhododendron* spp., bulbous species in such genera as *Crocus*, *Cyclamen*, *Iris* and *Tulipa*, and other herbaceous plants, such as *Centaurea* spp.

About 60 tree species are used as sources of timber. The most valuable timbers include the dominant montane forest trees, such as *Castanea sativa*, *Fagus orientalis*, *Fraxinus excelsior* and *Parrotia persica*.

Social and environmental values

The forests are extensively used for recreation. Health resorts and tourist camps are located along the sea coast as well as in the mountains. There are about 10,000 km² of forested recreation areas, visited by about 4.2 million people in 1990.

The forests support a rich fauna including brown bear, wild boar, lynx and marten. Hunting and apiculture are popular local trades. The forests are also important regulators of both climate and the hydrological cycle and play a major role in watershed protection and the prevention of soil erosion.

Threats

Logging is a major threat, especially in the northern Caucasus where about 50% of the forested area is subject to logging. Georgia and Azerbaijan are less affected, with about 2% of their forests being subjected to logging at present. With slow natural recovery and poorly developed reforestation techniques, cleared beech, oak, chestnut and spruce-fir forests are replaced by less productive (and floristically less diverse) oak-hornbeam or hornbeam woodlands and xerophytic shrublands.

Most of the steppes in the lowlands and on lower slopes have been ploughed, while the swampy Colchic forests have been cleared. Semi-desert areas are used as winter pastures for grazing sheep, while more than 40% of the montane tall grass meadows suffer from overgrazing. Further threats are uncontrolled plant collecting and inadequate controls on tourism.

340 vascular plant species are considered to be threatened, of which 77 are locally Endangered and 10 are locally Extinct; 155 species have been included in the Red Data Book of the former U.S.S.R. (Borodin *et al.* 1984). The Red Data Books of the Russian Federation, Georgia and Armenia include 155, 161 and 387 plant species, respectively.

Conservation

There are 37 Nature Reserves (Zapovedniki) protecting a total area of 8982 km² (c. 2% of the region). The Russian Federation and Armenia each have 5 reserves, while Georgia and Azerbaijan each have 14 reserves. Details of the larger reserves are summarized in Table 8.

TABLE 8. SUMMARY OF LARGER NATURE RESERVES IN THE CAUCASUS

Reserve	Vegetation	Area (km²)	Vascular plants Species	% endemic
Hircanian NR	Montane and lowland Hyrcanian forests	30	1167	21
Kabardino-Balkarskiy NR	Upper montane forest, alpine vegetation	741	1000	10
Kavkaz'skiy Zapovednik BR (includes several separate areas)	Broadleaved and coniferous forests, subalpine and alpine meadows, calcicole communities	2635	2000	36
Kazbegskiy NR	Birch, pine, beech forests, subalpine shrublands and meadows, cliff communities	87	1347	28
Khosrovskiy NR	Montane xerophytic woodlands	297	1800	26
Kintrishskiy NR	Relict chestnut-beech forests	139	1043	9
Lagodekhskiy NR	Oak-hornbeam and beech forests, montane meadows	178	1100	13
North Osetian NR	Pine-birch forests, montane meadows, cliff communities	367	1500	20
Teberdinskiy NR	Forest, subalpine and alpine vegetation	850	1200	20

Among the smaller protected areas, the Erebunian Reserve (89 ha) in Armenia was established in 1981 for the protection of wild wheats and other cereals. The Vavilov Institute of Plant Industry stores the world's largest collection of wild relatives of crop plants.

Despite considerable conservation efforts, some areas and vegetation types, notably in the Lesser Caucasus, Dagestan, the xerophytic woodlands of the Armenian Highlands, the Cis-Caucasian steppes, montane steppes and meadow formations, are insufficiently protected. The current network of protected areas needs to be substantially expanded.

References (Russian titles have been translated.)

Borodin, A.M. *et al.* (eds) (1984). *Red Data Book of the USSR. Rare and endangered species of animals and plants*, 2nd Ed. Lesnaya Promyshlennost, Moscow. 478 pp. (In Russian.)

Gabrielian, E. Tz. and Fajvush, G.M. (1989). Floristic links and endemism in the Armenian Highlands. In Kit Tan, Mill, R.R. and Elias, T.S. (eds), *The Davis and Hedge Festschrift: plant phytogeography and related subjects*. Edinburgh University Press, Edinburgh. Pp. 191–206.

Grossheim, A.A. (1948). *Rastitel'nyi pokrov Kavkaza.* [Caucasus vegetation cover.] Moskovskoe obshchestvo estestvoispitateley prirody, Moscow. 267 pp. (In Russian.)

Karadze, A.L. (1966). On the botanical-geographical divisions of the Greater Caucasus highlands. In Tolmachev, A.I. (ed.), *Problems of botany 8*. Nauka, Moscow. 358 pp. (In Russian.)

Kolakovskiy, A.A. (1961). *Plant world of the Kolchis*. Mysl', Moscow. 460 pp. (In Russian.)

Lvov, P.L. (1966). Regularities of the forest type distribution in Dagestan and their classification. *Bot. Zhurn.* 51(3): 396–402. (In Russian.)

Prilipko, L.I. and Gogina, E.E. (1978). Rare species in the natural flora of Talysh in need of protection. *Byull. Glavn. Bot. Sada* (Moscow) 107. (In Russian.)

Safarov, I.S. (1962). *Notable woody Tertiary relicts of Azerbaijan*. Baku. 263 pp. (In Russian.)

Takhtajan, A. (1986). *Floristic regions of the world*. University of California Press, Berkeley. 522 pp.

Vavilov, N.I. (translated by D. Löve) (1992). *Origin and geography of cultivated plants*. Cambridge University Press, Cambridge, U.K. 498 pp.

Acknowledgements

This Data Sheet was prepared by Dr G.A. Lomakina (Institute of Nature Conservation and Reserves, Moscow).

MOUNTAINS OF MIDDLE ASIA
Kazakhstan, Kirghizia, Tadzhikistan, Turkmenistan and Uzbekistan

Location: Mountain ranges of Kopetdag, Tien Shan, Pamiro-Alai, Pamir and Dzhungarian Alatau, between latitudes 35°00'–45°20'N and longitudes 55°10'–82°00'E.

Area: c. 550,000 km².

Altitude: c. 100–7495 m (summit of Pik Kommunizma).

Vegetation: Semi-desert vegetation, montane and subtropical steppe, cushion (tragacanthic) communities, shiblyak (maquis), broadleaved forest, coniferous forest, juniper and pistachio woodlands, alpine and subalpine meadows, nival vegetation.

Flora: c. 5500 vascular plant species, of which c. 1500 endemic.

Useful plants: c. 1000 species of useful plants, including timber trees, medicinal plants, fruit and nut trees, ornamental plants.

Other values: Tourism, genetic resources of cultivated plants, rich fauna.

Threats: Industrial and agricultural development in the lowlands, overgrazing, visitor pressure, over-collection of medicinal and ornamental plants.

Conservation: 18 reserves covering c. 5720 km² (c. 1% of region).

Geography

The mountain ranges covered here are the Kopetdag, Tien Shan, Pamiro-Alai, Pamir and Dzhungarian Alatau, between latitudes 35°00'–45°20'N and longitudes 55°10'–82°00'E, occupying about 550,000 km². The largest among them is Tien Shan, which extends for 2500 km. Its altitude mostly ranges from 3500–4000 m in the west to 4000–5000 m in the east. The highest peaks are Khan-Tengri (6995 m) and Pobedy (7439 m). The upper slopes are glaciated and permafrost occurs above 3200–3400 m.

Pamir is a mountain massif rising to 7495 m above sea-level. East Pamir has glaciers, narrow canyons and steep cliffs, while West Pamir is lower with broader, flat-bottomed valleys.

The Pamiro-Alai extend for 900 km between the Pamir and Fergana lowlands. The altitude is mostly about 5000 m above sea-level.

The Kopetdag extends 650 km from Turkestan to Iran, where it rises to 3300 m. Its gentle southern slopes face the Iranian Highlands, whereas the steeper northern slopes rise abruptly above the Turanian Plains. Characteristic of the Kopetdag are highland plateaux with cliff margins and dry valleys which are periodically flooded by mudflows.

The main geological features of the ranges were formed by mid-Palaeozoic tectonic movements, when thick masses of geosynclinal rocks were thrust over metamorphic basement rocks. The Herzinian thrust belt was peneplained in the Permian and Triassic and subsequently block-faulted in the Jurassic and Cretaceous. Lowlands were periodically inundated by warm seas in which coral reefs formed. In the Fergana depressions are Mesozoic marine and lagoonal deposits as much as 10–12 km thick. The mountain system was uplifted during the late Palaeogene to Neogene, and even more extensively raised in the Pliocene-Pleistocene when the modern relief was formed.

The mountains of Middle Asia have a dry, sunny continental climate. The western part of the region (Kopetdag, Pamiro-Alai, western Tien Shan) is influenced by strong westerly winds which bring hot air from the dry subtropical lowlands. Average July temperatures are 20–25°C in the lowlands and 15–17°C at middle elevations. Winter temperatures at high altitudes can fall to -30°C. Average annual precipitation ranges from 150–300 mm in the lowlands to 450–800 mm at mid-altitudes, and occasionally up to 1600 mm in the glacier belt. The snow-line is at 3600–3800 m above sea-level.

The eastern part of the region (Pamir, inner Tien Shan) is influenced by northerly winds which bring cold air from Siberia, resulting in severe frosts (down to -40°C) in winter. The average January temperature is -20°C. The thin covering of snow results in permafrost and solifluction processes. Summer cyclones bring tropical air, raising day-time temperatures to 30–40°C in intermontane depressions. In the Pamir, the annual precipitation is less than 70 mm even at high altitudes, but heavy downpours sometimes result in catastrophic mud flows. On the slopes of the inner Tien Shan precipitation increases to 300–500 mm.

Soils vary from rich chernozem-like soils, with comparatively high humus content, in the montane forest and subalpine meadow belts of the eastern Tien Shan, to brown carbonate soils in the western part of the region. Grey, locally saline, soils are typical of lower slopes. Montane desert soils, low in humus and high in carbonates, develop on highland plateaux.

The total population of the region is about 18.3 million. Average population density is about 30–35 people/km², the density varying from 400–500 people/km² in Fergana Valley to 1.3 people/km² in the Pamir highlands. The main traditional occupations were sheep, camel, and (at high altitudes) yak herding, with fishing on the Issyk-Kul and other larger lakes, and fruit and melon cultivation. In recent decades, cotton-growing and mining have become major industries.

Vegetation

The vegetation of the Middle Asian Mountains has evolved from the Arcto-Tertiary flora. Uplifting of the mountains gave rise to altitudinal variations which have allowed immigration of species from the Caucasus and Himalaya. Pleistocene climatic changes have fostered the development of highland cryophytic and xerophytic vegetation types. The following formations are recognized (Korovin 1961, 1962; Stanjukovich 1973; Pavlov 1985):

Subtropical steppe
This peculiar type of grassland is rich in ephemerals. Low grass savannas occur mostly in the eastern Tien Shan and Pamir lowlands and foothills. *Carex pachystylis* and *Poa bulbosa* are the main species, in association with species of *Eremurus*, *Ferula*, *Gagea* and *Tulipa*, and annual members of *Astragalus*, *Draba*, *Malcolmia* and *Trigonella*. *Artemisia ferganensis* and other wormwoods, together with *Stipa hohenackerana*, also occasionally occur. Tall grass savannas occur in the western Tien Shan, Pamiro-Alai and Kopetdag foothills up to about 2000 m. Dominant species are *Elytrigia trichophorum*, *Ferula kuhistanica* and *Hordeum bulbosum*.

Festucoid steppe
This consists mainly of xerophytic perennials and occurs at high altitudes, descending to mid-altitudes and foothills on northern slopes. Subalpine and alpine steppes include *Festuca valesiaca*, associated with such montane species as *Potentilla nervosa* and *Primula algida*. Steppes at mid-altitudes include members of such shrub genera as *Caragana*, *Cotoneaster*, *Lonicera*, *Rosa* and *Spiraea*. Cryophitic steppes of the Tien Shan and Pamir include dwarf grasses, such as *Stipa purpurea*, together with *Kobresia capilliformis* and *Puccinellia subspicata*.

Montane xerophytic vegetation
This endemic-rich vegetation comprises many cushion (tragacanthic) plants and grasses occurring on rocky outcrops of carbonate-rich metamorphic shales. Prominent plants are subshrubs, such as species of *Acantholimon*, *Artemisia* and *Ephedra*. In the Pamir, shrubs and trees sometimes form sparse xerophytic woodlands.

Shiblyak
This scrub formation, analagous to Mediterranean maquis, is dominated by thorny deciduous shrubs, such as species of *Amygdalus*, *Paliurus* and *Ziziphus*, and perennial herbaceous species. In the Kopetdag and western Tien Shan, shiblyak also contains *Pistacia vera* which forms sparse woodlands associated with semi-desert species of *Artemisia*.

Broadleaved forests
Forests form isolated "islands" among montane steppes and other vegetation types. Walnut (*Juglans regia*) forests are characteristic of the western Tien Shan, Pamiro-Alai and Kopetdag, at elevations of 1000–2300 m. They include species of *Lonicera*, *Malus*, *Prunus* and *Rhamnus* in the understorey. *Acer* spp. occur on drier slopes, whilst *Picea schrenkiana* occurs at the upper limits of the walnut forest.

Coniferous forests
These occur only in the Tien Shan and are dominated by *Picea schrenkiana*, *Abies semionovii* and *A. sibirica*. They may have a closed canopy, or form "parklands" with well-developed grass or moss layers. At high altitudes they form sparse woodlands.

Juniper woodlands
These are widespread at various elevations and are associated with other vegetation types. The main species are *Juniperus turkestanica*, *J. semiglobosa* and *J. sevarshanica*. In Kopetdag, they are common in the tragacanthic belt, while in the Tien Shan and Pamiro-Alai, the creeping *J. turkestanica* forms pure stands, or mingles with subalpine meadows.

Montane meadows
These occur in Tien Shan (being replaced by steppes in the other mountain ranges). Mixed subalpine meadows on northern slopes consist of species of *Geranium*, *Festuca*, *Phlomis*, *Ranunculus*, *Trisetum* and other herbs, while in the alpine belt they give way to *Kobresia* meadows which cover highland plateaux and moraines. The meadows contain such steppe elements as *Festuca valesiaca* and *Stipa regeliana*.

Cryophytic communities
These occur at the highest elevations of the Pamir and central Tien Shan. There are several types, the most widespread being low cushion vegetation of *Acantholimon diapensioides*, *Oxytropis* spp. and *Potentilla* spp. *Sibbaldia tetrandra* occurs on highland plateaux while *Ceratoides fruticulosa* occurs locally on various substrates.

Flora

The variety of land forms, rock types and climatic conditions over a wide altitudinal range has given rise to an immense diversity of habitats and genetic variation. Of about 7000 vascular plant species in the region, about 5500 species occur in the mountains. Endemism at the species level is exceptionally high: about 1500 species (or 30% of the total vascular flora) are endemic (Kamelin 1967, 1979, 1990; Goloskokov 1972, 1984). Most of the endemics are confined to xerophytic and cryophytic communities developed on geologically young substrates. Many of the montane endemics have lowland ancestral forms. This is evidence of the autochthonous development of the endemic montane flora.

Available data on the floristic diversity of the Middle Asian Mountains are summarized in Table 9 below.

There are 64 endemic genera, of which 21 belong to Umbelliferae and 12 to Compositae.

TABLE 9. FLORISTIC DIVERSITY OF THE MOUNTAINS OF MIDDLE ASIA

Range	Species	Genera	Families
Pamiro-Alai	4000	?	114
West Tien Shan	2812	690	99
Dzungarian Alatau	2130	?	?
Central Tien Shan	1870	?	?
Kopetdag	1770	620	102
Karatau	1666	576	100
West Pamir	1481	461	89
East Pamir	700	264	60

Useful plants

The Fergana Depression is one of the most ancient agricultural areas in the world with about 1000 useful plant species known. They include more than 300 species of wild fruit and nut trees, found mostly in broadleaved forests and in river valleys, in genera such as *Amygdalus, Crataegus, Juglans, Malus, Pistacia, Prunus* and *Pyrus*. Middle Asia is a centre of origin of melons (*Cucumis melo*).

53 species are of medicinal value, including *Artemisia cina*, endemic to the Karatau Mountains, and *Ephedra* spp., widespread in Tien Shan, Pamiro-Alai and Kopetdag. Also of value in pharmacy are members of such genera as *Crataegus, Melissa, Rosa* and *Thymus*. Some species are used as sources of both food and medicine (e.g. *Pistacia vera*). About 2000 tonnes of dried medicinal plant material are harvested each year from the wild.

About 200 species of grasses and legumes are important fodder plants. They are dominant in steppe, meadow and savanna-like formations.

Tannins, natural pigments and rubber (e.g. from *Chondrilla ambigua*) are among the industrial products obtained from the plant resources of the region.

There are numerous ornamental plants in the region, including species of *Amygdalus, Crocus, Eremurus, Fritillaria, Juniperus* and *Tulipa*.

Social and environmental values

Montane steppes, meadows and xerophytic formations play a vital role in the traditional economy, as pastures for sheep, cattle, horses, camels and yaks. Forests are no longer significant for their timber, but they are still important in preventing erosion and catastrophic mud flows. In recent years, forests have been intensely used for recreation. They are also the last refuge for a number of endemic animals, including 87 species of endemic mollusc. The region also includes 50 species of reptiles, 500 species of birds and 120 species of mammals.

Threats

Of 468 rare or threatened species in the region, 18 are Endangered (e.g. *Astragalus arianus* and *Salvia baldschuanica*). 174 species from the region are included in the Red Data Book of the former U.S.S.R. (Borodin *et al.* 1984). Major threats in the densely populated lowlands are industrial and agricultural pollution, while montane plant communities are modified, or seriously degraded, by overgrazing. Pastures have been lost as a result of erosion, or are replaced by unpalatable plants.

Forests have been extensively cleared in the past, but montane forests are now protected from logging throughout the region. However, forests are still adversely affected by uncontrolled development of recreation and by over-collection of medicinal and ornamental plants.

With the advent of mass tourism, the frequency of forest fires, especially in the juniper and pistachio woodlands (previously burnt for charcoal) has increased. Visitor pressure has resulted in excessive trampling and eventual loss of vegetation cover in some places, leaving areas vulnerable to erosion.

Conservation

There are 18 Nature Reserves (Zapovedniki) covering c. 5720 km² (c. 1% of region). They occur in Turkmenistan (8), Uzbekistan (6), Kirghizia (4), Tadzhikistan (3) and Kazakhstan (2). All contain examples of natural vegetation but are at risk from economic activities in surrounding areas and by excessive use by local people. Moreover, many vegetation types of outstanding plant diversity and high endemism remain unprotected in the region. Among these are broadleaved forest remnants, Tien Shan spruce forests, montane steppes, saxicolous communities, pistachio woodlands and the peculiar juniper shrublands which occur on various substrates.

The Karatau Range in Kazakhstan, Pyandj River in Tadzhikistan, Karakul Lake in Pamir, as well as the Kugitang Range in Turkmenistan, are considered to be the most important areas in need of conservation. Of special importance are the habitats of wild relatives of cultivated plants.

References (All titles translated from Russian.)

Borodin, A.M. *et al.* (eds) (1984). *Red Data Book of the USSR. Rare and endangered species of animals and plants*, 2nd ed. Lesnaya Promyshlennost, Moscow. 478 pp. (In Russian.)

Goloskokov, V.P. (1972). *Generic endemism in the Kazakhstan flora*. In Vasilchenko, I.T. (ed.), *History of the Eurasian flora and vegetation*. Nauka, Leningrad. Pp. 145–155.

Goloskokov, V.P. (1984). *Flora of the Dzhungarian Alatau*. Nauka, Alma-Ata. 222 pp.

Kamelin, R.V. (1967). On some notable anomalies in the montane Middle Asian Province flora. *Bot. Zhurn.* 52: 447–460.

Kamelin, R.V. (1973). *Florogenic analysis of the mountainous Middle Asia natural flora*. Nauka, Leningrad. 356 pp.

Kamelin, R.V. (1979). *Kukhistan District of the mountainous Middle Asia. Botanical-geographical analysis*. Nauka, Leningrad. 117 pp.

Kamelin, R.V. (1990). *Flora of the Syrdarjinskiy Karatau*. Nauka, Leningrad. 146 pp.

Korovin, E.P. (1961, 1962). *Vegetation of Middle Asia and south Kazakhstan*, 2 vols. 2nd Ed. Acad. Sci. Uzbek. SSR. Tashkent. (Vol. 1: 452 pp.; vol. 2: 547 pp.)

Pavlov, V.N. (1985). *Geographical affinities of dominant species and some problems in the origin of vegetation cover of the western Tien Shan*. In *Plants of Middle Asia*. Nauka, Moscow. Pp. 20–36.

Stanjukovich, K.V. (1973). *Montane vegetation of USSR*. Donish, Dushanbe. 416 pp.

Acknowledgements

This Data Sheet was prepared by Dr A.N. Kuliev (Institute of Nature Conservation and Reserves, Moscow).

CHUKOTSKIY PENINSULA
Russia

Location: Extreme north-east of the Asiatic continent between latitudes 64°00'–68°00'N and longitudes 169°00'–180°00'E.

Area: c. 117,000 km².

Altitude: 0–2300 m.

Vegetation: Tundra, relict steppe and arcto-boreal shrub communities, rare hot spring communities.

Flora: 939 vascular plant species, including c. 50 narrow Beringian endemics and 56 threatened species.

Useful plants: c. 40 species of food and medicinal plants used by Chukchi and Eskimo people; c. 400 fodder plant species.

Other values: Soil stabilization, wildlife refuge, landscape value.

Threats: Mining, fire, overgrazing by reindeer, waste disposal near villages, visitor pressure around hot springs.

Conservation: Proposed International Ethno-ecological Park to cover c. 50,000 km² of region.

Geography

The Chukotskiy Peninsula (Chukotskiy Poluostrov) forms the extreme north-east of the Asiatic continent between latitudes 64°00'–68°00'N and longitudes 169°00'–180°00'E. The region consists of a complex series of massifs and isolated mountains and depressions. The highest point is 2300 m but most of the mountains are less than 1000 m altitude. The Chukotskiy Khrebet forms the backbone of the region, extending some 650 km, while in the far east of the peninsula the Tenkanyy range of mountains is some 60 km long.

The largest inter-montane depressions are the Uljuveem Depression (110 km long) and the Mechigmen-Ioni Depression. Some depressions are filled with large lakes, e.g. Ioni (12 km × 3.5 km) and Koolen (15 km × 2 km). There are many smaller lakes in the coastal lowlands. In the southern and eastern parts of the peninsula, mountain slopes and valleys contain glacial troughs, solifluction terraces and other picturesque land forms. Lowland coastal plains (about 100 m above sea-level) occur along the coast to the east and south of Koljuchinski Bay, north-west of Mechigmenski Bay and east of Cross Bay.

The peninsula is part of the Beringian Plate, which consists of Precambrian metamorphic rocks overlain by clastic and carbonate deposits of lower to middle Palaeozoic age. The Mechigmenski Rift splits the Beringian Plate into almost two equal blocks, namely the Chukchi and Eskimo (or Beringian) blocks. The Rift itself is filled with late Palaeozoic to older Mesozoic geosynclinal rocks folded during the middle Jurassic. In the south, rocks of the Okhotsk-Chukotskian volcanic belt are superimposed upon the older structures.

Soil development is particularly influenced by seasonal freezing and melting of permafrost, giving rise to neutral to acid gley soils. Iron and aluminium hydroxides and humus accumulate under these conditions. In the highlands, Arctic soils typically exhibit a polygonal structure formed by a combination of the frost weathering and summer drying.

The climate is continental with cold winters. The January temperature in the mountains is mostly below -32°C. Winters in the coastal areas last for 7 months, from October to April. Summers last from early June to mid-August, with very short springs (one month only – May) and autumns (August to September). Snow storms occur on about 100 days per year. The average annual temperature is -5° to -7°C, the coldest months being January and February (-18° to -20°C), and the warmest being July and August (3–6°C). Temperatures range from a maximum of 24°C to a minimum of -40°C to -45°C.

Annual precipitation varies from 354 mm at Chaplino to 535 mm at Provideniya. Most occurs during the warmer months. Snow cover lasts from early October to mid-June. Most rivers freeze in winter. Floods occur after the spring thaw and during autumn as a result of heavy rains.

Vegetation

The Chukotskiy Peninsula lies within the hypo-arctic vegetation zone, subdivided into southern, middle and northern tundra subzones (Alexandrova 1977; Dervis-Sokolova 1961; Jurtsev 1981), the distributions of which are controlled by summer temperatures, precipitation and relief. Most of the area is occupied by the middle ("typical") tundra. Northern tundra occurs along the eastern and southern margins of the region, and as narrow strips along the north-western and south-western coasts, including the Konergin Plain and the south-eastern coast of Cross Bay. Southern tundra occurs as large enclaves in the eastern and south-eastern parts of the peninsula.

All the various tundra types include hypo-arctic and arcto-boreal shrubs, some weedy perennials, together with mosses and lichens which can tolerate acid soils. In southern lowland tundras, the main assemblages are floristically-poor shrub communities, dwarf shrub-cotton grass communities and shrub-sedge tussock tundras. Middle tundras are dominated by the both oligotrophic and eutrophic dwarf shrub and weed communities. Shrub communities are virtually lacking in northern hypo-arctic tundras (or there are creeping variants of some shrubs). Boreal species are exceedingly rare. Meadows and meadow tundras are more extensive near the coast.

Flora

The flora comprises 939 vascular plant species. Although not species-rich, the flora contains a relatively high proportion of local Beringian endemics (c. 50 species). Two floristic districts are recognized: Koljuchinski District in the west and centre, containing 485 species, and the floristically more diverse Extreme-Eastern District, containing 617 species. Rich areas include Yandrakinot (more than 450 vascular plant species), and Penkignej, Laurentia and Getlyangen (each with 350–450 species).

Species richness in the east is correlated with a more oceanic climate, diverse relief, and underlying geology. Inland massifs composed of carbonate-rich rocks support some Beringian relicts of Asiatic and American origin, while Arctic relicts, such as *Poa abbreviata* and *Puccinellia angustata*, occur on the north coast. Thermophilous and halophilous relicts occur in isolated sites associated with numerous hot springs. Some American species penetrate into the eastern margin of the region, while endemic species with narrow ranges occur mostly in central Beringia. The flora of the Koljuchinski District includes many species which extend further west into the Amguema Valley and beyond. There are also some hot springs which support thermophilic elements.

At least 56 plant species are considered to be rare or threatened. Most occur in the eastern part of the Chukotskiy Peninsula. Carbonate-rich substrates house refuge sites for the moss *Leptopterigynandrum austroalpinum*, along with *Arabidopsis czukczorum*, *Artemisia senjavinensis*, *Cardamine sphenophylla*, *Chrysosplenium rimosum-dezhnevii*, *Papaver walpolei* and *Primula beringensis*, all of which are rare or threatened. *Chrysosplenium rimosum-dezhnevii* and *Potentilla beringensis* are known from only one locality, while *Primula beringensis* is known from only eight localities in the peninsula and on St Lawrence Island (Alaska).

The Chukotskiy Peninsula is of phytogeographic interest as many North American species occur at their westernmost limit of distribution. Examples include *Cryptantha spiculifera*, *Phlox alaskensis*, *Polygonum alascanum* and *Populus balsamifera*.

Useful plants

Chukchi and Eskimo people use about 40 species of plants as sources of food, medicine and dyes. Berries of *Arctoüs*, *Empetrum*, *Ribes*, *Rosa*, *Rubus* and *Vaccinium*, leaves of *Dryas*, *Oxyria*, *Salix* and *Saxifraga*, and the roots and shoots of *Claytonia pedicularis* are eaten raw, dried or fermented. Medicinal plants include some widely used species, such as *Rhodiola rosea* (Tikhomirov 1958; Menovstchikov 1974). Mosses and lichens are used to insulate houses. About 400 species, mostly lichens, but also horsetails, many grasses, sedges, willows, some Ranunculaceae, Polygonaceae and Vacciniaceae, are used as sources of fodder for reindeer.

Social and environmental values

Tundras provide pastures for reindeer herds, as well as refuges for various herbivorous mammals, such as lemmings and gophers. The region is extremely important for breeding waterbirds, including the threatened spoon-billed sandpiper (*Eurynorhynchus pygmeus*) which breeds only in the region around Peninsular Chukotka.

The vegetation helps to prevent soil erosion, landslides and solifluction processes. The diversity of tundra landscapes adds to the scientific and aesthetic attraction of the region.

Threats

The thin cover of tundra vegetation is very vulnerable to disturbance by human activities. Locally, mining is a major threat, leaving devastated areas covered with rock debris. Vehicles, even if fitted with caterpillar tracks, can cause severe damage to vegetation leading to soil erosion.

The tundra is also threatened by fire and overgrazing. Uncontrolled reindeer herding results in the loss of lichen cover, which again renders the soil liable to erosion.

Small populations of rare plant species in the vicinity of Provideniya, Laurentia and other larger villages are threatened by construction, waste dumping and excessive trampling by reindeer. Rare species and communities associated with hot springs need special protection measures to prevent their extinction as a result of the visitor pressure.

At least 56 plant species have been included, or were considered for inclusion, in the Red Data Books of the former U.S.S.R.

Conservation

There are no existing protected areas in the peninsula. However, a Russian-American bilateral agreement on environmental protection proposes an International "Beringian Heritage" Park to be created in Chukotka and Alaska and will include c. 50,000 km² of the Chukotskiy Peninsula. The maintenance of traditional lifestyles of local people will be an important element in the management of the park, while high priority will also be given to protecting rare plant species and communities (Jurtsev, Katenin, and Korobkov 1985).

References (All titles translated from Russian.)

Alexandrova, V.D. (1977). Geobotanical regions of Arctic and Antarctic. In *Komarov Readings 29*. Nauka, Leningrad. 189 pp.

Dervis-Sokolova, T.G. (1961). Vegetation of the Chukotski Peninsula extreme north-east. *Problems in the North* 8: 74–82.

Jurtsev, B.A. (1981). *Relict steppe complexes of north-eastern Asia. (Problems in reconstruction of cryoxeric landscapes of Beringia)*. Nauka, Novosibirsk. 168 pp.

Jurtsev, B.A., Katenin, A.E., and Korobkov, A.A. (1985). Problems in plant protection in the Chukotskian tundra. In Chernov, Ju.I. (ed.), *Communities of the extreme north and man*. Nauka, Moscow. Pp. 245–271.

Menovstchikov, G.A. (1974). Wild plants in the native Chukotkan people's diet. *Soviet Ethnography* 2: 93–99.

Tikhomirov, B.A. (1958). Data on useful plants of the south-eastern Chukotski coast Eskimo peoples. *Bot. Zhurn.* 43: 242–246.

Acknowledgements

This Data Sheet was prepared by Dr O.A. Druzhinina and Professor V.A. Krassilov (Institute of Nature Conservation and Reserves, Moscow).

PRIMORYE
Russia

Location: Southern Far Eastern Russia, bordering on North Korea and China, approximately between latitudes 42°00'–48°00'N and longitudes 132°00'–141°00'E.

Area: c. 165,900 km².

Altitude: 0–1933 m.

Vegetation: Mixed coniferous-broadleaved montane forest, oak-pine woodlands, wetlands.

Flora: 1850 vascular plant species with high species endemism; association of north temperate and subtropical elements.

Useful plants: Medicinal plants, melliferous plants, food plants, timber trees, ornamental plants.

Other values: The forests are extensively used for recreational activities, including sport-hunting; they also protect watersheds and prevent soil erosion.

Threats: Logging, pollution, visitor pressure, fire, over-collection of medicinal and ornamental species.

Conservation: c. 6.5% of the region is protected in 5 Strict Nature Reserves (Zapovedniki) covering c. 5299 km², 8 Refuges (Zakazniki) covering c. 2032 km², and the Sikhote-Alin Biosphere Reserve Zapovednik covering 3402 km².

Geography

Primorye forms the extreme south-eastern corner of Far Eastern Russia, bordering on China, Korea and the Sea of Japan, approximately between latitudes 42°00'–48°00'N and longitudes 132°00'–141°00'E. The Sikhote-Alin Mountain Ranges, part of the circum-Pacific mountain belt, extend along the coast of the Sea of Japan. Most of the mountains are under 1000 m, but the highest peak reaches 1933 m.

Geologically, the Sikhote-Alin consist of successive thrust belts formed in the Palaeozoic and Mesozoic periods along the eastern periphery of the stable Khankian Massif. In the mid- to late Cretaceous, volcanic activity resulted in andesites and rhyolites being intruded over vast areas. Younger Tertiary basalts form the highland plateau, while thick sequences of coarse molassoid clastics accumulated in inter-montane depressions into which rivers have cut deep valleys.

In the west, Precambrian and Palaeozoic magmatic and metamorphic rocks of the Khankian Massif form the low East Manchurian mountains and plains. There are also broad inter-montane depressions, one of which contains Khanka Lake (Ozero Khanka) which straddles the border with China.

Major rivers of the region are the Ussuri, a tributary of the Amur River, which flows along part of the border with China, the Razdolnaya and the Partisanskaya. The western slopes of Sikhote-Alin are traversed by tributaries of the Ussuri, while much shorter mountain streams flow down the steep eastern slopes to the Sea of Japan.

Primorye has a monsoon summer-wet climate. The average annual precipitation is 600–900 mm, 75–90% of it falling in the summer and often causing catastrophic floods. In August, cyclones bring tropical typhoons with heavy rains. Winters are cold but there is little snowfall. Dry continental air masses force the average monthly temperature in January down to -20°C. The average monthly temperature in July is 20°C.

Soils vary from acid humic soils on mountain ridges, to rich brown soils on lower slopes. Subtropical yellow soils occur in some watersheds at lower altitudes, while gley, boggy soils occur in the Khankian lowlands.

Primorye is inhabited by 2,136,000 people (1985), about 78% of whom live in a few large cities. The average population density is 11.3 people/km², with 50 people/km² in southern districts and on the Khankian Plains. Russian and Ukrainian settlers constitute about 95% of the population. Native Udege, Nanaj, Tas and Orochon people (c. 1500 in total) live in the Sikhote-Alin forests and continue to practice traditional methods of hunting, fishing and plant-gathering.

Vegetation

The main vegetation formation of the Sikhote-Alin Mountains is mixed coniferous-broadleaved forest (Ussuri taiga), although very little remains in a truly pristine state. The forest is floristically rich and dominated by *Pinus koraiensis* (cedar pine). Associated tree species include *Acer* spp., *Fraxinus mandshurica*, *Juglans mandshurica*, *Phellodendron amurense* and *Tilia amurensis*. *Aralia*, *Eleutherococcus* and other Araliaceae are typical of the undergrowth. *Actinidia*, *Celastrus*, *Schizandra* and *Vitis* are common climbers which give the forest an almost subtropical appearance. Herbaceous communities include tall ferns, such as *Athyrium* spp. and *Dryopteris* spp. Riverine forest includes large specimens of *Chosenia* among the dominants.

Spruce-fir forests, dominated by species of *Abies* and *Picea*, occur above 800 m in southern Primorye. They contain a considerable broadleaved component at their lower altitudinal limits, including members of the genera

Acer, *Carpinus*, *Kalopanax* and *Tilia*, and some climbers. In the north, *Betula ermanii* forms a well-defined altitudinal belt above the mixed taiga.

Shrub or dwarf shrub-grass communities of *Rhododendron* spp., *Weigela* spp. and *Ledum* spp. occur above the tree-line. Higher still, the endemic creeping conifer, *Microbiota decussata*, forms mono-dominant carpets of vegetation at 750–1500 m. At 1800 m, *Pinus pumila* (which is 1.5 m tall at 1500 m) is dwarfed to a mere 30 cm. It covers vast areas of the highlands in the north, while it is comparatively rare in the south and virtually lacking on the East Manchurian Mountains. Montane tundras occur locally on the higher mountains (Vassiliev and Kolesnikov 1912; Rosenberg 1961; Kurentsova 1968).

The southern spurs of the East Manchurian Mountains were once covered with magnificent black fir-broadleaved forests. A few stands remain in the Ussuriyskiy Strict Nature Reserve, along the Artemovka River valley, and elsewhere. This forest is dominated by *Abies holophylla* and *Kalopanax* spp. and contains up to 200 different species of trees. Floristically, these are the most species-rich conifer forests in Russia. Vast areas of southern Primorye black fir forests have been cleared and replaced by oak woodlands of *Quercus mongolica* and *Q. dentata*, with a dense shrub layer of *Lespedeza bicolor*.

In western Primorye, patches of native grasslands remain in the Khankian Plains, the lower Rasdolnaya River valley, and the Khasan district west of Amurskiy Bay. Khanka Lake is surrounded by extensive wetlands, including sedge, sedge-cotton grass, tall grass bogs and wet meadow communities.

Flora

The flora of Primorye contains 1850 vascular plant species (Voroshilov 1966), including 460 Manchurian and local endemics, amongst them the monotypic *Microbiota decussata*. The floristic richness of the region is due to a peculiar mixture of temperate and subtropical elements. Coniferous forests extend south to 43°N contributing significantly to the outstanding conifer diversity of the region. In the south, black fir is associated with *Pueraria* and other subtropical lianas. Primitive angiosperms (e.g. *Schizandra chinensis*) are among the relict species. There is also an unusually high diversity of Araliaceae and woody legumes, many of them pioneer plants growing vigorously in forest clearings.

The Ussuri taiga is floristically similar to the Tertiary forests known from fossil records in the same region, though with different dominants. For example, *Fagus* spp. have totally disappeared since Pliocene or Pleistocene times. Orogenic events, mountain glaciation and eustatic sea-level fluctuations, orographic rain-shadow effects and associated climatic changes have all influenced the evolution of the autochthonous flora. Neo-endemics occur mostly among subalpine species (e.g. *Microbiota decussata*), carbonate cliff communities (e.g. *Hedysarum ussuriense*, *Sanguisorba magnifica* and *Sedum ussuriense*), psammophytes (e.g. *Euphorbia chankoana*, *Oxytropis chankaensis* and *Thymus mandsburicus*) and coastal vegetation (e.g. *Anemone brevipedunculata*, *Draba cardaminiflora* and *Peucedanum littorale*).

An enclave of the eastern Manchurian flora occurs in southern Primorye; 46 relict species occur here at the northernmost limit of their ranges. They include *Abelia coreana*, *Fritillaria ussuriensis* and *Thymus komarovii*.

Useful plants

Panax ginseng (ginseng) is celebrated in the Far East and known worldwide as a stimulant. It was found recently that other native Araliaceae, notably *Aralia elata*, *Eleutherococcus senticosus* and *Oplopanax elatus*, have apparently similar effects. In all, 57 species are used to make potent drugs and about 800 species are considered to be of potential use in medicine. Some of these also provide sources of food.

The fruits of the wild vine, *Vitis amurensis*, and other climbers, such as *Schizandra chinensis* and *Actinidia kolomikta*, are eaten by local inhabitants as sources of vitamins. Few of these species remain near to cities and large villages. *Juglans mandshurica* is used both for food and medicine, while cedar pine seeds ("nuts") are a high-quality food source used by both rural and urban communities.

About 212 species are used in the production of honey, more species than in any other area in Russia; apiculture in the region depends solely on wild plants.

In addition to the considerable timber reserves, the forests contain a number of species which provide various industrial products. About 80 species are of value as ornamental plants.

Social and environmental values

Traditional use of wild plant resources is perhaps more evident in Primorye than it is in any other region of Russia. Rural communities depend to a large extent on wild plant resources for their subsistence, and even city-dwellers occasionally spend a few weeks in the taiga gathering fruits and fungi.

Forestry is a major regional economic activity. There are an estimated 2000 million m³ of timber reserves. In addition, taiga is used extensively for recreation and hunting for sport. There is a rich variety of animal life, including wild boar, roe deer, badger and brown bear.

In the monsoonal summer-wet climate, dense taiga forests help to prevent catastrophic summer floods and soil erosion, which in deforested areas are major threats to human life and development.

Threats

Forest fires and commercial logging have left very few patches of undisturbed primary Ussuri taiga. Clearings in mountain forest are subject to erosion, making reforestation difficult if not impossible. Logging in cedar pine and black fir forests has not only caused the decline of these conifers, but has also caused the decline of populations of associated plants, such as ginseng. Secondary regrowth is floristically different and less diverse than the primary forest.

Over-collection is a threat to wild populations of some medicinal plant species, notably *Panax ginseng*, as well as some ornamental species.

Locally, some forests have been seriously damaged by toxic emissions of boron and other chemicals from industries, notably in the Dalnegorsk area. Pesticide pollution from rice fields, and other forms of pollution from agriculture and industry, are a major threat to the Khankian wetlands. Wetland species such as *Nelumbo komarovii* and *Euryale ferox* are considered to be Endangered.

The impact of visitors, and particularly fires, has replaced some south-western oak-pine woodlands by mono-dominant stands of *Lespedeza* shrublands and steppe-like herbaceous communities.

Of those species considered to be rare or threatened and/or those which occur in the Red Data Books of the former U.S.S.R., 29 occur in the Sikhote-Alin taiga, 16 in south Primorye black fir forests and 21 in oak woodlands.

Conservation

Existing reserves and refuges cover about 6.5% of the Primorye (Vassiliev, Pankratiev, and Parov 1965; Matjushkin 1985; Bogatov *et al.* 1989). The eastern slopes of the Sikhote-Alin are better protected than those in the west, with 2 Strict Nature Reserves (Zapovedniki), namely Lazovskiy (1165 km²) and Sikhote-Alinskiy (3470 km²), and 4 Refuges (Zakazniki), namely Chernye Skaly (260 km²), Goralovyj (82 km²), Losinyj (260 km²) and Vasilkovskiy (287 km²). However, some plant formations, notably in the subalpine belt, as well as the habitats of many threatened species, are not included within existing protected areas. About 13,180 km² (c. 9% of the region) are estimated to be required to adequately protect the flora and the various vegetation types of Primorye.

On the western slopes of the Sikhote-Alin are the Ussuriyskiy Strict Nature Reserve (404 km²), the Sikhote-Alin Zapovednik Biosphere Reserve (3402 km²), together with the Beresovyj (600 km²), Taiezhnyj (310 km²) and Tikhij (126 km²) Refuges.

The upper and middle reaches of the Bikin and Bolshaya Ussurka rivers, which contain cedar pine-broadleaved forests, including the endemics *Fraxinus mandshurica*, *Phellodendron amurense* and *Ulmus japonica*, together with spruce-fir forests (which contain no less than 54 rare or threatened plant species) are currently proposed for protection.

The Manchurian black fir-broadleaved forests are protected in the Kedrovaya Pad' Strict Nature Reserve (179 km²) and Barsovyj Refuge (107 km²). Upland variants of these forests, which contain the southernmost occurrence of larch and juniper on the Borisovskoye Plateau, are outside the existing protected areas network. The Khankian Reserve covers about 80 km² of wetlands around Khanka Lake. Other wetlands, notably in the Bikin River valley and Posiet estuarine-lagoonal complex, are not protected at present.

References (All titles translated from Russian.)

Bogatov, V.V., Krassilov, V.A., Krylov, A.G. *et al.* (1989). *System of protected areas in the Ecological Programme of Primorskiy Region.* Far Eastern Branch Acad. Sci. U.S.S.R., Vladivostok. 39 pp.

Kurentsova, G.E. (1968). *Vegetation of Primorskiy Region.* Far Eastern Publishing House, Vladivostok. 190 pp.

Matjushkin, E.N. (1985). Physico-geographical features and reserve network of the Far East. In Sokolov, V.E. and Syroyechkovskiy, E.E. (eds), *Far East Reserves.* Mysl', Moscow. Pp. 8–16.

Rosenberg, V.A. (1961). Some problems of the spruce-fir forest management in the southern Sikhote-Alin. In *Problems of agriculture and forestry in the Far East.* Vladivostok.

Vassiliev, N.G. and Kolesnikov, B.P. (1912). *Black fir-broadleaf forest of southern Primorye.* Acad. Sci. U.S.S.R., Moscow. 145 pp.

Vassiliev, N.G., Pankratiev, A., and Parov, E. (1965). *Kedrovaya Pad' Reserve.* Far Eastern Publishing House, Vladivostok. 58 pp.

Voroshilov, V.N. (1966). *Flora of the Soviet Far East.* Nauka, Moscow. 476 pp.

Acknowledgements

This Data Sheet was prepared by Professor V.A. Krassilov (Institute of Nature Conservation and Reserves, Moscow).

REGIONAL OVERVIEW: INDIAN SUBCONTINENT

ROBERT R. MILL

> **Total land area:** c. 4,850,000 km^2.
>
> **Population:** c. 1,160,000,000.
>
> **Altitude:** 0–8848 m (summit of Sagarmatha, Qomolangma Feng, or Mount Everest, the highest point on Earth).
>
> **Natural vegetation:** Tropical evergreen rain forest to high-altitude alpine vegetation; mixed broadleaved and/or coniferous forests, woodland, savanna, thorn scrub, dwarf shrub, alpine grassland and scree communities.
>
> **Number of vascular plants:** c. 25,000 species.
>
> **Number of regional endemics:** >11,330 species (a minimum number for single country endemics).
>
> **Number of vascular plant families:** >350.
>
> **Number of endemic families:** 0 (2 near-endemic families: Dipentodonaceae and Plagiopteraceae).
>
> **Number of genera:** c. 4000.
>
> **Number of endemic genera:** c. 200.
>
> **Important plant families:** In temperate habitats: Ericaceae, Primulaceae, Gentianaceae, Compositae, Cyperaceae, Gramineae, Leguminosae, Cruciferae, Rosaceae, Balsaminaceae, Labiatae, Liliaceae, Orchidaceae, Scrophulariaceae. In tropical habitats: Orchidaceae, Acanthaceae, Balsaminaceae, Dipterocarpaceae, Rubiaceae, Zingiberaceae, Compositae, Gramineae, Palmae, Leguminosae, Euphorbiaceae, Convolvulaceae, Solanaceae, Lauraceae.

Introduction

The Indian Subcontinent is bounded by the Tibetan Plateau and Tadzhikistan to the north, Afghanistan to the north-west, the Arabian Sea to the west, the Indian Ocean to the south and east, and Indochina (Thailand, Laos), China (Yunnan) and Malesia to the east and south-east. The region includes India, Pakistan, Nepal, Bhutan, Bangladesh, Myanmā (Burma), Sri Lanka (Ceylon), the British Indian Ocean Territory (Chagos Archipelago), the Republic of the Maldives, Lakshadweep (Laccadive Islands) and the Andaman and Nicobar Islands.

Geology

The Indian Subcontinent can be divided into two main units of very different age, namely: the ancient land mass of Peninsular India, and the geologically young Himalayas and associated ranges.

Peninsular India, including Sri Lanka, consists of a single tectonic structure, the Deccan Plate, which originally formed part of Gondwanaland. The Deccan Plate was one of the earliest blocks to separate from Gondwanaland, in the Lower Cretaceous some 165 million years ago. Initially, the Plate may also have included Madagascar (which may have broken free about 90 million years ago). Both Madagascar and the Deccan Plate remained close to Africa for a lengthy period. India migrated northwards during the Cretaceous and Tertiary, eventually coming near the southern shore of Eurasia in the Eocene (c. 45 million years ago). The cataclysmic collision of the Deccan Plate with Eurasia resulted in the uplift of the Himalayas and Tibetan Plateau. This was not a single event: at least four major Himalayan mountain-building phases can

be recognized between the Eocene and the Pleistocene and the process continues today.

Ridd (1971) has postulated that parts of South East Asia, including southern Myanmā, are also of Gondwanic origin. The northern part of Myanmā is geologically part of the Himalayas, while the Shan Plateau is geologically part of the Yunnan system.

Physical features

The Indian Subcontinent embraces a very wide range of topography, including Sagarmatha (Mount Everest), the world's highest terrestrial mountain, other peaks exceeding 8000 m altitude, low-lying swamps and mangroves (such as the Sundarbans, the largest area of mangrove forest in the world), island systems (such as the Andaman and Nicobar Islands), luxuriant rain forests (in Myanmā, southern Nepal, Bhutan, the Western Ghats of India, and Sri Lanka), fertile alluvial plains, arid areas (such as the Thar Desert in north-west India and southern Pakistan) and high-altitude cold deserts (such as the Deosai Plains in Kashmir).

Peninsular India includes mainland India south of the Indo-Gangetic Plain. It is an ancient land mass (the Deccan Plateau) of Archaean and Precambrian formations which are exposed over more than half of India. The remaining area is covered by Gondwanan and later formations, and Deccan lava flows. Major mountain-building events took place in the Precambrian, with few significant events other than minor folding and block-faulting since then. The area is generally seismically inactive but when earthquakes do occur, as in 1993 in Maharashtra, they can be severe. The region is highest in the south and west, the western edge of the plateau being formed by the Western Ghats (Sahyadri Mountains). The eastern edge is also marked by a range of hills, the Eastern Ghats.

The Himalayas are the product of intense mountain-building activity in the Cretaceous, Tertiary and Pleistocene. They extend for 3200 km, from the "Pamir Knot" on the Afghanistan border in the north-west, across the northern part of the Indian Subcontinent in an arc from Jammu and Kashmir, eastwards through Himachal Pradesh, Nepal, Sikkim, the Chumbi Valley (Tibet) and Bhutan, to Arunachal Pradesh in the east. They continue through northern Myanmā and into China, where they become a complex of mountain ranges.

The main range of the Himalayas (the Great Himalaya) includes, from west to east: the Kashmir Himalaya; the North-west Himalaya; the Kumaon Himalaya; the Nepal Himalaya (including several of Earth's highest mountains over 8000 m, including Mount Everest – 8848 m, Kanchenjunga – 8579 m, Makalu – 8470 m, Dhaulagiri – 8425 m, Annapurna – 8091 m, and Gosainthan – 8010 m); and the Assam Himalaya in Sikkim, Bhutan and Arunachal Pradesh.

The Cis-Himalayas lie to the south of the Great Himalaya, while the Trans-Himalaya lie to the north. The Cis-Himalayas include the Siwaliks and the Lesser Himalaya; the Trans-Himalayas comprise the Zanskar Range (in north-west Pakistan, reaching 7770 m at the summit of Mount Kamet), the Ladakh Range, and the Karakoram (which includes more than 30 peaks over 7300 m, including K2 at 8610 m).

In the west, the Baluchistan Arc of the Himalayas runs south-west from Kashmir through Baluchistan to the Arabian Sea. It continues through Makran as a low range of hills to finally join up with the Zagros Range in Iran (see Regional Overview on South West Asia and the Middle East in Volume 1).

The Indo-Gangetic Plain is 250–450 km wide and extends for 3000 km between the Himalayas and the Deccan Plateau, from the Arabian Sea to the Bay of Bengal. It is a flat plain with alluvial deposits which are thought to be at least 2 km thick.

Climate

The climate of almost the whole of the Indian Subcontinent is monsoonal, with typically three distinct seasons: a cool dry season, a hot dry season and a hot wet season. In Bangladesh, India, Nepal, Sikkim, Bhutan and much of Pakistan, the wet season arrives with the south-west monsoon. In South India the monsoon begins in late May or early June; it begins about 6 weeks later in Nepal and north-east India. In some years, the monsoon brings less rain than usual, resulting in drought and subsequent crop failure.

Parts of Sri Lanka, especially the north-east, are unusual in that the main rains are brought by the onshore north-east monsoon, which in the rest of the Indian Subcontinent heralds the dry season. Bangladesh, eastern India and Sri Lanka also receive rain in autumn and early winter during violent tropical cyclones which regularly cause severe flooding in the Ganges Delta. Parts of Jammu and Kashmir also receive appreciable winter rainfall. Rainfall in the Rajasthan and Sind Deserts (Pakistan and north-west India) is mostly below 500 mm p.a., many places receiving less than 250 mm.

The Indian Subcontinent includes the two wettest places on Earth (Cherrapunji and Mawphlang, both in Meghalaya, which receive about 11,000 mm of rainfall p.a.), one of the

hottest (Jacobabad in Pakistan: mean day July temperature 46°C, up to 53°C having been recorded), and some of the most extreme cold climatic conditions on Earth (in the permanent snowfields and glaciers of the Himalayas and in the cold deserts of Baltistan and Ladakh).

Vegetation

The Indian Subcontinent has probably the widest variety of vegetation types anywhere on Earth, as a result of the great diversity of latitude, altitude, climate and topography. The potential natural climax vegetation is forest, except in the higher parts of the Himalayas, and in the arid regions of Baluchistan and the Thar Desert. Less than 10% of the subcontinent remains forest covered, much of the original vegetation having been greatly modified as a result of at least 5 millennia of human activity.

The monsoon rainfall pattern is of prime importance in determining the type of vegetation that would occur naturally. Soils and topography play secondary roles (except in the Himalaya). Four principal rainfall-vegetation types can be distinguished, namely: evergreen forest (in areas with more than 2500 mm p.a.), deciduous (monsoon) forest (1000–2000 mm p.a.), dry forest and scrubland (500–1000 mm p.a.), and desert and semi-desert vegetation (less than 500 mm p.a.).

Champion (1936) divided the forest types of India into five main types, namely: tropical forests, montane subtropical forests, montane temperate forests, alpine forests and specialized types (mainly littoral or riverine formations).

Tropical forests

A recent assessment of the extent of tropical moist forests is provided by Collins, Sayer and Whitmore (1991), who give country-by-country surveys of the moist forest cover in the region, with maps compiled from satellite and radar imagery and aerial photography. Table 10 gives figures for the original and remaining extent of closed canopy tropical moist forest in the region (derived from Collins, Sayer and Whitmore 1991)

TABLE 10. ORIGINAL AND REMAINING EXTENT OF CLOSED CANOPY MOIST FORESTS (INCLUDING TROPICAL CONIFEROUS FORESTS) IN THE INDIAN SUBCONTINENT

Country	Approximate original extent of closed canopy tropical forest cover (km²) [a]	Remaining area of tropical moist forest (km²) [a]	Remaining moist forests as % of original closed canopy forest [a]	Average annual loss of closed canopy forest moist 1981–1985 (%) [b]
Bangladesh	130,000	9730	7	0.9
India	910,000	228,330	25	0.3
Myanmā	600,000	311,850	52	0.3
Sri Lanka	26,000	12,760	47	3.5

Sources:
[a] Collins, Sayer and Whitmore (1991).
[b] World Resources Institute (1992).

World Resources Institute (1994) gives the following statistics for natural closed forest in other parts of the region:

	Extent of original closed natural forest (1990) (km²)	Annual deforestation rate 1981–1990 (%)
Bhutan	28,090	0.6
Nepal	50,230	1.0
Pakistan	18,550	2.9

and the average annual deforestation rate of closed canopy forest between 1981 and 1985 (from World Resources Institute 1992).

Brief descriptions are given below of the main forest types (including tropical forests) found in the Indian Subcontinent.

Tropical wet evergreen and semi-evergreen forests occur in areas with more than 3000 mm annual rainfall and a short dry season. True evergreen rain forest occurs on the Western Ghats, on the Assam Hills, and in south-western Sri Lanka which has an aseasonal, perhumid climate. The forests are dense and multi-storied with emergents; many trees are buttressed. Epiphytes are abundant, but the herb layer is poorly developed. Species numbers are high.

Tropical deciduous (monsoon) forest is the natural cover over almost the whole of Peninsular India. Most trees are deciduous for about 6–8 weeks but the forest is hardly ever totally leafless. The most frequent trees include *Tectona grandis* (teak), *Shorea robusta* (sal), *Terminalia chebula* and *Acacia catechu*.

Thorn forest, dominated by *Acacia* spp., occurs where the average annual rainfall is less than 750 mm, such as in the north-west of the peninsula and in the lee of the Western Ghats. The vegetation is open and stunted, with trees generally less than 6 m tall. Thorn forest grades into xerophytic bushland and desert vegetation.

Tropical dry evergreen forest occurs only on the coast from Madras to Point Calimere, where most rainfall is from October to December in the north-east monsoon. The canopy is closed and low (1–13 m), with an understorey of spiny shrubs.

Montane subtropical and temperate forests occur in the Nilgiri Hills, Anaimalai Hills and Palni Hills of South India, in the outer Himalayan ranges of Nepal, Bhutan and Sikkim, and in Assam and Meghalaya. The southern forests are low (15–18 m) and have a dense undergrowth of laurels, rhododendrons and ferns. In the northern subtropical montane forests, the trees are typically 20–30 m tall. Evergreen Fagaceae and some *Fraxinus* species predominate, with *Shorea robusta* in favourable sites; climbers and epiphytes are common.

Subtropical moist pine forest occurs on the Khasia Hills, the mountains of Assam and northern Myanmā, and in a belt from 73–88°E between 900–1800 m on the southern slopes of the Himalayas.

Subtropical dry evergreen forest is only found on the Salt Range, Kashmir, the Himalayan foothills (1000–1525 m), and as scattered patches in Baluchistan. The forest resembles Mediterranean maquis, composed of low scrub, with the dwarf palm *Nannorrhops ritchieana* often being frequent, together with *Acacia modesta* and *Olea cuspidata*.

Northern wet temperate forest, a closed forest type dominated by *Quercus*, *Castanopsis* and *Laurus* with a dwarf bamboo undergrowth, occurs east of longitude 88°E, between 1800–2900 m, where rainfall is more than 2000 mm per annum.

Himalayan moist temperate forest, the commonest forest type in the Himalayas, occurs between 150–3050 m in areas which receive 1000–2500 mm annual rainfall. It is a mixed broadleaved evergreen and coniferous forest, with rhododendron, oak, laurel and bamboo undergrowth.

Alpine forest and scrub occur between 2895–3660 m in the Himalayas. Juniper, pine, birch and rhododendron are dominant. Above the tree-line, at about 4000 m, the vegetation changes to open *Rhododendron* scrub and alpine pasture. Wet areas have a very rich herb flora containing many species of *Primula* and *Pedicularis*. Chasmophytes and cushion plants, such as *Chionocharis hookeri*, occur on rocks. There is a community of extremely deep-rooted perennials and small annuals which help to stabilize scree slopes. The subalpine zones of the southern hill ranges have a similarly rich vegetation but with different floristic composition.

Tidal forests and mangroves occur in the Sundarbans (the largest area of mangrove forest in the world), the coast of Taninthayi (Tenasserim) in southern Myanmā, some of the offshore islands (especially the Myeik Kyunzu or Mergui Archipelago), and a few places elsewhere along the coast. Sand-dunes are often fringed with, and stabilized by, *Casuarina* spp.

Flora

The Indian Subcontinent contains about 25,000 species of vascular plants, of which at least half are endemic to the region. No modern Flora covering the whole region exists, the only such earlier work being Hooker's *Flora of British India* (Hooker 1872–1897) although that excluded much of northern Myanmā. Even now, India, the largest country, has no complete modern Flora, although the first three volumes of a new *Flora of India* (Sharma and Balakrishnan 1993a, b; Sharma and Sanjappa 1993) have recently appeared. The complete Flora is projected to be 32 volumes. Very little has been produced so far of the *Flora of Bangladesh* (Khan and Huq 1972–); a checklist exists for Nepal (Hara *et al.* 1978–1982). The *Flora of Pakistan* (Nasir and Ali 1970–) is substantially complete; the *Flora of Bhutan* (Grierson and

TABLE 11. FLORISTIC RICHNESS AND ENDEMISM

Territory	Number of vascular plant species	Endemic species	Endemic genera
Andaman and Nicobar Islands[a]	2270	225	?
Bangladesh[b]	5000	?	?
Bhutan[c]	5500	100	0
India[d]	17,000	6800–7650	140
Lakshadweep[e]	348	0	0
Maldives[f]	277	5	0
Myanmā[g]	12–14,000	1500–1700	?
Nepal[h]	7000	350	?
Pakistan[i]	5100	400	6
Sri Lanka[j]	3370	902	12

Sources:

[a] Balakrishnan (1977).
[b] Khan and Huq (1972–).
[c] Grierson and Long (1983–), and unpublished estimates by D.G. Long.
[d] Sharma and Balakrishnan (1993a).
[e] Raghavan (1977).
[f] Adams (1983).
[g] R.R. Mill personal estimates based on unpublished research and re-appraisal of previously published lists and estimates, including Kurz (1874, 1875, 1876, 1877a, 1877b), Lace (1913), Lace and Rodger (1922), Chatterjee (1940), Kingdon-Ward (1944–1945), Nath (1960), Hundley and Chit Ko Ko (1961), and Davis *et al.* (1986).
[h] Hara *et al.* (1978–1982).
[i] M.N. Chaudhri quoted in Davis *et al.* (1986); Ali (1978); Ali and Qaiser (1986). Figures include Jammu and Kashmir; figure for total species increases to at least 5800 when non-native taxa (653, *fide* Ali 1978) are taken into account. Ali (1978) quoted 203 endemic species; the figure given here allows for the description of numerous new taxa since 1978 as part of the *Flora of Pakistan* project.
[j] Ashton and Gunatilleke (1987).

63

Long 1983–), which also treats Sikkim, and the *Revised Handbook to the Flora of Ceylon* (Dassanayake and Fosberg 1980–) are about two-thirds complete. However, much of the subcontinent has still been insufficiently explored, or not at all (see map in Rao 1979). The very rich flora of Myanmā is the least known of the whole region; the one checklist that exists (Hundley and Chit Ko Ko 1961), which is frequently quoted as a source of information, is very incomplete and probably lists scarcely half the species that actually occur in Myanmā.

For these reasons, figures for the number of species and endemics for each country (Table 11) and phytochorion (Table 18) in the region have been difficult to compile. Estimates for the same area vary widely; for example, according to Dhar and Kachroo (1983a, b) the Himalayas are reckoned to have 4196 endemics, whereas Nayar (1987) considers they have 2532 endemic species. Peninsular India is estimated to have about 2200 endemic species, most of them (c. 1500) in the Western Ghats.

No families are endemic to the subcontinent, but Dipentodonaceae and Plagiopteraceae are near-endemic, extending to either China or Thailand.

Endemic genera, of which there are probably not more than c. 200, are concentrated on the periphery of the area: in the Himalayas (especially the Western Himalayas), in Myanmā and north-east India, and in the Western Ghats and Sri Lanka. Of the 58 genera endemic to Peninsular India, no less than 52 appear to be confined to the Western Ghats (cf. list in Ahmedullah and Nayar 1987). A further 27 endemic genera are confined to the Western Ghats and Sri Lanka (Nayar and Ahmed 1984).

No discussion of endemism covering the whole subcontinent appears to exist. The most comprehensive is still that of Chatterjee (1940), which only deals with India and Myanmā and needs considerable updating to take account of the many new taxa described over the past half-century. On the basis of Chatterjee (1940), which primarily discussed the dicotyledons, the families possessing the largest numbers of species and the largest numbers of endemics are given in Table 12.

The Indian Subcontinent is situated at a cross-roads of two floristic kingdoms, the Holarctic and the Palaeotropical. It is also the meeting point, on both its western and eastern sides, of major phytochoria within these kingdoms. On the west, the Irano-Turanian and Somalia-Masai floras meet in southern Pakistan and Rajasthan, while both these meet the Deccan flora at the Aravalli Range in Rajasthan. In the north-west, there is a meeting-point between the Central Asiatic and Tibetan flora and that of the Irano-Turanian Region. The eastern end of the Himalayas is an important meeting point of the Sino-Himalayan and Indomalayan floras, and of the Tibetan with the Sino-Himalayan. All these phytochoria have their main centres outside the subcontinent. The only phytochorion wholly contained within the subcontinent is the Indian Region.

Table 18 gives the numbers of species and endemics in each phytochorion in the Indian Subcontinent. Descriptions of the vegetation, flora, useful plants, threats and conservation status of each phytochorion are given later in this Overview.

Useful plants

India and neighbouring regions have supplied people with a wealth of timber trees, food plants, medicines, spices, fibres, oils, dyes and other useful plants for thousands of years. Wild plants continue to be extremely important for supplying basic needs and as sources of income generation. The Indian Subcontinent is a centre of genetic diversity for several crop plants and their wild relatives. These include:

Rice (*Oryza sativa* and many wild relatives)
Rice is the staple food crop throughout the subcontinent. Many thousands of local varieties of *O. sativa* have been cultivated for centuries, but the introduction of modern high-yielding cultivars has led to a dramatic decline in the number of local varieties grown. It is important for future breeding needs that the biodiversity of rice varieties and their wild relatives be conserved.

Mango (*Mangifera indica*)
The greatest diversity of mango cultivars is in India (at least 1000); many are also grown in Pakistan and Bangladesh. The cultivated mango probably originated in the Assam-Chittagong area (Maheshwari 1987).

Neem (*Azadirachta indica*)
Neem is one of the most widely used plants of the subcontinent. It occurs throughout the drier parts of the region, from the Carnatic to the Siwaliks, as well as in Myanmā. Neem has many traditional uses, e.g. its twigs are used to clean teeth and gums, and neem oil is used to kill head lice and in veterinary medicine. Recent analyses of extracts obtained from neem leaves and neem oil (cold-pressed from the kernels of the seed) have yielded a whole family of bioactive chemicals (limonoids) which have great potential as insect repellents, insecticides, fungicides, anti-bacterial and anti-viral agents, in dental hygiene, and as contraceptives and spermicides (National Research Council 1992).

Pulses
There are many wild relatives of leguminous crops, e.g. black gram, green gram, moth bean, rice bean and sword bean. Many wild *Vigna* species occur in the Western Ghats and the Deccan Plateau (Arora and Nayar 1983). Pigeonpea

TABLE 12. FAMILIES WITH THE LARGEST NUMBERS OF SPECIES AND ENDEMICS IN THE INDIAN SUBCONTINENT			
Family	Number of species	Number of endemics	% species endemism
Papilionaceae	867	505	58.2
Compositae	697	367	52.7
Rubiaceae	555	368	66.3
Acanthaceae	514	426	82.9
Euphorbiaceae	444	283	63.7
Labiatae	421	261	62.0
Rosaceae	257	179	69.7
Balsaminaceae	242	221	91.3
Asclepiadaceae	234	172	73.5
Primulaceae	208	177	85.1
Gentianaceae	189	147	77.8
Umbelliferae	180	131	72.8
Cruciferae	178	96	53.9
Lauraceae	172	139	80.8
Ranunculaceae	163	99	60.7
Boraginaceae	145	83	57.2

(*Cajanus cajan*), of which India grew 85% of the world crop in 1983, is related to the genus *Atylosia* of which the subcontinent is a major centre of diversity (van der Maesen *et al.* 1985).

Fruit crops

The subcontinent is a centre of diversity of many fruit crops, especially in the families Anacardiaceae, Euphorbiaceae, Guttiferae, Moraceae, Musaceae, Myrtaceae, Rhamnaceae, Rosaceae, Rutaceae and Vitaceae. North-east India and neighbouring Myanmā is a centre of diversity for *Citrus*. Diversity also exists in many species of *Musa*, *Mangifera*, *Spondias*, *Vitis* and other tropical genera with edible fruits. The Himalayas are a major centre for *Ribes* and various genera of Rosaceae, such as *Pyrus*, *Prunus* and *Rubus* (Arora and Nayar 1983). The genus *Ziziphus* exhibits maximum diversity in the semi-arid plains of the north-west of the subcontinent.

Vegetables

The subcontinent is a centre of diversity for *Abelmoschus esculentus* (okra) (of which wild relatives occur in the sub-Himalayan ranges, Karnataka and the Nilgiri Hills), many genera of Cucurbitaceae (such as *Cucumis*, *Citrullus*, *Luffa* and *Momordica*), *Solanum melongena* (egg plant) and *Dioscorea* spp. (yams).

Condiments and spices

Spices and flavourings, which are such a distinctive feature of the subcontinent's cuisine, are well-represented in the region's flora. *Amomum*, *Zingiber*, *Piper* and *Curcuma* show much genetic variation in the peninsula and in tropical areas, while the Himalayan region has numerous Umbelliferae and *Allium* spp.

Palms

21 genera and about 91 species of palms occur in India, mainly in Peninsular India and the Andaman and Nicobar Islands. Coconut (*Cocos nucifera*) and areca nut (*Areca catechu*) are extensively cultivated, coconuts being the prime component of Lakshadweep's economy.

Native palms have a wide range of uses, including house-building, thatching, making bags, fans and other items, and fibre for industrial purposes (80% of palmyra palm fibre is exported to Japan and the West). A comprehensive account of the utilization of palms in the subcontinent is given by Basu (1991).

Cultural and ornamental plants

A very wide range of plants is exploited for personal adornment at festivals and for religious or traditional purposes (see, for example, Francis 1984). There is a vast number of species of horticultural importance and potential, especially among rhododendrons, orchids and alpines. Some of the more important useful plants of the subcontinent are listed in Table 13 according to their category of use.

TABLE 13. SELECTED LIST OF NATIVE AND EXOTIC PLANTS OF ECONOMIC IMPORTANCE

a. Timber trees

Species name	Vernacular name	Species name	Vernacular name
Abies pindrow	rousla	Ehretia wallichiana	bohori
Abies webbiana	gobrasalla	Eriolaena candollei	botuku, salmon-wood
Acacia ferruginea	sonkhair	Fraxinus hookeri	angan, Hooker ash
Acacia latronum	karodei	Glochidion acuminatum	latikat
Acacia lenticularis	khin	Gmelina arborea	gambhar
Acacia leucophloea	safed kihar	Homalium spp.	
Acer mono	kainjli	Ilex spp.	
Acer oblongum	pengoi, Indian maple	Lagerstroemia floribunda	pyinma (Myanmā)
Acrocarpus fraxinifolius	red cidar, nundani	Lagerstroemia flos-reginae	jarul
Adenanthera pavonina		Lagerstroemia hypoleuca	pyinma (Andaman Islands)
Adina cordifolia	haldu, yellow wood	Lannea coromandelica	jhingan
Ailanthus excelsa	maharuk	Lithocarpus spp.	
Albizia lebbeck	siris	Lophopetalum wightianum	banate
Alnus nepalensis	utis	Lumnitzera racemosa	kripa (Andaman and Nicobar Islands)
Amoora rohituka	harin hara	Machilus spp.	
Amoora wallichii	lalchini	Melia azedarach	bakain, bead tree
Anogeissus latifolia	dhaura	Memecylon spp.	
Anogeissus pendula	dhaukra	Mesua ferrea	nagsekar, ironwood
Aquilaria agallocha	eaglewood	Michelia spp.	
Berrya cordifolia	sarladevdaru	Mimusops littoralis	golikath, bullet wood
Betula alnoides	saur	Olea ferruginea	kahu
Betula utilis	bhojpatra	Olea glandulifera	gulili
Calophyllum inophyllum	Sultana champa	Ougeinia oojeinensis	sandan
Calophyllum polyanthum	kandeb	Parastemon urophyllum	
Calophyllum soulattri	lalchuni	Parishia insignis	laldhoop, dhup
Canarium strictum	raldhoop, black dammer tree	Phyllostachys bambusoides	
Carapa granatum	Pussur, puzzle tree	Picea smithiana	rhai, Himalayan spruce
Careya arborea	kumbhi	Pinus spp.	
Cedrella toona	tun, red cedar	Planchonella longipetiolata	lambapatti (Andaman and Nicobar Islands)
Cedrus deodara	deodar		
Celtis australis	khark, nettle-wood	Podocarpus spp.	
Chamaecyparis lawsoniana	Lawson cypress	Polyalthia spp.	
Chloroxylon swietenia	bhirra, satin-wood	Pometia pinnata	Jhit kandu, kasai tree
Cinnamomum spp.		Premna spp.	
Cupressus torulosa	leauri	Prinsepia utilis	karanga
Dalbergia latifolia	lalshisham, rosewood	Prosopis spp.	
Dalbergia sisso	shisham	Prunus cerasoides	paddam
Diospyros chloroxylon	ninai, green ebony	Prunus ceylanica	galmorre
Diospyros kaki	tendu, persimmon	Pterocarpus dalbergioides	padauk
Ehretia acuminata	punyan	Pterocarpus santalinus	raktachandan, red saunders

TABLE 13 ...continued

Species name	Vernacular name	Species name	Vernacular name
Quercus spp.		Rhododendron spp.	
Rhodamnia trinervia	hathori kat, mallet wood tree	Sageraea listeri	chooi, bow wood tree

b. Food and beverages

According to Kaul *et al.* (1990), some 800 plant species are used in India alone for food or forage. The following list includes some of the more important species:

Species name	Vernacular name	Species name	Vernacular name
Abelmoschus esculentus	bhindi	Hibiscus sabdariffa	lal ambari
Acacia catechu	katha	Hitchenia caulina	tikhur, Indian arrowroot
Anacardium occidentale	cashew	Hovenia dulcis	sicka, raisin tree
Areca catechu	supari, betel nut	Ilex vomitoria	yaupon
Camellia sinensis	chai, tea	Ipomoea aquatica	mendka, nalichi, pandratonda
Castanopsis hystrix	mithi chestnut	Ipomoea cairica	chimnati
Castanopsis indica	Indian chestnut	Lansium domesticum	duku, langsat
Celtis australis	nettle wood	Luffa spp.	
Chloranthus officinalis		Madhuca spp.	
Citrus spp.		Maesa indica	ramjani
Clausena willdenowii	kariveppila	Manilkara hexandra	khirni
Curcuma amada	amada	Manilkara littoralis	dogola
Curcuma angustifolia	tilchur	Moringa oleifera	saunjana, horse radish tree
Cymbopogon citratus	lemon grass	Morus spp.	
Dioscorea spp.	yam	Murraya koenigii	kripatta, curry leaf tree
Diospyros kaki	tendu, persimmon	Nelumbo nucifera	Indian lotus, kamal
Diospyros lotus	amlok, dateplum persimmon	Nephelium lappaceum	ramlitchi
Diploknema butyracea	phulwara, Indian butter tree	Nymphaea spp.	
Dolichos lablab	sem, lablab bean	Orchis spp.	salep
Emblica officinalis	amla, Indian gooseberry	Pachyrhizus erosus	sankalu, yam bean
Eriobotrya japonica	loquat	Pandanus leram	Nicobari keoraphal, Nicobar bread fruit
Eugenia formosa	phuljamb	Phoenix acaulis	ban khajur
Euphoria longan	anshpal	Phoenix humilis	pahari khajur; hill date palm
Fragaria nilgerrensis	Nilgiri strawberry	Piper betle	betel
Garcinia atroviridis		Pisonia grandis	vilayati salet, lettuce tree
Garcinia cambogia	dharambe	Pometia pinnata	jhit kandu, kasai tree
Garcinia cowa	kaphal	Premna bengalensis	dauli
Garcinia indica	kokam	Premna latifolia	dandra
Garcinia mangostana	mangosteen	Prunus spp.	
Hedyotis scandens	haniktu, hylubi, lahora	Pyrus spp.	
Hemerocallis fulva	swarnlili	Rheum emodi	revatchini

c. Spices

Species name	Vernacular name	Species name	Vernacular name
Amomum aromatica	Bengal cardamom	Piper longum	peepal, long pepper
Amomum subulatum	Nepal cardamom	Piper nigrum	colmirich, black pepper
Myristica fragrans	jaiphal (nutmeg); javitri (mace)	Piper sylvaticum	paharipepul
Myristica malabarica	kanagi, Bombay mace		

d. Medicinal plants

An immense number of plants (probably about 7000 species) are used in ayurvedic, Tibetan and other traditional medicinal practices throughout the subcontinent (see, for example, Jain and DeFilipps 1991). Some products are exported in sizeable quantities for use in Western medicine. The most important medicinal plants include:

Species name	Vernacular name	Uses
Abelmoschus crinitus	dama-danmda-jata	aphrodisiac
Abelmoschus esculentus	bhindi	veterinary
Abrus precatorius	charmoi, ghumchi	aphrodisiac, menstrual complaints and many other uses
Acacia catechu	kattha, khair	toothache, nosebleeds, diarrhoea
Acacia gageana	changratong	fish poison
Acalypha indica	khokali, kuppameni	expectorant, laxative
Achillea millefolium	chbumentok, gandan	epilepsy
Achyranthes aspera	many local names	many uses
Albizia lebbeck	chinchola, siris, vaaka	gonorrhoea treatment, piles
Allamanda cathartica	pila-jara	jaundice
Alnus nepalensis	intsungtong, rupuo	vulnerary, diarrhoea
Alocasia montana		tiger poison
Alstonia scholaris	buchong, chhatian, lazarong	many uses
Andrographis paniculata	bhuilimb, chirata	liver and intestinal complaints
Angelica archangelica	buriwakhat	childbirth
Annona squamosa	ata, mandargom	many internal uses
Anthocephalus chinensis		treatment of cholera, dysentery
Arnebia benthamii	gaujaban, kahzaban	boils, cuts, headache
Artemisia nilagirica	chiena, nagadona, pina	treatment of epilepsy, gastric complaints, antiseptic, asthma
Azadirachta indica	neem	treatment of measles, piles, cholera, cancer, dysentery, malaria
Bacopa monnieri	brahmi	coughs, fever, epilepsy
Bauhinia variegata	guiral, tago	leprosy, scrofula, tumours, snake bite, worms
Bidens biternata	kuro, agedi	diarrhoea, inflammation, headache, toothache; used to ward off evil spirits
Bombax ceiba	saur, semal	aphrodisiac and many other uses
Boswellia serrata	salar, gugal, salga	epilepsy, snake and scorpion bites

TABLE 13 ...continued

Species name	Vernacular name	Uses
Buchanania lanzan	char, reka	cholera, anti-cancer, antidote to snake and scorpion bites/stings
Butea monosperma	dhak, khakro, palash	many uses
Calotropis gigantea	akado	many uses, including anti-cancer
Calotropis procera	ak, madar	many uses, including anti-cancer
Canscora decussata	katchirata	blood purifier
Cassia fistula	amaltas, bahava	many uses
Cedrus deodara	deodar	anthelminthic
Celastrus paniculatus	papdi, peng	fever, headache, tonic
Centella asiatica	mandukpurni	many uses
Cimicifuga foetida	rotong	sedative
Cissampelos pareira	akanbindi, barwant	many uses
Cleome spp.		
Clerodendron spp.		
Coptis teeta	teeta, ringo	backache, dysentery, wounds
Crotalaria spp.		
Cuscuta reflexa	akasbel	many uses
Cynoglossum lanceolatum	balraj, sungaban	aphrodisiac
Delphinium spp.		
Desmodium motorium	bhunakra, ote-atil	used to ensure fidelity
Drimia indica	koli-kanda, ran-kanda	abortifacient, anti-cancer
Ehretia laevis	mahudiyomunjar	treatment of syphilis
Euphorbia spp.		
Evolvulus alsinoides	Vishnu-krant	many uses
Excoecaria agallocha		fish poison
Ficus bengalensis	alamaram, bargad	many uses
Ficus racemosa	atti, loa	many uses
Gentianella moorcroftiana	changra, sweetisheeti	colds, coughs and fevers
Geranium spp.		
Gloriosa superba	chengarollagadda, puttichattaasthma	gonorrhoea, leprosy; cultivated as a source of colchicine
Hedyotis spp.		
Helicteres isora	maradsing	many uses
Holarrhena antidysenterica	dudhkhuri	many uses, incl. treatment of dysentery, eczema, epilepsy
Ipomoea spp.		
Iris kumaonensis	balupuchhya	treatment of epilepsy and urinary complaints
Jatrophis curcas	bharenda	anti-cancer, pleurisy
Kickxia ramosissima		treatment of diabetes
Leucas spp.		
Lindelofia longiflora	kararetsi	diarrhoea
Lindernia spp.		
Madhuca longifolia	garang, mahua, soso	many uses
Mangifera indica	amba, maka	many uses
Microula tibetica	charoknemna	pulmonary
Mucuna spp.		
Mussaenda spp.		
Nardostachys jatamansi	jatamansi	cholera, epilepsy, jaundice, hysteria
Neanotis hirsuta	dampara	eczema and other skin diseases
Nepenthes khasiana	memang-koksi	cataracts
Oroxylum indicum	arlu, kotor, tetoli	many uses
Ougeunia oojeinensis	sandan	cholera, dysentery
Paeonia emodi	udsalib	convulsions, dropsy, hysteria and other mental disorders
Parnassia spp.		
Pedicularis pectinata	lugro-marpo	sedative
Pedicularis pycnantha	langna	intoxicant
Persea gamblei	ongtat	used as massage
Peucedanum nagporense	bhojraj	aphrodisiac
Phyllanthus emblica	nelli	many uses
Physochlaina praealta	langtan	liver complaints and epilepsy
Picrorhiza kurrooa	kutki	diarrhoea and other digestive complaints; jaundice; promotes bile secretion
Picrorhiza scrophulariiflora	kutki	similar to *P. kurrooa*
Pimpinella bracteata	hansraj	aphrodisiac
Pinus roxburghii	chir	bone fractures, skin complaints
Piper betle	pan, vetta	antiseptic, dysentery, eye diseases, mental disorders
Piper nigrum	jaluk	carminative, stomachic; also recently reported to yield effective anti-convulsants to treat epilepsy
Plumbago zeylanica	agiyachit, chitrak	skin diseases, intestinal disorders
Podocarpus neriifolius		rheumatism
Polygonatum spp.		
Polygonum spp.		
Prunus spp.		
Pygmaeopremna herbacea	bhant-bharangi	aphrodisiac
Quercus acutissima	sulemtong	eye complaints
Rhododendron spp.		
Rumex nepalensis	jaba	purgative
Santalum album	chandan	abortifacient, skin disorders
Sapindus emarginata	ritha	aches, epilepsy
Saraca asoca	ashok	urinogenital and menstrual disorders
Scrophularia koelzii	yarma	sciatica
Scutellaria discolor	lali	constipation
Semecarpus anacardium	bhailawa, idumaram	many uses
Shorea robusta	sal	burns, anti-cancer, gonorrhoea

TABLE 13 ...continued

Species name	Vernacular name	Uses
Smilax spp.		
Smithia spp.		
Solanum spp.		
Streblus asper	khaksa, sheora	anti-cancer, cholera, urinary complaints
Tamarindus indica	amli, katara	coughs, colds, fevers, digestive disorders
Trichosanthes spp.		
Vaccinium spp.		
Vatica lancifolia	janmi rang-rang	dysentery
Ventilago denticulata	bongasarjom	many uses
Woodfordia fruticosa	dhai	many uses
Xantolis tomentosa	kantabar	malaria
Zingiber spp.		
Zornia gibbosa	hirankurni	cramps, sedative

e. Fodder and forage crops

Species name	Vernacular name	Notes
Bromus catharticus	jharughas	
Cajanus cajan	arhal	
Pegolettia senegalensis		good camel fodder
Planchonella longipetiolata	lambapatti	Andamans and Nicobars: leaves used as elephant fodder
Polygonum spp.		
Pueraria spp.	kudzu	

f. Dyes

Species name	Vernacular name	Part used	Colour of dye
Adina cordifolia	haldu	wood dust	yellow
Ardisia littoralis	molakka	berries	yellow
Arnebia euchroma	kahzaban	root	red
Bergia ammannioides	jalagni	flowers	red
Bixa orellana	latkan	seeds	orange
Butea monosperma	palas		yellow
Carapa granatum	pussur	wood	red
Cassia fistula	Indian laburnum	bark	pale
Chlorophora excelsa		bark	yellow
Chrozophora prostrata	subali	capsules	blue, purple
Clitoria ternata	aparjit	flowers, roots	blue
Curcuma aromatica	banhaldi	rhizome	orange
Curcuma longa	haldi, turmeric	rhizome	yellow
Delphinium zalil	guljalil	flowers	yellow
Desmos cochinchinensis		fruits	purple
Didymocarpus pedicellata	shilapushpa	leaves	red
Garcinia morella	tamal	cortex, pith, leaves, flowers, fruits	yellow
Gentiana kurrooa	nilkanthi	roots	
Geranium nepalense	bhanda	roots	red
Hedyotis scandens	bhedeli lata	leaves	green
Indigofera spp. (e.g. I. tinctoria)	indigo	leaves	indigo
Jasminum humile	pilichameli	roots	yellow
Lotus garcini		flowers, leaves	orange, yellow
Lychnis indica		flowers	scarlet
Lycopus europaeus	jalnim	fruit	green
Maclura pomifera	osage orange	wood extract	orange
Mallotus philippinensis	rohini, kamala tree	unripe fruits	red
Manilkara littoralis	dogola	bark	red
Marsdenia tinctoria	riyong	leaves	indigo
Morinda citrifolia	surangi	roots	rose-red
Onosma hispidum	ratanjyoti	roots	red
Pithecellobium clypearia	grasshopper tree	bark	black
Psychotria viridiflora		leaves	red
Pterocarpus dalbergioides	padauk	wood	red
Pterocarpus marsupium	kino	wood	red
Rinorea bengalensis	kali patta	leaves	brown
Rubia cordifolia	manjit, Indian madder		red
Rubia sikkimensis	naga madder		red

g. Fibre and latex

Species name	Vernacular name	Part used	Uses
Abroma augusta	ulatkamba, devil's cotton	bark	ropes
Abutilon indicum	atibala	stem	ropes
Aechmanthera tomentosa	latgha	bark	netting, weaving, ropes
Aeschynomene aspera	sola pith plant	stem	sun hats, toys
Anodendron paniculatum	lamtani	stem	mats
Antiaris toxicaria	karwat, upas tree	bark	tribal garments
Arundo donax	baranal	stem	musical pipes, fishing rods, baskets, toys
Bambusa tulda	peka	stem	basket work; also used in paper industry
Bombax ceiba	semul	fruit	pillows
Borassus flabellifer	tar, Palmyra palm	leaves	brooms, brushes, fans
Calotropis gigantea	madar	bark	nets, twine, string

TABLE 13 ...continued

Species name	Vernacular name	Part used	Uses
Calotropis procera	ak, madar	stem	mats
Cannabis indica	charas	stem	sackcloth, ropes
Cassia auriculata	tarwar, tanner's cassia	bark	hessian bags
Chlorophora excelsa	iroko	bark	yellow latex
Clinogyne dichotoma	sitalpati	leaves	baskets
Cyperus spp.			
Dalbergia extensa	takoli	bark	mats
Dalbergia sissoides	kalishisham	bark	ropes
Debregeasia hypoleuca	tushiari	stem	ropes, nets, cordage
Debregeasia longifolia	sansaru	stem	cordage
Dicranopteris linearis		leaf stalks	mats, chair-seats, baskets
Erinocarpus nimmonii	haladi	bark	ropes
Erythrina suberosa	dauldhak	bark	insulation
Ficus benghalensis	banyan	bark and aerial roots	yields latex
Ficus benjamina	pakur	sap	yields latex
Ficus elastica	attah, Assam rubber	sap	yields rubber
Gyrinops walla		bark	ropes, hats
Helicteres isora	marorphali	bark and stem	string, sacks, canvas, weighing machine pans
Hibiscus cannabinus	patsan, Ambari hemp	stem	paper pulp, cordage
Iris ensata	irisa	leaves	thatching
Marsdenia roylei	maruabel		nets, fine ropes
Musa textilis	naaru	stem	fabrics, mats
Nannorrhops ritchieana	mazari	leaves	mats, baskets
Ochrosia oppositifolia		sap	latex for caulking boats (Andaman Islands)
Palaquium gutta	percha	sap	gutta percha latex
Pandanus spp.			
Parameria barbata	tenga lata	sap	yields rubber-like latex (Andaman Islands)
Phragmites karka	bagnarri		
Phyllostachys bambusoides			used in paper industry, rayon manufacture

h. Gums, resins and waxes

Species name	Vernacular name	Notes
Acacia arabica	babul	gum arabic
Acacia dealbata	chikaka	
Acacia senegal	kher	true gum arabic
Albizia lebbeck	chinchola, siris, vaaka	
Albizia odoratissima	gadad	
Anogeissus latifolia	dhavada	edible gum
Aquilaria agallocha	eaglewood	oleoresin
Boswellia serrata	salai, Indian olibanum	oleoresin; also a medicinal gum and essential oil
Butea superba	latapalash	
Cochlospermum religiosum	katira	
Diospyros toposia	Assam ebony	
Dipterocarpus spp.		
e.g. D. griffithii	garjan balsam	
D. indicus	gteo resin	
D. tuberculatus	eng	
Dryobalanus aromatica	barus camphor	
Feronia limonia	elephant apple, kaithbel	
Ferula foetida	hing, asafoetida	
Gardenia gummifera	Cumbi gum tree	
Juniperus spp.		
Macaranga tanaria	mallata	gum kino
Melanorrhoea usitata	kheu, Burmese lacquer tree	bark resin (Manipur, Myanmā)
Odina modier	Indian ash tree	
Pinus spp.	pine	oleoresins used as turpentine in cosmetics, rubber and paint industries
Pterocarpus marsupium	kino	gum kino
Rhus succedanea	kakrasingi, wax tree	
Vateria indica	akjarna	amber-like oleoresin, used to make ornamental beads

i. Oils and soaps

Species name	Vernacular name	Notes
Acacia dealbata	chikaka	
Achras zapota	cheeku, sapota	
Adenanthera pavonina	bari-ghumchi	
Aleurites montana	chiniakhrot	
Azadirachta indica	neem	
Caesalpinia sappam	putag	
Cerbera manghas		
Cinnamomum camphora	kapoor	
Cymbopogon spp.		
Elettaria cardamomum	small cardamom, choti ilaichi	
Erioglossum rubiginosum	ritha, soap nut tree	
Erythrina arborescens	rungara	yields a soap
Evodia fraxinifolia	kannlipa	
Impatiens sulcata	khanchedargulmehdi	balsam oil
Jasminum sambac		
Limnophila aromatica	kuttra	
Melaleuca leucadendron	cajuputte	cajuput oil

TABLE 13 ...continued

Species name	Vernacular name	Notes
Mesua ferrea	nagsekar, ironwood	stamens used as pillow stuffing
Nardostachys jatamansi	jatamansi, spikenard	roots yield spikenard (essential oil)
Payena oleifera		seeds yield oils, used as illuminant
Pittosporum floribundum	tumri	essential oil from flowers; oleoresin (narcotic) from bark
Pogostemon cablin	patchouli	leaves yield commercial essential oil; flowers and leaves of other species also used
Pogostemon heyneanus	Indian patchouli	
Quillaja saponaria	sabunper, soap bark tree	powdered bark yields foam for shampoo, detergent

j. Perfumes

Species name	Vernacular name	Notes
Acacia farnesiana	gandbabool, cassie flower	
Cananga odorata	maladi	
Cinnamomum glanduliferum	malligiri	
Cinnamomum impressinervium	chotatejpatta	
Cinnamomum iners	janglidarchini	
Commiphora caudata	kiluvai, hill mango	
Commiphora mukul	Indian bdellium	
Deutzia corymbosa		
Iris kumaonensis	karkar	
Magnolia grandiflora	himchampa, bull bay	volatile oil
Magnolia griffithii	barachamp	
Mimusops elengi	maulsari	
Mimusops littoralis	golikath, bullet wood	flowers yield essential oil
Nyctanthes arbor-tristis	harsinghar, night jasmine	
Osmanthus fragrans	silang	
Pandanus spp.		
(especially P. odoratissimum)	keora attar oil	
Rosa spp.		

k. Tannins

Species name	Vernacular name	Species name	Vernacular name
Acacia decurrens	hara chikaka	Chrysobalanus icaco	coco plum
Acacia jacquemontii	kikas	Cyperus tuberosus	
Aegialitis rotundifolia		Dalbergia lanceolaria	bithua
Anogeissus latifolia	dhaura	Dysoxylum binectariflorum	
Bauhinia tomentosa	phalgu	Jatropha curcas	arand, bharenda, ratanjot
Buchanania lanzana	chiranji	Knema angustifolia	motapasuti
Caesalpinia digyna	rakeri mul	Lespedeza cuneata	khunju
Cassia auriculata	tarwar, tanner's cassia	Pongamia pinnata	karang

l. Ornamentals

Only a few of the very many ornamental plants of the subcontinent are listed below.

Species name	Species name
Amherstia nobilis	Ipomoea aculeatum
Buddleja asiatica	Jasminum spp.
Caesalpinia pulcher	Meconopsis spp.
Chrysanthemum indicum	Paeonia emodi
Cymbidium aloifolium	Paphiopedilum spp.
Desmotrichum fimbriatum	Pleione spp.
Erythrina crista-galli	Porana spp.
Gentiana spp.	Quisqualis indica
Gloriosa superba	Rhododendron spp.

m. Religious uses and sacred plants

Species name	Vernacular name	Notes
Adansonia digitata	gorakhimli	
Anodendron paniculatum		associated with tree spirits
Artemisia nilagirica	chiena, nagadona, pina	keeps spirits away
Butea monosperma	dhak	sacred tree
Calotropis gigantea	akado	
Calotropis procera	ak	
Cedrus deodara	deodar	
Evolvulus alsinoides		used in Santal religious ceremonies
Excoecaria agallocha		cultivated in Shiva temples
Ficus religiosa	peepal	
Goniothalamus cardiopetalus	sane	used as incense in temples
Gonystylus macrophyllus		temple incense (Nicobar Islands)
Madhuca longifolia	garang, mahua, soso	
Mangifera indica	amba, maka	used as festive decorations; Buddha is said to have rested under it
Melia azedarach	bakain; bead tree	fruits: rosaries
Rivea cuneata	bondwail	
Santalum album	chandan	offered to Shiva in worship
Saraca asoca	ashok	associated with Buddha
Shorea robusta	sal	associated with Buddha
Streblus asper	khaksa, sheora	

TABLE 13 ...continued

n. Soil binders

Species name	Species name
Acacia latronum	Eleusine flagellifera
Acrostichum aureum	Eremopogon foveolatus
Aeluropus lagopoides	Eremurus himalaicus
Azima tetracantha	Eulaliopsis binata
Breweria evolvuloides	Glyceria tonglensis
Brownlowia torsa	Halopyrum mucronatum
Bulbostylis barbata	Haplothismia exannulata
Canavalia maritima	Hubbardia heptaneuron
Casuarina equisetifolia	Ipomoea pes-caprae
Chrysopogon montanus	Ipomoea tuba
Cyperus rotundus	Justicia quinqueangularis
Dolichos spp.	Pachygone ovata
Echinochloa frumentacea	Spermacoce stricta

Factors causing loss of biodiversity

Natural environmental factors

Much of the region is subject to seismic activity or to the effects of violent storms and floods, which cause landslides or wash away topsoil and thus alter or destroy the vegetation. However, human impact on the environment (e.g. deforestation), results in a greater frequency of "natural" events such as erosion and flooding. Deforestation in the Himalayas, for example, is resulting in increased floods in the Ganges Delta in Bangladesh because of changes in river flow volumes.

Population pressure

Table 14 gives the area, present population, annual growth rate and expected population by 2025 for each country in the region.

The Indian Subcontinent has an area of about 4,850,000 km² (c. 3.6% of Earth's surface) and has a combined total population of 1,160 million (c. 20% of the world's population). The population is expected to almost double by 2025, to c. 2,100 million. Average per capita income in the subcontinent in 1985 was US$214 (1.5% of that in the U.S.A.) (Johnstone 1986), ranging from US$85 per annum in Bhutan to US$390 per annum in Pakistan. In some countries, such as Bangladesh, the majority of the population live below the local official poverty line. Many people are landless (especially in Bangladesh), and in some countries there are significant populations of refugees, e.g. Nepal (from Bhutan) and Bangladesh (from Myanmā). The population is very unevenly distributed. Most of the population of India, for example, live in two states (Kerala in the south and Uttar Pradesh in the north). Even where population densities are very low, as in Ladakh, Kashmir, the ecosystems may not be able to support population numbers much above present levels.

Cattle grazing

India supports 15% of the world's cattle (Kaul et al. 1990). Excessive grazing by cattle has led to serious land degradation in some areas, especially on the Deccan Plateau.

Fuelwood cutting

In India, 90% of cooking fuel is biomass (fuelwood, cow dung and crop waste). Even in urban areas, fuelwood is an essential commodity, accounting for an annual purchase value of 5,000 million rupees (Kaul et al. 1990). The average annual requirement in India alone is 130 million tonnes. More than 80% of firewood is gathered illegally from the countryside. Increased fuelwood needs have resulted in deforestation of many areas. Even sacred groves, which have been left untouched for countless generations, have been damaged or even cut down (Gadgil and Vartak 1975, 1976).

Shifting cultivation

Shifting cultivation, known as *jhumming* in India and *taungya* in Myanmā, is practised by hill tribes in north-east India, Myanmā, parts of Nepal and Pakistan, and to a lesser extent elsewhere (e.g. South India). Forest trees are felled

TABLE 14. POPULATION DATA

Country	Area (km²)	Population (millions) [a]		Annual growth rate (%) [a]		Expected population (millions) by 2025 [b]
Bangladesh	133,910	122.3	(1993)	2.5	(1990)	234.99
Bhutan	46,620	0.6	(1990)	2.0	(1985)	3.07
B.I.O.T.[c]	60	0.0		0.0		0.00
India	2,973,190	846.3	(1991)	2.2	(1985)	1442.39
Maldive Is.	298	0.02	(1990)	3.0		?
Myanmā	677,855	41.55	(1992)	1.8	(1992)	72.62
Nepal	141,415	19.36	(1991)	2.3	(1991)	34.97
Pakistan	803,940	114.0	(1991)	2.7		267.11
Sri Lanka	65,630	17.25	(1991)	2.1	(1985)	24.57

Sources:

[a] Hunter (1993) except Bhutan, India, Pakistan and Sri Lanka (Johnstone 1986).
[b] World Resources Institute (1992).
[c] British Indian Ocean Territory has no permanent population.

before the monsoon and the area then burned for cultivation. When the fertility of the cleared plot decreases, usually after 2–3 years, the area is abandoned and the process is repeated elsewhere, leaving the cleared site to regenerate for a number of years until it is cleared again. Jhumming cycles used to be 25–50 years, allowing sufficient time for forest to regenerate. However, population pressure has led to the shortening of jhumming cycles to 5–8 years. As a result, forest does not have sufficient time to regenerate and abandoned plots become dominated by bamboo scrub (Rao 1977).

Soil erosion

When an area has been deforested, the topsoil (which is often very thin) is frequently washed away by the first monsoon rains and the land becomes unsuitable for forest regeneration. The problem is particularly severe in montane areas, such as in Bhutan, Nepal, the Western Ghats of India, and parts of Myanmā, where slopes are steep, run-off considerable and landslides frequent. The Department of Soil and Water Conservation of Nepal estimates that each hectare of deforested land loses between 30 and 75 tonnes of soil per annum; some 249,000,000 m³ of soil are lost to India each year (Cool 1980).

Construction schemes

Several countries in the region are rapidly developing modern road networks. India, in particular, has embarked on a massive road-building programme in previously remote and inaccessible parts of Sikkim and Arunachal Pradesh. Road building opens up areas to logging, colonization and harvesting of wild species (Sahni 1980).

The construction of hydroelectric dams and subsequent submergence of forested valleys have caused large-scale deforestation in many montane areas. The intensive utilization of water resources in the Western Ghats of India gives particular cause for concern. Large stands of species-rich forests have already been submerged, such as along the Periyar River, and the activities associated with construction of dams (such as road building to provide access) has led to human encroachment and the fragmentation of the remaining forest.

Public opposition to dam construction was instrumental in halting the Silent Valley Hydroproject in January 1980. This would have resulted in the inundation of 5.4 km² of species-rich tropical rain forest along the Kunthipuzha River (Goodland 1985).

Plantation forestry

Large areas of land have been converted to forestry plantations, often monocultures of teak (*Tectona grandis*), sal (*Shorea robusta*), *Cryptomeria japonica*, *Eucalyptus* spp. and Mexican pine (*Pinus patula*). Some native species are used in afforestation schemes. For example, large tracts of *Pinus kesiya* are planted in north-east India.

Plant collecting

As noted above, some 800 native plant species are used for food or forage in India alone (Kaul *et al.* 1990); the figure for the whole region is likely to be well over 1000 species. Many other species are used for construction, furniture and other domestic purposes. About 7000 species have some use in indigenous folk medicine within the region. About 1500 different drugs used in India and Nepal are plant-derived (Chopra and Handa 1961). In Sri Lanka, about 500 species (c. 17% of the total flora) are used in Ayurvedic medicine (Lokubandara 1991). Many introduced species are also used in folk medicine.

In India and Nepal, many species are threatened with extinction as a result of commercial trade (Maheshwari 1977). Examples include: *Coptis teeta*, *Gentiana kurrooa*, *Nardostachys jatamansi*, *Rheum emodi* and *R. nobile* (all medicinal plants), and numerous orchids, such as *Paphiopedilum fairieanum*, *Pleione* spp. and *Cypripedium cordigerum*. *Vanda coerulea*, once common in the Khasia Hills, has been collected almost to extinction. *Colchicum luteum* and *Gloriosa superba* are valuable sources of colchicine and are heavily exploited.

Nepal's foreign earnings have risen dramatically since the mid-1970s; by far the principal component responsible for the rise is the huge increase in commercial exports of medicinal plants or their products. Principal species include: *Aconitum heterophyllum*, *Ephedra gerardiana*, *Nardostachys jatamansi*, *Orchis latifolia*, *Picrorhiza kurrooa* and *Rheum emodi*.

Introduced plants

A large number of introduced species has become naturalized over much of the region, mainly introduced in the 20th century. In some Indian states, exotic species now account for up to 40% of the total flora. In Sind (Pakistan), the proportion is even higher. Widespread exotics include: *Ageratum conyzoides*, *Alternanthera pungens*, *Croton bonplandianum*, *Lagascea mollis* and *Tridax procumbens* (all from South America or Mexico), and *Crassocephalum crepidioides* (from tropical Africa). Many introduced species are extremely aggressive and very quickly become established as the dominant species in disturbed habitats. Two of the most invasive species in the Indian Subcontinent are *Eupatorium adenophorum* (in north-east India) and *Parthenium hysterophorus* (in the South Indian plains), while *Eichhornia crassipes* (the water hyacinth) eliminates all other hydrophytes in any body of water in which it occurs.

Fire

Annual fires are a severe problem in some ecosystems, such as in *Pinus wallichiana* forest in Bhutan and in subtropical pine forest in Arunachal Pradesh.

Changes in agricultural practices

Agriculture has been practised in the region for thousands of years. A complex gene pool of thousands of land races of crop plants, each variety ideally suited to its particular local conditions, has been built up over the years. Often, several different varieties are planted in different seasons in a given area to minimize the risk of crop failure. For example, it has been estimated that, as recently as 50 years ago, Indian farmers were growing some 30,000 varieties of rice; however, Maheshwari (1986) predicts that the number of varieties grown will have been reduced to no more than 50 by the year 2000 as a result of agricultural modernization. These are likely to be "improved" cultivars with a narrow genetic base. Such a reduction in the genetic diversity of staple food crops could have serious consequences for future plant breeding programmes.

Rare or threatened plants

No single country in the region has a complete Red Data Book on threatened plants, although three volumes have been produced of the Indian Red Data Book (Nayar and Sastry 1987–1990). Many papers have been published on threatened plants of individual States of India. The most comprehensive compendia are Jain and Rao (1983) and Jain and Sastry (1983).

Conservation

Tables 15, 16 and 17 give the numbers and categories of protected areas in each country of the region and the percentage of land protected.

Note that the figures presented in the tables refer only to those areas which meet the criteria for inclusion in the *United Nations List of National Parks and Protected Areas* (IUCN 1990, 1992). The protected sites included are those which cover an area of 10 km² or more and which are assigned IUCN Management Categories. It is very important to note that, in some cases, this figure includes sites which are only partially protected. Therefore, in some cases, the figures imply a greater area protected than is actually the case. A further important consideration is that many protected areas have been established primarily for their fauna and are not necessarily the best areas for plants.

The importance of conservation of wild plant resources is officially recognized by most countries in the region; however, management of protected areas is often ineffective due to economic constraints. A review of the protected area systems and conservation legislation in each country is given by IUCN (1992).

A National Conservation Strategy (NCS) has been developed for Bangladesh. The strategy is currently before the Cabinet of Ministers for approval. The Ministry of Environment and Forests and the National Planning Commission, with advice from IUCN, are producing a document on the "NCS Implementation Project". Some of the key recommendations are the development and strengthening of the Forest Department, National Herbarium and Botanical Gardens, the development of a database on the status of biodiversity in Bangladesh and associated biodiversity surveys (Choudhury 1993). With the support of IUCN and others, the Government of Bangladesh has prepared a National Environmental Management Plan (NEMP).

Bhutan and Myanmā are not parties to any international convention concerned with protecting natural areas, and neither participates in the UNESCO Man and the Biosphere (MAB) Programme. However, the two countries have very different attitudes to conservation. Bhutan places great emphasis on maintaining at least 60% of its land area under closed forest in order to maintain climatic equilibrium

TABLE 15. PROTECTED AREAS SYSTEMS IN THE INDIAN SUBCONTINENT

Country	Total number of protected areas	Total area protected (km²)	% land area protected
Bangladesh	9	1084	0.8
Bhutan	8	9519	20.4
India	361	132,474	4.2
Maldives	0	0	0.0
Myanmā	14 [a]	4494 [a]	0.6 [a]
Nepal	12	10,910	7.7
Pakistan	53	36,550	4.5
Sri Lanka	45 [b]	7839	11.9

Notes:

[a] Excludes 11,207 km² of proposed protected areas. If established, they will bring the percentage land area protected to 2.3%.
[b] Gunatilleke and Gunatilleke (1990) list 96 protected areas; the figure of 45 refers to those recognized by IUCN (1992).

TABLE 16. NUMBER OF PROTECTED AREAS IN EACH OF THE IUCN MANAGEMENT CATEGORIES

Country	Total number of protected areas	IUCN Management Category [a]				
		I	II	IV	V	VIII
Bangladesh	9	0	0	6	2	1
Bhutan	8	0	1	4	0	3
India	361	2	59	299	1	0
Maldives	0	0	0	0	0	0
Myanmā	14 [b]	No IUCN Management Categories assigned				
Nepal	12	0	7	4	0	1
Pakistan	53	0	6	43	4	0
Sri Lanka	45	3	11	31	0	0

Notes:

[a] There are no protected areas in Categories III, VI or VII.
[b] Excludes proposed protected areas not yet established.

TABLE 17. PROTECTED AREAS BY IUCN MANAGEMENT CATEGORIES

Country	Total area protected (km²)	IUCN Management Category [a]				
		I	II	IV	V	VIII
Bangladesh	1084	0	833	135	0	116
Bhutan	9519	0	658	8403	0	458
India	132,474	1660	41,929	88,699	186	0
Maldives	0	0	0	0	0	0
Myanmā	4494 [b]	No IUCN Management Categories assigned				
Nepal	10,910	0	8644	941	0	1325
Pakistan	36,550	0	8822	27,007	721	0
Sri Lanka [c]	7839	316	4602	2921	0	0

Notes:

[a] There are no protected areas in Categories III, VI or VII.
[b] Excludes proposed protected areas not yet established.
[c] The area of one Category IV reserve (Mahakandaraywewa) was not available.

and to prevent soil erosion. The entire northern part of the country is a vast Wildlife Sanctuary (Jigme Dorji Wildlife Sanctuary) of 7905 km². Of all the countries in the subcontinent, Bhutan has by far the greatest percentage of its land classed as protected areas (20.4%). In Myanmā, by contrast, only 0.6% of the land surface is protected within legally protected areas. Furthermore, the degree of protection in many of the legally protected areas in Myanmā is questionable. The percentage land area protected will rise to 2.3% if 26 proposed protected areas are legally established.

Pakistan has developed a National Conservation Strategy. In 1993, Pakistan approved the proposal to designate the

Central Karakoram as a National Park and to put forward a proposal to UNESCO for its listing as a World Heritage Site (Anon. 1994). If accepted, this important area would become the first World Heritage Site in Pakistan.

India has a large network of some 361 protected areas but these still only protect 4.2% of the land surface and are inadequate to protect the biodiversity which is rapidly being lost. Two orchid reserves have been established in Sikkim to protect *Paphiopedilum fairieanum* and two pitcher plant reserves in Meghalaya have been established to protect *Nepenthes khasiana*. Thirteen areas have been identified as potential Biosphere Reserves under the UNESCO MAB Programme.

Conservation awareness in Nepal dates back many centuries. Many sacred forests have been preserved for countless generations according to deep-rooted religious tradition. A *National Conservation Stategy* has been prepared by the Government of Nepal in conjunction with IUCN. Nevertheless, deforestation continues, and forest loss has been particularly severe in the Middle Mountains.

Sri Lanka has an extensive network of 96 reserves and proposed reserves, summarized by Gunatilleke and Gunatilleke (1990). However, of the 15 floristic zones into which Sri Lanka has been classified (Ashton and Gunatilleke 1987), by far the largest number of reserves (58) are in the Dry Zone. Conservation of species diversity in two categories of protected area (Sanctuaries and Jungle Corridors) is threatened by recommendations for multiple use of these areas, including timber extraction. Only 9 reserves are in the floristically richest wet zones.

Centres of plant diversity and endemism

Gadgil and Meher-Homji (1986) provide estimates of the remaining extent of 43 vegetation types in India and suggest a series of localities (numbering more than 80) which should be accorded the highest priority to conserve the whole spectrum of India's biological diversity. Nayar (1987) provides a list of 26 centres of angiosperm endemism in India.

The most species-rich and endemic-rich areas for plants in the Indian Subcontinent are listed below. A total of 13 areas have been selected for Data Sheet treatment. Each site contains, or is estimated to contain, more than 1000 vascular plant species, of which more than 100 are endemic to the site or phytogeographic region.

TABLE 18. NUMBER OF CPD SITES SELECTED FOR EACH PHYTOCHORION

In the table below, the phytochoria are arranged according to the size of their floras.

Phytochorion	Vascular plant species	Endemic species	% Species endemism	Number of CPD sites	Number of Data Sheets
Indian	12,000	2000	17	7	6
Indochinese	10,000	1500	17	4	3
Eastern Asiatic	9000	3600	40	4	3
Irano-Turanian	6500	550	8	2	1
Somalia-Masai	1200	70–80	6–7	0	0
Malesian[a]	750–800	72	9–10	1	1

Note:

[a] CPD Site IS17 (Andaman and Nicobar Islands) represents the Malesian (Nicobar Islands) and Indian (Andaman Islands) phytochoria.

TABLE 19. SITES OF THE INDIAN SUBCONTINENT IDENTIFIED AS CENTRES OF PLANT DIVERSITY AND ENDEMISM

The list of sites is arranged below according to the sequence adopted in the Regional Overview. Sites selected for Data Sheet treatment appear in bold.

IRANO-TURANIAN REGIONAL CENTRE OF ENDEMISM
IS1. Kashmir Himalaya (Jammu and Kashmir, Pakistan/India)
IS2. **Nanda Devi** (Kumaon-Garhwal Himalaya, India)

EASTERN ASIATIC REGIONAL CENTRE OF ENDEMISM
IS3. Northern Sikkim and East Nepal (India, Nepal)
IS4. **Namdapha** (India)
IS5. **Natma Taung (Mount Victoria) and Rongklang (Chin Hills)** (Myanmā)
IS6. **North Myanmā** (Myanmā)

INDIAN REGIONAL CENTRE OF ENDEMISM
IS7. **Agastyamalai Hills** (India)
IS8. **Nilgiri Hills** (India)

IS9. **Nallamalai Hills** (India)
IS10. Sundarbans (Bangladesh, India)
IS11. **Knuckles** (Sri Lanka)
IS12. **Peak Wilderness and Horton Plains** (Sri Lanka)
IS13. **Sinharaja** (Sri Lanka)

INDOCHINESE REGION
IS14. **Bago (Pegu) Yomas** (Myanmā)
IS15. Shan Plateau (Myanmā)
IS16. **Taninthayi (Tenasserim)** (Myanmā)
IS17. **Andaman Islands** (India)

MALESIAN REGION
IS17. **Nicobar Islands** (India) (treated with Andaman Islands)

The list below is arranged by country for cross-reference purposes. Sites selected for Data Sheet treatment appear in bold.

BANGLADESH
IS10. Sundarbans

INDIA
IS1. Kashmir Himalaya
IS2. **Nanda Devi**
IS3. Northern Sikkim and East Nepal
IS4. **Namdapha**
IS7. **Agastyamalai Hills**
IS8. **Nilgiri Hills**
IS9. **Nallamalai Hills**
IS10. Sundarbans
IS17. **Andaman and Nicobar Islands**

MYANMĀ
IS5. **Natma Taung (Mount Victoria) and Rongklang (Chin Hills)**
IS6. **North Myanmā**
IS14. **Bago (Pegu) Yomas**
IS15. Shan Plateau
IS16. **Taninthayi (Tenasserim)**

NEPAL
IS3. Northern Sikkim and East Nepal

PAKISTAN
IS1. Kashmir Himalaya

SRI LANKA
IS11. **Knuckles**
IS12. **Peak Wilderness and Horton Plains**
IS13. **Sinharaja**

MAP 3. CENTRES OF PLANT DIVERSITY AND ENDEMISM: INDIAN SUBCONTINENT
The map shows the locations of the CPD Data Sheet sites for the region

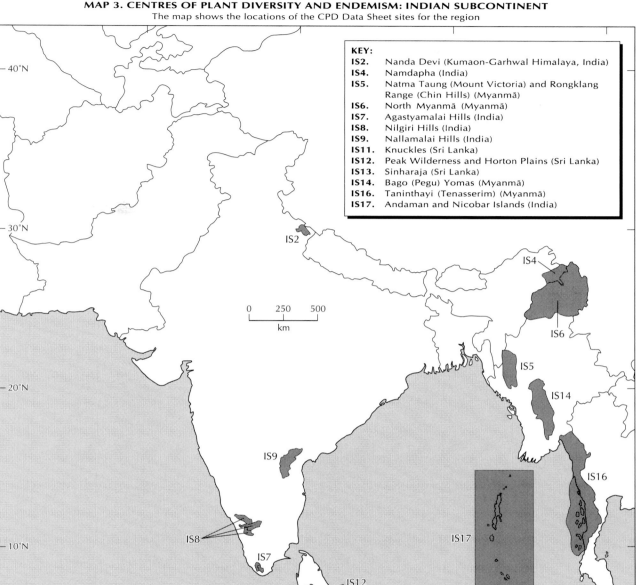

KEY:
IS2. Nanda Devi (Kumaon-Garhwal Himalaya, India)
IS4. Namdapha (India)
IS5. Natma Taung (Mount Victoria) and Rongklang Range (Chin Hills) (Myanmā)
IS6. North Myanmā (Myanmā)
IS7. Agastyamalai Hills (India)
IS8. Nilgiri Hills (India)
IS9. Nallamalai Hills (India)
IS11. Knuckles (Sri Lanka)
IS12. Peak Wilderness and Horton Plains (Sri Lanka)
IS13. Sinharaja (Sri Lanka)
IS14. Bago (Pegu) Yomas (Myanmā)
IS16. Taninthayi (Tenasserim) (Myanmā)
IS17. Andaman and Nicobar Islands (India)

SOMALIA-MASAI REGIONAL CENTRE OF ENDEMISM

This region extends from tropical north-east Africa and southern Arabian Peninsula (see the Regional Overviews on Africa, and South West Asia and the Middle East in Volume 1) to southern Baluchistan (Makran) and Sind in Pakistan, and north Gujarat, Haryana, west Rajasthan (Thar Desert) and the Punjab Plain of India.

Climate

Semi-arid to arid, many areas having a mean annual rainfall of less than 200 mm. Jacobabad is the hottest place on the subcontinent, and one of the hottest places on Earth, with summer temperatures in excess of 50°C.

The Thar Desert experiences extreme diurnal and seasonal temperature variations; winter temperatures sometimes drop below 0°C, summer maxima are over 47°C. Dust storms and desiccating winds are frequent in summer.

Flora

Number of species:	c. 1200
Endemic species:	c. 70–80
Regional endemism:	c. 6–7% (higher in Pakistan, lower in India)
Endemic genera:	0 or very few
Endemic families:	0
Figures refer to vascular plants.	

This is floristically the poorest region of the Indian Subcontinent. There are no CPD sites. Two phytochoria are represented: the South Iranian Province (in Makran) and the Sindian Province. The South Iranian Province includes the Makran Range of southern Baluchistan (which extends into Iran) and the adjacent coast. The region is mainly tropical desert with few endemic or near-endemic genera and species (e.g. *Grewia makranica*). Typical species of trees and shrubs include *Acacia nilotica*, *Mimosa hamata*, *Suaeda monoica* and *Grewia villosa* (Tasnif and Snead 1964). The Sindian Province includes Sind (Pakistan), the Punjab Plain and Thar Desert, Haryana, west Rajasthan and north Gujarat (India). The region is mostly desert, with thorn scrub, *Euphorbia* scrub and *Acacia senegal* forest. Hasanain and Rahman (1957) list 901 species from Sind, but of these scarcely 500 are native (Stewart 1982). There are no endemic genera and only a few endemic species. Kutch is under-explored and has only about 2.4% endemism. Endemics in western Rajasthan are mainly concentrated in the Jaisalmer and Barmer Districts.

Factors causing loss of biodiversity

Overgrazing, land clearing, collection of firewood and over-exploitation of medicinal plants such as *Cassia senna*.

Conservation

In Baluchistan and Sind there are 4 National Parks: Dhrum (1677 km²), Hazar-Ganji-Chiltan (155.6 km²), Mingol (1650 km²) and Kirthar (3087.3 km²) and 25 Wildlife Sanctuaries (of total area 16,671.8 km²). Of the Wildlife Sanctuaries, the largest are the Runn of Kutch (3204.6 km²), Nara Desert (2235.9 km²), Dureji (1782.6 km²), Buzi Makola (1451 km²) and Raghai Rakshan (1254.3 km²).

The main protected area in the Indian part of the region is the Desert National Park (3162 km²). About 50 species of angiosperms and one gymnosperm in this protected area are considered to be threatened (Pandey, Shetty and Verma 1985).

IRANO-TURANIAN REGIONAL CENTRE OF ENDEMISM

This vast region extends from Anatolia (Turkey) through most of South West Asia as far as the western spurs of the Himalayas (east to 83°E). Only some north-western parts of the subcontinent, in Pakistan and northern India, fall within this phytochorion. 45.6% of the total flora of Pakistan are Irano-Turanian elements (Ali and Qaiser 1986). The percentage for India is not known but will be very much smaller.

NORTH BALUCHISTANIAN PROVINCE

This covers the Sulaiman Range and much of upland central Pakistan. There is a transition to the Western Himalayan flora which begins at Kurram and Khyber.

Climate

This part of the subcontinent is the least influenced by the monsoon. The climate is extreme, with very hot summer temperatures (especially around Sibi) and cold winters. Some areas have only 25–75 mm annual rainfall; only in the Waziristan Ranges does rainfall exceed 250 mm.

Flora

Number of species:	3300
Endemic species:	120
Regional endemism:	3%
Endemic genera:	1
Endemic families:	0
Figures refer to vascular plants.	

Important plant families include: Boraginaceae, Chenopodiaceae, Convolvulaceae, Cruciferae, Liliaceae, Plumbaginaceae, Umbelliferae and Zygophyllaceae. There are many bulbous and tuberous species in such genera as *Eremurus*, *Ixiolirion* and *Hyacinthus*.

There is one endemic genus, *Sulaimania* (Labiatae), while the genus *Aitchisonia* (Rubiaceae) is a Pakistan endemic occurring both in this region and further north (Ali and Qaiser 1986). The Toba Range and the Quetta-Pishin Plateau are local centres of endemism. The foothills have a flora similar to that of Sind, with many Somalia-Masai elements, such as *Salvadora oleoides*. The northern part of the area, around Quetta, has much in common with the flora of eastern Afghanistan.

Main vegetation types

In low-lying areas subject to flooding from the Indus, *Tamarix articulata*, *T. gallica* and *Populus euphratica* occur. Common shrubs include *Ziziphus nummularia*, *Leptadenia spartium* and *Acacia jacquemontii*. Extensive "juniper tracts" dominated by *Juniperus macropoda* occur around Quetta and Ziarat between 2000–3000 m altitude. Here, there are many Himalayan elements, including *Acantholimon*, *Astragalus*, *Gypsophila* and *Onobrychis* species, which grow in association with *Iris*, *Allium* and *Ferula* species.

Species of economic importance

An account of the useful plants of Pakistan is given by Kazmi and Johan (1975, 1976, 1977). Psyllium (*Plantago ovata*) is an important medicinal plant of potential export importance on account of its laxative properties (Duke 1990).

Factors causing loss of biodiversity

Juniperus macropoda is virtually the only source of fuel and timber for the inhabitants of the Quetta region. Population growth, combined with the slow rate of growth and regeneration of the juniper, is placing increased pressure on this unique vegetation type.

Conservation

There are 3 National Parks and 14 Wildlife Sanctuaries in Baluchistan. Of these, probably the most significant botanically is the Ziarat Juniper Wildlife Sanctuary (372.5 km²).

Nasir (1991) has stated that at least 12% of the flora of Pakistan is threatened. Families with the most threatened taxa are Compositae (119 of 604 taxa), Papilionaceae (100 of 492), Gramineae (83 of 490), Cruciferae (52 of 236) and Umbelliferae (42 of 162).

WESTERN HIMALAYAN PROVINCE

This phytochorion includes the Kurram, Kunar, Swat and Gilgit valleys in northern Pakistan, Waziristan, and the southern slopes of the Western Himalayas (west of longitude 83°E) in Nepal westwards through Himachal Pradesh and including Kashmir, Simla, Mussoorie and Naini Tal. Part of the province extends outside the subcontinent to Nuristan in eastern Afghanistan (see entry on Safed Koh, CPD Site SWA21, in the Regional Overview on South West Asia and the Middle East in Volume 1). The Sutlej Defile (c. 78°E) forms an important biogeographical barrier to both fauna and, to a lesser extent, flora.

Climate

Unlike most of the Irano-Turanian region, the West Himalayan Province has a monsoon climate. This has an influence on the flora.

Flora

Number of species:	>5000
Endemic species:	>430
Regional endemism:	9%
Endemic families:	0
Endemic genera:	20
Figures refer to vascular plants.	

Although Takhtajan (1986) includes the whole of the Western Himalayas in the Irano-Turanian region, most authorities (cf. Kitamura 1960; Hara 1966; Zohary 1973; Ali and Qaiser 1986) regard the flora as Sino-Japanese. There are affinities with the flora of Central Asia.

Estimates of the number of species and endemics vary considerably. According to Ali and Qaiser (1986), there are at least 111 Sino-Himalayan endemics in the Pakistan flora; according to Ali (1978), 90% of Pakistan's endemics are confined to the northern and western mountains, i.e. the Pakistan sector of the Western Himalayan Province. Dhar and Kachroo (1983a,b) give a figure of 589 endemic taxa out of 1610 taxa for the Kashmir Himalaya. Nayar (1987) records c. 4800 species and 430 endemics (c. 9%) in the Indian sector. There are at least 19 endemic and near-endemic genera, including *Alexeya* (Ranunculaceae), *Clarkella* (Rubiaceae), *Decalepidanthus* and *Ivanjohnstonia* (Boraginaceae), *Meeboldia* (Umbelliferae), *Nervilia* and *Oreorchis* (Orchidaceae), *Parrotiopsis* (a monotypic endemic genus in Hamamelidaceae) and *Roylea* (Labiatae). Genera with numerous endemic species include *Taraxacum* (over 70) (see list in Naithani 1990), *Euphrasia* (at least 25), *Aconitum*, *Impatiens* (13) and *Astragalus* (12). There are at least 189 pteridophytes, of which 153 are Sino-Himalayan elements and 36 Euro-Siberian (Fraser-Jenkins 1991).

Main vegetation types

The vegetation types of the Western Himalayas are very varied, dependent on aridity and degree of influence of the monsoon. The main types in Kashmir are subtropical semi-desert (dominated by *Capparis*, *Calotropis*, *Ephedra* and *Pistacia*), *Artemisia* steppe, steppe forest (with *Salix*, *Lonicera*, *Juniperus*, *Hippophaë* and *Artemisia*, below 3000 m), West Himalayan coniferous forests (dominated by *Abies pindrow*, *A. spectabilis*, *Cedrus deodara*, *Picea smithiana*, *Pinus wallichiana* and *Taxus wallichiana*, between 3000–3600 m through the Vale of Kashmir to western Nepal), subalpine *Betula* forest (between 3800–4150 m), alpine herb vegetation (including *Aconitum*, *Aquilegia*, *Lloydia* and *Potentilla*) and "Kashmir scrub" (including the endemic *Parrotiopsis jacquemontii*).

On the Pir Panjal Range, *Acacia zizyphus* thorn scrub of Mediterranean affinity occurs on the foothills, with *Pinus roxburghii* between 900–1700 m altitude, mixed oak-conifer-rhododendron woodland, and *Betula utilis/Rhododendron campanulatum* from 3000 m to the tree-line. Subalpine and alpine Himalayan herb flora occur above the tree-line.

In the Sutlej valley, *Euphorbia royleana* is dominant on dry south-facing slopes; mixed evergreen forest (with *Euonymus*, *Ilex* and *Litsea*) occurs on northern slopes; stands of *Cupressus torulosa* occur on some limestone outcrops. There is a great belt of *Quercus semecarpifolia* in Bushahr Division, below the subalpine pasture. Along the Tibetan border there is an extremely arid *Artemisia-Ephedra* steppe.

Between the Sutlej and Kali valleys, *Shorea robusta* (sal) forest occurs on the Siwaliks and Lesser Himalaya below 1000 m. Other vegetation types here include freshwater swamp forests (dominated by *Bischofia javanica* and *Salix tetrasperma*), mixed deciduous forest (with *Lagerstroemia parviflora* and *Dalbergia sissoo*) on dry exposed sites above 1200 m, oak-rhododendron forest above 1500 m, *Betula utilis* forest between 3000–4000 m, juniper scrub and dwarf *Rhododendron-Betula* scrub above the tree-line, and subalpine meadows at higher altitudes.

Species of economic importance

Cereals include wheat, barley, *Paspalum scrobiculatum*, *Panicum miliaceum*, *Oplismenus frumentaceus*, *Eleusine coracana* and *Avena sativa*. Rice (*Oryza sativa*) can be grown up to 1980 m; at least 48 varieties were known in Kumaon alone (Atkinson 1980/1882).

Pulses include *Phaseolus torosus* (cultivated up to 1980 m), *Dolichos* spp. and *Cajanus cajan*. Edible vegetables and beverages used in Kashmir include *Bergenia ligulata* (a tea substitute), *Coronopus didymus*, *Dipsacus mitis*, *Eremurus persicus*, *Lamium amplexicaule*, *Silene conoidea*, *Tulipa clusiana* (bulbs fried or eaten raw) and *Indigofera gerardiana* (Koul, Karihaloo and Hamal 1982). Many species of Rosaceae and other families have edible fruits. *Morus serrata*, a mulberry, is a Garhwal-Himachal Pradesh endemic.

There are many native medicinal plants which are harvested, including *Aconitum falconeri, A. ferox, A. heterophyllum, Angelica glauca, Gentiana kurrooa, Nardostachys jatamansi, Picrorhiza kurrooa, Orchis* spp., *Rheum emodi* and *R. webbianum*. The rhizome of *Podophyllum emodi* yields podophyllol (a resin) and the drug podophyllin; the species is used in cancer research (Nasir 1991).

Factors causing loss of biodiversity

The main threats are deforestation, shifting cultivation, and urban and industrial development, especially in Himachal Pradesh. According to Rawat and Srivastava (1986), 40% of the flora of Himachal Pradesh comprises naturalized exotics. Some introduced species are spreading aggressively at the expense of the natural vegetation. Many plants of northern Pakistan are threatened, including *Cinnamomum tamala* (Endangered) and *Podophyllum emodi* (Vulnerable).

Conservation

In Himachal Pradesh there are 2 National Parks (of total area 1413 km²) and 26 Wildlife Sanctuaries (of total area 3865.5 km²); Uttar Pradesh has 7 National Parks and 12 Wildlife Sanctuaries (totalling 8510.5 km²). The protected areas include Nanda Devi World Heritage Site (630.3 km²) (CPD IS2, see Data Sheet). Jammu and Kashmir has 3 National Parks (of total area 4551 km²) and 14 Wildlife Sanctuaries (6978.6 km²).

In the Federal Capital Territory of Pakistan there is 1 National Park (Margalla Hills: 173.9 km²) and 1 Wildlife Sanctuary (70 km²). In the Northern Areas there is 1 National Park (Khunjerab: 2269.1 km²) and 5 Wildlife Sanctuaries (1855.4 km²). In North-West Frontier Province there are 2 National Parks (94.3 km²) and 4 Wildlife Sanctuaries (497.5 km²); 313.6 km² of Lal Suhanra National Park (Punjab) is a Biosphere Reserve.

In Nepal, there are 3 National Parks totalling 1299 km².

Centres of plant diversity and endemism

Pakistan

IS1. Kashmir Himalaya

The Vale of Kashmir and associated mountains is one of the most floristically rich regions of Pakistan. A high proportion of alpine and subalpine species in Fumariaceae, Primulaceae, Saxifragaceae and Scrophulariaceae are endemic. About 40 endemics are Endangered, including *Aconitum kashmiricum, Picrorhiza kurrooa, Saussurea sacra* (medicinal species), *Corydalis cashmeriana, Gentiana venusta, Primula minutissima* (all of which are ornamental species) and *Megacarpaea bifida* (used for cattle fodder) (Dhar and Kachroo 1983a,b).

India

IS2. Nanda Devi

– see Data Sheet. A representative site of the Kumaon-Garhwal Himalaya.

TIBETAN PROVINCE

Of the Tibetan Province, only the eastern slopes of the Karakoram, the northern slopes of the Himalayas, Ladakh and Baltistan (including the Deosai Plains) and the area of Lingzi Than-Aksai Chin on the border between China and India, fall within the area covered by this Regional Overview. (The Province also includes the whole of the Tibetan Plateau, the Pamirs and Trans-Alai Ranges, for which see the Regional Overview on Central and Northern Asia.)

The area is geologically young and a mixture of rugged high mountains and flat desert plains. There are many salt lakes in Ladakh. Almost the whole of Ladakh is above 2850 m; the Deosai Plains region of Baltistan is lower, but almost entirely above 2300 m. Baltistan includes the Karakoram Range, which has the greatest concentration of peaks above 7400 m anywhere on Earth, as well as the largest glacier system outside the Arctic (Stewart 1982). Most of the area is desert and very sparsely populated.

Climate

Tibetan-type, cold, arctic-desert with very low rainfall. The area around Dras (Ladakh) is the second coldest place in the world, after Siberia (Kachroo, Sapru and Dhar 1977).

Flora

Number of species:	1500–1600
Endemics species:	c. 70
Regional endemism:	5%
Endemic families:	0
Endemic genera:	0
Figures refer to vascular plants.	

The province consists of a post-Quaternary glaciation flora, and is floristically poor except in the southernmost parts. About 1223 species have been reported from Baltistan and slightly more from Ladakh. The Deosai Plains probably have not more than 800 species, with low endemism. Kachroo, Sapru and Dhar (1977) list 34 species endemic to Ladakh; the total number of endemics in the region may be about 70.

Main vegetation types

Snow-melt alpines exclusively on the Deosai Plains; a mixture of snow-melt alpines, desert and oasis species in Central Baltistan; halophytic vegetation around the Ladakh salt lakes. Some pockets of *Juniperus* and *Betula* forest occur in favoured spots, but otherwise trees are almost entirely absent.

Species of economic importance

Very few; crops cannot be grown without irrigation. There are a few medicinal species.

Factors causing loss of biodiversity

Sustainable forms of agriculture based on traditional irrigation practices are discontinued as the population in rural areas continues to migrate to the state capital, Leh. An excellent account of Ladakhi culture, agricultural practices and recent demographic changes is given by Norberg-Hodge (1991).

Conservation

Karakoram Wildlife Sanctuary (IUCN Management Category: IV) covers 1800 km². In 1993, a proposal to designate the Central Karakoram as a National Park was approved. The area is also to be proposed for listing as a World Heritage Site (Anon. 1994).

EASTERN ASIATIC REGIONAL CENTRE OF ENDEMISM

This region, as delimited by Takhtajan (1986), includes a vast area stretching from central Nepal to Taiwan, and from Manchuria to Manipur and Central China. It is divided into 13 floristic provinces of which 4 lie wholly or partly in the Indian Subcontinent.

EASTERN HIMALAYAN PROVINCE

This province lies almost entirely within the Indian Subcontinent, between 83°00'–97°00'E and 27°30'–29°30'N. It includes the following territories: Nepal east of the Kali River (83°00'E); Sikkim and Darjeeling; the Chumbi valley of southernmost Tibet, between Sikkim and Bhutan; Bhutan; Arunachal Pradesh; and south-eastern Tibet (the Tsangpo valley east of 92°00'E). It comprises all the mountainous country east of the Kali River and north of the Brahmaputra-Ganges flood plain, and includes the highest mountain on Earth (Sagarmatha, Qomolangma Feng, or Mount Everest at 8848 m) and, in the Nepal sector, many other peaks over 8000 m.

Climate

Monsoonal, with most rain during the south-west monsoon. There are great extremes of temperature dependent on season and altitude. The Siwaliks and lower valleys are subtropical to tropical, hot and wet, while some of the deep river valleys in the interior, particularly in central Bhutan (Thimphu-Wangdi Phodrang areas) are extremely arid and very hot. With increasing altitude the climate becomes progressively more temperate. Arctic conditions occur at the highest altitudes above the limit of perpetual snows. Although the phytochorion covers only 2° of latitude, the altitudinal effect leads to a range of climates more typical of about 40° of latitude. Throughout the phytochorion, but especially in Nepal, Sikkim and Bhutan, there are many very localized variations in climate, often of an abrupt nature.

Flora

The vascular flora of the Eastern Himalayas comprises about 9000 species, of which c. 39% are endemic (Myers 1988; Wilson 1992). Table 20 gives floristic data for the three main subdivisions of central and eastern Nepal, Bhutan/Sikkim/Chumbi valley and Arunachal Pradesh (north-east India).

TABLE 20. FLORISTIC DATA FOR THE MAIN SUBDIVISIONS OF THE EASTERN HIMALAYAN PROVINCE

	Central and eastern Nepal	Bhutan/ Sikkim/ Chumbi	Arunachal Pradesh [a]
Number of vascular species	6000	5500	>3000
Number of endemic species	250	100	?
Number of endemic families	0	0	0
Number of endemic genera	0	0	?
Regional species endemism (%)	4.2	1.8	?

Note:

[a] Although the size of the flora of Arunachal Pradesh is given as 3000 species in various publications (cf. Malhotra and Hajra 1977; Kaul and Haridasan 1987), it is undoubtedly richer.

The Eastern Himalayan Province, together with the Khasi-Manipur Province, has the richest flora of the Indian Subcontinent (with the possible exception of Myanmā) (Rao and Murti 1990). The province contains the largest number of families, endemic species and "primitive" species in the subcontinent (Barna, Chowdhury and Neogi 1988). The flora is transitional between those of the Central Himalayas and China, and includes several endemic or near-endemic genera, such as *Smithiella*, *Milula* and *Bryocarpum*. The main families are Orchidaceae, Gramineae, Leguminosae, Cyperaceae, Scrophulariaceae, Rubiaceae, Euphorbiaceae, Acanthaceae, Ericaceae, Primulaceae and Boraginaceae. Endemism is especially high in *Rhododendron*, *Pedicularis* (over 80 species from Sikkim and Bhutan alone: one of the major centres of diversity for the genus outside China), *Primula*, Orchidaceae and Acanthaceae. The Lohit area of easternmost Arunachal Pradesh contains some primitive genera at the edge of their ranges, e.g. *Amentotaxus* (Ferguson 1985).

The East Himalayas are the meeting point of the Indochinese and Indomalayan tropical lowland flora, the Sino-Himalayan/East Asiatic flora and the Western Himalayan flora. Towards the east, the alpine flora becomes similar to that of western China.

Nepal is of particular floristic interest, because it is here, at about longitude 83°00'E, that the differing floras (both alpine and lowland) of the Western and Eastern Himalayas meet. *Cedrus deodara*, a Western Himalayan element, reaches its easternmost limit at 82°50'E, while *Magnolia campbellii*, an East Asiatic element, reaches its westernmost limit at 83°15'E. The ranges that run NNE-SSW in eastern Nepal act as natural floristic barriers; many species of *Rhododendron* and Vacciniaceae do not extend further west than these ranges. Of the 63 species of *Pedicularis* in Nepal, some 43 are restricted, in Nepal, to the central and eastern regions, including all the strict Nepal endemics (Yamazaki 1988).

480 ferns have been recorded from the Himalayas; 137 (28%) are endemic, the majority being found in the Eastern Himalayas, where about 42 species are Endangered (Bir 1987). Of the 12 tree fern species (*Cyathea*) occurring in India, 7 are found in the Eastern Himalayas and neighbouring areas (Dixit 1986).

Sikkim and Darjeeling have 24 endemic liverworts – almost half the total endemic hepatic flora of the whole of India (Udar and Srivastava 1983).

Main vegetation types

Stainton (1972) gives a detailed account of the vegetation types of Nepal. In central Nepal, *Pinus roxburghii* (chir pine) forms the lowest zone on both north- and south-facing slopes. Mixed *Quercus incana-Q. lanuginosa* forest occurs between 1370–1930 m; *Q. semecarpifolia* replaces these species above 2440 m. *Abies spectabilis* (sometimes mixed with *Quercus semecarpifolia*) and *Betula utilis* occur from 3500 m to the tree-line. *Cedrus deodara*, *Cupressus torulosa* and *Abies pindrow* occur only west of the Karnali River.

Eastern Nepal is much wetter and supports *Schima-Castanopsis* and subtropical semi-evergreen hill forest. Tree ferns occur at lower altitudes. Temperate mixed broadleaved forest, with *Michelia doltsopa*, *Lithocarpus spicata*, *Quercus glauca* and many species of Lauraceae, occurs up to 1830 m. Between 1830–2900 m there is often a continuous belt of evergreen forest: *Castanopsis* spp. form the lowest zone, *Quercus lamellana* the middle zone and *Lithocarpus pachyphylla* the highest. Much of the *Castanopsis* forest has been converted to cultivation. *Rhododendron* spp. become abundant at higher altitudes from east Nepal eastwards through Sikkim and Bhutan.

In the central part of Nepal, there is a transitional zone between the vegetation types of the West and East Himalayas. Much of the subtropical forest is degraded.

Grierson and Long (1983) give an introduction to the vegetation types of Sikkim and Bhutan. Subtropical forest occurs on the foothills (200–1000 m); *Shorea robusta* (sal) is absent in Bhutan, but present in Sikkim. Warm mixed evergreen and deciduous broadleaved forest occurs between 1000–2000 m; *Pinus roxburghii* forest between 900–1800 m in Bhutan's inner dry valleys; cool broadleaved forest between 2000–2900 m, especially in eastern Bhutan; evergreen oak forest between 2000–2600 m in central Bhutan; blue pine (*Pinus wallichiana*) forest between 2100–3000 m in the dry valleys of inner Bhutan (the temperate equivalent of the chir pine forest); *Picea* forest in the montane cloud forest zone at 2700–3100 m; *Tsuga dumosa* in central and northern Bhutan at 2800–3300 m; and *Abies densa* forest on the highest ridges. Above the tree-line, *Juniperus* and *Rhododendron* scrub, and dry alpine scrub with *Caragana*, *Ephedra* and *Chesneya*, occur.

In Arunachal Pradesh, tropical broadleaved evergreen forest occurs up to 900 m where summer rainfall exceeds 3000 mm and where there is only a brief temperate winter. Typical species are *Castanopsis tribuloides*, *Terminalia myriocarpa* and *Canarium resiniferum*. There is an abundant epiphytic flora of orchids, aroids and ferns (Hegde 1985). On the north bank of the Brahmaputra, the forest is rich in species and contains many buttressed trees. No single species dominates. The lowest stratum includes *Mesua*

ferrea, *Altingia excelsa* and *Cinnamomum glaucescens*; the middle stratum includes *Sauravia cerea*, *Mallotus nepalensis* and *Sterculia hamiltonii*. Lianes include species of *Gnetum*, *Pothos* and *Piper*.

Tropical semi-evergreen forests occur on the foothills up to 600 m. Subtropical pine forest occurs between 1000–1800 m; three species predominate – *Pinus wallichiana*, *P. roxburghii* and *P. merkusii*. Temperate broadleaved and conifer forests occur as continuous belts between 1800–2800 m and 2800–3500 m, respectively. Alpine forests occur at 4000–5500 m. Tall trees are absent but there are many dwarf bushes and herbs which yield a profusion of brightly coloured flowers in the short growing season. Species include *Rhododendron nivale*, *Saxifraga* spp. and *Saussurea* spp. For further accounts of the vegetation of Arunachal Pradesh, see Champion (1936), Malhotra and Hajra (1977), and Kaul and Haridasan (1987).

Species of economic importance

Tropical wet evergreen forest contains many timber species of commercial importance, including *Dipterocarpus macrocarpus* and *Shorea assamica*. Many economically important trees also occur in the tropical semi-evergreen forests, including *Bombax ceiba*, *Canarium strictum* and *Ailanthus grandis*.

The juniper/rhododendron scrub of Bhutan and elsewhere in the region contain many horticulturally important plants, such as species of *Meconopsis*, *Primula* and *Rhododendron*.

Factors causing loss of biodiversity

In Nepal, and to a lesser extent Sikkim, logging of forests, either to convert the land to cultivation or to obtain timber, is causing serious erosion. The removal of forest is thought to be responsible for local climatic changes resulting in altered rainfall patterns and landslides.

There is still much intact forest in Bhutan and, in general, the forests are less disturbed than those in Nepal. However, population pressure is resulting in the clearance of forest for shifting cultivation, fuelwood and grazing of livestock in some areas. For example, the southernmost forest belt has been almost completely deforested.

In Arunachal Pradesh, there are still large areas of primary forest, but development is taking place rapidly and population growth is causing a shortening of the jhumming cycle to about 5–8 years. This does not give the forest sufficient time to regenerate and results in bamboo brakes developing rapidly in abandoned plots.

Annual winter fires can cause much devastation, especially to the *Pinus wallichiana* forest in Bhutan and the subtropical pine forest of Arunachal Pradesh. Throughout the region, many exotic weeds are spreading aggressively in disturbed habitats at the expense of the native flora.

Conservation

Four National Parks, the Annapurna Sanctuary, the Royal Dharpatan Hunting Sanctuary and 3 Wildlife Reserves protect 17.1% of the High Himalaya of Nepal, but only 1.4% of the ecologically important Middle Mountains physiographic zone. Royal Chitwan National Park (932 km²) and Sagarmatha National Park (1148 km²) are World Heritage Sites.

Sikkim has 1 National Park (Khangchendzonga: 849.5 km²) and 3 small Sanctuaries (totalling 119.6 km²). There is also a proposed rhododendron reserve, and a centre for the conservation of orchids.

Arunachal Pradesh has 2 National Parks (totalling 2468.2 km²) and 4 Sanctuaries (1473.8 km²). Namdapha National Park (1985.2 km²) (CPD Site IS4, see Data Sheet) has been proposed as a Biosphere Reserve.

In Bhutan, there are 1 National Park (Royal Manas: 658 km²), 4 Wildlife Reserves (458.4 km²), 2 Wildlife Sanctuaries (7945 km²) and 3 Reserved Forests (457.6 km²). Protected areas cover nearly 19% of the country, including the entire north of Bhutan. Conservation is covered only by the Bhutan Forest Act under which all non-privately owned forest is declared government reserved forest. Government policy emphasizes the need to maintain at least 60% forest cover to prevent soil erosion and to maintain climatic equilibrium.

Centres of plant diversity and endemism

India, Nepal

IS3. Northern Sikkim and East Nepal

Includes North District (Sikkim) and Arun Valley (Nepal), including Zemu and Llonakh valleys. Area: c. 11,250 km². Altitude: c. 200–8600 m. Most land is over 1000 m, except in river valleys. The region includes Kanchenjunga (8579 m).

❖ Vegetation: Subtropical forest to high-altitude alpine scree, subalpine meadows, rock and scree communities.
❖ Flora: c. 4000 vascular plant species; many endemics. An important centre of diversity for *Rhododendron* and the most important centre of diversity outside China for *Pedicularis* (c. 60 species, about 25% of which are strict endemics).
❖ Threats: Road building, plant collecting.
❖ Conservation: Khangchendzonga National Park (849.5 km²) (IUCN Management Category: II); 3 Sanctuaries (IUCN Management Category: IV) totalling 119.6 km²; 2 orchid sanctuaries.

India

IS4. Namdapha

– see Data Sheet.

KHASI-MANIPUR PROVINCE

Includes the Garo, Khasia and Jaintia Hills on the Shillong Plateau (Assam); Nagaland; Manipur; the Patkai Hills; the Mikir Hills; the Barail Range; Mizoram; south-east Arunachal Pradesh (Tirap Frontier Division south-west of the Noa Dihung valley); and the Chin Hills (Myanmā).

The area is topographically and geologically diverse. The Assam Plateau (the Garo, Khasia and Jaintia Hills of Meghalaya) is an upland area, 1000–2000 m in altitude, of ancient gneisses intruded by granites thinly covered by Cretaceous sandstone. It is considered to be a detached part of the Indian Shield. The ranges of the north-eastern states form part of the Burmese Arc, a southern extension of the Himalayas which continues south into the Andaman and Nicobar Islands and beyond. The Lower Brahmaputra valley (c. 800 × 80 km) consists of a braided river in a broad floodplain.

Climate

Tropical in the lowlands; warm subtropical to cool temperate in the uplands. Frosts occur at high altitudes in Nagaland but snow is rare. Some parts of the Shillong Plateau receive extremely heavy rainfall, Cherrapunji in Meghalaya being one of the wettest places on Earth. Studies of fossil wood have shown that the climate and ecology of the area have remained stable since the Miocene (Prakash, Du Nai-zheng and Tripathi 1992); this stability has influenced the present day phytogeography.

Flora

Number of species:	7000–8000
Endemic species:	2000
Regional endemism:	25–30%
Endemic families:	0 (1 near-endemic)
Endemic genera:	9; at least a further 5 near-endemic
Figures refer to vascular plants.	

About 50% of the total flora of India occurs in this region. The Khasi-Manipur Province is a centre of diversity for several primitive tree genera, such as *Magnolia* and *Michelia*, and of families such as Elaeocarpaceae and Elaeagnaceae. Major families are Orchidaceae, Gramineae, Leguminosae, Rubiaceae, Cyperaceae, Euphorbiaceae, Acanthaceae, Compositae, Labiatae and Zingiberaceae (34 of the world's 60 species of *Hedychium* grow in the region).

Eastern Asiatic and Indochinese elements form the bulk of the flora. There are strong affinities with the floras of the Eastern Himalayas, northern Myanmā and China. Takhtajan (1986), in a very incomplete enumeration, lists over 60 endemic species; the true figure for the phytochorion must be very much higher, but is as yet unknown due to incomplete exploration. The Khasia Hills are one of the most important centres of survival of the East Asiatic Tertiary flora. Endemism is high on the Shillong Plateau but apparently very low in Manipur.

The area is an important refuge for the Miocene flora which has persisted here virtually unchanged to the present day as a result of the stable climate (Prakash and Tripathi 1992). Examples include *Amentotaxus assamicus*, recently described by Ferguson (1985), and *Tetracentron sinense*, which occurs in Arunachal Pradesh and north Myanmā and westwards to Bhutan and Nepal (Hajra and Rao 1986). The area is also remarkable for the large number of disjunct elements. These include *Nymphaea pygmaea* (otherwise known from Siberia and northern China), *Mitrastemon yamamotoi* (known also from Japan and Sumatra), *Aphyllorchis montana* (Sri Lanka), *Illicium cambodium* (southern Indochina) and *Epipogium roseum* (Java, West Africa and Australia) (Rao and Murti 1990). The genus *Nepenthes* reaches its north-western limit in the Khasia Hills, where it is represented by the endemic and threatened *N. khasiana*.

There is an extremely rich pteridophyte flora of almost 600 species (Bir, Vasudeva and Kachroo 1990); 368 species are known from the Khasia and Jaintia Hills alone (Bir *et al.* 1991). The main floristic affinities are with the fern floras of hina, South India, Myanmā and the Wesern Himalayas. Onl 28 ferns (4.7%) are endemic to north-eastern India (Bir *et al.* 1991).

Main vegetation types

The vegetation is tropical below 900 m and belongs to the Bengal Province. Tropical evergreen forests, rich in species, occur in the Assam Valley, and in the lower parts of the Naga Hills and in Manipur. There are many Magnoliaceae and other primitive trees and vines (e.g. *Gnetum*) and a dense herb layer of *Impatiens*, *Pouzolzia* and many Zingiberaceae. Ferns and orchids, both terrestrial and epiphytic, are very abundant, and there is a rich bryophyte flora.

Deciduous forests, mainly of *Shorea robusta*, predominate on the northern lower slopes of the Garo and Khasia Hills in Meghalaya and in the North Cachar Hills. They have been heavily exploited. Tropical grassland occurs on flats inundated by the Brahmaputra.

Subtropical mixed forests occur in parts of Tirap District adjoining the Patkai Hills below 1500 m. The main associations are of *Schima*, *Ficus*, *Michelia*, *Cinnamomum* and *Castanopsis*.

A distinct type of savanna forest occurs in south-east Manipur (Mistry and Stott 1993), in which *Shorea robusta* is replaced by *S. siamensis* or *Dipterocarpus tuberculatus*. *Melanorrhoea usitata* (Burmese lacquer tree), *Pterocarpus marsupium* (bastard teak), *Tectona grandis* (teak) and *Cedrela toona* (tairel) are abundant. This forest type is similar to the *Tectona-Dipterocarpus* formations which occur in northern Myanmā.

Temperate vegetation grows between 1300–2500 m on the Shillong Plateau and in the Naga, Lushai and Mikir Hills. Large areas have been cleared for shifting cultivation, but primary forest relicts are preserved as "sacred forests" at Shillong Peak and some other localities (Rao and Haridasan 1982).

The summit of Natma Taung (Mount Victoria) (part of CPD Site IS5, see Data Sheet) in north-west Myanmā is notable for being a southern exclave of the Holarctic temperate flora and is a refugium for several species belonging to genera such as *Geranium*. Much of the Chin Hills is botanically poorly explored.

Species of economic importance

One of the most useful plants characteristic of the Khasi-Manipur Province is the neem tree, *Azadirachta indica*. Neem is thought to have originated in Assam and Myanmā, and hence this region is important as a gene pool for this valuable tree (National Research Council 1992).

The area is a centre of genetic diversity for mango (*Mangifera indica*), taro (*Colocasia esculenta*), *Cymbopogon* spp., *Garcinia* spp., ironwood (*Mesua ferrea*), banana (*Musa*

spp.) and many other plants of economic importance. There are 64 varieties of *Citrus*, belonging to at least 8 species (Bhattacharyya and Dutta 1951).

About 300 species are consumed locally as food. Examples include *Artocarpus lakoocha*, *Centella asiatica*, *Castanopsis indica*, *Rubus ellipticus*, *Nymphaea nouchali*, *Myrica farquharia*, *Solanum indicum*, *Dioscorea alata*, *Hedychium coronarium*, *Alpinia allughas* and *Eryngium foetidum* (Singh and Singh 1985; Singh, Singh and Singh 1988; Rao and Haridasan 1991). In Mizoram, varnish is obtained from *Mesua ferrea*; *Adhatoda vasica* is used as an insecticide (Shuleta, Baishya and Ali 1978).

Arora, Mehra and Nayar (1983) estimated that the North-East Region, including the Eastern Himalayas, contained 189 species of wild relatives of crop plants. Recent surveys of the hills of Meghalaya and Arunachal Pradesh yielded more than 5000 primitive rice cultivars, out of a total of 6730 (Rao and Murti 1990). Tea has been cultivated for at least 4000 years in the region. There are many different land races of jute on the Shillong Plateau and the region is the centre of origin of 5 commercially important species of palm.

There is a wide variety of medicinal herbs (Rao and Jamir 1982; Rao and Haridasan 1991), including *Allium chinense*, *Alpinia bracteosa*, *Garcinia lancifolia*, *Mangifera indica* and the rare endemic, *Nepenthes khasiana*. Trees and shrubs of horticultural importance include *Aesculus assamicus*, *Agapetes variegata*, *Buddleja asiatica*, *Engelhardtia spicata*, *Firmiana colorata*, *Luculia pinceana* and *Jasminum coarctatum* (Rao and Haridasan 1985).

Factors causing loss of biodiversity

The main threats are clearance for shifting cultivation, annual fires in subtropical pine forest, over-collecting of medicinal plants, some of which are threatened (e.g. *Nepenthes khasiana*), and collecting of horticulturally desirable species (Jain and Sastry 1980).

Conservation

Only 2725 km² (1.7%) of that part of the province lying in India, and only 88 ha in Myanmā, are protected.

In Assam, Kaziranga National Park and World Heritage Site covers 430 km². There are also 9 Sanctuaries totalling 999.9 km², including Manas World Heritage Site (391 km²). Manipur has 2 National Parks (totalling 81.30 km²) and 1 Sanctuary (IUCN Management Category: IV) covering 29 km².

Meghalaya has 2 National Parks (totalling 288 km²), and 1 Sanctuary. Rao and Haridasan (1982) enumerate 70 rare, endangered or endemic species, including the following which are Endangered: *Chirita hamosa* (endemic), *Clerodendron hastatum*, *Daphniphyllum himalayense* (now only in sacred groves), *Euonymus bullatus* and *Pittosporum humile*.

In Mizoram, 2 Sanctuaries (IUCN Management Category: IV) cover a combined area of 530 km²; in Nagaland, there is 1 Sanctuary covering 202 km²; in Tripura, there are 3 Sanctuaries (578.6 km²).

Two very small pitcher-plant sanctuaries, each of 2.5 ha or less, were established in the Garo Hills and Jaintia Hills, but the "sacred" status of the Jaintia Hills Sanctuary has not been maintained owing to shortage of both staff and funds (Rodgers and Gupta 1989). A further consideration is the prevailing land ownership system. In Meghalaya, only 3% of the land is State-controlled. The remaining forest in Meghalaya (over 34% of the State) is controlled by district councils (which are short of money), local villages and private individuals.

In Myanmā, Thamihla Kyun Wildlife Sanctuary (88 ha) protects a tiny island off the coast of Rakhine; the summit area of Natma Taung (364.2 km²) has been proposed as a National Park.

Centres of plant diversity and endemism

Myanmā

IS5. Natma Taung (Mount Victoria) and Rongklang (Chin Hills)

– see Data Sheet.

NORTH BURMESE PROVINCE

This covers Myanmā, north of about latitude 25°00'N (near Myitkina) to 29°30'N and between 94°30'–98°40'E. The flora is transitional between those of the East Himalayas, Assam and Yunnan, and includes Indomalayan elements. There are several monotypic endemic genera; species endemism is at least 25%. The whole region is covered by a Data Sheet (IS6 – North Myanmā).

Centres of plant diversity and endemism

Myanmā

IS6. North Myanmā

– see Data Sheet.

INDIAN REGIONAL CENTRE OF ENDEMISM

MALABAR PROVINCE

This covers the western coastal plain of Peninsular India, from Broach to Cape Comorin, the western side of the Western Ghats, the Nilgiri, Palni, Anaimalai and Cardamom Hills. It thus includes westernmost Maharashtra and Karnataka, most of Kerala, and western Tamil Nadu.

The Western Ghats (Sahyadri Mountains) run from near Bombay to near Mysore, where they meet the Eastern Ghats. A deep valley separates them from the Nilgiri Hills and another broad valley (the Patghal Gap) separates the Nilgiri Hills from the Cardamom Hills. The northern half of the Western Ghats are of Deccan Lavas but the southern half, and the Nilgiri, Cardamom, Palni and Anaimalai Hills, are of Archaean basement rocks, mainly gneisses and schists with intruded charnockite series granites. They reach their greatest elevation in the south (2695 m in the Anaimalai Hills).

Climate

The climate is wet-tropical. The Malabar Province receives the highest rainfall of the whole of Peninsular India (>2500 mm per annum). The highest rainfall on the Ghats occurs on the crest of the range (e.g. Mahabaleshwar: 6520 mm). There is a very marked rain-shadow effect. In the Nilgiri Hills, rainfall in areas exposed to the south-west monsoon (which usually breaks in late May or June) ranges from 3500 to 6000 mm p.a., but the driest parts of the Moyar Gorge, which lies in permanent rain shadow, receive less than 500 mm (Larsen 1987). Mean daily minimum and maximum temperatures vary little throughout the year (e.g. Malabar: 22.2–26.6°C minimum, 28.3–32.7°C maximum) (Pearce and Smith 1990).

The main soil types are red soils (poor in nitrogen and organic matter), laterites and black soils derived from Deccan Lavas.

Flora

Number of species:	>4000
Endemic species:	1500
Regional endemism:	37.5%
Endemic families:	0
Endemic genera:	>41
Figures refer to vascular plants.	

The Western Ghats are home to at least 4000 species, of which c. 1500 are endemic (Subramanyam and Nayar 1974). This represents nearly 75% of the total number of species endemic to the whole of Peninsular India. A large number of the endemics of the region appear to be the products of recent diversification, but there is also a significant proportion of palaeo-endemics, especially among trees and shrubs. About 800 lichens occur on the Western Ghats, including 90 species of *Parmelia*. More than 40 lichen species are endemic (Patwardhan 1983).

There is no single comprehensive modern Flora covering the whole of the Western Ghats, but a detailed inventory of the flora of the Mahabaleshwar has been published (Bole and Almeida 1980, 1981, 1983a, 1983b, 1984, 1985, 1987, 1988, 1989a, 1989b). Subramanyam and Nayar (1974) give a comprehensive account of the vegetation and phytogeography.

The most speciose families are Gramineae, Leguminosae, Acanthaceae, Orchidaceae, Compositae, Euphorbiaceae, Rubiaceae, Asclepiadaceae, Geraniaceae and Labiatae. Malesian elements, such as Dipterocarpaceae, Myristicaceae, Anacardiaceae, Gesneriaceae, Meliaceae, Melastomataceae, Myrtaceae, Orchidaceae and Sterculiaceae, are abundant.

There are at least 41 endemic genera, of which more than half are monotypic although *Nilgirianthus* has more than 20 species. Examples include *Adenoön, Bacolepis, Campbellia, Erinocarpus, Griffithella, Jerdonia, Meteoromyrtus, Nanothamnus, Octotropis, Pseudoglochidion* and *Willisia*. The genus *Impatiens* is well-represented, with at least 77 species out of about 175 known from India; many are endemic.

Apart from the clear phytogeographical links with the Indomalayan flora, there is evidence of a link between the flora of the northern part of the Western Ghats (Mahabaleshwar area) with that of Dhofar in southernmost Oman (CPD Site

SWA1, see Data Sheet in Volume 1). An example is the genus *Paracaryopsis* (Boraginaceae), which has 2 species endemic to Mahabaleshwar and one extending from there to Kanara, Gujarat and Dhofar (Mill 1991).

The Nilgiri Hills are very rich in species and have a high degree of endemism. There are strong phytogeographic connections between the Nilgiri Hills flora and that of the Shillong Plateau in Meghalaya. There are many trees and shrubs with disjunct distributions, including *Ternstroemia japonica*, *Rhododendron arboreum* and *Cotoneaster buxifolia*. *Nageia wallichiana* (Podocarpaceae), the only conifer to occur in South India, is disjunct between the Nilgiri Hills, China and north-east India. A particular curiosity of the Nilgiri Hills is *Lobelia leschenaultii* which has immensely tall, dense, cylindrical inflorescences. It resembles the pachycaul lobelias of East Africa.

The flora of the southernmost sector of the Malabar Province (the Anaimalai, Palni and Cardamom Hills) has strong affinities with that of Sri Lanka, which until recent geological time was united to southern Peninsular India. The monotypic genus *Kendrickia* occurs only on Anamudi (Anaimalai Hills), the highest point of the Western Ghats, and Adam's Peak in Sri Lanka.

Main vegetation types

The vegetation over most of the Western Ghats is tropical monsoon rain forest, but there are considerable variations dependent on latitude, local rainfall and soil type. Dry semi-deciduous scrub forests occur on the foothills between the Tapti River in the north and Goa. Dry deciduous hill forests occur on the eastern (lee) side of the Ghats, while moist deciduous forest occurs on the windward side. Montane subtropical evergreen forest, characterized by *Amoora lawii* and *Walsura trijuga*, occurs near Maheshtra. The forest contains many species of *Begonia*, *Impatiens* and orchids.

South of the Kalinadi the wettest areas are covered by tropical evergreen forest, with dipterocarps, *Alstonia scholaris*, *Strychnos nux-vomica* and *Artocarpus lalloocha* in the upper canopy, *Flacourtia montana*, *Leea indica* and *Memecylon* spp. in the lower canopy, and a dense undergrowth of shrubs and climbers.

Deciduous forests (12–24 m tall) occur between 650–1000 m in regions where the annual rainfall is between 1500–2000 mm. Typical species include *Emblica officinalis*, *Ehretia laevis*, *Lagerstroemia lanceolata*, *Shorea talwa* and *Tectona grandis*. Thorn scrub forest occurs along the eastern side of the Western Ghats, where rainfall is very low.

The Nilgiri Hills are covered with evergreen tropical and subtropical forest. Characteristic trees and shrubs are *Michelia nilagirica*, *Berberis tinctoria*, *Mahonia leschenaultii*, *Osyris wightiana*, *Macaranga indica* and *Cinnamomum wightii*. The undergrowth includes *Clematis wightiana*, *Viola serpens* and *Parthenocissus neilgherriensis*. There are many orchids and ferns, and a rich lichen flora. Insectivorous plants (*Drosera* and *Utricularia*) occur above 2000 m. Peat bogs, a rare feature in Peninsular India, occur above 2300 m.

The southernmost ranges are covered with dry semi-desert or dry deciduous hill forest. The grassland flora of these southern ranges is broadly similar to that of the Nilgiri Hills; typical species include *Dipsacus leschenaultii*, *Lilium neilgherrense* and *Lobelia nicotianifolia*.

Species of economic importance

Commercially important timber trees include *Mesua ferrea*, *Tectona grandis*, *Calophyllum tomentosum*, *Palaquium ellipticum*, *Dalbergia latifolia*, *Terminalia tomentosa*, *Pterocarpus marsupium*, *Anogeissus latifolia* and *Sterculia* spp. Of India's 29 dipterocarps and 25 species of rosewood (*Dalbergia*), 13 and 22 respectively occur in the Western Ghats (Synge 1990). Many other species are used locally for building purposes and furniture-making. Sandalwood, derived from *Santalum album*, is a major source of income.

Edible fruits include *Mangifera indica* (mango), *Elettaria cardamom* (cardamom) and *Syzygium cumini*. The area contains potentially valuable gene pools of many crop plants, including species of *Amomum* and *Atylosia* (relatives of pigeonpea, *Cajanus cajan*), *Coffea* (coffee), *Mangifera*, *Musa* (banana), *Oryza* (rice) and *Piper* (pepper).

A large number of species are used in ayurvedic and other traditional forms of medicine and some are considered sacred or are used in worship. Ornamental species with showy or fragrant flowers include *Butea monosperma*, *Lilium neilgherrense* and *Michelia nilagirica*.

Factors causing loss of biodiversity

The main threat is forest clearance for plantation crops (including tea, coffee and temperate vegetables), roads and hydroelectric power schemes, logging and conversion to *Eucalyptus* plantations. Large-scale planting of *Eucalyptus* began in Kerala in the 1950s; by the end of 1987, 441 km² had been converted to *Eucalyptus* plantations (Jayarama and Krishnankutty 1991).

Extensive logging has taken place in the Deccan Lavas Ghats; pockets of primary forest survive in "dev raies" (sacred groves). These are of botanical importance as they have become the last refuges for many species (Gadgil and Vartak 1975, 1976; Vartak 1983). Pressures on the sacred groves are mounting as a result of the expansion of arable agriculture and road building. Taboos which protected the groves are also changing (Sharma and Kulkarni 1980). For example, many villages now depend on the sacred groves as sources of fuel; some groves have been completely destroyed (Gadgil and Vartak 1976). According to Larsen (1988), there is increasing evidence that further deforestation of the Western Ghats will lead to problems of water supply, erosion, and possibly even long-term climatic effects.

Fires, invasive introduced plants and plant collecting, particularly of ornamentals, such as orchids and *Lilium neilgherrense*, are also threats to the flora.

Conservation

The Western Ghats contain 8 National Parks, covering an area of 2848 km² (1.8% of the Western Ghats), and 39 Wildlife Sanctuaries (13,862 km², or 8.7% of the land area). Goa has is 1 National Park (107 km²) and 2 Sanctuaries (253.5 km²). Kerala has 3 National Parks (491.5 km²), including Silent Valley National Park (89.5 km²), and 12 Sanctuaries (1860.2 km²). The main protected areas in Karnataka are in Bandipur and Nagarahole, totalling 1517.6 km² (IUCN Management Category: II). The whole of the Nilgiri Hills has been declared a Biosphere Reserve. An insufficient amount of the Ghats on the Deccan Lavas is protected.

Centres of plant diversity and endemism

India

IS7. Agastyamalai Hills

– see Data Sheet.

IS8. Nilgiri Hills

– see Data Sheet.

DECCAN PROVINCE

This covers most of Peninsular India east of the Malabar Province and south of the Indo-Gangetic Plain. It includes the whole of the Eastern Ghats and other lesser ranges in the interior. A vast area of the north-west is occupied by the Deccan Traps, a great tract of basaltic lavas, mainly of Eocene age, which erupted and spread over the pre-existing, ancient land surface. The Chota-Nagpur Plateau comprises Gondwanan rocks with patches of Archaean gneisses, Deccan Lavas and Permian marine beds. To the east of the Deccan Lavas, between the Chota-Nagpur Plateau and Maikal Hills to the north and the Orissa Hills to the south, is the Chhatisgarh or Upper Mahanadi Basin, about 130–160 km wide. The remainder of the interior of the peninsula is a peneplain of Archaean gneisses known as the Telangana, and bordered on the east by the Eastern Ghats. These are ancient, eroded mountains, including the Nallamalai, Velikonda, Palkonda, Pachamalai and Shevroy ranges, composed of highly metamorphosed sedimentary rocks, including mica schists, crystalline limestones and khondalite (a quartz-garnet-sillimanite-graphite schist).

Climate

The climate is tropical to subtropical. Rainfall is generally low as a result of the rain-shadow effect of the Western Ghats. The Eastern Ghats, however, receive rainfall from both the south-west and north-east monsoons, as do parts of the north-eastern tableland.

Flora

Number of species:	5000
Endemic species:	250–300
Regional endemism:	4%
Endemic genera:	0
Endemic families:	0
Figures refer to vascular plants.	

There are fewer Malesian elements than in the Malabar Province and the more arid parts contain a considerable proportion of Somalia-Masai elements. There are floristic links between the flora of the north-east tableland (Bihar and Orissa) and those of Assam and Myanmā.

The present flora is largely the product of migration into the peninsula from neighbouring floristic provinces following the collision of India and Eurasia. There are no endemic families and no endemic genera, although 9 genera are "pan-Peninsular Indian" endemics (cf. list in Nayar 1980). Pockets of endemism and floristic richness occur in the Chota-Nagpur Plateau and the Eastern Ghats. The latter have about 2000 species (c. 13% of India's flora), of which about 4% are strict endemics (Nayar, Ahmed and Raju 1984). Many of the endemic species of the Deccan Province are palaeo-endemics with small populations and restricted distributions. Endemics include *Cycas beddomei*, *Argyreia choisyana*, *Boswellia ovalifolia* and *Shorea tumbuggaia*. Some Pleistocene relicts occur on both the Eastern and Western Ghats, e.g. *Clematis wightiana*, *C. murroana*, *C. gouriana*, *Ranunculus reniformis*, *Viola patrinii* and *Viburnum officinale*.

The thickly wooded Chota-Nagpur Plateau in southern Bihar has a distinctive climate and flora different from that of the Indo-Gangetic Plain to the north and Orissa to the south. Wood (1907) enumerates 1424 vascular plant species.

Main vegetation types

Much of the Deccan Plateau is covered by thorn forest with *Acacia* spp., *Balanites roxburghii*, *Cordia myxa* and (in damp places) *Phoenix sylvestris*. Vast tracts are under short-grass savanna or semi-desert. Where forests remain, they are most typically composed of *Tectona grandis*, *Shorea robusta*, *Cedrela toona*, *Boswellia serrata*, *Acacia catechu*, *Gmelina arborea* and *Terminalia* spp.

On the Chota-Nagpur Plateau are species-rich forests of *Shorea robusta*, *Anogeissus latifolia*, *Terminalia alata*, *Lagerstroemia parviflora*, *Pterocarpus marsupium* and *Aegle marmelos*. Shola-type forests, characterized by *Phoenix robusta*, *Pterospermum acerifolium* and *Clematis nutans*, occur at higher altitudes.

The Eastern Ghats are covered with moist or dry deciduous forest depending on rainfall (see Mani 1974; Nayar, Ahmed and Raju 1984). The northern part is dominated by *Shorea robusta*; the central Deccan part (including the Nallamalai Hills, CPD Site IS9, see Data Sheet) by *Helicteres isora*, *Erythroxylon monogynum*, *Azadirachta indica* and various Leguminosae; the southern part, comprising the eastern scarps of the Nilgiri Hills and Anaimalai Hills, is included in the Malabar Province.

The coastal strip between the Eastern Ghats and the sea, between Orissa and Tirunelveli, is sometimes regarded as a separate phytochorion, the Coromandel Subprovince (or Carnatic Province), on account of its distinct vegetation, including evergreen shrubs and trees belonging to *Flacourtia*, *Randia*, *Diospyros*, *Sapindus* and *Strychnos*. On the extreme south coast there is an *Acacia-Cocculus-Cassia-Capparis* association and mangrove swamps.

TABLE 21. FOREST COVER AND PROTECTED AREAS FOR EACH STATE IN THE DECCAN PROVINCE

State	Area (km²)	Forest cover (km²) [a]	% land area	National Parks (km²) [b]	Sanctuaries (km²) [c]	% land area protected
Andhra Pradesh	276,820	47,911	17.3	0	156,725	2.4
Bihar	173,875	26,934	15.5	1213	144,839	2.9
Karnataka	191,775	32,100	16.7 [d]	2472 [e]	3345 [e]	3.0 [e]
Madhya Pradesh	442,840	133,191	30.0	911,185	314,321	3.4
Maharashtra	307,760	44,058	14.3 [d]	956 [e]	14,267 [e]	4.9 [e]
Orissa	155,780	4713	30.2	1846	205,979	4.3
Uttar Pradesh	294,411	33,844	11.5			

Notes:

[a] FSI (1989).
[b] IUCN Management Category: II.
[c] IUCN Management Category: IV.
[d] Most of this forest is on the Western Ghats and is, therefore, part of the Malabar Floristic Province.
[e] Figures include the Western Ghats.

Species of economic importance

The Eastern Ghats are important as a gene pool for many wild relatives of food plants, including: mountain rice (*Oryza granulata*) and other rice species such as *O. malampuzhaensis* and *O. jeyporense*; *Musa balbisiana*, a banana relative; *Curcuma* spp., allied to turmeric (*C. longa*); *Atylosia cajanifolia* (a relative of pigeonpea, *Cajanus cajan*) (Raju, Ahmedullah and Nayar 1987).

Many tree species are exploited for timber, for the paper and rayon industries, and for tanning. Red sanders (*Pterocarpus santalinus*) accounts for a considerable amount of foreign exchange.

Many species of the Eastern Ghats, such as *Gloriosa superba*, *Glycine max* and *Dolichos purpureus*, are used for food and medicine. The rest of the interior of the Deccan Plateau is of comparatively lesser importance as a pool of genetic material, much of the original natural vegetation having been long since degraded. However, many species are used medicinally by local people throughout the interior (Sharma and Malhotra 1984). Examples include *Abelmoschus esculentus*, *Helicteres isora* and *Sida cordata*. *Grewia tiliifolia* is used in rope-making; *Ventilago denticulata* yields an edible oil.

Six species of lichens (*Heterodermia tremulans*, *Parmelia cirrhata*, *P. reticulata*, *P. tinctorum*, *Ramalina subcomplanata* and *Usnea longissima*) are used by tribes in Madhya Pradesh as spices and flavouring agents (Lal, Upreti and Kalakoti 1985).

Factors causing loss of biodiversity

Much of the original vegetation of the Deccan interior has already been cleared or degraded. The main threats to the remainder are conversion to cash crop plantations, excessive cutting of fuelwood and overgrazing by cattle. The Nallamalai Hills (CPD Site IS9, see Data Sheet) are subjected to heavy cutting of trees and bamboos to supply paper and other industries. Hydroelectric schemes are a threat to some areas.

The mangrove species *Cassipourea ceylanica* is Endangered in Orissa as a result of clearance of mangrove forests which were once plentiful along the fringes of Chilka Lake. *Gloriosa superba* is Vulnerable because of the increasing demand for its seeds as a source of colchicine (Saxena and Brahmam 1983).

Conservation

Table 21 gives forest cover and protected areas for each State which lies wholly or partly in the Deccan Province.

Centres of plant diversity and endemism

India

IS9. Nallamalai Hills

– see Data Sheet. A representative site for the **Eastern Ghats**.

UPPER GANGETIC PLAIN PROVINCE

This extends from the Aravalli Hills and Yamuna River (Rajasthan) east to the Kosi River and includes the tropical foothills of the Siwaliks and the entire lowland of the Upper Ganges. It includes eastern Rajasthan, lowland Uttar Pradesh and the northern part of Bihar.

The Aravalli Hills are of Precambrian age and are one of the world's oldest mountain ranges. The highest peak is Mount Abu at 1721 m. From the Aravalli Hills, the Deccan Plateau of eastern Rajasthan slopes gently eastwards to the Indo-Gangetic Plain. The plain was formerly the eastern end of the Tethys Sea which lay been Eurasia and Gondwanaland. The Tethys Sea was gradually infilled with sediments eroded from the continents. Sediments are still accumulating on the Indo-Gangetic Plain, which presently covers an area of nearly 1,400,000 km². It is estimated that some 5 km of sedimentary material has been laid down since the Tertiary.

Climate

The climate is hot and dry from March to June. Rainfall decreases from east to west; semi-arid conditions prevail north-west of Delhi. The south-west monsoon arrives in July. In the west, the winter season (December–February) is dry and sunny, with warm days and chilly nights, but in the east the climate is more tropical.

Flora

Number of species:	2000–3000
Endemic species:	<100
Regional endemism:	3–5%
Endemic genera:	0 or very few
Endemic families:	0
Figures refer to vascular plants.	

There are probably no endemic genera and few endemic species. The endemics mostly occur in eastern Rajasthan, especially in the Aravalli Hills, including Mount Abu (e.g. *Dicliptera abuensis*, *Strobilanthes halbergii* and *Veronica anagallis* var. *bracteosa*) (Pandey, Shetty and Malhotra 1983) and in the Hadoti region of Kota, Jhalawar and Bundi districts. Mount Abu is the meeting point of the Himalayan and South Indian floras (Jain 1968).

Species endemic to the Upper Gangetic Plain include several species of *Acacia*, *Phaseolus mukerjeeanus*, *Diospyros holeana*, *Ceropegia borii* and *Sesamum mulayanum*. There is a Mediterranean-type component in the Indo-Gangetic flora, exemplified by many legumes such as *Trigonella*, *Melilotus*, *Medicago* and *Ebenus*.

Main vegetation types

Most of the area was formerly covered by sal (*Shorea robusta*) forest, but the majority has been cleared for agriculture. Only a few patches of forest survive on the Siwaliks, where they are surrounded by savanna and scrub. Mount Abu has dense subtropical evergreen forest (Jain 1968). Thorn scrub is the dominant vegetation on the rest of the Aravalli Hills and in south-east Rajasthan. Halophytic formations occupy considerable areas of the Upper Gangetic Plain.

Species of economic importance

The majority of India's estimated 18 million neem trees (*Azadirachta indica*) occur in the Deccan Province and especially in Uttar Pradesh within the Upper Gangetic Plain Province. The area therefore contains an important gene pool of this species, which shows considerable variation in its insecticidal and other properties. The region is also important as a gene pool for wild races of cultivated plants belonging to the genera *Aegle*, *Citrullus*, *Emblica*, *Feronia*, *Grewia*, *Luffa*, *Momordica*, *Morus*, *Panicum* and *Syzygium*.

Conservation

Rajasthan has 4 National Parks and 21 Sanctuaries; however, not all of these are within the Upper Gangetic Plains Province. Among those within the phytochorion are Keoladeo National Park and World Heritage Site (28.7 km²), Mount Abu Wildlife Sanctuary (50 km²), Sariska Wildlife Sanctuary (492 km²), Darrah Wildlife Sanctuary (265.8 km²) and Sawai Mansingh Wildlife Sanctuary (103.3 km²).

BENGAL PROVINCE

This comprises the lower Ganges, the Brahmaputra valley in Bangladesh, the Orissa lowlands of north-east Peninsular India, parts of northern Rakhine (Arakan) in Myanmā, as well as the tropical parts of Nagaland, Manipur, Tripura and Assam (discussed under the Khasi-Manipur Province).

The main topographical feature is the Ganges-Brahmaputra delta, which covers an area of some 130,000 km². Large areas have been drained for cultivation. The coastal region of the Ganges Delta is occupied by the Sundarbans, the world's largest expanse of mangrove forests, named after the most important mangrove species here, *Heritiera fomes* (sundri).

Climate

The climate is tropical monsoonal, with most of the rain occurring during the south-west monsoon. Some rainstorms also occur in the hot season (March–June). The Bay of Bengal is subjected to occasional devastating cyclones, mainly between September and November. Widespread flooding is a regular occurrence. The cool season (November–February) is warmer than in much of India. Daytime maxima vary from 25–26°C in the cold season to 32–35°C in the hot season.

Flora

Number of species:	>5000
Endemic species:	?
Regional endemism:	?
Endemic genera:	few
Endemic families:	0
Figures refer to vascular plants.	
Bangladesh and Rakhine are too poorly known to allow endemism statistics to be computed.	

The flora is very rich, with many endemic species and a few endemic genera. About 5000 species have been recorded from Bangladesh. The flora of most of Bangladesh has much in common with that of India, especially with the floras of Orissa and Bihar. However, the flora of the Chittagong Hill Tracts and northern Rakhine has affinities also with those of Indochina and west-central Myanmā.

Main vegetation types

Until the beginning of the 20th century much of this region was covered with thick tropical forests, swamp forest and mangroves. The largest extant rain forest is the Sundarbans, a vast coastal mangrove forest of more than 4000 km², the largest mangrove forest in the world. Tropical semi-evergreen rain forest still occurs in Sylhet in north-east Bangladesh, and on the Chittagong Hill Tracts and adjacent Rahkine (Arakan, Myanmā). Tropical moist semi-evergreen sal (*Shorea robusta*) forest occurs north of Dhaka, but is now mostly secondary in nature.

Species of economic importance

Commercial timber species include *Dipterocarpus* spp., *Sterculia alata*, *Swintonia floribunda* and *Tetrameles nudiflora*. Other forest products include honey, sungrass, wax, cane and golpata (leaves of *Nypa fruticans*).

Factors causing loss of biodiversity

Bangladesh, whose rain forests were described by Hooker (1906) as the richest in the whole of the Indian Subcontinent, is now almost totally deforested (Collins, Sayer and Whitmore 1991). The estimated amount of closed broadleaved forest about a decade ago was 9270 km², and its rate of depletion was 80 km²/annum (FAO/UNEP 1981). Assuming that a similar rate of deforestation has prevailed since, less than 6% of the land is now forested. Much of the remaining forest is degraded.

The population of Bangladesh (122,300,000 in 1993) is set to rise to 342,000,000 by 2150. The population density (>800/km²) is already one of the world's highest. The increase in population will place even greater pressures on remaining areas of natural vegetation.

Urbanization and industrialization in the Bengal Plains of India has increased the pressure on dry deciduous sal forests in the districts of Burdwan, Birbhum, Bankera and Purulia. *Olax nana* and three insectivorous species (*Aldrovanda vesiculosa*, *Drosera burmanii* and *D. indica*) are now Vulnerable (Giri and Nayar 1983).

Little is known about the threat to the vegetation of northern Rakhine in Myanmā, but shifting cultivation (taungya) is practised there, as well as in the north-eastern states of India and the Chittagaong Hill Tracts of Bangladesh.

Centres of plant diversity and endemism

Bangladesh, India

IS10. Sundarbans

Area: c. 4000 km². Altitude: Sea-level.
- ❖ Vegetation: The largest area of mangrove forest in the world.
- ❖ Flora: Prain (1903) enumerated 334 species of 245 genera in 75 families; c. 40 species are endemic to the Indian Subcontinent and at least 3 species are strict endemics (c. 1.5% strict endemism). The forest is rich in epiphytic ferns, parasitic plants (Loranthaceae and Cuscutaceae) and orchids. *Heritiera fomes*, *Excoecaria agallocha* and *Ceriops decandra* are commercially important mangrove species.
- ❖ Threats: Natural and man-made changes in the flow of the River Ganges; river diversions and abstraction of water for irrigation has resulted in a reduction in the amount of freshwater flowing into the Sundarbans. The resulting increased salinity is thought to be the cause of unusually high mortality of *Heritiera fomes* (Naskar and Guha Bakshi 1986). Mangrove forests are cleared for paddy cultivation and cut for fuelwood. There is large-scale removal of *Excoecaria agallocha* for the paper industry. As a result of forest clearance, large tracts of land are exposed to coastal erosion and inundation during cyclones and tidal bores (Giri and Nayar 1983).

- ❖ Conservation: The Sundarbans have been protected since 1875 as a Reserved Forest. In 1966 a mangrove planting programme was initiated. This is now financially supported by the World Bank.

SRI LANKA PROVINCE

The Sri Lanka Province, as defined by Takhtajan (1986), includes Sri Lanka and the Maldives. Lakshadweep (Laccadive Islands) and the Chagos Archipelago (British Indian Ocean Territory) are included here for convenience.

Sri Lanka comprises a central mountain mass and broad coastal plains. The highest peaks are Pidurutalagala (2527 m), Kirigalpotta (2393 m) and Adam's Peak (2243 m). The island was connected to South India until the late Pleistocene. Like South India, it consists of crystalline Precambrian rocks, largely metamorphosed quartzites, schists and crystalline limestones.

The Maldives are an archipelago of 1201 small coral atolls, none more than 2 m above sea-level, which extend for 800 km in the Indian Ocean. They have a total land area of 298 km². Lakshadweep (Laccadive Islands) comprises 27 coral atolls north of the Maldives, c. 300 km west of the Malabar Coast. Their total land area is 32 km². The Chagos Archipelago (British Indian Ocean Territory) lies between latitudes 5–10°S and longitudes 70–75°E. The total land area is 60 km²; the main island is Diego Garcia.

Climate

The climate of Sri Lanka is tropical, although temperatures are significantly reduced in the interior highlands. Most of the country receives moderate or abundant rainfall throughout the year. The wettest regions are the south-western coast and the mountains, the rainfall being greatest during the south-west and north-east monsoons (April–June and October–November, respectively). The north-eastern lowlands and the south-eastern coast are much drier, receiving their main rains during the north-east monsoon.

The climate of the Maldives, Lakshadweep and the Chagos Archipelago is tropical oceanic.

Flora

	Sri Lanka	Maldives	Lakshadweep	Chagos
Number of species:	3370	277 [a]	348	c.100
Endemic species:	902	5	0	0
Endemic genera:	12	0	0	0
Endemic families:	0	0	0	0
Regional species endemism (%):	24.5	1.8	0	0

Notes:

Figures refer to vascular plants.
[a] Excludes 450 introduced species.

Sources:

Sri Lanka: Ashton and Gunatilleke (1987). Maldives: World Conservation Monitoring Centre statistics (1994). Lakshadweep: Raghavan (1977). Chagos Archipelago: Davis *et al.* (1986).

Sri Lanka has high generic and specific endemism, although there are no endemic families. There are 12 endemic genera, and a further 27 which are endemic to Sri Lanka and Peninsular India (where nearly all are confined to the Western Ghats). About 845 species of angiosperms and 57 species of ferns are strict endemics to Sri Lanka; some 600 vascular plant species are endemic to Sri Lanka and Peninsular India. Most of these species are in India confined to the Western Ghats, Anaimalai Hills and Nilgiri Hills, indicating that Sri Lanka's strongest floristic affinity with mainland India is with the Malabar Province.

Many of Sri Lanka's 902 endemic plant species are relicts. Some 740 (89.1%) are concentrated in the south-western, perhumid zone (an area of some 15,000 km²) (Ashton and Gunatilleke 1987). They include many species of Dipterocarpaceae, including the endemic genus *Stemonoporus*.

The Maldives, an archipelago of coral atolls, has a small flora; the 5 endemics are all species of *Pandanus*. The other two island groups have very impoverished floras with many introduced species.

Main vegetation types

The wet and perhumid zones of south-western Sri Lanka support mixed dipterocarp forests. These forests differ from tropical forests elsewhere in the Indian Subcontinent which experience a short dry season. The nearest equivalents of Sri Lanka's evergreen rain forests are in western Malesia, eastern Madagascar and the Seychelles, although the species composition differs markedly in each.

The highlands of Sri Lanka support montane subtropical broadleaved hill forest and wet temperate forests. Tropical dry evergreen forest occurs in the dry zone (in areas receiving 1000–1400 mm annual rainfall), and tropical semi-evergreen forest in an intermediate zone (where the annual rainfall is 1400–2000 mm). Tropical thorn forest occurs in the arid zones of the east, south-east and far north of Sri Lanka in areas which have a dry season of more than five months and less than 1000 mm total annual rainfall (Gunatilleke and Ashton 1987).

The vegetation of Lakshadweep is mostly coconut palms, on which the culture and economy of the islands is based.

Species of economic importance

More than 700 vascular plant species have some value in indigenous medicine or are used as food. The forests contain many species of commercial timber importance. Various species of *Cyperus*, *Pandanus* and rattans are used for making mats, baskets and utensils.

Wild relatives of crop plants include members of the genera *Mangifera* (mango), *Cinnamomum* (cinnamon), *Piper* (pepper), *Myristica* (nutmeg), *Artocarpus* (breadfruit), *Syzygium* (clove), *Atalantia* (citrus) and *Cullonia* (allied to durian).

A host of orchids and other herbaceous plants have potential horticultural value.

Factors causing loss of biodiversity

Only 8% of Sri Lanka's wet zone remains forested. Primary lowland and hill forests now comprise less than 1% and 3%, respectively, of the wet zone (Ashton and Gunatilleke 1987). The area of closed canopy forest was reduced from 29,000 km² in 1956 to 16,590 km² in 1980, and to 12,260 km² in 1983, of which only 1440 km² was rain forest.

The main causes of deforestation and forest degradation are logging, mining for gemstones, shifting agriculture and urbanization. Some areas have been cleared and planted with Central American mahogany (*Swietenia macrophylla*).

Conservation

Conservation in Sri Lanka is of ancient, traditional origin; one of the world's first wildlife sanctuaries was established by King Devanampiyatissa in the 3rd century BC.

Gunatilleke and Gunatilleke (1990) list 96 protected areas. Of these, 45 meet the criteria for inclusion in the *United Nations List of National Parks and Protected Areas* (IUCN 1990, 1992), including 11 National Parks (totalling 4601.8 km²), 3 Strict Natural Reserves (315.7 km²), 2 Nature Reserves (325.5 km²) and 28 Sanctuaries (2519.5 km²). Sinharaja (112 km²) is a Biosphere Reserve and World Heritage Site as well as being Sri Lanka's only National Heritage Wilderness Area.

Most of the protected areas are in the dry zone, whereas by far the greatest amount of biodiversity in need of protection is in the wet zone where almost all the remaining forest is under threat. Many of Sri Lanka's endemic species are therefore threatened; Abeywickrama (1983) estimated that up to 160 non-endemic species were also rare or threatened.

Centres of plant diversity and endemism

Sri Lanka

IS11. Knuckles

– see Data Sheet.

IS12. Peak Wilderness and Horton Plains

– see Data Sheet.

IS13. Sinharaja

– see Data Sheet.

INDOCHINESE REGION

The Indochinese Region, as defined by Takhtajan (1986), extends from south-east Bangladesh, through central Myanmā and the Andaman Islands to Thailand, south-west and south China, and the island of Hainan. Of its seven floristic provinces, two lie entirely within the Indian Subcontinent, a third includes the southernmost part of Myanmā, and a fourth plays a very minor role in the shaping of the Subcontinent's flora.

SOUTH BURMESE PROVINCE

This phytochorion includes central Myanmā, from Myitkina south to Yangon (Rangoon) and Mawlamein (Moulmein), neighbouring small islands, a tropical part of the extreme east of India, and south-east Bangladesh. It includes the Rakhine Yoma, Bago (Pegu) Yoma, the Shan Plateau, the Ayeyarwady (Irrawaddy) Basin, part of the Chittagong Hill Tracts (Bangladesh) and Mizoram.

The Rakhine Yoma in north-west central Myanmā is part of a southward extension of the Himalayas, known as the Burmese Arc, and dates from the Mesozoic. Immediately inside and parallel to the Burmese Arc is a zone of Upper Tertiary to recent volcanoes, an extension of the volcanic regions of Java and Sumatra. The volcanoes in Myanmā and India were active from Miocene to Pleistocene times (Krishnan 1974).

Immediately to the east is the Ayeyarwady Basin, drained by the Chindwinn and Ayeyarwady rivers. Between the two main river valleys is the ancient mountain range of the Bago (Pegu) Yoma, which has some extinct volcanoes including Mount Popa. To the east of the Ayeyarwady Basin is the Shan Plateau. Geologically, this is part of Yunnan and is the most ancient part of the phytochorion. There are outcrops of Archaean gneiss in the west and granite in the east; slates, quartzites and limestone varying in age from Precambrian to Jurassic also occur. The Shan Plateau is rich in minerals and gemstones, including silver, zinc, jade, lapis lazuli and rubies.

Climate

The climate is tropical monsoonal, but the full effects of the south-west monsoon are only felt on the windward side of the Rakhine (Arakan) Yoma, Chin Hills and neighbouring areas. To leeward there is a pronounced rain-shadow effect which becomes progressively more marked further inland so that the interior of the Ayeyarwady Basin has a semi-desert climate. The Shan Plateau has a slightly cooler and wetter climate. The higher mountains on the west side of the phytochorion have a temperate climate.

Flora

Number of species:	>7000
Endemic species:	many
Regional endemism:	high
Endemic genera:	several
Endemic families:	0
Figures refer to vascular plants.	

This phytochorion is renowned for its high generic and specific endemism, but neither the total number of species (probably in excess of 7000) nor the number of endemics can be ascertained with certainty because of the absence of any up-to-date detailed botanical knowledge of Myanmā.

There are no endemic families; endemic genera include *Hypselandra*, *Tractopevodia*, *Pommereschia* and *Ratzeburgia*. The Chindwinn River acts as a natural floristic barrier leading to vicariant distributions. For example, *Rhododendron arizelum* of north Myanmā is replaced west of the Chindwinn by *R. macabeanum*; *Lilium mackliniae* (Manipur) and

L. wallichianum (Assam Himalaya) are replaced east of the Chindwinn by *L. primulinum* and *L. bakerianum* (Mackenzie 1952).

Main vegetation types

The vegetation of Myanmā was classified by Stamp (1925) into 36 types. Tropical semi-evergreen monsoon forest, subtropical evergreen forest (pine savanna and mixed broadleaved forest) and temperate semi-evergreen forest all occur on the Burmese Arc. Pyinkado (*Xylia dolabriformis*) semi-evergreen forest, moist teak forest, dry teak forest, pyinma (lower mixed) forest occur on the Bago Yoma, the leeward side of the Burmese Arc, and parts of the Shan Plateau. In the dry interior of Myanmā, various types of savanna forest, dominated by eng (*Dipterocarpus tuberculatus*) or te (*Diospyros burmanica*), dahal (*Tectona hamiltonii*) or than (*Terminalia oliveri*) occur. In particularly arid areas there are various types of thorn forest dominated by *Acacia catechu*, *Tectona hamiltonii* or *Ziziphus jujuba*. *Euphorbia* semi-desert thorn scrub grows on alkaline soils.

Freshwater swamp forests were formerly widespread in the Ayeyarwady Basin (Stamp and Lord 1923). The southern Shan States, especially around Inle Lake, have a rich freshwater swamp and lake-margin vegetation of aquatics and semi-aquatics. There is some *Heritiera* mangrove forest in Rakhine; *Heritiera* also formerly covered much of the Ayeyarwady Delta.

Factors causing loss of biodiversity

Shifting cultivation (taungya) is a serious problem in parts of the Rakhine (Arakan) Yoma, huge tracts of which have become degraded to bamboo brakes. The formerly rich and luxuriant freshwater swamp forests that grew widely in the Ayeyarwady valley, as well as much of the delta mangrove forest, have been all but totally cleared for agriculture and other uses.

Species of economic importance

Timber exports still provide 25% of Myanmā's foreign earnings. Teak is by far the most valuable timber tree. As well as being native, it is widely planted. Dipterocarps, such as *Dipterocarpus turbinatus*, yield kanyin, a type of oleoresin.

A large number of species, listed by Nordal (1963), are used in indigenous herbal medicine, including *Coptis teeta*, *Fritillaria roylei* and various relatives of ginseng (*Panax* and related genera). Myanmā is a centre of diversity for *Dioscorea* (yams), *Rubus* (brambles), *Sorbus*, *Prunus* and *Syzygium*.

Many species are of ornamental value, including species of *Rhododendron*, *Lilium* and *Primula*.

Conservation

Protected areas include Kelatha Hill Game Sanctuary (24.5 km²) in Mon State, Gyobyu Reservoir (38.6 km²), Mandalay Game Sanctuary (103 km²), Taunggyi Wildlife Sanctuary (16.9 km²), Wethigan Wildlife Sanctuary (4.4 km²)

in Magwe Division, and Minwun Taung Wildlife Sanctuary (201.2 km²) in Sagaing Division. The Bago Yomas (1462 km²), Inle Lake (158.1 km²) and Mong Pin Lake (622 km²) on the Shan Plateau, have been proposed as Wildlife Sanctuaries.

Centres of plant diversity and endemism

Myanmā

IS14. Bago (Pegu) Yomas

– see Data Sheet.

IS15. Shan Plateau

Comprises the Shan Plateau proper (c. 54,400 km²) and the Southern Shan States, including Inle Lake. Area: c. 150,000 km². Altitude: 800–1800 m.
- ❖ Vegetation: Some evergreen (*Quercus-Castanopsis*) forest, *Pinus kesiya* forest and dry hill forest. Rich aquatic and marsh vegetation on Inle Lake and neighbouring water bodies.
- ❖ Flora: Probably at least 2000 vascular plant species, many endemic or near-endemic (some extending into Thailand, China or Laos).
- ❖ Threats: Mining for jade and other precious stones and minerals; shifting cultivation.
- ❖ Conservation: Taunggyi Wildlife Sanctuary (16.9 km²) (IUCN Management Category: unassigned); Inle Lake Wildlife Sanctuary (proposed); Mong Tai Wildlife Sanctuary (proposed).

SOUTH CHINESE PROVINCE

This includes southern tropical Yunnan, northernmost Vietnam, coastal southern China, Macao, northern Thailand and Laos. The only part included within the Indian Subcontinent is easternmost Myanmā. The other parts of the phytochorion are treated in the Regional Overview on China and East Asia.

Climate

Similar to that of extreme south-west Yunnan, which receives between 1500–2250 mm rainfall per annum.

Flora

Number of species:	?
Endemic species:	?
Regional endemism:	?
Endemic genera:	probably 0
Endemic families:	0
Figures refer to vascular plants.	

The total number of vascular plant species in the phytochorion is probably in excess of 10,000. The number of species occurring in the Myanmā fraction of the phytochorion is not known, and neither is the number of Myanmā endemics. The present almost total lack of botanical knowledge of this part of Myanmā is unlikely to change in the foreseeable future as a result of the political situation and very restricted access to the area.

Main vegetation types

The vegetation is likely to be similar to that of extreme southwest Yunnan, where there is a mixture of montane and subtropical conifer forests, subtropical evergreen broadleaved forests and sclerophyllous forests. Descriptions of these forest types in Yunnan are given by Li Xiwen and Walker (1986) and can be assumed to apply also to this part of easternmost Myanmā.

Species of economic importance

No information available. The area is in the main opium-cultivation region of Myanmā and Thailand, known as the "Golden Triangle".

Conservation

No protected areas.

THAILANDIAN PROVINCE

This includes most of Thailand and western Laos, as well as Taninthayi (Tenasserim) in Myanmā. The whole of Taninthayi (CPD Site IS16) is treated in a Data Sheet.

Centres of plant diversity and endemism

Myanmā

IS16. Taninthayi (Tenasserim)

– see Data Sheet.

ANDAMANESE PROVINCE

This province comprises only the Andaman Islands (treated with the Nicobar Islands as CPD Data Sheet IS17). There is at least one endemic genus (*Pubistylus*) and about 10% specific endemism. Malesian elements are an important component of the flora but there are also strong affinities with the flora of southern Myanmā.

Centres of plant diversity and endemism

India

IS17. Andaman Islands

– see Data Sheet on the Andaman and Nicobar Islands.

MALESIAN REGION

Takhtajan (1986) includes the Nicobar Islands within the Sumatran Province of the Malesian Region. In the current treatment, the Nicobar Islands are considered as part of the Indian Subcontinent.

Centres of plant diversity and endemism

India

IS17. Nicobar Islands

– see Data Sheet on the Andaman and Nicobar Islands.

References

Abeywickrama, B.A. (1983). Threatened or endangered plants of Sri Lanka and the status of their conservation measures. In Jain, S.K. and Mehra, K.L. (eds), *Conservation of tropical plant resources*. Botanical Survey of India, Howrah. Pp. 11–18.

Adams, C.D. (1983). *Report to the Government of the Maldive Islands on flora identification*. FAO Project RAS 79/123, Rome.

Ahmedullah, M. and Nayar, M.P. (1987). *Endemic plants of the Indian Region. Vol. 1*. Botanical Survey of India, Calcutta. 261 pp.

Ali, S. (1978). The flora of Pakistan: some general and analytical remarks. *Notes Roy. Bot. Gard. Edinb.* 36: 427–439.

Ali, S.I. and Qaiser, M. (1986). A phytogeographical analysis of the phanerogams of Pakistan and Kashmir. *Proceedings of the Royal Society of Edinburgh* 89B: 89–101.

Anon. (1994). Good news from Pakistan. *IUCN Bulletin* 25(1): 8.

Arora, R.K., Mehra, K.C. and Nayar, E.R. (1983). Conservation of wild relatives of crop plants in India. *NBPCR Sci. Monograph* 6: 1–14.

Arora, R.K. and Nayar, M.P. (1983). Wild relatives and related species of crop plants in India – their diversity and distribution. *Bull. Bot. Surv. India* 25: 35–45.

Ashton, P.S. and Gunatilleke, C.V.S. (1987). New light on the plant geography of Ceylon. I. Historical plant geography. *J. Biogeography* 14: 249–285.

Atkinson, E.T. (1980/1882). *The economic botany of the Himalayas*. Cosmo Publications, New Delhi. [Reprint of pp. 672–923 only of a paper *The Himalayan Districts of the North Western Provinces*, first published in 1882.]

Balakrishnan, N.P. (1977). Recent botanical studies in Andaman and Nicobar Islands. *Bull. Bot. Surv. India* 19: 132–138.

Banerji, M. (1963). Outline of Nepal phytogeography. *Vegetatio* 11: 288–296.

BARC (1987). *National Conservation Strategy for Bangladesh. Draft prospectus (Phase I)*. Bangladesh Agricultural Research Council (BARC)/IUCN, Gland, Switzerland. 154 pp.

Barna, I.C., Chowdhury, S. and Neogi, B. (1988). Primitive land plants (angiosperms) and their distribution pattern in Assam. *J. Econ. Tax. Bot.* 12: 81–92.

Basu, S.K. (1991). India: palm utilization and conservation. In Johnson, D. (ed.), *Palms for human needs in Asia. Palm utilization and conservation in India, Indonesia, Malaysia and the Philippines*. Balkema, Rotterdam. Pp. 13–35.

Bhattacharyya, S.C. and Dutta, S.C.D. (1951). Citrus varieties of Assam. *Indian J. Genetics and Pl. Breeding* 11: 57–62.

Bir, S.S. (1987). Pteridophytic flora of India: rare and endangered elements and their conservation. *Indian Fern J.* 4: 95–101.

Bir, S.S., Vasudeva, S.M. and Kachroo, P. (1990). Pteridophytic flora of north-eastern India – IV. *Indian Fern J.* 7: 219–226.

Bir, S.S., Vasudeva, S.M., Kachroo, P. and Singh, Y. (1991). Pteridophytic flora of north-eastern India – V. Ecological, distributional and phytogeographical account. *Indian Fern J.* 8: 98–139.

Bole, P.V. and Almeida, M.R. (1980). Materials to the flora of Mahabaleshwar. *J. Bombay Nat. Hist. Soc.* 77: 450–464.

Bole, P.V. and Almeida, M.R. (1981). Materials to the flora of Mahabaleshwar. *J. Bombay Nat. Hist. Soc.* 78: 548–567.

Bole, P.V. and Almeida, M.R. (1983a). Materials to the flora of Mahabaleshwar – 3. *J. Bombay Nat. Hist. Soc.* 79: 307–323.

Bole, P.V. and Almeida, M.R. (1983b). Materials to the flora of Mahabaleshwar – 4. *J. Bombay Nat. Hist. Soc.* 79: 594–606.

Bole, P.V. and Almeida, M.R. (1984). Materials to the flora of Mahabaleshwar – 5. *J. Bombay Nat. Hist. Soc.* 81: 364–379.

Bole, P.V. and Almeida, M.R. (1985). Materials to the flora of Mahabaleshwar – 6. *J. Bombay Nat. Hist. Soc.* 82: 68–86.

Bole, P.V. and Almeida, M.R. (1987). Materials to the flora of Mahabaleshwar – 7. *J. Bombay Nat. Hist. Soc.* 83: 570–602.

Bole, P.V. and Almeida, M.R. (1988). Materials to the flora of Mahabaleshwar – 8. *J. Bombay Nat. Hist. Soc.* 84: 372–391.

Bole, P.V. and Almeida, M.R. (1989a). Materials to the flora of Mahabaleshwar – 6A. *J. Bombay Nat. Hist. Soc.* 86: 175–186.

Bole, P.V. and Almeida, M.R. (1989b). Materials to the flora of Mahabaleshwar – 8 [sic], Pteridophytes. *J. Bombay Nat. Hist. Soc.* 86: 400–407.

Champion, H.G. (1936). A preliminary survey of the forest types of India and Burma. *Indian Forest Rec. (n.s.), Silvicult.*, 1.

Chatterjee, D. (1940). Studies in the endemic flora of India and Burma. *J. Asiatic Soc. Bengal* 5: 19–69.

Chopra, I.C. and Handa, K.L. (1961). *Review of research on Indian medicinal and allied plants.* Indian Council of Agricultural Research, New Delhi.

Choudhury, A.M. (1993). Bangladesh: balancing numbers and needs. *IUCN Bulletin* 24(2): 25.

Collins, N.M., Sayer, J.A. and Whitmore, T.C. (eds) (1991). *The conservation atlas of tropical forests: Asia and the Pacific.* Macmillan, London. 256 pp.

Cool, J.C. (1980). *Stability and survival – the Himalayan challenge.* Ford Foundation, New York. 22 pp.

Dassanayake, M.D. and Fosberg, F.R. (eds) (1980-). *A revised handbook to the flora of Ceylon.* Amerind, New Delhi.

Davis, S.D., Droop, S.J., Gregerson, P., Henson, L., Leon, C.J., Lamlein Villa-Lobos, J., Synge, H. and Zantovska, J. (1986). *Plants in danger: what do we know?* IUCN, Gland, Switzerland and Cambridge, U.K. 461 pp.

Dhar, U. and Kachroo, P. (1983a). *Alpine flora of Kashmir Himalaya.* Scientific Publishers, Jodhpur. 280 pp.

Dhar, U. and Kachroo, P. (1983b). Some remarkable features of endemism in Kashmir Himalaya. In Jain, S.K. and Rao, R.R. (eds), *An assessment of threatened plants of India.* Botanical Survey of India (Department of Environment), Botanic Garden, Howrah. Pp. 18–22.

Dixit, R.D. (1986). Tree ferns – an urgent need of conservation. *Indian Fern J.* 3: 42–45.

Duke, J.A. (1990). Medicinal plants of Pakistan. In Ali, S.I. and Ghaffar, A. (eds), *Plant life of South Asia.* Department of Botany, University of Karachi, Karachi. Pp. 195–225.

FAO/UNEP (1981). *Tropical forest resources assessment project (in the framework of the Global Environment Monitoring System – GEMS).* UN 32/6.1301-78-04. Technical Report 3: *Forest Resources of Tropical Asia.* FAO, Rome. 475 pp.

Ferguson, D.K. (1985). A new species of *Amentotaxus* (Taxaceae) from northeastern India. *Kew Bull.* 40: 115–119.

Francis, P. (1984). Plants as human adornment in India. *Economic Botany* 38: 194–209.

Fraser-Jenkins, C.R. (1991). The ferns and allies of the Far West Himalaya. *Pakistan Systematics* 8(1–2): 85–120.

FSI (Forest Survey of India) (1989). *The state of forest report.* Government of India, Ministry of Environment and Forests.

Gadgil, M. and Meher-Homji (1986). Localities of great significance to conservation of India's biological diversity. In: *Proceedings of the Indian Academy of Sciences (Anim. Sci./Plant Sci.) Supplement, November 1986.* Pp. 165–180.

Gadgil, M. and Vartak, V.D. (1975). Sacred groves in India – a plea for conservation. *J. Bombay Nat. Hist. Soc.* 72: 314–320.

Gadgil, M. and Vartak, V.D. (1976). The sacred groves of Western Ghats in India. *Economic Botany* 30: 152–160.

Giri, G.S. and Nayar, M.P. (1983). Some threatened plants of Bengal Plains. In Jain, S.K. and Rao, R.R. (eds), *An assessment of threatened plants of India.* Botanical Survey of India (Department of Environment), Botanic Garden, Howrah. Pp. 91–93.

Goodland, R. (1985). Environmental aspects of hydroelectric power and water storage projects (with special reference to India). Paper presented at an International Seminar on the Environmental Impact Assessment of Water Resources, University of Roorkee, Uttar Pradesh, December 12–14, 1985. 30 pp.

Grierson, A.J.C. and Long, D.G. (eds) (1983-). *Flora of Bhutan including a record of plants from Sikkim.* Royal Botanic Garden, Edinburgh.

Gunatilleke, C.V.S. and Ashton, P.S. (1987). New light on the plant geography of Ceylon. II. The ecological biogeography of the lowland endemic tree flora. *J. Biogeography* 14: 295–327.

Gunatilleke, I.A.U.N. and Gunatilleke, C.V.S. (1990). Distribution of floristic richness and its conservation in Sri Lanka. *Conservation Biology* 4(1): 21–31.

Hajra, P.K. and Rao, R.S. (1986). Notes on *Tetracentron sinense* Oliver and *Schizophragma integrifolia* Oliver – two threatened plants from Kameng District, Arunachal Pradesh. *J. Econ. Tax. Bot.* 8: 455–459.

Hara, H. (1966). *The flora of eastern Himalaya. Report 1.* University of Tokyo Press, Tokyo. 744 pp.

Hara, H. *et al.* (1978-1982). *An enumeration of the flowering plants of Nepal.* British Museum, London. 3 vols.

Hasanain, S.Z. and Rahman, O. (1957). *Plants of Karachi and Sind.* Monograph no. 1. Department of Botany, University of Karachi.

Hegde, S.N. (1985). Observations on the habitat and distribution of orchids in Arunachal Pradesh. *J. Bombay Nat. Hist. Soc.* 82: 114–125.

Hooker, J.D. (1872-1897). *Flora of British India.* London. 7 vols.

Hooker, J.D. (1906). *A sketch of the flora of British India.* Ed. 3. Imperial Gazetteer, Oxford. (Reprinted in 1973 by Bishen Singh Mahendra Pal Singh, Dehra Dun.)

Hundley, H.G. and U Chit Ko Ko (1961). *List of trees, shrubs, herbs and principal climbers, etc. recorded from Burma with vernacular names.* Government Printing and Stationery, Rangoon. 532 pp.

Hunter, B. (ed.) (1993). *The Statesman's year-book.* Ed. 130. Macmillan, London.

IUCN (1990). *1990 United Nations list of national parks and protected areas.* IUCN, Gland, Switzerland and Cambridge, U.K. 284 pp.

IUCN (1992). *Protected areas of the world: a review of national systems. Volume 1: Indomalaya, Oceania, Australia and Antarctic.* IUCN, Gland, Switzerland and Cambridge, U.K. 352 pp. (Prepared by the World Conservation Monitoring Centre.)

Jain, S.K. (1968). Phytogeographical consideration on the flora of Mt. Abu. *Bull. Bot. Surv. India* 9: 68–78.

Jain, S.K. and DeFilipps, R.A. (1991). *Medicinal plants of India,* 2 vols. Algonac, Michigan, U.S.A. 849 pp.

Jain, S.K. and Rao, R.R. (eds) (1983). *An assessment of threatened plants of India.* Botanical Survey of India (Department of Environment), Botanic Garden, Howrah. 334 pp.

Jain, S.K. and Sastry, A.R.K. (1980). *Threatened plants of India. A state-of-the art report.* Botanical Survey of India and Man and Biosphere Committee, National Committee on Environmental Planning and Co-ordination, Department of Science and Technology, New Delhi. 48 pp.

Jain, S.K. and Sastry, A.R.K. (1983). *Materials for a catalogue of threatened plants of India.* Department of Environment, GOI, Calcutta.

Jayarama, K. and Krishnankuatty, C.N. (1991). Yield from eucalypt plantations in Kerala. *Indian J. Forestry* 14: 51–53.

Johnstone, P. (1986). *Operation World.* STL Books, Bromley, Kent. 501 pp.

Kachroo, U., Sapru, B.L. and Dhar, U. (1977). *Flora of Ladakh. An ecological and taxonomical appraisal.* Dehra Dun. 172 pp.

Kaul, M.K., Singh, V., Sharma, P.K. and Bhatia, A.K. (1990). Ethnobotanic studies in north-west and Trans-Himalaya. II. Approaches to the study of ethnobotany towards the human welfare in remote north-west and Trans-Himalaya. *J. Econ. Tax. Bot.* 14: 271–285.

Kaul, R.N. and Haridasan, K. (1987). Forest types of Arunachal Pradesh – a preliminary study. *J. Econ. Tax. Bot.* 9: 379–389.

Kazmi, S.M.A. and Johan, A. (1975). Useful plants of Pakistan. Part I. Gymnosperms. *Sultania* 1: 5–55.

Kazmi, S.M.A. and Johan, A. (1976). Useful plants of Pakistan. II. *Sultania* 2: 23–88.

Kazmi, S.M.A. and Johan, A. (1977). Useful plants of Pakistan. III. *Sultania* 3: 17–65.

Khan, M.S. and Huq, A.M. (1972-). *Flora of Bangladesh.* Dhaka.

Kingdon-Ward, F. (1944-1945). A sketch of the botany and geography of North Burma. *J. Bombay Nat. Hist. Soc.* 44: 550–574; 45: 16–30 (1944); 45: 133–148 (1945).

Kitamura, S. (1960). *Flora of Afghanistan. Results of the Kyoto Scientific Expedition to the Karakorum and Hindukush.* Kyoto University, Kyoto. 466 pp.

Koul, A.K., Karihaloo, J.L. and Hamal, I.A. (1982). Wild edible plants of Kashmir – some less known vegetable substitutes and beverages. *Bull. Bot. Surv. India* 24: 67–69.

Krishnan, M.S. (1974). Geology. In Mani, M.S. (ed.), *Ecology and biogeography in India.* Junk, The Hague. Pp. 60–98.

Kurz, W.S. (1874). Contributions towards a knowledge of the Burmese flora, 1. *J. Asiat. Soc. Bengal* 43(2): 39–141.

Kurz, W.S. (1875). Contributions towards a knowledge of the Burmese flora, 2. *J. Asiat. Soc. Bengal* 44(2, 3): 128–190.

Kurz, W.S. (1876). Contributions towards a knowledge of the Burmese flora, 3. *J. Asiat. Soc. Bengal* 45(2): 204–210.

Kurz, W.S. (1877a). Contributions towards a knowledge of the Burmese flora, 4. *J. Asiat. Soc. Bengal* 46(2): 49–250

Kurz, W.S. (1877b). *Forest flora of British Burma.* Calcutta. 2 vols. 549 and 613 pp.

Lace, J.H. (1913). *List of trees, shrubs, and principal climbers, etc. recorded from Burma with vernacular names.* Rangoon. 291 pp.

Lace, J.H. and Rodger, A. (1922). *List of trees, shrubs, and principal climbers, etc. recorded from Burma with vernacular names,* 2nd edition. Rangoon. 366 pp.

Lal, B., Upreti, D.K. and Kalakoti, B.S. (1985). Ethnobotanical utilization of lichens by the tribals of Madhya Pradesh. *J. Econ. Tax. Bot.* 7: 203–204.

Larsen, T.B. (1987). The butterflies of the Nilgiri Mountains of southern India (Lepidoptera: Rhopalocera). *J. Bombay Nat. Hist. Soc.* 84: 28–65.

Larsen, T.B. (1988). The butterflies of the Nilgiri Mountains of southern India (Lepidoptera: Rhopalocera). *J. Bombay Nat. Hist. Soc.* 85: 26–41.

Li Xiwen and Walker, D. (1986). The plant geography of Yunnan Province, southwest China. *J. Biogeography* 13: 367–397.

Lokubandara, W.J.M. (1991). Policies and organisation for medicinal plant conservation in Sri Lanka. In Akerele, O., Heywood, V.H. and Synge, H. (eds), *The conservation of medicinal plants*. Cambridge University Press, Cambridge, U.K. Pp. 241–247.

Mackenzie, J.M.D. (1952). A note on some natural barriers in Burma. *J. Bombay Nat. Hist. Soc.* 51: 189–199.

Maesen, L.J.G. van der, Remanandan, P.S., Rao, N.K. and Pundir, R.P.S. (1985). Occurrence of Cajaninae in the Indian Subcontinent, Burma and Thailand. *J. Bombay Nat. Hist. Soc.* 82: 489–500.

Maheshwari, J.K. (1977). Conservation of rare plants – Indian scene *vis-a-vis* world scene. *Bull. Bot. Surv. India* 19: 167–173.

Maheshwari, J.K. (1986). Editorial: progress of holotaxonomy. *J. Econ. Tax. Bot.* 8: iii–vii.

Maheshwari, J.K. (1987). Editorial: taxonomy of cultivated plants. *J. Econ. Tax. Bot.* 9: i–viii.

Malhotra, C.L. and Hajra, P.K. (1977). Status of floristic studies in Arunachal Pradesh. *Bull. Bot. Surv. India* 19: 61–63.

Mani, M.S. (1974). The vegetation and phytogeography of the Eastern Ghats. In Mani, M.S. (ed.), *Ecology and biogeography in India*. Junk, The Hague. Pp. 197–203.

Mani, M.S. (ed.) (1974). *Ecology and biogeography in India*. Junk, The Hague. 773 pp.

Mill, R.R. (1991). The generic position of C.B. Clarke's species of *Paracaryum*. *Edinburgh J. Bot.* 48: 55–61.

Mistry, J. and Stott, P. (1993). The savanna forests of Manipur State, India: an historical overview. *Global Ecology and Biogeography Letters* 3: 10–17.

Myers, N. (1988). Threatened biotas: "hotspots" in tropical forests. *Environmentalist* 8: 187–208.

Naithani, H.B. (1990). *Flowering plants of India, Nepal & Bhutan (not recorded in Sir J.D. Hooker's Flora of British India)*. Surya Publications, Dehra Dun. 711 pp.

Nasir, E. and Ali, S.I. (eds) (1970-). *Flora of West Pakistan*. Pakistan Agricultural Research Council, Islamabad. (Continued from 1980 as *Flora of Pakistan*.)

Nasir, Y.J. (1991). Threatened plants of Pakistan. In Ali, S.I. and Ghaffar, A. (eds), *Plant life of South Asia*. Department of Botany, University of Karachi, Karachi. Pp. 229–234.

Naskar, K. and Guha Bakshi, D.N. (1986). On the verge of extinction of some important mangrove species from the Sundarbans Delta in West Bengal. *J. Econ. Tax. Bot.* 8: 431–437.

Nath, D.M. (1960). Botanical survey of the Southern Shan States with a note on the vegetation of Inle Lake. *Burma Research Society Fiftieth Anniversary Publication* I: 161–418.

National Research Council (1992). *Neem: a tree for solving global problems*. BOSTID Report No. 71. National Academy Press, Washington, D.C. 141 pp.

Nayar, M.P. (1980). Endemism and patterns of distribution of endemic genera (angiosperms) in India. *J. Econ. Tax. Bot.* 1: 99–110.

Nayar, M.P. (1987). *In situ* conservation of wild flora resources. *Bull. Bot. Surv. India* 29(1–4): 319–333.

Nayar, M.P. and Ahmed, M. (1984). Phytogeographical significance of endemic genera (angiosperms) in Peninsular India and Sri Lanka. *Bull. Bot. Surv. India* 26: 63–70.

Nayar, M.P., Ahmed, M. and Raju, D.C.S. (1984). Endemic and rare plants of Eastern Ghats. *Indian J. Forestry* 7: 35–42.

Nayar, M.P. and Sastry, A.R.K. (eds) (1987-1990). *Red Data Book of Indian Plants*, 3 vols. Botanical Survey of India, Calcutta. (Vol. 1: 1987; vol. 2: 1988; vol. 3: 1990.)

Norberg-Hodge, H. (1991). *Ancient futures: learning from Ladakh*. Rider Books, London. 204 pp.

Nordal, A. (1963). *The medicinal plants and crude drugs of Burma. I. Collection of research material from indigenous sources during the years 1957–1961*. Oslo. 55 pp.

Pandey, R.P., Shetty, B.V. and Malhotra, S.K. (1983). A preliminary census of rare and threatened plants of Rajasthan. In Jain, S.K. and Rao, R.R. (eds), *An assessment of threatened plants of India*. Botanical Survey of India (Department of Environment), Botanic Garden, Howrah. Pp. 55–62.

Pandey, R.P., Shetty, B.V. and Verma, M.P. (1985). A checklist to the flora of the Desert National Park in Western Rajasthan. *J. Econ. Tax. Bot.* 6: 45–60.

Patwardhan, P.G. (1983). Rare and endemic lichens in the Western Ghats. In Jain, S.K. and Rao, R.R. (eds), *An assessment of threatened plants of India*. Botanical Survey of India (Department of Environment), Botanic Garden, Howrah. Pp. 318–322.

Pearce, E.A. and Smith, C.G. (1990). *The world weather guide*. Ed. 2. Hutchinson, London. 480 pp.

Prain, D. (1903). Flora of the Sundribuns. *Rec. Bot. Surv. India* 2: 231–370.

Prakash, U., Du Nai-zheng and Tripathi, P.P. (1992). Fossil woods from Tipam sandstones of northeast India with remarks on palaeoenvironment of the region during the middle Miocene. *Biological Memoirs* 18: 1–26.

Prakash, U. and Tripathi, P.P. (1992). Floral evolution and climatic changes during the Siwalik period. *Biological Memoirs* 18: 57–68.

Raghavan, R.S. (1977). Floristic studies in India – the Western Circle. *Bull. Bot. Surv. India* 19: 95–108.

Raju, D.C.S., Ahmedullah, M. and Nayar, M.P. (1987). Genetic potential in the flora of the Eastern Ghats of India. *J. Econ. Tax. Bot.* 9: 13–138.

Rao, R.R. (1977). Changing patterns in the Indian flora. *Bull. Bot. Surv. India* 19: 156–166.

Rao, R.R. and Haridasan, K. (1982). Notes on the distribution of certain rare, endangered or endemic plants of Meghalaya with a brief remark on the flora. *J. Bombay Nat. Hist. Soc.* 79: 93–99.

Rao, R.R. and Haridasan, K. (1985). A survey of wild plants of horticulture importance from Meghalaya, N.E. India. *J. Econ. Tax. Bot.* 6: 529–537.

Rao, R.R. and Haridasan, K. (1991). An ethnobotanical survey of medicinal and other useful plants from north-east India. *J. Econ. Tax. Bot.* 15: 423–436.

Rao, R.R. and Jamir, N.S. (1982). Ethnobotanical studies in Nagaland. II. 54 medicinal plants used by Nagas. *J. Econ. Tax. Bot.* 3: 11–17.

Rao, R.R. and Murti, S.K. (1990). North-east India – a major centre for plant diversity. *Indian J. Forestry* 13: 214–222.

Rao, R.S. (1979). Indian plant taxonomy. In Larsen, K. and Holm-Nielsen, L.B., *Tropical botany*. Academic Press, London. Pp. 153–163.

Rawat, G.S. and Srivastava, S.K. (1986). Recently introduced exotics in the flora of Himachal Pradesh. *J. Econ. Tax. Bot.* 8: 17–20.

Ridd, M.F. (1971). Faults in southeast Asia and the Andaman rhombochasm. *Nature, Physical Sciences* 229: 51–52.

Rodgers, W.A. and Gupta, S. (1989). The pitcher plant (*Nepenthes khasiana* Hk. f.) sanctuary of Jaintia Hills, Meghalaya: lessons for conservation. *J. Bombay Nat. Hist. Soc.* 86: 17–21.

Sahni, K.C. (1980). Vanishing Indian taxa and their conservation. In Nair, P.K.K. (ed.), *Glimpses in plant research. V. Modern methods in plant taxonomy*. Vikas Publishing House, New Delhi. Pp. 161–172.

Sharma, B.D. and Balakrishnan, N.P. (1993a). *Flora of India*, Vol. 1. Botanical Survey of India, Calcutta. 467 pp.

Sharma, B.D. and Balakrishnan, N.P. (1993b). *Flora of India*, Vol. 2. Botanical Survey of India, Calcutta. 625 pp.

Sharma, B.D. and Kulkarni, B.G. (1980). Floristic composition and peculiarities of Dev Raies (sacred groves) in Kolhapur District, Maharashtra. *J. Econ. Tax. Bot.* 1: 11–32.

Sharma, B.D. and Malhotra, S.K. (1984). A contribution to the ethnobotany of tribal areas in Maharashtra. *J. Econ. Tax. Bot.* 5: 533–537.

Sharma, B.D. and Sanjappa, M. (1993). *Flora of India*, Vol. 3. Botanical Survey of India, Calcutta. 639 pp.

Shen, S. (1991). Biological engineering for sustainable biomass production. In Wilson, E.O. (ed.), *Biodiversity*. National Academy Press, Washington, D.C. Pp. 377–389.

Shuleta, U., Baishya, A.K. and Ali, S. (1978). Observations on some economic plants of Mizoram. *Bull. Bot. Surv. India* 20: 48–52.

Singh, R.S. and Singh, N.I. (1985). A preliminary ethnobotanical studies [sic] on wild edible plants in the markets of Manipur I. *J. Econ. Tax. Bot.* 6: 699–703.

Singh, P.K., Singh, N.I. and Singh, L.J. (1988). Ethnobotanical studies on wild edible plants in the markets of Manipur II. *J. Econ. Tax. Bot.* 12: 113–119.

Stainton, J.D.A. (1972). *Forests of Nepal*. John Murray, London. 181 pp.

Stamp, L.D. (1925). *The vegetation of Burma*. University of Rangoon Research Monograph No. 1. Rangoon. 65 pp.

Stamp, L.D. and Lord, L. (1923). The ecology of part of the riverine tract of Burma. *J. Ecol.* 11: 129–159.

Stewart, R.R. (1982). *Flora of Pakistan. History and exploration of plants in Pakistan and adjoining areas*. Islamabad. 186 pp.

Subramanyam, K. and Nayar, M.P. (1974). Vegetation and phytogeography of the Western Ghats. In Mani, M.S. (ed.), *Ecology and biogeography in India*. Junk, The Hague. Pp. 178–196.

Synge, H. (1990). *Twenty opportunities for saving biological diversity. Priority places for possible U.K. aid*. WWF, Godalming. Pp. 25–26.

Takhtajan, A. (1986). *Floristic regions of the world*. University of California Press, Berkeley. 522 pp.

Tasnif, M. and Snead, R.E. (1964). An ecological survey of the vegetation of Las Bela area. *The Scientist, Pakistan* 42–48.

Udar, R. and Srivastava, S.C. (1983). Rare and endangered liverworts of India. In Jain, S.K. and Rao, R.R. (eds), *An assessment of threatened plants of India*. Botanical Survey of India (Department of Environment), Botanic Garden, Howrah. Pp. 303–312.

Vartak, V.D. (1983). Observations on rare, imperfectly known and endemic plants in the sacred groves of western Maharashtra. In Jain, S.K. and Rao, R.R. (eds), *An assessment of threatened plants of India*. Botanical Survey of India (Department of Environment), Botanic Garden, Howrah. Pp. 169–178.

Wilson, E.O. (1992). *The diversity of life*. Belknap Press of Harvard University Press, Cambridge, Massachusetts.

Wood, J.J. (1907). Plants of Chutia Nagpur including Jaspur and Sirguja. *Rec. Bot. Surv. India* 2: 1–170.

World Resources Institute (1992). *World resources 1992–93: a guide to the global environment*. Oxford University Press, New York. 385 pp. (Prepared in collaboration with UNEP and UNDP.)

World Resources Institute (1994). *World resources 1993–94: a guide to the global environment*. Oxford University Press, New York. (Prepared in collaboration with UNEP and UNDP.)

Yamazaki, T. (1988). A revision of the genus *Pedicularis* in Nepal. *The Himalayan Plants* 1: 91–161.

Zohary, M. (1973). *Geobotanical foundations of the Middle East*, 2 vols. Fischer, Stuttgart, and Swets and Zeitlinger, Amsterdam. 739 pp.

Acknowledgements

Grateful thanks are extended to M. Ahmedullah (Botanical Survey of India) for providing information on the Himalayas.

IRANO-TURANIAN REGIONAL CENTRE OF ENDEMISM: CPD SITE IS2

NANDA DEVI
India

Location: Western Himalaya, approximately between latitudes 30°16'–30°41'N and longitudes 79°40'–80°05'E, in the Chamoli District, Uttarkhand Division, Uttar Pradesh.

Area: 2000 km².

Altitude: 1000–7817 m (summit of Nanda Devi).

Vegetation: Temperate coniferous forests, subalpine conifer, birch and *Rhododendron* forests, alpine vegetation.

Flora: 900 flowering plant species so far recorded; rich lichen flora.

Useful plants: Many medicinal, edible and ornamental plants.

Other values: High wilderness quality, prevention of soil erosion, potential ecotourism.

Threats: No major existing threats, but proposed dam could adversely affect area.

Conservation: National Park (IUCN Management Category: I) and World Heritage Site status for 630.3 km². Proposed as a Biosphere Reserve.

Geography

The proposed Nanda Devi Biosphere Reserve lies approximately between latitudes 30°16'–30°41'N and longitudes 79°40'–80°05'E, at the junction of the Garhwal and Kumaon Himalayas, in the Chamoli District of Uttarkhand Division, Uttar Pradesh, in the upper watershed of the River Alaknanda.

The area comprises a glacial basin in the Western Himalayas, of approximately 799 km², enclosed by high mountain ranges, including such major peaks as Nanda Devi (7817 m), India's second highest mountain, Trisul (7120 m), Dunagiri (7066 m), Rishi Pahar (6992 m), Kalark (6931 m), Changbang (6864 m), Nanda Khat (6611 m), Mrigthuni (6855 m) and Berthartoli (6352 m).

Vegetation

As a result of its remoteness and relative inaccessibility, much of the area is still covered by pristine vegetation. Temperate coniferous forests, dominated by *Picea smithiana*, *Pinus wallichiana* and *Taxus wallichiana*, occur within the buffer zone. Subalpine forests are found near Latakhatak, Himtoli, Dibrugheta Deodi and Ramani, at an altitude of about 3350 m. Common tree species are *Abies pindrow*, *A. spectabilis*, *Betula utilis* and *Rhododendron campanulatum*. Shrubby and herbaceous species include *Rosa macrophylla*, *Senecio alatus*, *Smilacina pallida*, *Thalictrum reniforme* and *Viburnum cotonifolius*. Pure stands of *Betula utilis* and *Rhododendron campanulatum* occur up to the tree-line.

Alpine meadows are found only in the core zone of the reserve (which covers 300 km²). Common shrubs include *Cotoneaster* spp., *Juniperus* spp., *Rhododendron anthopogon* and *Salix* spp. The dominant herbaceous plants are *Anaphalis*

spp., *Aster* spp., *Cynanthus* spp., *Jurinea macrocephala*, *Morina longifolia*, *Potentilla* spp. and *Saussurea* spp., along with sedges and grasses.

CPD Site IS2: Nanda Devi, India. Photo: Botanical Survey of India.

Flora

The flora of the proposed Biosphere Reserve is very diverse and so far about 900 flowering plant species have been recorded (M. Ahmedullah *in litt.*). Certain groups, such as Ranunculaceae, Asteraceae, Rosaceae, Poaceae and Cyperaceae, are well-represented.

Rare endemics include *Carex nandadeviensis*, *Cypripedium elegans, C. himalaicum, Festuca nandadevica, Listera nandadeviensis, L. tenuis, Saussurea sudhanshui* and *Woodsia cycloloba*. The insectivorous *Pinguicula alpina* is common in alpine meadows, along with *Circaeaster agrestis*.

Forested areas are rich in fleshy species of fungi, including species in such genera as *Agaricus, Morchella* and *Polyporus*. Some of the species are edible. Festoons of lichens hang from trees in the temperate and subalpine forests. They include *Parmelia* spp. and *Usnea* spp.

Useful plants

The area is very rich in medicinal plants. Among the most important are *Aconitum balfourii, A. falconeri, Arnebia benthamii, Berberis aristata, Dactylorhiza hatagirea, Dioscorea deltoidea, Nardostachys grandiflora, Picrorhiza kurrooa* and *Podophyllum hexandrum*.

Many edible species are gathered from the wild by local villagers. Among them are *Allium wallichii* (both the leaves and bulbs of which are used as a vegetable), *Paeonia emodi* (tender shoots cooked and eaten as a vegetable), *Podophyllum hexandrum* (edible fruits) and *Viburnum cotonifolium* (edible fruits).

Many ornamental species are of potential value in horticulture. Some are already in cultivation, including *Cyananthus lobatus, Erigeron multiradiatus, Geranium* spp., *Hypericum* spp., *Primula macrophylla* and *Rhododendron campanulatum*.

Social and environmental values

Nanda Devi lies within the Western Himalayas Endemic Bird Area (EBA), which extends from western Pakistan and adjacent Afghanistan to central Nepal. Ten restricted-range bird species are endemic to this EBA; these are mainly confined to temperate and subalpine forests, although the threatened cheer pheasant (*Catreus wallichii*) occurs in grassland and scrub. As many as six of these species could occur in the Nanda Devi Biosphere Reserve.

The area is undoubtedly of high scenic value, with a dramatic backdrop of high mountain peaks and ridges, pristine forested slopes, and floristically-rich alpine meadows. There is great potential for developing ecotourism and mountain climbing in the region, but the core area has been closed to tourists since 1983.

Although the core zone (Nanda Devi National Park) of the proposed Biosphere Reserve is uninhabited, there are

CPD Site IS2: Nanda Devi, India. Photo: Botanical Survey of India.

settlements in the buffer zone. However, poaching persists within Nanda Devi National Park.

The forested mountain slopes help to prevent devastating avalanches and soil erosion.

Threats

There are no major threats to the region. Human interference is limited to the buffer zone where hill tribes practice terrace cultivation on mountain slopes. Local villagers also keep herds of goats and sheep which graze in large numbers in the area, but controls on grazing have now been introduced in most areas within the proposed Biosphere Reserve.

Between 1936–1982, increasing numbers of mountaineering expeditions visited the area. Their impact had local effects on the vegetation, as a result of trampling, route clearance and cutting of wood for fuel. Nanda Devi National Park has been closed to tourists (foreign and national) since 1983.

A proposal to build a dam across the River Ganga (formed by the confluence of the Alaknanda and Bhagirathi rivers) could adversely affect the Nanda Devi basin.

Conservation

The whole area is proposed as a Biosphere Reserve. Nanda Devi National Park (630.3 km²) (IUCN Management Category: I) was notified in 1982 and designated a World Heritage Site in 1988.

Several projects are underway to propagate rare plant species in *ex situ* cultivation. The Botanical Survey of India is currently engaged in surveying and plant inventory work to prepare a Flora of the proposed Biosphere Reserve.

References

Anon. (1987). The Nanda Devi Biosphere Reserve. Project document – 3. Department of Environment and Forests, New Delhi.

Hajra, P.K. (1983). A contribution to the botany of Nanda Devi National Park in Uttar Pradesh, India. Calcutta.

Khacher, Lavkumar (1978). The Nanda Devi Sanctuary – 1977. *J. Bombay Nat. Hist. Soc.* 75(3): 868–887.

Sandhu, B.S., Dorjee, L., and Purohit, N. (1982). *Nanda Devi Expedition – 1981.* Indian Mountaineering Foundation, Delhi.

Sarin, H.D. *et al.* (eds) (1982). *Indian mountaineer.* Special Nanda Devi Number 9. Indian Mountaineering Foundation, Delhi.

Acknowledgement

This Data Sheet was prepared by P.K. Hajra, Ministry of Environment and Forests, New Delhi.

EASTERN ASIATIC REGIONAL CENTRE OF ENDEMISM: CPD SITE IS4

NAMDAPHA
India

Location: Eastern Himalaya, between latitudes 27°00–28°51'N and longitudes 95°45'–97°30'E, in the Changlang and Lohit Districts of Arunachal Pradesh.

Area: c. 7000 km², of which the core area occupies c. 2500 km².

Altitude: 200–4578 m (summit of Dapha Bum).

Vegetation: Tropical evergreen and semi-evergreen rain forests, temperate to alpine vegetation.

Flora: At least 5000 vascular plant species, of which an estimated 2000–3000 species occur in the alpine zone; high endemism. Sino-Japanese, Indo-Burmese and Indo-Malayan affinities.

Useful plants: Many progenitors of cultivated plants, including wild relatives of bananas, citrus fruits, coffee, ginger, mango, pepper and yam; c. 150 timber tree species; medicinal and ornamental plants, particularly orchids and alpines.

Other values: Home for tribal inhabitants, rich fauna, forests provide protection for important water catchment area.

Threats: No major threats to core area, but command area and buffer zone threatened by local population pressure resulting from settlement of refugees and other settlers, firewood cutting, over-exploitation of agar and dhoop, shifting cultivation.

Conservation: Namdapha National Park (IUCN Management Category: II) covers 1985.2 km²; proposal to establish whole of region as a Biosphere Reserve now under consideration.

Geography

Namdapha is located at the junctions of the north-eastern Himalaya and outspurs of the Patkoi Ranges of Burma, in the Changlang and Lohit Districts of Arunachal Pradesh, between latitudes 27°00–28°51'N and longitudes 95°45'–97°30'E. The total area of the proposed reserve is approximately 7000 km², including a core area of about 2500 km², a buffer zone of 2000 km² and a command area of about 2500 km².

Altitude ranges from about 200 m in the lowlands to 4578 m at the summit of Dapha Bum. Other high mountain ridges in the area are: Champai Bum (2950 m), Yapawa Bum (2276 m), Litang Bum (1932 m), Teng Bum (1680 m), Ingkhu Bum (1827 m), Nanon Bum (1465 m) and Miao Bum (1198 m).

The region is drained by many perennial and seasonal rivers and streams. The four main rivers are the Lohit, Delei, Dihang and Dibang.

The Namdapha area is geologically recent in origin, dating back to the Pliocene period of the Tertiary era. The area is seismically active; a massive earthquake in the Lohit Valley in 1950 devastated much of the conifer forest in the valley (Kingdon-Ward 1953). The Tertiary and Quaternary rock sequences are an extension of those occurring in Nagaland and Upper Assam.

Namdapha adjoins North Myanmā (IS6), for which see separate Data Sheet.

Vegetation

Namdapha supports pristine and luxuriant tropical, temperate and alpine vegetation. Its unique geographical position, varied topography, high annual rainfall spread throughout the year, and the relatively little human impact, makes the area one of the richest botanical sites in India.

Tropical evergreen and semi-evergreen rain forests predominate. The lowland evergreen forests are among the largest remaining tracts of dipterocarp forest in India. The tallest trees of *Dipterocarpus retusus* sometimes attain a height of over 50 m at Namdapha. No single species dominates the lowland forest and there is no apparent clear-cut stratification. This is probably due to vigorous and continuous natural forest regeneration throughout the year in response to climatic and edaphic factors. The main trees present include (among others) *Albizia julibrissin* var. *mollis, Alnus nepalensis, Anthocephalus chinensis, Aquilaria malaccensis, Artocarpus chama, Bischofia javanica, Canarium strictum, Castanopsis* spp., *Celtis tetrandra, Dipterocarpus retusus, Duabanga grandiflora, Elaeocarpus* spp., *Ficus* spp., *Mangifera indica, Nauclea griffithii, Quercus* spp., *Shorea assamica, Terminalia myriocarpa* and *Toona ciliata*. Smaller trees include *Altingia excelsa, Castanopsis indica, Dalbergia assamica, Dysoxylum binectariferum, Elaeocarpus tectorius, Euodia trichotoma, Magnolia griffithii, Schima wallichii, Syzygium* spp., *Terminalia chebula* and *Turpinia pomifera*. The main shrubs present include *Aralia armata, Ardisia virens, Brassiopsis* spp., *Camellia caudata, Coffea khasiana, Morinda angustifolia* and *Saurauia* spp. There are many species of lianes and climbers, such as *Adenia trilobata, Argyreia argentea, Cayratia japonica, Cissus assamica, Dioscorea alata, Entada pursaetha, Gnetum* spp. and *Tetrastigma* spp. Epiphytes are common, and include species of *Aeschynanthes, Agapetes, Peperomia, Piper, Pothos,*

Raphidopora and *Schefflera*, as well as many orchids, ferns, bryophytes and lichens.

Kingdon-Ward (1930a, 1930b, 1953) made several expeditions into the area between 1926 and 1950 and published several accounts of the flora of the higher slopes. Temperate rain forest occurs at 1830–2745 m. The dominant tree genera are *Acer*, *Alnus*, *Betula*, *Castanopsis*, *Eriobotrya*, *Ilex*, *Illicium*, *Juniperus*, *Michelia*, *Pinus*, *Podocarpus*, *Populus*, *Pyrus*, *Quercus*, *Rhododendron*, *Schima* and *Tsuga*. Shrubs include species of *Corylopsis*, *Sorbus* and *Viburnum*, along with *Magnolia campbellii*, *M. globosa* and *M. rostrata* (Kaul and Haridasan 1987).

Tsuga forest, with numerous species of *Rhododendron*, occurs at higher altitudes; forests of *Pinus wallichiana* and *P. merkusii* occur in the Lohit District (Kaul and Haridasan 1987).

The alpine meadows above the tree-line are rich in species. Typical genera represented include *Aconitum*, *Corydalis*, *Diapensia*, *Meconopsis*, *Primula*, *Rheum* and *Rhododendron*. Malhotra and Hajra (1977) give a sketch of the vegetation of Arunachal Pradesh, including the alpine zone.

Flora

Namdapha has at least 5000 species of vascular plants (R. Mill 1993, *in litt.*), of which about 2000–3000 species occur in the alpine zone. Only about 60% of the area has been explored to date. Nevertheless, it is clear that the forests are very species-rich and contain important gene pools of crop relatives (see Useful Plants).

Namdapha harbours such botanical curiosities as the root parasites *Balanophora dioica* and *Rhopalocnemis phelloides* (Balanophoraceae), *Aegenetia acaulis* (Orobanchaceae) and *Sapria himalayana* (Rafflesiaceae). A number of primitive flowering plant genera are also represented, including *Exbucklandia*, *Houttuynia*, *Kadsura*, *Magnolia* and *Talauma*. The area is the north-western limit of the primitive conifer genus *Amentotaxus*, of which *A. assamicus* was recently described from the Delei Valley.

The flora is enriched with Sino-Japanese, Indo-Burmese, Indo-Malayan and Peninsular Indian elements. Chinese elements include such genera as *Actinidia*, *Anthocephalus*, *Camellia* and *Kadsura*; Indo-Malayan elements include *Balanophora*, *Engelhardtia* and *Exbucklandia*; Peninsular Indian elements include disjunct populations of *Butea parviflora*, *Cissampelos pareira*, *Dillenia indica*, *D. pentagyna*, *Eurya japonica*, *Elatostema platyphylla*, *Entada pursaetha*, *Mesua ferrea*, *Meliosma simplicifolia* and *Pavetta indica*.

Namdapha contains a number of rare and endangered taxa which are being depleted at an alarming rate in other parts of north-east India, including *Aeschynanthus superba*, *Angiopteris evecta*, *Aquilaria malaccensis*, *Balanophora dioica*, *Cyathea gigantea*, *Cymbidium eburneum*, *Gnetum gnemon*, *Liparis distans*, *Livistona jenkinsiana* and *Magnolia griffithii*. Local endemics include *Acer oblongum* var. *serrulatum*, *Aconitum lethale*, *Begonia arborensia*, *B. iridescens*, *Ceratostylis subulata*, *Chirita mishmensis*, *Paphiopedilum wardii*, *Piper clarkei*, *Rubus burkillii* and *Symplocos pealii*.

Useful plants

Namdapha has a wealth of plants of economic potential, including c. 150 timber tree species, wild relatives of cultivated crop plants, medicinal plants and ornamental species of potential value in horticulture.

Important timber species include *Ailanthus integrifolia* subsp. *calycina*, *Alnus nepalensis*, *Artocarpus* spp., *Canarium strictum*, *Dalbergia assamica*, *Duabanga grandiflora*, *Gmelina arborea*, *Terminalia myriocarpa*, and members of the family Dipterocarpaceae, including *Dipterocarpus macrocarpus*, *D. retusus* and *Shorea assamica*. *Aquilaria malaccensis* and *Canarium strictum* are in great demand for agar and dhoop (a type of resin), respectively.

Some of the most common medicinal plants used by local tribal people include *Achyranthes bidentata*, *Alpinia allughas*, *Amomum aromaticum*, *Aquilaria malaccensis*, *Barleria cristata*, *Callicarpa arborea*, *Citrus medica*, *Coptis teeta* (of which an endemic variety, var. *lohitensis*, has recently been described), *Costus speciosus*, *Dioscorea pentaphylla*, *Hedychium coronarium*, *Piper thomsonii* and *Solanum torvum*.

Namdapha includes important gene pools of crop relatives, including fruit tree relatives such as *Artocarpus* spp., *Citrus medica*, *Mangifera sylvatica*, and the banana relatives *Ensete glaucum*, *Musa rosacea* and *M. velutina*, as well as *Camellia caudata*, a relative of tea, and *Coffea benghalensis* and *C. khasiana*, wild relatives of coffee.

Considerable numbers of alpine species have been introduced into cultivation. There are many more ornamental plants of potential value in horticulture.

Social and environmental values

Most of the tribal groups of Arunachal Pradesh (e.g. Khamtis, Mishmis, Nocte, Singhpho, Tangsa and Wanchoo) live in the command area and gather products from the forest. They are not a threat to the core area.

Namdapha has a rich fauna, including more than 120 species of mammals, 560 species of birds, and 90 species of reptiles and amphibians. Tiger (*Panthera tigris*) (Endangered), leopard (*P. pardus*) (Vulnerable), snow leopard (*P. uncia*) (Endangered) and clouded leopard (*Neofelis nebulosa*) (Vulnerable) are present, an assemblage of large carnivores that is thought to be unique.

Namdapha lies within the Eastern Himalayas Endemic Bird Area (EBA), which comprises the main Himalayan range between east Nepal and west Yunnan, China, and the ranges between Nagaland, India, and Natma Taung, Myanmā. Fifteen of the 25 restricted-range bird species of this EBA have been recorded in this region, in subtropical, temperate and subalpine zone forests. They include the threatened Sclater's monal (*Lophophorus sclateri*), Blyth's tragopan (*Tragopan blythii*), rusty-bellied shortwing (*Brachypteryx hyperythra*), rusty-throated wren-babbler (*Spelaeornis badeigularis*), wedge-billed wren-babbler (*Sphenocichla humei*) and snowy-throated babbler (*Stachyris oglei*). More widespread threatened species which occur (or are likely to occur) here are white-bellied heron (*Ardea imperialis*), white-winged duck (*Cairina scutulata*), black-necked crane (*Grus nigricollis*) (non-breeding only), wood snipe (*Gallinago nemoricola*), Blyth's kingfisher (*Alcedo hercules*), rufous-necked hornbill (*Aceros nipalensis*) and beautiful nuthatch (*Sitta formosa*).

The forests of Namdapha protect important water catchment reserves.

Threats

Much of the area is still in a pristine condition and there are no major threats to the core area. However, a number of threats occur around the core area, particularly arising from local population pressure resulting from the settlement of refugees and other settlers. About 25,000 Chakma and Tibetan refugees have been settled on the western side of the Deban River in the buffer zone. They practice shifting cultivation. About 450 Lamas from Bhutan have been settled on the north bank of the Noa-Dihing River in close proximity to the core area. The State Forest Department of Arunachal Pradesh and Project Tiger Namdapha have proposed to the Arunachal Government that these refugees are resettled in more suitable areas.

Similar problems exist in the Gandhigram and Vijoynagar area on the south-eastern boundary of the proposed reserve, where the settlement of approximately 1600 Lisus and ex-servicemen has resulted in trees being cut for timber and fuelwood, and forests cleared for shifting cultivation. Illegal extraction of agar, dhoop and over-exploitation of several other forest products is a threat to some taxa.

A proposal exists to build a dam across the Noa-Dihing River at Burma Nala, as part of a hydroelectric power scheme. The Arunachal Chief Wildlife Warden and Project Tiger Namdapha have rejected the proposal.

Conservation

Scientific explorations of Namdapha began around the 1930s by Kingdon-Ward (1930a, b). Subsequently, numerous flora surveys have been carried out by the Botanical Survey of India and, since 1982, by a UNESCO MAB-sponsored project. However, the northern, north-eastern and south-eastern parts of Namdapha are yet to be thoroughly explored.

Namdapha was declared a Sanctuary under Assam Forest Regulation Act in 1972. Namdapha National Park (IUCN Management Category: II), covering an area of 1985.2 km², was notified in 1983 and designated a Tiger Reserve under Project Tiger that same year. A proposal to establish the whole of the region as a Biosphere Reserve is now under consideration. This would protect a core area of about 2500 km², and would include a buffer zone of about 2000 km² and command area of about 2500 km².

References

Anon. (1985, 1986). *Study and conservation of the plant resources of the proposed Namdapha Biosphere Reserve, Tirap District, Arunachal Pradesh*. Technical Report, Botanical Survey of India.

Deb, D.B. and Dutta, R.M. (1971). Contribution to the flora of Tirap Frontier Division. *J. Bombay Nat. Hist. Soc.* 68(3): 573–595.

Deb, D.B. and Dutta, R.M. (1972). Contribution to the flora of Tirap Frontier Division. *J. Bombay Nat. Hist. Soc.* 69(3): 547–573.

Deb, D.B. and Dutta, R.M. (1973). Contribution to the flora of Tirap Frontier Division. *J. Bombay Nat. Hist. Soc.* 70(1): 72–94.

Deb, D.B. and Dutta, R.M. (1974). Contribution to the flora of Tirap Frontier Division. *J. Bombay Nat. Hist. Soc.* 70: 266–294.

Joseph, J. and Chauhan, A.S. (1983). Namdapha Wildlife Sanctuary, Tirap, Arunachal Pradesh. In *Botany of some tiger habitats in India*. Pp. 26–29.

Kaul, R.N. and Haridasan, K. (1987). Forest types of Arunachal Pradesh – a preliminary study. *J. Econ. Tax. Bot.* 9: 379–389.

Kingdon-Ward, F. (1930a). *Plant hunting on the edge of the world*. Victor Gollancz, London. 383 pp. (Reprinted in 1985 by Cadogan Books, London. Part III, pp. 189–367, Assam, deals with the Delei Valley and Mishmi Hills.)

Kingdon-Ward, F. (1930b). The forests of the north-east frontier of India. *Empire Forestry J.* 9(1): 11–31.

Kingdon-Ward, F. (1953). The Lohit valley in 1950. *Proc. Linn. Soc. London* 164: 2–8.

Kulshrestha, V.K. and Shukla, B.K. (1987). Rare and interesting plant records of proposed Namdapha Biosphere Reserve, Arunachal Pradesh. *J. Econ. Tax. Bot.* 18: 61–63.

Malhotra, C.L. and Hajra, P.K. (1977). Status of floristic studies in Arunachal Pradesh. *J. Econ. Tax. Bot.* 18: 61–63.

Nair, S.C. (1981). *The Namdapha Biosphere Reserve*. Project Document, MAB Programme, Department of Environment, Government of India.

Panigrahi, G. and Joseph, J. (1966). A botanical tour to Tirap Frontier Division, NEFA. *Bull. Bot. Surv. India* 8: 142–157.

Sharma, B.D., Chauhan, A.S. and Wadhwa, B.M. (1990). *Study and conservation of the plant resources of the proposed Namdapha Biosphere Reserve, Arunachal Pradesh*. Technical Report (Part 1), t. 1–47. Botanical Survey of India. 650 pp.

Acknowledgements

This Data Sheet was prepared by Dr D.K. Singh and Dr A.S. Chauhan (Botanical Survey of India, Eastern Circle, Shillong), with additional information supplied by Dr Robert R. Mill (Royal Botanic Garden, Edinburgh).

EASTERN ASIATIC REGIONAL CENTRE OF ENDEMISM: CPD SITE IS5

NATMA TAUNG (MOUNT VICTORIA) AND RONGKLANG RANGE (CHIN HILLS) Myanmā

Location: The Rongklang Range (Chin Hills) lies in southern Chin State, western Myanmā, approximately between latitudes 20°45'–24°00'N and longitudes 93°20'–94°05'E. It forms part of the Burma Arc on Myanmā's western seaboard.

Area: c. 25,000 km².

Altitude: 500–3053 m (summit of Natma Taung, or Mount Victoria).

Vegetation: Tropical semi-evergreen forest below 1000 m; subtropical evergreen forest at 1000–2130 m, temperate semi-evergreen forest at 1830–3053 m, savanna and alpine vegetation.

Flora: Estimated 2500 vascular plant species. Endemics mainly in alpine zone, but some occur at mid-altitudes.

Useful plants: Local Chin population are known to use plants from lower forest zones, including orchids (possibly for decoration); there are many plants of horticultural value, especially rhododendrons, daphnes, primulas and *Ficus benjamina*.

Other values: Refuge for Himalayan bear, leopard, tiger, hoolock gibbon and other mammals; one endemic bird on Natma Taung (white-browed nuthatch) and four others whose only known Burmese locality is Natma Taung.

Threats: Slash and burn agriculture.

Conservation: Proposed protected area covers 364 km².

Geography

The Rongklang Range (the southern Chin Hills) lies in Chin State in west-central Myanmā, between latitudes 20°45'–24°00'N and longitudes 93°20'–94°05'E. The Rongklang forms part of the Burma Arc, a range of mountains extending for 700 km from the Eastern Himalaya through the Naga Hills and Manipur Hills of north-east India, the Letha Range (or northern Chin Hills), Rongklang and Arakan Yoma of western Myanmā, to the Andaman and Nicobar Islands. The Rongklang Range is separated from the Letha Range to the north by the Manipur River. The southern and northern Chin Hills have a combined length of about 400 km and their width varies from 160 to 250 km. There are several peaks over 2500 m, the highest being Natma Taung (Mount Victoria) (3053 m), the highest peak in southern and central Myanmā. Most of Chin State lies above 500 m. Drainage from the eastern slopes is into the Ayeyarwady (Irrawaddy), either directly or, in the northern part, by streams which flow into the Ayeyarwady's major western tributary, the Chindwinn. On the western side, the rivers drain into the Bay of Bengal. Most rivers are permanent.

The Rongklang were uplifted in the late Cretaceous or early Eocene. At that time the lower Ayeyarwady valley was a marine gulf between the Shan Plateau to the east and the newly raised Chin Plateau on the west. The Rongklang may have been joined to the older Shillong Plateau of Meghalaya or have been a separate island (Kingdon-Ward 1958). They show no signs of having been glaciated in the Pleistocene. There are, however, signs of injection of harder crystalline rocks into softer subcrystalline material.

The Rongklang have a typical Burmese monsoon climate. Annual rainfall varies from 1659 mm at Mindat, near Natma Taung, in the south-east part of the range, to about 3800 mm on the western seaboard (facing the Bay of Bengal). Together with the Arakan Yoma to the south, the Rongklang Range is responsible for the Dry Belt of inner Myanmā by blocking the intrusion of the south-west monsoon. Frost never occurs below 1676 m but above 2438 m it becomes an important factor in determining the vegetation.

Chin State had a population of 368,985 in 1983.

Vegetation

Apart from Natma Taung, the Rongklang Range is almost unexplored botanically. Small collections (deposited at Edinburgh) were made on short visits by Cooper in 1924 and by Unwin in 1926. Neither appears to have published anything concerning their expeditions. Kingdon-Ward (1958) published an informative account of the flora of Natma Taung and its environs. No other account of the vegetation of the area has been traced. Kingdon-Ward differentiated three principal types of forest on Natma Taung and the surrounding Rongklang: tropical semi-evergreen forest (monsoon forest), subtropical evergreen forest and temperate semi-evergreen forest.

Tropical semi-evergreen forest (monsoon forest), dominated by *Tectona grandis* (teak), together with *Bauhinia variegata*, *Lagerstroemia flos-reginae* and *Derris robusta*, occurs up to about 1000 m. The forest contains many strangling figs (*Ficus* spp.), species of *Hibiscus* and *Strobilanthes*. Epiphytes are few but there are many lianes, such as *Congea tomentosa* and *Mucuna pruriens*.

Subtropical evergreen forest occurs at 1000–2130 m. This is below the mist-line and mainly below the frost-line. Two distinct subtypes were recognized by Kingdon-Ward: a fire preclimax pine savanna and mixed evergreen broadleaved forest. Pine savanna, dominated by *Pinus kesiya* (= *P. insularis, P. khasia*), occurs at 1000–2130 m on south-facing slopes and ridges. The forest contains numerous lianes (e.g. species of *Aristolochia, Jasminum* and *Vitis*) and perennial twiners (e.g. species of *Codonopsis, Stephania* and *Thunbergia*). Terrestrial orchids, such as *Arundina bambusifolia*, and lilies, such as *Lilium wallichianum* (on Natma Taung), also occur.

Mixed evergreen broadleaved forest is composed of several species of oak, such as *Q. spicata*, and species of *Castanopsis, Eugenia, Saurauia, Eriobotrya* and *Schima*, together with a wide variety of other arboreal species including the cycad *Cycas circinalis*, the palm *Phoenix humilis* and dicotyledonous trees such as *Anneslea fragrans, Helicia erratica, Kydia calycina* and *Michelia baillonii*. There are several species of fig, including *Ficus benjamina*.

Temperate semi-evergreen forest occurs from 1830 m (above the mist-line) to the summit. Species of *Alnus, Betula, Carpinus, Prunus, Pyrus* and *Torreya* occur between 1830 and 2134 m. These are replaced between 2134–2438 m by species of *Castanea, Cornus, Eriobotrya, Laurus, Quercus, Schima* and *Taxus*. In contrast to the other forest types, epiphytes (including *Aeschynanthus, Agapetes, Rhododendron cuffeanum*, aroids, *Dendrobium* and *Pleione*) are numerous. Between 2438 and 2740 m, *Quercus xylocarpa* is the dominant oak; this is replaced above 2743 m by *Q. semecarpifolia, Pinus kesiya* and *Rhododendron arboreum* (the last two extending down to 1200 m).

Shrubs at the highest altitudes (c. 3000 m) include *Hypericum patulum* and *Rhododendron burmanicum*. Herbaceous plants of this alpine forest include species of *Aconitum, Lactuca, Pedicularis* and *Veronica*. On Natma Taung, large areas are covered by *Anemone obtusiloba, Iris kumaonensis, Primula denticulata, P. nudicaulis* and species of *Allium, Anaphalis, Potentilla, Roscoea, Sedum* and *Swertia*.

Parts of the summit ridge are covered by a temperate savanna composed of various shrubs (e.g. *Rhododendron arboreum, R. burmanicum, Buddleja fallowiana, B. paniculata, Colquhounia coccinea, Cornus oblonga*, and species of *Daphne, Leycesteria* and *Lonicera*), tall grasses and herbs (e.g. species of *Aconitum, Delphinium, Geranium* and *Thalictrum*).

Flora

It is estimated that there are about 2500 vascular plant species in the region. By reason of its altitude and isolation from peaks of comparable height, Natma Taung is an "ecological island" (Blower 1985) and a refuge for numerous temperate and subalpine species. Endemics occur mainly in the alpine zone, but there are some at mid-altitudes. Endemics include *Rhododendron burmanicum, R. cuffeanum* (Hutchinson 1919), *Agapetes unwinii* (Evans 1927), *Viola unwinii* (Becker 1931), *Mantisia wardii* (Burtt and Smith 1966), *Geranium wardii* (Yeo 1975), *Roscoea australis* (Cowley 1982) and at least four species of grasses (Bor 1958): *Agrostis burmanica, A. mackliniae, Apocopis anomalus* and *Tripogon wardii*. All these species occur above 1800 m on Natma Taung. Other species doubtless remain to be described; they include a peculiar member of the Boraginaceae, which may represent a genus new to science (R.R. Mill unpublished).

The Rongklang often provide the only Myanmā locality for plants occurring in neighbouring parts of Manipur, Tripura and Assam, such as *Trichodesma khasianum* and *Pyrus khasiana*. Other species have disjunct distributions, occurring on Natma Taung and localities further north. For example, *Rosa sericea* is known from Natma Taung and Htawgaw. Some species which may have spread northwards along the Burma Arc from more tropical forests to the south have their northernmost limit in the Rongklang.

Two floristic lists, Gage (1901) and Fischer (1938), enumerate 317 and 1360 species, respectively, for the neighbouring Lushai Hills of Mizoram in north-east India.

Useful plants

Very little information is available on economic plants of the Rongklang although IUCN Protected Areas Data Unit (1987) noted that the local Chin people collect orchids (see below). Gage (1901) noted that the fruits of *Vaccinium bancanum* are eaten. Local people make potent alcoholic beverages from the leaves and fruits of *Solanum verbascifolium*, the fruits of *S. indicum*, the bark of *Aporosa oblonga* and *Sideroxylon assamicum* or *S. tomentosum*, and the rhizomes of *Zingiber* spp.

Cinnamomum tamala was formerly used in tattooing (Gage 1901); the root of *Buddleja asiatica* is made into a paste and taken in rice water as a tonic.

There are many species of ornamental plants, including orchids, rhododendrons, buddleias, daphnes, primulas and the popular house plant *Ficus benjamina*.

Social and environmental values

Hunting and habitat loss have eliminated several mammals from the area during modern times, including gaur (*Bos gaurus*), elephant (*Elephas maximus*) and rhinoceros. However, tiger (*Panthera tigris*), leopard (*P. pardus*), Himalayan bear (*Ursus arctos*), serow (*Capricornis sumatrensis*), hoolock gibbon (*Hylobates hoolock*), sambar (*Cervus unicolor*), goral (*Nemorhaedus goral*) and mythin (*Bos frontalis*) still occur (Blower 1985; IUCN Protected Areas Data Unit 1987).

Natma Taung and Rongklang are included in the Eastern Himalayas Endemic Bird Area (EBA), which comprises the main Himalayan range between east Nepal and west Yunnan, China, and the ranges between Nagaland, India and Natma Taung. Nine of the 25 restricted-range bird species of this EBA have been recorded on Natma Taung and in the Rongklang, including the threatened Blyth's tragopan (*Tragopan blythii*), black-breasted parrotbill (*Paradoxornis flavirostris*) and white-browed nuthatch (*Sitta victoriae*). Four of the restricted-range species are endemic to the mountains between Nagaland, India, and Natma Taung, including the white-browed nuthatch which is only known from Natma Taung. All of the restricted-range species of this region are found in subtropical or temperate zone forests.

The small local population of Chin people, who live below 2134 m, practise shifting cultivation, growing rice and maize; they collect beeswax, firewood, fruit and orchids from the lower forests (IUCN Protected Areas Data Unit 1987).

Threats

Taunggya (shifting) cultivation is by far the most serious threat to the remaining undisturbed natural vegetation. Secondary bamboo scrub occurs when the cycle of forest clearance is too short to allow forest to regenerate. Primary climax vegetation below about 2500 m has been virtually eliminated, including that of the more accessible parts of Natma Taung (IUCN Protected Areas Data Unit 1987).

Conservation

No part of the Rongklang is at present officially protected. Part of Natma Taung was proposed as a National Park after an ecological survey undertaken by FAO (FAO 1983). The proposed protected area is the whole of the mountain, from the summit down to either 2134 m or 1829 m, the latter being the preferred contour line. If this lower level is accepted, the area of the proposed Natma Taung National Park would be approximately 364 km². Park management would require the support of local people and the curbing of taunggya in the immediate vicinity.

References

Becker, W. (1931). New species of *Viola* from south-east Asia. *Notes Roy. Bot. Gard. Edinb.* 16: 147–148.

Blower, J. (1985). Conservation priorities in Burma. *Oryx* 19(2): 79–85.

Bor, N.L. (1958). Notes on Asiatic grasses: XXIX. New species from Burma. *Kew Bull.* 12: 414–418.

Burtt, B.L. and Smith, R.M. (1966). *Mantisia wardii*: a new Burmese species of Zingiberaceae. *Notes Roy. Bot. Gard. Edinb.* 28: 287–290.

Carey, B.S. and Tucker, H.N. (1896). *The Chin Hills*, 2 vols. (Reprinted in 1983 by Cultural Publishing House, Delhi.)

Cowley, E.J. (1982). A revision of *Roscoea* (Zingiberaceae). *Kew Bull.* 36: 747–777.

Evans, W.E. (1927). Some interesting and undescribed Vacciniaceae from Burma and western China. *Notes Roy. Bot. Gard. Edinb.* 15: 199–208.

FAO (1983). *A survey of Natma Taung (Mount Victoria) southern Chin Hills. Nature conservation and national parks project FO/BUR/80/006.* Field Report 20/83. FAO, Rangoon. 18 pp.

Fischer, C.E.C. (1938). The flora of the Lushai Hills. *Rec. Bot. Surv. India* 12: 75–161.

Gage, A.T. (1898). The vegetation of the District of Minbu in Upper Burma. *Rec. Bot. Surv. India* 1: 1–141.

Gage, A.T. (1901). A botanical tour of the South Lushai Hills. *Rec. Bot. Surv. India* 1: 331–369.

Hutchinson, J. (1919). The Maddeni series of *Rhododendron*. *Notes Roy. Bot. Gard. Edinb.* 12: 1–84.

IUCN Protected Areas Data Unit (1987). IUCN Directory of Indomalayan Protected Areas. Burma: draft. World Conservation Monitoring Centre, Cambridge, U.K. (Unpublished typescript.)

Kingdon-Ward, F. (1958). A sketch of the flora and vegetation of Mount Victoria in Burma. *Acta Horti Gotoburgensis* 22: 53–74.

Yeo, P.F. (1975). *Geranium* species from Mount Victoria in Burma. *Notes Roy. Bot. Gard. Edinb.* 34: 195–200.

Acknowledgement

This Data Sheet was prepared by Dr Robert R. Mill (Royal Botanic Garden, Edinburgh).

NORTH MYANMĀ
Myanmā

Location: North of latitude 25°00'N and between longitudes 96°00' and 98°45'E, including the whole of Kachin State and the northern part of Sagaing Division. It comprises the Kachin Hills, the Angpawng Bum and associated ranges and river systems.

Area: 115,712 km².

Altitude: c. 150–5881 m (summit of Hka Kabo Razi).

Vegetation: Lowland tropical forest, various types of monsoon forest, mixed and coniferous temperate forest, *Rhododendron* forest and alpine meadows.

Flora: c. 6000 vascular plant species, of which perhaps 25% are endemic. The flora contains Indomalayan, Sino-Himalayan and arctic-alpine relicts. 1 near-endemic family (Dipentodonaceae); several endemic or near-endemic genera. Centre of diversity for *Rhododendron* (more than 80 species), *Agapetes, Vaccinium* and many other genera.

Useful plants: *Fritillaria roylei* and *Coptis teeta* are widely used medicinally; many species of ornamental plants, including rhododendrons, primulas, *Meconopsis betonicifolia, Ficus elastica* and *F. benjamina*.

Other values: Ethnic diversity, including an endangered hill tribe, the Daru; major bird migration route; major centre (together with Assam) for Lepidoptera.

Threats: Slash and burn agriculture below about 2400 m; increasing population pressure. Threats to vegetation above 2400 m are minimal and virtually all the vegetation is intact.

Conservation: Two small protected areas (Pidaung Game Sanctuary and Tamanthi Wildlife Sanctuary), both at low altitude and not protecting valuable botanical sites. More conservation areas needed, particularly to protect remaining areas of forest in the cultivation zone.

Geography

The area under consideration is "Upper Burma", as defined by Kingdon-Ward (1913, 1930, 1937, 1944, 1946, 1949, 1956, 1957). It is a mountainous region including the whole of Kachin State, together with the northern part of Sagaing Division, in the far north of Myanmā. There are four more or less parallel mountain ranges, orientated approximately north-south. From west to east, these are: the Angpawng Bum, which forms the west boundary between Myanmā and Nagaland (north-east India); the Kumon Taungdan and Shanngaw Taungdan, which together form the Kachin Hills proper; and the western slopes of the Gaoligong or Goligong Shan (Kingdon-Ward's "Irrawaddy-Salween divide"), whose main, eastern, slopes lie in Yunnan (China). The region therefore adjoins two other CPD sites, namely: Namdapha (IS4) in India and the Gaoligong Mountain, Nu Jiang River and Biluo Snow Mountains region (EA26) in China. These areas are treated in separate Data Sheets (the last named is included in the China and East Asia region).

There are only two extensive areas of lowland in North Myanmā: the Hnkawng Valley in the west, and the basin of the Mali Hka. Most land, apart from these valleys, is above 1500 m. Some of the highest peaks are Saramati (3826 m), Bumba Bum (3411 m), Chingwin Bum (3292 m) and Nanggum Bum (3204 m). The highest of all is Hka Kabo Razi (5881 m), the highest peak in Myanmā, located in the extreme north-west of the region. Principal rivers are the Chindwinn, Mali Hka and N'mai (Me) Hka. The area between the Mali Hka and the N'mai Hka near their confluence (north of Myitkyina) is known as The Triangle.

The population of the region is relatively small but ethnically varied, including the Shan (wet rice cultivators in the lowlands), Kachin and Chinese (originating from Yunnan and who practice permanent terraced rice cultivation) (Kingdon-Ward 1941; Leach 1954). The Kachin include numerous tribal groups with different dialects. They include Dulong, Basen, Gauri, Atsi, Maru, Lashi, Nung and Lisu, as well as some lesser known tribes. These various peoples are agriculturalists and utilize many wild plant species (see Useful plants).

Vegetation

The only detailed account of the vegetation is that of Kingdon-Ward (1944, 1945, 1946). This, together with information in his travel books (Kingdon-Ward 1913, 1923, 1930, 1937, 1949) and the much briefer account of the lower parts of the Kachin Hills by Pottinger and Prain (1898), form the basis of the present account.

Of all the regions of Myanmā, the north has by far the greatest variety of vegetation types. These include some which are not found elsewhere in Myanmā. Kingdon-Ward (1944, 1945) identified 13 climax vegetation types, falling into eight main classes. These are described briefly below.

Tropical evergreen rain forest occurs up to 600 m altitude on the Hkamti Plain (wherever it is not cultivated) and in the valley bottoms of the lower Mali Hka, the Nam Tisang and the N'mai Hka rivers. The forest is almost entirely Indomalayan in composition. Typical tree species are *Mesua ferrea* (ironwood), *Stereospermum personatum, Terminalia myriocarpa, Dipterocarpus alatus* and *D. turbinatus*. Pandans (such as *Pandanus furcatus*) and palms (such as *Caryota urens*) occur, along with numerous strangling figs (such as *Ficus elastica* and *F. benjamina*), tree ferns, lianes and climbers (including the spectacular *Thunbergia grandiflora*). Epiphytes increase in abundance with altitude.

Subtropical hill forest occurs at 450–1675 m. The upper limit of this zone is defined by the lower limit of *Bucklandia populnea*, which occurs only above about 1525 m. The forest includes Magnoliaceae, Lauraceae and some Dipterocarpaceae (below 915 m), while above this altitude are Fagaceae, Meliaceae, tree ferns and climbing palms. Characteristic tree species include *Acer pinnatinervium, Aesculus assamicus, Betula alnoides, Carpinus viminea, Castanopsis argentea* and *Magnolia pterocarpa*. Lianas include *Jasminum duclouxii, J. pericallianthum, Lonicera hildebrandii*, and species of *Bauhinia, Clematis, Mussaenda* and *Rubus*. Terrestrial orchids include *Cypripedium villosum* (endemic to Myanmā) and *Paphiopedilum wardii* (a strict endemic). Although Indomalayan in character, the flora above 1525 m includes many Eastern Asiatic elements.

Subtropical pine-oak forest occurs at 1000–1980 m in the Ngawchang valley between Htawgaw and Gangfang, on the border with Yunnan. Dominant trees are *Pinus kesiya, Quercus incana, Q. serrata* and *Q. griffithii*. These form an open parkland amongst bracken, grass and scattered shrubs. The herbaceous flora is rich and is almost unique in North Myanmā. It includes *Anemone begoniifolia, Gentiana cephalantha, Gerbera piloselloides, Inula cappa, Lilium bakerianum, L. ochraceum* var. *burmanicum, Primula denticulata* and *Senecio densiflora*. The forest is possibly a fire preclimax; increasing the fire regime on the hillsides favours the spread of *Primula denticulata* and the two species of *Lilium*.

Temperate rain forest (monsoon forest) includes warm temperate, cool temperate and temperate pine forests. Warm temperate rain forest occurs at 1525–2135 m in areas with distinct spring and winter seasons, with little snow in winter. Climbing palms, bamboos and tree ferns may reach the zenith of their abundance at the lower altitudinal limits of warm temperate rain forest. Tropical genera are less in evidence, while Northern and Eastern Asiatic species increase. Typical trees are *Alnus nepalensis, Betula cylindrostachya, Bucklandia populnea* (whose vertical range indicates the upper and lower levels of the warm temperate rain forest) and some palm-like arboreal Araliaceae. The epiphytic shrub flora is very rich, including species in the Maddenii and Vaccinioides series of *Rhododendron*.

Cool temperate rain forest occurs at 1830–2440 m. In some parts of North Myanmā the distinction between this and warm temperate rain forest is not very clear, but where the mountains are more than 4600 m high it is better defined. The indicator is the appearance of the main belt of large shrub rhododendrons, such as *R. decorum, R. magnificum, R. bullatum, R. crinitum* and *R. neriiflorum*. These flower mainly in February and March, coinciding with a major bird migration.

Temperate pine forest occurs at 1370–2440 m. The dominant species is *Pinus excelsa*, which forms open parkland on exposed slopes. This species also occurs as scattered trees within broadleaved forests of *Acer, Ilex, Laurus, Prunus* and *Quercus*. There is a thick bamboo undergrowth; woody climbers include *Aristolochia griffithii, Clematis forrestii* and *Paederia foetida*.

Mixed temperate forest occurs at 2135–2745 m. It is transitional between broadleaved temperate rain forest below and *Abies* (silver fir) forest above. Its limits appear to be defined by the lowest altitude at which winter frost is prevalent and (upper limit) that at which snow lies for an appreciable time. The dominant genera are *Quercus, Magnolia, Acer, Prunus, Ilex* and *Rhododendron*; coniferous species include *Picea brachytyla, Tsuga dumosa, Larix griffithiana* and *Taiwania flousiana*. The latter is disjunct from the allied *T. cryptomerioides* of Taiwan and adjacent eastern and central China. The shrub flora is very diverse, including species of *Acer, Berberis, Clethra, Enkianthus, Euonymus, Hydrangea, Photinia, Rhododendron, Rubus* and *Sorbus*, while a notable species of the ground flora is *Chamaepericlymenum suecicum*, an arctic-alpine relict. Moss forest is a special development of mixed temperate forest which occurs in localities such as Mungu Hkyet in the Tamai valley.

Silver fir forest occurs at 2745–3660 m. At this altitude, deep snow lies for at least a month. The forest is dominated by *Abies fargesii*, but there are also species of *Acer, Betula, Rhododendron* and *Magnolia*. At higher altitudes, the forest is more open and bamboo (*Arundinaria*) thickets occur. In open meadows, tall alpine herbs flourish. Species include *Lilium giganteum, Meconopsis paniculata* and *Notholirion campanulatum*. From 3050 m upwards, primulas increase in numbers and diversity; species include *P. agleniana* var. *thearosa* (the tea-rose primula endemic to the Seinghku Valley), *P. calthifolia, P. eucyclia* and *P. sikkimensis*.

Subalpine rhododendron scrub occurs between 3350–3960 m. There are many species of *Rhododendron* – at least 20 species are known to occur. The dominant above 3350 m is *R. selense* which forms dense thickets with pink and cream flowers in spring. Of at least 12 dwarf species of *Rhododendron* found in North Myanmā, about half are confined to subalpine scrub. A very wide range of herbaceous alpine plants is found. They include *Caltha palustris, Cypripedium tibeticum, Nomocharis souliei, Omphalogramma souliei*, and several primulas. Many of these species occur in single-species drifts.

Alpine vegetation occurs between 3660–4575 m. Shrubs include several dwarf rhododendrons (such as *R. calciphila, R. crebriflorum, R. chryseum, R. riparium, R. sanguineum* and *R. saluenense*), *Cassiope fastigiata, Potentilla fruticosa* and *Rosa sericea*. The main herbaceous genera include *Alchemilla, Androsace, Anemone, Diapensia, Draba, Gentiana, Leontopodium, Pedicularis, Saussurea, Saxifraga* and *Viola*. Screes are colonized by species which have very long tap roots. Examples include *Picrorhiza scrophulariiflora* and *Oreosolen wattii*.

Flora

Kingdon-Ward (1944) estimated that there were at least 6000 species of vascular plants in North Myanmā. Little exploration has taken place since his day, but in the heyday of plant hunting expeditions, Upper Myanmā was a favourite haunt of both Kingdon-Ward, who made eight journeys there between 1914 and 1942, and George Forrest, who explored the Upper Thanlwin (Salween), N'mai Hka and Shweli-Salween divides from the Yunnan side between 1917 and 1930. Reginald Farrer also made collections in the Htawgaw area of extreme north-east Myanmā; other collectors who have visited parts of the area include Pottinger and Prain (1898) and some Burmese such as U Tha Hla and U Chit Ko Ko.

Floristically, the area is one of the richest and most diverse in mainland Asia. This is explained partly by the tremendous range of topography and partly because of North Myanmā's geographical and biogeographical situation at the meeting point of at least four distinct floras: the Assam-Indian, the Eastern Himalayan, the Indomalayan and the Chinese. There are floristic (and faunistic) connections with Madagascar and South Africa, indicating that the area is the refuge for at least a few ancient Gondwanaland relicts. Kingdon-Ward (1957) emphasized the relictual nature of much of the flora, by describing it as a "Miocene reserved forest".

Unlike the rest of Myanmā, the whole of the area was affected by the Pleistocene glaciation. The result is that, compared with other areas of Myanmā, the Indomalayan element in the flora is less prevalent, and restricted to river valleys below 2440 m. Above 2440 m, the flora is mainly Indo-Himalayan in character. In the extreme north are Tibetan elements, while in the west there is a strong influence from Assam and Arunachal Pradesh. At high altitudes, above about 3500 m, the important families are mainly temperate, such as Caryophyllaceae, Gentianaceae, Geraniaceae, Primulaceae, Ranunculaceae, Rosaceae and Saxifragaceae.

Endemism is significant in most altitudinal zones. The endemics include some very remarkable species, such as a unique epiphytic lily, *Lilium arboricola*. The following are examples of endemics of each vegetation type:

❖ Tropical evergreen forest: *Agapetes wardii, Albizia vernayana, Camellia stenophylla, Strobilanthes arenicolus* and *Syzygium cuttingii*.

❖ Subtropical hill forest: *Agapetes adenobotrys, A. pubiflora, Brachytome wardii, Lactuca gracilipetiolata, Lasianthus wardii, Paphiopedilum wardii* and *Strobilanthes stramineus*.

❖ Subtropical pine forest: *Paphiopedilum wardii, Primula densa* and *Stemona wardii*.

❖ Warm-temperate rain forest: *Aeschynanthus wardii, Aster helenae, Diplycosia alboglauca, Ixora kingdon-wardii, Leycesteria insignis, Litsea cuttingii, Primula dictyophylla, Rhododendron dendricola* and *Sorbus paucinervis*.

❖ Cool-temperate rain forest: *Euonymus burmanica, Primula burmanica, Rhododendron agapetum, R. insculptum, R. magnificum, R. taggii* and *Rubus chaetocalyx*.

❖ Mixed temperate forest: *Acer taronense, Berberis hypokeriana, Ilex burmanica, Juniperus coxii, Prunus kingdon-wardii, Rhododendron butyricum* and *R. vesiculifolium*.

❖ Silver fir forest: *Berberis burmanica, Gaultheria minuta, Primula eucyclia, P. agleniana* var. *thearosa* and *Sorbus wardii*.

❖ Rhododendron scrub: *Cremanthodium wardii, C. farreri, Meconopsis violacea* and 4 species of *Rhododendron*.

❖ Alpine vegetation: Apparently few endemics, but among them *Primula fea*.

North Myanmā is a centre of diversity for several genera of Ericaceae, including *Agapetes* (G. Argent, pers. comm.), *Rhododendron* (more than 80 species present), *Vaccinium*, *Rubus* (some 24 species), *Sorbus* (at least 20), *Prunus* (at least 11) and *Pedicularis* (more than 10). There is one monotypic, near-endemic family, Dipentodonaceae (*Dipentodon sinicus*), which also occurs in adjacent China.

Useful plants

Pottinger and Prain (1898) provide some information on plants used by the Kachin Hills people. Kingdon-Ward also mentions numerous observations in many of his works; the treatment in Kingdon-Ward (1941) is particularly detailed but covers only the Hpimaw and Htawgaw Hills.

All Kachin tribes practice shifting cultivation. The main crops are rice, maize, marrows, pumpkins and *Dolichos lablab*. Cotton and tea (native) are grown for fibre and beverages, respectively. Above 1967 m, rice is replaced by maize, *Setaria italica, Eleusine coracana* and buckwheat (*Fagopyrum esculentum*). Tobacco is widely cultivated.

Oil from *Ricinus communis* is used in lamps; beer is obtained from rice, *Setaria* and *Eleusine*. *Caryota urens* is used by the Kachins to make a waterproof coat (li-kyeng) and also to construct the walls and floors of houses where bamboos are scarce. The Marus boil and eat the pith of the stem as a kind of sago. A dark blue dye is obtained from *Strobilanthes flaccidifolius*, while *Rubia manjith* yields a particularly deep red madder dye.

Rosaceae contains several plants of food value, including *Cydonia cathayensis, Fragaria elatior* and many species of *Rubus*. Bamboos are used for carrying water, for making ropes, matting and bows and arrows. *Arundinaria* is used to make walking sticks and pipe bowls. Some of the rattan palms of the tropical and subtropical forest zones are used to make suspension bridges.

Many plants are used medicinally, most being employed by specific tribes. Among the more widely used are *Fritillaria roylei* and *Coptis teeta* (used by Chinese for the treatment of malaria and as a tonic or aphrodisiac). These two species are dug up in vast quantities and exported to China.

One of the rarest and most heavily exploited trees is *Taiwania flousiana*. The wood is exported to China, where it is used to make coffins. The commonest sources of local timber are *Pinus kesiya* and some *Castanopsis* species.

The region contains a large number of plants of horticultural value. Many, especially rhododendrons and herbaceous species (such as primulas and *Meconopsis betonicifolia*), have been successfully introduced into horticulture.

Social and environmental values

The remoteness of the area, the wide range of habitats, from tropical forest to alpine scree, the very low population density (except in the few lowland areas), and the fact that, at least above 2400 m, much of the vegetation is intact, makes the Kachin Hills and other parts of North Myanmā of special environmental and conservation value. The area is home to many different tribal groups, including an endangered group, the Daru.

The mammal fauna includes at least 70 species, some of which are very rare and localized. There are several rare endemic or near-endemic species, including *Cemas cranbrookii* (a type of goral), a bat belonging to the genus *Myotis*, the shrew *Blarinella wardii* and an endemic rat. Other mammals include wild dogs, Himalayan bear, flying squirrels (*Petaurista yunnanensis* and *Hylopetes alboniger*), red-bellied squirrels (*Calliosciurus erythraeus*) and various civets and cats.

There are probably 300–400 species of birds (Kingdon-Ward 1937); the area is on a major bird migration route in the spring, when the rhododendrons are in bloom. The subtropical and temperate forests and the subalpine zones are part of the Eastern Himalayas Endemic Bird Area (EBA), which comprises the main Himalayan range between east Nepal and west Yunnan, China, and the ranges between Nagaland, India, and Natma Taung, Myanmā. Nine of the 25 restricted-range bird species of this EBA have been recorded in this region, including the threatened Sclater's monal (*Lophophorus sclateri*), Blyth's tragopan (*Tragopan blythii*) and wedge-billed wren-babbler (*Sphenocichla humei*). Another restricted-range bird species, the chestnut-backed laughingthrush (*Garrulax nuchalis*), is endemic to tropical and subtropical hill zone habitats in the valleys of North Myanmā and adjacent India.

North Myanmā is, with parts of neighbouring Assam, one of the richest areas for Lepidoptera in the world (Mani 1974).

There is great mineral wealth, including gold, silver, rubies and jade. The Kachin Hills (and the Shan Plateau) are one of the most important jade-producing areas in the world, much of the production being exported to China.

Threats

Kingdon-Ward (1944) graphically outlined the threat to the vegetation of the Triangle area of the Kachin Hills from the effects of taunggya cultivation. The main pressures are on the lower forest zones, but these are also the richest in species. Increasing population pressure has led to the shortening of forest clearance cycles from 12–20 years to 5–8 years. This has resulted in large areas being converted to bamboo scrub. However, the threat to the vegetation above about 2400 m (above the limit of cultivation) is minimal and virtually all the vegetation above this altitude remains intact.

The effects of warfare on the vegetation in this region are unknown.

Conservation

The IUCN draft of protected areas in Myanmā (IUCN Protected Areas Data Unit 1987) lists only two protected areas for North Myanmā: Pidaung Game Sanctuary (705 km²) and Tamanthi Wildlife Sanctuary (215 km²). Neither of these sanctuaries protect areas which are botanically rich.

The richest plant areas and habitats have no protection. These include the mid-altitude forests of The Triangle, which contain a large assemblage of trees and shrubs, including many endemic species (Kingdon-Ward 1957), and the herbaceous vegetation of the alpine and subalpine slopes of the upper river valleys (Nam Tamai, Adung, Taron, Seinghku, and others). The inaccessibility of both these areas to some extent affords protection, but Kingdon-Ward noted that much of the vegetation in the more accessible, cultivable parts of The Triangle was being destroyed as early as 1944. Designation of a protected area within The Triangle is one of the most important priorities for plant conservation in Myanmā.

References

IUCN Protected Areas Data Unit (1987). IUCN directory of Indomalayan protected areas. Burma: draft. World Conservation Monitoring Centre, Cambridge, U.K. (unpublished typescript).

Kingdon-Ward, F. (1913). *The land of the blue poppy*. Cambridge. 283 pp.

Kingdon-Ward, F. (1916). Further notes on the land of deep corrosions. *Geol. Mag.* 6(623): 209–219.

Kingdon-Ward, F. (1923). *The mystery rivers of Tibet*. London. 316 pp.

Kingdon-Ward, F. (1930). *Plant hunting on the edge of the world*. London. 383 pp.

Kingdon-Ward, F. (1933). A naturalist's journey to the sources of the Irrawaddy. *Himalayan J.* 5: 46–57.

Kingdon-Ward, F. (1937). *Plant hunter's paradise*. London. 347 pp.

Kingdon-Ward, F. (1941). The Vernay-Cutting Expedition, November, 1938, to April, 1939: report on the vegetation and flora of the Hpimaw and Htawgaw Hills, northern Burma. *Brittonia* 4: 1–19.

Kingdon-Ward, F. (1944). A sketch of the botany and geography of North Burma. *J. Bombay Nat. Hist. Soc.* 44: 550–574; 45: 16–30.

Kingdon-Ward, F. (1945). A sketch of the botany and geography of North Burma. *J. Bombay Nat. Hist. Soc.* 45: 133–148.

Kingdon-Ward, F. (1946). Additional notes on the botany of North Burma. *J. Bombay Nat. Hist. Soc.* 46: 381–390.

Kingdon-Ward, F. (1949). *Burma's icy mountains*. Oxford. 287 pp.

Kingdon-Ward, F. (1956). *Return to the Irrawaddy*. Andrew Melrose, London. 224 pp.

Kingdon-Ward, F. (1957). The great forest belt of North Burma. *Proc. Linn. Soc. London* 168: 87–96.

Leach, E.R. (1954). *Political systems of highland Burma. A study of Kachin social structure*. London School of Economics Monographs on Social Anthropology no. 44. Bell, London. (Reprinted in 1977 by the Athlone Press, London and Atlantic Highlands, New Jersey.) 324 pp.

Mani, M.S. (1974). Biogeography of the eastern borderlands. In Mani, M.S. (ed.), *Ecology and biogeography in India*. Junk, The Hague. Pp. 648–663.

Pottinger, E. and Prain, D. (1898). A note on the botany of the Kachin Hills north-east of Myitkyina. *Records Bot. Surv. India* 1(2): 215–310.

Acknowledgement

This Data Sheet was prepared by Dr Robert R. Mill (Royal Botanic Garden, Edinburgh).

AGASTYAMALAI HILLS
India

Location: Southern end of Western Ghats, between latitudes 8°20'–8°50'N and longitudes 77°05'–77°40'E.

Area: 2000 km².

Altitude: 67–1868 m (summit of Pothikaimudi Peak).

Vegetation: Southern Peninsular Indian variants of tropical thorn forest, tropical dry deciduous forest, tropical moist deciduous forest, tropical evergreen rain forest and subtropical montane forest; lowland and montane grasslands.

Flora: c. 2000 species of vascular plants, of which 100 are strict endemics.

Useful plants: Medicinal herbs, timber trees, bamboos, rattan, resins.

Other values: Tourism, watershed protection.

Threats: Clearance for plantation crops, hydroelectric power schemes, visitor pressure, fire, cattle grazing, fuelwood cutting.

Conservation: 3 Sanctuaries (IUCN Management Category: IV) and a number of Reserved Forests protect 918.5 km² (46% of the region); whole region proposed as Biosphere Reserve.

Geography

The Agastyamalai Hills are located in the Neillai-Kattabomman and Kanniyakumari Districts of Tamil Nadu, and the Thiruvananthapuram District of Kerala, between latitudes 8°20'–8°50'N and longitudes 77°05'–77°40'E. The highest point is Pothikaimudi Peak (or Agasthyarkudam), a towering peak reaching 1868 m. The rugged terrain is covered by relatively intact forest. Hill tribe settlements of the Kanis (or Kanikkars) occur around Inchikuzhi, Kanthaparal, Lower Kodayar and Anchunazhiathode.

Vegetation

Almost all the vegetation types found in the Western Ghats are represented in the Agastyamalai Hills. They include southern variants of tropical thorn forest, tropical dry deciduous forest, tropical moist deciduous forest, tropical evergreen rain forest and subtropical montane forest. There are also lowland and montane grasslands. For a detailed account of the vegetation, see Henry *et al.* (1984) and Henry and Subramanyam (1981). The Agastyamalai Hills represents a prime example of intact tropical moist forest, including "the finest remaining example of tropical wet evergreen forest (rain forest) in Western Ghats" (Henry *et al.* 1984; Nair and Daniel 1986).

Flora

The Agastyamalai Hills include a good overall representation of the flora of the Western Ghats. Of about 5000 vascular plant species occurring in southern Peninsular India (i.e. the former Madras Presidency), the Agastyamalai Hills harbour over 2000 species (Henry *et al.* 1984; Nair and Daniel 1986). Of these, 100 species are local endemics.

Among the endemics are such trees as *Aglaia elaegnoidea* var. *bourdillonii*, *Diospyros barberi*, *Elaeocarpus venustus*, *Eugenia floccosa*, *E. singampattiana*, *Garcinia travancorica*, *Humboldtia unijuga*, *Symplocos barberi*, *S. oligandra* and *Syzygium microphyllum*. Endemic herbs, shrubs and climbers include *Belosynapsis kewensis*, *Crotalaria scabra*, *Desmodium dolabriforme*, *Exacum travancoricum*, *Grewia pandaica*, *Hedyotis villosostipulata*, *Impatiens travancorica*, *Psychotria globicephala*, *Senecio calacadensis*, *Sonerila clarkei*, *Symplocos sessilis* and *Vernonia gossypina*.

A striking feature of the flora is the occurrence of several species typical of the Sri Lankan flora, including *Abarema subcoriacea*, *Biophytum nudum*, *Chrysoglossum maculatum*, *Eugenia rotundata*, *Fahrenheitia zeylanica*, *Filicium decipiens*, *Pavetta zeylanica* and *Rubus micropetalus*, along with several species which were once considered to be Sri Lankan endemics, such as *Andrographis ceylanica*, *Antidesma walkeri*, *Eugenia mabaeoides* and *Neanotis nummularia*.

About 50 species are considered to be rare or threatened. Among them are *Hedyotis barberi*, *H. travancorica*, *H. villosostipulata*, *Knoxia linearis*, *Paphiopedilum druryi*, *Piper barberi*, *Popowia beddomeana*, *Rhychosia jacobii*, *Toxocarpus beddomei* and *Vernonia heynei*.

New species are still being discovered in the region. About 30 new plant taxa have been recently recorded from the area, including *Cheilanthes keralensis*, *Euphorbia santapaui*, *Homalium jainii* and *Hoya kanyakumariana*. *Janakia arayalpathra* represents a new genus. The flora of the region is of ancient lineage (Subramanyam and Nayar 1974; Nair and Daniel 1986).

Useful plants

The ancient sage, Agastya, is said to have lived here on the leaves, tubers, fruits and sap of wild plants. Local inhabitants rely heavily on wild plants and animals for their subsistence. Many species are widely used in Ayurvedic medicines. They include species in such genera as *Aristolochia, Cardiospermum, Ceropegia, Dioscorea, Ficus, Gloriosa, Gymnema, Janakia, Knema, Leucas, Naregamia, Rauvolfia, Smilax, Solanum, Stephania, Strychnos* and *Tylophora*.

Important timber species include *Canarium strictum, Cullenia exarillata, Elaeocarpus* spp., *Gluta travancorica, Hopea* spp., *Hydnocarpus* spp., *Litsea* spp., *Mesua nagassarium, Myristica* spp. and *Pterocarpus marsupium*.

Wild fruit trees include *Antidesma* spp., *Artocarpus* spp., *Baccaurea courtallensis, Canthium travancoricum, Emblica officinalis, Ficus* spp., *Mangifera indica, Solanum* spp. and *Syzygium* spp.

There is a large number of wild relatives of cultivated plants, such as species of *Amomum, Atylosia, Canavalia, Cinnamomum, Coffea, Dioscorea, Elettaria, Garcinia, Mangifera, Musa, Myristica, Oryza, Piper* and *Rauvolfia*. The presence of such gene pools makes the Agastyamalai Hills a potentially very valuable source of genetic material.

Social and environmental values

The Agastyamalai Hills lie in the south of the South Indian Hills Endemic Bird Area (EBA), which includes the Western Ghats plus a few small ranges of hills to the east. Sixteen restricted-range bird species are endemic to this EBA, and are particularly associated with tropical evergreen rain forest, tropical moist deciduous forest, subtropical montane forest and montane grasslands. All of these habitats are represented in the Agastyamalai Hills and they support all except one of these species. They are likely to be a particularly important site for six restricted-range bird species which are found in subtropical montane forest and montane grassland, habitats which are confined to the higher peaks in the south of the Western Ghats.

The wildlife, plant life and scenic beauty of the region attract many tourists. Many visit the three Sanctuaries (see Conservation section), where such features as Agastyiyar Falls and Tiger Falls are popular. Pothikaimudi Peak attracts visitors who come to see the spectacular scenery and is also a place of pilgrimage for devotees of Agasthya Maharishi.

The forests protect important water catchment areas. There are five reservoirs in the region, which are used to produce hydroelectricity and supply water for irrigation.

Economic assessment

The current value of natural resources and ecological services which the area provides to the national economy on a

MAP 4. AGASTYAMALAI HILLS, INDIA (CPD SITE IS7)

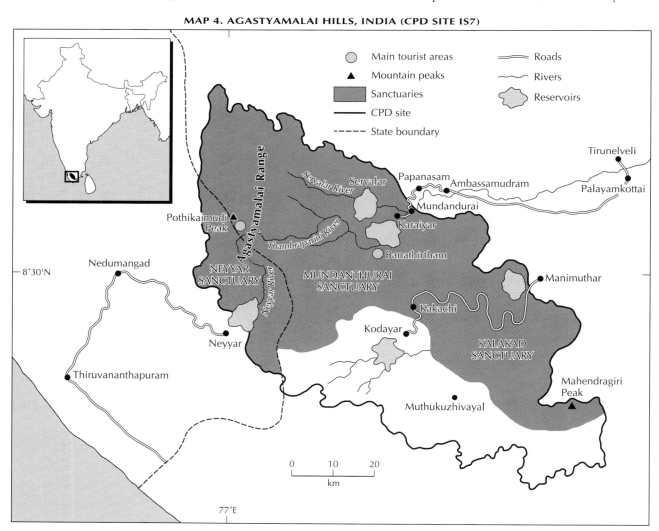

sustainable basis has yet to be fully assessed. Besides valuable timber trees, revenue is collected from the sale of minor forest products, such as bamboos (e.g. *Bambusa arundinacea, Dendrocalamus strictus* and *Ochlandra travancorica*) and rattan (*Calamus rotan*). Trees yielding gums, resins and dyes are also common in these forests; *Canarium strictum* yields the Alriba resin. The Kanis collect honey, cinnamon bark and resins, especially black damar. Hill slopes are used to grow commercial crops, such as coffee, tea, rubber, pepper and cardamom.

Threats

Forest clearance and degradation has occurred around a number of settlements and as a result of hydroelectricity and irrigation projects. For example, on the Mundanthurai Plateau, moist deciduous forest has been modified to dry deciduous forest, as a result of changes to the soil water balance, while the tropical evergreen rain forest at Muthukuzhivayal was cleared for the Kodayar hydroelectric project.

The Singampatti Forest Reserve has been considerably disturbed by tea cultivation and partly cleared for the cultivation of other plantation crops.

Increasing tourism, and particularly the increasing number of tourists and pilgrims who visit Pothikaimudi, has resulted in increased trampling and local modification and clearance of vegetation, for example by the widening of footpaths and bridle paths.

Intentional and accidental fires are a threat to seasonally dry forests. Most localities of *Euphorbia santapaui* and *Paphiopedilum druryi* have already been destroyed. Other major threats are cattle grazing and fuelwood cutting.

Conservation

There are three Sanctuaries (IUCN Management Category: IV) in the Agastyamalai Hills, namely: Mundanthurai (567.4 km²) and Kalakad (223.6 km²) in Tamil Nadu, and Neyyar (128 km²) in Kerala.

Intensive field studies have been carried out in the region during the last three decades by the Botanical Survey of India and the Zoological Survey of India. It has been recommended that the Man and Biosphere National Committee of the Government of India designate the whole region as a Biosphere Reserve, so that it may serve as an "ecological protectorate" (Henry *et al.* 1984).

Conservation work on the endangered flora of the Western Ghats is being undertaken by the Tropical Botanic Garden and Research Institute at Pachaa-Palode, Trivandrum. The Foundation for Revitalization of Local Health Traditions (FRLHT), based in Bangalore, has established centres in the Western Ghats for *in situ* and *ex situ* conservation of medicinal plants.

References

Henry, A.N., Chandrabose, M., Swaminathan, M.S. and Nair, N.C. (1984). Agastyamalai and its environs: a potential area for a Biosphere Reserve. *J. Bombay Nat. Hist. Soc.* 82: 282–290.

Henry, A.N. and Subramanyam, K. (1981). Studies on the flora of Agastyamalai and surrounding regions in Tirunelveli District, Tamil Nadu. *Bull. Bot. Surv. India* 23: 42–45.

MAB National Committee, Government of India (1979). *Preliminary inventory on potential areas for Biosphere Reserves.* New Delhi.

Nair, N.C. and Daniel, P. (1986). *The floristic diversity of Western Ghats and its conservation: a review.* Proceedings of the India Acad. Sci. (Animal Sci./Plant Sci.) Suppl. Pp. 127–163.

Subramanyam, K. and Nayar, M.P. (1974). Vegetation and phytogeography of the Western Ghats. In Mani, M.S. (ed.), *Ecology and biogeography in India.* Junk, The Hague. Pp. 178–196.

Acknowledgements

This Data Sheet was written by A.N. Henry and R. Goplan (Botanical Survey of India, Southern Circle, Coimbatore).

NILGIRI HILLS
India

Location: Southern Western Ghats between latitudes 10°45'–12°15'N and longitudes 76°00'–77°15'E, straddling the borders of Karnataka, Kerala and Tamil Nadu.

Area: 5520 km².

Altitude: 250–2500 m.

Vegetation: Tropical evergreen rain forest, tropical semi-evergreen forest, tropical moist deciduous forest, tropical dry thorn forest, tropical montane evergreen shola forest and grassland.

Flora: Estimated 3240 vascular plant species, of which c.100 are strict endemics; 2 endemic genera.

Useful plants: Medicinal plants, timber trees, fruit tree relatives, ornamental plants.

Other values: Watershed protection, rich fauna, tourism.

Threats: Clearance for plantation crops, timber and fuelwood extraction, over-collection of some medicinal and ornamental plant species, tourist pressure, overgrazing, fire.

Conservation: Several National Parks (IUCN Management Category: II), including Silent Valley (89.5 km²), Bandipur (874.2 km²) and Nagarahole (643.4 km²), and Sanctuaries (IUCN Management Category: IV), together with Reserved Forests. The whole region has been declared a Biosphere Reserve by the Government of India. Management needs strengthening; further establishment of National Parks and Sanctuaries is recommended.

Geography

The area under consideration includes the Nilgiri Biosphere Reserve (declared in 1988 by the Government of India, see Conservation section). The area covers 5520 km² in the Nilgiri Hills, part of the Western Ghats of Peninsular India, between latitudes 10°45'–12°15'N and longitudes 76°00'–77°15'E. The whole of the Western Ghats cover approximately 159,000 km². The reserve straddles the borders of the states of Karnataka, Kerala and Tamil Nadu, and stretches from the Coorg-Wynaad Plateau, east of the Brahmaagiri, south to the Attapadi-Bolampatti Hills at the northern edge of the Palghat Gap, and eastwards to the Talamalai-Hasanur Plateau of the Eastern Ghats.

The topography is extremely varied, ranging from an altitude of 250 m in the plains and rising steeply to over 2500 m in the hills; however, the highest peak in the Nilgiri Hills, Doda Betta (2636 m), is excluded from the Biosphere Reserve. Wynaad, Mysore, Sigur and Talamalai Plateaux are located to the north. They are between 700 and 1000 m altitude. On the west, the slopes of Nilambur, New Amarambalam and Silent Valley descend to the Calicut Plains at 250 m altitude. On the east, the Nilgiris slope down to the Coimbatore Plains.

The region drains both to the west and east. On the west, swift flowing streams drain into the Chaliyar, Kunthipuzha and Koraiyar rivers. The eastern portion is drained by tributaries of the Kabbini, Moyar and Bhavani rivers which ultimately join the Cauvery River. The area is subject to the influence of both south-west and north-east monsoons.

The following tribal people live in the area: Cholainaikas (hunter-gatherers in the New Amarambalam forests of Silent Valley), Todas (who live throughout the Nilgiri Hills and practice buffalo rearing and crop cultivation), Badagas (who cultivate the fertile slopes of the Nilgiri Hills), Irulas (who are mostly gatherers of minor forest products, although they also cultivate crops to a limited extent), Kurumbas and Soligas (who are gatherers of minor forest products in the Nilgiri Hills and Mysore Plateau, and the Mysore and Talamalai Plateaux, respectively), Chetties (who are farmers living in the Wynaad areas) and Pannias (landless labourers who carry out work for other communities).

Vegetation

Many types of vegetation can be found in the Biosphere Reserve. The major types are briefly described.

Tropical wet evergreen forest (rain forest)

This occurs along the western slopes up to 1500 m in areas receiving in excess of 2000 mm annual rainfall. Evergreen rain forest is found at Nilambur Kovilakam, New Amarambalam, Silent Valley and parts of Attapadi Reserved Forests. The forest is dense and multistoried, with the main canopy at over 35 m and emergents reaching 50 m. Lichens, mosses, epiphytes and climbers are common. Common trees include *Artocarpus hirsutus, Bischofia javanica, Cinnamomum verum, Diospyros montana, D. nilagirica, Elaeocarpus tuberculatus, Garcinia cowa, G. morella, G. xanthochymus, Hopea parviflora, Kingiodendron pinnatum, Litsea oleoides, Michelia nilagirica* and *Syzgium densiflorum.*

Tropical semi-evergreen forest

This is transitional between evergreen and moist deciduous forest types. It is found along the lower western slopes and on northern and western slopes. Common species include *Acrocarpus fraxinifolius, Bombax ceiba, Caryota urens, Holigarna arnottiana, Persea macrantha, Trewia nudiflora* and *Vitex altissima,* along with such deciduous tree species as *Lagerstroemia microcarpa, L. parviflora* and *Xylia xylocarpa.*

Tropical moist deciduous forest
Forests of this type are found on the Wynaad Plateau and Mukkali slopes. Typical trees are *Dalbergia latifolia, Kydia calycina, Lagerstroemia microcarpa, Schleichera oleosa, Tectona grandis* and *Terminalia coriacea. Bambusa arundinacea* forms large clumps in the forest. Tall grass species in the genera *Cymbopogon* and *Themeda* are also found.

Tropical dry deciduous forest
This type is found on the Mysore Plateau, Tamil Nadu Plateau and on the eastern slopes of the Nilgiri Hills. Common tree species include *Anogeissus latifolia, Albizia*

lebbeck, A. odoratissima, Grewia tiliifolia, Haldenia cordifolia, Sterculia urens, S. villosa, Terminalia chebula, T. crenulata and *T. paniculata.* These forests also contain a luxuriant grass cover, including species of *Cymbopogon, Heteropogon, Imperata* and *Themeda.*

Tropical dry thorn forest
This occurs in the Moyar Valley, Kundah Downs and in certain places on the Attapadi slopes. Thorny plants are frequent and include such species as *Acacia chundra, A. horrida, A. leucophloea, A. sinuata, Albizia amara, Capparis* spp. and *Dichrostachys cinerea.*

Tropical montane evergreen shola forest and grassland
This occurs above 1500 m on much of the upper Nilgiri Plateau and in the higher parts of the Siruvani Hills. Shola forests are restricted to the valleys and folds of hills and contain stunted trees, while the surrounding hill slopes are covered in grassland. The most common trees are *Cinnamomum wightii, Litsea glabrata, L. glutinosa, L. stocksii,*

MAP 5. NILGIRI BIOSPHERE RESERVE, INDIA (CPD SITE IS8)

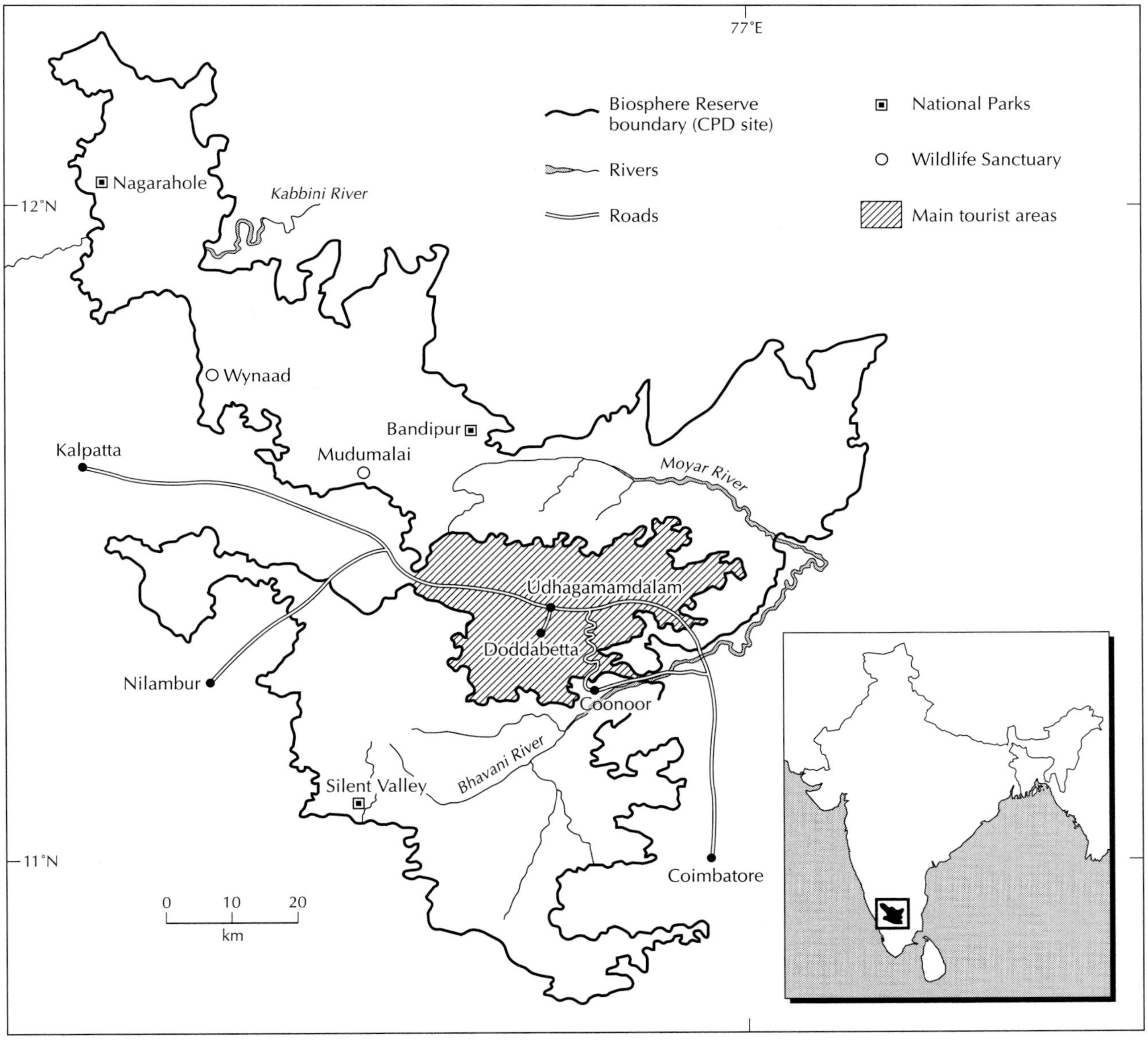

Elaeocarpus tectorius, E. recurvatus, Meliosma pinnata, M. simplicifolia, Ligustrum gamblei, Neolitsea cassia, Phoebe wightii, Schefflera capitata, S. racemosa, Symplocos foliosa, S. macrophylla ssp. *microphylla, S. obtusa, S. wynadense, Syzygium densiflorum* and *Viburnum punctatum. Rhododendron arboream* spp. *nilagiricum* is a common shola tree producing very attractive crimson flowers. Several species of *Strobilanthes* are commonly found in the undergrowth, along with species of Asteraceae and Rubiaceae. The grasslands include members of the grass genera *Bothriochloa, Cymbopogon, Eragrostis* and *Themeda.*

The occurrence of shola forests and grasslands in close juxtaposition and apparent equilibrium is of great ecological interest. The shola forests are relicts, whereas the grasslands have been variously considered as climax, sub-climax and successional communities.

Peat bog vegetation

Peat bogs, which are rare in India, are found in depressions in the Nilgiri Hills at c. 2000 m altitude. The vegetation includes grasses, sedges, mosses, rushes, *Pleiocraterium vertillare* (Rubiaceae), *Eriocaulon* spp., *Utricularia* spp. and *Xyris* spp.

Flora

There are an estimated 3240 species of vascular plants, including an extraordinary wealth of endemic and rare species. In addition to the diversity of plant communities, the presence of temperate elements and a large number of endemic taxa on the isolated peaks makes this area one of the most botanically rich and interesting areas of South India. Some areas appear to be particularly species-rich. For example, 966 species of flowering plants have been recorded from Silent Valley (89.5 km²), to the south-west of the Nilgiri Hills. Blasco (1970) drew attention to the abundance of endemic species on the South Indian massifs. He observed that 82 species are exclusively confined to the Nilgiris and points out that the Nilgiris appear to be an important centre of speciation in South India. There are now estimated to be about 100 strict endemic species, many of which are rare and threatened. Strict endemic genera include *Baelopsis* and *Silentvalleya*, while many other genera are restricted to the Western Ghats (e.g. *Ascophilos, Kanjarum* and *Meteoromyrtus*).

Certain groups, such as orchids, are well-represented in the flora. About 125 species of orchids have been recorded from the Nilgiri Hills alone, including such showy species as *Acanthephippium bicolor, Calanthe triplicata, Coelogyne mossiae, Habenaria* spp., *Pecteilis gigantea, Rhynchostylis retusa* and *Vanda tessellata* (among others). These add much to the beauty of the forests.

Endangered endemic species include the following: *Actinodaphne lanata, A. lawsonii, Amomum pterocarpum, Antistrophe serratifolia, Begonia aliciae, Bulbophyllum kaitiense, B. albidum, B. acutiflorum, B. elegantulum, Ceropegia barnesii, C. pusilla, Crotalaria longipes,*

CPD Site IS8: Nilgiri Hills, India. Photo: V.H. Heywood.

C. peduncularis, Clematis theobromina, Coelogyne mossiae, Corymborchis veratrifolia, Commelina wightii, Eria albiflora, Eriochrysis rangacharii, Euonymus angulatus, Habenaria barnesii, Hedyotis beddomei, Impatiens nilagirica, Ipsea malabarica, Liparis biloba, Memecylon sisparense, Meteoromyrtus wynaadensis, Melicope indica, Oberonia brachyphylla, Pogostemon atropurpureum, P. nilagiricus, Pavetta wightii, Smilax wightii, Toxocarpus palghatensis, Tephrosia wynaadensis, Vanilla walkeriae, Willisia selaginoides and *Youngia nilagiriensis* (among others). In recent years, such rare species as *Actinodaphne lawsonii, Hedyotis hirsutissima, Ophiorrhiza pykarensis* and *Senecio lawsonii* have been re-collected in the region.

About 160 species of ferns, fern-allies and gymnosperms have been recorded from the Nilgiri Hills, including the tree ferns *Cyathea gigantea,* and *C. schimidiana* which occur on the fringes of shola forests. Rare or threatened endemic ferns include *Cyathea nilgerensis, Elaphoglossum nilagiricum, E. stigmatolepis, Pseudocyclosorus gamblei* and *Pronephrium thwaitesii.* The primitive fern ally *Psilotum nudum* is now locally rare.

Mass flowering of *Phlebophyllum kunthianum* (*Strobilanthes kunthianus*) after an interval of several years attracts large numbers of tourists to the area. An interesting feature of the flora is its affinity with that of temperate regions of Khasia, Manipur and the Naga Hills in north-east India. Temperate elements include species of *Gaultheria, Geranium, Hypericum, Potentilla, Rubus* and *Vaccinium.*

CPD Site IS8: Nilgiri Hills, India. Photo: V.H. Heywood.

Useful plants

The timber of many tree species is used for building purposes and furniture making. Important timber species include *Acrocarpus fraxinifolius, Acronychia pedunculata, Actinodaphne malabarica, A. tadulingamii, Artocarpus heterophyllus, Canarium strictum, Cassine glauca, Elaeocarpus recurvatus, E. tuberculatus, Hopea parviflora, Mangifera indica, Mesua ferrea, Poeciloneuron indicum, Shorea roxburghii* and *Vateria indica.*

There are many plants which produce edible or otherwise useful fruits. Examples include *Acacia sinuata, Artocarpus heterophyllus, Canthium parviflorum, Capparis zeylanica, Carissa carandas, Citrus* spp., *Elettaria cardamomum, Flacourtia indica, Mangifera indica, Momordica charantea* var. *muricata, Passiflora edulis, Piper nigrum, Rhodomyrtus tomentosa, Syzygium cumini, S. jambos, Sapindus laurifolia* and *Solanum torvum.*

The tuberous roots of *Dioscorea* spp. are the staple food of the indigenous tribal people. The aromatic roots of *Decalepis hamiltonii* are used for pickles. Unripe fruits of *Carissa carandas* and ripe fruits of *Phyllanthus emblica* are also used for pickles, as well as for medicinal purposes. The aromatic roots of *Hemidesmus indicus* are used in making beverages.

There are many species of medicinal plants. Some of the most important are *Andrographis paniculata, Caesalpinia bonduc, Cardiospermum halicacabum, Centella asiatica, Cissus quadrangularis, Costus speciosus, Datura metel, Dodonaea viscosa, Gloriosa superba, Hydnocarpus laurifolia, Leucas* spp., *Ocimum* spp., *Piper longum, Pterospermum marsupium, Solanum virginianum, S. trilobatum* and *Tylophora indica.*

Ornamental plants with showy fragrant flowers include *Butea monosperma, Cochlospermum religiosum, Filicium decipiens* (with fern-like foliage), *Jasminum* spp., *Lilium wallichianum* var. *neilgherrense* (sometimes treated as a distinct species, *L. neilgherrense*), *Michelia nilagirica* and *Pongamia pinnata.*

Social and environmental values

The Nilgiri Biosphere Reserve is inhabited by many tribal people (see Geography section). Some practised shifting cultivation in the past but now practise terrace cultivation, growing such crops as millet (ragi), maize (sholam) and a variety of vegetables. Some also rear animals and many collect forest products. Many of the tribal people now live in permanent settlements, some in government quarters and others in huts.

The Nilgiri Biosphere Reserve is notable for its rich fauna, including many rare and threatened species, such as the lion-tailed macaque *Macaca silenus* (Endangered) and Nilgiri tahr (*Hemitragus hylocrius*) (Vulnerable), both of which are endemic to the Western Ghats. The Nilgiri Biosphere Reserve lies within the South Indian Hills Endemic Bird Area (EBA), which includes the Western Ghats plus a few small ranges of hills to the east. Sixteen restricted-range bird species are endemic to this EBA, and are particularly associated with tropical evergreen rain forest, tropical moist deciduous forest, subtropical montane forest and montane grasslands. All of these habitats are represented in the Nilgiri Biosphere Reserve and all except one of these species occurs here. This reserve is likely to be a particularly important site for six restricted-range bird species which are found in subtropical montane forest and montane grassland, habitats which are confined to the higher peaks in the south of the Western Ghats. These birds include the rufous-breasted laughing-thrush (*Garrulax cachinnans*) which is endemic to the Nilgiri Hills.

The rich flora and fauna of the region, and the natural beauty of the forests, are attracting increasing numbers of tourists. The Mudumalai Sanctuary, Botanical Garden, Ooty and Sim's Park, Coonoor, are among the most popular tourist destinations.

The forests are especially valuable for protecting watersheds and in soil conservation management.

Economic assessment

Apart from revenue derived from timber extraction, the Biosphere Reserve contributes to the local economy of the large population of tribal people who collect minor forest products. Sandalwood, derived from *Santalum album*, is a major source of revenue for the government, and is used in the manufacture of sandalwood oil, soap, incense sticks (agarbathies) and for many wooden artefacts. Other minor forest products are derived form *Anogeissus latifolia* (gum of anogeissus), *Piper nigrum* (wild pepper), *Pongamia glabra* (pungum seed) and *Pterocarpus chebula* (gallnuts). These are often collected and sold to forest contractors; honey and wax are collected by the Forest Department, and tanning materials are utilized by local tanneries. Lichens collected as "stone and tree moss" are used for medicinal and culinary purposes. The revenue derived from minor forest products in Nilgiri South Division during 1982–1983 was Rs.35,600/- and Rs.36,300/-, respectively.

Tamil Nadu Government Chinchona Department also produces many essential oils, such as geranium oil, citriodora oil, camphor and eucalyptus oil (the latter from introduced *Eucalyptus* spp., which also provide the basis for local cottage industries manufacturing eucalyptus oil).

Introduced species of wattles – *Acacia dealbata*, *A. decurrens* and *A. mearnsii* – and introduced *Eucalyptus globulus* (blue gum) are the basis of important viscose and wattle industries.

Threats

The major threats are forest clearance for plantation crops (including tea, coffee, potatoes and other temperate vegetables, and *Eucalyptus* trees), road construction, tourist accommodation, and potentially hydroelectric power schemes. Public opposition to the loss of habitat and the species extinctions which would have resulted from inundation of 5.4 km² of species-rich tropical rain forest along the Kunthipuzha River, was instrumental in halting the Silent Valley Hydroproject in January 1980 (Goodland 1985).

Timber extraction, fuelwood cutting, and cattle and sheep grazing affect some areas. Forest fires are a major problem in some areas, as in Silent Valley where 20% of the National Park has been degraded by fire in the last few years.

Some ornamental species, particularly those with showy flowers, are collected in large quantities and sold to tourists.

Flowers are also gathered by tourists out of curiosity, only to be discarded later. This is especially the case during the mass flowering of *Strobilanthes* spp. The Nilgiri Hills are frequently visited during botanical excursions. Many showy orchids, such as *Aerides crispum, Calanthe* spp., *Habenaria* spp., *Platanthera gigantea* and *Rhynchosia retusa*, along with the gigantic lily, *Lilium wallichianum* var. *neilgherrense*, once common in the forests, have now become rare owing to forest clearance and over-collecting.

Introduced plants, such as *Ageratum houstonianum*, *Erigeron karvinskianus*, *Helichrysum bracteatum*, *Sarothamnus scoparius, Solanum sisymbrifolium* and *Ulex europaeus*, are naturalized in some areas.

Conservation

The major protected areas are Silent Valley National Park (89.5 km²) in Kerala, and Bandipur (874.2 km²) and Nagarahole (643.4 km²) National Parks in Karnataka. In addition, there are several Sanctuaries (IUCN Management Category: IV) and many Reserved Forests. Of these, the most important are the Attapadi Reserved Forest, New Amarambalam Reserved Forest, Nilambur Vested Forests and Wynaad Sanctuary (344.4 km²). The whole of the region was declared a Man and Biosphere Reserve by UNESCO. Further establishment of National Parks and Sanctuaries to safeguard natural resources is recommended, notably the 255 km² proposed Katimpuzha National Park which presently forms part of New Amarambalam Reserved Forest.

The collection of orchids and rare plants without permission is prohibited by law. Re-introduction programmes of rare and threatened species propagated in *ex situ* collections should be carried out.

There is a critical need to strengthen the management of the Nilgiri Biosphere Reserve.

References

Allardyce, J. (1936). Remarks on the vegetation of the Nilgherries, Madras. *J. Lit. Sci.* 4:67–78.

Beddome, R.H. (1876). The forests and flora of the Nilgiris. *Indian Forester* 2: 17–28.

Blasco F. (1970). Aspects of the flora and the ecology of savannas of the South Indian hills. *J. Bombay Nat. Hist. Soc.* 67: 522–534.

Gadgil Madhav and Sukumar, R. (eds) (1986). Scientific programme for the Nilgiri Biosphere Reserve: report of a workshop, Bangalore, 7–8 March 1986. 48 pp.

Gamble, J.S. and Fischer, C.E.C. (1915-1936). *Flora of the Presidency of Madras*. Parts 1–11.

Goodland, R. (1985). Environmental aspects of hydroelectric power and water storage projects (with special reference to India). Paper presented at an International Seminar on the Environmental Impact Assessment of Water Resources Projects, University of Roorkee, Uttar Pradesh, 12–14 December 1985. 30 pp.

Gupta, R.K. (1962). Some observations on the plants of the South Indian hill tops (Nilgiri & Palani) and their distribution in the Himalayas. *J. Indian Bot. Soc.*41: 1–15.

Gupta, R.K. and Sankaranarayan, K.A. (1962). Ecological status of the grasslands in South India. *Tropical Ecology* 3: 75–78.

Jayaraman, V. (1974). Working plan for the Nilgiris South Forest Division, 1974–75 to 1983–84.

Manilal, K.S. (1988). *Flora of Silent Valley.* Mathrubhumi (MM) Press, Calicut. xl, 398 pp.

Meher-Homji, V.M. (1965). Ecological status of the montane grasslands of the South Indian hills. A phytogeographic reassessment. *Indian Forester* 91:210–215.

Nayar, M.P. and Sastry, A.R.K. (1987-1990). *Red Data Book of Indian Plants,* 3 vols. Botanical Survey of India, Calcutta. (Vol. I: 1987; vol. 2: 1988; vol. 3: 1990).

Rege, N.D., Devaraj, S.Y. and Nair, P.K. (1959). Botanical survey of the Nilgiris. *Indian Forester* 85: 287–291.

Sankaranarayan K.A. (1959). The vegetation of the Nilgiris – II. The shola and grassland. *J. Biol. Sci.* 2:14.

Sharma, B.D. *et al.* (1977). Studies on the flora of Nilgiris, Tamil Nadu: biological memoirs. *Angiosperm Taxonomy* 2 (1–2): 1–186.

Acknowledgement

This Data Sheet was prepared by E. Vajravelu (Botanical Survey of India, Southern Circle, Coimbatore).

INDIAN REGIONAL CENTRE OF ENDEMISM: CPD SITE IS9

NALLAMALAI HILLS
India

Location: Central part of the Eastern Ghats, between latitudes 15°20'–16°30'N and longitudes 78°30'–80°10'E, in Kurnool, Mahaboobnagar and Prakasam Districts of Andhra Pradesh.

Area: 7640 km².

Altitude: 300–939 m (summit of Virannakonda Peak).

Vegetation: Dry deciduous forest, moist deciduous forest, dry evergreen forest, riverine forest, scrub forest.

Flora: 758 vascular plant species so far recorded; many Eastern Ghats endemics and a few local endemics.

Useful plants: Many medicinal herbs, bamboos, timber trees, wild relatives of pepper and rice.

Other values: Cultural and religious significance, water catchment protection.

Threats: Large-scale cutting of bamboos, tree felling for fuelwood, dam construction, fire, tourist pressure.

Conservation: Nagarjunasagar Srisailam Sanctuary (IUCN Management Category: IV) covers 357 km² (c. 4.7% of region).

Geography

The Nallamalais are a group of moderately steep hills in the central part of the Eastern Ghats, between latitudes 15°20'–16°30'N and longitudes 78°30'–80°10'E, in Kurnool, Mahaboobnagar and Prakasam Districts of Andhra Pradesh. They cover an area of 7640 km². The highest point is Virannakonda Peak (939 m).

The Nallamalais form an almost unbroken chain of rugged hills with some precipitous cliffs. Two major passes (Mantralakanama and Nandikanama) and two minor passes (Veligonda and Hylokanama) dissect the hills from east to west. In the centre of the hills is the Gundlabrahmeswaram Plateau at an average altitude of about 800 m. The Nallamalais comprise two principal geological formations: the Kurnool and Cuddapah. The Kurnool Formation dates from the upper Precambrian period. A detailed account of the geological history is given in Ellis (1968) and Anon. (1986).

Chenchu tribal groups are found throughout the area.

Vegetation

Most of the forests of the interior region are still undisturbed and are very diverse, being located in an area of fertile, moist soils, and experiencing a favourable climate influenced by south-west and north-east monsoons. As a result, the Nallamalais contain a good representative sample of nearly all the major vegetation types known from the Eastern Ghats, namely dry deciduous forest, moist deciduous forest, dry evergreen forest, riverine forest and scrub forest.

Dry deciduous forest is the most common type of forest in the Nallamalais. Common species are *Antidesma acidum, Canthium parviflorum, Ceriscoides turgida, Cissus pallida, Cochlospermum religiosum, Colebrookea oppositifolia, Dalbergia lanceolaris, D. paniculata, Diospyros melanoxylon, Dolichondrone arcuata, Ehretia laevis, Eriolaena lushingtonii, Firmiana colorata, Indigofera mysorensis, Ixora pavetta, Lagerstroemia parviflora, Pterocarpus marsupium, Syzygium alternifolium, Tamilnadia uliginosa* and *Wrightia arborea*. In addition, a *Boswellia* forest type (with *Boswellia serrata* and *Chloroxylon swietenia* as the main species) occurs near Chelama, a *Terminalia* type (with *Terminalia coriacea* and *Anogeissus latifolia*) occurs in the Eastern Nallamalais, a *Phoenix* type (with *Phoenix loureirii* as the dominant species forming a pure stand on rocky substrates) occurs between Ramanapenta and Gundlabrahmeswaram, and a *Calamus* type (dominated by *Calamus rotang*) is restricted to the Krishnanandi area (Ellis 1987).

Moist deciduous forests are restricted to moist and sheltered sites with higher rainfall, such as at Gundlabrahmeswaram, Rollapenta and in the south of Nallamalais between upper and lower Ahobilum, Bairani, and on the Iskagundam, Morricheruvu and Guttachenu Plateaux of the Eastern Nallamalais. Common elements in the forest include *Adiantum lunulatum, Athyrium hohenackerianum, Barleria strigosa, Careya arborea, Casearia graveolens, Desmodium gangeticum, Dillenia pentagyna, Ficus hispida, Glochidion zeylanicum, Oroxylum indicum, Pimpinella wallichiana, Trema orientalis* and *Triumfetta pilosa*.

Scrub forest is confined to the base of hills and is dominated by *Atalantia monophylla, Balanites aegyptiaca, Cassine glauca, Dichrostachys cinerea, Diospyros chloroxylon, Maytenus emarginata, Moringa concanensis, Mundulea sericea* and *Ochna obtusata* var. *gamblei*. Dry evergreen and riverine forest types are also represented in the Nallamalais.

Flora

So far, 758 vascular plant species have been recorded from the Nallamalai Hills, including 743 of angiosperms and 15 ferns. A total of 109 families is represented in the flora (Ellis 1987, 1990). Grasses, with about 66 species, are well-represented (Ellis 1968).

The Nallamalai Hills harbour many Eastern Ghats endemics, as well as several local endemics, such as *Andrographis nallamalayana*, *Eriocaulon lushingtonii*, *Crotalaria madurensis* var. *kurnoolica*, *Dicliptera beddomei* and *Premna hamiltonii*. New taxa recently described from the area include *Euphorbia linearifolia* var. *nallamalayana* and *Rostellularia vahlii* var. *rupicola*.

An interesting feature of the flora is that many species exhibit gigantism. For example, the shrubby climber, *Marsdenia tenacissima*, has leaves measuring up to 32 cm by 30 cm, *Bauhinia vahlii* and *Entada pursetha* overtop other species to dominate the vegetation in places, and the vine *Cissus vitiginea* also acquires an arboreal habit (Ellis 1975).

Useful plants

Besides valuable timber trees, the forests provide minor forest products, such as bamboo (*Bambusa arundinacea* and *Dendrocalamus strictus*), dyes, gums and resins (particularly from *Boswellia serrata*, *Commiphora caudata*, *Mallotus philippensis* and *Sterculia urens*).

The indigenous tribes depend to a large extent on wild plants for their survival, as sources of food and medicines, and for shelter. The following are among some of the most important species utilized locally: *Albizia lebbeck*, *Bambusa arundinacea*, *Barleria strigosa*, *Bauhinia racemosa*, *B. vahlii*, *Calamus rotang*, *Calycopteris floribunda*, *Casearia graveolens*, *Cassine glauca*, *Corallocarpus epigaeus*, *Cordia dichotoma*, *C. monoica*, *Dalbergia latifolia*, *Dendrocalamus strictus*, *Dillenia pentagyna*, *Diospyros montana*, *Entada pursaetha*, *Erythroxylum monogynum*, *Ficus amplissima*, *F. hispida*, *Firmiana colorata*, *Gardenia gummifera*, *Grewia orbiculata*, *Gymnema sylvestre*, *Holarrhena antidysenterica*, *Maerua apetala*, *Mitragyna parvifolia*, *Mundulea sericea*, *Pavetta indica*, *Polyalthia cerasoides*, *Pterocarpus marsupium*, *Sterculia urens*, *Strychnos nux-vomica*, *Tectona grandis*, *Terminalia bellirica*, *Wrightia arborea*, *Xylia xylocarpa*, *Ziziphus oenoplia* and *Z. xylopyrus*.

The occurrence of wild rice relatives, namely *Oryza meyeriana* var. *granulata*, *O. officinalis* subsp. *malampuzhaensis* and *O. sativa*, the latter apparently an accidental introduction in and around Gundlabrahmeswaram (Ellis 1968, 1969), makes the area a prospective site for germplasm conservation (Ellis 1982; Nayar, Ahmed and Raju 1984; Ahmedullah and Nayar 1987). Wild relatives of pepper, namely *Piper hymenophyllum*, *P. nigrum* and *P. trioicum*, also occur in the forests.

Social and environmental values

The threatened bird, Jerdon's courser (*Cursorius bitorquatus*), was assumed to be extinct, but was rediscovered in the Eastern Ghats in 1986. All recent records are from the area to the south of Nallamalais, but it is possible that it occurs at Nallamalais.

The temples at Srisailam, Mahanandi and Ahobilam attract large numbers of pilgrims who also trek through the dense forests as part of their experience.

The forests protect important water catchment areas including several rivers and natural springs. The perennial natural tepid spring at Mahandi attracts hundreds of religious devotees each day (Ellis 1987).

Threats

Being in an "industrial catchment area", the Nallamalais are subjected to heavy cutting of bamboos and trees to supply paper industries in Kurnool (Mukhadkar 1978). Some areas of forest have also been degraded as a result of felling trees to supply local needs for fuelwood.

Cattle grazing and the accidental and intentional setting of fires are threats in some areas.

A large area of forest was destroyed at Srisailam as a result of dam construction.

Conservation

The Nagarjunasagar Srisailam Sanctuary (IUCN Management Category: IV) covers 356.9 km².

Afforestation programmes are to be implemented to augment the supply of raw materials for nearby industries. Alternative sources for cattle feed and fuelwood will relieve pressure on the natural vegetation.

The Botanical Survey of India and other institutions have undertaken intensive studies on the flora of the region over the last three decades.

References

Ahmedullah, M. and Nayar, M.P. (1987). *Endemic plants of the Indian region, Vol. 1*. Botanical Survey of India, Calcutta. 261 pp.

Anon. (1986). Eastern Ghats Eco-development Programme. *Eastern Eco.* (Visakhapatnam.)

Ellis, J.L. (1968). The Flora of Nallamalais on the Eastern Ghats of India – I: a preliminary list. *Bull. Bot. Surv. India* 10: 149–160.

Ellis, J.L. (1969). Notes on some interesting plants from South India – I. *J. Bombay Nat. Hist. Soc.* 66: 233.

Ellis, J.L. (1975). Notes on some interesting plants from South India – III. *J. Bombay Nat. Hist. Soc.* 72: 230–236.

Ellis, J.L. (1982). Wild plant resources of Nallamalais on the Eastern Ghats. In *National Seminar on Resources, Development and Environment of the Eastern Ghats*. Andhra University, Visakhapatnam. Pp. 65–67.

Ellis, J.L. (1987). *Flora of Nallamalais. Vol 1*. Botanical Survey of India, Calcutta.

Ellis, J.L. (1990). *Flora of Nallamalais. Vol 2*. Botanical Survey of India, Calcutta.

Krishnan, M.S. (1956). *Geology of India and Burma*. Madras.

Mukhadkar, P.A. (1978). *Andhra Pradesh forest souvenir*.

Nayar, M.P., Ahmed, M. and Raju, D.C.S. (1984). Endemic and rare plants of Eastern Ghats. *Indian J. Forestry* 7(1): 35–42.

Pushp Kumar (1982). Wildlife Sanctuaries in Andhra Pradesh with special reference to Eastern Region. In *National Seminar on Resources, Development and Environment of the Eastern Ghats*. Andhra University, Visakhapatnam. Pp. 98–99.

Acknowledgements

This Data Sheet was prepared by T. Ravisankar and V.B. Hosagoudar (Botanical Survey of India, Southern Circle, Coimbatore) with additional information from M. Ahmedullah (Botanical Survey of India, Howrah).

KNUCKLES
Sri Lanka

Location: North-east of the central mountain massif in Central Province; at latitudes 7°18'–7°34'N and longitudes 80°41'–80°55'E.

Area: 182 km².

Altitude: 1068–1906 m.

Vegetation: Lowland tropical dry semi-evergreen forest, riverine forest, savanna, submontane tropical wet semi-evergreen forest, submontane tropical dry semi-evergreen forest, montane wet evergreen forest, submontane and montane *pathana* grasslands.

Flora: Estimated >1000 vascular plant species (> 700 flowering plant species recorded so far, c. 20% of the angiosperm flora of Sri Lanka); high species endemism. Relict of Deccan-Gondwana flora, many montane and submontane taxa at the northern limits of their ranges in Sri Lanka, threatened species.

Useful plants: Ornamental and medicinal plants, timber and fruit trees, rattans, bamboos, wild relatives of crop plants.

Other values: Rich fauna, watershed protection, soil conservation, hydroelectric power generation, high landscape quality, tourism.

Threats: Cardamom cultivation, illegal firewood collection, mining for precious gem stones, agricultural encroachment, poaching.

Conservation: No legal conservation status, but a conservation management plan is in preparation.

Geography

Falling within the Kandy and Matale districts, and resembling the knuckles of a closed fist, the Knuckles group of mountains form a magnificent range of rugged, steep hills extending for 35 km. There are several prominent peaks along the main SE-NW range. They include Dotalugala, Gombaniya, Kirigalpotha, Knuckles and Kobonilagala. Two other prominent extensions (the Kalupahana-Wamarapugala-Lakkegala Range and the Dumbanagala-Galtuna Range) are at right angles to the main range. The latter extension is connected to another range of mountains running parallel to the main range. Many of the peaks have moderately-sloping, triangular-faceted western faces and east-facing scarps which are sometimes wedge-shaped (Cooray 1961).

The underlying rocks are crystalline, non-fossiliferous rocks of metamorphic origin belonging to the Precambrian Highland Series, comprising khondolites (garnetiferous gneisses, quartzites and quartz schists, garnet-sillimanite-graphite schists and gneisses, and crystalline limestone) and charnokites (quartz, feldspar and pyroxene). There are many tear faults and long parallel folds, ascribed to the Taprobanian Fold System. A number of different soil types occur, including Typic Tropudults (Red Yellow Podzols), Typic Troporthents (Mountain Regosols), Udic and Ultic Haplustalfs (Reddish Brown Earths), Typic Dystropepts and Lithic Ustropepts (Immature Brown Loams) and Lithic Troporthents (Lithosols) (Dimantha 1988).

The Knuckles range is the most northern and north-eastern outlier of the central mountain massif of Sri Lanka, from which it is separated by the Dumbara valley. This valley contains the Mahaweli River, the longest of all Sri Lankan rivers, and along which several major hydroelectric and irrigation reservoirs have been constructed. Several perennial streams (such as the Ambanganga, Suduganga, Kaluganga and Huluganga) which flow into the Mahaweli originate from the frequently mist-covered upper parts of the Knuckles.

The Knuckles are located in close proximity to the dry zone of Sri Lanka. They form an effective barrier to both south-west (May to July) and north-east (October to January) monsoons during which the range receives most of its rainfall. Other sources of rain are mist and inter-monsoonal convectional rains. The west and south-western parts of Knuckles have a submontane ever-wet climate, the eastern and north-eastern parts are seasonally dry, while the upper parts have a montane ever-wet climate. The annual rainfall in the wettest areas is 2725–4470 mm. Temperatures range between 25 and 27°C at lower altitudes and between 18 and 20°C at higher altitudes. The peaks are subject to strong winds and are frequently shrouded in mist. The relative humidity is often 80–90%.

Vegetation

Although the Knuckles cover a relatively small area, their altitudinal range and location at the ecotonal boundary between wet and intermediate climate zones has given rise to a diverse range of vegetation, which includes most of Sri Lanka's major formations.

Lowland dry semi-evergreen forests (intermediate zone forests), with a canopy height of 25–30 m, occur in the foothills (outside the National Heritage Wilderness Area). The dominant trees are *Filicium decipiens*, *Melia dubia*,

Semecarpus obscura, Dimocarpus longan, Vitex altissima, Mangifera zeylanica, Calophyllum tomentosum and *Nothopegia beddomei.*

Submontane tropical wet evergreen forests (canopy height: 20–25 m) occur at mid-altitudes and are dominated by *Cryptocarya wightiana, Myristica dactyloides, Aglaia congylos, Elaeocarpus glandulifer, Litsea gardneri, Bhesa montana, Cullenia rosayroana* and *Pseudocarapa championii.*

Submontane tropical dry evergreen forests (canopy height: 15–20 m) are dominated by *Calophyllum tomentosum, Mangifera zeylanica, Myristica dactyloides, Nothopegia beddomei, Syzygium zeylanicum* and *S. spathulatum.* Subcanopy species include *Pittosporum zeylanicum, Actinodaphne stenophylla* and *Scolopia schreberi.*

Montane tropical wet evergreen forests (cloud or mossy forests) attain 15–20 m in sheltered sites, but may only be 1–2 m high in exposed, wind-swept sites. The main tree species are *Calophyllum walkeri, C. trapezifolium, C. cuneifolium, Eugenia cotinifolia, Garcinia echinocarpa, Gordonia ceylanica, G. speciosa, Mastixia tetrandra* and *Palaquium rubiginosum.* Shrubs include *Alloephania decipiens, Hedyotis* spp., *Indocalamus* spp., *Osbeckia* spp., *Rhodomyrtus tomentosa* and *Strobilanthes* spp. There is a rich moss flora.

Riverine forests (canopy height: 25–30 m) are dominated by *Diospyros malabarica, Pongamia pinnata* and *Terminalia arjuna*; savannas are dominated by the fire-tolerant trees *Careya arborea* and *Phyllanthus emblica*, and the tussock grass *Cymbopogon nardus.* Grasslands of anthropogenic origin are dominated by *Cymbopogon* sp., *Imperata cylindrica* and *Themeda tremula*, and may include shrubs and herbaceous species, such as *Brachystelma lankensis* and *Dipcadi montanum*, and the insectivorous sundews *Drosera burmanii* (an Endangered endemic) and *D. indica.*

Flora

There are estimated to be more than 1000 vascular plant species in the area. So far, over 700 species of flowering plants have been recorded from Knuckles (about 20% of the total angiosperm flora of Sri Lanka) (Rosayro 1958; Werner 1981; Balasubramaniam 1988; Ratnayaka 1993). The Knuckles also carry a rich bryophyte and lichen flora.

The flora of Knuckles is so distinct that it is recognized as a separate floristic region (Ashton and Gunatilleke 1987) within Sri Lanka. It contains part of a relict flora of Deccan-Gondwanic origin with a high level of infra-generic endemism.

In the montane forests of the Knuckles region, 329 woody species belonging to 222 genera and 82 families have been recorded. Among the woody species, 51% are endemic to the island and they contribute 82% of the density of woody individuals in this vegetation type (Ratnayaka 1993).

Endangered species endemic to Knuckles include *Brachystelma lankensis, Dipcadi montanum, Drosera burmanii, Helicia ceylanica, Selaginella wightii, Stemonoporus affinis, Syzygium fergusonii* and *Xanthophyllum rhesta.*

Speciose genera in the Knuckles include *Calophyllum, Diospyros* and *Syzygium.* The family Dipterocarpaceae, which is well-represented in the perhumid south-western part of Sri Lanka (see, for example, the Data Sheet on Sinharaja, CPD Site IS13), is represented at Knuckles by just a single species (*Stemonoporus affinis*), which has a very restricted distribution in the area.

CPD Site IS11: Knuckles, Sri Lanka. Distant view of forest at Corbett's Gap. Photo: V.H. Heywood.

124

Useful plants

It is estimated that more than 20% of the tree species in Knuckles, and a similar proportion of shrubs and herbs, are used in indigenous medicine. Amongst these are *Anoectochilus setaceus, Careya arborea, Gordonia speciosa, Lycopodium phlegmaria, Madhuca longifolia, Munronia pumila, Phyllanthus emblica* and *Zeuxine* sp.

Ochlandra stridula, Pandanus spp. and several species of *Cyperus* are used by the villagers for making baskets, mats and a wide array of household containers. Rattans include *Calamus pseudotenuis* and *C. thwaitesii*.

Plants with edible fruits include *Garcinia quaesita, Phyllanthus emblica* and *Schleichera oleosa*. The inflorescences of the palm *Caryota urens* are tapped for phloem sap to make an alcoholic beverage, a common rural industry in the villages surrounding the forest. Wild relatives of crop plants found in the Knuckles include wild nutmeg (*Myristica dactyloides*), wild mango (*Mangifera zeylanica*), wild breadfruit (*Artocarpus nobilis*), cinnamon (*Cinnamomum* spp.) and wild peppers (*Piper* spp.), among others.

Ornamental plants of potential in horticulture include several orchid species, *Exacum macranthum, Gordonia speciosa* and *Kendrickia walkeri* (for their showy flowers), and ornamental bamboos, such as the endemic monotypic genus *Davidsea* and the endemic *Arundinaria walkeri*.

Social and environmental values

The Knuckles range is an important watershed and its perennial streams feed several major irrigation and/or hydroelectric power schemes (e.g. Victoria, Randenigala, Nalanda, Elahera and Dewahuwa). Two further hydroelectric power/irrigation reservoirs (Moragahakanda and Kaluganga) are also planned for the future.

The Knuckles has a rich fauna, including leopard, sambar, wild boar, barking deer, purple-faced leaf monkey, large Ceylon flying grey squirrel, black and yellow giant squirrel, jungle squirrel and several species of lizards endemic to the area. Sri Lanka is an Endemic Bird Area (EBA), with 23 endemic restricted-range bird species. At least 10 of these species occur in this area (Perera 1988), including several of the 13 species which are endemic to the wet and hill zones. A cavern, popularly known as Nitre Cave, is inhabited by flocks of predominantly insectivorous bats which feed in the forests. Deep layers of their droppings have accumulated and are reported to be used as fertilizer by the villagers (Edussuriya 1988).

The scenic qualities of the landscape, combined with a diversity of plant and animal communities within a relatively small area in close proximity to major cities in Central, North-Western and North-Central provinces, makes the Knuckles an important site for environmental education, research and recreation.

Economic assessment

The annual income from commercial cultivation of cardamom (*Elettaria cardamomum* var. *cardamomum*) in the Knuckles range has been estimated at US$300,000) (Gurusinghe 1988). The forests of the Knuckles protect important catchment areas for the multi-million dollar Mahaweli basin development

CPD Site IS11: Knuckles, Sri Lanka. Close-up of forest at Corbett's Gap. Photo: V.H. Heywood.

programmes which include several hydroelectric and irrigation reservoirs.

A preliminary economic assessment of non-timber forest products gathered by villagers from the Knuckles has been made in a sample of 60 households in three villages using both market and non-market valuation methods. The results revealed that the income generated from forest-related activities, including cardamom cultivation, is 62.5% of the total annual household income and 58.8% of the monetary income, suggesting a heavy dependence on forest-based resources. Non-timber forest products, excluding cardamom products, are estimated to constitute 16.2% of total income and 5.3% of monetary income (Goonatillaka 1992). A detailed economic assessment of the major goods and services provided by the forest, the economic benefits derived by conversion of the forest and grasslands to cash crop plantations, and the environmental costs associated with this shift in land use is being planned as a prerequisite for sustainable management of this complex ecosystem.

Threats

Within the forests at Knuckles, an area of 27.5 km^2 (15% of the total area) is under cardamom cultivation (as at 1988). In the past, land leased to both private and government agencies in the Knuckles contributed 55% of the land area under cardamom cultivation in Sri Lanka. Cardamom requires overhead shade, so it is planted within the forest after the undergrowth and ground vegetation has been cleared. Such clearance and subsequent weeding destroys the structure of the forest, reduces its floristic diversity and prevents natural forest regeneration. Furthermore, fuelwood is cut from the forest for drying harvested cardamom pods and for heating.

Illegal hunting of wild animals, such as wild boar, monkeys, sambar and deer, takes place, along with illicit mining for precious gem stones. Mining has degraded some areas of riverine forest.

Agricultural encroachment is occurring around the forest. People who live around the area practice shifting cultivation and contribute to illicit felling of trees for timber and fuelwood. More recently, some of the abandoned tea estates and grasslands (both within and immediately outside the area) have been converted to potato farming, leading to severe soil erosion.

Part of the buffer zone surrounding Knuckles is planted with *Pinus caribaea*. These trees are often burnt during dry periods, and fires could spread into the natural forest if left uncontrolled.

Conservation

As yet, the Knuckles has no legal status as a conservation area. A conservation management plan is being prepared by the Ministry of Lands and Land Development with assistance from IUCN. The plan is intended to identify critical areas within the Knuckles watershed that need to be protected from harmful activities, determine the socio-economic implications of sustainable management, initiate appropriate socio-economic programmes which do not conflict with conservation, improve the administrative infrastructure for implementing the programmes, and generate public support for conservation of the Knuckles through legislation, further research, education and extension activities. Future development of tourism should be regulated to ensure the protection of fragile sites.

References

Ashton, P.S. and Gunatilleke, C.V.S. (1987). New light on the plant geography of Ceylon, I. Historical plant geography. *J. Biogeography* 14: 249–285.

Balasubramaniam, S. (1988). Major forest formations of the Knuckles Region. Paper presented at a Workshop for the Preparation of a Conservation Plan for Knuckles Range of Forests.

Cooray, P.G. (1956). The Knuckles Expedition. *Bulletin of the Ceylon Geographical Society* 10(3–4): 50.

Cooray, P.G. (1961). Geographical aspects of the Knuckles area. *Bulletin of the Ceylon Geographical Society* 15(1–2).

Dimantha, S. (1988). Soils and land use of the Knuckles conservation zone. Paper presented at a Workshop for the Preparation of a Conservation Plan for Knuckles Range of Forests.

Edussuriya, S.C. (1988). Some physiographical and other related aspects of the Knuckles region. Paper presented at a Workshop for the Preparation of a Conservation Plan for Knuckles Range of Forests.

Goonatillaka, H. (1992). Impact of forest conservation programme for Knuckles on rural communities in the vicinity: a preliminary economic assessment. Paper presented at a Workshop on Methods for Social Science Research on Non-timber Forest Products, Bangkok.

Gurusinghe, P. de A. (1988). Cardamom cultivation in the Knuckles range. Paper presented at a Workshop for the Preparation of a Conservation Plan for Knuckles Range of Forests.

Perera, M.M.D. (1988). Wildlife in Knuckles range. Paper presented at a Workshop for the Preparation of a Conservation Plan for Knuckles Range of Forests.

Ratnayaka, H.D. (1993). A plant ecological study of the upper montane rain forests of the Knuckles region, Sri Lanka. University of Peradeniya, Sri Lanka. (M.Phil. thesis.)

Rosayro, R.A. de (1958). The climate and vegetation of the Knuckles region of Ceylon. (A reconnaissance study with special reference to aerial photographic interpretation). *Ceylon Forester* 3(3–4): 201–260.

Werner, W.L. (1981). *Die Hohen und Nebelwalder auf de Insel Ceylon (Sri Lanka)*. Tropische und Subtropische Pflanzenwelt 46. Akad. Wiss. Lit. Mainz.

Acknowledgements

This Data Sheet was prepared by Professors Nimal and Savitri Gunatilleke (Department of Botany, University of Peradeniya, Sri Lanka).

PEAK WILDERNESS AND HORTON PLAINS
Sri Lanka

Location: Contiguous areas on the western range of the main central mountain massif of Sri Lanka, between latitudes 6°44'–6°54'N and longitudes 80°25'–80°50'E.

Area: Peak Wilderness: 223.8 km²; Horton Plains: 31.6 km².

Altitude: Peak Wilderness: 700–2238 m (summit of Adam's Peak); Horton Plains: 1800–2389 m (summit of Mount Kirigalpota).

Vegetation: Lowland tropical wet evergreen rain forest, submontane and montane tropical wet evergreen forests, wet *pathana* grasslands.

Flora: Estimated >1000 vascular plant species; high species endemism; relict of Gondwanan flora; localized species distributions.

Other values: Watershed protection for all the major rivers of Sri Lanka, which include major irrigation and hydroelectric power schemes; tourism, religious significance.

Threats: Visitor pressure, mining for precious gem stones, extraction of timber and fuelwood, forest die-back, fire, invasive plants.

Conservation: The Peak Wilderness is a Sanctuary (IUCN Management Category: IV) and Horton Plains is a National Park (IUCN Management Category: II). The conservation value of the existing protected area would be enhanced by the addition of adjacent Forest Reserves.

Geography

The Peak Wilderness is a rugged mountain range on the western ridge of the main mountain massif of Sri Lanka. Horton Plains is an undulating plateau connected to Peak Wilderness at its eastern end. Both areas are located between latitudes 6°44'–6°54'N and longitudes 80°25'–80°50'E. Peak Wilderness covers 223.8 km² and has an altitidunal range of 700–2238 m, and includes several prominent peaks (such as Adam's Peak, the highest point), Benasamanala and Kunudiyaparvatha. Horton Plains covers 31.6 km² and has an altitudinal range of 1800–2389 m. It is the highest tableland in Sri Lanka and includes Mount Kirigalpota (Sri Lanka's second highest mountain, at 2389 m) and Thotupolakanda (the third highest, at 2357 m).

The underlying rocks are ancient crystalline, non-fossiliferous metamorphic rocks belonging to the Precambrian Highland Series, and comprise khondalites and charnokites (for further details see Data Sheet on Knuckles, CPD Site IS11). Soils are ultisols with a characteristic thick black organic A-horizon at high altitudes.

Peak Wilderness and Horton Plains, together with surrounding forested areas, comprise Sri Lanka's most important water catchments from which almost all the country's major perennial rivers originate. These include the Kalu Ganga, Kelani Ganga, Mahaweli Ganga and Walawe Ganga. There are extremely precipitous cliffs on the southern flanks of the area, with sheer drops to almost 1000 m, down which spectacular waterfalls cascade.

Peak Wilderness has a perhumid and aseasonal climate. Its southern and south-western slopes are the wettest parts of Asia west of Borneo (Ashton and Gunatilleke 1987). Horton Plains also has a perhumid climate, but there is a short dry spell between January and March. The mean annual rainfall ranges from 3080 mm (on the south-western slopes of Peak Wilderness) to 5120 mm (in the north-eastern high-altitude region towards Horton Plains). The region is influenced by both south-west (May–July) and north-east (October–January) monsoons, and also receives inter-monsoonal convectional rains. High-altitude areas are frequently shrouded in mists. The mean annual temperature is 13°–15°C. Ground frosts frequently occur at night in the grasslands of Horton Plains during January and February, but do not occur in forested areas. Both Peak Wilderness and Horton Plains are subject to strong winds.

Vegetation

Peak Wilderness is one of the few sites remaining in Sri Lanka with continuous tracts of forest altitudinally graded from lowland tropical wet evergreen rain forest to montane (cloud) forest.

Lowland tropical wet evergreen rain forest is dominated (in the canopy) by *Anisophyllea cinnamomoides, Palaquium petiolare* and *Shorea trapezifolia*, and by *Chaetocarpus castanocarpus, Cullenia rosayroana, Myristica dactyloides* and *Syzygium* spp. in the subcanopy. Understorey species include *Antidesma pyrifolium, Memecylon gardneri, Schumacheria castanifolia, Stemonoporus elegans* and *Psychotria* spp.

Submontane evergreen forest includes *Adinandra lasiopetala, Bhesa montana, Gordonia speciosa, Mastixia montana, Palaquium rubiginosum, Shorea gardneri, Stemonoporus cordifolius, S. gardneri, S. oblongifolius* and *S. rigidus*. The last four species are highly localized

CPD Site IS12: Peak Wilderness and Horton Plains, Sri Lanka. The Horton Plains area showing grassland and forest patches. Photo: V.H. Heywood.

but exhibit single-species dominance in their stands (Greller *et al.* 1987). Submontane evergreen forests are the uppermost distributional limit of dipterocarps, with *Stemonoporus gardneri* having been recorded at 1750 m altitude.

Montane forests are dominated by *Actinodaphne speciosa*, *Calophyllum walkeri*, *Garcinia echinocarpa*, *Rhododendron arboreum* var. *zeylanicum*, *Litsea* sp., *Michelia nilagirica*, *Syzygium cyclophyllum* and *S. revolutum*. The shrub layer includes *Strobilanthes* spp. and the bamboo *Indocalamus wightiana*. The herbaceous layer includes *Emilia glabra*, *Exacum trinerve*, *Impatiens* spp., the ground orchid *Phaius tancarvilleae* and *Sonerila* spp. (Greller *et al.* 1987). Montane forest at Horton Plains can attain 10–15 m but canopy height is reduced to about 1 m on ridges and the summit of Thotupolakanda. Dominant canopy species are the emergent *Calophyllum walkeri*, *Cinammomum ovalifolia*, *Eugenia mabaeoides*, *Litsea ovalifolia*, *Neolitsea fuscata*, *Syzygium revolutum*, *S. rotundifolium* and *Symplocos* spp. The trees are often gnarled and twisted and their trunks and lower branches are densely covered with epiphytic orchids, ferns (particularly of the family Hymenophyllaceae), bryophytes, foliose lichens and the fruticose lichen *Usnea barbata* (Ratnayeke and Balasubramaniam 1989; Wijesundara 1990). The understorey is very dense and dominated by *Strobilanthes* spp.; where gaps occur, the ground layer has *Coleus* spp., *Impatiens* spp. and *Selaginella* spp.

Grasslands cover about half the lower slopes and valleys of Horton Plains. The dominant grass is the tussock-forming *Chrysopogon zeylanicum*, which grows to about 1 m in height. A large number of semi-woody or herbaceous species occur in shallow depressions between the tussocks. The dwarf bamboo, *Arundinaria walkeri*, dominates along streamsides.

Flora

The flora of Peak Wilderness and Horton Plains has not been extensively studied. Apart from Adam's Peak, most other areas are botanically poorly known. The few localized phytosociological surveys that have been conducted, along with random collections of herbarium specimens, suggest that the Peak Wilderness/Horton Plains area is floristically rich. It is estimated that the flora of these two areas combined is likely to include more than 1000 species of vascular plants.

The most speciose genera are *Strobilanthes*, *Symplocos*, *Stemonoporus* and *Syzygium*. Genera with northern temperate affinities include (among others) *Anaphalis*, *Gaultheria*, *Pedicularis*, *Ranunculus*, *Rhododendron* and *Vaccinium*.

In a 5 ha sample of lowland wet evergreen rain forest (Gilimale) in Peak Wilderness, the tree component represents

CPD Site IS12: Peak Wilderness and Horton Plains, Sri Lanka. Peak Wilderness showing montane forest with *Rhododendron arboreum* var. *zeylanicum*.
Photo: V.H. Heywood.

41 families, 88 genera and 136 species. Of the species, 59% of those recorded were endemic to Sri Lanka (Gunatilleke and Ashton 1987). The endemics contributed 74% of the individuals in the stand. Of 54 woody species recorded in a preliminary survey in Horton Plains, 50% are endemic to Sri Lanka, 39% are restricted to forests of South India and Sri Lanka, and the remaining 11% are widely distributed throughout the forests of South East Asia (Ratnayeke and Balasubramaniam 1989).

A number of rare endemics are confined to Peak Wilderness and have localized distributions. For example, the endemic *Stemonoporus rigidus* was recently rediscovered after an interval of 150 years. Other rare species include *Schumacheria alnifolia*, the rare daffodil orchid *Ipsea speciosa* (both endemic to Sri Lanka), and the root parasites *Balanophora* spp. and *Christisonia* spp. The only genus of freshwater red alga in Sri Lanka, *Batracospermum*, is represented at Horton Plains.

Useful plants

Many species of trees, shrubs and climbers are used as sources of wood for fuel and poles, or used in the construction of small huts and seating along the pilgrim trails to Adam's Peak. *Indocalamus* sp. and *Ochlandra* sp. are dwarf bamboos used in basketry.

The young inflorescences of the palm *Caryota urens* are tapped for phloem sap which is used in the preparation of sugar candy and an alcoholic beverage. Fruits of *Garcinia quaesita* are used as a spice. Edible nuts and resin are obtained from *Canarium zeylanicum*.

Medicinal plants include *Asparagus* spp., *Gordonia speciosa*, *Rubia cordifolia* and the liane *Coscinium fenestratum*. The bark of *Kokoona zeylanica* is ground and pressed into biscuit-like discs which are sold as a cosmetic.

An oil is obtained from the Endangered endemic *Dipterocarpus glandulosus*. A hole is cut into the base of the trunk and fires are lit to extract damar. The oil is used for lighting lamps, as well as being used medicinally and as an insect repellant in paddy fields. Resins are obtained from the other dipterocarp species.

Ornamental plants include *Burmannia coelestis*, *Exacum trinerve*, *E. walkeri*, *Gordonia speciosa*, *Impatiens* spp., *Osbeckia* spp., *Medinella maculata*, *Rhododendrum arboreum* var. *zeylanicum* and the ground orchid *Phaius tancarvilleae* (for their showy flowers), and many species of ferns.

Social and environmental values

Peak Wilderness and Horton Plains have a rich fauna. Mammals recorded include Kelaart's long-clawed shrew (a monotypic genus endemic to the mountains of Sri Lanka), the torque monkey (endemic to Sri Lanka), purple-faced langur, leopard and wild boar. In addition, rusty spotted cat, fishing cat, stripe-necked mongoose, Indian spotted chevrotain, Indian muntjac, sambar and long-tailed giant squirrel have been reported from Horton Plains. The slender loris is restricted to Horton Plains. There is a herd of 30–50 elephants in Peak Wilderness (IUCN 1990).

Sri Lanka is an Endemic Bird Area (EBA), with 23 endemic restricted-range bird species. Six of these are confined to montane habitats in the hill zone in the centre of the island, two to the lowland rain forests of the wet zone and a further five to the forests of both of these zones. Together, the Peak Wilderness and Horton Plains contain suitable habitats for all of these wet and hill zone species, and are a key site for the conservation of many, particularly the threatened hill zone endemics, Sri Lanka wood-pigeon (*Columba torringtoni*) and Sri Lanka whistling-thrush (*Myiophonus blighi*).

About 70 species of insects have been recorded, including (at Peak Wilderness) the Sri Lankan relict ant, *Aneuretus simoni* (IUCN 1990). See Silva (1982) and Silva and Silva (1990) for details of the freshwater fauna.

Horton Plains, with its grasslands, rolling forested hills, fast-flowing streams and panoramic views (such as that from World's End, named for its sheer drop from 2100 m to 1000 m), attracts local and international tourists, and is frequently used for environmental studies and research. About 25 archaeological sites are known (Chandraratne 1990), some of which may also provide clues to the origin of the wet pathana grasslands.

Adam's Peak is an important religious site for Buddhists, Hindus and Muslims, and its spectacular landscapes attract other tourists.

The natural vegetation of Peak Wilderness and Horton Plains protects the watersheds of all the major river systems in Sri Lanka. The rivers are harnessed in major irrigation and hydroelectric power schemes.

Economic assessment

Hydroelectric power plants along rivers having their origins in Peak Wilderness and Horton Plains generate over 90% of Sri Lanka's electricity. The valleys of these major river systems are the most densely populated areas of the country. In addition, the rivers provide water for major irrigation schemes in the north-central, north-eastern and south-eastern parts of the country. Peak Wilderness and Horton Plains, along with adjacent Forest Reserves, therefore provide some of the most vital ecological services to the nation. It is essential that the native forests are conserved in order that their protective function is maintained.

Village-level surveys to determine the dependency on forest products for those people living in the Peak Wilderness area have been initiated by the Environmental Management Division of the Forest Department, with the assistance of IUCN and the U.K. Overseas Development Administration. Studies need to be undertaken at Horton Plains to assess the economic benefits derived form tourism and to determine the optimum level of visitation to prevent areas becoming degraded.

Threats

Man-made fires are a constant threat to Horton Plains during the dry season (Chambers 1980). Forest die-back is occurring on Thotupolakanda and in some stands on the plateau (Perera 1978; Werner 1988; Ratnayeke and Balasubramaniam 1989; Wijesundara 1990). It has yet to be established whether the die-back is caused by climate change, acid rain, deforestation in the valleys around the Horton Plains plateau or some other factor, including natural cycles of vegetation change.

In the 1970s, a small area of grassland in Horton Plains was converted to a seed potato farm. Although this practice was subsequently suspended, many grass species were accidentally introduced during this period and now compete with native grasses.

The sambar population appears to have increased considerably as a result of protection and reduction in the numbers of predators. This, together with the spread of invasive species, could lead to an overall change in the floristic composition of the forest-grassland ecosystem.

Illicit poaching, mining for precious gemstones, timber and fuelwood harvesting pose threats to Peak Wilderness and Horton Plains (Hoffmann 1988). A sizeable area of natural forest near the perimeter of Peak Wilderness has been extensively damaged as a result of mining for precious stones. This has led to severe soil erosion.

Visitor pressure poses a threat to some fragile areas at Horton Plains and especially to a number of rare grassland species. In addition, the number of visitors to Adam's Peak has increased dramatically over the last 4–5 decades. During annual pilgrimages fuelwood is cut from the natural forest. Although the authorities have now restricted the removal of wood from the forest, implementation is difficult. Most other parts of Peak Wilderness do not, however, suffer the same amount of disturbance.

Conservation

The Peak Wilderness is a Sanctuary (IUCN Management Category: IV) and Horton Plains is a National Park (IUCN Management Category: II). Both areas are under the jurisdiction of the Department of Wildlife Conservation. Both areas urgently need a management plan. Some initial steps in this direction have been taken by the Department of Wildlife Conservation in collaboration with other government and non-government agencies. In addition, long-term monitoring of ecosystem dynamics and possible changes in climate is required, along with more staff to manage and patrol the reserves.

Conservation education and awareness programmes, being conducted by the Department of Wildlife Conservation with assistance from non-governmental organizations, need to be expanded. Co-operative programmes with rural communities living around these forests need to be developed to ensure sustainable use of forest resources.

The conservation value of the Peak Wilderness/Horton Plains protected area would be significantly improved by the inclusion of some adjacent biologically rich and environmentally critical Forest Reserves, such as the upper regions of the Kelani Valley Proposed Reserve, Morahela-Bambarabotuwa and Walawe Basin Forest Reserves.

References

Ashton, P.S. and Gunatilleke, C.V.S. (1987). New light on the plant geography of Ceylon, II. The ecological biogeography of the lowland endemic tree flora. *J. Biogeography* 14: 295–327.

Chambers, M.R. (1980). Horton Plains – to burn or not to burn. *Loris* 15: 181–183.

Chandraratne, R.M.M. (1990). Archaeological explorations at Horton Plains. 8 pp. (Unpublished report.)

Deraniyagala, S.U. (1971). Archaeological explorations in Ceylon, Part I – Horton Plains. *Spolia Zeylanica* 32: 13–22.

Greller, A.M., Gunatilleke, I.A.U.N., Jayasuriya, A.H.M., Gunatilleke, C.V.S., Balasubramaniam, S., and Dassanayake, M.D. (1987). *Stemonoporus* (Dipterocarpaceae) – dominated montane forests in the Adam's Peak Wilderness, Sri Lanka. *J. Tropical Ecology* 3: 243–253.

Gunatilleke, C.V.S. and Ashton, P.S. (1987). New light on the plant geography of Ceylon, II. The ecological biogeography of the lowland endemic tree flora. *J. Biogeography* 14: 295–327.

Hoffmann, T. (1988). Report on the southern and the western boundaries of the Peak Wilderness Sanctuary. *Loris* 20: 10.

IUCN (1990). *IUCN directory of South Asian protected areas.* IUCN, Gland, Switzerland and Cambridge, U.K. xxiv, 294 pp. (Compiled by the World Conservation Monitoring Centre.)

Perera, W.R.H. (1978). Thotupolakanda – an environmental disaster? *Sri Lanka Forester* 13: 53–55.

Ratnayeke, S. and Balasubramaniam, S. (1989). The structure and floristic composition of the montane forest in the Horton Plains, Sri Lanka. Institute of Fundamental Studies, Kandy, Sri Lanka. 18 pp. (Unpublished report.)

Silva, K.H.G.M. de (1982). Aspects of the ecology and conservation of Sri Lanka's endemic freshwater shrimp *Caridina singhalensis. Biological Conservation* 24: 219–231.

Silva, K.H.G.M. de and Silva, P.K. de (1990). Stream fauna in Horton Plains and Peak Wilderness Areas. 18 pp. (Unpublished report.)

Werner, W.L. (1982). The upper montane rain forests of Sri Lanka. *Sri Lanka Forester* 15: 119–129.

Werner, W.L. (1988). Canopy die-back in the upper montane rain forests of Sri Lanka. *Geogr. Journal* 17: 245–248.

Wijesundara, D.S.A. (1990). Die-back in montane forests. Paper presented at NARESA Workshop on Conservation Management of Ritigala Kanda, Horton Plains and Peak Wilderness Wildlife Reserves and the Adjoining Areas. 10 pp.

Acknowledgements

This Data Sheet was prepared by Professors Nimal and Savitri Gunatilleke (Department of Botany, University of Peradeniya, Sri Lanka).

SINHARAJA
Sri Lanka

Location: South-west lowland wet zone of Sri Lanka, between latitudes 6°21'–6°27'N and longitudes 80°21'–80°38'E.

Area: 111.9 km² (including 23 km² of submontane forests and grasslands recently added to the conserved area).

Altitude: 210–1170 m (summit of Hinipitigala Peak).

Vegetation: Lowland and submontane tropical wet evergreen forests and submontane *pathana* grasslands. Sinharaja is the largest remaining tract of relatively undisturbed tropical lowland wet evergreen forest in Sri Lanka.

Flora: Estimated c. 700 species of flowering plants, c. 20% of the angiosperm flora of Sri Lanka; estimated >1000 species with inclusion of ferns, bryophytes and lichens. Relict of Deccan-Gondwana flora; many disjuncts, high species endemism, threatened species.

Useful plants: Timber trees, wild relatives of fruit and spice plants, rattans, food and medicinal plants.

Other values: Watershed protection, wildlife refuge, education and research centre, tourism.

Threats: Deforestation, agriculture, mining for precious stones, visitor pressure, potential hydroelectric scheme.

Conservation: National Heritage Wilderness Area, World Heritage Site and Biosphere Reserve.

Geography

Sinharaja is situated in the south-west lowland wet zone of Sri Lanka, between latitudes 6°21'–6°27'N and longitudes 80°21'–80°38'E, in Sabaragamuwa and Southern provinces. The total area of the National Heritage Wilderness Area is 111.9 km², of which 88.6 km² has been designated as a World Heritage Site and Biosphere Reserve. This includes an eastern extension of 23 km² of wet evergreen submontane forests, grasslands and some degraded and abandoned agricultural land, including abandoned tea and cardamom plantations.

The terrain is undulating, consisting of a series of ridges and valleys with a network of streams draining into the Gin Ganga on the southern boundary and the Kalu Ganga on the northern boundary. Altitude ranges from 210 m in the west to 1170 m at Hinipitigala Peak in the east. There are at least 10 prominent peaks scattered throughout the forest with a high-altitude plateau (Tangamale Plains) at 1100 m in the east.

Geologically, Sinharaja lies in the transition zone between two local geological formations, known as the Highland Group and the Southwestern Group, consisting predominantly of khondalites and charnokites of Precambrian crystalline origin (Cooray 1978). Sinharaja also represents a distinctive zone of basic rocks which include hornblendes, basic charnokites, pyroxene amphibolites and scapolite-bearing calc-granulites. The soils are mostly ultisols with abundant lateritic formations (Gunatilleke and Gunatilleke 1985; Zoysa and Raheem 1990).

An aseasonal perhumid climate prevails within Sinharaja forest. Mean annual precipitation ranges from 3600 to 5000 mm with distinct monsoonal peaks in May and November. There are relatively dry periods in January–March and August. Mean annual temperatures range from 19° to 31°C. The eastern highlands may be somewhat cooler, but no records are available. The eastern sector of the forest is frequently subject to mists and strong winds.

Nearly 40 small villages are scattered around the perimeter of the forest. Most of them are ancient hamlets, each with 20–50 or more families, most of whom are at least partially dependent on the forest for their subsistence (McDermott, Gunatilleke and Gunatilleke 1990).

Vegetation

Sinharaja is the largest tract of tropical lowland wet evergreen forest in Sri Lanka. Only 9% of this forest type remains on the island, and much of this is partially degraded and fragmented due to timber extraction and village expansion schemes.

Based on physiognomic, ecological and floristic criteria, the vegetation of Sinharaja can be divided into the following categories: lowland tropical wet evergreen forests (*Mesua-Doona* (*Shorea*) formation), submontane tropical wet evergreen forests (*Shorea-Calophyllum-Cullenia* formation), wet *pathana* grasslands, and secondary forests and fernlands of anthropogenic origin.

Lowland wet evergreen forests, 30–35 m in height, are dominated by the *Mesua-Doona* formation with no emergent layer. The canopy is co-dominated by several species each of *Shorea* and *Syzygium, Mesua nagassarium, Palaquium petiolare* and *Anisophyllea cinnamomoides*. The subcanopy is dominated by *Chaetocarpus castanocarpus, Cullenia rosayroana, Mesua ferrea* and *Myristica dactyloides*. An understorey tree stratum dominated by *Garcinia hermonii* and *Xylopia championii* is distinguishable. A sparse shrub and herbaceous layer is dominated by members of Rubiaceae, Euphorbiaceae and Zingiberaceae. *Artabotrys zeylanica, Coscinium fenestratum, Dalbergia championii* and *Entada* sp. are among the common woody climbers. A rich epiphytic flora of orchids, bryophytes and lichens is also present.

Submontane tropical wet evergreen forests, with a canopy height of 25–30 m, are dominated by *Shorea gardneri* and are physiognomically similar to their lowland counterparts in valleys and lower slopes. However, trees are often gnarled and twisted in higher, windswept areas.

Secondary scrub vegetation occurs on the periphery of the primary forests, and includes species of *Alstonia, Macaranga, Melastoma, Osbeckia*, and the ferns *Dicranopteris* and *Pteris*. Wet *pathana* grasslands are dominated by *Chrysopogon zeylanicum* and several species of *Eriocaulon*.

Flora

The rain forest flora of south-western Sri Lanka, represented by Sinharaja, is a relict of the ancient Gondwana flora. Both species richness and endemism are concentrated in these primeval forests. Endemicity is extraordinarily high at specific and intraspecific ranks, suggesting evolution during isolation of the Deccan Plate during the upper Cretaceous and early Eocene periods.

The phytogeographic affinities of Sri Lankan rain forest elements with those of Madagascar, Seychelles, South India and Malesia are of considerable interest to biogeographers. According to some phytogeographers, the Deccan Plate played a major role in the northward migration of Gondwanic families, such as Dipterocarpaceae and Dilleniaceae, and of supra-generic taxa, notably among the Palmae, Monimiaceae, Proteaceae, Myrtaceae and Bombacaceae. Sinharaja rain forest is among the last vestiges of this original Deccan-Gondwanic flora in South Asia (Ashton and Gunatilleke 1987).

The total angiosperm flora of Sinharaja, including all woody and non-woody life forms in both primary and secondary vegetation, is estimated at around 700 species (based on several floristic surveys and existing herbarium collections). This represents about 20% of the total angiosperm flora of Sri Lanka, of which nearly 90% is concentrated in the perhumid south-western sector of the island. Inclusion of ferns, bryophytes and lichens would probably bring the flora of Sinharaja to more than 1000 species. The epiphytic and epiphyllous flora is relatively poorly studied but considered to be very rich. For example, as many as 13 different epiphyllous bryophyte species have been observed on a single leaf of *Mesua ferrea*.

64% of the trees in Sinharaja forest are endemic to Sri Lanka and, as in other Sri Lankan rain forests, restricted or localized distribution of species is unusually high. An enumeration of woody species over 30 cm girth at breast height in 25 ha of lowland primary forest at Sinharaja revealed the presence of 211 species belonging to 119 genera and 43 families. Dominant tree families are Clusiaceae, Dipterocarpaceae, Sapotaceae, Bombacaceae and Myrtaceae. The shrub flora is dominated by Rubiaceae, Euphorbiaceae and Melastomataceae. Dipterocarpaceae, Myrtaceae, Euphorbiaceae, Clusiaceae and Rubiaceae are among the most speciose families within the forest.

In Dipterocarpaceae, the genus *Shorea* is best represented, with 13 species, all of which are endemic to the island. Other speciose genera with high endemism include *Calophyllum, Diospyros, Memecylon, Palaquium, Semecarpus, Stemonoporus* and *Syzygium*.

Since most other low and mid-altitude rain forests of Sri Lanka have been degraded by timber extraction, Sinharaja forest remains the main refugium for long-term survival of the endemic-rich lowland rain forest flora of Sri Lanka. Based on phytosociological surveys, it has been estimated that, out of 135 endemic woody species, 15 are Endangered, 48 are Vulnerable and 64 are Rare, according to IUCN Red Data Book category definitions (Gunatilleke and Gunatilleke 1991). The Endangered category includes *Diospyros quaesita*, the variegated ebony or calamander, one of Sri Lanka's most beautiful luxury hardwoods.

Useful plants

Over 80 species in both primary and secondary forests in Sinharaja are reported to have food and medicinal value (Gunatilleke and Gunatilleke 1993). In addition, a number of species are collected from the forest for a variety of other purposes (Gunatilleke 1988). Among the most sought-after plant species, other than for timber, are *Caryota urens* for its sugary sap, *Calamus* spp. for rattan cane, *Coscinium fenestratum* and *Elettaria cardamomum* for their medicinal and/or spice value, and a host of orchids and other herbaceous plants for their ornamental value.

Wild relatives of clove (*Syzygium* sp.), nutmeg (*Myristica* sp.), cinnamon (*Cinnamomum* spp.), cardamom (*Elettaria* sp.), pepper (*Piper* sp.), durian (*Cullenia* spp.), mango (*Mangifera* sp.), breadfruit (*Artocarpus* sp.) and citrus (*Atalantia* sp.) have been recorded from Sinharaja forest.

Social and environmental values

Tributaries of two rivers, the Gin Ganga and Kukulu Ganga, originate in Sinharaja forest, which is therefore of great hydrological importance to south-western Sri Lanka.

Sinharaja has a rich fauna, including 262 species of vertebrates (representing 36% of the Sri Lanka's vertebrate fauna), of which 43% are endemic to Sri Lanka (Zoysa and Raheem 1990), nearly half of the endemic amphibian fauna of Sri Lanka and, among the invertebrates, 65 species of butterflies (of which 2 species and 19 subspecies are endemic).

Sri Lanka is an Endemic Bird Area (EBA), with 23 endemic restricted-range bird species. Six of these are confined to montane habitats in the hill zone in the centre of the island (and do not occur or are of marginal occurrence in Sinharaja), two to the lowland rain forests of the wet zone and a further five to the forests of both of these zones. Sinharaja is a key site for the conservation of many of these species, particularly the threatened green-billed coucal (*Centropus chlororhynchus*), which is confined to the lowland rain forests of the wet zone, and ashy-headed laughing-thrush (*Garrulax cinereifrons*).

The north-western part of Sinharaja forest, with its road network, research and educational facilities, attracts large numbers of local and foreign tourists. It has become one of the most popular outdoor educational centres for school children in Sri Lanka. Similar facilities need to be established in other areas to spread the visitor load.

Economic assessment

Socio-economic profiles and demographic trends of the villages are being documented at present. Preliminary results have shown that 8% of the households in a few selected villages were completely dependent on the resources of the rain forest for their subsistence, while others depend on the forest to varying degrees for fuelwood, bathing and drinking water, food and medicine. Among the income-generating products gathered from the forest are sugar syrup and candy from the palm *Caryota urens*, rattans for basketry and furniture from species of *Calamus*, resins from dipterocarps, medicinal plants and gemstones.

An economic assessment of goods and services offered by the forest is underway. According to preliminary findings, the majority of peripheral households have indicated their unwillingness to pay for goods and services which they traditionally enjoyed for generations. Alternative methods of assessing the value of services and goods provided by the forest to the rural communities need to be employed to prevent gross under-valuation of these important local benefits (Gunatilleke, Gunatilleke and Abeygunawardena 1993).

Threats

The main threats to the forest are from agricultural encroachment, particularly on its southern boundary. The legal status provided under the Natural Wilderness Heritage Area Act prohibits the conversion of Sinharaja to other land uses. The forest boundary has been surveyed and clearly demarcated, using concrete posts and a buffer zone strip of planted *Pinus caribaea* and *Areca catechu*.

Collection of fuelwood and other non-timber forest products, including medicinal plants and rattans, and mining for precious stones pose a continued threat to the conservation of the forest.

The Gin Ganga and Kukulu Ganga have been ear-marked for hydroelectric power generation in the future. The likely impact of the proposed reservoirs on Sinharaja forest is claimed to be minimal. Environmental impact studies are currently being assessed.

During the period between 1970 and 1977, about 14 km² of forest in the north-western sector was selectively logged. 40 km of logging roads were constructed during the logging project. The roads are maintained to allow access to the interior forests for educational, research and tourism purposes. However, visitor pressure in this sector poses problems of pollution to streams, damage to fragile habitats (including ridge tops), collection of rare and ornamental plants, and litter accumulation.

Conservation

Logging in Sinharaja forest was banned in 1977 after considerable public pressure. Today, the conservation area has World Heritage status and is a National Heritage Wilderness Area and Biosphere Reserve. The forest is administered by the Forest Department under the Ministry of Lands and Land Development. A management plan was drawn up in 1985 by the Ministry of Lands and Land Development with assistance from IUCN. Its implementation is being carried out by the Forest Department of Sri Lanka under a cooperative agreement with IUCN and additional funding from the Norwegian Government. An educational and research centre, equipped with pamphlets, brochures and guides, and a field research station with basic facilities, have been established during the initial phase. The management plan was revised in 1993.

The creation of a buffer zone is planned outside the reserve to meet local needs for forest products, thereby relieving pressure on the Sinharaja forest.

The inclusion of the mist-clad, high-altitude forests and grasslands of the adjacent Handapan Ella Plains would add a further important area of conservation value to the Sinharaja National Heritage Wilderness Area.

References

Ashton, P.S. and Gunatilleke, C.V.S. (1987). New light on the plant geography of Ceylon, I. Historical plant geography. *J. Biogeography* 14: 249–285.

Cooray, P.G. (1978). Geology of Sri Lanka. In Nutalya, P. (ed.), *Proceedings of the Third Regional Conference on Geology and Mineral Resources of Southeast Asia, Bangkok.* Pp. 701–710.

Gunatilleke, C.V.S. (1988). Trees of the Sinharaja forest and their non-timber products. In Ng, F.S.P. (ed.), *Trees and mycorrhiza.* Forest Research Institute, Kuala Lumpur. Pp. 251–260.

Gunatilleke, I.A.U.N. and Gunatilleke, C.V.S. (1985). Phytosociology of Sinharaja – a contribution to rain forest conservation in Sri Lanka. *Biological Conservation* 31: 21–40.

Gunatilleke, I.A.U.N. and Gunatilleke, C.V.S. (1990). Distribution of floristic richness and its conservation in Sri Lanka (1990). *Conservation Biology* 4: 21–31.

Gunatilleke, I.A.U.N. and Gunatilleke, C.V.S. (1991). Threatened woody endemics of the wet lowlands of Sri Lanka and their conservation. *Biological Conservation* 55: 17–36.

Gunatilleke, I.A.U.N. and Gunatilleke, C.V.S. (1993). Under-utilized food plant resources of Sinharaja Rain Forest, Sri Lanka. In Hladik, C.M., Pagezy, H., Linares, O.F., Hladik, A. and Hadley, M. (eds), *Food and nutrition in the tropical forest: biocultural interactions.* Man and the Biosphere Series – Vol. 15.

Gunatilleke, I.A.U.N., Gunatilleke, C.V.S. and Abeygunawardena, P. (1993). Interdisciplinary research towards management of non-timber forest resources in lowland rain forests of Sri Lanka. *Economic Botany* 47(3): 282–290.

McDermott, M., Gunatilleke, C.V.S. and Gunatilleke, I.A.U.N. (1990). Conservation of biological and cultural diversity in Sinharaja rain forest. *Sri Lankan Forester* 20:

Zoysa, N. de and Raheem, R. (1990). *Sinharaja – a rain forest in Sri Lanka.* March for Conservation, Sri Lanka. 61 pp.

Acknowledgements

This Data Sheet was prepared by Professors Nimal and Savitri Gunatilleke (Department of Botany, University of Peradeniya, Sri Lanka).

BAGO (PEGU) YOMAS
Myanmā

Location: South-western central Myanmā between latitudes 17°25'–21°00'N and longitudes 95°00'–96°45'E; mainly in Bago (Pegu) Division but extending into northern Yangon (Rangoon) Division.

Area: c. 40,000 km².

Altitude: 100–821 m. (The Pyi Hills to the north attain 1518 m at the summit of Mount Popa.)

Vegetation: Wet evergreen dipterocarp forest, pyinkado forest, moist teak forest, dry teak forest, dry dipterocarp forest (eng or indaing), pyinma forest. Bamboo occurs where the canopy has been opened by logging or slash and burn agriculture.

Flora: Estimated 2000 vascular plant species, of which c. 100 species are endemic. At least one endemic genus (*Zollingeria*, Sapindaceae) and several other Burmese endemic genera also present.

Useful plants: Timber trees, including *Tectona grandis* (teak), *Pentace birmanica* and *Shorea robusta* (sal).

Other values: Spectacular landscape, high wilderness value, rich fauna.

Threats: Slash and burn agriculture, illegal logging, plans to build Yangon-Mandalay expressway through part of the area (including the proposed National Park), plans to dam the Lanwe Chaung and create a lake.

Conservation: Some Reserved Forests; proposed Bago Yomas National Park (1462 km²) in the southern part of the area. Laterite flora needs to be represented in reserve system.

Geography

Bago (formerly Pegu) Yoma is a range of low hills in south-western central Myanmā, mainly in Bago (Pegu) Division but extending south into Yangon (Rangoon) Division. The hills are orientated north-south between two important rivers, the Ayeyarwady (Irrawaddy) to the west and the Sittoung (Sittang) to the east, of which they form the watershed. They run northwards for about 500 km, with a width of 60–100 km, from near Taikkyi and Bago (Pegu) in the south to near Meiktila in the north. The main range lies between latitudes 17°25'–21°00'N and longitudes 95°00'–96°45'E and has an area of about 40,000 km²; there is a small northern extension (the Pyi or Prome Hills). The highest point of the main range is Bago Yoma (821 m). The Pyi Hills attain 1518 m at the summit of the sacred extinct volcano, Mount Popa or Nattoung ("Spirit Mountain"). The terrain is rugged and dissected by steep valleys, with many spurs intersected by ravines; this makes access difficult to much of the main Bago Yoma. The region is sparsely populated.

The hills of the Bago Yoma are composed of Tertiary sandstone formations, mostly dating from the Oligocene/Miocene period. Almost the whole of the southern part of the range, from the headwaters of the Hswa Choung to the Bago and Pazwoodoung (Poungli) valleys is formed of a soft, grey stratified sandstone. The highest crest of the main range, and the spurs of the Kanbala Taung, are of a coarser, pale brownish grey sandstone, and in the Yan valley there are alternating beds of highly folded sandstones and shales. These soft, very permeable sandstones have weathered into an intricate labyrinth of ridges and gorges with numerous waterfalls. Oligocene peridotite intrusions and a number of extinct volcanoes form distinct features in the landscape. In the north-west, the Bago Tertiary sandstones are replaced by older, greenish calcareous sandstone, which are very resistant to weathering. Along the base of the Bago Yoma are lateritic rocks, gravels and loams, with quartz or sandstone conglomerates frequent in the Pyi (Prome) area. The region is rich in fossils.

The climate is monsoonal with the heaviest rainfall between May and October (IUCN Protected Areas Data Unit 1987). Annual rainfall ranges from about 3400 mm in the wettest areas to about 1000 mm in the driest (Stamp 1925; IUCN Protected Areas Data Unit 1987).

Vegetation

The Bago Yomas massif supports the only extensive area of closed canopy forest in Bago (Pegu), Ayeyarwady (Irrawaddy) and Yangon (Rangoon) Divisions (Allen 1984, quoted in IUCN Protected Areas Data Unit 1987). The precise type of forest is determined by aspect, soil type and mean annual rainfall. Stamp (1925) distinguished six types occurring in the Bago Yomas, each of which is described briefly below.

Wet evergreen dipterocarp forest occurs in areas receiving at least 2000 mm rainfall per annum. Typical trees include *Dipterocarpus alatus*, *D. turbinatus*, *D. obtusifolius*, *D. pilosa*, *Anisoptera glabra*, *Hopea odorata*, *Lagerstroemia calyculata*, *L. floribunda*, *L. speciosa*, *Parashorea stellata*, *Pentace birmanica* and *Swintonia floribunda*, with undergrowth of *Calamus* palms and the creeping bamboo *Temostachyon helferi*. Mixed cane brake occurs along watercourses in wet dipterocarp forests. *Calamus arborescens*, *Licuala peltata*, *Zalacca wallichiana* and *Temostachyum helferi* (a creeping bamboo) are typical species.

Pyinkado forest occurs over much of the southern part of the Bago Yomas. It is intermediate in character between wet evergreen dipterocarp forest and moist teak forest. The dominant tree is pyinkado or Burmese ironwood, *Xylia dolabriformis*; subdominants are *Dipterocarpus alatus*, *D. turbinatus* and *Lagerstroemia floribunda*. Other typical species include *Careya arborea*, *Gmelina arborea*, *Homalium tomentosum* and *Schleichera trijuga*. The most abundant bamboo is *Bambusa polymorpha*.

Moist teak forest, sometimes referred to as moist upper mixed forest, covers large areas of the Bago Yomas on well-drained deep loams over Peguan Sandstone where the annual rainfall is 1500–2000 mm. Teak (*Tectona grandis*) and pyinkado (*Xylia dolabriformis*) are co-dominant.

Dry teak forest (dry upper mixed forest) occurs in the northern part of the Bago Yomas, where the annual rainfall is 1000–1500 mm. The dominant species is *Terminalia tomentosa*; *Tectona grandis* and *Xylia dolabriformis* are also present. *Dendrocalamus strictus* is the characteristic bamboo species.

Pyinma forest (lower mixed forest) occurs on alluvial flats and plains surrounding the Bago Yomas massif. The dominants are *Lagerstroemia* spp.; several species of *Terminalia* also occur.

Dry dipterocarp forest (eng or indaing) occurs on dry lateritic and light sandy soils where the annual rainfall is less than 1125 mm. It is poorer in species than wet evergreen dipterocarp forest. Dominant species are *Dipterocarpus tuberculatus* (eng), *Melanorrhoea usitata*, *Terminalia tomentosa* and *Pentacme suavis*. *Cycas siamensis* occurs in the undergrowth.

Extensive tracts of *Dendrocalamus* bamboo jungle replace pyinkado or moist teak forest where slash and burn agriculture has been practised.

Flora

There are an estimated 2000 vascular plant species, of which around 100 may be endemic. Endemic species include *Lysimachia fletcheri* (Hu and Bennell 1983), *Dendrobium peguanum* (Hunt 1970), *Apocopis peguensis* (Bor 1949, 1952a), *A. burmanicus* (Bor 1951), *Musa laterita* (Cheesman 1949), *Lygisma angustifolia*, *Canscora schultesii*, several species of *Argyreia*, *Breweria elegans* (Prome Hills), *Brandisia discolor* and several grasses, including *Eragrostis burmanica* (Bor 1951), *Eremochloa ciliaris* (Bor 1952c), *Microstegium eucnemis*, *M. ciliatum* and *M. delicatulum* (Bor 1952b). Some probable Burmese endemics occur both on Bago Yomas and in Taninthayi, e.g. *Exacum pteranthum*, *Argyreia barbata*, *Mimulus orbicularis*, *Gentiana crassa* and *Erycibe expansa*.

There is at least one endemic genus (*Zollingeria*, Sapindaceae); several other Burmese endemic genera are represented, e.g. *Cystacanthus* (Acanthaceae), which also occurs in Mawlamyine (Moulmein) and Myeik (Mergui). The most important families, in terms of species, are Leguminosae (*sensu lato*), Acanthaceae, Orchidaceae, Rubiaceae and Zingiberaceae.

Useful plants

By far the most important commercial timber tree is teak (*Tectona grandis*), which is still an important export-earner. The forests of the Bago Yoma have been carefully managed for some 130 years using traditional, low-technology methods of timber extraction, such as the use of elephants. Many of the forests are at present on the fourth or fifth extraction cycle (Collins, Sayer and Whitmore 1991).

Species of *Lagerstroemia* are used to make beams, carts, planks, oars and paddles (*L. speciosa*), bows, spear-heads and canoes (*L. tomentosa*). *Homalium tomentosum* is used in furniture making. Many of the dipterocarps, e.g. *D. alatus*, *D. turbinatus* and *D. tuberculatus*, are valued for house-building and cabinet-making; some, such as *D. turbinatus* and *D. alatus*, also yield high-quality wood oil and/or resin. *Shorea robusta* (sal) makes particularly good quality railway sleepers. The wood of *Pentacme siamensis* is reputed to be as durable as teak.

One of the local bamboos, *Bambusa tulda*, is widely cultivated. Jute fibre is obtained from *Corchorus capsularis*, native to Bago, and *C. olitorius* (cultivated), while a similar fibre which is used in rope-making is obtained from various species of *Sterculia*.

Social and environmental values

The area has spectacular scenery and a high wilderness value. There is a rich fauna, including two restricted-range bird species which are endemic to the rain-shadow zone of central Myanmā. Of these, the threatened hooded treepie (*Crypsirina cucullata*) occurs in dry dipterocarp forest. Other threatened bird species which occur, or formerly occurred, in this area are lesser adjutant (*Leptoptilus javanicus*), greater adjutant (*Leptoptilus dubius*), Pallas's fish eagle (*Haliaeetus leucoryphus*) and Jerdon's babbler (*Moupinia altirostris*), which are all wetland birds.

Threats

Taunggya (slash and burn) cultivation has opened the canopy in some areas, leading to the formation of bamboo brakes. Logging has also resulted in the degradation of some areas. There is a plan, so far not implemented, to dam the Lanwe Chaung and create a lake of up to 76 km² in the proposed Bago Yomas National Park. There is also a plan to build an expressway from Yangon to Mandalay. This would pass through the area (IUCN Protected Areas Data Unit 1987).

Conservation

The proposed Bago Yomas National Park (1462 km²) is situated in the southern part of the massif, between latitudes 17°45'–18°30'N and longitudes 95°55'–96°48'E. It has an altitude range of 100–488 m. It would comprise Zamayi Reserved Forest (691.7 km²), parts of Aingdon Kun Reserved Forest (135.8 km²), all but four compartments of Yenwe Reserved Forest (610.5 km²) and small parts of Bawbin and Gamon Reserved Forests (together 24 km²). These Reserved Forests are already protected under the provisions of the 1902

Forest Act and the 1936 Burma Wildlife Protection Act. The proposed National Park is valued on account of the small areas of completely undisturbed teak forest, the spectacular landscape and the wide range of mammals and birds. No information on the particular botanical value of the proposed National Park in relation to the rest of the Bago Yomas is available.

Kurz (1875) mentions the remarkable diversity of vegetation found on lateritic soils. It is recommended, therefore, that attention be paid to the importance of the flora on this type of substrate when conservation priorities are being assessed.

References

Bor, N.L. (1949). A new *Apocopis* from Burma. *Kew Bull.* 4: 28.

Bor, N.L. (1951). Some new species of Indian grasses. *Kew Bull.* 6: 166–171.

Bor, N.L. (1952a). The genus *Apocopis* Nees. *Kew Bull.* 7: 101–116.

Bor, N.L. (1952b). The genus *Microstegium* in India and Burma. *Kew Bull.* 7: 209–223.

Bor, N.L. (1952c). Notes on Asiatic grasses: VIII. The genus *Eremochloa* Büse in India and Burma. *Kew Bull.* 7: 309–317.

Cheesman, E.E. (1949). Classification of the bananas. III. Critical notes on species. *Kew Bull.* 4: 265–267.

Collins, N.M., Sayer, J.A. and Whitmore, T.C. (eds) (1991). *The conservation atlas of tropical forests: Asia and the Pacific.* Macmillan, London. 256 pp.

Hu, C.-H. and Bennell, A.P. (1983). Two new Asiatic species of *Lysimachia*. *Notes Roy. Bot. Gard. Edinb.* 40: 461–466.

Hunt, P.F. (1970). Notes on Asiatic orchids V. *Kew Bull.* 24: 75–99.

IUCN Protected Areas Data Unit (1987). IUCN Directory of Indomalayan Protected Areas. Burma: draft. World Conservation Monitoring Centre, Cambridge, U.K.

Kurz, W.S. (1875). *Preliminary report on the forest and other vegetation of Pegu.* Calcutta, India.

Stamp, L.D. (1925). *The vegetation of Burma.* University of Rangoon Research Monograph No. 1. Rangoon.

Acknowledgement

This Data Sheet was prepared by Dr Robert R. Mill (Royal Botanic Garden, Edinburgh).

INDOCHINESE REGION: CPD SITE IS16

TANINTHAYI (TENASSERIM)
Myanmā

Location: The southern "tail" of Myanmā, comprising Taninthayi (Tenasserim) Division, Mon State and the southern part of Karen State, including the Dawna Taungdan (Range), between latitudes 9°45'–17°45'N and longitudes 97°00'–99°40'E.

Area: 73,845 km².

Altitude: 0–2275 m (summit of Mulayit Taung).

Vegetation: Mainly wet evergreen dipterocarp forest with some small pockets of montane rain forest (moist upper mixed forest, dry upper mixed forest, lower mixed forest) on the higher peaks in the east and in the north; coastal communities include mangrove forests, fresh- and brackish swamp vegetation and pinle-kanazo tidal forest. Some areas of bamboo brake, where forest has been cleared and on poor soils.

Flora: Probably at least 3000 vascular plant species (more than 2100 species actually recorded); c. 500 endemic species. Flora mostly Indomalayan in south (with links with Sri Lanka, Tamil Nadu and Madagascar), Indochinese elements in north and east, some temperate elements in south.

Useful plants: Teak, rosewood and other timbers; numerous dye plants, medicinal plants, ornamentals.

Other values: Forest helps prevent fragile soils from being eroded by monsoon rains; offshore islands are breeding grounds for green turtles and edible-nest swiftlets; home of Salôn tribe (aquatic nomads).

Threats: Legal and illegal tree felling leading to soil erosion; resin tapping; charcoal burning.

Conservation: 2 established protected areas (Moscos Islands Wildlife Sanctuary and Mulayit Game Reserve) and 2 proposed (Lanbi Kyun Marine National Park and Pakchan Nature Reserve). However, these are inadequate to protect the plant diversity of the region. Several endemic or threatened species, e.g. *Amherstia nobilis*, have been placed on a list of plants recommended for legislative protection.

Geography

The area under consideration includes the southern "tail" of Myanmā, comprising Taninthayi (Tenasserim) Division, Mon State and the southern part of Karen State (formerly Kawthoolei State), including the Dawna Taungdan (Range), between latitudes 9°45'–17°45'N and longitudes 97°00'–99°40'E.

The topography consists of a narrow coastal plain bordering the Andaman Sea and ranges of mainly low hills. Of these, the principal ranges are the Tenghyo Range in Mon State (extending into south-western Karen State), the Dawna Taungdan (Range) forming the boundary between southern Karen State and Thailand, and the Taninthayi Taungdan, which forms the backbone of Taninthayi and whose eastern range marks the international boundary with Thailand. The main peaks are Sedaung Taung (1420 m) and Sadaik Taung (1283 m) in Mon State, Mulayit Taung (2275 m) in the Dawna Taungdan, and Myinmoylet'hkal Taung (2022 m), Paungchon Taung (1174 m) and Pya Taung (1089 m) in Taninthayi. Mean altitude rapidly decreases southwards from Myinmoylet'hkal Taung in central Taninthayi.

There are several groups of offshore islands, including the Moscos Islands (Heinze Island, Maungmagan Island and Launglon Bok Island) and the Myeik Kyunzu (Mergui Archipelago). The latter comprises 8 relatively large islands (Mali Kyun, Kadan Kyun, Daung Kyun, Saganthit Kyun, Letsôk-aw Kyun, Kanmaw Kyun, Lanbi Kyun and Zadetkyi Kyun) and some 900 smaller islets and island groups, such as the Great Western Torres Islands and the Lord Loughborough group.

The Thanlwin (Salween) River enters the Gulf of Martaban at the twin towns of Martaban (north bank) and Mawlamyine (Moulmein, south bank), after its journey of 2815 km from the mountains of Tibet. There are also several local streams.

The predominant geological formations are of Archaean granite which weathers to a coarse sandy soil which is easily eroded if unprotected. Most land above 900 m is granitic, as is much of the lowland and most of the hilly islands of the archipelago. Palaeozoic rocks of the Mergui Series occupy much of the remainder of Taninthayi and comprise a mixture of shale, kaolinized sandstone and quartzites, with some slates, phyllites, tuffs, agglomerates and quartz grits (IUCN Protected Areas Data Unit 1987). These rocks weather to a heavy clay soil. Limestones are widespread around Kyaikkami (Amherst) in the north of the area, but are uncommon in the south. Late Tertiary sandstones and shales occur in the lower valley of the Taninthayi River and near Kyaukmadaung and Myittha; various types of very fertile alluvia occur on the coastal strip and along the estuary of the Thanlwin (Salween).

The climate is monsoonal and transitional between that of most of Myanmā (which experiences distinct wet and dry seasons) and that of Peninsular Malaysia (which has more evenly distributed rainfall). The winds are west or south-west from May to September and north-east from October to April. Towards the south of the area, the proximity to the Isthmus of Kra (11°00'N) results in penetration of rain-bearing winds from the east as well, resulting in some exceptionally high annual rainfalls (3964 mm at Kawthang and more than

4100 mm on the watershed of the proposed Pakchan Nature Reserve) (IUCN Protected Areas Data Unit 1987). Mean minima and maxima temperatures are about 21°C and 34°C, respectively, in the south (IUCN Protected Areas Data Unit 1987).

The population of Mon State in 1983 was 1,682,041, and that of Taninthayi was 917,628. Principal towns are Thaton, Martaban, Mawlamyine (Moulmein) (the capital of Mon State), Kyaikkami (Amherst), Dawei (Tavoy) and Myeik (Mergui).

Vegetation

This account of the vegetation follows the terminology of Stamp (1925).

In Myanmā, evergreen dipterocarp forest (wet dipterocarp forest) reaches its maximum development and diversity in Taninthayi. The forest contains a large number of timber species, including *Dipterocarpus alatus* (kanyin), *D. griffithii* (kanyin-byin), *D. laevis* (kanyin-byan), *D. turbinatus* (kanyin-ni), *Shorea* spp. (kaban), *Parashorea stellata* (kaunghinu), *Hopea odorata* (thingan), *Fagraea fragrans* (anan), *Bassia longifolia* (kanzaw), *Mesua ferrea* (ironwood or gangaw), *Delina sarmentosa*, *Tetracera assa*, *Dillenia aurea*, *Talauma mutabilis*, *T. rabaniana*, *Uvaria hirsuta*, *U. merguensis*, *Fibraurea chloroleuca*, *Limacia cuspidata*, *Calophyllum kunstleri*, *C. parkeri*, *Durio zibethinus*, *Neesia synandra* and many others. There are numerous epiphytes, including filmy ferns, mosses, aroids and, according to Rao (1974), some 700 orchids, as well as woody climbers, including rattan palms.

Moist teak forest (moist upper mixed forest), dominated by *Tectona grandis* and *Xylia dolabriformis*, occurs in northern Taninthayi.

Dry teak forest (dry upper mixed forest) occurs very locally on the Thailand border in northern Taninthayi. Very little is known about its composition in Taninthayi.

Pyinma forest (lower mixed forest) occurs on plains and alluvial flats. *Lagerstroemia* (pyinma) is the dominant genus; *Terminalia* spp. also occur.

Heritiera (pinle-kanazo) forest occurs over large areas of Myeik (Mergui, central Taninthayi) and the archipelago, in brackish or nearly fresh water. The dominant species is *Heritiera fomes*. Stamp (1925) distinguished two variants: freshwater kanazo, with *Amoora cucullata*, *Dysophyllum cochinchinensis*, *D. turbinatus*, *Intsia bijuga*, *Barringtonia acutangula* and *Combretum trifoliatum*, and brackish water kanazo, with *Bruguiera parviflora*, *Aquilaria agallocha*, *Sonneratia griffithii*, *Cynometra mimosoides* and the marsh fern *Acrostichum aureum*.

Mixed delta scrub and low forest (ken-byauk) probably occurs over large tracts of Myeik (Mergui) district (Stamp 1925). The principal tree species are *Elaeocarpus hygrophilus*, *Calophyllum amoenum*, *Litsea nitida*, *Eugenia* spp. and *Diospyros burmanica*, with a dense undergrowth of *Calamus erectus* and *Pinanga gracilis*.

Bamboo brakes, composed of *Oxytenanthera albociliata*, occupy extensive areas on badly drained Tertiary soils.

Mangrove forests occur on the low islands of the Myeik Kyunzu (Mergui Archipelago); beach or dune forests occur near Dawei.

Flora

The incomplete standard Myanmā checklist (Hundley and Chit Ko Ko 1961) lists some 2100 species as occurring in Taninthayi, Mon and adjacent areas. The actual number of vascular species present is probably more than 3000. Of these, it is estimated that about 500 are endemic. There is one near-endemic mono- or ditypic family of lianes, Plagiopteraceae. Endemic genera include *Amherstia* (Fabaceae), *Schellenbergia* (Connaraceae), *Tractocopevodia* (Rutaceae), *Trisepalum* (Gesneriaceae, 3 spp.) and *Pommereschea* (Zingiberaceae, 2 spp.). Areas with particularly high endemism appear to be Kyaikkami (Amherst), Dawei (Tavoy) and Myeik (Mergui).

The main floristic affinities are with Thailand and Peninsular Malaysia to the south and east, the Shan States and western China in the north, and the Andaman Islands, Rakhine (Arakan) and Bangladesh in the west. There are also affinities with the floras of Sri Lanka and southernmost Tamil Nadu (India), many species being common to both areas (Rao 1974), and more distant floristic links with Madagascar, Australasia and the Cape Province of South Africa. Temperate families are not entirely unrepresented; the rather peculiar moderating effect of the sea on both sides of the Isthmus of Kra in the south has led to an unusually temperate climate for the latitude. This allows genera and species which, in Assam and northern Myanmā, are not found below 1200–1500 m, to grow at or near sea-level in Taninthayi. Examples include *Castanea martabanica*, *Michelia* spp., *Pyrus* spp., *Quercus fenestra* and *Rubus* ssp.

Access to the region has been prohibited for many areas for security reasons and problems of illegal smuggling of drugs between Thailand and Myanmā. As a result, the region is very poorly known botanically.

Useful plants

The most detailed account of the useful plants of Taninthayi and Mon is that of Mason (1850). Only a selection of useful species can be given here.

The most important commercial timber is teak (*Tectona grandis*), which is used locally and exported. Other hard timbers include *Heritiera fomes*, *Bassia longifolia*, *Diospyros* spp. (ebony), *Pterocarpus wallichii* (Tenasserim mahogany or rosewood) and *Shorea robusta* (sal). The woods of *Hopea odorata* and *Grewia* spp. are used by local Karen and Burmese boat-builders, while the Salôn use *Zalacca wallichiana* (*Z. edulis*) to construct their very light boats (Mason 1850). Some other timber trees have already been mentioned (see Vegetation).

Dyes are obtained from *Garcinia elliptica*, *G. pictoria*, *Terminalia chebula*, *Semecarpus anacardium*, *Strobilanthes flaccidifolius* (*Ruellia indigofera*), *Tamarindus indica*, *Adenanthera pavonina*, *Caesalpinia sappan* and *Gluta tavoyana*.

Native edible fruits and nuts include *Musa paradisiaca*, *Elaeagnus conferta*, *Syzygium malaccense*, *Sterculia foetida*, *S. alata*, *Sandoricum koetjape*, *Willughbeia edulis*, *Zalacca wallichiana*, *Artocarpus heterophyllus* (*A. integrifolius*), *A. echinatus*, *Durio zibethinus* and several variants of *Citrus aurantium*.

There are many locally valuable species of yam (*Dioscorea* spp.), including *D. atropurpurea* and *D. globosa*. Other important native vegetables include *Sesbania grandiflora*, *Vigna pilosa* and *Canavalia virosa*. Many other species have been introduced.

The fruit of *Cerbera manghas*, a mangrove tree, yields an oil used to anoint the head in Burmese ceremonies. The oil is also burned in lamps. The oil of *Dipterocarpus laevis* and *D. turbinatus* is used for torches. An edible oil is obtained from the seeds of *Bassia longifolia*. Soap and shampoo substitutes are obtained from *Acacia rugata* pods. *Gluta usitata* is the source of Burmese lacquer (Mabberley 1987).

Various species of *Pandanus* are employed to make mats and sails. Rope is made from *Hibiscus macrophyllus*, *H. tiliaceus* and *Sterculia* spp. The down from the seeds of *Bombax ceiba* (silk cotton tree) is used to stuff pillows and mattresses. Hemp substitutes include *Crotalaria juncea*, *Sida acuta* and *Urena lobata*.

The coast of Taninthayi abounds in medicinal plants. According to Mason (1850), more than 10% of those listed in John Lindley's *Flora Medica* (Lindley 1838) were to be found there. Some of the most important are *Blumea balsamifera* (Shan camphor), *Pterocarpus wallichii* and *P. dalbergioides* (gum kino, used as a vermifuge), *Butea frondosa*, *Altingia excelsa* (which yields a storax-like gum), *Terminalia bellirica*, *T. chebula*, *Calotropis gigantea* (used in the treatment of leprosy), *Dipterocarpus laevis* (which yields balsam-like oil), *Azadirachta indica* (neem; the bark is used as a quinine substitute, the seeds as an insecticide, the fruit oil as an anthelminthic, and also used in soaps and toothpaste) (Mason 1850; Mabberley 1987), *Caesalpinia bonduc* (a quinine substitute), *Elettaria cardamomum* (cardamom) and *Cymbopogon citratus*.

Ornamental plants include the endemic *Amherstia nobilis*, *Mesua ferrea* (ironwood tree, often planted in Burmese monasteries), *Clerodendron nutans*, *Michelia champac* (orange blossoms used as hair decoration), *Cassia nodosa*, *C. fistula* (laburnum-like flowers, pink in the former, yellow in the latter), *Lagerstroemia* spp., *Bignonia stipulata*, *Begonia* spp. and many orchids.

Social and environmental values

The fauna of the area is very varied and includes species not found elsewhere in Myanmā (Blower 1985), including two species of mouse deer (*Tragulus javanicus* and *T. napu*), tapir (*Tapirus indicus*) and the white-handed gibbon (*Hylobates lar*). There are at least four species of bats, including cave bats (*Scotophilus temminckii*).

Many species of bird, including several threatened species, which occur in the lowland rain forests of Borneo, Sumatra, Java and Peninsular Malaysia, reach the northern limits of their ranges in Taninthayi and Peninsular Thailand. Examples are Malaysian peacock-pheasant (*Polyplectron malacense*), which is endemic to the Malay Peninsula and the extreme south of Taninthayi, and Gurney's pitta (*Pitta gurneyi*), which is confined to Taninthayi and Peninsular Thailand. Three threatened waterbird species occur, or have occurred, in Taninthayi, namely: white-shouldered ibis (*Pseudibis davisoni*), white-winged duck (*Cairina scutulata*) and masked finfoot (*Heliopais personata*). Edible-nest swiftlets (*Aerodromus fuciphaga*) nest in the limestone caves on the islets off Dawei

and less commonly at Myeik; they occur on Lanbi Kyun in the proposed Marine National Park.

Threats

Threats include timber exploitation (legal and illegal), resin tapping and the burning of mangroves for charcoal (Blower 1985). Illegal extraction by Thai loggers on the eastern side of the region has become a problem in recent years. Legal concessions were granted by Myanmā to Thailand to extract timber from its forests after Thailand banned timber exploitation in its own forests in 1988. As noted above (see Geography), the soil on which these forests grow, although very fertile, is very vulnerable to erosion when it is exposed. The long-term ecological effects of large-scale clear-felling would be catastrophic.

The current rate of exploitation of Taninthayi's mineral wealth and the effects which this is having on the flora and vegetation are not known to the author.

Conservation

Four protected areas have been established, or have been proposed, in the area (IUCN Protected Areas Data Unit 1987). Moscos Islands Wildlife Sanctuary covers an area of 49.2 km² in the Andaman Sea off Dawei, and includes the South Moscos Islands which are covered with climax southern low tropical evergreen forest, partly degraded by illegal felling. The islands are important breeding grounds for green turtles (*Chelonia mydas*: Endangered) and edible-nest swiftlets (*Aerodromus fuciphaga*).

Mulayit Game Sanctuary, in Karen State, has an area of 138.7 km². The highest point within the Sanctuary is the sacred mountain of Mulayit Taung (2275 m). The Sanctuary was established in 1935 primarily to protect tiger (*Panthera tigris*), leopard (*P. pardus*), Indian muntjac (*Muntiacus muntjak*) and wild boar (*Sus scrofa*). The flora is also of interest. Dawna Taungdan includes some rare or endemic species, such as *Ardisia gracilis*, *Rhododendron parishii*, *Ixora arguta*, *Bauhinia scortechinii*, *Coelogyne cyanoches*, *Hydnocarpus dawnensis* (Hundley and Chit Ko Ko 1961), *Artabotrys multiflorus* and *Sloanea parkinsonii* (Fischer 1937).

Pakchan Nature Reserve (proposed) would comprise the west part of Pakchan Reserved Forest in southernmost Taninthayi. The Reserved Forest, established in 1931, has an area of 1454 km² and is contiguous with the Lenya Reserved Forest (648 km²). The proposed Nature Reserve would have an area of about 259 km² (FAO 1982, 1983) with an altitudinal range from sea-level to 904 m (at Khao Hkanbou) in the north. The Reserved Forest includes some of the finest, most intact evergreen rain forest in the whole of Myanmā (IUCN Protected Areas Data Unit 1987) and contains the near-endemic palm, *Calamus helferianus*. The area also has intact mangroves and freshwater swamp vegetation containing a wealth of ferns and orchids (FAO 1983; FAO/UNDP 1985a).

Lanbi Kyun (Lampi Island) Marine National Park (proposed) comprises about 3700 km² of sea plus Lanbi Kyun (Lampi or Sullivan Island, 168 km²) and associated smaller islets, opposite the proposed Pakchan Nature Reserve. The vegetation of Lanbi Kyun is relatively undisturbed climax tropical evergreen (mainly dipterocarp) forest and coastal *Casuarina equisetifolia* forest. The island is visited by the Salôn marine nomads. The establishment of a Nature Reserve would help to preserve their culture (FAO 1982).

These few established or proposed protected areas are inadequate to preserve the botanical diversity of southern Myanmā. Although most of the forest on the eastern side of the region appears to be reasonably intact, there has been degradation around Myeik (Mergui) and Dawei (Tavoy). Large tracts further north, formerly covered with forest, have been cleared; these include the gorges of the Thanlwin (Salween) River where it enters the Andaman Sea at Mawlamyine (Collins, Sayer and Whitmore 1991). As this area is known to have harboured many local or endemic species of orchids, begonias and other herbs, the consequences of these clearances, although unknown, must be severe.

Amherstia nobilis, Fagraea fragrans, Aquilaria agallocha and *Mansonia gagei*, all of which occur in Taninthayi and/or Mon, have been listed in a schedule of plants requiring legislative protection (J. Paine, pers. comm.).

References

Blower, J. (1985). Conservation priorities in Burma. *Oryx* 19(2): 79–85.

Collins, N.M., Sayer, J.A. and Whitmore, T.C. (eds) (1991). *The conservation atlas of tropical forests: Asia and the Pacific.* Macmillan, London. 256 pp.

FAO (1982). *Maungmagan, Moscos Islands and Mergui Archipelago: report on a preliminary survey.* Nature Conservation and National Parks Project FO/BUR/80/006. Field Report 4/82. FAO, Rangoon.

FAO (1983). *Report on a reconnaissance of part of the Pakchan Reserved Forest and Lampi island, Tenasserim.* Nature Conservation and National Parks Project FO/BUR/80/006. Field Report 21/83. FAO, Rangoon.

FAO/UNDP (1985a). *Burma: project findings and recommendations. Nature Conservation and National Parks Project FO/BUR/80/006.* Terminal Report. FAO, Rome.

FAO/UNDP (1985b). *Burma: survey data and conservation priorities.* Nature Conservation and National Parks Project FO/BUR/80/006. Technical Report no. 1. FAO, Rangoon.

Fischer, C.E.C. (1937). Contributions to the flora of Burma. XIII. *Bull. Misc. Inform. Kew* 1937(8): 436–440.

Hundley, H.G. and Chit Ko Ko (1961). *List of trees, shrubs, herbs and principal climbers, etc. recorded from Burma, with vernacular names.* 3rd edition. Rangoon.

IUCN Protected Areas Data Unit (1987). IUCN Directory of Indomalayan Protected Areas. Burma: draft. World Conservation Monitoring Centre, Cambridge, U.K.

Lindley, J. (1838). *Flora medica.* London. 656 pp.

Mabberley, D.J. (1987). *The plant-book.* Cambridge University Press, Cambridge, U.K. 706 pp.

Mani, M.S. (1974). Biogeography of the eastern borderlands. In Mani, M.S. (ed.), *Ecology and biogeography in India.* Junk, The Hague. Pp. 648–663.

Mason, F. (1850). *The natural productions of Burmah, or notes on the fauna, flora, and minerals of the Tenasserim Provinces, and the Burman Empire.* American Mission Press, Moulmein. 332 pp.

Rao, R.S. (1974). The vegetation and phytogeography of Assam-Burma. In Mani, M.S. (ed.), *Ecology and biogeography in India.* Junk, The Hague. Pp. 204–246.

Stamp, L.D. (1925). *The vegetation of Burma.* University of Rangoon Research Monograph No. 1. Rangoon. 65 pp.

Acknowledgement

This Data Sheet was prepared by Dr Robert R. Mill (Royal Botanic Garden, Edinburgh).

ANDAMAN AND NICOBAR ISLANDS
India

Location: 572 islands on the Arakan Yoma-Indonesian arch, eastern Indian Ocean, extending south from near the coast of Myanmā to Sumatra, between latitudes 6°00'–14°00'N and longitudes 92°00'–94°00'E'.

Area: 8249 km². (Andaman Islands: 6408 km²; Nicobar Islands: 1841 km².)

Altitude: 0–726 m (summit of Saddle Peak).

Vegetation: Tropical evergreen rain forest, semi-evergreen rain forest, moist deciduous forest, beach forest, swamp forest, bamboo scrub.

Flora: c. 2270 vascular plant species, of which c. 10% are endemic. There is at least 1 endemic genus in the Andamans: *Pubistylus*.

Useful plants: Wild relatives of cultivated plants, including a wild rice relative, *Oryza indandamanica*; valuable timber trees, including dipterocarps and teak (*Tectona grandis*).

Other values: Rich fauna, tourism.

Threats: Clearance of forests for agriculture, settlements, hydroelectric facilities; logging; tourist developments; population pressure.

Conservation: 6 National Parks and 94 Sanctuaries cover a total land area of c. 520 km² (c. 6% of the land area). However, most are small islets; only 9 cover more than 10 km². The biologically richest islands of the Andamans have only 3 small National Parks and 1 very small Sanctuary. Existing protected area system inadequate to protect the flora. Tribal Reserve on Middle Andaman; Great Nicobar Biosphere Reserve; North Andaman and adjoining islands proposed as a Biosphere Reserve (1375 km²).

Geography

The Andaman and Nicobar Islands consist of about 572 islands, reefs and rocks situated in the eastern Indian Ocean on the Arakan Yoma-Indonesian arch, between latitudes 6°00'–14°00'N and longitudes 92°00'–94°00'E. They have a total area of 8249 km².

The highest peak of the Andamans is Saddle Peak, North Andaman (726 m); that of the Nicobars is Mount Thullier (670 m). The terrain is mostly undulating; flat land occurs only in the Nicobars. The oldest rocks date from the Jurassic-Miocene period, and are found in the Andaman Islands. They include intrusive and volcanic igneous rocks. The volcanics are derived from submarine lava flows which occurred 75–100 million years ago. Sedimentary rocks were subsequently deposited on top of the volcanic rocks. The Nicobar Islands include serpentine gabbros, marine deposits of the late Tertiary (including sandstones, slates, clay marls and plastic clays) and coral reefs of recent origin. Barren Island is still volcanically active.

Thirty-eight islands are inhabited. The population of the Andamans has grown from 50,000 in 1960 to around 180,000 (Whitaker 1985). There are five indigenous tribes, three on the Andamans (Jarawas, Ongee and Andamanese) and two on the Nicobars (Nicobrese and Shompens).

The islands are influenced by the north-east and south-west monsoons. The mean annual rainfall is 3180 mm.

Vegetation

Forests occupy 7163 km² (86% of the land area). The main types are: tropical and semi-evergreen rain forests, tropical moist deciduous (monsoon) forest, riverine forest, beach forest, swamp forest, mangroves and bamboo scrub.

Tropical evergreen rain forest in the Andamans is only slightly less grand in stature and rich in species than its counterpart on the mainland. The main species include *Dipterocarpus griffithii*, *D. grandiflorus*, *Endospermum malaccense*, *Mesua ferrea*, *Pterocarpus* spp. and *Terminalia bialata*, while *D. kerrii* is prominent on some islands in the southern part of the archipelago. Tropical moist deciduous forest includes *Pterocarpus dalbergioides*, *Canarium* spp., *Chukrasia* spp., *Albizia* spp., *Terminalia* spp., *Tectona grandis* (teak) and *Shorea robusta* (sal).

In the Nicobars, the main forest genera include *Alstonia*, *Amoora*, *Artocarpus*, *Canarium*, *Calophyllum*, *Garcinia*, *Hopea*, *Horsfieldia*, *Mangifera*, *Miliusa*, *Syzygium* and *Terminalia*. The genera *Dipterocarpus* and *Pterocarpus* do not occur in the Nicobar Islands.

Coastal marshy areas and mangroves contain genera found in similar environments throughout the region, such as *Aquillaria*, *Bruguiera*, *Ceriops*, *Heritiera*, *Nypa*, *Pandanus*, *Rhizophora* and *Sonneratia*.

Unique among the islands is the presence of grass heaths in Car Nicobar and Nancowry Islands. Secondary vegetation includes coconut plantations, bamboo scrub and grasslands.

Flora

The flora of the Andaman and Nicobar Islands contains about 2270 vascular plant species, of which about 10% are endemic. There is at least one endemic genus in the Andamans, namely *Pubistylus*. Endemic species include *Ailanthus kurzii, Amoora mannii, Dichapetalum andamanicum, Mangifera andamanica, Planchonia andamanica, Pubistylus andamanensis* and *Strobilanthes glandulosus* (Thothathri 1962). Balakrishnan (1989) estimates that 144 taxa are endemic to the Andamans and 72 taxa are endemic to Great Nicobar. Many taxa occur on one group of islands but are absent elsewhere in the archipelago. This can be explained by the juxtaposition of the islands in the past and subsequent submergence and emergence above sea-level. It is estimated that there are about 50 lichen taxa and about 15 bryophyte taxa.

The flora of the Andamans belongs to the Andamanese Floristic Province of the Indochinese Floristic Region, while Takhtajan (1986) considers the Nicobar Islands to be part of the Malesian Region, the flora of the Nicobars being closely related to that of Sumatra.

Useful plants

The Andaman and Nicobar islands contain several plants of economic importance, including *Piper betel, Cocos nucifera, Areca catechu*, and several species of *Knema* and *Myristica*. In addition, there are many potentially valuable plants, such as *Elaeagnus latifolia, Baccaurea ramiflora* and *Garcinia cowa*. The discovery of a wild relative of rice, *Oryza indandamanica* (Ellis 1987a), indicates that the islands contain potentially important genetic resources.

Important timber trees include *Dipterocarpus* spp., *Pterocarpus dalbergioides, Artocarpus* spp. and *Terminalia* spp. The rattan, *Calamus pseudorivalis*, is widely used.

Social and environmental values

The islands have a rich fauna, including 17 restricted-range species of land birds. Of these, 8 species are endemic to the Andamans, 5 species are endemic to the Nicobars and 4 species are shared between the two island groups. Most of the birds are forest-dwelling species and the majority are threatened, given their small ranges and the threat of habitat destruction. Narcondam hornbill (*Aceros narcondami*) is especially vulnerable, being confined to the small, isolated island of Narcondam in the Andamans, and numbering only 400 individuals.

The islands have potential for the development of ecotourism.

Threats

The main threats are clearance of forests for agriculture, settlements and the construction of hydroelectric dams, logging, tourist developments and population pressure, exacerbated by the settlement of displaced people from mainland India and refugees from Sri Lanka.

Large-scale industrial logging is a threat to the forests of the Andaman Islands. Forests in North Andaman and Middle Andaman have already suffered severely, while the Jarawa Tribal Reserve contains the only pristine tract of forest remaining in the south (Centre for Science and Environment 1985). Parts of the Nicobar Islands still contain pristine forests (Collins, Sayer and Whitmore 1991).

The clearance and inundation of forests for the construction of hydroelectric facilities threatens a number of important sites. For example, a proposed dam on the Kalpong River (North Andaman) would flood 2 km² of forest on the west slope of Saddle Peak (M. Ahmedullah 1992, *in litt.*). The site of the recently discovered *Oryza indandamanica* has come under threat. Other threats include quarrying, and the cutting of mangroves for fuelwood.

Conservation

There are 6 National Parks (4 in the Andamans and 2 in the Nicobars) and 94 Sanctuaries covering a total area of 708 km², of which about 520 km² is terrestrial. This represents about 6% of the land area. However, most of the protected areas are small islets (57 have an area of less than 1 km², and only 9 cover more than 10 km²) (IUCN 1992).

The biologically richest islands of the Andamans (North Andaman, South Andaman, Middle Andaman, Little Andaman, Baratang and Rutland) have only 3 small National Parks and 1 very small Sanctuary. The largest island, Middle Andaman, has no protected area except the Jarawa Tribal Reserve. The protected area system is therefore inadequate to protect the plant diversity of the archipelagos. Proposals for upgrading and extending the reserve network have been made by Rodgers and Panwar (1988).

The following protected areas (Table 22) (greater than 50 km², and not including Forest Reserves) are listed in Collins, Sayer and Whitmore (1991) as having tropical moist forests within their boundaries.

TABLE 22. PROTECTED AREAS IN THE ANDAMAN AND NICOBAR ISLANDS

	Existing area (km²)	Proposed area (km²)
ANDAMAN ISLANDS		
National Parks		
Little Andaman		300
Mount Diavolo		200
Mount Harriet		110
West Rutland		50
Sanctuaries		
Austin-Kishorinagar Mangroves		50
Interview Island	134	
Mount Diavolo		200
North Andaman Peninsula		100
North Andaman Ridge	100	
Total	**134** [a]	**1100** [b]
NICOBAR ISLANDS		
National Parks		
Little Nicobar		159
Mount Thullier		100
Sanctuaries		
Great Nicobar		200
Total	**0**	**459** [c]

Notes:
[a] Smaller protected areas bring the total area of forest within existing protected areas to 520 km².
[b] Smaller proposed protected areas would bring the total area of forest within protected areas on the Andamans to 1140 km².
[c] Smaller proposed protected areas would bring the total area of forest within protected areas on the Nicobars to 469 km².

Part of Great Nicobar has been declared a Biosphere Reserve (Balakrishnam 1989), but so far this has not been accepted by the UNESCO MAB Programme; North Andaman and some adjoining islands are proposed as a Biosphere Reserve covering 1375 km² (Ellis 1989). Core areas will include Saddle Peak and a Mangrove Centre.

References

Balachandra, L. (1989). A comprehensive account of the mangrove vegetation of Andaman and Nicobar Islands. *Ind. For.* 114: 741–751.

Balakrishnan, N.P. (1987). Andaman Islands – vegetation and floristics. In Saldanha, C.J. (ed.), *The Andaman and Nicobar Islands – an environmental impact assessment.* New Delhi. Pp. 55–68.

Balakrishnan, N.P. (1989). *Great Nicobar Biosphere Reserve.* Project Document-11. Ministry of Environment and Forests, Government of India, New Delhi.

Balakrishnan, N.P., Hore, D.K. and Dwivedi, R.P. (1984). *Status survey of the flora constituents in the island ecosystems of Great Nicobar Island in the present context of changing habitats.* Botanical Survey of India, Howrah.

Bhargava, O.P. (1958). Tropical evergreen virgin forests of Andaman Islands. *Indian For.* 84: 20–29.

Centre for Science and Environment (1985). *The state of India's environment 1982: a Second Citizens' report.* Centre for Science and Environment, New Delhi. Pp. 343–351.

Collins, N.M., Sayer, J.A. and Whitmore, T.C. (eds) (1991). *The conservation atlas of tropical forests: Asia and the Pacific.* Macmillan, London. 256 pp.

Ellis, J.L. (1987a). *Oryza indandamanica* Ellis, a new rice plant from islands of Andaman. *Bull. Bot. Surv. India* 27: 225–227.

Ellis, J.L. (1987b). Plant diversity in the Andamans with emphasis on endangered and endemic species. In Saldanha, C.J. (ed.), *The Andaman and Nicobar Islands – an environmental impact assessment.* New Delhi. Pp. 69–73.

Ellis, J.L. (1987c). The pteridophytic flora of Andaman and Nicobar Islands. *Andaman Sci. Assoc.* 3(2): 59–79.

Ellis, J.L. (1988). The potentially exploitable wild nutmegs of Andaman and Nicobar Islands. *J. Andaman Sci. Assoc.* 4: 149–150.

Ellis, J.L. (1989). *North Andaman Biosphere Reserve.* Project Document-13. Ministry of Environment & Forests, Government of India, New Delhi.

Ellis, J.L. (1990). Exploitable souring plants of Andaman and Nicobar Islands. *J. Andaman Sci. Assoc.* 6: 52.

IUCN (1992). *Protected areas of the world: a review of national systems. Volume 1: Indomalaya, Oceania, Australia and Antarctic.* IUCN, Gland, Switzerland and Cambridge, U.K. xx, 352 pp. (Prepared by the World Conservation Monitoring Centre.)

Kurz, S. (1870). *Report on the vegetation of the Andaman Islands.* Calcutta.

Kurz, S. (1876). A sketch of the vegetation of the Nicobar Islands. *J. Asiatic Soc. Beng.* 45: 105–164.

Menon, M.G.K. (1986). *An integrated environmentally sound development strategy for the Andaman and Nicobar Islands.* Plan Comm., Government of India, New Delhi.

Parkinson, C.E. (1923). *A forest Flora of the Andaman Islands.* Simla. 325 pp.

Prain, D. (1893). On the flora of Narcondam and Barren Islands. *J. Asiatic Soc. Beng.* 62: 39–86.

Rodgers, W.A. and Panwar, H.S. (1988). *Planning a wildlife protected area network in India,* 2 vols. Wildlife Institute of India, Dehra Dun.

Sahni, K.C. (1953). Botanical exploration in the Great Nicobar. *Indian For.* 79: 3–7.

Saldanha, C.J. (ed.) (1987). *The Andaman and Nicobar Islands – an environmental impact assessment.* New Delhi.

Sree Kumar, P.V. and Ellis J.L. (1990). Six wild relatives of betel vine from Great Nicobar. *J. Andaman Sci. Assoc.* 6: 150–152.

Takhtajan, A. (1986). *Floristic regions of the world.* University of California Press, Berkeley. 522 pp.

Thothathri, K. (1962). Contributions to the flora of the Andaman and Nicobar Islands. *Bull. Bot. Surv. India* 4: 281–296.

Whitaker, R. (1985). *Endangered Andamans. Managing tropical moist forests.* Environmental Services Group, WWF India, MAB India and Department of Environment. 52 pp.

Acknowledgements

This Data Sheet was written by Stephen D. Davis, based on material provided by J.L. Ellis (Botanical Survey of India) and other sources.

REGIONAL OVERVIEW: CHINA AND EAST ASIA

WANG XIANPU, YANG ZHOUHUAI, HORNG JYE-SU, KUNIO IWATSUKI,
KIM YONG SHIK (CHINA, TAIWAN, KOREAN PENINSULA AND JAPAN),
ALAN C. HAMILTON AND STEPHEN D. DAVIS (INDOCHINA)

Total land area: 13,043,209 km².

Population: c. 1,484,490,000.

Altitude: -155 m (Turfan Basin, China) to 8848 m (summit of Qomolangma Feng, or Mount Everest, on the border between China and Nepal).

Vegetation: Very diverse: tropical evergreen and semi-evergreen rain forests in southern mainland China, Hainan, Taiwan and Indochina, tropical moist deciduous forest, limestone vegetation rich in endemic species (particularly in southern China and Thailand), temperate broadleaved deciduous and coniferous mixed forest, coniferous forest, extensive grasslands (steppe), desert vegetation (including the world's highest desert), alpine vegetation, mangroves.

Number of vascular plants: 45,000 species[a].

Number of regional endemics: 18,650 species[a].

Note: [a] Estimate based on available data.

Introduction

The region, as here defined, includes the floristically-rich areas of mainland China, the Korean Peninsula, the Japanese archipelago, the islands of Hainan and Taiwan, and mainland Indochina (Cambodia, Laos, Thailand and Vietnam). Hong Kong and Macau are also part of this region. The flora of eastern China, together with that of Korea and Japan, belongs to the Eastern Asiatic Floristic Region (Takhtajan 1986); the flora of western China mostly belongs to the Irano-Turanian Region. Most of Indochina falls within the Indochinese Floristic Region. The Indochinese Floristic Region also includes part of Myanmā (Burma) (which is treated in the Regional Overview on the Indian Subcontinent). Following this brief introduction to the whole region, separate overviews are given for China, Taiwan, the Korean Peninsula, Japan, and the countries of Indochina, followed by references for all areas.

The following tables summarize population data (Table 23) and floristics data (Table 24) for the whole region. Table 25 gives a full list of sites selected as centres of plant diversity and endemism throughout the entire region.

TABLE 23. POPULATION DATA

Country	Area (km²)	Population (millions)[a]	Average annual growth rate (%) 1985–1990[a]	Expected population (millions) by 2025[a]
Cambodia	176,520	8.25 (1990)	2.48	13.99
China	9,600,000	1,139.06 (1990)	1.45	1512.59
Japan	376,520	123.46 (1990)	0.43	127.50
Laos	230,800	4.14 (1990)	2.82	8.60
Mongolia	1,566,500	2.19 (1990)	2.74	4.83
North Korea	120,540	21.77 (1990)	2.82	33.06
South Korea	99,020	42.79 (1990)	0.95	51.63
Taiwan	36,179	20.44 (1991)[b]	>2.0[c]	-
Thailand	511,770	55.7 (1990)	1.53	80.91
Vietnam	325,360	66.69 (1990)	2.15	117.49

Notes:

[a] World Resources Institute (1992), unless otherwise indicated.
[b] IUCN (1992a).
[c] Estimated current annual growth rate.
- Data unavailable.

TABLE 24. SPECIES RICHNESS AND LEVELS OF ENDEMISM FOR COUNTRIES IN THE REGION

	Vascular plant species	Endemic species	% Endemism
Cambodia/Laos/Vietnam[a]	12–15,000	?	10.0[d]
China[a]	27,100	10,000	36.9
Hong Kong	1984	25	1.3
Japan[b]	5565	>222	>4.0
Korean Peninsula	2898	407[c]	14.0
Mongolia	2272	229	10.1
Taiwan	3577	1075	30.1
Thailand	12,000	?	10.0[d]
Vietnam	8000	>800	>10.0

Notes:
[a] Figures for China and Indochina are very approximate.
[b] Includes the main islands of Japan together with the Ryukyu Islands and Bonin (Ogasawara) Islands.
[c] Refers to taxa.
[d] These are very approximate estimates from K. Larsen (pers. comm.).

Sources: World Conservation Monitoring Centre, updated with statistics arising from the CPD project.

MAP 6. CENTRES OF PLANT DIVERSITY AND ENDEMISM: CHINA AND EAST ASIA
The map shows the location of CPD Data Sheet sites.

KEY:
EA1. Changbai Mountains region (China)
EA6. Taibai Mountain region of Qinling Mountains (China)
EA13. Nanling Mountain Range (China)
EA26. Gaoligong Mountains, Nu Jiang River and Biluo Snow Mountains (China)
EA27. Tropical forests of Hainan Island (China)
EA29. Xishuangbanna region (China)
EA31. Limestone region (China)
EA40. High Mountain and Deep Gorge region, Hengduan Mountains and Min Jiang River basin (China)
EA41. Kenting National Park (Taiwan)
EA44. Mount Halla (South Korea)

EA49. Mount Hakusan (Japan)
EA50. Yakushima (Japan)
EA53. Doi Chiang Dao Wildlife Sanctuary (Thailand)
EA55. Doi Suthep-Pui National Park (Thailand)
EA57. Khao Yai National Park (Thailand)
EA59. Thung Yai-Huai Kha Khaeng World Heritage Site (Thailand)
EA62. Bach Ma-Hai Van (Vietnam)
EA63. Cat Tien Biosphere Reserve (Vietnam)
EA64. Cuc Phuong National Park (Vietnam)
EA65. Langbian-Dalat Highland (Vietnam)
EA66. Yok Don National Park (Vietnam)

TABLE 25. LIST OF SITES IDENTIFIED AS CENTRES OF PLANT DIVERSITY AND ENDEMISM IN CHINA AND EAST ASIA

The list of sites is arranged below according to the sequence adopted in the Regional Overview. Sites selected for Data Sheet treatment appear in bold. The phytogeographical regions (*I–IX*) refer to China only.

CHINA, TAIWAN, KOREAN PENINSULA AND JAPAN

CHINA

I. CONIFEROUS FOREST REGION (COLD TEMPERATE ZONE)
No CPD sites.

II. MIXED CONIFEROUS-DECIDUOUS BROADLEAVED FOREST REGION (TEMPERATE ZONE)
EA1. **Changbai Mountains region** (Jilin Province)
EA2. Xizo Hinggan Mountain Range (Heilongjiang Province)
EA3. Gao Tai Mountain Range
EA4. Chang Guancai Mountain Range
EA5. Da Tuzi Mountain Range

III. MIXED DECIDUOUS BROADLEAVED FOREST REGION (WARM TEMPERATE ZONE)
EA6. **Taibai Mountain region of Qinling Mountains** (Shaanxi Province)
EA7. Zhongtiao Mountains (Shanxi Province)
EA8. Wutai Mountains (Shanxi Province)
EA9. Southern parts of Taihang Mountains (Henan Province)
EA10. Lingwu Mountain (Hebei Province)
EA11. Lao Mountains (Shandong Province)
EA12. Kunyu Mountains (Shandong Province)

IV. EVERGREEN BROADLEAVED FOREST REGION (SUBTROPICAL ZONE)
EA13. **Nanling Mountain Range** (Guangdong, Guangxi, Hunan and Jiangxi Provinces)
EA14. Wuyi Mountain (Fujian Province)
EA15. Jiulong Mountains (Zhejiang Province)
EA16. Fanjing Mountains (Guizhou Province)
EA17. Dabie and Guniu Mountains (Anhui Province)
EA19. Shennongjia (Hubei Province)
EA20. Funiu Mountains (Henan Province)
EA21. Daba Mountains (Sichuan Province)
EA22. Wolong Mountains, Da and Xiao Liang Shan Mountains (Sichuan Province)
EA23. South Yulong Mountains (Yunnan Province)
EA24. Haba Snow Mountains (Yunnan Province)
EA25. Ailao Shan (Yunnan Province)
EA26. **Gaoligong Mountains, Nu Jiang River and Biluo Snow Mountains** (Yunnan Province)

V. SEASONAL RAIN FOREST REGION (TROPICAL ZONE)
EA27. **Tropical forests of Hainan Island**
EA28. Southern Guangxi Province (Shiwanda Mountain and Nonggang Nature Reserves)
EA29. **Xishuangbanna region** (Yunnan Province)
EA30. Zayu, Medog, Yadon and Nyalam (Xizang Autonomous Region)
EA31. **Limestone region** (Zhuang Autonomous Region, Guangxi Province)

VI. EVERGREEN DWARF FOREST AND SCRUB ON TROPICAL CORAL ISLANDS
No CPD sites.

VII. GRASSLAND REGION (TEMPERATE ZONE)
EA32. Western slope of Da Hinggan Mountains, Horqin and Xilin Gol (Nei Mongol Zizhiqu)
EA33. Helan Mountains (Ningxia)
EA34. Huang Long Mountains (Shaanxi Province)
EA35. Mazui Mountain (Gansu Province)
EA36. Altai-Sayan (Xinjiang)

VIII. DESERT REGION (TEMPERATE ZONE)
EA37. Northern slopes of Tien Shan (Xinjiang Uygur Zizhiqu)
EA38. Tacheng Basin and Ili Valley (Xinjiang Uygur Zizhiqu)

IX. HIGH-ALTITUDE COLD VEGETATION OF THE QINGHAI-XIZANG PLATEAU
EA39. Mountains of west Sichuan
EA40. **High Mountain and Deep Gorge region, Hengduan Mountains and Min Jiang River basin** (Sichuan Province)

TAIWAN
EA18. Yushan National Park
EA41. **Kenting National Park**

KOREAN PENINSULA
EA42. Mount Sorak National Park and Biosphere Reserve (South Korea)
EA43. Mount Chiri National Park (South Korea)
EA44. **Mount Halla** (Cheju do, South Korea)
EA45. Mount Chilbo Nature Reserve (North Korea)

JAPAN
EA46. Rebun Island
EA47. Mount Hyachine (Honshu)
EA48. Shiroum Mountains (Honshu)
EA49. **Mount Hakusan** (Honshu)
EA50. **Yakushima**

INDOCHINA

CAMBODIA
EA51. Cardamom Mountains

LAOS
EA52. Bolovens Plateau

THAILAND
EA53. **Doi Chiang Dao Wildlife Sanctuary**
EA54. Doi Inthanon
EA55. **Doi Suthep-Pui National Park**
EA56. Khao Soi Dao Wildlife Sanctuary
EA57. **Khao Yai National Park**
EA58. Limestone flora
EA59. **Thung Yai-Huai Kha Khaeng World Heritage Site**
EA60. Tarutao National Park
EA61. Wet seasonal evergreen forests of south-east Thailand

VIETNAM
EA62. **Bach Ma-Hai Van**
EA63. **Cat Tien Biosphere Reserve**
EA64. **Cuc Phuong National Park**
EA65. **Langbian-Dalat Highland**
EA66. **Yok Don National Park**
EA67. Mount Fan Si Pan
EA68. Phu Khan

CHINA

Total land area: 9,600,000 km².

Population (1990): 1,139,060,000 (21.5% of the world's population).

Altitude: -155 m (Turfan Basin) to 8848 m (summit of Qomolangma Feng, or Mount Everest, on the border with Nepal).

Natural vegetation: Seasonal rain forest, monsoon forest, evergreen broadleaved forest, semi-deciduous broadleaved forest, mixed coniferous and broadleaved forest, subalpine coniferous forest, elfin forest, boreal coniferous forest, alpine scrub, alpine meadow, alpine tundra, steppe, desert, savanna, mangroves. Natural closed forests cover about 10% of China.

Number of vascular plants: c. 27,100 species, including c. 24,300 angiosperm species.

Number of country endemic species: c. 10,000.

Number of vascular plant families: 301 (seed plants).

Number of endemic families: 3 (Bretschneideraceae, Davidiaceae, Eucommiaceae).

Number of vascular plant genera: 3116.

Number of endemic genera: 243.

Geography

China, located in the east of the Eurasian continent, covers 9.6 million km² (nearly 7% of the world's land area). China extends about 5500 km from north to south, and 5200 km from west to east. The area is mainly mountainous: hills, mountains and plateaux cover two-thirds of the country, culminating in the highest place on Earth – Qomolangma Feng (Mount Everest) – on the border between China and Nepal. Many mountain regions, including limestone mountains, notably in Zhuang Autonomous Region (southern China), have distinctive floras. There is a wide range of habitats, including deep gorges, plains, high plateaux and basins, which influence the distribution of vegetation types and species.

Before its geologically recent uplift, the Qinghai-Xizang Plateau had a warm, humid climate and was covered by subtropical forest and savanna. Today, however, it is the world's highest desert, having been raised by 4500–5000 m. Its vegetation includes alpine meadow, high-altitude grassland and cold desert vegetation. This vast land mass has a major influence on the climate of the whole of South East Asia. Westerly air streams are forced to divide north and south of the plateau, resulting in an area of exceptionally high air pressure and low rainfall to the north, and creating the huge temperate desert of northern China and Mongolia extending as far north as latitude 50°N. In the absence of a barrier of high mountains in eastern China, cold dry air from this desert is able to penetrate far to the south, influencing the northern limits of tropical and subtropical vegetation in western China and in the eastern part of the Himalayas. In contrast, warm and very humid air flowing northwards from the Indian Ocean allows tropical vegetation to reach almost to 29°N in south-west China, the most northerly limit of tropical forest in the world.

Climate

There are 5 climatic zones, from north to south: cold temperate, temperate, warm temperate, subtropical and tropical. The climate of China is strongly influenced by the south-east monsoon from the Pacific Ocean and the south-west monsoon from the Indian Ocean. As a result, the southern and eastern sides of China are the wettest areas. Generally, precipitation decreases to the north-west; western China consists of the high-altitude desert of the Qinghai-Xizang (Tibet) Plateau and, to its north, arid basins adjoining Mongolia.

Vegetation

The main types of native vegetation in China are: seasonal rain forest, monsoon forest, evergreen broadleaved forest, semi-deciduous broadleaved forest, mixed coniferous and broadleaved forest, subalpine coniferous forest, elfin forest, boreal coniferous forest, alpine scrub, alpine meadow, alpine tundra, steppe, desert, savanna and mangrove forest. The distribution of dryland forests in the south-east is related to temperature: coniferous forest occurs in the cold temperate zone, mixed broadleaved forest in the temperate zone, deciduous broadleaved forest in the warm temperate zone, evergreen broadleaved forest in the subtropical zone, and seasonal rain forest and tropical evergreen forest in the tropical ·zone. The north-western region (including the Qinghai-Xizang Plateau) is mainly covered by dry xerophilous grassland and desert.

The total area of natural closed forest cover remaining in China is estimated at 978,470 km² (about 10% of the land area) (World Resources Institute 1992). Open forest covers a further 172,000 km². Massive afforestation programmes are underway. Currently there are about 127,330 km² of plantation forests in China, over four times the area of forestry plantations in the whole of Africa and representing 65% of the area under plantation forests in all of Asia (including the Middle East). Details of each of the major vegetation formations in China and areas of high plant diversity within them are given later in this chapter.

Flora

China has one of the richest floras in the world. There are an estimated 27,100 vascular plant species, including approximately 24,500 species of seed plants in 3116 genera and 301 families, and over 2600 species of ferns and fern allies (22% of the world's pteridophyte flora) in 52 families. Flowering plants number about 24,300 species (c. 10% of the world's total angiosperm flora) and there are 190 species of gymnosperms in 34 genera. In addition, there are 2100 species of bryophytes in 480 genera and 106 families, representing 10% of the world's total bryophyte flora. Floristic affinities are with Eurasia, India and Malaysia, as well as North America. Ancient Laurasian and Gondwanan elements are represented in the flora, along with pan-Arctic, pantropical and palaeotropical elements.

China has enjoyed a relatively stable climate since the Cretaceous, although the cold and/or dry areas in the north and north-west were once warmer and wetter than they are today. Apart from some mountain regions, China was little affected by changes in climate during the last glaciation, although large amounts of loess were deposited at the end of the last glacial period. There are some Pleistocene refugia which house relict species as well as being sites of speciation.

There are 16 families in China with monotypic genera, such as *Metasequoia* (*M. glyptostroboides*) (dawn redwood), *Ginkgo* (*G. biloba*) (maidenhair tree) and *Eucommia* (*E. ulmoides*). China not only has many primitive families and relict or monotypic genera, but also a large number of endemic genera, of which there are 243 among seed plants (7.8% generic endemism) (Tsun-shen Ying, Yu-long Zhang and Boufford 1993). Most belong to families which have disjunct distributions, occurring in the tropics or subtropics of East Asia and North America. Of the endemic genera, 8 (with 11 species) are gymnosperms, 31 (with 72 species) are monocotyledons and 204, with (444 species) are dicotyledons. The endemic genera belong to 72 families. The family with the largest number of endemic genera is Gesneriaceae, with 28. Of the larger families, those with the highest number of endemic genera are: Asteraceae (17), Apiaceae (17), Poaceae (15), Lamiaceae (13), Brassicaceae (10), Orchidaceae (10), Melastomataceae (8), Ranunculaceae (7) and Hamamelidaceae (5) (Tsun-shen Ying, Yu-long Zhang and Boufford 1993). Of the endemic genera, only a small proportion are neoendemics. There are 3 endemic families: Bretschneideraceae, Davidiaceae and Eucommiaceae.

Tsun-shen Ying, Yu-long Zhang and Boufford (1993) identify three major regions of generic endemism in China:

Eastern Sichuan – western Hubei
This region comprises eastern Sichuan, western Hubei, the northernmost part of Guizhou and the north-western part of Hubei. It contains 82 genera of seed plants which are endemic to China, of which 39 are monotypic. Among the 25 genera which are strictly endemic to the eastern Sichuan/ western Hubei region are *Cathaya*, *Metasequoia*, *Pseudolarix*, *Fortunearia*, *Sinowilsonia*, *Tapiscia*, *Dipteronia*, *Cyclocarya* and *Davidia*. Many of the genera reflect the ancient nature of the temperate flora of this particular part of China.

Western Sichuan – north-western Yunnan
This region, which lies within the Hengduan Mountain system, contains 101 genera of seed plants which are endemic to China, of which 30 are strictly endemic to western Sichuan/north-western Yunnan. The flora is considered to be much younger in origin than that of the previous region. Strictly endemic genera include *Anemoclema*, *Asteropyrum*, *Beesia*, *Calathodes*, *Kingdonia*, *Metanemone* (Ranunculaceae), *Sinofranchetia* (Lardizabalaceae), *Dysosma* (Berberidaceae), *Gymnotheca* (Saururaceae), *Sargentodoxa* (Sargentodoxaceae) and *Eucommia* (Eucommiaceae).

South-eastern Yunnan – western Guangxi
This region contains 56 genera which are endemic to China, of which 23 are strictly endemic to south-eastern Yunnan/ western Guangxi. Among the endemic genera of gymnosperms in China, *Glyptostrobus* occurs only in this region. Also found here are all of the endemic genera of the most primitive families of Magnoliales (*Tsoongiodendron*, *Manglietiastrum* and *Parakmeria*).

Useful plants

Approximately 2411 vascular plant species (nearly 10% of the vascular plant flora) are documented as having uses (Compilation Committee of *Flora of Economic Plants of China*, undated). A considerable number of species are used on an industrial scale, for the production of fibres, vegetable gums, tanning materials, aromatic oils (>300 kinds developed so far), industrial oils and dyes. The Xishuangbanna region alone (CPD Site EA29, see Data Sheet) is estimated to contain over 1000 species of plants with high economic potential. For example, more than 500 species have long been used there by local people for medicinal purposes, some 150 species are oil plants with seeds containing over 15% oil, and a further 150 species are fast-growing and valuable timber tree species or bamboos (Xu Zaifu 1987). China also contains many valuable germplasm resources. In the Yunnan tropics, for example, there are about 120 species of wild types or close relatives of cultivated crops.

Medicinal plants

Chinese traditional medicine dates back for thousands of years. Ma huang (*Ephedra sinica*), has been used for treating asthma for more than 5000 years. In China as a whole, more than 5000 plant species have been used medicinally, mostly on a local scale (see Table 26). There are about 500 species in widespread use, of which about 100 species are cultivated, the rest being harvested solely from the wild. The most important cultivated medicinal plants are *Panax ginseng*, *P. notoginseng*, *Astragalus mongholicus*, *Angelica sinensis*, *Coptis chinensis*, *Codonopsis pilosula*, *Rehmannia glutinosa*, *Paeonia suffruticosa*, *Cinnamomum cassia*, *Amomum villosum* and *Atractylodes macrocephala* (Xiao Pei-Gen 1991).

In China, the quantity of medicinal plants used for direct decoction in traditional Chinese doctors' prescriptions and as ingredients in officinal medicine is immense. The current annual demand (excluding other forms of traditional usage) is reported to be 700,000 tons (Xiao Pei-Gen 1991). Xiao Pei-Gen (1987) lists 5136 medicinal plants in China; Duke and Ayensu (1985) describe 1240 Chinese medicinal plants. For a general introduction to medicinal plants in China, see Xiao Pei-Gen (1981a, 1983, 1986, 1991); for pharmacologically active principles, see Xu Ren-Shen *et al.* (1985), Liang Xiao-Tian *et al.* (1986), Xiao Pei-Gen (1987), Xiao Pei-Gen and Fu Shan-Lin (1987), and Zhu Da-Yuan (1987); and for new drugs development, see Xiao Pei-Gen (1981b).

TABLE 26. CHINESE MEDICINAL PLANTS IDENTIFIED TO DATE

	Number of species
Thallophytes	281
Bryophytes	39
Pteridophytes	395
Gymnosperms	55
Angiosperms	
Dicotyledons	3690
Monocotyledons	676
Total	**5136**

Source: Xiao Pei-Gen (1987).

Crop plants

Crop plants which have their origins in China include: *Glycine max* (soya bean), *Cannabis sativa* (hemp), *Prunus persica* (peach), *P. armeniaca* (apricot), *Diospyros kaki* (persimmon), *Citrus medica* (citron), *C. reticulata* var. *deliciosa* (tangerine), *C. sinensis* (sweet orange), *Eriobotrya japonica* (loquat), *Camellia sinensis* (tea), *Litchi chinensis* (lychee), *Actinidia chinensis* (kiwi fruit) and *Eleocharis tuberosa* (Chinese water chestnut).

Ornamental plants

A vast wealth of horticulturally desirable plants is found in China and throughout East Asia and many have been introduced into cultivation, especially in Europe and North America and form important parts of the cultivated flora of those countries. The genus *Rhododendron* is the largest vascular plant genus in the flora of China, with c. 500 species. Other horticulturally important genera include *Berberis*, *Camellia*, *Cotoneaster*, *Mahonia*, *Ginkgo* (*G. biloba*), *Metasequoia* (*M. glyptostroboides*), *Wisteria*, *Davidia*, *Pleione* and *Primula*, among many others.

Factors causing loss of biodiversity

Natural environmental factors

Much of the eastern and southern part of the region is affected by storms and floods which cause landslides or wash away fragile topsoil, thus altering or destroying the vegetation. Human impact on the environment (e.g. deforestation) results in a greater frequency of catastrophic events, resulting in severe erosion in places.

Population pressure

The population of China in 1990 was estimated at 1,139,060,000, representing 21.5% of the world's population (World Resources Institute 1992). The annual average growth rate between 1985 and 1990 was 1.45%. The annual growth rate between 1995 and 1990 is expected to be 1.22%. By the year 2025, the population of China is expected to be about 1,512,590,000 (World Resources Institute 1992). Most of the population is rural. However, there has been a rapid increase in the urban population over the last 50 years. In 1949, 11% of the China's population lived in urban areas (Zhao Ji *et al.* 1990); by 1990, the percentage had increased to over 33.4% (World Resources Institute 1992).

China's population is heavily concentrated in the plains and riverine lands of the south-eastern half of the country, while most of the north-west is virtually uninhabited. Very high population densities occur in the Changjiang Delta and the Red Basin of Sichuan. 90% of the population inhabit just 15% of the total land area (Europa Publications 1987). The large and growing population, and the high population density of some regions, inevitably places enormous pressures on natural resources. Most of the major threats noted below arise from population pressure.

Soil erosion and desertification

About 1,500,000 km^2 (approximately one-sixth of China) suffers soil erosion problems. The amount of soil washed away annually is estimated at 50 billion tonnes (Zhao Ji *et al.* 1990). The problem is particularly severe on the Loess Plateau, where 80% of the land is subject to erosion. The problem is made worse by the clearance of native vegetation for crops and the cultivation of steep slopes.

Land degradation, desertification and salinization is particularly acute in arid and semi-arid regions. Of a total of 3,000,000 km^2 of grassland, some 500,000 km^2 have been degraded, and the area of desertification is increasing at the rate of 6600 km^2 per year (Zhao Ji *et al.* 1990). Most of this is caused by overgrazing.

Deforestation and timber cutting

China is one of the world's oldest civilizations. Agriculture began there about 5000 years BP. Conversion of natural and semi-natural habitats to agricultural land still continues today. Forests are under increasing pressure as more agricultural land is required to increase food production for the growing population. Those forests that remain are sometimes over-exploited for timber and fuelwood.

Over-collection of wild plant resources

Over-collection is a threat especially to medicinal plants (see discussion in the Useful Plants section). Many species, such as *Panax ginseng* (ginseng), are now Endangered in the wild. Over-collecting also threatens some ornamental species. In 1987, a list of more than 380 rare and threatened plant species was produced by the State Environmental Protection Bureau and the Institute of Botany of the Chinese Academy of Sciences. The majority of the listed species are under threat from habitat loss or over-exploitation.

Other threats

Clearance of land for industrial and urban developments, and the impacts of environmental pollution and tourism on key sites have become major threats recently.

Conservation

Nature protection is central to the philosophies of Confucianism, Taoism and Buddhism (Wang Xianpu 1980; Zhao Ji *et al.* 1990). The first Imperial temple gardens were established during the Xia Dynasty almost 4200 years BP. Many of these have been designated subsequently under the county or provincial park system.

To date, China has established more than 500 Nature Reserves (IUCN 1992b), covering 3% of the total land area. Over 300 of the reserves are in forested areas. The reserve system is designed to contain representative samples of many typical natural landscapes and ecosystems in different biogeographical zones, as well as to contain populations of many rare and threatened species. New reserves are created on a regular basis. The level of protection is, however, generally low and there is a great need to strengthen reserve management.

The following 8 areas are internationally recognized Biosphere Reserves in the UNESCO Man and Biosphere Programme:

❖ Bogdhad Mountain (21,700 km²);
❖ Changbai Mountain Nature Reserve (1906 km²) (see Data Sheet on Changbai Mountains region, CPD Site EA1);
❖ Dinghu Nature Reserve (12 km²);
❖ Fanjingshan Mountain (415.3 km²);
❖ Fujian Wuyishan Nature Reserve (565.3 km²);
❖ Shennongjia (1474.7 km²);
❖ Wolong (2072.1 km²) (see Data Sheet on the High Mountain and Deep Gorge region, Hengduan Mountains and Min Jiang River basin, CPD Site EA40);
❖ Xilin Gol Natural Steppe Protected Area (10,786 km²).

Mount Huangshan (296 km²) and Mount Taishan are World Heritage Sites.

Chinese botanic gardens have shown a remarkable development since 1950 when there were only 5. By 1980 the figure had reached 39 and the total today is 116 (He, Shan-an *et al.* 1993, 1994 in press). They play a major role in the conservation of rare and threatened Chinese species, including economically important trees and medicinal plants, subjects of major concern in China (He, Shan-an *et al.* 1990).

Centres of plant diversity and endemism

Map 7 shows the location of the CPD Data Sheet sites for China, together with the main vegetation (phytogeographical) regions. Table 27 presents some floristic data for each of the regions, which are described in more detail below.

MAP 7. CPD DATA SHEET SITES AND PHYTOGEOGRAPHICAL REGIONS OF CHINA

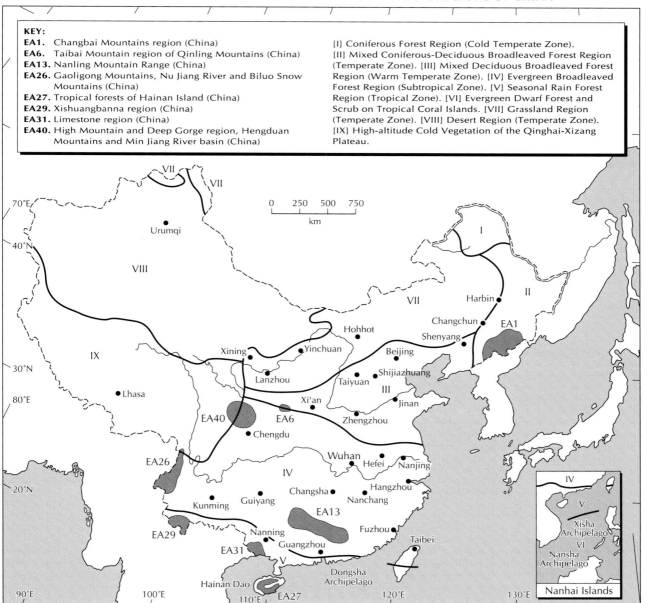

KEY:
EA1. Changbai Mountains region (China)
EA6. Taibai Mountain region of Qinling Mountains (China)
EA13. Nanling Mountain Range (China)
EA26. Gaoligong Mountains, Nu Jiang River and Biluo Snow Mountains (China)
EA27. Tropical forests of Hainan Island (China)
EA29. Xishuangbanna region (China)
EA31. Limestone region (China)
EA40. High Mountain and Deep Gorge region, Hengduan Mountains and Min Jiang River basin (China)

[I] Coniferous Forest Region (Cold Temperate Zone). [II] Mixed Coniferous-Deciduous Broadleaved Forest Region (Temperate Zone). [III] Mixed Deciduous Broadleaved Forest Region (Warm Temperate Zone). [IV] Evergreen Broadleaved Forest Region (Subtropical Zone). [V] Seasonal Rain Forest Region (Tropical Zone). [VI] Evergreen Dwarf Forest and Scrub on Tropical Coral Islands. [VII] Grassland Region (Temperate Zone). [VIII] Desert Region (Temperate Zone). [IX] High-altitude Cold Vegetation of the Qinghai-Xizang Plateau.

TABLE 27. PHYTOGEOGRAPHICAL REGIONS OF CHINA

Phytogeographical region	Climatic zone	Numbers of vascular plants		
		Species	Genera	Families
Coniferous forest	Cold temperate	800	>300	>60
Mixed coniferous-deciduous broadleaved forest	Temperate	1900	>700	>130
Mixed deciduous broadleaved forest	Warm temperate	3500	1000	200
Evergreen broadleaved forest	Tropical	15,600	2000	350
Seasonal rain forest	Tropical	>13,000	>1500	>300
Evergreen dwarf forest and scrub on tropical coral islands	Tropical	213	154	57
Grassland	Temperate	>3600	>760	125
Desert	Temperate	3900	817	130
Qinghai-Xizang Plateau	High-altitude desert	4400	1200	189

Note:

Figures are estimates, except for evergreen dwarf forest and scrub on tropical coral islands.

I. CONIFEROUS FOREST REGION (COLD TEMPERATE ZONE)

This region is in extreme northern China between latitudes 46°00'–54°00'N and longitudes 120°00'–127°00'E. It is an extension of the Siberian taiga, which stretches southwards in China along the Da Hinggan Mountain Range and to the southern tip of the Altai-Sayan. The region consists of low mountains and undulating hills with an average elevation of 700–1000 m (highest peak: Aukelidui, 1530 m).

Climate

The mean annual temperature is between -12°C and -5.6°C. The absolute minimum is <-40°C. Annual precipitation is 360–500 mm.

Vegetation

The main forest formations contain abundant *Quercus mongolicus* (Mongolian oak), intermixed with *Tilia amurensis* (Amur lime), *Fraxinus mandshurica* (Manchurian ash) and *Phellodendron amurensis*. At higher altitudes are *Pinus pumila* (Japanese stone pine) and *Betula ermanii* intermixed with *Larix gmelinii* (Dahurian larch), the main timber species. Cold temperate coniferous forest covers c. 150,000 km².

Flora

The area is relatively poor in species. There are about 800 species of vascular plants, almost none of which are endemic. 51% of the species occur widely throughout Siberia; 30% occur in mixed coniferous-deciduous broadleaved forest in the Changbai region. The mountains of Aukelidui, Yingili and Beigeli are of floristic interest. However, no sites qualify as globally important centres of plant diversity.

Conservation

There are 4 Nature Reserves. There is a great need for integrated management plans, considering the demands of growing industrial forestry interests.

II. MIXED CONIFEROUS-DECIDUOUS BROADLEAVED FOREST REGION (TEMPERATE ZONE)

This mountainous region covers 500,000 km² in north-east China, between latitudes 40°15'–50°20'N and longitudes 126°00'–135°00'E. The region adjoins Sikhote-Alin on the Pacific coast to the east and the Korean Peninsula to the south. The main mountain ranges are Xiao-Hinggan, Wan Da, Chang Guancai, Laoye and the Changbai Mountains. The average altitude is c. 300–800 m; the highest peak (Bei Yun Peak in the Changbai Mountains) is 2691 m. The region is one of the China's most important timber producing areas, but timber resources are being depleted rapidly.

Climate

The climate is monsoonal, with a mean annual temperature of 2–8°C. The absolute minimum is -35°C. Annual rainfall is 500–800 mm (locally 1000 mm).

Vegetation

The main forest formation throughout the region is mixed coniferous-deciduous broadleaved forest. The most abundant trees are *Pinus koraiensis* (Korean pine) and numerous deciduous species. Dense alpine coniferous forest occurs at 700–1800 m, with *Picea jezoensis*, *P. koraiensis* and *Abies nephrolepis*. The vegetation at 1100–2100 m is mainly dwarf *Betula ermanii* forest. Alpine tundra, similar to that of the Arctic, occurs above 2100 m; this is the only region in China with tundra.

Flora

The flora includes c. 1900 vascular plant species. This region, together with Amur, the coastal area of Far Eastern Russia and North Korea, carries a distinctive flora known as the Changbai. Typical species include *Panax ginseng*, *Astilboides tabularis*, *Trifolium lupinaster*, *Aristolochia moupinensis* and *Fritillaria ussuriensis*. *Pinus koraiensis* is endemic. Other conifers include *Abies holophylla* and

Taxus cuspidata var. *changpaiensis*. Deciduous broadleaved trees include *Juglans mandshurica* (Manchurian walnut), *Phellodendron amurense* and *Fraxinus mandshurica*, all Tertiary relicts. Species present which are more typical of southern China include *Actinidia* spp. and *Magnolia sieboldii*, which are believed to be survivors from a time when the region experienced a subtropical climate. There are also a number of Arctic elements, including *Salix tschanbaischanica* and *Pyrola tschanbaischanica*, both endemic.

Species of economic importance

The main timber species are *Abies holophylla*, *Juglans mandschurica*, *Phellodendron amurense* and *Pinus koraiensis*. Important medicinal plants include *Boschniakia rossica*, *Fritillaria ussuriensis* and *Panax ginseng*. Timber cutting and over-collection of medicinal plants are the main threats to the flora.

Conservation

There are over 30 Nature Reserves, the most famous of which is Changbai Mountains Nature Reserve (1906 km²).

Centres of plant diversity and endemism

EA1. Changbai Mountains region (Jilin Province)

– see Data Sheet.

EA2. Xizo Hinggan Mountain Range (Heilongjiang Province)

EA3. Gao Tai Mountain Range

EA4. Chang Guancai Mountain Range

EA5. Da Tuzi Mountain Range

III. MIXED DECIDUOUS BROADLEAVED FOREST REGION (WARM TEMPERATE ZONE)

This region is located in east central China, between latitudes 32°00'-43°00'N and longitudes 104°00'-124°00'E. The west of the region is mountainous, the central part is hilly, and the east consists of the North China Plain. The mountains have an average elevation of over 1500 m, but some, such as the Tai Bai Mountains in the Qinling Mountain Range, rise to over 3000 m. The hilly zone does not generally exceed 500 m, with some exceptions, such as Tai Shan Mountain (1546 m) and Lao Shan Mountain (1130 m). The North China Plain, mostly at 50–100 m altitude, is the largest plain in China.

Climate

The climate is very hot in summer and severely cold in winter. The mean annual temperature is 8–14°C; the absolute minimum is -38.4°C. Annual rainfall is 500–1000 mm, 75% falling in summer.

Vegetation

The vegetation of the North China Plain has been greatly modified over a long period to such an extent that almost all natural forest has been cleared for agriculture. Mixed deciduous broadleaved forest formed the original vegetation over most of the region; remnants survive in some valleys and on mountain foothills. The main species are *Acer ginnala*, *A. truncatum*, *Koelreuteria paniculata*, *Ulmus macrocarpa*, *Celtis korainensis*, *Tilia amurensis*, *T. mandschurica*, *Carpinus turczaninowii* and *Fraxinus bungeana*. Oak forests on dry mountain slopes contain, in the south, *Quercus acutissima*, *Q. variabilis* and *Q. serrata* and, in the north, *Q. mongolica*, *Q. liaotungensis* and *Q. aliena*. *Pinus densiflora* occurs in the Liaoton and Shandong peninsulas; *Pinus armandii* forest occurs in the south-west. Subalpine coniferous forest, at 2400–3300 m, includes, in the north, *Picea meyeri*, *P. wilsonii*, *Larix principis-rupprechtii* and *L. wulingshanensis* and, in the south, *Picea asperata*, *P. neoveitchii*, *Abies fargesii* and *Larix chinensis*. Alpine scrub and meadow occurs at higher altitudes.

Flora

It is estimated that there are c. 3500 species of seed plants, belonging to 1000 genera and 200 families. However, there are only 40 endemic species. The best represented families are Gramineae, Leguminosae and Rosaceae. 66% of the flora consists of herbaceous species; many have European and Siberian affinities. Some species and families are more typical of the tropics and subtropics. There are also many Himalayan and South West Asian elements. Japan was connected with China during the Tertiary period, resulting in the presence of a number of Japanese elements along the coast, including *Pinus densiflora* and *Camellia japonica*.

Conservation

There are almost 100 Nature Reserves in the region.

Centres of plant diversity and endemism

EA6. Taibai Mountain region of Qinling Mountains (Shaanxi Province)

– see Data Sheet.

EA7. Zhongtiao Mountains (Shanxi Province)

EA8. Wutai Mountains (Shanxi Province)

EA9. Southern part of Taihang Mountains (Henan Province)

EA10. Lingwu Mountain (Hebei Province)

EA11. Lao Mountains (Shandong Province)

EA12. Kunyu Mountains (Shandong Province)

IV. EVERGREEN BROADLEAVED FOREST REGION (SUBTROPICAL ZONE)

This is the largest region in China, covering about 2.4 million km² (c. 25% of the total land area of China). The northern boundary is the Hui River as far as Qinling Mountain Range at latitude c. 34°00'N. The southern boundary is near the Tropic of Cancer, extending eastwards to the island of Taiwan. The western boundary is formed by the eastern slopes of the Qinhai-Xizang Plateau. To the south, the vegetation continues into the Indian Subcontinent, including North Myanmā (Burma) (CPD Site IS6, see Data Sheet) and the foothills of the Eastern Himalayas in India (see, for example, the Data Sheet on Namdapha, CPD Site IS4, and the Regional Overview on the Indian Subcontinent). The topography is varied, including plains, basins, hills, plateaux and mountains. Most of the region is limestone.

Climate

The eastern part of the region is under the influence of the Pacific Monsoon. Cold air penetrates from Siberia. The western part of the region includes the Yungui Plateau and the mountains of West Sichuan. Here the climate is influenced by the Indian Ocean Monsoon which brings high rainfall during the summer and autumn; continental dry air ensures that winter and spring are dry and warm. The mean annual temperatures over the region as a whole are 15–21°C. In winter, temperatures can be as low as -10°C in the north and -6°C in the south. Annual rainfall is in excess of 1000 mm and sometimes over 2000 mm.

Vegetation

The main formation throughout the region is evergreen broadleaved forest. In valleys below 1000 m there are small areas of tropical monsoon forest and savanna woodland. Forest on limestone mountains is distinctive, consisting of both evergreen and deciduous broadleaved species, and coniferous species. The species composition of evergreen broadleaved forest varies considerably throughout the region. Typical species include: in the east, Cyclobalanopsis glauca, Castanopsis carlesii and C. sclerophylla; in the south, Cryptocarya concinna, C. chinensis, Machilus chinensis and

Beilschmiedia percoriacea; and in the west, Cyclobalanopsis glaucoides and C. delavayi. A unique type of deciduous evergreen broadleaved mixed forest is found in the north, consisting mainly of Quercus variabilis, Q. acutissima, Q. fabri and Q. glandulifera, as well as a number of evergreen broadleaved trees, such as Cyclobalanopsis glauca, C. gracilis and Castanopsis sclerophylla.

Montane deciduous broadleaved forest is found intermixed with montane semi-deciduous broadleaved forest at 1000–2200 m. Among the evergreen species are Cyclobalanopsis stewardiana, C. multinervis and Castanopsis platyacantha; the deciduous species include Fagus lucida, Betula austrosinensis, Tetracentron sinense and Davidia involucrata. In the west, montane evergreen broadleaved forest is sometimes dominated by Pinus yunnanensis and P. armandii. Subalpine coniferous forest with Tsuga chinensis, Abies fabri, A. kawakamii, Picea asperata and P. brachytyla is found at 2200–3200 m. Alpine Rhododendron scrub and meadow occurs at higher altitudes. There is scant vegetation above 4000 m.

Although this region has had a long history of cultivation, most of the vegetation on the mountains is still intact.

Flora

This region is situated at the meeting point of the pan-Arctic and palaeotropical floras. The climate has been relatively stable since the Tertiary Period, being comparatively little influenced by Quatenary climatic changes. As a result, there are many ancient relict species, such as Abies beshanzuensis, A. ziyuanensis, A. franjingshanensis and A. yuanbaoshanensis. Tropical families are well-represented in the flora. The region is the centre of origin of many East Asian species; it is possible that the region was the centre of origin of the angiosperms. Based on incomplete surveys, it is estimated that the flora contains 14,600 species of seed plants belonging to over 1730 genera. There are c. 14,500 species of flowering plants in over 1700 genera and c. 100 species of gymnosperms in 30 genera. There are estimated to be over 1000 species of ferns and fern allies. There are 155 genera of seed plants with disjunct distributions, occurring also in North America. Examples include Magnolia, Liriodendron and Sassafras.

Of China's 198 endemic genera, 148 occur in this region, including 77 which are monotypic. Examples include Ginkgo, Pseudolarix, Cathaya, Glyptostrobus, Eucommia and Cyclocarya. Relict species include Ginkgo biloba, Glyptostrobus pensilis, Metasequoia glyptostroboides, Pseudolarix kaempferi, Cathaya argyrophylla, Liriodendron chinense, Davidia involucrata and Camptotheca acuminata.

Species of economic importance

Important timber trees are the conifers Cunninghamia lanceolata and Pinus massoniana.

Conservation

More than 200 Nature Reserves have been established in the region.

Centres of plant diversity and endemism

EA13. Nanling Mountain Range (Guangdong, Guangxi, Hunan and Jiangxi Provinces)

– see Data Sheet.

EA14. Wuyi Mountain (Fujian Province)

EA15. Jiulong Mountains (Zhejiang Province)

EA16. Fanjing Mountains (Guizhou Province)

EA17. Dabie and Guniu Mountains (Anhui Province)

EA18. Yushan National Park (Taiwan)

Phytogeographically part of the evergreen broadleaved forest region (subtropical zone). See overview on Taiwan.

EA19. Shennongjia (Hubei Province)

EA20. Funiu Mountains (Henan Province)

EA21. Daba Mountains (Sichuan Province)

EA22. Wolong Mountains, Da and Xiao Liang Shan Mountains (Sichuan Province)

EA23. South Yulong Mountains (Yunnan Province)

EA24. Haba Snow Mountains (Yunnan Province)

EA25. Ailao Shan (Yunnan Province)

EA26. Gaoligong Mountains, Nu Jiang River and Biluo Snow Mountains (Yunnan Province)

– see Data Sheet.

V. SEASONAL RAIN FOREST REGION (TROPICAL ZONE)

This region covers c. 600,000 km², from Jingpu (Taiwan) and Hainan Island to Yadong and Nyalam (Xizang Province). The northern boundary is mostly between latitudes 21–24°N, but warm air from the Bay of Bengal allows rain forest to develop as far north as 25°N in Yunnan and 28–29°N in south-east Xizang. The region is geomorphologically complex, including alluvial plains, tablelands, hills, mountains, plateaux, limestone peaks and islands. There are a large number of karst peaks with distinctive floras in south-west Zhuang Autonomous Region (Guangxi Province). The western part of the region includes the southern part of the Yungui Plateau and the deeply dissected southern slopes of the Himalayan mountains at altitudes up to 1000–1500 m.

Climate

The climate is tropical monsoonal, with average annual temperatures of 20–22°C, but reaching 25–26°C in the south. Frost is very rare. Mean annual rainfall generally exceeds 1500 mm and can be as high as 3000–5000 mm locally. Rain-shadows can reduce rainfall to 900–1200 mm. Rain mostly falls between April and October. Typhoons occur between May and November.

Vegetation

Seasonal rain forest varies in species composition throughout the region. Prominent species on Hainan include *Heritiera parvifolia*, *Vatica astrotricha* and *Litchi chinensis*. *Myristica cagayanensis*, *Pleurospermum niveum* and *Artocarpus lanceolatus* are characteristic of southern Taiwan (which phytogeographically belongs to this region). In southern Guangxi, *Saraca chinensis*, *Artocarpus styracifolia* and *Hopea chinensis* are common. Typical species in Xishuangbanna (Yunnan Province) include *Dipterocarpus tonkinensis*, *Hopea mollissima*, *Terminalia myriocarpa*, *Antiaris toxicaria*, *Parashorea chinensis* and *Tetrameles nudiflora*. Western season rain forest includes *Dipterocarpus alatus*, *D. pilosus*, *D. turbinatus*, *Shorea assamica*, *S. robusta* and *Canarium strictum*. Limestone areas carry a distinctive flora, including *Burretiodendron hsienmu*, *Garcinia paucinervis* and *Cephalomappa sinensis*.

Montane seasonal rain forest occurs above 700–800 m in the south, with subtropical evergreen broadleaved forest at higher altitudes. However, in the north the forests are all of the evergreen broadleaved type, extending up to 2200–2400 m in the western part of Xizang. The main constituents are species of *Castanopsis*, *Lithocarpus* and *Cyclobalanopsis*. In south-east Zixang, the vegetation zonation at higher altitudes continues through montane coniferous forest, sclerophyll broadleaved forest, subalpine coniferous forest, to alpine *Rhododendron* scrub and meadow at 4000–5000 m. At 5000–5500 m, the vegetation consists of lichens and sparse cushion plants, comprising species of *Saussurea*, *Cremanthodium*, *Rhodiola* and *Saxifraga*. The permanent snow-line is at 5500–6200 m.

Coastal mangrove forests are not as rich in species as those of Malesia.

Flora

There are estimated to be more than 13,000 vascular plant species in the region. The flora is palaeotropical with affinities to that of Malesia (in the east of the region) and Indo-Burma (in the west). The flora was little affected by Quaternary climate change. As a result, there are many relict species. Dipterocarpaceae, typical of South East Asian forests, is represented by a number of genera. The flora of south-east Zizang is basically Indo-Himalayan and there are also, in the east, Pacific and Sino-Japanese floristic elements. Although there are some endemic species, many species are shared with tropical Asia. Although rich, the flora is an impoverished version of that found further south. There are fewer endemics than in the subtropical zone.

Species of economic importance

Important timber trees include *Burretiodendron hsienmu* and *Garcina paucinervis*. There are many medicinal plants, including *Amomum villosum*, *Aquilaria sinensis* and *Panax sanchii*.

Conservation

There are over 100 Nature Reserves in the region; however, more are required to provide adequate coverage of the flora, especially in south-west Yunnan and south-east Xizang.

Centres of plant diversity and endemism

EA27. Tropical forests of Hainan Island

– see Data Sheet.

EA28. Southern Guangxi Province (Shiwanda Mountain and Nonggang Nature Reserves)

EA29. Xishuangbanna region (Yunnan Province)

– see Data Sheet.

EA30. Zayu, Medog, Yadon and Nyalam (south part of Xizang Autonomous Region)

EA31. Limestone region (south-west Zhuang Autonomous Region, Guangxi Province)

– see Data Sheet.

EA41. Kenting National Park (Taiwan)

Phytogeographically part of the seasonal rain forest region (tropical zone). See overview on Taiwan.

VI. EVERGREEN DWARF FOREST AND SCRUB ON TROPICAL CORAL ISLANDS

This region includes the archipelagos of Dongsha, Zhongsha, Xisha and Nansha in the South China Sea. The islands are mostly small coral islands, the largest of which is Yong Xing Island (1.85 km²) and the highest of which is Shi Island (12.5 m altitude).

Climate

The climate of Dongsha, Zhonsha and Xisha is monsoonal oceanic, while that of the Xisha Archipelago is equatorial. Mean annual temperatures are 25–28°C. Annual rainfall is 1400–2200 mm, most falling in June–November.

Vegetation

Tropical evergreen dwarf forest and scrub is dominated by *Pisonia grandis*, *Guettarda speciosa*, *Scaevola sericea*, *Cordia subcordata*, *Tournefortia argentea* and other widespread littoral species. Large areas of intact vegetation remain on the islands of Yong Xing, Dong, Zhongjian, Jinyin, Ganquan (Xisha Archipelago) and Taiping Island (Nansha Archipelago).

Flora

The flora includes only 213 species of vascular plants belonging to 154 genera and 57 families. Most are tropical coastal plants belonging to Nyctaginaceae, Rubiaceae, Goodeniaceae, Verbenaceae, Lythraceae, Guttiferae and Gramineae. Many species occur throughout the Pacific.

VII. GRASSLAND REGION (TEMPERATE ZONE)

China has one of the most extensive areas of grassland on the Eurasian continent, extending from the Songliao Plain, across Inner Mongolia and the Loess plateaux, and including a small part of the Altai-Sayan in northern Xinjiang Uygur Zizhiqu. Altitude increases towards the south-west, ranging from 120 m to over 2000 m.

Climate

The climate is temperate arid and semi-arid with a distinct continental character. In the north, the mean annual temperature is -3°C and the absolute minimum is -30°C. In the south, the mean annual temperature is 5.6–9°C, with the absolute minimum being -20°C. Annual rainfall is 200–450 mm, decreasing from south-east to north-west. About 80–90% of the rain falls in summer. Sandstorms are a notable feature.

Vegetation

The dominant vegetation is steppe grassland. Species found on the eastern Songliao Plain include *Stipa baicalensis*, *Aneurolepidium chinese* and *Filifolium sibiricum*. Some of the typical grassland species of the Inner Mongolian Plateau and western Songliao Plain are *Stipa grandis*, *S. krylovii*,

Cleistogenes squarrosa, Aneurolepidium chinense, Filifolium sibiricum, Festuca ovina and *Agropyron cristatum*. Desert steppe of the Ulanqab Plateau includes *Stipa* spp., *Cleistogenes songorica* and *Allium mongolicum*. Montane desert steppe occurs on the Altai-Sayan. The flora of the central and eastern parts of the Loess Plateau includes *Stipa bungeana, Artemisia giraldii* and *Thymus mongolicus*. The desert grassland of the western Loess Plateau carries *Stipa breviflora, S. glareosa, Ajania achilleoides, Caragana tibetica* and *Reaumuria soongarica*. Low mountains, hills and ravines in the eastern part of the region carry trees of *Pinus sylvestris* var. *mongolica* and *Quercus mongolica*. Subalpine coniferous forest occurs on various mountain ranges within the region. Alpine scrub and meadow occur at higher elevations.

Much of the original grassland has been ploughed or severely degraded by overgrazing. No large areas of forest remain and those that survive are threatened.

Flora

It is estimated that there are over 3600 species of seed plants, representing over 760 genera and 125 families. The flora includes about 42% of China's plant families, about 24% of its genera and about 13% of its species. However, considering the large area of the region, the flora is not very rich. The best represented families are Compositae, Gramineae, Rosaceae, Leguminosae, Cyperaceae and Liliaceae. Most endemic species occur in the eastern part of the region (in forest steppe and meadow steppe). These include *Stipa baicalensis, Aneurolepidium chinense* and *Filifolium sibiricum*. Endemic genera include *Psammochloa, Pugionium* and *Anemarrhena*. Most other genera are widely distributed in north temperate regions of the world, including Central Asia and the Mongolian grasslands.

Species of economic importance

Important medicinal plants include *Astragalus hoantchi* and *Glycyrrhiza uralensis*. Many medicinal plants are threatened by habitat destruction and over-collection.

Conservation

Over 40 Nature Reserves have been established in the region.

Centres of plant diversity and endemism

EA32. Western slope of Da Hinggan Mountains, Horqin and Xilin Gol (Nei Mongol Zizhiqu)

EA33. Helan Mountains (Ningxia)

EA34. Huang Long Mountains (Shaanxi Province)

EA35. Mazui Mountain (Gansu Province)

EA36. Altai-Sayan (Xinjiang)

The extension of this mountain range into Russia and Kazakhstan is designated as CPD Site CA1 and described in a Data Sheet (see Regional Overview on Central and Northern Asia).

VIII. DESERT REGION (TEMPERATE ZONE)

The desert region is located in north-west China between latitudes 36°00'–49°00'N and longitudes 74°00'-108°00'E. It is the most easterly part of the world's largest desert region, which stretches across Asia and into Africa. Geomorphically, the region consists of high mountains separated by basins, including the Junggar and Tarim Basins (Xinjiang), the Qaidam Basin (Qinghai Province), the high plateaux of northern Gansu and Ningxia, and the western part of the tableland of Nei Mongol Zizhiqu (Inner Mongolia). The entire region in China covers 1.9 million km² (about 20% of the land area of China). At its centre, the desert is 2000–3000 km from the coast.

Climate

The annual and diurnal temperature ranges are the highest in China (26–42°C and 30–40°C respectively). Mean annual temperatures are 0–14°C, falling to below -5°C above 2500 m. The absolute maximum temperature is 47°C (in the Turfan Depression of Xinjiang) and the absolute minimum is -35°C. Annual rainfall is generally only c. 100 mm, with some locations having just 25–50 mm. In the mountains, annual rainfall can reach more than 500 mm. Rainfall increases from the central part of the region towards the west and east. Much of the region is subject to strong winds and sandstorms.

Vegetation

Much of the vegetation consists of sub-shrub communities. In the Junggar and Tacheng Basins and in the Ili Valley in the west, prominent species are *Haloxylon ammodendron, H. persicum, Nanophyton erinaceum, Anabasis brevifolia, A. salsa, Suaeda physophora, S. microphylla, Artemisia borotalensis, A. kaschgarica, Ephedra przewalskii* and *Salsola laricifolia*. At 800–1500 m on the northern slopes of the Tien Shan Mountains, there is a belt of *Stipa capillata* and *Festuca sulcata* grassland. Subalpine coniferous forest, dominated by *Picea schrenkiana*, is found at 1500–2700 m. *Juniperus sibirica* scrub occupies the southern slopes. Valleys at 1500–1900 m contain montane deciduous broadleaved forest with *Malus sieversii, Prunus armeniaca* (wild apricot), *Juglans regia* and *Cerasus tianschanica*. Alpine meadows, dominated by *Kobresia capillifolia*, occur at 2700–3600 m. At 3600–4000 m, alpine cushion vegetation and cryophytes are found. The snow-line is at 4000 m.

The hot dry deserts of the Turfan Basin, Hami Basin, Hashun Gobi and Tarim Basin carry only sparse vegetation, with *Nitraria sphaerocarpa, Ephedra przewalskii, Iljinia regelii, Halocneum strobilaceum, Alhagi sparsifolia, Calligonum mongolicum* and *Gymnocarpos przewalskii*.

Large areas of the southern slopes of the Tien Shan, Kunlun and Altun mountains are covered by *Stipa* grasslands. Subalpine coniferous forest occurs at 2400–3600 m, mostly in sheltered gullies and valleys on northern slopes. Alpine meadows extend up to 4000 m; cryophytes and cushion communities are found at higher altitudes. On some peaks above 6000 m, there is permanent snow and glaciers.

Timber cutting and collection of firewood have resulted in severe degradation to the vegetation in some places; some species are threatened as a result.

Flora

There are estimated to be 3900 species of vascular plants, belonging to 130 families and 817 genera. Although the region has a large number of species, it is floristically poor considering its huge area. More species occur in the mountains (2900) than on the plains (1000). The best represented families are Compositae, Gramineae, Leguminosae, Cruciferae and Chenopodiaceae. The flora has affinities with those of the Mediterranean, South West Asia and Central Asia. Most of the endemics are closely related to species found elsewhere in Central Asia. Among the endemic species are *Ammopiptanthus mongolicus*, *Potaninia mongolica*, *Calligonum roborowskii*, *Zygophyllum kaschgaricum*, *Reaumuria kaschgaricum*, *Kaschgaria komarovii* and *Picea crassifolia*.

Conservation

About 40 Nature Reserves have been established in the region.

Centres of plant diversity and endemism

EA37. Northern slopes of Tien Shan (Xinjiang Uygur Zizhiqu)

The mountains are an eastern extension into China of the area covered in the Data Sheet on the Mountains of Middle Asia (including the mountain ranges of Kopetdag, Tien Shan, Pamiro-Alai, Pamir and Dzhungarian Alatau) (CPD Site CA3, see Regional Overview on Central and Northern Asia).

EA38. Tacheng Basin and Ili Valley (Xinjiang Uygur Zizhiqu)

IX. HIGH-ALTITUDE COLD VEGETATION OF THE QINGHAI-XIZANG PLATEAU

The Qinghai-Xizang (Tibet) Plateau is a huge region covering 2.2 million km². The region is known as the "Roof of the World". It has an average altitude of 4000 m and is surrounded by and includes several high mountains. The plateau was created by massive uplifting which began some 40 million years ago, when the Indian Subcontinent collided with Asia and was carried beneath the Eurasian continental crust by the continuing northward movement of the Indo-Australian Plate. The Himalayas were also a product of these earth movements. At the same time, the Pacific Plate was being thrust beneath the Eurasian Plate, creating the dominant landforms in eastern China.

Climate

Mean annual temperatures over much of the region are between -5.8°C and 3.7°C, but higher mean temperatures (7–10°C) occur towards the south-east and in some river valleys. The absolute minimum temperatures are between -26°C and -46°C. The mean annual rainfall is 100–1000 mm, increasing from north-west to south-east. Sandstorms frequently occur. The plateau has a profound effect on climate of much of East and South East Asia, as described in the introduction to this Regional Overview.

Vegetation

From south-east to north-west, the following sequence occurs: tropical succulent thorn scrub, montane evergreen broadleaved forest, montane mixed broadleaved coniferous forest, subalpine coniferous forest, alpine scrub and meadow, alpine grassland, alpine desert and alpine sub-cryophytic vegetation. The vegetation of the peripheral mountains is very varied. In Yunnan, there are large areas of pine forest at 1800–2400 m, dominated by *Pinus yunnanensis* and *Pinus densata*. North-facing slopes at 2400–3200 m carry mixed forest of *Tsuga chinensis*, *T. dumosa*, *Acer* spp. and *Betula* spp.; south-facing slopes are dominated by *Pinus densata*. On northern slopes at 3200–4200 m, there are large areas of subalpine coniferous forest, including many species of fir, spruce and larch; southern slopes are covered by open sclerophyll evergreen broadleaved forest and scrub in which the main species are oaks and junipers. Alpine scrub and meadow occur at 4000–4800 m, with sparse alpine sub-cryophytic vegetation at 4800–5200 m. The snow-line is at 5200 m.

The north-east part of the region (south-east Qinghai, north-west Sichuan, south-west Gansu, the eastern part of the north Tibetan Plateau) is a transitional area between high mountain valleys and the inner part of the plateau. There are large areas of high-altitude cold scrub and meadow, in which the following species occur: *Rhododendron violaceum*, *R. capitatum*, *R. thymifolium*, *R. nivale*, *Potentilla fruticosa*, *Salix delaveyana* and *Caragana jubata*. The main species of high-altitude meadows are *Kobresia* spp., *Polygonum sphaerostachyum* and *P. viviparum*. Cushion plants include *Androsace tapete*, *Arenaria kansuensis* and *Saussurea medusa*.

The central part of the region includes south-west Qinghai, much of the Qiangta Plateau and the valley plain of southern Xizang. There are large areas of high-altitude steppe at 4300–5000 m, containing *Stipa purpurea*, *S. subsessiliflora* var. *basiplumosa*, *Carex moorcroftii* and many needle grasses, such as *Stipa bungeana*. Wormwoods (*Artemisia* spp.) are frequent.

The north-west part of the region includes the northern part of the Qiantang Plateau and the eastern part of the Pamir Plateau. The area above 4600–5000 m is the highest altitude desert in the world. The main species are *Ceratoides compacta, Ajania tibetica, Artemisia rhodantha, Hedinia tibetica, Pegaeophyton scapiflorum, Astragalus heydei, Myricaria prostrata, Ephedra gerardiana, E. fedtschenkoae* and *Acantholimon diapensioides.*

Overgrazing and, locally, mineral extraction, are severe threats to the natural vegetation over much of this region.

Flora

There are an estimated 4400 vascular plant species in about 1200 genera. So far, 4385 vascular plant species have been recorded in 1174 genera and 189 families. Most of the genera are found elsewhere in Asia, but 14 are endemic. There are also many species of Mediterranean, South West Asian and Central Asian affinities.

Conservation

There are more than 20 Nature Reserves in the region.

Centres of plant diversity and endemism

EA39. Mountains of west Sichuan

EA40. High Mountain and Deep Gorge region, Hengduan Mountains and Min Jiang River basin (Sichuan Province)

– see Data Sheet.

TAIWAN

Area: 35,990 km².

Population: 20,440,000 (1991); natural increase >2% per annum.

Altitude: 0–3997 m (summit of Yushan).

Natural vegetation: c. 52% of the land area is under forest cover, of which 68% was natural forest in 1978. The major types include tropical broadleaved forest, subtropical evergreen broadleaved forest, temperate broadleaved forest and coniferous forest.

Number of vascular plant species: 3577.

Number of country endemic species: 1075.

Number of vascular plant families: 28.

Number of genera: 1360.

Vegetation

The island of Taiwan lies off the south-east coast of mainland China. Phytogeographically, there are two regions, which are essentially continuations of the vegetation belts described for China (see also Map 7). The evergreen broadleaved forest region (subtropical zone) occurs in the northern two-thirds of Taiwan, while the southern third is occupied by the seasonal rain forest region (tropical zone). Most areas of more natural vegetation are found in montane areas, which also contain many of Taiwan's endemic

species. Much of the vegetation of the coastal plains (particularly in western Taiwan) has been cleared or highly modified, as a result of urban and industrial development. There is a floristically rich area of evergreen broadleaved rain forest and semi-deciduous (monsoon) forest in the Hengchun Peninsula of southern Taiwan. According to Collins, Sayer and Whitmore (1991), lowland rain forest covers 1660 km² (4.6% of the land area of Taiwan). A summary of the vegetation zones of Taiwan is given in Table 28.

TABLE 28. VEGETATION ZONES OF TAIWAN

Altitudinal zone	Vegetation	Altitude (m)	Mean annual temperature (°C)
Foothills	*Ficus-Machilus* zone (tropical rain forest, seasonal rain forest)	0–500	> 23
Submontane	*Machilus-Castanopsis* zone (subtropical broadleaved forest)	500–1500	17–23
Montane	Lower *Quercus* zone (warm temperate broadleaved forest)	1500–2000	14–17
Montane	Upper *Quercus* zone (temperate broadleaved-coniferous mixed forest)	2000–2500	
Upper montane zone	*Tsuga-Picea* (cool temperate coniferous forest, pine forest)	2500–3100	8–11
Subalpine	*Abies* zone (Cold temperate coniferous forest)	3100–3600	5–8
Alpine zone	*Juniperus-Rhododendron* scrub	3600–3997	<5

Flora

Taiwan occupies a special phytogeographical position. The montane flora has close affinities to that of the Eastern Asiatic Floristic Region (including the floras of the Eastern Himalayas, southern China and Japan). Malesian elements are especially evident in the Hengchun Peninsula, at the extreme southern tip of Taiwan, where many species reach the northern limits of their ranges. Indeed, Takhtajan (1986) places this part of Taiwan within the Malesian Floristic Region, although it is not included as such in the regional floristic account of the region, *Flora Malesiana*.

Conservation

Existing protected areas cover nearly 10% of the land area. There are 4 National Parks (covering 2267 km² in total, or 6.3% of the land area), 14 Nature Reserves (623 km², or 1.7%) and 20 National Forests (415 km², or 1.6%). The forests were subject to extensive logging over past decades but a total ban on cutting was introduced in 1990. Major areas of botanical importance in Taiwan are already protected within National Parks.

Centres of plant diversity and endemism

EA18. Yushan National Park

Situated in the subtropical zone and ranging in altitude from 300 to 3997 m. Area: 1055 km².
- ❖ Vegetation: Includes nearly all the vegetation zones of Taiwan, except tropical forest.
- ❖ Flora: 722 vascular species have been recorded in a preliminary inventory covering 25% of the area.
- ❖ Conservation: The largest National Park in Taiwan.

EA41. Kenting National Park

– see Data Sheet.

Areas of botanical interest

Taroko National Park

Area: 920 km², with an altitudinal range of 0–3740 m.
- ❖ Vegetation: Includes representative samples of all of Taiwan's vegetation types, limestone vegetation and alpine tundra being well-represented.
- ❖ Flora: 1163 vascular plants so far recorded.

Yangmingshan National Park

Area: 115 km², with an altitude range of 200–1120 m.
- ❖ Vegetation: Volcanic and solfatara vegetation.
- ❖ Flora: 1224 vascular plant species so far recorded; many Japanese and central Chinese elements.

Chiatienshan Nature Reserve

Area: 73 km², with an altitude range of 600–2100 m.
- ❖ Vegetation: A unique type of forest of beech (*Fagus hayatae*) and giant red cypress (*Chamaecyparis* spp.).

KOREAN PENINSULA

> **Total land area:** 122,312 km² (North Korea); 98,447 km² (South Korea).
>
> **Population:** c. 20 million (North Korea); c. 40 million (South Korea)
>
> **Altitude:** 0–2744 m.
>
> **Natural vegetation:** Evergreen broadleaved (subtropical) forest, mixed deciduous coniferous forests, alpine forest.
>
> **Number of vascular plant species:** 2898.
>
> **Number of endemic species:** 407 taxa endemic to the Korean Peninsula, of which 224 restricted to South Korea and 107 restricted to North Korea.

The Korean Peninsula lies at c. 34°00'–42°00'N and 124°00'–131°00'E, bordering China and Russia to the north-west and north, respectively. The main bioclimatic zones are warm temperate, temperate and cold temperate. The area is mountainous.

Vegetation

The natural vegetation of Korea is largely forest. Forest still covers 65,310 km² (66% of the land area) in South Korea. There are major variations in vegetation related to climate and topography. The main vegetation types of Korea are:

Evergreen broadleaved forest

Subtropical evergreen broadleaved forest occurs south of latitude 35°00'N in areas with mean annual temperatures greater than 14°C. It occurs also on offshore islands such as Cheju do. The main genera are *Quercus* and *Camellia*, together with species of bamboo.

Deciduous and mixed deciduous coniferous forests

These forests occur between 35° and 43°N in areas with mean annual temperatures of 5–14°C. This includes most of the peninsula, except for higher altitudes. Characteristic species in the south include *Acer* spp., *Carpinus laxiflora*, *Quercus* spp., *Pinus densiflora* and *P. thunbergii* and, towards the north, *Betula schmidtii*, *Tilia amurensis*, *Larix gmelini*,. *Pinus koraiensis*, *Abies holophylla* and *Betula platyphylla*. In North Korea, mixed deciduous coniferous forest is found at 700–1700 m altitude.

Alpine forest (taiga)

This occurs on high mountains with mean annual temperatures below 5°C. The lower altitude of this zone is at about 1500 m on Mount Halla, but can be as high as 2744 m (Mount Paektu). The main species are *Picea jezoenesis*, *Abies nephrolepis*, *Larix gmelini* var. *koreana*, *Pinus pumila* and *Juniperus chinensis* var. *sargentii*.

Many of the native plant communities of both South and North Korea, especially in the lowlands, have been destroyed or greatly modified by the expansion of cultivation and settlements. There are some primary forests in Paekdusan, Kwanmo-bong, Potaesan, Chail-bong and Puksubaek-san in North Korea (Kim 1977).

Flora

The Korean Peninsula has 2898 vascular plant species. There are 407 taxa endemic to the Korean Peninsula, of which 224 are restricted to South Korea (Lee 1973, 1976). Takhtajan (1986) places the Korean Peninsula within the Japanese-Korean Province of the Eastern Asiatic Floristic Region.

Conservation

In South Korea, the total coverage of protected areas is c. 6.7% of the land area, with several more protected areas proposed. The most important botanical areas in South Korea (listed below) are already protected within National Parks, Biosphere Reserves or other types of protected areas. There is little information available on conservation in North Korea. A review of the protected areas system and conservation legislation is given in IUCN (1992b).

Centres of plant diversity and endemism

EA42. Mount Sorak National Park and Biosphere Reserve (South Korea)

Located on the eastern coast of the Korean Peninsula, and reaching an altitude of 1060 m. Area: 3743 km².

- ❖ Flora: 1013 vascular plant taxa so far recorded, including a diverse cliff flora.
- ❖ Conservation: Designated a National Park in 1970 and a Biosphere Reserve in 1982.

EA43. Mount Chiri National Park (South Korea)

Area: 4405 km², with an altitude range of 400–1915 m.

- ❖ Vegetation: The park includes nearly all the vegetation zones of South Korea, except subtropical forest.
- ❖ Conservation: The largest National Park in South Korea.

EA44. Mount Halla (Cheju do, South Korea)

– see Data Sheet.

EA45. Mount Chilbo Nature Reserve (North Korea)

Area: c. 250 km²; reaching an altitude of 659 m.

- ❖ Flora: Contains rich cliff flora.

Area of botanical interest

Ullung Island

Situated off the east coast of South Korea and reaching 984 m altitude at the summit of Songinbong. Area: 72.5 km².

- ❖ Vegetation: Primary forest, well conserved on the Nari Plateau.
- ❖ Flora: 654 vascular plant species in 380 genera and 115 families recorded so far. The flora is intermediate between that of Korea and Japan.

JAPAN

> **Total land area:** 380,000 km².
>
> **Population:** 120,000,000.
>
> **Altitude:** 0–3776 m (summit of Mount Fuji).
>
> **Natural vegetation:** Cold temperate, warm temperate and subtropical forests; alpine meadows.
>
> **Number of vascular plant species:** 5565.
>
> **Number of country endemic species:** >222.
>
> **Number of vascular plant families:** 229.
>
> **Number of endemic genera:** 17.

The Japanese Archipelago extends for c. 1000 km off the east of the Eurasian continent. It falls predominantly into the Sino-Japanese Floristic Province. The archipelago extends from 45°30'N (northern tip of Hokkaido) to c. 24°00'N (Hateruma, Ryukyu Islands). The climate is influenced by the warm Black Current in the south and the cold Kuril Current in the north. It is humid and relatively warm for its latitude. The rugged and often mountainous topography means that less than 20% of the total land is cultivated. For this reason, much of Japan retains forest cover, although most of the forests are secondary. Most of the population lives in lowland coastal areas, particularly in eastern central Honshu. 80% of the total population lives in urban areas; the largest cities (Tokyo, Osaka and Nagoya) contain more than one-third of the population.

Vegetation

The Japanese archipelago displays a range of vegetation types associated with cold temperate, warm temperate and subtropical climates. The natural vegetation is mainly moist forest, with a high diversity of species. Forests cover nearly 67% of the land area, although some 40% of this total is commercial plantation (Stewart-Smith 1987). Xerophytic vegetation is restricted to areas such as coastal sand-dunes, recent volcanic deposits and alpine meadows. Numata, Yoshioka and Kato (1975) describe the main types of vegetation.

Flora

There are 5565 species of vascular plants recorded from the Japanese archipelago, including the Ryukyus and the Bonin (Ogaswara) Islands. In addition, there are 124 subspecies, 1612 varieties and 815 forms. The number of families is 228, including unusual families such as Trochondendraceae, Cercidiphyllaceae and Glaucidiaceae. About 4% of the flora is endemic. The flora belongs to the Eastern Asiatic Floristic Region (Takhtajan 1986) and is closely related to that of China, to which Japan has been joined at various times in the geologic past, allowing easy dispersal of plants. Additionally, some species are believed to have been transported from China through dispersal of seeds or spores by animals or by the wind.

Factors causing loss of biodiversity

895 species are considered threatened (Table 29). Types of threat are listed in Table 30. The main causes are habitat destruction and modification, and over-collection (especially for commercial purposes). An Endangered Species Act was put into effect in April 1993.

Conservation

As of March 1991, there were 28 National Parks covering 2,050,000 km² (5.4% of the land area), 55 quasi-National Parks covering 1,330,000 km² (3.5%) and 299 Prefectural Natural Parks covering 1,950,000 km² (5.2%). In total, legally designated protected areas covered 5,330,000 km² (14.1% of the land area) (IUCN 1992b). Tourism has always been a major reason for the creation of parks in Japan. In 1986 there were 363 million visitors to National Parks and 908 million

TABLE 29. THREATENED SPECIES OF VASCULAR PLANTS IN JAPAN

	Extinct	Endangered	Vulnerable	Indeterminate	Total
Pteridophytes	10	11	74	6	101
Gymnosperms	0	0	4	0	4
Angiosperms:					
Dicotyledons					
Sympetalae	5	41	138	4	188
Chloriopetalae	10	41	190	3	244
Monocotyledons					
Orchidaceae	6	40	94	4	144
Other than orchids	4	14	177	19	214
Total	**35**	**147**	**677**	**36**	**895**

TABLE 30. MAJOR THREATS TO THE FLORA OF JAPAN

	Extinct	Endangered	Vulnerable	Indeterminate	Total
Development					
Wetland development	8	19	110	5	142
Deforestation	5	23	97	1	126
Grassland development	1	7	28	2	38
Construction of roads	0	1	17	1	19
Construction of dams	1	2	8	0	11
Others	1	11	39	0	51
Over-collection					
Horticultural	3	71	178	2	254
Medicinal	0	0	3	0	3
Environmental crises					
Rare	0	22	252	2	276
Feeding by animals	0	3	8	0	11
Trampling by people	0	0	9	0	9
Volcanic ashes	3	0	1	0	4
Others (undetermined)	13	3	1	23	40

visitors to all categories of protected natural sites (Nature Conservation Bureau 1988). Careful management is required to prevent serious problems of erosion and pollution, and insensitive infrastructural development, which has already occurred in places.

Fundamental biological research into threatened plant species is underway. The Environment Agency has taken a lead in collaboration with the Japan Society of Plant Taxonomists. The Japan Association of Botanical Gardens is preparing a database of threatened species present in botanical gardens and is also intending to reintroduce some threatened species to their original habitats. There have already been some successful reintroductions, especially in the Bonin (Ogasawara) Islands (see the Data Sheet on the Bonin Islands, CPD PO1, treated in the Pacific Ocean Islands region).

The Osaka Exposition of Flower and Greenery in 1990 spawned a movement in cities in favour of a greener environment and a more harmonious relationship between people and nature.

Centres of plant diversity and endemism

EA46. Rebun Island

Area: 82 km²; located north of Hokkaido and reaching 490 m altitude.
❖ Vegetation: Sand-dunes, temperate grassland, coniferous forest.
❖ Flora: 364 vascular plant species recorded so far.
❖ Threats: Visitor pressure, over-collection of ornamental species.

❖ Conservation: National Park (whole island) and National Monument (part of island). No management plan; at risk.

EA47. Mount Hyachine

Area: 54.6 km²; located in northern Honshu, reaching an altitude of 1914 m.
❖ Vegetation: Cold temperate deciduous broadleaved forest; alpine serpentine vegetation.
❖ Flora: 650 vascular plant species.
❖ Threats: Some areas suffering from visitor pressure.
❖ Conservation: Hyachinesan Prefecture Wildlife Protection Area (IUCN Management Category: IV); the alpine vegetation on the south-facing slope is protected as a Special Natural Monument.

EA48. Shiroum Mountains

Area: 800 km²; located in central Honshu, with an altitude range of 800–2930 m.
❖ Vegetation: Montane beech forest, subalpine coniferous fir forest, alpine pine scrub, alpine grassland.
❖ Flora: 1500 vascular species, including 40 orchids.
❖ Threats: Population pressure, visitor pressure at summit.
❖ Conservation: National Park, National Monument (summit).

EA49. Mount Hakusan

– see Data Sheet.

EA50. Yakushima

– see Data Sheet.

INDOCHINA

Total land area: 1,244,450 km².

Population: c. 134,780,000.

Altitude: 0–3142 m (summit of Fan Si Pan, Vietnam).

Natural vegetation: Evergreen and semi-deciduous lowland rain forest, semi-deciduous forest, submontane and montane forests.

Number of vascular plants: Estimated 12,000 species in Thailand; 12,000–15,000 in Cambodia, Laos and Vietnam together (> 8000 in Vietnam).

Number of endemic species: > 800 (Vietnam).

Important plant families: Dipterocarpaceae, Fagaceae, Magnoliaceae, Gramineae (including bamboos).

Geography

The four countries of Indochina (Cambodia, Laos, Thailand and Vietnam) were once almost entirely covered by various types of forest. Much of the original vegetation has been cleared or modified. A priority for conservation of plant diversity is to ensure that sufficient examples of all main forest types are protected and well managed.

Most of the population of Indochina lives in the lowlands, which include extensive plains mostly under intense irrigated agriculture. Major plains are the Central Plain of the Chao Phraya River of Thailand, the plain of the Mekong River in Cambodia, south-western Laos and southern Vietnam, and the plain of the Red River in north-east Vietnam. The undulating Korat Plateau of north-east Thailand is a low-lying area, between 100–200 m altitude, surrounded by the Petchabun Range in the west, and the Dangrek Range in the south. These ranges reach 500–1400 m and meet in the highlands of Khao Yai National Park. The plateau is now largely treeless, but some forest remains on the hills.

The Northern Highlands of Thailand extend from the borders with Myanmā (Burma) and Laos to c. 18°N. They consist mainly of north/south-running ridges at 1500–2000 m separated by wide and now completely cultivated valleys at 300–500 m. The Central Plain of the Chao Phraya River is now the main concentration of agriculture and population, and is almost entirely cultivated. The South East Uplands are an extension of the Cardamom Mountains of Cambodia and still carry some evergreen rain forest in protected areas. The Tenasserim Hills extend along the western border with Myanmā (see Data Sheet on Taninthayi, CPD Site IS16, in the Indian Subcontinent region), from the Northern Highlands to the Kra Isthmus. Some semi-deciduous forest remains at higher altitudes. The Southern Peninsula extends to the Peninsular Malaysian border and is an area of heavy rainfall. Most lowland forest has been cleared, but there is some forest at higher altitudes.

Hills and mountains are prominent in northern Indochina (highest point: Fan Si Pan in Vietnam) and extend southwards, on the west, to form the spine of the southern peninsula of Thailand and, on the east, along the border of Laos and Vietnam and on towards the Mekong Delta. These hills and mountains are sometimes sparsely populated.

Most of Cambodia consists of the plain of the Lower Mekong River, which is densely populated and largely under rice cultivation. The isolated highlands of the Elephant and Cardamom Mountains lie in the south-west. The Cardamom Mountains reach 1563 m. The western slopes of the Annamite Range are situated in the east near the border with Vietnam.

Laos is a land-locked country with rugged hills in the north. The Annamite Mountains run down the south-east (along the border with Vietnam); the low-lying (<200 m altitude) plain of the Mekong River is on the west, adjacent to Thailand; and the isolated Bolovens Plateau rises to more than 1500 m in the south. The highest point is Phou Bia (2820 m).

Indochina has long-established settled civilizations based on paddy agriculture in the fertile plains and valleys. Hill tribes in more mountainous areas traditionally practice shifting agriculture. In recent years, population pressure has resulted in the periods between episodes of forest clearance under shifting agriculture being reduced to such an extent that large areas of land have become converted to grassland, bamboo scrub and fire-swept savanna. Opium is grown extensively in northern Thailand and Laos, resulting in considerable additional deforestation, since fresh forest soils are preferred for its cultivation.

Climate

The climate is monsoonal, with the wetter South-west and South-east monsoons dominating from May to October and the North-west Monsoon from November to April. The climate is wettest and more uniformly hot in the south, becoming seasonally cooler and also drier northwards. More inland parts and rain-shadow areas are relatively dry.

In Cambodia, the mean annual rainfall is generally 1200–1875 mm, with a dry season from November to March, but rainfall of up to 3000–4000 mm is experienced in the south-west. The lowlands of Laos receive about 1250 mm of rain per year, most of which falls between May and September.

Thailand experiences occasional typhoons from the South China Sea. Rainfall in the Northern Highlands and the Central Plains is approximately 1500 mm per year, that in the Korat Plateau about 1000 mm per year, while south-east Thailand and Peninsular Thailand receive more than 2000 mm per year (4000 mm locally). The mean monthly temperature ranges from about 25°C in the coolest months (December/January) to about 30°C in April/May, with seasonal differences in temperature being much more marked north of the peninsula.

Vietnam extends over a wide latitudinal range (from 8°30'N to 23°30'N) and the climate varies from humid tropical in the southern lowlands to temperate in the north. The mean annual temperature at sea-level ranges from 27 to 21°C accordingly. The mean annual rainfall is approximately 2000 mm, increasing in the narrow central mountain range to 3000 mm. There are three monsoons: the North-east winter Monsoon, and the South-east and the Western summer monsoons, with typhoons along the coast during hot weather.

Vegetation

Indochina was once almost entirely covered by forest, varying in type mainly according to rainfall, altitude and underlying geology. The most recent comprehensive assessment of the extent of remaining tropical moist forests in Indochina is that

TABLE 31. ORIGINAL AND REMAINING EXTENT OF CLOSED CANOPY MOIST FORESTS (INCLUDING TROPICAL CONIFEROUS FORESTS) IN INDOCHINA

Country	Approximate original area of closed canopy tropical moist forest cover (km²) [a]	Remaining area of tropical moist forest (km²) [a]	Remaining area of moist forest as % of original closed forest	Annual area of deforestation (total forest) 1981–1985 (km²) [b]
Cambodia	160,000	113,250	71	300
Laos	225,000	124,600	55	1300
Thailand	250,000	106,900	43	3790
Vietnam	280,000	56,680	20	650
Total	**915,000**	**401,430**	**47.25**	-

Sources:
[a] Collins, Sayer and Whitmore (1991).
[b] World Resources Institute (1994).

of Collins, Sayer and Whitmore (1991). They provide country-by-country surveys of moist forest cover in the region, with maps compiled from satellite and radar imagery and aerial photography. Table 31 gives figures for the original and remaining extent of closed canopy tropical moist forest in the region (derived from Collins, Sayer and Whitmore 1991) and the annual deforestation rate of all forest types between 1981 and 1985 (from World Resources Institute 1994).

Brief descriptions are given below of the main forest types found in Indochina.

Tropical wet evergreen and semi-evergreen forests occur in areas with more than 3000 mm annual rainfall. Lowland evergreen rain forest is the natural vegetation in Peninsular Thailand, extreme south-east Thailand and neighbouring south-west Cambodia, north-east Cambodia and parts of Laos, east-facing slopes in central Vietnam, and throughout the southern Vietnamese plains. Dipterocarpaceae are conspicuous components. In Cambodia, evergreen rain forests are best preserved on the western slopes of the Elephant and Cardamom Mountains, where population density is low. Lowland evergreen rain forest up to 700 m altitude contains abundant *Palaquium obovatum* and numerous widespread dipterocarp species, including *Anisoptera costata, A. glabra, Dipterocarpus costatus, Hopea odorata* and *Shorea hypochra* (Legris and Blasco 1972; Rollet 1972). Palms, especially rattans, are abundant, while Fagaceae (*Castanopsis* and *Lithocarpus*) are also present. Semi-evergreen rain forest was formerly extensive on the Annamite chain, but most has been cleared or severely damaged by shifting cultivation, as well as having suffered from defoliation and bombing during the Vietnam War.

Evergreen and semi-evergreen forests originally covered about 70% of Laos (Salter and Phanthavong 1989). Lowland and montane rain forests covered much of the Annamite Mountains and Bolovens Plateau; lowland forests were once extensive on the Mekong Plain.

Thai evergreen rain forests (mixed dipterocarp forests) represent the northern fringe of the great Malesian forests (see Regional Overview on South East Asia). The canopy contains many species of dipterocarps in the genera *Anisoptera, Balanocarpus, Dipterocarpus, Hopea, Parashorea* and *Shorea,* mixed with other species (notably members of the Bombacaceae, Sterculiaceae and Leguminosae). Semi-evergreen rain forests are Thailand's main forest formation. Two types of lowland wet seasonal evergreen forest occur in Thailand, namely peninsular wet seasonal evergreen forest (mainly occurring in Peninsular Thailand from Chumphon Province southwards) and south-eastern wet seasonal evergreen forest (which occurs in the extreme south-east of Thailand and south-west Cambodia). Wet seasonal forests occur in areas with less than 3 months dry season and more than 2000 mm mean annual rainfall.

Dry evergreen forest is poorer in species, shorter in stature and has more deciduous species than wet seasonal forest. Two-thirds of Vietnam were once covered by semi-evergreen and dry evergreen forest (IUCN 1985; MacKinnon and MacKinnon 1986).

Tropical moist deciduous and semi-deciduous monsoon forests naturally occur in lowland areas (occasionally to 1200 m) which have less than 1500 mm mean annual rainfall and a seasonal climate with three months dry season. They cover much of central, northern and eastern Thailand, central, eastern and northern Cambodia, probably much of Laos, and more northern parts of Vietnam. Some of these forests are rich in dipterocarps and teak (*Tectona grandis*). Much has been degraded by shifting cultivation and fire, and many areas have been converted to open savanna woodland and grassland. In Laos, valuable stands of teak still occur to the north and west of the Mekong.

Mixed deciduous forest is of moderate to low species richness. It has a distinctive flora in which Verbenaceae (including teak), Leguminosae and *Lagerstroemia* are abundant, the understorey consisting only of juvenile canopy trees or bamboo. It occurs throughout Thailand, north of the peninsula, on clay rich, relatively fertile, soils. Dense semi-deciduous and deciduous forests are the climax vegetation types of most of Cambodia, including the central area and the Annamite Mountains. Vast areas have been degraded by shifting agriculture and burning, the vegetation now consisting of open savanna woodland.

Dry dipterocarp forest is relatively poor in species. Its canopy is dominated by Dipterocarpaceae. It occurs on acid, infertile, sandy and lateritic soils.

Submontane and montane forests occur throughout Indochina above about 700 m altitude. They are evergreen forests, typically with species of Fagaceae, Lauraceae and Magnoliaceae. Gymnosperms, such as *Pinus* and *Podocarpus,* are also represented. Lower montane forest occurs at 700–1800 m; upper montane forest is confined to the highest peaks. Upper montane forest has fewer tree species than lower montane forest, but has a rich epiphytic flora.

In Laos, there are 10,000 km² of pine forest, found in the Xieng Khouang region and on sandy soils at 600–1400 m; bamboo forest is estimated to cover 6000 km² (Myers 1980). Pine forests occur in Cambodia on the Kirikom Plateau. Much of the uplands of Vietnam were originally covered by dense evergreen forest. Pine forests are mainly restricted to the Tay Nguyen Highlands. Fire has resulted in the creation of open montane woodland over extensive areas.

Limestone forest is a distinctive forest type on limestone substrates. The flora of karst limestone is rich in endemic herbs. There are many karst limestone outcrops in southern Thailand, including on the islands off the south-west coast. There are extensive limestone mountains in the north and west.

Permanent and seasonally inundated freshwater swamp forests once occurred in Cambodia in the Tonlé Gap and Mekong Delta, and were once also extensive in Thailand. The best remaining areas are in southern Peninsular Thailand.

Peat swamp forest is a distinctive type of evergreen forest of moderate stature found on peat in flat lowlands in Thailand where it is confined to areas south of the peninsula.

Beach forest fringes sandy coasts of the mainland and also occurs on offshore islands. It includes widespread Indo-Pacific elements and has been much degraded or cleared to make way for settlements and (in Thailand) tourist developments.

Thailand has the most extensive areas of **mangrove forest** remaining in Indochina. The largest remaining expanses are on the western (Andaman Sea) coast of Peninsular Thailand. Mangroves were once extensive along the Cambodian coast; the most extensive areas remaining in the country today are at Kas Kong. Mangrove forest occurs in the deltas of the Mekong and (but now almost entirely destroyed) the Red River in Vietnam. Over half of Vietnam's mangroves were destroyed through spraying with Agent Orange (Kemf 1986).

Flora

There are estimated to be 12,000 vascular plant species in Thailand, more than 8000 vascular plant species in Vietnam, and 12,000–15,000 species in Cambodia, Laos and Vietnam combined (Davis *et al.* 1986; Campbell and Hammond 1989; K. Larsen, pers. comm.). Cambodia, Laos and Vietnam have c. 600 fern species (Parris 1985); 600 tree and shrub species and 300 orchid species have been listed for Laos (Davis *et al.* 1986; Bochkov *et al.* 1988); more than 300 tree species and 1000 species of orchids occur in Thailand. Thailand and Vietnam have the largest numbers of endemics (more than 10% of the vascular flora of Vietnam is endemic to that country).

Mixed dipterocarp forests are the richest vegetation types in Thailand. However, they are not as rich in species as their Malaysian counterparts. West Malesian elements are well-represented in evergreen forests in Peninsular Thailand and in the forests of south-east Thailand/south-west Cambodia. Indo-Burmese, Indochinese and Sino-Himalayan elements (the latter including many species in Fagaceae, Lauraceae, Magnoliaceae and Ericaceae, notably in the genus *Rhododendron*) are prominent in montane areas. Some places of floristic importance in Indochina are mentioned in Campbell and Hammond (1989) and Santisuk *et al.* (1991).

There is a great need in all countries for fundamental work in plant taxonomy and floristic inventory, especially in Cambodia, Laos and Vietnam. There is no national herbarium in Cambodia and no botanical institute in Laos, and all countries lack modern Floras.

Useful plants

Very many species are used for a wide variety of purposes, including to provide food, construction materials, firewood, bamboo products, cane, household goods, medicines and many other products. In Vietnam alone, 2300 species of plants are known to be used for food, medicines, animal fodder, wood products or other purposes (IUCN 1985). Nguyen Van Duong (1993) lists more than 600 medicinal plant species of Cambodia, Laos and Vietnam. Many wild species, particularly timber trees and wild relatives of food plants (such as fruit trees), are valuable resources for forestry and agriculture. There are many valuable timber trees, though the commercial value of the standing timber crop has been severely reduced as a result of forestry practices, involving logging, taking little account of regeneration.

The forest reserves of Cambodia play an important role in the national economy. Cambodia produced 600,000 m³ of sawlogs and peeler logs in 1969, mostly for domestic use, and

TABLE 32. AREAS OF FOREST IN INDOCHINA

The following figures for forest cover are from Collins, Sayer and Whitmore (1991). The areas given are determined from maps and are not official statistics. They include both relatively undisturbed and disturbed forests, the latter having, for example, enclaves of cultivation and plantations occur within areas which are substantially forested.

	Area remaining (km²)	% of land area
CAMBODIA		
Rain forests		
Lowland	55,500	31.4
Montane	2250	1.3
Inland swamp	7500	4.2
Mangrove	250	0.1
Monsoon forests		
Lowland	47,750	27.1
Total	**113,250**	**64.1**
LAOS		
Rain forests		
Lowland	31,130	13.5
Montane	10,840	4.7
Monsoon forests		
Lowland	22,220	9.6
Montane	3590	1.6
Total	**67,780** [a]	**29.4**
THAILAND		
Rain forests		
Lowland	54,900	10.7
Montane	14,800	2.9
Mangrove	5700	1.1
Monsoon forests		
Lowland	29,500	5.8
Montane	2000	0.4
Total	**106,900**	**20.9** [b]
VIETNAM		
Rain forests		
Lowland	28,040	8.6
Montane	7520	2.3
Mangrove	1610	0.5
Monsoon forests		
Lowland	18,010	5.5
Montane	1500	0.5
Total	**56,680**	**17.4**

Notes:
[a] According to Collins, Sayer and Whitmore (1991), there are an additional 56,820 km² of degraded forest in Laos.
[b] According to official figures (1985), 28.8% of Thailand is forest land; however, this includes both closed and open canopy forest, and some areas of legally gazetted Forest Reserves, National Parks and Wildlife Sanctuaries which are severely degraded. K. Larsen (pers. comm.) estimates forest cover at about 20%.

mostly carried out by small-scale local enterprises. Little information is available on more recent logging volumes. Until 1970, considerable yields of rattan, bamboo, resin (from Dipterocarpaceae and *Pinus merkusii*), tannin, cardamom and other products were obtained from the forests, but there are no recent statistics.

In Thailand, the value of marketed charcoal and fuelwood has equalled that of commercial timber (c. 5 billion baht per year) (ONESDB 1989); recorded sales of raw bamboo are c. 250 million baht per year (Hoamuangkaew, undated). Various other figures showing the high value of non-timber forest products are given in Santisuk *et al.* (1991). For edible plants in Thailand, see Phengklai (1978) and Sanguantan *et al.* (1988); for medicinal plants, see Brun and Schumacher (1987).

Among notable timber species is teak (*Tectona grandis*), populations of which have been severely depleted. Some species are wild relatives of crops or horticultural plants (orchids are notable members of the latter group). There are also the possibilities of searching plants for new natural products, such as pharmaceutical drugs, a significant factor in a country in which the chemical and biotechnology industries are rapidly expanding. An example of benefits already harvested, quoted in Santisuk *et al.* (1991), is the discovery of a wild durian species that is resistant to soil-borne diseases; within 7–8 years of this discovery, this species was already being used as a rootstock in durian plantations throughout the country. Another example is a commercial anti-inflammation ointment developed from *Zingiber cassumunar*.

The forests of Indochina serve to protect water supplies and to ameliorate the climate. Forest degradation and destruction have caused adverse changes in river regimes and have disrupted rainfall patterns. Major flooding and landslides helped to trigger a ban on commercial logging in Thailand in 1989.

Factors causing loss of biodiversity

Population pressure

Thailand and Vietnam have large populations (55.7 million and 66.7 million in 1990, respectively) (see Table 23). Indeed, Vietnam is the most densely populated country in mainland tropical Asia. Some 80% of its population is rural. Partly as a consequence of population size, there has been large-scale conversion of forests to cultivated land and for settlements, both in Vietnam and Thailand. In Thailand, the last two decades have witnessed impressive socio-economic development, with a significant increase in *per capita* income. The population growth rate has declined by a third. In Vietnam, the population growth rate is still relatively high (2.15% between 1985 and 1990) (World Resources Institute 1992). Laos and Cambodia have even higher growth rates (2.82% and 2.48% for the same period, respectively).

Shifting cultivation

A major cause of forest loss in Indochina is shifting cultivation. As a result of population pressure, the cycles of land clearance no longer allow sufficient time for the development of secondary forest after the phase of cultivation. Fires related to agriculture, pastoralism or hunting are a major cause of degradation of semi-deciduous and deciduous forests.

In Laos, shifting cultivation is the main cause of forest loss, accompanied by fires started to encourage grazing for livestock and to aid hunting. The rate of deforestation is said to be 2000 km² per year. It is feared that a current road development programme will accelerate forest loss by opening up the forests to logging and slash and burn cultivation. Various systems of shifting cultivation are associated with the main ethnic groups. For example, the lowland Lao Loum people traditionally practised irrigated agriculture but, as a result of a growing population, they have recently spread into adjacent upland areas, resulting in clearance and deterioration of forests. The Lao Soung people of northern Thailand cultivate opium poppies, preferring primary forest sites; when the fields are abandoned, regeneration is to grassland and savanna rather than forest – this is said to be the major reason for deforestation in these upland areas.

Much of Cambodia was once forested, but there has been widespread deforestation for agriculture and settlement. There is considerable uncertainty about the extent and state of remaining forest in Cambodia. Clearance of some swamp forests for agriculture has not been successful, instead resulting in formation of treeless plains. Most loss of forest over recent years has probably been caused by slash and burn agriculture. Deciduous and semi-deciduous forests have been severely degraded by burning. Forest clearance in the catchment of the Mekong River, both inside and outside Cambodia, has caused major adverse changes in river regimes, leading to violent floods after heavy rain and very low flows at other times.

In Vietnam, many hill tribes practise shifting cultivation, clearing hillsides to plant hill rice and cassava. Warfare increased the pressure to convert forested land to agriculture.

Logging

Commercial logging has degraded many of the forests (<1% of Vietnam's forests are undisturbed). A ban on logging was introduced in Thailand in 1989. However, this has increased the pressure on natural forests in neighbouring countries and elsewhere, as production of timber from plantations in Thailand cannot as yet meet that country's demand. In Laos, logging is concentrated in more accessible areas on the Mekong Plain and adjacent areas. Annual roundwood timber production is 3.6 m³ (1988) (FAO 1990). Logging is virtually unregulated, though at times there have been restrictions on the export of logs from Laos.

Due to political and military disruption, the Forest Department of Cambodia has been virtually inactive over the last 20 years. Even prior to that, logging was carried out without any plans for regeneration. Little is known about current exploitation of the forests for timber, but unregulated logging for export to timber-starved Thailand and Vietnam is a possible threat. Indeed, there have been reports of recent contracts for large-scale export of timber and rattan to Thailand.

Warfare

Cambodia, Laos and Vietnam have been severely disrupted by years of warfare. During the Vietnam War, 22,000 km² of forest and farmland were destroyed in Vietnam, mainly in the south, by bombing, spraying and mechanical clearing; a further 1170 km² of forest were destroyed by cratering as a result of bombing. Over 50% of the country is classified as wasteland and in need of urgent rehabilitation. Bombing and defoliation has also caused widespread forest damage in Cambodia and Laos.

Plant collecting and fuelwood cutting

Over-collection of medicinal plants and ornamental plants is a threat to some species. For example, orchid collecting in Thailand threatens many species with restricted distributions, such as *Paphiopedilum godefroyae*, *P. sukhakulii*, *Pecteilis sagarikii* and *Vanda coerulescens* (Campbell and Hammond 1989). Fuelwood shortages cause over-harvesting of forests in some areas.

Conservation

The four countries are at different stages in the development of viable schemes to conserve biodiversity and to ensure sustainable use of plant resources. The establishment of a protected area system embracing adequate examples of all major vegetation types is best developed in Thailand (some suggestions regarding modifications are given in Santisuk *et al.* 1991) and steps are being taken towards the same objective in Vietnam. Cambodia and Laos lag far behind in conservation planning and action.

In Cambodia, 11.5% of the country is legally protected, but there is little active management. Angkor Wat, the famous archaeological site, was declared a National Park in 1925, the area being greatly enlarged in the 1960s (area 107 km²). Other reserved areas include Faunal Reserves and 172 Production Forest Reserves. There is a need to establish reserves for mangroves, at present legally unprotected.

There is no effective system of protected areas in Laos. A total of 17 Forest Reserves covering 1280 km² have been declared, but protective measures have never been implemented (FAO/UNEP 1981). Proposals for the establishment of a comprehensive protected area system have been made by Salter and Phanthavong (1989). They include 50 areas with moist forest within their boundaries (listed in Collins, Sayer and Whitmore 1991, which also suggests other conservation initiatives).

By 1989, 59 National Parks had been gazetted in Thailand, covering a total area of 31,505 km² (approximately 6% of the country). A further 21 areas (11,121 km², or 2.2% of the country) are proposed. There are 28 Wildlife Sanctuaries covering 21,394 km² (4.2% of the country); a further 7 areas (covering 2845 km², 0.6% of the country) are being gazetted. In addition, there are 48 Non-hunting Areas (4024 km²). In total, approximately 11% of the land area of Thailand is totally protected; however, it should be noted that there is considerable overlap in the functions of these various categories of protected areas. Thus, some sanctuaries are subject to considerable recreation pressure. Also, many protected areas are nevertheless under threat and suffering from various forms of degradation.

Although the present protected area system in Thailand constitutes an adequate framework for conserving the more important plant resources of the country, major shortfalls are the lack of significant representation of the wet seasonal evergreen forests in the south-east and of lowland evergreen

forests in general. A priority is to survey existing remnants, establish new protected areas and undertake restoration work. A suggested order of plant conservation priorities in Thai forest types in terms of species richness and regional endemism is given in Table 33 (Santisuk *et al.* 1991).

TABLE 33. THAILAND: FOREST TYPES RANKED BY CONSERVATION PRIORITIES

Forest type	Species richness	Regional endemism[a]
Mixed dipterocarp	1	10
Wet seasonal evergreen dipterocarp (Peninsular)	2	5
Wet seasonal evergreen dipterocarp (south-east)	3	4
Lower montane	4	3
Dry evergreen	5	6
Upper montane	6	2
Mixed deciduous	7	8
Limestone	8	1
Peat swamp forest	9	9
Dry dipterocarp	10	7
Mangrove	11	11

Notes:

1–11 High to low priority.

[a] Includes Myanmā, Thailand, Cambodia, Laos, Vietnam, Yunnan-Guangxi (China) and the Eastern Himalayas. Santisuk *et al.* (1991) considers that regional endemism should be given higher consideration than overall species richness.

Botanical research and conservation have not been given sufficient attention in Thailand. There is an urgent need for more work on plant taxonomy, ecology and ethnobotany. Apart from research to develop better ways of managing natural forests, planting and habitat restoration to meet some of the demands for forest products are urgently needed. There is some official recognition in Thailand of the need to allow local people to use forests for the extraction of non-timber products, if they are to have an incentive to participate in efforts at sustained forest management. However, there is clearly much further development needed in this field. Forests also provide recreation, tourism and watershed protection values. Their conservation, therefore, provides significant economic benefits. For example, the numbers of Thai and foreign visitors to National Parks have increased rapidly during recent years. At present, 90% of visitors to National Parks are Thai citizens (Arbhabhirama *et al.* 1987). Watershed protection is economically vital, both to secure supplies of fresh water, including for irrigated agriculture, and for hydroelectric generation. There are many degraded watersheds in Thailand and restoration is essential. Santisuk *et al.* (1991) recommend the development of mixed-species forests, which can additionally provide products desired by local people.

A total of 87 reserves has been approved by the Government of Vietnam. These areas include examples of most major forest types. They include 7 National Parks, 49 Nature Reserves and 31 Cultural and Environmental Reserves. A Nature Conservation Strategy (IUCN 1985) awaits approval; IUCN has produced a first draft of a Biodiversity Action Plan. Tree planting has been encouraged by the government, with plans to increase the rate of planting from 1600 km² (1987) to 3000 km² per year (Nguyen Nghia Thin 1991, *in litt.*). However, many species used in afforestation programmes are not indigenous to Vietnam. Experiments have been initiated to find methods for rehabilitation of land devastated by warfare.

Effective management of protected areas in all countries in Indochina requires massive investment in staff. There is a great need for more trained staff, financial resources and management. There is also an urgent need to bring local people fully into conservation efforts by working with them to determine their perceptions, uses and traditional methods of management of nature. Such collaborative research should aim at the identification of conservation issues and, where needed, search for improved methods of managing ecosystems or particular populations of plants. If necessary, alternatives to harvesting from the wild should be identified and promulgated. Legal rights over forest management by local people should be reviewed in many cases.

Programmes should be started or, where existent, intensified to establish tree plantations, preferably mixed plantations of indigenous species, to meet demands for timber, fuelwood, rattans and other forest products. Those areas devastated by warfare, especially in Vietnam, require major re-habilitation, which should involve use of a variety of native species, so that these areas can serve a variety of functions.

Trade in wild collected horticultural plants needs to be combated by further legislative measures, enforcement of regulations, campaigns to dissuade collectors and further establishment of nurseries to provide artificially propagated plants.

A review of the protected areas system and conservation legislation is given in IUCN (1992a).

Centres of plant diversity and endemism

Cambodia

EA51. Cardamom Mountains

The Cardamom Mountains are located in south-west Cambodia (at approximately 12°N and 103°E) and attain 1563 m (the highest point in Cambodia). Area: 130 km².
❖ Vegetation: Submontane semi-deciduous forest, pine forest.
❖ Flora: >100 endemic species.
❖ Threats: Logging (for export).
❖ Conservation: Wildlife Reserve (8.2 km²).

Laos

EA52. Bolovens Plateau

In Champassak, Attopeu and Saravane Provinces, southern Laos; between latitudes 14°40'–15°30'N and longitudes 106°00'–106°50'E, ranging in altitude from c. 200 m to 1716 m. Area: c. 4000 km².
❖ Vegetation: Lowland semi-evergreen forest, montane evergreen forest, wetlands.
❖ Threats: Shifting cultivation and fire damage to large remnant forest blocks, mainly in the south-west and north-east of the plateau; water pollution from coffee processing may be a possible future threat; forests have been reduced by warfare.

❖ Conservation: 3 protected areas have been proposed. Tha Teng (300 km²) in the north-east includes some intact forest but is relatively small. Bolovens Plateau (790 km²) consists largely of uninhabited savanna with patches of evergreen forest. Dong Hua Sao (710 km²) contains some dense contiguous forest (Twardy 1987; Johansson, Stromquist and Wickstrom 1988; Mekong Committee 1988; Young and Hyde 1988; Birgegard 1989).

Thailand

EA53. Doi Chiang Dao Wildlife Sanctuary

– see Data Sheet.

EA54. Doi Inthanon

This granitic massif is the highest mountain in Thailand, rising to 2595 m and located 60 km south-west of Chiang-Mai.
❖ Vegetation: Lowland dry dipterocarp forest with *Dipterocarpus obtusifolius*, *D. tuberculatus*, *Pentacme suavis* and *Shorea obtusa* up to 1000 m; montane forest, with *Castanopsis acuminatissima*, *C. tribuloides*, *Lithocarpus leucostachys*, *Pinus insularis*, *Quercus brandisiana* and *Q. kingiana* above c. 1000 m (Robbins and Smitinand 1966). The highest peaks above 1850 m are frequently cloud-covered and carry upper montane forest with small gnarled trees thickly covered with bryophytes.
❖ Flora: A number of species occurring on Doi Inthanon are mentioned in Robbins and Smitinand (1966).
❖ Threats: Shifting agriculture is practised up to c. 1850 m and has resulted in the clearance of much of the forest on the foothills and slopes, with large areas converted to grassland.
❖ Conservation: Doi Inthanon National Park (IUCN Management Category: II) covers 482.4 km².

EA55. Doi Suthep-Pui National Park

– see Data Sheet.

EA56. Khao Soi Dao Wildlife Sanctuary

Khao Soi Dao is an extension of the Cardamom Mountains in Chanthaburi Province. Geographical coordinates: c. 12°30'N, 102°10'E. Area: 4656 km².
❖ Vegetation: Mostly evergreen forest (84%), found up to 1000 m; submontane scrub (5%); hill evergreen forest (1000–2000 m). Together with adjacent Khao Kitchakut National Park, the lowland forests constitute a significant part of the remaining seasonal evergreen forests of south-east Thailand.
❖ Flora: A large number of endemic plant species and species of Indochinese affinity.
❖ Threats: Severe encroachment in the north-east. More than 10% of the land is degraded.
❖ Conservation: Of value for its fauna and as a catchment area, as well as for its plants. Land use zonation is recommended, as well as an extension to the west which would create a link with Khao Ang Ru Nai Wildlife Sanctuary (World Bank 1993).

EA57. Khao Yai National Park

– see Data Sheet.

EA58. Limestone flora

Karst limestone hills support a distinctive forest type, and contain an endemic-rich herbaceous flora. They are the highest conservation priority for plants in Thailand.

EA59. Thung Yai-Huai Kha Khaeng World Heritage Site

– see Data Sheet.

EA60. Tarutao National Park

An archipelago of 51 islands off the coast of Satun Province, between latitudes 6°60'–6°44'N and longitudes 99°44'–99°09'E. Area: 1490 km², of which 226 km² is terrestrial.
❖ Vegetation: Tropical evergreen forest (rare in the rest of Thailand and the richest forest type floristically), limestone forest and mangrove forest.
❖ Flora: There are an estimated 2000 species of vascular plants, including many which are very rare or absent from the rest of Thailand.
❖ Threats: Illegal logging; cutting of mangroves for fuelwood and construction.
❖ Conservation: National Park (IUCN Management Category: II), established in 1974. Conservation activities have been undertaken with the coastal fishing communities, aimed mainly at addressing marine issues. There is a management plan for 1990–1994 (UNESCO, undated).

EA61. Wet seasonal evergreen forests of south-east Thailand

See also Khao Soi Dao Wildlife Sanctuary (CPD Site EA56). Unique to Indo-Burma; the canopy contains many species of dipterocarps in the genera *Anisoptera*, *Balanocarpus*, *Dipterocarpus*, *Hopea*, *Parashorea* and *Shorea*, mixed with other species (notably members of the Bombacaceae, Sterculiaceae and Leguminosae). Many endemic species; high regional endemism and exceptional tree species richness.

Vietnam

There are 4 main endemic-rich areas, namely Hdang Lien Son Mountains, Ngoc Linh Mountains, Lam Vien Highlands and the rain forests of central Vietnam (IUCN 1985). Many species are rare and very local. CPD sites include the following:

EA62. Bach Ma-Hai Van

– see Data Sheet.

EA63. Cat Tien Biosphere Reserve

– see Data Sheet.

EA64. Cuc Phuong National Park

– see Data Sheet.

EA65. Langbian-Dalat Highland

– see Data Sheet.

EA66. Yok Don National Park

– see Data Sheet.

EA67. Mount Fan Si Pan

The highest mountain in Vietnam (3142 m), located at 22°20'N, 103°40'E. Area: 2000 km².
❖ Vegetation: Deciduous tropical montane forest, subtropical montane forest.
❖ Flora: Estimated >3000 vascular plant species, including many medicinal plants. Requires surveying.
❖ Threats: Shifting cultivation, over-collection of non-timber forest products, burning.
❖ Conservation: Hoang-Lien Son Nature Reserve (200 km²), established in 1986.

EA68. Phu Khan

Located in central Vietnam, at 11°42'–13°34'N and c. 108°20'–108°40'E; four summits exceed 2000 m. Area: 9807 km².
❖ Vegetation: Lower montane subtropical forest, montane tropical forest, pine forest, prairie steppe.
❖ Flora: Estimated 4000–5000 vascular plant species, of which 1035 so far recorded in 599 genera and 161 families. Many endemics; many timber, edible, medicinal and ornamental species.
❖ Threats: No information.
❖ Conservation: No information.

References

(Titles originally in Chinese, Korean or Japanese have been translated.)

Agriculture Planning Institute of Ningxia (1980). *Vegetation of Ningxia.* People Press of Ningxia.

Anon. (1977). Kuwol-san Nature Reserve. *Korean Nature* 3(46): 11–12.

Arbhabhirama, A. *et al*. (1987). *Thailand natural resources profile.* Thai Development Research Institute, Bangkok.

Bian Wenxuan (1959). Botanical regions of Shandong. *Journal of Shandong Normal University* 2: 15–20.

Birgegard, L. (1989). *Socio-economic study.* Xeset hydropower project, Laos. Prepared for the Mekong Secretariat.

Bochkov, I.M., Korolev, I.A. and Filipchuk, A.N. (1988). Inventory of tropical forests (case-study of Laos). In: *International Training Seminar on Forestry Applications of Remote Sensing, Moscow, 1988.* UNEP, Nairobi, Kenya. Pp. 277–295.

Botanic Gardens of China (1988). *Course on the function of botanic gardens in conservation of nature and natural resources.* Botanic Gardens of China.

Botany Institute of the Chinese Academy of Sciences (1988). *Vegetation in Xizang.* Science Press, Beijing.

Brun, V. and Schumacher, T. (1987). *Traditional herbal medicine in northern Thailand.* University of California Press, Berkeley, California. 349 pp.

Campbell, D.G. and Hammond, H.D. (eds) (1989). *Floristic inventory in tropical countries: the status of plant systematics, collections, and vegetation, plus recommendations for the future.* The New York Botanical Garden, New York. 545 pp.

Chen Binghao *et al.* (1959). *Xylosma forest on the south slope of Xiao Hinggan Mountains.* Collected Papers on Plants 4. Science Press, Beijing.

Cheng Dake (1982). An approach on the Korean pine of northeast China. *J. Northeastern Forestry Institute*: 1–177.

Cheng Lingzhao (1964). Some structural characteristics of the main plant communities in all altitudinal zones of the north slope of Changbai Mountains. *Acta Plant Ecology and Geobotany* 2(2): 207–225.

Collins, N.M., Sayer, J.A. and Whitmore, T.C. (eds) (1991). *The conservation atlas of tropical forests: Asia and the Pacific.* Macmillan, London. 256 pp.

Compilation Committee of "Flora of Economic Plants of China" (undated). *Flora of economic plants of China,* 2 vols. Science Press, Beijing.

Compilation Committee of "Natural Protection Outline of China" (1987). *Natural protection outline of China.* China Environmental Sciences Press.

Compilation Committee of "Vegetation of China" (1980). *Vegetation of China.* Science Press, Beijing.

Compilation Group on Yunnan Vegetation (1987). *Vegetation of Yunnan Province.* Science Press, Beijing.

Cooperation Group of Sichuan Botany (1980). *Vegetation of Sichuan Province.* People Press of Sichuan.

Davis, S.D., Droop, S.J., Gregerson, P., Henson, L., Leon, C.J., Lamlein Villa-Lobos, J., Synge, H. and Zantovska, J. (1986). *Plants in danger: what do we know?* IUCN, Gland, Switzerland and Cambridge, U.K. 461 pp.

Du Qing *et al.* (1990). *Vegetation and its economic utilization in the Chaidam Basin.* Science Press, Beijing.

Duke, J.A. and Ayensu, E.S. (1985). *Medicinal plants of China,* 2 vols. Algonac, Michigan, U.S.A.

Ecology and Geobotany Group of Biology Department of Yunnan University (1960). Vegetation in Natural Reserves of Yunnan. *Journal of Yunnan University* 1: 50–72.

Europa Publications (1987). *The Far East and Australasia 1988.* 19th edition. Europa, London. 1015 pp.

Expedition to Xinjiang of the Chinese Academy of Sciences (1978). *Vegetation and its economic utilization in Xinjiang.* Science Press, Beijing.

Fan Zheng *et al.* (1963). Vertical zonal spectrum of the vegetation on the northwest slope of Taibai Mountains in Qinling Range. *Series Reference Books on Phytoecology and Geobotany* 1/2: 162–163.

FAO (1987). *Special study on forest and utilisation of forest resources in the developing region. Asia-Pacific Region. Assessment of forest resources in six countries.* FAO Field Document 17. 104 pp.

FAO (1988). *An interim report on the state of tropical forest resources in the developing countries.* FAO, Rome. 18 pp.

FAO (1990). *FAO yearbook of forest products 1977–88.* FAO Forestry Series No. 23, FAO Statistics Series No. 90. FAO, Rome.

FAO/UNEP (1981). *Tropical forest resources assessment project (in the framework of the Global Environment Monitoring System – GEMS).* UN 32/6.1301-78-04. Technical Report 3: *Forest Resources of Tropical Asia.* FAO, Rome. 475 pp.

Forestry Department of Guangxi University (1978). Ecology and nutrient requirements of Hsienmu (*Burretiodendron hsienmu*). *Report of the Research on Phytoecology* no. 1. Science Press, Beijing.

Fu Zizhen *et al.* (1976). Analysis of vertical zonation of vegetation of mountains in Shanxi Province. *Forestry Sciences and Technology of Shanxi* 2: 1–10.

Gao Shangwu (1956). Forest in the west part of Shanxi Province. *Forestry Sciences* 2(2): 30–38.

Gu Yunchun (1986). *Forest resources in Da Hinggan Mountain Range.* Investigation and Planning Institute, Ministry of Forestry.

Han Linfeng *et al.* (1951). Report on the forest survey of Da Hinggan Mountain Range. *Journal of Harbib Agricultural College*: 163–164.

He, Shan-an, Gu, Yin and Sheng, Ning (1993). The role of Chinese botanical gardens in the development of the national economy. In: *Abstracts XI International Association of Botanic Gardens Conference.* Wuxi, China, p. 9.

He, Shan-an, Gu, Yin and Sheng, Ning (1994, in press). *Proceedings of the XI International Association of Botanic Gardens Conference.* Jiangsu Science and Technology Publishing House, Nanjing.

He, Shan-an, Yuan, Yi-Wei, Qin Hui Zhen and Dudley, T.R. (eds) (1990). *Present conservation status of rare and endangered species in Chinese botanical gardens.* Jiangsu Science and Technology Publishing House, Nanjing.

Hoamuangkaew, W. (undated). Country paper: Thailand. Fac. For., Kasetsart University. 60 pp. (Unpublished manuscript.)

Hou Kuanzhao *et al.* (1955). General situation of the continental vegetation in Guangdong and the plants and vegetation in Hainan Island. *Series Reference Books on Phytoecology and Geobotany* no. 4. Science Press, Beijing.

Huang Shengliang *et al.* (1988). *Vegetation of Guizhou Province.* People Press of Lanzhou.

Huang Xichou *et al.* (1959). Natural landscape belt of the north side of Changbai Mountains. *Acta Geography* 95(6): 315–328.

Inner Mongolia Expedition of the Chinese Academy of Sciences (1985). *Vegetation in Inner Mongolia.* Science Press, Beijing.

Institute of Botany of Guangdong (1976). *Vegetation of Guangdong Province.* Science Press, Beijing.

IUCN (1985). *Vietnam: National Conservation Strategy. Draft.* Prepared by the Programme for Rational Utilisation of Natural Resources and Environmental Protection (Programme 52-02) with assistance from IUCN. Environmental Services Group, WWF India, New Delhi. 71 pp.

IUCN (1992a). *Protected areas of the world: a review of national systems. Volume 1: Indomalaya, Oceania, Australia and Antarctic.* IUCN, Gland, Switzerland and Cambridge, U.K. xx, 352 pp. (Prepared by the World Conservation Monitoring Centre.)

IUCN (1992b). *Protected areas of the world: a review of national systems. Volume 2: Palaearctic.* IUCN, Gland, Switzerland and Cambridge, U.K. xxviii, 556 pp. (Prepared by the World Conservation Monitoring Centre.)

Johansson, D., L. Stromquist and H. Wickstrom (1988). *The environmental impacts of the Xeset hydropower project in the Lao PDR.* Prepared for the Mekong Secretariat by SWECO, Stockholm, Sweden.

Kemf, E. (1986). The re-greening of Vietnam. *WWF News* 41: 4–5.

Kemf, E. (1988). Dance of a thousand cranes. *New Scientist* 8 October: 34–36.

Kim, C.S. (1977). Chilbo-san Nature Reserve. *Korean Nature* 1: 26–29.

Kim, I. (1977). Primeval forests of Korea. *Korean Nature* 4: 17–18.

Kim, S.S. (1989). *Academic survey report of the rare plants in Mt. Chiri.* Sanchong-gun, Kyongsangnam-do, Korea. 100 pp.

Kim, T.W. and Chun, S.H. (1991). A comprehensive re-examination of endemic woody plants in Korea. *Bulletin of the Kwanak Arboretum, Seoul National University* 11: 1–37.

Lee, T.B. (1973). *Illustrated woody plants of Korea.* Forest Experimental Station, Seoul. 262 pp.

Lee, T.B. (1976). Vascular plants and their uses in Korea. *Bulletin of the Kwanak Arboretum, Seoul National University* 1: 137 pp.

Lee, T.B. (1980). Rare and endangered species in the area of Mt. Sorak. *Bulletin of the Kwanak Arboretum, Seoul National University* 3: 197–210.

Lee, W.T. and Yang, I.S. (1981). *The flora of Ulreung Island and Dogdo Island.* The Report of the KACN, No.19. A Report on the Scientific Survey of the Ulreung and Dogdo Islands. The Korean Association for Conservation of Nature. Pp. 61–95.

Legris, P. and Blasco, F. (1972). *Notice de la carte: Cambodge.* Carte International du Tapis Végétal. Extraits des travaux de la section scientifique et technique de l'Institut Français de Pondicherry: hors série no 1. Toulouse, France.

Liang Xiao-Tian, Yu De-Quan and Fang Qi-Cheng (1986). Structural chemistry of natural products in Chinese herbal medicine. In Tang You-Qi (ed.), *Advances in science of China, chemistry*, Vol. 1. Science Press, Beijing. Pp. 1–39.

Li Bosheng *et al.* (1987). A study of the cryophilous vegetation in the high mountains of Xizang. *Acta Botany* 23(2): 122–139.

Liu Shene (1955). *Pictoral handbook of Zylophyta in northeast China.* Science Press, Beijing.

MacKinnon, J. and MacKinnon, K. (1986). *Review of the protected areas system in the Indo-Malayan Realm.* IUCN, Gland, Switzerland and Cambridge, U.K. (in collaboration with UNEP). 284 pp.

Mekong Committee (1988). *Bolovens Plateau land use map (northern part).* Mekong Committee Secretariat, Bangkok.

Myers, N. (1980). *Conversion of tropical moist forests.* National Academy of Sciences, Washington, D.C. 205 pp.

Natural Protection Division of State Environmental Protection Bureau (1989). *List of natural reserves in China.* China Environmental Sciences Press.

Nature Conservation Bureau (1988). *Nature conservation in Japan.* Environment Agency, Tokyo. 45 pp.

Nguyen Van Duong (1993). *Medicinal plants of Vietnam, Cambodia and Laos*. Nguyen Van Duong. 528 pp.

Nie Shaoji (1963). Vegetation on the north side of Da Hinggan Mountain Range, northeast China. *Phytoecology and Geobotany* 21: 154–155.

Numata, M., Yoshioka, K. and Kato, M. (eds) (1975). *Studies in conservation of natural terrestrial ecosystems in Japan*. Japanese Committee for the International Biological Programme, JIBP Synthesis Vol. 8. *Part 1: Vegetation and its conservation*. University of Tokyo Press, Tokyo. 157 pp.

ONESDB (Office of the National Economic and Social Development Board) (1989). *National income of Thailand*. (1988 Ed.)

Parris, B.S. (1985). Ecological aspects of distribution and speciation in Old World tropical ferns. *Proc. Roy. Soc. Edinburgh* 86: 341–346.

Phengklai, C. (1978). Edible plants of Thailand. Paper presented at 8th World Forestry Congress, October 16–28, Jakarta.

Plant Survey Team of Botany Institute of Guangdong (1977). *Plants and vegetation in Xisha Archipelago of China*. Science Press, Beijing.

Poole, C. (1991). The gift of a No-Man's Land. *BBC Wildlife* 9 (9): 636–639.

Qi Jiade *et al.* (1990). *Vegetation of Hunan Province*. People Press of Hunan.

Qian Chongshu (1957). Botanical geography of northeast China. Physical geography materials of northeast China. *Book Series of Geographical Papers of China* 2: 60–71. Science Press, Beijing.

Qian Chongshu *et al.* (1957). Plant geography of north China. *Reference Materials on Physical Geography of North China* 3: 74–82.

Qian Jiaju (1956). Plants of the forest survey on the west side of Changbai Mountains. *Acta Plant Ecology and Geobotany* no. 10. Science Press, Beijing.

Qiao Zengjian (1964). Preliminary analysis of the flora of Beijing. *Journal of Beijing Normal University* 2: 35–40.

Robbins, K.G. and Smitinand, T. (1966). A botanical ascent of Doi Inthanond. *Nat. Hist. Bull. Siam Soc.* 21: 205–227.

Rollet, B. (1972). *La végétation du Cambodge bois et Forêts des Tropiqués*, nos. 144–146. Nogent-sur-Marne, France.

Rothe, P. (1947). La forêt d'Indochinie. *Bois et Forêts Tropicaux* 1: 25–30; 2: 18–23; 3: 17–23.

Salter, R.E. and Phanthavong, B. (1989). *Needs and priorities for a protected area system in Laos PDR*. Forest Resources Conservation Project, Lao/Swedish Forestry Conservation Project, Lao/Swedish Forestry Cooperation Programme, Vientiane, Laos.

Sanguantan, P. *et al.* (1988). *Multiresource inventories in Dong Mun forest communities, northeast Thailand*. Kasetsart University Ford Foundation 870–0535, Working Document No. 3. 69 pp.

Santisuk, T., Smitinand, T., Hoamuangkaew, W., Ashton, P., Sohmer, S. and Vincent, J.R. (1991). *Plants for our future: botanical research and conservation needs in Thailand*. Royal Forest Department, Thailand. 48 pp.

Shi Huamin (1960). Introduction to the flora of Henan Province. *Journal of Henan Agricultural College* 4: 18–27.

State Environmental Protection Bureau and Institute of Botany, the Chinese Academy of Sciences (1987). *List of the rare and endangered plants of China*. Science Press, Beijing.

State Environmental Protection Bureau and Institute of Botany, the Chinese Academy of Science (1990). *Red book of plants of China*, Vol. 1. Science Press, Beijing.

Stewart-Smith, J. (1987). *In the shadow of Fujisan, Japan and its wildlife*. Viking/Rainbird, London.

Takhtajan, A. (1986). *Floristic regions of the world*. University of California Press, Berkeley, California. 522 pp.

Tsun-shen Ying, Yu-long Zhang and Boufford, D.E. (1993). *The endemic genera of seed plants in China*. Science Press, Beijing. 824 pp.

Twardy, A.G. (1987). *Southern area development master plan. Soil resources and land capability*. Prepared for State Planning Committee, Lao PDR by Lavalin International Inc. and MPW Rural Development Pty.

UNESCO (undated). *Tarutao National Park*. Nomination of Natural Property to the World Heritage List submitted by Thailand. The National World Heritage Committee, Bangkok, Thailand.

Wang Xianpu (Wang Huen-pu) (1980). Nature conservation in China: the present situation. *Parks* 5(1): 1–10.

Wang Xianpu (1986). Protected natural areas in China. *Arnoldia* 46(4): 38–45.

Wang Xianpu, Chen Sing-chi and Wang Si-yu (1989). China. In Campbell, D.G. and Hammond, H.D. (eds), *Floristic inventory in tropical countries: the status of plant systematics, collections, and vegetation, plus recommendations for the future*. The New York Botanical Garden, New York. Pp. 35–43.

Wang Xianpu and Jin Xiaobai (1986). Plant conservation in China. *Species* 8: 5–6.

Wang Xianpu and Jin Xiaobai (1986). Beijing Botanic Garden – its contribution to conservation. *Species* 8: 29–30.

Wang Xianpu and Yu Dejan (1983). *The endangered plants in China and their conservation. Report and abstract.* Botanical Society of China. (Paper presented at a meeting commemorating the 50th anniversary of the Botanical Society of China.)

Wang Xianpu *et al.* (1983). *Rational utilization and conservation of natural plant resources. Report and abstract.* Botanical Society of China. (Paper presented at a meeting commemorating the 50th anniversary of the Botanical Society of China.)

Wang Xianpu *et al.* (1986). *Environmental and socio-economic aspects of tropical deforestation in Asia and Pacific.* ESCAP, Bangkok. Pp. 65–71.

Wang Xianpu *et al.* (1989). The achievement and future task of conservation phytoecology studies. *Proceedings of the International Symposium on Phytoecology Conservation.* Botanical Society of China. Pp. 30–34.

Wang Xianpu *et al.* (1989). *Theory and practice of natural reserves in China.* China Environmental Sciences Press.

Woo, B.M. (1990). Status of management of the protected areas in the Republic of Korea. Paper No. 13, delivered at FAO Conference. *Regional Expert Consultation on Management of Protected Areas in the Asia-Pacific Region,* 10–14 December 1990, Bangkok, Thailand. 43 pp.

Woo, B.M. (1991). Status of the management of the protected areas in the Republic of Korea. *Tiger Paper* 18(2): 14–20.

World Bank (1993). *Conservation forest area, protection, management and development project.* Pre-investment study, interim report. MDDAS Agronomics Company Ltd, Bangkok.

World Resources Institute (1992). *World resources 1992–93: a guide to the global environment.* Oxford University Press, New York. 385 pp.

World Resources Institute (1994). *World resources 1994–95: a guide to the global environment.* Oxford University Press, New York.

Wu Zhengyi (1979). About the division of the flora of China. *Research in Botany of Yunnan* 1(1): 1–22.

Wu Zhengyi *et al.* (1965). *Research report on the flora of tropical and sub-tropical zones in Yunnan no. 1.* Science Press, Beijing.

Xiao Pei-Gen (1981a). Some experience on the utilization of medicinal plants in China. *Fitoterapia* 52: 65–73.

Xiao Pei-Gen (1981b). Traditional experience of Chinese herb medicine, its application in drug research and new drug searching. In Beal, J. and Reinhard, E. (eds), *Natural products as medicinal agents.* Hippokrates Verlag, Stuttgart. Pp. 351–394.

Xiao Pei-Gen (1983). Recent developments on medicinal plants in China. *J. Ethnoparm.* 7: 95–109.

Xiao Pei-Gen (1986). Basic research on herbal medicine in China. *Herba Polonica* 32(3–4): 235–245.

Xiao Pei-Gen (1987). Ethnopharmacological investigation on pharmacologically active principles from Chinese medicinal plants. In Lei, H.P., Song, Z.Y., Zhang, J.T., Liu, G.Z. and Tian, H.Z. (eds), *Proceedings of the International Symposium on Traditional Medicines and Modern Pharmacology.* Beijing. Pp. 106–115.

Xiao Pei-Gen (1991). The Chinese approach to medicinal plants – their utilization and conservation. In Akerele, O., Heywood, V.H. and Synge, H. (eds), *The conservation of medicinal plants.* Cambridge University Press, Cambridge, U.K. Pp. 305–313.

Xiao Pei-Gen and Fu Shan-Lin (1987). Pharmacologically active substances of Chinese traditional and herb medicines. In Craker, L.E. and Simon, J.E. (eds), *Herbs, spices and medicinal plants,* vol. 2.

Xu Ren-Shen, Zhu Qiao-Zhen and Xie Yu-Yuan (1985). Recent advances in studies on Chinese medicinal herbs with physiological activity. *J. Ethnopharm.* 14: 223–253.

Xu Zaifu (1987). The work of Xishuangbanna Tropical Botanical Garden in conserving the threatened plants of the Yunnan tropics. In Bramwell, D., Hamann, O., Heywood, V. and Synge, H. (eds), *Botanic gardens and the World Conservation Strategy.* Academic Press, London. Pp. 239–253.

Xu Zaifu *et al.* (1982). Research on reservation of germplasm resources of tropical plants in Xishuangbanna. In: *Collected research papers on tropical botany.* Yunnan People Press, Kunming, China. Pp. 7–15.

Yang Hanxi *et al.* (1990). *Proceedings of the International Symposium on Grassland Vegetation.* Science Press, Beijing.

Yang Yujin *et al.* (1964). Classification and distribution of larch in Xiao Hinggan and Changbai Mountains of China. *Acta Plant Taxonomy* 9(2): 20–23.

Yim, Y.J. and Baik, S.D. (1985). *The vegetation of Mt. Seolrag.* The Chung-ang University Press, Seoul, Korea. 200 pp.

Young, V. and M.J. Hyde (1988). *Southern area development master plan. Sectoral report. Forestry.* Prepared for State Planning Committee, Lao PDR, by Lavalin International Inc. and MPW Rural Development Pty.

Zhang Hongda (1962). Character of flora of Guangdong. *Journal of Zhongshan University* 1: 1–34.

Zhang Hongda *et al.* (1957). Vegetation in Leizhou Peninsula. *Series Reference Books on Phytoecology and Geobotany* no. 17. Science Press, Beijing.

Zhang Jingwei (1963). Basic feature and the zonal meaning of the steppe in southeast of Qiangtong Plateau. *Series Reference Books on Phytoecology and Geobotany* 1: 1–2.

Zhang Jingwei *et al.* (1966). *Vegetation in Central Xizang.* Science Press, Beijing.

Zhang Jingwei *et al.* (1973). Preliminary research on the relation between vertical and horizontal belts of vegetation in Qomolangma area. *Acta Botany* 15(2): 221–238.

Zhang Jinquan (1954). Systematic classification of vegetation of Henan Province. *Normal University of South China* 1: 112–121.

Zhang Jinquan (1963). Vegetation survey report of Taihang Mountains in Henan Province. *Journal of Kaifeng Normal University* 2: 15–30.

Zhang Xinshi (1978). *About the zonation of vegetation on the Xizang Plateau.*

Zhang Xinshi *et al.* (1973). About the community and ecogeographic characteristics of the wild fruit forest in Ili. *Journal of Botany* 15(2): 239–254.

Zhang Xinshi *et al.* (1980). About the zonation of vegetation on the Qinghai-Xizang Plateau. *Science of China* 11: 1090–1098.

Zhang Yeliang *et al.* (1983). *Vegetation of Anhui Province.* Science Press of Anhui Province.

Zhang Yuliang (1955). *Plant communities in Da Hinggan Mountain Range.* Series Reference Books on Phytoecology and Geobotany No. 1. Science Press, Beijing.

Zhao Dachang (1958). Plant community in Muling River area. *Acta Plant Ecology and Geobotany* no. 1. Science Press, Beijing.

Zhao Ji, Zheng Guangmei, Wang Huadong and Xu Jialin (1990). *The natural history of China.* Collins, London. 224 pp.

Zhong Hongda (1974). Vegetation on Xisha Archipelago. *Botany Journal* 16(3): 183–192.

Zhou Guangchuang (1955). Plant geography of Shandong. *Journal of Shandong University* 2(1): 70–85.

Zhou Guangchuang (1963). Vegetation classification and distribution in Shandong Province. *Journal of Shandong University* 1: 58–70.

Zhou Yiliang (1990). *Forests of China.* Science Press, Beijing.

Zhou Yiliang *et al.* (1955). *Xylophyta in Xiao Hinggan Mountain Range.* China Forestry Publishing House.

Zhou Yiliang *et al.* (1964a). Distributional determinants and characteristics of the main vegetation types in mountain areas of east China. *Acta Plant Ecology and Geobotany* 2(2): 258–272.

Zhou Yiliang *et al.* (1964b). Successful regulation and the distribution of natural secondary forest in Xiao Hinggan – Changbai Mountain Area. *Acta Northeast China Institute of Forestry.*

Zhu Da-Yuan (1987). Recent advances on the active components in Chinese medicines. *Abstracts of Chinese Medicine* 1(2): 251–286.

Zhu Jimin (1958). Korean pine (*Pinus koraiensis*) broadleaved mixed forest in Xiao Hinggan Mountain Range. *Science Press* 4: 10–15.

Acknowledgements

The overview for China was prepared by Professors Wang Xianpu and Yang Zhouhuai (Commission for Integrated Survey and Natural Resources, Chinese Academy of Sciences, Beijing, China) and Professor He Shan-an (Director, Nanjing Botanic Garden Mem. Sun Yat-Sen, Jiangsu, China), with contributions from Li Zhiji (Forestry Sub-College, Agricultural College of Zhoung Autonomous Region of Guangxi), Qiu Xuezhong (Kunming Institute of Ecology, Chinese Academy of Sciences), Huang Shiman (Biological Research Centre, Hainan University), Su Zhixian (Biodiversity Research Centre of Sichuan Normal University), Pan Borong (Turfan Botanical Garden, Xinjiang Institute of Biology) and Zhou Yilian (Northeast Forestry University). The overview for Taiwan was prepared by Professor Horng-Jye Su (Department of Forestry, National Taiwan University, Taiwan). The overview for Japan was written by Professor Kunio Iwatsuki (Botanical Gardens, University of Tokyo, Japan), with some additional material from Professor T. Shimizu (Kanazawa University, Japan) and Professor H. Ohashi. The overview for Korea was written by Professor Kim Yong Shik (Yeungnam University, Kyongsan, Republic of Korea). All of these accounts have been edited by Alan C. Hamilton and Stephen D. Davis.

The overview for Indochina was prepared by Dr Alan C. Hamilton (WWF) from information submitted by Richard Salter (IUCN, Vientiane, Laos), Dr Ouk Syphan (Forest Department, Phnom Pen, Cambodia), Thawatchai Santisuk (Forest Herbarium, Bangkok, Thailand), and Professor Phan Ke Loc and Dr Nguyen Nghia Thin (University of Hanoi, Vietnam). Kai Larsen (Institute of Botanical Sciences, University of Aarhus, Denmark) provided some additional information. Stephen D. Davis made various contributions throughout the text and helped to edit the final account.

CHANGBAI MOUNTAINS REGION
Jilin Province, China

Location: Jilin Province, north-east China, between latitudes 40°40'–44°30′N and longitudes 125°20'–131°20′E.

Area: 30,000 km² (the area of high plant diversity), within a region covering 75,940 km².

Altitude: 300–2691 m (summit of Bei Yun Peak).

Vegetation: Deciduous broadleaved forest, mixed coniferous and deciduous broadleaved mixed forest, boreal coniferous forest, subalpine forest, alpine tundra. Meadows and swamps are found at various altitudes.

Flora: Estimated 2000–2500 vascular plant species, with 1478 flowering plant species so far recorded from Changbai Mountains Nature Reserve. The flora belongs to the Manchurian Floristic Province.

Useful plants: Timber trees, medicinal plants (>80 species used), edible fruits and vegetables, fodder plants, melliferous plants.

Other values: Water resource conservation, climate amelioration, scientific research, tourism.

Threats: Illegal logging, over-collection of medicinal plants, increasing tourism, poaching of animals.

Conservation: Changbai Mountains Nature Reserve (IUCN Management Category: IV) and Biosphere Reserve covers 1906 km².

Geography

The Changbai Mountains are located in Jilin Province, northeast China, between latitudes 40°40'–44°30′N and longitudes 125°20'–131°20'E. The total area of the administrative region is about 75,940 km² (c. 40% of Jilin Province), of which about 30,000 km² is rich in plant biodiversity. The eastern part of the region adjoins the coastal area of Primorskiy Kray (Russia), while the south-eastern part is bounded by the Tumen and Yalu rivers along the border with North Korea.

The region is geomorphologically complex, including mountains, hills, tablelands, valleys and a cluster of volcanoes. At the summit of Changbai Mountain there is a famous volcanic lake – Tien Chi – about 5–6 km in diameter and over 300 m deep. At the outlet of the lake there is a magnificent waterfall which forms the origin of the Songhua River. The altitude throughout much of the·region is between 300 and 1000 m, with peaks reaching over 1300 m. The mountains consist of granite, basalt and metamorphic limestone. Soils are dark brown forest soils with a slightly acid reaction. There is a deep, seasonally frozen, soil layer.

The climate is of a temperate continental monsoonal type, with low temperatures in spring, warm summers with high rainfall, and cool autumns. Winters are long and severe, with 200–400 mm snow cover on average. The mean annual temperature is 2–6°C, dropping to a mean monthly average of below -10°C in the winter. The hottest month is July when the mean monthly temperature is over 20°C. The absolute minimum temperature is -40.2°C. There are 700–900 mm of rain per year, over 60% of which falls in June, July and August.

In 1949, the population of the entire administrative district of the Changbai Mountain region was 1,974,000. This had risen to 5,180,000 by 1985, and is now increasing at approximately 0.3% per annum. A small number of people live in the Changbai Mountains Nature Reserve.

Vegetation

There is a wide range of vegetation types, including approximately 2680 km² of deciduous broadleaved forest, 43,050 km² of mixed coniferous and deciduous broadleaved forest and 2340 km² of subalpine forest. Forests of all these types cover about 63% of the entire mountain region; however, much has been modified by human activities. The least disturbed areas are the coniferous and deciduous broadleaved forest, and the boreal coniferous forest, within the Changbai Mountains Nature Reserve.

Typical deciduous broadleaved forest in mountain valleys, and on lower slopes where humidity is high, includes a mixture of trees with no one species dominating. Commonly occurring species are *Tilia amurensis* (Amur lime), *Fraxinus mandshurica* (Manchurian ash), *Ulmus propinqua* (Japanese elm) and *Acer mono*. In dry conditions on middle and upper slopes, *Quercus mongolica* (Mongolian oak) forest occurs, mixed with some *Betula dahurica* and other deciduous broadleaved trees.

At 500–1100 m, hills and tablelands are covered by mixed forest of deciduous broadleaved trees and the conifer *Pinus koraiensis* (Korean pine). Among the many deciduous species are *Tilia amurensis*, *T. mandshurica*, *Betula costata*, *Phellodendron amurense*, *Juglans mandshurica*, *Carpinus cordata*, *Populus ussuriensis* and *P. koreana*. At 1100–1800 m, boreal coniferous forest predominates, in which *Picea jezoensis*, *P. koraiensis*, *Abies nephrolepis* and *A. holophylla* (Manchurian fir) are the main components.

Alpine dwarf forest dominated by *Betula ermanii* occurs at 1800–2100 m. Above 2100 m, there is alpine tundra, the only place in China with this type of vegetation. *Dryas octopetala*, *Phyllodoce caerulea*, *Rhododendron redowskianum*, *R. aureum* and *Salix rotundifolia* are the main species. Endemic species include *Papaver pseudo-*

radicatum, Salix tschanbaichanica (Changbai willow) and *Pyrola tschanbaichanica.*

In the plains and lowlands, there are large areas of meadows and swamps. Sedges, such as *Carex meyeriana, C. tato* and *C. lasiocarpa,* birch (*Betula fruticosa*) and willows, such as *Salix brachypoda* and *S. myrtilloides,* are most frequently encountered, while the Changbai larch, *Larix olgensis* var. *changpaiensis,* occurs in some places. Subalpine meadows include such species as *Ligularia japonica, Sanguisorba sitchensis, Trollius japonica* and *Hieracium boreanum.*

Flora

The total number of plant species so far recorded in the Changbai Mountains Nature Reserve is 1794 (comprising 1478 species of flowering plants, 15 species of gymnosperms, 118 species of bryophytes and 183 species of lichens). In addition, 437 species of fungi have been recorded. It is estimated that the total vascular flora of the whole region contains 2000–2500 species.

Many species are endemic, either to the region, or to the region and neighbouring coastal areas of Far Eastern Russia and North Korea. Endemic herbs include *Panax ginseng* (ginseng), *Astilboides tabularis* and *Trifolium lupinaster,* the only representative of this genus in eastern China; endemic conifers include *Pinus koraiensis, Abies holophylla, Taxus cuspidata, Thuja koraiensis* and *Larix olgensis* var. *changpaiensis.* Broadleaved deciduous endemics include *Acer triflorum, A. mandshuricum, Fraxinus mandshurica, Maackia amurensis, Juglans mandshurica, Phellodendron amurense, Populus koreana* and *Syringa reticulata* var. *mandshurica.* There are many ancient Tertiary relicts represented in the flora, such as *Juglans mandshurica, Phellodendron amurense, Fraxinus mandshurica, Vitis amurensis* and *Schisandra chinensis.* Species more typical of southern China include *Actinidia arguta, A. kolomikta, Tripterygium regelii, Magnolia siebioldii* and *Daphne koreana.*

According to Takhtajan (1986), the flora belongs to the Manchurian Floristic Province of the Eastern Asiatic Region (Holarctic Kingdom). Endemic elements occur mainly below 1100 m; at higher elevations Arctic elements predominate.

Useful plants

The forests of the region include a vast wealth of useful and potentially useful plant resources. There are over 80 species of medicinal plants harvested from the wild, including *Panax ginseng, Gastrodia elata, Astragalus membranaceum, Codonopsis pilosula, Asarum hertropoides* var. *mandschuricum, Oplopanax elatus, Acanthopanax senticosus, Schisandra chinensis, Fritillaria ussuriensis, Aristolochia mandsuriensis, Boschniakia rossica* and *Rhododendron aureum.* Since 1952, the annual harvest of wild medicinal plants has amounted to about 40.6 tonnes dry weight.

Since 1980, the mean annual harvest of timber from the region has been 4.82 million m³. The main timber trees are *Pinus koraiensis, Juglans mandshurica, Phellodendron*

amurense, Fraxinus mandshurica, Quercus mongolica, Picea spp. and *Abies* spp.

Vitis amurensis is used to produce fruit juice, jams and wine. Other fruits include *Actinidia kolomikta, A. arguta, A. polygama, Crataegus pinnatifida, Pyrus ussuriensis, Malus baccata, Vaccinium uliginosum* and *Vaccinium vitis-idaea.* Many of these plants are used in plant breeding.

Carex meyeriana provides fibre, and over 30 species of legumes and over 40 species of grasses are used as fodder plants. Honey is produced from a number of trees in the Tiliaceae. There are many trees and shrubs of great ornamental value, particularly magnolias, ash, walnuts, daphnes and conifers.

Social and environmental values

The region is the source of many large rivers, such as the Songhua, Yalu, Tumen, Mudan, Suifen He and Hun Jiang. Natural forest plays a very important role in protecting the catchments of these and other rivers, as well as ameliorating the climate throughout the whole region. As a result, water supplies are assured for crop production in the lower and middle reaches of the river systems.

The landscape throughout the region is scenically attractive; many tourists visit the region to witness the mountain scenery, including volcanic landforms, the vast expanses of virgin forest, magnificent waterfalls and hot springs, as well as many cultural sites.

The threatened scaly-sided merganser (*Mergus squamatus*) breeds here, and it has been speculated that the area along the border with North Korea may be the breeding area of the threatened crested shelduck (*Tadorna cristata*), a species known from only a handful of records (Collar and Andrew 1988). The forests are also the habitat of tiger (*Panthera tigris*).

Economic assessment

The region supplies a large part of China's timber and forest products. Harvesting and utilization of forest products is now controlled. There are many edible and ornamental plants which have great potential for future use. Experimental stations should be established in the region to demonstrate sustainable utilization of forest resources.

Threats

Timber cutting is no longer allowed within the Changbai Mountains Nature Reserve, but trees are still cut illegally by both local and state forestry authorities. Forest regeneration is hampered by both timber cutters and collectors of medicinal plants who establish settlements within the forest (including inside Changbai Mountains Nature Reserve). In some areas, all the forest has been cleared.

Most of the medicinal plants in the region are over-collected and in grave danger of extinction. *Panax ginseng, Boschniakia rossica, Gastrodia elata, Astragalus membranaceum, Oplopanax elatus* and *Acanthopanax senticosus* are most at risk.

Tourism in the region is increasing and needs regulation in some places, especially to protect China's only tundra ecosystem. Unplanned roads and settlements are also a threat.

Conservation

Changbai Mountains Nature Reserve (1906 km²) was established in 1961 (IUCN Management Category IV: Nature Conservation Reserve/Managed Nature Reserve/Wildlife Sanctuary). It is one of the largest reserves in China and is designated as an UNESCO Man and Biosphere Reserve. Ecological monitoring of the temperate forest ecosystem has been underway for over 10 years and a great quantity of data has been obtained. Implementation of the core area, buffer zone and experimental area is required, and rational planning needed in the land surrounding the reserve. With these measures effective, resource conservation and sustainable utilization can be achieved.

References (Titles in Chinese have been translated.)

Collar, N.J. and Andrew, P. (1988). *Birds to watch: the ICBP world checklist of threatened birds*. Technical Publication No. 8. International Council for Bird Preservation, Cambridge, U.K.

Environmental Sciences Institute of Jilin Province (1988). *Natural resources exploitation and ecological environment protection in Changbai Mountain Area*. Science and Technology Press of Jilin Province.

Qian Jiajiu *et al.* (1980). Name list of the vertical distribution of plants in Changbai Mountains. *Appendix of the Journal of Northeast Normal University*.

Station of Ecological Orientation System in Forest of Changbai Mountain Area of the Chinese Academy of Sciences (1981). *An approach on forest ecological system* 1: 1–324.

Station of Ecological Orientation System in Forest of Changbai Mountain (1981). *An approach of forest ecological system* 2: 1–261.

Takhtajan, A. (1986). *Floristic regions of the world*. University of California Press, Berkeley. 522 pp.

Acknowledgements

This Data Sheet was prepared by Professors Wang Xianpu and Yang Zhouhuai (Commission for Integrated Survey of Natural Resources, Chinese Academy of Sciences, Beijing) and Professor He Shan-an (Nanjing Botanic Garden Mem. Sun Yat-Sen, Nanjing).

TAIBAI MOUNTAIN REGION OF QINLING MOUNTAINS
Shaanxi Province, China

Location: 120 km WSW of Xian City, in southern Meixian County, at c. 33°40'–34°10'N and 107°19'–107°58'E.

Area: 2779 km².

Altitude: 500–3767 m.

Vegetation: North slope: broadleaved deciduous forest, subalpine coniferous forest, alpine scrub and meadow. South slope: mixed deciduous evergreen broadleaved forest, deciduous broadleaved forest, alpine coniferous forest, alpine scrub and meadow.

Flora: Estimated 1900 species of vascular plants. Flora belongs to the Eastern Asiatic Region, at the junction between the Sino-Japanese and Sino-Himalayan Floristic Provinces.

Useful plants: Many medicinal plants; many other species are sources of starch, oil, fibre, tannin, perfumes, pigments, pesticides and fodder.

Other values: Scientific research, tourism, maintenance of ecological processes over a large region.

Threats: Deforestation, over-collecting of medicinal plants, illegal hunting, tourist developments.

Conservation: Taibai Mountain Nature Reserve (IUCN Management Category: IV) covers 540 km². Effective management is needed.

Geography

Qinling Mountain Range stretches across a vast area of three counties (Taibai, Zhouzhi and Meixian) in central China; it is effectively the divide between north and south China. The Taibai Mountain region is located in the central part of the range, in southern Meixian County. The Taibai Mountain region measures 39 km N-S and 61 km W-E, covering a total area of 2779 km² in Shaanxi Province. Landforms include plains, hilly areas, lower, mid- and upper mountain slopes, the river valley of the Weihe on the northern slopes and the river valleys of the Hanjuang on the southern slopes. The highest point is 3767 m. The mountain consists mainly of granite, gneiss and phyllite. Various glacial landforms were formed during the last Ice Age and are clearly visible on the mountain. Soils, from lower to higher altitudes, are: typical brown soil, brown forest soil, grey-brown forest soil and alpine meadow soil.

Taibai stands at the transition between the warm temperate and north subtropical climatic zones. There are climatic differences between southern and northern slopes. On the northern slopes at 500 m, the mean annual temperature is 12.9°C, the mean minimum temperature (January) is -1.1°C, the mean maximum temperature (July) is 26.3°C, the absolute minimum temperature is -17.2°C and annual precipitation is 606 mm. On southern slopes at 500 m, the mean annual temperature is 14.7°C, the mean minimum temperature (January) is 2.1°C, the mean maximum temperature (July) is 26.8°C, the absolute minimum temperature is -10.1°C and the annual precipitation is 804 mm. As altitude increases, temperature decreases, but rainfall increases. Annual rainfall is 650–800 mm at 800–1500 m altitude, 750–1000 mm at 1500–3000 m and 800–900 mm above 3000 m. The boundaries of altitudinal, climatic and vegetational zones are a little higher on the southern, compared with the northern, slopes.

Vegetation

Natural and semi-natural forest covers about 550 km². Deciduous broadleaved forest occurs up to 2600 m. Below 1500 m the forests contain *Quercus variabilis*, sometimes with *Q. dentata* and *Q. aliena* var. *acuteserrata*. There are differences in the floristic composition of northern and southern slopes below 1500 m, with more evergreen elements in the latter, including *Cyclobalanopsis glauca* and *Machilus thunbergii*. These lower altitude southern forests also contain evergreen shrubs and bamboos. In wet mountain valleys, there are some small patches of deciduous forest, composed of *Picrasma quassioides*, *Celtis bungeana*, *Pteroceltis tatarinowii*, *Eucommia ulmoides*, *Fraxinus mandshurica*, *Euptelea pleiospermum*, *Kolreuteria paniculata*, *Zelkova schneideriana* and *Pistacia chinensis*. Occasionally there are small, scattered areas of *Platycladus orientalis* (Chinese arbor-vitae).

At 1500–1800 m, the forest is dominated by *Quercus aliena* var. *acuteserrata*. Associated species include *Q. baronii* and *Q. aliena*. Wet montane valleys at this altitude also support deciduous broadleaved forest, but there are no dominant species. Common trees are *Acer griseum*, *A. palmatum*, *Carpinus cordata*, *C. turczaninowii*, *Dendrobenthamia kousa* var. *chinensis*, *Fraxinus paxiana*, *Tilia dictyoneura* and *T. oliveri*. The mountain range itself and steep slopes support small areas of coniferous forest dominated by *Pinus tabulaeformis*. At 1800–2300 m, there are large areas of mixed oak-pine forest dominated by *Quercus liaolungensis*, *Pinus armandii* and *Albies fargesii*,

178

along with hornbeams, dogwoods, maples, willows and mountain ashes (species include *Acer caudatum*, *Carpinus turczaninowii*, *Cornus macrophylla*, *Salix cathayana*, *S. wallichiana* and *Sorbus koehneana*).

Subalpine coniferous forest occurs at 2600–3350 m. At 2600–3000 m, the forest mainly comprises *Albies fargesii*; between 3000–3350 m, *Larix chinensis* is the dominant species. Subalpine forest forms a more continuous belt on northern slopes. The tree-line is reached at about 3500 m, above which the main vegetation is alpine scrub and meadow. Alpine scrub is mainly composed of *Rhododendron cupularis*, while the meadows consist of *Kobresia graminifolia*, *Polygonum sphaerostachyum* and *Deschampsia caespitosa*.

Flora

There are an estimated 1900 species of vascular plants. The Taibai Mountain region is located at the boundary of the Sino-Japanese and Sino-Himalayan Floristic Provinces. North China floristic elements are more typical of the northern slopes; central China floristic elements are more typical of the southern slopes. Himalayan elements are found throughout the region. At present, 1550 species of seed plants are known from Taibai Mountain, belonging to 628 genera and 121 families. Twenty-three of the genera are endemic to China. There are 40 species endemic to Taibai Mountain and a further 110 species endemic to the whole Qinling Mountain Range. Endemics include *Larix chinensis*, *Sorbus tapashana*, *Fritillaria taipaiensis*, *Lonicera tapeiensis*, *Anemone taipaiensis*, *Souliea vaginata*, *Angelica tsinlingensis*, *Primula giraldiana*, *Saxifraga giraldiana* and *Delphinium taibeicum*. *Kingdonia uniflora* is a relict element of the Himalayan flora, sometimes included in a separate family (Kingdoniaceae) within the Ranales. There are 320 species of bryophytes, belonging to 142 genera and 63 families.

Useful plants

The Taibai Mountain region abounds in plant resources. There are about 500 species, including trees, used medicinally. The total annual harvest of medicinal plants is c. 1 million kg, valued at c. US$0.5–1 million. Medicinal plants include *Fritillaria taipaiensis*, *Souliea vaginata*, *Notholirion hyacinthinum*, *Aster flaccidus*, *Daphne giraldii*, *Coeloglossum viride* var. *bracteatum*, *Codonopsis pilosula*, *Gastrodia elata*, *Rheum officinale* and *Eucommia ulmoides*, as well as the mosses *Haplocladium microphyllum* subsp. *capillatum* and *Sphagnum teres*. Medicinal plants also include species of *Betula*, *Pinus* and *Quercus*. Some plants are recognized as effective in the treatment of cancer, such as *Podophyllum emodi* var. *chinensis*, *Paris chinensis*, *Umbilicaria hypococcinea* and *Patrinia heterophylla*, as well as the fungi *Polyporus umbellatus*, *Pyropolyporus fomentarius* and *Hericium erinaceus*.

The most important timber trees are *Abies fargesii*, *Betula albo-sinensis*, *Pinus armandii*, *Quercus aliena*, *Q. liaolungensis* and *Q. variabilis*. There are many endemic poplars, such as *Populus davidiana*, *P. purdomii*, *P. tomentosa* and *P. wilsonii*. These are fast growing timber species, useful for tree breeding. There are also many plants used for other purposes, such as sources of starch (*Eastenea seguinii*, *Pueraria lobata*), fibre (*Broussonetia papyrifera*, *Iris lactea*), tannin (*Quercus* spp., *Rhus chinensis*), perfume (*Lindera obtusiloba*), lacquer (*Rhus verniciflua*), fodder (*Broussonetia papyrifera*) and pesticide (*Melia azedarach*).

Social and environmental values

The Taibai region has a rich fauna. There are 230 species of birds and about 40 species of mammals. Over 500 species of insects have so far been recorded. Representatives of both Palaearctic and Oriental faunas are present. Giant panda and golden-haired monkey are found on the southern slopes of the mountains at Huangboyuan and Houzhenzi.

The region is geologically very important with complete traces of the Quaternary glaciation, making it significant in the study of the glacial period. There are cirques, trough bottoms, glacial terraces, ice cross-walls, end-morraines, together with 5 moraine lakes: Large Taibai Lake, Second Taibai Lake, Third Taibai Lake, Yuhuang Pool and Sanqing Pool. The Taibai Mountain region is the dividing range of the Weihe and Hanjiang river systems, and is the source of many rivers. The dense forest cover plays an important role in water resource conservation and in the amelioration of climate, thereby helping to sustain agricultural production along the middle and lower reaches of the rivers.

Taibai Mountain is a very important religious centre for Taoism. There are many cultural relics, attracting the attentions of scholars, scientists and devotees. About 100,000 people annually visit the mountain. Further studies are needed to quantify the region's economic value and potential for tourism.

Threats

The most serious threat is illegal logging. Over-collection of medicinal plants (especially of *Fritillaria taipaiensis*, *Notholirion hyacinthum* and *Souliea vaginata*) and illegal hunting are also problems. The increasing amount of tourism is another potentially serious threat. Tourism is not yet controlled and needs to be regulated and planned.

Conservation

The Taibai Mountain Nature Reserve was established in 1965 with a total area of 540 km². Most of the reserve is above 1500 m. No people live in the reserve, but c. 50,000 live in the vicinity. The reserve should be enlarged to include representative samples of all the vegetation zones on the southern and northern slopes. A core area, buffer zone and an experimental area should be established. More effective management is needed, and conservation and scientific research should be strengthened. The region has great potential as a source of economic plants, including material for agroforestry. This role needs to be incorporated into a management plan for the reserve, so that the security of these plant resources can be guaranteed and so that the local population can benefit from and support its conservation.

References (Titles in Chinese have been translated.)

Fu Baopu *et al.* (1983). Characteristic of the climate in Qinling Mountains. *Meteorology of Shaanxi Province* 1: 10–15.

Liu Youmin *et al.* (1984). The function of the Quaternary glacier in the Qinling Mountains and the evolution of the Palaeo-environment. *Proceedings of the International Exchange of Geology.* Science Press.

Ma Naixi (1987). Main characteristics and preliminary assessment of Taibai Nature Reserve. *Journal of Northwest University* 71 (Suppl.): 132–140.

Natural Reserve of Taibai Mountains (1982). *The main peak of Qinling Mountains – Taibai Mountain.* Science Press, Shaanxi Province.

Tien Zesheng (1985). About the effects of the Quaternary glaciation on Taibai Mountains. *Proceedings of Symposium on Quaternary Glaciation.* Science Press.

Zhang Zhiying *et al.* (1984). Characteristics of the flora of Taibai Mountains. *Botany Research* 4: 50–56.

Acknowledgements

This Data Sheet was prepared by Professors Wang Xianpu and Yang Zhouhuai (Commission for Integrated Survey of Natural Resources, Chinese Academy of Sciences, Beijing) and Professor He Shan-an (Nanjing Botanic Garden Mem. Sun Yat-Sen, Nanjing).

NANLING MOUNTAIN RANGE
Guangdong, Guangxi, Hunan and Jiangxi Provinces, China

Location: South Hunan, south Jiangxi, north Guangdong and north-east Zhuang Autonomous Region of Guangxi. Approximate coordinates: 24°00'– 27°00'N, 110°00'–115°00'E.

Area: c. 30,000 km².

Altitude: 200–2142 m.

Vegetation: Evergreen broadleaved forest, montane semi-deciduous broadleaved mixed forest, some coniferous/broadleaved mixed forest.

Flora: >3000 species of vascular plants. The flora is mainly East Asian with many subtropical endemics. There are also many Sino-Japanese elements and some relict species.

Useful plants: More than 800 species are used by local people. Many plants are potentially important sources of oil, starch, fibre, aromatic compounds, medicines, pesticides, fruits, timbers, wild vegetables and dyestuffs.

Other values: Watershed protection, scientific research, tourism.

Threats: Clearance of steep slopes for shifting cultivation, over-collection of wild plants.

Conservation: 17 Nature Reserves cover about 5000 km². Management needs to be strengthened.

Geography

The Nanling Mountain Range forms the watershed between the Yangtze and Pearl (Zhu Jiang) rivers. There are 5 mountain ranges, namely Yuechengling, Dupong, Mingdu, Qitian and Dageng, which together stretch across south Hunan, south Jiangxi, north Guangdong and north-east Guangxi Provinces in a north-east/south-west direction. The total area is 137,000 km², with biological diversity concentrated in 30,000 km² of mountainous and hilly terrain between 500 and 1500 m. A number of peaks reach over 1800 m (the highest point is 2142 m). Most of the mountains consist of granite, metamorphic rocks and arenaceous shale, with limestone locally. Soil types include red earth, yellow earth, yellow brown earth and mountain meadow. The soils are generally acidic, with pH values of 4.5–5.5, though brown limestone soil and black limestone soil have pH values of 6.0–7.8.

The range is located at the southern periphery of the central subtropical zone of eastern China. The climate is humid subtropical, mainly under the influence of the Pacific Monsoon. There are four distinct seasons. In the hills and plains below 580 m, the mean annual temperature is 16.1–21.1°C, and the mean temperature of the coldest month (January) is 5.8–10°C and that of the hottest month (July) 25–30°C. Temperatures fall occasionally to -9.8°C. Annual rainfall is 1400–2000 mm, about 68% of which falls between April and September. The lapse rate with altitude is c. 0.47–0.63°C per 100 m, accompanied by an increase in annual rainfall. Snow occurs only in the northern part of the region.

The population of the region is about 27 million, with an annual growth rate of c. 2%.

Vegetation

The natural forest cover below 1300 m is evergreen broadleaved forest. Below 500 m, the main species are *Altingia chinensis, Castanopsis fissa, C. fordii* and *C. hystrix*; there are also some tropical floristic elements. At 500 and 700 m, the main species are *Castanopsis fargesii, Schima superba, Machilus cathayensis* and *M. decursinervis.* Between 700–1300 m, the main species are *Castanopsis carlesii, C. eyeri, C. fabri, C. tibetana, Machilus thunbergii, Pentaphylax euryoides* and *Schima argentea.* There are some areas of secondary subtropical deciduous broadleaved forests. In valleys and on the lower parts of the mountain, where it is humid, the main species are *Populus adenopode, Betula luminifera, Carpinus fargesii, Alniphyllum fortunei* and *Styrax subnivea.* On dry mountain slopes and valleys, important species are *Quercus acutissima, Q. fabri* and *Q. variabilis.* There is also a large area of artificial or naturally regenerated subtropical coniferous forest, the main species being *Pinus massoniana* and *Cunninghamia lanceolata.* Bamboo (*Phyllostachys pubescens*) forest also occurs.

Limestone occurs only below 1000 m and carries a special type of semi-deciduous broadleaved mixed forest of *Cyclobalanopsis glauca, Cinnamomum calcarea, Celtis austro-sinensis, C. sinensis, Ulmus parvifolia, Platycarya strobilacea, Pistacia chinensis* and *Bridelia fordii* in moist areas, and *Canthium dicoccum, Cornus fordii, Koelreuteria minor* and *Sapium rotundifolium* on shallow dry soils. Some species, such as *Cupressus funebris,* are suitable for local afforestation.

At 1300–1800 m, the forest is semi-deciduous. Dominant deciduous trees include *Fagus lucida, F. longipetiolata, Pterostyrax leveillei* and *Acer sinense.* Evergreen trees include

Castanopsis eyrei var. *caudata, C. lamontii, Cyclobalanopsis multinervis, C. nubium, Lithocarpus cleistocarpus* and *Cleyera japonica*. There are scattered areas of subtropical mid-montane coniferous forest, with *Pinus kwangtungensis, Cathaya argyrophylla, Fokienia hodginsii* and *Amesiodendron argotaenia*.

Above 1800 m, winds can be strong and soils are shallow. Elfin forest is present on summits. The trees are stunted (about 10 m tall) and covered in lichens and mosses. This forest type has been called semi-deciduous broadleaved mixed forest. Evergreen species include *Cyclobalanopsis stewardiana, Symplocos decora, Camellia pitardii, Illicium majus* and *Dendropanax dentiger*. Deciduous trees include *Litsea pedunculata, Sorbus folgneri, S. keissleri, Clethra kaipoensis* and *Enkianthus quinquegona*. There are small areas of coniferous and broadleaved mixed forest. Coniferous species include *Abies ziyuanensis, Tsuga chinensis, T. cuneiformis* and *T. longibracteata*. Much of the mountain summit is bare, with small patches of *Quercus phillyraeoides*, the presence of which indicates a phytogeographical relationship to the sclerophyllous broadleaved forest of the Mediterranean.

Flora

There are estimated to be more than 3000 species of vascular plants, including more than 600 trees and about 400 pteridophytes. The families Fagaceae, Lauraceae, Theaceae, Magnoliaceae, Symplocaceae, Aceraceae, Hamamelidaceae, Araliaceae, Rosaceae and Leguminosae are well-represented. The flora contains central, eastern and southern Chinese elements, together with Sino-Japanese elements. The majority of the species belong to the first of these categories. At lower elevations, in valleys south of 26°N, there are Indomalayan elements. North temperate elements are better represented at higher elevations.

Since the Jurassic Period, the region has experienced a stable, warm and humid climate. As a result, many ancient Tertiary relicts are present in the flora. Examples include *Cathaya argyrophylla, Amentotaxus argotaenia, Cephalotaxus oliveri, Liriodendron chinense, Cyclocarya paliurus, Tapiscia sinensis* and *Torricellia tiliifolia*. The presence of Tertiary elements suggests that climatic change during the Pleistocene glaciations did not have as severe an impact on the flora in this area as elsewhere.

Useful plants

The most valuable timber trees are *Castanopsis fargesii, Cinnamomum camphora, Cunninghamia lanceolata* and *Fagus lucida*.

A wide range of plants is gathered from the wild. These include species providing oils, starch, fibre, aromatic compounds, medicines, pesticides, vegetables and dyestuffs. Several species are valuable for making honey. 800 species are used locally, over 50 commonly. Species used include: as medicines – *Coptis teeta, Asarum longepedunculatum, Polygala aureocauda, Panax pseudo-ginseng* var. *japonicum, Tinospora sagitate, Uncaria rhynchophylla, Lonicera confusa, Dipsacus asper, Ophiopogon japonicus,*

Platycodon grandiflorus, Campaumosa japonica, Paris polyphylla, Ligusticum sinense and *Gynostemma pentaphyllum*; for their fruits – *Vitis pentagona, Myrica rubra, Dendrobanthamia hongkongense, D. melanotricha, Hovenia duclis* and many species of *Actinidia* (kiwi fruit); as vegetables – *Pteridium aquilinum* and *Houttynia cordata*, both of which are arousing considerable interest as food plants; for providing substrates for raising fungi – *Altingia chinensis, Carpinus davidii, Rhoiptelea chiliantha, Pentaphylax euryoides, Elaeocarpus* spp. and *Liquidambar acalycina*; for pesticides – *Macleya cordata* and *Illicium majus*; for starch – *Amorphophallus rivieri, Dioscorea bulbifera* and *Lilium giganteum*; for aromatic oils – *Lysimachia foenum-graecum* and *Litsea cubeba* (both of which are cultivated); and for dyestuffs – *Gardenia jasminoides* and *Polygonum yunnanensis*. The annual harvest of medicinal plants is 15,000–20,000 kg.

An oil-producing plant, *Camellia cuspidata*, is found above 1000 m. The oil content is as high as in the commonly cultivated *Camellia oleifera*. *Hydrangea paniculata* is an ornamental plant and also a good source of nectar for bees.

Social and environmental values

The Nanling Mountain Range is the source of the Yangtze and Pearl rivers and their tributaries. The forests have a significant and fundamental role to play in water resource conservation, and thereby for assuring water supplies for farmland irrigation, power generation, navigation and fisheries.

The Nanling Mountain region carries the best example of intact humid subtropical vegetation in East Asia and therefore has great research value and potential for tourism. Particular features of interest are the karst landscapes, dense forests, clean rivers and waterfalls. The region is also of cultural and religious importance, with many ancient temples. There are about 2 million visitors to the region annually.

Timber cutting has been carried out for many years, but the forest cannot be cut more than once without causing serious degradation. Important plantations of *Pinus massoniana* and *Cunninghamia lanceolata* have been established in the region. The native forest is a potentially valuable gene source for plant breeding. For example, the genetic resources of fast-growing trees, valuable timber trees, wild fruit trees and medicinal plants could be used to improve existing crops.

Threats

Large-scale tree cutting is now controlled. However, cultivation on steep slopes, shifting cultivation and over-collecting of wild plants continue. There is very serious soil erosion in some places. Water and air pollution are also becoming serious threats to the habitat, as a result of development of industries at both village and national levels. Many medicinal plant species are at risk of local extinction as a result of over-collection from the wild.

Conservation

The forest in this region is generally in good condition. There are 17 Nature Reserves, the most important of which are: Huaping Reserve (174 km²), Miao'er Mountain Reserve (451 km²), Laoshan Reserve (145 km²), Huashuichong Reserve (120 km²), Shunhuangshan Reserve, Mongshan Reserve, Qianjiadong Reserve, Jiulian Mountain Reserve (40.7 km²), Babao Mountain Reserve (32 km²) and Qingxige Reserve. Management of these areas should be strengthened.

References (Titles in Chinese have been translated.)

Comprehensive Survey Team of Huaping Region in Guangxi (1986). *Report of the Comprehensive Survey Team in Huaping Region.* Science Press of Hunan Province, Shandong Science Press.

Fu Likuo *et al.* (1980). The genus *Abies* discovered for the first time in Guangxi and Hunan. *Acta Phytotaxonomica Sinica* 18(2): 205–210.

Guangdon Botany Institute (1976). *Vegetation of Guangdong Province.* Science Press.

Qi Chengjing (ed.) (1988). *Hunan vegetation.* Hunan Science Press.

Second Team of the South China Mountainous Regions Comprehensive Expedition of the Chinese Academy of Sciences (1989). *Comprehensive study and survey of natural resources in Nanling Mountainous areas of Hunan Province.* Science Press of Science and Technology University.

Second Team of the South China Mountainous Regions Comprehensive Expedition of the Chinese Academy of Sciences (1990). *Study of the comprehensive terrestrial management and natural resources exploitation in Nanling Mountain regions of Hunan Province.* Academic Books Press.

Wang Xianpu (Wang Huen-pu) *et al.* (1984). General introduction to the forest vegetation in Longsheng County of Guangxi. *J. Agriculture College, Guangxi* 1: 75–85.

Wang Xianpu *et al.* (1986). General situation of vegetation in Miaoershan Reserve of Xingan County. *Guangxi Guihaia* 6(1/2): 79–91.

Acknowledgements

This Data Sheet was prepared by Professors Wang Xianpu and Yang Zhouhuai (Commission for Integrated Survey of Natural Resources, Chinese Academy of Sciences, Beijing) and Professor He Shan-an (Nanjing Botanic Garden Mem. Sun Yat-Sen, Nanjing).

GAOLIGONG MOUNTAINS, NU JIANG RIVER AND BILUO SNOW MOUNTAINS
Yunnan Province, China

Location: The mountains are on both sides of the Nu Jiang River in western Yunnan, between latitudes 24°56'–28°24'N and longitudes 98°34'–99°02'E.

Area: c. 10,000 km².

Altitude: 1090–5128 m.

Vegetation: Evergreen broadleaved forest, subalpine coniferous forest, alpine scrub and meadow, scree vegetation. There are small patches of savanna at low altitudes in hot and dry valleys.

Flora: c. 2000 species of vascular plants. The region is transitional between the Palaeotropical and Palaearctic phytogeographical regions; most of the flora is Palaearctic.

Useful plants: Timber trees, medicinal plants, ornamental plants.

Other values: Conservation of water resources, climatic amelioration, rich fauna and avifauna.

Threats: Cultivation on steep slopes, illegal timber cutting, hunting.

Conservation: This is one of the best preserved areas of subtropical forest in western China. Gaoligong Nature Reserve covers 1240 km²; Nu Jiang Nature Reserve covers 3754 km². Management needs to be strengthened. A regional management plan is needed.

Geography

There are four counties of Yunnan Province in this region: Lushui, Fugong, Bijiang and Drung-Nu Autonomous County of Gongshan. The eastern boundary is the watershed between the Nu Jiang and Lancang rivers; the western border is Nmai Hka River; the north-west boundary is the basin of the Dulungjiang River (which is the source of the Nmai Hka River); on the north, the region grades into subalpine coniferous forest on the south-eastern part of the Qinghai-Xizang Plateau; the southern boundary is Pianma and Luku. The region lies at the very western end of the Hengduan Mountains. It is 280 km from north to south and 30–50 km from east to west and has an area of 10,000 km². It includes the valley of the Nu Jiang River, the Gaoligong Mountains to the west and the Biluo Snow Mountains to the east. Both of these ranges rise to c. 3500 m, with some peaks reaching 4000–4500 m (the highest point is 5128 m). The Nu Jiang River lies at 1090–1200 m. Topography is very sharp, with the vertical distance from valleys to peaks being over 2500 m, but the distance from the ridge of the Gaoligong Mountains to the ridge of Nu Mountains is only 25–40 km. Rocks are granite and metamorphic (e.g. schist, gneiss, phyllite). The soils vary altitudinally and include the following types: red earth, yellow earth, yellow brown earth, brown forest soil, alpine shrub meadow soil and alpine cold desert soil. All the soils are acid, the pH being 4.5–5.5.

The climate is under the influence of the south-west Indian Ocean Monsoon and is warm and humid. Most rainfall occurs in summer and autumn; winter and spring are warm and dry. The annual temperature range is low. Temperatures decline from south to north, related to increasing latitude and altitude. The eastern slopes are warmer than the western slopes. The valley of the Nu Jiang River is subject to foehn winds and the climate is dry and hot. At 1200 m, 1700 m and 2000 m altitude, mean annual temperatures are 16.9°C, 15°C and 13.8°C respectively; the mean temperatures of the coldest month (January) are 9.5°C, 9.1°C and 7.6°C; and the mean temperatures of the hottest month (July) are 23.8°C, 19°C and 19.3°C. Annual precipitation is 1000–1500 mm.

Vegetation

Vegetation varies according to topography and altitude. About 900 km² of forest remains. Evergreen broadleaved forest occurs at 1100–2800 m. Below 1800 m, the most abundant species are *Castanopsis ferox*, *C. orthacantha* and *C. wattii*, while *Lithocarpus echinocarpa*, *L. polystachys*, *L. truncatus*, *Machilus longipedicellata* and *Schima argentea* are also common. At 1800–2800 m, *Cyclobalanopsis lamellosa*, *Lithocarpus hancei*, *L. leucostachys*, *L. polystachys* and *L. variolosus* are abundant. In some locations there are extensive stretches of *Pinus yunnanensis*, with smaller areas of *Taiwania floustana* forest and *Pinus griffithii*. In hot dry valleys in the south, below 1100 m, there are small patches of savanna. Trees include *Bombax malabaricum*, *Erythrina stricta*, *Albizia chinensis*, *Acrocarpus fraxinifolius*, *Garuga floribunda* var. *gamblei* and *Rabdosia yunnanensis*. Common herbs include *Heteropogon contortus* and *Bothriochloa pertusa*.

Alpine scrub and alpine meadows occur at 3800–4500 m. Alpine scrub occurs on slopes, consisting mainly of *Rhododendron neriiflorum*, *R. beesianum*, *Sinarundinaria nitida*, *Cotoneaster microphyllus* and *Rosa omiensis*. Above 4500 m there is sparse scree vegetation. Lichens and mosses are abundant, together with *Meconopsis pseudovenusta* and many species of *Pedicularis*.

Flora

The unique combination of high mountains and large rivers trending south to north, and the monsoonal climate, makes this a transitional region between Palaeotropical and Palaearctic floras. In general, the Palaearctic flora is dominant, most of its elements belonging to the Sino-Himalayan Province. The gorge was a refuge for tropical plants during the Quaternary glaciations. This mixing of floras seems to have resulted in a high rate of evolution of new species. Based on incomplete statistics, there are estimated to be more than 2000 species of vascular plants in Gaoligong Nature Reserve and possibly 500–1000 species of lower plants. Four families of gymnosperms are represented.

Many of China's endemic subtropical species occur in the region. Examples include *Abies delavayi*, *A. georgei*, *Cyclobalanopsis glaucoides* and *Castanopsis delavayi*. Notable species in this region are *Cephalotaxus lanceolata*, *Magnolia campbelii* and *Diphylax sinicus*.

Useful plants

This region abounds with plant resources. There are many valuable, fast-growing timber species, including *Phoebe nanmu*, *Machilus hurzii*, *Toona ciliata*, *Manglietia fordiana*, *Liriodendron chinensis*, *Exbucklandia populnea*, *Castanopsis fargesii* f. *ducluxii*, *C. hystrix* and *Taiwania flousiana*. The region also has about 500 species of medicinal plants, including *Angelica sinensis*, *Aucklandia lappa*, *Chaenomeles speciosa*, *Coptis teeta*, *Eucommia ulmoides*, *Gastrodia elata*, *Magnolia officinalis*, *Panax japonicus* var. *major*, *P. japonicus*, *Paeonia veitchii*, *Dipsacus asper*, *Akebia quinata* and *Dactylicapnos scandens*. The annual harvest of medicinal plants is c. 50,000 kg. There are many plants yielding oils or tannin. The region is also rich in ornamental plants, particularly in the families Orchidaceae, Theaceae and Magnoliaceae.

Social and environmental values

The region has some of the best preserved subtropical vegetation in western China and is therefore important for plant genetic resources. The region also has a rich fauna, including takin (*Budorcas taxicolor*), golden-haired monkey (*Rhinopithecus brelichi*), red goral (*Naemorhedus cranbrooki*), lesser panda (*Ailurus fulgens*) and gaur (*Bos frontalis*). The biological diversity of the whole region has great significance for scientific research.

The forest has important roles in catchment protection and climatic amelioration. The eastern slopes of the Gaoligong Mountains form the main catchment of the Nu Jiang River, the source of water for irrigation in the Nu Jiang River basin. The western slopes are the source of the Longchuan River, providing water for irrigation to Tengchong County. The magnificent landscape of high mountains, deep gorges, dense forests and fast streams attracts many tourists. The region is a natural classroom for teaching ecology.

Threats

Large-scale timber cutting has stopped, but some illegal timber cutting and hunting still occurs. The tradition of cultivating steep slopes continues, with the result that soil erosion is very serious in places.

Conservation

This is the second largest forested area in south-west China, and one of the best preserved areas of subtropical forest in China. Gaoligong Nature Reserve (IUCN Management Category: IV) covers 1240 km². About 1000 people live on the periphery of the reserve. Natural forest covers 922 km² (74% of the reserve area). Shrubland and open forest make up a further 15%. The timber stock is about 20,000,000 m³. Nu Jiang Nature Reserve includes the Nu Jiang River basin and the Dulong River basin, as well as the mountains of Nushan, Gaoligong and Dandanglika. This reserve is divided into two parts, Gangshan and Bijiang. The Gangshan part has an area of 2376 km², while the Bijiang part covers 1378 km². Natural forest covers 1488 km² (40% of the reserve area). Shrubland and open forest cover about 22% of the area. The timber stock is 47,198,385 m³.

The management of these reserves needs to strengthened. A regional management plan is also required. The priority for conservation is protection and restoration of evergreen broadleaved forest, especially at lower altitudes. The cultivation of wild economic plants would help to raise the living standards of local people.

References (Titles in Chinese have been translated.)

Compilation Group of Yunnan Vegetation (1987). *Vegetation of Yunnan*. Science Press.

Forest Survey and Planning Department of Yunnan Province (1987). *Nature Reserves of Yunnan Province*. Chinese Forest Press.

Acknowledgements

This Data Sheet was prepared by Professors Wang Xianpu and Yang Zhouhuai (Commission for Integrated Survey of Natural Resources, Chinese Academy of Sciences, Beijing) and Professor He Shan-an (Nanjing Botanic Garden Mem. Sun Yat-Sen, Nanjing).

TROPICAL FORESTS OF HAINAN ISLAND
Hainan Province, China

Location: Hainan Island is located in the north of the South China Sea, between latitudes 18°10'–20°10'N and longitudes 108°37'–111°03'E.

Area: 33,920 km².

Altitude: 0–1867 m (summit of Wuzhi Mountain).

Vegetation: Tropical lowland seasonal rain forest, monsoon forest, savanna, montane seasonal rain forest, mangrove forest.

Flora: c. 4200–4500 vascular plant species, of which over 80% are tropical. Affinities with the flora of Indomalaya, some pantropical elements and numerous Chinese endemic tropical species. 630 species are endemic to Hainan Island.

Useful plants: More than 2900 vascular plant species are commonly used by local people as important sources of timber, medicines and for handicrafts (e.g. rattan and bamboo).

Other values: Natural forest cover has a vital role in water resource conservation, climatic amelioration and prevention of soil erosion. Hainan's tropical forests are becoming a major tourist attraction and are important for scientific research.

Threats: Illegal clearance of forest, timber cutting, over-collection of medicinal plants, hunting, clearance for settled agriculture and shifting cultivation. Inadequate funding and lack of trained personnel prevent effective management of protected areas.

Conservation: 51 Nature Reserves cover a total area of c. 1500 km² (including marine reserves). The terrestrial protected areas system includes all the major plant-rich areas. The main requirement is for effective management.

Geography

Hainan Island is situated on the continental shelf of East Asia, about 24 km from the Leizhou Peninsula of mainland China, in the northern part of the South China Sea, between latitudes 18°10'–20°10'N and longitudes 108°37'–111°03'E. The total area of the island is 33,920 km².

Originally connected to the Leizhou Peninsula of mainland China, Hainan became an island about 500,000 years ago when the Qiongzhou Straits were formed along a fault-line. The island is mountainous, with the highest mountains occurring in the south. Land over 500 m occupies c. 25% of the total land area and there are 667 peaks over 1000 m, the highest being Wuzhi Mountain (1867 m). Low coastal plains occupy c. 29% of the island's land surface.

The island is mainly granite, with some sandstone, shale and limestone. The tableland in the north is mainly basalt; the coastal plain is mainly sedimentary, with a wide saltmarsh zone around the coast. Soils are lateritic red earths, lateritic red loams, mountain red earths and mountain yellow earths. In the coastal plain and tableland, there are large areas of sand. Saline soils occur on coastal mud flats.

The island has a tropical monsoonal climate, with a wider fluctuation in temperatures than is typical of other tropical regions. The mean annual temperature in the lowlands is between 22–26°C, but temperatures are lower in the mountains. In the lowlands, the mean temperature of the coldest months (January–February) is 16–21°C. In the north, winter temperatures drop below 0°C. During the hottest months (July–August), the mean monthly temperature is 25–29°C, but the maximum temperature reaches 40°C. Annual precipitation generally ranges between 800–2800 mm. On the windward (eastern) side of the island, the annual rainfall is between 1500–2800 mm. The lee (western) side of the island is drier and receives between 800–1200 mm (locally as low as 300 mm) of rain per year. Monsoon rain occurs between May–June. Typhoons occur between August–October. About 70% of the total annual rainfall occurs during this period.

The population of Hainan is 6,056,000 (1986). The annual growth rate before 1980 was over 2% per annum, but this decreased to 1.5% in 1980. By 1986, it had decreased again to 1.36%.

Vegetation

Hainan is at the northern periphery of the Asian moist tropics. Seasonal tropical rain forest is the main vegetation type below 500 m. The forest is rich in species; no one species dominates. The main trees are *Tarrietia parrifolia*, *Hopea hainanensis*, *Reevesia longipetiolata*, *Casearia aequilateralis* and *Litchi chinensis* (lychee). On middle and upper slopes, the main species include *Antiaris toxicaria*, *Pouteria annamensis*, *Nephelium topengii* (Hainan rambutan), *Hydnocarpus anthelminticus*, *Pseudostreblus indica*, *Gironniera cuspidata*, *Walsura robusta* and *Baccaurea ramiflora*.

In hilly areas and basin foothills, where the environment is drier (and particularly in the west and south of the island), there are large areas of monsoon forest. Where the forest is still intact, the main species are *Syzygium cuminii*, *Lannea grandis*, *Dillenia pentagyna*, *Pterospermum heterophyllum*,

Terminalia hainanensis, Meyna hainanensis, Albizia odoratissima, Cratoxylum ligustrinum and *Spondias pinnata*. In degraded areas, the environment is even drier and, as a result, the original forest constituents are replaced by subtropical elements, such as *Liquidambar formosana, Kleinhovia hospita, Macaranga denticulata, Quercus acutissima* and *Albizia chinensis*. If burned, the forest degenerates even further to scrub and grassland, after which forest regeneration is difficult to achieve.

On the west tableland there are large areas of savanna. The main tree is *Bombax malabaricum* (kapok), while grasses include *Heteropogon contortus* and *Imperata cylindrica* var. *major* (alang-alang).

At 500–1100 m, montane seasonal rain forest occurs. The main species are *Dacrydium pierrei, Podocarpus imbricatus, Lithocarpus fenzelianus, Castanopsis hystrix, Alseodaphne hainanensis, Madhuca hainanensis, Cryptocarya hainanensis* and *Altingia obovata*. At higher elevations the forest becomes stunted and includes conifers, such as *Pinus kwangtungensis, P. fenzeliana* and *Keteleeria hainanensis*, together with Ericaceae, Theaceae and Symplocaceae.

Coastal mud flats support mangrove forests, although these have been greatly reduced in extent. There are 18 species of mangrove trees in Hainan, representing 11 plant families. In terms of species numbers, the mangroves of Hainan are not as rich as those of Malesia.

In 1956, forest covered 8630 km² (or 25% of the land area). By 1980, the forest area had decreased to 3620 km² (10.5% of the land area). It is estimated that c. 3000 km² of natural tropical forest remain today. Mangrove forest covered 100 km² in 1956, but by 1980 it had been reduced to only 33 km². It has since been further reduced.

Flora

Although representing only 0.35% of the total land area of China, Hainan contains 7% of China's vascular flora. There are estimated to be c. 4200–4500 species of vascular plants, including 630 which are endemic to Hainan. Over 80% are tropical species. The main floristic affinities are with the Malay Peninsula (Indomalayan element). There are also many pantropical elements and tropical Chinese endemics. At higher elevations, there are some subtropical elements belonging to the families Theaceae, Aquifoliaceae, Magnoliaceae and Ericaceae. Some typically temperate species are also found in the tropical zone. There are many widely distributed species of Podocarpaceae, showing affinities to the flora of the Southern Hemisphere. Important plant families in terms of species numbers are Euphorbiaceae, Leguminosae, Annonaceae, Moraceae, Sapindaceae, Myrtaceae and Sapotaceae.

Useful plants

More than 2900 species of vascular plants (over 60% of the total vascular flora) are commonly used by local people. There are 458 species of commercial timber trees, including *Dalbergia obtusifolia, Hopea hainanensis, Madhuca hainanensis* and *Litchi chinensis*. 34 trees are listed as first grade timber, 48 as second grade and 119 as third grade.

Over 2500 species have been used for medicinal purposes. Of these, many have potential in cultivation, such as *Cephalotaxus mannii, Aquilaria sinensis, Maytenus tiaoloshanensis, M. hainanensis, Alpinia oxyphylla* and *Morinda officinalis*.

There are 76 species of wild fruit trees, more than 70 species of tropical ornamental plants, and a number of trees which are used for afforestation programmes. There are 100 species of fibre plants, over 30 species yielding oil, rubber and dyestuffs, more than 10 species used as sources of sugar for brewing and more than 200 species of fodder plants. Rattans and fan palms number about 10 species. Of the rattans, *Daemonorops* spp. and *Calamus* spp. have potential for cultivation in plantations. There are more than 150 species of bamboo and about 20 species of wild crop relatives, including wild rices (*Oryza meyeriana, O. granulata* and *O. officinalis*).

Social and environmental values

The Hainan Endemic Bird Area (EBA) supports four threatened and restricted-range bird species, of which two, the Hainan partridge (*Arborophila ardens*) and the recently described Hainan leaf-warbler (*Phylloscopus hainanus*) (Olsson, Alström and Colston 1993) are endemic to the island. They are all forest birds, apparently restricted to montane areas in the centre and south of the island.

Hainan is known as China's "Precious Island", mainly because of the occurrence of dense tropical forests. The many places of historical interest and the beauty of its scenery make the island one of China's most popular and famous tourist attractions. In fact, Hainan attracts about one million tourists each year, most of these visitors coming to view the island's magnificent natural landscapes, tropical forests and wildlife. The tropical forests of Hainan are also important for scientific research.

Agriculture on Hainan is dependent upon natural forest cover for the regulation of the hydrological cycle. Natural forest cover helps to prevent soil erosion and thereby increases the life of reservoirs which are important for irrigation systems. By regulating the water regime, forests help to maintain pools and wells. They also contribute to the formation of topographic rain in mountainous areas. The loss of forest cover results in less rain, lower water-tables, increased rates of siltation of reservoirs and sudden changes in river flows, thereby increasing the risk of flooding and erosion. Conservation and sustainable utilization of the tropical forest is therefore of the utmost importance for the future development of the Hainan economy.

Economic assessment

The economy of Hainan depends on the resources of its tropical forests. There is no overall figure available for the amounts of forest products harvested from the wild, but about 1.5 million kg of medicinal plants are purchased annually. Tropical forest lianas are a major component of this trade. The increasing number of tourists who visit the island also provide a valuable income to the local economy.

Threats

A major threat to the flora is over-collection of wild plant resources, particularly medicinal plants. Species which are threatened include *Alpinia oxyphylla*, *Amomum villosum*, *Aquilaria sinensis*, *Nervilia fordii*, *Morinda officinalis* and *Maytenus hainanensis*. Illegal hunting of wild animals also occurs.

The Development Plan for Hainan stipulates that large-scale cutting of forest is illegal. However, cutting continues because regulations are not enforced due to lack of resources. Deforestation continues as more land is cleared for settled agriculture and shifting cultivation, while illegal cutting of trees for fuelwood also takes place. Being at the northernmost limit of tropical rain and monsoon forest, the tropical forests of Hainan are particularly fragile. When the canopy is opened up, exposed seedlings of climax trees are unable to survive.

Conservation

51 Nature Reserves (including marine reserves) have been established, covering a total area of about 1500 km². The existing terrestrial reserve system includes the major areas of importance for plants and includes a range of forest types. Reserves containing moist forests include Wuzhi Mountain Nature Reserve (187 km²), Bawangling Natural Protected Area (20 km²) and Jianfengling Natural Protected Area (16 km²) (Collins, Whitmore and Sayer 1991). However, effective management of the existing protected areas requires allocation of more funds and trained personnel. There is also a serious need to develop an environmental education programme to make local people more aware of their actions, to educate them about the importance of conservation and to involve them in the management of reserves. At present, there are plans to use a World Bank loan to establish a "Biodiversity Conservation Region".

References (Titles in Chinese have been translated.)

Botany Institute of Guangdong Province (1977). *Flora Hainanica*. Science Press, Beijing.

Collins, N.M., Sayer, J.A. and Whitmore, T.C. (eds) (1991). *The conservation atlas of tropical forests: Asia and the Pacific*. Macmillan, London. 256 pp.

Olsson, U., Alström, P. and Colston, P.R. (1993). A new species of *Phylloscopus* warbler from Hainan Island, China. *Ibis* 135: 2–7.

Wang Xianpu (Wang Huen-pu) (1982). Present situation and prospect of natural reserves in Hainan Island. *Natural Resources* 1: 4–8.

Wang Xianpu (1984). Relation between natural resources and the development of tourism in Hainan Island. *Guihaja* 4: 89–92.

Wang Xianpu (1988). Relation between the creation of Nature Reserves and the development of the economy of Hainan Island. *Rural Ecology Environment* 2: 32–34.

Wang Xianpu *et al.* (1990). The approach and exploitation of terrestrial biological resources and comprehensive agriculture. *Journal Biology* 2: 1–5.

Zhu Rui *et al.* (1988). *Handbook for exploitation of Hainan Island*. Science and Technology Press.

Acknowledgements

This Data Sheet was prepared by Professors Wang Xianpu and Yang Zhouhuai (Commission for Integrated Survey of Natural Resources, Chinese Academy of Sciences, Beijing) and Professor He Shan-an (Nanjing Botanic Garden Mem. Sun Yat-Sen, Nanjing).

XISHUANGBANNA REGION
Yunnan Province, China

Location: Xishuangbanna is located in southern Yunnan Province, approximately between latitudes 21°09'–22°36'N and longitudes 99°58'–101°50'E.

Area: 19,690 km² (natural forest 1978 km²).

Altitude: 500–2429 m (summit of Huazhulingze).

Vegetation: Tropical lowland seasonal (semi-evergreen) rain forest, tropical evergreen dipterocarp forest, seasonal rain forest over limestone, monsoon forest, montane seasonal rain forest, montane evergreen broadleaved forest.

Flora: c. 4000–4500 vascular plant species, of which 120 species are strictly endemic. Affinities with the floras of Indochina, Myanmā and Thailand.

Useful plants: Over 800 species of medicinal plants; 128 timber tree species; wild relatives of crops and fruit trees.

Other values: The forests play an important role in water resource conservation and climatic amelioration, and have a rich fauna, including 25% of China's mammal species.

Threats: Slash and burn agriculture, population pressure, clearance for plantation crops, illegal logging, hunting.

Conservation: 5 Nature Reserves, with a total area of 2416 km², include all the major plant-rich areas. The main requirement is for effective management.

Geography

The Dai Autonomous Prefecture of Xishuangbanna is an undulating and mountainous region covering 19,690 km² in southern Yunnan Province, near the border with Myanmā and Laos. The region has many broad valleys and basins surrounded by low mountains and hills. The average elevation is 500–1000 m, with numerous peaks reaching 1500 m. The highest peak is Huazhulingze (2429 m). The mountains consist mainly of metamorphic rocks, phyllite, red sandstone and granite. Soils are acidic laterites and mountain red earths. In some places, there are limestone soils and purple soils with neutral to slightly alkaline reactions.

The climate is similar to that of north-east India and Myanmā. There are two distinct seasons. From April to October, the region is under the influence of the South-west Monsoon originating from the Bay of Bengal. This gives rise to tropical conditions of high humidity and high temperatures. From November to March, the region is under the influence of westerly winds from the subtropics. During this period the weather is drier with intense solar radiation. In the hottest month (June), temperatures range from 15.5° to 21.7°C, while, in the coldest month (January), temperatures drop to between 8.8° and 15.6°C. The mean annual rainfall varies from 1194 to 2492 mm, depending on location, with most of the region receiving 1200–1675 mm. Most of the rain occurs in July and August, with over 250 mm per month. February, the only dry month, has 20 mm of rain.

The total population of the region is about 644,000 and the annual rate of increase is 2% per annum. Some 200,000 people depend on slash and burn cultivation. Of these, about 14,000 live within Nature Reserves (Wadley 1990).

Vegetation

Xishuangbanna is the largest remaining area of tropical forest in China. It lies at the northern limit of the Asian moist tropics and, as a result of the seasonal pattern of rainfall, the vegetation is different from that in the everwet tropics in Malesia. Below 800 m, species-rich tropical lowland seasonal (semi-evergreen) rain forest occurs, in which no single species dominates. The main species present are *Barringtonia pendula*, *Dracontomelon macrocarpum*, *Epiprinus siletianus*, *Garcinia tinctoria*, *Homalium laoticum*, *Horsfieldia tetratepala*, *Knema linifolia*, *Myristica yunnanensis*, *Phaeanthus saccopeloides*, *Pometia tomentosa* and *Terminalia myriocarpa*. Tropical evergreen dipterocarp forest is confined to small, low-lying, moist valleys and is dominated by *Parashorea chinensis* and *Vatica xishuangbannaensis*.

Seasonal rain forest developed over limestone has a very different composition from the above forest types. The main species here are *Antiaris toxicaria*, *Celtis cinnamomifolia*, *C. wightii*, *Cleistanthus sumatranus*, *Garuga floribunda*, *Pterospermum menglunense*, *Tetrameles nudiflora*, *Ulmus lanceaefolia* and *Xantolis stenopetala*.

Between 800 and 1000 m, montane seasonal rain forest occurs. This includes *Dysoxylum gobara*, *Lithocarpus corneus*, *Mangifera sylvatica* (a mango), *Nephelium chryseum* (rambutan), *Phoebe nanmu*, *Podocarpus imbricatus*, *Pouteria grandifolia*, *Semecarpus reticulata* and *Xanthophyllum siamense*. Seasonal rain forests are often replaced by monsoon forest in drier areas. Common monsoon forest trees include *Bombax malabarica*, *Chukrasia tabularis* var. *velutina*, *Erythrina stricta*, *Ficus fulva*, *Gmelina arborea*, *Macaranga denticulata*, *Stereospermum tetragonum* and *Trema orientalis*.

At 1000–2000 m, montane evergreen broadleaved forest occurs. The species composition is quite different from that of tropical rain forest, with chestnuts (such as *Castanopsis carlesii* var. *spinulosa*, *C. echinocarpa*, *C. hystrix*, *C. indica* and *C. mekongensis*) and oaks (such as *Lithocarpus truncatus*, *L. fenestrata* and *Cyclobalanopsis kerrii*) much in evidence. The Szemao pine (*Pinus kesiya* var. *langbianensis*) also forms forests at these elevations. Clearance of montane forest has resulted in large areas becoming colonized by *Alnus nepalensis* (Nepal alder) forest.

Natural forest covers 1978 km² (10% of the total area), a stark figure in comparison with the 15,752 km² present in 1958. The total volume of standing timber is 39,600,000 m³, with each hectare of forest having an average of 200 m³ of standing timber. Standing timber stocks of *Parashorea chinensis* are up to 1000 m³ ha⁻¹.

Flora

The Xishuangbanna region is a meeting point of South Asian and East Asian tropical and subtropical climate zones. Its flora has a mixture of tropical and subtropical elements from South Asia and East Asia. Although occupying only 0.2% of the total land area of China, the region contains about 7% of China's vascular flora. There are estimated to be about 4000–4500 vascular plant species in Xishuangbanna, including 120 species which are endemic to the region.

The main floristic affinities are with Indochina, Myanmā and Thailand. Apart from Indomalayan elements, there are many tropical Chinese endemic elements and pantropical species. The flora also contains many ancient relict species. In terms of species numbers, the most important families are Meliaceae, Sapindaceae, Moraceae, Euphorbiaceae, Leguminosae, Rubiaceae, Sapotaceae, Annonaceae, Burseraceae and Guttiferae. Other important families are Dipterocarpaceae, Crypteroniaceae, Tetrameliaceae, Sterculiaceae and Combretaceae. At elevations over 1000 m, subtropical East Asian elements are found. Notable families include Fagaceae, Lauraceae, Magnoliaceae and Theaceae.

Useful plants

There are a large number of species used locally, sold in markets or which are of industrial importance. Among them are more than 800 medicinal plant species, 182 species of timber trees, 150 species yielding oils, 134 species of wild fruits and ornamental plants, 90 species supplying fibres, 62 species providing aromatic compounds, 39 species used as sources of starch, 38 species which are important crop germplasm resources and 32 species which supply resin.

Among important medicinal plants are: *Cephalotaxus mannii*, *Gloriosa superba*, *Marsdenia tenacissima*, *Maytenus hookeri* and *M. austroyunnanensis*, all used traditionally for the treatment of cancer; *Paris polyphylla* and *Hydnocarpus anthelminthicus* (the chaulmoogra tree), which form the basis of the product "Yunnan white medicine", a cure for leprosy; and the Yunnan devil pepper *Rauvolfia yunnanensis*.

Wild relatives of rice (*Oryza* spp.), tea (*Camellia* spp.), litchi (*Litchi* spp.), citrus fruits (*Citrus* spp.), mango (*Mangifera* spp.), balsam pear (*Momordica subangulata*), cucumber (*Cucurbita* spp.) and ginseng (*Panax zingiberensis*) are found throughout the region. In many places, the understorey of the forest has been cleared for the cultivation of medicinal wild ginger (*Amomum villosum*).

Social and environmental values

Xishuangbanna is known in China as "Green Treasure". The region has a rich avifauna of c. 410 species of birds (35% of the national total), including many South East Asian and East Himalayan species not found elsewhere in China. These include the threatened Hume's pheasant (*Syrmaticus humiae*), green peafowl (*Pavo muticus*), Blyth's kingfisher (*Alcedo hercules*), rufous-necked hornbill (*Aceros nipalensis*) and giant nuthatch (*Sitta magna*). The region also has about 200 species of fish (25% of the national total) and 120 species of mammal (25% of the national total, including 30% of the protected species). Among the mammals are Asian elephant (*Elephas maximus*) (one of the few places in China where this species is found), gaur (*Bos gaurus)* and gibbon (*Hylobates concolor leucogenys*).

The natural forests of this region have special significance for climate amelioration, water and soil conservation, crop improvement and scientific research.

The region is becoming increasingly important as a tourist attraction. Approximately 1 million people visit the region annually, mostly to experience the tropical forest scenery and wildlife.

Economic assessment

The economy of the region is largely dependent on forest products and the ecological services provided by a forest cover, but there are no figures available for the total monetary value of such products and services. The increasing number of tourists to the region also provides a valuable contribution to the local economy.

Threats

Large-scale deforestation began in 1950, mainly for agriculture. In the early 1950s, natural forest covered c. 60% of the area, but only 32% remained by 1981, a decrease of 2% per year (Jiang Youxu 1986). Today, some 28% of the region is forest covered, but natural forests cover just 1978 km² (c. 10% of the total area). About 2000 km² (10% of the area) is affected by shifting cultivation. In addition, there are 420 km² of paddy fields, c. 110 km² of tea plantations and 670 km² of rubber plantations. The current target is to expand rubber to cover an area of 1000 km² (about 5% of the whole Prefecture). Non-productive land (mostly degraded forest resulting from previous shifting cultivation) covers c. 47% of the entire region. Some of this will eventually regenerate to productive forest given time, but much will remain as *Imperata cylindrica* grassland or covered in weeds such as *Dendrocalamus* and *Eupatorium*. (Land use figures from Mackinnon 1987.)

The loss of rain forest and the increasingly large areas given over to shifting agriculture, unterraced dryland farming and plantations, have led to accelerated soil erosion in the

Xishuangbanna region. Although large-scale logging is now controlled, about 150 km² of forest are still cleared annually. The main threats are expanding agriculture, especially slash and burn cultivation, and illegal timber cutting. Hunting is a threat to some of the forest animals. Migration of peasant farmers to the region has been a long-term threat; the influx of migrants continues.

Conservation

In 1980, 5 Nature Reserves were established in the region. They have a combined total area of 2416 km² (c. 12% of the region). The reserves are: Mengla Natural Reserve (929 km²), Menglun Natural Reserve (112 km²), Shangyong Natural Reserve (305 km²), Mengyang Natural Reserve (997 km²) and Mangao Natural Reserve (73 km²). The existing reserve system includes all the major plant-rich areas, as well as representative samples of all the vegetation types. However, effective management of the reserves is needed to ensure conservation and sustainable utilization. Environmental education programmes are needed to increase awareness among local people concerning the importance of conservation and to involve them in the management of reserves and forested areas.

The Xishuangbanna rain forest has been the focus of a WWF project concentrating on elephant protection and assisting government efforts in the development of wildlife-based industries (such as butterfly farming), agroforestry, nature tourism, establishment of buffer zones around reserves and resettlement of villagers away from reserve core areas.

References (Titles in Chinese have been translated.)

Comprehensive Survey Team to Xishuangbanna Nature Reserve (1987). *Nature Reserve of Xishuangbanna.* Science Press of Yunnan Province.

Jiang Youxu (1986). Ecological exploitation of tropical plant resources in China. *INTERCOL Bulletin* 13: 13–75.

MacKinnon, J. (1987). Ecological guidelines for the development of Xishuangbanna Prefecture, Yunnan Province, China. WWF, Gland, Switzerland. (Unpublished draft report.)

Wadley, H.E. (1990). WWF 3194 – China, development of a management plan for Xishuangbanna (agroforestry). 10 pp. (Unpublished report for WWF.)

Wang Xianpu (Wang Huen-pu) (1984). From the information of Xishuangbanna to discuss the creation of the Nature Reserve. *Environmental Protection* 11: 2–5.

Wang Xianpu (1985). About the management and the basic characteristics of the Menglun Nature Reserve of Xishuangbanna, Yunnan Province. *Natural Resources* 4: 78–82.

Wang Xianpu (1985). About the concept and application of joint management of the Nature Reserve – taking the Menglun Nature Reserve as an example. *Vegetation of Guangxi* 5(4): 409–412.

Wang Xianpu (1986). Environmental and socio-economic aspects of tropical deforestation in China. In United Nations and ESCAP, *Environmental and social-economic aspects of tropical deforestation in Asia and the Pacific.* United Nations and ESCAP, Bangkok. Pp. 65–71.

Wang Xianpu *et al.* (1987). Prospect of the creation of Xishuangbanna Nature Reserve in Yunnan Province. *Vegetation of Guangxi* 7(3): 245–250.

Wang Xianpu, Sing-chi and Wang Si-yu (1989). China. In Campbell, D.G. and Hammond, D. (eds), *Floristic inventory of tropical countries: the status of plant systematics collections and vegetation, plus recommendations for the future.* New York Botanical Garden, New York. Pp. 35–43.

Xu Zaifu *et al.* (1982). *Research on reservation of germplasm resources of tropical plants in Xishuangbanna. Collected papers on tropical botany.* Yunnan Press.

Acknowledgements

This Data Sheet was prepared by Professors Wang Xianpu and Yang Zhouhuai (Commission for Integrated Survey of Natural Resources, Chinese Academy of Sciences, Beijing) and Professor He Shan-an (Nanjing Botanic Garden Mem. Sun Yat-Sen, Nanjing).

LIMESTONE REGION
Zhuang Autonomous Region, Guangxi Province, China

Location: South-western Zhuang Autonomous Region of Guangxi and the Zuojiang and Youjiang river basins, between latitudes 21°58'–23°28'N and longitudes 105°40'–108°06'E.

Area: 20,000 km².

Altitude: 100–1300 m.

Vegetation: Seasonal rain forest, monsoon forest, montane evergreen broadleaved forest, limestone semi-deciduous broadleaved mixed forest.

Flora: 2500–3000 vascular plant species, mostly tropical Indomalayan elements; many endemic species.

Useful plants: >1000 species used by local people. Timber trees, medicinal plants, ornamental plants.

Other values: The largest area of limestone in the tropics; spectacular karst landscape; many endemic animals.

Threats: Illegal felling of trees, illegal hunting, lack of conservation awareness programme for local people.

Conservation: 11 Nature Reserves (total area: 4000 km²). The urgent need is for effective management.

Geography

This area includes the whole limestone region of Zhuang Autonomous Region of Guangxi and the basins of the Zuojiang and Youjiang rivers. It is located between latitudes 21°58'–23°28'N and longitudes 105°40'–108°06'E, and has a total area of 20,000 km². The population of the region is 3,000,000, increasing by 2% annually.

The geology of the region is Devonian to Permian limestone of pure quality. The karst landforms include limestone peaks protruding from forest, occupying over 50% of the total area. There are also hills and low mountains composed of granite, metamorphic rock and sandy shale. Limestone outcrops have shallow brown rendzina and black limestone soils (pH 6.0–7.8). In the mountainous granitic and sandy shale areas, soils are laterites, lateritic red earth and yellow soils. Their reaction is acidic (pH 4.5–5.5). The region is highest in the north-west, where it attains 1300 m; the south-east is lower (200–500 m). Mountains encircle the area on three sides (east, west and south). The valleys of the Zuojiang, Youjiang and Yongjiang rivers are at 100–120 m.

The mean annual temperature is 19.1–22°C. In the coldest month (January) mean temperatures are 10.9–13.9°C. Mean monthly temperatures higher than 22°C occur from April/May to September/October, the hottest month (July) having temperatures of 25.1–28.4°C. Even though this region is at the same latitude as Xishuangbanna (CPD Site EA29, see Data Sheet), winters are cold and minimum temperatures can drop below 0°C. Annual precipitation is 1000–1500 mm. Most rainfall (80%) occurs between April–September.

The dry season occurs at the same time as the cold season, but the humidity of the air is high (relative humidity >75%), thus alleviating drought. As a result, evergreen broadleaved mesophytes are important components of the vegetation.

Vegetation

The region lies at the northern limit of the tropical zone. The dominant vegetation below 700 m is seasonal rain forest varying in species composition according to soils and microhabitat. The main species in lowland limestone areas surrounding limestone mountains and in wet valleys are *Horsfieldia hainanensis*, *Parashorea chinensis* var. *kwangsiensis*, *Deutzianthus tonkinensis*, *Dracontomelon duperreanum*, *Ailanthus guangxiensis* and *Saraca chinensis*. Species at mid-altitudes include *Burretiodendron hsienmu*, *Garcinia paucinervis*, *Cephalomappa sinensis*, *Drypetes perreticulata*, *Hydnocarpus hainanensis*, *Walsura robusta*, *Cleistanthus petelotii* and *Streblus tonkinensis*. Common species on the tops of lowland limestone hills are *Cleistanthus* sp., *Planchonella pedunculata* and *Sterculia euosma*. Seasonal rain forest on granite and sandy shale contains a different assemblage of tree species, including *Knema guangxiensis*, *Canarium pimela*, *C. album*, *Artocarpus styracifolius*, *Madhuca subquincurcialis*, *Xerospermum guangxiensis* and *Horsfieldia amygdalina*.

In areas where seasonal rain forest has been destroyed, the environment is drier and large areas of monsoon forest appear. The main species in limestone areas include *Sterculia lanceolata*, *Bischofia javanica*, *Mallotus philippinensis* and *Rademachera hainanensis*. On acid soils, these species are replaced by *Liquidambar formosana*, *Albizia chinensis*, *Schima wallichii*, *Macaranga denticulata*, *Trema orientalis* and *Schefflera octophylla*.

On acid soils above 700 m, the main trees are *Castanopsis hystrix*, *C. kawakami*, *Cryptocarya concinna* and *Beilschmiedia percoriacea*. Semi-deciduous forest on limestone mountains contains *Cyclobalanopsis glauca*, *Cinnamomum calcarea*, *Pteroceltis tatarinowii*, *Celtis sinensis*, *Ulmus parvifolia* and *Platycarya strobilacea*.

Flora

The region is transitional between the north tropical and subtropical zones and, as a result of variations in climate and soils, the flora is rich. There are an estimated 2500–3000 species of vascular plants, 88% being tropical, mainly components of the Indomalayan and Sino-Vietnam floras. There are many endemic species, including 30 endemic species of *Camellia* on the limestone mountains. Species in the following families are well-represented in the flora: Euphorbiaceae, Leguminosae, Moraceae, Meliaceae, Sapindaceae, Anacardiaceae, Annonaceae, Sapotaceae and Burseraceae. There are also some dipterocarps and members of the nutmeg family, Myristicaceae. On mountains over 700 m, tropical East Asian floristic elements are well-represented. The special character of the limestone flora is shown by the fact that only 28% of species occur also on acidic soils nearby. Over the whole region, over 80% of the genera are shared with the Sino-Indian region and Hainan Island; only 40% of the genera are shared with the subtropical zone of north-east Guangdong. This indicates that the flora of this north tropical zone has a special character of its own.

Useful plants

Local people use nearly 1000 species of plants for a variety of purposes. The numbers of species used for different purposes are as follows: medicine (74), timber (80), sources of starch (52), oil (70), fibre (150), rubber (25), fodder (82), wild fruits (38), brewing (21), tanning (32), host plants for lac insects (16), aromatic uses (60), ornamental plants (105), honey production (21), vegetables (26), pesticides (35), as green fertilizer (33), for dyeing (22) and resin (10). If these species come to be used industrially, there will be a shortage of wild plant resources and plantations will be required. So far, the following species are established in plantations: *Burretiodendron hsienmu* (timber), *Maytenus confertiflora* (medicinal), *Cleistanthus saichikii* (treating cancer), *Picria felterrae* (pain relief and reducing inflammation), *Stephania* spp., *Aristolochia longgangensis* and *Premna fulva*.

Social and environmental values

The limestone area of Guangxi extends over about 20,000 km², making it one of the largest areas of limestone anywhere in the tropics or subtropics. Endemic species are continually being discovered. The forests support a rich fauna, including the white-headed leaf monkey (*Presbytis leucocephalus*). Many newly discovered insects have yet to be named. Detailed surveys and other research are needed.

The landscape is comparable with that of Guilin in Guangxi Zhuang Autonomous Region, which also has spectacular karst features and steep peaks. There are many places of historical and cultural interest, including rock drawings more than 2000 years old. The area has great potential for archaeological research and tourism. Currently, there are about 150,000 visitors annually.

Economic assessment

This region abounds with valuable hardwood timber trees, such as *Burretiodendron hsienmu*, which is exported to South East Asia. Large trees of this species only occur today in remote places. Plantations are being established. Leaves of *Cepahalomappa sinensis* provide a valuable fodder and this species has an important role to play in the development of agriculture, particularly in the raising of cattle and goats. Many animals are hunted for food and skins, but this should be controlled to avoid over-exploitation.

Threats

Large-scale timber cutting and uncontrolled burning are no longer problems but small-scale illegal cutting of timber and illegal hunting still occur. As a result, large trees of *Burretiodendron hsienmu* have disappeared and many wild animals have been seriously reduced in numbers, including the white-headed leaf monkey, which is now threatened. One of the problems has been a lack of involvement of local people in efforts to conserve species and habitats. A conservation management plan and a public awareness programme needs to be developed.

Conservation

There are 11 Nature Reserves with a total area of about 4000 km². The main reserves are Nonggang Nature Reserve (80 km²), Longrui Nature Reserve (23 km²), Fusui Nature Reserve (80 km²), Chongzuo Nature Reserve (300 km²), Nongmei Nature Reserve (240 km²), Longhushan Nature Reserve (3 km²) and Xialei Nature Reserve (79 km²). A regional management plan is needed, including an awareness programme to involve local people in conservation efforts. There is a need for more conservation and scientific research, and environmental education. The plan needs to address the links between production, tourism and conservation, so that multiple uses can be properly planned. Further plantations of over-harvested wild plants should be established.

References (Titles in Chinese have been translated.)

Agriculture College of Guangxi, Department of Forestry (1978). *Ecology of Excentrodendron hsienmu and afforestation.* Research Report of Plant Ecology, Science Press. Pp. 1–96.

Comprehensive Survey Team of Nonggang Nature Reserve (1988). *Report on comprehensive survey of Nonggang Reserve, Guangxi, Guihaia Additamentum.* Pp. 1–293.

Hu Shunshi *et al.* (1980). Community characteristics of seasonal rainforest in the limestone area of Guangxi. *J. Northeast Forestry College* 4: 11–26.

Li Xiangdong (1982). *About the rational exploitation in limestone mountains of southwest of Guangxi.* Papers of Ecological Balance of the Construction in Mountainous and Hilly Areas of Tropical and Subtropical Zone, Science Popularization Press. Pp. 2–45.

Wang Xianpu (Wang Huen-pu) (1984). About the management in Nongmei Nature Reserve from the point of view of the function and meanings of the Nature Reserve. *Guihaia* 4(4): 353–354.

Wang Xianpu (1985). About the management of Longrui Mountain Nature Reserve of Guangxi. *Wild Animals* 4: 1–4.

Wang Xianpu (1988a). About management and character of the Juesui Precious Animals Reserve in Guangxi. *Wild Animals* 5: 15–16.

Wang Xianpu (1988b). The feature and management of the Precious Animals Reserve in Juesui of Guangxi. *Guihaia* 7(1): 53–70.

Wang Xianpu *et al.* (1985). The effective management and characteristics of the Longrui Nature Reserve of Guangxi. *World Environment* 2: 16–18.

Wang Xianpu *et al.* (1986). *Burretiodendron hsienmu*: its ecology and production. *Arnoldia* 46(4): 46–51.

Acknowledgements

This Data Sheet was prepared by Professors Wang Xianpu and Yang Zhouhuai (Commission for Integrated Survey of Natural Resources, Chinese Academy of Sciences, Beijing) and Professor He Shan-an (Nanjing Botanic Garden Mem. Sun Yat-Sen, Nanjing).

HIGH MOUNTAIN AND DEEP GORGE REGION, HENGDUAN MOUNTAINS AND MIN JIANG RIVER BASIN
Sichuan Province, China

Location: East slopes of Qiaolai Mountains, on the right bank of the upper reaches of Min Jiang River, in the northern part of the Hengduan Mountains, south-west Wenxian County, Sichuan Province; c. 30°40'–31°30'N, 102°30'–103°30'E.

Area: c. 4000 km² (area of high biological diversity).

Altitude: 600–6250 m.

Vegetation: Evergreen broadleaved forest, semi-deciduous broadleaved forest, mixed coniferous broadleaved forest, subalpine coniferous broadleaved mixed forest, scrub and meadow, alpine vegetation. In some lowland valleys, there are small areas of dry river valley scrub.

Flora: Estimated >4000 species of vascular plants; many Sino-Japanese and Sino-Himalayan elements; locally, some Mediterranean elements.

Useful plants: Medicinal plants, timber trees, oil and starch plants, plants yielding sugar.

Other values: Forests provide catchment protection for the Yangtze River basin and habitat for giant panda; scientific research; educational resource; locality for training park personnel; tourism.

Threats: Illegal cutting of trees, hunting, increasing tourism, road building through the core area.

Conservation: Wolong Nature Reserve (2000 km²), which forms part of the Wolong Biosphere Reserve (2072.1 km²), contains much of the floristic diversity of the region. Management needs strengthening.

Geography

The area under consideration includes the upper reaches of the Min Jiang River in south-west Wenxian County, Sichuan Province. The area includes the eastern slopes of Qiaolai Mountains in the northern part of the Hengduan Mountains, between latitudes 30°40'–31°30'N and longitudes 102°30'–103°30'E. The area is 60 km from east to west and 60 km from north to south. The total area of the High Mountain and Deep Gorge Region of Min Jiang River Basin is c. 200,000 km², of which c. 4000 km² has exceptionally high biological diversity. The region is transitional between the high mountain and deep valley region of the Sichuan Basin and the Qinghai-Xizang Plateau. The Longmen Mountain Range trends north-east/south-west across the whole region. The altitude ranges from 1200 m in the east at Majiangping to 6250 m in the north-west at Siguning Mountain (the second highest peak in Sichuan). This is a vertical difference of 5000 m over only 50 km. The river valley on the south-east periphery of the Wolong Reserve is at c. 600 m. The region is dissected by V-shaped valleys. The Qiaolai Mountains consist mainly of phyllite, quartzite, granite and limestone. Soil types include mountain yellow earth, yellow brown earth, brown forest soil, podzolized brown forest soil, alpine meadow soil and high mountain, cold desert soil. Most soils are acidic, with pH values of 4.5–6.0.

The climate is influenced by the proximity of the Qinghai-Xizang Plateau. Three sides are surrounded by mountains so that, in winter, cold currents from the north are blocked by the mountains. In summer, the South-east Monsoon brings high rainfall. As a result, winters are relatively mild and summers are warm and humid. The mean annual temperature at 1448 m (Wenchuan City) is 12.7°C and at 1920 m (Wolong Nature Reserve) 8.4°C. The coldest month is January, when mean monthly temperatures at 1448 m and 1920 m are 2.4°C and -6.4°C respectively; mean temperatures of the hottest month (July) are 21.9°C and 17.6°C at these two locations. Mean annual precipitation is 516 mm at Wenchuan and 861 mm at Wolong. However, rainfall in the south-east part of Wolong can reach 1419 mm.

Vegetation

The region lies at the transition between the subtropical zone and the Qinghai-Xizang Plateau. There is very distinct vegetational zonation. Generally, below 1600 m, evergreen broadleaved forest is predominant, but species composition varies. Some of the commonest species below 1000 m are *Castanopsis ceratacantha, C. fargesii, Lithocarpus megalophyllus, L. spicata* and *L. viridis.* There are also many Lauraceae, such as *Actinodaphne omeiensis, A. trichocarpa, Cinnamomum wilsonii, C. mairei, Lindera megaphylla, Machilus microcarpa, M. pingii, Phoebe zhannan, P. chinensis, Nothaphoebe cavaleriei* and *Neocinnamomum fargesii.* Between 1000 and 1600 m the dominant species are *Cyclobalanopsis glauca, C. oxyodon, Lithocarpus cleistocarpus, Cinnamomum longepaniculatum* and *Lindera limprichtii.* Dry hot valley scrub in the south-west of the region includes *Caryopteris mongholica, Ajania potaninii* and *Ceratostigma willmottianum.*

At 1600–2000 m, deciduous broadleaved trees gradually replace evergreen trees, forming a unique type of semi-deciduous broadleaved montane forest. Evergreen trees are mainly those already mentioned. Common deciduous trees

**CPD Site EA40: High Mountain and Deep Gorge region,
Hengduan Mountains and Min Jiang River Basin,
Sichuan Province, China. Wolong Biosphere Reserve.**
Photo: Jim Thorsell.

include *Aesculus wilsonii, Davidia involucrata, Tetracentron sinense* and *Juglans cathayensis.* At 2000–2600 m, the forest contains both coniferous and broadleaved trees, the former predominating, notably *Tsuga chinensis, T. dumosa* and *Picea brachytyla* var. *complanata.* Some hardy deciduous broadleaved trees are found among the conifers; these include *Acer caudatum* var. *pratii, A. maximowiczii, A. stachyophyllum* and *Betula utilis* var. *sinensis.*

Subalpine coniferous forest is found at 2600–3600 m, with coniferous species dominating on northern slopes. There is a large area of *Abies faxoniana,* while less abundant species include *Abies ernestii, A. faxoniana, A. recurvata, Picea asperata, P. purpurea, P. wilsonii* and, in some places, *Pinus densata.* Giant panda (*Ailuropoda melanoleuca*) live in this area.

At 3600–4600 m, the vegetation is alpine scrub and meadow. Common shrubs include *Rhododendron violaceum, Spiraea alpina, Cassiope fastigiata* and *Potentilla fruticosa.* Alpine meadows include *Kobresia humilis, Anaphalis flavescens* and *Meconopsis punicea.* At 4600–5200 m, the mean temperature in the hottest month (July) is below -3°C. There are only some scarce patches of grass and herbs among the rocks and scree. Common plants include *Saussurea obvollata, S. medusa, Saxifraga confertifolia, Eriophyton wallichii, Androsace tapete, Meconopsis horridula* and *Arenaria kansuensis.*

Flora

There are estimated to be more than 4000 species of vascular plants in the region, making it one of the richest areas for plants in East Asia. The region was little influenced by climatic changes during the Quaternary. As a result, the flora contains many relict species. There are many endemic elements of the subtropical zone of China, as well as many Sino-Japanese and Sino-Himalayan elements. Mediterranean elements are also present. Of the species endemic to the south-west mountain region, about 263 species belonging to 36 genera occur in Wolong Nature Reserve, including three endemic rhododendrons (*Rhododendron balangense, R. longesquamatum* var. *sessilifolium* and *R. wolongense*). Tertiary relicts include *Acer cappadocicum* var. *tricaudatum* and *A. fulvescens.* There are also more recently evolved species, such as *Acer caudatum, A. giraldii, A. maximowiczii* and *A. tetramerum.*

Useful plants

The High Mountain and Deep Gorge region of the Hengduan Mountains is part of the second largest forested area in China. It represents a vast genepool of valuable timber tree provenances, which could be used in plantation forestry elsewhere. Notable timber trees are *Abies fabri, A. faxoniana, Larix mastersiana* and *Picea brachytyla.*

More than 870 species of medicinal plants are known from the area, including *Gastrodia elata, Fritillaria cirrhosa, Coptis chinensis, Astragalus sinensis, Magnolia officinalis, Notopterygium incisum, Heracleum hemsleyanum, Saussurea medusa* and *Rheum palmatum.* The annual harvest of medicinal plants purchased for trade is 1.5 million kg. Other useful plants include: *Daphne retusa* and *Debregeasia edulis* for fibres; *Platycarpa strobilacea* and *Rhus chinensis* for tannins; *Cinnamomum longepaniculatum* and *Litsea pungens* for perfumes; *Corylus chinensis* and *Rosa roxburghii* for starch and carbohydrates; and *Coriaria sinica* and *Litsea cureba* for oils.

Social and environmental values

The forests are extremely important for the protection of water catchments. The protection afforded by forests ensures comparatively little difference between dry and rainy season river flows: river levels rise only slowly after about 12 hours of heavy rain and then gradually decrease. As a result, floods along the Min Jiang River are prevented, there is little run-off and therefore little erosion, and the water resources of 10 counties in the Cheng Du Plain are assured.

About 10% of the world's giant pandas live in the region. Many other rare animals occur here, including the golden-haired monkey (*Rhinopithecus bieti*), takin (*Budorcas taxicolor*) and Thorold's deer (*Cervus albirostris*). An estimated 20% of all of China's species of birds and mammal species occur in the region, making it of considerable importance for scientific research, ecological monitoring, education and training.

The spectacular mountain scenery, including deep gorges, steep cliffs, forest-clad mountain slopes and many rivers, makes this area of great value for tourism.

Economic assessment

The forest protects water resources along the whole Yangtze River basin. Hydroelectric power provides 750,000 kW every year. The rivers also supply water for drinking, irrigation and for the brewing industry. Although it is now illegal to cut timber trees or gather medicinal or other plants directly from the forests, wild plants can be used as germplasm resources and for supplying seedlings for introduction elsewhere, for agriculture, forestry and animal husbandry. There is also great potential for ecotourism; Wolong Nature Reserve (which is not formally open to visitors and is rather remote) receives about 250,000 visitors a year. Ecologically sensitive management of the region would provide long-lasting economic benefits to a large part of China.

Threats

Timber cutting, over-collection of medicinal plants, hunting and cultivation on steep slopes are all legally prohibited, but illegal cutting of timber trees, harvesting of medicinal plants and hunting still occur. Even giant panda are sometimes hunted. A highway from Chengdu to Aba County has been constructed in the core area of Wolong Nature Reserve. It is now the main highway from Sichuan to Xizang and is a serious cause of disturbance to giant panda. *Fritillaria* spp. and *Gastrodia elata* are seriously threatened by over-collection.

Conservation

Wolong Nature Reserve (2000 km²) was established in 1962; it is the largest reserve in China and forms part of the Wolong Biosphere Reserve (2072.1 km²). It contains much of the floristic diversity of the region, though a further 2000 km² nearby is also rich. A joint project was initiated in 1981 between the reserve authorities and WWF to establish "The

World Institute for Conservation of the Giant Panda" and to undertake research on the conservation of giant panda. The project is also concerned with sustainable utilization of the biological resources of the area and assistance with economic development, thus contributing to the raising of living standards of the local population (c. 1000 people) who live near the reserve. Management of the reserve still needs to be strengthened.

References (Titles in Chinese have been translated.)

Gao Chengzhun *et al.* (1986). *The characteristics of vertical natural zonation in the northern part of Mount Hengduan: studies in Qinghai-Xizang (Tibet) Plateau. Special Issue of Hengduan Mountains Scientific Expedition, 2.* Beijing Science and Technology Press. Pp. 156–167.

Management Bureau of Wolong Nature Reserve *et al.* (1987). *Wolong Nature Reserve and plant resources.* Sichuan Science Press.

Vegetation Cooperation Group of Sichuan (1980). *Vegetation of Sichuan Province.* Sichuan People Press.

Zhong Xianghao *et al.* (1983). *A preliminary study on the natural vertical zonation in the middle part of the eastern periphery of Qinghai-Xizang Plateau. Study on Qinghai-Xizang Plateau. Special Issue of Hengduan Mountains Scientific Expedition, 1.* Yunnan People Press. Pp. 106–113.

Acknowledgements

This Data Sheet was prepared by Professors Wang Xianpu and Yang Zhouhuai (Commission for Integrated Survey of Natural Resources, Chinese Academy of Sciences, Beijing) and Professor He Shan-an (Nanjing Botanic Garden Mem. Sun Yat-Sen, Nanjing).

KENTING NATIONAL PARK
Taiwan

Location: Southern tip of Taiwan; between latitudes 21°54'–22°05'N and longitudes 120°41'–120°53'E.

Area: 177 km² (a further 149 km² of Kenting National Park is marine).

Altitude: 0–526 m (summit of Nanjen Shan).

Vegetation: Evergreen broadleaved rain forest, semi-deciduous seasonal (monsoon) forest, littoral forest, grassland, coral reef vegetation, sclerophyll forest, scrub.

Flora: c. 1350 vascular plant species (c. 33% of Taiwan's flora), including c. 160 Taiwan endemic species (c. 15% of Taiwan's endemic species); c. 68 species (5% of the park's flora) are strictly endemic. Many taxa are at the northern limits of their ranges.

Useful plants: Timber trees, medicinal plants, ornamental plants, genetic resources for agriculture and forestry.

Other values: Watershed protection, wildlife refuge, tourism.

Threats: Visitor pressure at certain sites, grazing, illegal plant collection, military construction.

Conservation: National Park; generally well-protected but threatened in places by visitor pressure.

Geography

Kenting National Park is located at the southernmost tip of Hengchun Peninsula, which itself extends southwards from the mountains of the Central Range, the backbone of the island of Taiwan. It covers a land area of 177 km² (a further 149 km² are marine). The area includes hilly terrain and low mountains, ranging from sea-level to 526 m at the summit of Nanjen Shan.

There are two major physiographic regions separated by fault-lines: the north-east region (Nanjenshan Mountain region) and the south-west region. The north-east comprises Miocene sandstones and shales and has yellow-brown lateritic soils. The south-west region can be divided into two sub-regions. One of these, the Hengchun-Kenting area, is centrally situated and comprises Miocene to late Pleistocene turbidites overlain by mudstones, soft sandstones and limestone. Soils are reddish-brown laterites. There are also raised coral reefs. The second sub-region is the West Hengchun Hill area, comprising Pliocene to Pleistocene sediments with fringing reefs and limestone; there are large tracts of reddish-brown lateritic soil (Cheng, Huang and Liew 1986; Su and Su 1988).

The Hengchun Peninsula has two distinct climatic zones, everwet on the east coast and summer rain on the west (Su 1985a). In the south-west region of Kenting National Park, the mean annual temperature in the lowlands is 24°C, with the mean temperature of the hottest month (July) being 27.5°C and that of the coldest month (January) 20.5°C. The north-east mountain region is subject to a lapse rate of 0.8°C per 100 m in winter months (Su 1984a) and elevations above 200 m have a subtropical-type climate (Su 1984b). Rainfall is influenced by monsoons, with most (80%) occurring in summer months. The annual rainfall ranges from 2000 mm in the lowlands in the south-west to 3500 mm in the north-east. There is a distinct dry season of 4–5 months in the winter in the south-west due to rain-shadow effects. In contrast, there is no dry season in the north-east.

Vegetation

There are two main forest formations: monsoon rain forest in the north-east and moist monsoon forest in the south-west (Su and Su 1988). In addition, there are 4 other important forest formations and 7 more local forest formations as a result of local physiography (Su 1985b).

The north-east (Najenshan) region is mostly covered by evergreen broadleaved rain forests of tropical, subtropical and warm temperate types (Su and Su 1988; Hsieh and Hsieh 1990). *Ficus-Bischofia* forest is a type of tropical rain forest found only in valley bottoms and on south-facing leeward slopes near Chialoshui (Su and Su 1988). On the more exposed windward slopes, rain forest is replaced by maquis-like sclerophyll forest and scrub (*Pasania*, *Pouteria-Gordonia* and *Gordonia-Myrica* types). With increasing altitude, *Castanopsis-Schima* forest and *Machilus-Schefflera* forest are encountered. These represent warm temperate and subtropical rain forest types, respectively. Swamp and aquatic vegetation is found in the vicinity of Nanjuen Lake.

The south-west region has been subjected to more human interference (Su 1984a). Moist monsoon forest is represented by *Albizia-Kleinhovia* semi-evergreen, broadleaved forest restricted to undisturbed river valleys. The remaining forested area is dominated by sclerophyll forests of *Acacia* and mixed *Acacia-Vitex* types. Sclerophyll *Lindera-Cinnamomum* scrub occurs on exposed ridges, with thorn scrub on some rock outcrops. Fringing coral reefs and limestone outcrops are covered by sclerophyll forest dominated by species of *Ficus*, *Aglaia*, *Palaquium*, *Diospyros* and *Drypetes*. In sheltered sites, these forests take on the appearance of tropical rain forest. Throughout the south-west region many terraces and low hills are subject to livestock grazing. This results in tall *Miscanthus* and low *Chrysopogon-Paspalum* grasslands (Su and Yang 1988; Chen 1989).

Littoral vegetation includes *Pemphis* and *Scaevola* scrub developed on low coral reefs, and littoral forest comprising *Barringtonia*, *Hernandia* and *Heritiera*. It is now restricted to only a few localities (Chen 1985).

Flora

The flora contains both Boreal and Palaeotropical elements, including a large proportion of East Asiatic, Indochinese and Malesian elements. Indeed, the Hengchun Peninsula (including Kenting National Park) is considered to be a "phytogeographical island" (Li and Keng 1950) with many tropical species at the northern limits of their ranges. Takhtajan (1986) places the demarcation line between the Boreal and Paleotropical Kingdoms to the north of the peninsula.

A published inventory of the flora of Kenting National Park includes 1179 vascular plant species, representing 688 genera and 186 families (Liu and Liu 1977). Since this inventory was published, there have been numerous additional records, bringing the total count to at least 1350 vascular plant species, in 711 genera. This represents about 33% of the flora of Taiwan. Ferns account for more than 10% of the total vascular flora of the park (149 species belonging to 53 genera and 23 families) (Kuo 1986).

Among the flowering plants, 88 species of orchids, belonging to 43 genera (Su 1987b), have been recorded from Kenting National Park, out of a total of about 100 species recorded from the Hengchun Peninsula (Su 1987a). Other well-represented families include Leguminosae (124) (Huang 1990), Gramineae (116), Compositae (64) and Euphorbiaceae (49).

The flora of Kenting National Park is estimated to contain about 160 Taiwan endemic species (15% of Taiwan endemics); about 68 species (5% of Kenting's flora) are endemic to the National Park and its vicinity. A recent evaluation proposed that 41 species, including 10 Kenting endemics, are rare or threatened (Hsu 1985).

Useful plants

The forests of the north-eastern part of the park contain many timber trees, plants yielding edible fruits, medicinal plants, ornamentals (such as orchids), aromatic plants and rattans. The south-western part of the park includes many disturbed habitats with abundant legumes, grasses, and pioneer trees and shrubs. Among these, there are several species which have potential as food crops, forage plants, medicinal plants and plants with potential for reclaiming degraded land. Apart from being grazed by domestic animals, few plants are used locally.

Social and environmental values

The mountains of the north-east region are important interceptors of rainfall; the forest cover helps to prevent soil erosion and floods. Forests in the south-west, particularly

those on coral reef formations, are outstanding recreational resources, attracting both national and international tourists. Each year, Kenting National Park receives about 1,000,000 visitors.

The forests provide food and shelter for many threatened animals and migratory birds. There are more than 60 resident bird species. Of Taiwan's 14 restricted-range bird species, those recorded from Kenting National Park include the threatened Swinhoe's pheasant (*Lophura swinhoii*), Styan's bulbul (*Pycnonotus taivanus*) and Taiwan magpie (*Urocissa caerulea*). The national park agency has set up several breeding centres for endangered animals, including a breeding and reintroduction site for the endemic Formosan sika deer (*Cervus nippon taiouanus*), which became extinct in the wild in 1969.

Threats

Due to ease of accessibility, a few important sites within the park are suffering from visitor pressure. Both amateur and commercial collectors have illegally collected rare plants from the park. A number of important localities for rare species have been damaged by the construction of military facilities. A nuclear power station has been constructed in the vicinity of the park. The vegetation in the south-west has been degraded by livestock grazing. Coral reefs are under increasing pressure from silting.

Conservation

Kenting National Park (IUCN Management Category V: Protected Landscape or Seascape) was established in 1982. Prior to that, some vegetation types, such as the tropical forest at Kueitsuchia and the littoral forest near Kenting, were protected as Nature Reserves. Except for a few places suffering from visitor pressure, the park is generally well protected. There is a system of zoning which restricts mass tourism to a few sites, which serve as landscape and recreation areas. The north-east region is set aside as an ecological reserve. A restoration project for the Endangered moth orchid has been undertaken. More effective controls on visitor use and enforcement of park regulations is needed.

References (Titles in Chinese have been translated.)

Chen, Y.C. (1989). Studies on the vegetation of Sheting area as affected by the grazing of livestock. Master Thesis of the Graduate Institute of Forestry, National Taiwan University, Taipei. (In Chinese, with English summary.)

Chen, Y.F. (1985). Coastal vegetation of Kenting National Park. *Kenting National Park, Taiwan, Research Series* No. 1: 264 pp. (In Chinese.)

Cheng, Y.M., Huang, C.Y. and Liew, P.M. (1986). Investigation on the geology and paleobotany of Kenting National Park. *Conservation Report of Kenting National Park, Taiwan.* (In Chinese, with English summary.)

Hsieh, T.H. and Hsieh, C.F. (1990). Woody floristic composition and distribution pattern in the subtropical forest of Nanjenshan area. *Annals of the Taiwan Museum* 33: 121–146. (In Chinese, with English summary.)

Hsu, K.S., (1985). Investigation on the rare plants of Kenting National Park. *Joint Report of Kenting National Park and Taiwan Forestry Research Institute*. 101 pp. (In Chinese.)

Huang, T.C. (1990). Resource inventory on the legumes of Kenting National Park. *Conservation Report of Kenting National Park, Taiwan* No. 65. (In Chinese, with English summary.)

Kuo, C.M. (1986). Investigation on the ferns of Kenting National Park. *Conservation Report of Kenting National Park, Taiwan* No. 29. (In Chinese, with English summary.)

Li, H.L. and Keng, H. (1950). Phytogeographical affinities of southern Taiwan. *Taiwania* 1: 103–128.

Liu, T.S. and Liu, Z.Y. (1977). Studies on the vegetation and flora of Najenshan area on Hengchun Peninsula. *Annals of the Taiwan Museum* 20: 51–149. (In Chinese, with English summary.)

Su, H.C. (1987a). Native orchids of Hengchun Peninsula (southern Taiwan), I. New recorded plants and taxonomic revision. *Quarterly Journal of Chinese Forestry* 20(4): 95–114.

Su, H.-J. (1984a). Studies on the climate and vegetation types of the natural forests in Taiwan, I. Analysis of the variation in climatic factors. *Quarterly Journal of Chinese Forestry* 17(3) : 1–14.

Su, H.-J. (1984b). Studies on the climate and vegetation types of the natural forests in Taiwan, II. Altitudinal vegetation zones in relation to temperature gradient. *Quarterly Journal of Chinese Forestry* 17(4): 57–73.

Su, H.-J. (1985a). Studies on the climate and vegetation types of the natural forests in Taiwan, III. A scheme of geographical climatic regions. *Quarterly Journal of Chinese Forestry* 18(3): 33–44.

Su, H.-J. (1985b). Vegetation analysis on the native habitat of Formosan sika deer and proposal of its reintroduction area in Kenting National Park. In: Report on Formosan sika deer reintroduction programme for 1984. *Conservation Report of Kenting National Park, Taiwan* 18: 63–96. (In Chinese, with English summary.)

Su, H.-J. (1987b). Studies on the orchid flora of Kenting National Park and its conservation. *Conservation Report of Kenting National Park, Taiwan*. No. 41. (In Chinese, with English summary.)

Su, H.-J. and Su, C.Y. (1988). Multivariate analysis on the vegetation of Kenting National Park. *Quarterly Journal of Chinese Forestry* 21(4): 17–32. (In Chinese, with English summary.)

Su, H.-J. and Yang, S.Z. (1988). Vegetation ecology and succession of She-ting area in Kenting National Park. *Proceedings of Symposium on Formosan Sika Deer Reintroduction*. Pp. 141–163. (In Chinese, with English summary.)

Takhtajan, A. (1986). *Floristic regions of the world*. University of California Press, Berkeley. 522 pp.

Acknowledgements

This Data Sheet was prepared by Professor Horng-Jye Su (Department of Forestry, National Taiwan University, Taiwan).

MOUNT HALLA
Cheju do, Republic of Korea

Location: Located at the centre of the island of Cheju do, off the southern tip of the Korean Peninsula, between latitudes 33°15'–33°25'N and longitudes 128°03'–128°25'E.

Area: 1825 km² (whole mountain).

Altitude: 800–1950 m.

Vegetation: Deciduous broadleaved forest, evergreen coniferous forest and scrub, secondary grassland.

Flora: 1453 vascular plant species and 275 varieties in 663 genera and 158 families; 74 island endemic species among 230 Korean endemic species.

Useful plants: Medicinal plants, food plants, fibre plants, timber trees.

Other values: Rich insect and vertebrate fauna.

Threats: Tourism, over-collection of medicinal and ornamental species.

Conservation: The most species-rich areas are mostly within Mount Halla National Park (IUCN Management Category: V) (151 km²) which includes virtually all of Mount Halla Nature Reserve (IUCN Management Category: I) (91 km²). The protected area covers 8% of the island.

Geography

Mount Halla is an extinct volcano located in the centre of Cheju do (Quelpart Island) about 170 km south of the Korean Peninsula. The total area of the mountain is 1825 km², of which the richest botanical areas are mostly within Mount Halla National Park (151 km²) and Nature Reserve (91 km²). The altitude of the protected areas ranges from 800 m to the summit at 1950 m. The climate ranges from subtropical to alpine. Annual rainfall ranges from c. 1530 mm on the north side of the mountain to 1600–1800 mm on the south side. Most of the rainfall occurs during July, August and September.

There is a crater-lake (Paiknokdam) at the summit of the mountain and 360 volcanic cones, which together make an impressive landscape. The population of the island in 1991 was 515,000, with a growth rate of 5.1% per year. Most inhabitants live in the main cities, such as Cheju and Soguipo, and surrounding small villages.

Vegetation

The vegetation varies according to altitude and aspect. There are four main vegetation types: deciduous broadleaved forest, evergreen coniferous forest, scrub and heath communities and secondary grassland. Differences between the vegetation of the northern and southern slopes are a consequence of differences in rainfall and the altitude of the snow-line. The vegetation can be summarized as follows:

Northern slopes

Deciduous broadleaved forest occurs up to 1100 m. *Quercus serrata-Carpinus tschnoskii* community occurs at 250–750 m, while *Carpinus laxiflora-Quercus mongolica* var. *grosserrata* community occurs at 750–c. 1100 m. Evergreen coniferous forest of *Abies koreana* and *Pinus densiflora* occurs between 1200 and 1950 m. Scrub and heath communities occur above 1600 m. Important species are *Abies koreana*, *Betula ermanii* and *Empetrum nigrum* var. *japonicum*. One of the distinctive Korean endemics, *Diapensia lapponica* var. *obovata*, grows in scrub and heath.

Southern slopes

Deciduous broadleaved forest occurs at 700–1200 m. There are two types: *Carpinus tschonoskii-Quercus glauca* forest (700–800 m) and *Carpinus laxiflora-Quercus serrata* forest (1000–1200 m). Evergreen coniferous forest occurs at 1400–1800 m. The dominants are either *Pinus densiflora* or *Abies koreana*. Scrub communities are found up to 1700 m. The dominant taxa are *Ilex crenata* var. *microphylla* and *Rhododendron mucronulatum* var. *ciliatum*.

Secondary *Miscanthus sinensis* grassland occurs in the lowlands (between 0 and 250 m on the northern slopes and between 0 and 70 m on the southern slopes). Grazing by feral horses and domestic animals (especially cattle and sheep) has resulted in major changes to the vegetation in the lowlands, which are outside the boundary of the National Park.

Flora

Kim (1985) reported 1453 vascular plant species and 275 varieties in 663 genera and 158 families. 74 species are

CPD Site EA44: Mount Halla, Korea. Photo: Kong-Bin-Yim.

island endemics; 230 species are Korean endemics (Kim 1985; Lee 1985). The best represented families are Urticaceae (126 species), Gramineae (123), Cyperaceae (104), Aspleniaceae (82) and Liliaceae (59).

Useful plants

Many species are used traditionally for food, medicine, ship-building, fibre production and house construction. Examples of useful plants include: species of *Castanopsis*, *Diospyros*, *Machilus* and *Michelia* (timber trees); *Ficus* spp. and *Myrica* spp. (edible fruits); *Anoectochilus* spp., *Empetrum nigrum*, *Ephemerantha* spp., *Clerodendrum* spp. and *Gastrodia elata* (medicinal plants); *Cinnamomum* spp. (spices); and *Calamus* spp. (rattan). *Empetrum* and *Gastrodia* have declined due to over-collection and trampling.

Social and environmental values

The area attracts many national and international tourists. Paiknokdam, a crater-lake at the summit of the mountain, is considered to be sacred. Besides its rich flora, Mount Halla also has a rich fauna, including 873 species of insects and 198 species of birds so far recorded (Kim *et al.* 1968).

Threats

Mount Halla has suffered local deforestation as a result of timber cutting and collection of fuelwood. The vegetation has also been damaged by military activities. The rapid increase in the numbers of visitors since 1970 has caused major environmental problems (e.g. trampling, erosion and plant collecting), as has illegal collection of ornamental and medicinal plants. The community of *Empetrum nigrum* var. *japonicum* has been severely damaged by visitors, especially during times of snow-melt. Orchids in the Suak Valley are threatened by illegal collection.

The National Institute of Environmental Research recently listed 20 locally rare or threatened taxa, including *Psilotum nudum*, *Lycoris aurea*, *Sisyrinchium angustifolium* f. *album*, *Gastrodia elata*, *Bulbophyllum inconspicuum*, *Neofinetia falcata*, *Aerides japonicum*, *Goodyera schlechtendaliana*, *Calanthe discolor*, *C. reflexa*, *C. striata*, *Asarum maculatum*, *Albizia coreana*, *Empetrum nigrum* var. *japonicum*, *Diapensia lapponica* var. *obovata*, *Pedicularis verticillata*, *Leontopodium coreanum*, *Saururus chinensis*, *Hibiscus hamabo* and *Ligularia taquetii* (Koh *et al.* 1991). Of these, *Psilotum nudum*, *Gastrodia elata*, *Hibiscus hamabo* and *Ligularia taquetii* are considered to be locally endangered. *Saururus chinensis*, *Hibiscus hamabo* and *Ligularia taquetii* are not included within the protected areas.

Conservation

Mount Halla Nature Reserve covers 91 km². It includes virtually all of Mount Halla Nature Reserve (91 km²) and contains most of the botanically important sites. Walkways, footpaths and fences have been constructed to protect important plant communities. Erosion, caused by trampling of vegetation around Lake Paiknokdam, is a major threat. The park authority has recently taken measures to limit visitor access to a few sites and is investigating how to conserve the lake. There is a plan to enlarge the protected areas to include the High Rest Area (at 1100 m altitude) and the Suak Valley (Tae Wook Kim 1992, pers. comm.).

The National Institute of Environmental Research, in collaboration with the Korean Association for Conservation of Nature, as well as several botanists from Korean universities, recently carried out a survey to determine measures to protect the rare and endangered plant species.

References

Kim, C.H. *et al.* (1968). *Natural Conservatory Area Han La San and Hong Do (Natural Monument No. 162 & 170). Report of the Academic Survey of Mt Han La San and Is. Hong do.* Ministry of Culture and Information, Korea. 424 pp.

Kim, M.H. (1985). Flora of vascular plants in Cheju do. In: *Report of the Academic Survey of Hallasan (Mountain) Natural Preserve.* 424 pp.

Kim, T.W. and Chun, S.H. (1991). A comprehensive re-examination of endemic woody plants in Korea. *Bulletin of the Kwanak Arboretum, Seoul National University* 11: 1–37.

Kim, Y.S. and Kim, T.W. (1990). The conservation of Korean rare and endangered plant species and the role of the botanic gardens and arboreta. *Bulletin of the Kwanak Arboretum, Seoul National University* 10: 33–47.

Koh, H.S., Choi, D.I., Bae, J.O., Chung, S.W., Kim, D.H., Huh, I.A., Lee, J.B., Lee, Y.M., Lee, T.B., Chung, Y.H., Lee, W.T.G., Lee, J.S., Kim, S.S., Kim Y.S. and Lee, E.B. (1991). *The conservation of legally protected wildlife and plants (II).* National Institute of Environmental Research, Korea. 94 pp.

Koh, K.S., Lee, Y.M., Kim, T.W. and Bae, J.O. (1991). The endangered plants in Cheju do. *Bulletin of the Kwanak Arboretum, Seoul National University* 16: 71–81.

Lee, D.B. (1957). The Flora of Quelpart Island. *Thesis of the College of Art and Sciences, Korea University* 2: 339–412.

Lee, T.B. (1985). Endemic and rare plants of Mt. Halla. *Bulletin of the Kwanak Arboretum, Seoul National University* 6: 1–16.

Woo, B.M. (1990). *Status of management of the protected areas in the Republic of Korea.* FAO Regional Office for Asia and the Pacific, Bangkok, Thailand. 43 pp.

Acknowledgements

This Data Sheet was prepared by Professor Kim Yong Shik (Yeungnam University, Kyongsan, Republic of Korea). Dr Tae Wook Kim (Kwanak Arboretum, Seoul National University) and Professor Bo-Myeong Woo (Department of Forest Resources, Seoul National University) provided helpful comments on an earlier draft.

MOUNT HAKUSAN
Japan

Location: West-central Honshu; the main peak is at 36°10'N, 136°45'E.

Area: 480 km².

Altitude: 1700–2702 m.

Vegetation: Montane deciduous forests, subalpine coniferous forests, alpine scrub, alpine meadows, *Sasa* grassland, scree vegetation.

Flora: 1300 vascular plant species; 115 species at the western and southern limits of their distribution; a large number of disjunct alpine species.

Useful plants: Timber trees, ornamental plants.

Other values: Tourist attraction, watershed protection for water supply and hydroelectric power generation.

Threats: Increasing tourist pressure, over-collecting of orchids, introduced plants.

Conservation: National Park (477 km²); Biosphere Reserve (480 km²).

Geography

Mount Hakusan is located at 36°10'N, 136°45'E in west-central Honshu, on the border between the prefectures of Gifu, Ishikawa, Toyama and Fukui. The area consists mainly of highlands, bounded by the Sho River in the east, the Tedori River in the west, and the Ono Basin and upper part of the Kuzuryu River in the south. The land is owned by the National Government (67%) or local public authorities (8%) or is in private ownership (25%). However, there is no permanent population; a few people live in the area in summer, but return to the lowlands in winter.

Many of the rocks belong to the Tedori deposit of Jurassic age. Igneous rocks, such as hornblende andesite, pyroxene andesite and quartz trachyte, intrude into the Tedori. There are many deep, V-shaped valleys and waterfalls, along with volcanic lakes and craters.

The monthly minimum and maximum temperatures at Shiramine are, respectively, -3.3°C and 3.4°C in January and 18.1°C and 28.0°C in July. Annual precipitation is 3238 mm, winter being the wettest season. Snowfall is heavy; snowdrifts to 10 m deep are not uncommon on the mountain.

Vegetation

There is a zonation of vegetation, from warm temperate forests in the foothills to alpine vegetation at the summit. Extensive beech (*Fagus crenata*) forests occur in the cool temperate zone. Along the Tedori River, *F. crenata* is mixed with *Cryptomeria japonica*. *Abies mariesii*, *Tsuga diversifolia* and *Betula ermanii* are typical of the subalpine zone. Mount Hakusan has the most westerly occurrence of alpine vegetation in Japan, with *Pinus pumila* being abundant. There are various types of subalpine vegetation, including: dwarf shrubland with *Empetrum nigrum*, *Phyllodoce aleutica* and *Vaccinium vitis-idaea*; scree vegetation with *Arenaria arctica*

var. *hondoensis*, *Campanula lasiocarpa* and *Deschampsia flexuosa*; alpine vegetation with *Fritillaria camtschatcensis*, *Potentilla matsumurae* and *Primula cuneifolia* var. *hakusanensis*; and *Sasa* grassland with *Sasa kurilensis*.

Avalanches are a common feature throughout the area, preventing the growth of trees in some places. Such areas are often colonized by a community of plants dominated by *Angelica pubescens* and *Cirsium hakusanense*.

Flora

There are an estimated 1300 species of vascular plants. There are no strictly endemic species, although many of the alpine and subalpine plants are endemic to Japan. The local government of Ishikawa Prefecture is planning to make a detailed inventory of the alpine and subalpine zone. According to a preliminary list (Hakusan Integrated Scientific Reports Editorial Committee 1992), 79 species occur in the alpine zone and 126 species occur in the subalpine zone. 69% of the alpine species and 32% of the subalpine species are at the western and southern limits of their distribution. Examples include *Anemone narcissiflora*, *Campanula lasiocarpa*, *Cassiope lycopodioides*, *Diapensia lapponica*, *Empetrum nigrum*, *Fritillaria camtschatcensis*, *Pinus pumila*, *Polygonum viviparum*, *P. weyrichii* and *Stellaria nipponica* (alpine species) and *Abies mariesii*, *Adenophora nikoensis*, *Hedysarum ussuriense*, *Linnaea borealis*, *Pedicularis yesoensis*, *Rubus vernus*, *Smilacina yesoensis* and *Vaccinium ovalifolium* (subalpine species).

Useful plants

The forests contain many species of timber trees, most notably *Fagus crenata*, *Cryptomeria japonica*, *Abies* spp. and *Tsuga* spp. The forests of Mount Hakusan represent a potentially valuable genetic resource from which provenance material could be selected for forestry plantations elsewhere.

Many of the showy alpine and subalpine species, and the orchids, are of ornamental value and are important horticultural subjects.

Social and environmental values

The spectacular mountain scenery and forested slopes make Mount Hakusan highly attractive for tourism. Some 30,000 people visit the area each year, mostly for wilderness experiences and outdoor recreational pursuits, such as mountain-climbing. There is a visitor centre and several mountain lodges which provide accommodation. Besides its value for tourism, the area has been a centre for ecological studies on primates since 1962. This work continues under the auspices of the Primate Research Institute of Kyoto University and the Japan Monkey Centre. The forested slopes help to protect fragile mountain soils from erosion. The protection of the forests is also critical to safeguard vital watersheds for water supplies and existing hydroelectric plants.

Threats

Most of the vegetation is still in a pristine condition. There is some local disturbance to vegetation as a result of visitor pressure. Several species of orchids are threatened by excessive collecting for horticulture. There is some planting of non-native species under a vegetation reclamation programme. As a result some species, such as *Dicentra peregrina*, have become troublesome weeds.

Conservation

In 1974, Ishikawa Prefecture established a Hakusan Nature Conservation Centre for the purpose of starting a comprehensive protection programme for the natural environment. The centre conducts a wide range of studies, particularly on large animals, such as Japanese macaque (*Macaca fuscata*), and on plant species, together with studies on climate and folklore.

Mount Hakusan was designated a National Park (IUCN Management Category: II) in 1962. In 1982 Mount Hakusan was notified as a Biosphere Reserve (480 km²) under the UNESCO MAB Programme. The lack of financial support has prevented any activities taking place under this programme.

References (Titles in Japanese have been translated.)

Hakusan Integrated Scientific Reports Editorial Committee (1992). *Hakusan – nature and culture*. Hokkoku Press, Kanazawa.

Ishikawa Prefecture (1970). *Hakusan no Shizen* (Nature in Hakusan). Ishikawa Prefecture.

Acknowledgements

This Data Sheet was prepared by Professor T. Shimizu (Department of Biology and the Herbarium, Kanazawa University, Kanazawa, Japan).

JAPAN: CPD SITE EA50

YAKUSHIMA
Japan

Location: An island located south of Kyushu at 130°30'E and 30°20'N.

Area: 503 km².

Altitude: 0–1935 m (summit of Mount Miyanouradake).

Vegetation: 90% forest covered, with zones of evergreen forest, mixed *Cryptomeria* forest, *Rhododendron-Juniperus* scrub and subalpine vegetation.

Flora: 1343 vascular plant species and 100 varieties, of which 45 and 27 respectively are endemic to the island; 322 fern species.

Useful plants: Valuable provenance of *Crytomeria japonica* known as Yaku-sugi.

Other values: Forestry, tourism.

Threats: Tourism.

Conservation: Most of the island is a National Park; Yakushima Island Biosphere Reserve covers 190 km².

Geography

The island of Yakushima is situated some 80 km south of the southern end of Kyushu Island at c. 130°30'E and 30°20'N. The island covers some 503 km². There are more than 30 peaks over 1000 m in and around the higher central part of the island (highest point: Mount Miyanouradake, 1935 m).

The warm Kuroshio Current flows along the south-eastern coast. In the coastal zone, the mean annual temperature is between 19–21°C and the mean annual precipitation is 2500–4500 mm. The high rainfall gives rise to many streams. The floristically-richest area of the island is Kosugidani, about 650 m above sea-level. Here the mean annual precipitation is as high as 8600 mm, with a mean annual temperature of 15.9°C.

Vegetation

About 90% of the island is forested. Natural woody vegetation on the lower slopes has mostly been cleared for settlement, agriculture or plantations. Only fragments of the original vegetation of evergreen broadleaved forest and laurel forest remain. Evergreen broadleaved forest dominated by *Quercus*, *Castanopsis* and *Persea* occurs between 200 and 500 m, where there are also extensive plantations of *Cryptomeria japonica* (of the local provenance Yaku-sugi). The latter species also occurs as a native tree in forests above 650 m, reaching 30 m tall and accompanied by *Abies* and *Tsuga*. Between 1200 and 1500 m, native *Cryptomeria* is mixed with summer-green broadleaved species, such as *Stewartia monadelpha*, *Kalopanax pictus* and *Trochodendron* sp. This zone has exceptionally high precipitation and is often shrouded in mist, allowing the development of abundant epiphytes, including bryophytes. Above 1500 m, trees are stunted and *Cryptomeria* forest is replaced by *Rhododendron-Juniperus sargentii* scrub. The highest zone, above 1700 m, is subalpine.

The vegetation at this altitude consists of a scant covering of *Pseudosasa* and small patches of *Rhododendron*. There are marshy areas at c. 1600 m above sea-level, with *Sphagnum* and *Eriocaulon*.

Flora

The native flora of Yakushima includes 1343 vascular plant species and 100 varieties belonging to 608 genera and 165 families. The most species-rich families are Orchidaceae, Cyperaceae, Gramineae and Compositae. There is a rich fern flora (322 species and 39 varieties), almost a quarter of all vascular plants on the island. 45 vascular plant species and 27 varieties are endemic to the island, while 37% of the vascular flora is endemic to Japan. Plants at middle and higher elevations belong to the Sino-Himalayan phytogeographical element.

Useful plants

There is an important provenance (Yaku-sugi) of *Cryptomeria japonica*, one of the most important commercial timber trees in Japan; it is found only on ridges and moist slopes at 650–1850 m. Many trees are more than 200 years old. The biology of Yaku-sugi has yet to be thoroughly investigated. Introduced *Cryptomeria* grows quickly, but the timber is inferior to that of the native provenance. Most of the Yaku-sugi trees have been cut down and only small areas are left.

Social and environmental values

The island has been inhabited since the 7th century, with most people being employed in the logging industry. Major exploitation of Yaku-sugi dates from the 18th century. At times, more than 30,000 people lived on the island. Today the population is over 25,000, but the timber trade is decreasing. Most people now work in the tourism, agriculture or fishing industries. Many areas in the lowlands have been cleared to grow horticultural crops. Recently, a small airport was constructed. A daily air service brings increasing numbers of tourists. Some 300,000 people visit Yakushima annually, a figure which is expected to increase. Among the attractions of the island are its warm and humid climate, its forest-covered steep slopes and mountain scenery, clean and abundant streams, hot springs and coastal resorts.

Threats

The main threat is the density of the human population and the increasing number of visitors. Yaku-sugi was once seriously threatened by commercial logging, but this threat has receded. Most moderately steep slopes at lower elevations have been logged or cleared for settlements.

Conservation

The whole island, except residential areas (mostly coastal), is protected as a National Park. Yakushima Island Biosphere Reserve covers 190 km². The remaining populations of Yaku-sugi are protected. The recent increase in the number of tourists is a problem. Tourism needs to be controlled and effectively managed.

References (Titles in Japanese have been translated.)

Darnaedi, D. and Iwatsuki, K. (1987). On the structure and systematic position of the fern *Dryopteris yakusilvicola* Kurata. *J. Fac. Sci. Univ. Tokyo III* 14: 121–136.

Hatusima, S. (1991). *Flora of the northern Ryukyus.* Asahi, Kagoshima. (In Japanese.)

Miyawaki, A. (ed.) (1980). *Vegetation of Japan, vol. 1. Yakushima.* Shibundo, Tokyo. (In Japanese.)

Okada, H., Fujishima, H. and Yahara, T. (1985). Cytotaxonomical study of *Ranunculus yaegataakensis* Masam., an endemic species on Yakushima Island. *J. Jap. Bot.* 6: 296–302. (In Japanese.)

Yahara, T., Ohba, H., Murata, J. and Iwatsuki, K. (1987). Taxonomic review of vascular plants endemic to Yakushima Island, Japan. *J. Fac. Sci. Univ. Tokyo III* 14: 169–119.

Yahara, T., Yamaguchui, H. and Yumoto, T. (1986). Biology of hybridization between *Farfugium japonicum* and *F. hiberniflorum* (Compositae). In Iwatsuki, K., Raven, P.H. and Bock, W.J. (eds), *Modern aspects of species.* University of Tokyo Press, Tokyo. Pp. 183–193.

Acknowledgements

This Data Sheet was prepared by Professor Kunio Iwatsuki (University of Tokyo, Japan).

DOI CHIANG DAO WILDLIFE SANCTUARY
Thailand

Location: The sanctuary lies in Chiang Dao District, northern Thailand; c. 19°24'N, 98°54'E.

Area: 521 km².

Altitude: <800–2175 m.

Vegetation: Mixed evergreen-deciduous and deciduous dipterocarp-oak forest in the lowlands (<800 m); hill and open hill evergreen forest at higher altitudes; a unique form of upper montane scrub.

Flora: >1200 vascular plant species.

Useful plants: Formerly important for teak (*Tectona grandis*); *Baccaurea ramiflora* has edible fruits.

Other values: Threatened bird fauna.

Threats: Fire.

Conservation: Wildlife Sanctuary (IUCN Management Category: IV).

Geography

Doi Chiang Dao Wildlife Sanctuary lies in Chiang Dao District, Chiang Mai Province, Thailand. It has an area of 521 km² and includes Doi Chiang Dao (2175 m), one of Thailand's highest mountains and by far the largest limestone massif in the country. Granite and shale are found at lower altitudes around the limestone. The sanctuary is located at c. 19°24'N and 98°54'E.

Vegetation

Accounts of the vegetation are given by Smitinand (1966), Santisuk (1985) and Maxwell (1992), the following description coming from the latter source. There are two major lowland forest types (up to about 800 m altitude), namely mixed evergreen-deciduous forest and deciduous dipterocarp-oak (savanna) forest. Lower montane forest occurs at 800–1800 m. A unique form of upper montane scrub is found above 1800 m. Due to disturbance, such as forest destruction, the composition and limits of these two types are often indistinct. Bamboo is abundant in some disturbed areas. Secondary growth is found on abandoned agricultural land and along roads.

Mixed evergreen-deciduous forest
This is the most extensive lowland forest type and is found on shale, granite and limestone. Except for species which actually grow on limestone cliffs and outcrops, the general appearance and species composition of the vegetation seem to be unaffected by the nature of the geology. Mixed evergreen-deciduous forest includes both evergreen and deciduous trees. Emergents, up to 50 m tall, include *Dipterocarpus costatus*, *D. turbinatus*, *Melia toosenden*, *Pterocymbium laoticum* and *Tetrameles nudiflora*. Canopy trees, to 40 m, include *Acrocarpus fraxinifolius*, *Amoora polystachya*, *Anogeissus acuminata*, *Duabanga grandiflora*, *Knema linifolia*, *Parkia leiophylla*, *Pterocarpus macrocarpus*, *Pterospermum grande*, *Sapium baccatum*, *Terminalia bellirica* and *Xylia xylocarpa*. The understorey is richer in species than the higher tree strata. The shrub layer differs from the taller strata in consisting mostly of evergreen species; it also contains young individuals of species which grow to maturity in the upper strata. The herbaceous ground vegetation is generally dense, diverse and includes creepers, climbers and erect herbs. There are numerous Urticaceae and Zingiberaceae. Several species of bamboo (e.g. *Bambusa tulda*, *Dendrocalamus membranaceus* and *D. nudus*), more common in disturbed, fire-prone areas, are occasionally found within the forest, especially in disturbed places. A stemless cycad (*Cycas micholitzii* var. *simplicipinna*) has a scattered occurrence. Woody climbers, some of very large size, are abundant in mixed evergreen-deciduous forest. Epiphytes are abundant and include trees (*Ficus* spp.), an evergreen hemi-parasitic shrub (*Helixanthera parasitica*), ferns (e.g. *Asplenium nidus* var. *nidus*), numerous orchids (e.g. *Coelogyne trinervis*, *Dendrobium dixanthum*, *D. gratiosissimum*, *Pteroceras appendiculatum* and *Robiquetia paniculata*) and a few dicotyledonous herbs (e.g. *Aeschynanthus macranthus* and *Didymocarpus rodgeri* var. *siamensis*).

Extensive logging of teak and other timber species, combined with the effects of fire and the activities of charcoal burners and farmers, has led to a partially degraded and patchy forest, with open agricultural areas, bamboo thickets, fire-prone deciduous dipterocarp-oak (savanna) associations and undisturbed stands of the original forest.

Deciduous dipterocarp-oak forest
This is a secondary forest type which develops after logging of mixed evergreen-deciduous forest for teak. Annual fires occur in this forest type during the dry season. These forests

are similar to the deciduous dipterocarp-oak forests in Doi Suthep-Pui National Park (CPD Site EA55, see Data Sheet). The general appearance is of well-spaced, single-canopied (to 20 m) deciduous trees, over a thin and rocky soil carrying grasses and sedges. Seedlings and saplings of the canopy trees are common, but there is essentially no layer of shrubs or treelets. There are few climbers, but vascular epiphytes are common and include several succulent Asclepiadaceae (e.g. *Dischidia imbricata* and *D. major*), orchids (e.g. *Aerides falcata, Coelogyne prolifera, C. trinervis* and *Dendrobium fimbriatum*) and ferns (especially *Drynaria rigidula*). The hemi-parasite *Scurrula feruginea* (Loranthaceae) becomes conspicuous during the dry season when the host trees are leafless.

Deciduous dipterocarp forest is dominated by trees of the family Dipterocarpaceae, mixed with a variety of other trees. Common dipterocarps are *Dipterocarpus obtusifolius* var. *obtusifolius*, *D. tuberculatus* var. *tuberculatus*, *Shorea farinosa*, *S. roxburghii* and *S. siamensis* var. *siamensis*. There are several monocotyledonous herbs which produce flowers at the height of the dry season before they leaf (e.g. *Curcuma zedoaria, Gagnepainia godefroyi* and *Murdannia scapiflora*). Also noteworthy are the aroids *Amorphophallus kerrii* and *A. macrorhizus* and the orchids *Geodorum siamense* and *Nervilia aragoana*. Sedges (*Scleria* spp.), grow up to 1 m tall and form a dense covering in many areas, while grasses (e.g. *Imperata cylindrica, Narenga fallax, Panicum notatum*, and also bamboos) are particularly characteristic of formerly clear-cut and subsequently regularly burnt places.

Hill evergreen forest
Hill evergreen forest occurs from 700 to 1900 m. Open hill evergreen forest occurs from 1900 m to the summit (Smitinand 1966). According to Maxwell (1992), little information is available about these forest types.

Flora

The total vascular flora is estimated to be over 1200 species (Maxwell 1992). Smitinand (1966) enumerated 109 families, based on a much shorter species list. A number of the more prominent species in the lowland forests are mentioned in Maxwell (1992) (see also preceding section on Vegetation).

Although the floras of lowland forests developed over calcareous and non-calcareous rocks are similar, certain plants are restricted to limestone outcrops. These include *Begonia fibrosa*, *Chlamydoboea* aff. *sinensis* and *Ornithoboea arachnoidea*.

Useful plants

Teak (*Tectona grandis*) was once a common tree throughout the lowland forests of northern Thailand, but was logged out of the area now covered by the Wildlife Sanctuary several decades ago. The understorey tree *Baccaurea ramiflora* yields edible fruits.

Social and environmental values

The globally threatened Deignan's babbler (*Stachyris rodolphei*) is only known from Doi Chiang Dao, where it is found in bamboo forest between 1000 and 1700 m. Other threatened species which occur here are Hume's pheasant (*Syrmaticus humiae*) and giant nuthatch (*Sitta magna*).

Threats

Fires sweep up to the summit, following grassy slopes and open ridges (Smitinand 1966).

Conservation

Doi Chiang Dao Wildlife Sanctuary was established by the Royal Forest Department in 1978. The highest water-hole is at 910 m (Smitinand 1966), which restricts the possibilities for settlement at higher altitudes.

References

Maxwell, J.F. (1988). The vegetation of Doi Sutep-Pui National Park, Chiang Mai Province, Thailand. *Tigerpaper* 15: 7–9.

Maxwell, J.F. (1989). Botanical notes on the vascular flora of Chiang Mai Province, Thailand. *Nat. Hist. Bull. Siam Soc.* 37: 177–185.

Maxwell, J.F. (1991). Botanical notes on the vascular flora of Chiang Mai Province, Thailand: 2. *Nat. Hist. Bull. Siam Soc.* 39: 71–83.

Maxwell, J.F. (1992). Lowland vegetation (450–c.800 m) of Doi Chiang Dao Wildlife Sanctuary, Chiang Mai Province. *Tigerpaper* 19: 21–25.

Santisuk, T. (1985). Conservation of temperate and subalpine vegetation on the mountain summits and ridges of Doi Chiang Dao. In Siam Society: *Nature conservation in Thailand*. Bangkok. Pp. 237–242.

Smitinand, T. (1966). The vegetation of Doi Chiengdao, a limestone massive in Chiengmai, north Thailand. *Nat. Hist. Bull. Siam Soc.* 21: 93–128.

Acknowledgements

This account was prepared by Dr Alan C. Hamilton (WWF), with the assistance of Ros Coles (WWF), largely based on the account in Maxwell (1992).

DOI SUTHEP-PUI NATIONAL PARK
Thailand

Location: The park lies immediately to the west of Chiang Mai, Thailand's second largest city. The summit of Doi Pui is at 18°50' N, 98°54'E.

Area: 261 km².

Altitude: 360–1685 m.

Vegetation: Monsoonal forests, including dipterocarp-oak and mixed evergreen-deciduous associations, in the lowlands; evergreen forest (locally with pine) above c. 950 m.

Flora: 2063 vascular plant taxa belonging to 193 families recorded since 1987.

Useful plants: Timber trees, bamboos, fruit trees, mushrooms and other edible plants, medicinal plants, ornamental plants.

Other values: Very high cultural and religious significance; northern Thailand's biggest tourist attraction; water catchment area for Chiang Mai City; long history of scientific research; high educational value. Animal species include 326 birds, 61 mammals, 28 amphibians, 50 reptiles, c. 500 butterflies and c. 300 moths.

Threats: Encroachment by tourism development, government offices and villagers; road building; tree felling; hunting, leading to extirpation of pollinators and seed dispersers; commercial collection of ornamental plants; forest fires.

Conservation: National Park (IUCN Management Category: II), Biosphere Reserve.

Geography

Doi Suthep-Pui National Park covers 261 km² and lies to the west of Chiang Mai, Thailand's second largest city. The summit of Doi Pui is at 18°50'N, 98°54'E. The more or less isolated mountain forms the western side of the Ping River valley. Rocks are mostly granitic, but shale occurs in some places. Soils are generally deep, highly weathered, sandy loams or sandy clay loams.

Annual rainfall ranges from about 1000 mm per annum at the base of the mountain to about 2000 mm near the summit. There is a marked dry season from December to March, during which virtually no rain falls. The rainy season extends from May to November, with peak rainfall in August (about 250 mm). The cool season is from November to February, when mean temperatures at the base of the mountain are 20–24°C, after which mean temperatures rise sharply to peak in April at 30°C. Temperatures at higher elevations are considerably cooler.

In 1981, when Doi Suthep was declared a National Park, 1956 people belonging to four ethnic groups were living within the park's boundaries. By 1988, this number had increased, mostly through immigration, to 13,694 (Kasetsart University 1988). Two villages of the Hmong hill tribe have been established in the middle of the area for about 60 years. The largest tracts of forest survive on the eastern side of the mountain. In other areas, the forest is fragmented, mostly due to agricultural development and the effects of fire.

Vegetation

For descriptions of the vegetation of Doi Suthep, see Maxwell (1988) and Küchler and Sawyer (1967). There are two basic kinds of forest, deciduous forest up to about 950 m and evergreen forest at higher altitudes. The deciduous forest can be divided into two associations, described by Elliot, Maxwell and Beaver (1989).

A deciduous dipterocarp-oak association (dominated by members of the Dipterocarpaceae and Fagaceae) occurs in the drier areas, especially on ridges. The largest trees (up to about 15 m high) are *Dipterocarpus obtusifolius* and *D. tuberculatus*. The main canopy is dominated by *Quercus kerrii, Q. kingiana, Shorea siamensis* and *S. obtusa*, with *Anneslea fragrans, Craibiodendron stellatum* and *Tristaniopsis burmanica* at higher elevations. Typical shrubs include *Ellipeia cherrevensis, Pavetta fruticosa* and *Enkleia malaccensis*. The ground layer is mostly formed of grasses and sedges (e.g. *Arundinella setosa, Carex continua* and *Themeda triandra*) with members of the Orchidaceae and Zingiberaceae also fairly common.

A mixed evergreen-deciduous association (in which 43% of the individual trees are evergreen) is found in the moister gullies, interspersed with the deciduous dipterocarp-oak association, from which it differs in having taller trees, mostly of different species, a denser understorey and a ground layer rich in herbs and seedlings. No families or species dominate this forest type. *Dipterocarpus costatus* occurs as an emergent. Other characteristic canopy trees include *Engelhardtia serrata, Eugenia albiflora, Metadina trichotoma, Terminalia mucronata, Vitex peduncularis* and *Xylia xylocarpa*. Lianes are common (e.g. *Millettia extensa* and *Spatholobus parviflorus*), as are treelets and shrubs (e.g. *Antidesma acidum, Desmodium heterocarpon, Helicteres plebeja, Leea indica* and *Pavetta petiolaris*) and bamboos (e.g. *Bambusa tulda* and *Dendrocalamus membranaceus*). Typical members of the ground flora include *Boesenbergia rotunda, Desmodium heterocarpon* and *Justicia procumbens*.

Above about 950 m altitude, the evergreen forest contains some very large trees 30–40 m high, including *Acrocarpus fraxinifolius*, *Sapium baccatum* and *Tetrameles nudiflora*. Although no family dominates this forest, the Fagaceae (e.g. *Castanopsis armata*, *C. acuminatissima* and *Quercus semiserrata*) and Magnoliaceae (e.g. *Manglietia garrettii*, *Michelia champaca* and *Talauma hodgsonii*) are well-represented. The understorey is dense and includes *Osbeckia stellatum*, *Pandanus penetrans* and *Psychotria ophioxyloides*. Giant lianes include *Diploclisia glaucescens* and *Mucuna macrocarpa*. The herbaceous ground flora is diverse, with members of the Zingiberaceae (e.g. *Hedychium ellipticum* and *Zingiber smilesianum*) and Araceae (e.g. *Amorphophallus yunnanensis*) well-represented.

Towards the summit, the evergreen forest becomes less tall and dense (due at least partly to tree felling and fire) and the trees become covered in epiphytes, including ferns (e.g. *Mecodium exsertum* and *Microsorum membranaceum*), orchids (e.g. *Bulbophyllum sauvissimum* and *Coelogyne flavida*), members of the Ericaceae (e.g. *Aeschynanthus hosseussii* and *Agapetes variegata*), bryophytes, lichens and algae. Pine (*Pinus kesiya*) occurs naturally and has also been planted. Other characteristic tree species include *Helicia nilagirica*, *Rhododendron oxyphyllum* and *Ternstroemia gymnanthera*. Unusual species in the ground flora include *Hedychium coccineum* and *Lilium primulinum*.

Flora

Doi Suthep's vascular flora is probably one of the best documented of any tropical mountain. Records of 2063 vascular plant taxa (an estimated 17% of Thailand's vascular flora) belonging to 193 families, based on the collections of J.F. Maxwell since 1987, are held in a computer database at the Department of Biology, Chiang Mai University (CMU). Specimens are preserved in the university's herbaria. Doi Suthep's flora includes several undescribed species and 13 recent new records for Thailand, including one new family record (Maxwell 1989, 1991, and in press; Bänziger 1989).

The total numbers of species recorded in each major habitat are presented in Table 34. The best represented families (with numbers of species so far recorded) are Leguminosae (187), Orchidaceae (149), Gramineae (113), Rubiaceae (88), Compositae (79), Euphorbiaceae (73), Cyperaceae (54), Acanthaceae (48), Moraceae (43) and Zingiberaceae (43). Epiphytes are well-represented in Doi Suthep's vascular flora. There are 149 species from 18 families, mostly orchids (67 species) and ferns (49 species). One of the most interesting epiphytes is the ant plant *Dischidia major*. There are 25 parasitic plant species in the families Balanophoraceae, Loranthaceae, Orobanchaceae, Rafflesiaceae and Scrophulariaceae. There are at least 9 saprophytic orchid species and two carnivorous plants, *Drosera burmannii* and *D. peltata*.

Doi Suthep has the highest tree species richness so far recorded for any of the drier types of tropical forest in the world. A 1.38-km transect survey at 670–960 m altitude, traversing both of the deciduous forest associations, revealed a mean tree species richness (for trees of diameter at breast height 10 cm) of 90 species per hectare (Elliott, Maxwell and Beaver 1989), a figure comparable to, or exceeding, that of many tropical rain forests. Further analysis and subsequent

surveys, focusing on specific habitats, have recorded tree species richness figures for deciduous dipterocarp-oak, evergreen and mixed evergreen-deciduous forests of 65, 100 and 132 species respectively per 0.5 ha (Wong 1992).

Lower plants have hardly been studied, although recent surveys by scientists from The Natural History Museum, London, indicate a high species richness among lichens (P. Wolseley and B. Aguirre-Hudson, pers. comm.).

One reason for the mountain's outstanding biodiversity is that it lies at the meeting point of several biogeographical zones. Its flora includes representatives of Himalayan (e.g. rhododendrons, Magnoliaceae), Yunnanese (e.g. *Begonia yunnanensis*), Indochinese (e.g. *Macrosolen cochinchinensis*) and Indomalesian (e.g. figs and palms) floristic elements. The mountain's wide altitude range (360–1685 m) and its sharply contrasting topography of moist gullies and dry ridges provide a diverse range of plant niches. The high species' count is also related to its long history of scientific study.

TABLE 34. NUMBER OF TAXA OF VASCULAR PLANTS IN DOI SUTHEP-PUI NATIONAL PARK RECORDED IN THE CMU DATABASE

Habit	Total	Deciduous dipterocarp-oak association	Mixed evergreen-deciduous association	Evergreen forest	Secondary growth and disturbed areas
Trees and treelets	605	141	399	319	56
Shrubs	90	29	47	44	7
Lianas	141	16	92	71	8
Vines	218	35	119	100	55
Herbs	1009	280	469	493	186
Total	**2063**	**501**	**1126**	**1027**	**312**

Useful plants

Doi Suthep supports a wide range of useful plants which are still collected in large quantities by local residents, although National Park regulations officially forbid such activity. Major products from the forest include bamboo shoots, mushrooms, medicinal plants (e.g. *Holarrhena pubescens*) and edible fruits (e.g. *Baccaurea ramiflora*, *Castanopsis* spp. and *Phyllanthus emblica*) (Trisonthi 1986). Collection of such products is usually sustainable, but collection of ornamental plants for the horticultural trade has caused the local extinction of several species. The park provides a gene pool of timber trees (e.g. Dipterocarpaceae) of potential value in tree-breeding programmes.

Social and environmental values

Doi Suthep provides a spectacular backdrop to the city of Chiang Mai. The mountain is regarded as sacred and has very high cultural significance for most Thai people (Eeowsriwong 1993; Bänziger, in press). The highly revered Phra Taht Temple is situated at about 1000 m; a palace at about 1400 m is occupied periodically by the Royal Family.

Doi Suthep is northern Thailand's most important tourist attraction with more than half a million visitors annually. Although the vast majority visit the temple, palace and

Hmong villages, a high demand for ecotourism in the park has been clearly demonstrated (Elliott 1992b and 1993, in press). This demand is not being satisfied with existing facilities.

The mountain is an important water catchment area, providing much of the western side of Chiang Mai City with its water supply. It is classified as a "B-1" watershed, the second highest category. Any construction on it requires Cabinet approval.

One of Doi Suthep's most important values is its long history of botanical research (e.g. Hosseus 1908; Kerr 1911; Cockerell 1929; Ogawa, Yoda and Kira 1961; Küchler and Sawyer 1967; Sawyer and Chermsirivathana 1969; Bhumibhamon and Wasuwanich 1970; Beaver and Jinorose 1974; Cheke, Nanakorn and Yankoses 1979). This is important in providing baseline data to monitor expected changes as a result of the rapid development of northern Thailand. As the remaining forests in northern Thailand fast disappear, Doi Suthep will become increasingly important as a site where ecologists can carry out the crucial scientific research needed to restore native forest to degraded areas (Elliott and Beaver 1992). Current research projects in this field on Doi Suthep cover seed germination (Hardwick and Elliott 1992), phenology (Elliott, Promkutkaew and Maxwell 1993, in press), seedling morphology, mycorrhiza, soil-tree relationships and the effects of air pollution on the lichen community. Doi Suthep is also important to research on plant taxonomy, since it is the type locality of at least 293 species.

Situated so close to a major urban area, Doi Suthep is an ideal site for environmental education. It provides opportunities for field excursions and acts as an outdoor laboratory for Chiang Mai's many schools and two universities. CMU and several NGOs organize nature education camps for school children in the park, some of which cater especially for disabled children.

Doi Suthep supports a diverse fauna. Animal species include 328 birds (Round 1984), 500 butterflies, 300 moths (Bänziger 1988), 61 mammals (Conservation Data Centre, Mahidol University, pers. comm.; Elliott, Ua-Apisitwong and Beaver 1989), 28 amphibians and 50 reptiles (Nabhitabhata 1987).

Economic assessment

Since tourism is Chiang Mai's most important industry and Doi Suthep is the area's most important tourist attraction, the National Park contributes significantly to the local economy. Accommodation for tourists within the park is run by the Royal Forest Department, but there are also many privately owned resorts around the park's boundaries, several of which encroach on National Park land.

No information is available on the value of products collected from the forest.

Threats

Fifty of Doi Suthep's orchid species are Rare, Vulnerable or Endangered and seven of them have never been found growing elsewhere (Bänziger 1988). Two of the park's parasitic *Balanophora* species are considered to be threatened with extinction (Bain and Humphrey 1982) and *Sapria himalayana* is Endangered (Elliott 1992a). The CMU database lists 39 species as being in imminent danger of local extinction, including five orchids (*Anoectochilus trotus, Dendrobium* sp. nov., *Nervilia calcicola, Pecteilis susannae* and *Tainia viridifusca*), a palm *Plectocomia kerrana* and the gymnosperm *Podocarpus neriifolius*. Species already locally extinct include *Mussaenda sanderiana* (collected for its ornamental value), *Psilotum nudum* (one of the world's most primitive vascular plants) and at least three species of orchids, *Paphiopedilum callosum, P. villosum* and *Phaius tankervilleae* (mostly collected for the horticultural trade).

The main threat to the flora of Doi Suthep is encroachment by tourist development, government offices and villagers, which have already destroyed about 44% of the park's forest. The resulting disturbed areas and secondary growth support only about 15% of the park's total vascular flora (Table 34). Construction activities include tourist resorts, TV relay stations, police and army posts and two large agricultural research stations. The presence of villages and the continuance of slash and burn agriculture have all contributed to the park's deterioration. Moist gullies at lower elevations are particularly favoured for the construction of roads and tourist resorts, in the process destroying forest of the mixed evergreen-deciduous association, the most species-rich habitat in the park.

Encroachment has been encouraged by the rapid development of Chiang Mai as a tourist centre and big increases in land prices. Prosecution of encroachers is difficult, due to interference with park boundary markers and ambiguous land rights' documents, often acquired illegally. Another major threat to the park is a road improvement programme. Dirt tracks all over the park are being widened and surfaced, opening up previously inaccessible areas to motor vehicles. This greatly facilitates hunting, tree felling, garbage dumping and other illegal activities within the park.

Hunting has caused the local extinction of all large mammals (except barking deer) (Elliott, Ua-Apisitwong and Beaver 1989) and at least 10 bird species (Round 1984) within the past 20 years. Of particular concern is the loss of all primates and hornbills. Over the next few decades, plant species, which once depended on these animals for pollination or seed dispersal, will gradually disappear. Loss of primates alone will probably reduce tree species richness by about 10% in the deciduous association and in evergreen forest (Wong 1992). Hunting of remaining animals continues unabated (Elliott and Beaver 1992).

Man-made forest fires burn over large areas of the park every dry season. The deciduous dipterocarp-oak association recovers quickly after fire, but other forest types suffer loss of ground flora and understorey species, death of some adult trees and invasion by grasses and weeds, following opening up of the canopy. The overall impression is that recent increases in the frequency and extent of fires are having a significant adverse effect on Doi Suthep's biodiversity (Maxwell 1993).

A survey of Doi Suthep's visitors revealed that more than half thought the park was threatened by garbage dumping (77%), deforestation (69%) and tourist development (58%) (Elliott 1992b and 1993, in press). Any further deterioration of the park's condition could therefore have significant implications for Chiang Mai's tourism industry.

Conservation

Doi Suthep was made a Forest Reserve in 1967 and upgraded to a National Park in 1981. Parts of the park have also been declared a Biosphere Reserve and a Non-Hunting Area. The park is administered by the National Parks Division of the Royal Forest Department (RFD). Due to lack of funding, inadequate training, an ineffective legal system and lack of support from politicians and local people, the RFD has been unable to prevent rapid deterioration of the park. A management plan for the park, including a zoning system, has been prepared (Kasetsart University 1988), but few of its recommendations have been implemented. In particular, construction and road improvement is continuing in areas marked by the plan as "primitive zone" (no disturbance permitted).

The RFD has implemented tree planting projects in degraded areas, involving local school children and villagers. However, the seedlings planted are mostly of commercial species. Other government agencies have planted *Eucalyptus*, purportedly to protect watershed areas.

A visitors' centre has been constructed but, apart from an infrequently run audiovisual show, it contains very little educational material. Government regulations do not permit the RFD to sell guidebooks or maps, so there is no promotion of ecotourism. Chiang Mai University is planning to build a second visitors' centre on university land immediately adjacent to the park.

There is a fire control unit within the park, but it lacks sufficient resources to make a significant impact on the forest fire problem.

One local NGO, the For Chiang Mai Group, has made a significant contribution to conservation in the National Park. It has campaigned successfully against proposals to construct a cable car system and an international conference centre in the park. The group has also mass-produced a poster entitled "The Biodiversity of Doi Suthep" which has been donated to local schools and sold to tourists to raise awareness of the park's importance for nature conservation. In 1991 the group organized a seminar which brought together all agencies, local villagers and academics involved in the park's management (Eeowsriwong 1993). Recommendations arising from the seminar included:

- limit the number of tourists entering the park and the construction of tourist facilities;
- find ways to control population growth within the park;
- develop alternative farming methods for existing communities within the park that preserve the environment;
- permission should no longer be given for government agencies to use the park's area for building offices;
- an organization, including representatives from every agency involved in the park's management, should be established to restore Doi Suthep and devise a master plan;
- check-points should be set up to inspect vehicles in the park;
- guns should not be allowed in the park;
- forest restoration should take the form of trying to re-establish the original forest ecosystem. All reforestation for commercial purposes should be halted.

China and East Asia

References

Bain, J.R. and Humphrey, S.R. (1982). *A profile of the endangered species of Thailand*. Florida State Museum. 367 pp.

Bänziger, H. (1988). How wildlife is helping to save Doi Suthep: Buddhist Sanctuary and National Park of Thailand. *Symb. Bot. Uppsala* 23: 255–267.

Bänziger, H (1989). Lardizabalaceae: new plant family for Thailand "predicted" by rare moth on Doi Suthep. *Nat. Hist. Bull. Siam Soc.* 37: 187–208.

Bänziger, H. (in press). Biodiversity, Buddhism and bulldozers in Thailand's Doi Suthop sanctuary. *Proc. 2nd Princess Chulabhorn Sci. Congress* 2–6 November 1992, Bangkok.

Beaver, R.A. and Jinorose U. (1974). A comparison of some forest types in northern Thailand. *J. Sci. Fac. Chiangmai Univ.* 1: 1–36.

Bhjumibhamon, S. and Wasuwanich, P. (1970). The structural characteristics of Huay Kog-Ma Forest. *Kog-Ma Watershed Bull.* 4: 20 pp. Kasetsart University, Bangkok. (In Thai.)

Cheke, A.S., Nanakorn, W. and Yankoses, C. (1979). Dormancy and dispersal of seeds of secondary forest species under the canopy of a primary rain forest in northern Thailand. *Biotropica* 11: 88–95.

Chiang Mai University, Culture Centre (1993). *Doi Suthep-Pui National Park: management and conservation*. Proceedings of a seminar held at Chiang Mai University, 14–15 May 1991. (In Thai with summary in English.)

Cockerell, T.D.A. (1929). The flora of Doi Sutep, Siam. *Torreya* 29: 159–162.

Eeowsriwong, N. (1993). The cultural and historical importance of Doi Suthep-Pui National Park. In Chiang Mai University, Culture Centre: *Doi Suthep-Pui National Park: management and conservation*. Proceedings of a seminar held at Chiang Mai University, 14–15 May 1991. (In Thai with summary in English.) Pp. 10–14.

Elliott, S.D. (1992a). The status, ecology and conservation of *Sapria himalayana* Griff. in Thailand. *J. Wildlife in Thailand* 2: 44–52.

Elliott, S.D. (1992b). National parks; protect or promote? *Chiang Mai Newsletter and Advertiser* 1(9): 1, 3, 12.

Elliott, S.D. (1993, in press). Tourists' perceptions of wildlife and national parks in northern Thailand. *J. Wildlife in Thailand* 3(1). Paper presented at the 13th Annual Wildlife Symposium, Kasetsart University, Bangkok.

Elliott, S.D. and Beaver, O. (1992). The importance of Doi Suthep-Pui National Park for wildlife conservation, scientific research and education. *Tigerpaper* 14: 1–6.

Elliott S.D., Maxwell, J.F. and Beaver O.P. (1989). A transect survey of monsoon forest in Doi Suthep-Pui National Park. *Nat. Hist. Bull. Siam Soc.* 37: 137–171.

Elliott, S.D., Promkutkaew, S. and Maxwell, J.F. (in press). The phenology of flowering and seed production of dry tropical forest trees in northern Thailand. *Proc. ASEAN-Canada Int. Symp. on Genetic Conservation and Production of Tropical Forest Tree Seed.* Chiang Mai, 14–16 June 1993.

Elliott, S.D., Ua-Apisitwong S. and Beaver, O. (1989). The small mammal communities of Doi Suthep-Pui National Park. *Proc. 10th Ann. Wildlife Symposium.* Pp. 2/1–2/12. Kasetsart University, Bangkok.

Hardwick, K. and Elliott, S.D. (1992). Factors affecting germination of tree seeds from dry tropical forests in northern Thailand. Department of Biology, Chiang Mai University. (Unpublished research report.)

Hosseus, C.C. (1908). Beitrage zur Flora des Doi Sutap. *Bot. Jahrb.* 40 Beibl., 92–99.

Kasetsart University (1988). Provisional management plan for Doi Suthep-Pui National Park. Faculty of Forestry, Kasetsart University, Bangkok. (Unpublished report in Thai.)

Kerr, A.F.G. (1911). Sketch of the vegetation of Chiengmai. *Bull. Misc. Infor. Kew.* 1: 1–6.

Küchler, A.W. and Sawyer, J.O. (1967). A study of the vegetation near Chiang Mai Thailand. *Trans. Kansas Acad. Sci.* 70: 281–348.

Maxwell, J.F. (1988). The vegetation of Doi Sutep-Pui National Park, Chiang Mai Province, Thailand. *Tigerpaper* 15: 6–14.

Maxwell, J.F. (1989). Botanical notes on the vascular flora of Chiang Mai Province, Thailand. *Nat. Hist. Bull. Siam Soc.* 37: 177–185.

Maxwell, J.F. (1991). Botanical notes on the vascular flora of Chiang Mai Province, Thailand: 2. *Nat. Hist. Bull. Siam Soc.* 39: 71–83.

Maxwell, J.F. (in press). Botanical notes on the vascular flora of Chiang Mai Province, Thailand: 3. *Nat. Hist. Bull. Siam Soc.*

Maxwell, J.F. (1993). More rot, less fire for Doi Suthep. *Chiang Mai Newsletter and Advertiser* 2(6): 1, 3.

Nabhitabhata, J. (1987). Wildlife of Doi Suthep-Pui National Park. *Kog-Ma Watershed Bull.* 48: 42 pp. Kasetsart University, Bangkok. (In Thai.)

Ogawa, K., Yoda, K. and Kira, T. (1961). A preliminary survey of the vegetation of Thailand. *Nature and Life in S.E. Asia* 1: 21–157.

Round, P.D. (1984). The status and conservation of the bird community in Doi Suthep-Pui National Park, North-West Thailand. *Nat. Hist. Bull. Siam Soc.* 32: 21–46.

Sawyer, J.O. and Chermsirivathana, C. (1969). A flora of Doi Suthep, Doi Pui, Chiang Mai, north Thailand. *Nat. Hist. Bull. Siam Soc.* 23: 99–132.

Trisonthi, C. (1986). Edible wild fruits in Chiang Mai. *J. Sci. Fac. Chiang Mai Univ.* 13: 67–88. (In Thai.)

Wong, J. (1992). Seed dispersal mechanisms of flora in the forests of Doi-Suthep-Pui National Park, Chiang Mai, Thailand. University of California/Chiang Mai University. (Unpublished research paper.)

Acknowledgements

This Data Sheet was prepared by Dr Stephen Elliott and J.F. Maxwell (Department of Biology, Faculty of Science, Chiang Mai University). Additional information was provided by Dr Hans Bänziger (Department of Entomology, Faculty of Agriculture, Chiang Mai University).

KHAO YAI NATIONAL PARK
Thailand

Location: North-east of Bangkok, on the Dongrek Mountain Range; 14°05'–14°15'N , 101°05'–101°50'E.

Area: 2168.6 km².

Altitude: Near sea-level along the south-eastern boundary, to 1351 m in the central region.

Vegetation: Mostly moist evergreen forest, with dry evergreen forest, hill evergreen forest, dry mixed deciduous forest, grassland and secondary regrowth.

Flora: 2000–2500 vascular plant species, of which 7 are strictly endemic.

Useful plants: Medicinal plants, rattans; populations of species valuable as genetic resources.

Other values: Rich fauna, catchment protection, tourism.

Threats: Some agricultural encroachment and illegal logging; the collection of some forest products by local people is reported to be a problem; potential dam construction; poaching.

Conservation: National Park (IUCN Management Category: II). Management plan has served as a model for other parks and sanctuaries; development and educational work with local communities.

Geography

Khao Yai National Park lies in the heart of Thailand, between latitudes 14°05'–14°15'N and longitudes 101°05'–101°50'E, on the Dongrek Mountain Range, adjoining the provinces of Saruburi, Nakorn Nayok, Nakorn Rachisima and Prachinburi. The total area is 2168.6 km². The altitude ranges from near sea-level along the south-eastern boundary, to 1351 m in the central region. The major peaks are: Khao Laem (1326 m) in the north; Khao Rom and Khao Khleo (1292 m) near the centre; Khao Kamphaeng (875 m) in the north-east; and Khao Sam Yot (1142 m) and Khao Fa Pha (1078 m) in the north-west. Palaeozoic sediments of the Kanchanburi Series form the bedrock, overlain with marine limestone and shales (exposed in the north). Sediments of the Korat Series (of the Korat Plateau), including red sandstones, shales, gypsum and salt, are found along the eastern edge of the park. The majority of the substrate is, however, made up of rhyolite, the product of volcanic activity.

Soils vary from deep, well-drained clay/lateritic soils and shallow, loamy non-calcareous soils of low fertility, to podsols and laterites derived from old alluvial deposits underlain by marine sediments. The east and central parts of the park are predominantly podzolic and lateritic and have a sandy texture.

The climate is heavily influenced by topography and the South-west and North-east monsoons. The average annual rainfall recorded at the Park Headquarters is 2770 mm. Rainfall ranges, however, from less than 1600 mm in the south-west and west, to over 3000 mm in the Khlang Tha Dam Basin, which is located below Khao Khieo and Khao Rom. Most rain falls during the mid-May to October South-west Monsoon (up to 1917 mm), while the driest months are December and January (only 15 mm per month). The mean annual temperature is 23°C, with the hottest months being April and May (mean temperature: 28°C) and the coolest being December and January (17°C).

Vegetation

There are five main vegetation types, namely tropical evergreen rain forest, dry evergreen forest, hill evergreen forest, dry mixed deciduous forest, and grassland and secondary regrowth. The most widespread forest type is tropical evergreen rain forest, which covers more than 60% of the area of the park at altitudes from 400 to 1000 m. It is one of Thailand's last remaining tracts of this forest type. Important canopy species include *Dipterocarpus alatus*, *D. gracilis*, *D. costatus* and *Schima wallichii*.

Dry evergreen forest covers about 25% of the park, mostly in the west, north and south of the park at 100–400 m altitude. Typical tree species include *Dipterocarpus alatus*, *Shorea roxburghii*, *Hopea odorata*, *Hydnocarpus ilicifolius* and *Aglaia* spp. Much of this forest type has been disturbed by timber extraction.

Hill evergreen forest occurs on mountain tops above 1000 m where dipterocarps are replaced by gymnosperms (such as species of *Podocarpus* and *Dacrydium*) and oaks (of the genera *Lithocarpus* and *Quercus*). Epiphytes are especially abundant and there a few bogs in this formation.

Dry mixed deciduous forest is found in the north-west at 400–600 m. Typical tree species include *Afzelia xylocarpus*, *Xylia kerrii* and *Lagerstroemia calyculata*. The ground flora includes *Bambusa arundinacea* and several species of grasses. Only isolated patches of this forest type remain.

Secondary grassland and regrowth resulting from human disturbance covers about 5% of the park area. The most widespread grasses are *Imperata cylindrica*,

Saccharum spontaneum and *Themeda* spp. Common pioneer trees include *Trema orientalis* and *Hibiscus macrophyllus.*

Flora

The vascular flora is estimated at 2000–2500 species, including 7 strictly endemic species. In the montane forests at higher altitudes, there are some temperate elements, such as *Betula alnoides,* a Himalayan species.

Useful plants

The park contains many valuable timber tree species, especially dipterocarps, as well as many medicinal and other locally useful plants, such as rattans.

Social and environmental values

The wildlife of the park is particularly rich and has been extensively studied. 318 species of birds (35% of Thailand's total) are recorded from Khao Yai, including the globally threatened Siamese fireback (*Lophura diardi*), which is found in the moist evergreen forest in the lower parts of the park. There are at least 67 species of mammals (about a third of Thailand's total).

The park is one of the few remaining places in Thailand supporting large populations of such mammals as sambar (*Cervus unicolor*), muntjac (*Muntiacus muntjak*) and wild boar (*Sus scrofa*), along with common gibbon (*Hylobates lar*) and pileated gibbon (*H. pileatus*) (Endangered), elephant (*Elephas maximus*) (Endangered), gaur (*Bos gaurus*) (Vulnerable), tiger (*Panthera tigris*) (Endangered), leopard (*P. pardus*) (Vulnerable) and Asiatic black bear (*Selenarctos thibetanus*).

The park contains four major watersheds, namely Prachin Buri, Nakam Nayok, Lam Takhong and Lam Phra Phloeng, all important to regional industry and agriculture. Total run-off discharge from Khao Yai is about 1900 million m³ per year.

The park is readily accessible and is the most famous protected area in Thailand, attracting a large number of visitors.

Before the National Park was created in 1961, part of a deforested area around the present Park Headquarters (a result of earlier agriculture) had been developed for recreation, including visitors' facilities and a golf course, all now administered by the Tourism Authority of Thailand. A zone for intensive tourist use has been maintained, covering about 39 km².

Threats

There is agricultural encroachment and illegal logging within the forest, especially along the park's perimeter. The rate of deforestation has been slowing due to increasing difficulties of access. Wildlife poaching is a serious problem, the main targets being barking deer and wild pig, traded by villagers; there are also some poachers from outside. There is some illegal collection of medicinal plants, rattans and other forest plants. There is a threat of dam construction in the Nakorn Nayok watershed. The dam proposal has been opposed by environmentalists.

Conservation

Formerly a National Forest Reserve, Khao Yai became Thailand's first National Park in 1962. It is administered by the National Park Division of the Royal Forest Department and enjoys the best institutional support of any National Park in Thailand. The National Park has been nominated for inclusion as a World Heritage Site. Work on a management plan commenced in 1984, resulting in an initial plan covering 1987–1991. This plan has served as a model for other parks and wildlife sanctuaries in Thailand. When the park was created, reserve forests remained as surrounding buffers, but these have since disappeared except for a relict portion on the north-west. According to UNESCO (undated), there are threats from the collection of plants and animals by local people, who are among the poorest in Thailand. In 1985, a pilot rural development project was initiated at Sup Tai village adjacent to the park to incorporate socio-economic development with park conservation. Activities include promotion of income-generation (e.g. from trekking by tourists), improvements in health and nutrition, and environmental education. In addition to the Sup Tai project, WWF Thailand has initiated rural economic development and conservation education in a further 47 villages on the periphery of the park.

References

UNESCO (undated). *Khao Yai National Park. Nomination of natural property to the World Heritage List submitted by Thailand.* The National World Heritage Committee, Bangkok, Thailand.

Acknowledgements

This account was written by Dr Alan C. Hamilton (WWF), assisted by Ros Coles (WWF), based on UNESCO (undated).

THUNG YAI-HUAI KHA KHAENG WORLD HERITAGE SITE
Thailand

Location: West central Thailand; 14°56'–15°48'N, 98°27'–99°28'E.
Area: 6427 km².
Altitude: c. 200–1811 m.
Vegetation: Evergreen and deciduous lowland forests, evergreen montane forest.
Flora: >2500 vascular plant species.
Useful plants: Wild relatives of many agricultural and horticultural crops.
Threats: Agricultural encroachment, logging, building and other development activities, potential dam construction.
Conservation: Strictly protected legally; management under-resourced.

Geography

Thung Yai-Huai Kha Khaeng World Heritage Site contains the largest remaining area of forest in western Thailand and is one of the largest protected areas in mainland South East Asia. It is one of Thailand's least accessible and least disturbed forests and stands at the core of various protected areas with a total area of 12,966 km². It lies in the provinces of Kanchanaburi, Tak and Uthai Thani between latitudes 14°56'–15°48'N and longitudes 98°27'–99°28' E. The western part of the sanctuary is known as Thung Yai Naresuan and the eastern part as Huai Kha Khaeng.

The sanctuary straddles the Shan-Thai fold mountains and contains three north/south-running ridges. Altitudes range from c. 200 to 1811 m.

Vegetation

This site contains near-pristine examples of many of the principal inland forest formations of Indochina; there are also wetlands. There are significant variations related to topography, altitude, rainfall, soil type and biotic factors. According to Smitinand and Santisuk (undated), there are two main lowland forest types (c. 200–1000 m): deciduous forest (deciduous dipterocarp forest and mixed deciduous forest) and evergreen forest (seasonal rain forest or dry evergreen forest). Deciduous forest is regularly subject to fires started deliberately or accidentally by people. The two forest types in the montane zone (1000–1800 m), both evergreen, are lower montane rain forest and lower montane oak forest. According to UNESCO (undated), the dry lowland forest here forms the most secure example of this forest type in South East Asia. Savanna forest is found in Thung Yai, where grassland areas contain some large-sized cycads.

Flora

Over 2500 vascular plants occur, with floristic elements belonging to four phytogeographical zones: Sundaic, Indo-Burmese, Indochinese and Sino-Himalayan (Smitinand and Santisuk, undated). Many species reach the northern, southern, western or eastern limits of their ranges here, not occurring together elsewhere. There are many rare or endemic species not known from outside western Thailand (e.g. *Afgekia mahidolae*).

Plant families typical of lowland forest include Annonaceae, Dipterocarpaceae, Meliaceae and Sapindaceae, while those typical of montane forest include Fagaceae, Lauraceae, Magnoliaceae and Theaceae.

Useful plants

The sanctuary supports wild relatives of many agricultural and horticultural crops and is an important site for conservation of genetic resources. Examples include *Amorphophallus*, *Citrus*, *Dimocarpus*, *Mangifera*, *Nephelium* and *Xerospermum*.

Social and environmental values

Caves just to the south of the sanctuary were occupied by hominids 500,000 years ago. There are a number of archaeological sites in the sanctuary. The Hmong and Karen peoples lived recently inside the sanctuary but, since 1987, most of them have moved elsewhere.

The sanctuary is an important catchment and contains many lakes. Two of the river systems are protected in their entireties by intact and well-protected forest, which is rare in South East Asia today. Wetlands provide an important habitat for birds. Thung Yai-Huai Kha Khaeng is important for the globally threatened white-winged duck (*Cairina scutulata*), green peafowl (*Pavo muticus*), masked finfoot (*Heliopais personata*), plain-pouched hornbill (*Aceros subruficollis*) and rufous-necked hornbill (*A. nipalensis*). At least one-third of all terrestrial vertebrates known from mainland South East Asia are present, including almost two-thirds of the region's large mammal species. Conspicuous mammals include leopard, gaur, banteng, tapir, elephant, wild buffalo, serow and red dog. 28 vertebrate species are regarded as internationally threatened, including 15 species of mammal and 4 reptiles.

Threats

Nakhasathien and Stewart-Cox (1990) state that logging and collection of other forest products from near settlements in the buffer zone are the greatest threats to the integrity of the sanctuary. Fire is a further threat, as is the presence of domestic animals, including cattle, within the sanctuary. There is a mining concession (Phu Jur) near the north-west boundary. Smitinand and Santisuk (undated) state that the sanctuary is also threatened by encroachment and a multitude of detrimental development projects, including expansion tourist facilities, road developments, the construction of various government stations and the continuation of slash and burn agriculture.

Proposals were made in 1982, and again in 1986, to build a hydroelectric dam across the Upper Khwae Yai at the southern boundary of Thung Yai. If built, the reservoir would have split the sanctuary into three parts, thereby destroying its integrity, and would have inevitably resulted in encroachment and deforestation, as has happened around every other reservoir in Thailand. The dam scheme was shelved in 1988 following vociferous public protest. There is the possibility that the dam project may be revived.

Conservation

When created, the protected area combined two contiguous Wildlife Sanctuaries, Huai Kha Khaeng and Thung Yai Naresuan, established respectively in 1972 and 1974, with some additions. Administration is by the Wildlife Conservation Division of the Royal Forest Department. Guard posts and a research station have been established. Personal and material resources are inadequate to prevent a certain amount of poaching and illegal logging. Conservation efforts have been supported by WWF.

Thung Yai-Huai Kha Khaeng Wildlife Sanctuary has been inscribed as a World Heritage Site.

References

Nakhasathien, S. and Stewart-Cox, B. (1990). *Thung Yai-Huai Kha Khaeng Wildlife Sanctuary: Nomination of natural property to the UNESCO World Heritage List submitted by Thailand*. The National World Heritage Committee, Bangkok, Thailand.

Santisuk, T. (1988). An account of vegetation of northern Thailand. *Geoecological Research* 5: 1–101.

Smitinand, T. and Santisuk, T. (undated). Plant and ecological diversity in western Thailand. (Unpublished manuscript.)

Acknowledgements

This account was written by Dr Alan C. Hamilton (WWF), assisted by Ros Coles (WWF), largely based on Nakhasathien and Stewart-Cox (1990).

BACH MA-HAI VAN
Vietnam

Location: Bach Ma-Hai Van is located in the centre of Vietnam, between latitudes 16°05'–16°16'N and longitudes 107°43'–108°15'E.

Area: c. 600 km².

Altitude: 0–1450 m.

Vegetation: The main types are tropical lowland evergreen forest and tropical montane evergreen forest; some forest has been badly damaged by application of herbicides.

Flora: Estimated c. 2500 species of vascular plants. Dipterocarpaceae (under 1000 m altitude) and Podocarpaceae (above 1000 m) are major components of the vegetation.

Useful plants: Many species yielding timber and non-timber products.

Other values: Important bird fauna; forests protect watersheds supplying water for drinking and for rice field irrigation; a famous resort; tourism.

Threats: Cutting of hardwood timbers, collection of fuelwood and non-wood forest products, illegal hunting; high population pressure.

Conservation: Bach Ma National Park and 2 other protected areas were established in 1986.

Geography

Bach Ma-Hai Van is located on the boundary between Thua Thien-Hue and Quang Nam-Danang Provinces in the centre of Vietnam. It is 50 km to the south of Hue, between latitudes 16°05'–16°16' and longitudes 107°43'–108°15'E. The terrain is steep, with slopes averaging 15–25°. The altitude ranges from sea-level to 1450 m. There are many long, narrow valleys in the foothills. The bedrock is granite. Soils are mainly red or yellow ferralite (in the lowlands) and humic yellow ferralite (on higher ground). The climate is tropical monsoonal. The mean annual temperature at low altitudes is 24–25°C, with a maximum of 40°C (April) and a minimum of 6°C (January). The mean annual rainfall is 2800 mm in the north and 3490 mm in the south-west (Nam Dong District). The rainy season lasts for 4 months (September–December).

Vegetation

Tropical lowland evergreen forest occurs below 1000 m. This is dominated by Dipterocarpaceae, Leguminosae and Sapindaceae. A dipterocarp, *Parashorea stellata*, is the most common tree. Tropical montane evergreen forest occurs above 1000 m. This is dominated by Podocarpaceae and Theaceae. *Dacrydium pierrei* (Podocarpaceae) is the most common species.

Some areas sprayed by herbicides remain devoid of mature forest trees. These areas are dominated by genera such as *Mallotus*, *Macaranga* and *Cratoxylum*. Elsewhere, areas poisoned by herbicides carry bamboo forest, dominated by *Neohouzeaua dullooa*, and grasslands dominated by *Imperata cylindrica*.

Flora

501 species of vascular plants, belonging to 344 genera and 124 families, were listed in an initial survey in 1989. They comprise 31 species of pteridophyte, 11 species of gymnosperm and 459 species of angiosperm. It is estimated that the total number of vascular plant species is about 2500. The best represented families are Euphorbiaceae, Lauraceae, Orchidaceae and Palmae. Dipterocarpaceae and Podocarpaceae are also important elements. There are 3 Endangered species: *Dalbergia cochinchinensis*, *Aquilaria crassna* and *Podocarpus fleuryi*.

Useful plants

An initial list of forest resources includes the following numbers of useful species: timber trees – 200; medicinal plants – 108; ornamental plants – 35; wild fruits – 22; rattans – 7.

Social and environmental values

Bach Ma-Hai Van is in the southern part of the Annamese Lowlands Endemic Bird Area (EBA), where 8 restricted-range bird species occur, 4 of them endemic. They are found in lowland evergreen forest, some ranging as high as 1500 m altitude in the foothills, but others apparently confined to lowland forest below 300 m. There has been extensive lowland deforestation in this part of Vietnam, and 6 of the restricted-range species are listed as globally threatened, notably extreme lowland specialists such as Edward's pheasant (*Lophura edwardsi*), which formerly occurred in this area, but is now feared extinct in the wild (Eames *et al.* 1992). More widespread threatened species which occur in this area are Siamese fireback (*Lophura diardi*), green peafowl (*Pavo muticus*) and Blyth's kingfisher (*Alcedo hercules*).

The forests protect watersheds supplying water for drinking and for rice field irrigation. A resort was constructed in 1928–1940 at 1000 m on Bach Ma Mountain. The railway and highway from Hanoi to Ho Chi Minh pass through the eastern part of Hai Van.

Threats

About 40,000 people live around the area. Many collect fuelwood, rattans, resin and honey from within the protected area. Forest fires sometimes occur. Park wardens are attempting to prevent the exploitation of forest products and hunting within the protected area.

Conservation

Bach Ma-Hai Van Protected Area was declared in 1986. In 1991, it was divided into 3 protected areas: Bach Ma National Park (220 km²), North Hai Van Environment Protection Forest and South Hai Van Environment Protection Forest. A buffer zone has been proposed.

References

Eames, J.C., Robson, C.R., Nguyen Cu and Truong Van La (1992). *Vietnam Forest Project forest bird surveys in Vietnam*. ICBP Study Report 51. ICBP, Cambridge. 69 pp.

Acknowledgements

This Data Sheet was prepared by Dr Vu Van Dung (Forest Inventory and Planning Institute, Ministry of Forestry, Hanoi, Vietnam).

CAT TIEN BIOSPHERE RESERVE
Vietnam

Location: South-west Vietnam at the intersection of 4 provinces: Dong Nai, Lam Dong, Song Be and Dac Lak; between latitudes 11°20'–11°50'N and longitudes 107°11'–107°38'E.

Area: 1372 km².

Altitude: 60–754 m.

Vegetation: Tropical lowland evergreen forest, lowland semi-deciduous forest, bamboo forest, riverine forest, freshwater swamp vegetation.

Flora: c. 2500 species of vascular plants.

Useful plants: Timber trees, medicinal plants, rattans, fruit trees, ornamental plants.

Other values: Important fauna, including the last Javan rhinoceros in Vietnam; tourism.

Threats: Illegal logging, collection of rattans, resins, poaching of animals.

Conservation: Nam Cat Tien National Park (379 km²) and Rhino Sanctuary (360 km²).

Geography

Cat Tien Biosphere Reserve is situated at the intersection of Dong Nai, Song Be, Lam Dong and Dac Lak provinces. It lies to the south of Truong Son Mountain Range, in the transition area between the High Plateau and the south-eastern region of Vietnam. Dong Nai River, originating from the mountain of Lam Dong, flows along the north-west boundary of the Biosphere Reserve, separating it into 2 areas, the Rhino Sanctuary in the north and Nam Cat Tien National Park in the south.

The area is located between latitudes 11°20'–11°50'N and longitudes 107°11'–107°38'E. The mean altitude in the north is 200 m and, in the south, 100 m. Low-lying areas are flooded in the rainy season. In the dry season the water only remains in the lowest lying areas, forming a system of swamps, such as Crocodile Swamp and Brigade 600 Swamp.

Cat Tien Biosphere Reserve is hilly. During the Quaternary, the area was covered by basaltic lavas. Both pyroclastic and sedimentary deposits are present. The main soils are alluvium, podzols and latosols.

The area has a tropical monsoon climate. The mean annual temperature is 25°C, the highest mean monthly temperature being 27°C (April) and the lowest 23°C (December). Maximum and minimum recorded temperatures are 38°C and 13°C respectively. Mean annual precipitation is 2205 mm. Rainfall is seasonal, with a rainy season from April to November, during which over 90% of the total annual rainfall occurs. The dry season is from December to March.

Vegetation

Tropical lowland evergreen broadleaved forest is dominated by *Hopea odorata*, *Dipterocarpus alatus*, *D. turbinatus*, *Vatica odorata* and *Irvingia malayana*. Semi-deciduous forest is dominated by *Lagerstroemia calyculata*, *Tetrameles nudiflora*, *Sindora siamensis* and *Anogeissus acuminata*. Bamboo and mixed bamboo-tree forest is dominated by *Bambusa blumeana*, *B. procera* and *Oxytenanthera nigro-ciliata*. Riverine evergreen forest is dominated by *Barringtonia racemosa*, *Lagerstroemia flos-reginae*, *Hydnocarpus anthelmintica*, *Xanthophyllum* spp., *Saccharum spontaneum* and *Phragmites australis*.

Flora

An initial survey of the area in 1991 recorded 652 vascular plant species belonging to 442 genera and 126 families, including 32 species of pteridophytes belonging to 28 genera and 19 families, 5 species of gymnosperms belonging to 3 genera and 3 families, and 615 species of angiosperms belonging to 414 genera and 104 families. The largest families are Orchidaceae, Euphorbiaceae, Gramineae, Moraceae, Rubiaceae, Fabaceae, Mimosaceae and Dipterocarpaceae (of which 15 species have been recorded). Endangered species include *Dalbergia bariaensis*, *D. mammosa*, *Cycas micholitzii*, *Aquilaria crassna* and *Afzelia xylocarpa*. The total number of vascular plant species is estimated at about 2500.

Useful plants

Among 652 species listed in the initial survey of 1991 are timber trees (200 species), medicinal plants (120), orchids (59), rattans (11), bamboos (7) and oil and resin plants (12). The main forest products are hardwood timbers, oils, resins, bamboos and rattans.

Social and environmental values

Cat Tien is in the South Vietnamese Lowlands Endemic Bird Area (EBA), where 3 restricted-range bird species occur, of which 2 are endemic: the globally threatened orange-necked partridge (*Arborophila davidi*) and Germain's peacock-pheasant (*Polyplectron germaini*). They are found in evergreen forest in the lowlands and foothills. More widespread threatened species which occur in this area are Siamese fireback (*Lophura diardi*), green peafowl (*Pavo muticus*), lesser adjutant (*Leptotilus javanicus*), white-shouldered ibis (*Pseudibis davisoni*) and white-winged duck (*Cairina scutulata*).

The area is the watershed of the Dong Nai River. The forest protects the catchment of the biggest hydroelectric plant in southern Vietnam.

The area has many of the characteristic vegetation types of south-east Vietnam, and has many endangered mammals, such as Javan rhinoceros (*Rhinoceros sundaicus*), elephant, gaur and banteng.

About 650 indigenous people live in the core zone and 5000 in the buffer zone. They use many forest products.

Threats

The main threats are shifting cultivation by indigenous people living in the core zone, illegal exploitation of valuable hardwood trees and other plant resources, and illegal hunting. These activities are now declining.

Conservation

The south of the area was declared a Nature Reserve in 1979. Nam Cat Tien National Park was established in 1986. A management plant was accepted in 1991. Cat Tien Biosphere Reserve was nominated as a Man and Biosphere Reserve in 1991. A management plant for Cat Loc Rhino Sanctuary has been prepared by the Ministry of Forestry.

Acknowledgements

This Data Sheet was prepared by Dr Vu Van Dung (Forest Inventory and Planning Institute, Ministry of Forestry, Hanoi, Vietnam).

CUC PHUONG NATIONAL PARK
Vietnam

Location: Cuc Phuong is located south of Hanoi, between latitudes 20°14'–20°24'N and longitudes 105°29'–105°44'E.

Area: 300 km².

Altitude: 200–636 m (summit of Silver Cloud Peak).

Vegetation: Various lowland evergreen forest types, including limestone forest; some semi-deciduous forest.

Flora: 1980 species of vascular plants recorded so far, belonging to 887 genera and 221 families.

Useful plants: Very rich in medicinal plants, timber trees, ornamental plants.

Other values: High landscape value, including caves; tourism.

Threats: Cutting of hardwood timbers, fuelwood collection, poaching.

Conservation: National Park (222 km²) established in 1962.

Geography

Cuc Phuong is located south of Hanoi at the intersection of Ninh Binh, Ha Tay and Thanh Hoa provinces, between latitudes 20°14'–20°24'N and longitudes 105°29'–105°44'E. It lies at the end of a limestone mountain range eminating from the Son La Plateau and orientated north-west to south-east. It is about 25 km long and over 10 km wide, with an area of about 300 km². Cuc Phuong is surrounded by rice fields on three sides. The main landscape feature is a limestone mountain (highest point: Silver Cloud Peak, at 636 m). In the middle of Cuc Phuong there is a long and narrow valley. Buci River flows along the north-west boundary of the area. Most streams in Cuc Phuong are temporary, water flowing only after heavy showers. There are two main soil types, developed respectively on limestone and clay schist.

Cuc Phuong has a tropical monsoon climate. The mean annual temperature is 20°C, with a maximum of 39°C (March) and a minimum of 7°C (January). The mean annual rainfall is 2157 mm, the rainy season lasting from May to November.

Vegetation

Cuc Phuong contains a large area of primary tropical rain forest on valley slopes and on the slopes of the limestone mountain. The tallest trees are more than 30 m in height. The main forest types are lowland semi-deciduous forest on limestone, closed broadleaved tropical evergreen seasonal lowland forest (dominated by Dipterocarpaceae, Fabaceae, Meliaceae and Sapindaceae), closed broadleaved tropical evergreen lowland forest (dominated by Fabaceae and Lauraceae) and submontane forest on limestone. The forest contains parasitic species, many epiphytic species (especially Orchidaceae) and woody lianes.

Flora

1980 vascular plant species have been recorded so far, representing 887 genera and 221 families. The largest families (with the numbers of species so far recorded) are: Euphorbiaceae (102 species), Gramineae (86), Fabaceae (72), Rubiaceae (72), Compositae (65), Moraceae (54), Lauraceae

CPD Site EA64: Cuc Phuong National Park, with Silver Cloud Peak in the background. Photo: Jim Thorsell.

(54), Cyperaceae (54), Orchidaceae (51) and Acanthaceae (36). The most abundant families in terms of individuals are Moraceae, Euphorbiaceae, Compositae, Rubiaceae, Sapindaceae, Meliaceae and Lauraceae.

Useful plants

The forests of Cuc Phuong are very rich in medicinal plants, timber trees and ornamental plants. Medicinal plants include *Morinda officinalis*, *Amomum xanthoides*, *Schefflera octophylla* and *Aralia armata*. Timber trees include *Parashorea chinensis*, *Pometia pinnata*, *Aglaia gigantea*, *Michelia mediocris*, *Dracontomelon duperreanum* and *Terminalia myriocarpa*. Orchids of ornamental value include *Dendrobium nobile*, *D. aggregatum* and *Aerides odoratum*.

Social and environmental values

Cuc Phuong forms the watershed of the Buoi River. Many streams supply water for drinking and irrigation. The forest also supplies fuelwood and many kinds of non-wood forest products for local people. The park receives c. 100,000 visitors every year.

The area supports populations of several birds species which are endemic to northern Indochina, including the globally threatened red-collared woodpecker (*Picus rabieri*).

Threats

30,000 people live around the area and about 100 live inside the National Park. Threats include clearance of forest for agriculture by the local Muong people, hunting of large mammals and illegal cutting of valuable hardwood trees.

Conservation

Cuc Phuong National Park (IUCN Management Category: II) was established in 1962. It was the first protected area in Vietnam. In 1988, a management plan for Cuc Phuong National Park was accepted by the government.

Acknowledgements

This Data Sheet was prepared by Dr Vu Van Dung (Forest Inventory and Planning Institute, Ministry of Forestry, Hanoi, Vietnam).

CPD Site EA64: Cuc Phuong National Park, showing interior of forest. Photo: Jim Thorsell.

INDOCHINA: CPD SITE EA65

LANGBIAN-DALAT HIGHLAND
Vietnam

Location: Langbian-Dalat Highland (11°56'N, 108°25'E), is in Lam Dong Province in the south of the Truong Son Mountain Range.

Area: 4000 km².

Altitude: 1400–2289 m (summit of Bidoup).

Vegetation: Tropical montane evergreen forest, subtropical montane forest.

Flora: Estimated 2000 vascular plant species; high endemism. A centre of diversity for orchids in Vietnam.

Useful plants: 100 medicinal plant species, ornamental plants (especially orchids), resin trees, timber trees, rattans.

Other values: Endemic bird fauna, watershed protection for drinking water, hydroelectric scheme, tourism.

Threats: Logging, slash and burn cultivation, fire.

Conservation: Dalat Nature Reserve (425 km²); Langbian Plateau Nature Reserve (40 km²); Thuong Da Nhim Nature Reserve (70 km²).

Geography

Langbian-Dalat Highland is situated in the north-east of Lam Dong Province and in the south of the Truong Son Mountain Range. It is a highland massif extending over 4000 km². The highest points are Bidoup (2289 m) and Langbian (2167 m). Most of the land is below 1500 m. The bedrock is granite; mountainous yellow ferralite soil predominates.

This highland region has a subtropical climate. The mean annual temperature is 18°C, with a maximum of 31°C (April) and a minimum of 0°C (January). The mean annual rainfall is 1792 mm, concentrated in the rainy season (April–October).

Vegetation

The vegetation of this extensive area varies greatly according to altitude. Most land below 1700 m is covered by coniferous forest (*Pinus khasya* and *P. merkusii*). This pine forest is currently being exploited by the local authorities. Tropical montane evergreen forest and subtropical montane forest occur above 1700 m.

The conifers, *Dacrydium pierrei*, *Fokienia hodginsii*, *Libocedrus macrolepis*, *Pinus krempfii* and *P. dalatensis*, are characteristic strict endemics. The area is one of the richest centres of diversity for orchids in Vietnam, more than 100 species having been recorded so far.

Useful plants

Pinus khasya and *P. merkusii* supply timber and resin. *Fokienia hodginsii* and *Libocedrus macrolepis* are the most valuable timber trees in Vietnam. Local people also collect rattan. Approximately 100 medicinal plant species are used locally. Some species of *Cinnamomum* and *Illicium* are used for medicines and essential oils. Ornamental plants include many species of orchids.

Social and environmental values

This is a very important watershed area. The area protects the catchment of the Da Nhim hydroelectric scheme. Local people continue to exploit resin from *Pinus khasya* and *P. merkusii*. A large tree planting programme has been launched to restore pine forests in the area.

The Dalat Plateau Endemic Bird Area (EBA) supports 8 restricted-range bird species, of which 4 are endemic, namely grey-crowned crocias (*Crocias langbianis*), black-hooded laughing-thrush (*Garrulax milleti*), collared laughing-thrush (*Garrulax yersini*) and Vietnamese greenfinch (*Carduelis monguilloti*). Apart from the Vietnamese greenfinch, which is found in pine forest, these species are found in montane evergreen forest above 900 m. Seven of the restricted-range species, including all four endemics, are considered to be globally threatened.

Threats

The forest is subject to commercial logging by the Provincial Forest Department and to slash and burn cultivation by hill tribes. Both of these activities have reduced and modified the forests. Fires often occur in the dry season and are an additional threat to the forest.

Conservation

Dalat Nature Reserve (425 km²) was declared in 1977; Langbian Plateau Nature Reserve (IUCN Management Category: IV) (40 km²) was declared in 1977; and Thuong Da Nhim Nature Reserve (IUCN Management Category: IV) (70 km²) was declared in 1986. A management plan for Da Nhim Watershed Forest was accepted in 1991. A Provincial Nature Reserve was established in Cong Troi to protect *Pinus krempfii* forest.

Acknowledgements

This Data Sheet was prepared by Dr Vu Van Dung (Forest Inventory and Planning Institute, Ministry of Forestry, Hanoi, Vietnam).

YOK DON NATIONAL PARK
Vietnam

Location: South-west Vietnam, between latitudes 12°45'–13°00'N and 107°29'–107°50'E.

Area: 650 km².

Altitude: 200–482 m (summit of Yok Don Hill).

Vegetation: Dry dipterocarp forest, lowland semi-deciduous forest, riverine evergreen forest, swamp forest.

Flora: c. 1500 vascular plant species; many endemic and threatened species.

Other values: Watershed protection for drinking water and rice production; rich fauna; tourist attraction.

Threats: Illegal logging, hunting, forest fires.

Conservation: National Park (580 km²).

Geography

Yok Don is located between latitudes 12°45'–13°00'N and longitudes 107°29'–107°50'E in the centre of the Srepok River basin, which forms the eastern branch of the Lower Mekong basin of Indochina. The area under consideration covers 650 km². Yok Don is a relatively flat area interspersed by several small rivers which drain northwards into the Srepok River. The altitude is mostly 200–300 m; the highest point (Yok Don Hill, 482 m) is in the centre. The bedrock consists predominantly Jurassic sediments. Soils are mainly grey or yellow-red soils rich in sialite and ferralite.

Yok Don has a tropical monsoon climate. The mean annual rainfall is 1540 mm. The rainy season lasts from May to November, during which 76% of the rain falls. The mean monthly temperature ranges between 24°C and 26°C, with a maximum in May and minimum in January.

Vegetation

The area is dominated by dry dipterocarp forest, with widely spaced trees over grassland. The most common trees are *Dipterocarpus obtusifolius*, *D. intricatus*, *D. tuberculatus*, *Shorea obtusa*, *S. siamensis* and *Terminalia chebula*. All of these are valuable hardwood timbers, but rarely grow taller than 22 m. Other forest types are tall riverine evergreen forest and hill evergreen forest. River banks are lined by tall clumps of *Bambusa blumeana* and *B. arundinacea*. On higher ground and along rivers are *Hopea odorata*, *H. ferrea*, *Sindora siamensis* and (on lower slopes) *Lagerstroemia* spp. Grassland is found in open clearings and around seasonal water-holes and salt-licks. More than 60 species of grasses are recorded. Grasslands are regularly burned in the dry season.

The areas of the various vegetation types in the National Park are: dry dipterocarp forest (390 km²), mixed deciduous forest (123 km²), riverine evergreen forest (11 km²), hill evergreen forest (18 km²) and grassland (26 km²).

Flora

A list of 464 vascular plant species (representing 97 families) was recorded in an initial survey. It is estimated that the total number of vascular plant species is 1500–1700. The most important families are Dipterocarpaceae, Lythraceae, Combretaceae and Gramineae. Locally threatened species in this area include *Dalbergia barianensis*, *Afzelia xylocarpa* and *Hopea ferrea*.

Useful plants

About 150 species are valuable for their timber. 10 species are also valuable for turpentine resin, especially species of dipterocarps in the genera *Dipterocarpus*, *Shorea* and *Hopea*. A few species (20) provide tannin or edible fruits (e.g. *Ziziphus*, *Grewia*), while some have medicinal value (e.g. *Dillenia tetracera*). Others are useful for thatch (*Imperata*, *Livistona*) or fibre (*Calamus*, *Bambusa*). The area is also rich in orchids; 40 orchid species are of horticultural value.

Social and environmental values

Yok Don is the only reserve in Vietnam protecting dry dipterocarp forest. This vegetation is highly vulnerable to fire damage. The area has a rich fauna. Notable mammals include such large ungulates as kouprey, banteng, gaur, wild buffalo, hog deer, muntjak, lesser mouse deer and Asian elephant. The reserve also contains several species of primates, including Concolor gibbon, douc langur and silver leaf monkey. The area is potentially attractive for scientific research and tourism. The forest trees of Yok Don are likely to be an important seed source of valuable timber trees for tree plantations.

The area is likely to be important for a number of globally threatened bird species, such as green peafowl

(*Pavo muticus*), which favours riverine forests, and Siamese fireback (*Lophura diardi*). A number of grassland and savanna bird species have extremely poorly known Indochinese populations, but could occur in this part of Vietnam, notably the threatened Bengal florican (*Houbaropsis bengalensis*).

Threats

There are about 1500 villagers living around Yok Don National Park. These people keep about 1000 buffalo and 300 cattle. In addition, there are about 20 domestic elephants. Hunting and collecting of resin, honey and other forest products occurs within the park. Hunters set fire to grasslands in the reserve in the dry season to encourage growth of grass shoots to attract animals. Some forest fires are started by resin collectors, who use fire to start resin flow from dipterocarps.

Conservation

In 1977 Yok Don was declared a Nature Reserve and, in 1991, a management plan for Yok Don National Park (580 km^2) was accepted by the Vietnamese Government.

Acknowledgements

This Data Sheet was prepared by Dr Vu Van Dung (Forest Inventory and Planning Institute, Ministry of Forestry, Hanoi, Vietnam).

REGIONAL OVERVIEW: SOUTH EAST ASIA (MALESIA)

STEPHEN D. DAVIS

WITH MAJOR CONTRIBUTIONS FROM PETER S. ASHTON AND ROBERT J. JOHNS

Total land area: c. 3,070,000 km².

Population (1990): 271,820,000[a].

Number of islands: c. 15 major islands and c. 20,000 smaller islands.

Maximum altitude: In West Malesia – Mount Kinabalu, Sabah (4101 m). In Papuasia – Puncak Jaya, Irian Jaya (4884 m).

Natural vegetation: c. 1,842,662 km² of tropical moist forests[b] (c. 61% of the land area); second most extensive area of rain forest in the world. Main forest types: lowland evergreen rain forest, dominated by dipterocarps in the west, moist deciduous forest, semi-evergreen rain forest, montane forest, heath forest (kerangas), limestone forest, ultramafic vegetation, alluvial and peat swamp forests, mangroves, remnants of coastal forest, alpine and subalpine vegetation extensive on high mountains of New Guinea and on Mount Kinabalu in Borneo.

Number of vascular plants: c. 42,000 species[c], possibly as many as 50,000 species[d].

Species endemism: 70–80%[d].

Vascular plant families: 310[e].

Number of endemic families: 4 (Lophopyxidaceae, Matoniaceae, Pentastemonaceae, Scyphostegiaceae).

Number of genera: c. 3250.

Number of regional endemic genera: >900[e].

Important plant families: Orchidaceae: 208 Malesian genera; c. 6500 species. Palmae: 52 Malesian genera; c. 975 species. Dipterocarpaceae: 10 Malesian genera; 386 species.

Sources:
[a] World Resources Institute (1994); [b] Collins, Sayer and Whitmore (1991); [c] Roos (1993); [d] R.J. Johns (1992, pers. comm.); [e] M. Roos (1993, *in litt.*).

Introduction

The phytogeographic region of Malesia is floristically the richest region of the Indomalesian Subkingdom (Takhtajan 1986). It consists of the Malay Peninsula and the Malesian archipelago of some 20,000 islands, which extend over 6000 km from the south-eastern coast of continental Asia eastwards to the north of Australia and the western edge of the Pacific Ocean. The region spans two continental shelves: the Sunda shelf (the largest continental shelf in the world) in the west, and the Sahul shelf in the east. The Sunda shelf includes the Malay Peninsula and the islands of Sumatra, Java, Borneo and Palawan. The Sahul shelf includes New Guinea (the largest tropical island in the world) and its surrounding islands. The two shelves are separated by deep seas in which lie most of the Philippines (except Palawan), Sulawesi (Celebes) and Nusa Tenggara (the Lesser Sunda Islands). In the east, the region includes the Bismarck Archipelago, the Louisiade Archipelago and the Solomon Islands.

Geology

The geological history of the region forms the background to why the floras of Sundaland and Sahul differ so markedly. While Sundaland was originally part of Laurasia, the Sahul shelf is Gondwanic in origin, the two land masses having

collided at Sulawesi about 15 million years ago in the mid-Miocene. The islands of Sumatra and Java, the Lesser Sunda Islands and Papua New Guinea all lie on the line of impact, which is one of the most actively volcanic regions of the world and the site of some of the most dramatic volcanic events known (e.g. the eruption of Krakatau in 1883, midway between Java and Sumatra, the loudest reported explosion in historical times, and the eruption of Sumbawa's highest mountain, Gunung Tambora, in 1815, the most massive recorded eruption). Another line of volcanoes occurs along the eastern and northern parts of Sulawesi, extending north to the Philippines. By contrast, the Malay Peninsula and Borneo have experienced relatively little volcanic activity in their recent history.

During the Pleistocene glaciations, sea-levels were as much as 180 m lower than today and the climate was drier and more seasonal. The rain forest blocks would have contracted, but to what extent remains unknown. However, it is thought that the contraction of rain forest in South East Asia was less severe than in Africa and South America (Whitmore 1985), which helps to explain the very high floristic richness of the present rain forest flora of Malesia. During periods of glaciations, the islands of the Sunda shelf (Java, Borneo, Sumatra and Palawan) were joined by land-bridges to mainland Asia at various times, though Java and Palawan, at the extremities of the shelf, were connected less often and less recently than Borneo and Sumatra. This explains the present day similarities and differences of their floras.

The region's mountainous terrain, reaching over 4500 m in New Guinea, and its predominantly insular character, has provided the conditions for many local speciation events. For a detailed discussion on the geological history of the region, see Whitmore (1981).

Climate

South East Asia straddles the Equator and experiences a tropical climate. Areas nearest the Equator (the Malay Peninsula, Borneo, Sulawesi, the southern parts of the Philippines, and parts of New Guinea) are generally hot, wet and humid throughout the year, with annual rainfalls averaging over 2000 mm, with at least 100 mm falling in every month. For example, Singapore (1°20'N, 103°49'E) receives 2282 mm of rainfall per year, and has mean monthly temperatures of 26°C in January and 27°C in July (at sea-level). These hot and humid conditions allow the development of rich tropical rain forest over much of the region. In general, the climate becomes drier and rainfall patterns are more seasonal as one travels further from the Equator. This is due to seasonal changes in winds (monsoons). Areas to the north, such as Luzon in the Philippines, experience their wettest months from June to August, whereas areas in the south, such as Java, have their wettest months from December to February. Jakarta (6°08'S, 106°45'E), for example, receives on average 1755 mm of rain each year, with an average of 335 mm falling in January but only 61 mm in July. Mean monthly temperatures are similar to those of Singapore (26°C in January and 27°C in July, at sea-level). Monsoon areas generally support less luxuriant forest cover than those nearer the Equator. Deciduous woodlands, savanna and grasslands may predominate, as in parts of the Lesser Sunda Islands and southern New Guinea.

These general patterns of climate are affected by altitude. In some years, the general pattern is also affected by El Niño Southern Oscillation events. These have caused serious droughts and have had marked affects on the vegetation in parts of Borneo (see Factors Causing Loss of Biodiversity, below). Typhoons (tropical storms known elsewhere as hurricanes), as well as heavy monsoon and equatorial rainfalls, can also have devastating effects. On the islands in the east of the region, and in the Philippines, in particular, typhoons can cause extensive destruction of forests through wind damage and tree felling, while heavy rainfalls throughout the region can result in serious erosion, landslides and flooding.

Population

The population of the South East Asian region is estimated at 271.82 million for 1990, and is set to rise to 420.66 million by 2025 (see Table 35). Most of the population lives in the western part of the region; New Guinea has only about 5.4 million inhabitants (see section on Papuasia). Malesia includes two of the world's most densely populated islands: Singapore (4463 people/km²) and Java (>700 people/km²), while many of the smaller islands in the region are uninhabited. Whereas Singapore's population is totally urbanized, nearly 75% of Papua New Guinea's population is rural.

Indonesia, with over 184 million people (in 1990) is the fifth most populated country in the world. As a means of alleviating the over-crowding on Java, Bali, Madura and Lombok, nearly three million people have been moved to the "outer" islands (Sumatra, Kalimantan, Sulawesi and to Irian Jaya) as part of the Indonesian Government's transmigration scheme – the world's largest programme of assisted migration. The land to which the transmigrants have moved has often suffered degradation as a result of the unsuitability of some areas for agriculture. Furthermore, the population of Java has been increasing at a faster rate than the numbers of people resettled elsewhere.

Settlement schemes are also ongoing in Malaysia. In 1956 the Malaysian Government began a large land development and settlement programme and established the Federal Land Development Authority (FELDA). By the end of 1984, 89,000 landless families (about 500,000 people) had been moved into 367 schemes covering over 6000 km² in Peninsular Malaysia. Many of the areas settled had been forested before the schemes commenced (Collins, Sayer and Whitmore 1991). The Sahabat Project, in the Dent Peninsula, is the largest land development scheme in Sabah, entailing the conversion of approximately 1030 km² of unpopulated forest into oil palm and other plantations,

TABLE 35. POPULATION DATA

| Country | Population (millions) | | | Average annual incremental rates (%) | | Urban population as % of total [d] | Density 1990 per km² |
	1950	1990	2025	1985–1990	1995–2000		
Brunei	-	0.3[a]	0.6[b]	2.7[c]	-	-	38.5[c]
Indonesia	79.54	184.28	282.32	2.1	1.8	31	101.7[d]
Malaysia	6.11	17.89	20.13	2.6	2.4	43	54.5[d]
Papua New Guinea	1.61	3.88	7.77	2.3	2.3	16	8.4[d]
Philippines	20.99	62.44	105.15	2.6	2.1	43	209.3[d]
Singapore	1.02	2.71	3.31	1.2	1.0	100	4463.9[d]
Solomon Islands	0.09	0.32	0.38	3.5	3.3	-	11.6[d]
Totals		271.82	420.66				

Sources:

Figures quoted are from World Resources Institute (1994), except where indicated by notes below.
[a] 1989 figure (from Collins, Sayer and Whitmore 1991).
[b] Maximum expected in year 2075 (from Collins, Sayer and Whitmore 1991).
[c] 1985 estimate (from Europa Publications 1987).
[d] World Resources Institute (1992).

TABLE 36. ORIGINAL AND REMAINING EXTENT OF CLOSED CANOPY MOIST FORESTS IN SOUTH EAST ASIA

Country	Approximate original extent of closed canopy tropical moist forests (km²)[a]	Remaining extent of moist forests (km²)			Rain forest (km²)[b]	% moist forest remaining	
		WCMC atlas data; rain and monsoon forests[a]	Publication date of maps[a]	FAO(1988a) data for 1980, closed broad-leaved plus coniferous forests[a]		WCMC map data[a]	From FAO (1988a) data[a]
Brunei	5000	4692	1988	3230	4580	94	65
Indonesia	1,700,000	1,179,140	1985–89	1,138,950	938,270	69	67
Malaysia	320,000	200,450	-	209,960	163,390	63	66
Peninsular Malaysia	(130,000)	(69,780)	1986	-	-	(53)	-
Sabah	(70,000)	(36,000)	1984	-	-	(51)	-
Sarawak	(120,000)	(94,670)	1979	-	-	(79)	-
Papua New Guinea	450,000	366,750	1975	342,300	293,230	82	76
Philippines	295,000	66,020	1988	95,100	37,280	22	32
Singapore	500	20	(1980s)	-	40	4	-
Solomon Islands	28,500	25,590	(1980s)	24,230	-	90	90
Totals	2,799,000	1,842,662		1,813,770		66	65

Sources:

[a] Collins, Sayer and Whitmore (1991). The remaining extent of closed canopy moist forests (including tropical coniferous forests), as derived from recently published maps, is compared with FAO statistics for 1980.

[b] World Resources Institute (1994).

together with a number of townships, a port, and several farming industries, served by a resident population of about 900,000 (Collins, Sayer and Whitmore 1991). The project is close to the Tabin Wildlife Reserve (see Data Sheet on East Sabah Lowland/Hill Dipterocarp Forests, SEA22).

Agricultural expansion and the number of land development schemes are likely to increase as the population continues to grow. However, large areas of the region have poor soils and will not sustain intensive agricultural production. Careful planning, environmental impact assessments, and the adoption of ecological principles in land management are essential to minimize soil erosion and degradation. Land development schemes need to be integrated with the protected areas network and areas of high biological diversity to avoid unnecessary damage.

The forests of the region are the home of many groups of tribal people some of whom, such as the Penan of Kalimantan and Sarawak, rely on hunting and gathering food from the forest for their subsistence. For these people, the destruction or degradation of forest brings economic impoverishment and the loss of their culture and ways of life. Often, the destruction of the forest forces indigenous tribes to migrate to the towns where they contribute to the growing numbers of unemployed and landless. With them too goes ethnobotanical knowledge built up over many generations.

Vegetation

The tropical rain forests of South East Asia together comprise the second largest area of tropical rain forest in the world (after that of Central and South America). Originally, closed canopy tropical moist forests of Malesia are estimated to have covered 2,799,000 km² (MacKinnon and MacKinnon 1986; Collins, Sayer and Whitmore 1991), about 92% of the total land area, extending from Sumatra in the west to the Solomon Islands in the east. North of the isthmus of Kra (latitude 10°30'N) in southern Thailand, rain forest only occurs as scattered patches in the wettest of sites, although there is a substantial area in south-eastern peninsular

Thailand. To the east, tropical rain forest extends into the Pacific region (Fiji, Samoa, Polynesia).

Estimates of the remaining extent of tropical moist forests vary according to definitions of forest type, estimated rates of deforestation, definitions of the various types of disturbances and the methods used in determining how much forest remains. Using recently available maps, WCMC estimate that there are 1,842,662 km² of moist forest (rain and monsoon forest types) remaining in the region (or 66% of the original area of closed canopy tropical moist forest (Collins, Sayer and Whitmore 1991). Table 36 provides the latest FAO and WCMC statistics on closed canopy tropical moist forest cover in South East Asia, and those for "rain forest" from World Resources Institute (World Resources Institute 1994).

The various types of forest in South East Asia have been well described by Whitmore (1985). The following section gives an overview of the main types; more detailed discussion on the extent of forest types in each part of the region can be found later in this chapter. Note that the forests of East Malesia are floristically distinct from those of West Malesia and are described in more detail in the section on Papuasia.

Lowland tropical evergreen rain forest

This is the most species-rich forest formation of the region and structurally the most complex. Species composition varies according to local soil and drainage conditions. The best sites are those which are not excessively drained and not excessively poor in mineral nutrients. Where environmental conditions are less favourable, the forest is generally less species-rich. In West Malesia, the dominant species are members of the economically important plant family Dipterocarpaceae. These often have clean boles of up to 40 m and occur as emergents as well as forming the upper canopy of the forest. Overall, Malesia contains 386 of the 550 species of dipterocarp. The greatest concentration of species within the family are in Borneo (which also has the highest number of endemic dipterocarp species), Peninsular Malaysia, Sumatra and the Philippines.

TABLE 37. DISTRIBUTION AND ENDEMISM IN MALESIAN DIPTEROCARPACEAE			
Area	Species	Endemics	% endemism
Borneo	267	155	58
Peninsular Malaysia	156	26	17
Sumatra	95	10	10
Philippines	45	21	45
New Guinea	15	11	73
Java	8	2	20
Sulawesi	7	2	29
Moluccas	6	1	16
Lesser Sunda Islands	3	0	0
Bismarck Archipelago	0	0	0
Solomon Islands	0	0	0

Sources: Jacobs (1981); Ashton (1982).

Table 37 shows the pattern of species distribution and endemism within the Dipterocarpaceae for the Malesian region.

In Peninsular Malaysian and Sumatran forests, trees belonging to families other than Dipterocarpaceae occur as emergents along with dipterocarps to a much greater degree than elsewhere in West Malesia. Thus, *Dialium*, *Koompassia* and *Sindora* (in the Leguminosae) and *Dyera costulata* (Apocynaceae) frequently occur as emergents in Peninsular Malaysia and Sumatra. In the east of the region, the forests of Papuasia have relatively few dipterocarp species.

Dipterocarps are highly valued by commercial loggers. Although the impact of logging varies according to the techniques used and levels of harvesting, logging often allows access for colonization and shifting cultivation. For example, virtually all primary forests outside of protected areas will have gone by the end of the century in the Philippines as a result of commercial logging followed by conversion to oil palm plantations and slash and burn cultivation. Little lowland forest is also expected to remain within 20 years in most parts of Malaysia and Indonesia, outside of Kalimantan and Irian Jaya, if the current rate of deforestation continues (see Factors Causing Loss of Biodiversity).

In contrast to those of West Malesia, the forests of Papuasia are dominated by a diverse mixture of tree species. The pressures on New Guinea forests are not yet as great as those on the forests elsewhere in the region; however, as elsewhere in the region, the impact of logging, shifting cultivation and associated fire damage, agricultural encroachment, road building and resettlement programmes, is increasing (see section on Papuasia).

Besides their value as sources of timber, the lowland forests of South East Asia contain a vast wealth of other useful plant resources (see Useful Plants). In view of their species diversity, economic importance and the increasing rate of forest clearance, lowland dipterocarp forests are a top priority for conservation throughout the region.

Tropical moist deciduous forest (Monsoon forest)

This occurs in areas with a marked dry season, e.g. northern parts of Sumatra, the Malay Peninsula and the Philippines, the Lesser Sunda Islands, east and central Java, southern Sulawesi and Timor. Tropical moist deciduous forests are not as rich in species as the lowland evergreen forests.

Dry evergreen forest

This occurs in southern New Guinea, and includes Australian floristic elements such as *Eucalyptus*, *Banksia* and *Grevillea* (see section on Papuasia).

Tropical semi-evergreen rain forest

This is the climax vegetation in transition areas between wet evergreen and deciduous forests and occurs, for example, in the Kra isthmus of the Malay Peninsula. It includes both evergreen and deciduous trees. These forests are not as rich in species as evergreen rain forests. Because of the dry season, both monsoon and semi-evergreen forest types are more easily destroyed by fire and, as a consequence, have been extensively cleared for shifting cultivation or have been logged, so that now only fragments of these forest types remain intact.

Heath forest (Kerangas)

Evergreen rain forest is replaced by heath forest (kerangas) on well-drained acidic soils derived from siliceous rocks. The main centre of development of heath forest is in southern Borneo, Sarawak, Brunei and along the eastern coast of Peninsular Malaysia (where they have all but disappeared due to burning). Many species found in heath forest also occur in lowland evergreen rain forest. However, there a number of differences in species composition, notably the predominance of members of such families as Myrtaceae and Casuarinaceae in heath forests, as well as the abundance of conifers such as *Agathis* (in numbers, but not species). In this respect, heath forests are similar to montane forests. Often, heath forest will occur in close proximity to lowland tropical evergreen rain forest, the latter occurring on more fertile soils.

Forest over limestone

In contrast to tropical Africa and much of Latin America (except the Caribbean region), South East Asia has many distinctive limestone outcrops. In Peninsular Malaysia and Sabah, these outcrops take the form of isolated precipitous outcrops, often in the lowlands. Elsewhere in the region, limestone occurs as extensive uplands, for example in New Guinea, and at Gunung Mulu National Park in Sarawak (where they form precipitous outcrops on Gunung Api and Gunung Benarat, which rise to over 1200 m). Forest over limestone generally supports a rich flora with a high degree of endemism, especially among herbs (see, for example, Chin 1977, 1979; and the Data Sheets covering the limestone floras of Peninsular Malaysia, Borneo, Sumatra and Sulawesi – SEA3, SEA18, SEA43 and SEA47, respectively, and the Data Sheet on Gunung Mulu National Park, CPD Site SEA33). In some outcrops, acidic conditions may develop in pockets where a deep mat of peat-like humus accumulates, supporting vegetation similar to heath forest, and including *Rhododendron*, *Vaccinium* and *Nepenthes*. A further distinct type of limestone is that of recently emerged, pericoastal coral platforms (for example in the Solomons) on which the flora is similar to adjacent lowland evergreen rain forest.

Ultramafic vegetation

Ultramafic (ultrabasic) outcrops support a distinct vegetation type. The best known areas of ultramafic vegetation are those found on Mount Kinabalu and Mt Tembuyuken (Mt Tambuyukon) in Sabah (see Data Sheet on Kinabalu Park, CPD Site SEA24), but other important outcrops are scattered throughout eastern Sabah (see Data Sheet on North-east Borneo Ultramafic Flora – SEA27). Other large areas of ultramafic rock outcrops include the northern foothills of the Cyclops Mountains and the north coast of Waigeo Island, Irian Jaya (CPD Site SEA71, see Data Sheet), substantial areas of Palawan (CPD Site SEA60, see Data Sheet), around Lake Matano in southern Sulawesi, and in Morowali Nature Reserve (see Data Sheet on the Ultramafic Flora of Sulawesi, CPD Site SEA48) in eastern Sulawesi. In Peninsular Malaysia, forest over ultramafic rocks is less distinctive (for example where it occurs on the eastern side of the Main Range). In the Solomon Islands ultramafic vegetation is mainly dominated by widespread *Casuarina papuana* and *Dillenia crenata*, with few endemic species. A general account of the vegetation of ultramafic areas in the region is given by Proctor (1992).

Montane vegetation

With increasing altitude, the structure, physiognomy and floristic composition of rain forest changes. Above 750–1200 m, lowland and hill forests merge into **lower montane rain forest**. This has a lower canopy than forests at lower elevations, and contains an increasing abundance of vascular epiphytes with altitude. Above approximately 1500 m (depending on location), there is a sharp decrease in the occurrence of mesophyllous species and an increase in the number of microphyllous species in the canopy. This is the **upper montane forest**, which may include variants such as "elfin forest", "cloud forest" and "mossy forest" depending on the characteristics of the forest on any particular mountain. Generally, upper montane forest has a stunted appearance with a canopy height of 10–20 m, and is especially rich in epiphytes (including a rich bryophyte flora), ericaceous species, Myrtaceae (particularly *Leptospermum flavescens*, which is replaced above 2450 m on Mount Kinabalu by *L. recurvum*) and orchids. Lower montane rain forest is generally richer in species than upper montane forest. In East Malesia, mid-montane forests are often dominated by *Nothofagus*, and the conifers *Dacrycarpus*, *Libocedrus* (*Papuacedrus*) and *Podocarpus* (see section on Papuasia).

On the higher mountains of the region, such as Puncak Jaya (Mount Carstensz, 4884 m) in Irian Jaya, Mt Wilhelm (4449 m) in Papua New Guinea, and Mt Kinabalu (4101 m) in Sabah, **subalpine** and **alpine zones** are encountered. The flora in these high elevations is less diverse than at lower altitudes. What vegetation exists includes low-growing herbaceous species and very stunted shrubs and subshrubs which may also be found in the upper montane zone.

In West Malesia, montane areas are generally less disturbed and not as seriously threatened as lowland areas. The forests are less attractive commercially for logging. The species composition of the forests, the steepness of slopes and inaccessibility are factors which prevent such large-scale clearances as those occurring in the lowlands. However, some very rich montane areas are under threat. In Peninsular Malaysia, for example, a number of important botanical sites along the Main Range (such as the Cameron Highlands and, further south, the Genting Highlands) are under increasing pressure from the development and extension of resorts and leisure complexes (see Data Sheet on the Montane Flora of Peninsular Malaysia, SEA4). At Taman Negara there were recent plans to construct a jeep track to open up the summit of Gunung Tahan to more visitors, and although plans for a chairlift to the summit of Mt Kinabalu (Sabah) have now been withdrawn, part of the Pinosuk Plateau, an area with a rich endemic flora, was excised in 1984 for the construction of a golf course and cattle farm.

Beach vegetation

The original vegetation along sandy shores included forests of pandans (*Pandanus* spp.), *Hibiscus tiliaceus*, *Thespesia populnea* and *Barringtonia asiatica*. *Terminalia catappa* often occurs along rich river valleys, and *Casuarina equisetifolia* forms pure stands on sandy floodplains. Most of the plants associated with these types of forest are almost entirely restricted to it. However, they are generally widespread, pantropical species (the so-called "Indo-Pacific strand flora"). In terms of species diversity, beach vegetation cannot be regarded as a priority for conservation. However, remnant stands of beach forest are, nevertheless, important habitats and contribute to coastal protection. Furthermore, since most has been cleared or greatly modified, remaining areas should be protected as samples of a severely threatened habitat type.

Wetland forests

The main wetland forest formations are: **mangrove forest**, **brackish-water forest**, and **periodically inundated freshwater swamp forests**. Each has a characteristic flora, but diversity is low when compared to dryland rain forest. Information on important wetland sites in South East Asia is given in Scott (1989). The status and importance of mangrove communities worldwide is reviewed by Saenger, Hegerl and Davie (1983). See also Collins, Sayer and Whitmore (1991) for more recent statistics and maps showing the extent of mangroves and swamp forests in South East Asia.

Mangrove forest occurs in silt-rich, saline, coastal waters, and is usually dominated by only a few species in families such as Rhizophoraceae (e.g. *Bruguiera*, *Rhizophora*), Avicenniaceae (e.g. *Avicennia*), Combretaceae (e.g. *Lumnitzera*) and Sonneratiaceae. Likewise, species diversity of **brackish-water forest** is low, often consisting of pure stands of nypa palm (*Nypa fruticans*).

Periodically inundated freshwater swamp forests are of two kinds: those developed on alluvial soils, and those developed on acidic peat. **Alluvial freshwater swamp forests** occur extensively in New Guinea (especially around the large rivers Fly and Sepik), and are scattered throughout the region on river floodplains, such as that of the Kinabatangan River in eastern Sabah. Where flooding is brief, the forest takes on the character of lowland tropical evergreen rain forest. In other areas (for example around lakes in Borneo) there are extensive floating grass mats. Open sedge or grass plains, possibly maintained by fire, are found in New Guinea. Also in New Guinea, pandan or palm swamp forest is extensive (see section on Papuasia).

Lowland peat swamp forests are extensive in east Sumatra, on the east and west coasts of Peninsular Malaysia, in Borneo (especially in Sarawak), and in the southern part of west New Guinea. Most of the tree families of lowland evergreen rain forest are found in peat swamp forest. Nearly all species are also common to both heath and peat swamp forest types (Anderson 1963; Brünig 1973).

Over much of their range (particularly in Java, the Philippines and in the Malay Peninsula), wetland forests (especially mangroves and alluvial freshwater swamp forests) have been over-exploited for timber, fuelwood and charcoal production, or to supply paper pulp industries, or have been reclaimed for agriculture and urban developments. In the Malay Peninsula much of the former alluvial wetland forests have been cleared to make way for rice paddies and, in places, rubber plantations; only fragments of alluvial freshwater swamp forests remain. Though not centres of plant diversity, wetland forests are nevertheless of major economic and ecological significance. Besides timber and fuelwood, they can supply a range of other products, such as alcohol from the sap of *Nypa fruticans*. Some species of mangrove are used as sources of medicines, glues, green manure and fodder for livestock. They also perform important ecological functions. For example, mangroves help to protect coastlines from erosion, and freshwater swamp forests help alleviate floods along river courses. Mangroves also play a crucial role in acting as breeding areas for many species of fish, prawns and molluscs. A recent estimate of mangrove-dependent fish and prawn catches in Peninsular Malaysia is well over US$30 million per year (Cubitt and Payne 1990).

Flora

Malesia is one of the richest botanical regions of the world. Earlier estimates for the size of the flora suggested that approximately 25,000–30,000 vascular plant species occurred in Malesia (van Steenis 1971). As work on *Flora Malesiana* has progressed, the estimate has been revised. Specialists now consider the region to have approximately 42,000 vascular plant species (Roos 1993). Some estimates put the figure as high as 50,000 vascular plant species (R.J. Johns 1992, pers. comm.). The flora is therefore estimated to include between 16–20% of the world's vascular plant species on just c. 2% of the world's land surface. Possibly 30% of the world's fern flora occurs in the region (Roos 1993).

About two-thirds of the flora of Malesia is found *only* in lowland rain forests; however, certain groups, such as orchids and ferns are primarily found in montane areas. Therefore, effective conservation of the flora requires a network of both lowland and montane sites throughout the archipelago.

The high floristic diversity of South East Asia is attributed by many authors to the prevailing climate and a diversity of microhabitats resulting from past and recent geological events. In addition, the existence of differing reproductive systems among sympatric plants of different taxa, and the frequent occurrence of natural disturbances in the region (e.g. earthquakes, cyclones, landslides, prolonged drought) may also have contributed to speciation. The region, especially Papuasia, is also notable as a refuge of many ancient, archaic angiosperms (Takhtajan 1986).

Flora Malesiana, the first part of which appeared in 1947, has so far covered 6231 species in 165 families (Roos 1993). The boundaries of Malesia are defined by generic "demarcation knots" which form the limits beyond which many genera do not occur (van Steenis 1950). These demarcation knots closely coincide with the limits of tropical evergreen rain forest. The first lies to the west, at the Isthmus of Kra in southern Thailand. Van Steenis (1950) found that 375 Malesian genera reach their northern limit here, while 200 continental Asian genera reach their southernmost limit of distribution. A second demarcation knot occurs in the north between the Philippines and Taiwan and mainland China. 421 genera were found to reach their northern limit here, while 265 genera reach their southern limit. The sharpest division occurs between New Guinea and Australia. This is the dividing line for 984 genera; 644 Malesian genera do not occur in northern Australia, and 340 Australian genera do not cross the Torres Strait into New Guinea. The eastern boundary of the region is not sharply defined, but *Flora Malesiana* accounts now include the Bismarck Archipelago, Louisiade Archipelago and the Solomon Islands.

A feature of the flora of Malesia is the presence of many species-rich families dominating the vegetation, including the important family of timber trees which dominate the canopies of western Malesian forests, the Dipterocarpaceae, which is represented by 10 genera and 386 species in the region (see Table 37).

There are at least 16 families of flowering plants in Malesia each with more than 500 species (van Steenis 1987; Dransfield 1990 for palms; Soepadmo 1992; Roos 1993, and *in litt.*). They include the following:

Family	Number of indigenous genera	Number of species
Orchidaceae	208	6500
Rubiaceae	149	2000
Euphorbiaceae	103	1000
Melastomataceae	35	1000
Palmae	52	975
Gesneriaceae	34	900
Annonaceae	56	875
Ericaceae	12	750
Araceae	41	725
Myrtaceae	34	725
Zingiberaceae	26	700
Lauraceae	20	700
Acanthaceae	54	625
Moraceae	16	575
Scrophulariaceae	44	500
Myrsinaceae	16	500

Malesia has 4 endemic families (Lophopyxidaceae, Matoniaceae, Pentastemonaceae and Scyphostegiaceae) and about 228 single-island endemic genera (see also van Steenis 1987; Johns 1989b; Soepadmo 1992).

Distribution of Endemic Genera

Area	Endemic genera
New Guinea	<140
Borneo	61
Peninsular Malaysia	24
Philippines	23
Sumatra	13
Sulawesi	5
Java	5
Moluccas	4
Solomon Islands	4
Lesser Sunda Islands	1
Bismarck Archipelago	1

Sources: van Steenis (1987); Soepadmo (1992).

18 genera are represented in Malesia by more than 200 species. They include the following:

Genus	Approximate number of Malesian species
Bulbophyllum (Orchidaceae)	1000
Dendrobium (Orchidaceae)	700
Selaginella (Selaginellaceae)	500
Syzygium (Myrtaceae)	500
Schefflera (Araliaceae)	490
Ficus (Moraceae)	475
Asplenium (Aspleniaceae)	400
Cyrtandra (Gesneriaceae)	400
Pandanus (Pandanaceae)	400
Diplazium (Dryopteridaceae)	300
Rhododendron (Ericaceae)	290
Calamus (Palmae)	280
Diospyros (Ebenaceae)	250
Eria (Orchidaceae)	250
Memecylon (Melastomataceae)	250
Vaccinium (Ericaceae)	240
Ardisia (Myrsinaceae)	220
Grammitis (Grammitidaceae)	215

(Data kindly supplied by M. Roos, *Flora Malesiana* project, based on a survey of specialists in 1991–1992.)

Some important plant groups in South East Asia

Orchidaceae
The largest family represented in the Malesian flora, with an estimated 6500 species (Roos 1993).

Palmae
Malesia and surrounding areas have the richest palm flora in the world, with c. 975 species in 52 genera, including 560 species of rattans. Rich palm floras include:

	Number of palm species	Endemic species
Indonesia	477	225 (47%)
Sarawak	213	56 (26%)
Peninsular Malaysia	195	83 (43%)
Philippines	157	109 (69%)
Sabah	131	14 (11%)

Dipterocarpaceae
386 out of the family's 550 species grow in Malesian forests, mostly in West Malesia. 346 species are endemic to Malesia. Borneo has 267 species, of which 58% are endemic; Sarawak and Brunei alone have 245 species; Peninsular Malaysia has 156 species, of which 17% are endemic.

Floristic divisions of Malesia

The floristic divisions of Malesia are described below, each of the main land masses within the region closely corresponding with the limits of floristic divisions. The distinctness of the floras of each of the main land masses underlines the need to protect a range of sites of high plant diversity throughout the region.

Malayan Sub-region
❖ *Malay Province*: includes the Malay Peninsula, the south-east part of peninsular Thailand, Singapore and Kepulauan Riau (Riau Archipelago). The flora is allied to Sumatra and Borneo and characterized by high generic endemism.
❖ *Bornean Province*: includes Borneo and its smaller surrounding islands, and Palawan (politically part of the Philippines). Floristically very rich, it has the highest generic and species endemism within the Malayan sub-region. The flora has much in common with that of the Malay Province; indeed a few genera, such as *Ashtonia* and *Stemmatodaphne* are confined to the Malay and Bornean provinces.
❖ *Philippinean Province*: includes the Philippine islands (excluding Palawan), the Babuyan and Batan Islands to the north of Luzon. The flora includes Malesian and Eastern Asiatic elements (the latter especially well-represented in montane areas), and also includes some Australian elements. Takhtajan (1986) includes the southern extremity of Taiwan in the Philippinean Province, although it is not included in *Flora Malesiana*. (Taiwan is treated in the Regional Overview on China and East Asia, elsewhere in this volume.) Generic and species endemism is very high in the Philippinean Province. According to Takhtajan (1986), there are over 30 endemic genera, and specific endemism approximates 68%. In primary forests, specific endemism is estimated at 84%. These figures are based on Merrill (1946); more accurate assessments await the completion of *Flora Malesiana*.
❖ *Sumatran Province*: includes Sumatra and its surrounding islands, and the Nicobar Islands (politically part of India, and treated in the Regional Overview on the Indian Subcontinent).
❖ *South Malesian Province*: includes Java and the Lesser Sunda Islands, as well as Christmas Island (300 km south of Java in the Indian Ocean). The latter is politically part of Australia, and is included in the Regional Overview on Australia. The flora of the South Malesian Province has low generic and specific endemism. Many Malesian rain forest genera are absent.

Central Malesian Sub-region
❖ *Celebesian (Sulawesian) Province*: includes Sulawesi and its neighbouring islands.
❖ *Moluccan Province*: includes Maluku (Moluccas) and the Banda Islands. There are no endemic genera.

Papuan Sub-region
❖ *Papuan Province*: includes New Guinea and its surrounding islands, the D'Entrecasteaux Islands and the Louisiade Archipelago. It is the richest province in all of the Indomalesian Subkingdom with high generic and species endemism.
❖ *Bismarckian Province*: includes the Bismarck Archipelago, the Admiralty Islands, and the Solomon Islands. The flora is an attenuated version of that of the Papuan Province.

Of the floristic provinces, the richest are the Bornean and the Papuan. The New Guinea mainland alone has an estimated 15–20,000 vascular plant species (R.J. Johns 1992, pers. comm.) and has exceptionally high rates of specific and generic endemism. Whilst being floristically very rich, Borneo and New Guinea are also the two great centres of rain forest in the region.

TABLE 38. FLORA STATISTICS OF INDIGENOUS VASCULAR PLANTS FOR PARTS OF SOUTH EAST ASIA

	Land area (km²)	Number of genera	Endemic genera	Number of vascular plant species	Number of endemic species [a]	% endemism
Papuasia	950,000	-	-	20,000–25,000 [b]	-	-
New Guinea	808,510	1465	<140	15,000–20,000 [b]	10,500–16,000	70–80 [b]
Solomon Islands	29,790	-	4	3172 [c]	30 [c]	0.9 [c]
Bismarck Archipelago	49,658	-	1	-	-	-
D'Entrecasteaux	3142	-	0	>2500 [d]	-	-
Louisiade Archipelago	1300	-	0	>3000 [d]	-	-
Bougainville	10,620	-	0	-	-	-
Borneo	738,864	-	61 [l]	20,000–25,000	6000–7500	c. 30 [f]
Brunei	5765	-	-	c. 6000 [f]	-	-
Sabah	73,710	-	-	>10,000 [m]	-	-
Sarawak	124,499	-	-	>10,000 [m]	-	-
Kalimantan	534,890	-	-	-	-	-
Malay Peninsula						
Peninsular Malaysia	131,598	1500 [g]	24 [l]	>9000 [h]	2700–4500	30–50 [h]
Singapore	570	577 [o]	0 [o]	1293 [o]	2 [o]	0.1
Sumatra	472,610	-	13 [l]	>10,000 [e]	>1200	12
Philippines	298,170	-	23 [l]	8931 [c,k]	3500 [c]	39 [c]
Sulawesi	184,840	-	5 [l]	c. 5000 [e]	-	-
Java	134,044	-	5 [l]	4598 [i]	230	5 [n]
Lesser Sunda Islands	89,770	-	1 [l]	-	-	1 [j]
Moluccas	69,230	0	4 [l]	3000 [p]	-	Low

Notes:
[a] The numbers of endemic species are mostly derived from the percentage estimate of species endemism, except where notes indicate.
[b] R.J. Johns (1992, pers. comm.).
[c] World Conservation Monitoring Centre (1992), approximate counts and/or extrapolations.
[d] Johns (1992).
[e] Whitten, Muslimin Mustafa and Henderson (1987).
[f] P.S. Ashton (1991, pers. comm.).
[g] Flowering plants.
[h] R. Kiew (1993, pers. comm.).
[i] Backer and Bakhuizen van den Brink (1963–1968).
[j] MacKinnon and MacKinnon (1986), estimates based on families so far revised for *Flora Malesiana*.
[k] Altoveros, Rosario, Sanico and Santos (1989) estimate >8600 vascular plant species for the Philippines.
[l] van Steenis (1987).
[m] Idris Mohd. Said (1989). Combined figures for number of species in Sabah and Sarawak.
[n] Soepadmo (1992).
[o] Keng (1990); the figures are for gymnosperms and dicots only.
[p] de Vogel (1989b).

Table 38 provides summary data on the richness and endemism of the various land masses in the region. The floras of the Sunda islands (Sumatra, Borneo) and that of Peninsular Malaysia, which also lies on the Sunda shelf, have close floristic similarities, though there are many differences at the species level. The Philippines, Peninsular Malaysia and Sumatra, though not quite as rich as Borneo or New Guinea, all contain in excess of 8000 species and numerous endemic genera. Sulawesi may be as rich, but at present its flora is poorly known. The southern island arc, from Java to the Lesser Sunda Islands, has a rather impoverished flora. The flora of the Moluccas is poorly known, but recent expeditions to Ceram indicate a very rich flora on that island. The islands of the southern arc have suffered greatly from deforestation. For example, virtually all Javan lowland forest has been converted to agriculture or cleared for settlements. What little forest remains in Java is restricted to the slopes of volcanoes and has been modified to a certain extent.

In addition to the above, figures quoted in World Conservation Monitoring Centre (1992) give 22,500 vascular plant species for the whole of Indonesia, with 15,000 endemics (i.e. 67% species endemism), and 12,500 vascular plant species for Malaysia (Peninsular Malaysia, Sabah and Sarawak). The figure for Malaysia is probably an underestimate bearing in mind that 30–50% of Peninsular Malaysia's 9000 vascular plant species are endemic and the richest areas of Borneo are in the north-western and northern parts of the island which include Sabah and Sarawak.

Useful plants

A significant number of village people in South East Asia depend on plants for their subsistence and well-being. It is estimated that between 5000 and 10,000 plant species in South East Asia are used in one way or another (Westphal and Jansen 1989). Heyne (1913–1917) described some 3000 useful species in Indonesia, and Burkill (1966) described 2432 species of the Malay Peninsula which have non-timber uses. Of the latter, Jacobs (1982) determined that 1283 flowering plant species are indigenous to primary lowland rain forests. From this he calculated that a minimum of 1 in 6 species native to this habitat are directly useful to man. At least 4.5% of the indigenous South East Asian flora has been used in traditional medicine. Of those species which have so far been used medicinally, between 560–900 species occur in the lowland rain forests of Borneo, New Guinea and Peninsular Malaysia (Jacobs 1982).

In order to update earlier studies on useful plants in the region, a major international project was initiated in 1985 by

Wageningen Agricultural University. This project, called PROSEA (*Plant Resources of South-East Asia*), is scheduled to last 10 years and will result in a database on the useful plants of the region and a multi-volume publication, each volume dealing with a particular commodity group. At the beginning of the PROSEA project, a "Basic list of species and commodity groupings" was made by Lemmens, Jansen and Siemonsma (1989). This initial list included the following among the largest commodity groups (excluding records from Papuasia):

Products/Commodity groups	Number of species
Timber trees	1517
Medicinal plants	1182
Ornamental plants	528
Edible fruits and nuts	414
Fibre plants	328
Forages	287
Vegetables	238
Plants producing exudates	184
Rattans	170
Dye and tannin-producing plants	121
Spices and condiments	112
Bamboos	58

The numbers in this list refer only to the primary uses of plants (and include introductions to the South East Asian region). Since only about a fifth of the plants on the "Basic list" belong to families so far treated in *Flora Malesiana*, the figures given for each commodity group must be treated with caution. Moreover, the "Basic list" was derived from only a few published sources and is, therefore, likely to change as PROSEA proceeds. However, the list does provide a reasonable estimate of the numbers of plants useful to man in the region.

The discussion below focuses attention on some of the most important commodity groups, particularly emphasizing the role of wild collected species in sustainable development.

Timber

By far the most immediate and visible cash benefit of tropical forests is in their exploitation as timber resources. Indeed, since the early 1970s the South East Asia-Pacific region has been the main source of the tropical timber trade (Nectoux and Dudley 1987). Of a total of 25 million m³ of tropical hardwood logs traded internationally in 1986, 21.4 million m³ originated from South East Asia and the Pacific region. The average annual export trade in forest products (i.e. roundwood, industrial wood, fuelwood and charcoal) amounted to US$3,713,902,000 for the whole of South East Asia between 1981 and 1983 (World Resources Institute and IIED 1986). In the same period, the highest earning countries in the region for exporting forest products were Malaysia (US$1,975,786,000), Indonesia (US$917,156,000) and Singapore (US$435,254,000). The figure for Singapore reflects that country's position at the centre of much of the region's trade with such importers of wood products as Japan. Out of a total world trade of 7.9 million m³ of sawn tropical hardwood in 1986, South East Asia accounted for 6.7 million m³. In Indonesia, timber is the second largest export earner after oil and natural gas combined, and foreign exchange earnings from timber rose to US$2,500,000,000 in 1987.

Nearly all industrial wood is extracted from closed broadleaved forests ("natural forests"). For example, the annual production of logs averaged 80,020,000 m³ during the years 1976–1979 in tropical Asia, of which 76,300,000 m³ were from "natural forests" (FAO 1982). About a quarter of all commercial hardwood cut today consists of dipterocarps, especially species of the genera *Shorea* (meranti), *Dipterocarpus* (keruing), *Vatica* and *Hopea* (giam) (Jacobs 1982). Certain types of *Shorea*, together with *Neobalanocarpus heimii* (chengal) and some species of *Hopea*, are used locally for construction; the light hardwoods of other species of *Shorea* (yellow meranti, red meranti and red seraya) and *Parashorea* are the basis of the export trade in logs, sawn timber and plywood. *Dipterocarpus* (keruing, apitong) and *Dryobalanops* (kapor) are used for railway sleepers and in construction.

Dipterocarp forests are now among the most threatened in the world; almost all dipterocarp forests outside of protected areas up to 800 m altitude have been leased to timber companies for exploitation. The situation is most acute in the Philippines where almost all dipterocarp forests have been logged. In 1986, the Philippines Government imposed a ban on all log exports. Previously, in the 1920s and 1930s, its forests yielded up to 450 m³/ha in Negros Province and Mindanao. In primary forests in Borneo, current fellings over limited areas yield more than 100 m³/ha; the regional average is c. 45 m³/ha (Collins, Sayer and Whitmore 1991).

In the late 1970s, Indonesia sought to reduce the preponderance of foreign interests in the export of its timber, and imposed a ban on export of all unprocessed logs in 1980; a large-scale plywood industry supplying North America and Europe established instead. Consequently, Indonesia is now the world's major tropical plywood producer and exporter. In Peninsular Malaysia, log exports are severely restricted and, in effect, non-existent. However, in Sabah, Sarawak and Papua New Guinea, the majority of forest products exported still consists of unprocessed timber. At the end of 1992, the federal government of Malaysia began negotiations to plan for banning all exports of unprocessed logs from Sabah. (This initiative was apparently aimed toward saving the sawmill industry.) According to FAO, nearly 68% of all wood removals in Malaysia (the leading world trader) are exported (FAO 1988b). Together, the two Malaysian states of Sabah and Sarawak exported 19 million m³ of logs in 1986, and 22.8 million ³ in 1987. Other major exporters are Papua New Guinea (1.44 million m³ of exported logs in 1987) and the Solomon islands (c. 0.3 million m³). The forests of New Guinea, as in other parts of the region east of Wallace's line (which runs between Borneo and Sulawesi), are sometimes entirely lacking in dipterocarps, the main timber trees being *Dracontomelum, Intsia, Pometia, Terminalia* and *Vitex* (see section on Papuasia).

A major review of commercial timber trees in the region is given by Soerianegara and Lemmens (1993). It deals with about 700 tree species.

Non-timber forest products

While their economic value as timber resources is beyond doubt, traditional societies and rural people have used dipterocarps and other forest products sustainably over long periods of time for a variety of purposes, and without the destruction of the resource base. For example, before the advent of synthetic materials, damar (a type of resin) was collected from dipterocarps and exported to Europe for use in the production of paints, varnish and linoleum. The Malays also collected damar for use as a fuel for lamps. The resin can also be used for waterproofing, as a glue, as a fumigant, and in medicine.

Some forest-dwelling peoples of South East Asia do not have access to substitutes for non-timber forest products they have traditionally used, or have no cash income with which to purchase substitutes. The value of non-timber forest resources cannot therefore be quantified simply in monetary terms. Furthermore, the cultural value of some forest products cannot be transferred to substitutes. Where trade occurs, non-timber forests products can contribute significantly to local and national economies, as demonstrated by a recent study made by Beer and McDermott (1989). For example, villagers in some parts of Lampung, Sumatra, earn about US$1000 per ha each year from tapping damar from cultivated trees of *Shorea javanica*. This is about one-quarter of the value of the trees if exploited for timber (Collins, Sayer and Whitmore 1991). However, damar can be tapped from a single tree for an estimated 15–20 years, whereas timber exploitation is a one-off event. Oleoresins are currently in demand for use as a perfume base. In Peninsular Malaysia, the Semelai used to tap *Dipterocarpus kerrii* for an oleoresin from which they would sell the essential oil fraction. About 20 different species of dipterocarp are known to have potentially valuable resins. Edible oils are obtained from illipe nuts of about 20 species of *Shorea*, all of which are also highly prized by loggers for their valuable timber (Beer and McDermott 1989).

In Sabah, it is estimated that a single mature wild tree of the durian *Durio zibethinus* could produce between 100–1000 kg of fruit per year, selling in local markets for between M$3–5/kg. Estimates for the other two main edible species of durian (which are rarely cultivated or only semi-cultivated) are, for *D. oxleyanus*, 300–500 kg of fruit/tree/year, and also selling for M$3–5/kg, and for *D. graveolens*, 200–800 kg/of fruit/tree/year selling at M$1–3/kg (A. Lamb 1993, *in litt.*).

At the national scale, Beer and McDermott (1989) calculate that the export value of non-timber forest products amounted to at least US$238 million for Indonesia in 1987, and US$11 million for Malaysia in 1986. It is important to note that these figures do not include items derived primarily from cultivated sources, and are probably under-estimates as official figures often exclude or under-report many non-timber items. The figures also omit local trade and those items which are used and consumed locally and which do not enter trade.

Rattan is by far the most important commercial non-timber forest product in South East Asia (see below). In Sarawak, however, illipe nuts are among the most important non-timber forest products in terms of export income. The market for illipe nuts, however, fluctuates widely. In 1982, the total value of illipe nuts entering export trade from Sarawak amounted to M$31,880,831 (approximately US$13 million), whereas in 1985 the value was M$326,816 (Department of Statistics, Sarawak, figures quoted in Beer and McDermott 1989).

Table 39 presents some Indonesian trade statistics for a number of non-timber forest products, including those from dipterocarps. (These figures refer to export trade and exclude locally consumed and traded products.)

At least 29 million people (the approximate number of forest dwellers in South East Asia) are critically dependent on forest resources, while the total number of people deriving benefits from them is substantially greater. The value of forest products other than timber is mostly underestimated since many of the products are consumed locally without entering the monetary economy. Even so, official exports of bamboo,

TABLE 39. INDONESIAN EXPORTS OF SOME NON-TIMBER FOREST PRODUCTS IN 1987

Species	Commodity	Value (US$)
Dipterocarps		
Shorea spp.	Illipe nuts	5,130,958
	Illipe oil	2,946,075
Dipterocarpus spp.	Damar oleoresin	651,883
Dipterocarpaceae spp.	Gum damar	506,743
Dryobalanops aromatica	Camphor	1293 [a]
Non-dipterocarps		
Rattans (all forms)	Rattan	211,560,000
Pinus merkusii	Pine resin	5,660,312 [b]
	Gum turpentine	789,823 [b]
Dyera costulata	Jelutong	2,183,462
Agathis dammara	Copal resin	1,541,714
Arenga spp.	Aren fibre	851,435

Notes:
[a] Includes camphor derived from *Cinnamomum camphora* (Taiwan camphor wood), most of which is obtained from cultivated sources.
[b] A significant amount of pine resin and gum turpentine is obtained from cultivated sources.
Source: Beer and McDermott (1989).

rattan, tannins, honey, wood oils, pharmaceuticals and wildlife earned more than US$100 million in foreign exchange for Indonesia in 1980 (IIED 1985) and US$238 million in 1987 (UNEP 1981). It is estimated that in Indonesia there were 150,000 people in 1979 involved on a full-time basis in collecting non-timber forest products for sale. (This figure excludes a much larger number who are engaged in part-time collecting.) In comparison, total employment in the logging industry was only 70,000 in 1982 for Indonesia (IIED 1985).

Primary rain forests in the region, particularly primary lowland evergreen rain forests, contain the greatest number of plant species (Soepadmo 1983), including those which are currently the most valued non-timber forest resources by indigenous and rural people (as sources of food, medicines and a host of other products). Primary forests represent a vast pool of potentially useful species, as well as a more or less untapped pool of genetic material for breeding or selecting improved varieties of existing fruit and timber trees (for example). This last point is particularly important for tropical forestry, in view of its shrinking resource base, and the danger of "genetic erosion" resulting from the continual harvesting of the best timber trees through selective logging. The protection of the best remaining, species-rich areas of forest is therefore not only biologically important, but in the long-term, a sound commercial expedient.

Besides the loss of useful plant resources, deforestation results in the reduction, or total loss, of many other economic benefits, such as watershed protection and climate amelioration, which would have been provided by the forest on a long-term and sustainable basis. In addition, tropical rain forests and montane areas are becoming increasingly attractive resources for national and international tourism. Yet the value of these potential and actual economic benefits, which could accrue from conservation and sustainable use of the resource, is often not taken fully into account. Often this is a result of the difficulties of valuing the range of goods and services which rain forest provides, although the study by Beer and McDermott (1989) clearly demonstrates the importance of non-timber forest resources to the economies of the region.

A number of important non-timber forest products are discussed in more detail below. Particular emphasis is given to West Malesia. For examples of useful plants in East Malesia, see the later section on Papuasia.

Rattans

There are about 600 species of rattans, all of which are confined to the Old World. They favour wet evergreen rain forests, their greatest concentration being in Borneo (which has at least 151 rattan species) and Peninsular Malaysia (at least 104 species) (Dransfield 1979, 1981). At the local level, people living near to forests may have uses for almost all the species encountered. They are used for matting, thatching, basketry, and as sources of dyes and medicines. Some species of rattan have edible fruits (such as *Daemonorops ingens* and *D. scapigera*); others are valued for their edible palm "cabbage" (*D. longipes* and *D. microstachys*, for example), while *D. micracantha* is said to produce the best quality Dragon's Blood in Sarawak and was formerly used in dyes and medicines. By contrast, relatively few species enter world trade in rattan for the furniture industry (Dransfield 1992).

The total value of world trade in rattan is difficult to quantify but estimates of US$2.5 billion per annum are probably conservative (Dransfield, Mogea and Manokaran 1989). This makes rattan the most important commercial forest product after timber in South East Asia. Between 70–90% of rattan that enters trade comes from Indonesia, which exported about 145,000 tonnes of raw, processed and manufactured rattan in 1987. Most rattan is harvested from the wild. For example, of the 104 species of rattans in Peninsular Malaysia, only about 20 species are commercially important, and all rattan entering commerce is collected from the wild (Kiew 1989, 1991).

Rural people throughout the region have relied for their rattan supplies on the diversity of species occurring naturally in the forest, but decreasing forest cover and commercial collecting have resulted in spiralling over-exploitation, and some species are now threatened. This is particularly the case in the Philippines, where little legally harvestable wild rattan now remains. Export restrictions on unmanufactured rattan introduced by neighbouring countries, such as Indonesia, have exacerbated the shortages. As a result, in a few areas where primary forest cover is much depleted and there is a strong tradition of rattan handicrafts, rattan cultivation is beginning. In Kalimantan, where whole villages rely on rattan production as an economic activity, there has been rattan cultivation for over 100 years.

The first large-scale rattan plantations outside of Kalimantan were in Sabah in the late 1970s. Since then, government forest agencies have set up plantations in Sarawak and in parts of Indonesia. In the Philippines, most rattan plantations are private concerns. Trials are underway in other parts of the region, such as in Peninsular Malaysia, where recently the Forest Department has encouraged rattan planting in both logged forests and rubber plantations (Kiew 1989, 1991). Clearly, there is great potential for future development of commercial rattan cultivation in South East Asia, and this will depend on areas of intact forest supplying the source material from which commercial ventures can be set up.

Further information on the rattan trade is given in Beer and McDermott (1989) and in Johnson (1991) which covers all aspects of palm utilization and conservation (including rattans) in Asia. A comprehensive guide to rattan ecology, uses and cultivation, including economic aspects, is given in Wan Razali Wan Mohd., Dransfield and Manokaran (1992). See also Dransfield and Manokaran (1993) which deals with 24 major and 106 minor rattans in the region. For Malaysia, see also the *Malayan Naturalist* (1989) special issue entitled: *Conservation and utilization of Malaysian palms* (Vol. 43, Nos. 1–2).

Fruits

South East Asia, and the forests of West Malesia in particular, contains one of the world's largest gene pools of tropical fruit trees. Examples include:

❖ *Artocarpus integer* (cempedak), with 45 wild relatives;
❖ *Citrus* spp., of which there are at least 45 wild relatives;
❖ *Durio zibethinus* (durian), with about 25 wild relatives, 5 of which have edible fruits;
❖ *Garcinia mangostana* (mangosteen), with about 10 edible wild relatives;
❖ *Mangifera* spp. (mangoes) of which there are 65 species, many with edible fruits (Kostermans and Bompard 1989);
❖ *Musa* spp. (bananas and plantains), with about 10 edible species;
❖ *Salacca zalacca* (snakefruit), with 12 wild relatives.

There are about 800 species in the region which bear edible fruits, nuts or seeds (Verhey and Coronel 1989), including introductions. Of these, about 400 species are primarily used as sources of these products, and about 250 of them are trees. Loh (1975) reported that, of the estimated 100 species of fruit trees grown in Peninsular Malaysia on an area of 500 km^2, 80 species are native, and nearly all come from the lowland forests of Peninsular Malaysia and Borneo.

Most fruit in South East Asia is produced in home gardens, fruit growing presumably originating at the time of settled agriculture. However, a considerable amount of fruit is still gathered directly from the forests and sold locally. For example, of the 17 species of mango native to Indonesia, 14 are sold in local markets. Of the species sold, 5 occur only in the wild, while others are either cultivated or "semi-cultivated" within the forest (Bompard 1988). In shifting agriculture, fruit trees are often planted to enrich fallows, or are "semi-cultivated" in areas of forest close to settlements, while indigenous hunter-gathering tribes harvest fruits directly from wild trees in the forest. Both urban dwellers and settled rural agriculturalists plant fruit trees in their gardens while, on a commercial scale, fruit trees are grown in plantations to supply an increasing urban and tourist market, as well as for export trade.

Despite the apparent abundance of fruits in South East Asia, the commodity is often too expensive for local people (Verhey and Cronel 1989). Part of the reason for this is relatively low yields. Growing fruit in home gardens is a solution to this, enabling rural societies to enjoy fruit without having to pay. However, the demands of a growing population and, particularly, the increasing number of people living in towns and cities, where land is in short supply, continue to make fruit expensive.

There is no doubt that methods of cultivation and selection of high-yielding cultivars can increase yields, but there is also the possibility that wild species as yet uncultivated could hold promise for cultivation. However, Verhey and Coronel (1989) suggest that the number of such species is likely to be small. They believe that the long tradition of shifting cultivation in the region has probably resulted in most fruit trees having been tried in cultivation. For evidence of this, they point to the lists of species found in fallow plots, which reveal only well-known fruit species. They argue that this may be an indication that in South East Asia there is not much scope for bringing new species of fruits into cultivation. However, some species that have good fruits are virtually unknown in cultivation because their requirements have not been determined (for example, they may require specific mycorrhizal fungi). When their cultivation requirements are known they could have great potential. Another reason why some species may not have been tried in cultivation is that traditionally it has been easier to collect the fruits every year from nearby forest trees. This is the case for some wild *Durio* and *Artocarpus* spp.

South East Asian forests contain a large number of wild relatives of existing fruit crops which offer potential for utilization in breeding programmes, or as rootstocks, to improve the yields of existing crops. This particularly applies to such fruits as durian (*Durio* spp.), rambutan (*Nephelium* spp.) and mangoes (*Mangifera* spp.). Furthermore, many existing species of economic value are under-utilized, such as mangosteen (*Garcinia mangostana*) and cempedak (*Artocarpus integer*). The long-term contribution of these and other non-timber plant-derived forest products to the economies of South East Asia is threatened by the current rate of forest loss and, in the case of fruit trees, by erosion of their gene-pools by selective felling of good fruiting specimens. This is principally carried out by loggers and hunters visiting areas temporarily.

Bamboos

Bamboos represent one of the major plant resources of South East Asia, particularly for people living in rural areas. It is estimated that there are about 180 species of bamboo in South East Asia (Widjaja and Dransfield 1989). About 100 species are indigenous to monsoon areas and have limited distributions. About 30 species are found only in cultivation, while 125 species are cultivated and are also known in the wild. Some important bamboos in the region have been introduced from elsewhere, such as *Gigantochloa apus* from Burma, and *Bambusa multiplex* from China.

Bamboos have many uses and are sometimes grown on a large-scale for specific purposes, e.g. *Dendrocalamus asper* for canning as a vegetable, *Gigantochloa atroviolacea* for musical instruments, *G. atter* for toothpicks and chopsticks, and *Bambusa vulgaris* for furniture. More recently, bamboos have also been used in the paper pulp industry, and for the production of ply-bamboo.

A number of genera are particularly important, such as *Dendrocalamus*, of which 17 species occur in South East Asia, 9 species being of economic importance; members of the genus *Gigantochloa* are the most widely used by Malays and Indonesians for construction, basketry and other household utensils (Widjaja 1984).

The most important use of bamboos is for building materials. It is estimated that 80% of the bamboo consumed in Indonesia is used in the construction of buildings (for floors, walls, pillars, rafters and ceilings for example) (Widjaja and Dransfield 1989). *Bambusa*, *Dendrocalamus* and *Gigantochloa* are the most widely used, but in the Philippines and Sulawesi, *Schizostachyum brachycladum* and *S. lumampao* are also used (Widjaja and Dransfield 1989). Another important use of bamboos is in the production of handicrafts and furniture.

Bamboos have often been planted along rivers to prevent soil erosion, and as windbreaks, and for ornamental purposes. In Indonesia, they are increasingly planted on degraded land to prevent soil erosion, as well as providing an economic crop for the paper industry.

The many uses of bamboos offer opportunities and income to rural people. Production comes from two sources: harvesting species in cultivation and collecting directly from the wild. The majority of bamboo is harvested from plantations established especially for this purpose. However, there is scope for increasing the area under plantations. The average annual production of bamboo poles in Thailand in 1981–1984 was about 52 million culms, whereas in Indonesia the annual average production was only about 52,089 tons or 53,105 culms for the period 1974–1981.

Staple foods

For many rural households, forests supply staple foods, or others which are gathered in times of shortage. One of the most important staples is wild and semi-wild sago (*Metroxylon sagu*), especially in the freshwater swamp areas of New Guinea (see section on Papuasia), the Mentawai Islands and Sabah. The traditional staple of the Punan and Penan, hunter-gatherer tribes in Borneo, is sago from *Eugeissona utilis*, a calamoid palm. This is also used as a reserve food by the Kenyah of Sarawak, as are palm hearts. Other palms also provide sago in times of hardship.

Factors causing loss of biodiversity

Volcanoes, earthquakes and typhoons

Indonesia is one of the most active volcanic regions of the world. Java alone has over 50 active volcanoes out of Indonesia's total of 150. Earthquakes are also common, mostly occurring along the outer edges of the island arcs, especially in the Mentawai Islands to the south of Sumatra. The damage caused by these events, along with occasional typhoons, in the Philippines, northern Borneo and Papua New Guinea, in particular, is at times catastrophic and it is quite possible that extinctions of locally restricted endemics have occurred as a result (though as far as is known there is no documentary evidence of such cases in the region). On the other hand, the forests have co-evolved with these natural disturbance factors over long periods of time, and such disturbances are part of the overall dynamics of the forest ecosystem and give rise to habitat diversity (see, for example, Johns 1986, 1990).

Droughts and fires

The El Niño Southern Oscillation appears to have had a major impact on ecosystem stability in West Malesian and Papuasian rain forest communities (see, for example, Johns 1986, 1989b, 1990). The significance of droughts associated with periodic El Niño Southern Oscillation events was not fully realized until the 1982–1983 droughts (and associated fires) which decimated extensive areas of rain forest in Kalimantan and Sabah (Beaman, Beaman, Marsh and Woods 1985; Woods 1987). The fire became known as "The Great Forest Fire of Borneo". East Kalimantan was the worst affected area. Here, 8000 km² of unlogged primary forest, 5500 km² of peat swamp forest, and 12,000 km² of selectively logged forest were severely damaged (Malingreau, Stephens and Fellows 1985). The fire began during the drought in areas which had been converted to shifting cultivation following logging. It spread rapidly as a result of the dry litter in logged-over forests, and also as a result of burning surface peat and underground coal deposits. In Sabah, nearly all the fires which began at that time were the result of human activities (deliberate and accidental). Many fires "escaped" from areas being burnt for shifting cultivation, or were started by hunters and road-cutters. Fires then funnelled along logging roads, feeding on bark and leaf litter.

1986 was another period of major El Niño-related droughts; less serious drought occurred in 1987, which resulted in fires in south Kalimantan. Another in 1991 witnessed fires in several regions of Borneo, apart from the north-west.

The link between forest disturbance and fires suggests that damaging fires during prolonged dry spells are likely to become an even greater problem in the future. However, fires are not restricted to disturbed forests; extensive areas of natural forest are subjected to fires resulting from lightning strikes.

Logging

FAO/UNEP (1981) estimates that deforestation of closed forest during the period 1981–1985 averaged 2550 km² per year (or 1.2% of the total) for Malaysia and 6000 km² per year (0.5% of the total) for Indonesia. These figures refer to outright conversion of forest land for subsequent use for permanent agriculture or settlement. The figures do not include modifications made to the forest by selective logging and active management of production stands, or modifications made during shifting cultivation. Even selective logging of primary forest areas can leave between one-third and two-thirds of the residual trees severely damaged if logging operations are not done with adequate care. In addition to the direct effects of logging operations, the forest is opened up to illegal squatters and/or shifting cultivators, resulting in further modification and, at worse, total elimination of the forest resource.

According to a recent study for the ITTO, less than 1% of natural forests in South East Asia undergo silvicultural management to ensure sustainable yields (IIED 1988; Poore, Burgess, Palmer, Rietbergen and Synott 1989).

Shifting cultivation

When shifting cultivation is carried out at a low intensity with adequate periods of fallow, it is a successful and sustainable way of cultivating areas with poor soils, steep gradients and heavy rainfall. In the most stable and productive systems, crops are grown on cleared land for one or two years, after which weed growth and lack of nutrients in the soil makes further cultivation difficult. Secondary forest colonizes the abandoned fields from adjacent primary forest patches. This woody vegetation provides a number of useful products (such as fruits) and provides the habitat for deer, primates,

and other animals which are hunted for food. Often, over 100 crops (including medicinal plants) may become naturalized, or are planted, in swiddens and regenerating fallow forest. In East Kalimantan, for example, rattans are planted in old swiddens, while, in the Chimbu valley in New Guinea, agroforestry has been based on *Casuarina oligodon*, a nitrogen-fixing tree of secondary-regrowth, for some 700 years. Gradually, the fertility of the soil is restored until after about 10–15 years plots can be brought back into cultivation.

Traditional shifting cultivation is well-adapted to tropical moist forest environments, and in any one area results in a mosaic of vegetation types from cleared land to secondary and primary forest patches. In its traditional form, therefore, it does not lead to outright deforestation. However, as the human population has grown, and in areas where smallholders have been forced to migrate to uplands as a result of competition over land use in the lowlands, traditional forms of shifting cultivation have been replaced by more destructive systems in which fallow periods are shortened and areas unsuited to cultivation are cleared of forests. These destructive forms of shifting cultivation, perhaps better described as "slash and burn" agriculture, have resulted in vast areas of land becoming degraded throughout the region. As a result, *Imperata cylindrica* grasslands, bamboo and other types of scrub, and weed-infested landscapes have replaced the original forest cover in many areas, notably in south and central Borneo, in the New Guinea uplands, the Philippines and in the Lesser Sunda Islands.

Myers (1980) estimated that forest farmers (including traditional shifting cultivators, smallholder agriculturalists and squatters) accounted for a minimum of 85,000 km² of land cleared for agriculture in South East Asia each year. (Some of this land would be allowed to regenerate.) This makes shifting cultivation, in all its forms, the most significant factor in deforestation in South East Asia. According to Lanly (1982), shifting cultivation accounts for 50% of all forest loss in the whole of Asia. Often, slash and burn agriculture follows in the wake of commercial logging as access and forest clearance is made easier by logging tracks and the opening up of the forest during logging operations.

Plantation agriculture

Conversion of forests for large-scale commercial plantations of oil palm, rubber, sugar cane, tea, coffee and cacao is occurring throughout the region. In Peninsular Malaysia, much of the original forest has been cleared for rubber plantations. Today, oil palm is replacing rubber as a leading plantation crop throughout much of West Malesia, while in Papua New Guinea coffee is more important. Although some plantations are established on land which has long since been cleared of forests, many new ones result in the direct loss of primary forest.

Transmigration and settlement schemes

Indonesia has the world's largest programme of assisted migration. Since the programme began, over 26,000 migrants from western Indonesia (principally from the over-crowded island of Java) have been moved to new settlements in less-crowded islands, such as Sumatra, Borneo (Kalimantan), Sulawesi, and to Irian Jaya. Transmigrants are settled in pre-selected development regions usually after the sites have

been evaluated by foreign consultants and national professionals (Petocz 1984, 1989). The effects of these re-settlement schemes on the environment differ from place to place, but in many cases have been adverse as a result of the areas selected being marginal and unsuitable for sustained agriculture (Hanson 1981). The actual deforested area arising from the transmigration programme is, however, small relative to the total forest estate and, in almost all cases, the areas allocated were already scheduled as "Conversion Forest". Designated land for transmigration sites amounts to 28,804 km^2 in Sumatra, 14,872 km^2 in Kalimantan, 9063 km^2 in Irian Jaya and 4174 km^2 in Sulawesi (figures from ODA 1990, quoted in Collins, Sayer and Whitmore 1991).

In addition to the actual area deforested for transmigration settlements, associated road developments open up formerly undisturbed areas to agriculture and settlement, and ribbon development often occurs along the newly constructed roads. The requirements of resettled people for fuelwood and building materials also places additional pressures on surrounding areas of forest.

Earlier problems associated with transmigration schemes taking place in unsuitable areas should be alleviated by the Regional Physical Planning Programme for Transmigration project (ODA 1990). This has been preparing land use maps of Indonesia since 1988 to enable identification of areas most suited for possible future development as transmigration sites. Ensuring the integrity of protected areas is one of the priorities of the project (ODA 1990).

Road building

Roads are a major threat to wildlife conservation in general. Besides the direct effects of forest destruction during their construction, roads increase accessibility for hunters, settlers, plant collectors, and for agricultural expansion, and affect the movement and distribution of species (especially animals). Cuttings increase the risk of soil erosion, and localized flooding can occur as a result of compaction and alteration of drainage patterns resulting in the death of forests in inundated areas. Major road building programmes are of particular concern at present in Peninsular Malaysia, where many montane areas of high endemism are threatened (see Data Sheet on Montane Flora of Peninsular Malaysia, SEA4). In Irian Jaya a number of reserves have been damaged or are threatened by major road-building schemes (see section on Papuasia). They include the proposed National Parks of Gunung Lorentz (CPD Site SEA69, see Data Sheet) and Mamberamo-Foja (see Data Sheet on Mamberamo – Pegunungan Jayawijaya, CPD Site SEA70), both of which are important centres of plant diversity.

Mining and quarrying

Mining and quarrying have a marked impact locally, but often do not result in large areas being deforested. Large-scale gold, copper and nickel mining occur in New Guinea and Bougainville (see section on Papuasia). Nickel mining occurs near Malili in Sulawesi. Copper is also mined on a large scale in an area once within Kinabalu Park (CPD Site SEA24, see Data Sheet) in Sabah; quarrying of limestone is one of the main threats to a number of endemic-rich limestone outcrops in Peninsular Malaysia (see Data Sheet on the Limestone Flora of Peninsular Malaysia, SEA3).

Over-collecting of plants

A number of plant groups, especially useful plants, such as rattans (see above) and ornamental plants, such as orchids and *Nepenthes* (pitcher plants), are threatened by over-collecting for commercial purposes. Collection of forest products frequently takes place illegally within established protected areas. However, in some cases, collecting such products within national parks is a statutory right of indigenous people who retain traditional hunting and gathering rights.

There is a significant international demand for ornamental species, especially orchids. While around 80% of internationally-traded orchids are reported to be artificially propagated, a large part of the trade is satisfied through the collection and export of wild plants. Among the sought-after genera are *Paphiopedilum* and *Dendrobium*. The genus *Paphiopedilum* is now included in Appendix I of CITES which effectively bans commercial international trade in wild-collected plants (Oldfield 1992). *Nepenthes rajah* is also on Appendix I, while all other species of *Nepenthes* are on Appendix II.

Conservation

A number of reviews have been made of the protected areas system and recommendations for its further development in the region. For example, a comprehensive National Conservation for Indonesia (FAO 1981–1982) outlined the development of a protected areas network covering 112,000 km^2 of Indonesia's terrestrial area, and subsequently formed the basis of the Indonesian section of an IUCN System Review of the Indomalayan Realm (MacKinnon and MacKinnon 1986) and all subsequent reviews. A conservation strategy for Irian Jaya has subsequently been expanded and updated by WWF/IUCN (Petocz 1984, 1989). IUCN (1992) provides a recent review of the protected areas system of the region and legislation relating to conservation in each country.

Many studies have primarily focused on large mammals as a means of assessing priorities for expanding the protected areas network, as well as indicating major habitat types which are inadequately protected. An analysis of the areas selected in the present study indicate the urgent need to protect more samples of lowland rain forest formations throughout the region, increased protection for specialized edaphic communities, particularly limestone and ultramafic vegetation, and the need to ensure protection of montane sites, many of which harbour local endemics. Wetland sites are generally under-represented in the areas selected as CPDs, but their conservation is important for other ecological and economic reasons (including sometimes their importance as fish-breeding areas and their role in coastal protection).

Management of protected areas throughout much of the region is constrained by insufficient trained personnel and a frequent absence of clearly and accurately defined protected areas boundaries. Frequently, there are conflicting land use objectives of national and local governments, the conservation administration, and local people living within and around the reserves. As a result of pressures for land to grow crops and the encroachment of logging concessions, few of the legally designated protected areas are, in practice, under complete protection. In recent years, governments have excised some important areas from national parks and reserves for land development and resource exploitation, while slash and burn agriculture is a threat to many protected areas in Indonesia, the Philippines and Sarawak.

Recognizing the important role that local people can play in managing the areas they utilize, and often on which they depend for their survival, protected area management in the region is increasingly concerned with improving the welfare of local inhabitants and developing buffer zones around reserves.

In Malaysia, WWF Malaysia, the Malaysian Nature Society (formerly the Malayan Nature Society), and other local NGOs, frequently work with government agencies on matters relating to conservation. A National Conservation Strategy (NCS) was commissioned by the Economic Planning

Unit of the Prime Minister's Department in 1991, and completed at the end of 1992. The Malaysian Nature Society has recently produced baseline data on Malaysia's flora, fauna and ecosystems (Kiew 1991) and is currently developing a computerized database on threatened species, sites and habitats throughout Malaysia.

Centres of plant diversity and endemism

South East Asia sites identified as centres of plant diversity and endemism are listed in Table 40. The location of the CPD Data Sheet sites are shown on Map 8.

MAP 8. CENTRES OF PLANT DIVERSITY AND ENDEMISM: SOUTH EAST ASIA

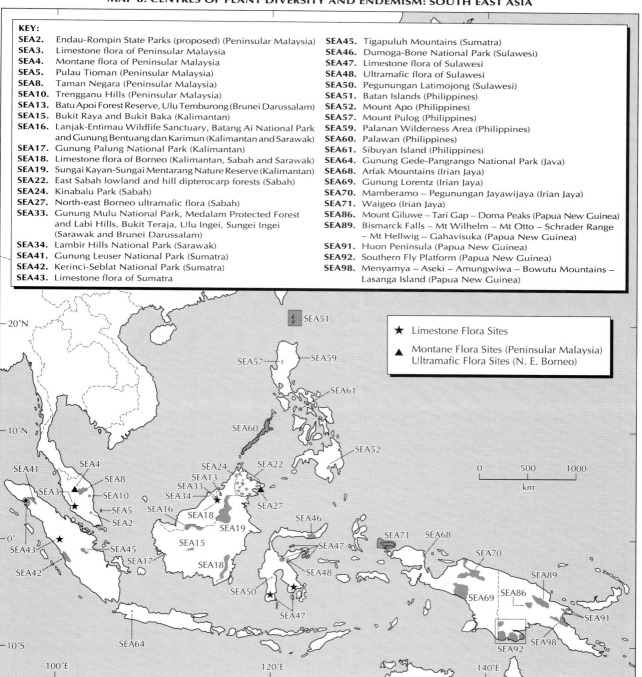

TABLE 40. SOUTH EAST ASIA SITES IDENTIFIED AS CENTRES OF PLANT DIVERSITY AND ENDEMISM

The list of sites is arranged according to the sequence adopted in the Regional Overview. Sites selected for Data Sheet treatment appear in bold.

PENINSULAR MALAYSIA
SEA1. Dindings, Segari Melintang and Larut Hills
SEA2. **Endau-Rompin State Parks (proposed)**
SEA3. **Limestone flora of Peninsular Malaysia**
SEA4. **Montane flora of Peninsular Malaysia**
SEA5. **Pulau Tioman**
SEA6. Sedili Kecil Swamp Forest
SEA7. South-east Pahang Swamp Forests
SEA8. **Taman Negara**
SEA9. Tasek Berah Forest Reserve
SEA10. **Trengganu Hills**
SEA11. Ulu Belum

BORNEO – BRUNEI DARUSSALAM
SEA12. Andulau Forest Reserve
SEA13. **Batu Apoi Forest Reserve, Ulu Temburong**
SEA14. Labi Hills, including Bukit Teraja and Ulu Ingei, Batu Patam-Sungei Ingei (See also SEA33.)

BORNEO – KALIMANTAN, INDONESIA
SEA15. **Bukit Raya and Bukit Baka**
SEA16. **Lanjak-Entimau Wildlife Sanctuary, Batang Ai National Park and Gunung Bentuang dan Karimun** (also in Sarawak)
SEA17. **Gunung Palung National Park**
SEA18. **Limestone flora of Borneo** (also covers limestone areas in Sabah and Sarawak)
SEA19. **Sungai Kayan-Sungai Mentarang Nature Reserve**
SEA20. Ulu Sembakung

BORNEO – SABAH, MALAYSIA
SEA21. Crocker Range/Mount Trus Madi
SEA22. **East Sabah lowland and hill dipterocarp forests**
SEA23. Gunong Lotung/Maliau Basin
SEA24. **Kinabalu Park**
SEA25/26. Ulu Meligan/Ulu Long Pasia
SEA27. **North-east Borneo ultramafic flora**
Note: For limestone sites in Sabah, see SEA18

BORNEO – SARAWAK, MALAYSIA
SEA28. Bako National Park
SEA29. Batu Laga, Linau Balui Plateau
SEA30. Bukit Mersing, Anap, Tatau region
SEA31. Gunung Gading National Park
SEA32. Gunong Gaharu, Gunong Apeng and Gunong Silantek, Sabal Forest Reserve
SEA33. **Gunung Mulu National Park, Medalam Protected Forest and Labi Hills, Bukit Teraja, Ulu Ingei, Sungei Ingei** (also in Brunei Darussalam)
SEA34. **Lambir Hills National Park**
SEA35. Mixed dipterocarp forests on humult ultisols on coastal hills
SEA36. Nieuwenhuis Mountains
SEA37. Pueh Range (Gunung Pueh, Bukit Kanyi, Bukit Berumput to Bukit Berpayong)
SEA38. Pulong Tau, Gunung Murud
SEA39. Usun Apau Plateau
Note: For Lanjak-Entimau Wildlife Sanctuary, see SEA16

SUMATRA, INDONESIA
SEA40. Barisan Selatan National Park
SEA41. **Gunung Leuser National Park**
SEA42. **Kerinci-Seblat National Park**
SEA43. **Limestone flora of Sumatra**
SEA44 Berbak Game Reserve
SEA45. **Tigapuluh Mountains**

SULAWESI, INDONESIA
SEA46. **Dumoga-Bone National Park**
SEA47. **Limestone flora of Sulawesi**
SEA48. **Ultramafic flora of Sulawesi**
SEA49. Lore Lindu National Park
SEA50. **Pegunungan Latimojong**

PHILIPPINES
SEA51. **Batan Islands**
SEA52. **Mount Apo**
SEA53. Mount Baloy
SEA54. Mount Isarog
SEA55. Mount Kitanglad
SEA56. Mount Makiling and Mount Banahaw
SEA57. **Mount Pulog**
SEA58. Mount Talines and Lake Balinsasayao
SEA59. **Palanan Wilderness Area**
SEA60. **Palawan**
SEA61. **Sibuyan Island**
SEA62. Southern Samar

JAVA, INDONESIA
SEA63. Baluran National Park
SEA64. **Gunung Gede-Pangrango National Park**
SEA65. Gunung Halimun Nature Reserve
SEA66. Ujong Kulon National Park

MOLUCCAS, INDONESIA
SEA67. Manusela National Park (Seram)

IRIAN JAYA, INDONESIA
SEA68. **Arfak Mountains**
SEA69. **Gunung Lorentz**
SEA70. **Mamberamo – Pegunungan Jayawijaya**
SEA71. **Waigeo**
SEA72. Cagar Alam Pulau Salawati Utara (North Salawati Island Nature Reserve)
SEA73. Pegunungan Tamrau Utara (Northern Tamrau Mountains)
SEA74. Pegunungan Tamrau Selatan (Southern Tamrau Mountains)
SEA75. Pegunungan Wandamen-Wondiwoi (Wandamen-Wondiwoi Mountains, Wandamen Peninsula)
SEA76. Gunung Wagura-Kote (Mount Wagura-Kote)
SEA77. Pegunungan Kumawa (Kumawa Mountains)
SEA78. Pegunungan Weyland (Weyland Mountains)
SEA79. Cagar Alam Pegunungan Cyclops (Cyclops Mountains Nature Reserve)
SEA80. Cagar Alam Pulau Supiori (Supiori Island Nature Reserve) – Cagar Alam Pulau Numfor (proposed Numfor Island Nature Reserve) – Cagar Alam Pulau Biak Utara (North Biak Island Nature Reserve)
SEA81. Cagar Alam Pulau Yapen Tenggah (Japen Island Nature Reserve)

PAPUA NEW GUINEA
SEA82. Torricelli Mountains – Bewani Mountains – Prince Alexander Range
SEA83. Star Mountains – Telefomin – Tifalmin – Strickland Gorge
SEA84. Hunstein Range – Burgers Mountains – Schatterburg
SEA85. Kiunga – Palmer River – Victor Emmanuel Range
SEA86. **Mount Giluwe – Tari Gap – Doma Peaks**
SEA87. Kubor Ranges
SEA88. Adelbert Ranges
SEA89. **Bismarck Falls – Mt Wilhelm – Mt Otto – Schrader Range – Mt Hellwig – Gahavisuka**
SEA90. Finisterre Ranges
SEA91. **Huon Peninsula** (Mount Bangeta – Rawlinson Range; Cromwell Ranges and Sialum Terraces)
SEA92. **Southern Fly Platform** (Lake Daviumbu – Oriomo – Wassi Kussa – Tonda Wildlife Management Area)
SEA93. Mount Bosavi – Nomad River
SEA94. Tower Limestone Region: Leonard Murray Mountains – Darai Hills – Great Papuan Plateau
SEA95. Gulf – Ihu
SEA96. Mount Michael – Okapa – Crater Mountain
SEA97. Galley Reach
SEA98. **Menyamya – Aseki – Amungwiwa – Bowutu Mountains – Lasanga Island**
SEA99. Milne Bay – Collinwood Bay to southern coast
SEA100. Owen Stanley Mountains
SEA101. Varirata and Astrolabe Ranges
SEA102. Safia Savanna
SEA103. Topographer's Range
SEA104. Lake Wanum – Red Hill Swamp – Oomsis Ridge
SEA105. Porgera Peaks
SEA106. Gogol – Sogeron Headwaters
SEA107. Lower Watut
SEA108. Cloud Mountains

BISMARCK ARCHIPELAGO, PAPUA NEW GUINEA
SEA109. Willaumez Peninsula – Lake Dakataua
SEA110. Whiteman Range to southern coast of New Britain
SEA111. Nakanai Mountains
SEA112. Mounts Sinewit and Burringa
SEA113. Hans Meyer Range
SEA114. Southern Namatanai
SEA115. Schleinitz Range – Lelet Plateau
SEA116. Central Manus – Mount Dremsel

BOUGAINVILLE, PAPUA NEW GUINEA
SEA117. Mount Balbi to southern coast
SEA118. Mount Takuan – Tonolei Harbour

D'ENTRECASTEAUX ISLANDS, PAPUA NEW GUINEA
SEA119. D'Entrecasteaux Islands
SEA120. Louisiade Archipelago

THE MALAY PENINSULA

The area under consideration includes Peninsular Malaysia (comprising 11 of the 13 states of Malaysia) (see section on Borneo, later, for treatments of the Malaysian states of Sabah and Sarawak), and the island of Singapore. Peninsular Thailand, which is geographically part of the Malay Peninsula, is treated with Thailand (see Regional Overview on China and East Asia elsewhere in this volume). Since Singapore has only a very small area of its former forest remaining, the main emphasis here is on Peninsular Malaysia which still contains some of the most species-rich rain forests and other plant communities in the region.

Total land area: Peninsular Malaysia – 131, 598 km². Singapore – 570 km².

Population: Peninsular Malaysia – c. 18,000,000 (1992), with an annual growth rate of 2.3%.
Singapore – 2,710,000 (1990), with an annual growth rate of 1.2%.

Altitude: 0–2188 m (summit of Gunung Tahan, Peninsular Malaysia).

Natural vegetation: Estimates of forest cover for Peninsular Malaysia vary from 61,456 km² (Forestry Department 1990) to 69,780 km² (Collins, Sayer and Whitmore 1991). About 44% is lowland and hill forest, 5% montane forest, 3% swamp forest, 1% mangrove forest. Limestone outcrops cover 0.3% of the land area and support an endemic-rich flora. Annual deforestation rate (1985–1990): 956 km². Most of the original tropical lowland rain forest, mangrove forest and freshwater swamp forest of Singapore has been cleared for urban, industrial and agricultural developments.

Number of vascular plants: Peninsular Malaysia – >9000 species. Singapore – 8 gymnosperm species, 1285 dicot species (no recent figure available for monocots).

Species endemism: Peninsular Malaysia – 30–50% strictly endemic to Peninsular Malaysia.
Singapore – 0.1% strictly endemic to Singapore.

Number of endemic families: 0.

Number of genera: Peninsular Malaysia – 1500 (flowering plants). Singapore – 577 (gymnosperms and dicots only; no recent figure available for monocots).

Number of endemic genera: Peninsular Malaysia – 24. Singapore – 0.

Important plant families: Orchidaceae: c. 850 species of which c. 50% endemic. Dipterocarpaceae: 156 species of which 17% endemic. Palmae: 195 species in 31 genera, of which 83 species (43%) and 1 genus (*Calospatha*) are endemic. (Figures refer to Peninsular Malaysia only.)

Threats: In Peninsular Malaysia, large-scale agricultural development schemes (particularly oil palm and rubber plantations), logging, mining and quarrying, resort development in montane areas, construction of hydroelectric dams. There is only a small amount of shifting cultivation.

Conservation: Peninsular Malaysia – 1 National Park (IUCN Management Category: II) covering 4344 km² (3.3% of the land area); 1 State Park (IUCN Management Category: II) covering c. 500 km² (not yet gazetted); 8 Wildlife Reserves (IUCN Management Category: IV) covering 2395 km²; Wildlife Sanctuaries (IUCN Management Category: IV) covering 650 km²; 1 Park (IUCN Management Category: V) covering 10 km²; 81 Virgin Jungle Reserves (IUCN Management Category: I) covering 910 km². Note that these figures refer only to protected areas over 10 km², and that some areas have overlapping designations. Existing conservation areas cover 6.3% of the land area.
Singapore – All primary forest remnants are protected, including Bukit Timah Nature Reserve (81 ha) and the Central Catchment Area Nature Reserve (27 km²) (IUCN Management Category: IV).

Geology

A series of mountain ranges run the length of Peninsular Malaysia, with summits between 1200 and 2000 m. The main period of folding which created these mountains took place during the Mesozoic period. Today, the granitic cores of the mountains are widely exposed through weathering and erosion. The most continuous range is the Main Range, which forms the main divide between the relatively narrow western coastal plain draining to the Straits of Malacca, and the larger eastern area of mountains and lowlands draining into the South China Sea. Gunung Tahan (2188 m) is the highest mountain.

Isolated limestone hills (tower karsts) are a distinctive landscape feature in some parts of Peninsular Malaysia. They contain a rich endemic flora (see Data Sheet on the Limestone Flora of Peninsular Malaysia – SEA3). Their origins are pre-Cenozoic, and the rock is recrystallized into marble which is quarried in some places.

Climate

The climate is equatorial, with average annual rainfall ranging from 2500 mm in drier locations to 4000 mm on the east coast, which experiences monsoon rain between September and March. Rainfall on the west coast is more evenly spread, with the heaviest rain falling in inter-monsoon periods. There is no dry season. The mean annual temperature is 26.7°C, with a diurnal range of 8.9°C. The difference between mean monthly maxima and minima is only 3.3°C.

Population

Peninsular Malaysia's population is about 18 million (1992), with a predicted annual growth rate between 1987 and 2000 of 2.3%. There are some 50,000 Orang Asli (aboriginal people). The majority of the population are Malays (54%), Chinese (35%) and Indians (10%). The population of Peninsular Malaysia is rapidly becoming urbanized; there are at least 10 cities of over 100,000 people, including Kuala Lumpur, the national capital, which had a population of 912,610 in 1984 (Europa Publications 1987).

Singapore had a population of 2,710,000 in 1990 (World Resources Institute 1994), with an average annual growth rate of 1.2% between 1985 and 1990.

Economy

Rich tin deposits occur in alluvial gravel along the western foothills of the Main Range and have given rise to massive opencast tin-mining operations. Indeed, Malaysia may still have the largest deposits of tin in the world. Other major economic activities include plantation crops, mainly oil palm and rubber (Malaysia being the world's top producer of these products), but also some cacao and forestry. Nearly one-half of Malaysia's export earnings were derived from rubber in 1961, but by 1986 earnings had declined to 8.9%. Oil palm accounted for 8.6% of Malaysia's export earnings in 1986, while the agricultural sector as a whole contributed 21% of Malaysia's GDP and employed 34% of the labour force

(Europa Publications 1987). The biggest share of the export market is now in manufactured goods (40.5% of all export earnings in 1986).

Vegetation

According to the Forestry Department (1990), 41.5% of a land area of Peninsular Malaysia is covered by forests. However, subsequent figures released by the Forestry Department give 46.7% of the land area under forest cover (G. Davison 1993, *in litt.*). Collins, Sayer and Whitmore (1991) give a figure for forest cover of 69,780 km² (53% of a land area of 131,598 km²), based on a Forestry Department map of 1989. About 44% is lowland (0–300 m altitude) and hill forests (300–1300 m), 5% montane forest, 3% swamp forest and 1% mangrove forest. Limestone outcrops cover 0.3% of the land area and support an endemic-rich flora (see Data Sheet on the Limestone Flora of Peninsular Malaysia – SEA3).

Lowland evergreen rain forest is dominated by members of the Dipterocarpaceae; Peninsular Malaysia has 156 species of dipterocarps, of which 17% are endemic. The largest area of pristine lowland dipterocarp forest lies within Taman Negara (CPD Site SEA8, see Data Sheet), with a further substantial area in Endau Rompin (CPD Site SEA2, see Data Sheet). Other areas identified below as centres of plant diversity which contain important areas of natural lowland forests are the Dindings, Segari Melintang and Larut Hills (Perak) (CPD Site SEA1), the Trengganu Hills (Trengganu) (CPD Site SEA10, see Data Sheet) and Ulu Belum (Perak) (CPD Site SEA11).

There is a small area of semi-evergreen forest in the extreme north-west of Peninsular Malaysia along the border with Thailand. Along the east coast there are a few patches of heath forest, but, along with peat swamp and alluvial swamp forests that were formerly extensive, they are now reduced to fragments as a result of being cleared for agriculture. There are approximately 1200 km² of mangroves remaining (much having been cleared for agriculture, urbanization and fish ponds). Most mangrove forests occur along the west coast, where much is used for timber production.

All the main mountains are covered by montane rain forests. However, some areas are critically threatened by expansion of hill resort development and road building schemes (see Data Sheet on the Montane Flora of Peninsular Malaysia – SEA4).

The annual deforestation rate (1985–1990) was predicted to be 956 km² (FAO 1987). Most of the lowland and hill dipterocarp forests outside of protected areas have been logged; the remaining primary forests are mostly confined to upland areas along the Main Range. The major cause of forest depletion of lowland and hill dipterocarp forests is clearance for large-scale agricultural development schemes, particularly for plantation crops such as oil palm and rubber. Montane forests are seriously threatened by resort developments and road building schemes.

One of the important consequences of the great changes in land use in Peninsular Malaysia over the last 100 years is that much of the forest has become fragmented. This is one reason why Malaysia may need to protect a larger number of areas to safeguard its plant wealth than some other tropical countries or regions where there are still large contiguous blocks of intact forest.

Most of the original tropical lowland rain forest, mangrove forest and freshwater swamp forest of Singapore has been cleared for urban, industrial and agricultural developments.

Flora

The flora of Peninsular Malaysia includes at least 9000 vascular plant species, of which about 500 are ferns (Keng 1983). Between 30–50% of the flora is strictly endemic to Peninsular Malaysia (R. Kiew 1993, pers. comm.). Endemism is particularly high among trees (30% species endemism for the whole of the tree flora of the Malay Peninsula, including southern Thailand and Singapore) (Ng and Low 1982). Among the flowering plants, there are 1500 genera, of which 24 are endemic to Peninsular Malaysia (van Steenis 1987). There are no endemic families, but the level of species endemism within some families is high (e.g. 90% of Peninsular Malaysian Begoniaceae are strictly endemic; corresponding figures for Gesneriaceae and Orchidaceae are 80% and 50%, respectively – Kiew 1983).

The flora of Singapore was estimated to contain 2030 species (Ridley 1900). A more recent analysis (Keng 1990) gives 8 gymnosperm species and 1285 dicot species (no recent figure available for monocots). Singapore has 2 strictly endemic species: *Polyosma kingiana* and *Sabia erratica*.

The flora of the Malay Peninsula shows closest affinities with those of Borneo and Sumatra.

Useful plants

See account in General Overview on South East Asia (Malesia).

Factors causing loss of biodiversity

The main threats are large-scale agricultural development schemes (particularly oil palm and rubber plantations), logging, mining and quarrying, hydroelectric schemes and clearance of forests for urban developments, including road schemes. Montane areas are particularly threatened by large-scale resort development. There is only a small amount of shifting cultivation. For a general review of the main threats to the flora, see Kiew (1990a). For more detailed discussion of how the various threats affect individual CPD sites, see Data Sheets SEA2, SEA3, SEA4, SEA5, SEA8 and SEA10.

Conservation

In Peninsular Malaysia, the Permanent Forest Estate covered 47,500 km² (14% of the land area) in 1985 (Ministry of Primary Industries 1988). This comprises productive forests (28,500 km²) managed for timber production, protective forests to prevent erosion, silting and flooding and to maintain water supplies, and amenity forests for conservation, recreation, education and research purposes. Protective forests are mainly found in mountainous areas and, together with amenity forests, cover 19,000 km². In addition, there are many Forest Reserves set up by the Forest Department. With the exception of the small Virgin Jungle Reserves, Forest Reserves are not managed for conservation of nature and it is easy for State governments to reduce or degazette them.

Although there is an impressive network of totally protected areas, now covering 8293 km² of Peninsular Malaysia (6.3% of the land area), the network is far from complete in terms of its coverage of the more than 9000 vascular plant species in the peninsula and the diverse range of plant communities. Many Forest Reserves are damaged or under threat. Only approximately 5452 km² (about 4% of Peninsular Malaysia's land area) is primary forest legally protected by National Park or Wildlife Sanctuary status (Kiew 1991).

The National Conservation Strategy (NCS) for Malaysia was commissioned by the Economic Planning Unit of the Prime Minister's Department in 1991, and completed at the end of 1992. It covers Peninsular Malaysia, Sabah and Sarawak, concentrating on: the administration of nature and natural resources (law, planning, policy, management, enforcement, information, education, awareness and training); "critical sites", with a complete listing of all protected and managed areas (over 1000 sites); and economics, with special reference to natural resources accounting. The NCS provides a framework which can be used by the government, private sector and NGOs, as a guide to planning and action for conservation and sustainable development. A review of the protected areas system and conservation legislation is given in IUCN (1992).

In Singapore, all primary forest remnants are protected, including Bukit Timah Nature Reserve (81 ha) and the Central Catchment Area Nature Reserve (27 km²) (IUCN Management Category: IV).

Singapore Botanic Garden was established in 1859. It contains about 3000 living taxa, including important collections of orchids, palms and bamboos, and other plants of economic importance.

In Peninsular Malaysia, the **Forest Research Institute Malaysia** (FRIM) maintains an arboretum (600 ha) at Kepong, which includes 722 woody plant taxa, mostly from South East Asia, including many dipterocarp species. There is an associated reserve (Bukit Lagong Forest Reserve) covering 5 km².

The **Fernarium of the Botany Department, Universiti Kebangsaan Malaysia** (Bangi, Selangor) covers 13 ha and contains 150 fern taxa of South East Asia; **Penang Botanic Gardens** (29 ha) includes an arboretum and collections of orchids, ferns, gingers and other ornamental species (c. 1000 taxa in total), while **Rimba Ilmu Universiti Malaysia** (the botanic garden of the University of Malaya, Kuala Lumpur) has c. 1200 taxa (mostly Malaysian accessions), including medicinal plants, fruit trees (including *Citrus* spp. and relatives) and palms (Jones 1987; Heywood, Heywood and Wyse Jackson 1990).

Centres of plant diversity and endemism

Peninsular Malaysia

The sites below cover a range of forest types, including various lowland and montane forests from different floristic regions within the peninsula, special forest types (such as coastal and swamp forests) and communities adapted to specialized edaphic conditions (the limestone flora). They have been determined by conservation biologists as the *minimum* needed for conserving Peninsular Malaysia's plant wealth. Such a range of sites needs to be protected in order to include a representative sample of Peninsular Malaysia's high plant diversity.

Some of the sites are already established as protected areas, but most are not and are severely threatened. Some, such as Endau-Rompin and Taman Negara, are of such outstanding importance as to warrant individual Data Sheets. Others, such as the limestone and montane sites, are individually quite small but their floras, nevertheless, contain important endemic elements. There are too many limestone and montane sites to treat individually and data for some are very scant, so the approach adopted here is to treat them collectively in Data Sheets covering the whole of these community types.

SEA1. Dindings, Segari Melintang and Larut Hills (Perak)

❖ Vegetation: Some of the last remnants of coastal dipterocarp forest in Peninsular Malaysia.
❖ Flora: A mixture of widespread lowland dipterocarp forest flora, Indo-Burmese seasonal elements, Sumatran elements (such as *Vatica lowii* and *Parashorea globosa*), species more closely associated with humult ultisols of Sarawak and north-west Kalimantan in Borneo, and endemic relicts (e.g. *Maingaya*).
❖ Threats: The forests are close to urban areas and therefore highly at risk. As land becomes scarce, remaining coastal forests are threatened by de-gazettement for clear-felling (P. Ashton, pers. comm.).
❖ Conservation: Forest Reserves, including Virgin Jungle Reserves.

SEA2. Endau-Rompin State Parks (proposed)

– see Data Sheet.

SEA3. Limestone flora of Peninsular Malaysia

– see Data Sheet.

SEA4. Montane flora of Peninsular Malaysia

– see Data Sheet.

SEA5. Pulau Tioman

– see Data Sheet.

SEA6. Sedili Kecil Swamp Forest (Johore)

Area: c. 50 km².
❖ Vegetation: Seasonally inundated freshwater alluvial swamp forest.
❖ Threats: Most of the swamp forest occurs within Chandangan Forest Reserve. Virtually all remaining virgin forest areas in the reserve were licensed out for logging in 1986 and 1987. Logging commenced in 1988 and will be followed by total clearance for oil palm plantations by FELDA (the Malaysian Government agricultural development agency) (Scott 1989). Sedili Kecil is critically threatened since it falls within an area earmarked for industrial and commercial development.
❖ Conservation: No area of alluvial swamp forest is protected in Peninsular Malaysia.

SEA7. South-east Pahang Swamp Forests (Pahang)

This is the largest remaining peat swamp in the peninsula. The area consists of six blocks (Pahang Swamp Forest, Pekan Swamp Forest, Nenasi Swamp Forest, Rosak Swamp Forest, Rompin Swamp Forest and Endau Swamp Forest) between latitudes 2°32'–3°48'N and longitudes 103°05'–103°38'E. Area: 3250 km². Altitude: Mostly low-lying, >76 m, with occasional hills.

❖ Vegetation: At least 900 km² is peat swamp; the other principal vegetation types are alluvial freshwater swamp forest and lowland rain forest.

❖ Threats: The remaining swamp forests in south-east Pahang are critically threatened by logging, tin-mining, and clearance for agriculture, rice, rubber and coconut plantations. Coastal swamp forests continue to be cleared for development.

❖ Conservation: About 800 km² of swamp forest occurs in Forest Reserves. However, no swamp forest in Peninsular Malaysia is totally protected from logging.

SEA8. Taman Negara

– see Data Sheet.

SEA9. Tasek Berah Forest Reserve (Pahang)

Area: 400 km², between latitudes 2°47'–3°09'N and longitudes 102°23'–102°47'E.

❖ Vegetation: Includes the largest natural lake in Peninsular Malaysia (Tasek Berah) and surrounding wetlands (of approximate total area 62 km²).

❖ Flora: Among the useful plants of the area is *Dipterocarpus kerrii* which yields an oil from which local Orang Asli derive an income.

MAP 9. CENTRES OF PLANT DIVERSITY AND ENDEMISM: THE MALAY PENINSULA

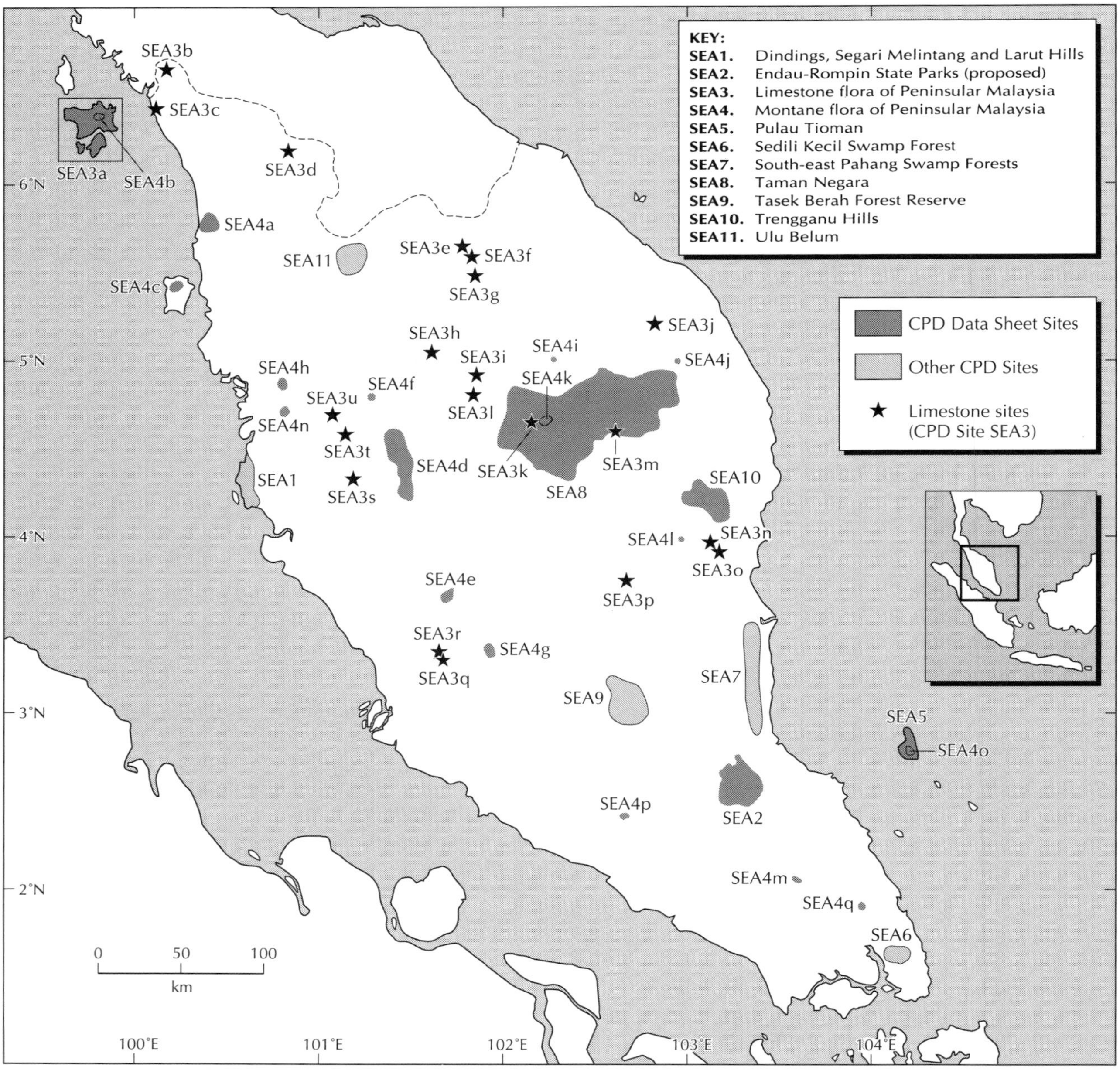

KEY:
SEA1.   Dindings, Segari Melintang and Larut Hills
SEA2.   Endau-Rompin State Parks (proposed)
SEA3.   Limestone flora of Peninsular Malaysia
SEA4.   Montane flora of Peninsular Malaysia
SEA5.   Pulau Tioman
SEA6.   Sedili Kecil Swamp Forest
SEA7.   South-east Pahang Swamp Forests
SEA8.   Taman Negara
SEA9.   Tasek Berah Forest Reserve
SEA10. Trengganu Hills
SEA11. Ulu Belum

CPD Data Sheet Sites

Other CPD Sites

★ Limestone sites (CPD Site SEA3)

❖ Threats: Large-scale agricultural development has resulted in clear-felling of much of the surrounding forest and this threatens the water regime of the wetland ecosystem.

SEA10. Trengganu Hills

– see Data Sheet.

SEA11. Ulu Belum (Perak)

Located in the north-east part of Upper Perak and situated within the Northern Floristic Zone, between latitudes 5°13'–5°55'N and longitudes 101°14'–101°45'E on the border with Thailand. Area: c. 2740 km². Altitude: 100–1889 m.

❖ Vegetation: Small area of lowland dipterocarp forest dominated by *Shorea leprosula*, *S. parviflora*, *Intsia palembanica* and *Koompassia excelsa* (among others), hill and ridge dipterocarp forest (occupying c. 60% of the area) and lower montane forest (above 1500 m).

❖ Flora: Little known; the area appears to be very rich and a meeting point of Burmese-Thai and Malesian elements. Perak itself contains 212 tree species which are endemic to Peninsular Malaysia, of which 103 species are endemic to Perak (Ng 1991); 57 of these are rare or endangered, including *Actinodaphne cuspidata*, *Ardisia perakensis* and *Mangifera whitmorei*, which are restricted to Upper Perak.

❖ Threats: Some of the lowland forest has been logged or cleared for shifting cultivation, or was drowned by Temenggor Hydroelectric Lake. However, much of the remainder is intact and has been inaccessible due to security reasons until recently. Selective logging has recently begun in various places; Belum is also earmarked as a potential land development area, and prospecting for gold is a potential threat (Malaysian Nature Society 1993).

❖ Conservation: The area falls within the Belum Forest Reserve (c. 2170 km²), Grik Forest Reserve (c. 200 km², in part) and Temenggor Forest Reserve (370 km², in part); logging licenses currently being issued. Scientific investigations are underway to help provide the basis for protecting the area (Malaysian Nature Society 1993).

Areas of botanical interest

The following sites contain important samples of lowland rain forests.

Peninsular Malaysia

Pasoh Forest Reserve (Negri Sembilan)

Area: 24 km².
❖ Vegetation: Lowland dipterocarp forest.
❖ Flora: Scientific studies have been on-going since the 1960s International Biological Programme (IBP) and continues under the UNESCO Man and Biosphere (MAB) programme and the Forest Research Institute (FRIM). Enumeration of trees (>10 cm dbh) in 11 ha at Pasoh identified 460 species in a total sample of 5907 (Soepadmo 1978); more recently a 50 ha plot yielded 820 species of

trees (>1 cm dbh) (Kochummen, LaFrankie and Manokaran 1990).
❖ Threats: Surrounded by oil palm plantations, increasing edge effects and possibly alteration of the water-table.
❖ Conservation: Pasoh is now managed by the Forestry Research Institute, Malaysia (FRIM).

Singapore

Bukit Timah Nature Reserve

Area: 81 ha.
❖ Vegetation: The largest remaining contiguous block (c. 50 ha) of mainly primary tropical lowland rain forest in Singapore.
❖ Flora: It is estimated that about 20% of Singapore's native vascular flora is now extinct. The forests around Bukit Timah, Singapore's highest hill (163 m) and the adjacent Central Catchment Area Nature Reserve (18 km²) retain a large proportion of the remainder.
❖ Threats: Isolation, edge effects, small population sizes of individual species, visitor pressure.
❖ Conservation: Nature Reserve; the area has an important educational role (being easily accessible to a large urban population) and scientific role (for studying the effects of forest fragmentation, isolation and edge effects) and, together with the Central Catchment Area, protects the water catchment of Singapore City.

BORNEO

Total land area: 738,864 km².

Population: c. 10,000,000.

Altitude: 0–4101 m (summit of Mount Kinabalu).

Natural vegetation: c. 67% of the island is still covered by tropical rain forests of varying sorts, including logged forests. Main forest types: lowland tropical evergreen rain forest dominated by dipterocarps, montane forest, heath forest (kerangas), limestone forest, ultramafic vegetation, alluvial and peat swamp forests, mangroves, beach forest, subalpine and alpine vegetation on Mount Kinabalu.

Number of vascular plants: 20,000–25,000 species.

Species endemism: c. 30% endemic to Borneo; regional endemism higher.

Number of endemic genera: 61.

Important plant families: Orchidaceae: c. 1500 species, over 10% of the world total, in 149 genera. About 40% of the orchid flora is endemic to the island. Dipterocarpaceae: 267 species, of which 58% are endemic. Palmae: c. 290 species, of which at least 40% endemic.

Introduction

Borneo is the third largest island in the world, straddling the Equator in the Sundaic biogeographical sub-region, which also includes Peninsular Malaysia, Sumatra and Java. About 67% of the land area is forested, with extensive areas of peat swamps, heath forest, lowland and hill dipterocarp forests, ironwood forests and various types of montane forests. The island is mostly geomorphologically young. Coastal swampy plains give way to hilly lowlands and mountains in the interior. The central and northern parts of Borneo are the most mountainous, with the highest peak, Mount Kinabalu, rising to 4101 m, in the north-east. This is the highest mountain between the Himalayas and New Guinea. Most of Borneo's rocks are Cretaceous and Tertiary sedimentaries, with subordinate volcanics and limestones. Basement granites protrude from the west and are exposed on the higher hills.

The population of Borneo remains at a relatively low density, at approximately 10 million. This includes indigenous proto-Malay tribes who still hunt and gather using traditional methods in the forests of some parts of Borneo. However, their forest habitat, especially that in the lowlands, has been drastically reduced and is under continuing threat as a result of shifting cultivation (the dominant form of agriculture), fires and (since the 1960s) extensive timber exploitation of the rich dipterocarp flora. The forest cover of Borneo has, as a consequence, been reduced, today, to about 67% of the land area. (This figure is for all forest types, including secondary forest; the area of primary forest is likely to be much less.)

Flora

The varied topography and geology give rise to a landscape of higher habitat diversity than in most other parts of equatorial Asia. Borneo also has the greatest diversity of forest types in the Sunda islands, and includes the richest forest types. As such, it is the centre of diversity for many Malesian genera. Based on a comparison of species richness between Peninsular Malaysia and Borneo of selected plant families revised in *Flora Malesiana*, it is estimated that there are likely to be between 20,000 and 25,000 vascular plant species in Borneo. The largest family represented is the Orchidaceae. Wood and Cribb (1994) estimate that Borneo has c. 1500 species of orchids in 149 genera, almost 10% of the world's orchid flora. About 40% of Bornean orchids are endemic (Lamb 1991a). Mount Kinabalu alone is estimated to have about 700 orchid species in 121 genera (Wood, Beaman and Beaman 1993).

The most species-rich communities are lowland evergreen rain forests (mixed dipterocarp forests, or MDF). Variations in species richness and composition of MDF result from variations in environmental conditions, notably soils and rainfall. In general, it can be predicted that the richest areas (as elsewhere in Malesia) are likely to be those receiving a mean monthly rainfall in excess of 100 mm. These conditions provide the equable climate necessary for the development of the richest evergreen tropical rain forest. Individual community types, particularly on distinct soils occurring in ecological islands, are richest north-west of the main mountains, perhaps for historical reasons and perhaps because this region is sheltered by the mountains from occasional catastrophic droughts associated with the El Niño Southern Oscillation which affects the east and south-east lowlands in particular (P.S. Ashton 1991, *in litt.*). However, very bad droughts associated with the El Niño phenomenon occurred in Sabah, in the north, in 1983 when over 10,000 km² of forest were burned, 85% of which was logged forest (Beaman, Beaman, Marsh and Woods 1985).

Within MDF, species diversity and endemism is highest in areas of relatively poor yellow sandy and yellow-red dryland soils. Very nutrient-poor or highly fertile soils, by contrast, tend to be species-poor, although they have their own distinct floras which may include point endemics. The dipterocarp

forests developed on the widespread clay soils, which cover much of East Kalimantan, have a generalized flora, which, although rich, contains relatively few endemics. The main variations in forest composition in the latter are determined largely by topography. On the other hand, forests developed on less nutrient-rich humult ultisols vary continuously with, and in relation to, nutrient concentration (Ashton 1990). These forests are also among the most fragile ecosystems, having developed on poor yellow soils over young rocks which are poorly consolidated and easily eroded following removal of the vegetation cover. In general, these types of forests are found from west-central Borneo (north of the Kapuas River) north-east to Sarawak, Brunei and Sabah. North-western Borneo, therefore, contains a variety of edaphic and topographical conditions, supporting the most species-rich and endemic-rich MDF communities in the whole of Borneo, including mixed dipterocarp forests developed on subcoastal hills with yellow leached soils.

Generic endemism is low, as in all parts of Malesia, but species endemism is high. This may be explained by the possible connection of Borneo to continental Asia and Sumatra during most of its history, interrupted by periods of isolation as a result of sea-level changes. The richness of north-west Borneo may suggest that the area was a "refugium" which has not experienced drastic climate change for a considerable period of geological time.

Heath forests are scattered throughout Borneo on raised beaches, sandstone plateaux and ridges. Those of Sarawak and Brunei, and the Nabawan heath forests of Sabah, are richer in species and endemics than elsewhere. Other lowland forest types, namely mangroves and swamp forests, are relatively species-poor communities, though species adapted to these environments tend to be restricted to them.

An area of exceptional richness is the Kinabalu massif (see Data Sheet on Kinabalu Park, CPD Site SEA24). Mount Kinabalu is, for its area, undoubtedly the richest locality in species in Asia west of New Guinea, and one of the few mountains in the Old World to compare in species diversity with the Andes of Colombia and Ecuador (Ashton 1990). However, comparable figures are not yet available for any mountain in New Guinea. The few figures that are available from high altitudes on Mount Wilhelm (see Data Sheet on Bismarck Falls – Mt Wilhelm – Mt Otto – Schrader Range – Mt Hellwig – Gahavisuka, CPD Site SEA89) seem to indicate the flora there is equally as rich as Kinabalu (R.J. Johns, pers. comm.; see also section on Papuasia).

Kinabalu contains a diversity of vegetation types, resulting not only from the large altitudinal range, but also from the varying geology of the mountain. The massif includes a distinctive flora, rich in endemics, developed on ultramafic rocks. Ultramafic outcrops occur elsewhere in the north-east part of Borneo where they also often support endemic-rich floras (see Data Sheet on North-east Borneo Ultramafic Flora, SEA27).

Another specialized flora, rich in endemics, is that of limestone outcrops. The most extensive areas occur in west Sarawak, in the Gunung Mulu National Park, in north-east and east Sabah, and in the Sangkulirang Peninsula (see Data Sheets on the Limestone Flora of Borneo and Gunung Mulu National Park, CPD Sites SEA18 and SEA33, respectively). The isolated nature of these outcrops has promoted speciation in certain families, particularly in certain herbaceous plant families, such as Orchidaceae, Gesneriaceae and Begoniaceae.

The following sections deal with each of the political divisions of Borneo in more detail. Lists of individual sites of global importance for plant conservation are given, from which a range of sites covering the diversity of plant-rich vegetation types are selected for detailed treatment in Data Sheets.

BRUNEI DARUSSALAM

Total land area: 5765 km².

Population (1989): 300,000; growth rate 2.7%.

Altitude: 0–1850 m (summit of Gunung Pagon).

Natural vegetation: About 81% of the land area is still under forest cover, of which 59% is primary forest. The main types are: tropical evergreen rain forest, rich in dipterocarps; tropical submontane and montane rain forests to 1850 m; heath (kerangas) forest on sandy alluvial soils and sandstone ridges; mangroves; extensive peat swamp forest near the coast in Belait and Tutong districts.

Flora: c. 6000 vascular plant species (P.S. Ashton 1991, pers. comm.), including an estimated 2000 tree species.

Threats: Clearance of forest as a result of coastal developments, oil and gas industries, urban development and road building; deforestation rate low.

Conservation: All existing protected areas occur within Forest Reserves. They include:
1 Wildlife Sanctuary (90 km²)
3 Conservation Areas (735 km²)
4 Secondary Conservation Areas (50 km²)
5 Protection Forests (185 km²)
5 Recreation Areas (18 km²)

Forest Reserves (IUCN Management Category: IV) cover 3190 km² (c. 55% of the land area). About 25% of the remaining moist forest is included within existing and proposed protected areas.

Brunei Darussalam, in north-west Borneo, lies within one of the most floristically diverse regions in the world and, unlike many other areas in the region, its forests are still relatively intact. Much of Brunei consists of a low alluvial and swampy coastal plain, mostly below 90 m. The plain is backed by low hills, the main mountains occurring in the south along the Sarawak border. Gunung Pagon (1850 m) is Brunei's highest mountain.

Investigation of the Brunei flora is still at a preliminary stage, apart from pioneering studies on mixed dipterocarp forest by Ashton (1964a) and on Dipterocarpaceae (Ashton 1964b). Initial results from the compilation of a new checklist of the vascular plants of Brunei Darussalam, a collaborative venture between the Forestry Department in Brunei and the Royal Botanic Gardens, Kew, suggest that the flora of the country may be far richer than formerly supposed (Dransfield, Kirkup and Coode 1993). P.S. Ashton (1991, pers. comm.) provided a current estimate of 6000 vascular plant species.

The economy of Brunei is largely dependent on oil and gas production. There has, therefore, been less need to extract timber for export. Most timber extracted from the forest has been used for local purposes and, even then, strict controls have been enforced. Some clearance has taken place as a result of oil and gas exploration, and the need to construct roads and develop towns, particularly near the coast. However, the rate of logging and deforestation is generally agreed to be very low, at approximately 50 km² per year for closed broadleaved forests (FAO/UNEP 1981).

Climate

Brunei has a consistently hot and humid climate, with mean monthly temperatures of c. 27°C, and annual rainfall varying from 2310 mm on the coast to more than 5080 mm in the mountains. The wettest period is during the south-west monsoon, usually between May–October.

Population

The population in 1989 was estimated to be 300,000 with an annual growth rate of 2.7%. The majority of the population live in the capital, Bandar Seri Begawan, and in the oil-producing areas along the western coast. The economy is based mostly on the production of oil and natural gas from rich reserves. This, together with the low population, has ensured that much of Brunei's forests remain intact.

Vegetation

The natural vegetation throughout much of Brunei is tropical evergreen rain forest. About 81% of the land area is still covered by forest, of which about 59% is under primary forest cover (Anderson and Marsden 1988). The main types of forest are:

❖ Lowland and hill evergreen rain forest, rich in dipterocarps, comprising about half the forest cover.
❖ Lower montane forest, above 700 m, where dipterocarps give way to Fagaceae and Lauraceae.
❖ Upper montane forest, generally above 1200 m, principally on Gunung Pagon in the Temburong area, rich in Dipterocarpaceae, Clusiaceae and Ericaceae.
❖ Peat swamp forest, comprising about 25% of the forest cover.
❖ Periodically flooded riverine alluvial forests.
❖ Heath (kerangas) forests, which grade directly into upper montane forests at altitude.
❖ Mangroves cover about 200 km² and are best developed in Brunei Bay, one of the best preserved and richest mangrove areas in Asia (P.S. Ashton 1991, *in litt.*), and extending into neighbouring Sarawak and Sabah.

Estimates of forest cover

The following estimates are taken from Collins, Sayer and Whitmore (1991). The areas given are determined from maps and are not official statistics. They include relatively undisturbed, and disturbed, forests where, for example, enclaves of cultivation and plantations occur within areas of forest.

	Area (km²)	% of land area
Lowland rain forests	2760	46.3
Montane rain forests	70	1.2
Inland swamp forests	1750	30.4
Mangroves	200	3.5
Totals	**4690**	**81.4**

The figures given for *lowland rain forests* include: tropical evergreen rain forest, tropical semi-evergreen rain forest, heath forest, limestone forest, ultramafic forest and beach forest; those for *montane rain forests* include: lower and upper montane rain forests and subalpine forests; and those for *inland swamp forests* include peat swamp forest, freshwater swamp forest and periodically inundated freshwater swamp forest.

Flora

Brunei has an estimated 6000 vascular plant species (P.S. Ashton 1991, pers. comm.), including an estimated 2000 tree species.

Useful plants

See account in General Overview on South East Asia (Malesia).

Factors causing loss of biodiversity

The deforestation rate is low. The main pressure on forests is clearance for coastal developments, oil and gas industries, urban development and road building.

Conservation

About 25% of the remaining moist forests of Brunei is included within existing and proposed protected areas (see Collins, Sayer and Whitmore 1991). All notified protected areas are within Forest Reserves. Presently, Forest Reserves cover about 3190 km² (c. 55% of the land area) (IUCN 1992). A quarter of this total is considered unexploitable or has been allocated for protection or conservation purposes. There is no legislation at present for the establishment of National Parks.

Most significant among the existing protected areas are the three Conservation Areas: Ulu Temburong/Batu Apoi (488 km²), Sungei Ingei (185 km²) and Ulu Mendaram (62 km²). Each of these areas protect large samples of rain forest; the last two include the best examples of primary peat swamp forest in Borneo, with a full range of community types (P.S. Ashton 1991, *in litt.*). Other smaller conservation units protect important samples of a range of Brunei's vegetation, but peat swamp forest is identified in Collins, Sayer and Whitmore (1991) as under-represented in the existing protected areas system.

A review of the protected areas system and conservation legislation is given in IUCN (1992).

Centres of plant diversity and endemism

The following three areas contain good examples of the richest vegetation types in Borneo, namely dipterocarp forests on deep yellow sands.

SEA12. Andulau Forest Reserve

Area: 13 km².
- ❖ Vegetation: Coastal mixed dipterocarp forest. Now entirely selectively logged, this area has poor, erodible soils carrying many tree species, including point and regional endemics. Proving very slow to regenerate, it is clearly not economic as a production forest and should be preserved to gradually restore naturally. The forest is of a type similar to Lambir Hills, Sarawak (CPD Site SEA34 – see Data Sheet), which remains primary.

SEA13. Batu Apoi Forest Reserve, Ulu Temburong

– see Data Sheet.

SEA14. Labi Hills, including Bukit Teraja and Ulu Ingei, Batu Patam-Sungei Ingei

– see also Data Sheet on Gunung Mulu National Park/ Medalam Protected Forest (Sarawak) and Labi Hills/Bukit Teraja/Ulu Ingei/Sungei Ingei (Brunei) – CPD Site SEA33.
- ❖ Vegetation: A diverse mosaic of forests on podzols and sandy yellow soils, rich in endemics. It is an important area of forest contiguous with Gunung Mulu National Park and Medalam Protected Forest (Sarawak).
- ❖ Flora: The area includes two palms endemic to Brunei, *Livistona exigua* and *Pinanga yassinii*, known only from podzolized ridges in the Ulu Ingei area.

Areas of botanical interest

The following sites and vegetation types, though not meeting the global criteria for selection as centres of plant diversity are, nevertheless, extremely important and require protection:

Brunei Bay mangrove forests

Although not species-rich compared with inland forests, the mangrove forests of Brunei are among the most significant in the world and especially important since they have been less disturbed than those in other parts of South East Asia; Brunei probably has the largest remaining intact patches in the whole of northern Borneo (Collins, Sayer and Whitmore 1991). The most extensive and best-preserved areas are to be found in Brunei Bay, where they are used to a limited extent for fuelwood and poles. Brunei Bay mangroves are, however, seriously threatened by pollution, both from oil spills and industry. There are proposals to create mangrove conservation areas on Pulau Berambang (7 km²) and Pulau Siarau (5 km²).

Belait River peat swamp forests

Although representing only a small proportion of the total forest cover, peat swamp forests in Brunei are, like mangrove forests, less disturbed than those elsewhere in the region. Some of the forests in the Belait River basin are still in a pristine condition, and will soon be the only peat swamp forests in the region not to have been highly disturbed. Peat swamp forests in Brunei could be under threat if plans to extend forestry operations result in over-exploitation of forests rich in *Shorea albida*. So far, peat swamps are under-represented in the existing reserve network. Proposals have been made for a Belait Peat Swamp Forest Reserve containing c. 617 km² of peat swamp (Anderson and Marsden 1984).

MAP 10. CENTRES OF PLANT DIVERSITY AND ENDEMISM: BORNEO

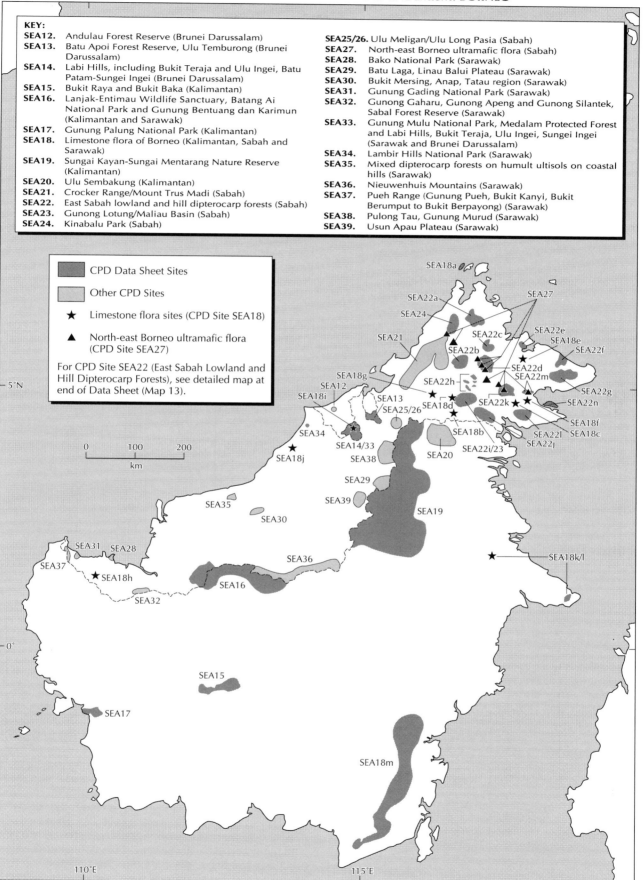

KEY:

SEA12. Andulau Forest Reserve (Brunei Darussalam)
SEA13. Batu Apoi Forest Reserve, Ulu Temburong (Brunei Darussalam)
SEA14. Labi Hills, including Bukit Teraja and Ulu Ingei, Batu Patam-Sungei Ingei (Brunei Darussalam)
SEA15. Bukit Raya and Bukit Baka (Kalimantan)
SEA16. Lanjak-Entimau Wildlife Sanctuary, Batang Ai National Park and Gunung Bentuang dan Karimun (Kalimantan and Sarawak)
SEA17. Gunung Palung National Park (Kalimantan)
SEA18. Limestone flora of Borneo (Kalimantan, Sabah and Sarawak)
SEA19. Sungai Kayan-Sungai Mentarang Nature Reserve (Kalimantan)
SEA20. Ulu Sembakung (Kalimantan)
SEA21. Crocker Range/Mount Trus Madi (Sabah)
SEA22. East Sabah lowland and hill dipterocarp forests (Sabah)
SEA23. Gunong Lotung/Maliau Basin (Sabah)
SEA24. Kinabalu Park (Sabah)

SEA25/26. Ulu Meligan/Ulu Long Pasia (Sabah)
SEA27. North-east Borneo ultramafic flora (Sabah)
SEA28. Bako National Park (Sarawak)
SEA29. Batu Laga, Linau Balui Plateau (Sarawak)
SEA30. Bukit Mersing, Anap, Tatau region (Sarawak)
SEA31. Gunung Gading National Park (Sarawak)
SEA32. Gunong Gaharu, Gunong Apeng and Gunong Silantek, Sabal Forest Reserve (Sarawak)
SEA33. Gunung Mulu National Park, Medalam Protected Forest and Labi Hills, Bukit Teraja, Ulu Ingei, Sungei Ingei (Sarawak and Brunei Darussalam)
SEA34. Lambir Hills National Park (Sarawak)
SEA35. Mixed dipterocarp forests on humult ultisols on coastal hills (Sarawak)
SEA36. Nieuwenhuis Mountains (Sarawak)
SEA37. Pueh Range (Gunung Pueh, Bukit Kanyi, Bukit Berumput to Bukit Berpayong) (Sarawak)
SEA38. Pulong Tau, Gunung Murud (Sarawak)
SEA39. Usun Apau Plateau (Sarawak)

KALIMANTAN (INDONESIA)

Total land area: 534,890 km².

Population (1980): 6,700,000.

Altitude: 0–2556 m (unnamed peak in the headwaters of Bahau River).

Natural vegetation: About 74% of the land area is estimated to be under forest cover, the largest expanse of tropical rain forest in South East Asia. Lowland evergreen rain forests, dominated by Dipterocarpaceae, up to c. 1000 m; various montane forests above c. 700 m; extensive peat and riverine swamp forests, particularly in the west and south; the largest expanse of heath (kerangas) forest in Malesia in the south; extensive mangroves; some important outcrops of limestone and ultramafic rocks with endemic-rich flora.

Threats: Logging, slash and burn cultivation, fire.

Conservation: 5 National Parks (IUCN Management Category: II) covering 15,711 km² (2.9% of the land area).
8 Nature Reserves (IUCN Management Category: I) covering 17,115 km² (3.2% of the land area).
7 Game Reserves (IUCN Management Category: IV) covering 7780 km².
2 Recreation Parks (IUCN Management Category: V) covering 272 km².
4 Protection Forests (IUCN Management Category: VI) covering 11,438 km².

In addition, proposed Nature Reserves would increase the total coverage of Nature Reserves to 10.5% of the land area.

Note that these figures refer only to protected areas over 10 km², and that some areas may have overlapping designations.

The Indonesian province of Kalimantan forms the southern part and much of the eastern part of Borneo. The southern coastal plain is characterized by vast areas of coastal swamps, extending inland along the major river systems. Much of the central and northern parts of Kalimantan is mountainous. The Schwaner and Muller Ranges extend north-west to join the Nieuwenhuis Mountains along the border with Sarawak. The Meratus Mountains are an isolated (small) group in the extreme south-east.

Climate

Kalimantan has a relatively constant warm humid climate with year-round rainfall and very few dry months (except during drought periods associated with El Niño Southern Oscillation phenomena). November to April is generally the wettest period. Most of the hilly inland areas receive between 2000 and 4000 mm of rain per year. Rainfall is more seasonal on the east coast, but poor drainage ensures that the forests are evergreen. Within the forest, ground temperatures remain close to 27°C at sea-level. (Climate details from FAO 1981–1982.)

Population

The population of Kalimantan was estimated to be 6,700,000 in 1980. The dominant form of agriculture is shifting cultivation. About 20% of the transmigrants from Indonesia's inner islands have been settled in Kalimantan. Since 1950, over 136,000 people have been moved to Kalimantan under the Indonesian Government's transmigration scheme; a further 33,714 have spontaneously moved to Kalimantan (Ministry of Transmigration Indonesia figures, quoted in Collins, Whitmore

and Sayer 1991). Problems have arisen in the choice of sites for settlements and in the fact that many of the transmigrants have no previous experience of owning and managing land. Unplanned settlement and lack of resources have often led to destructive forms of shifting agriculture. In South Kalimantan, "spontaneous transmigrants" include an increasing proportion of "multiple-timers" – transmigrants who have been through the process more than once, having previously exhausted areas where they had settled before (Davidson 1987).

Vegetation

Kalimantan supports the largest expanse of tropical rain forest in South East Asia. The lowland rain forests are dominated by dipterocarps. In Kalimantan, 179 species of dipterocarps, out of a world total of c. 550 species, have so far been described. As a result of the wealth of valuable tropical timber trees, the forests (particularly the lowland forests) have been heavily exploited for timber since the late 1960s. Although Indonesia prohibited log exports in 1980, sawn timber and plywood are still exported, Indonesia being a major supplier of these products. In 1987, the export of tropical hardwoods earned Indonesia US$2.5 billion, to which Kalimantan contributed a large part.

Although there are extensive areas of former forest which have been seriously degraded as a result of excessive logging, fire damage and slash and burn cultivation, there are, nevertheless, extensive tracts of pristine lowland and montane rain forests remaining. Collins, Sayer and Whitmore (1991) estimate the following extent of various types of rain forest in Kalimantan:

	Area (km²)	% of land area
Lowland rain forests	298,070	55.7
Montane rain forests	25,540	4.8
Inland swamp forests	62,210	11.6
Mangroves	11,500	2.1
Totals	**397,320**	**74.3**

These figures are based on analyses of maps prepared from data supplied by the regional Physical Planning Programme for Transmigration (ODA 1990) and do not distinguish between logged and otherwise degraded forest and primary rain forest. FAO estimated the closed forest area to be 353,950 km² in 1980 (FAO/UNEP 1981). Much of the land officially classed as forest is secondary in nature, or supports grasslands dominated by *Imperata cylindrica*.

The spread of *Imperata* grasslands is increasing, as more and more areas are being abandoned following failure of transmigration programmes and abandonment of cultivation plots. Typically, shifting cultivators move into areas, often illegally, after logging operations have opened up the forests. Whereas traditional swidden agriculture at low population densities generally results in small areas of forest being cleared, and often allows forest regeneration to take place after several years of cultivation, the present unplanned spread of shifting cultivation often results in complete deforestation and soil erosion. Throughout the whole of Kalimantan, the area under shifting cultivation is estimated by the Land Resources Development Centre to be 112,000 km², and it is now the dominant form of land use in Kalimantan.

Slash and burn agriculture and logging also increase the risk of devastating forest fires. For example, in 1983,

33,000 km^2 of Kalimantan's forest was destroyed either by drought or fire as described earlier in the General Overview of Malesia. A less serious drought in 1987 resulted in fires in South Kalimantan, and another in 1991 witnessed fires in several regions of the island, but not in the north-west.

Useful plants

See account in General Overview on South East Asia (Malesia).

Conservation

At present, there are five National Parks covering 15,711 km^2, or 2.9% of the land area. In addition, there are 8 Nature Reserves with a combined area of 17,115 km^2, or 3.2% of the land area. (Note that these figures refer only to protected areas over 10 km^2, and that some areas may have overlapping designations.)

FAO and IUCN collaborated on a major review of the requirements for conservation (see FAO 1981–1982 and MacKinnon and MacKinnon 1986). One of the main findings of the 1986 review was the lack of coverage of lowland rain forests in the reserve system throughout Borneo. Existing and proposed protected areas following these reviews would bring the coverage of legally protected areas to about 14% of Kalimantan's land area. If effectively implemented, these, together with the other forms of protected areas, are thought to go a long way toward conserving Kalimantan's rich biological heritage, although the criteria for choice rests on vertebrates alone. Priority areas for plants, currently inadequately known, do not always correlate with those for large vertebrates in some parts of the island (P.S. Ashton 1991, *in litt.*). The 1986 review also highlighted the opportunities for international cooperation in the planned establishment of large transfrontier parks between Indonesian Kalimantan and the neighbouring Malaysian states of Sabah and Sarawak. Such reserves would include both lowland and montane rain forests, and would be linked by watershed protection forests. They would result in extremely important areas for biological conservation as well as protecting most of the major watersheds of Borneo. Several of these areas are included in the list of sites selected as centres of plant diversity, below.

A review of the protected areas system and conservation legislation is given in IUCN (1992).

Centres of plant diversity and endemism

SEA15. Bukit Raya, Bukit Baka

– see Data Sheet.

SEA16. Gunung Bentuang dan Karimun

– see Data Sheet on Lanjak-Entimau Wildlife Sanctuary, Batang Ai National Park (Sarawak) and Cagar Alam Gunung Bentuang dan Karimun.

SEA17. Gunung Palung

– see Data Sheet.

SEA18. Limestone flora, including the Sankulirang Peninsula (Nyapa Mountains and Peg. Mangkalihat) and the southern part of the Meratus Mountains

– see Data Sheet entitled **Limestone Flora of Borneo**.

SEA19. Sungai Kayan-Sungai Mentarang Nature Reserve

– see Data Sheet.

SEA20. Ulu Sembakung

Area: 5000 km^2, in northern Kalimantan. Altitude: 130–2143 m.
❖ Vegetation: Rich lowland, hill and montane forest. Lowland and hill forests cover c. 4000 km^2. Botanically unexplored.
❖ Conservation: Proposed Nature Reserve.

Areas of botanical interest

The following are good examples of specialized communities under threat throughout the region and although not meeting the global criteria for selection as centres of plant diversity are, nevertheless, extremely important and require protection:

Tanjung Puting

National Park and Game Reserve, of area 3000 km^2, with proposed extension of 700 km^2. Although not rich in species or endemics, it includes a complete spectrum of the coastal and lowland habitats of south-central Kalimantan (although only a very small amount of lowland forest). Altitude: 0–100 m. Existing reserve includes heath forest (1100 km^2), peat swamp forest (950 km^2), freshwater swamp forest (550 km^2), lowland rain forest (100 km^2) and mangroves (100 km^2). The proposed extension includes adjacent areas of swamp forests, heath forest and mangroves along the Sungei Kumai.
❖ Threats: Illegal logging. Botanically under-collected.

Danau Sentarum freshwater swamp forests

Danau Sentarum is a Game Reserve of 800 km^2, based around a series of interconnecting lakes. Of importance primarily for its bird life and endemic freshwater fish, the area also encompasses freshwater swamp forests, peat swamp forests and some lowland forest. Though not yet evaluated botanically, the lowland hills of soft sandstones are predicted to have high point endemism, and are representative of the rich flora of north-west Borneo. Because this would be the only reserve in Indonesia to include what is the richest lowland flora in the republic, botanical exploration is of the highest priority (P.S. Ashton 1991, *in litt.*).

Muara Sebuku mangroves

Muara Sebuku, in the extreme north-east of Kalimantan, contains some of the best remaining, and least disturbed, areas of mangroves in the province. Besides mangroves, which cover 550 km², the area also includes 427 km² of lowland rain forest, 250 km² of heath forest and 100 km² of freshwater swamp forest.

Gunung Penrisen/Gunung Nyiut

Game Reserve, of area 1800 km². Altitude: 150–1701 m.
❖ Vegetation: Lowland dipterocarp forest on clay soils (1250 km²), heath forest (70 km²), montane forest. Most of the area has been logged (K. MacKinnon 1990, pers. comm.).
❖ Threats: Shifting cultivation, dam construction.

Kutai

National Park and Game Reserve, of area 2000 km². Altitude: 0–398 m. Contains a good example of the East Kalimantan lowland flora developed on argillaceous sediments, and the only protected area in Kalimantan to include MDF developed on Tertiary (Miocene) sedimentary deposits. The flora is relatively low in endemics compared to that of north-west Borneo. 180 species have been recorded in a 1.2 ha plot. Nengah Wirawan (1986) lists 659 species of flowering plants and 19 species of ferns recorded in 52 sample plots of total area 10.4 ha. Large areas of forest were burnt in 1982; however, there are still about 1000 km² of forests in the Suaka Margasatura Kutai area that have not been logged or affected by fire. These include dipterocarp, "ulin" and c. 7000 km² of mangrove forest. Threats include logging, which has been continuing in the Santan catchment since the 1970s, fire, shifting cultivation, and surrounding development activities associated with oil, gas, timber and coal industries (Nengah Wirawan 1985).

SABAH (MALAYSIA)

Total land areas: 73,710 km².

Population (1991): 1,736,902; growth rate >5%.

Altitude: 0–4101 m (summit of Mount Kinabalu).

Natural vegetation: About 49% of the land area is estimated to be under forest cover. Lowland and hill evergreen rain forests, dominated by Dipterocarpaceae; peat swamp forest in the south-west; heath (kerangas) forest; a few outcrops of limestone, supporting a distinct forest, particularly on the east coast; lower and upper montane vegetation; forest on ultramafic rocks; alpine vegetation on Mount Kinabalu.

Flora: >10,000 vascular plant species in Sabah and Sarawak combined.

Threats: Logging, shifting cultivation, fire, settled agriculture.

Conservation: 1 National Park (IUCN Management Category: II) covering 1399 km².
5 State Parks (IUCN Management Category: II) covering 1259 km².
2 Wildlife Reserves (1412 km²).
2 Sabah Foundation Conservation Areas (818 km²).
18 Virgin Jungle Reserves (IUCN Management Category: I) cover 764 km².
Existing National and State Parks cover 3.6% of the land area; other categories cover 3% of the land area. In addition, there are c. 1000 km² of protection forests, which play an important role in conserving biodiversity.

Sabah lies in the northern tip of Borneo, bounded by the South China Sea to the west and the Sulu Sea to the east. It is the second largest state of Malaysia, with a coastline of approximately 1500 km. From the coastal plains, the interior of Sabah rises abruptly on the western coast to the central mountain ranges, culminating in the granodiorite peak of Mount Kinabalu which, at 4101 m, is the highest peak in Borneo. The Crocker Range, extending south-west, and Trus Madi (2649 m), are also notable mountain features of the western side of Sabah. In the east, few hills rise above 500 m, whereas central Sabah is mountainous. The largest river in Sabah is the Kinabatangan, which flows eastwards. Some 95% of Sabah's land area consists of sedimentary and sedimentary-volcanic rock formations. There are also some exposed volcanic, intrusive igneous and crystalline basement rocks.

Climate

The average maximum daytime temperature in the lowlands is 30°C, although midday temperatures on hot days can be up to 34°C. The average nightime minimum temperature is 25°C. There is little seasonal variation in temperature, but there are distinct seasonal variations in rainfall. From November to February the wet north-east monsoon blows across Sabah carrying heavy rain into the interior. Sabah's western coast has its least amount of rainfall during this period. The south-west monsoon blows from May to August, carrying heavy rain to the west coast. In the north-east, annual rainfall is c. 3000–3500 mm (e.g. Beluran 3300 mm; Sandakan 3200 mm); in the centre, it is 2500–3000 mm (e.g. Lamag 2800 mm; Litang 2900 mm; Tangkulap 2500 mm); and in the south, it is 1800–2500 mm (e.g. Lahad Datu 1900 mm; Semporna 2200 mm; Tawau 1800 mm). Rainfall is fairly evenly distributed in the south, heaviest in December–January in the north. In the central part, there is a tendency to bimodal distribution, with contributions from both monsoons. Between the two monsoon periods there can be little rainfall; April is generally the driest month.

In some years, the general pattern is also affected by El Niño Southern Oscillation phenomena. These events caused serious droughts from June 1982 to April 1983, with marked effects on the vegetation in many parts of Borneo. At the height of the drought, in February–April 1983, rainfall was only 15% of normal. Fires caused by man began in January of that year and burned over 10,000 km² of forest in Sabah (Beaman, Beaman, Marsh and Woods 1985). Logged forests were more seriously affected than primary forests, as a result of the litter that had accumulated following logging operations. About 85% of the forest that was destroyed by the fires had previously been logged.

Population

Sabah's population was 1,736,902 in 1991 (census figures). Although a relatively low figure, the growth rate is high, at around 5% or more. Most urban centres are found around the coast, but the majority of people are rural. Because of the steepness of the terrain, only a maximum of 30% of the land area has been assessed as suitable for agriculture. Nevertheless, settled agriculture is more extensive than in Sarawak, and large areas in the lowlands of eastern Sabah are being converted to settled agriculture. However, shifting cultivation is less extensive than in Sarawak, covering about 11,000 km² or 15% of the land area. This is mostly in the west and centre of the state.

Vegetation

Collins, Sayer and Whitmore (1991) give the following estimates of forest cover, based on analysis of maps provided by the Sabah Forest Department:

	Area (km²)	% of land area
Lowland rain forests	29,500	40.4
Montane rain forests	3100	4.5
Mangroves	3400	5.0
Totals	**36,000**	**49.9**

Lowland and hill evergreen rain forest is rich in dipterocarps, and therefore highly valued as a commercial source of timber. Floristically, these are also the richest communities. Some of the most valuable and productive forests once occurred on the extensive lowlands in the middle and lower reaches of the major river systems. Between 1973 and 1983, the area of undisturbed forest in Sabah was halved. By 1980, virtually all of Sabah's productive forests had either been logged or licensed for logging (FAO/UNEP 1981). Remaining areas of lowland and hill dipterocarp forests in east Sabah are particularly important for conservation (see Data Sheet on East Sabah Lowland and Hill Dipterocarp Forests, CPD Site SEA22).

Sabah has some small areas of peat swamp forests, the most important of which occur in the south-west around Beaufort, covering a few thousands of hectares, most of which are now within Protection Forest Reserves (J. Payne 1992, *in litt.*). A distinctive high-altitude peat swamp forest, rich in orchids and rhododendrons, occurs south of Sipitang, in the highlands on the Sarawak border in the Ulu Meligan (A. Lamb and A. Phillipps 1990, pers. comm.).

There are various types of heath forest exhibiting altitudinal variation. Coastal lowland heath forest, mostly cleared, occurs at Sipitang; mid-altitude heath forest, rich in orchids, including several endemics, occurs at Nabawan at around 500 m, while high-altitude heath forest occurs at Ulu Long Pasia above 1000 m, and in the Maliau Basin.

Limestone outcrops are less extensive than in Sarawak and Kalimantan, and remain poorly known botanically. However, their flora is very distinct and undoubtedly rich, and each outcrop is likely to have its own suite of endemics (A. Lamb 1990, pers. comm.). See Data Sheet on Limestone Flora of Borneo (CPD Site SEA18).

Lower and upper montane forests are best developed in the upper Padas Valley (in the Sabah/Sarawak/Kalimantan border area), on Trus Madi, the Crocker Range and Mount Kinabalu. As in montane forests elsewhere in Borneo, the families Fagaceae, Flacourtiaceae, Myrtaceae, Ericaceae, Orchidaceae and Nepenthaceae are well-represented. At higher altitudes, conifers in the Podocarpaceae and Phyllocladaceae (*Phyllocladus* spp.) are common.

Forests on ultramafic (ultrabasic) rocks are, in some cases, floristically and structurally distinct. Ultramafic rocks outcrop in an arc of mountains extending from Mount Kinabalu to the east coast. Those of the Mount Kinabalu mountain complex are particularly rich in endemics (see Data Sheet on Kinabalu Park, CPD Site SEA24). The ultramafic flora of north-east Borneo (SEA27) is also the subject of a separate Data Sheet.

In addition to the above, mangrove forests cover about 3400 km², principally on the east coast, along with coastal swamp forests. A mosaic of wetlands, consisting of peat swamp, freshwater alluvium, mangrove forests, and nipa swamps, cover 900 km² at the Klias Peninsula bordering Brunei Bay in south-western Sabah.

Flora

The flora of Sabah and Sarawak combined is estimated to include more than 10,000 vascular plant species (Idris Mohd. Said 1989).

Useful plants

See account in General Overview on South East Asia (Malesia).

Conservation

At present, there is only one National Park (the Crocker Range National Park) which covers 1399 km² of mainly hill and montane forests; however, the park is reserved under State, not National, Parks legislation. In addition, there are five State Parks, including Kinabalu Park. Other reserves include two areas (Danum Valley and Gunong Lotung/Maliau Basin) in which the timber rights are owned by the Sabah Foundation.

In addition to these areas, there are 18 Virgin Jungle Reserves (VJRs) covering 764 km² (IUCN 1992) and Protection Forests which cover c. 1000 km² (Collins, Sayer and Whitmore 1991). These are part of the Permanent Forest Estate (PFE) of Sabah, managed by the Forest Department. The PFE covers 45% (33,500 km²) of the land area of Sabah. Ultimately, the majority of this area will be commercially exploited for its timber. Although timber legislation determines a lower girth limit for a number of timber tree species, in practice the residual damage to the timber stand can be between 40–70% when 4–6 trees/acre are extracted.

VJRs and Wildlife Reserves are not totally protected. For example, the Tabin Wildlife Reserve (1205 km²) (formerly a commercial Forest Reserve, and one of the few remaining areas of lowland forest below 300 m in eastern Sabah) has been heavily logged in the past. There is still a core area of approximately 85 km² of intact forest. Illegal logging has also occurred within Kinabalu Park and Crocker Range National Park.

The inadequate representation of lowland dipterocarp forest has been identified as a deficiency of the protected areas system in Sabah (MacKinnon and MacKinnon 1986). Existing reserves are mostly below 1000 m (and thereby technically lowland) but forests below 200 m are the richest. It is precisely these areas which are most valuable for logging and at risk from land development. For both Sabah and Sarawak combined, existing and proposed protected areas which contain tropical moist forests include just 11.4% of all remaining moist forests in the two states (Collins, Sayer and Whitmore 1991).

A review of the protected areas system and conservation legislation is given in IUCN (1992).

There are several important *ex situ* conservation collections focusing on native rare and threatened plants. The **Forest Research Centre, Sepilok** includes about 200 lowland species of orchids, while the **Tenom Orchid Centre** contains the largest collection of lowland Borneo orchids, estimated at over 460 species in 72 genera in 1990 (Lamb 1991a). The **Mountain Garden, Kinabalu Park** (at c. 1520 m altitude), and the **Poring Orchid Centre** based at the Poring Hot Springs Ranger Station (at c. 487 m) within Kinabalu Park, includes a collection of orchids and other species collected in the park. A collection of montane species is being established at the **Sinsuron Mountain Garden**, near Mount Alab, in the Crocker Range, under the jurisdiction of the Tambunan District Council.

The **Agricultural Research Station at Lagud Sebrang**, Tenom, has what is probably the best germplasm collection of wild fruit trees in Borneo. Most are planted in the Living Museum of Economic Crop Plants which also contains many examples of other economic plants of value, both native and introduced.

Centres of plant diversity and endemism

SEA21. Crocker Range/Mount Trus Madi

Geomorphologically (but not geologically) an extension of the Kinabalu massif, which runs parallel to the western coast of Sabah. Mount Trus Madi (2649 m) is the second highest mountain in Borneo. Area: Crocker Range – 1399 km²; Gunung Trus Madi – 1840 km². Altitude: 1000–2423 m (Crocker Range) –2649 m (Gunung Trus Madi).
* Vegetation: Montane forest.
* Flora: A rich area, but many plants also found on Mount Kinabalu. Exceptions include *Rafflesia tengku-adlinii* (which occurs only on Trus Madi and in the Maliau Basin) and several new species of orchids discovered in the Crocker Range but not yet recorded from Mount Kinabalu (A. Lamb and A. Phillipps 1990, pers. comm.).
* Threats: The lower slopes of the Crocker Range are threatened by illegal shifting cultivation. In 1984, the designation of Trus Madi was changed from a watershed protection forest to that of a commercial forest reserve. As a result, it has been logged, and serious soil erosion has occurred in places. However, intact forests still remain on the upper slopes and on some of the lower slopes. Ornamental plants, such as orchids, are collected from the forests.
* Conservation: The Crocker Range is a National Park; Gunung Trus Madi is within a Forest Reserve.

SEA22. East Sabah Lowland and Hill Dipterocarp Forests, including Danum Valley, Sepilok Forest Reserve, Tabin Wildlife Reserve, Tawau Hills

– see Data Sheet.

SEA23. Gunong Lotung/Maliau Basin

An area of interbedded sandstones and mudstones, with some coal deposits, in south-central Sabah, about 40 km north of the Indonesian border between latitudes 4°40'–4°50'N and longitudes 116°40'–117°2'E. Area: 390 km². Altitude: 400–1900 m (although the highest point, Gunong Lotung has yet to be accurately surveyed).
* Vegetation: Lowland (hill) dipterocarp forest up to 700 m; ridge forest of dipterocarps and Fagaceae on ridge crests up to 950 m; lower and upper montane heath forests, best developed at c. 1000 m; montane conifer forest; small area of upper montane forest above 1200 m dominated by Ericaceae. 88% of the basin comprises montane forests; 12% is lowland/hill forest (Marsh 1989; Marsh and Gasis 1990). An expedition in early 1992 discovered a montane conifer/*Casuarina* (*Gymnostoma*) forest (dominated by a new species of the latter) (A. Lamb and A. Phillipps 1990, pers. comm.).
* Flora: An expedition made in April–May 1988 made an incomplete collection of plants totalling 460 vascular species (Marsh 1989; Marsh and Gasis 1990), including 38 dipterocarp species, representing about 21% of Sabah's dipterocarp flora (Marsh 1989). The heath forests contain a rich orchid and *Nepenthes* flora. *Rafflesia tengku-adlinii* occurs in ridge forests, one of only two Sabah localities.
* Threats: Exploration for oil and coal is a potential major threat.
* Conservation: The area is designated and maintained as a Conservation Area by the Sabah Foundation.

SEA24. Kinabalu Park

– see Data Sheet.

By far the most important botanical site in Borneo, Mount Kinabalu is protected within Kinabalu Park. Although it does not contain any substantial areas of lowland forest, its altitudinal range and variety of edaphic conditions provide a diversity of habitat types for an extraordinary wealth of species (including about 4500 vascular plant species), many of which are only known from this one mountain, the highest in Borneo.

SEA25/26. Ulu Meligan/Ulu Long Pasia

A montane area in south-western Sabah, south of Sipitang near the border with Sarawak, between latitudes 4°30'–4°32'N and longitudes 115°33'–115°42'E. Area: c. 500 km². Altitude: c. 1450 m.
* Vegetation: Heath forest and a unique high-altitude peat swamp forest (covering c. 8 km²), the only high-altitude swamp forest in Sabah, and therefore of considerable scientific interest. The swamp forest performs a valuable function in regulating water supply to areas downstream.
* Flora: A rich flora, including many species of orchids and rhododendrons not found elsewhere in Sabah. The flora has affinities to that of neighbouring Sarawak.
* Threats: Logging has occurred in the hinterland with the intention of replanting with fast-growing exotic trees (Scott 1989; A. Lamb and A. Phillipps 1990, pers. comm.).
* Conservation: The area is partly State-owned and partly owned by Sabah Forest Industries. Part of the area is within a Virgin Jungle Reserve of over 90 km².

SEA27. North-east Borneo ultramafic flora (eastern Sabah)

– see Data Sheet.

Note: Numerous limestone sites in Sabah are included in the Data Sheet on the **Limestone flora of Borneo**, CPD Site SEA18.

Areas of botanical interest

Although not meeting the criteria for selection as centres of plant species diversity, the following sites nevertheless contain important examples of vegetation types requiring protection:

Kinabatangan freshwater swamp forests

At 560 km long, the Kinabatangan is Sabah's longest river, arising from steep mountains in the south-west and flowing into the Sulu Sea through the largest tract of mangrove forest in Malaysia. The flood plain of the river covers c. 2800 km². There is a variety of vegetation types, including logged dipterocarp forest, seasonally inundated alluvial swamp forest, peat swamp forest, coastal mangroves and nipa swamps. Much of the forest is of low stature with little timber of commercial value; inundation creates problems for permanent agriculture. As a result, the swamp forests are largely intact (although the lowland dipterocarp forests have been logged). Indeed, the alluvial swamp forests are the largest remaining tracts of such forest in Malaysia, those elsewhere having been converted mainly to paddi or oil palm plantations. A large rattan plantation has been established by the Sabah Forest Development Authority (SAFODA) under thinned secondary forest in the Batu Putih region (Scott 1989). The Kinabatangan forests remain poorly known botanically.

Klias Peninsula

A large mosaic of wetland and dryland vegetation covering 900 km² on the coast of south-western Sabah, around Brunei and Kimanis bays, between latitudes 5°12'–5°30'N and longitudes 115°22'–115°.42'E. Altitude: 0–10 m. Vegetation: peat swamp (607 km²), freshwater alluvial swamp (145 km²), mangrove and nipa swamps, heath (kerangas) forest rich in myrmecophytes, grassland, scrub and secondary forest, with tall gallery dipterocarp forest along the Sebuboh River.

Five Forest Reserves have been established: Sungai Binsuluk (121 km², mainly peat swamp forest), Klias (36 km², mainly peat swamp forest), Padas Damit (90 km², mixed swamp forest and nipa swamp), Kampung Hindian (6 km², mostly mangrove), and Menumbak (57 km² of mangrove). In 1978, 309 km² were gazetted as a National Park, but de-gazetted in 1980. Small-scale logging has occurred; there is also some clearance for agriculture. However, proposed development schemes involving wetland drainage for agriculture are a more serious threat. The mangrove swamps of Klias are important breeding areas for fish and prawns, and support the marine fisheries of western Sabah and Brunei. In 1973, prawn landings in Brunei Bay alone fetched M$3 million (Scott 1989).

SARAWAK (MALAYSIA)

Total land area: 124,499 km².

Population (1991): 1,648,217.

Altitude: 0–2438 m (summit of Gunung Murud).

Natural vegetation: About 76% of the land area is estimated to be forest covered. Lowland evergreen rain forests (MDF) throughout much of the interior lowlands; extensive peat swamp forests on the coastal plains, much degraded by logging; heath (kerangas) forest; forest on limestone; lower and upper montane rain forests on the north-eastern border with Sabah and along part of the Indonesian frontier south-west to the Lupar valley, with outliers in the west, centre and north-east.

Flora: >10,000 vascular plant species in Sarawak and Sabah combined.

Threats: Logging, shifting cultivation.

Conservation: 9 National Parks (IUCN Management Category: II) covering 1041 km² (0.8% of land area).
3 Wildlife Sanctuaries (IUCN Management Category: II) covering 1749 km² (1.4% of land area).
There are proposals to establish a further 13 areas as National Parks, covering an additional 4516 km², 6 Wildlife Sanctuaries covering 2476 km², and 6 Nature Reserves covering 16 km². This would bring the area under total protection to 9896 km² (c. 8% of the land area).

Sarawak contains the most diverse range of vegetation types and the richest lowland flora of Malesia. Like its neighbour, Brunei, it lies in an optimum area of humid-insular equatorial climate on the north-western side of Borneo in one of the richest floristic regions of the world. Brünig (1973) estimated the total tree flora of Sarawak and Brunei combined to be between 2800 and 3300 species. However, this range is now thought to be too low.

Geologically, Sarawak consists mainly of relatively young, very deep sedimentary rocks that have been subject to complex and localized folding, although some ancient formations of Pre-Permian age do occur, such as in the extreme west. While mountains extend along two-thirds of the boundary with Kalimantan (rising to 2438 m at Gunung Murud in the Kelabit Highlands), 14% of Sarawak's land area is covered by low-lying coastal swamps, extending some way inland from the 1050 km-long South China Sea coastline. The mountains and coastal plain are dissected by many rivers which generally flow in a northerly or westerly direction. Large areas of Sarawak, therefore, are unsuitable for cultivation, either because of permanent or seasonal inundation, the fragile nature of acidic, sandy *kerangas* soils, or else because of the steepness of the terrain in the interior mountains. Indeed, about 70% of the land area consists of mountainous country with slopes of more than 30° (Hatch 1982), while a further 12% is covered by peat swamps, and approximately 1.3% by mangroves and nipa swamps.

Climate

The climate is warm and humid throughout the year. The mean annual temperature at sea-level is about 27°C. The seasonal variation is slight (1–2°C), the diurnal variation being greater (6–7°C). There is a lapse rate of 0.5–0.7°C per 100 m elevation. The annual rainfall varies considerably from year to year, and between different regions. The average annual rainfall is 3000–4000 mm, with extremes of 2571 mm (at Long Semado) and 6661 mm (at Lingga). The wettest areas are in the south and west, and in the interior of Sarawak. Rainfall exceeding 100 mm in a day is not exceptional, the highest daily total recorded in recent years being 283 mm at Kuching (JPM 1984). High rainfall usually occurs between November and February (the rainy or "landas" season), with a drier period from June to August. Seasonal variations are more pronounced in the coastal and western parts of Sarawak than in the north (which is drier) and the interior (Scott 1989).

Population

According to the 1991 census, the population of Sarawak stood at 1,648,217. The population includes 28 different tribal groups; 30% of the population consists of Ibans, who along with other Orang Ulu groups are mainly confined to inland areas where they now farm. Many still retain a culture and livelihood which is associated closely with the forest. Penan, from the interior of Borneo, traditionally hunted and gathered forest products. Today, there are c. 9000 Penan in Sarawak, of whom c. 25% are permanently settled. Of the remainder, most are semi-settled, and less than 400 are nomadic (figures from the State Planning Unit, quoted in Kavanagh, Abdul Rahim and Hails 1989). Most nomadic Penans dwell in the Magoh and Sepayang river basins, tributaries of the Baram. Most of Sarawak's urban centres have developed along the coast.

Vegetation

Collins, Sayer and Whitmore (1991) give the following estimates of the extent of rain forest in Sarawak, based on analysis of maps published in 1979 by the Sarawak Forest Department:

	Area (km²)	% of land area
Lowland rain forests	61,170	49.1
Montane rain forests	17,060	13.7
Inland swamp forests	14,080	11.9
Mangroves	1640	1.3
Totals	**94,670**	**76.0**

In addition, there are important areas of forest on limestone, as well as heath forests, which cover about 3.9% of the land area (FAO/UNEP 1981). There are also areas of high-altitude heath forests at Bario. As of 1990, approximately 60,000 km² of forest was primary forest (ITTO 1990; Primack and Hall 1992). Myers (1980) estimated the area of undisturbed forest (including montane forests) to be 55,687 km². Probably less than 2% of lowland forest remains in a pristine state (Lamb 1991a).

Floristically, the richest vegetation formation is lowland tropical evergreen rain forest (MDF). Of the various types of lowland forest, the remaining areas of MDF on humult ultisols on the coastal hills are especially important for conservation. They are floristically distinct from forests on the prevailing udult ultisols and are particularly rich in endemics (Ashton 1990). These coastal forests also tend to be easily accessible and extremely fragile. Throughout Sarawak, lowland dipterocarp forests are under increasing pressure, with about 60% already having been licensed for logging. Each year approximately 2500 km² are logged (Collins, Sayer and Whitmore 1991).

Peat swamp forests were the first forests to be logged on a commercial scale, and for many years provided most of Sarawak's timber. By 1972, they had all been licensed for timber extraction, and virtually all are due to be logged by the year 2000 (WWF Malaysia 1985). Each year, about 350 km² of peat swamp forest are logged. Among the important timber species present are:

Gonystylus bancanus (ramin)
Dactylocladus stenostachys (jongkong)
Dyera polyphylla (swamp jelutong, also provides latexes)
Copaifera palustris (sepetir paya)
Shorea albida (alan bunga).

About 32,000 km² of peat swamp and dipterocarp forests have been logged so far (State Planning Unit figures), and each year 300 km² is being cut for a second time (Collins, Sayer and Whitmore 1991). Often the rotation cycle is just 10 years, and concern has been expressed by a 1989/1990 ITTO mission that such levels of logging are unsustainable. The current rate of harvesting in Sarawak's hill forest (where most of the timber extraction is currently taking place) is more than 13 million m³ per year. At this rate, which ITTO (1990) considers to be three times the rate that could provide a sustainable timber yield, almost all of the hill forests will have been selectively logged for commercial timber by the year 2000.

Although timber extraction does not cause outright deforestation by itself, second cuts at less than 40-year intervals radically alter and simplify forest composition. Logging also allows the spread of shifting cultivation. By 1978, about 23% of the state's land area had been used for shifting agriculture at some time, and the amount was growing by 0.5% to 1% per annum (Collins, Sayer and Whitmore 1991). By a combination of logging and shifting cultivation, primary forests are being replaced by secondary forests of lower stature and altered species composition, and by non-forest vegetation.

According to the State Planning Unit, forestry employed 582,580 people in Sarawak in 1985, and was projected to employ 870,060 by 1995. In 1988, the revenue generated from exported timber was M$2100 million (out of a total export trade of M$7300 million for Sarawak), while the revenue earned from domestic timber trade was M$491.3 million. Unless Sarawak's forests are managed sustainably, there will be a decline in timber production, employment and timber royalties paid to government in the future.

Flora

The flora of Sabah and Sarawak combined is estimated to include more than 10,000 vascular plant species (Idris Mohd. Said 1989).

Useful plants

See account in General Overview on South East Asia (Malesia).

Conservation

In Sarawak, the Forest Department is responsible for designating and managing the Permanent Forest Estate (PFE) which currently covers about 60,000 km² (48% of the land area). This includes production forests for timber production, and "protection forests" (about 30% of the PFE) set aside on steep land where logging is not possible, and for watershed protection. Totally protected areas (9 National Parks and 3 Wildlife Sanctuaries) currently cover just 2.2% of the land area. There are, however, proposals for an additional 13 areas to be designated as National Parks, and proposals for 6 more Wildlife Sanctuaries and 6 Nature Reserves. The proposed system would bring the area under total protection to c. 8% of the land area (Abang H.K. Morshidi and Gumal 1992).

While all the major vegetation types in Sarawak are represented in the existing and proposed protected areas system (Table 41), some types are currently under-represented. This is particularly the case for mangroves, peat swamp forest, and the full range of lowland mixed dipterocarp forests, the richest plant communities. The major lowland forest type of the region, mixed dipterocarp forest on shale and clay, is very rich in regional endemics and so far is inadequately represented in the present protected areas system, except possibly in Lanjak-Entimau Wildlife Sanctuary, part of which has been logged (P.S. Ashton 1990, *in litt.*). With the exception of relatively small areas of lowland forest in Lanjak-Entimau Wildlife Sanctuary, Lambir Hills National Park, and Gunung Mulu National Park the present protected areas system shows a bias toward montane forest types.

TABLE 41. AREAS OF MAJOR VEGETATION TYPES IN EXISTING AND PROPOSED NATIONAL PARKS, WILDLIFE SANCTUARIES, AND NATURE RESERVES IN SARAWAK (Areas in km²)

	MDF	PSF	Mangrove	"Heath"	Kerangas
National Parks					
Existing areas	559	86	2	32	326
Proposed areas	*2858*	*-*	*103*	*114*	*166*
Total	**3417**	**86**	**105**	**146**	**492**
Wildlife Sanctuaries					
Existing areas	1397	-	2	39	292
Proposed areas	*1542*	*97*	*23*	*142*	*221*
Total	**2939**	**97**	**25**	**181**	**513**
Nature Reserves					
Existing areas	-	-	-	-	-
Proposed areas	*11*	*-*	*-*	*-*	*-*
Total	**11**	**-**	**-**	**-**	**-**
Grand total	**6367**	**183**	**130**	**327**	**1005**

MDF – Mixed dipterocarp forest
PSF – Peat swamp forest

Source: Abang H.K. Morshidi and Gumal 1992.

Lanjak-Entimau (CPD Site SEA16, in part), because of its size (1688 km²), is particularly important, but its status as a Wildlife Sanctuary has not prevented incursions from logging in the lowlands (see Data Sheet). Gunung Mulu National Park (529 km²) (CPD Site SEA33, in part) includes all the major inland vegetation formations of Sarawak, except those which occur on volcanic soils. It contains a wide altitudinal range and varied geology, resulting in complex forest zonation, from lowland mixed dipterocarp forest, through lower montane forests, to upper montane forests with conifers. Mulu also contains good representation of riverine forests, with an extraordinary richness of epiphytes, many of which are locally endemic. In addition, the Melinau

limestone formation supports a distinct calcicolous flora, with many endemics and the best conserved example of MDF on humult ultisols (P.S. Ashton 1991, *in litt.*).

Of other sites identified below, Bako National Park (CPD Site SEA28) includes dipterocarp forest on sandy soils, heath (kerangas) forest on sandstone, and coastal cliff vegetation which is otherwise rare in Sarawak. Lambir Hills (CPD Site SEA34 – see Data Sheet), although small in area, contains a remarkably rich flora with many locally restricted species.

In 1991, 188,135 people visited Sarawak and receipts from tourism were worth M$180.6 million (Abang H.K. Morshidi and Gumal 1992). 23,228 foreign visitors visited one or more of the four National Parks. This represents 12% of all visitors entering the state. Chung (1987) calculated that the recreational value (through the travel cost method) of three National Parks (Bako, Lambir Hills and Niah) in any one year is worth several million Malaysian dollars. Revenue received from visitors to these three areas (excluding food purchases) in 1985 was c. M$2.5 million.

The *ex situ* conservation of rare and threatened plants is undertaken at the Botany Research Centre, Kuching. Currently it has collected and planted over 3000 local plants, with special emphasis on orchids, of which there are probably over 200 lowland species represented in the collection (Lamb 1991a), pitcher plants, palms, wild fruits, local medicinal plants and other economically important species.

In 1985, a Sarawak Conservation Strategy was completed (WWF Malaysia 1985) – a comprehensive report on all natural resources. It included numerous recommendations for conservation action, some of which have already been acted upon. The Strategy called for surveys of coastal forests to determine which areas of mangrove and peat swamp should be protected.

Centres of plant diversity and endemism

SEA28. Bako National Park

Area: 27 km², and a proposed extension of 8.7 km². Altitude: 0–244 m.

❖ Vegetation: Beach forest, mangroves, coastal cliff vegetation, heath (kerangas) forests (16.4 km²), lowland MDF on sandy loam soils (3.6 km²), riverine forest, peat swamp forest and "padang" vegetation.

❖ Flora: Four study plots in coastal dipterocarp forest (of total area 5.6 ha) contained 519 tree species, including seedlings (height 20 cm at least but dbh less than 1 cm), saplings (height at least 20 cm and dbh between 1.0 and 9.9 cm), and trees greater than or equal to 10 cm diameter dbh (Primack and Hall 1992). 35% of the species recorded in the sample plots were represented by just one individual.

❖ Threats: Some disturbance in the past from man-induced fires has occurred; some areas of swamp forest may have been logged or selectively cut (Ashton 1971).

❖ Conservation: Bako has had National Park status since 1957. The park is a growing tourist attraction, with an information centre which offers a range of educational exhibits. There were 29,675 visitors in 1984. Revenue generated from tourism (excluding food purchases) was M$218,191 in 1984 and M$990,436 in 1985 (G. Davison 1993, *in litt.*).

SEA29. Batu Laga, Linau Balui Plateau

A large basalt tableland area including Lina Balui Plateau and a steep rocky basalt mountain (Batu Laga).

❖ Vegetation: MDF on basic volcanic rocks on slopes and on the plateau, heath (kerangas) forest, lower and upper montane forests.

❖ Flora: Botanically unexplored but certain to be rich in rare and endemic species (P.S. Ashton 1991, *in litt.*).

❖ Conservation: Batu Laga is proposed as a Wildlife Sanctuary of area 2000 km² (Ngui 1991).

SEA30. Bukit Mersing, Anap, Tatau region

An isolated basalt range, rich in rare and endemic species (P.S. Ashton 1990, *in litt.*).

❖ Vegetation: MDF.

❖ Flora: Five study plots in mixed dipterocarp forest (of total area 7 ha) at Bukit Mersing contained 341 tree species, including seedlings (height at least 20 cm but dbh less than 1 cm), saplings (height at least 20 cm and dbh between 1.0 and 9.9 cm), and trees greater than or equal to 10 cm diameter dbh (Primack and Hall 1992). About half the species recorded in the sample plots were represented by just one individual.

❖ Conservation: Currently no legal protection; Bukit Mersing is proposed as a Nature Reserve of 12 km² (Ngui 1991).

SEA31. Gunung Gading National Park

Area: 42 km². Altitude: 500–1560 m.

❖ Vegetation: Lowland MDF, submontane rain forest and heath forest on granodiorite.

❖ Flora: Rich in endemics; site of *Rafflesia tuan-mudae*.

❖ Conservation: Declared a National Park in 1983. Important for watershed protection.

SEA32. Gunong Gaharu, Gunong Apeng and Gunong Silantek, Sabal Forest Reserve

Sandstone mountains in the Klingkang Range in west Sarawak.

❖ Vegetation: A mosaic of MDF, heath (kerangas) forest and cliff flora (P.S. Ashton 1990, *in litt.*).

❖ Flora: The palm flora is exceptionally rich (J. Dransfield 1992, *in litt.*).

SEA33. Gunung Mulu National Park

– see Data Sheet on Gunung Mulu National Park, Medalam Protected Forest (Sarawak) and Labi Hills, Bukit Teraja, Ulu Ingei, Sungei Ingei (Brunei).

SEA34. Lambir Hills National Park

– see Data Sheet.

SEA35. Mixed dipterocarp forests on humult ultisols on coastal hills

MDF on humult ultisols in Sarawak are particularly rich in local endemics and, as mentioned above, are floristically distinct from forests on udult ultisols. It has been recommended by Ashton (1990) that relict forest islands at **Bukit Undan** (First Division), **Sabal Forest Reserve**, and the **low coastal hills between the rivers Balingian and Muka**, should be added to the system of totally protected areas in Sarawak.

SEA36. Nieuwenhuis Mountains

The frontier ranges of the Balleh headwaters, from Gunung Lawit along the shale and sandstone divide eastward to Bukit Bulan and Batu Tiban, including the Sarawak part of the andesitic Nieuwenhuis Mountains; from the peaks at 1500 m to the headwaters of the Balleh. This biologically rich, but mostly unexplored, major watershed at the centre of Borneo is not protected at present. The area is adjacent to Lanjak-Entimau Wildlife Sanctuary and Gunung Bentuang dan Karimun (Kalimantan) (CPD Site SEA16, see Data Sheet), and therefore offers the potential for the establishment of a transfrontier park, including the Kalimantan Nieuwenhuis Mountains (P.S. Ashton 1990, *in litt.*).

SEA37. Pueh Range (Gunung Pueh, Bukit Kanyi, Bukit Berumput to Bukit Berpayong)

Granodiorite peaks at 1300–1600 m in west Sarawak with an isolated flora rich in endemics.

❖ Vegetation: MDF and heath (kerangas) forest at lower elevations (P.S. Ashton 1990, *in litt.*).

❖ Conservation: Gunung Pueh Forest Reserve includes the coastal terraces and Pueh-Berumput Range.

SEA38. Pulong Tau, Gunung Murud

Gunung Murud (2438 m) is Sarawak's highest mountain.

❖ Vegetation: The region includes 890 km² of lower and upper montane rain forests and 750 km² of lowland MDF. The foothills of Gunung Murud contain important areas of kerangas forest (Brünig 1991).

❖ Conservation: The proposed Pulong Tau National Park covers 637 km² (Abang H.K. Morshidi and Gumal 1992). The region is adjacent to **Cagar Alam Sungai Kayan-Sungai Mentarang** (CPD Site SEA19, see Data Sheet) in Kalimantan, and is likely to be richer (P.S. Ashton 1991, *in litt.*).

SEA39. Usun Apau Plateau

A volcanic highland plateau, south-west of the Kelabit Highlands, encompassing the upper reaches of the Batang Baram, Batang Tinjar and Batang Rajang rivers. Altitude: 1100–1400 m.

❖ Vegetation: MDF, lower and upper montane forests, high-altitude heath (kerangas) forest on ultramafic substrates (Brünig 1991; P. Chai 1990, *in litt.*). Localized upland peat bogs almost certainly support a highly specialized flora of considerable botanical interest, but detailed investigations have yet to be made (Scott 1989).

❖ Conservation: The proposed Usun Apau National Park covers 498 km² (Abang H.K. Morshidi and Gumal 1992). The area deserves nomination as a World Heritage Site according to the State Conservation Strategy of Sarawak (WWF Malaysia 1985).

Note: For **Batang Ai National Park** and **Lanjak-Entimau Wildlife Sanctuary**, see Data Sheet on **Lanjak-Entimau Wildlife Sanctuary, Batang Ai National Park (Sarawak) and Cagar Alam Gunung Bentuang dan Karimun (Kalimantan)**, CPD Site SEA16.

Note: Numerous limestone sites in Sarawak are included in the Data Sheet on the **Limestone flora of Borneo**, SEA18.

For **Ulu Medalam**, see Data Sheet on **Gunung Mulu National Park, Medalam Protected Forest (Sarawak) and Labi Hills, Bukit Teraja, Ulu Ingei, Sungei Ingei (Brunei)**, CPD Site SEA33.

Areas of botanical interest

The following sites contain important examples of vegetation types requiring protection:

Kubah National Park, formerly known as Matang, covers an area of 22.3 km² close to the state capital, Kuching. The vegetation includes MDF, heath forest and areas of submontane hill dipterocarp forest. The park is of considerable historic importance as it is the type locality for many Bornean plants. It is particularly rich in palms, with about 100 species recorded, making it one of the richest palm sites in the whole world (J. Dransfield 1993, *in litt.*).

Mangrove forests

These are of limited extent in Sarawak, covering 1640 km² (1.3% of the land area), of which 370 km² (22%) is gazetted as Permanent Forest Estate by the Forest Department. Within the PFE, large areas have been clear-cut (e.g. Rajang Mangrove Forest). Only 3.7 km² of mangrove forest is represented in the current protected areas system (Abang K.K. Morshidi and Gumal 1992). The only sizeable unlogged area is the **Sarawak Mangroves Forest Reserve** (area: 117 km², of which 87 km² is proposed as a National Park). Scott (1989) refers to some 15 km² of mangrove forest within the Forest Reserve being clear-felled for an aquaculture project, adversely affecting natural fisheries and wildlife.

Other principal areas of mangrove/nipa forests include:

❖ **Rajang delta**, comprising Matu-Daro and Sibu Swamp Forest – a large block (2670 km²) of peat swamp forest, mangroves and nipa swamp, mostly within Protected Forest Reserves; Pulau Bruit, a low-lying island in the delta of the Rajang River, predominantly mangrove forest; and Rajang Mangrove Forest Reserve (1250 km²), which according to Scott (1989) is one of the most diverse mangrove forests in Sarawak.

❖ **Lawas-Limbang estuaries** (proposed as a Wildlife Sanctuary of 45 km²) in the north-east bordering Brunei.

In 1988 it was recommended that a national Mangrove Management Committee be established which should include the creation of a mangrove biosphere reserve.

Kerangas (heath) forests

Some important areas of kerangas which warrant protection occur in the **Merurong Plateau**, the **Binio basin** south-east of Bintulu, and the **Bungoh Range**, south of Kuching (Brünig 1991).

Peat swamp forests

Borneo is one of the main centres of development of peat swamp forests in South East Asia (Sumatra and New Guinea being the other main areas). In Sarawak, peat swamp forests cover much of the broad, flat coastal plain. According to Forest Department figures (quoted in WWF Malaysia 1985), there are 14,736 km² of peat swamp forests (i.e. c. 12% of the state's area), of which 6836 km² (46%) is gazetted as Permanent Forest Estate. However, all inland swamp forests (including peat swamp forest) cover 14,080 km² according to Collins, Sayer and Whitmore (1991). This total was based on an analysis of maps published in 1979 by the Sarawak Forest Department. Elsewhere in Malaysia, peat swamp forests, especially those of Peninsular Malaysia, have practically all gone as a result of land use changes.

The peat swamp flora is not rich in endemics, most if not all of the species present being found in MDF and heath forests. However, there are structural differences in peat swamp forests as a result of differing responses to soil and site conditions; Anderson (1961, 1963, 1983), for example, recognizes six phasic community types. (See also Brünig 1969, 1989.) It is important that some areas of undisturbed peat swamp forest, exhibiting the full range of successional types, are protected. The best areas remaining unlogged are in the **Baulai tributary** of the Belait river in Brunei, south-west to the **Baram River** in Sarawak (P.S. Ashton 1991, *in litt.*). The **Binio basin**, south-east of Bintulu, also contains important areas of peat swamp and kerangas forests (Brünig 1991).

Currently, only 86 km² of peat swamp forest is protected, the largest area (about 79 km²) being within **Loagan Bunut National Park**. Very small areas also exist within Bako, Gunung Mulu, Niah and Similajau National Parks. The **proposed Maludam Wildlife Sanctuary** includes 87 km² of peat swamp forest, and a further 10 km² occurs within **proposed Sibuti Wildlife Sanctuary**.

SUMATRA, INDONESIA

Total land area: 472,610 km².

Population: c. 28,000,000.

Altitude: 0–3805 m (summit of Gunung Kerinci).

Natural vegetation: Lowland evergreen rain forest (123,150 km²); peat swamp forest and mangroves extensive along eastern coast; montane rain forest (32,190 km²), mostly still intact; limestone vegetation; heath forest; montane grasslands and subalpine vegetation. About 49% of the land area is still covered by forests.

Number of vascular plants: >10,000.

Species endemism: 12%.

Number of endemic genera: 13.

Threats: Large areas of rain forest have been cleared for agriculture and industrial plantations; legally protected areas are suffering from encroachment.

Conservation: 5 National Parks (IUCN Management Category: II) cover 27,723 km²; 13 Nature Reserves (IUCN Management Category: I) cover 3929 km²; 20 Game Reserves (IUCN Management Category: IV) cover 22,503 km². In addition, there are 5 Hunting Parks (IUCN Management Category: VI) (2003 km²), 35 Protection Forests (IUCN Management Category: VI) (17,683 km²); 1 Recreation Park (IUCN Management Category: V) (13 km²). 5 areas are designated as UNESCO Man and Biosphere Reserves (14,829 km²). Note that these figures refer only to protected areas over 10 km², and that some areas have overlapping designations.

Geology

Most of the land area was raised from the sea in the last 15 million years as a result of tectonic and volcanic activity. The Barisan Mountain Range, which forms the backbone of the island, lies along the volcanic arc that also passes through Java and the Lesser Sunda Islands. There are many active volcanoes and associated features, such as hot streams and sulphur fumaroles. Raised sedimentary rocks date mostly from the Miocene and Pliocene, although some are older. They are mostly of marine origin, and include limestone, sandstone and shales. To the west, the Barisan Range falls steeply into a deep ocean trough, whereas to the east the land drops gradually across alluvial plains supporting vast areas of swamp.

Climate

Sumatra has a tropical, everwet climate. Rainfall ranges from over 5000 mm in areas to the west of the Barisan Range, to less than 1500 mm in some areas in the east. The wettest months are May to September; over much of the island the driest months are normally associated with the north-easterly monsoon between December and March.

Population

Sumatra has a population of about 28 million. The most densely populated areas are northern Aceh, the Medan-Karo Batak area (north Sumatra), and the Padang area (west Sumatra). The annual growth rate is 3.3% (FAO 1981–1982). There are large transmigration settlements, especially in south Sumatra and in south-west Aceh in the north.

Vegetation

Rain forests still cover 230,660 km² of Sumatra (48.8% of the land area). Of this total, 123,150 km² (26.1% of the land area) is lowland rain forest mostly dominated by dipterocarps. Much of the lowland forest has been cleared, and much of what remains is degraded to some extent. On the flat lowlands of southern Sumatra, once great stands of ironwood (*Eusideroxylon zwageri*) have been almost entirely destroyed.

Inland freshwater swamp forests cover 65,310 km² (13.8% of the land area). Peat swamp forest is extensive in the eastern lowlands. Mangroves and nipa swamps occur extensively along the eastern coast.

Much of the montane forest in Sumatra is still intact. The Barisan Range receives the most precipitation (>3000 mm rainfall per year in many places) and contains various types of submontane and montane forests, including upper montane (cloud) forests. The only natural *Pinus merkusii* forest in Indonesia occur in the drier central intermontane valley in the far north (FAO 1981–1982; Whitten *et al.* 1984). This pine is widely used for reforestation of montane grasslands in north and central Sumatra. *Agathis dammara* is characteristic in the Kerinci area. For more detailed descriptions of the main vegetation types, see Whitten *et al.* (1984).

Collins, Sayer and Whitmore (1991) give the following estimates for forest cover. The areas given are determined from maps and are not official statistics. They include relatively undisturbed, and disturbed, forests where, for example, enclaves of cultivation and plantations occur within areas of forest.

	Area (km²)	% of land area
Lowland rain forests	123,150	26.1
Montane rain forests	32,190	6.8
Inland swamp forest	65,310	13.8
Mangroves	10,010	2.1
Totals	**230,660**	**48.8**

The figures given for *lowland rain forests* include: tropical evergreen rain forest, tropical semi-evergreen rain forest, heath forest, limestone forest and beach forest; those for *montane rain forests* include: lower and upper montane rain forests and subalpine forests; and those for *inland swamp forests* include peat swamp forest, freshwater swamp forest and periodically inundated freshwater swamp forest.

Flora

There are estimated to be more than 10,000 vascular plant species, of which c. 12% are endemic. There are 13 endemic genera. The flora has affinities with those of Peninsular Malaysia and Java.

Useful plants

See account in General Overview on South East Asia (Malesia).

Factors causing loss of biodiversity

Population pressure

Population pressure imposes severe threats on the forests. The population density on Sumatra (averaging 59 people/km²) is one of the highest in Indonesia. As a result, the forests, particularly those in the lowlands, are under increasing pressure from agriculture and settlements. Encroachment and illegal settlements affect many protected areas. Relatively large areas of peat swamp forest have been drained and cleared to provide farmland for transmigrants from Java.

Logging

Logging has been heavy in recent years in the lowlands east of the Barisan range. Estimates from 1975 indicated that 42% of Sumatra was covered with primary forests at that time (FAO/UNEP 1981), but the figure is certainly much lower now, and today the rate of loss of natural vegetation is probably faster in Sumatra than elsewhere in Indonesia (Collins, Sayer and Whitmore 1991).

Conservation

The protected areas system covers approximately 5.3% of the land area (MacKinnon and MacKinnon 1986). Protected areas over 10 km² include: 5 National Parks (IUCN Management

Category: II), covering 27,723 km^2; 13 Nature Reserves (IUCN Management Category: I), covering 3929 km^2; 20 Game Reserves (IUCN Management Category: IV), covering 22,503 km^2. In addition, there are 5 Hunting Parks (IUCN Management Category: VI) (2003 km^2), 35 Protection Forests (IUCN Management Category: VI) (17,683 km^2); 1 Recreation Park (IUCN Management Category: V) (13 km^2). 5 areas are designated as UNESCO Man and Biosphere Reserves (14,829 km^2). Note that these figures refer only to protected areas over 10 km^2, and that some areas may have overlapping designations.

In the existing protected areas system, there is a significant bias in the coverage of the least threatened habitat types (e.g. montane forests), whereas the most threatened habitats (e.g. the ironwood forests and other types of lowland rain forests, including evergreen and semi-evergreen rain forests) are the least protected. Most of the existing reserves are under intense pressure and lack sufficient resources and manpower for effective management (MacKinnon and MacKinnon 1986).

The spectacular wildlife and scenery of Sumatra's protected areas are described and vividly illustrated in Cubitt, Whitten and Whitten (1992). Sumatra is also included in the review of the Indonesian protected areas system and conservation legislation given in IUCN (1992).

Centres of plant diversity and endemism

Local endemism is relatively high in some areas, including the mountains of Aceh (e.g. Gunung Leuser); the Indragiri foothills, the flora of which has affinities with those of north-western and eastern Peninsular Malaysia (Ashton 1989); and the Tigapuluh Mountains (Indragiri Province). In addition, there are numerous areas of limestone which support a distinct and endemic-rich flora. These, and other areas, urgently require further botanical exploration (de Wilde 1989).

SEA40. Barisan Selatan National Park

Area: 3650 km^2. Altitude: 0–1964 m (summit of Gunung Pugung).
❖ Vegetation: Lowland tropical rain forest, hill forest, lower and upper montane forests, beach forest, mangroves, secondary forest and grasslands.
❖ Flora: No estimate for the size of the flora, but includes dipterocarps, durian relatives and *Rafflesia arnoldii*.
❖ Threats: Agricultural encroachment, influx of transmigrants around perimeter.
❖ Conservation: Barisan Selatan National Park (IUCN Management Category: II).

SEA41. Gunung Leuser National Park

– see Data Sheet.

SEA42. Kerinci-Seblat National Park

– see Data Sheet.

SEA43. Limestone flora of Sumatra

– see Data Sheet.

SEA44. Berbak Game Reserve

Area: 1750 km^2. Altitude: 0–16 m.
❖ Vegetation: Seasonally inundated freshwater swamp forest (600 km^2); peat swamp forest (1100 km^2), the best example of eastern peat swamp forest in Sumatra; riverine forest; mangroves (200 km^2); beach forest.
❖ Threats: Fire, fuelwood collection, illegal logging (two major logging concessions cover 675 km^2 in the south-east), lack of sufficient funds for staff and equipment to manage the reserve.
❖ Conservation: Berbak Game Reserve (IUCN Management Category: IV).

SEA45. Tigapuluh Mountains

– see Data Sheet.

Area of botanical interest

The following site contains an important sample of lowland dipterocarp forest, freshwater swamp forest and mangrove forest:

Siberut

This is the largest of the Mentawai Islands off the west coast of central Sumatra. Siberut is rugged and attains 384 m altitude. The most serious threats to the forest are: 1) the breakdown of traditional cultural practices mainly as a result of the influx of settlers from mainland Sumatra; 2) land clearance for cash crops; and 3) logging. About half the island's area has been designated as oil palm plantations (McCarthy 1991). Siberut (Tai-tai Batti) Game Reserve (IUCN Management Category: IV), covering 565 km^2, is an UNESCO Man and Biosphere Reserve.

SULAWESI (CELEBES), INDONESIA

Total land area: 184,840 km^2.

Population: 12,700,000.

Altitude: 0–3455 m (summit of Mount Rantemario).

Natural vegetation: About 61% of the land area is covered with forests. Extensive tracts of lowland rain forest (42% of the land area); the largest tracts of forest on ultramafic rocks in the tropics; limestone forest; lowland tropical moist deciduous (monsoon) forest; montane forests; small areas of inland swamp forest and mangroves.

Number of vascular plants: c. 5000 species.

Species endemism: No estimate available.

Number of endemic genera: 5.

Threats: Clearance for permanent and shifting cultivation.

Conservation: 4 National Parks (IUCN Management Category: II) cover 8200.7 km^2; 14 Nature Reserves (IUCN Management Category: I) cover 3610.4 km^2; 12 Game Reserves (IUCN Management Category: IV) cover 6229.2 km^2; 2 Hunting Parks (IUCN Management Category: IV) cover 720 km^2; 1 Research Forest (IUCN Management Category: IV) covers 13 km^2; 9 Protection Forests (IUCN Management Category: VI) cover 1936.4 km^2; 2 Recreation Parks (IUCN Management Category: V) cover 950 km^2. Note that these figures refer only to protected areas over 10 km^2, and that some areas have overlapping designations.

Geology

Sulawesi is geologically complex. The western arc of the main island consists of basic volcanic rocks and granite of Tertiary and Quaternary age, and Quaternary sediments. Volcanic rocks of the Minahasa Peninsula (in the north) are more recent; there is still some volcanic activity today. The central part of Sulawesi comprises blue schists and limestone outcrops. The eastern arc has the largest areas of ultramafic rocks (including ophioliotes, peridotites and serpentinites) in the tropics, together with Mesozoic and Tertiary sediments, and alluvial deposits. The Banggai Islands (in the east) consist of Palaeozoic and Jurassic rocks and Quaternary deposits.

Population

Sulawesi has a population of c. 12.7 million and an annual growth rate of about 2%. The average density is 68.7 people/km², however, more than half the population live in the fertile plains and valleys of south Sulawesi, while about one million people live in the capital, Manado, in the north. In these densely populated areas, the natural vegetation has been cleared for settlements and shifting cultivation (de Vogel 1989a). The Buginese are the dominant ethnic group. They travel around the archipelago to establish coastal settlements.

Climate

The central highlands and parts of the north are everwet, while a highly seasonal climate exists in the "arms" of the island, particularly in the south. Areas on the west coast have their highest rainfall in December, while those on the east coast have their wettest month around May. The Palu Valley (with an annual rainfall of less than 600 mm) is one of the driest parts of Indonesia.

Vegetation

Sulawesi was originally almost entirely covered by forest. Today, about 56.4% of the land area is covered by rain forests of various sorts (see Table 42) according to Collins, Sayer and Whitmore (1991), while tropical moist deciduous forest (monsoon forest) covers an additional 4.4% of the land area. Lowland rain forests cover 77,680 km² (42% of the land area).

Sulawesi has the largest tract of forest on ultramafic rocks in the tropics (see Data Sheet of the Ultramafic Flora of Sulawesi, CPD Site SEA48), and also has the largest area of karst limestone, which is found particularly in the south-west. There are large areas of montane forest, c. 2170 km² of mangroves (mostly in the south), and 2510 km² of inland swamp forest.

The dry Palu Valley is partly covered with low shrubby, xeromorphic vegetation; several parts of the valley are totally devoid of vegetation.

For a more detailed account of the main vegetation types, see Whitten, Muslimin Mustafa and Henderson (1987).

Table 42 gives estimates for the extent of forest cover (taken from Collins, Sayer and Whitmore 1991). The areas given are determined from maps and are not official statistics. They include relatively undisturbed, and disturbed, forests where, for example, enclaves of cultivation and plantations occur within areas of forest.

TABLE 42. ESTIMATED FOREST COVER IN SULAWESI

	Area (km²)	% of land area
Rain forests		
Lowland rain forests	77,680	42.0
Montane rain forests	21,920	11.9
Inland swamp forests	2510	1.4
Mangroves	2170	1.2
Sub totals	**104,280**	**56.4**
Monsoon forests		
Lowland monsoon forests	8120	4.4
Sub totals	**8120**	**4.4**
Totals	**112,400**	**60.8**

The figures given for *lowland rain forests* include: tropical evergreen rain forest, tropical semi-evergreen rain forest, heath forest, limestone forest, ultramafic forest and beach forest; those for *montane rain forests* include: lower and upper montane rain forests and subalpine forests; and those for *inland swamp forests* include peat swamp forest, freshwater swamp forest and periodically inundated freshwater swamp forest.

Flora

Sulawesi has an estimated 5000 vascular plant species (de Vogel 1989a). There are floristic affinities with both West Malesia and Papuasia. Van Balgooy (1987) indicates a stronger relationship of the flora of Sulawesi with the drier areas of Malesia (Philippines, Java, Lesser Sunda Islands and Moluccas) than with the wetter areas (Borneo and New Guinea).

Palms are a characteristic feature of the forests in Sulawesi. In dry coastal areas *Corypha* predominates; on lowland sandy soils the fan palm *Livistona rotundifolia* is common; *Pigafetta filaris* is found in wetter upland forests; stands of sago palm (*Metroxylon sagu*) occur in the south-west.

High levels of endemism have been claimed in the past for some families, for example c. 80% for Orchidaceae (Schlechter 1925), but recent investigations have shown these figures are much too high. The level of endemism has yet to be estimated for most families. There are 5 endemic genera. Of 27 species of *Rhododendron*, 21 are endemic to Sulawesi (de Vogel 1989a).

Useful plants

The main timber species are *Agathis dammara* and *Diospyros* spp. *Santalum album* (sandalwood) used to occur in the Palu Valley, but few trees remain as a result of over-exploitation. See also the account in the General Overview on South East Asia (Malesia).

Factors causing loss of biodiversity

Most of the natural forest has been cleared around population centres. Much of the south-west peninsula has been cleared for agriculture and, to some extent, cattle grazing. A number of areas have been cleared for transmigration settlements. In addition, there are extensive nickel mining operations which have affected large areas of forest on ultramafic rocks.

Much of the rest of the forest remains intact, owing (in part) to the general steepness of the terrain which makes cultivation difficult. Also, many areas are remote and difficult of access, particularly in the central massif region.

Conservation

About 3.2% of the land area is included in the protected areas system (MacKinnon and MacKinnon 1986). Protected areas over 10 km² include: 4 National Parks (IUCN Management Category: II), covering 8200.7 km²; 14 Nature Reserves (IUCN Management Category: I), covering 3610.4 km²; 12 Game Reserves (IUCN Management Category: IV), covering 6229.2 km²; 2 Hunting Parks (IUCN Management Category: IV), covering 720 km²; 1 Research Forest (IUCN Management Category: IV), covering 13 km²; 9 Protection Forests (IUCN Management Category: VI), covering 1936.4 km²; and 2 Recreation Parks (IUCN Management Category: V), covering 950 km².

The spectacular wildlife and scenery of Sulawesi's protected areas are described and vividly illustrated in Cubitt, Whitten and Whitten (1992). Sulawesi is also included in the review of the Indonesian protected areas system and conservation legislation given in IUCN (1992).

Centres of plant diversity and endemism

SEA46. Dumoga-Bone National Park

– see Data Sheet.

SEA47. Limestone flora of Sulawesi

– see Data Sheet.

SEA48. Ultramafic flora of Sulawesi

– see Data Sheet.

SEA49. Lore Lindu National Park

Area: 2310 km². Altitude: 200–2610 m (summit of Gunung Roreka Timbu).
❖ Vegetation: Mostly tropical montane forest, with small area of tropical lowland evergreen rain forest.
❖ Flora: No estimate available for size of flora; affinity with the floras of Philippines, Moluccas and New Guinea.
❖ Threats: Agricultural encroachment, over-exploitation of forest products (e.g. rattans), proposed hydroelectric scheme.
❖ Conservation: National Park (IUCN Management Category: II), UNESCO Man and Biosphere Reserve; proposed World Heritage Site (in 1991).

SEA50. Pegunungan Latimojong

– see Data Sheet.

PHILIPPINES

Total land area: 298,170 km².

Population (1990): 62,440,000.

Altitude: 0–2954 m (summit of Mount Apo).

Natural vegetation: A recent survey found that only 64,606 km² (21.7% of the land area) remains under forest. Near-natural dipterocarp rain forest remains on just 9880 km², of which 7000 km² are accessible to logging. Forest types include: lowland rain forest (various types), forest on ultramafic rocks, limestone forest, montane forests, mangroves, remnants of beach vegetation.

Number of vascular plants: c. 8900 species.

Species endemism: 39%.

Number of endemic genera: 23.

Threats: Logging, clearance for slash and burn agriculture (kaingin) and plantations (of oil palm, coconut, banana and sugar cane), over-collection of forest products (e.g. rattans), inadequate staffing and funds for effective management of protected areas, illegal encroachment in protected areas.

Conservation: 34 National Parks (IUCN Management Categories: II, III, IV, V, VII and VIII) cover 4493 km² (including marine areas); 3 Wildlife Sanctuaries (IUCN Management Category: IV) cover 1899.3 km² and 1 Faunal Reserve (Mount Makiling) (IUCN Management Category: VII) covers 33.3 km². There are 2 UNESCO Man and Biosphere Reserves: Palawan (11,508 km²) and Puerto Galera (235.5 km²). Note that these figures refer only to protected areas over 10 km², and that some areas have overlapping designations.

Geology

The Philippines comprise 7107 islands and islets. The two largest islands, Luzon and Mindanao, comprise about 70% of the total land area of the country. Most of the area is mountainous, but there are also vast plains, extensive rolling hills, broad plateaux and undulating valleys. The steep slopes of upland areas make them particularly susceptible to erosion, especially if their natural vegetation cover is removed.

Structurally, the Philippines may be considered to be the crumpled edge of the Asiatic continental platform. The Mariana Trench, 85 km east of Mindanao, is the deepest known part of the world. There is no evidence of former land connections between the Philippines and Taiwan. There may have been land connections between the Palawan-Mindoro islands and the Indochina-Hainan area during the Oligocene.

Andesite, basalt and agglomerates are found mostly in the uplands of the Philippines; volcanic tuffs are found in the provinces of Manila, in Albay and Negros Occidental; shales and sandstones occur throughout the archipelago; and limestone occurs from the northernmost part of Luzon to the southernmost part of Mindanao. Important outcrops of limestone and ultramafics also occur on Palawan and in southern Samar. Alluvial deposits are found particularly in the Central Plain of Luzon, parts of the Cagayan Valley and the Rio Grande of Mindanao. Alluvial soils are the most fertile in the country and most of the original vegetation they supported has been cleared for agriculture, especially rice and sugar cane plantations.

Climate

There are three main seasons, namely: a hot, dry season from March to May; a rainy season from June to November;

and a cool, dry season from December to February. Rainfall is high. Luzon receives 2479 mm of rain annually; Visayas, 2419 mm; and Mindanao, 2326 mm. Generally, July and August are the wettest months, while April is the driest. The eastern Pacific coasts have a prolonged wet season, while the western coasts of Luzon, Mindoro, Panay, Negros and Palawan receive little rainfall between November and February, during the north-eastern monsoon, because of intervening mountain ranges. Tropical storms (typhoons) occur frequently between July and November. The coolest month is January, with a mean temperature of 25.8°C, and the warmest month is May, with a mean temperature of 28.3°C.

Population

The Philippines had a population of 62,440,000 in 1990 (World Resources Institute 1994). The annual growth rate between 1985 and 1990 averaged 2.6%, one of the highest in the region. With approximately 209 people/km², the archipelago is one of the most densely populated areas in South East Asia. About 93% of the population live on 11 islands; Luzon and Mindanao account for over half the population. There are 111 cultural and linguistic groups, including more than 50 tribal groups, almost all of whom live in areas designated as "forest lands" by the government. Their land rights are enshrined in a multitude of religious beliefs and traditional laws that pre-date the creation of the Philippines state. Also, the socio-economic systems of these groups are closely linked to the forest through hunting and the collection of forest products. As deforestation continues, minority tribal groups have come into conflict with the authorities.

Vegetation

The Philippines were originally covered with forests. Generally, the western parts of the islands supported lowland and montane moist deciduous and semi-deciduous (monsoon) forests, while the wetter eastern sides were covered by lowland and montane evergreen rain forests.

Today, remnants of the original lowland evergreen rain forest survive on well-drained soils and on the lower slopes of mountains where the dry season is not pronounced. They are rich in dipterocarps. A number of distinct types of dipterocarp forest are recognized, including: lauan (*Shorea*) forest in lowlands and foothills up to 400 m; lauan-apitong (*Dipterocarpus*) forest between the foothills and lower montane forest; lauan-yakal (*Hopea*) forest on volcanic soils, including deciduous and semi-deciduous species, and now mostly cleared for cultivation; and lauan-hagakhak (*Dipterocarpus warburghii*) forest, now almost completely cleared for rice production.

Molave forest is more open than primary lowland forest and occurs in regions with a distinct dry season. The forest is semi-deciduous and includes such timber trees as *Vitex parviflora*, *Pterocarpus indicus*, *Dracontomelon dao* and *Intsia bijuga*. Much has been completely logged. A relatively well-preserved molave forest still occurs on the narrow plain west of the Zambales Mountains in Luzon.

Extensive pine forests, dominated by *Pinus insularis* (*P. kesiya*) or by *P. merkusii*, occur as almost pure stands, or mixed with broadleaved species in areas protected from fire, especially on ridges at lower altitudes. There are extensive stands of *P. insularis* in the mountains of northern and central Luzon between 450 and 2450 m.

Mid-montane and mossy forests occur in rugged mountain regions. Mossy forests cover about 8% of the land area and are best developed on mountains above 1200 m (Tan and Rojo 1989). Good examples are found on the Makiling, Banahaw, Halcon and Apo mountains. The forests include (as the principal trees) species of *Dacrycarpus*, *Engelhardtia*, *Lithocarpus*, *Podocarpus*, *Syzygium*, *Ternstroemia* and *Tristania*. There are an abundance of mosses and liverworts.

Grasslands and secondary forests and scrub are widespread. Grasslands are usually dominated by *Imperata cylindrica* and *Saccharum spontaneum*. They are extensive in Kalinga and Ifugao (part of the Zambales Mountains), in the western part of the Sierra Madre, the southern Bonduc Peninsula, Visayas, Masbate, the Buria Islands, Bukidnon, Cotabato, western Mindoro and Bohol. In many of these areas, the land is almost completely grass-covered.

Mangroves and nipa (*Nypa fruticans*) swamps occur along tidal flats and protected shores. Beach vegetation is found on sandy shores above high tide, but little remains in a natural state.

Estimates of forest cover

The Philippine-German Forest Resources Inventory Project recorded 64,606 km² of closed broadleaved and coniferous forest remaining in the Philippines, of which 9880 km² comprised near-natural (old-growth) dipterocarp rain forest (Forest Management Bureau 1988), 7000 km² of which are accessible to logging. Collins, Sayer and Whitmore (1991) expected all accessible dipterocarp forests to have been logged by 1995.

The Forest Resources Inventory Project found "good regeneration" in 20,000 km² of forest. The project considered such forests to be suitable for silvicultural treatment to produce 2 m³/ha/year of timber growth. Collins, Sayer and Whitmore (1991) conclude that even if this rather high output could be achieved, the current state of the forests in the Philippines is perhaps the worst in tropical Asia. They state that in less than 20 years the production of tropical timber has declined by 90%. As a result of agricultural encroachment and the absence of forest management, the entire timber industry, from logging to furniture-making, is reduced to a shadow of its former status, and is increasingly dependent upon imports from other Asian nations. The Government of the Philippines is now seeking external assistance to rehabilitate its forest resources and to protect remaining forest fragments. Logging has already been banned in all provinces with less than 40% forest cover. Only 9 of the nation's 73 provinces have forest resources in excess of this figure, but enforcing the ban in the remaining 64 provinces will undoubtedly prove difficult.

The estimates of forest cover given in Table 43 are taken from Collins, Sayer and Whitmore (1991). The areas given are determined from maps and are not official statistics. They include relatively undisturbed, and disturbed, forests where, for example, enclaves of cultivation and plantations occur within areas of forest.

TABLE 43. ESTIMATED FOREST COVER IN THE PHILIPPINES

	Area intact (km²)	% of land area	Area degraded (km²)	% of land area (km²)	Totals (km²)	% of land area (km²)
Rain forests						
Lowland rain forests	13,870	4.6	29,185 *	9.8 *	50,715 *	17.0 *
Montane rain forests	7660	2.6	*	*	*	*
Mangroves	25	<0.1	-	-	25	<0.1
Sub totals	**21,555**	**7.2**	**29,185**	**9.8**	**50,740**	**17.0**
Monsoon forests						
Lowland monsoon forests	3930	1.3	6530 *	2.2 *	15,280 *	5.1 *
Montane monsoon forests	4820	1.6	*	*	*	*
Sub totals	**8750**	**2.9**	**6530**	**2.2**	**15,280**	**5.1**
Totals	**30,305**	**10.1**	**35,715**	**12.0**	**66,020**	**22.1**

* = combined figures for lowland and montane forests. The figures given for *lowland rain forests* include: tropical evergreen rain forest, tropical semi-evergreen rain forest, heath forest, limestone forest, ultramafic forest and beach forest.

Flora

There are approximately 8900 vascular plant species, of which about 3500 species (39%) are endemic. There are 23 endemic genera (van Steenis 1987). Earlier studies on the flora gave much higher levels of species endemism. Merrill (1923–1926), for example, included an annotated list of 5532 species which were thought to be endemic to the Philippines. In 1990, the *Flora of the Philippines Project* began. This is a joint venture of the Botanical Research Institute of Texas, U.S.A. and the Philippines National Museum, Manila. The main component of the project is the Philippine Plant Inventory (PPI) Project which involves exploration, collecting and identification of Philippines flowering plants. The PPI is supported with funds from the U.S. National Science Foundation and the U.S. Agency for International Development. Field collecting under the PPI began in 1991 and is expected to continue until the year 2000 (J. Cunningham 1995, *in litt.*).

Useful plants

See account in General Overview on South East Asia (Malesia).

Factors causing loss of biodiversity

Deforestation

Forest loss between 1969 and 1988 was, on average, 2100 km²/year (2 ha every 5 minutes, about three times the average for all tropical rain forests over the same period) (Collins, Sayer and Whitmore 1991). Some islands have been completely deforested.

Most of the remaining forest estate outside the protected areas system is leased to private timber companies for logging. A selective logging system has been in operation since 1955, but it is not closely followed in practice and residual stands are often severely damaged by the use of poor log extraction techniques. As a result, many critical watersheds are severely eroded and siltation has affected water quality and hindered the operation of hydroelectric dams (Collins, Sayer and Whitmore 1991).

Although logging has contributed substantially to forest degradation, it rarely leads (by itself) to outright clearance;

however, logging opens up the forests to slash and burn agriculture (kaingin). Traditional, low intensity shifting cultivation was once widely practised by indigenous tribal groups. However, as the population has increased in recent years, and with the influx of large numbers of unemployed migrants into rural areas, traditional methods have been replaced by more intensive and unsustainable forms of agriculture. It is estimated that between 800 and 1400 km² of forest, including previously logged forest, are destroyed annually by inappropriate agricultural practices in the Philippines (Myers 1980). There is a risk of more frequent and damaging forest fires as land is cleared for cultivation.

Soil erosion

Soil erosion is a serious threat, particularly in the uplands, and is likely to become worse as deforestation continues (Myers 1988). The largest cities, Manila and Cebu, now periodically experience water shortages due to deforestation of their catchments (Ganapin 1987). Some major hydroelectric schemes have also been adversely affected by silting.

Conservation

Existing protected areas cover just 1.3% of the total land area of the country and are inadequate to protect the country's biodiversity (MacKinnon and MacKinnon 1986). Moreover, the levels of management of protected areas have been poor as a result of insufficient trained staff and funds. Indeed, in 1986 the Haribon Foundation claimed that no protected areas would satisfy international standards established by IUCN. Most park boundaries are not demarcated and law enforcement is lacking. Many protected areas are under threat from logging, and from encroachment by agriculture and settlement.

Recognizing the limitations of the protected areas system, the Haribon Foundation and the Department of the Environment and Natural Resources, with help from WWF U.S. and the World Bank, has put forward an Integrated Protected Areas System (IPAS) to implement management plans and provide staff training in protected area management. The IPAS identified an "Indicative List" of 330 sites, including 27 "priority one" potential protected areas and a further 41 "priority two" sites. Only 19 existing National Parks were included in the list. The specific recommendations of the study were not accepted by the Philippines Government.

IUCN (1992) lists the following protected areas: 34 National Parks (IUCN Management Categories: II, III, IV, V, VII and VIII), covering 4493 km² (including marine areas); 3 Wildlife Sanctuaries (IUCN Management Category: IV), covering 1899.3 km²; and 1 Faunal Reserve (Mount Makiling) (IUCN Management Category: VII), covering 33.3 km². There are 2 UNESCO Man and Biosphere Reserves: Palawan (11,508 km²) and Puerto Galera (235.5 km²). Note that these figures refer only to protected areas over 10 km², and that some areas have overlapping designations.

Centres of plant diversity and endemism

The following is based on information supplied by Dr Domingo A. Madulid.

SEA51. Batan Islands

– see Data Sheet.

SEA52. Mount Apo

– see Data Sheet.

SEA53. Mount Baloy

Located in central Panay. Area: 11,515 km². Altitude: Attains 2049 m.
❖ Vegetation: Lowland evergreen rain forest and montane forest.
❖ Flora: No estimate available for size of flora, but the area is rich in gymnosperm and tree fern species.
❖ Threats: Illegal logging, shifting cultivation (kaingin).
❖ Conservation: No legal protection.

SEA54. Mount Isarog

Located on Camarines Sur. Area: 101.1 km². Altitude: Attains 1966 m.
❖ Vegetation: Lowland dipterocarp forest and montane forest.
❖ Flora: No estimate available for the size of the flora, but includes rattans, timber trees, almaciga and bamboos among the useful plants.
❖ Threats: Illegal logging.
❖ Conservation: Mount Isarog National Park (IUCN Management Category: II).

SEA55. Mount Kitanglad

Area: 312.8 km². Altitude: Attains 2378 m.
❖ Vegetation: Lowland semi-deciduous forest and montane forest.
❖ Flora: No estimate available for the size of the flora, but the area is rich in gymnosperms and tree ferns.
❖ Threats: Fire, tourism.
❖ Conservation: National Park.

SEA56. Mount Makiling and Mount Banahaw

Area: Mount Makiling – 42.5 km²; Mount Banahaw – 111.3 km². Altitude: 1030–1250 m.
❖ Vegetation: Lowland dipterocarp forest and montane forest.
❖ Flora: 2038 species of flowering plants so far recorded.
❖ Threats: Illegal conversion to agriculture, illegal squatting, geothermal plant.
❖ Conservation: Mount Makiling Faunal Reserve (IUCN Management Category: VII) covers 33.3 km²; Mount Makiling Botanic Garden; Mount Banahaw – Cristobal National Park.

SEA57. Mount Pulog

– see Data Sheet.

SEA58. Mount Talines and Lake Balinsasayao

❖ Vegetation: Lowland dipterocarp forest, lower montane forest and aquatic communities.
❖ Threat: Kaingin agriculture and conversion to vegetable gardens.
❖ Conservation: Provincial Watershed.

SEA59. Palanan Wilderness Area

– see Data Sheet.

SEA60. Palawan

– see Data Sheet.

SEA61. Sibuyan Island

– see Data Sheet.

SEA62. Southern Samar

Area: 13,080 km². Altitude: 0–1000 m.
❖ Vegetation: Forest on ultramafic rocks, limestone forest, lowland dipterocarp forest, mangroves.
❖ Flora: Rich in timber trees, rattans, palms and pandans.
❖ Threats: Illegal logging, kaingin agriculture.
❖ Conservation: Mount Sohoton National Park covers a small area; no legal protection for remainder.

Area of botanical interest

Basilan

Basilan island contains basaltic and volcanic outcrops. The lowland forests are exceptionally rich and may include the highest levels of endemicity in the whole of the Philippines. The area is currently affected by civil disorder (P.S. Ashton 1991, *in litt.*). Basilan National Park (IUCN Management Category: II) covers just 39 km².

JAVA, INDONESIA

Total land area: 138,204 km².

Population: 109,000,000.

Altitude: 0–3676 m (summit of Gunung Mahameru).

Natural vegetation: The remaining natural forests consist largely of submontane and montane forests, most of the lowland forests having been converted to agriculture.

Number of vascular plants: c. 5000 species.

Species endemism: c. 5%.

Number of endemic genera: 5.

Threats: Population pressure, clearance for agriculture, illegal timber and fuelwood cutting, over-collection of forest products.

Conservation: 8 National Parks (IUCN Management Category: II) cover 5333.2 km²; 22 Nature Reserves (IUCN Management Category: I) cover 1388.7 km²; 8 Game Reserves (IUCN Management Category: IV) cover 1959.8 km²; 2 Hunting Parks (IUCN Management Category: VI) cover 824.2 km²; 3 Recreation Parks (IUCN Management Category: V) cover 36.4 km². Note that these figures refer only to protected areas over 10 km², and that some areas may have overlapping designations.

Geology

Java is the most volcanically active island in the Indonesian archipelago, having 23 of the 78 Indonesian volcanoes which have been active since 1600. All of Java's mountains are volcanic in origin and most are of Tertiary age. Almost half the island consists of volcanic deposits, while the remainder consists mainly of raised Tertiary marine deposits and alluvial plains.

Climate

The climate of most of west Java and the mountains in central and east Java is everwet. The area around Mount Slamet, in central Java, is the wettest place in Indonesia, receiving more than 7000 mm of rain annually. The lowlands in east, north-west and central Java experience a dry season lasting nine months.

Population

Java is one of the most densely populated areas in the world, with a total population of about 109 million. Most of the population is concentrated in the fertile alluvial lowlands and hills. The fertile volcanic soils have allowed the growth of a large rural population. The Indonesian Government has made efforts to reduce the pressure on the land by introducing large transmigration schemes (see section on Factors Causing Loss of Biodiversity in the General Overview of South East Asia) and the promotion of birth control. Population pressure has resulted in the clearance of most of the forests (see following section on Vegetation).

Vegetation

The remaining patches of natural forest on Java are mostly submontane and montane forests above 1400 m altitude. Almost all of the original lowland forest, particularly in the drier areas of Java (the northern coast and east Java), and most of the forest over limestone, have been converted to agriculture and teak

plantations, respectively. Mangroves and freshwater swamp forests also occur as scattered remnants. Most of moist deciduous (monsoon) forests in eastern Java have been cleared or subjected to frequent burning. Baluran National Park (CPD Site SEA63) has the only large area of this vegetation type remaining in Java, but even here it is fragmented by fire-climax grasslands.

Montane forests cover 3.9% of the land area (Collins, Sayer and Whitmore 1991). Extensive areas of montane forest have been converted to montane grasslands. Some protected areas still contain good examples of montane and subalpine forest, rich in Ericaceae. Natural montane grasslands (grass plains) and open volcanic debris ("alon-aloon plains") occur on high mountains.

At the end of 1980, closed broadleaved forest was estimated to cover about 8% of the land area (FAO/UNEP 1981). A recent study by Collins, Sayer and Whitmore (1991) indicates that 9.9% of the land area of Java and Bali is covered by forests. This area was determined from maps and is not an official statistic. The figure includes relatively undisturbed, and disturbed, forests where, for example, enclaves of cultivation and plantations occur within areas of forest. The following areas are taken from Collins, Whitmore and Sayer (1991) and refer to Java and the island of Bali.

	Area (km²)	% of land area
Rain forests		
Lowland rain forests	7370	5.3
Montane rain forests	5450	3.9
Inland swamp forests	70	0.1
Mangroves	850	0.6
Totals	**13,740**	**9.9**

Flora

The flora includes 4598 vascular plant species according to Backer and Bakhuizen van den Brink (1963–1968), of which 5% (230 species) are endemic (Soepadmo 1992).

Useful plants

Among the most important deciduous tree species is teak (*Tectona grandis*) which is often planted in reforestation schemes. For a general account on useful plants in the region, see the General Overview on South East Asia (Malesia).

Factors causing loss of biodiversity

Most of the original forest has been logged, cleared for agriculture or severely degraded by fuelwood cutting and frequent fires. Remaining forests, including those within legally protected areas, are (to varying degrees) increasingly under pressure from encroachment. Deforestation has resulted in severe soil erosion in places. Erosion is a particular problem in areas under annual cropping systems where the soil is disturbed and exposed during critical periods (e.g. during the transition from the dry to wet season). The government has promoted changes in land use and management to alleviate this problem, but the measures are not fully implemented.

Of the legally protected areas identified as CPD sites, logging and encroachment of agriculture has affected the rich forests of Gunung Halimun (CPD Site SEA65) and parts of Ujong Kulon (CPD Site SEA66). Agricultural encroachment, illegal timber and fuelwood cutting, and visitor pressure is a threat to Gunung Gede-Pangrango National Park (CPD Site SEA64).

Conservation

Protected areas cover about 2% of the land area (MacKinnon and MacKinnon 1986). IUCN (1992) lists the following areas: 8 National Parks (IUCN Management Category: II), covering 5333.2 km²; 22 Nature Reserves (IUCN Management Category: I), covering 1388.7 km²; 8 Game Reserves (IUCN Management Category: IV), covering 1959.8 km²; 2 Hunting Parks (IUCN Management Category: VI), covering 824.2 km² and 3 Recreation Parks (IUCN Management Category: V), covering 36.4 km². Note that these figures refer only to protected areas over 10 km², and that some areas may have overlapping designations.

Many of the protected areas are under considerable pressure, as already mentioned. There is an urgent need for major education and conservation awareness campaigns, as well as extensive reforestation programmes to alleviate pressures on the remaining natural forests. The protection of existing reserves needs to be strengthened (MacKinnon and MacKinnon 1986).

The spectacular wildlife and scenery of Java's protected areas are described and vividly illustrated in Cubitt, Whitten and Whitten (1992). Java is also included in the review of the Indonesian protected areas system and conservation legislation given in IUCN (1992).

Kebun Raya Bogor (Bogor Botanic Garden) (87 ha) was established in 1817 for the promotion of botanical investigation in Indonesia and for experimentation on important crops. It is one of the oldest botanic gardens in the tropics and was Indonesia's first. Three other associated gardens have been established: **Cibodas Garden** (82 ha), **Purwodadi Garden** (90 ha) and **Bali Garden** (129 ha). In addition, the **Serpong Garden** covers 150 ha around the science and technology research and development centre at Serpong. The gardens are under the administration of the Indonesian Institute of Science (LIPI) and have an important role to play in conservation and development (Sastrapradja, Sastrapradja and Usep Soetisna 1987; Riswan, Irawati and Sukendar 1991).

Centres of plant diversity and endemism

SEA63. Baluran National Park

Area: 250 km². Altitude: 0–1247 m (summit of Gunung Baluran).
❖ Vegetation: Seasonally inundated freshwater swamp forest, monsoon (tropical moist semi-deciduous) forest, riverine forest, mangroves and extensive secondary savanna and grasslands.
❖ Threats: Cattle grazing; introduced exotic plant species (e.g. *Acacia arabica* and *Lantana camara*).
❖ Conservation: Baluran National Park (IUCN Management Category: II).

SEA64. Gunung Gede-Pangrango National Park

– see Data Sheet.

SEA65. Gunung Halimun Nature Reserve

Area: 400 km². Altitude: 500–1929 m (summit of Gunung Halimun).
❖ Vegetation: Lowland rain forest, lower montane (submontane) rain forest. The drier, western part of the reserve includes open canopy forest.
❖ Flora: Estimated 1000 vascular plant species (McCarthy 1991), including numerous West Javan endemics.
❖ Threats: Fewer than other areas in Java due to local superstitions; however, agricultural encroachment occurs, as well as illegal logging (Wind and Soesilo 1978).
❖ Conservation: Gunung Halimun Nature Reserve (IUCN Management Category: I).

SEA66. Ujong Kulon National Park

Area: 783.6 km². Altitude: 0–576 m.
❖ Vegetation: Primary tropical lowland rain forest covers about 50% of the area; the higher slopes are dominated by *Castanopsis* spp. and *Podocarpus neriifolius*; the Telanca Plateau and central lowlands are covered in palm forest (secondary forest) with *Arenga pinnata* and *Caryota mitis*. In addition, there are mangroves and seasonally-inundated freshwater swamp forests, and coastal vegetation, including beach forest.
❖ Threats: Agricultural encroachment, illegal logging, fuelwood collection; oil pollution from passing tankers is a potential threat to marine and coastal communities.
❖ Conservation: Ujong Kulon National Park (IUCN Management Category: II).

MOLUCCAS (MALUKU), INDONESIA

Total land area: 69,230 km².

Population (1980): 1,400,000.

Altitude: 0–3019 m (summit of Mount Binaya, Seram).

Natural vegetation: 81% of the land area is covered by tropical rain forests and monsoon forests. Forest types include tropical evergreen rain forest, seasonal monsoon forest, forest on limestone, freshwater swamp forest, lower montane forest, upper montane forest and mangroves. Also present are rhododendron scrub, tree fern savanna and alpine grasslands.

Number of vascular plants: Estimated 3000 species, of which an estimated 2000 species (including more than 700 fern species) occur on the island of Seram.

Species endemism: No estimate available.

Number of endemic genera: 4.

Threats: Logging, clearance of forests for transmigration schemes, oil exploration, hydroelectric schemes.

Conservation: 1 National Park (Manusela National Park, Seram) (IUCN Management Category: II) covers 1890 km²; 4 Nature Reserves (IUCN Management Category: I) cover 562.5 km²; 3 terrestrial Game Reserves (IUCN Management Category: IV) cover 140 km². Note that these figures refer only to protected areas over 10 km².

The Moluccas include several hundred small islets, scattered up to as much as 1300 km apart. The largest islands are Seram (18,000 km²) and Halmahera; the smallest are uninhabited islets of only a few hundred hectares. Some islands are active volcanoes, others are non-volcanic but mountainous, others (such as the Aru group) are flat, coralline limestone islands.

Vegetation

Seram, which has a semi-everwet climate without a pronounced dry season, with 2100–4500 mm annual rainfall and the driest month having only slightly less than 100 mm, supports tropical evergreen rain forest. Evergreen forests also occur in north-west Halmahera. Seasonal monsoon forest occurs in south Halmahera, Obi and north-east Buru. Seram also supports forest on limestone, freshwater swamp forest, lower montane forest, upper montane forest, rhododendron scrub, tree fern savanna and alpine grasslands. Montane forests are also found on Halmahera, Obi, Bura, Sula and Morotai. Mangroves and nipa (*Nypa fruticans*) swamps occur in tidal creeks; sago palm (*Metroxylon sagu*) is cultivated as an important source of starch. For a more detailed description of the vegetation, see de Vogel (1989b).

Collins, Sayer and Whitmore (1991) give the following estimates for the extent of forest cover. The areas given are determined from maps and are not official statistics. They include relatively undisturbed, and disturbed, forests where, for example, enclaves of cultivation and plantations occur within areas of forest.

	Area (km²)	% of land area
Rain forests		
Lowland rain forests	44,160	63.8
Montane rain forests	1310	1.9
Inland swamp forests	60	0.1
Mangroves	1610	2.3
Sub totals	**47,140**	**68.1**
Monsoon forests		
Lowland monsoon forests	8820	12.7
Montane monsoon forests	110	0.2
Sub totals	**8930**	**12.9**
Totals	**56,070**	**81.0**

Flora

The Moluccas have an estimated 3000 species of vascular plants (de Vogel 1989b), of which about 2000 (including more than 700 ferns) occur on the island of Seram (Kato 1990). There are 4 endemic genera.

Useful plants

Important commercial timber trees include several species of dipterocarps, *Agathis* spp., *Pterocarpus indicus*, *Octomeles sumatrana* and various ebonies (*Diospyros* spp.). Various other species which occur in the Moluccas are of high commercial value, including cloves (*Eugenia aromatica*), candle-nuts (*Aleurites moluccana*) and nutmeg (*Myristica fragrans*). See also the account in the General Overview on South East Asia (Malesia).

Factors causing loss of biodiversity

Most inland forests throughout the archipelago are in logging concessions, but much forest is still intact. Deforestation by settlers following logging occurs less frequently than in other parts of Indonesia. On the smaller islands of the Banda Arc, most lowland forests seem to have been converted to savanna. Clearance of forests for transmigration schemes, oil exploration

and a hydroelectric scheme are threats surrounding Manusela National Park on Seram (see CPD Site SEA67).

Conservation

IUCN (1992) lists the following: 1 National Park (Manusela National Park, Seram) (IUCN Management Category: II), covering 1890 km²; 4 Nature Reserves (IUCN Management Category: I), covering 562.5 km²; and 3 terrestrial Game Reserves (IUCN Management Category: IV), covering 140 km². Note that these figures refer only to protected areas over 10 km².

The spectacular wildlife and scenery of the protected areas of the Moluccas are described and vividly illustrated in Cubitt, Whitten and Whitten (1992). The Moluccas are also included in the review of the Indonesian protected areas system and conservation legislation given in IUCN (1992).

Centres of plant diversity and endemism

SEA67. Manusela National Park (Seram)

Area: 1890 km². Altitude: 0–3019 m.
- ❖ Vegetation: Samples of all the major vegetation types on the island of Seram, including lowland alluvial forest, forest on limestone, species-poor dipterocarp forest, lower montane forest, upper montane, rhododendron scrub, tree fern savanna, alpine grasslands and mangroves.
- ❖ Flora: Estimated 2000 vascular plant species (J. Proctor 1992, pers. comm.). Includes elements from both West Malesia and Papuasia.
- ❖ Threats: Vegetation outside the park is threatened by logging (mainly of *Shorea*), transmigration schemes, oil exploration and a proposed hydroelectric dam; potentially the park may also be threatened by encroachment.
- ❖ Conservation: National Park (IUCN Management Category: II).
(Source: I.D. Edwards, Mount Coot-Tha Botanic Garden, Queensland, Australia.)

LESSER SUNDA ISLANDS (NUSA TENGGARA), INDONESIA

Total land area: 89,770 km².

Population (1980): 6,000,000.

Altitude: 0–2400 m (summit of Ruteng, Flores).

Vegetation: Savanna woodland, with *Casuarina* and *Eucalyptus*, now covers most of the islands; tropical evergreen rain forest (never extensive) only survives in isolated patches in steep valleys on south-facing sides of mountain ranges; monsoon forests; montane forests; extensive areas of grassland.

Number of vascular plants: No estimate available for size of flora, but poor in species and few endemics.

Species endemism: No estimate available.

Number of endemic genera: 1.

Conservation: 2 National Parks (IUCN Management Category: II) cover 807.3 km²; 5 Nature Reserves (IUCN Management Category: I) cover 1010.3 km²; 2 Hunting Parks (IUCN Management Category: 413.7 km²; 1 Forest Reserve (IUCN Management Category: VI) covers 150 km²; 5 Protection Forests (IUCN Management Category: VI) cover 802 km²; 2 Recreation Parks (IUCN Management Category: V) cover 99.8 km². Note that these figures refer only to protected areas over 10 km².

The Lesser Sunda Islands are a group of oceanic islands spread over approximately 900 km² in the south-eastern part of the Indonesian archipelago, between latitudes 8°00'–11°00'S and longitudes 115°00'–132°00'E. As a geographical unit, the Lesser Sunda Islands include Bali, Lombok, Sumba, Sumbawa, Flores, Alor, Wetar, Timor and the Tanimbar Islands. The inner arc of islands (Lombok, Sumbawa, Flores, Alor and Wetar) is volcanic in origin; Alor and Flores are mountainous with numerous active volcanoes.

Climate

The Lesser Sunda Islands lie in a rainshadow of the Australian continent and, hence, receive little rain in the summer monsoon (April–November) when the winds are from the south-east. As a consequence, the islands have the most seasonal climate in all of Indonesia.

Vegetation

Tropical evergreen rain forests were never extensive and survive only in small isolated patches on Flores. Seasonal monsoon forests are more widespread, covering 13,690 km² (15.2% of the land area) (Collins, Sayer and Whitmore (1991). Much of the original forest cover has been degraded by human activity to open savanna woodlands or converted to agriculture. Timor once had extensive sandalwood (*Santalum album*) forests (FAO 1981–1982). Patches of mangrove occur around the coasts, notably on Timor, Sumba and the Tanimbar Islands.

Collins, Sayer and Whitmore (1991) give the following estimates for the extent of forest cover. The areas given are determined from maps and are not official statistics. They include relatively undisturbed, and disturbed, forests where, for example, enclaves of cultivation and plantations occur within areas of forest.

	Area (km²)	% of land area
Rain forests		
Lowland rain forests	130	0.1
Montane rain forests	210	0.2
Inland swamp forests	70	0.1
Mangroves	490	0.5
Sub totals	**900**	**1.0**
Monsoon forests		
Lowland monsoon forests	12,590	14.0
Montane monsoon forests	1100	1.2
Sub totals	**13,690**	**15.2**
Totals	**14,590**	**16.2**

Flora

The flora of Lesser Sunda Islands is rather impoverished compared to other parts of Malesia. Although Malesian in composition, there are some Australian elements in the flora. There are few endemic species and only one endemic genus.

Useful plants

See account in General Overview on South East Asia (Malesia).

Conservation

See preceding summary, adapted from IUCN (1992). The wildlife and scenery of the protected areas of the Lesser Sunda Islands are described and vividly illustrated in Cubitt, Whitten and Whitten (1992).

Centres of plant diversity and endemism

No sites qualify as CPD sites; however, the following sites contain representative samples of various forest types on the islands: **Ruteng** (Flores), **Gunung Wanggameti** (Sumba), **Gunung Mutis** and **Gunung Timau** (Timor), and **Gunung Rinjani** (Lombok).

PAPUASIA

Area: c. 950,000 km².

Population (1990): c. 5,373,800 (Irian Jaya: 1,173,800; Papua New Guinea: 3,880,000; Solomon Islands: 320,000).

Altitude: 0–4884 m (summit of Puncak Jaya, or Mount Carstensz, in Irian Jaya).

Natural vegetation: Tropical lowland evergreen and semi-evergreen rain forests, montane forests, subalpine and alpine vegetation, extensive swamp forests, the richest mangrove communities in South East Asia, important areas of ultramafic and limestone vegetation (both poorly collected).

Number of vascular plants: 20,000–25,000 species, including at least 2000 pteridophytes (15% of the world's total).

Species endemism: Exceptionally high (70–80%) for mainland New Guinea, but decreasing further east.

Vascular plant families: 246 (217 seed plant families, 29 pteridophyte families).

Number of endemic families: 0.

Number of genera: 1465 angiosperm genera recorded for mainland New Guinea.

Number of endemic genera: At least 86 Papua New Guinean angiosperm genera are endemic to mainland New Guinea, whereas endemism is lower further east (just 4 genera are endemic to the Solomon Islands).

Important plant families: Orchidaceae: 2000–3000 species.

Introduction

Papuasia (East Malesia) includes the main island of New Guinea (the largest tropical island in the world) and its surrounding islands. In the west, the region includes the Indonesian islands of Waigeo, Biak, Yapen and Kepulauan Aru, and in the east it includes the Bismarck Archipelago (New Britain, New Ireland, the Admiralty Islands and their outliers), the Trobriand Islands, the D'Entrecasteaux Islands, the Louisiade Archipelago and Bougainville, all of which are politically part of Papua New Guinea, together with the Solomon Islands. The Santa Cruz Islands (politically part of Solomon Islands) are not included in Papuasia; biogeographically they are part of the New Hebridean group. Initially, *Flora Malesiana* excluded the eastern islands, but more recently the Bismarck Archipelago and Louisiade Archipelago have been included in the Flora accounts.

The total land area of Papuasia, is approximately 950,000 km², of which over 90% is accounted for by the island of New Guinea.

TABLE 44. PAPUASIA: GEOGRAPHICAL DATA			
Island or island group	Area (km²)	Maximum altitude (m)	
New Guinea	808,510		
Irian Jaya	421,980	4884	Puncak Jaya (Mt Carstensz)
Papua New Guinea*	462,840	4449	Mt Wilhelm
Biak-Supiori	3100	1034	
Kepulauan Aru	8270	70	
Waigeo	14,784	999	Mt Samlor
Bismarck Archipelago	49,658	2438	Mt Sinewit
D'Entrecasteaux	3142	2400	
Louisiade Archipelago	1300	800	Mt Tau
Bougainville	10,620	2743	Mt Balbi
Solomon Islands	29,790	2331	Mt Popomaneseu

* Note that the figure for Papua New Guinea refers to the political entity and not just the eastern part of the island of New Guinea.

Geology and topography

During the Cretaceous period (about 100 million years BP), southern New Guinea was (in part) joined with Australia, India, Antarctica and South America as the super-continent of Gondwanaland. At around 50 million years ago, Australia broke away and moved progressively northwards from the polar region, with New Guinea attached to it but beneath the sea. New Guinea finally began to emerge above the sea in the late Eocene, moving progressively northwards into the tropics and colliding with the proto-Indonesian island arc during the middle of the Miocene (c. 15 million years BP). During the last 2 million years, New Guinea has been intermittently joined to the Australian mainland as a result of sea-level fluctuations during the Pleistocene. The final separation from Australia was relatively recent, about 8000–6500 years ago. New Guinea's present position is on the northern face of the Australian Continental Shelf (Sahul Shelf).

These geological events have influenced the evolution of the flora of New Guinea. Thus, New Guinea's ancestral flora is shared with Australia, but the subsequent northern drift into tropical latitudes, and its collision with the Malesian archipelago, also allowed tropical Malesian elements to colonize the island's lowlands. Many Australasian elements occur in montane areas and in the drier south (see Flora section). There is still much debate about the geological history of Papuasia, and other interpretations to those given above are placed on the available evidence. For a review of the geological events in the region and how they may help to explain the origins and affinities of the present day flora, see Axelrod and Raven (1982) and Pieters (1982).

Six main topographic areas can be recognized (Stevens 1989): the Main Range, the Northern Basins and Ranges, the Southern Plain, the Vogelkop Peninsula and islands, North-eastern Islands and South-eastern Islands.

The Main Range is the dominant feature of the island of New Guinea, running the entire length of the island and exceeding 2000 m altitude for over 1600 km. This makes it the most extensive mountain region in the whole of South East Asia. The range includes South East Asia's highest mountain, Puncak Jaya (Mount Carstensz) at 4884 m, and all of South East Asia's present glaciers: Puncak Jaya, Mount Idenburg, Puncak Mandala (Mount Juliana) (4680 m) and Puncak Trikora

(Mount Wilhelmina, 4725 m). The range is geologically complex: Puncak Jaya is limestone, Mount Wilhelm (4449 m, the highest point in Papua New Guinea) is granodiorite, while many other mountains in the south-east comprise metamorphic rocks. A small area of sedimentary rocks occurs in the Aure Trough in Papua New Guinea around 146°E where the mountains are below 2000 m. There are numerous volcanoes, mostly inactive, such as Mount Giluwe (4088 m) and parts of the Owen Stanley Range, which forms the backbone of eastern New Guinea. A long belt of ultramafic outcrops occurs in Irian Jaya, running from the island of Waigeo in the west, through the Vogelkop Peninsula. Gunung Doorman (3580 m), Mount Suckling (3676 m) in the Owen Stanley Range, and parts of the Bowutu Mountains also comprise ultramafic rocks. A feature of the mountain ranges in both Irian Jaya and Papua New Guinea are the intermontane valleys which may drop to 500 m above sea-level. The diverse geology and large altitudinal range contributes to making the Main Range floristically rich and a centre of endemism.

The Northern Ranges lie to the north of an intermontane depression including the valleys of the Mamberamo, Sepik, Ramu and Markham. The ranges include Pegunungan Van Rees, the isolated Cyclops Mountains (2160 m) and Foja Mountains in Irian Jaya (both of which have ultramafic outcrops), the Bewani-Torricelli Mountains, straddling the political border between Irian Jaya and Papua New Guinea, and the Adelbert, Finisterre (highest point: Mount Finisterre, 3917 m) and Saruwaged Mountains (highest point: Mount Bangeta, 4120 m) in Papua New Guinea. The last five are still being uplifted and are seismically active; the Saruwaged Mountains are among the most actively uplifting in the world (1 m/100 years). These Northern Ranges are separated from the Main Range by large intermontane troughs occupied by the river basins of the Mamberamo (in Irian Jaya), the Sepik (mostly in Papua New Guinea), and the Ramu and Markham rivers (in Papua New Guinea).

The Southern Plain is an extensive area of low relief extending from the foothills of the Main Range south to the coast and through which a large number of rivers flow. The two largest river systems are those of the Digul (in Irian Jaya) and Fly (in Papua New Guinea). At its southernmost point, the Southern Plain is separated from Australia by only 150 km. During the last glaciation, when sea-levels were lower, the Torres Strait, to the south of the Southern Plains, was dry land and New Guinea was connected to Australia and the Aru Islands.

The Vogelkop Peninsula lies at the western end of Irian Jaya and consists of a heterogeneous mixture of mountain ranges (highest point: Gunung Lina, 3100 m) and low-lying swampy terrain. Many of the mountains exhibit karst topography, in particular the Weyland Mountains, the Tamrau Mountains, the Fakfak Mountains (1619 m) and Kumawa Mountains (1432 m).

The North-eastern Islands include the Bismarck Archipelago, and further to the south-east, the Solomon Islands. The area is one of extreme seismic activity with numerous active volcanoes. The Solomon Islands consist of a double chain of volcanic islands and raised coral islands. New Britain and New Ireland in the Bismarck Archipelago also contain raised limestones and rocks of sea-floor origin.

The South-eastern Islands are a heterogeneous mixture of mountainous islands (D'Entrecasteaux and Louisiade Archipelago) and raised coral atolls (Trobriand Islands and

Woodlark Island). The mountainous islands are floristically more diverse than the low atolls and fringing reefs.

Climate

New Guinea has a humid tropical climate with relatively high rainfall and mostly with little or no dry season. Parts of the south-central and south-eastern coastal strip are the only places which receive low amounts of rainfall (1000–1300 mm) and which are distinctly seasonal (Gressitt 1982). These areas are characterized by savanna vegetation with floristic affinities to Australia, whereas much of the rest of New Guinea supports rain forest of various sorts. In general, the wettest periods are from November to April. Parts of the Main Range and southern New Britain have 6000–8000 mm of rain per annum; some locations in the Main Range experience up to 10,000 mm per annum. The Southern Plains, the Sepik, Mamberamo and Markham basins (or intermontane depressions), together with parts of the Vogelkop Peninsula, receive less than 2500 mm, while parts of the south coast are drier, receiving less than 1500 mm annual rainfall. Temperatures in the lowlands are usually between 29° and 32°C during daytime and 5–8°C cooler at night. At 1500–2000 m, the temperatures during the day are 5–10°C cooler than the lowlands and there is a greater diurnal range than that experienced in the lowlands. At Mount Wilhelm and other peaks over c. 3960 m, occasional falls of snow occur. Humidity is generally high (75–80%).

Population

Irian Jaya, with a population of 1,173,800 in 1980, has one of the lowest population densities in the world (just 2.8 people/km²). About 40% of the population is settled in agricultural communities in the cool, temperate central highlands region around Baliem Valley, and the Paniai and Anggi Lakes regions. In some intermontane valleys the population density can be as high as 150/km². Irian Jaya's low population density is one factor which has contributed to the relatively slow rate of forest conversion. However, the number of transmigrants has increased steadily over recent years as a result of Indonesia's resettlement programme. Over 26,000 migrants from western Indonesia have settled in Irian Jaya since 1979.

Papua New Guinea has a population of 3,880,000 (1990 figures quoted in World Resources Institute 1994) and an overall population density of 8.4 people/km². Although this is a relatively low density, the population is increasing by about 2.3% per annum. Already this is placing traditional methods of shifting cultivation under pressure in some areas. About 84% of the population is rural; the highest concentrations are in high valleys of the Main Range, in Chimbu Province and in coastal areas. In some intermontane valleys, population densities of 200/km² occur. The urban areas of Port Moresby in the south, Goroka and Lae are expanding as a result of migration from rural areas. Although a few hunter-gathering tribes survive, most rural people practice subsistence agriculture. In coastal areas, this may be supplemented by fishing. Sago, yam, rice, sweet potato, bananas and taro are the main staple food crops. More recently, there has been a move towards planting cash crops, such as coconut, coffee, cocoa and oil palm.

The Solomon Islands have a population of 320,000 (1990 figures, quoted in World Resources Institute 1994) with 11.6 people/km². Population is increasing at around 3.5% per annum (IUCN 1992). Apart from Honiara, most of the people live in rural communities. About 87% of the land area is subject to customary or tribal tenure (IUCN 1991).

Vegetation

New Guinea contains one of the largest expanses of relatively pristine tropical rain forest in South East Asia. Detailed descriptions of the main vegetation types are given in Paijmans (1976), Johns (1982) and Grubb and Stevens (1985). A brief synopsis of the main vegetation types is given below.

Along the coasts are found *Casuarina* and mixed littoral forests. These have been reduced to fragments owing to relatively dense coastal populations and clearance for cultivation, especially in Papua New Guinea. Mangrove forests are the best developed and the richest in all of South East Asia. The largest areas are in the south, around the Gulf of Papua, Papua New Guinea (where they cover 1620–2000 km²) (Collins, Sayer and Whitmore 1991) and at the Ramu and Sepik estuaries. 36 tree species were recorded from New Guinea mangroves by Percival and Womersley (1975), but several additional species have been collected, including some lowland rain forest elements. Irian Jaya contains Indonesia's largest and most extensive areas of mangroves, the largest areas of which are at Bintuni Bay, and from Pulau Kimamam west to the Mikima River. Dense nipa swamps, comprising pure stands of *Nypa fruticans*, occur extensively in brackish areas of estuaries and tidal creeks.

Lowland freshwater swamp forests are extensive, particularly in the south, from the Gulf of Papua to Etna Bay in the southern lowlands of the Vogelkop Peninsula. On the north coast they extend from Mamberamo delta west to the Teluk Cenderwasih. Extensive inland swamps occur along the Idenburg and Rouffaer rivers in Irian Jaya, and along the Sepik, Fly, Ramu, Purari, Kikori and Turama rivers in Papua New Guinea. The swamps include a range of communities: aquatic, herbaceous, grass swamp, savanna, woodland and swamp forest. *Melaleuca*, sago palms (*Metroxylon sagu*) and pandans (*Pandanus* spp.) form distinct types of swamp woodland. *Campnosperma* spp. and *Terminalia brassii* are common dominants of mixed swamp forests, which also include such genera as *Mangifera*, *Garcinia* and *Acacia*. Irian Jaya contains the world's largest areas of sago palms, sago being an important staple food in many parts of lowland New Guinea.

Lowland rain forests of alluvial plains and fans in New Guinea differ markedly from those elsewhere in Malesia because of the paucity of dipterocarps; only 3 genera and 15 species of dipterocarps are found on the island of New Guinea. Lowland rain forests can be divided into a number of different types based on the dominant trees (e.g. *Pometia pinnata*, *Intsia bijuga*, *Anisoptera* and *Hopea*). They extend from the plains into the foothills and low mountains up to an altitude of approximately 700 m (Johns 1982). Lowland forests have the richest tree floras in New Guinea, containing more than 80 genera and 1200 species of trees (Womersley 1978–). Many important timber trees occur here, such as *Dracontomelon mangiferum* (black walnut) and *Intsia bijuga* and *I. palembanica* (ironwood). Dipterocarps (*Anisoptera*,

276

Vatica and *Hopea*) occur sporadically but, in general, they do not dominate lowland rain forest as in Borneo and other parts of West Malesia (Sundaland). Typical trees of the upper canopy are *Pometia*, *Ficus*, *Alstonia* and *Terminalia*, while lower storey trees include *Garcinia*, *Diospyros*, *Myristica* and *Maniltoa*. Palms (including rattans), ferns and orchids are abundant. The canopy trees are often densely covered by epiphytic ferns, mosses and orchids. The most common epiphytes are *Myrmecodia*, *Lecanopteris*, *Platycerium wandae* and *Dendrobium* spp. (Johns 1982).

Dry evergreen monsoon forests occur in south-east Irian Jaya and south-west Papua New Guinea. These forests include *Tristania*, *Syzygium*, *Acacia*, *Xanthostemon* and members of the Proteaceae. They intergrade with open woodland and savannas, in which *Eucalyptus* and *Melaleuca* are found. There is also an extensive belt of *Schizostachyum* bamboo forest in Irian Jaya at the transition between rain forest and savanna.

The montane zone occurs between approximately 700 and 3000 m. Montane forests reach their greatest extent on the Main Range, the Northern Ranges and the isolated mountain ranges of the Vogelkop Peninsula.

Lower montane forests are characterized by the prominence of *Castanopsis acuminatissima* and species of *Lithocarpus* (oaks), Elaeocarpaceae and Lauraceae. In some places, these forests are intermixed with *Nothofagus* forests. Ferns, including tree ferns, are less common than in the mid- and upper montane zones. *Araucaria* forest occurs in the Bulolo-Wau region, the Hydrographer's Range and the Jimi Valley at altitudes ranging from 550 to 1500 m (Paijmans 1970; Johns 1982, 1986). It is especially the lower montane zone which has received the most disturbance of all New Guinea's vegetation due to its suitability for traditional subsistence agriculture. Anthropogenic grasslands of *Themeda* and *Imperata*, and tree fern savannas, occur in many montane valleys, especially in Papua New Guinea, resulting from forest clearances for shifting cultivation and repeated fires. About 10,000 km² of former forest has been converted to grassland in Papua New Guinea as a result of intensive shifting agriculture.

Mid-montane forests occur between (1500–) 1700 and 2700 (–3000) m. They differ from lower montane forests both in species composition and in structure and physiognomy. They are dominated by conifers – *Podocarpus*, *Dacrycarpus*, *Libocedrus* (*Papuacedrus*), *Phyllocladus hypophyllus* – and members of the Araliaceae (such as *Harmsiopanax*) (Johns 1982). Forests dominated by *Nothofagus* are common throughout the mid-montane zone.

As altitude increases, the diversity of trees decreases. The **upper montane zone** occurs on ridges, peaks and plateaux above 2700 m and extends up to about 3300 m. There is a mosaic of forests and grasslands. Upper montane forests comprise mainly stunted, moss-covered trees and bushes. The main species include *Phyllocladus* and *Xanthomyrtus*, Ericaceae (including *Rhododendron* and *Vaccinium*), Myrtaceae and Rubiaceae, and conifers in the genera *Dacrycarpus*, *Dacrydium*, *Libocedrus* and *Phyllocladus* (Johns 1982).

The **subalpine zone** is floristically rather poor, and includes stunted forests with abundant Ericaceae, tree ferns (*Cyathea*) and the conifers *Dacrycarpus compactus* and *Libocedrus papuana*. Grasslands, bogs and fens also typify the subalpine zone, the latter between 3200 m and 4270 m on mountains such as Mount Wilhelm and Mount Giluwe.

Above c. 2500 m altitude there are areas of natural or semi-natural herbaceous vegetation in depressions (so-called "frost hollows"), which are caused by a combination of poor drainage, infrequent but severe frosts, and burning. Areas of herbaceous vegetation become progressively more extensive at higher altitudes. In the alpine zone (above about 3960 m on Mount Wilhelm), the vegetation is made up entirely of low, stunted heaths, grasses (particularly the tussock grass *Deschampsia klossii*) and low herbs such as *Ranunculus*, *Potentilla*, *Gentiana*, *Centrolepis*, *Oreomyrrhis*, *Tetramolopium* and *Epilobium*. Bryophytes and lichens are also common, the latter sometimes dominating the vegetation. Small pools contain species in such genera as *Isoetes* and *Eriocaulon*, and there are large areas of tussock vegetation in swamps. The highest peaks of New Guinea are capped by snow and icefields, but these are receding rapidly (P.F. Stevens 1992, *in litt.*).

Besides the altitudinal zonation of vegetation, there are also distinctive types of forest developed on ultramafic and limestone substrates. Important ultramafic forests occur in a belt along the Sepik River, in the Owen Stanley Range, Bowutu Mountains, and in a belt which runs from the island of Waigeo through the Vogelkop in Irian Jaya, with outliers in the Cyclops and Foja Mountains. Important limestone forests occur on Puncak Jaya and in the Vogelkop Peninsula in Irian Jaya, and are extensive also on the Great Papuan Plateau in Papua New Guinea.

Of the other islands, **Bougainville** contains large areas of freshwater swamp forest (particularly in the south), lowland rain forest (including *Calophyllum peekelii* forest and *Neonauclea/Sloanea* forest at 450–750 m), montane forest, and swamp forest in the south. Along the coast are beach forests and mangroves.

The three principal islands of the volcanic **D'Entrecasteaux group** (Normanby, Fergusson and Goodenough) still retain substantial stands of primary tropical rain forest, while the Bismarck Archipelago supports lowland, montane, freshwater swamp and mangrove forests. **New Britain** has the largest areas of tropical lowland rain forest in the D'Entrecasteaux group, together with *Eucalyptus deglupta* forests established on volcanic lapilli following disturbance (Johns 1986), submontane *Agathis* forest and montane *Nothofagus* forest above 1500 m, as well as swamp forest, beach forest and mangroves. Montane forests occur in the Whiteman Ranges (which contain ultramafic substrates), Nakanai Mountains and on Mount Sinewit. **New Ireland** supports lowland rain forest and some montane forest containing *Nothofagus* in the south. On Manus Island there is a unique forest dominated by *Calophyllum* (Guttiferae).

The **Louisiade Archipelago** consists of about 100 small islands, the majority of which are low coral islands. The three largest islands (Tagula, Misima and Rossel) are partly volcanic and support lowland tropical rain forest. The **Trobriand Islands** are low coral islands with small areas of limestone rain forest and fringing mangroves.

Tropical rain forest is the natural vegetation over most of the **Solomon Islands**; however, the forests are relatively species-poor when compared to those of New Guinea and West Malesia. The main emergent species are *Terminalia calamansanai* and *Ficus* spp. On Santa Cruz, kauri pine (*Agathis macrophylla*) once dominated, but these have now been logged. On Guadalcanal, mixed deciduous forest occurs, now mostly degraded to savanna woodland by fires. Montane forests are best developed on Guadalcanal around Mount Popomanaseu (the highest point at 2331 m) and Mount Kaichui. Small pockets of swamp forest occur mainly along the coast, and there are also areas of beach forest which have escaped clearances. The most distinctive forest type is found on ultramafic rocks, though this is species-poor and has been reduced to scrub and fern thickets in some places, probably as a result of man-made fires (Whitmore 1969). The forests are subject to frequent catastrophic events, such as cyclones, lightning strikes and landslips and increasingly by logging (see below).

Estimates of forest cover

The forests of Irian Jaya are still relatively undisturbed and botanically little known. They are the most extensive in all of Indonesia. Closed broadleaved forests of all kinds in Irian Jaya were estimated to cover 380,050 km² (or 92% of the land area) at the end of 1980 (FAO/UNEP 1981). Collins, Sayer and Whitmore (1991) estimate there to be 354,360 km² of rain forest (or 86.3% of the land area), of which lowland forest covers 232,610 km² (or 56.6% of the land area). According to the same study, rain forests (including lowland, montane, inland swamp forests and mangroves) cover 363,530 km² in Papua New Guinea (or 80.5% of the land area). Of this, lowland rain forest comprises 229,870 km² (or 50.9% of the land area). A further 3220 km² are covered by lowland monsoon forests (see Table 45).

World Resources Institute (1994) gives 293,230 km² of "rain forest", 7050 km² of "moist deciduous forest", 53,700 km² of "hill and montane forests", 4170 km² of "dry deciduous forest" in Papua New Guinea for 1990.

The estimates of forest cover for Papuasia given in Table 45 are taken from Collins, Sayer and Whitmore (1991). The areas given are determined from maps and are not official statistics. They include relatively undisturbed and disturbed forests where, for example, enclaves of cultivation and plantations occur within areas of forest.

TABLE 45. PAPUASIA: ESTIMATES OF FOREST COVER

	Area (km²)	% of land area
PAPUA NEW GUINEA*		
Rain forests		
Lowland	229,870	50.9
Montane	63,840	14.1
Inland swamp	64,420	14.3
Mangrove	5400	1.2
Sub totals	**363,530**	**80.5**
Monsoon forests		
Lowland	3220	0.7
Totals	**366,750**	**81.2**
IRIAN JAYA		
Rain forests		
Lowland	232,610	56.6
Montane	54,660	13.3
Inland swamp	49,590	12.1
Mangrove	17,500	4.3
Totals	**354,360**	**86.3**
SOLOMON ISLANDS		
Rain forests		
Lowland	24,810	90.1
Montane	780	2.8
Totals	**25,590**	**92.9**

* Refers to the political entity, therefore including associated islands and island groups.

The figures given in Table 45 for *lowland rain forests* include: tropical evergreen rain forest, tropical semi-evergreen rain forest, limestone forest, ultramafic forest and beach forest; those for *montane rain forests* include: lower, mid-montane and upper montane rain forests and subalpine forests; and those for *inland swamp forests* include peat swamp forest, freshwater swamp forest and periodically inundated freshwater swamp forest.

Flora

Papuasia is the easternmost limit of the Malesian floristic region. The island of New Guinea is now widely accepted as a biological "hot spot" deserving a concentrated conservation strategy because of its rich biodiversity. The forest flora, in particular, represents one of the most diverse biological ecosystems in the Old World Tropics. It is estimated that there are between 15,000–20,000 species of vascular plants on mainland New Guinea, including over 2000 species of orchids (Johns 1992) and at least 2000 species of ferns (or 15% of the world's fern flora) (Parris 1985), with 70–80% endemism. This is substantially more than an earlier estimate by Good (1960) of 9000 species (of flowering plants) in New Guinea. Taking Papuasia as a whole, the vascular flora is estimated to include 20,000–25,000 vascular plant species (R.J. Johns 1992, pers. comm.). Table 38 gives a breakdown of available statistics for each of the main islands and island groups of Papuasia.

Despite its richness and high levels of endemism at the species level, New Guinea has no endemic vascular plant families. This can be explained by the geographical position of New Guinea in a continuous series of islands between South East Asia and Australia. A different pattern of endemism emerges when examining the flora of Papua New Guinea at the generic level. A total of 86 angiosperm genera are endemic to New Guinea (W. Vink 1992, *in litt.*), although the actual figure will be greatly affected by systematic realignments and also by future botanical discoveries (Johns 1989b). Even in families that are the subject of taxonomic study, knowledge of many of the species, and critically of intra- and inter-specific variation, is rudimentary (Stevens 1989, 1990); many taxa are represented by a single or only a few collections. Herbs, sub-canopy trees, ferns and, especially, climbers are under-represented in herbaria. This situation creates fundamental problems in arriving at estimates of species endemism.

The affinities of the New Guinea flora are mainly with Malesia and Australia, although at a specific level there is a high degree of endemism. Certain lowland rain forest elements are considered to have their origins in Asia and the West Malesian region, for example the dipterocarps. However, recent studies suggest that rain forest covered extensive areas of northern Australia in the Miocene-Pliocene period, and that perhaps this is the origin for some of New Guinea's rain forest flora. There is also a small Pacific and South American component (e.g. the genera *Heliconia, Dimorphanthera* and *Eugenia*). Ancient Gondwanan relicts include the cycads, araucarias, Cunoniaceae, Monimiaceae and *Nothofagus*. These are especially well-represented in the montane flora (e.g. *Araucaria, Nothofagus*), while more recent Australian elements are mostly confined to the drier south.

The islands to the east of New Guinea are an attenuated version of that island's rich flora. There is only 1 monotypic endemic genus in the Bismarcks (*Clymenia*) and 4 such genera in the Solomons (*Allowoodsonia, Cassidispermum, Kajewskiella* and *Whitmorea*).

Useful plants

Throughout Papuasia, a wide range of plant resources are used both in hunter-gathering and more settled lifestyles. Many native (and introduced) plants provide food, medicines, poisons, raw materials for building houses and shelters, canoes, tools, weapons, clothing and containers. Plants also play an important part in cultural ceremonies, ritual and magic throughout the region. Powell (1976) lists 1035 useful plant species (wild and cultivated) representing 470 genera in 146 families, mostly for Papua New Guinea. This is by no means the total number of plants which are used, but indicates the wide range of plant species utilized. A very small selection of these is given below.

Timber trees

The lowland forests of New Guinea contain important timber trees. As noted previously, dipterocarps are poorly represented. Although of local importance, they never dominate the forests over extensive areas as they do elsewhere in Malesia. In addition, the average volumes per hectare of timber (suitable for extraction) is often less than 35 m³ (Johns 1990) and this (especially in combination with extraction difficulties caused by inaccessibility due to the steepness of terrain in many areas) has resulted in relatively low intensity of logging in New Guinea. Important timber trees include *Agathis* (kauri pine) and *Araucaria* spp., both genera providing a source of high quality softwood, *Palaquium* spp. (pencil cedars), *Dracontomelon mangiferum* (New Guinea black walnut), valuable in cabinet making, *Intsia bijuga* and *I. palembanica* (ironwoods), *Pometia tomentosa* (taun), *Pterocarpus indicus* (New Guinea rosewood), *Octomeles sumatrana* (erima), *Eucalyptus deglupta* (kamarere) and members of the genera *Canarium, Calophyllum* and *Dialium*. Both *Araucaria hunsteinii* and *A. cunninghamii* have been heavily exploited in New Guinea. For example, many of the former rich stands of *Araucaria* in the Wau-Bulolo-Watut valleys have been harvested for plywood export (Gagne and Gressitt 1982). Table 46 provides a list of the major timber genera exported from Papua New Guinea.

In Papua New Guinea, the timber industry has developed rapidly over the last 30 years. Total output of sawlogs and veneer logs has increased from 46,000 m³ in 1952 to 910,000 m³ in 1979, and almost 2.5 million m³ in 1988. Approximately three-quarters are exported, most (about 90%) going to Japan, Korea and Taiwan. In 1988, Papua New Guinea earned US$111 million from forest products, of which US$94 million was for logs. The importance of the Papua New Guinea timber trade is likely to increase in the future as the forests of other countries in the region are depleted. Ten species of trees are banned from being exported as unprocessed logs to guard against the rapid depletion of high-quality timber and to encourage local processing. The Solomon Islands export around 0.3 million m³ of logs. In 1987, Japan imported 0.17 million m³ from the Solomons.

The main indigenous species used in plantation forestry are: *Eucalyptus deglupta, Araucaria cunninghamii,* *A. hunsteinii* and (on swampy ground) *Terminalia brassii*. Increasingly, introduced *Acacia mangium* is used. The total area of plantations remains small. For example, in Papua New Guinea just 360 km² are covered by forestry plantations (FAO 1987). Fuller use of some species depends on selection of superior strains adapted to a range of ecological conditions. This in turn requires the protection of natural stands to conserve genetic diversity of ecotypes adapted to a variety of environmental conditions.

TABLE 46. MAJOR TIMBER GENERA EXPORTED FROM PAPUA NEW GUINEA (1988)

Genus	Trade name	Volume (%)	Average price (US$/m³)
Pometia	Taun	21.24	95.50
Calophyllum	Kalofilum	6.57	97.00
Homalium	Malas	6.21	56.00
Terminalia	Terminalia	5.08	82.00
Palaquium	Pencil Cedar	4.20	124.50
Dillenia	Simpoh	3.74	58.00
Intsia	Kwila	3.50	154.50
Anisoptera	Mersawa	3.42	97.50
Canarium	Red Canarium	3.09	67.00
Octomeles	Erima	2.98	58.00
Pterocymbium	Amberoi	2.89	56.00
Celtis	Light Celtis	2.86	56.00
Syzygium	Water Gum	2.17	59.00
Endospermum	Basswood	2.02	69.00
Eucalyptus	Kamarere	1.66	63.00
Burckella	Nyathoh	1.55	78.50
Dracontomelon	Walnut	1.52	94.00
Planchonella	Red Planchonella	1.34	121.00
Various genera	Mixed Red	1.24	50.00
Buchanania	Pink Satinwood	1.05	57.00

The total volume of timber exported in 1988 was approximately 1.16 million m³.

Source: Forest Industries Council of Papua New Guinea.

Other plants used in construction

Plants traditionally used in house building include *Metroxylon sagu* (sago palm), *Nypa fruticans* (nipa palm) and *Pandanus* spp., whose leaves are used for roofing. *Archontophoenix, Nypa fruticans, Caryota rumphiana* and other palms supply wood for floors. *Calophyllum inophyllum, Dysoxylum* spp., *Castanopsis acuminatissima* and *Nothofagus* spp. are preferred for house posts and beams, while *Libocedrus papuana, Buchanania arborescens* and *Pandanus* spp. (among others) are used for house walls. Powell (1976) lists over 130 species used in constructing and for decorating houses.

Mangroves throughout the coastal region provide traditional sources of building materials, as well as playing an important part in shore protection, land reclamation and in providing breeding grounds for prawns, fish and other wildlife which are traditionally hunted for food.

Albizia falcataria, Campnosperma, Canarium, Gmelina, Macaranga, Octomeles sumatrana and the mangrove *Bruguiera*, are among 39 species listed by Powell (1976) as providing wood used in constructing canoes and rafts in Papuasia.

Food plants

The staple foods are mainly starchy, comprising tubers such as edible yams (*Dioscorea* spp.) and sweet potato (*Ipomoea batatas*), corms such as taro (*Colocasia esculenta*) and wild bananas (*Musa* spp.) and sago from *Metroxylon sagu*. Sago is an important staple food of rural communities in swampy and lowland areas of New Guinea, while taro and sweet potato are staple crops in rain forest areas and on the major islands, sweet potato also being grown in the highlands. Of these staple foods, the edible yams grown in New Guinea are possibly introduced from elsewhere in South East Asia (though some species may be indigenous), taro is Indian or Indonesian in origin, and sweet potato originates from South America. Sago and some of the bananas are native. In addition, the winged bean (*Psophocarpus tetragonolobus*) is a traditional nitrogen-fixing legume crop in the New Guinea highlands. As well as providing a protein-rich food source, the plant also produces an oil which is used in cooking and in soap-making (Verdcourt 1979).

Powell (1976) lists over 200 species and genera as the main sources of supplementary foods in New Guinea. Most are native; some are gathered directly from the wild; some are tended in forests; while others are transplanted and cultivated. Table 47 lists only a small selection of those which are gathered from the wild in various parts of the region.

Medicinal plants

Plants are used widely in traditional medicine in the region. Powell (1976) provides extensive lists of species used in the treatment of a variety of illnesses and ailments, or as narcotics and stimulants. They include 25 plant species used for treating fevers, including malaria, in various parts of Papua New Guinea, 40 species recorded for the treatment of coughs, colds and sore throats, and 25 species associated with control of fertility and childbirth. A very small selection of medicinal plants is given in Table 48.

TABLE 47. SOME OF THE FOOD PLANTS GATHERED FROM THE WILD IN NEW GUINEA

Genus or species	Family	Part eaten and other notes
Alocasia macrorrhiza	Araceae	Tuber, leaves; also cultivated
Alpinia spp.	Zingiberaceae	Leaves, rhizome; also cultivated
Arenga spp.	Palmae	"Cabbage"
Artocarpus altilis	Moraceae	Fruit, seeds; also cultivated
Other *Artocarpus* spp.	Moraceae	Seeds, pulp
Bambusa spp.	Poaceae	Shoots; also cultivated
Begonia spp.	Begoniaceae	Leaves, stems
Canarium salomonense	Burseraceae	Nut; also cultivated
Caryota rumphiana	Palmae	Pith of young trunk
Cocos nucifera	Palmae	Nut, milk, "cabbage"; wild and cultivated
Cyathea spp.	Cyatheaceae	Fronds
Diospyros spp.	Ebenaceae	Fruit
Ficus spp.	Moraceae	Leaves, fruit; some species also cultivated
Libocedrus papuana	Cupressaceae	Leaves
Mangifera spp.	Anacardiaceae	Fruit; *M. indica* is cultivated
Pandanus spp.	Pandanaceae	Fruit, nut; some species also cultivated
Rhodomyrtus novoguinensis	Myrtaceae	Leaves, fruit
Sloanea archboldiana	Elaeocarpaceae	Nut
Syzygium spp.	Myrtaceae	Fruit; *S. malaccense* also cultivated
Zingiber spp.	Zingiberaceae	Rhizome, leaves; *Z. zerumbet* also cultivated

TABLE 48. SOME PLANTS USED FOR MEDICINAL PURPOSES IN NEW GUINEA

Genus or species	Family	Part used and complaint
Alpinia spp.	Zingiberaceae	Rhizome sap applied to cuts; also used to relieve headaches and toothache
Alstonia brassii	Apocynaceae	Used for relieving headaches
Alstonia scholaris	Apocynaceae	Stem sap diluted for coughs; bark shredded and diluted extract for dysentery, diarrhoea and stomach aches
Canarium indicum	Burseraceae	Bark masticated and applied to burns
Cinnamomum sp.	Lauraceae	Chest pains and treatment of fevers
Dolichandrone spathacea	Bignoniaceae	Sap mixed with lime for treatment of conjunctivitis
Endospermum formicarum	Euphorbiaceae	General pains
Ficus septica	Moraceae	Sap diluted, taken as a preventive dose against fevers, including malaria, dysentery and diarrhoea; apical leaves eaten with ginger for coughs
Ficus sp.	Moraceae	Headaches
Hibiscus tiliaceus	Malvaceae	"Pod" cotton used to bathe wounds; leaves crushed and sap diluted for sore throats and coughs; young leaf tips used on Manus to treat tuberculosis
Kaempferia galanga	Zingiberaceae	Abortifacient
Musa sp.	Musaceae	Leaves eaten to cause abortion; soup made to treat stomach disorders, dysentery; also used in treatment of fevers and general body pains
Parartocarpus venenosa	Moraceae	Powdered seeds and ovules applied to sores
Sida rhombifolia	Malvaceae	Used to relieve toothache, mouth infections and to ease childbirth
Smilax sp.	Smilacaceae	Sap used to treat ear infections
Syzygium spp.	Myrtaceae	Bark masticated for sore throats; leaves eaten for coughs; leaves boiled and eaten for treating dysentery, diarrhoea and stomach aches
Tournefortia sarmentosa	Boraginaceae	Leaf chewed in treatment of fevers, including malaria, also dysentery and diarrhoea
Vatica rassak	Dipterocarpaceae	Stops bleeding
Wendlandia paniculata	Rubiaceae	Muscle and joint pains
Zingiber spp.	Zingiberaceae	Rhizome sap stops bleeding; rhizome crushed and applied to burns; rhizome masticated to relieve headaches, toothache and general pains

Textiles

Ropes made from plant materials are used widely in all construction jobs. Rattans, pandans and the bark of such species as *Hibiscus tiliaceus* and *Triumfetta pilosa* are used for ropes and ties. Trees such as *Artocarpus altilis* and *Gnetum gnemon*, which are cultivated around settlements primarily for food, also supply bark and fibre, while *Broussonetia papyrifera* (introduced from eastern Asia) and *Phaleria macrocarpa* are planted especially for these products.

Fuelwood

Fuelwood collection amounted to 5.5 million m^3 in 1988 in Papua New Guinea alone (Collins, Sayer and Whitmore 1991). Many species are used, but special mention is made here of casuarinas. *Casuarina equisetifolia*, *C. papuana* (*Gymnostoma papuana*), *C. nodiflora* and *C. oligodon* are used to increase soil fertility and as wood crops. *C. oligodon* has formed the basis of the intensive agricultural system in the Chimbu valley for c. 700 years due to its nitrogen-fixing properties and rapid growth (R.J. Johns 1992, pers. comm.). Its wood is used for building and as firewood.

Ornamental plants

Over 50 species of plants are recorded by Powell (1976) for use in everyday and ceremonial dress, while 25 species are recorded for personal adornment, such as seed necklaces.

Among the many species of horticultural value or potential are orchids (of which New Guinea has over 2000 species), a large number of Ericaceae, in particular *Rhododendron* of which there are more than 120 species, many endemic to the montane zones and subalpine zones, and the decorative *Cordyline terminalis*.

Factors causing loss of biodiversity

Natural environmental factors

The forests of Papuasia are subjected to frequent damage and disturbance by cyclones, landslides (as a result of the steepness of the terrain in many montane areas), fires and changing river courses. Earthquakes and volcanoes also occur in the region. A further significant factor in ecosystem disturbance is drought (and associated fires) resulting from periodic El Niño (Southern Oscillation) events (Johns 1989c). The damage caused by these events is often catastrophic, and it is quite possible that extinctions of locally restricted endemics have occurred as a result (though as far as is known there is no documentary evidence of such cases in the region). On the other hand, the forests have co-evolved with these natural disturbance factors over long periods of time, and such disturbances are part of the overall dynamics of the forest ecosystem and give rise to habitat diversity (see Johns 1986, 1990).

Human factors

Estimates of outright deforestation for Papua New Guinea vary from 120 km^2 per annum for the period 1986–1990 (FAO 1987) to 220 km^2 per annum for the period 1981–1985 (FAO 1988a). These are rather conservative when compared to estimates from the Wau Ecology Institute of 800 km^2 of forests cleared annually.

Agriculture

The traditional form of subsistence agriculture is shifting cultivation, supplemented by hunting of wild animals and the collection of fruits and nuts from the forest. Traditional forms of agriculture have been practiced for the last 40,000 years in Papua New Guinea (R.J. Johns 1992, pers. comm.), and extensive areas have been converted to secondary forests, savanna and grassland as a result of repeated burning. According to Saulei (1987), 200,000 km^2 of Papuan forest is secondary; about 10,000 km^2 of man-made grasslands occur in the highland regions of Papua New Guinea as a result of repeated burning. Myers (1980) estimated the amount of forest cut down each year as a result of shifting agriculture to be 2500 km^2, including at least 250 km^2 of primary forest. Repetto (1988) estimates that 220 km^2 of forest are destroyed by shifting cultivation each year. Not all of this area will be permanently deforested. Some will grow back and some may be used subsequently for plantations.

Many rural settlements in Papua New Guinea are becoming more settled, and cash crop plantations, such as cocoa, coffee, oil palm, rubber and tea, are becoming established.

The forests of Irian Jaya are generally less disturbed than those of Papua New Guinea, due to a lower population density; however, transmigration has increased in recent years due to Indonesia's policy of resettling people from more crowded western islands. The total amount of forest lost so far through resettlement schemes is, however, small compared to the total forested area.

Logging

In Papua New Guinea, the first large-scale logging industry was based on *Araucaria* in the 1950s. The timber was used for plywood and mostly exported. The first large wood-chip industry began in the Gogol Valley, Madang Province in 1973. By the end of 1984, some 62,000 km^2 of Papua New Guinea was under logging concessions; about one-sixth of the total forest area. However, not all of the forests within timber concessions are logged. Often, up to 30–40% of the timber concession will be excluded from logging as a result of topography or low stocking rates (R.J. Johns, 1992 pers. comm.).

Apart from large agricultural projects, clearfelling is mostly confined on mainland Papua New Guinea to Madang Province to provide logs for chip production (Lamb 1991b). Where selective logging takes place, it is often the clearing operations and burning after logging which pose the main threats to the forest, rather than timber extraction itself. For example, in selective logging, typically only 20–35 m^3/ha of timber (5–6 trees) are removed (R.J. Johns 1992, pers. comm.).

Today, the main areas of logging activity are along the north coast of mainland Papua New Guinea, and on New Britain and New Ireland (Collins, Sayer and Whitmore 1991). Wau Ecology Institute estimates that commercial logging accounts for 600 km^2 of forest out of a total of 800 km^2 destroyed each year, although this is a higher figure than recent FAO estimates. There is concern that logging in Papua New Guinea (as elsewhere in the tropics) is not being carried out on a sustained yield basis and that logged forests show a lowering of tree species diversity (according to a TFAP 1989 mission).

A recent trend is the introduction of selective logging using helicopters. "Heli-logging" is already taking place in the Cromwell Mountains of the Huon Peninsula. This method restricts damage resulting from road construction during logging operations but could increase the rate of resource depletion (R.J. Johns 1992 pers. comm.). Furthermore, tree cutting is made possible in areas which may have been inaccessible using conventional logging methods, and the impact that this may have on wildlife needs to be monitored (Arentz 1992).

About 86% of Irian Jaya is still covered by relatively intact forests; however, logging has begun and is set to increase as sources of supply of timber from other parts of the region are diminished.

The rain forests of the Solomon Islands have been subjected to heavy exploitation from logging interests since the 1970s. As a result, primary forest has been lost from several islands, notably Ghizo and Kolombangara. Historically, there has been little regard for the ecological effects of logging, such as erosion, or to retaining small trees to allow forest regeneration. However, since 1986 logging companies have been allowed to fell only trees with a diameter in excess of 600 mm dbh. Approximately 15 km² of forest plantations are established annually (Collins, Sayer and Whitmore 1991), and it is hoped that plantations of fast-growing and commercially-valuable species will eventually replace the need to fell indigenous forests.

Road building

Roads are a major threat to wildlife conservation in general. Besides the direct effects of forest destruction during their construction, roads increase accessibility for hunters, settlers, agricultural expansion and plant collecting, and affect the movement and distribution of species (especially animals). Cuttings increase the risk of soil erosion, and localized flooding can occur as a result of compaction and alteration of drainage patterns resulting in the death of forests in inundated areas. Major road building programmes are of particular concern in Irian Jaya where a number of reserves have been damaged or are threatened by major road building schemes. The Wasur Wildlife Reserve has been damaged as a result of constructing part of the trans-Irian highway. It has opened up the area for hunting and increased the incidence of fire, and to timber and fuelwood cutting (Petocz 1984, 1989). Plans for roads affect Irian Jaya's two proposed National Parks (Gunung Lorentz and Mamberamo-Foja, CPD Sites SEA69 and SEA70, in part, respectively – see Data Sheets), as well as a number of other reserves.

Transmigration and resettlement schemes

The number of transmigrants to Irian Jaya has increased steadily over recent years as a result of Indonesia's resettlement programme designed to relieve pressure on Java's burgeoning population. Over 26,000 migrants from western Indonesia have so far settled in Irian Jaya since 1979. They are settled in pre-selected development regions usually after the sites have been evaluated by foreign consultants and national professionals (Petocz 1984, 1989). Despite the general low fertility of soils, large numbers of people have been settled, particularly on the lowlands of the south coast plains of Irian Jaya. The effect of these re-settlement schemes, along with road developments, is to open up formerly undisturbed areas to agriculture and settlement. The requirements for fuelwood and building materials have placed additional pressures on surrounding areas of forest. Earlier conflicts between transmigration schemes and protected areas have been avoided. For example, development regions designated within the Kumbe-Merauke Nature Reserve of the south coastal plains and in the proposed Mamberamo-Foja National Park (CPD Site SEA70, in part – see Data Sheet) have been cancelled by the Indonesian Government.

Resettlement schemes are designed to provide better housing and facilities to local people living in rural areas, to move people from areas which conflict with development, and to assist in centralizing the rural population. Along with housing, land is usually allocated for cultivation. In Irian Jaya, four protected areas are affected by resettlement schemes (Petocz 1984, 1989): Lorentz Nature Reserve (CPD Site SEA69, see Data Sheet), Arfak Mountains Nature Reserve (CPD Site SEA68, see Data Sheet), North Salawati Island Nature (CPD Site SEA72) and Wasur Wildlife Reserve.

Mining

Considerable areas are deforested as a result of mining activities. Among the areas most affected by large-scale mining activities are the Wau region, Porgera and Misima Island (for gold), and Bougainville (for copper). In Irian Jaya, mining operations are currently centred in two areas: the remote island of Gag, south-west of Waigeo, where there is a concession to mine nickel, and Gunung Lorentz, where 45% of the area mined for copper lies within the proposed Gunung Lorentz National Park (CPD Site SEA69, see Data Sheet). A possible economic deposit of nickel occurs in the Cyclops Mountains (CPD Site SEA79) (Petocz 1984, 1989).

Oil exploration

Oil exploration began in 1992 in the Lake Kutubu region. A pipeline has been constructed to the southern coast (Gulf Province). Drilling is excluded from the Lake Kutubu catchment and, so far, the impact of drilling operations has been on a local scale (R.J. Johns 1993, pers. comm.).

Tourism

Tourism can provide significant benefits to the local and national economy, and generate income for protected areas; however, there is a need to control and plan carefully for tourism to prevent irreparable damage to certain vegetation types which are vulnerable to trampling. High-altitude vegetation, for example on Puncak Trikora, is at risk. This area is not protected at present and local tour operators have no responsibility towards ensuring the protection of the vegetation (W. Vink 1992, in litt.). There is a need to regulate the number of visitors to particularly sensitive areas and to ensure that tour operators are aware of their environmental obligations.

Plant collecting

There have been a number of cases of illegal collection of ornamental plants, by amateur and commercial growers. Particularly at risk are orchids, Ericaceae and tree ferns.

Conservation

Papua New Guinea

About 97% of the land is held by ethnic groups under customary forms of land ownership. Traditional methods of cultivation and many of the customs adopted by rural communities have helped to ensure that wildlife resources have not been over-exploited. For example, the traditional shifting cultivation system allows 10–35 years to lapse between successive periods of cultivation on the same plot and prevents any tree felling along river banks. There are also some safeguards against cutting trees which are of particular importance to the local economy. Some areas may be protected permanently as burial grounds (Eaton 1985). Such customs are coming under growing pressure as the population increases and adopts more "western" lifestyles.

As a result of the complex system of land tenure, the establishment of legally protected areas is made difficult. Just 2% of Papua New Guinea has any legal form of protection. Following a policy study led by the World Bank in 1990, a National Forestry and Conservation Action Plan (NFCAP) has been drawn up by government departments. One NFCAP proposal calls for the creation of large, multiple use Conservation Areas, to be planned as a national system encompassing about 20% of the country's total area and providing protection to a representative cross section of PNG's terrestrial, marine and estuarine biodiversity (World Bank 1991).

A review of the protected areas system and conservation legislation is given in IUCN (1992).

The majority of Papua New Guinea's protected areas are small and do not cover adequately the full range of environments. Previous proposals for establishing new protected areas have been made based primarily on analyses of birds and birdwing butterflies. For example, Diamond (1976) proposed a system of 22 areas incorporating almost a complete range of environments; most remain unprotected. Of the areas identified for Data Sheet treatment in this present study, only Mount Wilhelm (CPD Site SEA89, in part) is an approved National Park, but even this has not been fully gazetted. There is an urgent need for more fully protected areas, as well as the establishment of areas where conservation and controlled utilization can take place.

An action strategy for protected areas in the South Pacific region (including Papua New Guinea) has been launched by SPREP (the South Pacific Regional Environment Programme) (SPREP 1985). Among its recommendations is the need to develop national conservation strategies and priorities for the establishment of a comprehensive protected areas network. Two important plant sites being established but which await final approval include Mount Wilhelm National Park (as noted above) and Mount Gahavisuka Provincial Park, both of which occur within CPD Site SEA89.

Irian Jaya

The current terrestrial protected areas system (excluding proposed protected areas) covers 49,593 km² or approximately 11.8% of the land area (including offshore islands). In addition to the gazetted reserves, a number of proposals have been made to extend the reserve system. Among the most important of these are the National Conservation Plan (FAO 1981–1982), covering the whole of Indonesia, and proposals arising from the Irian Jaya Conservation Development Strategy (Petocz 1984, 1989). Many of the areas proposed for protection in these studies are large and chosen for their water catchment functions as well as their biological richness. The Nature Conservation Plan also tried to include representatives of all the major habitat types found in Indonesia. Practical

TABLE 49. SUMMARY OF PROTECTED AREA COVERAGE IN PAPUA NEW GUINEA

Protected area	IUCN management category	Number and comments
National Parks	II	3 established, covering 73 km². 2 further parks to be gazetted, one of which (Mt Wilhelm) is identified below as a centre of plant diversity.
Wildlife Sanctuaries	Unassigned	1 (Moitaka), so far not gazetted.
Nature Reserves	IV	1 (Talele Islands, Bismarck Archipelago, 40 ha).
Reserves	Unassigned	1 (Namanatabu Historic Reserve, 27 ha).
Sanctuaries	Unassigned	1 (Baiyer River S, 1.2 km²).
Scenic Reserves	Unassigned	1 (Paga Hill ScR, 10 ha).
Marine Parks	Unassigned	1 (Horseshoe Reef MP, 3.9 km²), so far not gazetted.
Parks	Unassigned	1 (Cape Wom International Memorial Park, 1 km²).
Wildlife Management Areas	IV/VIII	21, covering 9739 km².
Provincial Parks	IV	2, covering 52 ha.
	Unassigned	1 (Mount Gahavisuka, 77 ha).

Note that IUCN (1991) also lists 81 proposed protected areas, mostly islands and marine areas.

Source: IUCN (1991). Note that this only includes protected areas of over 10 km², with the exception of islands of at least 1 km² where the whole island is protected.

TABLE 50. SUMMARY OF PROTECTED AREA COVERAGE IN IRIAN JAYA

Protected area	IUCN management category	Number and comments
National Parks	II	2 existing, but only 1 terrestrial covering 3080 km². 2 proposed (Gunung Lorentz, Mamberamo-Pegunungan Foja), covering 29,257 km², both of which are identified here as centres of plant diversity.
Nature Reserves	I	12 existing, covering 29,375 km². 18 proposed, covering >15,846 km².
Game Reserves	IV	4 existing, covering 17,105 km². 7 proposed, covering 2288 km².
Recreation Parks	V	5 existing, covering 33 km². 5 proposed, covering 269 km².

Sources: McCarthy (1991); IUCN (1992). Note that this only includes protected areas of over 10 km², with the exception of islands of at least 1 km² where the whole island is protected.

considerations were also taken into account. As a result, the Plan offers excellent coverage and, if implemented, would result in one of the finest and most comprehensive protected areas networks in South East Asia (MacKinnon and MacKinnon 1986). Five of the priority areas identified in the Plan are undoubtedly rich areas for plants, namely the proposed Lorentz and Mamberamo-Foja National Parks (CPD Sites SEA69 and SEA70, in part), the proposed Tamrau Mountains (SEA73/SEA74) and Arfak Mountains Nature Reserves (SEA68, see Data Sheet) and the Cyclops Mountains Nature Reserve (SEA79). In addition to these areas, the Irian Jaya Conservation Development Strategy (Petocz 1984, 1989) includes the Wasur Wildlife Reserve among terrestrial priorities for conservation. This reserve is an important wetland site, including *Melaleuca-Eucalyptus* woodland, savanna, swamps, lowland forests and mangroves.

A review of the protected areas system and conservation legislation covering the whole of Indonesia, including Irian Jaya, is given in IUCN (1992). The spectacular wildlife and scenery of the protected areas of Irian Jaya are described and vividly illustrated in Cubitt, Whitten and Whitten (1992).

As in other parts of the region, a functional system of conservation areas is essential to preserve ecosystems and biodiversity. Irian Jaya is fortunate to have the design of a comprehensive protected areas system which has been approved (if not yet fully implemented) by the Indonesian Government. But what is also needed, particularly where the population relies on subsistence agriculture to meet its basic needs, is a programme to encourage local communities to manage, together with local government, conservation areas located on their traditional lands. This is one of the main areas of focus for the WWF Irian Jaya Conservation Programme.

Solomon Islands

About 87% of the land area is subject to customary or tribal tenure (IUCN 1991), and only 9% (257 km²) is state-owned land. Of this, almost all (240 km²) is committed to forestry. As a result, only 0.2% of the land area of the Solomons is legally protected within the present reserve system, and the establishment of further protected areas is difficult. Furthermore, those areas which are established as protected areas have little conservation significance. For example, the Queen Elizabeth National Park comprises roughly equal proportions of grassland and degraded secondary woodland. The best conservation practice at present is that carried out by some of the customary land-owning groups which manage areas outside of the formal protected areas system (IUCN 1991).

An action strategy for protected areas in the South Pacific region (including the Solomon Islands) has been launched by SPREP (the South Pacific Regional Environment Programme) (SPREP 1985). Among its recommendations is the need to develop a national conservation strategy and the establishment of 5 protected areas.

A review of the protected areas system and conservation legislation is given in IUCN (1992).

Centres of plant diversity and endemism

The island of New Guinea has one of the richest floras in the world and also has one of the highest levels of species endemism (see Flora section). Floristic richness in the Papuasian region decreases further eastwards.

TABLE 51. SUMMARY OF PROTECTED AREA COVERAGE IN THE SOLOMON ISLANDS

Protected area	IUCN management category	Number and comments
National Parks	Unassigned	1 (Queen Elizabeth National Park, 11 km²).
Wildlife Sanctuaries	Unassigned	1 (Arnavon, 10 km²).
Bird Sanctuaries	Unassigned	1 (Tulagi).
Forest Reserves	Unassigned	1 (Kolombangara, 5 km²).
Other unclassified areas	Unassigned	4.

Source: IUCN (1991). Note that this only includes protected areas of over 10 km², with the exception of islands of at least 1 km² where the whole island is protected.

This general pattern of species richness and endemism is reflected in the distribution of sites considered to be globally important centres of plant diversity and endemism in this present survey. Thus, 41 individual sites and larger areas of exceptional diversity (based on current floristic knowledge) are listed for the main island of New Guinea, a further 8 areas are listed for the Bismarck Archipelago, 2 for Bougainville, while the D'Entrecasteaux Islands and Louisiade Archipelago are included in their entirety as general areas exhibiting local endemism. Of these, 9 areas in New Guinea have been chosen for Data Sheet treatment (5 from Papua New Guinea and 4 from Irian Jaya, including Waigeo, one of the offshore islands).

It should be stressed that most areas are poorly known and may not have been botanically investigated. In the rest of Malesia, only Sulawesi and Sumatra have comparable low figures of collecting density of <50 collections from 100 km². Probably the only area within Papua New Guinea, where the flora could be considered adequately known, is the Pindaunde valley on Mount Wilhelm. This formed the basis of one of the first comprehensive species' lists prepared for Papua New Guinea (Johns and Stevens 1972). Foreman (1971) produced a checklist of the plants of Bougainville. A species list has also been prepared for the Watut valley (Streimann 1983) but with only 1789 flowering plant species this list is obviously incomplete. Borrell (1989) published a detailed list of the plants of Kairuru Island in the East Sepik Province. In addition, there are a number of unpublished lists for certain areas.

The *Alpine Flora of New Guinea* by van Royen (1980–1983) represents in essence a listing of the high-altitude flora (upper montane, subalpine and alpine) of New Guinea, covering only a few species from the upper montane zone, namely those that have a larger altitudinal range and occur both above and below 3000 m. Many of the higher mountains and isolated mountain ranges support very high levels of local endemism.

With the exceptions of those areas mentioned above, there are no detailed lists of species for any area in Papua New Guinea. The situation is similar for Irian Jaya, making New Guinea as a whole one of the worse-collected areas in Malesia (Stevens 1989). Areas identified by Stevens (1989) as particularly in need of collecting are the following:

❖ Limestone areas (e.g. those of New Britain and the Great Papuan Plateau).
❖ Montane zones between 1000 and 2500 m of the Irian Jaya Main Range and Pegunungan Van Rees.
❖ Baining Mountains, including Mount Birinia, south-east Gazelle Peninsula (New Britain).
❖ The Main Range between Puncak Trikora and the Star Mountains (between 139° and 141°E) (CPD Site SEA83, in part).
❖ Pegunungan Tamrau (CPD Sites SEA73/SEA74).
❖ The lowland to lower montane forests at the headwaters of the Digul and Fly rivers, the eastern branch of the Mamberamo River and the headwaters of the Sepik, May and Horden rivers are noted as of "considerable diversity", but are little collected.
❖ The northern and most extensive outcrops of the Papuan Ultramafic Belt, for example east of Garaina.

❖ Forests west of 137°E in Irian Jaya need further collecting, in part because many taxa from West Malesia reach their easternmost limits there. The area includes numerous isolated ranges that are poorly known, with the exception of the Arfak Mountains (CPD Site SEA68) which are already known to be species-rich (see Data Sheet).
❖ Hilly islands to the west of the Vogelkop Peninsula, such as Salawati (CPD Site SEA72, in part), Batanta, Waigeo (SEA71, see Data Sheet) and Gebe.

Some of these areas are already known to be exceptionally rich in species and most are likely to qualify as important centres of plant diversity and endemism as more information becomes available. Throughout the region, and on the island of New Guinea in particular, further collecting is necessary before any meaningful statements can be made about the numbers of species present and the levels of endemism at the local level.

Bearing these points in mind, the following areas are listed as centres of plant diversity and endemism, since they appear to have exceptional richness based on present field knowledge, principally that of Professor Robert Johns (Royal Botanic Gardens, Kew), Dr Peter Stevens (Harvard University Herbaria) and their colleagues. The areas listed for Papua New Guinea are those considered to be of outstanding biological diversity and are listed in the conservation needs assessment for Papua New Guinea (Johns 1992). This list was based on that which Johns prepared as Annex 6 of the Tropical Forestry Action Plan Review (World Bank 1990) under the title "Suggested Areas for Conservation/Preservation". It includes a few modifications and updates (by Johns) to that list. Between them, the areas cover all the major vegetation types in Papua New Guinea.

The sites listed for Irian Jaya can only be regarded as a very preliminary list of outstanding areas of plant diversity. This is clearly illustrated by reference to the map for New Guinea, which shows very few areas in Irian Jaya compared to neighbouring Papua New Guinea. Some sites are shown as apparently ending at the border between Papua New Guinea and Irian Jaya. This is an artefact resulting from the lack of available information about the extension of these sites into Irian Jaya. It is important to note that many more individual sites within Irian Jaya are likely to qualify for listing as CPD sites, and many would be worthy of Data Sheet treatment in their own right. Indeed, virtually every sizeable tract of native vegetation is likely to contain at least some endemic plants. It is hoped that further identification and documentation of important plant sites will be forthcoming in the near future.

Irian Jaya

The following are selected for Data Sheets treatment:

SEA68. Arfak Mountains

– see Data Sheet.

SEA69. Gunung Lorentz

– see Data Sheet.

MAP 11. CENTRES OF PLANT DIVERSITY AND ENDEMISM: PAPUASIA

CPD Data Sheet Sites

Other CPD Sites

KEY:

SEA68. Arfak Mountains (Irian Jaya)
SEA69. Gunung Lorentz (Irian Jaya)
SEA70. Mamberamo – Pegunungan Jayawijaya (Irian Jaya)
SEA71. Waigeo (Irian Jaya)
SEA72. Cagar Alam Pulau Salawati Utara (North Salawati Island Nature Reserve) (Irian Jaya)
SEA73. Pegunungan Tamrau Utara (Northern Tamrau Mountains) (Irian Jaya)
SEA74. Pegunungan Tamrau Selatan (Southern Tamrau Mountains) (Irian Jaya)
SEA75. Pegunungan Wandamen-Wondiwoi (Wandamen-Wondiwoi Mountains, Wandamen Peninsula) (Irian Jaya)
SEA76. Gunung Wagura-Kote (Mount Wagura-Kote) (Irian Jaya)
SEA77. Pegunungan Kumawa (Kumawa Mountains) (Irian Jaya)
SEA78. Pegunungan Weyland (Weyland Mountains) (Irian Jaya)
SEA79. Cagar Alam Pegunungan Cyclops (Cyclops Mountains Nature Reserve) (Irian Jaya)
SEA80. Cagar Alam Pulau Supiori (Supiori Island Nature Reserve) – Cagar Alam Pulau Numfor (proposed Numfor Island Nature Reserve) – Cagar Alam Pulau Biak Utara (North Biak Island Nature Reserve) (Irian Jaya)
SEA81. Cagar Alam Pulau Yapen Tenggah (Japen Island Nature Reserve) (Irian Jaya)
SEA82. Torricelli Mountains – Bewani Mountains – Prince Alexander Range (Papua New Guinea)
SEA83. Star Mountains – Telefomin – Tifalmin – Strickland Gorge (Papua New Guinea)
SEA84. Hunstein Range – Burgers Mountains – Schatterburg (Papua New Guinea)
SEA85. Kiunga – Palmer River – Victor Emmanuel Range (Papua New Guinea)
SEA86. Mount Giluwe – Tari Gap – Doma Peaks (Papua New Guinea)
SEA87. Kubor Ranges (Papua New Guinea)
SEA88. Adelbert Ranges (Papua New Guinea)
SEA89. Bismarck Falls – Mt Wilhelm – Mt Otto – Schrader Range – Mt Hellwig – Gahavisuka (Papua New Guinea)

SEA90. Finisterre Ranges (Papua New Guinea)
SEA91. Huon Peninsula (Mount Bangeta – Rawlinson Range; Cromwell Ranges and Sialum Terraces) (Papua New Guinea)
SEA92. Southern Fly Platform (Lake Daviumbu – Oriomo – Wassi Kussa – Tonda Wildlife Management Area) (Papua New Guinea)
SEA93. Mount Bosavi – Nomad River (Papua New Guinea)
SEA94. Tower Limestone Region: Leonard Murray Mountains – Darai Hills – Great Papuan Plateau (Papua New Guinea)
SEA95. Gulf – Ihu (Papua New Guinea)
SEA96. Mount Michael – Okapa – Crater Mountain (Papua New Guinea)
SEA97. Galley Reach (Papua New Guinea)
SEA98. Menyamya – Aseki – Amungwiwa – Bowutu Mountains – Lasanga Island (Papua New Guinea)
SEA99. Milne Bay – Collinwood Bay to southern coast (Papua New Guinea)
SEA100. Owen Stanley Mountains (Papua New Guinea)
SEA101. Varirata and Astrolabe Ranges (Papua New Guinea)
SEA102. Safia Savanna (Papua New Guinea)
SEA103. Topographer's Range (Papua New Guinea)
SEA104. Lake Wanum – Red Hill Swamp – Oomsis Ridge (Papua New Guinea)
SEA105. Porgera Peaks (Papua New Guinea)
SEA106. Gogol – Sogeron Headwaters (Papua New Guinea)
SEA107. Lower Watut (Papua New Guinea)
SEA108. Cloud Mountains (Papua New Guinea)
SEA109. Willaumez Peninsula – Lake Dakataua (Bismarck Archipelago)
SEA110. Whiteman Range to southern coast of New Britain (Bismarck Archipelago)
SEA111. Nakanai Mountains (Bismarck Archipelago)
SEA112. Mounts Sinewit and Burringa (Bismarck Archipelago)
SEA113. Hans Meyer Range (Bismarck Archipelago)
SEA114. Southern Namatanai (Bismarck Archipelago)
SEA115. Schleinitz Range – Lelet Plateau (Bismarck Archipelago)
SEA116. Central Manus – Mount Dremsel (Bismarck Archipelago)
SEA117. Mount Balbi to southern coast (Bougainville)
SEA118. Mount Takuan – Tonolei Harbour (Bougainville)
SEA119. D'Entrecasteaux Islands (D'Entrecasteaux Islands)
SEA120. Louisiade Archipelago (D'Entrecasteaux Islands)

SEA70. Mamberamo – Pegunungan Jayawijaya

– see Data Sheet.

SEA71. Waigeo

– see Data Sheet.

In addition, on the basis of present (very incomplete) botanical knowledge, the following areas are identified as centres of plant endemism and diversity:

SEA72. Cagar Alam Pulau Salawati Utara (North Salawati Island Nature Reserve)

A small isolated mountain block in the north of Salawati Island between latitudes 0°54'–1°14'S and longitudes 130°03'–130°39'E. Area: 570 km². Altitude: 0–931 m.
- ❖ Vegetation: Lowland and lower montane rain forests.
- ❖ Flora: The island is a meeting point of Moluccan and New Guinean lowland floras; this is elsewhere heavily threatened as a result of high population density.
- ❖ Threats: Logging, road building, transmigration settlement (though subsequently this was halted) (Petocz 1983) and gravel extraction.
- ❖ Conservation: Nature Reserve (IUCN Management Category: I).

SEA73. Pegunungan Tamrau Utara (Northern Tamrau Mountains)

Area: 2657 km². Altitude: Sea-level to c. 3000 m.
- ❖ Vegetation: Coastal to montane forests, with montane shrubberies and podzol vegetation at higher altitudes.
- ❖ Flora: The Kebar Valley and southern slopes of the Tamrau block appear to have very diverse vegetation and a high degree of local endemism.
- ❖ Threats: Logging, firewood cutting, with shifting cultivation along the coast.
- ❖ Conservation: Proposed Nature Reserve.

SEA74. Pegunungan Tamrau Selatan (Southern Tamrau Mountains)

A mountain block occupying the centre of the Vogelkop, south and west of the Sorong and Ransiki Fault Zones, between latitudes 0°47'–1°19'S and longitudes 132°48'–133°34'E. The underlying geology includes argillaceous sediments, limestones, intrusive plutonic rocks, shales and slates. Area: 2479 km². Altitude: 300–2842 m.
- ❖ Vegetation: Lowland, lower montane and montane forest predominantly of conifers and Myrtaceae.
- ❖ Flora: Virtually unknown, but suspected to be very rich.
- ❖ Threats: Primary forests not threatened at present. Very low human population density.
- ❖ Conservation: Proposed Nature Reserve.

SEA75. Pegunungan Wandamen-Wondiwoi (Wandamen-Wondiwoi Mountains, Wandamen Peninsula)

Area: 795 km², located between latitudes 2°27'–3°05'S and longitudes 134°28'–134°41'E. Altitude: 0–2220 m.
- ❖ Vegetation: Lowland to mid-montane forests on a wide variation of base rocks. The forests protect the fishery resources of Cenderawasih Bay; these form the basis of the local economy (Petocz 1983; Gilkes and Adipati 1987).
- ❖ Flora: The area contains local and Vogelkop endemics.
- ❖ Threats: Some forested areas were damaged by a fire in 1982, particularly the slopes above Wandamen Bay and those on the east and west of the central mountain spine (Diamond *et al.* 1983). The area has been considered for mining development.
- ❖ Conservation: Proposed Nature Reserve, contiguous with Cagar Alam Cenderawasih (Cenderawasih Nature Reserve). An area to the south is also of interest and should be included.

SEA76. Gunung Wagura-Kote (Mount Wagura-Kote)

Located between Teluk Bintuni and Teluk Arguni, to the south-west of the narrow isthmus connecting the Vogelkop Peninsula to the mainland, between latitudes 2°41'–2°53'S and longitudes 133°46'–133°53'E. Area: 150 km². Altitude: 50–1134 m (summit of Gunung Kote).
- ❖ Vegetation: Important lowland *Agathis-Araucaria* coniferous forest complex on acid sands below 100 m altitude. This type of vegetation is usually associated with higher altitudes. The forest includes dipterocarps, such as *Hopea* spp., as well as montane genera, such as *Rhododendron*, *Vaccinium* and *Zygogynum* (*Bubbia*) which descend almost to sea-level.
- ❖ Threats: Logging.
- ❖ Conservation: Proposed Nature Reserve.

SEA77. Pegunungan Kumawa (Kumawa Mountains)

A small, rugged, uninhabited limestone block in the south of the Vogelkop Peninsula, located between latitudes 3°41'–4°07'S and longitudes 132°48'–133°21'E. Area: 1180 km². Altitude: 0–1432 m.
- ❖ Vegetation: Coastal vegetation, lowland, lower montane and montane forests on limestone, bordered by *Melaleuca* swamps in the north.
- ❖ Flora: No detailed botanical surveys have been made.
- ❖ Threats: Logging.
- ❖ Conservation: Proposed Nature Reserve; if implemented, this area (along with Pulau Supiori) would be among the few lowland limestone areas in the reserve system.

SEA78. Pegunungan Weyland (Weyland Mountains)

An isolated mountain range west of Paniai Lakes. Area: 2230 km². Altitude: 900–3892 m.
- ❖ Vegetation: Montane to subalpine vegetation.
- ❖ Flora: Virtually unknown but probably highly diverse; a meeting point of the floras of the Eastern Cordillera and the western mid-mountains. In need of botanical exploration.
- ❖ Threats: Not seriously threatened at present.
- ❖ Conservation: Proposed Nature Reserve.

SEA79. Cagar Alam Pegunungan Cyclops (Cyclops Mountains Nature Reserve)

Area: 225 km². Altitude: 90–2160 m.
* ❖ Vegetation: A small isolated mountain range with varied lowland to montane forests, including *Araucaria*. A dense and stunted forest occurs on ultramafic soils in the north-east, at Cape Tanah Merak and, to a lesser extent, in the south-east. High-altitude moss forest includes stunted *Nothofagus flaviramea*. Forests important for protection of major water catchment for Jayapura and as a basis for ecotourism.
* ❖ Flora: Many local endemics.
* ❖ Threats: Agricultural encroachment on southern and eastern boundaries; collecting of orchids; potential mining of nickel and marble.
* ❖ Conservation: Nature Reserve (IUCN Management Category: I).

SEA80. Cagar Alam Pulau Supiori (Supiori Island Nature Reserve) – Cagar Alam Pulau Numfor (proposed Numfor Island Nature Reserve) – Cagar Alam Pulau Biak Utara (North Biak Island Nature Reserve)

Islands of the Schouten Islands group in Cenderawasih Bay, northern Irian Jaya.

Cagar Alam Pulau Biak Utara is located between latitudes 0°42'–0°48' and longitudes 135°48'–135°55'E, and covers 110 km² of the island. Altitude ranges from sea-level to 695 m in the reserve.

Biak is the most densely populated of the Irian Jaya islands, and a considerable amount of land has been converted to agriculture. There are, however, remnants of lowland rain forest, and these are also important for birds. Some 82 species of bird have been recorded from the reserve of which 7 are endemic (McCarthy 1991).
* ❖ Threats: Logging, agricultural encroachment and poaching of forest species (Petocz 1983).

Cagar Alam Pulau Supiori covers 445 km² and is located between latitudes 0°37–0°47'S and longitudes 135°21'–135°49'E. Altitude ranges from sea-level to 1034 m (summit of Gunung Bonsupiori). Together with the Kumawa Mountains, this is one of the few lowland limestone areas in Irian Jaya's reserve system.
* ❖ Vegetation: coastal to lower montane forests of high interest because they are isolated from the mainland. The flora, however, is almost unknown. The island is also important for its avifauna, with 82 species expected to occur of which 9 are endemic (McCarthy 1991).
* ❖ Threats: logging (W. Vink 1992, *in litt.*) and some agricultural clearance by local villagers (Silvius 1989).

Pulau Numfor is the westernmost island of the Schouten Islands group. The proposed Nature Reserve covers 15 km² and is located between latitudes 0°59'–1°02'S and longitudes 134°50'–134°52'E. Altitude ranges from 100 to 200 m. There are remnants of primary lowland rain forest with several endemic trees. The forests are also important for birds: 52 bird species have been recorded, including several endemic to the Schouten Islands (McCarthy 1991).

SEA81. Cagar Alam Pulau Yapen Tenggah (Japen Island Nature Reserve)

A mountainous tilted fault block with varied lithology, including magmatites, metamorphic rocks and limestones. Area: 590 km². Altitude: 500–1496 m.
* ❖ Vegetation: Lowland, lower montane and mid-montane forests, including ultramafic vegetation. Forests important for watershed protection.
* ❖ Flora: Local endemics in both conifer and broadleaved forests.
* ❖ Threats: Logging, firewood cutting, shifting cultivation.
* ❖ Conservation: Nature Reserve (IUCN Management Category: I).

Papua New Guinea

(Based on Johns 1992.)

SEA82. Torricelli Mountains – Bewani Mountains – Prince Alexander Range (East and West Sepik Provinces)

Altitude: 0–2000 m.
* ❖ Vegetation: Limestone forest, which extends to the north coast where limestone communities are adjacent to coastal rain forest; lowland rain forest; montane forest.
* ❖ Flora: Estimated >2000 vascular plant species. It includes the known distribution of the only endemic genus of ferns in New Guinea, which is monotypic: *Rheopteris cheesmannii*. This is found on the limestone. Further botanical study is required in the area.
* ❖ Conservation: Listed in the Forestry Action Plan Review (World Bank 1990) as a potential World Heritage Site.

SEA83. Star Mountains – Telefomin – Tifalmin – Strickland Gorge (East and West Sepik Provinces, Western Province)

Altitude: 1800–3500 m.
* ❖ Vegetation: Very rich montane and high-altitude vegetation.
* ❖ Flora: Estimated >3000 vascular plant species; many species in common with Irian Jaya.
* ❖ Conservation: No formal protection; considerable potential for ecotourism. The low population means that extensive areas of lower montane forest could be preserved in this area. (See Kalkman 1963; Moi and Johns 1977.)

SEA84. Hunstein Range – Burgers Mountains – Schatterburg (East Sepik Province, Enga Province)

Altitude: 0–2000 m.
* ❖ Vegetation: Extensive stands of *Agathis labillardieri* (kauri pine) which support a rich epiphytic flora.

❖ Flora: Estimated >2500 vascular plant species; virtually unknown botanically.

SEA85. Kiunga – Palmer River – Victor Emmanuel Range (Western Province)

A very diverse area of lowland rain forest with lower montane elements such as *Podocarpus* and *Lithocarpus*. It includes significant numbers of species in common with Irian Jaya. Generally poorly known.

SEA86. Mount Giluwe – Tari Gap – Doma Peaks (Southern Highlands Province, Enga Province)

– see Data Sheet.

SEA87. Kubor Ranges (Simbu Province, Western Highlands Province)

An extensive area of high-altitude (to 3969 m) vegetation, much on limestone capped with volcanic ash. A fragile ecosystem likely to contain local endemics. The area is poorly known. (See Smith 1972.)

SEA88. Adelbert Ranges (Madang Province)

Altitude: 0–1800 m.
❖ Flora: Poorly known; estimated >2000 vascular plant species.
❖ Threats: Local village gardening activities. The area has received considerable disturbance from earthquakes. Requires urgent appraisal. (See Johns 1986.)

SEA89. Bismarck Falls (Ramu to Bundi) – Mt Wilhelm – Mt Otto – Schrader Range – Mt Hellwig – Gahavisuka (Madang, Eastern and Western Provinces)

– see Data Sheet.

SEA90. Finisterre Ranges (Madang Province)

The Finisterres consist of a narrow steep-sided ridge of limestone. Important high-altitude forests. Altitude: 0–3917 m (summit of Mount Finisterre).

SEA91. Huon Peninsula (Mount Bangeta – Rawlinson Range; Cromwell Ranges and Sialum Terraces) (Morobe Province)

– see Data Sheet.

SEA92. Southern Fly Platform (Lake Daviumbu – Oriomo – Wassi Kussa – Tonda Wildlife Management Area) (Western Province)

– see Data Sheet.

SEA93. Mount Bosavi – Nomad River (Western and Southern Highlands Provinces)

Mount Bosavi is an isolated volcanic mountain. Altitude: 2000–3000 m.
❖ Vegetation: Lowland rain forests dominated by *Hopea celtidifolia* and *Vatica rassak*; lower montane forest. Diverse lowland forest, little known. M. Coode (pers. comm.) notes that nearly all specimens from Bosavi are "tiresomely different" without actually being distinct.
❖ Flora: Estimated >3000 vascular plant species; local endemic trees, such as *Gnetum* spp. Important area for traditional edible and medicinal plants.
❖ Threats: Clearance for agriculture, logging in dipterocarp forests.

SEA94. Tower Limestone Region: Leonard Murray Mountains – Darai Hills – Great Papuan Plateau (Gulf and Southern Highlands Provinces)

Altitude: 0–1500 m.
❖ Vegetation: Includes a large area of tower limestone, with individual towers over 200–400 m tall, each capped with limestone rain forest.
❖ Flora: Botanically unexplored. The limestone can be predicted to have an endemic-rich flora. Detailed studies are needed.

SEA95. Gulf – Ihu (Gulf Province)

❖ Vegetation: A very diverse area of mangrove and swamp vegetation, with lowland rain forest on small limestone hills.
❖ Flora: The limestone evidently supports many local endemics, but the area is virtually unknown botanically. The area includes numerous species of *Pandanus* and has a rich palm flora, including many species of *Calamus*.
❖ Threats: Some logging.

SEA96. Mount Michael – Okapa – Crater Mountain (Simbu and Eastern Highlands Province)

Altitude: 300–650 m.
❖ Vegetation: An important area of lower montane forest, including *Araucaria* and *Castanopsis* forest and mixed lower montane forest. Useful plants include *Araucaria cunninghamii* (hoop pine) and *A. hunsteinii* (klinki pine), oaks, traditional medicinal and food plants, nutmeg and traditional spirit trees.
❖ Flora: Estimated >2000 vascular plant species.
❖ Threats: Potential threats from logging, traditional agriculture and expansion of subsistence coffee areas. The area is used for traditional hunting of Raggiana bird-of-paradise for sale and trade.
❖ Conservation: Not protected except by traditional owners.

SEA97. Galley Reach (Central Province)

Altitude: 0–30 m.
❖ Vegetation: Coastal mangrove, *Nypa* and lowland swamp

forest, coastal scrub. Mangrove communities reach their greatest diversity in Papuasia, and Galley Reach contains most of the species.
- ❖ Flora: Estimated 1000–1500 vascular plant species.
- ❖ Threats: Firewood collecting, tourism; logging potential due to accessibility from Port Moresby. (See Johnstone and Frodin 1982.)

SEA98. Menyamya – Aseki – Amungwiwa – Bowutu Mountains – Lasanga Island (Morobe District)

– see Data Sheet.

SEA99. Milne Bay – Collinwood Bay to southern coast (Milne Bay Province)

An important area of lowland rain forest, rising to 3676 m at Mount Suckling, 2980 m at Mount Simpson and 2880 m at Mount Dayman. Also included are important areas of lowland rain forest in Collinwood Bay and on the southern coast (see Brass 1956; Stevens and Veldkamp 1980). Mount Suckling has a number of narrow endemics, such as *Oreomyrrhis plicata* which is restricted to exposed ultramafic rocks (P.F. Stevens 1992, *in litt.*).

SEA100. Owen Stanley Mountains (Northern and Central Provinces)

This area includes all the high-altitude (upper montane) areas from 1600 m to the summits of the mountains along the chain from Mount Albert Edward and Victoria to Mount Suckling and Mount Dayman. Altitude: 1600–3500 m.
- ❖ Flora: Estimated >4000 vascular plant species; many local endemics. The Owen Stanley Mountains are also the centre of diversity of *Agapetes* (subgenus *Paphia*). (See Brass 1956; Coode and Stevens 1972; Paijmans and Löffler 1972.)
- ❖ Conservation: Area identified in the Tropical Forestry Action Plan Review (World Bank 1990) as a potential World Heritage Site.

SEA101. Varirata and Astrolabe Ranges (Central Province)

- ❖ Conservation: Includes Varirata National Park (10.6 km²) (IUCN Management Category: II). Requires more detailed botanical study.

SEA102. Safia Savanna (Northern Province)

A little known area of savanna to the north of the Owen Stanley Mountains.

SEA103. Topographer's Range (Northern Province)

A little known region of lowland rain forest to the north of the Owen Stanley Range. (See for example Paijmans 1970; Taylor 1957, 1959.)

SEA104. Lake Wanum – Red Hill Swamp – Oomsis Ridge (Morobe Province)

Grasslands surrounding Lake Wanum, swamp vegetation including swamp forest dominated by *Alstonia spatulata* at Red Hill swamp, ridge forest on Oomsis Ridge with considerable genetic variation in local populations of *Anisoptera thurifera* var. *polyandra*.

SEA105. Porgera Peaks (Enga Province)

A high-altitude plateau above 3000 m. No collections known from this area.

SEA106. Gogol – Sogeron Headwaters (Madang Province)

An important area of lowland forest requiring further study; many local endemics suspected to occur in upper catchments. (See Johns 1975; Saulei and Swaine 1988.)

SEA107. Lower Watut (Morobe Province)

A little known area of lowland swamp and rain forests, with populations of the endemic root parasite *Langsdorfia papuana*, a genus otherwise known only from Madagascar and Central and South America. Some mining is occurring in the area.

SEA108. Cloud Mountains (Milne Bay Province)

The most southerly montane area in Papua New Guinea. No collections are known from the area. Needs urgent study.

Papua New Guinea – Bismarck Archipelago

SEA109. Willaumez Peninsula – Lake Dakataua (West New Britain Province)

Altitude: 0–1155 m.
- ❖ Vegetation: A very diverse area, including lowland rain forest on recent, rich volcanic soils. High landscape quality; potential as a major tourist attraction.
- ❖ Flora: Estimated >2000 vascular plant species. Detailed botanical surveys needed to ascertain the diversity of the flora throughout the area.
- ❖ Threats: Logging and proposed development of oil palm plantations. (See Arentz *et al.* 1989.)

SEA110. Whiteman Range to southern coast of New Britain (West New Britain Province)

Estimated >3000 vascular plant species. Altitude: 0–2000 m.
- ❖ Vegetation: Together with their foothills, the Whiteman Mountains are an important area for limestone flora, surrounded by forests developed on sedimentary deposits. Extensive *Nothofagus* forests occur on the higher plateaux. Further botanical exploration required. (See Arentz *et al.* 1989.)

SEA111. Nakanai Mountains (East New Britain Province)

Altitude: 0–1900 m. (The most extensive high-altitude area in the Bismarck Archipelago.)
- ❖ Vegetation: Lowland rain forest and montane forest, including areas dominated by *Lithocarpus* and *Nothofagus* on limestone.
- ❖ Flora: Estimated >2500 vascular plant species. A little known area requiring more detailed studies. (See Clunie 1976; Arentz *et al.* 1989.)
- ❖ Threats: Logging; agricultural development.

SEA112. Mounts Sinewit and Burringa (East New Britain Province)

High-altitude mountains on the Gazelle Peninsula. Altitude: to 2438 m (summit of Mount Sinewit).
- ❖ Flora: Poorly known; historical collections, but no recent field investigations.

SEA113. Hans Meyer Range (New Ireland Province)

Altitude: 0–2399 m.
- ❖ Vegetation: Lowland and montane vegetation, including stands of *Terminalia brassii*.
- ❖ Flora: Estimated >2000 vascular plant species. Further botanical surveys needed.

SEA114. Southern Namatanai (New Ireland Province)

- ❖ Vegetation: Diverse hill and lowland rain forests; lower montane forest.
- ❖ Threats: Lowlands threatened by logging.

SEA115. Schleinitz Range – Lelet Plateau (New Ireland Province)

Altitude: 200–1500 m.
- ❖ Vegetation: Representative areas of New Ireland hill and lowland rain forests, with some lower montane elements on the Lelet Plateau.
- ❖ Flora: Estimated >1500 vascular plant species. The area is poorly known but is probably quite rich and is likely to contain many endemics. Biogeographical relationships with Manus, the Philippines and Solomon Islands. Requires more botanical studies.
- ❖ Threats: Lowlands threatened by logging.

SEA116. Central Manus – Mount Dremsel (Manus Province)

The area includes the central part of Manus Island in the Admiralty Islands group. Altitude: 0–719 m.
- ❖ Vegetation: An area from Mount Dremsel to the northern coast includes unique *Calophyllum* forests and requires further study and protection.
- ❖ Flora: Estimated >1500 vascular plant species. Important stands of 2 endemic *Calophyllum* species (both of which are of economic importance) and *Sararanga*. The island has several endemic species, including an undescribed

species of *Dillenia* which is apparently a food plant for the endemic green land snail *Papustyla pulcherrima*. (See Johns 1989a.)
- ❖ Threats: Logging.

Papua New Guinea – Bougainville

SEA117. Mount Balbi to southern coast

Altitude: 0–2743 m, Bougainville's highest mountain.
- ❖ Vegetation: Includes the largest stands of bamboo forest in Papuasia; other vegetation types include remnant stands of *Terminalia brassii*.
- ❖ Threats: Logging; possibly sulphur mining.

SEA118. Mount Takuan – Tonolei Harbour

Altitude: 0–2210 m.
- ❖ Vegetation: Natural stands of the economically important species *Terminalia brassii*.
- ❖ Flora: Estimated >1000 vascular plant species, with a large Pacific element.

Papua New Guinea – D'Entrecasteaux Islands (Milne Bay Province)

SEA119. D'Entrecasteaux Islands

Altitude: 0–2500 m.
- ❖ Flora: Estimated >2500 vascular plant species; the island chain includes many locally endemic species.
- ❖ Conservation: It is recommended in the Tropical Forestry Action Plan Review (World Bank 1990) that all areas over 700–1000 m altitude on the islands of Goodenough, Normanby and Fergusson should be protected. These islands are of outstanding scientific interest with many plants represented at lower altitudes than on the mainland. This is due to the Massenerhebung effect whereby smaller mountains and outliers are cooler at any given altitude than large mountains or the central parts of large ranges.

Papua New Guinea – Louisiade Archipelago (Milne Bay Province)

SEA120. Louisiade Archipelago

Altitude: 0–2200 m.
- ❖ Flora: Estimated >3000 vascular plant species, with high rates of local endemism, particularly at the species level. Includes important stands of endemic ebony *Diospyros* (2 undescribed species) and several locally endemic species of *Hopea*. Many other local endemics are known, e.g. Misima has some endemic *Pandanus* and ant-plants; Tagula and Rossel have locally endemic *Cyrtosperma*. There are several species with commercial potential for establishment of forest plantations. The flora has affinities with that of New Caledonia.

❖ Threats: Gold mining on Misima, copper mining, logging.
❖ Conservation: Area identified by Tropical Forestry Action Plan Review (World Bank 1990) as a potential World Heritage Site.

In addition to those areas listed above, Stevens (1989) lists the following as "particularly high in endemics":

❖ **Pegunungan Maoke** (Irian Jaya).
❖ **Headwaters of the Fly and Sepik rivers** (Papua New Guinea).
❖ **Lake Kutubu** (Papua New Guinea).

Areas of botanical interest

It should be emphasized that many distinctive vegetation types and plants with restricted distributions occur outside of the areas listed above but are, nevertheless, important to conserve. The following are examples:

❖ **Woodlark Island**, a raised coral atoll to the north-east of D'Entrecasteaux, has a slightly depauperate flora but contains several endemics (including two undescribed species of *Diospyros*). The southern peninsula of Woodlark Island includes the most diverse forests and contains most of the island's endemics. Threats: logging.
❖ **Forest dominated by *Dacrydium nidulum* var. *araucoides*** occurs in a small area of grassland plains south of Mendi in Papua New Guinea (Johns 1980). Similar stands which once occurred in the Tari region have been extensively logged. The extant stand in the Mendi region deserves protection.
❖ **Remnant stands of *Eucalyptus deglupta*** on New Britain are also worthy of protection.

All the above areas deserve protection, and more fieldwork and collecting programmes are urgently required to document the biodiversity of each.

References

Abang H.K. Morshidi and Gumal, M.T. (1992). Role of totally protected areas in protecting biological diversity in Sarawak. Paper prepared for the International Workshop on Ecology, Conservation, and Management of the Southeast Asian Rainforests, Kuching, Sarawak, 12–14 October 1992.

Altoveros, N.C., Rosario, B.P. del, Sanico, A.L. and Santos, M.T.F. (1989). Country report Philippines. In Siemonsma, J.S. and Wulijarni-Soetjipto, N. (eds), *Plant resources of South-East Asia. Proceedings of the First PROSEA International Symposium, May 22–25, 1989, Jakarta, Indonesia*. Pudoc, Wageningen. Pp. 201–205.

Anderson, J.A.R. (1961). *The ecology and forest types of the peat swamp forests of Sarawak and Brunei in relation to their silviculture*. Ph.D. thesis, University of Edinburgh, Edinburgh. 117 pp.

Anderson, J.A.R. (1963). The flora of the peat swamp forests of Sarawak and Brunei, including a catalogue of all recorded species. *Gard. Bull. Singapore* 20: 131–228.

Anderson, J.A.R. (1983). The tropical peat swamps of western Malesia. In Gore, A.J.P. (ed.), *Mires: swamp, bog, fen and moor*. Ecosystems of the World 14, Part B. Elsevier, Amsterdam. Pp. 181–199.

Anderson, J.A.R. and Marsden, D. (1984). *Brunei forest resources and strategic planning study. Final report*, 2 vols. (Unpublished report to the Government of His Majesty the Sultan and Yang Di-Pertuan of Negara Brunei Darussalam. Vol. 1: *The forest resources of Negara Brunei Darussalam*; vol. 2: *Strategic planning for the forests and forest resources*.)

Anderson, J.A.R. and Marsden, D. (1988). *Brunei forest resources and strategic planning study*. (Unpublished report to the Government of His Majesty the Sultan and Yang Di-Pertuan of Negara Brunei Darussalam.)

Arentz, F. (1992). Low impact logging – helicopter logging in Papua New Guinea. *Tropical Forest Management Update* 2(6): 6.

Arentz, F., Johns, R., Matcham, E. and Simaga, J. (1989). *The vegetation of central New Britain*. Consultancy report for Department of Environment and Conservation, Port Moresby.

Ashton, P.S. (1964a). *A manual of the dipterocarp trees of Brunei State*. Oxford University Press, Oxford.

Ashton, P.S. (1964b). Ecological studies in the mixed dipterocarp forests of Brunei State. *Oxford Forestry Memoirs* 25. Clarendon Press, Oxford. 75 pp.

Ashton, P.S. (1971). The plants and vegetation of Bako National Park. *Malay. Nat. J.*, 24(3–4): 151–162.

Ashton, P.S. (1982). Dipterocarpaceae. *Flora Malesiana* 9(2): 552 pp.

Ashton, P.S. (1989). Sundaland. In Campbell, D.G. and Hammond, H.D. (eds), *Floristic inventory in tropical countries: the status of plant systematics, collections, and vegetation, plus recommendations for the future*. The New York Botanical Garden, New York. Pp. 91–99.

Ashton, P.S. (1990). Plant conservation in the Malaysian region. Paper prepared for the Symposium on the State of Nature Conservation in Malaysia, Kuala Lumpur, 24–26 August 1990.

Axelrod, D.I. and Raven, P.H. (1982). Paleobiogeography and origin of the New Guinea flora. In J.L. Gressitt (ed.), *Biogeography and ecology of New Guinea*, Vol. 2. Junk, The Hague. Pp. 919–941.

Baas, P., Kalkman, K. and Geesink, R. (eds) (1990). *The plant diversity of Malesia. Proceedings of the Flora Malesiana Symposium commemorating Professor Dr. C.G.G.J. van Steenis, Leiden, August 1989*. Kluwer Academic Press, Dordrecht. 420 pp.

Backer, C.A. and Bakhuizen van den Brink, R.C. (1963-1968). *Flora of Java (Spermatophytes only)*, 3 vols. Noordhoff (Vols 1, 2) and Wolters-Noordhoff, Groningen.

Balgooy, M.M.J, van (1987). A plant geographical analysis of Sulawesi. In Whitmore, T.C. (ed.), *Biogeographic evolution in the Malay archipelago.* Clarendon Press and Oxford University Press, New York and London. Pp. 94–102.

Beaman, R.S., Beaman, J.H., Marsh, C.W. and Woods, P.V. (1985). Drought and forest fires in Sabah in 1983. *Sabah Society Journal* 8(1): 10–30.

Beer, J.H. de and McDermott, M.J. (1989). *The economic value of non-timber forest products in Southeast Asia with emphasis on Indonesia, Malaysia and Thailand.* Netherlands Committee for IUCN, Amsterdam. 175 pp.

Bompard, J.M. (1988). *Wild Mangifera species in Kalimantan (Indonesia) and in Malaysia.* Report prepared for IBPGR and IUCN-WWF.

Borrell, O.W. (1989). *An annotated checklist of the flora of Kairuru Island, New Guinea.* Victoria, Australia.

Brass, L.J. (1938). Notes on the vegetation of the Fly and Wassi Kussa rivers, British New Guinea. *J. Arnold Arboretum* 19: 190, 221–223.

Brass, L.J. (1956). Results of the Archbold expeditions No. 75. Summary of the fourth Archbold expedition to New Guinea 1953. *Bull. Amer. Mus. Nat. Hist.* 111: 77–152.

Brünig, E.F. (1969). Forest classification in Sarawak. *Malay. For.* 32(2): 143–179.

Brünig, E.F. (1973). Species richness and stand diversity in relation to site and succession of forests in Sarawak and Brunei (Borneo). *Amazoniana* 4(3): 293–320.

Brünig, E.F. (1989). Oligotrophic forested wetlands in Borneo. In Lugo, A.E., Brinson, M. and Brown, S. (eds), *Forested wetlands.* Ecosystems of the World 15. Elsevier, Amsterdam. Pp. 299–334.

Brünig, E.F. (1991). Kerangas and kerapah forests of Sarawak. In Kiew, R. (ed.), *The state of nature conservation in Malaysia.* Malayan Nature Society, Kuala Lumpur. Pp. 29–41.

Bureau of Forest Development (1982). *Philippine forestry statistics 1982.* Bureau of Forest Development.

Burkill, I.H. (1966). *A dictionary of the economic products of the Malay Peninsula.* 2nd Edition. 2 vols. Ministry of Agriculture, Kuala Lumpur.

Chin, S.C. (1977). The limestone hill flora of Malaya I. *Gard. Bull. Singapore* 30: 165–219.

Chin, S.C. (1979). The limestone hill flora of Malaya II. *Gard. Bull. Singapore* 32: 64–203.

Chung, K.S. (1987). *Estimating the demand curves of Bako, Niah and Lambir Hills National Parks of Sarawak.* Forestry Department, Kuching, Sarawak.

Clunie, N.M.U. (1976). *Botanical and ecological survey of the Nakanai Plateau, New Britain.* Ecol. Progress Report No. 2. Division of Botany, Department of Forests, Lae, Papua New Guinea.

Collins, N.M., Sayer, J.A. and Whitmore, T.C. (eds) (1991). *The conservation atlas of tropical forests: Asia and the Pacific.* Macmillan, London. 256 pp.

Coode, M.J.E. and Stevens, P.F. (1972). Notes on the flora of two Papuan mountains. *Papua New Guinea Sci. Soc. Proc.* 23: 18–25.

Cubitt, G. and Payne, J. (1990). *Wild Malaysia: the wildlife and scenery of Peninsular Malaysia, Sarawak and Sabah.* New Holland, London and WWF Malaysia. 208 pp.

Cubitt, G., Whitten, T. and Whitten, J. (1992). *Wild Indonesia: the wildlife and scenery of the Indonesian archipelago.* New Holland, London. 208 pp.

Davidson, J. (1987). *Conservation planning in Indonesia's transmigration programme: case studies from Kalimantan.* IUCN, Gland, Switzerland and Cambridge, U.K. 136 pp.

Diamond, J.M. (1976). *A proposed natural reserve system for Papua New Guinea.* 16 pp. (Unpublished report.)

Diamond, J.M., Irwanto, A., Kayoi, A., Rumboirusi, K., Ratcliffe, J., Sadsuitubun, F. and Samangun, A. (1983). *Surveys of five proposed reserves in Irian Jaya, Indonesia: Kumawa Mountains, Wandamen Mountains, Yapen Island, Salawati Island, and Bantanta Island, July–October 1983.* WWF Indonesia, Jayapura. Pp. 21–29. (Unpublished report.)

Dransfield, J. (1979). *A manual of the rattans of the Malay Peninsula.* Forest Department, Malaysia.

Dransfield, J. (1981). The biology of Asiatic rattans in relation to the rattan trade and conservation. In Synge, H. (ed.), *The biological aspects of rare plant conservation.* Wiley, London. Pp. 179–186.

Dransfield, J. (1990). Outstanding problems in Malesian palms. In Baas, P., Kalkman, K. and Geesink, R. (eds), *The plant diversity of Malesia. Proceedings of the Flora Malesiana Symposium commemorating Professor Dr. C.G.G.J. van Steenis, Leiden, August 1989.* Kluwer Academic Press, Dordrecht. Pp. 17–25.

Dransfield, J. (1992). Traditional uses of rattan. In Wan Razali Wan Mohd., Dransfield, J. and Manokaran, N. (eds), *A guide to the cultivation of rattan.* Malayan Forest Record No. 35. Forest Research Institute Malaysia, Kepong, Kuala Lumpur. Pp. 47–49.

Dransfield, J., Kirkup, D. and Coode, M. (1993). Brunei and biodiversity – the Kew-Brunei checklist project. Paper prepared for the Conference on "Tropical Rainforest Research: Current Issues", Bandar Seri Begawan, Brunei Darussalam, 9–17 April 1993.

Dransfield, J. and Manokaran, N. (eds) (1993). *Rattans.* Pudoc, Wageningen.

Dransfield, J., Mogea, J.P. and Manokaran, N. (1989). Rattans. In Siemonsma, J.S. and Wulijarni-Soetjipto, N. (eds), *Plant resources of South-East Asia. Proceedings of the First PROSEA International Symposium, May 22–25, 1989, Jakarta, Indonesia.* Pudoc, Wageningen. Pp. 130–141.

Eaton, P. (1985). Land tenure and conservation: protected areas in the South Pacific. *SPREP Topic Review* No. 17. South Pacific Commission, Noumea, New Caledonia. 103 pp.

Europa Publications (1987). *The Far East and Australasia 1988.* 19th edition. Europa, London. 1015 pp.

FAO (1981-1982). *National Conservation Plan for Indonesia.* 8 vols. Field report of UNDP/FAO National Parks Development Project INS/78/061. FAO, Bogor, Indonesia. (1 – Introduction; 2 – Sumatra; 3 – Java and Bali; 4 – Lesser Sunda Islands; 5 – Kalimantan; 6 – Sulawesi; 7 – Maluku; 8 – General topics.)

FAO (1982). *Tropical forest resources.* FAO Forestry Paper No. 30. FAO, Rome.

FAO (1987). *Special study on forest management, afforestation and utilization of forest resources in the developing regions. Asia-Pacific region. Assessment of forest resources in six countries.* FAO, Bangkok. 104 pp.

FAO (1988a). *An interim report on the state of forest resources in the developing countries.* FAO, Rome. 18 pp.

FAO (1988b). *FAO yearbook of forestry products, 1975–1986.* FAO, Rome.

FAO/UNEP (1981). *Tropical forest resources assessment project (in the framework of the Global Environment Monitoring System – GEMS).* UN 32/6.1301-78-04. Technical Report 3: *Forest Resources of Tropical Asia.* FAO, Rome. 475 pp.

Foreman, D.B. (1971). *A check list of the vascular plants of Bougainville with descriptions of some common forest trees.* Botany Bulletin 5, Division of Botany, Department of Forests, Lae, Papua New Guinea. 194 pp.

Forest Management Bureau (1988). *Natural forest resources of the Philippines. Philippine-German Forest Resources Inventory Project.* Forest Management Bureau, Department of Environment and Natural Resources, Manila, Philippines. 62 pp.

Forestry Department (1990). *Forest conservation and management practices.* (Paper produced by the Forestry Department, Malaysia.)

Gagne, W.C. and Gressitt, J.L. (1982). Conservation in New Guinea. In Gressitt, J.L. (ed.), *Biogeography and ecology of New Guinea,* vol. 2. Junk, The Hague. Pp. 945–966.

Ganapin, J.D. (1987). Forest resources and timber trade in the Philippines. In *Proceedings of the Conference in Forest Resources Crisis in the Third World, 6–8 September 1986, Kuala Lumpur, Malaysia.* Sahabat Alam Malaysia. Pp. 54–70.

Gilkes, L. and Adipati, E. (1987). *Teluk Cenderawasih Marine Conservation Area, Irian Jaya: management plan 1988–1992.* WWF/IUCN Project No. 3770. WWF Indonesia, Jayapura. 145 pp.

Godoy, R.A. and Tan Ching Feaw (1988). *Smallholder rattan cultivation in southern Borneo, Indonesia.* Harvard University for International Development, Cambridge, Massachusetts.

Good, R. (1960). On the geographical relationships of the angiosperm flora of New Guinea. *Bull. Br. Mus. Nat. Hist. Botany* 2: 205–226.

Gressitt, J.L. (ed.) (1982). *Biogeography and ecology of New Guinea,* 2 vols. Junk, The Hague. 983 pp.

Grubb, P.J. and Stevens, P.F. (1985). *The forests of the Fatima and Mt Kerigomma, Papua New Guinea, with a review of montane and subalpine forests in Papuasia.* Research School of Pacific Studies, Publication BG/5 (1985). Australian National University, Canberra.

Hanson, A.J. (1981). Transmigration and marginal land development. In Hansen, G.E. (ed.), *Agricultural and rural development in Indonesia.* Westview Press, Boulder, Colorado.

Hatch, T. (1982). *Shifting cultivation in Sarawak – a review.* Soils Division Research Branch, Department of Agriculture, Sarawak. 165 pp.

Heyne, K. (1913-1917). *De nuttige planten van Nederlandsch Indië,* 4 vols. Ruygrok, Batavia. (2nd edition, 1927, Departement van Landbouw, Nijverheid en handel in Nederlandsch Indië. 3rd edition, 1950. W. van Hoeve, 's-Gravenhage, Bandung.)

Heywood, C.A., Heywood, V.H. and Wyse Jackson, P.S. (comps) (1990). *International directory of botanical gardens.* 5th edition. Koeltz Scientific Books, Koenigstein, Germany. 1021 pp.

Idris Mohd. Said (1989). Country report Malaysia. In Siemonsma, J.S. and Wulijarni-Soetjipto, N. (eds), *Plant resources of South-East Asia. Proceedings of the First PROSEA International Symposium, May 22–25, 1989, Jakarta, Indonesia.* Pudoc, Wageningen. Pp. 186–191.

IIED (1985). *Forest policies in Indonesia: the sustainable development of forest lands,* 4 vols. Jakarta.

IIED (1988). *Natural forest management for sustainable timber production,* 2 vols. Pre-project report for the ITTO. IIED, London.

ITTO (1990). The promotion of sustainable forest management; a case study in Sarawak, Malaysia. (Unpublished report.)

IUCN (1986). *Review of the protected areas system in Oceania.* IUCN, Gland, Switzerland and Cambridge, U.K. 239 pp.

IUCN (1991). *IUCN directory of protected areas in Oceania.* IUCN, Gland, Switzerland and Cambridge, U.K. xxiii, 447 pp. (Prepared by the World Conservation Monitoring Centre.)

IUCN (1992). *Protected areas of the world: a review of national systems. Volume 1: Indomalaya, Oceania, Australia and Antarctic.* IUCN, Gland, Switzerland and Cambridge, U.K. xx, 352 pp. (Prepared by the World Conservation Monitoring Centre.)

Jacobs, M. (1981). Dipterocarpaceae: the taxonomic and distributional framework. *Malaysian Forester* 44(2/3): 168–189.

Jacobs, M. (1982). The study of minor forest products. *Flora Malesiana Bull.* 35: 3768–3782.

Johns, R.J. (1975). Natural regeneration following chip logging in the lowland tropical rainforest – a case study from the Gogol River valley. Paper presented to the 2nd meeting of the Papua New Guinea Botanical Society. UPNG Library.

Johns, R.J. (1980). Notes on the forest types of Papua New Guinea. The *Dacrydium* swamp forests of the Southern Highlands. *Klinkii* 1(4): 3–9.

Johns, R.J. (1982). Plant zonation. In Gressitt, J.L. (ed.), Biogeography and ecology of New Guinea. *Monographiae Biologicae* 42: 309–330.

Johns, R.J. (1986). The instability of the tropical ecosystem in New Guinea. *Blumea* 31: 341–371.

Johns, R.J. (1989a). *A check list of the species of Manus Province.* Training course on Environmental Assessment, Lae, Papua New Guinea.

Johns, R.J. (1989b). The endemic plant genera of Papuasia. Paper presented to the 16th Papua New Guinea Botanical Society meeting, Christensen Research Institute, Madang. UPNG Library.

Johns, R.J. (1989c). The influence of drought on tropical rain forest vegetation in Papua New Guinea. *Mountain Research and Development* 9(3): 248–251.

Johns, R.J. (1990). The illusionary concept of the climax. In Baas, P., Kalkman, K. and Geesink, R. (eds), *The plant diversity of Malesia. Proceedings of the Flora Malesiana Symposium commemorating Professor Dr. C.G.G.J. van Steenis, Leiden, August 1989.* Kluwer Academic Press, Dordrecht. Pp. 133–146.

Johns, R.J. (1992). Biodiversity and conservation of the native flora of Papua New Guinea. In Beehler, B.M. (ed.), *Papua New Guinea conservation needs assessment. Volume 2: A biodiversity analysis for Papua New Guinea.* Government of Papua New Guinea, Department of Environment and Conservation, Papua New Guinea. Pp. 15–32.

Johns, R.J. and Stevens, P.F. (1972). *Mount Wilhelm flora: a check list of the species.* Botany Bulletin No. 6, Division of Botany, Department of Forests, Lae, Papua New Guinea. 60 pp.

Johnson, D. (ed.) (1991). *Palms for human needs in Asia. Palm utilization and conservation in India, Indonesia, Malaysia and the Philippines.* Balkema, Rotterdam. 258 pp.

Johnstone, I.M. and Frodin, D.G. (1982). Mangroves of the Papuan subregion. In Gressitt, J.L. (ed.), *Biogeography and ecology of New Guinea,* vol. 1. Junk, The Hague. Pp. 513–528.

Jones, D.T. (1987). Rimba Ilmu Universiti Malaya – preserving the natural plant heritage of the world's oldest rain forest. In Bramwell, D., Hamann, O., Heywood, V. and Synge, H. (eds), *Botanic gardens and the World Conservation Strategy.* Academic Press, London. Pp. 345–346.

JPM (1984). *Siaran Perangkaan Tahunan Sarawak 1983.* Jabatan Perangkaan Malaysia (Cawangan Sarawak), Kuching, Sarawak.

Kalkman, C. (1963). Description of the vegetation in the Star Mountains region, West New Guinea. *Nova Guinea Botany No. 15.*

Kato, M. (1990). The fern flora of Seram. In Baas, P., Kalkman, K. and Geesink, R. (eds), *The plant diversity of Malesia. Proceedings of the Flora Malesiana Symposium commemorating Professor Dr. C.G.G.J. van Steenis, Leiden, August 1989.* Kluwer Academic Press, Dordrecht. Pp. 225–234.

Kavanagh, M., Abdul Rahim, A. and Hails, C.J. (1989). *Rainforest conservation in Sarawak. An international policy for WWF.* WWF Malaysia, Kuala Lumpur and WWF International, Gland, Switzerland. 70 pp.

Keng, H. (1983). *Orders and families of Malayan seed plants.* Singapore University Press, Singapore. 441 pp.

Keng, H. (1990). *The concise flora of Singapore. Gymnos and dicots.* Singapore University Press, Singapore.

Kiew, R. (1983). Conservation of Malaysian plant species. *Malayan Naturalist* 37: 2–5.

Kiew, R. (1989). Utilization of palms in Peninsular Malaysia. *Malayan Naturalist* 43(1–2): 43–67.

Kiew, R. (1990a). Conservation of plants in Malaysia. In Baas, P., Kalkman, K. and Geesink, R. (eds), *The plant diversity of Malesia. Proceedings of the Flora Malesiana Symposium commemorating Professor Dr. C.G.G.J. van Steenis, Leiden, August 1989.* Kluwer Academic Press, Dordrecht. Pp. 313–322.

Kiew, R. (ed.) (1990b). The state of nature conservation in Malaysia. Malayan Nature Society, Kuala Lumpur. 238 pp.

Kiew, R. (1991). Palm utilization and conservation in Peninsular Malaysia. In Johnson, D. (ed.), *Palms for human needs in Asia. Palm utilization and conservation in India, Indonesia, Malaysia and the Philippines*. Balkema, Rotterdam. Pp. 75–130.

Knowland, W. (1985). Rates of change of forest cover in South East Asia and implications for national economies. *The Environmentalist* 5: Suppl. 10. *The future of the tropical rain forests in South East Asia*. IUCN Commission on Ecology Papers No. 10: 27–35.

Kochummen, K.M., LaFrankie, J.V., jr and Manokaran, N. (1990). Floristic composition of Pasoh Forest Reserve, a lowland rain forest in Peninsular Malaysia. *Journal of Tropical Forest Science* 3(1): 1–13.

Kostermans, A.J.G.H. and Bompard, J.M. (1989). Mangoes. In Siemonsma, J.S. and Wulijarni-Soetjipto, N. (eds), *Plant resources of South-East Asia. Proceedings of the First PROSEA International Symposium, May 22–25, 1989, Jakarta, Indonesia*. Pudoc, Wageningen. Pp. 269–217.

Lamb, A. (1991a). Orchids of Sabah and Sarawak. In Kiew, R. (ed.), *The state of nature conservation in Malaysia*. Malayan Nature Society, Kuala Lumpur. Pp. 78–88.

Lamb, D. (1991b). Conservation and management of tropical rain forest: a dilemma of development in Papua New Guinea. *Environmental Conservation* 4(2): 121–129.

Lamb, A. (in press). The orchids. In *Kinabalu – summit of Borneo* (revised edition). Sabah Society, Kota Kinabalu, Malaysia.

Lanly, J.-P. (1982). *Tropical forest resources*. FAO Forestry Paper 30. FAO, Rome.

Lemmens, R.H.M.J., Jansen, P.C.M. and Siemonsma, J.S. (1989). Basic list of species and commodity groupings. In Siemonsma, J.S. and Wulijarni-Soetjipto, N. (eds), *Plant resources of South-East Asia. Proceedings of the First PROSEA International Symposium, May 22–25, 1989, Jakarta, Indonesia*. Pudoc, Wageningen. Pp. 71–75.

Loh, C.L. (1975). Fruits in Peninsular Malaysia. In Williams, J.T., Lamoureux, C.H. and Wulijarni-Soetjipto, N. (eds), *South East Asian plant genetic resources*. BIOTROP, Bogor, Indonesia. Pp. 47–52.

MacKinnon, J. and MacKinnon, K. (1986). *Review of the protected areas system in the Indo-Malayan Realm*. IUCN, Gland, Switzerland and Cambridge, U.K. (in collaboration with UNEP). 284 pp.

Malayan Naturalist (1989). Conservation and utilization of Malaysian palms. *Malayan Naturalist (Special Issue)* 43(1–2): 92 pp.

Malaysian Nature Society (1993). *Malaysian Heritage and Scientific Expedition Belum-Hulu Perak 1993–94. Scientific Committee of the Expedition*. Malaysian Nature Society, Kuala Lumpur. 7 pp.

Malingreau, J.P., Stephens, G. and Fellows, L. (1985). Remote sensing of forest fires: Kalimantan and north Borneo in 1982–83. *Ambio* 14: 314–321.

Marsh, C. and Gasis, J. (1990). An expedition to Sabah's lost world: the Maliau Basin. *Malayan Naturalist* 43(3): 15–22.

Marsh, C.W. (1989). *Expedition to Maliau Basin, Sabah, April–May 1988. Final report*. Yayasan Sabah, Kota Kinabalu. 172 pp. (Yayasan Sabah Forestry Division in conjunction with WWF Malaysia Project No. MY5 126/88.)

McCarthy, A.J. (comp.) (1991). *Conservation areas of Indonesia. Final draft*. World Conservation Monitoring Centre, Cambridge, U.K. in collaboration with Directorate General of Forest Protection and Nature Conservation (PHPA), Ministry of Forestry, Republic of Indonesia, and IUCN Commission on National Parks and Protected Areas, Gland, Switzerland.

Merrill, E.D. (1923-1926). *An enumeration of Philippine flowering plants*, 3 vols. Bureau of Forestry, Manila, Philippines.

Merrill, E.D. (1946). *Plant life of the Pacific world*. Macmillan, New York. 295 pp.

Ministry of Primary Industries (1988). *Forestry in Malaysia*. Ministry of Primary Industries, Malaysia.

Moi, W. and Johns, R.J. (1977). The vegetation of the Telefomin area. Paper presented at the 5th meeting of the Papua New Guinea Botanical Society. UPNG Library.

Myers, N. (1980). *Conversion of tropical moist forests*. National Academy of Sciences, Washington, D.C. 205 pp.

Myers, N. (1988). Environmental degradation and some economic consequences in the Philippines. *Environmental Conservation* 15: 205–214.

Myers, N. (1989). *Deforestation rates in tropical forests and their climatic implications*. Friends of the Earth, London. 116 pp.

Nectoux, F. and Dudley, N. (1987). *A hard wood story. Europe's involvement in the tropical timber trade*. Friends of the Earth, London.

Nengah Wirawan (1985). *Kutai National Park management plan 1985–1990*. Prepared for The Directorate General of Forest Protection and Nature Conservation (PHPA), Department of Forestry, Bogor, Indonesia. WWF/IUCN Report No. 10. WWF/IUCN Conservation for Development Programme, Indonesia. 124 pp.

Nengah Wirawan (1986). *Checklist of plants of Kutai National Park*. Prepared for The Directorate General of Forest Protection and Nature Conservation (PHPA), Department of Forestry, Bogor, Indonesia. WWF/IUCN Conservation for Development Programme, Indonesia. 13 pp.

Ng, F.S.P. (1991). Trees of Peninsular Malaysia. In Kiew, R. (ed.), *The state of nature conservation in Malaysia*. Malayan Nature Society, Kuala Lumpur. Pp. 67–70.

Ng, F.S.P. and Low, C.M. (1982). *Check list of endemic trees of the Malay Peninsula*. Forest Research Institute Research Pamphlet 88. Forest Research Institute, Kepong, Malaysia.

Ngui, S.K. (1991). National parks and wildlife sanctuaries in Sarawak. In Kiew, R. (ed.), *The state of nature conservation in Malaysia*. Malayan Nature Society, Kuala Lumpur. Pp. 190–198.

ODA (1990). *National overview of the Regional Physical Planning Programme for Transmigration in Indonesia*. Overseas Development Natural Resources Institute (ODA), Chatham, U.K.

Oldfield, S. (1992). Plant use. In World Conservation Monitoring Centre, *Global biodiversity: status of the Earth's living resources*. Chapman and Hall, London. Pp. 331–358.

Paijmans, K. (1970). An analysis of four tropical rain forest sites in New Guinea. *J. Ecology* 58: 77–101.

Paijmans, K. (ed.) (1976). *New Guinea vegetation*. Elsevier, Amsterdam. 213 pp.

Paijmans, K. and Löffler, E. (1972). High-altitude forests and grasslands of Mt. Albert Edward, New Guinea. *J. Trop. Geogr.* 34: 58–64.

Parris, B.S. (1985). Ecological aspects of distribution and speciation in Old World tropical ferns. *Proc. R. Soc. Edin.* 86: 341–346.

Percival, M. and Womersley, J.S. (1975). *Floristics and ecology of the mangrove vegetation of Papua New Guinea*. Botany Bulletin 8. PNG Department of Forests, Division of Botany, Lae, Papua New Guinea. 96 pp.

Petocz, R.G. (1983). *Recommended reserves for Irian Jaya Province: statements prepared for the formal gazettement of thirty-one conservation areas*. WWF/IUCN Conservation for Development Programme in Indonesia. WWF Indonesia, Jayapura.

Petocz, R.G. (1984). *Conservation and development in Irian Jaya: a strategy for rational resources utilisation*. WWF/IUCN Conservation for Development Programme in Indonesia Report. PHPA, Bogor, Indonesia. 279 pp.

Petocz, R.G. (1989). *Conservation and development in Irian Jaya: a strategy for rational resources utilisation*. Brill, Leiden. 218 pp.

Pieters, P.E. (1982). Geology of New Guinea. In Gressitt, J.L. (ed.), *Biogeography and ecology of New Guinea*, Vol. 1. Junk, The Hague. Pp. 15–38.

Poore, D., Burgess, P., Palmer, J., Rietbergen, S. and Synott, T. (1989). *No timber without trees: sustainabililty in the tropical forest*. Earthscan, London. 252 pp.

Powell, J.M. (1976). Ethnobotany. In Paijmans, K. (ed.), *New Guinea vegetation*. Elsevier, Amsterdam. Pp. 106–183.

Primack, R.B. and Hall, P. (1992). Biodiversity and forest change in Malaysian Borneo. *BioScience* 42(11): 829–837.

Proctor, J. (1992). The vegetation over ultramafic rocks in the tropical Far East. In Roberts, B.A. and Proctor, J. (eds), *The ecology of areas with serpentinized rocks. A world view*. Kluwer. Pp. 249–270.

Repetto, R. (1988). *The forest for the trees? Government policies and the misuse of forest resources*. World Resources Institute, Washington, D.C. 105 pp.

Ridley, H.N. (1900). The flora of Singapore. *J. Roy. Asiatic Soc.* 33: 1–178.

Riswan, S., Irawati and Sukendar (1991). Orchid conservation in Bogor Botanic Garden and its associated gardens. In Heywood, V.H. and Wyse Jackson, P.S. (eds), *Tropical botanic gardens: their role in conservation and development*. Academic Press, London. Pp. 297–306.

Roos, M.C. (1993). State of affairs regarding *Flora Malesiana*: progress in revision work and publication schedule. *Flora Malesiana Bulletin* 11(2): 133–142.

Royen, P. van (1980-1983). *The alpine flora of New Guinea*, 4 vols. Cramer, Vaduz.

Saenger, P., Hegerl, E.J. and Davie, J.D.S. (1983). *Global status of mangrove ecosystems*. IUCN Commission on Ecology Papers No. 3. IUCN, Gland, Switzerland. 88 pp.

Sastrapradja, S., Sastrapradja, D.S. and Usep Soetisna (1987). Botanic gardens in the process of national development: the case of Indonesia. In Bramwell, D., Hamann, O., Heywood, V. and Synge, H. (eds), *Botanic gardens and the World Conservation Strategy*. Academic Press, London. Pp. 217–226.

Saulei, S.M. (1987). The forest resource development crisis in Papua New Guinea. In: *Forest resources crisis in the Third World*. Sahabay Alam, Penang. Pp. 81–92.

Saulei, S.M. and Swaine, M.D. (1988). Rainforest seed dynamics during succession at Gogol, Papua New Guinea. *J. Ecology* 76: 1133–1152.

Schlechter, R. (1925). Die Orchidaceen der Insel Celebes. *Fedde's Repert.* 21: 113–212.

Scott, D.A. (ed.) (1989). *A directory of Asian wetlands*. IUCN, Gland, Switzerland and Cambridge, U.K. 1197 pp.

Silvius, M.J. (1989). Pulau Supiori, Indonesia. In Scott, D.A. (ed.), *A directory of Asian wetlands*. IUCN, Gland, Switzerland and Cambridge, U.K. Pp. 1087.

Smith, J.M.B. (1972). *Flora of Sigul Mugal, Kubor Range, Papua New Guinea*. Report for the Department of Biogeography and Geomorphology, Australian National University, Canberra.

Soepadmo, E. (1978). Introduction to the Malaysian I.B.P. synthesis meetings. *Malayan Nature Journal* 30: 119–125.

Soepadmo, E. (1983). Genetic resources of Malaysian fruit trees. *Malaysian Applied Biology* 8(1): 33–42.

Soepadmo, E. (1992). Floristic diversity of Southeast Asian tropical rain forest and its ecogeographical significance. Paper presented at the International Workshop on Ecology, Conservation, and Management of Southeast Asian Rainforests, Kuching, Malaysia, 12–14 October 1992.

Soerianegara, I. and Lemmens, R.H.M.J. (eds) (1993). *Timber trees: major commercial timbers*. Pudoc, Wageningen.

SPREP (1985). *Action strategy for protected areas in the South Pacific region*. South Pacific Commission, Noumea, New Caledonia. 21 pp.

Steenis, C.G.G.J. van (1950). The delimitation of Malaysia and its main geographical divisions. *Flora Malesiana* ser. I, 1, lxx–lxxv.

Steenis, C.G.G.J. van (1971). Plant conservation in Malesia. *Bull. Jard. Bot. Nat. Belg.* 41: 189–202.

Steenis, C.G.G.J. van (1979). Plant-geography of east Malesia. *Bot. J. Linn. Soc.* 79(2): 97–178.

Steenis, C.G.G.J. van (1987). *Checklist of generic names used for Spermatophytes in Malesian botany*. Flora Malesiana Foundation, Leiden.

Stevens, P.F. (1989). New Guinea. In Campbell, D.G. and Hammond, H.D. (eds), *Floristic inventory in tropical countries: the status of plant systematics, collections, and vegetation, plus recommendations for the future*. The New York Botanical Garden, New York. Pp. 120–132.

Stevens, P.F. (1990). Nomenclatural stability, taxonomic instinct, and flora writing – a recipe for disaster? In Baas, P., Kalkman, K. and Geesink, R. (eds), *The plant diversity of Malesia. Proceedings of the Flora Malesiana Symposium commemorating Professor Dr. C.G.G.J. van Steenis, Leiden, August 1989*. Kluwer Academic Press, Dordrecht. Pp. 387–410.

Stevens, P.F. and Veldkamp, J.F. (1980). *Report of the Lae-Leiden Mt Suckling Expedition, 1972*. Office of Forests, Division of Botany, Lae, Papua New Guinea.

Streimann, H. (1983). *The plants of the upper Watut watershed of Papua New Guinea*. National Botanic Gardens, Canberra.

Takhtajan, A. (1986). *Floristic regions of the world*. University of California Press, Berkeley. 522 pp.

Tan, B.C. and Rojo, J.P. (1989). The Philippines. In Campbell, D.G. and Hammond, H.D. (eds), *Floristic inventory in tropical countries: the status of plant systematics, collections, and vegetation, plus recommendations for the future*. The New York Botanical Garden, New York. Pp. 44–62.

Taylor, B.W. (1957). Plant succession on recent volcanoes in Papua. *J. Ecology* 45: 233–234.

Taylor, B.W. (1959). The classification of lowland swamp communities in north eastern Papua. *Ecology* 40: 703–711.

UNEP (1981). *Annual report 1981*. UNEP.

Verdcourt, B. (1979). *A manual of New Guinea legumes*. Botany Bulletin No. 11. Office of Forests, Department of Botany, Lae, Papua New Guinea. 645 pp.

Verhey, E.W.M. and Coronel, R.E. (1989). Edible fruits and nuts in South-East Asia. In Siemonsma, J.S. and Wulijarni-Soetjipto, N. (eds), *Plant resources of South-East Asia. Proceedings of the First PROSEA International Symposium, May 22–25, 1989, Jakarta, Indonesia*. Pudoc, Wageningen. Pp. 97–106.

Vogel, E.F. de (1989a). Sulawesi (Celebes). In Campbell, D.G. and Hammond, H.D. (eds), *Floristic inventory in tropical countries: the status of plant systematics, collections, and vegetation, plus recommendations for the future*. The New York Botanical Garden, New York. Pp. 108–112.

Vogel, E.F. de (1989b). The Moluccas. In Campbell, D.G. and Hammond, H.D. (eds), *Floristic inventory in tropical countries: the status of plant systematics, collections, and vegetation, plus recommendations for the future*. The New York Botanical Garden, New York. Pp. 113–119.

Wan Razali Wan Mohd., Dransfield, J. and Manokaran, N. (eds) (1992). *A guide to the cultivation of rattan*. Malayan Forest Record No. 35. Forest Research Institute Malaysia, Kepong, Kuala Lumpur. 293 pp.

Westphal, E. and Jansen, P.C.M. (eds) (1989). *Plant resources of South-East Asia. A selection*. Pudoc, Wageningen. 322 pp.

Whitmore, T.C. (1969). The vegetation of the Solomon Islands. *Philosophical Transactions of the Royal Society* B 255: 259–270.

Whitmore, T.C. (ed.) (1981). *Wallace's line and plate tectonics*. Clarendon Press, Oxford.

Whitmore, T.C. (1985). *Tropical rain forests of the Far East*. 2nd Edition. Clarendon Press, Oxford. 352 pp. (1st edition, 1975; 2nd edition reprinted with corrections, 1985.)

Whitten, A.J., Damanik, S.J., Anwar, J. and Hisyam, N. (1984). *The ecology of Sumatra*. Gadjah Mada University Press. 583 pp.

Whitten, A.J., Muslimin Mustafa and Henderson, G.S. (1987). *The ecology of Sulawesi*. Gadjah Mada University Press. 777 pp.

Widjaja, E.A. (1984). Ethnobotanical notes on *Gigantochloa* in Indonesia with special reference to *G. apus*. *J. American Bamboo Soc.* 5(3–4): 57–68.

Widjaja, E.A. and Dransfield, S. (1989). Bamboos of South-East Asia. In Siemonsma, J.S. and Wulijarni-Soetjipto, N. (eds), *Plant resources of South-East Asia. Proceedings of the First PROSEA International Symposium, May 22–25, 1989, Jakarta, Indonesia.* Pudoc, Wageningen. Pp. 107–120.

Wilde, W.J.J.O. de (1989). Sumatra. In Campbell, D.G. and Hammond, H.D. (eds), *Floristic inventory in tropical countries: the status of plant systematics, collections, and vegetation, plus recommendations for the future.* The New York Botanical Garden, New York. Pp. 103–107.

Wind, J. and Soesilo, B.K. (1978). *Proposed Halimun Nature Reserve management plan 1979–1982.* UNDP/FAO Nature Conservation and Wildlife Management Project INS/73/013. Field report no. 10. FAO, Bogor, Indonesia. 67 pp.

Womersley, J.S. (ed.) (1978–). *Handbooks of the flora of Papua New Guinea.* Melbourne University Press, Melbourne.

Wood, J.J., Beaman, R.S. and Beaman, J.H. (1993). *The plants of Mount Kinabalu: 2. Orchids.* Royal Botanic Gardens, Kew. 411 pp.

Wood, J.J. and Cribb, P.J. (1994). *A checklist of the orchids of Borneo.* Royal Botanic Gardens, Kew. 409 pp.

Woods, P. (1987). Drought and fire in tropical rain forests in Sabah: an analysis of rainfall patterns and some ecological effects. In Kostermans, A.J.G.H. (ed.), *Proceedings of the Third Round Table Conference on Dipterocarps.* MAB/UNESCO. Pp. 367–387.

World Bank (1990). *Papua New Guinea. The forestry sector: a tropical forestry action plan review.* A report prepared under the auspices of the Tropical Forestry Action Plan.

World Bank (1991). *Papua New Guinea – National Conservation & Resource Management Programme. Global Environment Facility project briefs GEF FY92 technical assistance projects – Second Tranche.* World Bank. Pp. 99–106.

World Conservation Monitoring Centre (1992). *Global biodiversity: status of the Earth's living resources.* Chapman and Hall, London. xx, 549 pp.

World Resources Institute (1992). *World resources 1992–93: a guide to the global environment.* Oxford University Press, New York. 385 pp.

World Resources Institute (1994). *World resources 1994–95: a guide to the global environment.* Oxford University Press, New York. 400 pp.

World Resources Institute and IIED (1986). *World resources 1986. An assessment of the resource base that supports the global economy.* Basic Books, New York. 353 pp.

WWF Malaysia (1985). *Strategi Pemeliharaan Sumber Semulajadi Malaysia.* (Proposals for a Conservation Strategy for Sarawak.) WWF Malaysia, Kuala Lumpur. 210 pp.

Acknowledgements

The preparation of this regional text has involved contributions and help from many individuals. The author wishes to thank the following for much help and advice on site selection: Professor Peter S. Ashton (Harvard University Herbaria, Cambridge, Massachusetts, U.S.A.) for valuable help and advice on site selection for the whole region and major contributions to the text for Borneo; Professor Robert J. Johns (Royal Botanic Gardens, Kew, U.K.) for site selection and major contributions to the text on Papuasia, and for providing much valuable information on sites in Papua New Guinea in particular; Dr Ruth Kiew (Universiti Pertanian Malaysia, Selangor, Malaysia) for site selection and help with the regional text on the Malay Peninsula; Dr Tony Lamb (Agricultural Research Centre, Tenom, Malaysia) for valuable contributions and advice on site selection for Sabah, Malaysia; Dr Domingo A. Madulid (National Museum, Manila, Philippines) for help with site selection and information on the Philippines; Anthea Phillipps (former Park Ecologist, Sabah Parks, Malaysia) for valuable advice and information on sites in Sabah, Malaysia; Dr Peter F. Stevens (Harvard University Herbaria, Cambridge, Massachusetts, U.S.A.) for valuable contributions and advice on site selection for Papuasia.

Special thanks are also extended to the following for contributing information and for commenting on earlier drafts: Professor M.M.J. van Balgooy (Rijksherbarium, Leiden, The Netherlands), Dr Paul Chai (Ministry of Environment and Tourism, Sarawak, Malaysia), Dr Phil Cribb (Royal Botanic Gardens, Kew, U.K.), Dr G.W.H. Davison (WWF Malaysia), Dr John Dransfield (Royal Botanic Gardens, Kew, U.K.), Dr Kathy MacKinnon (WWF Indonesia), Dr Jeff McNeely (IUCN, Gland, Switzerland), Dr Junaidi Payne (WWF Malaysia), Dr R. Petocz (Metro Manila, Philippines), Professor Duncan Poore (U.K.), Dr H.P. Nooteboom (Rijksherbarium, Leiden, The Netherlands) and Dr W. Vink (Rijksherbarium, Leiden, The Netherlands).

Dr Marco Roos, co-ordinator, *Flora Malesiana* project (Rijksherbarium, Leiden) kindly checked and provided updates on the flora statistics for the region, and June Cunningham (Botanical Research Institute of Texas) provided an update on the *Philippines Flora Project*.

Author's note:

Most of this Regional Overview was written between 1991 and 1993. A few updates to the original text were made prior to publication.

ENDAU-ROMPIN STATE PARKS (PROPOSED)
Johore and Pahang, Peninsular Malaysia, Malaysia

Location: Headwaters of the Endau and Rompin Rivers, Johore-Pahang, centred on 2°41'N and 103°14'E.

Area: Proposed State Parks covering c. 500 km².

Altitude: 100–1000 m.

Vegetation: Lowland rain forest, hill dipterocarp forest, hill swamp forest, riverine forest.

Flora: Southern flora of Peninsular Malaysia, including Bornean element flora.

Useful plants: Many timber trees, rattans and fruits of economic importance; ornamentals, such as pitcher plants, orchids, palms, bananas and aquatic plants.

Other values: Contains the largest breeding population of the Sumatran rhinoceros, Malaysia's most endangered mammal; tourism.

Threats: Logging and land clearance; tourist development and visitor pressure; commercial collection of ornamental plants.

Conservation: Forest Reserves, but proposed as two contiguous State Parks.

Geography

Endau-Rompin is situated 240 km south-east of Kuala Lumpur and 160 km north of Singapore, straddling the borders of the Malaysian states of Johore and Pahang. The area covers the headwaters of the Endau and Rompin rivers which drain into the South China Sea, and is bounded on the west by a north-south range of granite hills dominated by Gunung Besar (1132 m). Within the proposed parks, G. Janing (710 m) and G. Beremban (917 m) are capped with sandstone; otherwise the area comprises plutonic, volcanic, metamorphic and sedimentary rocks (Idris, Azman and Rosedean 1987). To the east, Triassic volcanic rocks of andesitic to rhyolitic composition are intruded by granite; in the north-east the younger late Jurassic-Cretaceous sandstones of the Tebak Formation overlie older granites of the late Triassic period, forming distinctive mesas, plateaux and escarpments.

Vegetation

The flora and vegetation are described in the results of expeditions to the Endau (1985–1986) and Rompin (1989) areas [*Malayan Nature Journal* 41(2–3), 1987; 43(4), 1990]. The principal forest types are broadly classified as lowland mixed dipterocarp forests (MDF) and edaphic hill forests (Wong, Saw and Kochummen 1987). Much of the lowland MDF are concentrated in the central and south-western parts of the area (roughly between the Endau, Selai and Jasin rivers) as well as on steep hilly terrain. The MDF is represented by the keruing-red meranti (*Dipterocarpus-Shorea*) and kapur (*Dryobalanops aromatica*) subtypes. The keruing-red meranti subtype mostly occurs below 250 m, and along the valleys of the Endau and Rompin rivers and their principal tributaries; the kapur subtype occurs only in a few localities below 300 m and is most common in the north-east and eastern parts

along the Kinchin and Lamakoh valleys. Logging has taken place along the Endau and Jasin rivers within the proposed park area during the last 15 years. All accessible forest surrounding the park has also been logged or cleared for agriculture.

Riverine forests include *Dipterocarpus costulatus*, *Shorea singkawang* and *Ficus variegata*, and plant communities adapted to river and stream edges, where *Tristania whiteana* is common. The rheophytic flora is well-represented on rocky rapids and stream banks.

Edaphic hill forests include: seraya (*Shorea curtisii*) ridge forest; fan palm forest (dominated by *Livistona endauensis*, endemic to the area) on ridges and on the sandstone plateaux (G. Keriong, G. Janing, Padang Temambun); and heath forests of various types on shallow podzols and plateaux. Kerapah (a type of heath forest occurring on swampy ground) is known in the peninsula only from Johore, and most of it occurs within Endau-Rompin. On waterlogged plateaux, forest is replaced by an open swamp dominated by sedges, such as *Machaerina maingayi*.

Flora

Endau-Rompin contains an important sample of the southern flora of Peninsular Malaysia. Species characteristic of the southern element include the dipterocarps *Shorea bentongensis*, *Parashorea densiflora*, *Vatica bella* and *V. bullettii*, the rare bamboo *Racemobambos setifera*, and the banana *Musa gracilis*.

The Endau-Rompin area is rich in endemic species. Among them are the rheophyte *Phyllanthus watsonii* (Euphorbiaceae); herbs, such as *Didissandra kiewii*, *Didymocarpus corneri*, *D. craspedodromus*, *D. davisonii*, *D. furcata*, *Loxocarpus tunkuii* (Gesneriaceae), *Phyllagathis cordata* (Melastomataceae) and *Staurogyne scopulicola*

(Acanthaceae); the climber *Hoya endauensis* (Asclepiadaceae); trees, such as *Schoutenia furfuracea*; and the palms *Calamus endauensis*, *Licuala dransfieldii*, *L. thoana* and *Livistona endauensis*. Plants found in Endau-Rompin, which are very rare elsewhere in the peninsula, include *Racemobambos setifera*, *Arthrophyllum alternifolium* (Araliaceae), *Euthemis minor* (Ochnaceae) and *Thismia arachnites* (Burmanniaceae).

The flora of Endau-Rompin also contains a Bornean element which includes species that are not found elsewhere in the peninsula, such as *Chionanthus lucens*, *Croton rheophyticus*, *Rothmannia kuchingensis* and *Sebastiana borneensis*, the palms *Daemonorops scapigera* and *Korthalsia hispida*, and the ferns *Lindsaea borneenis* and *Syngramma borneensis*. The area is also part of the "Riau pocket", a characteristic floristic element confined to south-east Peninsular Malaysia, the Riau Islands and west Borneo (Corner 1958), and which includes such species as *Croton ensifolius*, *Dillenia albiflos* and *Pandanus epiphyticus*.

The edaphic forest types on heath, sandy and rocky riverine sites have a characteristic flora which contains species usually found at above 1000 m elsewhere in the peninsula, but which are found between 100–750 m at Endau-Rompin. Examples include *Leptospermum flavescens* and *Dipteris conjugata*. Ant plants are common on these nutrient-poor sites.

Plant groups of particular note at Endau-Rompin are:

❖ Orchidaceae: 78 species so far recorded (Shaharin Yussof *et al.* 1987) but representing only a small proportion of the total orchid flora in the area.
❖ Herbs other than orchids: More than 150 species (Kiew 1987, 1990).
❖ Palmae: 74 species, representing about a third of the peninsula's palm flora and over half of its rattan species (Dransfield and Kiew 1987).
❖ Ferns: 81 species, representing about a third of the lowland fern flora of Peninsular Malaysia (Kiew *et al.* 1987).
❖ Mosses: 66 species, i.e. about 14% of the peninsula's flora, and much more diverse than any other locality of comparable size and altitudinal range in the peninsula (Haji Mohamed and Ahmad Damanhuri Mohamad 1987).

Useful plants

The presence of the diminutive banana *Musa gracilis*, together with the large number of orchid, rattan and timber tree (dipterocarp) species, has already been noted. Other species with potential as ornamental plants include the pitcher plants (*Nepenthes* spp.), *Dracaena aurantica*, herbs such as *Didissandra kiewii*, *Labisia acuta*, *Sonerila picta*, and gingers. Currently, hundreds of plants of *Piptospatha ridleyi* are collected for the aquarium trade; rattans (in particular *Calamus caesius*), and well-established seedlings of the endemic fan palm *Livistona endauensis*, are collected commercially.

In addition, 52 species are recorded as used in traditional herbal medicine by the local Orang Hulu community of Kampung Peta in the Endau Valley. Of these, 13 species are used in the preparation of aphrodisiacs and tonics, 4 as abortifacients and 3 for contraception (Taylor and Wong 1987).

Social and environmental values

Two recent Malaysian Heritage and Scientific Expeditions to Endau-Rompin have shown the great scientific importance of the area in terms of its rich and unique flora with a high number of endemic species (*Malayan Nature Journal* 1987, 1990). No other sites provide legal protection for the southern element of Peninsular Malaysia's flora.

Endau-Rompin contains one of the last remaining viable breeding populations in Peninsular Malaysia of the Sumatran rhinoceros, *Didermocerus sumatrensis*, the most endangered mammal in Malaysia. The Endau population is estimated at between 11 and 15 animals. The area also contains characteristic elements of the Malayan fauna, including elephant (*Elephas maximus*), Malayan gaur (*Bos gaurus hubbacki*), bearded pig (which in Peninsular Malaysia is found only in the south and whose population is seriously reduced by hunting), 3 species of deer, several species of primates, and predatory cats, including tiger (*Panthera tigris*). The alluvial forests are particularly rich in bird species and are an important, but critically endangered, habitat for birds in the peninsula. The river system is still pristine and is home to the endangered fish *Scleropages formosus*, which is exploited commercially for the aquarium trade. An endemic trap-door spider (*Liphistius endau*) is known only from the banks of the Endau River.

The Orang Hulu (one of the groups of aboriginal peoples in Peninsular Malaysia) live in the nearest village Kampung Peta downstream on the Endau River of the proposed State Park. They have traditionally hunted and gathered forest products for sale (e.g. rattan, fish and frogs) from the proposed park area (Kiew and Hood Salleh 1991). Many of their legends relate to sites within the park. With their intimate knowledge of the area, they could be involved in aspects of park management and could sell handicrafts direct to visitors. This would replace their incomes derived from traditional exploitation of the park area, which will cease once the area is gazetted.

The Endau-Rompin area is an important watershed; two major rivers, the Endau and Rompin, have their sources in the area.

Economic assessment

Tourist potential is excellent as the proposed parks are well-located to exploit the Singapore tourist market. Park facilities have not yet been set up, so economic values are not known. The area is well-known to sport fishermen, but how heavily this resource can be exploited is not known.

Rattan could be exploited on a sustainable basis if some type of long-term tenure is given to local villagers. Unfortunately, there is no legislation for this.

Threats

Originally proposed as a National Park in 1975 with an area of 2000 km², logging and land development schemes have seriously reduced the area. By 1980, the proposed park was to cover 480 km² in Johore and 360 km² in Pahang. By 1992, the areas had still not been gazetted under state legislation nor had the boundaries been established. The areas to be gazetted are likely to be much smaller than the 1980 figures, probably in the region of about 500 km^2 in total.

Logging within the proposed park area occurred in 1977 but was halted after considerable national protest. Logging continued in the Sg Jasin areas and between the Sg Kinchin and Sg Kemapan. Large-scale logging of surrounding forests has also occurred. Besides the direct effects of logging, massive siltation to some of the tributaries of the Endau River has occurred. The construction of logging roads allows access to the area for hunting and fishing (including a case of poisoning one river with insecticide) and the collection of forest products, such as rattans and the endemic fan palm.

There is currently concern that insensitive development of tourist facilities will degrade the pristine nature of the area. Unfortunately, current park boundaries exclude the important Gunung Janing and the western flanks of Padang Temambong.

Conservation

Endau-Rompin was proposed as a National Park in Third Malaysia Plan (1975) and then included parts of Labis Forest Reserve, Endau-Mas Forest Reserve, Endau-Kluang Wildlife Reserve (Johore) and Lesong Forest Reserve (Pahang). Because of the reluctance of states to relinquish land in perpetuity to the Federal Government under the National Parks Act, the Johore and Pahang State Governments proposed that the area be gazetted as State Parks. This has caused considerable delays in legal gazettement as State Park legislation had first to be enacted. By 1992 Johore had enacted its State Park Act but the Endau area had yet to be gazetted, while Pahang still had no State Park Act. However, publicity generated by the two Malaysian Heritage and Scientific Expeditions, and continued monitoring by the Malaysian Nature Society, helps to maintain the momentum to get the areas legally protected.

References

Corner, E.J.H. (1958). The Malayan flora. In Purchon, R.D. (ed.), *Proceedings Centen. and Bicent. Congr. Biology, Singapore*. Pp. 21–24.

Dransfield, J. and Kiew, R. (1987). An annotated checklist of palms at Ulu Endau, Johore, Malaysia. *Malayan Nature Journal* 41: 183–189.

Haji Mohamed and Ahmad Damanhuri Mohamad (1987). The moss flora of Ulu Endau, Johore, Malaysia. *Malayan Nature Journal* 41: 183–189.

Idris, M.B., Azman, S. and Rosedean, Z. (1987). Geology of the Ulu Endau area, Johore-Pahang, Malaysia. *Malayan Nature Journal* 41: 93–105.

Kiew, R. (1987). The herbaceous flora of Ulu Endau, Johore-Pahang, Malaysia, including taxonomic notes and descriptions of new species. *Malayan Nature Journal* 41: 201–234.

Kiew, R. (1990). Notes on the ground flora of Gunung Keriong, Pahang, Malaysia, including two new species. *Malayan Nature Journal* 43(4): 240–249.

Kiew, R. and Hood Salleh (1991). The future of rattan collecting as a source of income for Orang Asli communities. In Appanah, S., Ng, F.S.P. and Roslan Ismail (eds), *Malaysian forestry and forest products research*. Forest Research Institute Malaysia, Kuala Lumpur. Pp. 121–129.

Kiew, R., Parris, B.S., Madhavan, S., Edwards, P.J. and Wong, K.M. (1987). The ferns and fern-allies of Ulu Endau, Johore, Malaysia. *Malayan Nature Journal* 41: 191–200.

Malayan Nature Journal (1987). The Malaysian Heritage and Scientific Expedition: Endau-Rompin 1985–1986. *Malayan Nature Journal* 41(2/3): 446 pp.

Malayan Nature Journal (1990). Rompin-Endau Expedition: 1989. *Malayan Nature Journal* 43(4): 336 pp.; 44(1): 75 pp.

Shaharin Yussof, Kiew, R., Lim, W.H. and Nuraini Ibrahim (1987). A preliminary checklist of orchids from Ulu Endau, Johore, Malaysia. *Malayan Nature Journal* 41: 235–237.

Taylor, C.E. and Wong, K.M. (1987). Some aspects of herbal medicine among the Orang Hulu community of Kampung Peta, Johore, Malaysia. *Malayan Nature Journal* 41: 317–328.

Wong, K.M., Saw, L.G. and Kochummen, K.M. (1987). A survey of the forests of the Endau-Rompin area, Peninsular Malaysia: principal forest types and floristic notes. *Malayan Nature Journal* 41: 125–144.

Acknowledgements

This Data Sheet was prepared by Dr Ruth Kiew (Universiti Pertanian Malaysia, Serdang, Selangor, Malaysia).

LIMESTONE FLORA OF PENINSULAR MALAYSIA
Peninsular Malaysia, Malaysia

Location: About 300 scattered outcrops on the mainland and 99 limestone islands in the Langkawi group.

Area: 260 km².

Altitude: 0–713 m (summit of Gua Peningat).

Vegetation: Forest over limestone, limestone scrub, cliff vegetation.

Flora: >1300 vascular plant species, about 10% of which are endemic to Peninsular Malaysia and are restricted to limestone, including the monotypic genus Stenothrysus (*S. ridleyi*).

Useful plants: Ornamental plants, including white slipper orchid (*Paphiopedilum niveum*), Amorphophallus, balsams, begonias, hoyas, orchids and ferns; Stemona is sold for medicine in Langkawi.

Other values: Many outcrops are of great scenic beauty; Buddhist, Hindu and Taoist cave temples have religious significance as well as being tourist attractions; caves are the major archaeological sites in Peninsular Malaysia and a few contain ancient cave paintings; diverse cave fauna, including endemic snails; source of marble and limestone, particularly for the cement industry.

Threats: Burning, quarrying (particularly in the Ipoh area), agriculture at hill bases, construction of temples (Pahang, Perak and Selangor), flooding by hydroelectric dams (Kelantan, Pahang, Trengganu); illegal plant collection; mining; tourism.

Conservation: Only the limestone hills within Taman Negara (CPD Site SEA8, see also separate Data Sheet) are protected; the majority are on state land with no legal protection or are in Forest Reserves. A network of sites is recommended to protect Peninsular Malaysia's limestone flora.

Geography

The limestone landscape of Peninsular Malaysia is very distinctive. It consists of many isolated and often spectacular, tower-karst hills with sheer cliffs and jagged summits. There are about 300 hills on the mainland, the majority (about 210) in Kelantan, the rest scattered in Perlis, Kedah, Perak (with about 45 hills in the Ipoh area), Pahang and Selangor. Langkawi (Kedah) consists of about 99 limestone islands. Most of the hills are 75 m, or more, high; Gua Peningat in Taman Negara, reaches 723 m and is the tallest outcrop. (See Map 9.)

The limestones range from Ordovician to Permian in age (Hutchison 1978) and many are rich in fossils (Jones 1961). Most hills are perforated by caves, potholes, gullies and wangs (collapsed caves), which provide a great diversity of microhabitats. This is one reason why the limestone flora is so rich in species.

Vegetation

The vegetation forms a characteristic and easily recognized forest type. The structure of the vegetation depends on the topography of the hill and the abundance or scarcity of soil, moisture and shelter (Chin 1977). At the base of hills on talus slopes and in gullies and valleys where the deepest soil may be found, the vegetation often exceeds 10 m in height and is closed. Typical species include *Villebrunea sylvatica* and *Gmelina asiatica*. Where water drips from steep rocky slopes or overhanging cliffs, a distinct herb community develops, including such species as *Chirita caliginosa* and *Monophyllaea*

horsfieldii. On hill slopes of less than 60°, there is usually sufficient soil to support closed vegetation of 5–10 m. On vertical cliffs, very steep rock slopes and rock faces, the vegetation is restricted to cracks and crevices; it may be herbaceous (e.g. *Paraboea* spp.) or shrubby. Cliff faces with no cracks or crevices are bare of vegetation.

The summits of the hills are generally rocky and the vegetation is often stunted, 2–7 m tall, and may be closed or open. Occasional emergent trees include *Mangifera* sp. (on G. Pondok), *Madhuca ridleyi* (on Bukit Serdam) and *Garcinia murdochii* (on Gua Kechil). Beneath closed canopies, there is usually a rich ground layer, including ferns, orchids and bryophytes. In contrast, the vegetation of rocky summits (e.g. Bukit Takun in Selangor) is sparse and open. The plants on such hills include some herbs (e.g. *Amorphophallus* spp., *Paraboea* spp.), *Pandanus* spp., and stunted trees and shrubs (e.g. *Buxus malayanus*, *Ficus calcicola*). Considerable layers of peat (with pH as low as 4.5) develop on some hills.

Coastal limestone vegetation with *Shorea siamensis* is found on the Langkawi islands. Drought-tolerant species such as *Impatiens mirabilis* and *Euphorbia antiquorum* also occur on Langkawi. Distinctive subtypes of vegetation are found in and around lakes in limestone outcrops (Balgooy *et al.* 1977).

Flora

The total number of vascular plants exceeds 1300, distributed in 582 genera and 124 families. Chin (1977, 1979, 1983a, 1983b) provides a complete inventory of the flora. The best represented family is Orchidaceae with 136 species, followed by Euphorbiaceae (81 species), Rubiaceae (66 species), Gesneriaceae (44 species) and Annonaceae (39 species). 257 species (21%) are restricted to limestone in the peninsula and 130 species (10%) are endemic to the peninsula and are restricted to limestone (Chin 1977). These include two endemic genera, *Stenothyrsus* (Acanthaceae) and an as yet undescribed genus of the Gesneriaceae.

The distribution of limestone species is not uniform: regional differences exist (between Langkawi, Perak and Selangor, and Kelantan and Pahang), composition varies from hill to hill (probably due to chance dispersal and establishment and/or extinction), and several of the endemic species are known from a single hill or group of hills. For example, 34 species are endemic to the Ipoh limestone, 30 species to Langkawi and 11 species to Batu Caves and Bukit Takun. No single hill harbours more than a fraction of the flora. For example, 170 species were recorded from Batu Caves (Chin 1977) and 225 species from Bukit Takun (Chia 1983), two of the best collected hills. This means that, in order to conserve a representative part of the limestone flora, a network of hills needs to be conserved (see list of priority sites under Conservation).

Besides the large endemic and Malayan element, several Indochinese species reach their southernmost limit on limestone in the peninsula, e.g. *Buxus* spp. and *Ligustrum confusum*. Kiew (1991a) lists rare or endangered species by location.

Useful plants

The white slipper orchid (*Paphiopedilum niveum*) has commercial value. Easily accessible populations were decimated many years ago. However, at present it appears that wild-collected plants for sale in Bangkok markets are collected from Thai limestone islands not from Langkawi (R. Kiew, pers. obs.). The fleshy roots of *Stemona tuberosa* are collected and sold for medicine.

The limestone flora includes a number of wild relatives of economic plants, which have potential in breeding programmes. These include *Mangifera* spp. and *Atalantia roxburghiana* (an endemic citroid species). Many species have potential economic value as ornamentals, such as *Amorphophallus* spp., balsams, begonias, clerodendrons, ferns, gesneriads, hoyas and orchids. Besides slipper orchids, the spider orchid *Arachnis flos-regia* is found wild on limestone (Kiew and Chin 1982).

Social and environmental values

Limestone hills are important scenic features, particularly Bukit Takun (near Kuala Lumpur), the Ipoh Hills and the Gua Musang Hills. The most spectacular hills tower above the Nenggiri River (Davison and Kiew 1990). Limestone caves are becoming popular for recreational purposes and attract growing numbers of tourists.

Caves that contain temples are of religious significance. Batu Caves, near Kuala Lumpur, attracts over 100,000 people for the Thaipusam Festival. The Perak Tong Temple in Ipoh is visited by at least 10,000 people a year. Several caves around Ipoh (near Kuantan) and at Kota Gelanggi (Pahang) contain Bhuddist or Taoist temples.

Limestone hills are also important geological and archaeological sites (Peacock 1965). The oldest human bones in Peninsular Malaysia (13,000 years BP), as well as stone tools dated to 14,000 years BP, have been recovered from archaeological sites from under overhanging rocks in limestone. Bones of hippopotamus and antelope (both now extinct in Malaysia) have also been found. In addition, cave paintings several thousand years old, as well as more modern painting by aboriginal people (c. 50 years BP), persist on the walls of caves and rock overhangs in Perak and Pahang.

The rich cave fauna (Bullock 1965) includes large populations of bats, which are important pollinators of forest trees as well as the commercially valuable durian, and an endemic-rich snail fauna, many species of snails being endemic to particular hills (Davison 1991a).

Economic assessment

Limestone is an economic asset with more than 100 uses. Major sources of revenue are obtained from the extraction of marble (including terrazzo), road metal aggregate, white cement and calcium carbonate. In 1982, 8.1 million tonnes of limestone were extracted, and 53 limestone quarries were operational in 1988. 35 of the quarries occurred in the Ipoh area (Davison 1991b). In 1988, over 2000 people were employed in limestone quarries.

Removal of guano also yields a revenue, but in some cases this is illegal and has caused damage to archaeological sites. Tourism is a major source of revenue for temples. Commercial collection of plants yields only minor revenue.

Threats

The major threat to the limestone flora is from fires. Most at risk are the sensitive shade- and damp-loving plant communities that grow at the base of the limestone outcrops (Davison and Kiew 1990). These basal communities are the most endangered of the limestone communities and include species which are threatened by extinction (Kiew 1990, 1991a, 1991b). Fires can also sweep up the hills and burn summit vegetation, which, if the soil structure is damaged, may never recover. There is hardly a limestone hill that has not been damaged by fire. Agriculture too often encroaches right up to the base of the hill and has destroyed the hill base communities. This has caused the probable extinction of about 18 species in the Ipoh area (Kiew 1991b).

Quarrying for limestone is a major threat to many hills in the Ipoh area. Some of the outcrops are likely to be entirely destroyed. Quarrying also occurs on a large scale in Langkawi. Prolonged public protest finally stopped quarrying on Batu Caves in 1981. In the past, mining for iron-rich soil from the hills and tin from around the base of the hills caused widespread damage in the Ipoh area (Molesworth-Allen 1961). At present, such activities are a minor threat.

Temple building is particularly damaging in the Ipoh area (Davison 1991b). Tourism is also causing damage to some summits where trees have been chopped down, e.g. on Bukit Takun and Gua Musang. Major tourist resort development on Langkawi threatens its limestone flora; Langkawi has more endemics than any other area of limestone in the peninsula (Kiew 1991a).

The plant communities around the base of some hills (e.g. Batu Biwa, Trengganu) have been flooded by hydroelectric schemes, or are threatened by proposals for hydroelectric schemes (e.g. the limestone areas in Nenggiri Valley, Kelantan). Summit vegetation on some hills has been destroyed by the installation of trigonometrical points and, in one case, by a communication transmitter.

Orchids, particularly slipper orchids, and other plants are not protected by local legislation and are therefore at risk from commercial collection, except where they are protected within Taman Negara (see Conservation).

Almost all accessible caves have been plundered of their guano and cave soil to the detriment of archaeological remains and the cave fauna.

Conservation

The limestone hills within Taman Negara are protected by National Park status (see separate Data Sheet on Taman Negara, CPD Site SEA8). A few, e.g. in Kelantan, Pahang and Selangor, fall within Forest Reserves. The majority are on state land and are totally unprotected. Bukit Anak Takun, which lies within Templer Park, is now surrounded by a golf course and is very vulnerable. Licensed temples have the status of Temple Reserve, but such designation provides no protection whatever for the flora and fauna. Many temples are unlicensed.

A network of hills (see list below) is needed to protect: (a) a representative part of the limestone flora, (b) the endemic species, and (c) representative samples of the limestone flora of each phytogeographical region. In addition, protected hills must be surrounded by an adequate buffer zone of forest to prevent fire from damaging the limestone ecosystem and particularly the endangered microhabitat at the hill base.

Botanically important limestone sites of Peninsular Malaysia

Each of the following sites contains samples of lowland forest over limestone, scrub and cliff communities. Langkawi is the only limestone area in Peninsular Malaysia supporting coastal limestone forest. All the following sites contain about 300 vascular plant species, except Langkawi which has an estimated 500 vascular plant species. All the sites listed contain endemics (apart from Gunung Baling). Because of the floristic differences between each of the zones, a network of protected hills (21 of more than 200 hills are recommended here) is required to ensure that a representative part of the flora is conserved.

Northern Zone

Sites in this zone show floristic similarities to the Thai limestone flora.

SEA3a. Langkawi, Kedah

The only limestone in Peninsular Malaysia which supports coastal limestone forest. It also has more endemics than any other limestone area in the peninsula. Area: 40 km² (whole island).

- Flora: c. 500 vascular plant species, of which 30 species are endemic to Langkawi and the limestone in the extreme south of Thailand (Kiew 1991a). Plants of economic importance include *Paphiopedilum niveum* (white slipper orchid) and medicinal plants.
- Threats: Severely threatened by cement quarrying and large-scale tourist developments. *Paphiopedilum niveum* is threatened by commercial collecting.
- Conservation: Not protected.

SEA3b. Kaki Bukit, Perlis

6°39'N, 100°12'E. Area: >2.5 km²; >75 m high outcrop.
- Threats: Severely threatened by fires from surrounding agricultural land. Buffer zone of trees mostly cleared.
- Conservation: Not protected.

SEA3c. Bukit Lagi, Perlis

6°25'N, 100°06'E. Area: >2.5 km²; >75 m high outcrop.
- Threats: Severely threatened by fires from surrounding agricultural land. Buffer zone of trees mostly cleared.
- Conservation: Not protected.

SEA3d. Gunung Baling, Kedah

5°41'N, 100°54'E. Area: c. 2.5 km²; >75 m high outcrop.
- Flora: c. 300 vascular plant species, including the palm *Calamus balingensis*, which is strictly endemic.
- Threats: Severely threatened by fires from surrounding agricultural land. There is a microwave station on the peak.
- Conservation: Not protected.

SEA3e. Gunung Reng, Kelantan

5°43'N, 101°44'E. Area: >2.5 km²; >75 m high outcrop.
- Threats: Severely threatened by visitor pressure, cave tourism and encroachment by agriculture.
- Conservation: Not protected.

Kelantan-Pahang Zone

SEA3f. Gua Setir, Kelantan

5°40'N, 101°55'E. Area: c. 5 km²; >75 m high outcrop.
- Threats: Illegal cultivation; recent logging has opened up the area. Clearing and burning of the forest prior to illegal cultivation is rapidly approaching the hill.
- Conservation: Forest Reserve.

SEA3g. Gua Ikan, Kelantan

5°21'N, 102°01'E. Area: >2.5 km²; >75 m high outcrop.
- Threats: Severely threatened by agricultural encroachment and visitor pressure.
- Conservation: Forest Recreational Area, still partly surrounded by forest.

SEA3h. Gua Jaya, Kelantan

5°05'N, 101°46'E. Area: c. 3 km²; >75 m high outcrop.

- Conservation: Forest Reserve, still surrounded by undisturbed primary forest.

SEA3i. Gua Musang (including Batu Neng and Batu Boh), Kelantan

4°53'N, 101°58'E. Area: c. 5 km²; c. 75 m high outcrops.
- Threats: Illegal cultivation, squatter housing around the base of the hills. The summit vegetation of Gua Musang is suffering from visitor pressure and has been badly burned in the past.
- Conservation: Not protected.

SEA3j. Batu Biwa, Trengganu

4°51'N, 102°43'E. Area: c. 5 km²; >75 m high outcrop.
- Threats: The area is a Forest Reserve and has been logged. The base of hill has been submerged by a hydroelectric scheme. Further disturbance is unlikely.

SEA3k. Gua Peningat, Pahang

4°36'N, 102°10'E. Area: c. 5 km²; >75 m high outcrop. It is the highest limestone peak in Peninsular Malaysia, reaching 713 m altitude.
- Conservation: Totally protected within Taman Negara (CPD Site SEA8, see separate Data Sheet).

SEA3l. Gua Gagak, Kelantan

4°46'N, 101°58'E. Area: c. 2.5 km²; c. 75 m high outcrop.
- Threats: Some of the forest has been illegally logged. Other parts are severely threatened by agriculture and fire.
- Conservation: Part (about one-third) is within a Forest Reserve.

SEA3m. Batu Luas, Pahang

4°28'N, 102°30'E. Area: c. 5 km²; c. 75 m high outcrop.
- Conservation: Totally protected within Taman Nagara (CPD Site SEA8, see separate Data Sheet), but would be submerged if proposal to build a hydroelectric dam ever proceeds.

SEA3n. Bukit Sagu, Pahang

3°58'N, 103°10'E. Area: >2.5 km²; >75 m high outcrop.
- Threats: Surrounded by agriculture and severely threatened by fire.
- Conservation: Not protected.

SEA3o. Bukit Cheras, Pahang

3°56'N, 103°08'E. Area: >2.5 km²; >75 m high outcrop.
- Threats: Surrounded by agriculture, a rubber estate, and severely threatened by fire. Some disturbance from tourism associated with cave temple.
- Conservation: Not protected.

SEA3p. Gunung Senyum, Pahang

3°44'N, 102°30'E. Area: c. 2.5 km²; >75 m high outcrop.
- Threats: Surrounded by agriculture and severely threatened;

has been badly burned in the past. Some disturbance from cave tourism.
- Conservation: Not protected.

West Coast Zone

SEA3q. Batu Caves, Selangor

3°16'N, 101°39'E. Area: >2.5 km²; >75 m high outcrop.
- Flora: 170 vascular plant species recorded so far. Eleven species of vascular plants are endemic to Batu Caves and Bukit Takun (Kiew 1991a).
- Threats: Quarrying, residential and industrial developments, agriculture and tin mining have removed all the surrounding vegetation. Disturbance from cave tourism. An important cave temple. Renovation works on the temple threatened some rare plant populations.
- Conservation: Not protected; severely threatened.

SEA3r. Bukit Takun, Selangor

3°18'N, 101°42'E. Area: >2.5 km²; >75 m high outcrop.
- Flora: 225 vascular plant species recorded so far.
- Conservation: Located within Serendah Forest Reserve and still surrounded by forest, but threatened. **Anak Bukit Takun** is not protected, and is surrounded by a golf course and is particularly vulnerable.

CPD Site SEA3r: Bukit Takun, Selangor, Peninsular Malaysia, showing the dramatic vertical limestone cliffs and forest of this outcrop within the Serendah Forest Reserve. Photo: Stephen D. Davis.

SEA3s. Gunung Tempurong, Perak

4°28'N, 101°18'E. Area: c. 5 km²; >75 m high outcrop.
- ❖ Flora: c. 300 vascular plant species, including an economically important bamboos.
- ❖ Threats: Gross disturbance in the past from tin mining. Severely threatened now by agriculture, quarrying and unlicensed temple building.
- ❖ Conservation: Not protected.

SEA3t. Gunung Rapat, Perak

4°34'N, 101°07'E. Area: c. 4 km²; >75 m high outcrop.
- ❖ Flora: c. 300 vascular plant species, including an economically important bamboos.
- ❖ Threats: Gross disturbance in the past from tin and iron-ore mining. Severely threatened now by quarrying, agriculture and squatters from nearby town.
- ❖ Conservation: Not protected.

SEA3u. Gunung Datok, Perak

4°37'N, 101°10'E. Area: c. 3.5 km²; >75 m high outcrop.
- ❖ Flora: c. 300 vascular plant species, including an economically important bamboos.
- ❖ Threats: Almost all the surrounding forest has been cleared. Severely threatened by agricultural clearance and burning.
- ❖ Conservation: Not protected.

References

Balgooy, M.M.J. van, Kurtak, B.H., Kurtak, D.C., Littke, W.R., Parjatmo, W. and Weinheimer, E.A. (1977). A biological reconnaissance of Tasek Pulau Laggun, a sinkhole lake in the Langkawi district, Kedah, Malaysia. *Sains Malaysiana* 56: 1–29.

Bullock, J.A. (1965). Malaysian caves: introduction. *Malayan Nature Journal* 19: 1–3.

Chia, S.C. (1983). The lure of Bukit Takun. *Malayan Naturalist* 37(2): 18–25.

Chin, L.T. (1977). The limestone hill flora of Malaya, 1. *Gardens' Bulletin of Singapore* 30: 165–219.

Chin, L.T. (1979). The limestone hill flora of Malaya, 2. *Gardens' Bulletin of Singapore* 32: 64–203.

Chin, L.T. (1983a). The limestone hill flora of Malaya, 3. *Gardens' Bulletin of Singapore* 35: 137–190.

Chin, L.T. (1983b). The limestone hill flora of Malaya, 4. *Gardens' Bulletin of Singapore* 36: 31–91.

Davison, G.W.H. (1991a). Terrestrial molluscs in Peninsular Malaysia. In Kiew, R. (ed.), *The state of nature conservation in Malaysia*. Malayan Nature Society, Malaysia. Pp. 101–104.

Davison, G.W.H. (ed.) (1991b). *A conservation assessment of limestone hills in the Kinta Valley*. Malayan Nature Society, Malaysia. Project 1/90. 202 pp.

Davison, G.W.H. and Kiew, R. (1990). Survey of the flora and fauna of limestone hills in Kelantan with recommendation for conservation. Unpublished report for WWF-Malaysia. Malayan Nature Society, Malaysia. 98 pp.

Henderson, M.R. (1939). The flora of the limestone hills of the Malay Peninsula. *Journal of the Malayan Branch of the Royal Asiatic Society* 17: 13–87.

Hutchison, C.S. (1978). Physical and chemical differentiation of West Malaysian limestone formations. *Bull. Geo. Soc. Malaya* 1: 45–56.

Jones, C.R. (1961). Fossils in Malaya: their use to the geologist and the case for the conservation of certain fossil localities. In Wyatt-Smith, J. and Wycherley, P.R. (eds), *Nature conservation in western Malaysia*. Malayan Nature Society, Malaysia. Pp. 83–88.

Kiew, R. (1990). The flora. In Davison, G.W.H. and Kiew, R. (eds), Survey of the flora and fauna of limestone hills in Kelantan with recommendation for conservation. Unpublished report for WWF-Malaysia. Malayan Nature Society, Malaysia. 98 pp.

Kiew, R. (1991a). The limestone flora. In Kiew, R. (ed.), *The state of nature conservation in Malaysia*. Malayan Nature Society, Malaysia. Pp. 42–50.

Kiew, R. (1991b). Botanical survey of the limestone hills in Perak. In Davison, G.W.H. (ed.), *A conservation assessment of limestone hills in the Kinta Valley*. Malayan Nature Society, Malaysia. Project 1/90. Pp. 82–108.

Kiew, R. and Chin S.C. (1982). The effect of dam building on plant life in Taman Negara. *Malayan Naturalist* 35(4): 23–25.

Molesworth-Allen, B. (1961). Limestone hills near Ipoh. In Wyatt-Smith, J. and Wycherley, P.R. (ed.), *Nature conservation in western Malaysia*. Malayan Nature Society, Malaysia. Pp. 68–72.

Peacock, B.A.V. (1965). The prehistoric archaeology of Malayan caves. *Malayan Nature Journal* 19: 40–56.

Acknowledgements

This Data Sheet was prepared by Dr Ruth Kiew (Universiti Pertanian Malaysia, Serdang, Selangor, Malaysia) based on an earlier draft by Dr Chin See Chung.

MONTANE FLORA OF PENINSULAR MALAYSIA
Peninsular Malaysia, Malaysia

Location: Mostly along the Main Range, the Bintang Range, and isolated hills on west coast, and off-shore islands (see listed sites under Conservation).

Area: 17 localities recommended here for protection cover 2180 km².

Altitude: Mostly 810–1200 m; Gunung Tahan reaches 2188 m.

Vegetation: Lower and upper montane forests.

Flora: At least 3000 species of vascular plants, of which c. 2125 species confined to montane forests.

Useful plants: Ornamental plants, particularly orchids (including slipper orchids), pitcher plants and rhododendrons.

Other values: Tourism (as hill resorts), watershed protection, important catchment areas.

Threats: Large-scale hill resort development, agriculture (tea gardens, temperate flowers and vegetables), road building proposal, commercial collecting of some species.

Conservation: Gunung Tahan lies within the Taman Negara (National Park) (CPD Site SEA8, see also separate Data Sheet); Cameron Highlands Wildlife Sanctuary covers 650 km²; Gunung Kajang is part of Pulau Tioman Wildlife Reserve; however, protection is minimal at last two named sites. Other peaks mostly fall within Forest Reserves. A network of sites is recommended to protect Peninsular Malaysia's montane flora.

Geography

Most mountain peaks in Peninsular Malaysia lie on the Main Range (the Titiwangsa Range) parallel to the west coast (see Map 9). There is a shorter range (the Bintang Range), which runs parallel to the east coast, and which divides to form a shorter range to the west which culminates in Gunung Tahan and G. Rabung. Lower isolated hills are found along the west coast plain. They include G. Jerai (Kedah Peak), G. Bubu, G. Ledang (Mt Ophir) and G. Pulai. G. Raya occurs on Pulau Langkawi, and Penang Hill is on Penang Island. In the south are G. Belumut and G. Panti; G. Kajang occurs on Pulau Tioman off the east coast of Peninsular Malaysia. (Pulau Tioman, CPD Site SEA5, is the subject of a separate Data Sheet.)

Peaks in the Main Range and the Bintang Range mostly reach 1400 m. G. Korbu (2125 m) is the highest peak in the Main Range and G. Tahan (2188 m) the highest in Peninsular Malaysia. The isolated hills are much lower, ranging from 500 m (G. Panti) to 1613 m (G. Bubu), but most barely reach 1000 m.

The Main Range and Bintang Range are heavily weathered granite mountains, but some, such as G. Panti and G. Tahan, are sandstone capped. A well-developed peat layer occurs in upper montane forest. Some sandstone-capped peaks (e.g. G. Panti) have waterlogged plateaux where hill swamp forest is found.

Vegetation

Montane forest is generally divided into lower montane forest (between 1200–1500 m) and upper montane forest (above 1500 m). However, on the isolated peaks, upper montane forest abuts directly on hill forest as low as 800 m.

Lower montane forest is characterized by a tree canopy 15–33 m tall, with emergent trees (if present) reaching 37 m. The canopy is formed of rounded tree crowns of mesophyllous and microphyllous species. There are abundant vascular epiphytes but the ground layer is sparse. In contrast, upper montane forest is lower (1.5–18 m tall), the tree crowns are flatter, leaves are microphylls or pachyphylls, vascular epiphytes are abundant and the ground layer is rich in mosses and herbs (Whitmore 1985). A conspicuous facies of upper montane forest is "mossy" (or "elfin") forest, in which the canopy is low, trees are gnarled and non-vascular epiphytes (especially leafy liverworts) are particularly abundant.

Species composition differs between lower and upper montane forest types. Lower montane forest, also called oak-laurel forest, is characterized by an abundance of individuals or species of Fagaceae and Lauraceae, and of *Eugenia* (*Syzygium*) spp. and Balanophoraceae. Large Hamamelidaceae (*Exbucklandia, Altingia*) are characteristic but local. Compared with hill and lowland dipterocarp forest there is a marked absence of species of Anacardiaceae, Bombacaceae, Burseraceae, Dipterocarpaceae, Flacourtiaceae, Guttiferae and Myristicaceae. Upper montane forest, also called ericaceous forest, is characterized by the presence of species belonging to Cunoniaceae, Ericaceae, Myrtaceae, Nepenthaceae, Orchidaceae (particularly epiphytic species), Pentaphylacaceae, Podocarpaceae, Symplocaceae and Theaceae. Wyatt-Smith (1963) gives a list of the common and characteristic species of these two forest types.

Flora

The montane flora of Peninsular Malaysia is estimated to include at least 3000 vascular plant species, of which about

2125 species are confined to montane forest. The size of the flora could be larger because many species occur over a wide altitudinal range. For example, whereas 32% (157 species) of ferns in the peninsula only occur above 1000 m (i.e. are exclusively montane), 56% (275 species) of the peninsula's fern species are known to occur above 1000 m (Kiew *et al.* 1987).

Few detailed floristic studies have been published. Exceptions include the flora of Taiping Hills (Burkill and Henderson 1925; now out-of-date), where 1939 species were recorded (of which 48 and 7 species were reported as endemic to the lower and upper montane forest of this peak, respectively); and upper montane forest on G. Ulu Kali, where 460 species were recorded (Stone 1981). However, new species continue to be recorded from these localities.

Endemism is very high in the montane flora. In the larger herbaceous dicot genera, *Argostemma*, *Didymocarpus* and *Sonerila*, with more than 40 species in the peninsula, 71%, 72% and 56% of their species, respectively, are confined to mountains (Kiew 1991a). Families of trees, which are well-represented by montane species, also show high levels of endemism (53% for Aquifoliaceae, 57% for Araliaceae and Theaceae, and 65% for Myrsinaceae) compared with an average of 26.4% endemic species for all tree families in the peninsula (Ng, Low and Mat Asri Ngah Sanah 1990).

In addition, many endemics are confined to a single peak or adjacent peaks. For example, for *Argostemma*, *Didymocarpus* and *Sonerila*, 59%, 73% and 80% of their

Interior of montane forest at Gunung Ulu Kali, Pahang (CPD Site SEA4g), showing *Pandanus klossii* in foreground. This forest was only metres away from an area cleared for the construction of a large resort complex. Photo: Stephen D. Davis.

species are known from a single peak (Kiew 1991a). Orchids are particularly well-represented in the montane forest and also show this same phenomenon. For example, of the 10 species of *Corybas*, 6 are known from a single peak and 2 from just two peaks (Dransfield, Comber and Smith 1986).

Phytogeographically, the Sino-Himalayan element is well-represented in montane forest by species in such families as the Aceraceae, Ericaceae, Fagaceae, Hamamelidaceae and Lauraceae, and by genera such as *Anemone*, *Gentiana*, *Lonicera*, *Sanicula* and *Viola*. The southern element, which includes common species in families such as Cunoniaceae, Epacridaceae, Myrtaceae (*Baeckia*, *Leptospermum* and *Rhodamnia*) and Podocarpaceae, are species whose distribution is determined more by edaphic factors (they are species that can grow on poor, acid leached sands) than by altitude, as they may also be found in the lowlands on this soil type. The herb *Nertera* is an example of a southern genus confined to mountains.

Useful plants

In lower montane forest on ridges, the timber tree *Agathis borneensis* (damar minyak) may be locally abundant. Montane forest is particularly rich in species which have potential as ornamentals, such as ferns, orchids (slipper orchids in particular), gesneriads, pitcher plants and rhododendrons. Some species have commercial potential as sources of medicines, spices and essential oils.

Social and environmental values

The amenity value of hill resorts is rising both with increasing affluence and urbanization (Kiew 1991b). Most accessible areas are either developed as resorts or there are plans afoot to develop such areas. Extensive vegetation cover in the mountains maintains cool temperatures, which are a prime attraction of hill resorts in the tropics.

Montane forests protect water catchment areas and, by regulating water flow, maintain a supply of water during dry periods and prevent flooding, erosion, heavy silting and landslips during periods of heavy rain.

The montane forest is also important for the protection of montane animals. Four mammal species are restricted to montane forest (Ratnam, Nor Azman Hussein and Lim 1991) of which two are Endangered (the marmoset rat and the spotted giant flying squirrel) and two are extremely rare (Himalayan watershrew and the short-tailed mole, the latter in the peninsula being only known from Cameron Highlands). 75 montane species of bird are recorded for the peninsula (Davison 1991) of which only 45 species are protected within Taman Negara. The mountains of Peninsular Malaysia are included in the Sumatra and Peninsular Malaysia Endemic Bird Area (EBA), and support eight restricted-range bird species of which two are endemic, the mountain peacock-pheasant (*Polyplectron inopinatum*) and Malayan whistling-thrush (*Myophonus robinsoni*). The only known non-breeding record of the globally threatened rufous-headed robin (*Luscinia ruficeps*), endemic to south-west China as a breeding bird, was from Cameron Highlands. About half the species of Malayan butterflies (514 species) are found in the mountains (Kirton 1991), among which 9 distinct montane races are recognized. Mountain peaks are also important for the reproductive behaviour of butterflies (the phenomenon known as hill-topping).

Threats

Hill and montane forests in Peninsular Malaysia have recently come under severe threat; hill forests are being logged and montane forests are threatened by planned hill resort developments. Agriculture is encroaching into the foothills in many cases, and even extends into the highlands in some areas.

At present, the greatest threat is from hill resort development. There are plans to build new hotels, condominiums, bungalows, roads and recreational facilities (including golf courses, equestrian centres and theme parks). The development proposals are on such a large scale that irreversible damage to the environment and montane vegetation will inevitably result if the schemes go ahead (Kiew 1991b, 1992). None of the planned developments make provision for areas set aside as nature reserves. Mountains that are currently threatened include: G. Raya, G. Jerai, Maxwell Hill, G. Korbu (Kinta Highlands development), Fraser's Hill, G. Ulu Kali, G. Bunga Buah, G. Ledang and G. Kajang. Penang Hill was only saved from total destruction by vigorous and persistent public protest.

Clearing for agricultural practices, in particular for cut-flowers to supply the international trade, is another major threat. For example, at Cameron Highlands, land is now being cleared on G. Brinchang on steep slopes, extending into upper montane forest.

A mountain road is planned to link Cameron Highlands in the north, passing through Fraser's Hill, and continuing to G. Ulu Kali in the south. The purpose of this road is to open up land for logging, residential housing and agriculture. As it is planned to build the road along the ridges, it is likely to cause widespread damage to the fragile upper montane forest and montane ridge forest, besides causing landslips, soil erosion and siltation downstream.

Clearing the summit for microwave and trigonometrical points has destroyed the summit vegetation of several peaks. Tourist pressure is also a threat to summit vegetation of some peaks. For example, on G. Ledang much of the summit vegetation has been chopped down to fuel camp fires.

Most of the accessible orchids have been stripped from forests surrounding resorts such as Genting Highlands (G. Ulu Kali); pitcher plants are now difficult to find at Fraser's Hill and rhododendrons have also been collected. Much of the collection of orchids is by local visitors who do not understand that highland orchids will languish and die in their lowland gardens. Pitcher plants are also collected for the overseas trade. Slipper orchids appear on CITES Appendix I and pitcher plants on Appendix II. However, there is little enforcement of CITES regulations and there is no local wildlife legislation to protect plants.

Many important areas of montane forest in Peninsular Malaysia are threatened by hill resort development and road schemes. This photograph shows road development around the Genting Highlands hill resort complex at Gunung Ulu Kali (CPD Site SEA4g). The adjoining forest is rich in orchids and *Nepenthes* spp. Photo: Stephen D. Davis.

Conservation

Besides harbouring a significant proportion of the Peninsular Malaysian flora, montane vegetation has one of the highest levels of species endemism of any vegetation type of Peninsular Malaysia. Because many endemics are confined to a single peak, they are particularly vulnerable to small-scale disturbance. To conserve this flora it is necessary to protect a network of sites in each of the major floristic regions within the peninsula (see list of priority sites, below).

Upper montane forest grows extremely slowly (Kiew 1992) and its regeneration after disturbance is slow, if it occurs at all. Because of this, and because it has no value for timber, it would be wise to conserve all upper montane forest. This would not only protect species but would also provide a long-term gene pool for plants with commercial value, provide watershed protection and prevent erosion, as well as contributing to the amenity value of hill resorts (compared with other forest types, the canopy of upper montane forest is lower and is attractively gnarled, many plants are perpetually in flower, and orchids and pitcher plants are highly visible).

Botanically important montane sites of Peninsular Malaysia

All the sites listed below contain locally endemic species. There are also floristic differences between sites in different regions. As a result, a network of protected sites is required to conserve a representative part of the flora. The sites listed below are considered to be of the utmost priority for protection.

Northern Region

SEA4a. Gunung Jerai (Kedah Peak), Kedah

5°47'N, 100°26'E. Area: 30 km². Altitude: 75–1002 m.
- ❖ Vegetation: Hill dipterocarp forest and lower montane forest.
- ❖ Flora: c. 1000 vascular plant species.
- ❖ Threats: A Forest Reserve which is threatened by visitor pressure associated with tourism. There is also a microwave station at the summit. The forests are vitally important for water catchment protection.

SEA4b. Gunung Raya, Kedah

6°22'N, 99°49'E. Area: 50 km². Altitude: 75–858 m.
- ❖ Vegetation: Hill dipterocarp forest, containing trees used for wild honey harvesting.
- ❖ Flora: c. 1000 vascular plant species.
- ❖ Threats: A Forest Reserve which is critically endangered by large-scale hill resort development. The forests are vitally important for water catchment protection.

SEA4c. Penang Hill, Penang

5°26'N, 100°16'E. Area: 25 km². Altitude: 300–830 m.
- ❖ Vegetation: Hill dipterocarp forest and lower montane forest. The forests are vitally important for water catchment protection.
- ❖ Flora: c. 1000 vascular plant species.

- ❖ Threats: A Forest Reserve which was critically endangered by large-scale hill resort development which threatened to cover the entire summit. The area was saved after the scheme failed to get its EIA approved by the Department of Environment, and following widespread public protest against the scheme. An economically important slipper orchid (*Paphiopedilum barbatum*) has been over-collected almost to extinction locally.

Main range

SEA4d. Cameron Highlands (including Gunung Brinchang, Gunung Jasar, Gunung Beremban), Pahang

4°30'N, 101°34'E. Altitude: 800–1909 m.
- ❖ Vegetation: Hill dipterocarp forest, lower and upper montane forests, with rhododendrons, *Nepenthes*, orchids and rattans.
- ❖ Flora: c. 1500 vascular plant species.
- ❖ Threats: Gunung Brinchang is severely threatened by clearance of lower montane forest to make way for commercial cut-flower farms. There are also problems of land clearance resulting from inadequate boundary marking and enforcement of the Wildlife Sanctuary status. There is some disturbance from tourism, and there is a microwave station at the summit of Gunung Brinchang. Gunung Beremban and Gunung Jasar are not threatened.
- ❖ Conservation: Cameron Highlands Wildlife Sanctuary (IUCN Management Category: IV) covers 650 km², partly overlapping with Forest Reserves.

SEA4e. Fraser's Hill, Pahang

3°43'N, 101°45'E. Area: 50 km². Altitude: 800–1424 m.
- ❖ Vegetation: Hill dipterocarp forest and lower montane forest, with numerous orchids and *Nepenthes*.
- ❖ Flora: c. 1000 vascular plant species (836 species of seed plants recorded so far).
- ❖ Threats: Severely threatened by a large-scale hill resort development which is underway. *Nepenthes* spp. are almost locally extinct due to commercial collecting.
- ❖ Conservation: Forest Reserve; the Selangor side is also a Wildlife Reserve (reported to be de-gazetted in 1992).

SEA4f. Gunung Korbu, Perak

4°41'N, 101°18'E. Area: 150 km². Altitude: 800–2125 m.
- ❖ Vegetation: Hill dipterocarp forest, lower and upper montane forests.
- ❖ Flora: c. 1500 vascular plant species.
- ❖ Threats: A Forest Reserve whose vegetation is still undisturbed but could be severely threatened by a planned large-scale hill resort development.

SEA4g. Gunung Ulu Kali, Pahang and Gunung Bunga Buah, Selangor

3°23'N, 101°50'E. Area: 200 km². Altitude: 800–1725 m.
- ❖ Vegetation: Hill dipterocarp forest, lower and upper montane forests, with many orchids, rhododendrons, *Nepenthes* spp. and rattans.

❖ Flora: c. 1500 vascular plant species (500 species recorded so far from upper montane forest).
❖ Threats: Privately-owned, the forests are critically endangered. On Gunung Ulu Kali, the forest has been sold for residential development and roads have been built along ridges. There has been heavy over-collecting of orchids. Part of Gunung Bunga Buah was cleared for a ginseng farm which failed within one year.

SEA4h. Maxwell Hill (Gunung Hijau), Perak

4°52'N, 100°48'E. Area: 100 km². Altitude: 75–1410 m.
❖ Vegetation: Hill dipterocarp forest, lower and upper montane forests. The forests are vitally important for water catchment protection.
❖ Flora: c. 1500 vascular plant species.
❖ Threats: A Forest Reserve which is threatened by possible extension of the existing hill resort. There is also a microwave station at the summit.

Eastern Region

There are probably further sites to those listed below that qualify for inclusion, but the region is still poorly known botanically. Sites which are known to be of outstanding importance are:

SEA4i. Gunung Lawit, Kelantan

5°25'N, 102°35'E. Area: 150 km². Altitude: 75–1421 m.
❖ Vegetation: Hill dipterocarp forest and lower montane forest.
❖ Flora: c. 1500 vascular plant species. Several endemic palms and gesneriads, and the Endangered *Begonia rajah*, are known to occur in the area (including the lowland area of Ulu Setui).
❖ Threats: Logging has probably extended into the hill forest of this Forest Reserve, but the extent is not precisely known to the author and a ground survey is needed. Agriculture is encroaching into the foothills.
❖ Conservation: Not protected.

SEA4j. Gunung Mandi Angin, Trengganu

4°41'N, 102°51'E. Area: 100 km². Altitude: 75–1421 m.
❖ Vegetation: Hill dipterocarp forest and lower montane forest.
❖ Flora: c. 1500 vascular plant species.
❖ Threats: Logging has probably occurred into the hill forest of this Forest Reserve, but the extent is unknown to the author and a ground survey is needed.

SEA4k. Gunung Tahan, Pahang

4°34'N, 102°17'E. Area: 300 km². Altitude: 75–2188 m (Peninsular Malaysia's highest mountain).
❖ Vegetation: Hill dipterocarp forest, lower and upper montane forests, "padang" vegetation.
❖ Flora: c. 2000 vascular plant species.

❖ Conservation: Protected within Taman Negara (CPD Site SEA8, see separate Data Sheet). Plans to build a jeep track to the summit have been withdrawn. No collecting of flora is allowed in the National Park.

SEA4l. Gunung Tapis, Pahang

4°02'N, 102°54'E. Area: 150 km². Altitude: 75–1472 m.
❖ Vegetation: Hill dipterocarp forest and lower montane forest.
❖ Flora: c. 1500 vascular plant species.
❖ Threats: Logging has probably occurred into the hill forest of this Forest Reserve, but the extent is unknown to the author and a ground survey is needed.

Isolated lower peaks

SEA4m. Gunung Belumut, Johore

2°02'N, 103°31'E. Area: 50 km². Altitude: 75–1009 m.
❖ Vegetation: Hill dipterocarp forest and lower montane forest.
❖ Flora: c. 1500 vascular plant species.
❖ Threats: The lowlands of this Forest Reserve have been cleared for agriculture. The extent of logging in the hill forest is unknown to the author and a ground survey is needed.

SEA4n. Gunung Bubu, Perak

4°44'N, 100°50'E. Area: 50 km². Altitude: 300–1613 m.
❖ Vegetation: Hill dipterocarp forest and lower montane forest.
❖ Flora: c. 1000 vascular plant species.
❖ Threats: Encroachment from development is occurring around the perimeter of this Forest Reserve, which is severely threatened as a result.

SEA4o. Gunung Kajang, Pulau Tioman, Pahang

2°46'N, 104°10'E. Area: 50 km². Altitude: 75–1038 m.
❖ Vegetation: Hill dipterocarp forest and lower montane forest; upper (mossy) montane forest occurs on the crest above 1000 m (Henderson 1930).
❖ Flora: c. 1000 vascular plant species (658 species recorded so far).
❖ Threats: Plant collecting is a threat in this Forest Reserve. *Rafflesia cantleyi* is collected for medicine by local villagers, and the slipper orchid *Paphiopedilum barbatum* is commercially collected and may already be extinct locally.
❖ Conservation: The whole of Pulau Tioman is a Wildlife Reserve (IUCN Management Category: VIII); see also separate Data Sheet on Pulau Tioman (CPD Site SEA5).

SEA4p. Gunung Ledang (Mt Ophir), Johore

2°22'N, 102°36'E. Area: 50 km². Altitude: 75–1243 m.
❖ Vegetation: Hill dipterocarp forest and lower montane forest. The forests are vitally important for water catchment protection.

- Flora: c. 1000 vascular plant species.
- Threats: All summit vegetation of this Forest Reserve has been destroyed by campers. There is also some disturbance from a microwave station. The area is severely threatened by a planned large-scale hill resort development.

SEA4q. Gunung Panti, Johore

1°50'N, 103°53'E. Area: 25 km². Altitude: 75–500 m.
- Vegetation: Hill dipterocarp forest and hill swamp forest. The forests are vitally important for water catchment protection.
- Flora: c. 1000 vascular plant species.
- Threats: There is some disturbance around the waterfall area due to tourist developments, and the slipper orchid *Paphiopedilum bullenianum* has been over-collected almost to extinction locally.
- Conservation: Forest Reserve; a small part (at the base) is a Wildlife Reserve.

References

Burkill, I.H. and Henderson, M.R. (1925). The flowering plants of Taiping in the Malay Peninsula. *Gardens' Bulletin of the Strait's Settlements* 3: 303–458.

Davison, G.W.H. (1991). Birds. In Kiew, R. (ed.), *The state of nature conservation in Malaysia*. Malayan Nature Society, Malaysia. Pp. 135–142.

Dransfield, J., Comber, J.B. and Smith, G. (1986). A synopsis of *Corybas* (Orchidaceae) in West Malesia and Asia. *Kew Bulletin* 41: 575–613.

Henderson, M.R. (1930). Notes on the flora of Pulau Tioman and neighbouring islands. *Gardens' Bulletin of the Straits Settlements* 5: 80–93.

Keng, H. (1970). Size and affinities of the flora of the Malay Peninsula. *Journal of Tropical Geography* 31: 43–56.

Kiew, R. (1991a). Herbaceous plants. In Kiew, R. (ed.), *The state of nature conservation in Malaysia*. Malayan Nature Society, Malaysia. Pp. 71–77.

Kiew, R. (1991b). Fraser's Hill – resort to nature. Paper presented at the Seminar on Hill Development in Malaysia, Kuala Lumpur, Malaysia.

Kiew, R. (1992). The montane flora of Peninsular Malaysia: threats and conservation. Unpublished report for National Conservation Strategy, WWF-Malaysia.

Kiew, R., Parris, B.S., Madhavan, S., Edwards, P.J. and Wong K.M. (1987). The ferns and fern-allies of Ulu Endau, Johore, Malaysia. *Malayan Nature Journal* 41: 191–200.

Kirton, L.G. (1991). Butterflies in Peninsular Malaysia. In Kiew, R. (ed.), *The state of nature conservation in Malaysia*. Malayan Nature Society, Malaysia. Pp. 105–110.

Ng, F.S.P., Low, C.M. and Mat Asri Ngah Sanah (1990). *Endemic trees of the Malay Peninsula*. FRIM Research Pamphlet. No. 106.

Ratnam, L., Nor Azman Hussein and Lim, B.L. (1991). Small mammals in Peninsular Malaysia. In Kiew, R. (ed.), *The state of nature conservation in Malaysia*. Malayan Nature Society, Malaysia. Pp. 143–149.

Soepadmo, E. (1991). The impact of man's activities on the unique floras of Malaysian mountains. In Yusof Hadi *et al.* (eds), *Proceedings, Impact of Man's Activities on Tropical Upland Forest Ecosystems*. Universiti Pertanian Malaysia. Pp. 7–23.

Stone, B.C. (1981). The summit flora of Gunung Ulu Kali, Pahang, Malaysia. *Fed. Mus. J.* 26: 1–157.

Whitmore, T.C. (1985). *Tropical rain forests of the Far East*. 2nd Edition. Clarendon Press, Oxford. 352 pp. (1st edition, 1975; 2nd edition reprinted with corrections, 1985.)

Wyatt-Smith, J. (1963). Lower montane and upper montane forest. In *Manual of Malayan silviculture for inland forests*. Malay. For. Records 23. Vol. II. Pp. 23–24.

Acknowledgements

This Data Sheet was prepared by Dr Ruth Kiew (Universiti Pertanian Malaysia, Serdang, Selangor, Malaysia).

PULAU TIOMAN
Pahang, Peninsular Malaysia, Malaysia

Location: 32 km east from the coast of Johore; centred on latitude 2°46'N and longitude 104°13'E.

Area: 71.6 km².

Altitude: 0–1038 m (summit of Gunung Kajang).

Vegetation: Coastal forest, hill forest, upper montane forest, some mangroves.

Flora: Estimated c. 1500 vascular plant species, including some strictly endemic species; unique phytogeographical relationships.

Useful plants: *Rafflesia cantleyi*, used medicinally; ornamental plants such as slipper orchids.

Other values: Beach resort, the forests are critically important as a water catchment area.

Threats: Large-scale resort development (1992); *Rafflesia* and slipper orchids threatened by commercial collection.

Conservation: Wildlife Reserve (IUCN Management Category: VIII), but protected status is not enforced. Associated islands, Pulau Chebeh, Tulai, Sembilang and Seri Buat are proposed as a Marine Park (August 1992).

Geography

Situated 32 km east from the coast of Johore, Pulau Tioman is a pear-shaped island approximately 19 km long and 12 km wide. A central line of hills runs north-south, with peaks rising from 390 m in the north to 1038 m at Gunung Kajang in the south. Most of the island is rugged with a little flat land around the coast. The west coast comprises sandy bays and rocky headlands, while there are cliffs on the east coast.

The western half of the island (including G. Kajang) comprises granitic rocks of Upper Cretaceous age, while the eastern half is mostly made up of volcanic and plutonic rocks of Permian-Triassic age, which are distinctly different from other rock types in Peninsular Malaysia (Lee 1977). The western flanks support thin soil and are boulder-strewn and prone to landslips or are sheer rock faces devoid of soil. Coastal formations, such as raised beach ridges with coralline debris, show clear evidence that the sea-level was 6.2 m higher about 6000 years ago.

Vegetation

Forest up to about 70 m has been cleared for cultivation, including coconut groves and rubber plantations, and for villages. Small pockets of mangroves occur on the west of the island (e.g. at Kampung Paya) (Lee 1977).

Hill forest on the slopes includes pristine, tall seraya (*Shorea curtisii*) forest along ridges. The forest has never been logged commercially. The sparsity of the undergrowth is presumably caused by the drought-prone, thin soils. Landslips on steep slopes support pioneer species. The crest of Gunung Kajang (above about 1000 m) is covered by upper (mossy) montane forest (Henderson 1930).

Flora

The island's flora is of particular scientific importance, both for its endemic species as well as its unique phytogeographic links. It is estimated that there are approximately 1500 vascular plant species, but the precise figure is not known since there have been only two short botanical expeditions (Henderson 1930; Lee 1977) to Gunung Kajang. These have resulted in preliminary lists for ferns and fern allies (113 species) and seed plants (545 species), of which the dominant families are Rubiaceae (46 species), Euphorbiaceae (34 species, with pioneer species particularly well-represented) and Orchidaceae (31 species) (Lee 1977). Much of the rest of the island remains unexplored botanically. The flora of Gunung Kajang itself is estimated to contain approximately 1000 vascular plant species (see Data Sheet on Montane Flora of Peninsular Malaysia, SEA4, and the entry on Gunung Kajang, CPD Site SEA4o, in particular).

Endemic or near-endemic species (i.e. species restricted to Pulau Tioman and adjacent islands) include: *Begonia tiomanensis, Carex leucostachys, Coelogyne tiomanensis, Didymocarpus tiomanicus, Eugenia tiumanensis* and *Justicia ovalis. Lasianthus barbellatus* is a rare near-endemic also known from Pulau Pemanggil.

The flora of Pulau Tioman includes elements from the monsoon region of southern Thailand and the extreme north of Peninsular Malaysia. It has been suggested that this unique phytogeographical pattern is the result of species which are able to withstand a severe dry season on the mainland being able to survive on the shallow soils of Pulau Tioman. Such species include: *Atalantia monophylla, Chrysopogon fulvus, Glycosmis rupestris, Solanum decemdentatum* and *Stauranthera grandiflora*.

Several other species are known from north-west Peninsular Malaysia and from Pulau Tioman, such as *Oberonia tiomanensis* (also known from Gunung Jerai) and *Balanophora abbreviata* (also known from Lenggong, Perak, and elsewhere distributed from Indochina to Africa and Tahiti). The flora of Pulau Tioman also shows links with those of Borneo and Java, for which species Pulau Tioman is the only locality known for the Malay Peninsula. Such species include the tree ferns *Cyathea oosora* and *C. tripinnata*; and *Boehmeria malabarica* and *Loxonia acuminata*.

The coastal flora of Pulau Tioman and adjacent islands was investigated by Corner (1985). Again, the flora shows interesting distribution patterns: species, such as *Manilkara kauki*, *Pisonia grandis* and the fern *Quercifilix zeylanica*, are widespread on coasts from Indochina to Queensland, but are only found on the east coast islands and infrequently on the mainland of Peninsular Malaysia. *Q. zeylanica* is not found on the mainland at all.

Useful plants

Two species are collected commercially: *Rafflesia cantleyi* (collected for medicine by local villagers) and the slipper orchid (*Paphiopedilum barbatum*). Henderson (1930) reported this slipper orchid as common in the mossy forest on G. Kajang, but Stone (in Lee 1977) did not note its presence. This suggests that most of its population had already been stripped off.

The strand plant *Vitex triflora* ssp. *littoralis* has fine potential as an ornamental plant.

Social and environmental values

Besides its flora with unique phytogeographical links, the fauna of Pulau Tioman also shows important differences from that of the mainland. There is an endemic frog (*Ansonia tiomanica*) and the anglehead lizard (*Goniocephalus chalmaeleontus*) is common on the island but absent from the mainland. 15 of the 24 species of mammals found on the island are considered to be distinct varieties, of which the island variety of porcupine is particularly common (Lee 1977); the trident horseshoe bat (*Aselliscus stoliczkanus*) reaches its southern limit on Pulau Tioman (it is otherwise known from south China, Indochina, Burma, Thailand and a single record from Penang) (Zubaid 1988). A total of 206 butterfly species (about 20% of Peninsular Malaysia's butterfly fauna) are known from Pulau Tioman, of which 33 are represented by a geographic race distinct from the mainland races; 4 species range from Taiwan and Borneo as far as Pulau Tioman but are not found on the mainland (Kirton 1991). In 1988, an expedition recorded 3 new endemic species: a blind catfish (*Noemachilus* sp.), a snake (*Oligodon* sp.) and a gecko (*Cyrtodactylus* sp.) (G. Davison 1993, *in litt.*).

Pulau Tioman is a popular beach resort and film location. 145,000 tourist arrivals were reported for 1991. The local population is about 2500. Villages are confined to the narrow coastal areas of flat land. Traditionally, fishing was the main source of income; today tourism (renting of beach chalets) is more important.

Economic assessment

Tourism is the major source of revenue on the island, the attraction of the island being its landscape (a green, unspoilt mountain rising out of the sea), coral and sandy beaches. Conserving the vegetation of the island is, therefore, critical to: (a) preserve the ambience of the resort, (b) provide a reliable water supply from forested catchment areas and (c) protect the surrounding sea from siltation which would destroy the coral.

A minor source of income is derived from the sale of birds' nests of the black-nest swiftlet and (to a lesser extent) white-nest swiftlet which nest in caves on G. Kajang. Forest products, such as rattans, *Rafflesia* and orchids, are of marginal value economically as their supply is very restricted.

Threats

Pulau Tioman is currently (1992) threatened by a large-scale development plan which includes the construction of an airstrip (to take medium-sized planes), a new hotel complex and bungalows. The island is too small to absorb the impact of such a development, which is likely to result in destruction of the coral (a major attraction) and lead to water shortages. Already, coral is severely degraded by silting, organic pollution and the dragging of anchors. The coastal and mangrove forests are likely to be destroyed on a significant scale if the planned development proceeds.

The population of *Paphiopedilum barbatum* should be monitored to assess whether over-collection is a threat to its survival or indeed whether it can still be found at this locality.

Conservation

The whole island is a Wildlife Reserve (IUCN Management Category: VIII), originally established in 1972.

References

Corner, E.J.H. (1985). The botany of some islets east of Pahang and Johore. *Gardens' Bulletin of Singapore* 38: 1–42.

Henderson, M.R. (1930). Notes on the flora of Pulau Tioman and neighbouring islands. *Gardens' Bulletin of the Straits Settlements* 5: 80–93.

Kirton, L.G. (1991). Butterflies in Peninsular Malaysia. In Kiew, R. (ed.), *The state of nature conservation in Malaysia*. Malayan Nature Society, Kuala Lumpur. Pp. 105–110.

Lee, D.W. (1976). Pulau Tioman: Malaysian natural history in miniature. *Malayan Naturalist* 2 (3/4): 28–29.

Lee, D.W. (ed.) (1977). *The natural history of Pulau Tioman*. Merlin Samudra Tioman, Malaysia. 69 pp.

Zubaid, A. (1988). The second record of a trident horseshoe bat, *Aselliscus stoliczkanus* (Hipposiderinae) from Peninsular Malaysia. *Malayan Nature Journal* 42: 29–30.

Acknowledgements

This Data Sheet was prepared by Dr Ruth Kiew (Universiti Pertanian Malaysia, Serdang, Selangor, Malaysia).

TAMAN NEGARA
Kelantan, Pahang and Trengganu, Peninsular Malaysia, Malaysia

Location: South-east Kelantan, west Trengganu and north-east Pahang. The summit of Gunung Tahan is at 4°34'N, 102°17'E.

Area: 4343.5 km².

Altitude: 75–2188 m (summit of Gunung Tahan).

Vegetation: The largest expanse of pristine lowland tropical evergreen rain forest protected in perpetuity in Peninsular Malaysia; hill forest; lower and upper montane forests (including "padang" vegetation); limestone and quartzite vegetation; riverine forest; rheophyte vegetation.

Flora: Estimated >3000 vascular plant species, many endemic species.

Useful plants: Timber trees, indigenous fruit trees, rattans, orchids; many plants of potential medicinal and ornamental value.

Other values: Tourism, flood protection, cultural importance for the indigenous Batek people, home for all of Peninsular Malaysia's large mammal species, including a breeding population of Sumatran rhinoceros.

Threats: Logging, potential threats from hydroelectric dams and development of tourist facilities, e.g. jeep track to Gunung Tahan; lack of a buffer zone to protect against encroachment.

Conservation: National Park (IUCN Management Category: II).

Geography

Taman Negara lies in three states: 57% is within Pahang, 24% in Kelantan and 19% in Trengganu. Several rivers have their headwaters within the park: the River Tembeling forms the southern boundary and flows west before joining the Pahang River; to the north-east, tributaries drain into the Trengganu River; and to the north of Gunung Tahan, the Relai-Aring-Lebir Rivers drain to the north. Rivers afford some spectacular gorges, such as the Teku Gorge (south of Gunung Tahan) and the Tembeling Gorge. The Tahan River, which drains from the peat soils of the montane forest, is one of the few black water rivers in Peninsular Malaysia.

In the north and east of the park is a range of mountains with peaks over 1000 m, of which Gunung Tahan is the highest mountain in Peninsular Malaysia at 2188 m. Gunung Tahan is a sandstone mountain with quartzite intrusions. The summit is either bare rock or is covered by a thin layer of soil, which from February for about 8 weeks when there is little rain and cloud cover, suffers severe water stress.

In general, the area comprises sedimentary rocks (sandstone and shales) with just 17% granite in the northeast. Limestone is quite extensive, including the highest limestone hill in Peninsular Malaysia (Gua Peningat, 723 m), located in the west of the park, and the Kenyam and Gunung Besar groups of limestone hills in the central lowland area. The Kenyam limestone is known to be of Permian age.

58% of the land area is below 300 m. 2260 mm of rainfall is recorded per annum at Kuala Tahan.

Vegetation

Taman Negara contains the largest protected tract of pristine lowland tropical evergreen rain forest in Peninsular Malaysia. Most of the peninsula's vegetation types are found within the park, with the exception of coastal and swamp forest formations. Most of the forest is still pristine. General descriptions of the vegetation found on the ascent of Gunung Tahan are provided by Ridley (1915) and Soepadmo (1971). Forest types comprise lowland dipterocarp forest of the red meranti-keruing (*Dipterocarpus-Shorea*) type (in which *Koompassia excelsa*, tualang, is conspicuous), hill forest, forest on ridges (where *Shorea curtisii* and *Agathis borneensis* may be common), lower montane oak-laurel forest, upper montane forest (where below the ridges *Livistona tahanensis* is conspicuous), and "padang" vegetation on the summit. The padang vegetation occurs over bare rocks and is very stunted. It comprises shrubs about 1 m in height (e.g. *Leptospermum flavescens*) and includes a number of orchid species. Dense thickets of trees grow to about 10–17 m tall in sheltered valleys, with a boggy, mossy layer beneath.

The most spectacular riparian vegetation consists of neram (*Dipterocarpus oblongifolius*) trees which overhang the tributaries of the Sg Tembeling. On rocky banks and gravel spits a diverse assemblage of rheophytes is found.

Edaphic formations include the limestone flora (Kiew and Yong 1985; and see Data Sheet on the Limestone Flora of Peninsular Malaysia – SEA3) and the flora of quartzite outcrops.

Flora

It is estimated that there are more than 3000 vascular plant species in Taman Negara (i.e. an estimated one-third of the total flora of Peninsular Malaysia). No inventory exists and the only checklists available are for Gunung Tahan (Ridley 1908, 1915) and the limestone (Kiew and Yong 1985). Botanical exploration has concentrated on G. Tahan and accessible tributaries of Sg Tembeling. Large areas in the centre of the park and to the north (Kelantan) and east (Trengganu) have not been explored botanically. However, from the number of new and interesting species described, Taman Negara is particularly important, for it not only includes a significant area of pristine lowland forest, riparian forest, and the unique padang flora, but is also a centre of endemism.

The lowland forest is particularly important as a gene pool for commercially important species of timber trees, indigenous fruit trees (of which 43 species are reported; Kochummen 1990) and rattans (Dransfield and Kiew 1990). The 1303 km² of lowland forest is probably sufficient to maintain breeding populations of these species.

Studies on particular plant groups in the park include that of Parris and Edwards (1987) in which 134 species of ferns and fern allies are reported, representing about 40% of Peninsular Malaysia's fern flora, and of which 2 species are endemic to Taman Negara (*Selaginella mirabilis* and *Tectaria translucens*) and 8 species in Peninsular Malaysia are only known from Taman Negara. For palms (Dransfield and Kiew 1990), 70 species are recorded, representing about 30% of the peninsula's palm flora, of which one is endemic to Taman Negara (*Livistona tahanensis*). Ng (1990) reports that, of the 22 species of trees which are endemic to the park, 4 species are from riverine forest and the rest from G. Tahan; many of these are known only from the padang vegetation. Taman Negara is rich in species of *Didymocarpus* with 20 species recorded (Kiew 1989). This represents about 24% of the peninsula's species of this genus, of which 10 are endemic to Taman Negara.

Besides those endemics mentioned above, other endemic species include: *Anerincleistus fruticosa*, *Argostemma albociliatum*, *A. elongatum*, *A. muscicola*, *Begonia longicaulis*, *B. rheifolia*, *Loxocarpus angustifolia*, *Didissandra castaneifolia*, *Gentiana malayana*, *Podocarpus deflexus*, *Rhododendron seimundii*, *Sonerila calycula*, *S. patula*, *S. setosa*, *Utricularia nigricaulis* and *Xyris grandis*. (Until a complete checklist is available, the exact number of endemics cannot be calculated. The examples noted here illustrate the high level of endemism; the inclusion of other groups, such as orchids, would increase the number significantly.) In addition, G. Tahan is home to several distinct forms, such as the mountain form of *Agathis borneenis* (*A. flavescens*) and the white form of the pitcher plant *Nepenthes gracillima* (Kiew 1990).

The neram rivers are sites of high endemism, including such endemics as *Ardisia cardiophylla*, *Glycosmis perakensis* (which is probably now Extinct in Perak) and

CPD Site SEA8: Forest interior, Taman Negara, Peninsular Malaysia with *Licuala*, *Daemonorops* and *Nenga*.
Photo: T.C. Whitmore.

Hoya pusilla. In addition, neram trees harbour a wealth of epiphytic species, including the spectacular tiger orchid, *Grammatophyllum speciosum.* Henderson (1935) recorded 87 orchid species and a further 40 fern and dicot species from a few neram trees. The rheophytic flora is also diverse. *Indotristicha malayana,* the only representative of the Podostemonaceae in the peninsula, is found on submerged boulders in the shallower rivers (its range also extends east into Trengganu).

125 species have been recorded from the Kenyam limestone (Kiew and Yong 1985), including 16 species which are Rare and one undescribed species which belongs to a new genus. The Taman Negara limestone is of especial conservation importance as it is still surrounded by forest which protects the particularly vulnerable shade and damp-loving balsams and begonias. (Elsewhere in the peninsula, this shade-loving community is severely threatened; see Data Sheet on the Limestone Flora of Peninsular Malaysia – SEA3.)

The flora of Gunung Tahan is somewhat of a phytogeographical puzzle in that several temperate genera found on the Main Range (e.g. at Cameron Highlands) are absent. These include *Anemone, Sanicula, Sarcopyramis* and *Viola.* Ridley (1915) considered that the flora of Taman Negara shows more affinities with that of Borneo, particularly with that of Mount Kinabalu, than with the flora of the Main Range. Species such as *Pentaphragma aurantiaca, Itea macrophylla* (also from India and Java), *Eriocaulon hookerianum, Scirpus clarkei* and *Gentiana malayana* (which is closely related to *Gentiana borneensis*) led him to this conclusion. However, subsequent exploration of the Main Range shows that G. Tahan shares many species (including the massive *Pandanus klossii*) with the G. Benom-Fraser's Hill-G. Ulu Kali area of the Main Range.

Useful plants

Taman Negara contains important gene pools of timber and fruit tree species, and rattan species. Other plants with commercial importance include the incense wood, kayu gaharu (*Aquilaria malaccensis*), orchids, for example *Arachnis flos-aeris* (on limestone) and *Grammatophyllum speciosum,* and ornamental plants such as *Rhododendron seimundii* and the white forms of *Impatiens inopinata* and *Nepenthes gracillima,* which are endemic to the park.

Social and environmental values

Taman Negara is becoming a refuge for the nomadic Batek peoples who are being displaced from the north and west of the park by land schemes. There are approximately 600 Orang Asli in or around Taman Negara (as of 1990). A cave in Batu Luas contains recent aboriginal drawings.

Taman Negara is becoming more popular with both overseas and local visitors. In 1990, 15,000 tourists visited the park and numbers are increasing (G. Davison 1993, *in litt.*).

Taman Negara is the only National Park in Peninsular Malaysia and the only protected area in Peninsular Malaysia that conserves a significant area of pristine lowland forest. It is, therefore, invaluable as a permanent resource for nature and environmental education and for long-term scientific research.

Besides being a gene pool for plants, it is also a gene pool for indigenous fish species with commercial importance (Zakaria 1984).

The park ameliorates rainfall and is a significant factor in flood mitigation.

Threats

In spite of being protected by federal law, the integrity of Taman Negara has been threatened from time to time. Illegal logging encroaches within the boundaries of the park, there being no buffer zone around the park. In the early 1970s, the lowland heart of the park in Pahang was threatened by commercial logging. In 1982, a hydroelectric dam was proposed to be built in the Tembeling Gorge, which would have flooded the central lowland area. In 1986, a proposal to build a jeep tract along the banks of Tahan River threatened this black water river. Only by vigorous public protest were these schemes prevented. However, in 1983 the building of the Kenyir Dam (Trengganu) flooded some lowland areas, including species-rich neram rivers in the north-west.

The displacement of Batek people into the park has increased pressure on animals hunted for food (a native right) and the commercial collection of rattan (illegal).

Conservation

Taman Negara is the largest area of lowland forest protected in perpetuity in Peninsular Malaysia, so it is particularly important as a refuge for breeding populations of large mammals, such as elephants, seladang (gaur) and tigers, which elsewhere are threatened by the loss of their forest habitats. This is particularly the case for the Sumatran rhinoceros, the Taman Negara population being one of only two viable breeding populations left in Peninsular Malaysia.

260 species of birds are recorded from Taman Negara (Davison 1982), of which 17% are montane or hill-slope species and 10% are dependent on the rivers. Gunung Tahan is part of the Sumatra and Peninsular Malaysia Endemic Bird Area (EBA) and supports two restricted-range bird species, the globally threatened mountain peacock-pheasant (*Polyplectron inopinatum*), which is endemic to Peninsular Malaysia and the crested argus (*Rheinartia ocellata*), of the subspecies *nigrescens,* which is virtually endemic to Taman Negara. A number of other globally threatened species occur in lowland rain forests in this area, including the Malaysian peacock-pheasant (*Polyplectron malacense*), endemic to the Malay Peninsula, and the storm's stork (*Ciconia stormi*). The subspecies *waterstradti* of the hill prinia (*Prinia atrogularis*) is endemic to G. Tahan.

109 species of fish, more than are recorded from any other locality in the peninsula, are reported from Taman Negara (Zakaria 1984). For Peninsular Malaysia, 15 of these are only known from Taman Negara and, of these, 3 are Endangered and 12 are Rare.

55 species of amphibians (62% of the peninsula's species) are recorded from the park (Kiew 1990), the vast majority of which live in the lowlands. 67 species of snakes (58% of the peninsula's species) are recorded, of which *Cylindrophis rufus* and *Xenopeltis unicolor* are extremely rare and another 10 are uncommon (Lim, Ratnam and Saharudin Anan 1990).

248 species (24%) of Peninsular Malaysia's butterflies are known from Taman Negara (Kirton, Kirton and Tan 1990), of which 208 species were collected from the lowlands.

References

Davison, G.W.H. (1982). The birds of Taman Negara. *Malayan Naturalist* 35(4): 18–23.

Dransfield, J. and Kiew, R. (1990). The palms of Taman Negara. *Journal of Wildlife and Parks* 10: 38–45.

Henderson, M.R. (1935). The epiphytic flora of *Dipterocarpus oblongifolius. Gardens' Bulletin of the Straits Settlements* 9: 93–97.

Kiew, B.H. (1990). Amphibian fauna of Taman Negara. *Journal of Wildlife and Parks* 10: 96–108.

Kiew, R. (1989). *Didymocarpus* (Gesneriaceae) on Gunung Tahan, Malaysia. *Gardens' Bulletin of Singapore* 42: 47–64.

Kiew, R. (1990). Pitcher plants of Taman Negara. *Journal of Wildlife and Parks* 10: 34–37.

Kiew, R. and Yong, G.C. (1985). The limestone flora of the Batu Luas area, Taman Negara. *Malayan Naturalist* 38(3): 30–36.

Kirton, L.G., Kirton, C.G. and Tan M.W. (1990). Butterflies of Kuala Tahan and Gunung Tahan in Taman Negara. *Journal of Wildlife and Parks* 10: 62–77.

Kochummen, K.M. (1990). Wild fruit trees of Taman Negara. *Journal of Wildlife and Parks* 10: 30–33.

Lim, B.L., Ratnam, L. and Saharudin Anan (1990). A study on the collection of snakes from Taman Negara, Malaysia. *Journal of Wildlife and Parks* 10: 116–134.

Ng, F.S.P. (1990). Taman Negara as a centre of endemicity for trees. *Journal of Wildlife and Parks* 10: 52–53.

Parris, B.S. and Edwards, P.J. (1987). A provisional checklist of ferns and fern allies in Taman Negara, Peninsular Malaysia. *Malayan Naturalist* 41(2): 5–10.

Ridley, H.N. (1908). On a collection of plants made by H.C. Robinson and L. Wray from Gunong Tahan, Pahang. *Journal of the Linnean Society* 38: 301–336.

Ridley, H.N. (1915). The botany of Gunong Tahan, Pahang. *Journal of the Federated Malay States Museum* 4: 128–336.

Soepadmo, E. (1971). Plants and vegetation along the paths from Kuala Tahan to Gunong Tahan. *Malayan Nature Journal* 24: 118–124.

Zakaria, M.I. (1984). Checklist of fishes of Taman Negara. *Malayan Naturalist* 37: 21–26.

Acknowledgements

This Data Sheet was prepared by Dr Ruth Kiew (Universiti Pertanian Malaysia, Serdang, Selangor, Malaysia). Professor Peter S. Ashton (Harvard University Herbaria, Cambridge, Massachusetts), Dr G.W.H. Davison (WWF Malaysia) and Dr John Dransfield (Royal Botanic Gardens, Kew) provided additional information.

TRENGGANU HILLS
Trengganu, Peninsular Malaysia, Malaysia

Location: Eastern Peninsular Malaysia; centred on latitude 4°10'N and longitude 102°05'E.

Area: 150 km².

Altitude: 60–920 m.

Vegetation: Lowland and hill forest.

Flora: Estimated c. 1500 vascular plant species; particularly rich in palms and herbs; riverine forest.

Useful plants: Timber trees, rattans, ornamental plants.

Other values: Protection of water catchment areas.

Threats: Logging; land clearance for cultivation.

Conservation: Forest Reserve; Virgin Jungle Reserves (Bukit Bandi, Bukit Bauk and Ulu Chukai).

Geography

The Trengganu Hills (Ulu Kemaman) are situated in the low hills at the southern end of the Bintang Range on the east coast of Peninsular Malaysia. Its western boundary rises to 920 m on the watershed of these mountains. Bukit Bandi (520 m) is a small hill in the south of this area.

The hills are granitic and are drained by tributaries of the Kemaman River, which runs east and enters the South China Sea at Chukai. In the upper reaches, these streams fall steeply and have a rocky bed, but at lower altitudes they are shallow (a few metres deep) and have a sandy bed with gravel or sand bars and banks.

Vegetation

The area is covered in lowland rain forest of the red meranti-keruing (*Dipterocarpus-Shorea*) type, and hill forest. Riverine forests are well-represented and include *Dipterocarpus oblongifolius* (neram). There is a diverse rheophyte flora (Corner 1978).

Flora

Holttum (1936), based on the results of two expeditions by E.J.H. Corner, drew attention to the extraordinarily rich flora, which is distinctly different from that of other parts of the Malay Peninsula. Corner (1960) suggested this area contained the richest, and maybe the oldest, part of the flora of the peninsula. Since then, the area has not been subject to any detailed botanical investigation. In the absence of detailed investigations, it is estimated that the flora contains about 1500 vascular plant species.

Since Corner's expeditions, new species have been described which are endemic to the area. These include:

Ardisia tumida, Begonia corneri, Cleistanthus major, Didissandra sp., *Didymocarpus corneri, D. floribundus, D. geitleri, Garcinia cataractalis, Goniothalamus calycinus, Heliciopsis whitmorei, Licuala corneri, L. kemamanensis, Scaphochlamys breviscapa, S. tenuis, S. grandis* and *S. rubomaculata* (see, for example, Kiew 1991a).

The area is particularly rich in palm species and has been recommended as in need of protection (Kiew 1991b). *Licuala kemamanensis* is Endangered, and *L. corneri, Calamus corneri, C. pandanosmus* and *Pinanga cleistantha* are examples of species vulnerable to logging and habitat disturbance (Kiew 1989). In addition, there is also an undescribed species of *Livistona* (J. Dransfield, pers. comm.) which, although widespread on the Trengganu Hills, is protected only in the small (28 ha) coastal Virgin Jungle Reserve on Bukit Bauk. Other extremely rare species include *Begonia corneri*, known only from a single collection from a river bank.

Useful plants

Several palms and gesneriads have economic potential as ornamental plants. Asam paya or kelubi (*Eleiodoxa conferta*) fruits are pickled and sold in Chukai (Kiew 1991b). This palm grows in swampy areas and can be managed on a sustained basis to generate income locally. Much of the valuable timber and rattans have already been extracted.

Social and environmental values

The Trengganu Hills encompass the drainage basin of the Kemaman River. Protection of the forests is vital to maintain water supplies for Chukai town and for flood mitigation.

Economic assessment

Valuable timber and rattan has already been extracted from the area. The main value of the forests today lies in their significant role in maintaining water supplies and preventing soil erosion, and their importance as a valuable gene pool of timber tree species, fruit trees, rattans and potential medicinal plant species.

Threats

The area was heavily logged in the 1980s, and extensive damage was caused by the construction of logging roads and loading areas. In addition, a tinmine operated at Bukit Kajang from the 1930s until the 1970s. This, too, has created waste ground which will not regenerate into dipterocarp forest. Future threats are likely to be from land clearance for agriculture.

Conservation

In spite of being poorly known botanically, at least 20 strict endemic species are recorded from a relatively small area, which indicates its importance as a centre of endemism. In addition, apart from the Ulu Chukai Virgin Jungle Reserve (41 ha), protected as a seed stand and 2 other small Virgin Jungle Reserves, no are in the Trengganu Hills is protected by law either as a National Park, State Park or as a Virgin Jungle Reserve, which means that this rich and unique flora, which forms part of the eastern element of the peninsula's flora, is not protected.

References

Corner, E.J.H. (1960). The Malayan flora. In Purchon, R.D. (ed.), *Proceedings, Centen. and Bicenten. Congress Biol., Singapore.* Pp. 21–24.

Corner, E.J.H. (1978). The freshwater swamp-forest of southern Johore and Singapore. *Gardens' Bulletin of Singapore.* Suppl. 1: 40–45.

Holttum, R.E. (1936). *Annual report of gardens, Straits Settlements, for the year 1935.* Government Printing Office, Singapore.

Kiew, R. (1989). Conservation status of palms in Peninsular Malaysia. *Malayan Naturalist* 43(1/2): 3–15.

Kiew, R. (1991a). *Begonia corneri* (Begoniaceae), a new species from Kemaman, Malaysia. *Bot. Jahrb. Syst.* 113: 271–275.

Kiew, R. (1991b). Palm utilization and conservation in Peninsular Malaysia. In Johnson, D. (ed.), *Palms for human needs in Asia. Palm utilization and conservation in India, Indonesia, Malaysia and the Philippines.* Balkema, Rotterdam. Pp. 75–130.

Acknowledgements

This Data Sheet was prepared by Dr Ruth Kiew (Universiti Pertanian Malaysia, Serdang, Selangor, Malaysia). Dr John Dransfield (Royal Botanic Gardens, Kew) provided helpful comments on an earlier draft.

BATU APOI FOREST RESERVE, ULU TEMBURONG
Brunei Darussalam

Location: Southern part of eastern Brunei; Bukit Belalong is located at 4°29'N and 115°12'E.

Area: 488 km².

Altitude: 50–1850 m (summit of Gunung Pagon); most of the area lies above 100 m.

Vegetation: Lowland rain forest dominated by dipterocarps, lower montane forest on the hills (including heath forest elements), upper montane forest on the higher slopes of Gunung Pagon and Gunung Retak.

Flora: c. 3000 vascular plant species.

Useful plants: Timber trees (dipterocarps, *Agathis*), medicinal plants, ornamental plants.

Other values: Tourism (to be developed as Brunei's first National Park), watershed protection, educational and research values.

Threats: Illegal logging (encroachment from neighbouring state of Sarawak); possible exploitation for hydroelectric and water supply schemes.

Conservation: Forest Reserve (Conservation Area); planned National Park.

Geography

The Batu Apoi Forest Reserve includes the complete watershed of 3 main rivers: the Temburong, the Belalong and the Temawai. Four peaks rise to over 1000 m: Gunung Pagon (1850 m), on the south-east border, Gunung Retak (1618 m), on the south-west border, Bukit Lesong (1192 m) and Bukit Tudal (1181 m). Most of the remaining land is below 1000 m, with Bukit Belalong (915 m) prominent in the northern half of the reserve.

The whole area consists entirely of Tertiary sedimentary rocks – the relatively soft shales and interbedded harder sandstones of the Temburong Formation in the northern part, and the more massive sandstones of the Melingan Formation in the south. The Temburong Formation was deposited in an offshore basin, while the Melingan Formation is deltaic in origin. Both formations were subsequently uplifted and folded, and the erosional processes associated with the uplift have produced a very sharp topography in which very steep valleys are separated by narrow ridges (James 1984; Dykes 1994).

Detailed climate records are not available, the only study to date being that of Dykes (1994), using automatic weather stations over a 10-month period (May/June 1991 – April 1992) at Kuala Belalong, in the north (50 m altitude), and on the summit of Bukit Belalong (915 m altitude), 8 km distant. Although the monthly rainfall pattern was similar at the two sites, there was extreme localization of individual rainfall events.

Vegetation

The whole of the Batu Apoi Forest Reserve is covered in primary forest, with little or no human interference apart from a minimal amount of hunting, fishing and collecting of plant products. Two main vegetation types can be found: mixed dipterocarp forest covers most of the northern part, while montane rain forest covers the higher parts in the south, and the tops of the isolated peaks from about 750–800 m altitude.

The dipterocarp forest is fairly uniform (Anderson and Marsden 1988) due to the relative uniformity of soil types, and is an excellent example of north-east Borneo clay soil dipterocarp forest (P.S. Ashton 1991, *in litt.*). *Shorea parvifolia*, together with other species of *Shorea*, and *Dryobalanops lanceolata* dominate the mixed dipterocarp forest. A 1 ha plot near Kuala Belalong contained 231 tree species (minimum diameter 10 cm) belonging to 43 families, with *Shorea parvifolia*, *S. laevis*, *Elateriospermum tapos* and *Gluta laxiflora* the most important species (Poulsen *et al.* 1993). It is estimated that nearly 75% of all dipterocarp species in Brunei are represented in the Batu Apoi Forest Reserve. Of the non-dipterocarp trees, *Koompassia malaccensis* and *K. excelsa* are notable for their large size and emergent status; *Eusideroxylon* spp. (belian or Borneo ironwood) is also locally abundant.

The herb flora is comparable in richness to that of Amazonia, with 92 and 68 species recorded from two 1 ha plots enumerated near Kuala Belalong at an altitude of 250 m (Poulsen 1993). *Rhizanthes* sp. (Rafflesiaceae) occurs on rocky slopes in dipterocarp forest at an altitude of c. 150 m near Kuala Belalong.

The total area of montane forest is c. 71 km², mostly restricted to the southernmost part of the reserve (which is underlain by the Melingan Formation), and including the foothills and peaks of Gunung Pagon and Gunung Retak. Montane forest develops at an altitude of between 700–900 m, although there is no sudden transition from mixed dipterocarp forest (Wong 1990). An interesting area of montane forest (yet to be fully explored) covers the summit ridge of Bukit Belalong (on Setap Shales of the Temburong Formation), from an altitude of about 800 m. Smaller areas of montane forest are found on other isolated peaks of the reserve to the north of the main montane forest area.

Lower montane forest is developed above 900–1200 m (depending on local topography). Three subtypes have been recognized (Anderson and Marsden 1988). Mixed-species forest includes *Quercus* spp., *Lithocarpus* spp., Sapotaceae and *Podocarpus neriifolius* as significant components. Lauraceae, common in this type of forest in other areas of Malesia, is poorly represented. *Rafflesia pricei* (Rafflesiaceae) has been found at an altitude of c. 750 m in the valley between Gunung Pagon and Gunung Retak. Tolong forest occurs in small patches (maximum 1 km²). This forest is dominated by *Agathis dammara*; oaks and *Dacrydium beccarii* are also present. This subtype is replaced in certain areas (on ridges with shallow white sandy soils) by a forest dominated by *Shorea coriacea*. Heath forest species, such as *Casuarina* spp., also occur in this subtype, which may cover a large area in the headwaters region of the Sungai Temawai (Ashton 1964).

Tall and short facies can be recognized in upper montane forest, which develops at altitudes between 1000 m (on isolated ridges and knolls) and 1200 m (on broader ridges). Tall facies montane forest comprises small trees with a canopy height of c. 10–15 m. *Dacrydium beccarii*, *Phyllocladus hypophyllus*, *Lithocarpus* spp. and *Quercus percoriacea*, are frequent. The high-climbing pitcher plant *Nepenthes veitchii* also occurs in this forest type. Short-facies montane forest includes a similar range of woody species, but they grow as bushy shrubs on skeletal peat-covered soils in exposed situations. Ericaceae (*Rhododendron* spp., *Vaccinium* spp.) and pitcher plants (*Nepenthes* spp., including *N. stenophylla*, *N. tentaculata* and *N. lowii*) are noticeable components of short-facies montane forest. *Balanophora* (Balanophoraceae) has been found on Gunung Pagon.

Flora

It is estimated that the Batu Apoi Forest Reserve contains approximately 3000 vascular plant species. The palm flora of the reserve includes over half of those known from Brunei, with 49 species of rattan represented near Kuala Belalong (Dransfield 1994). Within the Batu Apoi Forest Reserve a new genus of bamboo has been recognized.

A small area (500 km²) of the Batu Apoi Reserve near Kuala Belalong, near the northern part of the reserve, was the focus for a detailed study known as The Brunei Rainforest Project 1991–92, jointly carried out by Universiti Brunei Darussalam and the Royal Geographical Society. The full results of this expedition have yet to be published, but are summarized by Cranbrook and Edwards (1994). Significant findings include several new Zingiberaceae (e.g. *Boisenbergia* sp.). The richness of this relatively small area, and the reserve as a whole, is indicated by the occurrence of over 150 species of ferns and fern allies (I. Edwards, in prep.), including the rare *Tectaria inopinata*, found at 850 m on Bukit Belalong (Poulsen 1993).

Useful plants

Much of the reserve is a significant timber resource, with many species of dipterocarps, particularly *Shorea* spp. (red merantis),

including *S. parvifolia*, *S. leptoclados*, *S. ferruginea* and *S. macroptera*, together with *Dryobalanops lanceolata* (kapur) (Anderson and Marsden 1988). The montane forests include several rather small stands of *Agathis dammara* (tolong).

The reserve contains a wide range of native fruit trees, including *Durio* spp., *Garcinia* spp. and *Nephelium* spp., offering potential for crop improvement and domestication of new species.

Many plants have been used in traditional medicine (K.A. Salim, pers. comm.). The montane forest includes plants of potential economic importance as ornamentals, but care will be needed to prevent over-harvesting from the small populations in the area.

Social and environmental values

The reserve is an important water catchment area, with the Sungai Temburong supplying water to the main town of the district.

Apart from the Universiti Brunei Darussalam/Royal Geographical Society (UBD-RGS) expedition to the Kuala Belalong area, there have been several short expeditions to the reserve, particularly to Gunung Retak. Long-term research will benefit from the establishment of the Kuala Belalong Field Studies Centre, located in the north of the reserve, which is a permanent facility run by Universiti Brunei Darussalam.

The Reserve has a rich fauna, with many of northern Borneo's larger mammals represented, including sun bear (*Helarctis malayanus*), Borneo gibbon (*Hylobates muelleri*), red leaf monkey (*Presbytis rubicunda*) and clouded leopard (*Neofelis nebulosa*). Hose's civet (*Hemigalus hosei*) occurs near Bukit Belalong; Savi's pigmy shrew (*Suncus etruscus*) has been found near Kuala Belalong. The following records obtained during the UBD-RGS Brunei Rainforest Project 1991–92 (which was limited to a maximum of 500 km² around the Kuala Belalong Field Studies Centre) provide an indication of the faunistic richness of the reserve: over 50 species of amphibians (of a Borneo total of c. 120), including only the second known locality for the intermediate sticky frog (*Kalophrynus intermedius*) and three previously unknown amphibians (Das 1993), 48 species of reptiles, including the sinister water snake (*Opisthotropis typica*), previously recorded only from Mount Kinabalu (I. Das, pers. comm.), 350 species of butterflies (Orr 1993), 32 species of bats and 198 species of birds (Mann 1993), including large populations of 7 species of hornbills.

The educational value of the reserve will be increased once facilities have been provided at the National Park headquarters, to be sited within the reserve on the Sg Temburong near Kuala Belalong. Short courses for secondary school children are presently run at the Kuala Belalong Field Centre. A balance between conservation, research, education and tourism will be required, and is presently being addressed by the Department of Forestry with the demarcation of zones within the reserve.

Economic assessment

Anderson and Marsden (1988) includes a review of the economic potential of the Batu Apoi Forest Reserve.

Threats

The rugged nature of the terrain makes commercial logging without serious environmental consequences very difficult, and it is unlikely that timber extraction will ever be feasible in the main part of the reserve. Cross-border incursions for timber extraction have damaged some areas in the southwest and north-east of the reserve.

Increased visitor pressure from the development of the National Park may pose problems in view of the very restricted number of routes through the forest, particularly to the summit of Bukit Belalong. Strict observance of zoning should prevent damage to much of the reserve, while the inaccessibility of the montane forest in the south should provide protection to this habitat.

The narrow valleys of the main rivers, and the relatively constant water supply, make the northern portion of the reserve one of the few areas in Brunei which would permit the development of hydroelectric power. Damming the Sg Temburong and/or the Sg Belalong would also increase water availability for the country as a whole (although this would entail a pipeline across Brunei Bay). Creation of a lake in the northernmost valleys of the reserve would have significant effects on the low-altitude flora and fauna, which is otherwise poorly represented in protected areas in Brunei, and in Borneo as a whole.

Conservation

Batu Apoi Forest Reserve was gazetted in 1950 and was designated as a Primary Conservation Area by the Department of Forestry in 1989. The reserve includes one of the largest areas of protected forest below 1000 m in north Borneo.

Plans to develop the area as a National Park are well-advanced, although the necessary legal framework has yet to be drafted. There are plans to extend the designated Forest Reserve to the north (Morni 1993), although the additional area will be designated as production forest and will be logged.

References

Anderson, J.A.R. and Marsden D. (1988). Brunei forest resources and strategic planning study. Unpublished report to the Government of His Majesty the Sultan and Yang Di-Pertuan of Negara Brunei Darussalam.

Ashton, P.S. (1964). Ecological studies in the mixed dipterocarp forests of Brunei State. *Oxford Forestry Memoirs* 25. Clarendon Press, Oxford. 75 pp.

Cranbrook, Earl of, and Edwards, D.S. (eds) (1994). *Belalong: a tropical rainforest.* Sun Tree Publishing, Singapore.

Das, I. (1993). The amphibians of Batu Apoi. Paper prepared for the Conference on "Tropical Rainforest Research: Current Issues", Bandar Seri Begawan, Brunei Darussalam, 9–17 April 1993.

Dransfield, J. (1994). Palms. In Cranbrook, Earl of, and Edwards, D.S. (eds), *Belalong: a tropical rainforest.* Sun Tree Press, Singapore.

Dykes, A.P. (1994). The tropical climate. In Cranbrook, Earl of, and Edwards, D.S. (eds), *Belalong: a tropical rainforest.* Sun Tree Press, Singapore.

James, D.M.D. (1984). *The geology and hydrocarbon resources of Negara Brunei Darussalam.* Muzium Brunei, Brunei Darussalam. 165 pp.

Mann, C.F. (1993). The avifauna of the Belalong forest. Paper prepared for the Conference on "Tropical Rainforest Research: Current Issues", Bandar Seri Begawan, Brunei Darussalam, 9–17 April 1993.

Morni, O. (1993). Forestry in Brunei Darussalam: meeting the challenges of the future. Paper prepared for the Conference on "Tropical Rainforest Research: Current Issues", Bandar Seri Begawan, Brunei Darussalam, 9–17 April 1993.

Orr, A.G. (1993). Spatial and temporal patterns of butterfly diversity at Kuala Belalong. Butterflies of Batu Apoi. Paper prepared for the Conference on "Tropical Rainforest Research: Current Issues", Bandar Seri Begawan, Brunei Darussalam, 9–17 April 1993.

Poulsen, A.D. (1993). The herbaceous ground flora of the Batu Apoi Forest Reserve, Brunei. Paper prepared for the Conference on "Tropical Rainforest Research: Current Issues", Bandar Seri Begawan, Brunei Darussalam, 9–17 April 1993.

Poulsen, A.D., Nielsen I.C., Tan, S. and Balslev, H. (1993). A quantitative inventory of trees in one hectare of mixed dipterocarp forest in Temburong, Brunei. Paper prepared for the Conference on "Tropical Rainforest Research: Current Issues", Bandar Seri Begawan, Brunei Darussalam, 9–17 April 1993.

Wong, K.M. (1990). *In Brunei forests: an introduction to the plant life of Brunei Darussalam.* Forestry Department, Brunei Darussalam. 108 pp.

Acknowledgements

This Data Sheet was written by Dr David S. Edwards (Universiti Brunei Darussalam), with thanks to the following members of Universiti Brunei Darussalam for their help and contributions: Joe Charles (mammals, birds), Indraneil Das (amphibia and reptiles), Kamariah A. Salim (medicinal plants), Chris Kofron (bats), Bert Orr (butterflies) and Samhan Nyawa (mammals).

BORNEO: CPD SITE SEA15

BUKIT RAYA AND BUKIT BAKA
Kalimantan, Indonesia

Location: Schwaner mountain range of central Borneo, spanning the provincial borders of Central and West Kalimantan. Bukit Raya lies between latitudes 0°00'–1°30'S and longitudes 112°00'–113°20'E; Bukit Baka lies between latitudes 0°30'–0°45'S and longitudes 112°15'–113°00'E.

Area: 7705 km².

Altitude: 100–2278 m (summit of Bukit Raya).

Vegetation: Lowland tropical rain forest dominated by dipterocarps, swamp forest, montane forest, upper montane forest (mossy forest), ericaceous scrub.

Flora: Botanical investigation very incomplete; vascular flora estimated at between 2000 and 4000 species.

Useful plants: Many species of wild fruit trees, such as mangoes; illipe nuts, rattans.

Other values: Watershed protection, rich fauna, source of forest products for hunter-gatherers and surrounding shifting cultivators.

Threats: Logging, road construction, some encroachment on the western side from shifting cultivation.

Conservation: Bukit Baka-Bukit Raya National Park (IUCN Management Category: II) covers 1810.9 km².

Geography

Bukit Raya (2278 m), one of the highest mountains in Indonesian Kalimantan, and Bukit Baka (1617 m) are part of the Schwaner mountain range (Pegunungan Schwaner) in central Borneo. They lie near the southernmost part of the great central mountain ranges that extend into southern Borneo and trend north-east along the border between Kalimantan and Sarawak, and continue into Sabah. Bukit Raya lies within the administrative province of Kalimantan Tengah (Central Kalimantan), and Bukit Baka within Kalimantan Barat (West Kalimantan).

The Schwaner mountain range consists mostly of a quartz diorite plutonic massif. The Bukit Raya area consists of mid-Tertiary volcanics. In the undulating lowlands and foothills of Bukit Raya, slopes of over 30% are encountered. Above 550 m there is an abrupt change to a very rugged landscape with very steep, deeply dissected slopes of the mountain proper (Nooteboom 1987).

No climatic data are available for the Bukit Raya area, but it is estimated to receive an annual rainfall of over 4000 mm. A dry period of several months (June–October) occurs in the Schwaner range, but heavy orographic rain can fall even in this period (ORSTOM 1981). Average temperatures are estimated to range from 12°C at the higher altitudes to 25°C at the lower altitudes.

Vegetation

The area includes fine examples of lowland and hill tropical rain forest, dominated by members of the Dipterocarpaceae. In some areas, a type of swamp forest has developed on clayey peat soils which are almost permanently flooded (Nooteboom 1987). Montane forest occurs above 1000 m, showing great similarity to that of Gunung Mulu in Sarawak, and dominated by Fagaceae, Guttiferae, Myrtaceae, Flacourtiaceae, Sapotaceae and numerous species of *Rhododendron*. From around 1600 m upper montane forest ("mossy forest") is encountered, again with various Ericaceae, such as *Rhododendron* and *Vaccinium*, and Guttiferae, as well as *Phyllocladus hypophyllus* (Phyllocladaceae), *Elaeocarpus* (Elaeocarpaceae), *Embelia* (Embeliaceae), *Nepenthes* (Nepenthaceae) and tree ferns. Toward the summit, above 2150 m, the vegetation is an ericaceous scrub, with *Leptospermum flavescens* and (on Bukit Raya) *Lycopodium cernuum* and *Myrica javanica*.

Flora

Botanical exploration of the area is still very incomplete, but the total vascular flora could be in the region of 4000 species (H.P. Nooteboom 1991, *in litt.*); however, P.S. Ashton (1991, *in litt.*) predicts about 2000 vascular plant species are present. Initial investigations were made by the 1982–1983 Bukit Raya Expedition, which collected nearly 1000 species of vascular plants from Bukit Raya. Over 400 species of phanerogams were found in an area of lowland rain forest of 1 km radius from the base camp at Tumbang Riang. In addition, 300 species of phanerogams were collected in the timber concessions at 50–100 m altitude, 20–70 km south of the base camp. Of these, more than 120 species were not collected at Tumbang Riang, suggesting that more than 30% of taxa are of very local occurrence throughout the area (Nooteboom 1987). Among the taxa collected to the north-west of the base camp area are the following which are apparently rare throughout Borneo: *Dichapetalum geloniodes* subsp. *sumatranum*, (Dichapetalaceae), *Fagraea macroscypha* (Loganiaceae) and *Lycopodium nummularifolium* (Lycopodiaceae).

The lowland flora is certainly diverse. Within a 600 m² plot, over 55 tree species of more than 0.15 m girth were recorded. These represent at least 38 genera in 25 families (Nooteboom 1987). Among the dipterocarps found on the alluvial soils in the bottomlands include: *Shorea seminis*, *Hopea centipeda* (a species confined to river banks, and endemic to Borneo) and *Dipterocarpus oblongifolius*, a true rheophyte. *Shorea polyandra*, *S. macrophylla*, *S. parvistipulata* subsp. *albifolia* and *S. palembanica* are also abundant on, although not restricted to, alluvial soils in the lowlands. The first three of these are endemic to Borneo.

The 1982–1983 expedition also collected more than 300 species of angiosperms and 35 species of ferns at 250–2270 m on Bukit Raya. Most of these species were different from those collected in the lowlands (Nooteboom 1987). *Rafflesia arnoldii* was also found here.

Palms found by the 1982–1983 expedition include several species which have been rarely collected elsewhere in Kalimantan, including: *Calamus divaricatus*, *C. flabellatus*, *C. mattanensis*, *C. marginatus*, *Daemonorops atra* (endemic to Borneo), *D. micrantha*, *D. korthalsii* (endemic to Borneo), *D. microstachya* (endemic to Borneo), *Iguanura prolifera*, *Pinanga* aff. *capitata*, *P. sessilifolia* and *Plectocomiopsis mira* (Mogea 1987).

Useful plants

The lowland forests contain a number of wild fruit tree species, such as *Artocarpus* spp. (jackfruit), *Durio* spp. (durians), *Litchi chinensis* (litchi), *Nephelium* spp., *Litsea* spp. and numerous species of *Mangifera* (mangoes). Illipe nuts are obtained from species of *Shorea*. Among the rattans present are *Calamus caesius*, *C. javensis* and *Daemonorops didymophylla*. Many medicinal plants are still used by the local population. An inventory of these is needed before this local ethnobotanical knowledge is lost (H.P. Nooteboom 1991, pers. comm.).

Social and environmental issues

The forests protect part of the catchment of the Melawi River which forms a major tributary of the Kapuas river system of West Kalimantan. The area also protects the headwaters of rivers flowing south into the Mendawai system which flows through southern Kalimantan.

A traditional tribe, the Ud, subsist by hunting and collecting forest products. Numerous groups of indigenous Otdanum Dayaks practice shifting agriculture (ladang) around the perimeter of the area. The 1982–1983 expedition reported ladang agriculture along the river near Tumbang Liang, but beyond a narrow strip of 500 m either side of the river the terrain becomes too rugged and poor to support agriculture (Nooteboom 1987).

The area contains a rich fauna, including a large number of mammals. Notable among these are the primates: orang-utan (*Pongo pygmaeus*) (Endangered), agile gibbon (*Hylobates agilis*), macaques (*Macaca* ssp.), maroon leaf monkey (*Presbytis rubicunda*) and slow loris (*Nycticebus coucang*). Other notable animals include clouded leopard

(*Neofelis nebulosa*) (Vulnerable), bearded pig (*Sus barbatus*), civets and several species of deer. A rich avifauna includes tree swifts, pheasants (including the rare Bulwer's pheasant, *Lophura bulweri*, a Bornean endemic) and hornbills. The montane forests of Bukit Raya and Bukit Baka lie within the Bornean Mountains Endemic Bird Area (EBA), which supports 28 restricted-range bird species, of which 24 are endemic.

Economic assessment

The local population depends on the forest for part of their food requirements and as a source of medicines. Additional income is obtained from rattan collection. Illipe nuts are exported to Singapore and provide an additional source of income (H.P. Nooteboom 1991, pers. comm.).

Threats

The most serious threats are logging and road construction. There is a large logging concession in the northern part of Bukit Baka, and some logging has taken place (K. MacKinnon 1991, *in litt.*). Logging concessions also overlap with an area that had previously been proposed as an extension to the protected area. Illegal logging is always a threat: 50–60 km² of lowland rain forest were logged illegally between 1982 and 1985 in the (then) Bukit Raya Nature Reserve. The proposed trans-Kalimantan highway would follow an existing logging road across the Schwaner Mountains to West Kalimantan and would run through lowland forests within the protected area.

Ladang agriculture is encroaching on the west (MacKinnon 1988). The nature of the terrain imposes limits on the amount of agriculture which is possible.

Conservation

Bukit Raya was established as a Nature Reserve (IUCN Management Category: I) covering 1100 km² in 1979; Bukit Baka was established as a Nature Reserve (also IUCN Management Category: I) covering 705 km² in 1987. They were re-established as the Bukit Baka-Bukit Raya National Park (IUCN Management Category: II) in 1992. The total area protected is 1810.9 km². A proposed extension to the Bukit Raya reserve covered 5900 km².

Bukit Raya was the focus of a major multidisciplinary expedition in 1982–1983, which included members from the Rijksherbarium (Leiden), Herbarium Bogoriense, the Forest Research Institute (Bogor), University of Wageningen, BIOTROP and UNESCO. No management had apparently been carried out in the reserve (up to 1988), although Tantra, Oldemann and Torquebiau (1982) had made several recommendations, including the implementation of a system of buffer zoning, boundary marking, gazettement of the proposed Bukit Raya extension and development of a scientific field station.

USAID are establishing a research station in Bukit Baka and will assist with projects involving community participation and buffer zone management to relieve pressure on the reserves.

References

MacKinnon, K. (1988). Consultant's report of biodiversity specialist, for USAID PID mission: natural resource management in Kalimantan. (Unpublished report.)

MacKinnon, J. and Artha, M.B. (1981). *A National Conservation Plan for Indonesia, Vol. V: Kalimantan*. FAO, Bogor. UNDP/FAO National Parks Development Project INS/78/061. Field report 17.

McCarthy, A.J. (comp.) (1991). Conservation areas of Indonesia. Final draft. World Conservation Monitoring Centre, Cambridge, U.K. in collaboration with Directorate General of Forest Protection and Nature Conservation (PHPA), Ministry of Forestry, Republic of Indonesia, and IUCN Commission on National Parks and Protected Areas, Gland, Switzerland.

Mogea, J.P. (1987). Notes on Palmae collected during the expedition. In Nooteboom, H.P. (ed.), *Report of the 1982–1983 Bukit Raya Expedition*. Rijksherbarium, Leiden. Pp. 67–70.

Nooteboom, H.P. (ed.) (1987). *Report of the 1982–1983 Bukit Raya Expedition*. Rijksherbarium, Leiden. 93 pp.

ORSTOM (1981). *Reconnaissance survey for the selection of transmigration sites in Central Kalimantan*. Indonesia-ORSTOM Transmigration Project PTA 44. Jakarta. 130 pp.

Tantra, I.G.M., Oldeman, R.A.A. and Torquebiau, E. (1982). Some preliminary remarks on the Bukit Raya Nature Reserve and its proposed extension. Palangkaraya, Indonesia. 9 pp. (Unpublished report.)

Acknowledgements

This Data Sheet was written by Stephen D. Davis, with grateful thanks to Dr Hans P. Nooteboom (Rijksherbarium, Leiden), Professor Peter S. Ashton (Harvard University Herbaria, Cambridge, Massachusetts), Dr Kathy MacKinnon (WWF Indonesia) and Dr John Dransfield (Royal Botanic Gardens, Kew) for helpful comments on an earlier draft.

LANJAK-ENTIMAU WILDLIFE SANCTUARY, BATANG AI NATIONAL PARK AND GUNUNG BENTUANG DAN KARIMUN
Sarawak, Malaysia and Kalimantan, Indonesia

Location: Lanjak-Entimau and Batang Ai are in south-western Sarawak, on the border with Kalimantan, in the Second, Third, Sixth and Seventh Divisions; Gunung Bentuang dan Karimun is in Kalimantan Barat (West Kalimantan).

Area: 10,112 km², comprising Lanjak-Entimau Wildlife Sanctuary (1688 km²), proposed extensions (184 km²), Batang Ai National Park (240 km²), Cagar Alam Gunung Bentuang dan Karimun (8000 km²).

Altitude: 500–1284 m (summit of Bukit Lanjak).

Vegetation: Tropical lowland and hill evergreen rain forest (mixed dipterocarp forest), heath (kerangas) forest, montane forest, small areas of swamp forest (Lanjak-Entimau).

Flora: No detailed botanical exploration, but flora predicted to be typical of the inland Bornean shale flora on lower slopes, with heath elements on ridges and submontane elements on upper slopes.

Useful plants: Many useful plants are utilized by the Ibans (Dayaks), including illipe nuts (*Shorea*), rattans and fruits.

Other values: Watershed protection, rich mammal and bird fauna, wide range of forest products utilized by Ibans.

Threats: Agricultural encroachment and illegal logging on western side.

Conservation: Lanjak-Entimau Wildlife Sanctuary (IUCN Management Category: IV), proposals to upgrade to National Park status and extend to link with Gunung Bentuang dan Karimun Nature Reserve in Kalimantan to form a Border Park or Transfrontier Reserve. Batang Ai National Park (IUCN Management Category: II) notified in 1990.

Geography

This region is a contiguous tract of rain forest in the rugged, steeply dissected mountainous border between the Second, Third, Sixth and Seventh Divisions of south-western Sarawak and Kalimantan Barat (West Kalimantan). There are no roads; access is by river. The whole area (>10,000 km²) comprises Lanjak-Entimau Wildlife Sanctuary (1687.6 km²) and proposed extensions (184 km²) and Batang Ai National Park (240 km²) in Sarawak (Malaysia), and Cagar Alam Gunung Bentuang dan Karimun (Gunung Bentuang dan Karimun Nature Reserve) (8000 km²) in Kalimantan (Indonesia).

The area covers part of the Boven Kapuas Mountains. In the east, the Gunung Bentuang dan Karimun Nature Reserve would extend as far as the Muller Range. The highest points in Lanjak-Entimau are Bukit Lanjak (1284 m), Bukit Entimau (975 m) and Gunong Spali (966 m). Most of the soils are immature, shallow, nutrient-poor regosols. In many areas, the steepness of the slopes prevents development of a soil profile as a result of soil movement downslope. Large-scale removal of vegetation would rapidly increase the rate of soil erosion.

The climate of Lanjak-Entimau is typical of much of Sarawak, being generally hot and humid throughout the year. Average annual rainfall is c. 3500 mm, with the heaviest rainfall between September and January (average monthly rainfall c. 300–350 mm). No climatic details are available for the other parts of the area.

Vegetation

Much of Lanjak-Entimau Wildlife Sanctuary (about 84%) is covered by tropical lowland and hill evergreen rain forest dominated by dipterocarps (mixed dipterocarp forest), with a small amount of montane forest (WWF-Malaysia 1982). However, this is based on remote sensing, and probably over-estimates the amount of lowland forest, which may cover as little as c. 15% of the area (P.S. Ashton 1991, *in litt.*). Lanjak-Entimau possibly includes some mixed dipterocarp forest on shale and clay, the region's major formation, and is presently under-represented in the protected areas system (P.S. Ashton 1990, *in litt.*). In the northern half of Lanjak-Entimau the forest is fairly uniform, of medium density on undulating terrain, mixed with small patches of mixed dipterocarp remnant forest that has been selectively logged for local use. There are some areas of shifting cultivation near the northern boundary. In the south, the terrain is more mountainous; the vegetation shows more variation, with less uniform mixed dipterocarp forest and substantial areas of heath (kerangas) forest (WWF-Malaysia 1982). There is a small area of swamp forest.

The Batang Ai National Park includes the catchment area of the Batang Ai Hydroelectric Scheme. This area is mostly covered by regenerating old secondary forest.

Gunung Bentuang dan Karimun is mostly covered by hill and montane forest, and some lowland forest. The area is predicted to have a flora typical of the central hills of the island.

TABLE 52. VEGETATION CLASSIFICATION OF LANJAK-ENTIMAU, BASED ON AERIAL SURVEYS OF 1975–1977.

Forest type	Area (km²)	% total area
Mixed dipterocarp forest	1428	84.6 *
Mixed dipterocarp remnant forest	14	0.8
Heath (kerangas) forest	203	12.0
Shifting cultivation	43	2.5
Totals	**1688**	**99.9**

* Note. Most of this amount is thought to be submontane non-dipterocarp forest (P.S. Ashton 1991, *in litt.*).

Source: WWF-Malaysia 1982.

Flora

The region is botanically unexplored. It is predicted that Lanjak-Entimau contains a representative sample of the inland Bornean flora on shale soils on the lower slopes, with heath forest elements on ridges and submontane elements on upper slopes. Endemism is probably low. The flora of Gunung Bentuang dan Karimun is predicted to be similar to that of Kutai, Gunung Penrisen and Gunung Nyiut (see Borneo section of Regional Overview), and is part of a region to the north of the Kapuas River which is rapidly losing its forests.

Useful plants

The Iban collect a wide variety of forest products, including wild fruits, illipe (engkabang) nuts (*Shorea* spp.), wood (some of which is used in construction of boats) and rattans. Oil from illipe nuts is used for culinary purposes by the Iban and is also sold commercially (WWF-Malaysia 1982). The area contains many timber trees (especially dipterocarps) and probably many species of wild fruit trees.

Social and environmental values

Lanjak-Entimau Wildlife Sanctuary was established to protect one of the few remaining viable populations of orang-utan (*Pongo pygmaeus*) (Endangered) in Sarawak. The reserve also contains Bornean gibbon (*Hylobates muelleri*), pangolin (*Manis javanica*), porcupines, sun bear (*Helarctos malayanus*), bearded pig (*Sus barbatus*) and deer. It is the only reserve in Malaysia with the white-fronted langur (*Presbytis frontata*), a Bornean endemic.

165 bird species have been recorded in Lanjak-Entimau (WWF-Malaysia 1982), including hawk eagles, pheasants (such as Bulwer's pheasant, which is Vulnerable), lorikeets, flycatchers, trogans and kingfishers. 6 of Sarawak's 8 species of hornbill occur within Lanjak-Entimau, and a seventh has been recorded nearby.

Lanjak-Entimau provides protection for much of the upper water catchment areas of the Batang Ai/Sungai Engkari, Batang Lemanak, Batang Skrang, Sungai Kanowit/Sg Mujok, Sg Poi, Sg Ngemah and Sg Katibas river systems. Essential benefits are therefore provided by the forested slopes to people living in the neighbouring parts of the Second, Third, Sixth and Seventh Divisions of Sarawak.

Iban (Dayaks) live in the surrounding area and practice shifting cultivation. They use the forest to collect a range of plant products and for hunting. Some Iban have established illipe (*Shorea*) plantations (K. MacKinnon 1991, *in litt.*).

In an evaluation of the importance of protected areas in the Indo-Malayan Realm (MacKinnon and MacKinnon 1986), Lanjak-Entimau Wildlife Sanctuary is given an "A" priority rating as an area of supreme importance for conservation based on vertebrate criteria. It probably protects a typical sample of mixed dipterocarp forest on shale and clay. This vegetation type, the major forest type of the region, is presently inadequately protected in the national park system in Sarawak (P.S. Ashton 1990, *in litt.*).

Threats

The main threats are illegal agricultural encroachment and illegal logging on the more accessible western side of Lanjak-Entimau and in the lower parts of Gunung Bentuang dan Karimun. Access to Lanjak-Entimau has been made easier from the south as a result of the creation of an artificial lake at Batang Ai in connection with a hydroelectric scheme.

Conservation

Lanjak-Entimau was gazetted as a Wildlife Sanctuary (IUCN Management Category: IV) in 1983. For about 40 years prior to this the area was administered as a protected forest. During this time, local Iban people legally hunted, collected and fished in the area. There are proposals to upgrade the area of the Wildlife Sanctuary to National Park status.

A management plan for Lanjak-Entimau, prepared in 1982 for the National Parks and Wildlife Office by WWF Malaysia (WWF-Malaysia 1982), identified the need to zone the area. In some areas human activity would be prohibited, with varying degrees of human use permitted in others. Agricultural encroachment would be stopped, reserve boundaries marked and a local education programme established. Local people could be recruited as guards and wardens. A research programme would include botanical surveys.

The plan also recommended that Batang Ai National Park be developed to the south of Lanjak-Entimau in order to protect its southern access following the construction of the Batang Ai dam, as well as to provide a leisure and recreation facility and to protect the Batang Ai water catchment area. In 1990, 240 km² of the Batang Ai area was notified as a National Park (IUCN Management Category: II).

There are also proposals to link Lanjak-Entimau with Cagar Alam Gunung Bentuang dan Karimun (Gunung Bentuang dan Karimun Nature Reserve) (IUCN Management Category: I) in Kalimantan to form a Border Park or Transfrontier Reserve.

References

MacKinnon, J. and MacKinnon, K. (1986). *Review of the protected areas system in the Indo-Malayan Realm.* IUCN, Gland, Switzerland and Cambridge, U.K. (in collaboration with UNEP). 284 pp.

Synge, H. (1990). *Twenty opportunities for saving biological diversity. Priority places for possible U.K. aid.* WWF, Godalming. Pp. 27–28.

WWF-Malaysia (1982). *Lanjak-Entimau Orang-Utan Sanctuary. A management plan.* IUCN/WWF Project No. 1995. WWF, Kuala Lumpur. 136 pp. (Prepared for The National Parks and Wildlife Office, Sarawak Forest Department, Kuching.)

Acknowledgements

This Data Sheet was prepared by Stephen D. Davis. Dr Kathy MacKinnon (WWF-Indonesia) and Professor P.S. Ashton (Harvard University Herbaria, Cambridge, Massachusetts) provided helpful comments.

BORNEO: CPD SITE SEA17

GUNUNG PALUNG NATIONAL PARK
Kalimantan, Indonesia

Location: An isolated massif to the north of the Kapuas River in Kalimantan Barat (West Kalimantan), between latitudes 1°05–1°33'S and longitudes 110°12'–110°36'E.

Area: 900 km².

Altitude: 0–1160 m (summit of Gunung Palung).

Vegetation: Lowland and hill dipterocarp forests, lower and upper montane rain forests, alluvial and peat swamp forests, beach forest, mangroves.

Useful plants: Timber trees, fruit trees, ornamental plants, especially orchids, ferns and pitcher plants.

Other values: Rich bird and mammal flora, many threatened animal species, watershed protection, potential tourism.

Threats: Logging, shifting cultivation, potential transmigration settlement to north of area.

Conservation: National Park (IUCN Management Category: II).

Geography

Gunung Palung is an isolated massif to the north of the Kapuas River in West Kalimantan (Kalimantan Barat). Access is from Pontianak, some 150 km to the north-west, via the coastal towns of Teluk Melanau and Sukadana. The National Park comprises the twin mountains of Gunung Palung and Gunung Panti, and surrounding swampy plains which isolate the mountains from other high ground. The park also includes a small stretch of coastline. Gunung Palung (1160 m) is the highest peak. The park lies between latitudes 1°05–1°33'S and longitudes 110°12'–110°36'E.

The closest town to the park is Monggo Jering, some 10 km to the north. Some 64,549 people were living in the three surrounding Kecamatan (administrative districts) in 1982, although there were no settlements within the reserve itself (MacKinnon and Warsito 1982). Population density in the immediate surrounding area is low, and ranges from 4.2 people/km² in the Simpang Hilir area to 31.9/km² in the Matan Hilir area (Silvius and Djurharsa 1989).

The geology consists of acid intrusive and plutonic siliceous rocks on the main massif, while the surrounding lowlands are composed of Quaternary alluvial deposits. Soils are predominantly organic latosols with peat deposits on the surrounding plains (MacKinnon and Warsito 1982).

The mean annual rainfall is 3000 mm, evenly distributed throughout the year (MacKinnon and Warsito 1982).

Vegetation and flora

The park contains a spectrum of Bornean vegetation types, ranging from coastal mangrove and nipa swamps and beach forests to montane forests.

Mangroves, *Nypa fruticans* swamps and beach forests are typical of those occurring elsewhere in Borneo. There are alluvial freshwater swamp forests and peat swamp forests in permanently and seasonally inundated areas. Peat swamp forests contain the commercially valuable timber tree *Gonystylus bancanus* (raman), along with *Litsea amara*, *Parastemon* sp., *Hopea sangal*, *Shorea leprosula*, *Calophyllum* sp. and *Ganua motleyana*. Over 40 species of trees have been recorded in 0.5 per ha, a reasonably high figure for peatswamp forest (MacKinnon and Warsito 1982).

Gunung Palung National Park contains a good sample of species-rich lowland tropical evergreen rain forest. Hill dipterocarp forest occurs on the lower slopes of the Gunung Palung massif. The forest is dominated by *Hopea ferruginea*, *Shorea* spp., *Calophyllum* spp., *Palaquium* spp. and *Gonystylus* spp., interspersed with occasional *Agathis beccari*.

A narrow zone of lower montane rain forest occurs, typified by smaller specimens of tree species found at lower altitudes. On the summits of the mountains, a stunted, bryophyte-encrusted upper montane rain forest is found. The dominant tree species are *Vaccinium* spp. (Ericaceae) and *Leptospermum* spp. (Myrtaceae). Pitcher plants (*Nepenthes* spp.), numerous species of orchids and ferns, and many species of mosses occur in the forest (MacKinnon and Warsito 1982). A preliminary inventory of the flora is given in MacKinnon and Warsito (1982).

Useful plants

The forests contain many fruit tree species, including species of *Durio* (durians), *Garcinia*, *Mangostana* (mangosteen), *Ficus* (figs), *Nephelium* (rambutans), *Artocarpus* (jackfruit), *Dialium* (keranji) and *Euphorbia malayana* (mata kucing).

The reserve contains many useful timber trees, especially dipterocarps, as well as ornamental plants, such as orchids, ferns and pitcher plants.

Social and environmental values

The park contains a rich mammalian fauna, including common civet (*Tangalunga tangalunga*), clouded leopard (*Neofelis nebulosa*) (Vulnerable), sun bear (*Helarctos malayanus*) (Vulnerable), and the primates: slow loris (*Nycticebus coucang*), crab-eating macaque (*Macaca fascicularis*), maroon leaf monkey (*Presbytis rubicunda*), silvered langur (*P. cristata*), agile gibbon (*Hylobates agilis*), proboscis monkey (*Nasalis larvatus*) (Vulnerable) and orang-utan (*Pongo pygmaeus*) (Endangered), for which the park supports the largest known population density of any Indonesian protected area. Sumatran rhinoceros (*Dicerorhinus sumatrensis*) (Endangered) is probably now extinct in the area, with the last known individual having been shot in 1939.

The park supports an extremely rich avifauna, with some 192 species recorded, including representatives of all the Bornean bird families. Notable species include rhinoceros hornbill (*Buceros rhinoceros*), helmeted hornbill (*Rhinoplax virgil*), Argus pheasant (*Argusianus argus*), trogon (*Harpectes kasumba*), honey-guide (*Indicator archipelagicus*), pitta (*Pitta baudi*) and long-tailed parakeet (*Psittacula longicauda*). An inventory of endemic mammalian and avifauna can be found in MacKinnon (1990).

Other notable fauna include, among reptiles, the false ghavial (*Tomistoma schlegelii*) (Endangered), monitor lizard (*Varanus borneensis*) and reticulated python (*Python reticulatus*), and, among invertebrates, the birdwing and swallowtail butterflies (MacKinnon and Warsito 1982).

As well as harbouring good populations of numerous endemic and endangered taxa, the park also contains many trees of silvicultural importance, and provides watershed protection to the surrounding area.

Local people depend on the forest as a source of wood for fuel, building poles, ramin logs (which are sold), resins, honey and other forest products.

MacKinnon and Warsito (1982) have conducted preliminary ecological surveys. Primate research studies have been carried out since 1984 at the Cabang Panti research camp.

Gunung Palung is scenically outstanding, and there is potential for developing ecotourism.

Threats

Little disturbance had been reported around the Gunung Palung massif up to 1988, other than the collection of minor forest products and some illegal logging of *Gonystylus bancanus*. Some of the adjacent lowland habitats have, however, been cleared for ladang agriculture (shifting cultivation), settlements and (particularly along the coast)

plantation agriculture. Some illegal logging of mangroves was occurring in 1985/1986 (W. Giesen 1991, pers. comm. to WCMC). Most of the reserve, however, is relatively undamaged, effective protection having been conferred by a local belief that the Gunung Palung massif is haunted.

The main current threats are logging concessions (which overlap to some extent with the park boundaries) and shifting cultivation pressure on the eastern side of the area (MacKinnon 1988). According to MacKinnon and Warsito (1982), areas to the north of the park have been scheduled for transmigration settlement. Buffer zones are required to adequately protect the reserve.

Conservation

The park protects a broad spectrum of representative Bornean habitats. Originally declared as a Natuur Monument in 1937, and later established as a Game Reserve in 1981 (covering 600 km²), the reserve was extended by 300 km² and declared a National Park in 1990.

References

Anon. (1982). *Indonesia: national parks and nature reserves*. Directorate General of Tourism, Jakarta. Pp. 93–94.

MacKinnon, J. and Warsito, I. (1982). *Gunung Palung Reserve Kalimantan Barat: preliminary management plan*. UNDP/FAO, National Parks Development Project INS/78/061. Field Report No. 27. FAO, Bogor. 40 pp.

MacKinnon, K. (1988). *Consultant's report of biodiversity specialist, for USAID PID mission: natural resource management in Kalimantan*. (Unpublished report.)

MacKinnon, K. (1990). *Biological diversity in Indonesia: a resource inventory*. WWF Indonesia, Bogor.

Silvius, M.J. and Djuharsa, E. (1989). Gunung Palung and surrounding swamps, Indonesia. In Scott, D.A. (ed.) *A directory of Asian wetlands*. IUCN, Gland, Switzerland and Cambridge, U.K. Pp. 1054–1056.

Acknowledgements

This Data Sheet was written by Stephen D. Davis, based on material prepared at WCMC by Andrew J. McCarthy, with some supplementary data.

LIMESTONE FLORA OF BORNEO
Sarawak and Sabah, Malaysia and Kalimantan, Indonesia

Location: In Malaysia, the most extensive outcrops occur in Gunung Mulu National Park, other significant outcrops being the Bau-Serian Formation and isolated sites, such as Niah; Sabah has many small scattered outcrops. In Indonesia, the main areas are the Meratus Mountains in Kalimantan Selatan (South Kalimantan) and the Sangkulirang Peninsula in Kalimantan Timur (East Kalimantan).

Altitude: The Melinau limestone to the north of Gunung Mulu (Sarawak) is the highest limestone area between northern Thailand and New Guinea, reaching 1710 m at the summit of Gunung Api and 1585 m at the summit of Gunung Benarat. All the scattered limestone areas in Sabah are in lowland areas.

Vegetation: Lowland forest over limestone, lower and upper montane limestone forest, limestone scrub, cliff and scree vegetation. In places where a deep leaf-litter has accumulated, a calcifuge flora develops.

Flora: Very poorly known; very rich in endemics; many local endemics.

Useful plants: Many species of potential horticultural value, particularly orchids, gesneriads, begonias, balsams, ferns.

Other values: Landscape value, tourist attraction, archaeological sites; some of the world's largest known caves occur in Gunung Mulu National Park (Sarawak); some caves are sources of edible birds' nests.

Threats: Quarrying, fire, clearance of surrounding forests for agriculture, potential damage of forests by development of tourist facilities, visitor pressure.

Conservation: In Sarawak, Gunung Mulu National Park (CPD Site SEA33, see separate Data Sheet) provides protection to major limestone areas of the Melinau Formation; a few small outcrops in Sabah are within Forest Reserves, but threatened nevertheless. The proposed Hutan Kapur Sangkulirang Nature Reserve and Sangkulirang National Park in Kalimantan would protect some areas of limestone.

Geography

Limestone outcrops in Borneo occur in the Malaysian states of Sarawak and Sabah, and the Indonesian province of Kalimantan. The main areas of limestone in Kalimantan are in the Meratus Mountains in Kalimantan Selatan (South Kalimantan), and the Sangkulirang Peninsula in Kalimantan Timur (East Kalimantan) on the eastern coast of Borneo (see Map 10, page 253).

There are two main limestone areas in Sarawak: the Melinau Formation, most of which is protected within Gunung Mulu National Park (CPD Site SEA33, covered in its entirety in a separate Data Sheet) and the Bau-Serian Formation in the First Division, in western Sarawak. In addition, there are several isolated outcrops, mainly in the Fourth Division, such as those at Subis/Niah, Kakus, Beluru and along the Baram. The Bau-Serian limestone areas, First Division, are floristically distinct from other limestone outcrops in the north of the state. In Sabah, there are a large number of small, isolated outcrops which are mostly vertical-sided hills.

Borneo limestone includes both old (pre-Cenozoic) and young (Tertiary) limestone formations. The Melinau limestone in Gunung Mulu National Park consists of massive limestone of white or grey calcilutite and fine calcarenite, locally recrystallized to marble. It is extremely pure, although some outcrops, as at Bukit Berau, are of almost pure dolomite (Waltham and Webb 1982). The limestone has been dated to the Lower Miocene (Adams 1965).

Vegetation

The vegetation ranges from lowland forest over limestone to lower and upper montane limestone forest on the major outcrops (as at Gunung Api and Gunung Benarat in Gunung Mulu National Park), and includes limestone scrub, cliff and scree vegetation.

A wide range of limestone vegetation types is found in Gunung Mulu National Park (CPD Site SEA33, see separate Data Sheet). Gunung Api and Gunung Benarat contain the only area of montane limestone forest in Malaysia. It is described in detail in Anderson and Chai (1982). Interestingly, where deep peat deposits have accumulated on the forest floor, calcifuge species dominate. Among them are the conifers *Dacrydium beccarii* and *Phyllocladus hypophyllus*, *Rhododendron* spp., the pitcher plant *Nepenthes stenophylla*, and other species found on the neighbouring granitic mountain, Gunung Mulu.

In Sabah, all the outcrops, except those on Balembangan Island, are more or less vertical-sided hills rising out of lowland forest. The vegetation on most of this type of outcrop is best described as limestone scrub, rather than forest, and includes a rich herbaceous flora associated with cracks and crevices. The herbaceous flora, in particular, includes many endemics.

Flora

The flora of limestone is very specialized and diverse and contains many local endemics (Anderson and Chai 1982; Chai

1982; Proctor, Anderson and Vallack 1982). Remarkably little is known botanically about the limestone areas of Borneo. Anderson (1965), in a brief account of limestone areas in Sarawak, mentioned that 600 species had been recorded from limestone at that time. More collections have been made since, but most areas remain poorly known. The best known localities are in Sarawak, and of these the extensive outcrops in Gunung Mulu National Park are of major importance.

In Mulu, the limestone flora of Gunung Api and Gunung Benarat is particularly rich in endemics. For example, 7 of the 8 species of *Monophyllaea* found on the Melinau limestone are newly described and not found anywhere else. Other calcicolous species which are restricted to this formation include other gesneriads, such as 3 species of *Cyrtandra* (*C. benaratica*, *C. calciphila* and *C. incrustata*), 3 species of *Paraboea* (*P. banyengiana*, *P. effusa* and *P. meiophylla*), the palm *Salacca rupicola* and 2 species of pandans (*Pandanus calcinatus* and *P. leptophilus*).

The isolated limestone outcrops at Bau, in western Sarawak, contain the Endangered endemic *Nepenthes northiana*. Other species restricted to these outcrops include *Cyrtandra thamnodes* and *C. urceolata*, 7 species of *Monophyllaea* and *Paraboea havilandii* (Kiew 1991), and the slipper orchid *Paphiopedilum stonei*.

Very little is known about the flora of the Sabah limestone outcrops (see list of sites, below).

At the family level there are some similarities between the limestone floras of Sabah and Sarawak and those of Peninsular Malaysia (see Data Sheet on the Limestone Flora of Peninsular Malaysia, SEA3). For example, Annonaceae, Balsaminaceae (*Impatiens*), Begoniaceae, Gesneriaceae (*Epithema*, *Monophyllaea* and *Paraboea*), Euphorbiaceae, Moraceae, Pandanaceae and Urticaceae (*Elatostema*, *Pilea*) are well-represented in the floras, whereas dipterocarps are poorly represented (Kiew 1991). However, there are many differences between the floras at the generic and species levels. For example, whereas the endemic pitcher plant, *Nepenthes northiana*, grows on limestone in Sarawak, pitcher plants are not found on limestone in Peninsular Malaysia (Kiew 1991).

Each limestone outcrop is likely to be of individual botanical interest and to contain endemics. Botanical exploration is urgently required.

Useful plants

Many limestone species, especially those among the herbaceous flora, are of potential horticultural value. They include orchids, gesneriads, balsams, begonias and ferns.

Social and environmental values

Limestone outcrops often include spectacular karst landscape features, and may exhibit sheer rock faces, potholes, caves, limestone pinnacles (those on Gunung Api in Gunung Mulu National Park reaching an exceptional 50 m tall) and other landforms associated with weathering and erosion. Often, limestone outcrops tower vertically above surrounding forests, which provide a dramatic backcloth to the rock features.

Some limestone areas are becoming very popular tourist attractions. For example, Niah was among three National

Parks in Sarawak (the other two being Bako and Lambir Hills) included in a study by Chung (1987), who calculated that the recreational value (through the travel cost method) of the three parks in any one year is worth several million Malaysian dollars. Revenue received from visitors to these three areas (excluding food purchases) in 1985 was c. M$2.5 million.

Limestone caves are regularly included on visitor itineraries at Gunung Mulu National Park, as well as attracting scientific expeditions. A visit to the limestone pinnacles on Gunung Api is a demanding adventure for ecotourists. In such recreational activities, the experience of adventure is heightened by the walk up through primary limestone forest.

The Subis limestone complex in Sarawak contains sites of archaeological importance, including the famous Niah Caves that were inhabited more than 40,000 years ago.

Borneo's limestone areas contain a diverse and endemic-rich fauna, including many species of endemic snails and an endemic-rich cave fauna. Of particular note are the large populations of fruit-eating and insect-eating bats and cave swifts which use limestone caves (such as those in Gunung Mulu National Park and at Niah, Sarawak, and Gomantong, Sabah) as roost sites, and depend on surrounding forests for foraging. Bats, depending on species, provide economic benefits by pollinating fruit trees (such as durians) and controlling insect populations.

Many limestone areas contain caves which are sources of edible birds' nests.

Threats

In some cases, fire spreading from surrounding logged forests threatens the limestone vegetation. Extensive areas of the Sangkulirang Peninsula were damaged by fire during "The Great Forest Fire of Borneo" in 1982–1983 (see Factors Causing Loss of Biodiversity in the Regional Overview for South East Asia).

Probably the greatest threat to limestone sites outside of protected areas is from quarrying. In Sarawak, gold and antimony mining in the Bau area began over a century ago and has caused serious disturbance to the limestone flora there (Anderson 1965). Quarrying of limestone for cement and roadstone threatens entire hillsides.

In Kalimantan, the principal threats are from logging, illegal small-scale tree removal and over-collecting of forest products. Potential threats to limestone areas in the Sangkulirang Peninsula include proposed transmigration settlements and quarrying. A road extension to Tanjung Redeb to the north of the proposed Hutan Kapur Sangkulirang Nature Reserve is proposed for quarrying operations (K. MacKinnon 1988, pers. comm. to WCMC).

There is a potential threat of local damage to forests by the increase in tourism, as new facilities and footpaths are created. Increased visitation brings an increase in the risk of fire, and possibly of plant collecting, especially of the more showy species.

Conservation

In Sarawak, Gunung Mulu National Park (CPD Site SEA33, see separate Data Sheet) provides protection to major limestone areas. Some limestone forest also occurs in the proposed Ulu Medalam National Park, a 350 km² extension to Gunung Mulu National Park. About 12 km² of forest on limestone occurs in Niah National Park (Abang H.K. Morshidi and Gumal 1992).

None of the limestone outcrops in western Sarawak are protected. This is an important omission from the existing and proposed protected area system in Sarawak. The State Conservation Strategy for Sarawak calls for further protection of limestone areas within the protected areas system, and ecological survey work to be undertaken to assess their conservation value (WWF Malaysia 1985). The Strategy also calls for steps to be taken to ensure that the conservation value of each site is determined before any quarrying operations are carried out.

Ex situ conservation of some rare and threatened limestone plants of Sarawak is being undertaken at the Botany Research Centre, Kuching.

A few small outcrops in Sabah are within Forest Reserves, but threatened nevertheless (A. Lamb and A. Phillipps 1993, *in litt.*).

In Kalimantan, the proposed Hutan Kapur Sangkulirang Nature Reserve (2000 km²) and the proposed Sangkulirang National Park (1000 km²) would protect an area of limestone karst hills and escarpments that stretch across the Sangkulirang Peninsula westward to the north of Muara Ma'au.

Because of the endemic-rich nature of the flora of limestone areas, a network of protected limestone sites is needed throughout Borneo. At present, very few botanical data are available to denote which sites are the major priorities. It is likely that most, if not all, the areas listed below, contain endemics. However, many more areas may qualify for inclusion on the list. There is an urgent requirement for more botanical exploration of limestone sites in all of Borneo.

Botanically important limestone sites of Borneo

Sabah (Malaysia)

The following areas are those which are likely to be the most important for plants. There are many more minor limestone outcrops in Sabah, but so far very little, if anything, is known about their plant life.

SEA18a. Balembangan Island limestone outcops

c. 7°17'N, 116°54'E. Area: The limestone occurs in two outcrops in the southern half of the island, totalling about 15 km². Altitude: 0–120 m.
- ❖ Vegetation: Lowland forest on limestone, merging on the coast with strand vegetation.
- ❖ Flora: c. 280 vascular plant species recorded from Balembangan (whole island, 120 km²), of which *Pandanus occultus* is restricted to the limestone there, and is recorded nowhere else in Borneo, although there is one record from Palawan (Philippines).
- ❖ Threats: Quarrying for proposed cement factory on the west coast of Sabah.

- ❖ Conservation: Parts of Balembangan (including much of the limestone area) have been proposed as conservation areas to the State Government recently. The outcrops are important historical and archaeological sites and some collection of birds' nests takes place on a minor scale (Wells, undated).

SEA18b. Batu Punggul (Batu Ponggol)

4°38'N, 116°37'E. Area: >1 km². Altitude: 0–250 m.
- ❖ Vegetation: Lowland forest, limestone scrub.
- ❖ Flora: This is the only known Borneo locality for the orchids *Phalaenopsis modesta* var. *alba, Spongiola lobokii* (in press), *Staurochilus fasciatus, Tainia poggollensis* and two unnamed species of *Trichoglottis*. Sands (1990) described the bizarre *Begonia amphioxus* from Batu Punggul.
- ❖ Threats: Fires from surrounding logged-over forest. Possible degradation from over-development of tourist facilities in the future.
- ❖ Conservation: Batu Punggul is located within the Sg Sansiang Virgin Jungle Reserve. Batu Punggul itself is a spectacular limestone pinnacle, and contains caves with other interesting limestone formations. It is becoming a popular tourist destination.

SEA18c. Baturong

4°42'N, 118°1'E. Area: >1 km². Altitude: 0–300 m.
- ❖ Vegetation: Lowland forest, limestone scrub.
- ❖ Threats: Fire from nearby logged-over forest.
- ❖ Conservation: Baturong is situated in the Madai-Baturong Forest Reserve. The caves are a minor source of edible birds' nests. The caves are also of archaeological and historical value.

SEA18d. Bukit Sinobang (Senobang)/Batu Urun

c. 4°48'N, 116°39'E. Area: c. 1 km².
- ❖ Vegetation: Lowland forest, limestone scrub.
- ❖ Threats: Fire spreading from nearby logged-over forest.
- ❖ Conservation: No formal protection. The caves are a minor source of edible birds' nests for which the collecting rights are privately-owned.

SEA18e. Gomantong

5°31'N, 118°4'E. Area: >1 km². Altitude: 0–230 m.
- ❖ Vegetation: Lowland forest, limestone scrub.
- ❖ Flora: The pink-spotted *Begonia malachosticta* has been described from the Gomantong limestone (Sands 1990).
- ❖ Threats: Fire from surrounding logged-over forest; possible degradation from over-development of tourist facilities in future.
- ❖ Conservation: Gomantong lies within the Gomantong Forest Reserve, and is managed by the Wildlife Department for the collection of edible birds' nests, for which it is the most important source in Sabah. Gomantong is also becoming a popular tourist attraction, particularly for the evening flight of bats and swifts out of the caves.

SEA18f. Madai

4°43'N, 118°9'E. Area: >1 km². Altitude: 0–600 m.
- ❖ Vegetation: Lowland forest, limestone scrub.
- ❖ Threats: Fire from nearby logged-over forest.
- ❖ Conservation: Madai is situated in the Madai-Baturong Forest Reserve and is a major source of edible birds' nests. The caves are of archaeological and historical value, and also have some tourism potential.

SEA18g. Pun Batu (Pohon Batu, Punan Batu)

4°47'N, 116°11'E. Area: >1 km².
- ❖ Vegetation: Lowland forest, limestone scrub.
- ❖ Threats: Fire from logged-over forest nearby.
- ❖ Conservation: No formal protection. The caves are a minor source of birds' nests for which the collecting rights are privately-owned.

Sarawak (Malaysia)

SEA18h. Bau-Serian limestone

Isolated limestone areas in the First Division, in western Sarawak, and floristically distinct from other limestone outcrops in the state. Includes Gunung Bra'ang, Gunung Selabor and Gunung Serapat. (See discussion in Flora section, above, for examples of local endemics.)

SEA18i. Melinau limestone

Extensive limestone area protected in Gunung Mulu National Park and extending into Ulu Medalam proposed National Park. Extremely important botanically. (See sections on Vegetation and Flora, above, and the separate Data Sheet on Gunung Mulu National Park, CPD Site SEA33.)

SEA18j. Niah National Park

Gunung Subis harbours some local endemics, e.g. *Cyrtandra spelaea* and *Paraboea speluncarum* (Kiew 1991).

Kalimantan (Indonesia)

Little information, apart from scattered records of plants collected from limestone, is available on sites in Kalimantan. Much more botanical exploration is needed before a comprehensive list of important sites can be drawn up. The list and information given below is very preliminary.

SEA18k/l. Sangkulirang Peninsula

Extensive area of limestone in Kalimantan Timur (East Kalimantan). Outcrops at **SEA18k - Gunung Antu** and **SEA18l - Gunung Nyat**.
- ❖ Threats: Logging plans, illegal logging, potential quarrying, badly damaged by fire.
- ❖ Conservation: The proposed Hutan Kapur Sangkulirang Nature Reserve (2000 km²) and the proposed Sangkulirang National Park (1000 km²) would protect an area of

limestone karst hills. The proposed Nature Reserve includes 1280 km² of forest on limestone, 300 km² of heath forest and the same amount of lowland rain forest. Altitude range: 100–1385 m.

SEA18m. Meratus Mountains

An isolated massif, of area 9505 km², in the extreme south-east of Borneo, of high botanical interest with numerous endemics. The underlying geology consists of a complex of sedimentary rocks, including karst limestone, igneous and volcanic rocks (including ultramafic outcrops). The south-western slopes are unusually dry.
- ❖ Threats: Shifting cultivation; logging.

References

Abang H.K. Morshidi and Gumal, M.T. (1992). Role of totally protected areas in protecting biological diversity in Sarawak. Paper prepared for the International Workshop on Ecology, Conservation and Management of the Southeast Asian Rainforests, Kuching, Sarawak, 12–14 October 1992.

Adams, C.G. (1965). The foraminifera and stratigraphy of the Melinau limestone, Sarawak, and its importance in Tertiary correlation. *Quart. J. Geol. Sci. Lond.* 121: 283–338.

Anderson, J.A.R. (1965). Limestone habitat in Sarawak. *Symp. Ecol. Research in Humid Tropics Vegetation, Kuching, Sarawak.* Government of Sarawak and UNESCO. Pp. 49–57.

Anderson, J.A.R. and Chai, P.P.K. (1982). Vegetation. In Jermy, A.C. and Kavanagh, K.P. (eds), Gunung Mulu National Park, Sarawak: an account of its environment and biota being the results of The Royal Geographical Society/ Sarawak Government Expedition and Survey 1977–1978. Part I. *Sarawak Mus. J.* 30(51) (New Series) (Special Issue No. 2): 195–206.

Chai, P.P.K. (1982). Flora and fauna of Sarawak. *Sarawak Gazette* 108(1480): 19–24.

Chung, K.S. (1987). *Estimating the demand curves of Bako, Niah and Lambir Hills National Parks of Sarawak.* Forestry Department, Kuching, Sarawak.

Francis, C. (1987). *The management of edible birds' nest caves in Sabah.* Wildlife Section, Sabah Forest Department.

Kiew, R. (1991). The limestone flora. In Kiew, R. (ed.), *The state of nature conservation in Malaysia.* Malayan Nature Society, Malaysia. Pp. 42–50.

Proctor, J., Anderson, J.A.R. and Vallack, H.W. (1982). Ecological studies in four forest types. In Jermy, A.C. and Kavanagh, K.P. (eds), Gunung Mulu National Park, Sarawak: an account of its environment and biota being the results of The Royal Geographical Society/Sarawak Government Expedition and Survey 1977–1978. Part I. *Sarawak Mus. J.* 30(51) (New Series) (Special Issue No. 2): 207–225.

Sands, M.J. (1990). Six new begonias from Sabah. *Kew Magazine* 7: 57–85.

Waltham, A.C. and Webb, B. (1982). Geology. In Jermy, A.C. and Kavanagh, K.P. (eds), Gunung Mulu National Park, Sarawak: an account of its environment and biota being the results of The Royal Geographical Society/Sarawak Government Expedition and Survey 1977–1978. Part I. *Sarawak Mus. J.* 30(51) (New Series) (Special Issue No. 2): 68–74.

Wells, D.R. (undated). *The Balembangan Report. A survey of the proposed Pulau Balembangan National Park Sabah.* WWF Malaysia.

WWF Malaysia (1985). *Strategi Pemeliharaan Sumber Semulajadi Malaysia.* (Proposals for a Conservation Strategy for Sarawak.) WWF Malaysia, Kuala Lumpur. 210 pp.

Acknowledgements

This Data Sheet was written by Stephen D. Davis. Anthea Phillipps (former Park Ecologist, Sabah Parks) and Tony Lamb (Agricultural Research Station, Tenom, Sabah) kindly provided information on Sabah limestone sites. Dr Jaap Vermuelen (Rijksherbarium, Leiden) provided a geological base map which was used to locate limestone outcrops throughout Borneo.

SUNGAI KAYAN-SUNGAI MENTARANG NATURE RESERVE
Kalimantan, Indonesia

Location: Kalimantan Timur (East Kalimantan), extending over 265 km along the border with Sarawak (Malaysia), between latitudes 2°00'–4°22'N and longitudes 114°30'–116°00'E.

Area: 16,000 km² (29,000 km² including proposed extensions).

Altitude: 100–2556 m.

Vegetation: Lowland and hill dipterocarp forest; lower and upper montane rain forest; heath (kerangas) forest; "mossy" riverine forest; small areas of freshwater swamp forest.

Flora: In the absence of any detailed botanical surveys, it is estimated that the flora contains c. 2000 vascular plant species.

Useful plants: Wild fruit trees, including durians, mangoes and bananas; gingers, rattans and many valuable timber species. A wide range of plants is utilized by tribal groups.

Other values: Rich fauna, including perhaps 100 species of mammals; 97 species of birds recorded. Watershed protection for a large area of East Kalimantan. Home of a diversity of tribal groups. Potential for planned, small-scale ecotourism.

Threats: Logging, mining, encroachment by shifting agriculturalists on the eastern side of the reserve.

Conservation: Established as a Nature Reserve (Cagar Alam) (IUCN Management Category: I) in 1980; management plan project underway. Adjacent to the proposed Pulong Tau National Park in Sarawak (Malaysia) (CPD Site SEA38, see entry in Borneo section of Regional Overview).

Geography

Cagar Alam Sungai Kayan-Sungai Mentarang (Sungai Kayan-Sungai Mentarang Nature Reserve) covers a vast area of 16,000 km² in the interior of Borneo, stretching for over 500 km along the mountainous international border between the Indonesian province of East Kalimantan (Kalimantan Timur) and the Malaysian states of Sabah and Sarawak. In the south, the reserve is bounded by Sungai Kayan, and from here it stretches north to the Sabah border. The site is adjacent to the proposed Pulong Tau National Park in Sarawak (CPD Site SEA38; see the entry in the Borneo section of the Regional Overview). In addition, the following areas have been proposed as extensions to the reserve within Kalimantan:

❖ Proposed Ulu Kayan Nature Reserve (Cagar Alam Perluasan Ulu Kayan) (8000 km²);
❖ Proposed Ulu Sembakung Nature Reserve (Cagar Alam Perluasan Ulu Sembakung) (5000 km²).

These extensions would bring the total area protected to 29,000 km² in Kalimantan alone.

Approximately 70% of the reserve lies below 1000 m, but it also includes some of Kalimantan's highest peaks, while across the international border Gunung Murud (2438 m) is Sarawak's highest mountain.

The geology of the region is complex, including basaltic plateaux, old volcanic highlands (which are unusual in Borneo) and small pockets of karst limestone. The reserve comprises the major water catchment area for East Kalimantan. The complex geology and landforms provide a diverse range of habitats and vegetation types.

The climate is perhumid and equatorial with an annual rainfall of approximately 4000 mm. Prolonged dry periods may occur in July and August, although rainfall rarely drops below 100 mm per month. The area was not seriously affected by the 1982–1983 El Niño drought, although some localized fires occurred and emergent trees died from water stress in some areas.

Vegetation

The reserve encompasses the largest continuous block of protected rain forest in Borneo. The most important and richest vegetation is lowland tropical rain forest below 300 m. The canopy is dominated by members of the Dipterocarpaceae, including species of *Dipterocarpus*, *Dryobalanops*, *Parashorea* and *Shorea*, Meliaceae, such as *Amoora* spp. and *Dysoxylum* spp., Bombacaceae, such as *Coelostegia chartacea*, and at least half the 14 species of *Durio* endemic to Kalimantan. Other canopy trees include: *Eusideroxylon zwageri* (Lauraceae), and species of *Canarium* (Burseraceae), *Myristica* and *Knema* (Myristicaceae). Sub-canopy trees include species of *Garcinia*, *Calophyllum*, *Gynotroches*, *Cinnamomum* and *Baccaurea*. Understorey palms include members of the genera *Caryota* and *Pinanga*; there are at least 20 species of rattans.

At higher altitudes, lowland rain forest gives way to hill dipterocarp forest; between 800 and 1500 m lower montane rain forest (with a canopy height of 35 m) occurs. Fagaceae are the main dominants here, including: *Castanopsis tunggrut*, *Lithocarpus sundaicus*, *L. pseudomolucca* and

L. indutus, Quercus gmellina and *Q. cyclocarpa*. Other canopy species are: *Elmerrillia mollis* and *Aromadendron elegans* (members of the Magnoliaceae), *Podocarpus imbricatus, Agathis, Dipterocarpus, Eugenia* and *Calophyllum* species. The understorey contains several species of Zingiberaceae and Palmae (such as *Licuala* and *Calamus* spp.). Upper montane forest occurs above 1500 m.

Heath forest (kerangas), which occurs on severely leached sandy soils, varies in structure from open to closed scrub with scattered trees, or low forest 5–8 m high. The canopy layer includes: *Dacrydium elatum, Tristania* spp., *Veronia arborea, Rapanea* and *Eugenia* spp. The shrub and herb layers include: *Vaccinium* spp., *Melastoma* spp., *Lycopodium* spp., *Nepenthes* and several rhododendrons (Blower, Wirawan and Watling 1981).

Other distinct plant assemblages occur on cliff tops, plateaux and ridge tops (where stands of *Tristania* dominate). Orchid-rich "mossy" forest occurs in river gorges. Wetland formations occur in and around oxbow lakes and small freshwater swamps in the upper Iwan River catchment. Here are found small areas of freshwater swamp forest.

In addition to the natural vegetation types, there are extensive areas of alang-alang (*Imperata cylindrica*) grassland and secondary forest, particularly in the centre of the reserve in areas of human activity (Blower, Wirawan and Watling 1981).

Flora

Botanical investigations have hardly begun, but, as with many other sites in Borneo, floristic richness is likely to be high. P.S. Ashton (1991, *in litt.*) provided an estimate of c. 2000 vascular plant species. The reserve is contiguous with the proposed Pulong Tau National Park (in Sarawak) (CPD Site SEA38), which includes Gunung Murud (Sarawak's highest mountain) and which contains tracts of lower and upper montane rain forest, as well as a some lowland mixed dipterocarp forest and kerangas. The Pulong Tau area is likely to be richer in species than Sungai Kayan-Sungai Mentarang (P.S. Ashton 1991, *in litt.*) but botanical exploration is needed.

In the Sungai Kayan-Sungai Mentarang Reserve, 179 species of trees (dbh >10 cm) were recorded on one 0.8 ha plot at around 750 m altitude in the upper Kayan River catchment, while at nearly 2000 m a similar sized plot contained 106 species of trees. The reserve includes a large number of orchids, palms, bamboos, gingers, tropical oaks, wild figs and numerous other wild fruit trees and related species in the genera *Durio* (durians), *Mangifera* (mangoes), *Nephelium* (rambutan), *Mangostana* (mangosteen), *Artocarpus* (jackfruit) and *Musa* (bananas and plantains).

There have not been sufficient botanical investigations to determine whether the forest is floristically richer relative to other forested sites in the region; the conservation significance of the area is that it contains a large, continuous block of rain forest, and therefore includes a representative sample of this vegetation.

Useful plants

The reserve contains a vast range of potentially useful and valuable genetic resources. In particular, the presence of a large variety of wild fruit tree relatives and timber trees has been noted above. The cultivated flora of the region is also rich, particularly in the number of rice varieties and domesticated fruit trees. A large number of rattans occurs in the reserve. A wide range of plants are utilized by tribal groups, including *Aquilaria malaccensis* which yields an aromatic gum (gharu).

Social and environmental values

Besides its botanical richness, the reserve is also notable for its fauna. Preliminary surveys confirmed the presence of 23 mammal species (although as many as 100 species may occur) (Petocz 1989). Notable species include: the Kalimantan endemic bearded pig (*Sus barbatus*), banteng (*Bos javanicus*) (Vulnerable), clouded leopard (*Neofelis nebulosa*) (Vulnerable), civets, sun bear (*Helarctos malayanus*) (Vulnerable) and pangolin (*Manis javanica*). In addition, numerous primates occur, including slow loris (*Nycticebus coucang*), tarsier (*Tarsius bancanus*), macaques, leaf monkeys and the Bornean gibbon (*Hylobates mulleri*). Some 97 species of birds have been recorded, including rhinoceros hornbill (*Buceros rhinoceros*) and helmetted hornbill (*Rhinoplax vigil*) (Blower, Wirawan and Watling 1981).

There is a diversity of peoples within the reserve, including some 12 distinct ethnic or linguistic groups (Jessup *et al.* 1991). These include the Penan, Kelabit and Kenyah tribes. About 9000 people live in the reserve, and a further 3000 people live in the areas proposed as reserve extensions. Approximately 13,000 people may inhabit areas to be included in buffer zones (Anon. 1990). Land use is predominantly ladang agriculture (shifting cultivation), supplemented by subsistence hunting and collection of forest products such as rattans and gharu. In the north, there are Lun Dayeh wet-rice (sawah) farmers, while in the south shifting cultivation is carried out by Kenyah people.

A number of villages manufacture iodized salt from saline groundwater for trade across the Malaysian border.

Not only does the reserve provide the basis of an extensive local subsistence economy, but it also protects the major watershed of East Kalimantan.

The reserve contains a number of sites of archaeological interest, including stone burial chambers.

In an evaluation of the importance of protected areas in the Indomalayan Realm (MacKinnon and MacKinnon 1986), Sungai Kayan-Mentarang is given an "A" priority rating as an area of supreme importance for conservation, based primarily on vertebrate criteria and the size of the protected area.

Threats

The population within the reserve boundaries and to the south has decreased because of emigration from the border region of East Kalimantan to the lowlands. Expansion of shifting cultivation into primary forest within the reserve is therefore not a problem here. The effects of present levels of subsistence agriculture, hunting and collection of forest products in the reserve are unknown.

The main threat comes from encroachment by loggers, miners and farmers in the lowlands on the eastern side of the reserve. This could endanger some of the richest areas of lowland dipterocarp forest. Some manual logging has already taken place in the past along the Sungai Kayan and Bahua, and possibly also along the Tubu, Mentarang and other rivers, but there are plans for commercial logging operations along the Tubu River, close to, or within the eastern boundary of the reserve (Jessup *et al.* 1991).

Conservation

The reserve was established in 1980 and is currently the focus of a collaborative programme of the Department of Forestry of Indonesia (PHPA), the Indonesia Academy of Sciences (LIPI), UNESCO and the WWF Indonesia Programme. The programme will redefine the boundaries of the area, justify possible extensions, and will develop a 5-year community participatory management plan. The plan includes the following elements:

❖ biological inventories for monitoring human impact on resources;
❖ integration of conservation with regional economic development in cooperation with East Kalimantan's provincial planning authority (BAPPEDA);
❖ redefining and securing reserve boundaries to exclude farmland and settlements;
❖ resolving land-use conflicts arising from logging and other commercial activities;
❖ local participation in conservation and resource management, and local recruitment of trained staff to carry out conservation and resource management activities;
❖ establishing a long-term management plan that provides local benefits;
❖ setting up village development projects in community forestry and agroforestry, and implementing a zoning system of strict protection areas and traditional use zones that reflects conservation priorities and the economic needs of local communities;
❖ helping to develop a programme of research, inventory and monitoring;
❖ establishing an international park with Pulong Tau on the border with Malaysia.

The presence of Dayak people in and around the reserve is an advantage for conservation because they know the region well and have an extensive ethnobotanical knowledge. The reserve has been cited as one of the best sites in Indonesia for the development of adventure tourism, based on the cultural and ecological diversity of the region. This needs to be carefully planned to ensure that the present social and environmental values of the reserve are maintained. People from the native tribes could be recruited to act as rangers, guards, guides, researchers, foresters and managers within the reserve.

Botanical exploration of the area is needed.

References

Anon. (1990). *WWF 4505 Project Outline. Indonesia (256) – E. Kalimantan, Sungai Kayan Mentarang Nature Reserve.* WWF, Gland, Switzerland. 9 pp.

Blower, J.H., Wirawan, N. and Watling, R. (1981). *Preliminary survey of Sungai Kayan – S. Mentarang Nature Reserve in East Kalimantan.* WWF Indonesia, Bogor. 20 pp.

Jessup, T.C., Soedjito, H., Amin, B.H. and Wirawan, N. (1991). *A short report on the Kayan-Mentarang Reserve, East Kalimantan.* February 1991. WWF Indonesia, Bogor. 4 pp. (Unpublished report.)

Jessup, T.C., Vayda, A.P. and Kartawinata, K. (in press). *Ecotourism, biological conservation, and sustainable development: some needs and possibilities in East Kalimantan, Indonesia.*

MacKinnon, J. and Artha, M.B. (1981). *A National Conservation Plan for Indonesia, Vol. V: Kalimantan.* Field report of UNDP/FAO National Parks Development Project INS/78/061. FAO, Bogor, Indonesia.

MacKinnon, J. and MacKinnon, K. (1986). *Review of the protected areas system in the Indo-Malayan Realm.* IUCN, Gland, Switzerland and Cambridge, U.K. (in collaboration with UNEP). 284 pp.

McCarthy, A.J. (comp.) (1991). *Conservation areas of Indonesia. Final draft.* World Conservation Monitoring Centre, Cambridge, U.K. in collaboration with Directorate General of Forest Protection and Nature Conservation (PHPA), Ministry of Forestry, Republic of Indonesia, and IUCN Commission on National Parks and Protected Areas, Gland, Switzerland.

Petocz, R. (1989). *Strategic planning for the WWF Indonesia conservation programme: a review of current programme components, planning strategy, recommended project concepts.* WWF Indonesia, Bogor. Pp. 73–77. (Unpublished report.)

Synge, H. (1990). *Twenty opportunities for saving biological diversity. Priority places for possible U.K. aid.* WWF, Godalming. Pp. 29–30.

Acknowledgements

This Data Sheet was written by Stephen D. Davis. Dr Kathy MacKinnon (WWF Indonesia) and Professor Peter S. Ashton (Harvard University Herbaria, Cambridge, Massachusetts) provided helpful comments on an earlier draft.

EAST SABAH LOWLAND AND HILL DIPTEROCARP FORESTS
Sabah, Malaysia

Location: Between latitudes 4°00'–7°00'N and longitudes 117°00'–119°00'E.

Area: c. 20,000 km².

Altitude: 0–1298 m (summit of Mount Tribulation).

Vegetation: Evergreen tropical rain forest dominated by large trees in the family Dipterocarpaceae.

Flora: 5000–6000 vascular plant species, including >2000 tree species in 80 families.

Useful plants: Many timber trees (seraya, keruing, kapur), rattans, native fruit trees, ornamental plants.

Other values: Rich fauna, resins, birds' nests, tourism.

Threats: Conversion to agriculture, human settlement and exotic tree plantations; unsustainable logging.

Conservation: 4077 km² protected in conservation areas; including several Protection Forest Reserves, 2 Wildlife Reserves, >20 small areas reserved as "Virgin Jungle Reserves", and a Conservation Area within a concession Forest Reserve. Many forests outside of protected areas are seriously threatened.

Geography

The forest areas described here lie to the east of longitude 117°00'E and occur within an area of some 37,500 km² (see Map 12). Apart from those living in coastal and riverside settlements, few people lived in eastern Sabah until after the Second World War. The natural forest cover was predominantly lowland dipterocarp forest, fringed by coastal mangroves with hill dipterocarp forest on higher ground. Commercially important forests were interspersed with swamp forests, and some other types on less fertile, or excessively well-drained sites. The forests formed an unbroken mass from the coast inland, giving way to oak forests in high country and to relatively fertile upland valley systems, in the west of the country, where shifting cultivation was practised. There were no forest-dwelling peoples in the forests of eastern Sabah.

In 1960, half the Sabah population of 0.45 million inhabited coastal areas (mostly in the west). The population had increased to 1.3 million by the late 1980s, largely driven by a boom in timber production for export and land settlement schemes involving plantation crops in logged-over forest. Many immigrants arrived from the Philippines and Indonesia (mostly Sulawesi). Some 30% of eastern Sabah has now been cleared of forest. About 21,200 km² of forest may be contained within areas designated as exploitable Forest Reserves. Most of these forest reserves have been logged over at least once.

The most productive and valuable dipterocarp forests occur on the extensive lowlands in the middle to lower reaches of the major rivers, such as the Kinabatangan, Paitan, Sugut, Labuk, Segama and Kalabakan. Until about 1970 most of these forests were managed in large Forest Reserves for the sustained yield of timber. A reorganization of tenure removed the then 12 concessionaires and replaced the bulk of the extant, unexploited forests into one multi-locational grouping under the Sabah Foundation (Innoprise Corporation). By 1992, the bulk of the land in the lower Kinabatangan, Labuk

and Segama rivers had been logged, de-reserved and allocated to non-forest land use. Replacement Forest Reserves had been created in the hillier inland sector of the state. Many of these in turn have been placed in the Sabah Foundation concession area.

The climate of Sabah is described in the Borneo section of the Regional Overview. There is some correlation between the main species of the forests and underlying geology. The north-east is mainly below 300 m altitude and consists of dissected peneplains of red and yellow sandstone, shales and mudstone, with some limestone and sand or gravel terraces. There are ultramafic and basaltic mountains in the upper Labuk and Karamuak valleys (see separate Data Sheet on the North-east Borneo Ultramafic Flora, SEA27). The Lokan Peneplain has mainly red sandstone and shales with terrace features of sand or gravel, probably representing dissected marine platforms. Concentric arcs of sandstone cliffs form the Sandakan Formation.

In the south-east, mountains comprising igneous rocks are found west of Tawau in an area which has undergone periodic uplift and river rejuvenation. Igneous rocks of the crystalline basement include gabbro and granodiorites. There are narrow areas of alluvium in the middle and upper reaches of the rivers. Ultramafic and metamorphic rocks occur as intrusive belts through a formation of chert, spilite, greywacke and limestone with numerous small volcanic outcrops. East of Tawau intrusive and volcanic activity have dominated the land-forming features such that erosion surfaces within 100 m of sea-level have hills of more resistant rocks rising from them, and in which volcanic landforms are superimposed.

In the central region volcanic dacites and andesites occur in the Bakapit area. East of Lahad Datu, rocks are mixed volcanics and sedimentaries, giving tuffaceous sandstones and conglomerates mixed with shales, mudstones and sandstones. Inner necritic to littoral deposits at the east of Dent Peninsula consist of mudstone, clay and coral limestone with lignite, marl and conglomerate. The main soils of the forest areas are lithosols and acrisols. The central and southern forests of Gunong Rara, Kalabakan and Silabukan occur on these soils, on steep land derived from volcanic ash and conglomerate. In the north-east, the main soils supporting dipterocarp forest are red/yellow acrisols. Red/yellow podsols occur where vegetation is grassy or sparse in trees.

Vegetation

The island of Borneo is the richest centre of dipterocarp tree species, with 58% being endemic (Ashton 1982). Dipterocarps dominate the lowland and hill forests of the eastern part of the state, with some 160 species found in Sabah as a whole, and 132 in eastern Sabah (see Table 53). Not all dipterocarps are large emergent trees; of the eight genera represented, *Vatica* and *Hopea* species are often of small to medium size.

TABLE 53. NUMBERS OF SPECIES WITHIN GENERA OF DIPTEROCARPACEAE

	Species present				Endemic species	
	Malesia	Borneo	Sabah	East Sabah	Borneo	East Sabah
Anisoptera	10	5	5	4	2	0
Cotylelobium	3	3	2	2	1	0
Dipterocarpus	53	41	25	23	15	1
Dryobalanops	7	7	6	4	5	1
Hopea	84	42	19	18	22	0
Parashorea	10	6	4	4	4	1
Shorea	163	127	84	65	82	4
Upuna	1	1	1	0	1	0
Vatica	55	35	14	12	23	0
Totals	**386**	**267**	**160**	**132**	**155**	**7**

Species endemic to the eastern part of Sabah are: *Dipterocarpus fusiformis, Dryobalanops keithii, Parashorea tomentella, Shorea kudatensis, S. leptoderma, S. symingtonii* and *S. waltonii*. Compared to the total number of Bornean dipterocarp endemics, the level of dipterocarp endemism in east Sabah is not high, and reflects the generalized nature of the forests, best considered as a continuum with generally common species giving way to others. There is a certain amount of specialization with changes in habitat type, particularly major changes in soil moisture regime and underlying rock type, but also more subtly with soil fertility and elevation.

Species of the genus *Shorea* may be divided into 4 sections, which correspond with timber groups (Table 54). The Rubroshorea (red seraya) section has most species.

TABLE 54. SPECIES OF *SHOREA* BY TIMBER GROUPS

Section	Timber	Number of species	
		Sabah	East Sabah
Anthoshorea	Melapi	7	7
Richetia	Yellow seraya	12	10
Rubroshorea	Red seraya	45	31
Shorea	Selangan batu	20	17

Other native vegetation types, besides the dipterocarp forests, occupy small areas (Fox 1979). Of these, the coastal and estuarine mangrove forests, covering some 3000 km² and containing 27 different species, are the most extensive. The lowland forests are characterized by an abundance of trees of the genus *Parashorea* (white seraya, or urat mata). These, and members of the section Rubroshorea of the

genus *Shorea*, are used to describe the broad forest types. The Borneo ironwood, *Eusideroxylon zwageri* (belian), today one of the most valuable of Sabah's timbers (Tsuruoka 1991), was also a common species of lowland formations prior to their commercial exploitation for timber. In contrast to the relatively fast-growing dipterocarps, ironwood is a slow-growing species and will be much less common in stands which have been exploited for the second or third time (Fox 1984). Exports of this timber from Sabah have now almost ceased (W. Meijer 1992, *in litt.*).

Distinction of forest types within the overall formation has been made on the basis of detailed enumerations over wide areas (Fox 1979) and are defined as follows:

❖ Lowland Dipterocarp Forests (0–300/600 m a.s.l.)
  Parashorea malaanonan forest
  Parashorea tomentella/Eusideroxylon zwageri forest
  Shorea (Rubroshorea)/*Eusideroxylon zwageri* forest
  Shorea (Rubroshorea)/*Dipterocarpus* forest
❖ Hill Dipterocarp Forests (300/600–900, or more, m a.s.l.)
  Shorea (Shorea) forest
  Dipterocarpus/Shorea (Richetia) forest

These six types are broad and generalized. Differences in floristics related to both texture and fertility of soil have been noted for the forests of Brunei (Ashton 1982), and similar contrasts probably exist for Sabah. Certainly species found on relatively well-drained sandstone ridges differ from forests on heavier soils, with more *Dipterocarpus* species on the former and more *Parashorea* (section Rubroshorea) on the latter. Perhaps the most striking contrast in floristics is that between species of the lowlands on soils derived from shales and sandstones, and those occurring on ultramafic hills (Meijer 1974).

Dipterocarps exhibit irregular gregarious flowering and poor fruit dispersal. Fallen seeds lack dormancy and will readily germinate and establish in moist, friable soil, but need suitable mycorrhiza to establish. Seedlings are shade tolerant and will persist for many years in dense shade, only moving to the sapling stage when adequate light becomes available which can then allow rapid growth. Adequate regeneration persists between the fruiting years. These general characteristics have allowed the development of silvicultural systems which secure forest renewal after exploitation through natural regeneration. The removal of large trees in felling, and selective removal of undesirable trees (defectives, damaged, diseased or useless species) by poisoning, created favourable light conditions for the dipterocarp seedlings. Second-growth stands would have a simpler composition with individuals of mainly valuable species of similar size and age. Provision was made for fruit tree retention. The fast-growing red seraya species and *Parashorea* species were favoured by such silvicultural management and could be recropped in cycles of 60–80 years.

This management requires the assessment of regeneration potential prior to opening of coupes for felling. Modifications are required for some stands in hilly areas or where particular species predominate. The forests of eastern Sabah cannot, however, be managed on a sustained basis using the types of short felling cycles (30 years) advocated in the Philippines and in Indonesian Borneo (Kalimantan).

Flora

The size of the flora of the forest area is unknown, but it is expected that the hill and lowland dipterocarp forests of eastern Sabah contain approximately 50–65% of Sabah's total vascular plant flora. A conservative estimate would be in the range of 5000–6000 vascular plant species. Most information is available concerning the taller synusiae, particularly tree species, and estimates for various groups of economically interesting plants are available. There are in excess of 2000 species, from some 80 families, which have tree form (Fox 1970). The wood properties of 400 species have been described by Burgess (1966). Botanical attention has necessarily concentrated on economic species groups. The possibilities of species not yet known to be of utility to man are considerable, and increased attention to the description and classification of plants should be an important priority.

In addition to a range of timber trees from such families as the Mimosaceae, Caesalpiniaceae, Sapotaceae, Anacardiaceae and Sterculiaceae, the forests contain a vast treasure trove of potentially edible fruits, with many congeners of the well-known cultivated fruit trees of South East Asia (Meijer 1969). There are some 49 species from 17 genera of palms in eastern Sabah, of which 4 are endemic. Some 60% of the rattan species found in Borneo occur in eastern Sabah (Dransfield 1984), with the genera *Calamus* (40 species) and *Daemonorops* (18 species) having the highest representation (Dransfield and Johnson 1989). Of the 14 rattan species endemic to Sabah, 11 are found in the forests of eastern Sabah, often on islands or ultramafic mountains.

Large numbers of orchid species are also present. The crowns of felled trees are often a mass of intermixtures of several species. A recent survey in the Tawau Hills State Park recorded some 107 species of orchids from 31 genera in a period of 6 days. At least two species were new to science.

Lianes are well-represented in primary forests. It is estimated that there may be some 150 genera and 300–350 species (Meijer 1965). Families well-represented include Asclepiadaceae (13 genera), Menispermaceae (12), Rubiaceae (10), Apocynaceae and Leguminosae (9 each).

The Kabili-Sepilok Reserve (see Table 55), just west of Sandakan, is perhaps the most well-known area in terms of tree species (Fox 1973). It has a range of vegetation types in the lowland and hill dipterocarp sequences, and, although much of the coastal areas of lowland forest have been logged in the past, there are areas of primary *Dipterocarpus* forest on sandstone hills within it. There is also a good sequence of mangrove forest associations. This reserve of 43 km² has some 700 tree species (W. Meijer, pers. comm. to J. Payne 1991) from over 60 families. This includes at least 54 dipterocarp species (from 8 genera), representing 33% of the dipterocarp species found in Sabah. Research Plot 17 has 190 species of tree >10 cm diameter on 1.84 ha.

Useful plants

There is an abundance of fruit trees in the dipterocarp forests of eastern Sabah, including 13 species of *Artocarpus* (jack- and breadfruits), *Durio* (15 species) and *Mangifera*

(17 species). A number of these also provide valuable timber. There are numerous understorey species, including several poorly known species of *Citrus*, 12 species of *Garcinia*, 3 of *Lansium* and 9 of *Nephelium*. Several understorey trees of the genus *Baccaurea* produce cauliflorous bunches of fruits with a taste similar to apples; there are at least 17 species in this genus in Sabah (Fox 1970). The mesocarp of *Dialium* (8 species) is eaten, as are the fruits of a number of species in the palm genus *Salacca*. Edible nuts include members of the genera *Canarium* (19 species) and *Terminalia* (8 species). Most of these are medium to large-sized timber trees. There are some 8 species of *Myristica* (nutmegs), none of which appear to have been examined for their utility.

The largest forest tree, *Koompassia excelsa*, is favoured by honey bees (*Apis dorsata*). Honey is collected from the nests for local consumption and medicine. A wide range of trees have medicinal uses, including *Alstonia* bark infusion for fever, *Garcinia*, as a purgative, *Dryobalanops* oil for rheumatism, *Canarium* resin for dressing sores, and *Heritiera* leaf and bark for fever. Fruits of some species of *Shorea* are rich in fat; formerly these were collected and entered world trade, especially in heavy mast-fruiting years, under the collective name "illipe nuts". Species so used, named "kawang", were *Shorea amplexicaulis*, *S. macrophylla*, *S. mecistopteryx* and *S. pinanga*. These went for tallow or vegetable fat, in candles, cooking and for machinery lubricants. Fruits of *Palaquium* are also a source of fat. Damar resin, from bole wounds, used for lighting, fuel or caulking boats, was taken from *Agathis dammara*, *Shorea faguetiana*, *S. mecistopteryx* and some *Hopea* spp. Resin from boles of the large tree *Antiaris toxicaria* is a hunting poison, and extracts from *Derris* are traditionally used to stun fish. Stems of the small tree *Goniothalamus* are used as walking sticks to ward off snakes and spirits. Incense wood was obtained from *Aquilaria*. Gutta jelutong, a low grade rubber, has been taken from *Dyera costulata*. Vegetable dyes are obtainable from the bark of *Morinda*, as well as *Garcinia*, *Intsia*, *Pterocarpus* and *Diospyros* fruits.

Rattan is an important forest product. Rattans provide materials for local use, such as binding ties, mats and basketwork, and are the source material for the cane furniture industry. *Korthalsia echinometra* is one of several species used in weaving baskets. Some of the best canes for furniture are *Calamus caesius* and *C. subinermis*. Fruits of some species are edible and new shoots are taken as "cabbage" (e.g. *Daemonorops microstachys*). The fruit scales of *Daemonorops didymophylla* and *D. micracantha* produce a resin ("dragon's blood") formerly exported to China for varnish.

Dipterocarp forests contain many species of ornamental value, including aroids, begonias, gingers and orchids.

Social and environmental values

The forests of eastern Sabah are a collective asset for all people of the state. There are no indigenous tribes in eastern Sabah which are able to claim large areas of pristine forest (although individuals who are indigenous may claim customary rights to specific areas of land, other than Forest Reserves, Parks or government reserves). Most of the forest did not have people living in it, although many moved through from time to time on hunting or gathering expeditions. In some areas of the central, inland western part of the region, indigenous people still use the forest in traditional ways. In parts of western Sabah, this has led to severe damage to the vegetation through repeated burning for shifting cultivation, and shortened rotations between crops. Along the alluvial banks of the major rivers some groups maintain a more benign relationship with the forests, using them for hunting, fishing, and the collection of fruits and tubers to supplement food obtained from cultivating relatively fertile soils near the rivers. Some nuts and rattans enter commercial trade. These activities have fluctuated with markets and the presence of traders in response to world demand. However, in general, the collection of "minor" forest products is now much reduced in Sabah (with the exception of rattan harvesting) as more people are attracted to urban areas, roadside communities and a regular wage income (J. Payne 1992, *in litt.*).

Most of the better soils, particularly on the more fertile volcanic locations, have been cleared of forest and used for cultivation of cocoa, oil palm and other plantation crops. The State has used much of the enormous revenues derived from forest liquidation to provide benefits to the people, and particularly so with a strong emphasis on enhanced educational opportunities.

The residual unexploited forests now have immense and immeasurable value simply because of their existence. For the production Forest Reserves it is inevitable that a decline in production is now underway.

The lowlands forests of Sabah are an Endemic Bird Area (EBA) with two endemic, restricted-range bird species, white-fronted falconet (*Microhierax latifrons*) and white-crowned shama (*Copsychus stricklandii*).

Economic assessment

Hard, heavy and durable timber was in most demand at the early stages of forest exploitation. The forests contain a wide range of timbers with all kinds of properties. Those species of dipterocarps attaining relatively large sizes provide timber of general utility. With the development of large-scale mechanized processing operations over the last 30 years, these became useful raw materials for veneer and plywood manufacture.

Several phases of economic development have run their course in Sabah, with forest exploitation, mainly producing logs for export, providing the main source of revenue. Between 1915 and 1926 production was static at 40–80,000 m³ per annum. A pre-war peak was achieved in 1937 at 0.25 million m³, and this was not equalled again until 1954. With the organization of concession agreements, and of special licenses outside the concession areas, production steadily increased from 2.8 million m³ in 1965, peaking at 12 million m³ in 1983. Subsequently production declined, hovering around 10 million m³ during the 1980s. Recent figures for exports include 6.1 million m³ in 1989 (Department of Statistics 1990) and 8.9 million m³ in 1991 (J. Payne 1992, *in litt.*). These levels cannot be sustained and the forthcoming period must be one of irreversible decline.

The dipterocarp forests of Sabah held the potential for sustained yield management on a scale of productivity which may have been the highest in the tropical world. Unfortunately,

that possibility was largely given away in the 1970s when the original system of Forest Reserves, worked over on long rotations, under the principle of sustained yield, was altered. Had the original aim of conserving 10,000 square miles (25,900 km²) of productive Forest Reserve been adhered to, using a felling cycle of 100 years, or 80 years on 80% of the area, then the annual yield in perpetuity could have been in the order of US$350–400 million in monetary terms. This could have been doubled if silvicultural practices had been undertaken in all areas. It must be stressed that this yield would have been of high value, general purpose dipterocarp logs. Any comparison with the present production prospects is clouded by uncertainty over the style of logging used, the areas involved and the long-term security of the estate. The government monopoly Sabah Foundation (Innoprise Corporation) has an area of 9730 km², of which 8900 km² is available for cutting. Should this be the remaining forest area to be managed, it could yield 1.2 million m³ per annum on a sustained basis, if silviculture were to be used. If the export price of logs is taken as US$100 per m³, then the "value" of the estate would be US$120 million per annum. However, as this 8900 km² includes all the residual areas of unexploited natural dipterocarp forests, much of it should be preserved. Also, there are concerns that current logging practices are not sustainable. A World Bank report used by the Malaysian Federal Government to gauge Sabah's forest management, estimated that most of the state's rain forests will be depleted by 1995 because of indiscriminate logging (Tsuruoka 1991). There is no reason for doubting or disputing this estimate. It is to be hoped that the State Government continues to support forest management efforts so that the depleted parts of the productive estate can be allowed to recover, to regenerate and to be improved by positive silvicultural investments. However, re-logging 10–20 years after the first logging seems to be increasing (W. Meijer 1992, *in litt.*).

As natural supplies of rattans have diminished in recent years, so prices have risen and interest has increased in the potential of commercial plantings. Plantings of rattans have been initiated by the Sabah Forestry Development Authority in a block of 100 km² (J. Dransfield 1992, *in litt.*). Harvesting from planted materials commenced in 1989. Two private companies have also developed significant estates. At present, collection is largely from the wild, with some village communities of the upper Kinabatangan River deriving a substantial part of their income from rattan collection (Marsh and Gait 1988). An estimate of income to a riverside settlement (Kampong Kuala Keramuak) made for 1987 was of M$150,000, representing a per capita income (for all residents) of M$171 (Marsh and Gait 1988). This figure can be multiplied by 30 for those who are actually involved. Rattan is sold in bundles (galongs) of 100 pieces of 18 feet (c. 5.5 m). Karamuak was estimated to have traded out 4000 galongs in 1987, at prices of M$30–40 per galong.

There is no doubt that the harvesting of rattan from the wild has not been carried out on a sustainable basis for many years. Prices have risen enormously, and the Indonesian government has recently banned exports (and more recently allowed them) to counter illicit trade and smuggling between the Malaysian states and Kalimantan. The recent interest in planting rattan is a symptom of the increasing shortages and cost of collection. The important species being tried in cultivation are *Calamus caesius*, *C. manan*, *C. subinermis* and *C. trachycoleus*.

Threats

Forest clearance not only removes the big tree species but also orchids, rattans, lianes, understorey species and animal life dependent on the forests. The potential uses of all these imperfectly known groups have scarcely been examined. Fortunately, there is a growing awareness in Sabah of the values associated with the forest inheritance and, today, large areas of the state remain unalienated and are allocated to reserve status of one kind or another. The position requires continuing vigilance, particularly in the face of changing political fashions and internal pressures for granting of resource rights to individuals.

Forest fires associated with speculative forest clearance, especially by migrant plantation workers, and the building of roads in previously remote areas are particular threats. Burning of dipterocarp forests for cropping effectively removes dipterocarps from the area affected. The main forest areas lack large populations of traditional swidden agriculturists and, where such people live in the western parts of the state, the forests had been deprived of their valuable tall tree components well before the modern timber exploitation era. Within the forest areas new settlers may squat on land already cleared by legal commercial harvesting. Village settlements may extend their areas of cultivation from traditional riverine sites into logged forest. Marsh and Gait (1988) describe how riverside village communities can become involved in accelerated forest destruction through participation in illegal activities.

An unprecedented drought, associated with an El Niño Southern Oscillation event, affected much of Borneo from June 1982 to April 1983, leading to considerable tree death in many forest areas (Mackie 1984). Man-induced fires burned over 10,000 km^2 of forest in Sabah alone, especially affecting areas which had been previously logged. It has been estimated that 85% of the fire damage occurred in logged forest (Beaman, Beaman, Marsh and Woods 1985). These fires undoubtedly destroyed dipterocarp regeneration in many areas. There may well be irreparable loss to future timber yields from affected forests. Although such severe droughts may have a periodicity of 1 in 100 years, it is possible that other fires may develop on shorter cycles in response to less severe droughts in the future. Indeed, there have been relatively long dry spells and localized but significant forest fires in several parts of Sabah in the years 1987, 1989, 1990–1991 and 1991–1992 (J. Payne 1992, in litt.). There is clearly an important amount of research to be undertaken to develop methods of minimizing any future fires, as well as to devise appropriate silvicultural and management procedures to restore those areas already damaged.

Much of the most productive lowland dipterocarp forest has already been alienated to private or group use and cleared for agricultural plantations. This has not been directly driven by land hunger nor the need to resettle overcrowded local Sabah populations. Indeed settlers and plantation workers have had to be actively recruited, and people on schemes or private plantations come from many places outside the state. The main economic force has been the knowledge of the timber values that accrue on liquidating the forest, coupled with the desire of politicians to develop land to what they suppose to be a higher land-use value. This has occurred despite the fact that timber workers command far higher income levels than do settlers or workers on agricultural plantation estates. Because conversion of forest to agricultural plantation crops involves land clearing and vegetation burning, the extent of land settlement schemes poses a real threat to the long-term integrity of the forest areas. Where schemes fail or are subsequently abandoned, then settlers may revert to subsistence farming using fire, further postponing the longer-term succession back to a form of high forest.

Several large areas of former Forest Reserve lands have been designated as timber plantation areas. These will contain mainly fast-growing, light weight and low utility species, such as the currently fashionable *Acacia mangium*. These forests will be species-poor compared to native forests. Unfortunately, there is no comparable work being undertaken on any of the multitude of very valuable, promising and naturally occurring species of timber tree.

With an increased awareness of the conservation value of the original vegetation, some designated areas have been set aside as strict conservation reserves. Sadly these areas have not been spared illegal activity, the most notorious examples perhaps being illegal logging in the Tabin Wildlife Reserve and in the Kalumpang area (Tsuruoka 1991). These transgressions do not appear to have been remedied by legal means, and hence similar illegal activities are a continuing threat in the near future. Other illegal practices documented by Tsuruoka (1991) include bribes and false documentation of both species and log volumes loaded at ports.

A misconception accentuating forest destruction is that lesser known species should become exploited. The more material removed in a logging operation, the greater the logging damage to the residual stands. Lightly logged dipterocarp forest will regenerate and can be managed for timber production in perpetuity. Heavier logging destroys more of the soil surface, more of the reproductive potential and leads to calls for enrichment planting, a largely unproven and certainly expensive silvicultural technique. So-called enrichment with alien species, of low stature, will further change the forest environment.

Conservation

At present a total complement of some 4077 km^2 is set aside for conservation purposes in the forest area of eastern Sabah (see Table 55). Few of these areas contain unexploited dipterocarp forest; their main value is their official designation as protected areas.

Commercial stands on the Tawau Hills had been cut out well before its designation as a State Park; the majority of the protection reserves occur in high hills with difficult terrain. The commercial stands on Timbun Mata were exploited in 1969. The modes of selection of "Virgin Jungle Reserves" tend to belie the name; many of the 49 areas set aside include sample plots established to assess regrowth in the much larger Forest Reserves of which they were once representative, but which have now been logged over several times and/or revoked. Sepilok is a special case, with an Orang Utan Sanctuary, a Forest Research Centre and numerous long-standing research plots. It has many practical uses in addition to its status as a Reserve.

The state logging undertaking (Innoprise Corporation Sdn. Bhd.) has a total logging concession area of 9730 km^2. Two conservation areas, Danum Valley (438 km^2) and Maliau Basin (390 km^2), comprise 8.5% of the logging concession.

These are perhaps the most significant dipterocarp forest sites in the state. At Danum Valley a Field Centre and laboratory complex, completed in 1984, is the site of a major international research programme. Maliau Basin (CPD Site SEA22i/23 – see entry in the Borneo section of the Regional Overview) lies to the west of the area covered by this Data Sheet. It is to be hoped that legislation will be effected to designate Danum Valley and the Maliau Basin as reserves in perpetuity.

Similar centres merit establishment in the Paitan, Segaliud-Lokan and Gunung Rara/Kalabakan forest areas, and in other areas with different vegetation types. All such developments would have great value for future tourism, an important current aim of the State Government of Sabah. Areas of unexploited virgin forest must be adequately conserved urgently to ensure that some, at least, of the immense biological diversity of Sabah is retained.

Despite the damage to the forests of eastern Sabah described above, there are some encouraging signs. In March 1992, the State Government converted about 1020 km² of former Commercial Forest Reserve to Protection Forest in eastern Sabah. This re-designation prohibits logging, although most, but not all of the areas concerned, had been previously logged (J. Payne 1992, *in litt.*). The largest single block of east Sabah lowland/hill dipterocarp forest which is totally protected and has not been logged is a core area of about 85 km² (recently redesignated as Protection Forest Reserve) within the Tabin Wildlife Reserve. Also in 1992, a "Sabah Conservation Strategy" was completed under the purview of the government; this stresses the need for forest conservation and management in relation to water, soil, biodiversity and the future needs of the timber industry.

TABLE 55. IMPORTANT PROTECTED AREAS IN EASTERN SABAH

Designation	Location	Area (km²)	Total (km²) East Sabah
State Park (1)			280
	Tawau Hills	280	
Protection Forest Reserves (12 areas)			1870
	Tavai Plateau	227	
	Bidu Bidu Hills	161	
	Timbun Mata Island	115	
	Tabin (core area)	85	
Virgin Jungle Reserves (total 49 areas)			600
	Sepilok	43	
	Sungei Imbak	181	
	Sepagaya/Silam	41	
Wildlife Reserves			1327
	Tabin (outer area)	1120	
	Kulamba	206	
Sabah Foundation Concession Area			
	Danum Valley	438	
Total area in formal reserves (excluding Danum Valley)			**4077**

MAP 12. EAST SABAH LOWLAND AND HILL DIPTEROCARP FORESTS (CPD SITE SEA22)

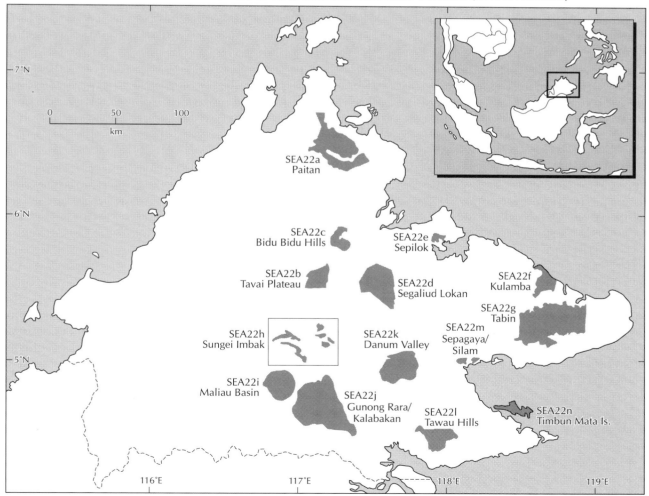

Important forest areas

SEA22a. Paitan area
SEA22b. Tavai Plateau Protection Forest
SEA22c. Bidu Bidu Hills Protection Forest
SEA22d. Segaliud Lokan area
SEA22e. Sepilok Virgin Forest Reserve
SEA22f. Kulamba Wildlife Reserve
SEA22g. Tabin Wildlife Reserve
SEA22h. Sungei Imbak Virgin Jungle Reserve
SEA22i. Maliau Basin (see also entry under SEA23 in the
         Borneo section of the Regional Overview)
SEA22j. Gunong Rara/Kalabakan Forest Reserve
SEA22k. Danum Valley
SEA22l. Tawau Hills State Park
SEA22m. Sepagaya/Silam Virgin Jungle Reserve
SEA22n. Timbun Mata Island Protection Forest

References

Anon. (1990). International Conference on Forest Biology and Conservation in Borneo, July 30 – August 3, 1990. Kota Kinabalu, Sabah. Extended abstracts of papers. 152 pp.

Anon. (1991). *Annual report for 1990.* Danum Valley Rain Forest Research and Training Programme. 49 pp.

Ashton, P. S. (1982). Dipterocarpaceae. *Flora Malesiana* Series 1, vol. 9 (2): 237–552.

Beaman, R.S., Beaman, J.H., Marsh, C.W. and Woods, P.V. (1985). Drought and forest fires in Sabah in 1983. *Sabah Society Journal* 8(1): 10–30.

Burgess, P.F. (1966). *Timbers of Sabah.* Sabah Forest Record No. 6. Forests Department, Sabah. 501 pp.

Cockburn, P.F. (1976). *Trees of Sabah*, vol. 1. Sabah Forest Record No. 10. Borneo Literature Bureau, Kuching. 261 pp.

Cockburn, P.F. (1980). *Trees of Sabah*, vol. 2. Sabah Forest Record No. 10. Dewan Bahasa dan Pustaka Cawangan, Kuching. 124 pp.

Department of Statistics (1990). *Annual bulletin of statistics, Sabah, 1990.* Department of Statistics, Malaysia, Sabah Branch.

Dransfield, J. (1984). *The rattans of Sabah.* Sabah Forest Record No. 13. Forest Department, Sabah. 182 pp.

Dransfield, J. and Johnson, D. (1989). The conservation status of palms in Sabah. *Malayan Naturalist* 43: 16–19.

Fox, J.E.D. (1970). *Preferred check-list of Sabah trees.* Sabah Forest Record No. 7. Borneo Literature Bureau, Kuching. 65 pp.

Fox, J.E.D. (1973). *A handbook to Kabili-Sepilok Forest Reserve.* Sabah Forest Record No. 9. Borneo Literature Bureau, Kuching. 102, 45 pp.

Fox, J.E.D. (1979). The natural vegetation of Sabah, Malaysia. 1. The physical environment and classification. *Tropical Ecology* 19: 218–239.

Fox, J.E.D. (1984). The natural vegetation of Sabah, Malaysia. 2. The *Parashorea* forests of the lowlands. *Tropical Ecology* 24: 94–112.

Innoprise Corporation Sdn. Bhd. (1989). Forestry, conservation and land-use in Sabah: a commercial perspective. Paper to International Hardwood Products Association, San Diego. 7 pp.

Jacobs, M. (1981). Dipterocarpaceae: the taxonomic and distributional framework. *Malaysian Forester* 44: 168–189.

Mackie, S. (1984). The lessons behind East Kalimantan's forest fires. *Borneo Research Bulletin* 16: 63–74

Marsh, C. and Gait, B. (1988). The effects of logging on rural communities: a comparative study of two villages in Ulu Kinabatangan. *Sabah Society J.* 8: 394–434.

Meijer, W. (1965). *Botanical News Bulletin No. 4.* Forest Department, Sabah. Pp. 123–129.

Meijer, W. (1969). Notes on some Malaysian fruit trees in Malesia. *Sabah Society J.* 5: 53–66.

Meijer, W. (1974). Plant geographic studies on Dipterocarpaceae in Malesia. *Annals Missouri Bot. Gard.* 61: 806–818.

Tsuruoka, D. (1991). Cutting down to size. *Far Eastern Economic Review* 4th July 1991: 43–46.

Wood, G.H.S. and Meijer, W. (1964). *Dipterocarps of Sabah.* Sabah Forest Record No. 5. Forests Department, Sabah. 344 pp.

Acknowledgements

This Data Sheet was prepared by Professor J.E.D. Fox (University of Technology, Perth, Australia). Professor P.S. Ashton (Harvard University Herbaria, Cambridge, Massachusetts), Professor J. Beaman (Beal-Darlington Herbarium, University of Michigan), Dr J. Dransfield (Royal Botanic Gardens, Kew), Dr W. Meijer (T.H. Morgan School of Biological Sciences, University of Kentucky), Dr J. Payne (WWF Malaysia), Dr A. Lamb (Agricultural Research Station, Tenom, Sabah) and Anthea Phillipps (former Park Ecologist, Sabah Parks) provided additional information.

KINABALU PARK
Sabah, Malaysia

Location: 6°5'N 160°33'E (summit of Low's Peak, Mount Kinabalu).

Area: 753.7 km².

Altitude: 150–4101 m, though mostly above 500 m.

Vegetation: Mostly tropical montane, with some lowland rain forest, ultramafic (serpentine) forest, tropical subalpine forest and scrub, cliff communities, tropical alpine vegetation.

Flora: More than 4000, and possibly more than 4500 vascular plant species in over 180 families and 950 genera.

Useful plants: Timber trees (especially dipterocarps, *Agathis*), ornamental plants (e.g. *Nepenthes*, orchids, rhododendrons), medicinal plants.

Other values: Tourism (the mountain attracts over 200,000 visitors, national and international, every year), cultural importance (the mountain is regarded as sacred by local Dusun), rich fauna, watershed protection, education and research values.

Threats: Visitor pressure in some areas, mining, clearance for cultivation, illegal plant collecting, commercial logging encroachment.

Conservation: State Park (IUCN Management Category: II).

Geography

Kinabalu Park is situated approximately 50 km east-north-east of Kota Kinabalu in northern Borneo. The park includes three main mountains: Mt Kinabalu (4101 m, the highest mountain in South East Asia between the Himalayas and New Guinea), Mt Tembuyuken (Mt Tambuyukon) (2579 m, Malaysia's third highest mountain) and Mt Templer (1133 m). Mt Kinabalu is a plutonic intrusion of adamellite (a type of granite) surrounded by metamorphosed and fractured country rocks consisting of schist, gneiss, ultramafic rocks and Tertiary sedimentary rocks. Radiometric dating indicates that cooling of the intrusion took place from 9 to 4.9 million years ago. The pluton remained deeply buried until 1–2 million years ago when it began to be uplifted at a geologically rapid rate and is still rising today. Quaternary sedimentary rocks (dating from the early Pleistocene) cover a small portion of the south face at c. 2000 m and the entire Pinosuk Plateau, whilst ultramafic rocks occur in numerous places on the Kinabalu massif, as well as forming the whole of Mt Tembuyuken except for the very lowest slopes. These various rock types have given rise to distinct vegetation types and floral assemblages.

The summit area of Kinabalu (above c. 3200 m) clearly shows the effects of glaciation. The whole summit area has been smoothed by the action of ice, and "nunataks" left above the glacier form the jagged peaks (such as Low's Peak and South Peak) along Kinabalu's distinctive skyline today. Denuded rock surfaces of the summit area support rock-desert or sparse vegetation. Soil development is hampered by high rates of erosion by surface run-off following torrential downpours. A more detailed account of Kinabalu's geological history is given by Collenette (1964).

Rainfall is generally high (up to 3800 mm) but occasionally there are prolonged dry spells (as in 1977, 1979 and 1983). The drought recurs periodically in relation to the El Niño-Southern Oscillation and has severe effects on the vegetation (see, for example, Lowry, Lee and Stone 1973).

Vegetation

The vegetation of Kinabalu Park has been mapped and described by Kitayama (1991) who recognizes 18 natural vegetation types. Mt Kinabalu itself supports mainly tropical montane rain forest, tropical subalpine forest, and scrub, cliff and tropical alpine vegetation. Important edaphic variants are the endemic-rich scrub and graminoid communities on ultramafic rocks (see, also, the Data Sheet on the North-east Borneo Ultramafic Flora – SEA27).

Natural vegetation covers about 93% of the park area (Kitayama 1991). Rich tropical lowland and hill rain forest (dominated by dipterocarps) covers about 35% of the park, occurring to the east of Mt Kinabalu and in the north around Mt Templer. Small areas also exist along the west boundary of the park (much cleared by shifting cultivation) and around Mt Nungkek (Mt Sadok Sadok). Among the important trees are the dipterocarps *Parashorea*, *Dipterocarpus* and *Shorea*, as well as members of the Sapindaceae, Sterculiaceae, Leguminosae, Anacardiaceae and Ebenaceae. Other abundant families include Xanthophyllaceae, Gonystylaceae, Meliaceae, Moraceae, Burseraceae and Bombacaceae. The parasitic *Rafflesia pricei*, *R. keithii* and *Mitrastemon* (Rafflesiaceae) are also present in lowland forests.

The upper limit of lowland rain forest is reached at around 1200 m, above which tropical montane rain forest occurs up to about 3000 m. Montane forest is the dominant vegetation over about 37% of Kinabalu Park. The lower montane zone has a number of species belonging to families better represented in the lowlands. They include *Palaquium gutta* (Sapotaceae), *Shorea monticola* (Dipterocarpaceae), *Knema kinabaluensis* (Myristicaceae) and *Santiria apiculata* (Burseraceae). With increasing altitude these species are replaced by species of *Lithocarpus* (oaks) and other members of the Fagaceae, Ericaceae, Myrtaceae, Lauraceae, Magnoliaceae and Guttiferae, along with conifers such as *Agathis*, *Dacrycarpus*, *Podocarpus*, *Phyllocladus* and *Dacrydium*. The oak *Trigonobalanus verticillata* (once thought to be endemic, but now also known from Gunung Leuser, Sumatra) is present on Mt Kinabalu in this zone (but much of its former habitat on the Pinosuk Plateau has been destroyed). Also present here are members of the Nepenthaceae, including *Nepenthes rajah*, a Mt Kinabalu endemic and the most spectacular species in the genus. The parasitic *Balanophora* (Balanophoraceae) is also found in montane forests.

Variations in the composition of montane rain forest communities arise in response to local patterns of cloud formation, topography and edaphic conditions. Of particular conservation significance are vegetation types developed on ultramafic rocks. Ultramafic (serpentine) vegetation covers 16% of the park, occurring from the lowlands to the upper montane zone and containing a large number of species which are restricted entirely to this substrate. Large expanses of evergreen microphyllous forest, dominated by *Gymnostoma*

sumatrana and *Tristania elliptica*, and scrub dominated by *Leptospermum flavescens* and *Tristania elliptica*, occur on Mt Tembuyuken and on the upper parts of Pinosuk Plateau (although it has been mostly cleared at this locality). On Marai Parai (the west part of the Kinabalu massif), the dominants are *Dacrydium* and *Podocarpus* spp. On the Summit Trail of Mt Kinabalu, the ultramafic zone extends between 2450 m and 3050 m and is dominated by *Dacrydium gibbsiae*, *Lithocarpus havilandii*, *Leptospermum recurvum* and *Schima brevifolia*. The summit of Mt Tembuyuken and parts of Marai Parai support graminoid communities on serpentine.

Tropical subalpine forest occurs only on Mt Kinabalu between 3000 and 3700 m, where the limit of tree growth is reached. This vegetation is a mixture of evergreen coniferous and broadleaved elements, including *Phyllocladus*, *Dacrydium*, *Schima*, *Eurya*, *Symplocos* and *Eugenia*.

The summit area of Kinabalu includes evergreen ericaceous scrub, where soil development is sufficient to support it, and large expanses of bare rock and scree with low-growing alpine communities. The main shrub species present are *Leptospermum recurvum*, *Vaccinium stapfianum*, *Rhododendron buxifolium* and *R. ericoides*. Often these become very stunted and restricted to crevices in the rock surface. Alpine herbaceous plants belonging to genera which are usually associated with temperate regions occur in the summit zone. They include *Ranunculus lowii*, *Euphrasia borneensis* and *Potentilla borneensis*.

CPD Site SEA24: The peaks of Mount Kinabalu with lower montane forest in the foreground.
Photo: Stephen D. Davis.

Flora

Kinabalu is one of the most remarkable and spectacular centres of plant diversity and endemism in the world. Despite its geological youth, the Kinabalu massif is remarkably rich in species, with elements from the Himalayas, China, Australia, New Zealand and Malesia, as well as pantropical species. Lee and Lowry (1980) estimated that the mountain and rain forests at its base contain approximately 4500 vascular plant species. This estimate of diversity is borne out by the recent work of Professor J. Beaman (Michigan State University) and collaborators who have developed a computer database of plant collections from the mountain. Their work, which provides the basis for much of this present account on the flora, indicates that nearly 4000 species of vascular plants have been collected from the mountain, but that this figure could rise to over 4500 species when work on orchids and other groups has been completed.

The high species diversity of Kinabalu results from a number of factors, including: 1) the great altitudinal and climatic range from tropical rain forest to alpine conditions; 2) precipitous topography causing effective geographic isolation over short distances; 3) the diverse geology with many localized edaphic conditions, particularly the ultramafic substrates; 4) the frequent climatic oscillations influenced by El Niño events; and 5) the geological history of the Malay Archipelago itself. The close proximity of the geologically older Crocker Range mountains, from which taxa could disperse to Kinabalu, is also a possible factor in explaining the high diversity of Kinabalu's flora (Argent 1992, *in litt.*).

Over 180 families and 950 genera occur in the flora (Beaman and Beaman 1990). Certain groups are well-represented, such as orchids, of which there are 711 named taxa (out of a total orchid flora estimated to be up to 800 taxa) on the mountain (Wood, Beaman and Beaman 1993). Of these, 77 taxa are endemic to Mt Kinabalu, 177 taxa are endemic to Sabah and 283 taxa are endemic to Borneo (Wood, Beaman and Beaman 1993).

The largest genus represented on the mountain is *Ficus* with 98 taxa (over half the number that occur in the whole of Borneo). Other genera with extraordinary numbers of taxa on Kinabalu include *Syzygium* (66 taxa), *Litsea* (53 taxa) and *Lithocarpus* (46 taxa) (Beaman and Beaman 1990). In Ericaceae, the genus *Diplycosia*, with approximately 100 species, has 26 taxa recorded from Kinabalu (about half the Bornean species) (Argent 1992, *in litt.*). Among orchids, the two largest genera are *Bulbophyllum* and *Dendrobium*, with 85 and 60 taxa respectively. So far, it is known that there are 73 genera with 10 or more species on the mountain and 30 genera which have 20 or more Kinabalu representatives. In view of the fact that nearly one third of Mt Kinabalu and a large proportion of the remainder of the park remain unexplored, the numbers of taxa are likely to

Leptospermum recurvum, **one of the main shrub species found on the summit area of Mount Kinabalu (CPD Site SEA24).** Photo: Sarah Fowler.

increase as further botanical exploration takes place. It is already clear, however, that rapid adaptive radiation has taken place among certain genera on the mountain.

So far, 26 species of gymnosperms (and 2 additional varieties) are recognized in the Kinabalu flora, of which 5 species (and one variety) are thought to be endemic to Mt Kinabalu, while 5 others are endemic to Borneo (Beaman and Beaman 1993). Considering the limited area of Kinabalu, the mountain contains a diverse and endemic-rich component of the world's gymnosperm flora. In addition, 609 species of pteridophytes belonging to 145 genera have been collected from Mt Kinabalu (Parris, Beaman and Beaman 1992). This is 5% of the world's total pteridophyte flora from an area of about 700 km^2, and more than the pteridophyte flora of the whole of tropical mainland Africa (totalling c. 500 species) (Parris, Beaman and Beaman 1992). About 50 pteridophytes (8% of the Kinabalu pteridophyte flora) are endemic to the mountain.

Many endemic taxa have extremely restricted distributions on the mountain. Statistics from the Kinabalu database indicate that 40% of the flora is presently known from just a single locality; 1336 species have been collected only once. Only 104 species (2.6% of the flora) are so far known from more than 10 localities (Beaman and Beaman 1990). Many of the rarest species (i.e. those known only from one to five localities on the mountain) are restricted to ultramafic outcrops.

Nepenthes × *kinabaluensis* **in montane forest on Mount Kinabalu (CPD Site SEA24) at 2820 m. The plant is the product of hybridization between** *N. rajah* **(endemic to Mount Kinabalu) and** *N. villosa.* Photo: Stephen D. Davis.

Important ultramafic localities

Among the most important ultramafic localities, based on existing collections, are:

- ❖ Penibukan/Marai Parai
- ❖ Summit Trail outcrops
- ❖ Mt Tembuyuken
- ❖ Gurulau Spur
- ❖ Mesilau Cave
- ❖ Penataran River
- ❖ Bambangan River

Other important localities (which have now been excised from the park and have lost much of their natural plant cover) include the Lohan River area, Hempuen Hill (Hampuan Hill) and Kulung Hill. (Further details on the North-east Borneo Ultramafic Flora are given in a separate Data Sheet – SEA27.)

The affinities of the flora of the lower slopes and foothills of Kinabalu are generally to local regions and to areas in Malesia west of Wallace's line (i.e. Peninsular Malaysia, Sumatra, Java and the Philippines). Distinctly fewer genera are shared with Sulawesi and New Guinea. At higher elevations, above 3000 m, the floristic relationships are more towards New Guinea, Australia and New Zealand. The communities of the summit zone of Mt Kinabalu have close affinities with alpine vegetation on New Guinea's high mountains.

Useful plants

Kinabalu has a wealth of horticulturally important plants, including orchids, pitcher plants and Ericaceae. Orchids, in particular, could become the basis of thriving commercial enterprises, based on local and export trade. However, there should be strict controls on collecting from the wild, and growers should be encouraged to propagate rare and endangered species from seeds, in collaboration with orchidaria and reference collections of both highland and lowland species established at Kinabalu and Tenom.

The lowland forests of Kinabalu contain important timber species, including members of the Dipterocarpaceae, such as *Shorea macroptera*, *S. rubra* and *S. johorensis*, while the "kampongs" of lower slopes in the hill zone (between 500–1000 m) contain a number of fruit tree species, such as langsat (*Lansium edule*), durian (*Durio graveolens, D. oxleyanus*) and rambutan (*Nephelium lappaceum*). Many of these have been selected by man from the surrounding forests and are semi-domesticated. The hill and montane forests also contain *Agathis*, another important timber tree.

People living in the surrounding foothills once used many species in the past for medicinal uses. Today, however, relatively few species are gathered from the wild for medicinal uses. Among them are *Pangium edule*, whose seeds and bark are externally used for killing parasites and for preserving meat, and *Ficus* sp., used as an abortifacient (K. Kitayama 1992, *in litt.*). In 1992, the Kinabalu Ethnobotany Project, funded by WWF, UNESCO and the Tropical Forestry Program of the U.S. Department of Agriculture Forest Service, began ethnobotanical surveys of kampongs and forests on the perimeter of the park with a view towards documenting the uses of plants.

Social and environmental values

Mt Kinabalu has long been regarded as a sacred mountain by the native Dusun people of the foothills region.

European exploration of the mountain dates from Sir Hugh Low's first ascent to the summit on 11 March 1851. Subsequently, the first major accounts on the flora were made by Stapf (1894) and Gibbs (1914). There have been numerous major expeditions in more recent years, including those sponsored by the Royal Society in 1961 and 1964. There are still large portions of the park which remain unexplored, especially the north and east slopes.

The park has a rich fauna including 289 species of birds, of which 254 are resident (Jenkins and Silva 1978), and 290 species of butterflies and moths (Holloway 1978) The montane habitats of Kinabalu Park lie within the Bornean Mountains Endemic Bird Area (EBA), which supports 28 restricted-range bird species, of which 24 are endemic. They include several species which are restricted to the mountains in the northern part of the EBA in Sabah and Sarawak, notably the globally threatened Mountain Serpent-eagle (*Spilornis kinabaluensis*). Kinabalu has 7 species of tree shrew and 28 of the 34 Bornean species of squirrels (Lim Boo Liat and Illar Muul 1978). Notable among the mammals are tarsier (*Tarsius bancanus*), Malay bear (*Helarctis malayanus*), orang utan (*Pongo pygmaeus*), Borneo gibbon (*Hylobates molloch*), grey-leaf monkey (*Presbytis aygula*) and red-leaf monkey (*P. rubicunda*).

Apart from its religious and scientific importance, Kinabalu greatly benefits the local and national economy through tourism. Today, Kinabalu Park caters for a growing number of both national and international tourists. In 1990, the park received 233,965 visitors (Nais 1992, *in litt.*). Visitors are attracted to the mountain for its spectacular scenery, to climb the Summit Trail, to experience the feeling of "wilderness", or to undertake relaxing activities at the Park Headquarters and Poring Hot Springs. Kinabalu Park is Sabah's major tourist attraction. Inevitably a balance needs to be struck between conservation and tourism to ensure that the natural interest and long-term benefits which could be gained from carefully planned tourism are not jeopardized by ill-conceived development projects.

The forests of Kinabalu act as a very important water catchment reserve.

Threats

Road construction has resulted in an increasing number of tourists, which in turn has led to pressures to build more facilities. Along with perfectly reasonable improvements to the visitor centre and tourist accommodation facilities at the Park Headquarters, there have been a number of unfortunate and less well planned developments. In particular, in 1984 a large area of alluvial Pinosuk Plateau, which supported one of the most species-rich lower montane forests in the park, was removed from park protection for government development projects which include a golf course, dairy farm, expensive house sites, experimental gardens and plantations. Several localities of the threatened *Rafflesia pricei* have already been destroyed on Pinosuk Plateau as a result of forest clearances.

Much of the lower slopes to the west of Kinabalu have been cleared by shifting cultivators. Areas to the south of the park have been largely converted to temperate vegetable gardens, particularly after the construction of the trans-Sabah highway to the south of the park in 1972. Forests on Hempuen (Hampuan) Hill and Kulung Hill were partially destroyed in 1987 or 1988 by illegal and unsuccessful shifting agriculture (Beaman and Beaman 1990). There is also encroachment into the park from commercial logging (K. Kitayama 1992, *in litt.*).

In 1963, a U.N. team detected copper while working in the headwater area of the Mamut River. Subsequent prospecting revealed the existence of a 77 million ton deposit of porphyry copper at 0.4–0.7% grade. A mining lease was granted over 25.5 km² to a joint Japanese-Sabahan mining company. Commercial production began in 1975 and the impact in the area further legitimized by the de-gazettement of a large portion of Pinosuk Plateau. Today, the Mamut Copper Mine has despoiled a large area on the east side of the mountain.

The rapid disappearance of the forests on the lower slopes of Mt Kinabalu over the last 25 years (much of which was formerly within the park) causes serious concern about the future of remaining forests below 2000 m. Sensitive planning and strict control of further encroachments are required if further damage to Kinabalu's unique flora is to be avoided.

A number of species have been threatened by over-collecting. For example, the slipper orchid *Paphiopedilum rothschildeanum* is endangered as a result of over-collecting for local and export trade, and the endemic Rajah Brooke's pitcher plant (*Nepenthes rajah*) has suffered a similar fate.

Conservation

In 1964 the mountain, and some of the surrounding rain forests above 150 m, were gazetted as a National Park of 712 km². In 1974 an additional 93 km² were gazetted in return for taking out the Mamut Copper Mine concession, bringing the Mt Templer Forest Reserve in the north within the National Park boundary. This increased the area of lowland habitat within the park, as 90% of the former Mt Templer Forest Reserve is under 1000 m. Several boundary changes have occurred since then, as described above. In 1984 Kinabalu was re-designated a State Park covering a total area of 753.7 km².

An ethnobotanical project, involving Sabah Parks, the Institute of Biodiversity and Environmental Conservation (Universiti Malaysia Sarawak), and the People and Plants initiative (WWF, UNESCO, Royal Botanic Gardens, Kew) was initiated in 1993 with funding from the MacArthur Foundation. The Park is now working closely with members of local communities to evaluate local uses of plant resources.

References

Beaman, J.H. and Beaman, R.S. (1990). Diversity and distribution patterns in the flora of Mount Kinabalu. In Baas, P., Kalkman, K. and Geesink, R. (eds), *The plant diversity of Malesia*. Kluwer Academic Publishers, Dordrecht. Pp. 147–160.

Beaman, J.H. and Beaman, R.S. (1990). The gymnosperms of Mount Kinabalu. *Contrib. Univ. Michigan Herb.* 19: 307–340.

Beaman, J.H. and Regalado, J.C., jr (1989). Development and management of a microcomputer specimen-oriented database for the flora of Mount Kinabalu. *Taxon* 38: 27–42.

Christensen, C. and Holttum, R.E. (1934). The ferns of Mount Kinabalu. *Gardens' Bull. Singapore* 7: 191–324.

Cockburn, P.F. (1978). Plant life. In Luping, D.M., Wen, C. and Dingley, E.R. (eds), *Kinabalu: summit of Borneo.* Sabah Soc. Monog., Malaysia. Pp. 255–263.

Collenette, P. (1964). A short account of the geology and geological history of Mount Kinabalu. *Proc. Roy. Soc. B.* 161: 56–63.

Corner, E.J.H. (1978). Plant life. In Luping, D.M., Wen, C. and Dingley, E.R. (eds), *Kinabalu: summit of Borneo.* Sabah Soc. Monog., Malaysia. Pp. 113–178.

Gibbs, L.S. (1914). A contribution to the flora and plant formations of Mount Kinabalu and the highlands of British North Borneo. *J. Linn. Soc. Bot.* 42: 1–240.

Grubb, P.J. (1977). Control of forest growth and distribution on wet tropical mountains. *Ann. Rev. Ecol. Systematics* 8: 83–107.

Harrison, T. (1978). Kinabalu – the wonderful mountain of change. In Luping, D.M., Wen, C. and Dingley, E.R. (eds), *Kinabalu: summit of Borneo.* Sabah Soc. Monog., Malaysia. Pp. 23–44.

Holloway, J.D. (1978). Butterflies and moths. In Luping, D.M., Wen. C. and Dingley, E.R. (eds), *Kinabalu: summit of Borneo.* Sabah Soc. Monog., Malaysia. Pp. 255–263.

Holttum, R.E. (1978). The ferns of Kinabalu National Park. In Luping, D.M., Wen. C. and Dingley, E.R. (eds), *Kinabalu: summit of Borneo.* Sabah Soc. Monog., Malaysia. Pp. 199–210.

Jenkins, D.V. and Silva, G.S. de (1978). An annotated check list of the birds of the Mount Kinabalu National Park, Sabah, Malaysia. In Luping, D.M., Wen, C. and Dingley, E.R. (eds), *Kinabalu: summit of Borneo.* Sabah Soc. Monog., Malaysia. Pp. 347–402.

Kitayama, K. (1991). *Vegetation of Mount Kinabalu Park, Sabah, Malaysia. Map of physiognomically classified vegetation, scale 1: 100,000.* East-West Center, Honolulu. 45 pp., map.

Kurata, S. (1976). *Nepenthes of Mount Kinabalu.* Sabah National Parks Publ. 2. Sabah National Park Trustees, Kota Kinabalu. 80 pp.

Lee, D.W. and Lowry, J.B. (1980). Plant speciation on tropical mountains: *Leptospermum* (Myrtaceae) on Mount Kinabalu, Borneo. *Bot. J. Linn. Soc.* 80: 223–242.

Lim Boo Liat and Illar Muul (1978). Small mammals. In Luping, D.M., Wen, C. and Dingley, E.R. (eds), *Kinabalu: summit of Borneo.* Sabah Soc. Monog., Malaysia. Pp. 403–457.

Lowry, J.B., Lee, D.W. and Stone, B.C. (1973). Effects of drought on Mount Kinabalu. *Malay Nature J.* 26: 178–179.

Meijer, W. (1965). A botanical guide to the flora of Mount Kinabalu. In *Symposium on Ecological Research in Humid Tropics Vegetation.* Kuching, Sarawak, July 1965. Government of Sarawak and UNESCO. Pp. 325–364.

Parris, B.S., Beaman, R.S. and Beaman, J.H. (1992). *The plants of Mount Kinabalu: 1. Ferns and fern allies.* Royal Botanic Gardens, Kew. 165 pp.

Smith, J.M.B. (1970). Herbaceous plant communities in the summit zone of Mount Kinabalu. *Malay Nature J.* 24: 16–29.

Stapf, O. (1894). On the flora of Mount Kinabalu, in north Borneo. *Trans. Linn. Soc. London, Bot.* 4: 69–263.

Steenis, C.G.G.J. van (1964). Plant geography of the mountain flora of Mount Kinabalu. *Proc. Roy. Soc. B.* 161: 7–38.

Wood, J.J., Beaman, R.S. and Beaman, J.H. (1993). *The plants of Mount Kinabalu: 2. Orchids.* Royal Botanic Gardens, Kew. 411 pp.

Acknowledgements

This Data Sheet was written by Stephen D. Davis, with grateful thanks to the following for their help and contributions: Professor John Beaman (Beal-Darlington Herbarium, University of Michigan), Anthea Phillipps (former Park Ecologist, Sabah Parks), Dr Kanehiro Kitayama (University of Hawaii at Manoa), Dr G. Argent (Royal Botanic Garden, Edinburgh) and Jamili Nais (Park Ecologist, Sabah Parks).

NORTH-EAST BORNEO ULTRAMAFIC FLORA
Sabah, Malaysia

Location: Several scattered localities within Sabah.

Area: c. 3500 km².

Altitude: Sea-level to c. 3000 m.

Vegetation: Facies of forest over ultramafic rocks, corresponding to tropical lowland evergreen rain forest, tropical lower montane forest and tropical upper montane forest; grassland.

Flora: Poorly known; likely to be rich in hitherto unrecognized endemic specific and sub-specific taxa.

Useful plants: Timber trees, plants of potential value for rehabilitating degraded sites.

Other values: Tourist attraction, wildlife refuge, watershed protection.

Threats: Logging, deforestation, colonization, agriculture, fire, grazing, dam construction, road building.

Conservation: Kinabalu Park (CPD Site: SEA24, see separate Data Sheet) protects outcrops of major importance; small areas occur within Danum Valley Conservation Area; Gunung Silam is a protected watershed, but has suffered disturbance and its conservation needs strengthening.

Geography

Ultramafic rocks are rich in magnesium and nickel. They are often referred to as "ultrabasic" or serpentine rocks, but ultramafic is now the preferred term. They outcrop in many places in Sabah (see Map 13) and occur at a range of altitudes, from sea-level up to 3000 m, in an area where rainfall is generally high, with annual means varying from about 2000 to 4000 mm. Hamilton (1979) has given a guide to their geology and provided a map of their occurrence in South East Asia. Elsewhere in Borneo their principal occurrence is in south-east Kalimantan, where they seem to be unknown botanically.

Vegetation

The most famous ultramafic rock outcrops in Sabah are in the area of Mount Kinabalu (see separate Data Sheet on Kinabalu Park, CPD Site SEA24). Their vegetation has recently been briefly described and mapped by Kitayama (1991). Ultramafic vegetation covers about 16% (c. 120 km²) of the area of Kinabalu Park. It is found largely on Mount Tembuyuken (Mt Tambuyukon), Marai Parai (the west corner of Mount Kinabalu massif) and the upper Pinosuk Plateau. Small mosaics of ultramafic vegetation are found between 2700 and 3000 m along the Summit Trail on Kinabalu itself. The summit of Mount Tembuyuken and the spur of Marai Parai support an ultramafic graminoid community which is somewhat boggy.

Kitayama (1991) recognizes at least three sub-divisions of the woody serpentine vegetation, which are, in order of their increasing typical altitude: *Tristania elliptica*-dominated evergreen microphyllous forest; *Leptospermum flavescens-Tristania elliptica*-dominated evergreen nano-microphyllous scrub (with conifers admixed); and *Leptospermum recurvum-Dacrydium gibbsiae*-dominated evergreen leptophyllous scrub (with conifers admixed). The first is the most widespread and

occupies 110.5 km², the second about 7.7 km²; and the third about 1.3 km². Most visitors to Kinabalu Park get an erroneous impression of the relative abundance of these vegetation types since the Summit Trail passes through a large area of the highly local third type of woodland. Earlier references dealing with the Kinabalu ultramafic vegetation are summarized in Kitayama (1991) and Proctor (1992).

The vegetation of the ultramafic Gunung Silam (altitude 884 m) is in many ways the most intensively investigated on this substratum in Sabah. Proctor *et al.* (1988) studied the structure and floristics of 10 plots ranging from 280 m to 870 m on a main ridge of the mountain. Over this narrow altitudinal range, the vegetation changed from large stature lowland dipterocarp forest to stunted myrtaceous forest from which Dipterocarpaceae were absent. Proctor *et al.* (1988) could find no obvious edaphic causes for the rapid vegetation changes and ascribed them to an unexplained "Massenerhebung effect", which refers to the general lowering of altitudinal limits of forest types on small mountains. They quantified many features of the forest and it was established that the lower forest had emergent mesophyllous trees with broad crowns. Leaf size tended to decrease with altitude and there was a rapid reduction of crown width above 330 m altitude. Proctor *et al.* (1988) pointed out that the distinctive features shown by forests on ultramafic soils may often involve the Massenerhebung effect, since ultramafic rocks often occur on small mountains. Bruijnzeel *et al* (1993) have recently discussed further the causes of forest stunting on Gunung Silam and related it to the cloud cap. However, the phenomenon of forest stunting has been noticed (personal observations from the air) on undescribed ultramafics elsewhere in Sabah where a cloud cap is unlikely to be the cause.

There is contrast between the vegetation on Gunung Silam and that described for other ultramafic rock outcrops in the Western Tawau and Lahad Datu Districts of Sabah. Wright (1975) described these forests as having a similar appearance on aerial photographs to heath forests. The trees are low and dense, and few exceed 120 cm in girth or 12 m in height. One forest was described by Wright (1975) as being rich in *Tristania grandifolia*, a species which is frequent in heath forest. Fox (1972) has recorded pure stands of *Casuarina nobilis* from low-lying sites on ultramafic rocks on islands in Darvel Bay, a few kilometres from Gunung Silam.

Flora

The flora of ultramafic areas is poorly known. Beaman and Beaman (1990) regard the areas of ultramafic outcrops on Mount Kinabalu as very important localities, harbouring many rare or endemic species (see Data Sheet on Kinabalu Park, SEA24, for list of important ultramafic localities). They believe that the unusual chemical conditions, in conjunction with the scattered nature of the outcrops and climatic fluctuations, have contributed to the development of endemism.

Proctor *et al.* (1988) found Gunung Silam to be very species-rich; two 0.24 ha plots at 610 m and 700 m both contained 91 species of tree (10 cm dbh). Only two of the tree species (*Borneodendron anaegmatica* and *Buchaniana arborescens*) on Gunung Silam are known to be restricted to ultramafic soils. However, 15 species of palms have been recorded from the mountain (J. Dransfield, pers. comm.), of

which one (*Salacca* sp. nov.) is apparently endemic to Gunung Silam; a further six species or varieties occur elsewhere but only on ultramafic soils; and one is variable, but suspected to have varieties restricted to ultramafic soils. S. Dransfield (pers. comm.) recorded a bamboo on Gunung Silam which is confined to ultramafic soils.

There is little doubt that if the flora were better known then many more ultramafic endemics would be recognized. There is the strong possibility, judging from analogies in temperate areas (Proctor and Woodell 1975), that many of the widespread species on ultramafics may have specially adapted races which may or may not have the morphological distinction to merit recognition in a formal taxonomic way. They may, nevertheless, be profoundly different biochemically and physiologically from other ecotypes.

Useful plants

The ultramafic areas are not inhabited and no medicinal plants are known. There are many potentially useful horticultural plants. The first report of a nickel-accumulating and manganese-accumulating species from Sabah (albeit weak ones) by Proctor *et al.* (1989) suggests that some of the plants may have an unusual and potentially valuable chemistry. The phenomenon of nickel accumulation has recently been

MAP 13. ULTRAMAFIC ROCKS: NORTH-EAST BORNEO

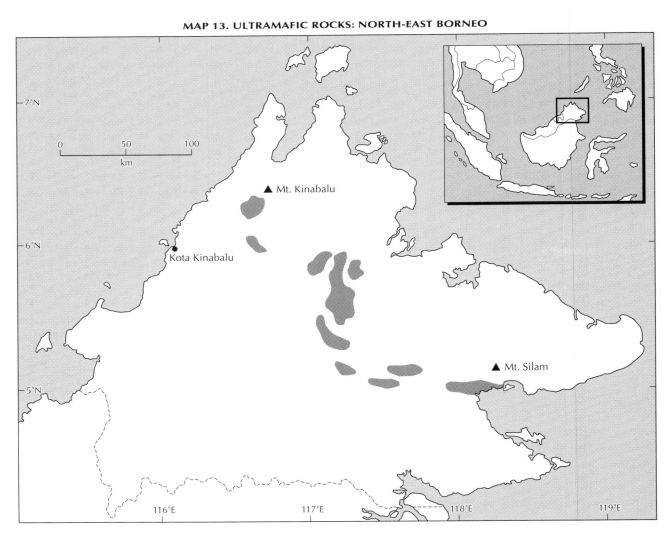

reviewed by Reeves (1992). Such plants may be useful for rehabilitating degraded sites elsewhere. Some tall ultramafic forests have valuable timber species.

Social and environmental values

The social and environmental importance of Mt Kinabalu (of which the ultramafic vegetation forms a part) is discussed in a separate Data Sheet on Kinabalu Park (CPD Site SEA24). Elsewhere, there is much potential for developing Gunung Silam as an educational and research resource, along with carefully planned ecotourism. There is an access road already to 700 m (to service the Telecom Booster Station), and it is possible to walk from there to the summit, passing through superb examples of stunted forest, to a spectacular viewing point. Lower montane and large stature lowland forest are accessible along the Lahad Datu to Tawau road. Nowhere in Sabah is it possible to see such a range of forests over such a short distance, and the proximity of the mountain to Lahad Datu, and the fact that it is on the way to the Danum Valley Conservation Centre, enhances the potential of Gunung Silam for tourism.

Threats

On Kinabalu, the area in the upper Pinosuk Plateau has already suffered land clearance, and its adjacent areas have been converted to a golf course and temperate vegetable farms. Concern has been expressed about the ultramafic grassland on the summit of Mount Tembuyuken and the spur of Marai Parai. Kitayama (1991) regards this community as "one of the most fragile ecosystems and (it) is susceptible to damage from human interference ...". He suggests that high priority should be given to protecting this community.

On ultramafics elsewhere in Sabah there are threats from logging, fires, deforestation, colonization, agriculture, grazing, dam construction and road building. The forests at the base of Gunung Silam have been destroyed and planted, and illegal logging has occurred in some places in surviving primary forest on the lower slopes.

Conservation

The Kinabalu ultramafic vegetation is within Kinabalu Park (CPD Site SEA24, see separate Data Sheet). Elsewhere, no formal full protection has been given. There are small areas of ultramafic forest within the Danum Valley Conservation Area, and the Gunung Silam area is a protected watershed but its conservation needs strengthening.

References

Beaman, J.H. and Beaman, R.S. (1990). Diversity and distribution patterns in the flora of Mount Kinabalu. In Baas, P., Kalkman, K. and Geesink, R. (eds), *The plant diversity of Malesia*. Kluwer Academic Publishers, Dordrecht. Pp. 147–160.

Bruijnzeel, L.A., Waterloo, M.J., Proctor, J., Kuiters, A.T. and Kotterink, B. (1993). Hydrological observations in montane forests on Gunung Silam, Sabah, Malaysia, with special reference to the "Massenerhebung" effect. *Journal of Ecology* 81: 145–167.

Fox, J.E.D. (1972). *The natural vegetation of Sabah and natural regeneration of the dipterocarp forests.* Ph.D. thesis, University of Wales, U.K.

Hamilton, W. (1979). *Tectonics of the Indonesian region.* Geological Survey Professional Paper 1078, United States Government Printing Office, Washington, D.C.

Kitayama, K. (1991). *Vegetation of Mount Kinabalu Park, Sabah, Malaysia. Map of physiognomically classified vegetation, scale 1: 100,000.* East-West Center, Honolulu. 45 pp., map.

Proctor, J. (1992). The vegetation over ultramafic rocks in the tropical far east. In Roberts, B.A. and Proctor, J. (eds), *The ecology of areas with serpentinized rocks. A world view.* Kluwer Academic Press, Dordrecht. Pp. 249–270.

Proctor, J., Lee, Y.F., Langley, A.M., Munro, W.R.C. and Nelson, T. (1988). Ecological studies on Gunung Silam, a small ultrabasic mountain in Sabah, Malaysia. I: Environment, forest structure and floristics. *Journal of Ecology* 76: 320–340.

Proctor, J., Phillipps, C., Duff, G.K., Heaney, A. and Robertson, F.M. (1989). Ecological studies on Gunung Silam, a small ultrabasic mountain in Sabah, Malaysia. II: Some forest processes. *Journal of Ecology* 77: 317–331.

Proctor, J. and Woodell, S.R.J. (1975). The ecology of serpentine soils. *Adv. Ecol. Res.* 9: 255–366.

Reeves, R. (1992). The hyperaccumulation of nickel by serpentine plants. In Baker, A.J.M., Proctor, J. and Reeves, R. (eds), *The ecology of ultramafic (serpentine) soils.* Intercept, Andover, U.K. Pp. 253–277.

Whitmore, T.C. (1985). *Tropical rain forests of the Far East.* 2nd Edition. Clarendon Press, Oxford. 352 pp. (1st edition, 1975; 2nd edition reprinted with corrections, 1985.)

Wright, P.S. (1975). *Western parts of Tawau and Lahad Datu Districts. The soils of Sabah volume 3.* Land Resource Study 20, Ministry of Overseas Development, Surbiton, U.K.

Acknowledgements

This Data Sheet was written by Dr John Proctor (University of Stirling, U.K.).

GUNUNG MULU NATIONAL PARK, MEDALAM PROTECTED FOREST AND LABI HILLS, BUKIT TERAJA, ULU INGEI, SUNGEI INGEI
Sarawak, Malaysia and Brunei Darussalam

Location: Northern Sarawak/southern Brunei.

Area: 1521.5 km²; comprising Gunung Mulu National Park (528.7 km²) and Medalam Protected Forest (350 km²) in Sarawak, and Bukit Teraja Protection Forest (68.3 km²) and Sungei Ingei Conservation Area (184.9 km²), both within the Labi Hills Forest Reserve (642.8 km²), in Brunei.

Altitude: 30–2376 m (summit of Gunung Mulu).

Vegetation: Gunung Mulu National Park contains all the inland vegetation formations of Sarawak, including lowland mixed dipterocarp forest, lowland limestone forest, lower and upper montane forests on sandstones, shales and limestone, limestone cliff and scree vegetation, riverine and alluvial forests, heath (kerangas) forest, peat swamp forest; Sungei Ingei includes one of the best examples of peat swamp forest in Borneo.

Flora: Gunung Mulu National Park has an estimated 3500 vascular plant species, of which c. 2500 species recorded so far; high endemism, especially on the Melinau limestone; the park contains possibly the world's richest palm flora, with some 109 species recorded so far. Rich bryophyte flora.

Useful plants: Wide range of plants used by indigenous groups, including wild sago palm, rattans, pandans, nuts, fruits, medicinal plants. Reservoir of important timber trees, particularly dipterocarps.

Other values: Indigenous semi-settled and nomadic ethnic groups live in and around Gunung Mulu National Park and are allowed to hunt and fish within its boundaries, watershed protection, rich fauna, spectacular montane scenery, karst landforms and caves, increasing potential for ecotourism, extensive scientific research.

Threats: Logging around perimeter of Gunung Mulu National Park, shifting cultivation along some rivers in Sarawak, hunting pressure on large animals, road construction is a potential threat.

Conservation: Gunung Mulu gazetted as a National Park in 1974; proposed extension would include Medalam Protected Forest in north. In Brunei, Sungei Ingei is designated a Conservation Area (IUCN Management Category: I) within the Labi Hills Forest Reserve; Bukit Teraja is a Protection Forest (IUCN Management Category I), also within Labi Hills Forest Reserve.

Geography

Gunung Mulu National Park spans the border of the Fourth and Fifth Divisions of northern Sarawak on the border with Brunei Darussalam, about 70 km south of Limbang. Mulu forms the watershed between the Tutuh and Limbang rivers. Medalam Protected Forest is contiguous with Gunung Mulu National Park in Sarawak, while Sungei Ingei Conservation Area, part of the larger Labi Hills Forest Reserve, adjoins Mulu on the Brunei side of the international border. The area under consideration also includes Ulu Ingei and Bukit Teraja. These areas form a continuous forested block and are treated here as one CPD site. Most of the available information concerns Gunung Mulu National Park and is summarized below.

The area lies within the north-west Borneo geosynclinal belt, all the major lithological units of which are represented within the Gunung Mulu National Park. The south-west part of the park includes Gunung Mulu massif, part of the Mulu Formation, comprising shales and sandstones which were laid down in the Tertiary, folded into their present form in the Pliocene and later uplifted. Gunung Mulu itself (4°02'N 114°54'E) attains 2376 m and is the second highest mountain in Sarawak. The massif consists of deeply dissected slopes with sandy soils and a dendritic gully drainage pattern.

To the north-west of Gunung Mulu is the Melinau Limestone Formation, the highest limestone area between north Thailand and New Guinea. It consists of white or grey calcilutite and calcarenite. The karst landscape includes a series of spectacular, precipitous mountains running south-west/north-east across the centre of the park. The highest peaks are Gunung Api (c. 1700 m) and Gunung Benarat, which are separated by the Melinau Gorge which has 600 m high vertical walls. Razor-edged pinnacles are a feature of the mountains, particularly on the north-east side of Gunung Api, where they reach up to 50 m high at around 1200 m altitude (Collins, Holloway and Proctor 1984). The Melinau Formation also includes an extensive cave system (a network of well over 100 km, and possibly the largest in the world). The most north-easterly part of the Melinau limestone massif is Bukit Buda, which is located within the Medalam Protected Forest, which adjoins the National Park.

In the north-west corner of the Gunung Mulu National Park is the Setap Shale Formation which consists of fine clay-shales in valleys and siltstones and quartzite sandstone on scarps. Along the border with Brunei is a narrow outcrop of the Belait Formation with alternating bands of shales and sandstones. The topography in the northern part of the park is one of low, sharply dissected hills and extensive Quaternary river terraces with white sandy soils.

Rainfall is high with an annual average of over 5000 mm. Although there is no dry season, there are distinct seasonal variations in rainfall. The wettest periods are October–November and April–May, with August and September being drier as a result of the SW monsoon (Walsh 1982). For more details on the climate, hydrology, geology, geomorphology and soils of Gunung Mulu National Park, see

Anderson, Jermy and Cranbrook (1979, 1982), and Jermy and Kavanagh (1982, 1984).

Vegetation

Gunung Mulu National Park contains all the inland vegetation formations of Sarawak, with the exception of vegetation on soils of volcanic origin. This diversity of vegetation is primarily the result of the variations in geology, topography and altitudinal range, giving rise to a complex zonation of some 18 vegetation formations (see Table 56). More detailed descriptions of the vegetation types within the National Park can be found in the Royal Geographical Society/Sarawak Government expedition report (Anderson and Chai 1982).

Lowland mixed dipterocarp forest occurs at low altitudes up to 800 m on the steep dissected terrain of Gunung Mulu and on alluvial floodplains of the Melinau, Tarikan and Medalam rivers. Approximately 40% of Gunung Mulu National Park is covered by lowland rain forest. The most species-rich form of mixed dipterocarp forest on humult ultisols over Miocene sandstone is confined to a narrow strip bordering Brunei. It contains several local species of dipterocarps. The most abundant dipterocarps are *Dryobalanops beccarii* and *Shorea scaberrima*. Species in the genera *Calophyllum*, *Diospyros*, *Durio*, *Eugenia* and *Garcinia* also occur here. Floristically the lowland forests are very rich; 284 species of trees, exceeding 30 cm girth, were recorded in three sample plots, totalling 1.2 ha, during the Royal Geographical Society/ Sarawak Government expedition (Anderson and Chai 1982).

About 20% of the area of Gunung Mulu National Park is covered by lower and upper montane rain forest types, in roughly equal proportions. Lower montane forest occurs at about 800 m on Gunung Mulu, as a transition zone between lowland dipterocarp forest and upper montane forest. It is floristically rich – 226 species of trees exceeding 20 cm girth were recorded in four plots totalling 0.5 ha (Anderson and Chai 1982) – though lower in stature than lowland forest (30 m maximum canopy height, as opposed to 55 m in lowland dipterocarp forest). Dipterocarps are less abundant, the families Fagaceae, Guttiferae and Myrtaceae being much more in evidence. *Quercus subsericea*, *Calophyllum nodosum*, *Eugenia* spp. and *Garcinia dulcis* are the most common trees.

At 1200 m, the lower limit of upper montane rain forest (mossy forest) is encountered. This is generally low in stature (normally around 15 m canopy height with occasional emergents reaching 21 m). Oaks (particularly *Lithocarpus hatusimae*), conifers (*Dacrydium beccarii* and *Phyllocladus hypophyllus*) and members of the Guttiferae and Myrtaceae are well-represented. Bryophytes are extremely abundant. The moss flora includes many Bornean endemics (such as *Hypnodendron beccarii* and *Ptychophyllum borneense*). Spectacular growth forms occur, such as the mosses Meteoriaceae and *Dicranoloma*, and the liverworts Lejeuniaceae, which drape from branches. The ferns *Plagiogyria* and *Coryphopteris* are frequent in ridge forest. At

CPD Site SEA33: Limestone pinnacles and forest on Gunung Api, Gunung Mulu National Park, Sarawak.
Photo: Clive Jermy

about 1600 m up to 1900 m, a short facies of upper montane forest occurs. The forest is stunted, and members of the Ericaceae are more evident along with the pitcher plants *Nepenthes lowii*, *N. muluensis* and *N. tentaculata*. Bryophytes are abundant in the stunted forest of the higher mountain ridges and in the summit area. The bryophyte flora largely consists of the hepatics *Bazzania* spp., *Frullania* spp. and *Plagiochila* spp., mosses being represented mainly by species of *Acroporium*, *Dicranoloma* and *Macrohymenium* (A. Touw 1992, *in litt.*). Summit vegetation is mostly dense and shrubby with a few stunted trees of *Leptospermum flavescens* and *Dacrydium beccarii*.

A parallel series of forest types is found on the Melinau Limestone Formation occurring on Benarat and Api; however, the species composition differs from the forests of the Gunung Mulu massif. Lowland forest over limestone covers about 10% of the park area. In places it is dominated by dipterocarps, but the overall species diversity is lower than mixed dipterocarp forests on alluvial soils. Lower montane limestone forest is found between 800 and 1200 m. It contains many epiphytic orchids, ferns and aroids. Bryophytes abound in rock crevices and on trees and shrubs, sometimes forming large tussocks at their base. The genera *Acroporium*, *Macromitrium*, *Schlotheimia*, *Pseudosymblepharis*, *Dicranoloma* and *Mastigophora* are well-represented. Upper montane limestone forest occurs above 1200 m. It includes *Dacrydium*, *Phyllocladus* and at least three species of *Pandanus*.

The alluvial plains in the north-west of Gunung Mulu National Park support lowland alluvial forest, heath (kerangas) forest and a small area of peat swamp forest. The largest trees in the lowland alluvial forest are Bornean ironwood *Eusideroxylon melagangai*. Riparian vegetation includes species characteristic of unstable and disturbed conditions, such as *Macaranga* spp., the ebony *Diospyros diepenhorstii*, *Octomeles sumatrana* and *Pometia pinnata*. Of particular note are a number of endemic and strictly rheophytic species of bryophytes which are confined to periodically inundated habitats. For example, *Neckeropsis beccariana* is confined to the muddy alluvial forests along the Melinau River, and the rare monotypic genus *Sclerohypnum* is only known from the Melinau Gorge at the base of Gunung Api (Touw 1992, *in litt.*). In general, the kerangas consists of medium to small straight pole-like trees mostly 200 cm in girth, and with an abundance of palms, pandans and pitcher plants. In places, taller forest is encountered, the main trees being *Shorea albida*, *S. scabrida*, *Melanorrhoea macrocarpa*, *Calophyllum* spp. and *Casuarina nobilis* (*Gymnostoma nobile*). Peat swamp forest occurs between the Tarikan and Medalam rivers. It covers only 1.8 km² and is similar to the vast coastal swamp forests found elsewhere in Sarawak (but now heavily logged).

The adjoining Medalam Protected Forest consists mainly of rich alluvial forest (presently used for timber extraction), as well as forest on limestone at Bukit Buda. In Brunei, the adjoining area of Labi Hills Forest Reserve, including Sungei Ingei Conservation Area, Bukit Teraja Protection Forest and Ulu Ingei, contains a diverse mosaic of forests on podsols and sandy yellow soils, rich in endemics. The Labi Hills reach 400 m and are covered by lowland forest; Sungei Ingei is one of the best examples of primary peat swamp forest in Borneo, with a full range of community types (P.S. Ashton 1991, *in litt.*). These areas are contiguous with Gunung Mulu National Park forming a forested block of 1521.5 km².

TABLE 56. MAIN VEGETATION FORMATIONS IN GUNUNG MULU NATIONAL PARK (AFTER ANDERSON AND CHAI 1982)

Land type/altitude	Vegetation formation
1. Gunung Mulu massif sandstone/shales	
i. Low altitude to 800 m	Lowland mixed dipterocarp forest
ii. 800–1200 m altitude	Lower montane forest
iii. 1200–1900 m altitude	Upper montane forest (tall facies)
iv. 1600–2177 m altitude	Upper montane forest (short facies)
v. 2177 m – summit	Upper montane forest (summit facies)
2. Limestone (Gunung Benarat/Gunung Api)	
i. Scree slopes	Limestone scree forest
ii. Cliffs	Limestone cliff vegetation
iii. Slopes, low altitude to 800 m	Lowland limestone forest
iv. 800–1200 m altitude	Lower montane limestone forest
v. 1200 m – summit	Upper montane limestone forest
vi. Caves	Limestone cave vegetation
3. Alluvial plains	
i. Alluvium	Alluvial forest
ii. Quaternary terraces	Heath (kerangas) forest
iii. Peat swamps	Peat swamp forest
4. Setap shales/Mentawai drainage	
i. Setap shale formation	Mixed dipterocarp forest (*Shorea parvifolia* type)
ii. Mentawai drainage	Heath (kerangas) forest
5. Belait formation/Mentawai drainage	
i. Low hills	Mixed dipterocarp forest (*Dryobalanops aromatica* type)
ii. Pleistocene terraces	Heath (kerangas) forest

Flora

Regular botanical collections have been made in Gunung Mulu National Park since 1958, specimens from which are housed in the Forest Herbarium, Kuching, and elsewhere. A checklist of the gymnosperms and angiosperms recorded from Gunung Mulu National Park is given in Anderson, Jermy and Cranbrook (1979, 1982). It is thought the park could contain up to 3500 species of vascular plants, of which about 2500 species have so far been recorded (Jermy 1983). To date, about 425 species of pteridophytes are known to occur on Mulu (Parris *et al.* 1984). There is a rich bryophyte flora. The park probably contains nearly all moss species so far known to occur in Borneo, with the exception of those confined to the higher parts of Sabah (A. Touw 1992, *in litt.*). In addition, there are thought to be over 8000 species of fungi (C. Jermy 1992, *in litt.*).

Gunung Mulu National Park is considered to be one of the richest sites in the world for palms, with some 109 species of 20 genera recorded. Among the most notable species are: *Iguanura melinauensis* and *Licuala lanata*, both of which are endemic to the alluvial plain; *Calamus neilsonii* and *Salacca rupicola*, which are endemic to the limestone; and *Areca abdulrahmanii* which occurs on the Setap shales. All the Bornean rattan genera are represented in the park.

Dipterocarps are represented by 8 genera and 115 species (Anderson, Jermy and Cranbrook 1979), 43% of Bornean species of dipterocarps.

The limestone is particularly rich in endemics. Here are found a number of endemic orchids and gesneriads. For example, 7 of the 8 species of *Monophyllaea* found on the Melinau limestone are newly described and not found anywhere else. Other notable calcicolous species which are restricted to this formation include other gesneriads such as *Cyrtandra* and *Paraboea* spp. (Kiew 1991), and the palm *Salacca rupicola*. In places where rich organic soil has accumulated, a calcifuge flora develops on the limestone, with rhododendrons prominent.

As in other rain forests, there are many examples of complex inter-relationships between plants and animals, many of which have yet to be unravelled. To give just two examples: the endemic fruit tree *Sandoricum borneense* (the river sentul), a tree inhabiting riverine forest, produces seeds which are said to be swallowed and dispersed by fish, which in turn provide a food source for the Penan who inhabit Gunung Mulu National Park; lowland forests also contain many species of banyans (*Ficus* spp.) which are a food source for arboreal vertebrates and ground dwellers such as the bearded pig *Sus barbatus*, which are hunted by the Penan.

Useful plants

The indigenous Penan of Gunung Mulu National Park utilize a range of forest products. The primary source of sago is the palm *Eugeissona utilis*. This forms their staple food source. The "cabbage" of the palm is also eaten. Another, though less important, source of sago is *Eugeissona insignis*. This also has an edible "cabbage", and its leaves are used for thatch. The endemic *Licuala lanata* is also used for thatching. Nuts and fruits are collected from the forest. Some fruit trees, such as papaya, rambutan, banana and durians, along with sago, tapioca and sweet potatoes, are sometimes planted by the Penan close to their houses or along river banks. Rattans (such as *Calamus* spp.) are another important item collected from the forest, being used to make baskets, mats, cord for tying, as well as in hut construction. Baskets and mats are often sold or exchanged for other goods. Mats are also made from the leaves of *Pandanus* spp.

Other products collected from the forest include damar (*Shorea* spp.), jelutong (*Dyera costulata*), gutta percha (*Palaquium* spp.), gaharu (an incense wood obtained from *Aquilaria microcarpa*) and latex from the Ipoh tree (*Antiaris toxicaria*), which is used for making blowpipe poison. Up to 20 species of trees, shrubs, epiphytes, climbers and herbs are used by the Penan and Berawan for medicinal purposes. Preliminary lists of plants used by Penan, giving Penan names and uses, are given in Kedit (1982).

Besides the wealth of dipterocarps, important timber species include ebonies (*Diospyros* spp.) and *Pometia pinnata*, which are found along river banks.

Social and environmental values

Gunung Mulu has an exceedingly rich fauna. Of the 60 species of mammal recorded in the National Park, among the most notable are: common gibbon (*Hylobates lar*), macaques (*Macaca* spp.), leaf monkeys (*Presbytis* spp.), sunbear (*Helarctos malayanus*), and numerous species of bats, including tail-less horseshoe bat (*Coelops robinsonii*) and round-eared tube-nosed bat (*Murina cyclotis*), both of which are confined to the region of the park.

Over 260 species of bird are recorded from the park, including all 8 species of hornbill found in Borneo. The montane forests of Gunung Mulu National Park are in the Bornean Mountains Endemic Bird Area (EBA), which supports 28 restricted-range bird species, of which 24 are endemic. They include several species which are restricted to the mountains in the northern part of the EBA in Sabah and Sarawak, notably the globally threatened mountain serpent-eagle (*Spilornis kinabaluensis*).

In addition, 320 species of fish, 23 species of lizards and 25 species of snakes have been recorded. The total number of invertebrates species in the park has been estimated at 20,000, including some 8000 coleopteran and 3000 lepidopteran species (Anderson, Jermy and Cranbrook 1979, 1982).

Mulu has been the subject of considerable scientific research. The Royal Geographical Society/Sarawak Forest Department undertook an extensive 15-month expedition to the park in 1977–1978. A checklist of mammals, birds, reptiles, amphibians, fish and butterflies recorded from the park is given in Anderson, Jermy and Cranbrook (1979, 1982).

Around 300 indigenous Penan, both semi-settled and nomadic groups, range widely throughout the park, and have official hunting and fishing rights within the park boundary. Their main settlements are on the south-west perimeter of the park at Long Iman along Sungai Tutuh, at Batu Bungan on the Sg Melinau (where there are about 200 inhabitants) and in the Ubung River area. Until recently, they used traditional blowpipe techniques for hunting, but shotguns are now also used (Earl of Cranbrook 1992, *in litt.*). Iban, Kenyah, Kayan and Kelabit tribes along the Baram and Limbang rivers also make use of the park for hunting and gathering forest products. Many Penan and Berawan are now employed by the National Park as labourers and guides.

The forests of Mulu protect the watersheds of the Tutuh and Medalam rivers. Without the forests, siltation and flooding would occur downstream resulting in the loss of towns and villages. Indeed, siltation is already a serious problem on the Tutuh river, where forests on the bank opposite the park have been logged (C. Jermy 1991, pers. comm.).

Economic assessment

Gunung Mulu National Park is now attracting thousands of visitors each year, both from overseas and from within Malaysia. Several caves have now been developed as highly successful tourist attractions and there is a labour force of well-trained guides. Many tourists come for the opportunity of experiencing pristine rain forest. There are well-marked trails, raised walkways, an information centre, several helipads and an airstrip, to cater for the demands of ecotourism. The number of visitors to Mulu has increased from 628 in 1986 to 8027 in 1991. It is expected that the number of visitors will increase to 20,000 in 1992 (Ngui Siew Kong 1992, *in litt.*). The revenue generated by tourism has not been quantified, but is likely to increase now that an airstrip has been opened (in 1992).

Plant products are a vital part of the economy of the Penan. Baskets and mats made from rattans are often sold and exchanged for other goods. The price of rattan products varies. In 1982, Kedit reported that baskets made by the Tepoh Basong community, for example, sold for M$5–18 at that particular time, whereas rattan mats ranged from M$35 to M$51 (Kedit 1982). *Tamu* (government organized and price controlled market) could be one way of allowing the Penan to obtain better prices for their goods.

Threats

There are incursions into Gunung Mulu National Park from the north by Ibans (C. Jermy 1991, pers. comm.). Along the north-western border (along the Melinau river) land has been cleared and settled up to the park boundary (Earl of Cranbrook 1992, *in litt.*).

Logging is occurring at an alarming rate around the park. All the surrounding forest is licensed for logging, and much of the forest has already been cut up to the boundary rivers (e.g. to the south along the Tutuh and to the east along the Ubung rivers). This has destroyed the traditional areas of the Penan who have, as a consequence, moved into the park. Increasing erosion in that area has increased the silt-load of the rivers, making them almost sterile (C. Jermy 1991, pers. comm.). Hunting pressure is increasing on large animals, such as pigs, primates and hornbills (Earl of Cranbrook 1992, *in litt.*).

Road building is a potential threat. The Beluru-Limbang highway has been proposed for a number of years, although it has now been dropped from state plans. If construction of the road were to proceed at some future date, inevitably this would give rise to forest clearance along the line of the highway, with the risks of altering surface drainage patterns and soil compaction, leading to ponding and subsequent tree deaths, the possibility of rock blasting, which might affect cave structures, and opening up of the forest increasing the threat of illegal hunting and plant collecting.

Conservation

Gunung Mulu was gazetted as a National Park in 1974. A management and development plan was prepared under an IUCN/WWF project in 1982 (Anderson, Jermy and Cranbrook 1979, 1982), but only preliminary management measures have so far been implemented. The Penan are an integral part of the ecosystem and their traditional hunting and gathering techniques ensure that the natural resources which they utilize are harvested on a sustainable basis.

The State Conservation Strategy for Sarawak (WWF Malaysia 1985) includes a proposal to include the Medalam Protected Forest within the National Park area. This would add a further 350 km² to the National Park, mainly lowland rain forest. The area also includes more traditional lands of the Penan. In addition, Mulu is contiguous with the Labi Hills Forest Reserve in Brunei, including Sungei Ingei Conservation Area (184.9 km²) and Bukit Teraja Protection Forest (68.3 km²), which includes a substantial area of pristine rain forest (Dransfield 1991, pers. comm.).

In the evaluation of the importance of protected areas in the Indo-Malayan Realm (MacKinnon and MacKinnon 1986), Gunung Mulu National Park is given an "A" priority rating as an area of supreme importance for conservation. The State Conservation Strategy for Sarawak considers that Gunung Mulu National Park deserves to be nominated as a World Heritage Site (WWF Malaysia 1985).

References

Anderson, J.A.R. and Chai, P.P.K. (1982). Vegetation. In Jermy, A.C., Kavanagh, K.P. (eds), Gunung Mulu National Park, Sarawak: an account of its environment and biota being the results of The Royal Geographical Society/Sarawak Government Expedition and Survey 1977–1978. Part I. *Sarawak Mus. J.*, 30 (51) (New Series) (Special Issue No. 2): 195–206.

Anderson, J.A.R., Jermy, A.C. and Cranbrook, Earl of (1979, 1982). *Gunung Mulu National Park. A management and development plan.* IUCN/WWF Project 1576. Royal Geographical Society. 345 pp.

Andersen, J.M., Proctor, J. and Vallack, H.W. (1983). Ecological studies in four contrasting lowland rain forests in Gunung Mulu National Park, Sarawak. III. Decomposition processes and nutrient losses from leaf litter. *J. Ecology* 71: 503–527.

Ashton, P.S. (1964). Ecological studies in the mixed dipterocarp forests of Brunei State. *Oxford Forestry Memoirs* 24. Clarendon Press, Oxford. 75 pp.

Collins, N.M., Holloway, J.D. and Proctor, J. (1984). Notes on the ascent and natural history of Gunung Api, a limestone mountain in Sarawak. *Sarawak Mus. J.* 33(54): 219–234.

Dransfield, J. (1984). The palm flora of the Gunung Mulu National Park. In Jermy, A.C. (ed.), *Studies on the flora of Gunung Mulu National Park, Sarawak.* Sarawak Forest Department, Kuching. Pp. 41–75.

Hanbury-Tenison, A.R. (1980). *Mulu: the rain forest.* Weidenfeld and Nicolson, London. 176 pp.

Jermy, C. (1983). Gunung Mulu National Park, Sarawak. *Oryx* 17(1): 6–14.

Jermy, A.C. (ed.) (1984). *Studies on the flora of Gunung Mulu National Park, Sarawak.* Sarawak Forest Department, Kuching. 233 pp.

Jermy, A.C. and Kavanagh, K.P. (eds) (1982, 1984). Gunung Mulu National Park, Sarawak: an account of its environment and biota being the results of The Royal Geographical Society/Sarawak Government Expedition and Survey 1977–1978. *Sarawak Mus. J.* 30 (51) (New Series) (Special Issue No. 2, Part I, July 1982): 279 pp.; *Sarawak Mus. J.* 30(51) (New Series) (Special Issue No. 2, Part II) (July 1984): 192 pp.

Kedit, P.M. (1982). An ecological survey of the Penan. In Jermy, A.C., Kavanagh, K.P. (eds), The Gunung Mulu National Park, Sarawak: an account of its environment and biota being the results of The Royal Geographical Society/Sarawak Government Expedition and Survey 1977–1978. Part I. *Sarawak Mus. J.* 30 (51) (New Series) (Special Issue No. 2): 225–279.

Kiew, R. (1991). The limestone flora. In Kiew, R. (ed.), *The state of nature conservation in Malaysia*. Malayan Nature Society, Malaysia. Pp. 42–50.

MacKinnon, J. and MacKinnon, K. (1986). *Review of the protected areas system in the Indo-Malayan Realm*. IUCN, Gland, Switzerland and Cambridge, U.K. and UNEP. 284 pp.

Newbery, D.McC. and Proctor, J. (1984). Ecological studies in four contrasting lowland rain forests in Gunung Mulu National Park, Sarawak. IV. Associations between tree distribution and soil factors. *J. Ecology* 72: 475–493.

Parris, B.S., Jermy, A.C., Camus, J.M. and Paul, A.M. (1984). The pteridophytes of Gunung Mulu National Park. In Jermy, A.C. (ed.), *Studies on the flora of Gunung Mulu National Park, Sarawak*. Forest Department, Sarawak, Kuching. Pp. 145–233.

Proctor, J., Anderson, J.M., Chai, P. and Vallack, H.W. (1983). Ecological studies in four contrasting lowland rain forests in Gunung Mulu National Park, Sarawak. I. Forest environment, structure and floristics. *J. Ecology* 71: 237–260.

Proctor, J., Anderson, J.M., Fogden, S.C.L. and Vallack, H.W. (1983). Ecological studies in four contrasting lowland rain forests in Gunung Mulu National Park, Sarawak. II. Litterfall, litter standing crop and preliminary observations on herbivory. *J. Ecology* 71: 261–283.

Walsh, R.P.D. (1982). Climate. In Jermy, A.C. and Kavanagh, K.P. (eds). Gunung Mulu National Park, Sarawak: an account of its environment and biota being the results of The Royal Geographical Society/Sarawak Government Expedition and Survey 1977–1978. Part I. *Sarawak Mus. J.* 30 (51) (Special Issue No. 2): 29–67.

Wood, J.J. (1984). A preliminary annotated checklist of the orchids of Gunung Mulu National Park with a key to the genera. In Jermy, A.C. (ed.), *Studies on the flora of Gunung Mulu National Park, Sarawak*. Sarawak Forest Department, Kuching. Pp. 1–39.

Wells, S.M., Pyle, R.M. and Collins, N.M. (comps) (1983). Rain forests of Gunung Mulu. In Wells, S.M., Pyle, R.M. and Collins, N.M. (comps), *The IUCN Invertebrate Red Data Book*. IUCN, Gland, Switzerland. Pp. 567–576.

WWF Malaysia (1985). *Strategi Pemeliharaan Sumber Semulajadi Malaysia*. (Proposals for a Conservation Strategy for Sarawak.) WWF Malaysia, Kuala Lumpur. 210 pp.

Acknowledgements

This Data Sheet was written by Stephen D. Davis, with grateful thanks to The Earl of Cranbrook, Dr Clive Jermy (The Natural History Museum, London), Dr Paul Chai (Ministry of Environment and Tourism, Sarawak), Professor Peter S. Ashton (Harvard University Herbaria, Cambridge, Massachesetts), Dr Andries Touw (Rijksherbarium, Leiden), Ngui Siew Kong (Forest Department, Sarawak) and Dr John Dransfield (Royal Botanic Gardens, Kew) for comments on an earlier draft.

LAMBIR HILLS NATIONAL PARK
Sarawak, Malaysia

Location: 30 km south of Miri, in the Fourth Division of Sarawak at 4°30'N, 113°55'–114°05'E.

Area: 69.5 km².

Altitude: 30–457 m.

Vegetation: Lowland mixed dipterocarp forest, heath (kerangas) forest, summit shrub vegetation.

Flora: c. 1500 vascular plant species (very high for an exclusively lowland area); c. 1000 species of trees so far recorded, including 69 dipterocarp species.

Useful plants: Timber trees, wild fruit trees (including mango and durian relatives), many rattans.

Other values: Watershed protection, potential educational and amenity role.

Threats: Encroachment from logging and agriculture, hunting.

Conservation: Gazetted as a National Park (IUCN Management Category: II) in 1975.

Geography

Lambir Hills National Park is situated about 30 km south of Miri, along the Miri-Bintulu road, in the Fourth Division of Sarawak. Most of the park consists of hilly terrain with steep slopes of 25–30°. The highest point is Bukit Lambir, which reaches 457 m in the centre of the park. The topography has resulted from three separate periods of uplifting, followed by north-west tilting, and subsequent erosion by rejuvenated rivers. Lambir Hills forms an east-west watershed; the Sungai Liam flows south to join the Batang Baram, while streams flowing north join the Sungai Miri. Westerly flowing streams drain to the sea at Kuala Sungai Bakam.

The oldest rocks are the Setap shales and clays deposited about 20–30 million years BP during the Miocene. The Lambir Formation consists of fine-grained sandstones and shales, deposited about 15–20 million years BP. The youngest formation, the Tukau Formation, consists of sand and poorly consolidated sandstone and clay, deposited about 15–20 million years BP during the Pliocene. The soils of Lambir Hills vary from red-yellow sandy humult ultisols (which cover most of the park), through udult clay ultisols to tropical spodosols. Generally, the soils have a low nutrient status and are easily leached. Because of the steepness of the terrain, any removal of vegetation greatly accelerates erosion.

The mean annual temperature is about 26°C with little seasonal variation. Mean annual rainfall is c. 3000 mm with most falling between September and January. Dry spells occasionally occur; for example, there were 25 consecutive rainless days in August 1972.

Vegetation

Lambir Hills is of outstanding regional and global significance as a relict coastal lowland mixed dipterocarp rain forest which is extraordinarily species-rich. According to Watson (1985), there are 37 km² of lowland mixed dipterocarp forest in the park. This is approximately 54% of the park area. Stature and physiognomy vary according to changes in altitude, soil type and drainage conditions. The tallest and most species-rich forest occurs from 100 to 250 m altitude, and includes (among the dipterocarps) *Anisoptera grossivenia*, *Dipterocarpus globosus*, *D. kunstleri*, *Dryobalanops beccarii*, *D. aromatica*, *Hopea pterygota* and numerous species of *Shorea*, such as *S. curtisii*, *S. macroptera*, *S. maxwelliana* and *S. ochracea*. Other important trees include *Lithocarpus conocarpus*, *Castanopsis motleyi* and *Koompassia malaccensis*. Between 260 and 350 m, dipterocarps are still dominant, but there are no emergents and the number of epiphytes, climbers and herbaceous species is reduced. This is partly explained by drier conditions coupled with sandier soils at this altitude. The undergrowth on ridges is dominated by the distinctive, stilt-rooted palm *Eugeissona minor*.

Kerangas (heath forest) covers approximately 15% of the park area, especially between 360 and 400 m on steep slopes and sandstone outcrops. Kerangas is relatively species-poor and is dominated by *Casuarina nobilis* (*Gymnostoma nobile*), *Dacrydium* sp., *Podocarpus neriifolius*, *Calophyllum* spp., *Tristania obovata* and *Ploiarium alternifolium*.

At the summit of Bukit Lambir the vegetation consists of shrub communities around 2 m tall, including *Ilex sclerophylloides*, *Elaeocarpus clementis*, *Calophyllum lowii*, *Rhododendron chamaepitys* (endemic to Lambir Hills), *Diplycosia heterophylla*, *Austrobuxus nitidus* and *Urophyllum hirsutum*.

Flora

Considering its relatively small size, Lambir Hills contains a remarkable diversity of species, principally due to the varied nature of the soils and topography. Up to 1984, 684 species of trees had been recorded in Lambir Hills National Park (Soepdamo *et al.* 1984), representing 253 genera and 77 families, but 1000 species exceeding 1 cm dbh were found in a recent census of only 5 ha. The total flora is estimated at 1500 vascular plant species (P. Ashton 1991, *in litt.*). This is very high for an exclusively lowland area and includes many species which are rare and endemic to Sarawak. The park is thought to contain more endangered tree species than any other park in Sarawak, and possibly in the whole of South East Asia.

Four study plots in mixed dipterocarp forest (of total area 5.6 ha) contained 742 tree species exceeding 10 cm dbh, including seedlings (height 20 cm at least but dbh less than 1 cm), saplings (height at least 20 cm and dbh between 1.0 and 9.9 cm), and trees equal to or greater than 10 cm diameter dbh (Primack and Hall 1992). Nearly half the species (44.3%) in the sample plots were represented by just a single individual.

While the total flora may be somewhat smaller than that of other areas selected in Borneo, Lambir Hills is nevertheless of significance for conservation as more than one in five of species found in the National Park are either rare or very locally distributed and generally not adequately protected elsewhere in Sarawak (Soepadmo *et al.* 1984).

Among the canopy and emergent trees, the dominant family is Dipterocarpaceae, of which there are 69 species recorded so far in the park (Soepadmo *et al.*, 1984). Dipterocarps accounted for c. 25% of all individuals recorded in two study plots of 0.5 ha each established during the 1981 ecological survey. Other important plant families include Anacardiaceae, Burseraceae, Euphorbiaceae, Lauraceae, Myristicaceae,

CPD Site SEA34: Lambir Hills National Park, Sarawak, showing interior of lowland mixed dipterocarp forest.
Photo: Stephen D. Davis.

Myrtaceae, Sterculiaceae and Tiliaceae. Of the 20 species of ebonies (*Diospyros* spp.) so far collected from the park, three have turned out to be new to science.

The area has a rich palm flora of c. 60 species, many of which have subsequently been collected from Brunei (Dransfield 1991 and pers. comm.). Rattans are well-represented; a one hectare sample revealed more than 100 canes of rattan, representing more than 32 species (LaFrankie 1993, *in litt.*).

Useful plants

Apart from the wealth of timber trees, the park is rich in wild fruit trees. Over 70 fruit tree species have so far been recorded. Besides providing an essential food supply for the park's fauna, they may also prove to be a valuable genetic resource for improving existing fruit tree crops, and developing new ones. Among the fruit trees, three species of mango (*Mangifera havilandii*, *M. pajang* and *M.* sp. nov.) are listed by Soepadmo *et al.* (1984), together with six species of durian, namely: *Durio acutifolius*, *D. graveolens*, *D. crassipes*, *D. griffithii*, *D. excelsus* and *D. testudinarium*. The herbaceous flora includes gingers (Zingiberaceae).

Many species of rattans are used locally for handicrafts. These are often sold at local markets or along roadsides, generating income for the local people (Dransfield 1991, pers. comm.). Bindang (*Borassodendron borneense*) provides edible palm shoots; wild sago (*Eugeissona utilis*) is also present, favouring dry ridges and clifftops. Lambir Hills is used by local Iban as a source of medicinal plants.

Social and environmental values

The fauna of Lambir Hills is less well known than the flora. Preliminary surveys undertaken during the 1981 ecological survey, revealed 13 species of mammals, 58 of birds, 10 of lizards, 7 of snakes and 13 of frogs. The scarcity of large mammals is probably due to intense hunting by local people.

Lambir Hills offers the potential for developing local education and teaching programmes in a rain forest ecosystem. The area is already a great recreational amenity for the population of the Miri area, attracting large numbers of people, especially at weekends. In 1985, the revenue generated from tourism amounted to M$1,011,611 (Chung 1987).

The forested slopes of Lambir Hills protect the watersheds of several rivers, including the Sungai Miri. The catchment area supplies about 38 million litres of water daily to Miri (Ngui 1991). Any removal of the forest cover, for example by logging or clearance for agriculture, would result in increased levels of soil erosion and flooding, which could in turn have devastating effects on surrounding areas.

Lambir Hills provides local Iban inhabitants with a source of timber (though legally only outside the park), rattans, fruits and other forest products. Some of the fruits are sold at roadside markets.

Threats

Lambir Hills National Park is an island of forest surrounded by shifting cultivation, settlements and logging. During the last

20 years, all the surrounding forest area has been licensed for logging and selectively logged. According to Watson (1985), about 23% of the park has been selectively logged since the 1960s.

Logging roads around the park perimeter allow easy access for illegal hunting and collection of forest products. Illegal hunting within the park is certainly a factor which affects the faunal diversity of the area; no doubt such incursions also result in the indiscriminate trampling and cutting of vegetation, vandalism and up-rooting of flora.

Shifting cultivation now reaches to the park boundary along the south-eastern side. There is a small amount of shifting cultivation within the park boundaries, affecting about 0.6% of the park area (Watson 1985). Much of the land to the south-west has been planted with oil palm.

The park is bisected by the Miri-Bintulu road.

Conservation

Lambir Hills was gazetted as a National Park in 1975. With the uncertainty over the minimal viable size necessary to sustain a tropical rain forest ecosystem, the boundary of the park needs to be adequately marked and patrolled. Watson (1985) suggests establishing a buffer zone around the park in some of the areas which have been logged. This could provide local inhabitants with a source of forest products as well as protecting the watershed.

A local education programme is needed to increase public awareness of the importance of the area and the need to ensure its conservation.

References

Chung, K.S. (1987). *Estimating the demand curves of Bako, Niah and Lambir Hills National Parks of Sarawak.* Forestry Department, Kuching, Sarawak.

Dransfield, J.D. (1991). Manuscript list of palms of Lambir Hills. Royal Botanic Gardens, Kew, U.K.

Ngui, S.K. (1991). National parks and wildlife sanctuaries in Sarawak. In Kiew, R. (ed.), *The state of nature conservation in Malaysia.* Malayan Nature Society, United Selangor Press, Kuala Lumpur. Pp. 190–198.

Primack, R.B. and Hall, P. (1992). Biodiversity and forest change in Malaysian Borneo. *BioScience* 42(11).

Soepadmo, E., Fong Foo Woon, Kiew Bong Heang, Mohamad Zakaria Ismail and Sudderuddin, K.I. (1984). *An ecological survey of Lambir Hill National Park, Sarawak.* WWF Malaysia, Kuala Lumpur. 83 pp.

Watson, H. (1985). *Lambir Hills National Park. Resource inventory with management recommendations.* National Parks and Wildlife Office, Kuching. 193 pp.

Acknowledgements

This Data Sheet was written by Stephen D. Davis with valuable help and information from Professor Peter S. Ashton (Harvard University Herbaria, Cambridge, Massachusetts) and Dr John Dransfield (Royal Botanic Gardens, Kew).

GUNUNG LEUSER NATIONAL PARK
Sumatra, Indonesia

Location: North-west Sumatra, between latitudes 2°55'–4°05'N and longitudes 96°55'–98°30'E.

Area: The whole area covers >9000 km², of which the National Park covers 7926.8 km².

Altitude: 0–3466 m (summit of Gunung Leuser).

Vegetation: Lowland dipterocarp forest, submontane forest, lower and upper montane forests, local montane wetland vegetation, subalpine vegetation, small areas of freshwater swamp forest and coastal dunes.

Flora: Estimated 2000–3000 vascular plant species, including several local endemics.

Useful plants: Timber trees, medicinal plants.

Other values: Watershed protection, high landscape value, rich bird and mammal fauna (including 60% of Sumatran species of each), potential for developing tourism.

Threats: Local population pressure leading to encroachment, slash and burn agriculture, illegal logging, over-collection of rattans and other forest products.

Conservation: Gunung Leuser National Park (IUCN Management Category: II) covers 7926.8 km²; Gunung Leuser Biosphere Reserve covers 9464 km². Lowland areas under increasing pressure.

Geography

Gunung Leuser National Park is situated in north-west Sumatra in the provinces of Aceh Tenggara and Sumatra Selatan, extending over more than 100 km of the Bukit Barisan Range and containing several of Sumatra's highest non-volcanic peaks. The Gunung Leuser-Sekundur-Langkat-Kluet mountain blocks form one of the most important and probably best known areas of the park. The total area covered is more than 9000 km².

One of the most striking features is the Alas Valley, a rift valley extending for c. 100 km in a south-easterly direction. The valley divides the Gunung Leuser complex into two parts: the Serbolangit-Langkat reserve and the Gunung Leuser proper. Apart from the Alas Valley, much of the area is rugged and mountainous. Gunung Leuser is the highest point, reaching 3466 m. To the south of the park are the lower Karo and Tapanuli Highlands surrounding Lake Toba.

Geologically, the Bukit Barasan Range is part of the Sumatra orogeny, having been uplifted, folded and faulted during the Miocene. The Alas Valley and Blangkejeren basin are a downwarped Eocene grabben structure. The downwarping was accompanied by vulcanism and, later, sedimentation during the Oligocene, Miocene and Pliocene periods, giving rise to the marine sediments of the present foothills and lowlands. Phyllites, metamorphic rocks, sandstones, quartzite, marble, conglomerates and limestones (with distinctive karst features in the Kluet Valley) form the main rocks in the park, with crystalline schists, black shale, slate, siltstone and limestone in the West Alas Range.

The region has a high rainfall with no pronounced dry season. The highest altitudes receive 4500 mm of rain per annum (Van Strien 1985). Nearer the coast, at lower altitude, the average annual rainfall is 3000–3500 mm, and can be as low as 1500 m in the central Alas Valley due to a rainshadow effect.

The majority of the rapidly growing population is located in the central Alas Valley. The population in 1980 was 100,000, most people living in the town of Kutacane. To the north of the park is the town of Blangkejeren. Most of the highlands are free from settlement. A 1987 census revealed almost 6000 people living in the park (Wells 1989).

Vegetation

In the eastern hills (300–800 m), a low-canopy forest occurs along river banks and on the lower terraces, and includes *Paranephelium nitidum, Rinorea sclerocarpa, Dendrocnide sinuata* and many species of Euphorbiaceae. A medium-canopy forest develops on higher terraces. This forest is dominated by Meliaceae (*Dysoxylum alliaceum, Aglaia cauliflora*), along with many species of *Ficus* and a few species of Dipterocarpaceae, such as *Shorea leprosula*.

Lowland dipterocarp forest occurs below 600 m, and covers approximately 12% of the park. It has a canopy of 30–40 m, and includes a number of species of Dipterocarpaceae. *Amorphophallus titanum, Rafflesia arnoldii* and *R. micropilorum* occur in the area. Considerable differences in the flora exist from one valley to the next. In the west, there are forests dominated by *Dryobalanops oblongifolia*. Emergent trees can reach heights of 40–45 m. Besides *D. oblongifolia*, are species encountered elsewhere on low hillsides, such as *Shorea maxwelliana, S. ovalis, S. ovata* and *Hopea* cf. *beccariana*.

The submontane and montane vegetation are poorly known. Submontane forests cover about 48% of the park and occur (in general) between 600 m and 1500 m. Above about 1500 m, montane forest develops, with low-branched trees rarely exceeding 20 m tall. Above 1700 m, upper montane forest (cloud or moss forest) occurs, in which the forest floor and trees are carpeted by mosses.

Of particular note is the "blang" marsh vegetation which develops in damp hollows at around 2000 m. The vegetation includes grasses, sedges, and dwarf herbs and shrubs with temperate affinities, including species of *Rhododendron*, *Vaccinium*, *Parnassia* and *Gentiana*. Above 2500 m, and on some exposed ridges, subalpine vegetation occurs, comprising stunted trees and low shrubs.

Gunung Leuser National Park also contains some freshwater swamp forest and marshes, and a small stretch of coastal dunes.

Flora

The total vascular flora is estimated at 2000–3000 species; the level of endemism is not known.

Gunung Leuser is the only locality in Indonesia for *Trigonobalanus verticillata* (formerly thought to be endemic to Mount Kinabalu in Borneo), and several endemic Ericaceae (e.g. *Rhododendron atjehensis*) occur on peaks within the National Park. Of particular note is the presence in the lowland forests of the giant parasitic *Rafflesia arnoldii* and the local endemic *R. micropilorum*. Further botanical surveys are urgently needed. Some species may already be extinct, including *Passiflora sumatrana* and *Ulmus lanceaefolia*.

Useful plants

Commercially important timber trees present in the park, and which could be important genetic resources in the future, include: *Shorea leprosula*, *S. maxwelliana*, *S. ovalis*, *S. ovata* and *Dryobalanops sumatrensis*. The park contains many species of wild fruit trees, including the durians *Durio oxleyanus* and *D. zibethinus*, duku (*Lansium domesticum*) and rambutan (*Nephelium lappaceum*).

Medicinal plants include: *Alstonia scholaris, Cinnamomum iners, Litsea* spp., *Sindora sumatrana, Ficus variegata, Nephelium lappaceum, Styrax benzoin, Vernonia arborea, Monophyllaea horsfieldii* and *Wedelia montana* (Elliott and Brimacombe 1985).

Social and environmental values

According to Van Strien (1985), 105 species of mammal (60% of the Sumatran mammalian fauna) have been recorded from the park. The most significant is the Sumatran rhinoceros (*Dicerorhinus sumatrensis*) (Endangered), of which Van Strien (1985) estimated the park contained 130–200 individuals at that time. Of the primates, the most notable and best studied is the orang utan (*Pongo pygmaeus*) (Endangered). Other large mammals present include the Asian elephant (*Elephas maximus*) (Endangered) and several species of cats, including the Sumatran tiger (*Panthera tigris*) (Endangered), of which Van Strien (1985) estimated a population of approximately 90.

A rich avifauna includes 313 species of birds (60% of Sumatran bird species). A species inventory is given by Van Strien (1985). The montane forests of Gunung Leuser National Park lie within the Sumatra and Peninsular Malaysia Endemic Bird Area (EBA) which supports 38 restricted-range bird species, of which 20 are endemic. The majority of these species occur in this park, including the globally threatened Sumatran pheasant (*Lophura hoorerwerfi*), which is only known from the mountains of northern Sumatra.

The park is an important catchment area on which a large number of people depend for their water supplies. Local people also depend on the forests as a source of minor forest products.

The area has high scenic value and has potential for ecotourism. Gunung Leuser is receiving increasingly large numbers of both domestic and international visitors. The principal attraction is the Borohok Orang Utan Rehabilitation Centre at Bukit Lawang. The site, together with the nearby forest recreation area, attracted over 5000 foreign tourists, and a large, but unrecorded, number of domestic tourists in 1987. A WWF development programme included the completion of a large visitor centre and plans for guided forest walks.

A large number of scientific studies have been made or are underway, particularly on the Sumatran rhinoceros and orang utan, but also on geology, vegetation and flora of the park.

Threats

The major threats are from encroachment as a result of the expanding population along the Alas River, which cuts through the centre of the park. Around Kutacane, wet rice cultivation or slash and burn agriculture prevails. The buffer zone, which was delineated when the park was established had already disappeared by 1980 and incursions were being made into hill forest by 1989 (R. Ives 1989, pers. comm. to WCMC). Improvements to the Kutacane-Blangkejeren road have allowed access to settlers who have cleared a strip of forest along the road, essentially bisecting the park (McCarthy 1991).

Several species of dipterocarp found growing along rivers are important sources of keruing oil, which is refined and then used as a perfume fixative. However, deep cuts are made in the trunk on alternate sides until the tree stops producing the sap. Ultimately, the tree is killed.

There is also over-collection of rattans and illegal logging in the lowlands to supply local sawmills. Another problem is poaching, particularly of Sumatran rhinoceros.

Conservation

Gunung Leuser National Park (IUCN Management Category: II) covers 7926.8 km²; Gunung Leuser Biosphere Reserve covers 9464 km². Effective conservation is hampered by the ever-increasing local population, resulting in a shortage of agricultural land, lack of funds, equipment and trained park personnel, inadequate demarcation of the park boundaries, and a general lack of awareness among the local population about the importance of conservation.

To address some of these problems, the park is currently the focus of a WWF project to harmonize the activities and perceptions of those living adjacent to the protected area with the needs of conservation.

References

Abdulhadi, R., Mirmanto, E. and Kartawinata, K. (1985). A lowland dipterocarp forest in Sekundur, north Sumatra, Indonesia: five years after logging. In *3rd Dipterocarp Round Table, Samarinda.* Samarinda.

Beek, C.G.G. van (1982). *A geomorphological and pedological study of the Gunung Leuser National Park, north Sumatra.* Wageningen Agricultural University, Wageningen.

Elliott, S. and Brimacombe, J. (1985). *The medicinal plants of Gunung Leuser National Park.* WWF, Switzerland.

McCarthy, A.J. (comp.) (1991). *Conservation areas of Indonesia. Final draft.* World Conservation Monitoring Centre, Cambridge, U.K. in collaboration with Directorate General of Forest Protection and Nature Conservation (PHPA), Ministry of Forestry, Republic of Indonesia, and IUCN Commission on National Parks and Protected Areas, Gland, Switzerland.

Rijksen, H.D. (1978). A field study on Sumatran orang-utan (*Pongo pygmaeus abelii* Lesson 1827). Ecology, behaviour and conservation. Veenman and Zonen, Wageningen.

Schaik, C.P. van (1986). Phenological changes in a Sumatran rain forest. *J. Trop. Ecol.* 2: 327–347.

Schaik, C.P. van and Mirmanto, E. (1985). Spatial variation in the structure and litterfall of a Sumatran rain forest. *Biotropica* 17(3): 196–205.

Steenis, C.G.G.J. van (1938). Exploratie in de Gajo-Landen. Algemeene resultaten der Loser expeditie 1937. *Tijdschr. Kon. Ned. Aard. Genootschap* 55: 728–801.

Van Strien, N.J. (1985). *The Sumatran rhinoceros in the Gunung Leuser National Park, Sumatra, Indonesia: its distribution, ecology and conservation.* Doorn, The Netherlands. 207 pp.

Wells, M.P. (1989). *Can Indonesia's biological diversity be protected by linking economic development with national park management? Three case studies from the outer islands.* World Bank Report. 59 pp.

Wilde, W.J.J.O. de (1989). Sumatra. In Campbell, D.G. and Hammond, H.D. (eds), *Floristic inventory in tropical countries: the status of plant systematics, collections, and vegetation, plus recommendations for the future.* The New York Botanical Garden, New York. Pp. 103–107.

Acknowledgements

This Data Sheet was written by Stephen D. Davis based on material provided by Yves Laumonier (BIOTROP, Bogor, Indonesia) and Andrew J. McCarthy (WCMC).

KERINCI-SEBLAT NATIONAL PARK
Sumatra, Indonesia

Location: West-central Sumatra, between latitudes 1°30'–2°40'S and longitudes 101°00'–101°50'E.

Area: 1484.7 km².

Altitude: 200–3805 m (summit of Gunung Kerinci).

Vegetation: Lowland dipterocarp forest, hill and submontane forests, montane and montane swamp forests, subalpine forest.

Flora: Estimated 2000–3000 vascular plant species.

Useful plants: Timber trees (e.g. dipterocarps, *Agathis dammara*), medicinal plants, fruit tree relatives, rattans.

Other values: Rich fauna, high landscape value.

Threats: Local population pressure leading to encroachment of settlements and agriculture, illegal logging, over-collection of rattans.

Conservation: National Park (IUCN Management Category: II); integrated conservation and development project.

Geography

The Kerinci-Seblat National Park is located in west-central Sumatra and extends for some 345 km along the Bukit Barasan Range within the administrative provinces of Sumatra Barat, Jambi, Bengkulu and Sumatra Selatan. Gunung (Mount) Kerinci (3805 m) is the highest peak of Sumatra. It is an active volcanic cone and dominates the landscape of the park. A rift valley, part of a tectonic structure that extends from north to south through the island of Sumatra, divides the Barisan into two parallel ranges within the park, enclosing the "Sungaipenuh enclave" (c. 1450 km²) which contains Lake Kerinci.

The western range of mountains is mostly volcanic, but the eastern Barisan consists mainly of metamorphic rocks, karst limestone (outside the park boundary) and large granite massifs, intermixed with volcanic ejections from nearby volcanoes. The volcanic material is rich in plagioclase and generally acidic (dacitic-liparitic). Ferralitic soils predominate at lower altitudes, while at higher altitudes cambisols are most common. These tropical brown soils are leached to varying degrees, but they often have a very high humus content. In the upper parts of the mountains, andosols have developed on volcanic materials. Kerinci Valley contains relatively fertile alluvial soils.

The region has a very humid climate, with most of the area receiving 2500–3000 mm rainfall per year. The eastern slopes and most of the foothills on the west receive more than 3000 mm rainfall per year, while the west coast almost always receives more than 4000 mm. The number of rainy days there varies from 180 to 220 per annum.

The earliest record of human presence in the region (in the south of Kerinci Valley) is dated to c. 4000 years ago, but it was not until the 18th century that a large population migrated into the interior. Today, the majority of the population of about 270,000 is centred on the market town of Sungai Penuh, within the Kerinci Valley, and around the park perimeter. Population growth is estimated at 2.2% per year (Aumeeruddy 1992).

Agricultural land use is either wet rice cultivation (sawah), or shifting cultivation (ladang) and plantation crops on the hillsides (see Threats section). Several illegal settlements are situated within the National Park.

Vegetation

The following main types of vegetation occur in the National Park:

Lowland dipterocarp rain forest

Lowland dipterocarp rain forest occurs up to about 300 m. This formation is rapidly disappearing elsewhere along the west coast. It is characterized by an abundance of *Dipterocarpus* spp., *Shorea atrinervosa* and *S. multiflora*, associated with *Koompassia* and emergent Anacardiaceae, such as *Swintonia schwenkii*. Other notable species include *Mangifera torquenda*, *Hopea dryobalanoides*, *Lithocarpus sundaicus*, *Endospermum quadriloculare*, *Horsfieldia majuscula*, *Heliciopsis* cf. *incisa* and *Pentace curtisii*, as well as many tree species which are common throughout Sumatra. *Koilodepas longifolium* is extremely abundant in the understorey, together with rattans, such as *Calamus leloi*. *Buettneria curtisii* is a small, creeping member of the Sterculiaceae.

On the eastern side of Kerinci, lowland rain forest can still be found in some areas along the park boundary. On granite substrates, the flora is relatively poor in certain families which are better represented on sedimentary rocks. This is the case for Dipterocarpaceae, Clusiaceae and Fabaceae. Conversely, the presence of many Meliaceae on granite outcrops is noteworthy. The dominant dipterocarp species on granite is *Parashorea lucida*, whereas *Hopea* and *Dipterocarpus* are poorly represented.

Hill forest

Hill forest occurs between 300 and 800 m. On the eastern volcanic rocks and slopes, the canopy is high (35–40 m) with emergent trees often reaching heights of 55 m. Dipterocarps are less abundant than in lowland forest, but remain co-dominant with Fagaceae and Burseraceae. *Shorea platyclados* occurs from an altitude of 500 m, but the most abundant and dominant species is *Hopea* cf. *beccariana*, which becomes the major component of the canopy, reaching impressive sizes on hill crests. These giants are accompanied by *Shorea ovalis* subsp. *sericea*, *S. ovata*, *Quercus argentata* and *Santiria laevigata*.

Dipterocarpaceae, which are abundant on neighbouring volcanic formations, are practically non-existent on metamorphic rocks, their ecological niche being mainly occupied by large Meliaceae, particularly *Dysoxylum acutangulum* and *Chisocheton ceramicus*, Sapindaceae, such as *Pometia pinnata*, and Anacardiaceae, such as *Dracontomelon costatum*. *Lansium domesticum* (Meliaceae), *Artocarpus anisophyllus* (Moraceae) and *Celtis rigescens* (Ulmaceae) are found in the lower strata of the forest. *Amorphophallus titanum* and *Trevesia burckii*, together with the parasitic *Rafflesia hasseltii*, *R. arnoldii* and *Rhizanthes zipellii*, are also found in hill forest. *Casuarina nobilis* (*Gymnostoma nobile*) is abundant on scree and boulder-strewn steep slopes.

Riverine hill forest

This occurs in valleys and is typified by *Pometia pinnata*, *Pterospermum javanicum*, *Aglaia argentea*, *Octomeles sumatrana*, *Bombax valetonii* and *Terminalia* spp. There are also numerous species of *Macaranga*, *Mallotus*, *Ficus* and *Dendrocnide*, together with *Nauclea officinalis*, *N. orientalis*, *N. subdita*, *Bischofia javanica*, *Firmiana malayana* and *Harpullia arborea* (kayu pacet), the last named being an uncommon tree and sought after in the Kerinci region for its veined sapwood.

Submontane forests

At altitudes ranging from 800 to 1400 m, species of Myrtaceae, Clusiaceae and Euphorbiaceae are abundant, while the main structural dominants are species of Fagaceae, Myrtaceae, Moraceae and Clusiaceae. Emergent trees approaching heights of 50 m are frequently encountered, as are trees with large buttresses, lianes, hemi-epiphytic and epiphytic figs.

The emergent *Agathis borneensis* is only found on the ridges west of the Lake Kerinci, between 1000 and 1300 m, often in association with natural populations of *Pinus merkusii*. The most characteristic species elsewhere are *Shorea platyclados*, *Altingia excelsa*, *Quercus oidocarpa*, *Neesia altissima*, *Podocarpus imbricatus*, *P. neriifolius*, *P. wallichianus* and numerous species of strangling figs (*Ficus* cf. *binnendykii*, *F. disticha* and *F. elastica*).

Montane swamp forest

A few mid-altitude swamp forests exist. The largest of these, currently being cleared and converted to rice paddi, are located north-east of the Kayu Aro tea plantation, south-east of Gunung Kerinci. Jacobs (1958) mentions *Antidesma tetrandrum*, *Symplocos cochinchinensis*, *Celtis timorensis* and *Lithocarpus hystrix* occurring here. Other swamps on the north-west of Gunung Kerinci are unexplored.

Montane forests

Lower montane forest occurs between 1400 and 1900 m. Its canopy is 25–30 m high, and the main tree species are members of Fagaceae (e.g. *Lithocarpus pallidus*, *Quercus gemelliflora*, *Castanopsis* spp.), Lauraceae (e.g. *Litsea* cf. *tuberculata*), Myrtaceae (three species of *Eugenia*), Theaceae (*Haemocharis buxifolia*, *Schima wallichii*) and Sapotaceae (*Payena* spp. and *Madhuca* spp.). *Eugenia longiflora*, *Magnolia macklottii*, *Garcinia gaudichaudii*, *Actinodaphne glomerulata*, *Cinnamomum subavenium*, *Cryptocarya densiflora*, *Lindera subumbelliflora*, *Urophyllum corymbosum* and *U. arboreum* occur in the understorey.

On Gunung Kerinci, upper montane forest occurs between 1900 and 2500 m altitude. The canopy is between 15–25 m tall and is very open, with small crowns shaped by the prevailing winds. The forest is often cloud-covered and bryophytes and lichens (*Usnea*) cover the trees. *Symingtonia populnea*, *Manglietia calophylla*, *Lithocarpus oreophilus*, *Quercus* cf. *steenisii* and *Glochidion lutescens* are the main canopy species.

Tropical subalpine forests

Subalpine forest occurs above 2500 m. A fern belt (comprising *Gleichenia* and *Dicranopteris*) occurs between 2400–2700 m on Gunung Kerinci. The origin of this belt has yet to be explained. Above the fern belt, twisted and stunted trees of about 15 m are found. The dominant genera are *Myrsine*, *Ardisia* and *Vaccinium*. At 2800 m, slopes are very steep. Many trees grow out horizontally from the slopes before bending upwards. Typically, the vegetation is moss-covered and most of the species are microphyllous. Notable species include *Symplocos cochinchinensis* var. *sessilifolia* and *Ilex pleiobrachiata* (*I. cymosa*), *Myrsine affinis*, *Ardisia laevigata*, *Meliosma lanceolata* and *Cyathea trachypoda*. The ground is covered by the fern *Plagiogyria pycnophylla* and brambles, such as *Rubus elongatus* and *R. alpestris*.

Above 3000 m the vegetation is reduced to a dense thicket 3–6 m high, dominated by Ericaceae (such as *Rhododendron retusum*, *Vaccinium miquelii* and *Gaultheria nummularioides*), Symplocaceae (*Symplocos cochinchinensis*) and *Anaphalis javanica*.

Flora

It is estimated that Kerinci-Seblat contains 2000–3000 vascular plant species. The flora is still poorly known.

Useful plants

Kerinci-Seblat contains important gene pools of such good-quality timber trees as the dipterocarps *Shorea atrinervosa*, *Shorea platyclados* and *Parashorea lucida*, as well as non-dipterocarp timber trees, such as *Agathis dammara*, *Altingia excelsa* and *Harpullia arborea*.

Wild fruit tree relatives include species of *Mangifera* (mangoes), *Durio* (durians), *Lansium* (langsat) and *Nephelium* (rambutan).

Medicinal plants, which are sought after locally, include *Parashorea lucida*, *Sindora* spp., *Lansium domesticum*, *Aglaia argentea*, *Eurycoma longifolia* and *Monophyllaea horsfieldii*, along with several members of the Lauraceae and

Rutaceae, several species of *Ficus* and *Piper*, and the fern *Lomagramma* sp.

Social and environmental values

Kerinci-Seblat has a rich fauna quite different from that of Gunung Leuser National Park (CPD Site SEA41, see Data Sheet) to the north (McCarthy 1991). Notable species in Kerinci-Seblat which do not occur in Gunung Leuser include (among others) Malayan tapir (*Tapirus indicus*) (Endangered), western tarsier (*Tarsius bancanus*), marbled cat (*Felis marmorata*) (Indeterminate), pangolin (*Manis javanica*) and Sumatran rabbit (*Nesolagus netscheri*) (Rare). Other notable mammals in Kerinci-Seblat include Asian elephant (*Elephas maximus*) (Endangered), tiger (*Panthera tigris*) (Endangered), Malayan sunbear (*Helarctos malayanus*) (Vulnerable), clouded leopard (*Neofelis nebulosa*) (Vulnerable) and the Sumatran rhinoceros (*Dicerorhinus sumatrensis*) (Endangered), of which there is estimated to be a population of 200–500 animals (Van Strien 1985). 167 species of birds have been recorded, including 5 species of hornbill, 3 species of pheasant, 9 species of dove and pigeon, 9 species of bulbul and 6 species of kingfisher. The montane forests of Kerinci-Seblat National Park lie within the Sumatra and Peninsular Malaysia Endemic Bird Area (EBA), which supports 38 restricted-range bird species, of which 20 are endemic. The majority of these species occur in this park, including the globally threatened Salvadori's pheasant (*Lophura inornata*), which is only known from the mountains of southern Sumatra, Schneider's pitta (*Pitta schneideri*) and probably Sumatran cochoa (*Cochoa beccarii*). An inventory of mammal and bird species is given in MacKinnon (1990).

The park is an important catchment area on which a large number of people depend for their water supplies. Local people also depend on the forests as a source of minor forest products, including medicinal plants and rattans.

The area has high scenic value, with a great diversity of scenery, including several mountain lakes. The park attracts a steady and increasing number of visitors, including about 360 international visitors annually. A programme is underway to develop nature-oriented tourism (McCarthy 1991).

Scientific studies at the park have included remote sensing vegetation studies (Purnadjaja 1988). The reserve has been selected as a study area under the Tropenbos programme, a joint venture between several Dutch research institutes and Indonesian universities.

Threats

The main threat is from encroachment as a result of an expanding local population. Several illegal settlements are located within the National Park and a census carried out in 1987 by PHPA found over 21,000 people cultivating an area of 115 km² within the park. There are also a number of expanding settlements to the east and south of the park (WWF 1989).

Besides the encroachment of settlements and agriculture, illegal logging along access roads and around the perimeter of the park is another threat (Wells 1989).

Hill valleys are traditionally occupied by local people who own rubber, coffee and cinnamon plantations. Traditional exploitation of the forests on hillsides has mainly involved the collection of rattan. Over-exploitation of rattan species, such as *Calamus manan* (manau), once an important source of income, has occurred (Siebert 1989). Other species of rattan which are now sought after include *Korthalsia echinometra* (rotan udang), *Calamus javensis* (rotan lilin) and *C. caesius* (rotan sega).

Many of the park's management problems arise from a lack of financial resources and trained personnel (McCarthy 1991).

Conservation

Kerinci-Seblat is a National Park (IUCN Management Category: II). A management plan has been prepared (Wulf, Supomo and Rauf 1981) in which the establishment of wilderness, sanctuary and buffer zones was included as an objective. Management activities have concentrated on demarcating the boundary of the reserve and negotiation with local government to find alternative sites for illegal settlers. A series of proposals for buffer zone management, and the development of manpower training, has been developed in conjunction with WWF (McCarthy 1991).

There is a feasibility study for the first phase of an integrated conservation and development project (ICDP), which will aim to conserve Kerinci-Seblat's biodiversity through a comprehensive management plan while maintaining the area's economic and social development. The study is one of the projects receiving a grant from the Global Environment Facility (GEF), and follows an agreement on biodiversity conservation signed by the Government of Indonesia, UNDP and the World Bank in 1992.

References

Aumeeruddy, Y. (1992). *Agroforestry in the Kerinci valley: a support to buffer zone management for Kerinci Seblat National Park – Sumatra, Indonesia.* Institut de Botanique, Montpellier and PHPA, Bogor, Indonesia.

Dransfield, J. (1974). Notes on the palm flora of central Sumatra. *Reinwardtia* 8(4): 519–531.

Jacobs, M. (1958). Contribution to the botany of Mount Kerinci and adjacent area in west central Sumatra. *Ann. Bogor* 3(1).

James, F. (1985). *The late Quaternary vegetational history of the upper Kerinci valley, Sumatra, Indonesia.* M.Sc. thesis, University of Hull.

MacKinnon, K. (1990). *Biological diversity in Indonesia: a resource inventory.* WWF Indonesia, Bogor, Indonesia.

McCarthy, A.J. (comp.) (1991). *Conservation areas of Indonesia. Final draft.* World Conservation Monitoring Centre, Cambridge, U.K. in collaboration with Directorate General of Forest Protection and Nature Conservation (PHPA), Ministry of Forestry, Republic of Indonesia, and IUCN Commission on National Parks and Protected Areas, Gland, Switzerland.

Mijn, van der, E. and Rahman, D. (eds) (1992). *Environmental profile of the wetland area of Jambi Province, Sumatra, Indonesia*. Asian Wetland Bureau, Bogor, Indonesia.

Morley, R.J. (1980). Changes of dry-land vegetation in the Kerinci area of Sumatra during the late Quaternary period. In *Proc. IV Int. Palynol. Conf. Lucknow*. 3: 2–10.

Oshawa, M., Nainggolan, P.H.J., Tanaka, N. and Anwar, C. (1985). Altitudinal zonation of forest vegetation on Mount Kerinci, Sumatra: with comparisons to zonation in the temperate region of east Asia. *Journal of Tropical Ecology* 1: 193–216.

Purnadjaja (1988). *Vegetation analysis and mapping by remote sensing techniques as a data base for management of the Kerinci-Seblat National Park, Sumatra. Field report January–September 1988*. SEAMEO-BIOTROP, Bogor, Indonesia. 9 pp. (Unpublished.)

Purnadjaja (1991). *Mise en place d'une base de données phytoécologique et cartographique pour l'aménagement du parc national de Kerinci Seblat, Sumatera, Indonésie*. Université, Paul Sabatier, Toulouse.

Ridley, H.N. (1917). Results of an expedition to Kerinci peak, Sumatra. Botany. *Journal of the Federated Malay State Museums* 8: 1–145.

Siebert, S.F. (1989). The dilemma of a dwindling resource: rattan in Kerinci, Sumatra. *Principes* 33(2): 79–87.

Siebert, S.F. (1990). Hillside farming, soil erosion and forest conservation in two southeast Asian national parks. *Mountain Research and Development* 10(1): 64–72.

Tantra, G.M. and Jafarsidik, Y.S. (1979). *Inventarisasi Flora Suaka Alam Bukit Tapan, Kerinci, Jambi*. Lembaga Penelitian Hutan, Bogor. Report no. 318.

Van Strien, N.J. (1985). *The Sumatran rhinoceros in the Gunung Leuser National Park, Sumatra, Indonesia: its distribution, ecology and conservation*. Doorn, The Netherlands. 207 pp.

Watson, C.W. (1984). *Kerinci: two historical studies*. Centre of South-East Asia Studies, University of Kent. Occasional paper no. 4.

Wells, M.P. (1989). *Can Indonesia's biological diversity be protected by linking economic development with national park management? Three case studies from the outer islands*. World Bank Report. 59 pp.

Wilde, W.J.J.O. de (1989). Sumatra. In Campbell, D.G. and Hammond, H.D. (eds), *Floristic inventory in tropical countries: the status of plant systematics, collections, and vegetation, plus recommendations for the future*. The New York Botanical Garden, New York. Pp. 103–107.

Wulf, R. de, Supomo, D. and Rauf, K. (1981). *Kerinci-Seblat proposed national park preliminary management plan 1982–1987*. Directorate General of Forest Protection and Nature Conservation, Bogor, Indonesia. 56 pp.

WWF (1989). *Project 3769: progress report, July–September 1989*. WWF Indonesia, Bogor, Indonesia. 4 pp. (Unpublished.)

Acknowledgements

This Data Sheet was written by Yves Laumonier (BIOTROP, Bogor, Indonesia). Supplementary material was provided by Andrew J. McCarthy (WCMC).

LIMESTONE FLORA OF SUMATRA
Sumatra, Indonesia

Location: Scattered outcrops, mostly in north-west Aceh Province; also in central Sumatra, in the massifs located between Payakumbuh and Sijunjung, and north-east of Gunung Kerinci, at Bukit Cermin and Gunung Sunggiri.

Area: c. 5000 km² (although few individual outcrops are more than 10 km²).

Altitude: 150–1500 m (mostly lowland).

Vegetation: Forest over limestone, limestone scrub, cliff vegetation.

Flora: Estimated 1500–2000 vascular plant species; very poorly known.

Useful plants: Ornamental plants, wild fruit tree relatives.

Threats: Quarrying.

Conservation: Very few outcrops protected.

Geography

Limestone outcrops mainly occur in the north-west of Aceh Province, and to a less extent in the central Sumatra, in the massifs located between Payakumbuh and Sijunjung (see Map 14). Limestone also outcrops to the north-east of Gunung Kerinci, at Bukit Cermin and Gunung Sunggiri. Although collectively covering about 5000 km², few outcrops exceed 10 km².

In Sumatra, karst limestone areas are often rugged tablelands with numerous rocky outcrops, frequently alternating with veins of quartzite or slate. Five morphological units are recognized: lower slopes from 30–45°, upper slopes steeper than 45°, crevassed pinnacles (e.g. at Lho'Nga), cliffs and "mesa" type summits. Soils are generally shallow on summits and pinnacles. They are dark brown-red, fine-textured, and have a granular structure. Drainage is rapid, resulting in a water deficiency during short dry periods. The calcium carbonate content is high, giving a top-soil pH of about 7. Lower down on moderate slopes, soils become brown-yellow and the texture is coarser. The pH here is 6.4–6.7.

Limestone areas in the eastern part of the Barisan Range receive less rain than those near the west coast. The differences in the amount of rainfall doubtlessly have a considerable effect on the geomorphology and pedogenesis of the karst limestone areas.

Vegetation

TABLE 57. LIMESTONE FOREST IN SUMATRA

	Natural area (km²)	Remaining area (km²) (and % of original area)
Montane forest on limestone	12,250	10,780 (88%)
Wet lowland forest on limestone	27,900	16,630 (60%)
Moist lowland forest on limestone	3000	154 (51%)

Source: FAO (1982).

On the west coast, the structure of forests developed on limestone is noticeably different from neighbouring forests developed on non-calcareous substrates. Generally, the canopy of limestone forest is more open. Emergent trees are mainly *Shorea maxwelliana*, *S. atrinervosa* and *Xanthophyllum amoenum*, which often exceed heights of 40–50 m. The main canopy of the forest is at 30–40 m, and consists mainly of *Artocarpus lanceifolius* and *Myristica iners*. The lower canopy (20–30 m) includes *Diospyros fasciculosa*, *Pometia pinnata*, *Calophyllum rubiginosum*, *Aidia cochinchinensis*, *Neonauclea* cf. *cyrtopoda*, *Knema laurina*, *Whitfordiodendron purpuraceum*, *Aglaia odoratissima* and *A. eximia*.

In the central eastern hills, the structure of the forest on the lower slopes around 500 m altitude is similar to that found at the same altitude on non-karstic hills. The canopy seldom exceeds a height of 25–30 m, but the occasional emergent tree can reach a height of 50 to 55 m. The emergents are mainly *Parashorea lucida*, *Pometia pinnata* and a number of hemi-epiphytic figs. The main canopy of the forest is also dominated by these species, together with many species of Meliaceae, such as *Aglaia oligocarpa*, *A. argentea*, *A. ganggo* and *Dysoxylum macrocarpum*, together with *Cratoxylum sumatranum*, *Schoutenia furfuracea*, *Margaritaria indica*, *Diospyros toposoides*, *D. apiculata*, *Celtis philippensis* and *Vatica* cf. *cinerea*. The rattan, *Calamus pandanosmus* and the palm tree *Arenga obtusifolia* are amongst the most common species on the lower slopes. The gesneriads *Monophyllaea hirtella* and *M. horsfieldii*, as well as *Amorphophallus titanum*, occur in damp places.

On ridges and rocky outcrops, the forest is reduced in size, with a few isolated emergent trees reaching 20 m. They include *Cratoxylum sumatranum*, *Distyliopsis dunnii*, *Drypetes* sp., *Ganua* sp., *Eugenia* sp., but most trees only reach a height of 5–10 m (or rarely 15 m). The flora is poorer in species, with the most abundant species being *Distyliopsis dunnii*, *Celtis philippensis*, *Memecylon* cf. *edule* and *Cratoxylum maingayi*, often associated with species of *Drypetes*, *Chionanthus* and an as yet undetermined *Pandanus*. This same *Pandanus* is sometimes very abundant on cliff faces, accompanied by numerous species of Gesneriaceae (*Boea*), Begoniaceae and Lycopodiaceae (*Lycopodium squamosum*), together with *Diploclisia glaucescens* (Menispermaceae), *Ventilago* sp. (Rhamnaceae) and *Vallariopsis lanceifolia*, a hemi-epiphytic member of the Apocynaceae.

Above the cliff faces, the canopy of the forest is still high. On these 55° slopes, at an altitude of 800 m, one encounters *Shorea platyclados*, well-developed but rare, while the dominant canopy species are *Schima wallichii*, *Quercus gemelliflora*, *Santiria apiculata*, *Casuarina nobilis* (*Gymnostoma nobile*), *Hopea dryobalanoides* and *Bhesa robusta*. *Calophyllum teijsmannii*, *C. canum*, *Litsea grandis*, *Magnolia villosa*, *Knema mandaraban*, *Mallotus penangensis*, *Macaranga gigantea* and *Pandanus* sp. make up the understorey, together with numerous undetermined species in such genera as *Morinda*, *Hullettia*, *Flacourtia*, *Euodia* and *Cynometra*.

The vegetation on the tops of limestone pinnacles consists of a sparse shrub cover, mostly of *Schima wallichii*, *Glochidion pubicapsa*, *Podocarpus polystachyus*, *Decaspermum* sp., *Daphniphyllum* sp., *Eugenia* sp. and *Ganua* sp.

Flora

The limestone flora is estimated to include about 1500–2000 species of vascular plants. Undoubtedly, the flora includes many Sumatran endemic and local endemic species. However, the flora is still very poorly known and no estimate of the level of endemism can be given.

Useful plants

The limestone flora includes many ornamental species of potential value in horticulture, including many species in the Gesneriaceae, Orchidaceae, Balsaminaceae and Begoniaceae. There are also a number of wild relatives of fruit trees.

Threats

The main threat is quarrying of limestone for making cement.

Conservation

The whole limestone vegetation only accounts for approximately 1% of the island's surface area, but the suspected high level of species endemism, and the natural beauty of the scenery, make it a priority habitat for conservation. Virtually all karstic mountain ranges are located outside the existing protected areas system.

References

FAO (1982). *National Conservation Plan for Indonesia, vol 2. Sumatra*. Field report of UNDP/FAO National Parks Development Project INS/78/061. FAO, Bogor, Indonesia.

Whitten, A.J., Damanik, S.J., Anwar, J. and Hisyam, N. (1984). *The ecology of Sumatra*. Gadjah Mada University Press. 583 pp.

Acknowledgements

This Data Sheet was written by Yves Laumonier (BIOTROP, Bogor, Indonesia).

MAP 14. LIMESTONE OUTCROPS: NORTH-WEST AND CENTRAL SUMATRA

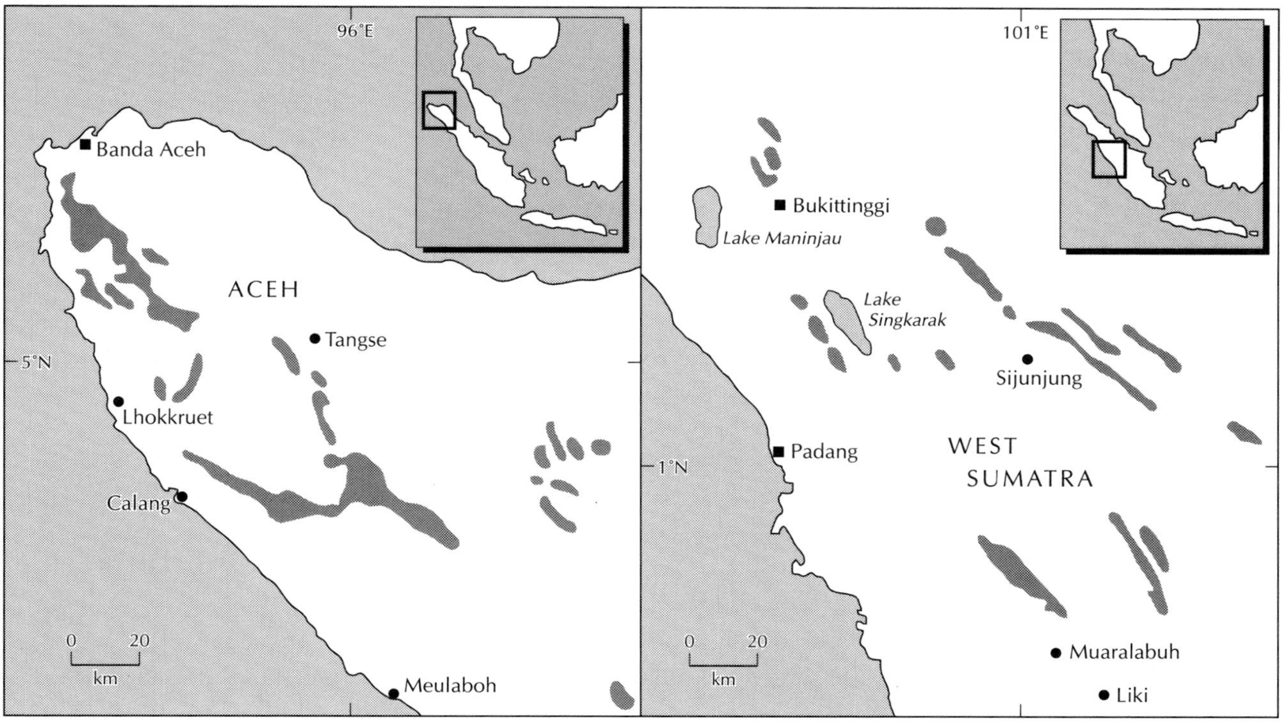

TIGAPULUH MOUNTAINS
Sumatra, Indonesia

Location: Jambi and Riau provinces, centred on latitude 1°05'S and longitude 102°30'E.

Area: c. 2000 km².

Altitude: 150–800 m (mostly between 400 and 800 m).

Vegetation: Tropical evergreen lowland and hill dipterocarp rain forests.

Flora: Estimated 2000–3000 vascular plant species; rich in elements of the "Riau pocket" flora, a distinct floristic assemblage containing species which are also found in parts of west and north-west Borneo and east Peninsular Malaysia.

Useful plants: Timber trees.

Threats: Logging; conversion to forestry and rubber plantations; shifting cultivation; local population pressure, particularly in eastern lowlands.

Conservation: No legal protection.

Geography

The Tigapuluh Mountains are located in central Sumatra, between Jambi and Riau provinces, centred on latitude 1°05'S and longitude 102°30'E. They are a pre-Tertiary metamorphic range of mountains which extend for approximately 100 km and are surrounded by eastern lowlands. They range from about 150 to 800 m altitude.

Vegetation

Tropical evergreen dipterocarp rain forest occurs in the lowlands and hills from 150 to 800 m altitude. Lowland rain forest occurs up to about 300 m. The canopy is 30–40 m high, with emergent trees reaching 45–55 m. The dominant tree species in lowland forest belong to Dipterocarpaceae, Myrtaceae, Burseraceae and Euphorbiaceae. Among the dipterocarps are *Shorea lumutensis, S. acuminata, S. macroptera* and *Shorea parvifolia. Koompassia, Dyera costulata, Fagraea gigantea, Heritiera sumatrana* and *Scaphium macropodum* are also present.

The forests are floristically very rich, with no single species dominant. The most abundant species are those belonging to the lower canopy, mainly *Gironniera hirta* (Ulmaceae), *Neoscortechinia kingii* (Euphorbiaceae), *Palaquium oxleyanum* (Sapotaceae), *Monocarpia marginalis* (Annonaceae), *Ixonanthes icosandra* (Linaceae) and *Gymnacranthera bancana* (Myristicaceae). There are a few species of palms in the lower strata of the forest, including *Oncosperma horridum* and *Livistona kingiana. Fordia* cf. *johorensis* (Fabaceae) dominates the lower layers of the forest.

Flora

The flora of the Tigapuluh Mountains is estimated to contain 2000–3000 vascular plant species.

The Tigapuluh area is noteworthy for its richness in elements of the "Riau pocket" flora, a distinct floristic assemblage containing species which are also found in parts of west and north-west Borneo and eastern Peninsular Malaysia. In Sumatra, the Riau pocket flora is confined to eastern central Sumatra and offshore islands, but the highest concentration of the flora is in the Tigapuluh Mountains. The area near the upper reach of the River Bulan is probably the most representative. Constituent species include the dipterocarp *Shorea peltata* (found only in south-east Peninsular Malaysia, east Sumatra and west Borneo) and the palm *Teijsmanniodendron altifrons*, which dominates the undergrowth. Other common species belonging to this floristic assemblage include: *Shorea lumutensis, S. gibbosa, Dipterocarpus lowii, Dryobanalops oblongifolia, Goniothalamus malayanus, Cyathocalyx ramuliflorus, Dacryodes macrocarpa, Dillenia albiflos, Lophopetalum pachyphyllum, Ptychopyxis kingii, Calophyllum flavoramulum* and *Brucea bruceadelpha*.

Useful plants

The forests contain a rich gene pool of important timber trees, such as *Shorea lumutensis, S. acuminata, S. macroptera, S. parvifolia, Dryobalanops oblongifolia, Dipterocarpus lowii* and *Anisoptera laevis; Eusideroxylon zwageri* (bulian) occurs in several localities.

Among fruit tree relatives are several species of *Durio* and *Mangifera* which appear to be restricted to the area.

Social and environmental values

There are still several hunter-gatherer groups of the Kubu tribal people who live in the area and depend on forest products for their subsistence. However, there is increasing pressure from a growing population (c. 2.5% growth rate per annum) in the surrounding lowlands, especially on the east. This is causing several conservation problems (see Threats section).

Threats

The main threats are from logging, conversion of primary forests to forestry plantations and shifting cultivation.

Conservation

The Tigapuluh Mountains are not currently protected.

Acknowledgements

This Data Sheet was written by Yves Laumonier (BIOTROP, Bogor, Indonesia).

DUMOGA-BONE NATIONAL PARK
Sulawesi, Indonesia

Location: Northern (Minahassa) peninsula, in the administrative province of Sulawesi Utara, between latitudes 0°21'–0°44'N and longitudes 123°05'–124°05'E.

Area: 3000 km².

Altitude: 200–1968 m (summit of Gunung Ganbuta).

Vegetation: Tropical lowland semi-evergreen rain forest, riverine forest, montane forest, small area of forest on limestone.

Flora: No estimate available for size of flora.

Useful plants: Gene pool of timber trees, rattans.

Other values: Watershed protection, rich fauna, tourism, scientific research.

Threats: Population pressure leading to over-exploitation of forest products and encroachment of shifting (ladang) agriculture; illegal hunting; potential threats from copper mining and road building.

Conservation: National Park (IUCN Management Category: II), having been established previously as 3 reserves: Dumoga Game Reserve (935 km², declared in 1979), Bone Game Reserve (1100 km², declared 1979) and Bulawa Nature Reserve (752 km², declared 1980).

This site is included as a representative site in Sulawesi containing some lowland rain forest. The flora of Sulawesi is generally considered to be of more recent origin than that of neighbouring Borneo and therefore contains fewer species and endemics. Further botanical surveys are needed to determine the relative richness of lowland forest sites within Sulawesi.

Geography

Dumoga-Bone comprises a number of steep mountain ranges in the east of the northern peninsula of Sulawesi, between Dumoga Valley and Gorantalo, and including some lowlands. The Bulawan Mountains divide the park into distinct catchment areas, ultimately draining into the Dumoga and Bone rift valleys to the east and west, respectively. The Perantanaan, Tilong, Kabila and Ali mountain blocks consist of sandstones, siltstones, shales, limestones and intermediate to basic volcanic rocks; the Bulawan Mountains were formed by volcanic activity. Granite and diorite intrusions form outcrops locally in the southern coastal mountains, and in the north. Spectacular limestone and tufa formations occur in areas of hot springs to the north-east of Gunung Renga and at Honajongo in the Bone Valley. The highest point is Gunung Ganbuta (1968 m).

Dumoga-Bone has a slightly seasonal climate, and only small areas can be said to be perhumid. Average annual rainfall is 1700–2200 mm, depending on altitude and aspect. November–January and March–May are the wettest periods. Lowest monthly rainfall is September and October, but no month has less than 100 mm.

Vegetation

Lowland forest makes up about 60% of the park area (McCarthy 1991); 1650 km² comprises primary tropical lowland semi-evergreen rain forest (MacKinnon and MacKinnon 1986). This is approximately 14% of the remaining lowland semi-evergreen rain forest in the northern peninsula of Sulawesi. The lowland forests are the richest communities.

Whitmore and Sidiyasa (1986) studied an area of forest at Toraut, at the north-west end of the Dumoga Valley. The main canopy of the forest is 30–40 m high, with no emergent trees. The commonest families represented amongst trees of 10 cm dbh or more at Toraut are Lauraceae, Guttiferae and Anacardiaceae (dipterocarps being absent). Canopy trees include members of the genera *Sandoricum*, *Dysoxylum*, *Pterospermum* and *Heritiera*. Common trees include *Bischofia javanica*, *Dracontomelon mangiferum* and the fan palm *Livistona rotundifolia*, which Whitmore and Sidiyasa (1986) measured at 30 m or more high at Toraut. The forest floor is also rich in rattans (notably *Calamus* spp. and *Daemonorops* spp.). Riverine forest and alluvial plains are dominated by *Eucalyptus deglupta*, which may reach 70 m in height, *Dracontomelon dao* and *Octomeles sumatrana*.

At higher elevations in Dumoga-Bone, the forest is dominated by *Eugenia*, *Shorea* and *Agathis*; there is an abundance of rattans in the understorey. Montane rain forest occurs above 1000 m, covering approximately 604 km². Limestone forest covers some 50 km² (FAO 1982; MacKinnon and MacKinnon 1986).

Flora

Floristic studies were made by Whitmore and Sidiyasa (1986) in lowland rain forest at Toraut. Their general impression is that the primary forest flora is of considerable floristic diversity at any one place, but overall the flora is not very rich, i.e. high α and low β diversity. Different parts of the forest were found to have different species of large trees, mostly related to habitat preferences. A one hectare sample plot yielded 109 species of trees with dbh of 10 cm or more. This compares with three 1 ha plots at Mulu (CPD Site SEA33, see Data Sheet) with 223, 214 and 123 species, and a fourth at Mulu (on limestone) with 73 species (the richest alluvium and poorest limestone Malesian forests yet enumerated).

At Toraut, the forest contains few climbers (except for large rattans, the aroid *Pothos hermaphroditica* and the climbing pandan *Freycinetia* sp.) and few epiphytes, including orchids. There are few herbs in the ground layer (which is usual for lowland tropical rain forest).

An overall figure for the size of the vascular flora is not available. Dumoga-Bone is included here as a representative site, but further botanical studies are needed.

Useful plants

Dumoga-Bone contains an important gene pool of timber tree species, especially of *Eucalyptus deglupta* and *Agathis*, as well as many rattans.

Social and environmental values

Dumoga-Bone has a remarkably diverse fauna. All the endemic mammal species of Sulawesi occur in the park, among them: two endemic species of macaques (*Macaca nigrescens* and *M. heckii*), babirusa (*Babyrousa babyrussa*) (Vulnerable), lowland anoa (*Bubalus depressicornis*) (Endangered), mountain anoa (*B. quarlesi*) (Endangered), Celebes cuscus (*Strigocuscus celebensis*), Celebes tarsier (*Tarsius spectrum*) and Celebes giant palm civet (*Macrogalidia musschenbroeki*) (Rare). 170 species of birds have been recorded from the park, including many of the 55 restricted-range species which occur in the Sulawesi Endemic Bird Area (EBA), notably the globally threatened Matinan flycatcher (*Cyornis sanfordi*) and perhaps satanic eared-nightjar (*Eurostopoduc diabolicus*), which are both only known from the Minahassa Peninsula. The threatened maleo (*Macrocephalon maleo*) also occurs here. Estuarine crocodile (*Crocodylus porosus*) (Endangered) occurs along the Bone River.

Dumoga-Bone has an important water catchment protection role for irrigation schemes in the Dumoga Valley. Without the protection of the catchment to ensure the quantity and quality of the water supply, the agricultural potential of the rich soils of this former lake bed could not be realized.

Scientific research on the flora and fauna has been carried out at Dumoga-Bone over a number of years notably through Project Wallace and Project Linnaeus. A growing number of tourists visit the park and there is potential for developing ecotourism as a means of generating income for the local and national economies.

Threats

The main threat results from increasing local population, with encroachment of agriculture and settlements. In 1980, there was a population of approximately 47,750 people living in the Dumoga Valley (Wind and Sumardja 1987). There are now considerably more people due to the influx of transmigrants from Bali and Java, and as a result of local population growth

(K. MacKinnon 1991, pers. comm.). In addition, there is a rapidly growing human population along the coastal plains, in the Bone Valley and in the Gorontalo area. Gorontalo itself has a population of approximately 222,000. Shifting cultivation (ladang) is encroaching, particularly on the western boundary of the park (Hitchcock, Sedensticker and Sumardja 1988). Illegal hunting for mammals also occurs.

One of the most serious potential threats is the possibility of copper mining in the Bone River catchment. However, permission has not been granted for the exploitation of the deposit (Whitten, Muslimin Mustafa and Henderson 1987). Other formations of economic value include gold and kaolinite. Gold is exploited illegally on a small-scale. Road development, local demand for forest products and logging of adjacent forests are potential threats (Wells 1989).

Conservation

Dumoga-Bone was proposed as a National Park in 1982, having been established previously as 3 reserves: Dumoga Game Reserve (935 km², declared in 1979), Bone Game Reserve (1100 km², declared 1979) and Bulawa Nature Reserve (752 km², declared 1980). The World Bank supported the establishment of the National Park principally to protect the watershed of the Dumoga Valley to protect investments in an irrigation scheme (Whitten, Muslimin Mustafa and Henderson 1987). Subsequently, there have been proposals put forward to extend the protected area to include the swamp lands and floodplain of Keringgolan, principally to protect populations of wildfowl and wading birds (see Wind 1984; Hitchcock, Sedensticker and Sumardja 1988).

A management plan has been formulated (Wind 1984). The principal management objectives are to maintain a fully functional forested ecosystem to maintain species diversity and to protect the watershed for the local population. This is to be achieved by zoning, including the establishment of intensive use zones, buffer zones, boundary fuelwood plantations, experimental forestry plantations in areas which have suffered from previous encroachment, wilderness zones with recreation facilities and a strictly protected core area.

So far, management activities have included boundary marking and patrols, development of tourism and research facilities, and the removal and subsequent relocation of illegal settlers in 1983. The growing number of tourists has been catered for by the development of an interpretation centre, marked trails, camping grounds, a guest house and shelters. In addition, there are scientific research facilities at Toraut, established by the Wallace expedition.

Dumoga-Bone is the largest lowland reserve in Sulawesi and is also one of the best managed protected areas in Indonesia (MacKinnon and MacKinnon 1986). In the evaluation of the importance of protected areas in the Indomalayan Realm (MacKinnon and MacKinnon 1986), Dumoga-Bone is given an "A" priority rating as an area of supreme importance for conservation, with the highest biological diversity value of any protected area in Sulawesi. This assessment was mainly based on its importance for vertebrate animals and its large area with a forest cover.

The loan from the World Bank for irrigation projects in Dumoga Valley laid down stringent environmental conditions to protect the forests (Whitten, Muslimin Mustafa and Henderson 1987). Boundary demarcation is also being improved with funds from the World Bank. The park is therefore a good example of how conservation and development can go hand in hand, if political will and adequate funds are forthcoming.

References

FAO (1982). *National Conservation Plan for Indonesia, vol. 6. Sulawesi.* Field report of UNDP/FAO National Parks Development Project INS/78/061). FAO, Bogor, Indonesia.

Hitchcock, P., Sedensticker, J. and Sumardja, E. (1988). *Dumoga-Bone National Park: conservation for development in north Sulawesi.* IUCN Mission Report. WWF Indonesia, Bogor, Indonesia. 64 pp.

MacKinnon, J. and MacKinnon, K. (1986). *Review of the protected areas system in the Indo-Malayan Realm.* IUCN, Gland, Switzerland and Cambridge, U.K. (in collaboration with UNEP). 284 pp.

McCarthy, A.J. (comp.) (1991). *Conservation areas of Indonesia. Final draft.* World Conservation Monitoring Centre, Cambridge, U.K. in collaboration with Directorate General of Forest Protection and Nature Conservation (PHPA), Ministry of Forestry, Republic of Indonesia, and IUCN Commission on National Parks and Protected Areas, Gland, Switzerland.

Wells, M.P. (1989). *Can Indonesia's biological diversity be protected by linking economic development with national park management? Three case studies from the outer islands.* World Bank Report. 59 pp.

Whitmore, T.C. and Sidiyasa, K. (1986). Composition and structure of a lowland rain forest at Toraut, northern Sulawesi. *Kew Bulletin* 41(3): 747–756.

Whitten, A.J., Muslimin Mustafa and Henderson, G.S. (1987). *The ecology of Sulawesi.* Gadjah Mada University Press, Yogyakarta. 777 pp.

Wind, J. (1984). *Management plan 1984–1989, Dumoga-Bone National Park.* WWF/IUCN Conservation for Development Programme in Indonesia. 133 pp.

Wind, J. and Sumardja, E.A. (1987). *Dumoga-Bone. World Bank project for irrigation and water catchment protection.* IIED Conference on Sustainable Development, 28–30 April. IIED, London.

Acknowledgements

This Data Sheet was written by Stephen D. Davis, with thanks to Andrew J. McCarthy (WCMC) for providing much valuable information, and to Drs Kathy MacKinnon (WWF Indonesia) and Tony Whitten for their comments on an earlier draft.

LIMESTONE FLORA OF SULAWESI
Sulawesi, Indonesia

Location: Scattered throughout Sulawesi; the most extensive outcrops are in the south (including the offshore islands of Buton and Muna), central and eastern Sulawesi (including the offshore islands of Banggai and Togian). Scattered outcrops in the Minahassa Peninsula in the north.

Area: No figure available.

Altitude: c. 150–1000 m. (Barrier reef and atoll limestones, not considered as part of the CPD area, occur at sea-level.)

Vegetation: Forest over limestone, limestone scrub, cliff vegetation.

Flora: Very poorly known; no estimate for size of flora available.

Useful plants: Sugar palm, fruit tree relatives, ornamental plants, rattans, species in secondary vegetation may have potential use for rehabilitating degraded limestone sites.

Threats: Virtually all limestone areas of the Maros Hills area are disturbed to some extent by collection of firewood and other forest products; those at Tonasa are being quarried. Clearance for agriculture and fire threaten some areas.

Conservation: Most outcrops unprotected.

Geography

The limestone areas of Sulawesi are scattered throughout the island, but the most extensive outcrops occur in the south (including the offshore island of Buton), central and eastern Sulawesi (including the offshore islands of Banggai and Togian). There are also scattered smaller outcrops in the Minahassa Peninsula in the north.

The limestone outcrops of Sulawesi comprise rocks of various origins. Those found over much of Banggai, Togian, Muna, Buton and the north coast north of Palu are Quaternary-Tertiary reef limestones, those in the south-west and north-east are Tertiary limestones formed from the Eocene to mid-Miocene, and the limestones found near Lake Matano and on Buton date from the Cretaceous.

There are two main types of karst landscapes in Sulawesi: conical hill karst, such as that found in the north of Bone, on the islands of Buton and Muna in the south, and tower karst, such as that found near Maros, in the south-west, and at Tonasa. The Maros/Tonasa Hills comprise 300 km² of Eocene and Miocene coral limestone. The Maros Hills are mostly between 150 and 300 m high, but the tallest reaches 575 m. The topography includes steep-sided valleys, probably formed by cave-roof collapse following erosion by rivers.

Conical hill karst landscapes may have been formed by streams flowing between blocks of limestone. In some areas, such as north of Bone, steep canyons have formed where a previous subterranean river has dissolved away the roof of its course until final collapse (Verstappen 1957).

On steep slopes and rocky hilltops, the soil is very shallow. Rendzinas are known from the conical hills of Kambara and Muna Island. Moderate slopes have clay-rich, leached brownish-red latosols (Burnham 1985), while crests and shelves may develop an acid, humus-rich peaty soil, as a result of the high rainfall and local accumulation of leaf-litter.

Vegetation

Table 58 gives the areas for limestone forest in Sulawesi. In addition, there are areas of montane limestone forest.

TABLE 58. LIMESTONE FOREST IN SULAWESI

	Natural area (km²)	Remaining area (km²) (and % of original area)
Wet lowland forest on limestone	330	30 (9%)
Moist lowland forest on limestone	5070	1650 (33%)
Dry lowland forest on limestone	2770	200 (7%)

Source: FAO (1982).

Although limestone forest generally contains fewer large trees and is poorer in tree species compared with lowland forests on deeper soils, they contain a specialized flora which is tolerant of the edaphic conditions. The vegetation of limestone areas in Sulawesi is also influenced by the relatively long dry periods. Few studies have been made of the vegetation of limestone areas in Sulawesi; most of the available information concerns part of the Maros Hills (south-west Sulawesi) and the Rantepo/Makale (Toraja) area in south-central Sulawesi (Whitten, Muslimin Mustafa and Henderson 1987).

Common trees in undisturbed valleys at Maros include *Pangium edule*, *Artocarpus* spp. and *Ficus* spp. A number of species of *Ficus* also cling to rocks on very steep slopes and cliff faces. Scrub vegetation and low-canopy forest (7–10 m tall) occur on the upper parts of the hills.

The forest at 1000 m on Mount Wawonseru, west of Soroako, reaches 40–45 m. No single family dominates, although species of Lauraceae and Annonaceae are the most abundant. The largest trees are *Bischofia* (Euphorbiaceae), *Eugenia* (Myrtaceae), *Podocarpus* (Podocarpaceae) and *Vernonia* (Asteraceae). The lower canopy includes *Polyalthia*

(Annonaceae, many species) and *Antidesma* (Euphorbiaceae). Orchids, *Piper* (wild pepper) and the gesneriad *Rynchoglossum* grow over bare rocks (van Balgooy and Tantra 1986).

Though not considered here as a centre of plant diversity and endemism, coastal reef limestone systems are nevertheless important barriers against coastal erosion and support a rich marine fauna. The reefs of Taka Bone Rate Archipelago (comprising one of the largest atolls in the world) include extensive beds of the sea grass *Thalassodendron ciliatum* (Djohani 1989), but much of the terrestrial vegetation of the larger islands of the reef system has been extensively modified.

Flora

The limestone flora is very poorly known. Most limestone areas remain to be botanically explored, and only miscellaneous records of plants from limestone areas are available. No estimate of the size of the flora and level of endemism can be given at present, but, on the basis of studies elsewhere in the region (see Data Sheet on the Limestone Flora of Peninsular Malaysia, SEA3, for example), it can be expected that the level of endemism is high, particularly among the herbaceous flora. The Maros Hills, in particular, are thought to harbour many rare species (Whitten, Muslimin Mustafa and Henderson 1987). More botanical surveys are needed to determine which outcrops support distinctive floras.

Useful plants

The sap of the sugar palm (*Arenga* sp.) is collected and fermented. Leaves of *Garcinia* and fruits of *Aleurites moluccana* (candlenut) are added to the brew. Rattans and the edible fruits of *Pangium edule* are collected. There are a number of wild fruit tree relatives, including *Ficus* spp. (figs) and *Artocarpus* spp. (jackfruits). Ornamental plants include Gesneriaceae, orchids and ferns.

Some tree species which are components of secondary vegetation following disturbance (such as quarrying operations) could be useful for re-vegetating degraded limestone areas. Among the trees are species of *Homalanthus*, *Lagerstroemia*, *Pterospermum*, *Kleinhovia* and *Villebrunea*.

Social and environmental values

Besides having a distinct flora, it can be expected that limestone areas in Sulawesi support a distinct fauna. One of the more spectacular butterflies, the large swallowtail *Graphium androcles*, is known largely from Sulawesi limestone, presumably because its food plant is restricted to limestone (Haugum, Ebner and Racheli 1980). No studies on snails are known; however, based on studies elsewhere in the region, it is likely that studies will reveal species which are restricted to the limestone.

A total of 55 restricted-range species occur in the Sulawesi Endemic Bird Area (EBA) of which 42 are endemic. They are all forest species, and many have localized distributions which are likely to be related to soil type (Whitten, Muslimin Mustafa and Henderson 1987), but this aspect of their ecology is poorly understood. Forest on limestone is likely to be important for a number of species.

The limestone scenery offers a spectacular landscape with many features of geological interest.

Threats

Virtually all accessible parts of the Maros and Toraja Hills have been exploited to a certain extent. Local people cut firewood and other forest products, such as rattan and fruits of *Pangium edule* and *Aleurites moluccana* (candlenut). Many trees of the latter species are planted (Whitten, Muslimin Mustafa and Henderson 1987). Some areas of limestone forest are threatened by clearance for agriculture and by fires spreading from surrounding cultivated areas (A.J. Whitten 1991, pers. comm.).

The Tonasa limestone supports large cement factories which supply almost all the cement needs of eastern Indonesia. The area affected is relatively small compared to the total area of limestone in Sulawesi. However, extensions to existing quarries and siting of new ones should take environmental considerations into account. Surveys need to be undertaken to determine which limestone areas are critically important to protect.

Disturbance to natural vegetation allows the establishment of introduced weeds (such as *Eupatorium* and *Lantana*) which can then compete with the native flora.

Conservation

About 70% of all limestone outcrops are unprotected (A.J. Whitten 1991, pers. comm.). About 50 km² of limestone forest, together with some spectacular karst limestone scenery, occurs within Dumoga-Bone National Park (CPD Site SEA46, see separate Data Sheet). The Morowali Nature Reserve includes some Tertiary limestone deposits, although the site is predominantly composed of ultramafic and metamorphic rocks. About 20 km² of limestone forest occurs in Bantimurung Nature Reserve and about 50 km² of limestone forest occurs in Kakinawe Game Reserve (FAO 1982). Limestone reef systems occur in a number of existing or proposed Marine Nature Reserves. For example, Taka Bone Rata Archipelago Marine Nature Reserve includes a large area of coastal reef limestone; however, vegetation on the larger islands of this system has been extensively modified (McCarthy 1991).

References

Balgooy, M.M.J. van and Tantra, I.G.M. (1986). *The vegetation in two areas in Sulawesi (Indonesia)*. Forest Research Bulletin (Special Edition), Bogor, Indonesia.

Burnham, C.P. (1985). The forest environment: soils. In Whitmore, T.C. (ed.), *Tropical rain forests of the Far East*. 2nd Edition. Clarendon Press, Oxford. Pp. 137–154. (1st edition, 1975; 2nd edition reprinted with corrections, 1985.)

Djohani, R. (1989). *Marine conservation development of Indonesia – coral reef policy. Recommendations and project concepts for the implementation of management of marine protected areas in Indonesia*. WWF Indonesia, Bogor, Indonesia. 113 pp.

FAO (1982). *National Conservation Plan for Indonesia, vol. 6. Sulawesi*. Field report of UNDP/FAO National Parks Development Project INS/78/061). FAO, Bogor, Indonesia.

Haugum, J., Ebner, J. and Racheli, T. (1980). *The Papillionidae of Celebes (Sulawesi)*. Lepidoptera Group of 1968, Supplement 9.

McCarthy, A.J. (comp.) (1991). *Conservation areas of Indonesia. Final draft*. World Conservation Monitoring Centre, Cambridge, U.K. in collaboration with Directorate General of Forest Protection and Nature Conservation (PHPA), Ministry of Forestry, Republic of Indonesia, and IUCN Commission on National Parks and Protected Areas, Gland, Switzerland.

Verstappen, H.Th. (1957). Some observations on karst development in the Malay Archipelago. *J. Trop. Geogr.* 14: 1–10.

Whitten, A.J., Muslimin Mustafa and Henderson, G.S. (1987). *The ecology of Sulawesi*. Gadjah Mada University Press, Yogyakarta. 777 pp.

Acknowledgements

This Data Sheet was written by Stephen D. Davis, based mainly on Whitten, Muslimin Mustafa and Henderson (1987).

ULTRAMAFIC FLORA OF SULAWESI
Sulawesi, Indonesia

Location: Large areas of ultramafic outcrops occur in central and south-eastern Sulawesi, including offshore islands of Buton and Wowoni, and the Talaud Islands.

Area: c. 12,000 km², of which 8500 km² is contiguous (the most extensive contiguous ultramafic outcrop in the world).

Altitude: Mostly lowland.

Vegetation: Mostly lowland forest and scrub, some montane vegetation.

Flora: Very poorly known. No reliable figures can be given for size of flora or level of endemism.

Useful plants: Plants of potential for rehabilitating degraded sites elsewhere.

Other values: Wildlife habitat.

Threats: Most areas intact, but many threatened by planned agricultural development.

Conservation: Most areas are outside the existing protected areas system, but have escaped clearance for agriculture due to poor soil conditions. Morowali Nature Reserve contains some ultramafic vegetation.

Geography

Central, south, and south-eastern Sulawesi contain the most extensive areas of ultramafic rock outcrops in the world (Whitten, Muslimin Mustafa and Henderson 1987; Proctor 1992). They cover at least 12,000 km², including parts of some offshore islands in the Buton complex to the south-east of the main island. They are mainly lowland. To the north-east of Sulawesi, ultramafic outcrops also occur on Gunung Piapi (690 m) in the Talaud Islands.

The rocks are largely composed of peridotite and serpentinite minerals. Soils are highly weathered, well-drained and of a reddish colour. Concentrations of heavy metals are relatively high.

Vegetation

The vegetation of ultramafic outcrops in the tropics has not been examined in any great detail, apart from studies undertaken in New Caledonia (see, for example, Jaffré and Veillon 1990) and at Gunung Silam in Sabah (Borneo) (Proctor *et al.* 1988, 1989). The reader is also referred to the Data Sheets on New Caledonia (CPD Site PO2) and the Ultramafic Flora of North-east Borneo (CPD Site SEA27) in this volume, and a recent overview on ultramafic vegetation in the tropical Far East by Proctor (1992). Much of the available information on ultramafic vegetation in Sulawesi concerns areas in Morowali Nature Reserve and outcrops around Soroake. Based on data available to the present authors, only sketches of the vegetation are possible for a few individual sites.

The high concentrations of metals such as magnesium and nickel, together with the relatively thin and nutrient-poor soils on ultramafic outcrops, result in a low, scrubby vegetation. Around Soroake, the forest consists of *Metrosideros* (ironwood), some *Agathis*, an abundance of *Calophyllum*, numerous Burseraceae and Sapotaceae, and at least two species of dipterocarp (*Hopea celebica* and a species of *Vatica*). The main canopy comprises Myrtaceae, such as *Eugenia*, *Kjellbergiodendron* and *Metrosideros*. The nutmegs, *Horsfieldia*, *Gymnacranthera* and *Knema* (including the endemic *K. celebica*), occur in the understorey (de Wilde 1981; Meijer 1984; van Balgooy and Tantra 1986).

On Mount Konde, west of Soroake, the forest has a closed canopy around 30–35 m high. No single family dominates; the most common large trees are species of *Eugenia*, *Ficus*, *Kjellbergiodendron*, *Lithocarpus* and *Santiria*. However, the ultramafic forest on the southern shores of Lake Matano is dominated by species of Myrtaceae (particularly *Metrosideros petiolata*). The forest here is mostly less than 15 m tall; among the tallest trees are *Gymnostoma sumatranum* (a she-oak) and *Terminalia supitiana* (a local endemic).

The forest at Batu Besi occurs on iron-rich ultramafic soils (Proctor 1992) and resembles some types of heath (kerangas) forests in Borneo. The forest is 10–15 m tall and consists of trees with straight trunks rarely exceeding 20 cm dbh. The forest has few climbers and epiphytes. The tallest trees are *Hopea celebica*, while *Austrobuxus nitida* is the most abundant species.

Lam (1927) describes the summit vegetation of Gunung Piapi (an ultramafic mountain reaching about 600 m altitude in the Talaud Islands) as remarkable. Even at 150 m, the vegetation resembles an alpine type, with a dense covering of grasses, ferns, sedges and orchids, a pandan (*Pandanus tectorius*) and occasional shrubs and small trees. Proctor (1992) provides a translation of Lam's account of the vegetation. The mountain was revisited in August 1991 (Proctor 1994 *et al.*). Although much of the vegetation is intact, the tall forests of lower slopes and surrounding areas are threatened by clearance for cultivation, and there is a potential risk of fire spreading into the vegetation of higher altitudes.

Flora

The ultramafic flora of Sulawesi is very poorly known. Botanical surveys are urgently needed. No figure can be given with any degree of certainty for the size of the flora or level of endemism. Some forests over ultramafic outcrops appear to be particularly rich in endemics, such as those around the Lake Matano area (van Balgooy and Tantra 1986).

Ultramafic vegetation contains a number of interesting myrmecophilous plants (ant-plants), such as *Myrmecodia* spp.

Useful plants

Some species found on ultramafic sites may have potential for rehabilitating degraded or polluted sites elsewhere, for example old mine workings. Some of the best colonizers and fastest growing trees on disturbed, and relatively flat, ultramafic sites appear to be species of *Alphitonia*, *Homalanthus* and *Callicarpa*, together with *Macaranga gigantea* and *Trema amboinensis*. On steep ground, the grass *Miscanthus sinensis* eventually forms a dense cover.

An ornamental shrub which could be useful for planting in gardens is the endemic gardenia, *Gardenia celebica* (W. Meijer, pers. comm. to Whitten, Muslimin Mustafa and Henderson 1987).

Social and environmental values

Little is known about the fauna of ultramafic outcrops in Sulawesi. However, available information indicates some interesting peculiarities (Whitten, Muslimin Mustafa and Henderson 1987). For example, a survey of birds around Soroake revealed that the ultramafic vegetation had the least number of species. However, 5 species, 3 of which are endemic to Sulawesi, are found only in ultramafic areas. Some species of flycatchers and starlings have a preference for ultramafic vegetation. Because of the brevity of the survey, and the lack off comparable data, no real conclusion about the relative importance of various sites can be drawn from the available records (Holmes and Wood 1980).

Threats

Ultramafic vegetation has suffered less disturbance and clearance than other lowland forest types because of the poor agricultural potential of the soils on which it occurs. However, Proctor (1992) reports that many ultramafic areas are designated by the Government of Indonesia for agricultural development.

Conservation

At present, very little lowland ultramafic vegetation occurs within the existing protected areas system. According to the National Conservation Plan for Indonesia (FAO 1982), existing reserves contained 230 km^2 of montane ultramafic forest (about 10% of the remaining total), whereas only 455 km^2 of lowland ultramafic forest (about 4% of the remaining total) occurred within protected areas.

Important areas of ultramafic vegetation are protected within Morowali Nature Reserve (Cagar Alam Morowali) (IUCN Management Category: I). The forest includes semi-deciduous lowland rain forest on ultramafic substrates, with *Calophyllum soulattri*, *Kjellbergiodendron celebicum*, *Gonystylus macrophyllus*, *Alstonia scholaris* and *Garcinia dulcis*, among other species. The reserve also includes forests on sandy substrates, and lower and upper montane forests (McCarthy 1991). According to Silvius and Djuharsa (1989), the majority of the lowland region within Morowali is threatened by logging.

References

Balgooy, M.M.J. van and Tantra, I.G.M. (1986). *The vegetation in two areas in Sulawesi*. Forest Research Bulletin (Special Edition), Bogor, Indonesia.

FAO (1982). *National Conservation Plan for Indonesia, vol. 6. Sulawesi*. Field report of UNDP/FAO National Parks Development Project INS/78/061). FAO, Bogor, Indonesia.

Holmes, P. and Wood, H. (1980). *The report of the Ornithological Expedition to Sulawesi 1979*. (Unpublished report.)

Jaffré, T. and Veillon, J.M. (1990). Etude floristique et structurale de deux forêts denses humides sur roches ultrabasiques en Nouvelle-Calédonie. *Bull. Mus. natn. Hist. nat., Paris*, 4e série, 12 (publ. 1991), section B, *Adansonia* 3–4: 243–273.

Lam, H.J. (1927). Een plantengeografisch Dorado. Handelingen. *IV Nederlandsch-Indisch natuurwetenschappelijk congres, Welteneden*. Pp. 386–397.

McCarthy, A.J. (comp.) (1991). *Conservation areas of Indonesia. Final draft*. World Conservation Monitoring Centre, Cambridge, U.K. in collaboration with Directorate General of Forest Protection and Nature Conservation (PHPA), Ministry of Forestry, Republic of Indonesia, and IUCN Commission on National Parks and Protected Areas, Gland, Switzerland.

Meijer, W. (1984). Botanical explorations in Celebes and Bali. *Nat. Geog. Soc. Rep.* 1976: 583–605.

Proctor, J. (1992). The vegetation over ultramafic rocks in the tropical far east. In Roberts, B.A. and Proctor, J. (eds), *The ecology of areas with serpentinized rocks. A world view*. Kluwer Academic Press, Dordrecht. Pp. 249–270.

Proctor, J., Fairweather, G.M., Balgooy, M.M.J. van, Nagy, L. and Reeves, R.D. (1994). "A plant geographical Dorado" revisited. (Unpublished manuscript to be submitted for publication.)

Proctor, J., Lee, Y.F., Langley, A.M., Munro, W.R.C. and Nelson, T. (1988). Ecological studies on Gunung Silam, a small ultrabasic mountain in Sabah, Malaysia. I: Environment, forest structure and floristics. *Journal of Ecology* 76: 320–340.

Proctor, J., Phillipps, C., Duff, G.K., Heaney, A. and Robertson, F.M. (1989). Ecological studies on Gunung Silam, a small ultrabasic mountain in Sabah, Malaysia. II: Some forest processes. *Journal of Ecology* 77: 317–331.

Silvius, M.J. and Djuharsa, E. (1989). Morowali, Indonesia. In Scott, D.A. (ed.), *A directory of Asian wetlands*. IUCN, Gland, Switzerland and Cambridge, U.K. Pp. 1061–1063.

Whitten, A.J., Muslimin Mustafa and Henderson, G.S. (1987). *The ecology of Sulawesi*. Gadjah Mada University Press, Yogyakarta. 777 pp.

Wilde, W.J.J.O. de (1981). Supplementary data on Malesian *Knema* (Myristicaceae), including three new taxa. *Blumea* 27: 223–234.

Acknowledgements

This Data Sheet was written by Dr John Proctor (University of Stirling, U.K.) and Stephen D. Davis.

PEGUNUNGAN LATIMOJONG
Sulawesi, Indonesia

Location: Northern part of the south-western peninsula of Sulawesi, about 60 km from the peninsula's eastern coast. The highest point (Mount Rantemario) is centred on latitude 3°23'S and longitude 120°02'E.

Area: c. 580 km².

Altitude: 1000–3455 m (summit of Mount Rantemario).

Vegetation: Mostly lower and upper montane rain forests; small area of hill forest on lower slopes; montane grasslands; subalpine vegetation.

Flora: Very poorly known; no estimates for size of the flora or level of endemism available.

Useful plants: Many ornamental shrubs and herbs.

Other values: Watershed protection; rich mammal and bird fauna.

Threats: Clearance of lower slopes for agriculture; mostly not threatened.

Conservation: Protection Forest (IUCN Management Category: IV); proposals have been made to strengthen protection to Cagar Alam (Nature Reserve) status.

Geography

Pegunungan Latimojong (the Latimojong Mountains) are located in the north-western part of the south-western peninsula of Sulawesi, about 60 km inland from Teluk Bone (Bone Bay). The range includes Mount Rantemario (centred on latitude 3°23'S and longitude 120°02'E), Sulawesi's highest mountain (3455 m). The mountains are largely unexplored.

Vegetation

Pristine montane forests cover the upper slopes of the range. In places, the lower slopes have been cleared for cultivation. For example, the lower slopes of south-west Mount Rantemario have been cleared up to 1650 m, where lower montane forest begins. No extensive botanical studies have been made. The following is a brief sketch of the vegetation on Mount Rantemario (based on the account in Whitten, Muslimin Mustafa and Henderson 1987).

Lower montane forest includes *Lithocarpus* (oaks) and the conifers *Phyllocladus hypophyllus*, *Podocarpus steupi* and *Taxus sumatrana*. Elements of upper montane forest are found from about 2150 m, although lower montane forest elements still dominate at that altitude. Upper montane forest proper occurs above 2650 m. It includes members of the Ericaceae, such as *Vaccinium* and *Rhododendron*, along with *Phyllocladus hypophyllus*. Nearly pure stands of the endemic yellow-orange flowered *Rhododendron vanvuurenii* can be found in fire-generated grassland (Sleumer 1966–1967). The bright yellow-flowered *Hypericum leschenaultii* also occurs in upper montane forest, along with *Drimys piperata* and a giant moss (*Dawsonia* sp.). The first subalpine herbs, such as *Gentiana laterifolia*, occur above 2650 m, although the subalpine zone proper begins at around 3200 m. At 3000 m, on the south-western slopes of Mount

Rantemario, the endemic tree fern *Cyathea pallidipaleata* occurs.

Subalpine vegetation includes species of *Decaspermum*, *Hedyotis* and *Rhododendron*, shrubby *Gaultheria* and *Styphelia*, the composite *Keysseria*, *Alpinia* (a relative of ginger), *Viola kjellbergii*, *Potentilla leuconata* and *P. parvus*. Locally, along streamsides, montane grasslands include club mosses (*Lycopodium* spp.) and sedges, along with such herbs as *Swertia* spp. and *Epilobium prostratum*. Cushion plants occur on biotite schists. Among the species present are *Centrolepis philippinensis*, *Monostachys oreoboloides*, *Eriocaulon celebicum* and *Oreobolus ambiguus*.

Flora

The flora is very poorly known and no estimates for the size of the flora or level of endemism are available. A brief botanical expedition in 1981 collected 57 high-altitude species on Mount Rantemario, of which more than 10% were new to science, while others were known from only one or two previous collections (Smith 1981; van Steenis and Veldkamp 1984). The flora has some Australasian affinities (Smith 1981). More botanical surveys are needed throughout Pegunungan Latimojong, as well as on other mountains in Sulawesi.

Useful plants

The montane flora contains many ornamental flowering shrubs and herbs of potential value in horticulture. In particular, there are many showy species of *Rhododendron*, particularly the endemic *R. vanvuurenii*, and the yellow-flowered *Hypericum leschenaultii*, described as "the jewel" of the mountain flora in Java (van Steenis 1972). Among the subalpine flora are ornamental species of *Gentiana* and *Potentilla*.

Social and environmental values

The forests are vital for the protection of watersheds and prevention of soil erosion. This function is recognized by the area's status as a Protection Forest (see Conservation).

The forests are largely unexplored but they are suspected to have a rich bird and mammal fauna.

Threats

The main threat is from clearance of the lower slopes for agriculture. The south-western slopes of Mount Rantemario have already been cleared for cultivation up to about 1650 m (Whitten, Muslimin Mustafa and Henderson 1987). However, most of the montane forests are still intact and are not threatened.

Conservation

Pegunungan Latimojong was designated a Protection Forest (IUCN Management Category: IV) in 1940. Proposals have been made to strengthen its protection to Cagar Alam (Nature Reserve) status.

References

Sleumer, H. (1966-1967). Ericaceae. *Flora Malesiana I*, 7: 265–403. Flora Malesiana Foundation, Leiden, The Netherlands.

Smith, J.M.B. (1981). *Vegetation and flora of Gunung Rantemario, Latimojong Range, Sulawesi (Celebes)*. (Unpublished report.)

Steenis, C.G.G.J. van (1972). *The mountain flora of Java*. Brill, Leiden. 90 pp.

Steenis, C.G.G.J. van and Veldkamp, J. (1984). Miscellaneous botanical notes XXVII. *Blumea* 29: 399–408.

Whitten, A.J., Muslimin Mustafa and Henderson, G.S. (1987). *The ecology of Sulawesi*. Gadjah Mada University Press. 777 pp.

Acknowledgements

This Data Sheet was written by Stephen D. Davis, based mainly on Whitten, Muslimin Mustafa and Henderson (1987).

BATAN ISLANDS
Batanes, Philippines

Location: 10 small islands and 13 islets at the northern tip of the Philippines, at latitude 20°30'N and longitude 121°50'E.

Area: 209 km².

Altitude: 0–1008 m (summit of Mount Iraya).

Vegetation: Lowland evergreen rain forest, mid-montane forest, summit grassland, beach forest, secondary forest and man-made pastures.

Flora: Estimated >500 vascular plant species; of which 16 species (c. 3%) are endemic to Batanes, at least 47 species (c. 9%) are endemic to Batanes and neighbouring Babuyan Islands, and 110 species (c. 22%) are endemic to the Philippines as a whole.

Useful plants: Many species used by local people to provide construction materials, clothing, food and medicines.

Other values: Home of Ivatans, high landscape quality, rich fauna.

Threats: Typhoons, forest clearance for cattle grazing and crops, shifting cultivation (kaingin), over-exploitation of forest products.

Conservation: Revised Fisheries Code (Presidential Decree 704) and Revised Forestry Code (Presidential Decree 705) provide limited protection of forested lands; the Batanes Islands are currently being proposed for inclusion in the National Integrated Protected Area System under IUCN Management Category: V (Protected Landscape and Seascape); proposal to designate Mt Iraya and Mt Matarem as "critical watersheds".

Geography

The Batan Islands are a group of 10 small islands and 13 islets with a total area of approximately 209 km², located at the northernmost part of the Philippines, and bounded by the Bashi Channel in the north, the Pacific Ocean on the east, the Balintang Channel in the south, and the China Sea in the west. The islands form the province of Batanes. The location is latitude 20°30'N and longitude 121°50'E.

The inhabited islands are Batan, Itbayat, Sabtang and Ibuhos. The uninhabited islands are Mavolis (Yami), Ditarem (Mavudis), Misanga (North Island), Siayan, San Diego (Dinem) and Dequey. Batan is the most densely populated island and has four towns, namely: Basco (the provincial capital), Mahatao, Ivana and Uyugan. The island has two mountains: Mount Matarem and Mount Iraya, an extinct volcano, which rises to about 1008 m.

The topography ranges from flat to rolling hills and steep mountainsides. Itbayat comprises rolling grasslands, with Mount Santa Rosa (277 m) in the north of the island and Mount Riposet (229 m) in the south. Sabtang Island has higher mountains with sharp ridges on its southern and western sides. Mount Alapad (347 m) and Mt Tungaru (346 m) dominate the landscape. Soils vary throughout the islands from loam to silt and clay loans (Simon and de Jesus 1974).

There is a very pronounced wet season, with cyclonic (summer rains) and north-east monsoonal rains. The average annual rainfall is 2918 mm. The annual number of rainy days per year is 202. The average annual temperature is around 25.7°C. The coolest months are December to February. Batanes is within the typhoon belt and often experiences strong winds (Kintanar 1985).

Vegetation

There are 6 distinct habitat types: beach forest, secondary forest and man-made pastures, lowland evergreen rain forest, mid-montane forest and summit grassland. Agricultural lands are found in and around the towns of Basco and Mahatao. About 64% of the land area of Batanes is classified as forest land.

The vegetation of Mount Iraya, Batan Island, includes lowland evergreen rain forest (200–500 m), lower montane rain forest (500–800 m) and grassland (800–1008 m). Forests cover about 50–60% of the land area of Mount Iraya and approximately 30–40% of Mount Matarem. Secondary forests are found on the western fringes of the latter; communal forests are found in ravines.

The general low stature of forest trees of Mt Iraya, and other mountains in Batanes, can be attributed to the effect of the strong typhoons that frequently occur in the province. The Batanes Socio-Economic Profile in 1988 determined that there are 135 km² of forest land in Batanes. Of these, 56 km² are reforested areas, 3 km² are grasslands and require reforestation, 12 km² are protection areas for watersheds, 3 km² are under pasture lease agreements, 1 km² are production forests, and the remainder are designated for other uses, including municipal forest parks.

The forests of Itbayat have been mostly converted to grassland or agricultural land. A few fragmented primary forests remain. Secondary forests are found in abandoned kaingin clearings. Mount Riposet in the south-western part of the island is totally cleared of trees and is now covered by rolling grasslands. Mount Santa Rosa, in the north of the island, is almost without forest cover except on its western slopes.

Sabtang Island is almost entirely bare of trees except on steep ridge slopes. A large part of the island is covered with grasslands of *Imperata cylindrica*, *Saccharum spontaneum* and *Themeda* spp. The rest of the area is cultivated, mainly by kaingin agriculturalists. On the rolling hills in the western part of the island there are patches of the endemic palm *Phoenix hanceana* var. *philippinensis* (Gruezo and Fernando 1985). Ibahos and Dequey Islands are mainly grasslands. Some native pandans and palm trees are found in coastal areas. Small patches of forests occur on the islands of Diogo, Mabudis, Maysanga and Siaya. The rest of the islets are almost devoid of trees.

Flora

The flora of the Batan Islands (Hatusima 1966) includes more than 500 vascular plant species, of which Quisumbing (undated) reported that at least 47 species are endemic to Batanes and the Babuyan Islands (a group of islands to the south of Batanes). 16 species (c. 3% of the total vascular flora) are endemic to Batanes (based on Merrill 1926) and 110 species (c. 22%) are endemic to the Philippines as a whole. Although these figures will inevitably change as a result of taxonomic changes and botanical exploration in the region, they nevertheless indicate that the level of local and regional species endemism is high considering the total land area involved. Rare and threatened species are: *Lilium philippinensis*, *Schefflera octophylla*, *Astronia luzoniensis* and *Persea thunbergii*.

Despite its location, the flora of Batanes is (surprisingly) not closely related to that of Taiwan (Quisumbing, undated; Merrill 1926) because connections between the Philippines and Taiwan, and the rest of South East Asia, were broken in the early Tertiary period. There are about 37 species of flowering plants which are found exclusively in Taiwan and the Philippines (Merrill 1926). Of these, the following are among those that occur in Batanes: *Bergia serrata*, *Illigera luzonensis*, *Gynura elliptica*, *Gaultheria cumingiana*, *Isanthera discolor*, *Callicarpa formosana*, *Scutellaria luzonica*, *Ainslea reflexa*, *Dicksonia smithii* and *Aglaia formosana*. Some of these species may have been disseminated by wind or birds.

On Batan Island, the forests on the lower slopes of Mount Matarem appear to be richer in species than those on Mount Iraya. Several species appear to be common on Mount Matarem, but are absent or rarely found on Mount Iraya. Notable examples include *Ardisia confertiflora* and *Ficus nitida* subsp. *nitida*. The former species is endemic to Batan Island.

Useful plants

Quisumbing (undated) lists 9 species of useful trees in Batan Island and the Babuyan Islands. A number of plants have been utilized by local people for a variety of purposes. Some of the indigenous species which the inhabitants of Batanes Islands use for vegetables are *Elatostema* spp., *Athyrium esculentum*, *Helminthostachys zeylanica*, *Cycas circinalis*, *Gnetum gnemon*, *Schizostachyum diffusum*, *Bambusa* spp., *Diplodiscus paniculatus* and *Pometia pinnata*.

The local Ivatan use the leaves of palms and bananas for making yakul and kanai, while the leaves of the threatened endemic palm *Phoenix hanceana* var. *philippinensis* are made into hats, cloaks and raincoats. *Pipturus arborescens* is used for ropes.

Toona calantas (cedar) is used for building houses and making chests, while *Artocarpus* spp. are used for flooring and planking, and *Miscanthus sinensis* for roofing and ceiling materials.

Chrysanthemum indicum is one of many medicinal plants harvested from the wild. It is used to relieve pain from fractures.

Social and environmental values

The population of Batanes in 1990 was 15,026 (National Statistics Office records). During the last decade, population growth was 2.2% per annum. The local Ivatan are of Malayan and mixed Malayan-Papuan descent (Hornedo 1976).

The islands have a rich fauna, including a number of endemic species of birds. Some of the shore birds present are shearwaters, frigatebirds, herons, hawks, eagles, buzzards, falcons, plovers, sandpipers, terns, noddies and kingfishers.

Batanes is a popular destination for tourists and hikers, offering attractive coastal scenery. Broad U-shaped valleys are a feature of the eastern side of Batan and Itbayat, and wave-cut cliffs, sea caves and secluded white sandy beaches are common alluring sights throughout the islands. Batanes is also famous for its distinctive architecture.

Threats

The forests of Batanes are threatened by clearance for cattle grazing and agricultural crops. Being isolated from the rest of the Philippines, the local people have come to rely on products derived from the forests. There is a danger that this could lead to over-exploitation, especially as the proximity of Taiwan invites illegal trade in natural products. Already, ornamental plants, such as *Podocarpus costalis* and *P. polystachyus*, are being depleted as a result of export trade. Those on Itbayat, for example, are dug up and sent to Batan Island, Luzon, or exported to Taiwan.

Typhoons and strong winds have modified the vegetation to a low stature forest. Heavy rains cause soil erosion problems in pasture lands on hills where there is only a thin cover of grasses and sedges.

Conservation

The revised Fisheries Code (Presidential Decree 704) and Revised Forestry code (Presidential Decree 705) provide limited protection of forests lands.

The Batan Islands are currently being proposed for inclusion in the National Integrated Protected Areas System (Integrated Protected Areas System 1991) under the IUCN Management Category: V (Protected Landscape and Seascape). Though its declaration as a protected area under such a category does not ensure the abatement of (public) forest land conversion, it would, nevertheless, promote sustainable development which would benefit the local inhabitants, and would impose strict controls on illegal activities. Effective management of the protected area may be hampered by the geographic isolation of the islands and inadequate transportation and communication facilities.

Environmental consciousness among the local people has been noticeably increasing in recent years. For example, there has been a drive to replant forest trees for firewood and lumber. Critical watersheds at Mount Iraya and Mount Matarem are also being proposed for forest-land status. An area of 12 km² already serves as a protection area for watersheds, and 5.8 ha are municipal forest parks. The local population appreciate the value of retaining forest cover to protect their water supplies and to supply them with forest products. This awareness is an encouraging basis for developing sustainable ways of using the forests whilst ensuring the protection of the flora.

References

Gruezo, W.S. and Fernando, E.S. (1985). Notes on *Phoenix hanceana* var. *philippinensis* in the Batanes Islands, Philippines. *Principes* 29(4): 170–176.

Hatusima, S. (1966). An enumeration of the plants of Batan Islands, northern Philippines. *Mem. Fac. Agric. Kagoshima Univ.* 5: 13–70.

Hornedo, F.H. (1976). *Batanes ethnographic history: a survey.* Ateneo de Manila, Philippines.

Integrated Protected Areas System (1991). *Integrated protected areas system technical report: Batanes biogeographic area.* WWF-UPSRF-FSDI.

Kintanar, R. (1985). *Climate of the Philippines.* PAGASA, Quezon City, Philippines.

Merrill, E.D. (1908). On a collection of plants from the Batanes and Babuyanes Islands. *Philippines Journal of Science* 3(6): 385–442.

Merrill, E.D. (1926). *Enumeration of Philippine flowering plants, (Vol. 4).* Bureau of Printing, Manila, Philippines.

Quisumbing, E. (undated). *The vegetation of Batan and Babuyan Islands.* (Unpublished report.)

Simon, A. and Jesus, F. de (1974). *Soil survey of Batanes Province.* Soil Report No. 40, Department of Agriculture and Natural Resources, Manila, Philippines.

Acknowledgements

This Data Sheet was written by Dr Domingo A. Madulid (Botany Division, National Museum, Manila, Philippines).

MOUNT APO
Mindanao, Philippines

Location: Southern part of the Central Cordillera of Mindanao, at latitude 6°59'N and longitude 125°12'E.

Area: 769 km².

Altitude: c. 500–2954 m.

Vegetation: Lowland primary forest (mostly cleared for cultivation), secondary forest, lower and upper montane forests, "elfin woodland", scrub and summit grassland.

Flora: Estimated >800 vascular plant species; local endemics.

Useful plants: Ornamental plants, especially orchids, begonias, aroids and ferns; gene pool of timber trees.

Other values: Home for six ethnic tribes; endangered fauna, e.g. Philippines eagle; high landscape quality.

Threats: Construction of geothermal plant, conversion to agricultural land, illegal and indiscriminate logging, kaingin activities.

Conservation: National Park (IUCN Management Category: II).

Geography

Mount Apo, an extinct volcano, is the highest peak in the Philippines, reaching 2954 m above sea-level. It is located in the southern part of the Central Cordillera of Mindanao (the Bukidnon-Davao Cordillera). This extends across the entire island from Diwata and Sipaca Points in the north to Sarangani Bay in the south.

The northern and north-eastern slopes of Mount Apo and neighbouring mountains are gradual, but those on the west descend abruptly to Cotabato Valley and those on the east abruptly to the lowlands of Davao. The south-eastern slope is bisected by the Marawin and Sibulan rivers. At 2400 m, there is a flat, plateau-like area which covers 6–7 km² and a cone of about 500 m in height. The north-eastern slopes of Mount Apo drain into the Davao and Talo rivers and their tributaries.

Mount Apo belongs to the Carmen Formation, which includes sequences of volcanic flows, shallow marine deposits of poorly consolidated tuffaceous sandstone and claystone, with interbedded conglomerates, basalt and andesite of Pleistocene age. The soils of the lower eastern slopes belong to the Tugbok Series, comprising brown to reddish-brown clays derived from the weathering of volcanic andesitic rocks. Those on the southern slopes belong to the Miral Series, derived from a mixture of igneous rocks and consolidated gravelly sand. The soils of the south-western lower slopes belong to the Kidapawan Series, developed mainly from andesitic igneous rocks. The upper slopes and summit of Mount Apo consist of a mixture of igneous and metamorphic rocks.

Mount Apo is one of the wettest places in the Philippines, with a mean annual rainfall of 2500 mm. The climate is slightly seasonal, with May to October being the wettest months. Temperatures range from 4° to 21°C, with 15°C being the average.

Vegetation

Forests extend up to 2700 m and cover about 50 km². The lower slopes, between 300 and 500 m, have been cleared for crops, including both lowland and upland varieties of rice, cassava and bananas. Durians (*Durio zibethinus*) and coconuts are often planted in gardens. Secondary woodland develops in areas not utilized for cultivation.

Primary rain forest occurs at 1000–1600 m, and includes the dipterocarps *Hopea plagata*, *Shorea guiso* and *Dipterocarpus grandiflorus*, along with species of *Cinnamomum*, *Lithocarpus* (Elmer 1910b), *Homalanthus* and *Musa*. The forests are festooned with epiphytes, the most abundant of which are ferns (e.g. Polypodiaceae, Aspleniaceae, Davalliaceae) and orchids (e.g. *Vanda sanderiana*, Endangered, and endemic to Mount Apo). The understorey consists of dipterocarps, tree ferns (*Cyathea*) and palms (*Areca*). Ferns, begonias, orchids and aroids occur in the ground layer.

With increasing altitude, *Angiopteris*, tree ferns, pandans and rattans (e.g. species of *Calamus* and *Daemonorops*) become abundant, while among the larger trees are *Shorea almon*, *S. polysperma* and *Lithocarpus* spp. There are prominent stands of the endemic *Agathis philippinensis* up to 1830 m.

Montane forest occurs above c. 2000 m and includes species of *Lithocarpus*, *Cinnamomum*, *Melastoma*, *Caryota*, *Calamus*, *Ficus*, *Agathis* and many Lauraceae (Elmer 1910a). Epiphytes abound; the forest and forest floor are clothed in lichens, bryophytes, begonias, orchids, aroids, *Selaginella* and *Nephrolepis* ferns. At 2400 m, the trees take on a stunted appearance and the vegetation is more open ("elfin woodland"). Scrub thickets occur above 2700 m on the steep walls of fumaroles, and include sedges, Cyperaceae and the fern *Gleichenia decarpa*. Ericaceae, such as species of *Rhododendron* and *Vaccinium*, are abundant here (Elmer 1911).

Flora

There are estimated to be more than 800 vascular plant species, and an abundance of bryophytes. For example, Schoenig *et al.* (1975) collected more than 30 species of cryptogams.

Among Mount Apo endemics collected between 300 and 1000 m are members of the genera *Pipturus*, *Saurauia* and *Poikilospermum*, as well as *Homalanthus populneus*, *Elephantopus spicatus*, *Piper apoanum* and *Vanda sanderiana* (the latter may possibly be extinct in the wild) (Madulid and Agoo 1991). Endemics at mid-altitudes include *Agathis philippinensis* (also found in upper montane forest on Mount Apo), *Lithocarpus submunticolus* (Endangered) and *Peperomia elmeri* (Endangered). Upper montane forest endemics are *Cypholopus microphyllus* and *Nepenthes copelandii*.

Social and environmental values

Mount Apo is a majestic mountain with spectacular scenery which makes it a popular destination for adventure tourism and hiking. Hiking to the summit usually takes four days from the Kidapawan side. However, the construction of a service road to the geothermal site has made access easier. Apart from its lush vegetation and diverse wildlife, the attractions of Mount Apo include several hot springs and lakes (including Agko Blue Lake at 1200 m and three summit lakes), the sulphurous volcanic cone, Marbel River (with its milky white water), several waterfalls, including Todaya Falls on the eastern flank, and the semi-circular summits of Mount Talomo and Mount Sibulan.

Six ethnic tribes live in the area. Mount Apo is a sacred place for the 450,000 Lumad tribal people and is their last remaining home.

The fauna of Mount Apo includes several threatened animals. Mount Apo falls within two Endemic Bird Areas (EBAs) (one lowland and one highland EBA) which cover Mindanao. Seven lowland and 24 highland restricted-range birds occur on Mount Apo respectively making it a very important site. The Mount Apo National Park also harbours a small population of the highly threatened, Philippines eagle (*Pithecophaga jeffreyi*).

Threats

A major threat is the planned construction of a geothermal power station. If this proceeds it could lead to the development of settlements, commercial areas and cultivated lands around the plant. Already roads have been built to allow access to drill sites.

At present, there are more than 7000 families occupying c. 258 km² within the park. Much of this area is used for shifting cultivation, which is itself another major threat. Illegal logging, and the increase of squatters who pan for gold, are also threats to the park.

Conservation

Mount Apo has long been a focus for botanical and zoological expeditions. The first attempt at the summit was in 1859. However, it was not until the third expedition in 1880, undertaken by Don Joaquin Rajal, Dr Joseph Montano and Father Gisbert, that the summit was reached and the first biological specimens collected (Bernard 1959). Subsequently, there have been many botanical and zoological expeditions (see, for example, Schoenig 1984; Schoenig *et al.* 1974, 1975).

Mount Apo was declared a reserved forest and National Park in 1936. The park is now under the management of the Protected Areas and Wildlife Bureau (DENR). Mount Apo has been listed in the ASEAN List of Critical Areas for Conservation.

References

Bernard, M.A. (1959). The ascent of Mt Apo, 1859–1958. *Philippine Studies* 7(1): 7–67.

Department of Environment and Natural Resources (1987). *Five year development plan for Mt Pulog, Mt Apo and Mt Iglit-Baco National Parks*. Quezon City, Philippines. (Unpublished manuscript.)

Elmer, A.D.E. (1910a). Lauraceae from Mt Apo and Mt Giting-giting. *Leafl. Philippines Botany* 2(41): 703–728.

Elmer, A.D.E. (1910b). The oaks of Mt Apo. *Leafl. Philippines Botany* 3(52): 935–946.

Elmer, A.D.E. (1911). The Ericaceae of Mt Apo. *Leafl. Philippines Botany* 3(59): 1089–1107.

Lewis, R.E. (undated). *The status of Mt Apo and other national parks in the Philippines*. 14 pp. (Unpublished manuscript.)

Madulid, D.A. and Agoo, E.M.G. (1991). Conservation status of rare and endangered Philippine plants, III. *Vanda sanderiana* Reichb. f. *National Museum Papers* (Manila).

Schoenig, E. (1984). Mt Apo revisited. *Philippine Scientist* 21: 172–174.

Schoenig, E., Plateros, C., Colina, A. and Jumalon, J. (1974). Mt Apo expedition: a preliminary report. *Philippine Scientist* 11: 32–97.

Schoenig, E., Plateros, C., Colina, A. and Jumalon, J. (1975). Mt Apo expedition: a botanical and ethnological survey. *Philippine Scientist* 12: 32–59.

Acknowledgements

This Data Sheet was written by Dr Domingo A. Madulid (Botany Division, National Museum, Manila, Philippines).

MOUNT PULOG
Luzon, Philippines

Location: Southern part of Cordillera Central, Benguet Province, Luzon, at latitude 16°35'N and longitude 120°53'E.

Area: 115.5 km².

Altitude: 2929 m (the highest mountain in Luzon).

Vegetation: Montane forest, pine forest, summit grassland, secondary grasslands in lowlands.

Flora: Estimated 800 vascular plant species; many local endemics; affinities with the flora of temperate continental Asia and Australasia.

Useful plants: Important potential source of forest tree provenances, especially of pines; ornamental plants.

Other values: High landscape value, archaeological importance, tourism, watershed protection, rich fauna.

Threats: Natural and man-made fires, conversion of forest to vegetable and cut-flower gardens.

Conservation: National Park (IUCN Management Category: VII), declared in 1987.

Geography

Mount Pulog is an extinct volcano in north-eastern Benguet, Luzon. It reaches a height of 2929 m, making it the highest mountain in Luzon, and covers an area of 115.5 km². Its geographical location is latitude 16°35'N and longitude 120°53'E.

The cone comprises Quaternary volcanics of igneous origin. The rim and upper slopes are very steep, and are thought to have been developed from eruptions during the late Pliocene to early Pleistocene. The lava flows consist of andesite and dacite interbedded with pyroclastics. The mountain has fine-loamy to clayey soils which have only a low to moderate fertility.

The mean annual rainfall ranges from 3600 to 4500 mm (which is much higher than adjacent areas). Heavy rainfall occurs during June to November; January to April are drier months. Frosts occur on the summit in January.

Vegetation

The area below 1200 m is mainly secondary grassland, primarily of *Themeda triandra*. A few broadleaved shrubs and small trees occur in moist ravines and gullies. Settlements and agricultural lands are extensive in this zone, e.g. around Babadak. The lower fringes of pine forest have also been converted to farmlands for the cultivation of vegetables and cut-flowers. Cattle grazing occurs on less rugged slopes. Lake Babadak, used as a water source for the settlers in this area, is the habitat for *Callitriche* spp., *Scirpus mucronatus* and *Eleocharis retroflexa*.

At an altitude of 1000 m, pine forests occur along river banks. An almost pure stand of pines (*Pinus insularis*) occurs from 1000 to 2000 m. In gullies and stream depressions, broadleaved trees and shrubs are intermixed with the pines. Typical trees and shrubs are *Pipturus asper*, *Melicope luzonensis*, *Bischofia javanica*, *Mallotus ricinoides*, *Acalypha stipulacea*, *Ficus hauili* and *Pittosporum pentandrum*. Ferns,

herbaceous plants, and woody species, such as *Saurauia elegans*, *Vaccinium benguetense*, *Itea macrophylla* and *Wendlandia glabrata*, are found in ravines at higher altitudes.

Pine forests and grasslands cover extensive tracts as a result of fire. *Pinus insularis* occurs as a pioneer in drier areas especially on bare soils. Seedlings of other forest species later colonize these areas beneath the cover of pines; however, man-made and natural fires kill many of the flowering plant species, while sparing the adult pine trees. As a result, pines may often occur in pure stands. Jacobs (1972) regarded pine forest on Mount Pulog as a regeneration stage of montane forest. He based this observation on *Pinus merkusii* in northern Sumatra which he believed behaved similarly to *P. insularis*.

The transition zone between the pine and montane forests occurs at about 2000 m. Most of the trees in transitional montane forest are irregularly shaped and short, but some reach a height of 15–30 m. The upper storey comprises *Symplocos* spp., *Leptospermum* spp., and *Quercus* spp., among others. The understorey includes *Debregeasia longifolia*, *Daphne luzonica*, *Aralia hypoleuca* and *Polyosma philippinensis*. Mosses and lichens cover the trunks of these trees in damp areas. Epiphytic ferns and orchids are also abundant. At its upper limit, montane forest comprises shrubby vegetation, mainly of *Rhododendron subsessile*, *R. taxifolium* and *Anaphalis* spp., and is gradually replaced by grassland.

Above 2600 m, summit grassland includes 37 species of grasses, along with a few mosses, scale-mosses and lichens. This type of vegetation covers approximately 20 km². Among the grasses found here are *Agrostis elmeri*, *Deschampsia flexuosa*, *Deyeuxia stenophylla*, *Hierochloë horsfieldii*, *Isachne kunthiana*, *Miscanthus* spp. and *Monostachya oroboloides*. Species of *Gentiana* and *Gnaphalium* are common. The dominant grass is *Yushania niitikayamensis*, which usually grows to a height of 1–3 m. In areas where montane vegetation has been burned, bamboos are often found. Small marshland areas also occur, and include such species as *Monostachya* spp. and *Haloragis* spp.

Flora

There are an estimated 800 vascular plant species on Mount Pulog, including many local endemics. Merrill and Merritt (1910) list 57 bryophyte species, 91 fern species, 3 gymnosperms and 377 flowering plant species for Mount Pulog. Of these, 19 bryophytes, 30 ferns, 1 gymnosperm and 174 angiosperms are listed as Philippine endemics. Although these figures are out of date, they give some indication of the level of endemism in the flora, but need to be treated with caution as a result of taxonomic changes.

Approximately 23% of the total number of genera represented in the flora are endemic to Mount Pulog and its vicinities. Some of these are: *Merrilliobryum, Curania, Aniselytron, Monostachya, Cleistoloranthus* and *Loheria*.

The flora of Mount Pulog has affinities with those of temperate continental Asia, Australasia and, to some extent, Peninsular Malaysia (although dipterocarps, pandans and palms are notably absent from Mount Pulog). *Carex graeffeana, Kyllinga intermedia, Schoenus apogon, S. axillaris* and *Uncinia rupestris* are among the Australasian elements; *Taxus wallichiana, Pinus insularis* and *Yushania niitakayamensis* are Asiatic elements.

Useful plants

Mount Pulog is an important potential source of forest tree provenances, especially of pines.

Jacobs (1974) notes several decorative species, including *Begonia merrittii* and *Daphne luzonica*.

Social and environmental values

Kabayan, which is at the eastern lower part of Mount Pulog, is a popular destination for both local and foreign tourists. The caves are the traditional burial grounds of the native people. Mount Pulog, being the highest peak in Luzon and the second highest mountain in the Philippines, is a favourite destination for mountain trekking.

Among the notable animals which occur on Mount Pulog are the cloud rat (*Crageromys shadenbergii*), which is a near-endemic, the swift *Collocalia whiteheadi*, flycatchers (*Rhipidura cyaniceps, Cryptolopha nigrorum* and *Eumyias nigrimentalis*), bullfinches (*Pyrrhula leicogenys, Prioniturus montanus* and *Brachypteryx poliogyna*) and, in the lower grasslands, fruit thrushes (*Iole gularis*) and silvereyes (*Zopterops whiteheadi*).

The montane forests of Pulog protect fragile mountain slopes from erosion. They also protect an important water catchment area for towns in the lowlands.

Threats

The lower slopes of Mount Pulog are densely populated in places and most of the forest has been cleared for cultivation. Cattle raising also occurs in the lowlands.

Forest fires are a natural occurrence within pine forests. However, the fires often spare adult trees while destroying the undergrowth. Man-made fires, for forest clearance or burning grasslands, are a threat to primary montane forests, especially where grasses have already penetrated into the forests.

Regeneration of the forest after burning can be hampered by aggressive invading species of grasses which compete with, and prevent, the growth of tree seedlings. As a result, slopes are left vulnerable to erosion.

Conservation

Expeditions to Mount Pulog have been undertaken since the early 1900s. The earliest of these expeditions was undertaken by E.B. Copeland and E.D. Merrill in 1905. The first ascent of the mountain itself was by Charles Benson. Later, botanical expeditions were made by H.M. Curran, M.L. Merritt, T.C. Zschokie, E.B. Copeland, E.D. Merrill and others. In 1968, Marius Jacobs visited the mountain and strong recommendations for conservation were subsequently made by the National Museum of the Philippines and the Rijksherbarium, Leiden (Jacobs 1972, 1974, and undated).

It was not until 1987 that Mount Pulog was declared a National Park. However, its exact boundaries have not yet been clearly established. Management zones are being proposed. The pine forests, montane forests and summit grasslands are recommended as strict conservation zones. The grassland areas of the lower slopes are proposed as buffer zones, since they are already disturbed and settlers have already established themselves there.

References

Jacobs, M. (1972). *The plant world on Luzon's highest mountains*. Rijksherbarium, Leiden, The Netherlands. 32 pp.

Jacobs, M. (1974). Luzon's highest mountains – conservation proposed. *Environmental Conservation* 1(3): 232–233.

Jacobs, M. (undated). *Luzon's highest mountains National Park, a proposal for conservation elaborated*. Rijksherbarium, Leiden, The Netherlands. 10 pp. (Mimeographed.)

Kintanar, R.L. (1984). *Climate of the Philippines*. PAGASA, Quezon City, Philippines.

McGregor, R.C. (1905). Birds from Pauai and Mt. Pulog, Subprovince of Benguet, Luzon. *Philippine Journal of Science* 5: 135–138.

Mendoza, D.R. and Jacbos, M. (1968). A preliminary report of the botanical exploration of Mt Pulog and Tabayoc, Kabayan, Benguet and the Sierra Madre Mountain Ranges of Dingalan and Baler, Quezon. *Proceedings of the 1968 National Science and Technology Week, Part 3*. Pp. 411–439.

Merrill, E.D. and Merritt, M.L. (1910). The flora of Mount Pulog. *Philippine Journal of Science* 5: 287–403.

Panot, I.A. (1983). Floristic composition of Mt Pulog. *Canopy* 6.

Acknowledgements

This Data Sheet was written by Dr Domingo A. Madulid (Botany Division, National Museum, Manila, Philippines).

PALANAN WILDERNESS AREA
Luzon, Philippines

Location: Palanan Wilderness Area is located in the central part of the Sierra Madre on the eastern side of Luzon in the province of Isabela.

Area: 2168 km².

Altitude: 0–1672 m (summit of Mount Cresta).

Vegetation: Predominantly lowland and hill evergreen rain forests, with lower montane rain forest, forest over limestone, forest over ultramafic rocks, mangroves, beach forest.

Flora: Estimated 1500 vascular plant species, of which it is estimated that more than 50 species are locally endemic and over 100 species are endemic to the Philippines.

Useful plants: Timber trees, rattans.

Other values: Rich fauna, including 84 species of birds of which 29 are endemic to the Philippines; home to indigenous Negritoes; watershed protection; high landscape quality; potential for tourism.

Threats: Expansion of towns, shifting cultivation, over-collection of plants and plant products, selective logging; potential threats are large-scale commercial logging, mining, road-building.

Conservation: Declared as a Wilderness Area; currently proposed as a National Park under the Integrated Protected Areas System for the Philippines.

Geography

Palanan Wilderness Area covers 2168 km² of the eastern side of Isabela Province in the central part of the Sierra Madre mountain range in Luzon. It is bounded on the north by the Dikatayan River, on the south by the Disabungan River, on the west by the Cagayan Valley, and on the east by the Philippine Sea. The towns of Palanan and Divilacan, and portions of the towns of Maconacon, Tumawuini, Ilagan, San Mariano and Dinapigue occur within the boundaries of the Wilderness Area. The area encompasses all forested lands within a 45 km arc from Palanan Point (latitude 17°08'N, longitude 122°30'E).

The highest peaks are Mount Cresta (1672 m), Mt Divilacan (1311 m) and Mt Palanan (1184 m). Relatively low hills with moderately steep slopes occur on the east. Towards the centre of the Sierra Madre, the mountains are higher and the slopes steeper, with many gulleys, ravines and V-shaped valleys. The Palanan River drains about 29% of the Wilderness Area; other major rivers are the Abuan River and the Catalangan River. There are 11 other river systems within the Wilderness Area.

The dominant rock type in the centre of the Wilderness Area is the Abuan Formation, a series of clastic marine sediments with alternating layers of volcanic breccia. Ultramafic rocks occur in the east, quartz diorite, an intermediate igneous intrusive rock, in the west, and a reef limestone formation (the Kanaipang Limestone) occurs in the south. Alluvial deposits occur in the floodplain of the Palanan River. Soils are clay to sandy loams, but many parts of the Wilderness Area have yet to be surveyed.

Rainfall is evenly distributed throughout the year, November to December being the wettest period and February to April the driest. Temperature averages 26.1°C, dropping to 24°C in January and February, and rising to 28°C in June.

Vegetation

The Palanan Wilderness Area contains one of the few remaining extensive blocks of rain forest in the Philippines. A variety of vegetation types occur within Palanan Wilderness Area, including lowland evergreen rain forest, lower montane forest, forest over limestone, forest over ultramafic soils, beach forest and mangroves.

Lowland and hill evergreen rain forests are the dominant forest types, covering an estimated 70% of the area, and occurring between 200 and 800 m. Dipterocarps, such as *Hopea negrosensis*, *Shorea polysperma*, *S. squamata* and *Anisoptera thurifera*, dominate the canopy. *Pterocarpus indicus* occurs in marginal areas. *Diospyros philippinensis* is also abundant. Epiphytes, especially orchids, are common.

Lower montane rain forest covers an estimated 15% of the area, and occurs from 900 m to the summit. Dominants include members of the genera *Lithocarpus*, *Syzygium*, *Schefflera*, *Rhododendron* and *Vaccinium*. Theaceae, Clethraceae and Elaeocarpaceae are also well-represented. *Pinus insularis* occurs in significant numbers. Emergent trees, such as *Agathis philippinensis*, grow to 30 m or more, but generally montane forests are lower in stature than lowland forests. Terrestrial and epiphytic ferns and mosses are abundant.

Forest over limestone covers about 10% of the area, and is found in coastal areas, particularly at the southern part of Palanan Point. The dominant species are *Vitex parviflora*, *Pterocarpus indicus* and *Garuga floribunda*. These are semi-deciduous, shedding their leaves from February to April.

Forest over ultramafic soils also occurs in coastal areas, such as at Dinapigue, where the soil is shallow, with poor water holding capacity, and has a high concentration of metals, but is poor in nutrients. The forest is stunted and the ground layer is dominated by members of the Cyperaceae and Compositae.

Mangroves are confined to inlets in the estuary of Palanan River, the intertidal mudflats, sandflats and saline lagoons in Callawan and Sabang, near the mouth of the Palanan River, and in the lagoons and coves at Bicobian and Dimasalansan. Nipa swamps, dominated by *Nypa fruticans*, also occur here.

Beach forest occurs along the coast on sandy or rocky substrates. The dominant species are *Casuarina equisetifolia*, *Terminalia catappa*, *Barringtonia asiaticum*, *Caesalpinia nuga*, *Erythrina variegata* and *Pterocarpus indicus*. *Crinum asiaticum*, *Acacia farnesiana*, *Ipomoea pes-caprae*, *Wedelia biflora* and *Mikania scandens* are also common.

Flora

It is estimated that there are 1500 species of vascular plants in Palanan Wilderness Area and that, of these, more than 50 species are locally endemic and over 100 species are endemic to the Philippines. Numerous endemic and rare species are restricted to the Sierra Madre mountain range. Many species are restricted to particular vegetation types within the area.

Useful plants

The forests of the Palanan Wilderness Area contain important gene pools of many species of timber trees, including dipterocarps, *Pterocarpus indicus* (narra) and *Diospyros* spp. (kamagong). Species of rattans, belonging to such genera as *Calamus* and *Daemonorops*, are also plentiful in the forests. *Agathis philippinensis* provides a resin which is collected by the local inhabitants. The highly attractive (and Endangered) jade vine, *Strongylodon macrobotrys*, which has vivid turquoise flowers, grows in the area. Orchids, peperomias and aroids are among other highly attractive ornamental species.

Social and environmental values

84 species of birds and 16 species of mammals have been recorded from the area. Sightings of the Philippines eagle (*Pithecophaga jeffreyi*) have been reported. Whistling duck (*Dendrocygna arcuta*), egret (*Egretta garzetta*) and Philippine mallard (*Anas luzonica*) occur in the wetlands. Reticulated python (*Python reticulatus*) and monitor lizard (*Varanaus salvator*) are two endangered reptiles found within the area. Estuarine or saltwater crocodile (*Crocodylus porosus*) and the green sea turtle (*Chelonie mydas*) have been reported in mangroves and wetlands.

The Palanan Wilderness Area falls within the Luzon Endemic Bird Area (EBA) (40 restricted-range landbirds of which 24 are endemic) and is a very important site for restricted-range species. The majority of these birds are likely to be threatened by forest destruction and are described as rare or uncommon, often with patchy distribution and many little known. A recent survey in the Sierra Madre recorded three of these very poorly known species, namely long-billed rhabornis (*Rhabdornis grandis*), Rabor's wren-babbler (*Napthera rabori*) and whiskered pitta (*Pitta kochi*).

Rich deposits of gold, chromite, copper, zinc, manganese and nickel occur within Palanan Wilderness Area, and are exploited by the indigenous Negritos, who still practice a nomadic lifestyle. Negritos are considered to be the original inhabitants of the area; their population is estimated to be more than 400. About 8525 Pala'wan also live in the Wilderness Area.

The coastline of Palanan is scenically attractive and offers potential for tourism. The forests are also important for watershed protection.

Threats

Palanan Wilderness Area is threatened by the expansion of towns, illegal squatters, over-exploitation of forest products, and by selective logging by local people.

The main towns (Maconacon, Palanan and Divilacan) had an estimated population of around 21,170 in 1990. Between 1980 and 1990, the annual growth rate was 2.93%, mainly as a result of immigration. The expansion of settlements and agricultural lands encroaches upon tropical lowland evergreen rain forest and other adjacent vegetation types. Technically, the settlements are illegal, since the Timber License Agreements (TLAs) of the three logging companies previously operating in the area were cancelled, and the Letter of Instruction which established the Wilderness Area prohibits human occupancy for development activities. Most agriculture around the settlements is permanent, but kaingin (shifting cultivation) occurs on a small-scale.

A major threat is over-collection of ornamental plants (such as orchids) and plant products (such as rattan and resin, the latter primarily collected from *Agathis philippinensis*). Such over-exploitation has increased at an uncontrolled rate as demand and prices have risen. So far, there have been no restrictions imposed by the government.

Illegal logging, though selective and small-scale, is expected to intensify. Dipterocarps are the favoured timber trees. If left uncontrolled, such logging will further degrade the forests of Palanan. The possibility of granting Timber Licence Agreements to meet domestic and world demands for timber or wood products cannot be ruled out, since the Wilderness Area contains one of the last remaining dense primary forests in the country. With insufficient supply of timber now coming from the country's secondary growth forests and tree plantations, primary forests, such as those of Palanan Wilderness Area, are in imminent danger from large-scale commercial logging activities.

Mining of chromite, gold, copper, manganese and nickel is a potential threat, but fluctuating export prices have so far prevented further exploration in the area.

Feasibility studies on building roads to enhance the accessibility of towns isolated by the Sierra Madre range are currently underway. If roads were to be built there would be both direct and indirect impacts on the forest, and the area would be opened to squatters and further illegal tree cutting.

Conservation

Palanan was declared a Wilderness Area in 1979. The area includes within its boundaries various forms of protected areas, including "mossy" forests, protection forests, critical watersheds, proclaimed watershed reservations which support existing government dam projects or domestic water supply facilities, mangrove forests needed for foreshore protection and for the maintenance of estuarine and marine life, and "species forests" (exclusive habitats of rare and endangered species). The Letter of Instruction which established the Wilderness Area prohibits human occupancy and other development activities within the boundaries of the protected area, except for the purposes of recreation, education, research and conservation.

In 1964, the Divilacan Forest Reserve (249.7 km²) was established to serve the needs of wood production, watershed protection, soil protection and other forest uses. The reserve includes forests within the Palanan Wilderness Area in the municipalities of Ilagan, Palanan and Tumainini.

In 1986, mining and prospecting permits were suspended within Palanan Wilderness Area. However, despite the above measures, illegal occupancy and extractive activities still occur within the protected area.

Palanan is proposed as a National Park in the National Integrated Protected Areas System for the Philippines. National Park status will help to strengthen its protection. It is planned to train forest managers and rangers to help implement conservation measures, and to involve local people in sustainable management of natural resources. Zoning, currently lacking in all protected areas in the country, will help to define prescribed uses within specific areas within Palanan. These will include protection zones, regeneration zones, areas of settlement and public service zones.

References

IPAS Project (1991). *Technical report: Palanan Wilderness Area*. WWF-UPSRF-FSDI, Philippines.

Jacobs, M. and Mendoza, D.R. (1968). *Opportunities and suggestions for botanical exploration work in the Sierra Madre Mountains, Luzon*. National Museum, Manila, Philippines.

Mendoza, D.R. and Jacobs, M. (1968). A preliminary report of the botanical exploration of Mt Pulog and Tabayoc, Kabayan, Benguet and the Sierra Madre Mountain Ranges at Dingalan and Baler, Quezon. *Proceedings of the 1968 National Science and Technology Week, Part 3*. Pp. 411–439.

Philippine-German Forest Resources Inventory Project (1987). *Forest resources of Region II*. FRI, Philippines.

Acknowledgements

This Data Sheet was written by Dr Domingo A. Madulid (Botany Division, National Museum, Manila, Philippines).

PALAWAN
Palawan, Philippines

Location: Palawan is located between the islands of Mindoro and Borneo, between latitudes 8°30'–12°45'N and longitudes 117°30'–121°45'E. It is bounded to the west by the South China Sea and to the east by the Sulu Sea.

Area: 14,896.3 km².

Altitude: 0–2085 m (summit of Mount Mantalingajan).

Vegetation: Lowland evergreen dipterocarp rain forest, lowland semi-deciduous forest, montane forest, forest over limestone, forest over ultramafic rocks, mangroves, beach forest.

Flora: 1522 flowering plant species recorded so far, estimated >2000 vascular plant species in total; 15–20% endemic to Palawan. 1 endemic genus.

Useful plants: Rattans, timber, *Agathis* for turpentine, ornamental plants (especially orchids, aroids, palms, bamboos), fruit tree relatives.

Other values: Home of 5 distinct ethnic groups; rich fauna with numerous endemics.

Threats: Deforestation due to logging and shifting cultivation (kaingin), road building through primary forests, mining, over-collection of plants and plant products for subsistence and commercial purposes.

Conservation: St Paul Subterranean River (39 km²) declared a National Park in 1971; Mangrove Swamp Forest Reserve (600 km²); various other protected areas cover 508.7 km² (3.4% of the area). The main island of Palawan is also a Biosphere Reserve (11,508 km²), and has been declared a Game Refuge and Bird Sanctuary.

Geography

The province of Palawan consists of the main island of Palawan and a group of 1767 smaller islands and islets bounded on the east by the Sulu Sea and on the west by the South China Sea. To the north is the island of Mindoro, and on to the south is the Malaysian state of Sabah in northern Borneo. Palawan is located between latitudes 8°30'–12°45' N and longitudes 117°30'–121°45' E. The land area of the province is 14,896 km² and there is a shoreline of 2000 km (including the offshore islands and islets). The following text refers to the main island of Palawan, unless otherwise stated.

About 45.6% of Palawan is mountainous, with slopes greater than or equal to 30%. The three highest peaks are Mount Mantalingajan (2085 m), Victoria Peak (1798 m) and Cleopatra's Needle (1593 m). Steep hills with slopes of 18–30% cover 2153 km², while low hills with slopes of 8–18% cover 2013 km². Swamps and lowland zones cover 2081 km².

There are 4 major geological zones:

❖ Metamorphic rocks of the Basement Complex occur north of the Mount St Paul region. Volcanics occur around Cleopatra's Needle, to the west of which are sedimentary rocks of the Bangley Formation. Slightly metamorphosed limestones are found in the karst landscape around Mount St Paul and the El Nido cliffs.

❖ Ultramafic outcrops dominate the region to the south of the Quezon-Abo-abo gap region; these are mixed with undifferentiated volcanics and Tertiary limestone.

❖ Tertiary sandstones and shales occur along the south-west coast.

❖ Alluvial plains and terraces occur in the lowlands fringing the above three regions.

Palawan contains a number of mineral deposits, such as chromite and minerals yielding nickel, mercury, copper, iron and manganese, as well as silica, talc, marble, limestone and guano deposits. Soils vary from well-drained, gravelly or stony soils found on older colluvial-alluvial fans, to clay and fine loamy soils of variable depth on hills and mountains.

North-west Palawan has two pronounced seasons: a dry season from November to May, and a wet season from June to October. The wettest period is from June to September during the south-west monsoon. The rest of Palawan has no pronounced maximum rainfall period, although there is a short dry season of 1–3 months. The west coast experiences orographic rainfall from May to December. The east coast, on the other hand, is shielded from heavy rains by the mountains and experiences four dry months. The mean annual rainfall for the east coast is 1600 mm; that for the north of Palawan is 2500 mm. In the north, the mountains do not influence rainfall patterns significantly, so there is less difference between the east and west coasts. Central and south-west coasts receive 3000 mm rainfall per annum, while the mountains receive 3000–5000 mm. The mean temperature for the province is 27.5°C with little seasonal variation. For a more detailed account of the climate of Palawan, see Kintanar (1989).

Vegetation

The vegetation of Palawan is one of the most diverse of any island within the Philippines. Lowland evergreen dipterocarp rain forests cover 3610 km² (comprising c. 31% of the mainland area). Among the dominants are *Aglaia* sp., *Dipterocarpus gracilis*, *D. grandiflorus*, *Ficus* spp., *Tristania* spp., *Exocarpus latifolius* and *Swintonia foxworthyi*. Emergents include *Syzygium* spp., *Dracontomelon dao* and *Pongamia pinnata*. Lianes, such as *Diplectria divaricata*, are also common, as are cycads (*Cycas* spp.). *Casuarina* sp. (*Gymnostoma* sp.), a large emergent pine-like tree, dominates the lowland forest of Victoria Peak in south Palawan.

Lowland semi-deciduous forest occurs on the steeper slopes of the mountains of the Irawan River Valley. The topsoil is usually thin and supports widely-spaced, small to medium-sized trees up to 15 m tall, which partially or totally shed their leaves during March–May and produce new leaves at the onset of the rainy season (June–July). Common trees include *Pterocymbium tinctorium*, *Pterospermum diversifolium*, *Hymenodictyon* sp. and *Garuga floribunda*. Numerous lianes, ferns, herbaceous epiphytes and ground herbs occur among loose rocks and boulders.

Montane forests occur between 800 and 1500 m. Dominants in lower montane forest are *Tristania* spp., *Casuarina* sp., *Swietenia foxworthyi* and *Litsea* spp. Common species of upper montane forest are *Agathis philippinensis*, *Dacrydium pectinatum*, *Podocarpus polystachyus*, *Gnetum latifolium*, *Cycas wadei*, *Cinnamomum rupestre*, *Nepenthes philippinensis* and *Angiopteris* spp.

Forests over limestone occur on most of the islets and over large areas of the southern part of the main island. There are many lithophytes and xerophytes which are found in pockets of thin soil and leaf litter in crevices in the limestone. Among the genera represented are *Euphorbia trigona*, *Aglaia argentea* and members of the genera *Antidesma*, *Drypetes*, *Gomphandra*, *Sterculia*, *Pleomele* and *Begonia*.

Trees in forests over ultramafic rocks are mostly up to 15 m tall. Many tree species are the same as those found in semi-deciduous vegetation. Several species, such as *Scaevola micrantha*, *Brackenridgea palustris* var. *foxworthyi*, *Exocarpus latifolius* and *Phyllanthus lamprophyllus*, are believed to be heavy metal indicators. Victoria Peak carries the largest region of ultramafic forest on Palawan.

Coastal forests include *Calophyllum inophyllum*, *Canarium asperum* var. *asperum*, *Pometia pinnata*, *Palaquium dubardii* and *Ficus* spp. At St Paul's Bay and Langen Island, coastal forest adjoins and overlaps with forest over limestone. Mangroves comprise species in the genera *Rhizophora*, *Aegiceras*, *Bruguiera* and *Sonneratia*.

Flora

An annotated checklist of the flowering plants of Palawan has been compiled by Madulid (1987). So far, 1522 species of flowering plants have been recorded in 649 genera and 138 families, of which about 15–20% are endemic to Palawan. The total vascular flora is estimated at more than 2000 species.

Most of the species-rich sites (see Table 59) include a mosaic of several vegetation types. Of the areas explored by the 1984 Swedish Match-Hilleshög Expedition, the Irawan River Valley-Mount Beaufort-Thumb Peak area was the richest in terms of species and vegetation types, followed by Lake Manguao in northern Palawan and Victoria Peak in the south. However, other sites of botanical interest have yet to be fully explored, and include the mountains of Palawan's northern islands, Mount Capaos (Coron Island) and Mount Mantalingajan and Babuyan River Valley in southern Palawan. A more intensive exploration of St Paul Subterranean National Park may also yield further new species.

Useful plants

The forests of Palawan are rich in timber trees, especially dipterocarps. Trees felled for local use include *Dipterocarpus gracilis*, *D. grandiflorus*, *D. hasseltii*, *Xanthostemon verdugonianus*, *Diospyros discolor*, *D. pilosanthera* and *Intsia bijuga*. Palawan is one of the biggest suppliers of rattans in the Philippines; *Calamus merrillii* (palasan) and *C. caesius* (sika) are among the most important rattan species.

Medicinal plants, used by the Tagbanuas, Palawanon, Tau't Bato and other ethnic tribes, include *Astronia cumingianus* for treating wounds and *Cassia alata* for skin infections. *Agathis philippinensis* yields resin (almaciga or Manila copal) which local people extract from the bark of mature trees, providing an income during the drier months. Tannins, dyes, gums and ornamental plants are also collected from the forest. Among potentially valuable genetic resources are wild relatives of fruit trees, such as citrus and mango relatives.

Several plants are used in cultural ceremonies. For example, *Thunbergia fragrans* and *Hypolytrum latifolium* are sprinkled on to paddis in the belief that they will ward off rice diseases.

TABLE 59. SITES IN PALAWAN RICH IN VASCULAR PLANT SPECIES

Site	Vegetation	Number of vascular plant species recorded
Irawan River Valley	Semi-deciduous forest, riverine forest, lowland forest, forest on rocky slopes	268
Mount Beaufort	Ridge forest, upper montane forest, dry forest on summit	225
Puerto Princessa (N)	Ultramafic vegetation	
Mount Bloomfield	Dry semi-deciduous and stunted forest on heavy metal-rich soils	58
St Paul's Bay	Lowland evergreen rain forest, forest on limestone, coastal forest	161
Pagdanan Range	Lowland evergreen rain forest	106
San Vicente	Hill rain forest	
Lake Manguao (Danao)	Lake and wetland vegetation, forest on limestone, valley forest	162
Calauag	Semi-deciduous forest	32
Langen (Malapakan) Island	Coastal forest, forest on limestone	106
Victoria Peak	Lowland evergreen rain forest, lower and upper montane rain forests, forest on ultramafic rocks	230
Infanta Mining Area	Lowland riverine forest	150
Quezon and Pulot Tres forests		31
Pancol forest		24
Igang Plain		10

The roots of *Croton tiglium* are tied around the wrists and ankles to drive away spirits inhabiting rivers.

Many forest species have potential in horticulture and in tropical landscape gardening. In particular, there is a host of ornamental figs, begonias, orchids, aroids and palms, including the endemic *Veitchia merrillii*, one of the most popular ornamental palms.

Social and environmental values

The province of Palawan is home to many species of animals known to be rare or endangered. These include the Palawan bearcat, scaly anteater, Balabac mouse deer, flying lemurs, Philippine palm civet, small leopard cat, Luzon white-toothed shrew, flying squirrel, armadillo and swallow-tailed butterflies. Among the avifauna are Palawan hornbills, Palawan eagle, Palawan racket-tailed parrot, hooded pitta, blue-naped parrots, black-naped orioles and talking mynas. A total of 19 restricted-range birds occur in this Endemic Bird Area (EBA) (which includes the islands of the Calamian Group and Balabac) of which 17 are endemic. Five species occur on Palawan alone, including the Palawan peacock-pheasant (*Polypectron emphanum*) which is heavily hunted. The island is also an important route for bird migration, forming a link across the Sulu Sea between Mindoro and Borneo.

Palawan is the home of five ethnic tribes: the Batak (estimated population in 1986: 8770), Tagbanua (76,830), Palawanon (76,830), Cuyonon (5130) and Tau't Bato (130).

Threats

Two of the most serious threats are logging and shifting cultivation. As of August 1989, three logging companies held licences over 1807 km². Large-scale logging, without reforestation, has severely damaged some areas. There are also smaller logging operations and "carabao" logging using water buffalo to haul logs out of the forest.

Mangroves are exploited by local people for firewood and for construction timber, and as sources of dyes and tannins. Records show that, between 1968 and 1980, mangroves were being depleted by 12 km² per year despite the designation of forest reserve status (PNSS-UNESCO MAB 1988). Dryland forests are also being cleared by kaingin agriculturalists (shifting cultivators), particularly in upland areas.

Over-collecting is a threat to some ornamental species, particularly the orchids *Phalaenopsis amabilis* and *Paphiopedilum argus*, pitcher plants (*Nepenthes* spp.), palms (such as *Veitchia merrillii*) and some aroids (especially *Amorphophallus* spp. and *Alocasia* spp.). Local populations of *Agathis philippinensis* are under threat as a result of excessive tapping of resin by local people. Ring-barking has left some trees vulnerable to pests and diseases.

Urbanization, and particularly road building, has destroyed a significant portion of primary forest, especially in the northern and southern parts of the island.

Conservation

Palawan forms a distinct region within the Bornean Floristic Province and contains a diversity of relatively intact vegetation types. The whole of mainland Palawan has been declared a Biosphere Reserve, Game Refuge and Bird Sanctuary. Mangroves are protected within a Mangrove Swamp Forest Reserve (of area 600 km², covering mangroves around the island). Various other kinds of protected areas cover 508.7 km² (c. 3.4% of Palawan). They include National Parks, Wilderness Areas, Experimental Forests, Forest Research Reserves, Game Refuges, Wildlife Sanctuaries, Museum Reservations and Research Sites, Tourist Zones and Marine Reserves.

St Paul's Bay (St Paul Subterranean National Park) and Irawan Flora and Fauna Reserve are two of the richest botanical sites with the highest recorded level of local endemism. However, strict conservation zones, buffer zones and agro-forestry zones have yet to be established. Mount Beaufort, Lake Manguao, Victoria Peak, Mount Bloomfield, Pagdanan Range, Mount Mantalingajan and the islets in northern Palawan are also priority areas for plant conservation.

Under the Integrated Protected Areas System, protected areas in the Philippines are being re-surveyed and legislation is being revised in order to achieve a viable protected areas system throughout the country. In Palawan, ineffective implementation of the law has resulted in encroachment and illegal activities within park boundaries.

In recent years, Palawan has been the focus of two major botanical expeditions. The 1984 Swedish Match-Hilleshög Forestry AB expedition involved botanists from the National Museum, Manila, the Rijksherbarium, Leiden, and the Royal Botanic Gardens, Kew, in a survey of the whole island to identify areas for conservation using the MAB concept. Since 1988, the University of Illinois at Chicago, College of Pharmacy, and the National Museum, Manila, have conducted intensive botanical explorations of the island in search of medicinal plants with potential for treatment of AIDS and cancer. To date, 1500 different plant samples have been collected and are currently being tested at the National Cancer Institute in Frederick, Maryland, U.S.A.

Proposals for selective logging within the concession areas are pending approval by the Philippines legislative body. The Haribon Foundation campained in 1988 for a total logging ban on Palawan; there were a million signatories to a petition.

Palawan is one of the most botanically important islands in the Philippines. Measures need to be implemented urgently to ensure strict protection of the most important botanical sites and the sustainable use of resources.

References

Bañez, G. (1991). *Forest structure of Irawan Forest Reserve, Palawan*. M.Sc. thesis, De La Salle University.

Elmer, A.D.E. (1911). A fascicle of Palawan figs. *Leafl. Philipp. Bot.* 4(71): 1363–1397.

Elmer, A.D.E. (1911). Euphorbiaceae collected on Palawan Island. *Leafl. Philipp. Bot.* 4: 1271–1306.

Elmer, A.D.E. (1912). Palawan Rubiaceae. *Leafl. Philipp. Bot.* 4: 1327–1362.

Florido, L. (1986). *Species composition of logged over area of Palawan Experimental Forest*. UPLB. (Unpublished report.)

Fox, R.B. (undated). The ethnobotany of Tagbanuas. (Unpublished manuscript.)

Jamer, S. (1987). *Forest vegetation and leaf characteristics of Mt Bloomfield, Palawan*. (Degree thesis, University of Stirling, Scotland.)

Kintanar, R.L. (1989). *Climate of the Philippines*. PAGASA, Quezon City, Philippines.

Madulid, D.A. (1987). A checklist of the rare, endemic, and endangered plants of Palawan. *Philipp. Scientist* 24: 55–66.

Madulid, D.A. (1989). Conservation of the natural heritage of Palawan, a case study. (Paper presented at the 5th Asian-American Conference of Environmental Protection, Singapore.)

Madulid, D.A. (1991). The flora of Palawan. In *Bountiful Palawan*. Aurora Publications, Philippines.

Merrill, E.D. (1920). *Myrmeconauclea*, a genus of rubiaceous plants from Palawan and Borneo. *Philipp. J. Sci.* 17: 375–376.

PIADPO-IEP (1985). *The strategic environmental plan of Palawan mainland report*. PIADPO-IEP.

PNSS-UNESCO (MAB) (1988). *Survey and feasibility study for the establishment of a Biosphere Reserve in Palawan, Philippines, a final report*. PNSS-UNESCO (MAB).

Podzorski, A. (1987). *Palawan Botanical Expedition Report*. Swedish Match-Hilleshög Forestry AB, Philippines.

Rice, P. and Margareth, G. (1987). *Ecological studies on a tropical forest site on Mt Bloomfield, Palawan*. (Degree thesis, University of Stirling, Scotland.)

Steenis, C.G.G.J. van (1987). *Checklist of generic names in Malesian botany (Spermatophytes)*. Flora Malesiana Foundation, Leiden, The Netherlands.

Acknowledgements

This Data Sheet was written by Dr Domingo A. Madulid (Botany Division, National Museum, Manila, Philippines). Professor Peter S. Ashton (Harvard University Herbaria, Cambridge, Massachusetts) and Dr John Dransfield (Royal Botanic Gardens, Kew) provided helpful comments on an earlier draft.

SIBUYAN ISLAND
Romblon, Philippines

Location: Sibuyan Island is located in the centre of the Philippines archipelago between the islands of Tablas, Masbate and Panay, at latitude 12°21'N and longitude 122°39'E, in the Sibuyan Sea.

Area: 445 km².

Altitude: 0–2052 m (summit of Mount Guiting-guiting).

Vegetation: Lowland primary rain forest, montane forests, summit grassland, heath forest, mangroves, beach vegetation.

Flora: Estimated 700 vascular plant species, including 54 species which are endemic to Sibuyan Island and 180 species which are endemic to the Philippines archipelago.

Useful plants: Timber trees, almaciga (*Agathis philippinensis*) resin, ornamental plants.

Other values: Rich fauna, attractive landscape, tourism.

Threats: Logging, slash-and-burn agriculture on lower slopes, fire, over-collecting of rattans.

Conservation: The whole island is proposed as a Nature Reserve under the Integrated Protected Areas System for the Philippines.

Geography

Sibuyan is the second largest island of Romblon Province and has an area of 445 km². It is surrounded by the islands of Marinduque in the north, Panay in the south, Masbate in the east, and Tablas and Romblon Islands in the west. Its location is latitude 12°21'N and longitude 122°39'E, in the centre of the Philippines archipelago. Mount Guiting-guiting (2052 m) and Mount Nailog are the highest peaks. The Cantingas, Punog, Olango, Cambajao and Pato-o rivers are found on Sibuyan.

The whole of Sibuyan, as well as Romblon and Tablas, consists of pre-Tertiary rocks. On Sibuyan there are schists, marble, volcanics, ultramafics and (in the eastern part of the island) metamorphic green schists. Soils range from sandy clay-loams to metamorphic sandy and stony soils, and loams underlain by coarse sands and gravels. Alluvial deposits occur along the coasts, where they support 6 km² of nipa swamps and mangroves. Mountain soils are undifferentiated, and cover a total area of 149 km².

Sibuyan Island experiences a short dry season lasting for one to three months. It is humid throughout the year.

Vegetation

Primary forests cover 149 km² (about 33% of the land area). The vegetation includes lowland primary rain forest, montane forest, summit grassland, heath forest, mangroves and beach vegetation. Lowland primary rain forest occurs from 200 to 700 m and is dominated by *Shorea* spp., *Hopea* spp., *Dipterocarpus* spp., *Pterocarpus indicus* and pandans, such as *Sararanga philippinensis*, *Pandanus cubicus* and *P. gracilis*. Other genera represented are *Xanthostemon, Canarium, Gymnostoma,* *Ardisia, Litsea, Ficus, Elaeocarpus, Croton, Ervatamia* and *Litsea*.

The transition to montane forest occurs between 700 and 900 m. Montane forest includes small to medium-sized trees, such as *Dacrydium elatum, Vaccinium gitingensis, Agathis* spp. and *Podocarpus* spp. Mountain summits are covered by grassland/heath communities dominated by grasses, sedges and ericaceous shrubs.

Sibuyan has extensive, well-developed and relatively undisturbed mangroves. Communities at the mouths of rivers and on the extensive mudflats of coastal areas.

Flora

There are an estimated 700 vascular plant species, including 54 species which are endemic to Sibuyan Island and 180 species which are endemic to the Philippines archipelago. The Sibuyan flora is closely related to that of the east coast of Luzon, and especially to the floras of Atimonan and Casiguran provinces of Aurora. Notable species include *Sararanga philippinensis*, a rare pandan found in swampy ground at the base of Mount Guiting-guiting.

Useful plants

Mount Guiting-guiting is home to many useful plants including almaciga (*Agathis philippinensis*), a source of resin, *Gymnostoma* spp. and *Casuarina equisetifolia*, which are used for house-posts, *Flagellaria* spp. and *Calamus* spp., used for making handicrafts and furniture, and *Gnetum gnemon, Amomum* spp. and *Alpinia* spp, which are sources of food. The montane forests include several ornamental species of *Rhododendron*.

Social and environmental values

Utzurrum (1991) considers Sibuyan to be an active centre of speciation and genetic evolution. Faunal diversity is low, but endemism is high.

Sibuyan is not included in an Endemic Bird Area (EBA). However, three restricted-range birds do occur on the islands of Sibuyan, Tablas and Romblon: Mantanani scops-owl (*Otus mantananensis*), streak-breasted bulbul (*Ixos siquijorensis*) and celestial monarch (*Hypothymis coelestis*).

The population of Sibuyan Island depends on the forests for watershed protection as well as for a range of forest products. Romblon Province (of which Sibuyan is the second largest island) had a population of 227,621 in 1990, and a mean annual growth rate of 1.7% during the period 1980–1990.

Threats

Until recently, the use of natural resources by indigenous inhabitants has been on a sustainable basis. For example, the value of forests for watershed protection has long been recognized, and resources such as timber, rattans and other minor forest products were traditionally harvested in a manner that did not drastically deplete them. Recently, however, "carabao" logging has begun and other resources, such as rattans, have been over-collected at lower altitudes. Carabao logging is a crude practice of selectively cutting high-grade timber trees with motorized chainsaws and thereafter using carabaos (water buffaloes) to drag the timber out of the forest. If this is allowed to continue in an uncontrolled way, logging may extend to higher parts of the mountains and to the steeper slopes of Mount Guiting-guiting, where the remaining large-boled trees are found. Gathering of rattan has now extended to the higher parts of the mountains because there are no more harvestable rattan poles at lower altitudes.

Slash-and-burn (kaingin) agriculture and seasonal fires are also threats. At present, these are confined to the lower fringes of the mountains (rarely above 200 m) where lowland primary forest is at risk (Stone 1992).

At present, forest exploitation on Mount Guiting-guiting is minimal and it has not drastically reduced forest cover. However, close monitoring is essential to ensure the conservation of the rich biodiversity of the island.

Conservation

The entire island of Sibuyan is proposed as a Nature Reserve under the Integrated Protected Areas System for the Philippines. This has yet to be evaluated by the government.

Stone (1992) recommends that the northern part of Sibuyan Island, including the Guiting-guiting massif down to the coastal mangroves, should be given nature reserve status since the vegetation in this part of the island is the most intact.

The island inhabitants are beginning to understand the importance and value of sustainable forest utilization. Because of this, conservation efforts are gaining local support.

References

Castillo, D., Quiro, I. and Marcella, H. (1973). *Soil survey of Romblon Province, Philippines-reconnaisance soil survey and soil erosion survey*. Soil Report No. 45. Government Printing Office, Manila, Philippines.

Elmer, A.D.E. (1910). Euphorbiaceae collected on Sibuyan Island. *Leafl. Philipp. Bot.* 3(51): 903–931.

Elmer, A.D.E. (1910). Lauraceae from Mt Apo and Mt Guiting-guiting. *Leafl. Philipp. Bot.* 2(41): 703–728.

Elmer, A.D.E. (1910). Sapotaceae from Sibuyan Island. *Leafl. Philipp. Bot.* 3(49): 869–874.

Elmer, A.D.E. (1911). A fascicle of Sibuyan figs. *Leafl. Philipp. Bot.* 4(69): 1307–1325.

Elmer, A.D.E. (1911). *Garcinia* from Sibuyan Island. *Leafl. Philipp. Bot.* 3(55): 1047–1055.

Stone, B.C. (1992). *Report on the field collecting trip to Mt Guiting-guiting, Sibuyan Island, under the Philippine Plant Inventory Project*. (Unpublished report.)

Utzurrum, R.C.B. (1991). *Philippine island biogeographic patterns: practical applications for resource conservation and management*. ASBP Comm. 3.

Acknowledgements

This Data Sheet was written by Dr Domingo A. Madulid (Botany Division, National Museum, Manila, Philippines).

GUNUNG GEDE-PANGRANGO NATIONAL PARK
Java, Indonesia

Location: West Java, within the administrative districts of Bogor, Cianjur and Sukabumi. The summit of Gunung Pangrango is at latitude 6°48'S and longitude 106°56'E.

Area: 150 km².

Altitude: 1000–3019 m (summit of Gunung Pangrango).

Vegetation: Mostly montane and submontane rain forest, with subalpine forest, grass plains, open volcanic debris ("alon-aloon" plains) in summit area.

Flora: >1000 vascular plant species.

Useful plants: Timber trees, ornamental plants, a few medicinal plants.

Other values: Rich fauna, including a number of threatened mammals, 245 species of birds; watershed protection; tourism; educational value.

Threats: Timber exploitation, agricultural encroachment, visitor pressure, over-collecting of mountain flora, fuelwood gathering.

Conservation: National Park (IUCN Management Category: II) declared in 1980, including Cibodas-Gunung Gede Nature Reserve (10.4 km²), Cimungkat Nature Reserve (0.5 km²), Situ Gunung Recreation Park (1.2 km²), and adjacent Protection Forest (137.8 km²). 140 km² of Gede-Pangrango was declared a UNESCO-MAB Biosphere Reserve in 1977. Cibodas Botanical Garden (25 ha) at the foot of Gede was established in 1862.

Geography

Gunung Gede-Pangrango National Park (Taman Nasional Gunung-Gede Pangrango) is located approximately 20 km south-east of Bogor, West Java, within the administrative districts of Bogor, Cianjur and Sukabumi. The summit of Gunung Pangrango is at latitude 6°48'S and longitude 106°56'E. The twin volcanoes of Gunung Pangrango (3019 m) and Gunung Gede (2958 m) dominate the area. They are connected by a saddle at around 2400 m at Kandang Badak. Geologically, Gunung Gede and Pangrango are part of the great belt of Quaternary to Recent volcanoes that extend in an arc from Sumatra, through Java, to the Lesser Sunda Islands. Pangrango, the older of the two volcanoes, is now extinct, but Gede remains semi-active. Hot-water springs, fumaroles, and several recent craters occur within the main crater rim. One of the craters, Kawah Lanang, produced lava beds as late as 1748, and ejected stones and ash in 1947.

Numerous rivers originate from the steep mountain slopes, including the Ciliwung, Cisadane and Cilaku. While the soils of the higher slopes are very porous andosols, the more weathered soils lower down are highly fertile latosols.

Cibodas is in the wettest part of Java, with an annual rainfall of 3000–4200 mm equally distributed throughout the year. On Pangrango, there is a 4-month drier season (June to September) when less than 200 mm falls per month. For the rest of the year, rainfall is usually between 300–500 mm per month. Average temperatures range from 18°C at Cibodas to 4°C at the summit of Pangrango (UNDP/FAO 1978).

Vegetation

Gede-Pangrango has the finest extant example of upper montane and subalpine forest in West Java. Submontane forest (or tropical lower montane forest) occurs between 1000 and 1500 m. The dominant components are the conifers *Podocarpus (Dacrycarpus) imbricatus* and *Podocarpus neriifolius*, along with laurels (*Litsea* spp.), oaks (*Lithocarpus* and *Quercus* spp.), chestnuts (*Castanopsis* spp.) and *Schima wallichii*. The most abundant emergent trees are *Podocarpus imbricatus*, *P. neriifolius* and *Altingia excelsa*. Lianas and epiphytes abound, particularly mosses, orchids and ferns. *Begonia robusta*, the pandan *Freycinetia javanica*, *Strobilanthes cernua* and terrestrial orchids, such as *Paphiopedilum javanicum* and *Phaius flavus*, are conspicuous in the forest. Meijer (1959) enumerated 78 trees, 40 shrubs, 30 climbers, and 100 epiphytes, among 333 species of vascular plants recorded in 1 ha of montane rain forest at Cibodas at 1500 m.

Upper montane forest occurs at 1500–2400 m. *Leptospermum flavescens* occurs above 1750 m and dominates at the upper limits. Conifers, such as *Podocarpus imbricatus* and *P. neriifolius*, and the chestnut *Castanopsis javanica* also dominate. Montane and submontane forests together cover about 85% of the park area.

Above 2400 m, subalpine forest occurs. The forest takes on a stunted appearance and includes many temperate genera such as *Vaccinium, Myrsine, Myrica, Sanicula, Primula, Ranunculus* and *Viola*. *Vaccinium varingiaefolium* is the main tree species, growing up to 10 m tall but often more stunted. It occurs throughout Java from 1800 to 3340 m, and is also found in Peninsular Malaysia and Sumatra. Trees are covered in mosses (such as *Aerobryum*), liverworts and lichens (especially *Usnea* spp.). These mossy facies are often termed "mossy forest".

The summit area and crater walls of Gunung Gede consist of bare, loose volcanic rock debris (sometimes referred to as "sand seas") and grass plains dominated by Javan edelweiss (*Anaphalis javanica*) and including *Agrostis infirma*, *Carex hypsophylla* and *Gentiana quadrifida*. (Such open areas are referred to locally as "alon-aloon", irrespective of whether there is any vegetation cover.)

Numerous waterfalls occur on the mountain slopes at 1000–2000 m. At Tjibeureum, on Gunung Gede, the vertical walls of the falls support *Nepenthes*, *Elatostemma* and *Pilea*, while at the foot of the falls a small area of marsh has developed, with *Gunnera macrophylla*, *Phragmites* and *Scirpus*.

Flora

Koorders (1918–1923) treats 850 species of flowering plants (indigenous and naturalized species) occurring at Cibodas. Considering the number of additional species found since then on Gunung Gede-Pangrango, and with the addition of ferns to the total, the native vascular plant flora is likely to contain well over 1000 species. A feature of the forest is its rich variety of herbs, shrubs, ferns and epiphytes.

CPD Site SEA64: Gede-Pangrango National Park, showing the summit of Gunung Pangrango with *Cyathea contaminans* in the foreground. Photo: Stephen D. Davis.

There are 208 species of orchids, of which *Corybas praetermissus*, *Liparis bilobulata* and *Malaxis sagittata* are endemic to Gunung Gede. A number of species are shared with Mount Kinabalu in Sabah; *Dendrophthoë magna* (Loranthaceae), a parasite of *Castanopsis acuminatissima*, is found only on Gunung Gede and Mount Kinabalu. Above 2800 m, the vegetation includes temperate elements, such as *Anaphalis javanica*, *Gentiana quadrifida* and species of Ericaceae. With so little natural vegetation remaining on Java, Gede-Pangrango is now a refuge for many rare and threatened species.

Useful plants

There are many species of timber trees, especially *Altingia excelsa* and species of *Podocarpus*, *Magnolia* and *Michelia*. *Gaultheria fragrantissima* ssp. *punctata* is used as a source of oil for hair-oil and for the treatment of rheumatism. The seeds of *Castanopsis* are eaten.

There are many ornamental species, including the bird's nest fern (*Asplenium nidus*) and many species of orchids, aroids, *Hedychium* and *Begonia*.

Social and environmental values

The forests of Gede-Pangrango are an important refuge for many threatened species of animals, including the Javan gibbon (*Hylobates moloch*) (Endangered) and Javan leaf monkey (*Presbytis comata*) (both confined to the lower slopes). 245 species of birds have been recorded from the park and surrounding regions. The National Park is one of the key sites for the conservation of the Javan and Balinese Forest Endemic Bird Area (EBA). A total of 22 birds are endemic to the area and eight endemic to western Java alone. All but one of these species are known from this park, including such poorly known globally threatened species as Javan scops-owl (*Otus angelinae*), Salvadori's nightjar (*Caprimulgus pulchellus*) and Javan cochoa (*Cochea azurea*).

Gede-Pangrango is the source of several major rivers, including the Ciliwung, Cisadane and Cilaku. The forested slopes of the mountains therefore play a vital role in protecting the catchments of these rivers, as well as preventing serious flooding and soil erosion problems which could affect the tea gardens, and vegetable and rice fields which have been developed on the fertile soils on the lower slopes and surrounding areas.

The park has an enormous value (and further potential) as a centre for tourism, recreation and education. It is close to such large population centres as Jakarta, Bandung and Bogor, and, as such, attracts many visitors. The park received more than 30,000 per year during the late 1970s, while the Cibodas Botanical Garden received 200,000 visitors per year at that time. The majority of visitors to Gede climb the summit trail to the crater rim. Being so close to large population centres, Gede-Pangrango and the adjoining botanic garden offer enormous possibilities for environmental education (an Environmental Education Centre has been built near the park entrance). Increasing visitor use of the area in the future needs to be carefully planned and managed (see Conservation section).

In an evaluation of the importance of protected areas in the Indomalayan Realm (MacKinnon and MacKinnon 1986), Gede-Pangrango is given an "A" priority rating on account of its spectacular mountain scenery, rich forests and as a valuable research site.

Threats

The most serious threats are agricultural encroachment and felling of timber trees on the lower slopes. Commercial logging is no longer a threat, but legal and illegal tree cutting still occurs in the southern parts of the park (A.J.G.H. Kostermans 1992, *in litt.*). The surrounding area is one of the most densely settled regions in Java, and local people still use the forests for the collection of firewood and other forest products. The boundaries of the reserve are inadequately marked. Vandalism and the collecting of wild flora (especially Javan edelweiss) by visitors are particular problems.

In 1985, a heavy storm caused considerable damage to the forest above Cibodas. This has opened up the canopy in places and allowed the spread of many alien elements and weedy species into the lower parts of the forest (M.M.J. van Balgooy 1992, *in litt.*).

Conservation

The area has a long history of scientific research dating from the early 19th century (UNDP/FAO 1978; van Steenis 1972). Apart from botanical collecting on the mountain, experimental plots were established in a number of places to study the behaviour of economically important plants at different altitudes.

The first area to be officially protected was the primary forest above Cibodas Botanical Garden. This was incorporated into the garden in 1889, and later became part of the much larger Cibodas-Gunung Gede Nature Reserve (Cagar Alam). National Park status for Gede-Pangrango was proposed in 1980. The park includes both peaks and the vegetation of their surrounding slopes, and encompasses Cibodas-Gunung Gede Nature Reserve (10.4 km²) and Cimungkat Nature Reserve (0.5 km²) (both of which are Strict Nature Reserves, IUCN Management Category: I), as well as the Situ Gunung Recreation Park (1.2 km² of secondary vegetation). There is also an adjacent area of Protection Forest (137.8 km²) incorporated into the National Park. In 1977, 140 km² of Gunung Gede-Pangrango was declared a Biosphere Reserve (Cibodas Biosphere Reserve) under the UNESCO-MAB Programme (McCarthy 1991).

A management plan has been prepared for the park (UNDP/FAO 1978) which sets out the following objectives:

❖ conservation of the montane forest and other ecosystems;
❖ conservation of rare and threatened species;
❖ encouragement of research programmes to achieve these aims;
❖ encouragement of tourism, in so far as this is compatible with conservation objectives;
❖ education programme to foster an understanding of the importance of the park among local people and visitors.

The plan recommends zoning to allow for: an intensive use area (3 ha), including a visitor centre; a wilderness zone, in which minimal development for tourism is allowed; and a sanctuary zone, to which access is restricted to scientists with permission. A buffer zone around the National Park would allow for local people to continue to collect firewood and other forest products on a sustainable basis.

Cibodas Botanical Garden (Cabang Balai Kebun Raya Cibodas), a satellite garden of Bogor Botanic Gardens, covers 25 ha of the lower slopes of Gunung Gede at 1425 m, and was first established in 1862. The gardens include some conservation collections, including plants from the mountain, and maintains a small herbarium of 5000 specimens.

References

Koorders, S.H. (1918-1923). *Flora van Tjibodas umfassend die Blütenpflanzen*, 3 vols. Boekhandel Visser, Batavia.

MacKinnon, J. and MacKinnon, K. (1986). *Review of the protected areas system in the Indo-Malayan Realm*. IUCN, Gland, Switzerland and Cambridge, U.K. (in collaboration with UNEP). 284 pp.

McCarthy, A.J. (comp.) (1991). *Conservation areas of Indonesia. Final draft*. World Conservation Monitoring Centre, Cambridge, U.K. in collaboration with Directorate General of Forest Protection and Nature Conservation (PHPA), Ministry of Forestry, Republic of Indonesia, and IUCN Commission on National Parks and Protected Areas, Gland, Switzerland.

Meijer, W. (1959). Plant sociological analysis of the mountain rain forest near Tjibodas, West Java. *Acta. Bot. Neerl.* 8: 277–291.

Seifriz, W. (1923). The altitudinal distribution of plants on Mt Gedeh, Java. *Bull. Torrey Bot. Club* 50(9): 283–306.

Steenis, C.G.G.J. van (1972). *The mountain flora of Java*. Brill, Leiden, The Netherlands. 90 pp.

UNDP/FAO (1978). *Proposed Gunung Gede-Pangrango National Park management plan*. FO/INS/73/013 Field Report 11. UNDP/FAO Nature Conservation and Wildlife Management Project, Bogor, Indonesia. 96 pp. (Includes a detailed bibliography.)

Acknowledgements

This Data Sheet was written by Stephen D. Davis, with grateful thanks to the late Professor A.J.G.H. Kostermans (Herbarium Bogoriense, Bogor, Indonesia) and Dr M.M.J. van Balgooy (Rijksherbarium, Leiden, The Netherlands) for commenting on an earlier draft.

ARFAK MOUNTAINS
Irian Jaya, Indonesia

Location: North-east Vogelkop Peninsula, to the south of Manokwari, and 750 km west of Jayapura. The Arfak Mountains Strict Nature Reserve (Cagar Alam Pegunungan Arfak) is located 25 km south-west of Manokwari, between latitudes 1°00'–1°29'S and longitudes 133°53'–134°15'E.

Area: The Arfak Mountains cover 2200 km², of which 450 km² is currently protected.

Altitude: 100–3100 m (at summit of Gunung Lina).

Vegetation: Primary and secondary tropical lowland and hill rain forests, lower montane rain forest, grassland/heath communities, lake vegetation.

Flora: Estimated 3000–4000 vascular plant species (or approximately 20% of the total vascular plant flora of mainland New Guinea); many local and Vogelkop endemics.

Useful plants: Timber trees, rattans, wild fruit tree relatives, ornamental plants (especially rhododendrons).

Other values: Watershed protection, rich fauna (including 320 species of birds, about half the total number recorded for Irian Jaya), centre of diversity for birdwing butterflies, home for indigenous tribal people.

Threats: Pressure from increasing local population, transmigration and resettlement schemes, logging and clearance for agriculture in lowlands, road building.

Conservation: The Arfak Mountains Nature Reserve (IUCN Management Category: I) covers 450 km²; it is proposed to enlarge this to 653 km² and change status to Nature Conservation Area.

Geography

The Arfak Mountains (the name being given by early settlers, "Arfak" meaning "interior") rise up steeply behind the coastal settlements of Manokwari, Oransbari and Ransiki on the north-east of the Vogelkop Peninsula, within the Manokwari District. The mountains cover an area of 2200 km² and are bounded by the coastal plain and Geelvink Bay in the east, the Mapar Plain in the south, the Lina Mountains in the south-west, the Warjori valley in the west, and hills near Andai in the north. They lie to the east of the Ransiki fault, an active subduction zone where the Pacific Ocean Plate descends below the Australian continental crust. The massif comprises mainly andesitic and basaltic volcanics, with conglomerates, sandstones and mudstones in the lowlands. An area of limestone (Maruni limestone) occurs to the north-east of the Arfak Mountains Nature Reserve (Cagar Alam Pegunungan Arfak).

The Arfak Mountains are generally steep-sided with undulating ridges and sharp crests. The region is dissected by V-shaped valleys. Low rolling hills form cliffs along the coastline of the Sarera Bay. Major catchments are those of the Ransiki, Warjori and Prafi rivers in the west, and the steeper Mupi, Warnasse, Massawui, Warbiadi and Moari catchments in the east. The highest mountains are Gunung Lina (3100 m), Pegunungan Arfak (2939 m) and Pegunungan Togwomeri (2680 m). To the north and east of Gunung Lina are the Anggi Lakes (Anggi Gigi at 1920 m and Anggi Gita at 1840 m). To the north-east of the lakes is the Arfak Mountains Nature Reserve, located 25 km south-west of Manokwari, between latitudes 1°00'–1°29'S and longitudes 133°53'–134°15'E. Its altitude ranges from 100 m to 2820 m at the summit of Gunung Humeibou.

Access to the reserve area is by road from Manokwari to the transmigration settlement of Prafi. Small boats also travel regularly between Manokwari, Ransiki and Oransbari. The western areas can only be reached by light aircraft landing at Minyambou, Makwam and Ransiki. The completion of a road from Manokwari to Ransiki will provide access to the east of the reserve.

The region experiences a wet tropical climate with high humidity. Mean maximum and minimum temperatures at 2050 m (Anggi Lake Station) are 22.5°C and 16°C, respectively. At this elevation, ground frosts can occur in depressions. At Manokwari, on the coast, the mean maximum temperature is 31°C, the mean minimum temperature 24°C. Annual rainfall varies from 14,014 mm at Ransiki to 3038 mm at Manokwari as a result of rain shadow effects. Rainfall is seasonal; Vink (1965) recorded 169 rainy days in one year at Manokwari, while at Momi there were only 116 days. The driest period is from June to October; there is a wet period from January to May (Craven and de Fretes 1987).

Prior to the Miocene (before 6 million years BP), the Arfak Mountains were separate from mainland New Guinea and were part of an island arc situated on the Pacific Ocean Plate. The former period of isolation helps to explain the high incidence of endemic flora and fauna in the Arfak Mountains (Craven and de Fretes 1987).

Vegetation

The notes below are condensed from the account given in Craven and de Fretes (1987) and refer to the Arfak Mountains Nature Reserve and extensions comprising the proposed Nature Conservation Area (see Conservation section).

Lowland tropical rain forest occurs between 100 and 300 m altitude. The canopy is 50 m or more high and includes *Mallotus, Aglaia, Pometia, Intsia, Palaquium* and *Ficus*. Climbers include species of *Aristolochia* (the food plant of the birdwing butterflies), *Piper, Freycinetia, Lygodium* and pitcher plants (*Nepenthes*). There are abundant epiphytes including the bird's nest fern *Asplenium nidus*. Among the understorey plants are tree ferns (*Cyathea*) and the spectacular "corpse flower", *Amorphophallus paeoniifolius*. At about 300 m, lowland forest grades into hill forest which has a lower canopy. Among the tree genera are numerous commercial timber trees, but the steepness of terrain ensures they are mostly inaccessible for logging. They include: *Pometia, Intsia, Ficus, Alstonia, Canarium, Syzygium* and *Araucaria*. Gingers (Zingiberaceae) and tree ferns are also found.

At 1000 m, lower montane rain forest is encountered. The forest is much cooler and wetter, and there is persistent cloud cover around 1700 m. The forest is dominated by oaks (*Lithocarpus*) and laurels (*Cryptocarya* and *Litsea*) up to 1500 m, giving way to *Nothofagus* forest from 1500 m to 2800 m. Other common tree genera are *Castanopsis* and the conifers *Dacrycarpus, Dacrydium, Podocarpus, Libocedrus* and *Araucaria cunninghamii*. Ericaceae (*Rhododendron* and *Dimorphanthera*) are also abundant, together with orchids (such as *Dendrobium* spp., used by the Vogelkop bower bird *Amblyornis inortatus* to decorate its bowers), tree ferns (*Cyathea* spp.), gingers, palms and selaginellas. Above 2400 m the forest floor and tree trunks are covered in a thick layer of mosses, such as *Sphagnum* and *Dawsonia*. The vegetation becomes stunted; at the summits of the highest mountains the canopy is only 15 m high.

In high, open, unstable areas, grasses predominate (e.g. *Imperata*) with rhododendrons (such as *R. konori*), edelweiss (*Anaphalis*) and *Dimorphanthera*.

The proposed Arfak Mountains Nature Conservation Area includes a complete altitudinal range of habitats except those below 100 m on the coastal plains; however, the majority of the forest below 400 m within the proposed boundary between Oransbari and Ransiki has been selectively logged.

Flora

The first botanical collections in the Arfak Mountains were made by Beccari in 1875, three years after the zoologist D'Albertis had been the first European to penetrate the Arfaks. Even today, the area remains under-collected and poorly known botanically. Vink (1965) provides a chronological account of botanical expeditions in the Arfaks up to 1962. A provisional list of vascular plants occurring in the Arfak Mountains, mainly compiled from Anon. (1961), with additions, is given in Craven and de Fretes (1987). It lists 116 flowering plant and 32 fern species. Nearly all the collections have been made south-west (around the Anggi Lakes) and west of the Nature Reserve (W. Vink 1992, *in litt.*). The total vascular plant flora of the Arfak Mountains is estimated at 3000–4000 species (P.F. Stevens 1993, personal estimate), or approximately 20% of the total vascular plant flora of mainland New Guinea.

The flora of the Arfak Mountains contains many local and Vogelkop endemics (W. Vink 1992, *in litt.*). Some remarkable plants of the Arfaks are *Discocalyx dissecta*, which looks rather like a fern when not in flower or fruit, and the local form of *Acsmithia pulleana*, which has thick and deeply concave leaflets. There are numerous endemic species in genera such as *Dimorphanthera* (including one species as yet undescribed), *Drimys, Vaccinium, Rhododendron* and *Diplycosia*.

Useful plants

Among the plants so far recorded are wild relatives of a number of fruit trees, including *Mangifera mucronulata, Artocarpus communis* and *A. fretissii*. Among important timber trees are *Araucaria cunninghamii, Pometia pinnata* (taun), *Dracontomelon mangiferum* (New Guinea black walnut), *Octomeles sumatrana* (erim) and the legumes *Pterocarpus indicus* (New Guinea rosewood), *Intsia palembanica* and *I. bijuga* (ironwood). *Pandanus* spp., which occur widely in the lowland rain forest, are used extensively by local people; the fruits provide food and the leaves are used for roofing. Rattans (*Calamus* spp.) are used to secure poles and walls of buildings. The palm *Gronophyllum* (*Kentia*) *gibbsianum* is used for making rafts (W. Vink 1992, *in litt.*).

The area is rich in species of *Rhododendron*, which have been introduced to horticulture as ornamental shrubs, or have been used in developing garden hybrids.

Social and environmental values

The Arfak Mountains are the home of three indigenous tribal groups: the Hatam, Sougb (Manikiong) and Meyah. The proposed Arfak Mountains Nature Conservation Area encompasses about 80% of the Hatam tribal land (Craven and de Fretes 1987). In total, about 75,000 people live in and around the Arfak Mountains (Craven and de Fretes 1987) in 5 main settlements (Manokwari, Ransiki, Warmare, Oransbari and Anggi). About 3590 people live in the expanding town of Ransiki, situated just 5 km south of the reserve. There are transmigration settlements at Prafi and Oransbari.

The preservation of forest cover in the Arfak Mountains is essential to protect and regulate water supplies within the catchment ecosystem. The protection afforded by forests to steep-sided and unstable mountain slopes ensures less risk of soil erosion and landslides associated with heavy tropical rainfall, and reduces the risk of flooding of settlements in the lowlands and siltation of coastal fisheries. They also help to stabilize mountain slopes in a region which is an earthquake zone.

The forest also provides a range of resources for isolated rural people without any reliable source of cash income. Unless they move to towns, where employment is difficult to find, most rural people derive their income from garden produce or the exploitation of forest resources (WWF 1992). The conservation of the forests and wildlife resources of areas such as the Arfaks would therefore help to contribute towards sustainable rural economic activity, and would help to reduce the numbers of people migrating to already over-crowded urban areas.

The proposed Nature Conservation Area will ensure a large area of protected forest providing indigenous people with the opportunity to continue certain traditional ecologically non-disruptive practices which are essential parts of their culture and subsistence economy, and will provide the basis for sustainable use of natural resources.

The Arfak Mountains are noted as a centre of diversity for birdwing butterflies. Species present include *Ornithoptera rothschildi*, known only from around the village of Hingk and possibly the Anggi Lakes. A total of 323 butterflies have so far been recorded from the Arfak Mountains (Craven and de Fretes 1987). Birds-of-paradise are also present, including *Astrapia nigra* (the Arfak Astrapia).

The Arfak Mountains are included in the Vogelkop Mountains Endemic Bird Area (EBA) (which also includes the Tamrau, Fakfak, Kumawa and Wandammen ranges). This EBA includes 20 restricted-range land bird species, of which 9 species are endemic. Nearly all the species can be found in the Arfak Mountains, including 3 near-endemics shared with the Tamrau Mountains: the Vogelkop whistler (*Pachycephala meyeri*), grey-banded munia (*Lonchura vana*) and the Arfak astrapia (*Astrapia nigra*).

A total of 110 species of mammal are expected to occur within the proposed Arfak Mountains Nature Conservation Area (Petocz and de Fretes 1983; Craven and de Fretes 1987). Of these, 44 are confirmed records. They include the locally endemic Arfak Mountains ringtail (*Pseudocheirus schlegeli*). 50 mammal species occurring in the Arfak Mountains are endemic to New Guinea.

The Arfak Mountains are historically and scientifically important, since early exploration of New Guinea's montane fauna and flora began here, the first collections of plants in the area being those of Lesson at Dorey Bay, Manokwari, in 1824 and 1827. Wallace visited the area in 1858, D'Albertis in 1872, and Beccari climbed into the mountains to around 2040 m in 1875. Gibbs visited the mountains at the end of 1913. As a result, the Arfak Mountains are the type locality for many species. The area's proximity to Manokwari and to UNCEN's Environmental Studies Center (PSL) provides the opportunity for biological and sociological research.

Because of the ruggedness and inaccessibility of much of the Arfak Mountains, there are few opportunities for developing tourism. However, the mountain scenery is spectacular and some areas, including the Anggi Lakes, the lower Ransiki River and Gribou Ridge, could be included in ecotourist itineraries.

Threats

Population increase in and around the Arfak Mountains is a threat, especially in the lowlands. Much of the lowland rain forest surrounding the Arfak Mountains has already been cleared for transmigration and resettlement schemes, plantations and subsistence cultivation. In the Minyambou area, for example, agriculture is expanding rapidly (Craven and de Fretes 1987), resulting in shortened fallow periods between cultivation. This in turn leads to reduced soil fertility, increased soil erosion and reduction in crop yields, which leads to more forest being cleared for cultivation. The loss of forests around Minyambou has resulted in reduction in the availability of building materials for local inhabitants (Craven and de Fretes 1987).

In the northern Arfaks, the concentration of people in the valleys is resulting in progressive forest clearance of the lower slopes. A transmigration settlement has been established at Oransbari. This threatens the only section of the proposed conservation area below 200 m. There are also plans to expand rubber and cocoa plantations in the eastern lowlands

bordering the proposed Nature Conservation Area (Petocz 1984, 1989). The demand for cash crops is increasing in the Manokwari area, reducing the area available for subsistence agriculture and giving rise to further forest clearances. In the Ransiki valley, agriculture is extensive, and occurs up to 2200 m in some parts. In addition, a cocoa plantation has been established, and part of this is within the proposed Arfak Mountains Nature Conservation Area (Craven and de Fretes 1987). It is expected that this enterprise will lead to wood shortages for fuel and building as a result of the numbers of people attracted to Ransiki for employment and because of the use of wood in the drying process for cocoa production. The expected wood shortage is recognized as the greatest threat to the integrity of the Arfak Mountains Nature Conservation Area and surrounding forests in this district (Craven and de Fretes 1987).

Logging in the Arfak region is only economically feasible on the coastal plains and foothills because of the steepness of slopes and inaccessibility of much of the interior. The Forestry Department recognizes this and has classified all land above 500 m as Hutan Lindung (Protection Forest). Under this category, no commercial timber extraction can take place, although limited extraction is permitted. Nevertheless, selective logging in the vicinity of the proposed Arfak Mountains Nature Conservation Area has taken place since 1980. A total area of 35 km² has been logged, mostly below 400 m, and concentrating on the removal of just three timber groups: *Intsia*, *Pometia* and *Palaquium* (Craven and de Fretes 1987); of this 35 km², 21 km² falls within the proposed conservation area. The building of roads for logging vehicles increases the risk of illegal incursions and forest fires. Clearance and/or modification of the forests cover allows light-demanding species to spread gregariously (especially members of the Ericaceae).

The Arfak Mountains Nature Reserve (area: 450 km²), as currently gazetted, does not include the full range of altitudinal habitats, and is considered to be too small for the maintenance of viable populations of Arfak flora and fauna (Craven and de Fretes 1987). The reserve currently has no marked boundaries and there are no staff to prevent illegal exploitation. Furthermore, its current status (Cagar Alam, or Strict Nature Reserve) places restrictions on the use of the area by local people. This could create local tensions which could be detrimental to the long-term security of the reserve. Craven and de Fretes (1987) therefore recommend an enlargement of the area to include a greater range of habitats and a change in status to Nature Conservation Area (see Conservation section).

Traditional hunting and cultivation practices were once less destructive due to customary controls, the absence of a market outside the mountains for vegetables and inefficient methods of hunting. These practices are now beginning to change and more modern techniques are being introduced which are leading to degradation of forest resources in some areas.

The use of fire, as an aid to hunting, has extensively damaged some areas within the conservation area. Vink (1965) noted that during dry spells (even in wet periods) large fires burned the slopes. Severely burnt areas were covered by ferns and Cyperaceae, whereas shrubs occurred in areas less severely burned.

Accessibility to the eastern and northern sections of the conservation area is increasing due to nearby road construction.

When the Manokwari-Ransiki road comes into service, settlements and small plantations are expected to follow rapidly. The road will increase accessibility to the forest which will be at risk from larger scale timber extraction (Craven and de Fretes 1987).

The Maruni limestone is quarried for road aggregate. The quarry is situated 5 km north-east of the nature reserve and poses no threat to it (Craven and de Fretes 1987).

Conservation

A Strict Nature Reserve (Cagar Alam) was first declared in the Arfak Mountains in 1957. This covered 100 km^2 and was later extended to 450 km^2. As such, the area was identified as one of four priority sites for conservation in Irian Jaya in the National Conservation Plan for Indonesia (FAO 1981–1982), and one of the seven priority sites identified in the Irian Jaya Conservation Development Strategy (Petocz 1984, 1989).

Through its Irian Jaya Conservation Programme, WWF is developing a management plan for the reserve for the Directorate General of Forest Protection and Nature Conservation (PHPA), Ministry of Forests. The plan aims to progress towards community-run conservation management and attempts to provide economic alternatives for local inhabitants in order to displace destructive activities and improve standards of living. The 5-year management plan for the Arfak Mountains for the period 1988–1992 (Craven and de Fretes 1987) recommends an enlargement of the nature reserve to 653 km^2 and a change in status from Strict Nature Reserve (Cagar Alam) to Nature Conservation Area (Kawasan Pelestarian Alam) to enable a flexible approach to indigenous peoples' use of the area whilst conserving its biodiversity. The authors of the plan argue that strict enforcement of the Cagar Alam status would be unworkable as it would alienate indigenous people and would prevent their use of resources on their traditional lands. As the management plan for the proposed Nature Conservation Area states: "By providing indigenous people with the opportunity to continue certain ecologically non-disruptive, forest-based practices, essential to their culture and subsistence economy, the conservation area will provide important socio-cultural benefits and will secure their lands and forest resources for sustainable use in the future" (Craven and de Fretes 1987).

Craven and de Fretes (1987) propose that certain inaccessible areas, or areas of rare habitats within the Nature Conservation Area, could be zoned as Strict Nature Reserves, while creating a "Community Development Zone" as a buffer zone around the conservation area. Agro-forestry programmes, and ventures such as butterfly farming, developed in the buffer zone, could help to gradually replace the dependence on forest resources within the conservation area with more intensive activities outside the boundary.

References

Anon. (1961). *Boomnamenlijst Manikiong van de inzameling masni.* Forestry Department, Manokwari.

Craven, I. and Fretes, Y. de (1987). *The Arfak Mountains Nature Conservation Area, Irian Jaya. Management plan, 1988–1992.* WWF project report, Bogor, Indonesia. 175 pp.

FAO (1981-1982). *National Conservation Plan for Indonesia.* Field Report of UNDP/FAO National Parks Development Project INS/78/061. 8 volumes. FAO, Bogor, Indonesia.

Petocz, R.G. (1984). *Conservation and development in Irian Jaya: a strategy for rational resources utilisation.* WWF/IUCN Conservation for Development Programme in Indonesia Report. PHPA, Bogor, Indonesia. 279 pp.

Petocz, R.G. (1989). *Conservation and development in Irian Jaya: a strategy for rational resources utilisation.* Brill, Leiden, The Netherlands. 218 pp.

Petocz, R.G. and Fretes, Y. de (1983). *Mammals of the reserves in Irian Jaya.* WWF/IUCN Project 1528. WWF/IUCN, Jayapura, Indonesia.

Vink, W. (1965). Botanical exploration of the Arfak Mountains. *Nova Guinea, Botany* 22: 471–494.

WWF (1992). *Butterfly farming in the Arfak Mountains of Irian Jaya, a project update.* WWF, Manokwari, Indonesia. 13 pp. (Unpublished report.)

Acknowledgements

This Data Sheet was written by Stephen D. Davis and Dr Peter F. Stevens (Harvard University Herbaria, Cambridge, Massachusetts), with thanks to Dr Wim Vink (Rijksherbarium, Leiden) for commenting on an earlier draft.

GUNUNG LORENTZ
Irian Jaya, Indonesia

Location: Southern Irian Jaya, stretching from the Central Cordillera to the New Guinea coast in the administrative regencies of Jayawijaya, Paniai, Fak-fak and Merauke, between latitudes 3°52'–5°17'S and longitudes 136°50'–138°25'E.

Area: 21,500 km².

Altitude: 0–4884 m (Puncak Jaya, Indonesia's highest mountain).

Vegetation: All the major environments of Irian Jaya represented. Lowland alluvial and hill rain forest, lower and upper montane rain forests, mangroves, freshwater and peatswamp forests, riparian forest, bogs, grasslands, sedgelands, heathlands, alpine/tundra vegetation.

Flora: Estimated 3000–4000 vascular plant species (or approximately 20% of the flora of mainland New Guinea); 258 vascular plant species so far recorded above 3200 m, together with 60 bryophyte species and 33 lichen species. Many local endemics; 60 vascular plant species so far known to be strictly endemic to the alpine and subalpine zones.

Useful plants: Fruits, vegetables, fibres, building materials.

Other values: Rich fauna, including 123 mammals and 411 species of birds. Inhabited by six tribal groups whose economies are dependent upon the biological resources of the area. Potential for ecotourism.

Threats: Mining, logging, petroleum exploration, road building, transmigration, tourism (high-altitude vegetation is particularly vulnerable to trampling).

Conservation: Established as a Nature Reserve (Cagar Alam) in 1978; proposals to upgrade to National Park and World Heritage status. Proposed as UNESCO Man and Biosphere Reserve. A management plan is in preparation.

Geography

Gunung Lorentz Nature Reserve (Cagar Alam Gunung Lorentz) lies within the administrative regencies of Jayawijaya, Paniai, Fak-fak and Merauke, and stretches for over 150 km from the equatorial glaciers of New Guinea's Central Cordillera, the highest mountains in South East Asia, to the south coast bordering the Arafura Sea. It is the largest protected area in Irian Jaya, extending from sea-level up to 4884 m at the summit of Puncak Jaya (also known as Mt Carstensz), the highest mountain in New Guinea and the whole of Indonesia. There are some 6.9 km² of glacier in the summit region, one of only three places in the world where glaciers are to be found in equatorial latitudes. The reserve, which includes part of Pegunungan Sudirman (the Sudirman Range), has a large number of streams and rivers which have cut deep valleys in the mountains and foothills as they drain south to the coastal plain. Here they form extensive areas of swamps with numerous permanent and seasonal lakes.

The area has a complex geology. In the north, moraines overlie an extremely rugged karst limestone topography; the Central Cordillera mountains are folded and metamorphosed oceanic sediments of Cretaceous (100 million years BP) and Eocene (40 million years BP) origin. Alluvial deposits cover the southern coastal plain.

Vegetation

All the main environments found in Irian Jaya occur within Gunung Lorentz Nature Reserve. Some 34 vegetation types have been identified (Kartawinata and Widjaja 1988). The coastal plain has extensive areas of wetlands, including mangroves along the coast, tidal and freshwater swamp and riparian forests, sedgelands, *Pandanus* and sago palm formations, and permanently and seasonally flooded peatswamp forests. Lowland rain forest, the richest community, occurs up to 1000 m. There are two main types of lowland forest: lowland alluvial rain forest and lowland hill rain forest. Lowland alluvial rain forest features high species diversity, with a multi-layered canopy, including emergent trees attaining 50 m. Representative trees include: *Pometia, Ficus, Alstonia* and *Terminalia*; the understorey contains *Garcinia, Diospyros, Myristica* and *Maniltoa*, as well as numerous palms, rattans, orchids, ferns, climbers and epiphytes. Lowland hill rain forest differs structurally from alluvial forest in being somewhat lower and closed, although species composition is similar. Emergents on hills and ridge crests include the gymnosperms *Araucaria* and *Agathis*, while the dipterocarps *Anisoptera, Vatica* and *Hopea* occur in more sheltered areas.

Lower montane rain forest, which is less rich in tree species than lowland alluvial and hill forests, occurs between 1000 and 3000 m. At the lower limit of montane forest, *Castanopsis* is the dominant tree. This is replaced at higher elevations by moss-covered, monotypic stands of *Nothofagus*, and eventually by dense conifer forests comprising *Podocarpus, Dacrydium, Dacrycarpus* and *Papuacedrus*.

An abrupt change in vegetation occurs at 3000 m. Tree ferns (*Cyathea* spp.), bogs, grasslands and heath vegetation predominate, until at 4000 m the alpine zone is reached. This includes the grasses *Deschampsia* and *Poa*, herbs such as *Ranunculus, Potentilla, Gentiana* and *Epilobium*, heaths and tundra vegetation, including lichens and bryophytes. The highest areas are permanently snow-covered.

Flora

The flora is estimated to contain 3000–4000 vascular plant species (or approximately 20% of the flora of mainland New Guinea) (P.F. Stevens 1993, personal estimate). All altitudes are poorly known; the lower altitudes are virtually unknown botanically but likely to be of exceptional botanical importance (P.S. Ashton 1991, *in litt.*). Many endemics occur at higher altitudes. Hope (1976) gives a list of collections made above 3200 m; it includes 258 species of vascular plants (221 angiosperms, 4 gymnosperms, and 33 ferns and fern allies), 90 bryophyte species and 33 species of lichens. From a study of van Royen (1980–1983) and subsequently published work, about 60 vascular plant species from 35 genera are currently known only from the alpine and subalpine areas of Gunung Lorentz. These include such striking species as *Tetramolopium distichum*. Other local endemics occur in the genera *Isoetes*, *Grammitis*, *Gentiana*, *Euphrasia*, *Rhododendron*, *Vaccinium*, *Corybas*, *Pilea* and *Ranunculus*. Possible endemics at lower altitudes include *Dimorphanthera* section *Pteridosiphon*, which is known only from the Utakwa area.

Useful plants

None recorded, but considering the wide range of habitats, there is predicted to be a large number of species used by local people (e.g. as sources of food, fibres and building materials).

Social and environmental values

The region has been inhabited for over 24,000 years. Six tribes inhabit the Lorentz area (Manembu 1991). The largest groups are the Nduga, the Amungme (Damal), the Nakai (Asmat Keenok) and the Sempan. The Nduga and Amungme inhabit the highlands above 1000 m; the Nakai and Sempan inhabit the lowlands. In addition, there are two smaller groups: the West Dani tribe of the Baliem valley, and the Kamoro. Traditional cultures have evolved a complex system of taboos and rituals which ensure that forest resources are not over-exploited (Petocz 1984; Kartawinata and Widjaja 1988).

The Nduga are one of the least known peoples in Irian Jaya, inhabiting the Central Highlands. The entire Nduga population is estimated at 10,000, of which approximately half live within the proposed Biosphere Reserve boundary (Manembu 1991). The Nduga are agriculturalists, cultivating sweet potatoes, taro, sugar cane, bananas and beans. Their form of gardening is called "yabu", and involves the use of pigs to help enrich the soil after garden plots have been cultivated for up to one year. The plots (which can be on flat ground or on hill slopes) are then allowed to remain fallow, returning to grass and tree cover, before being cultivated once more when the soil has regained its fertility. The diet of the Nduga is supplemented by hunting. The Amungme tribe is also found in the Central Highlands. There are about 14,000 who live in and around the reserve. Like the Nduga, the Amungme are cultivators and pig farmers, who supplement their diet by hunting. Their main crops are sweet potato and cassava, as well as a wide variety of fruits and vegetables (including many local varieties and introduced species). The Sempan people number about 1000 (Manembu 1991), mostly living in lowland swampy areas. Their subsistence is based on sago gathering and vegetable gardening, supplemented by hunting and fishing. The Nakai people live along the Topap River, and have a similar lifestyle to that of the Sempan. There were 310 Nakai in 1990 (Manembu 1991).

The majority of the population is located in the numerous settlements in the Baliem valley to the north-east, in the large towns of Atamanop and Tembagapura to the west, and in the towns of Jila, Bulialangki, Aramsolki and Akimuga in the centre of the reserve. The mining town of Freeport lies close to the north-western boundary below the Carstensz massif.

Some 123 mammals have been recorded from the reserve, representing 80% of the total mammalian fauna of Irian Jaya. The swamplands are home to two species of crocodile, both of which are threatened: the estuarine crocodile (*Crocodylus porosus*) (Endangered) and the New Guinea crocodile (*C. novaeguineae*) (Vulnerable) (Silvius 1989). The avifauna is likewise extremely rich, with 411 species recorded, including at least 20 species endemic to Irian Jaya. Notable species include 2 species of cassowary, 4 megapodes, 30 parrots, 20 birds-of-paradise and 6 species of bowerbirds. The Gunung Lorentz National Park straddles two Endemic Bird Areas (EBAs) which run parallel to each other: the Central New Guinean mountains (c.500–4900 m, 55 restricted-range birds occurring) and the South New Guinean lowlands and foothills (0–c.1000 m, eight restricted-range birds occurring). In total some 50 of the restricted-range landbirds are likely to occur in the park with seven endemic to the region. A number of these endemics are regarded as near-threatened, largely as a result of their small ranges. They include short-bearded melidectes (*Melidectes nouhuysi*), orange-cheeked honeyeater (*Oreornis chrysogenys*) and Archbold's bowerbird (*Archboldia papuensis*). Snow mountain quail (*Anurophasis monorthonyx*), another endemic, is confined to alpine grasslands and may be hunted.

Lorentz has great potential for ecotourism, offering magnificent scenery and a rich flora and fauna.

Threats

The Freeport copper mine is located within the existing Lorentz Strict Nature Reserve, and adjacent to the proposed Lorentz National Park, on the slopes of the Carstensz Massif near Puncak Jaya. Some endemics, such as a species of *Glossorhyncha* and an undescribed species of *Drimys*, may be restricted to the ore bodies. Freeport was extracting some 20,000 tonnes of copper ore per day from this site in 1990, and there were plans at that stage to increase extraction to 52,000 tonnes per day by 1992 (WWF 1991). Opencast mining has created a number of social and environmental problems, including forest clearance and logging for fuel supplies and building development for the 4000-strong work force, displacement of the indigenous Amungme tribe, river pollution and oil spillages. Proposed boundary changes to the reserve (see Conservation section) would still leave 45% of the mining concession within the reserve. As well as this, over half the reserve is currently under concession for petroleum exploitation (Silvius 1989). These developments bring with them the pressure to build more roads and open up the area further.

Already a road is planned between Timika on the western boundary and Aramsolki in the centre of the reserve (Kartawinata and Widjaja 1988).

Logging concessions border the reserve on the east. Logging poses a direct threat to the integrity of the reserve, and could induce long-term changes to the traditional lifestyles of some of the tribal inhabitants. Already, some of the Nakai tribe are engaged in logging activities. This could result in a shortage of suitable trees for making canoes, dependency on a consumer economy, and food shortages, as more and more people are engaged in logging at the expense of their garden plots (Manembu 1991). There is likely to be further pressure to provide farming land in the reserve for transmigrants from other parts of Indonesia.

Uncontrolled tourism is a threat to the high-altitude vegetation which is particularly vulnerable to trampling (W. Vink 1992, *in litt.*). Ecotourism should therefore be restricted in certain areas.

Conservation

Gunung Lorentz was declared a Nature Reserve (Cagar Alam) in 1978. It is the largest protected area (21,500 km^2) in Irian Jaya and probably the most important reserve for biodiversity in Indonesia (K. MacKinnon 1991, *in litt.*). It is one of four priority areas for conservation identified in the National Conservation Plan for Indonesia (FAO 1981–1982). Recent proposals by the Department of Forestry, supported by WWF, suggest upgrading the area to National Park status and reducing the size to 14,832 km^2 (thereby excluding part of the mining area). The Governor of Irian Jaya intends to nominate Gunung Lorentz for inscription under the World Heritage Convention. The area has been proposed as an UNESCO Man and Biosphere Reserve, in which the inhabitants of the area would remain and be assisted in improving their living conditions, contribute to management planning, and be invited to participate in the management of the reserve (Manembu 1991).

A management plan is in preparation, which recommends the regulation of mining activities on the reserve boundaries. A sociological study is currently in progress (WWF 1990) which it is hoped will facilitate the design of a culturally acceptable management plan.

References

Hope, G.S. (1976). Vegetation. In Hope, G.S., Peterson, J.A., Radok, U. and Allison, I. (eds), *The equatorial glaciers of New Guinea*. Balkema, Rotterdam, The Netherlands. Pp. 113–172.

Kartawinata, K. and Widjaja, E. (1988). *Consultants' report on preparation for development of Lorentz National Park, Irian Jaya*. UNESCO/Government of Indonesia UNDP/IBRD Project INS/83/013. 73 pp.

Manembu, N. (1991). *The Sempan, Nduga, Nakai, and Amungme peoples of the Lorentz area*. WWF Irian Jaya Conservation Programme Report. WWF Project 4521. WWF, Jayapura, Indonesia. 117 pp.

McCarthy, A.J. (comp.) (1991). *Conservation areas of Indonesia. Final draft*. World Conservation Monitoring Centre, Cambridge, U.K. in collaboration with Directorate General of Forest Protection and Nature Conservation (PHPA), Ministry of Forestry, Republic of Indonesia, and IUCN Commission on National Parks and Protected Areas, Gland, Switzerland.

Petocz, R. (1984). *Conservation in Irian Jaya: a strategy for rational resource utilization*. WWF/IUCN Conservation for Development Programme in Indonesia, Bogor, Indonesia. WWF/IUCN Project 1528: Irian Jaya Conservation Programme. 279 pp.

Royen, P. van (1980-1983). *The alpine flora of New Guinea*, 4 vols. Cramer, Vaduz.

Silvius, M. (1989). Indonesia. In Scott, D.A. (ed.), *A directory of Asian wetlands*. IUCN, Gland, Switzerland and Cambridge, U.K. Pp. 1091–1092.

Synge, H. (1990). *Twenty opportunities for saving biological diversity. Priority places for possible U.K. aid*. WWF, Godalming, U.K. Pp. 31–32.

WWF (1990). *Implementation of conservation in Irian Jaya. Project No. 2770. Progress report*. WWF Indonesia. 29 pp.

WWF (1991). *The WWF Irian Jaya Conservation Programme. November 1990–January 1991 progress report*. WWF, Jayapura, Indonesia. 33 pp.

Acknowledgements

This Data Sheet was written by Stephen D. Davis and Dr Peter F. Stevens (Harvard University Herbaria, Cambridge, Massachusetts), with thanks to Dr Kathy MacKinnon (WWF Indonesia) and Dr Wim Vink (Rijksherbarium, Leiden) for commenting on an earlier draft.

MAMBERAMO – PEGUNUNGAN JAYAWIJAYA
Irian Jaya, Indonesia

Location: Northern Irian Jaya from the Mamberamo River in the west to the Sobger River in the east. The proposed Mamberamo-Foja Mountains National Park is located between latitudes 1°28'–3°45'S and longitudes 137°46'–140°19'E.

Area: 23,244 km².

Altitude: 0–4680 m (summit of Puncak Mandala, = Mt Juliana).

Vegetation: Mangroves, lowland swamp forest, lowland tropical rain forest, montane rain forest.

Flora: Very poorly known; no estimate available for size of flora; likely to be at least 2000–3000 vascular plant species.

Useful plants: Timber trees, especially *Intsia, Pometia, Nothofagus, Araucaria, Agathis, Podocarpus* and *Calophyllum*.

Other values: Rich in birds and mammals; home of nomadic hunter-gatherers.

Threats: Petroleum exploration, logging at lower elevations.

Conservation: The entire region falls within existing and proposed protected areas. Mamberamo-Foja Mountains National Park (proposed) covers 14,425 km² and is contiguous with Pegunungan Jayawijaya Game Reserve (8000 km²) and the proposed Sungai Rouffaer Game Reserve (819 km²). The proposed National Park has also been proposed as a World Heritage Site.

Geography

The area under consideration includes the Gauttier-Foja, the Mamberamo-Idenburg river system and the Pegunungan Jayawijaya (Jayawijaya Mountains). Gauttier-Foja, the main massif north of the Main Range in Irian Jaya, comprises a resistant, intrusive pluton of metamorphic rocks surrounded by sedimentary rocks. The mountains are rugged and deeply incised by numerous streams that drain to the Apawar and Tor rivers in the north, and the Lakes Plains in the south. The large depression of the Mamberamo River basin and its tributaries (the Rouffaer, or Tariku, and the Idenburg) extend for several hundred kilometres in an east-west direction below the northern foothills of the Main Range. The region includes Irian Jaya's largest permanent freshwater lake – Danau Rombebai (140 km²). Along the northern coastal plain, below the foothills, are alluvial deposits of the coastal swamplands.

The Foja Mountains are very insufficiently known and difficult of access. The majority of the local inhabitants live in small villages on the coastal plains to the north, and in the Mamberamo basin. A small number of indigenous hunter-gatherers live in the Lakes Plains area and to the north of the Foja Mountains, but the main mountain massif remains uninhabited.

The proposed Mamberamo-Foja Mountains National Park covers 14,425 km² from Tanjung d'Urville to the Sobger River, 70 km west of the international border with Papua New Guinea. The altitude range within the park is from sea-level to 2193 m.

Vegetation

The region includes a complete range of northern Irian Jaya habitats, from mangroves and lowland swamp forest along the north coast and on the coastal plains, to lowland tropical rain forest, montane rain forest and lake vegetation. The vegetation along much of the Mamberamo is subject to inundation. The forest canopy is at about 45 m, and includes several species of *Ficus* and also *Pittosporum ramiflorum* in the canopy. Epiphytes are numerous, particularly ferns and orchids, as well as the ant-plants *Myrmecodia* and *Hydnophytum*.

Meervlakte is a large area of swamps and lakes, with *Adina* and *Barringtonia spicata* swamp forests, large areas of *Metroxylon sagu* (sago palm), and marsh vegetation with *Echinochloa stagnina*. Some other forests may be inundated for months at a time; these may be dominated by species of *Timonius, Dillenia* or *Nauclea*. South from Meervlakte, the land rises up to Doormantop. Montane forests are already covered in mosses at about 1350 m. The vegetation includes a diverse epiphytic flora, including a species of *Utricularia*.

Doormantop consists of ultramafic rocks, and has a remarkable vegetation, including the highest-altitude forest in New Guinea, with an admixture of locally endemic species, including *Casuarina orophila*. Pitcher plants (*Nepenthes*) are found climbing in the high-altitude shrubbery, and also form rosettes in grasslands.

A brief impression of the forests of Foja Mountains is given in an unpublished report by Diamond (1981). The mountains are covered with forest up to their summits. At an elevation of 1200 m the forest canopy is 30–40 m high, with the tallest trees 46 m. Dominant tall trees include *Araucaria cunninghamii, Podocarpus neriifolius, Agathis labillardieri, Calophyllum* spp. and *Palaquium* spp. Van Eechoud (1940) describes an *Intsia-Pometia-Vatica-Anisoptera-Teysmanniodendron* forest along the lower Mamberamo. *Nothofagus* spp. are dominant above 1400 m, the trunks and branches of the trees being clothed in bryophytes. Above 1900 m, the bryophyte cover is dense both on trees and on the forest floor. At 1900–2000 m, the canopy is about 25 m high, except for emergent *Araucaria* and *Podocarpus*. By 2000 m, tall trees are scattered and the canopy is open. The forests contain abundant tree ferns, palms and lianes. Secondary growth in areas of landslippage is dominated by *Sterculia macrophyllum*, *Elaeocarpus sphaericus* and (below 1550 m) *Casuarina montana*.

Flora

Botanically, the region is very poorly known. Much of the area remains unexplored. No estimates are available for the size of the flora, but a conservative estimate would be in the region of 2000–3000 vascular plant species. Details of the endemicity of the flora, particularly the lowland flora, are largely unknown. Doormantop possibly has more endemic species per unit area than any other comparable mountain in New Guinea. Endemics include *Casuarina orophila*, and numerous herbs and shrubs, including species of *Gentiana*, *Trachymene*, *Hedyotis*, *Drimys*, *Diplycosia* and *Rhododendron*.

Useful plants

The forests represent a vast storehouse of timber tree provenances, especially of *Intsia*, *Pometia*, *Nothofagus*, *Araucaria*, *Agathis*, *Podocarpus* and *Calophyllum*.

During Dutch colonial times, the people of Bora-Bora (a cluster of four villages along the Tor River) collected resins to make damar and kopal which they then floated on rafts to sell at the coast (Diamond 1981). This activity no longer takes place.

Sago palms (*Metroxylon sagu*) are a staple for many nomadic tribal people who live in the region. Breadfruits (*Artocarpus*) may be planted along banks of waterways.

Social and environmental values

The Foja Mountains support the richest variety of birds of Irian Jaya's isolated mountain ranges, except for those of the Vogelkop Peninsula (Diamond 1981). Mamberamo – Pegunungan Jayawijaya falls within three Endemic Bird Areas (EBAs): North New Guinean lowlands, North New Guinean Mountains and Central New Guinean Mountains. Some 35 restricted-range landbirds are likely to occur in this area with one species endemic to the Gauttier-Foya Mountains golden-fronted bowerbird (*Amblyornis flavifrons*) and three to the coastal and Mamberamo/Idenberg/Rouffaer lowlands, including Brass's friarbird (*Philemon brassi*), a poorly known species.

61 species of mammals are expected to occur in the Mamberamo-Foja area (Petocz and de Fretes 1983).

The region is the home of nomadic hunter-gatherer tribes (Diamond 1981) who are dependent on the biological resources of the region for their sustenance.

Economic assessment

At middle elevations in the Foja Mountains, Diamond (1981) estimated the useful timber at 45 m³/ha (especially of *Nothofagus*, *Podocarpus* and *Calophyllum*). *Araucaria* emergents each represent 7–8 m³ of timber. However, above 1900 m there is little usable timber except for Lauraceae. However, Diamond adds that discussion of the timber potential of the Foja Mountains is irrelevant for practical reasons. Firstly, there are no roads within 65 km of the mountains, and the steep slopes would make road building prohibitively expensive; and secondly many of the tall trees are concentrated on the crests of steep-sided ridges and would shatter when felled. However, the area on the east bank of the lower Mamberamo is easily accessible.

Threats

Petroleum exploration has taken place in the northern Mamberamo area and there are proposals for exploitation within the boundary of the proposed National Park (Petocz 1984). The steepness of the terrain in the Foja Mountains makes them unsuitable for logging (Diamond 1981); however, the use of helicopters for timber extraction is becoming more widespread in neighbouring Papua New Guinea (R.J. Johns 1992, pers. comm.) and such means of timber extraction could conceivably be used here in the future if more readily available supplies are exhausted. Forests at lower elevations are at risk; a 6000 km² concession has been granted to a forestry consortium along the west bank of the Mamberamo River. Operations proposed include a saw mill, pulp mill and chip mill (WWF 1989; McCarthy 1991). Road building is also a threat to the proposed Mamberamo-Foja Mountains National Park.

Doormantop contains mineral-rich ultramafic rocks with bands of magnetite and may prove to be commercially attractive.

In 1985, the Mamberamo-Foja Mountains National Park (proposed) was added to the IUCN/CNPPA's world list of threatened protected areas.

Conservation

The Mamberamo-Foja Mountains Proposed National Park (Taman Nasional Mamberamo Pegunungan Foja) is not yet gazetted but will cover 14,425 km² making it Indonesia's second largest National Park (Petocz 1984). It will contain a complete range of northern New Guinea habitats, from mangroves and swamps at the mouth of the Mamberamo River, through lowland rain forest and montane zones to Foja-Gauttier mountain complex (2193 m), then down through the lowlands of the Idenburg river system of the Lakes Plains region. The proposed park is contiguous with Pegunungan Jayawijaya Game Reserve and the proposed Sungai Rouffaer Game Reserve (8000 km² and 819 km², respectively). The proposed National Park has also been proposed as a World Heritage Site (Petocz 1984).

The Mamberamo-Foja Proposed National Park is one of the seven priority sites identified in the Irian Jaya Conservation Development Strategy (Petocz 1984, 1989).

Due to its inaccessibility, the only feasible entry to much of the Foja Mountains is by helicopter (Diamond 1981), and therefore its remoteness assures protection over most of the montane areas for the foreseeable future.

References

Archbold, R., Rand, A.L. and Brass, L.J. (1942). Results of the Archbold expeditions. Summary of the 1938–1939 New Guinea expedition. *Bull. Amer. Mus. Nat. Hist.* 79: 197–228.

Diamond, J.M. (1981). *Surveys of proposed reserves in the Foja Mountains and Fakfak Mountains, Irian Jaya, Indonesia. A report to World Wildlife Fund and to the Directorate of Nature Conservation, Indonesia.* (Unpublished report.)

Eechoud, J.P.K. van (1940). *Verslag van de exploratie naar Centraal Nieuw Guinea. Dienstrapport van de resident der Molukken.* (Unpublished.)

FAO (1981-1982). *National conservation plan for Indonesia.* Field Report of UNDP/FAO National Parks Development Project INS/78/061. 8 volumes. FAO, Bogor.

Lam, H.J. (1965). *Fragmenta papuana. Sargentia* 5: 1–196.

McCarthy, A.J. (comp.) (1991). *Conservation areas of Indonesia. Final draft.* World Conservation Monitoring Centre, Cambridge, U.K. in collaboration with Directorate General of Forest Protection and Nature Conservation (PHPA), Ministry of Forestry, Republic of Indonesia, and IUCN Commission on National Parks and Protected Areas, Gland, Switzerland.

Petocz, R.G. (1984). *Conservation and development in Irian Jaya: a strategy for rational resources utilisation.* WWF/IUCN Conservation for Development Programme in Indonesia Report. PHPA, Bogor, Indonesia. 279 pp.

Petocz, R.G. (1989). *Conservation and development in Irian Jaya: a strategy for rational resources utilisation.* Brill, Leiden, The Netherlands. 218 pp.

Petocz, R.G. and Fretes, Y. de (1983). *Mammals of the reserves in Irian Jaya.* WWF Indonesia, Jayapura, Indonesia. Pp. 19–22.

Petocz, R.G., Kirenius, M. and Fretes, Y. de (1983). *Avifauna of the reserves in Irian Jaya.* WWF Indonesia, Jayapura, Indonesia. Pp. 25–36.

Stevens, P.F. (1989). New Guinea. In Campbell, D.G., Hammond, H.D. (eds), *Floristic inventory in tropical countries: the status of plant systematics, collections, and vegetation, plus recommendations for the future.* The New York Botanical Garden, New York. Pp. 120–132.

WWF (1989). *World Wide Fund for Nature progress/financial report, April–June 1989.* WWF Indonesia, Jayapura, Indonesia. 18 pp.

Acknowledgements

This Data Sheet was written by Stephen D. Davis and Dr Peter F. Stevens (Harvard University Herbaria, Cambridge, Massachusetts), with thanks to Dr Wim Vink (Rijksherbarium, Leiden) for commenting on an earlier draft.

WAIGEO
Irian Jaya, Indonesia

Location: Island off the north-west coast of the Vogelkop Peninsula, between latitudes 0°00'–0°28'S and longitudes 130°10'–131°20'E.

Area: 14,784 km².

Altitude: 0–999 m (summit of Mount Samlor).

Vegetation: Lowland tropical rain forest, riverine forest, lower montane rain forest, mangroves, xeromorphic scrub on limestone and ultramafic rocks.

Flora: Few botanical studies, but many local endemics described. A published account (van Royen 1960) includes 322 vascular plant species (including some introduced species). This is clearly an incomplete list of the total flora.

Useful plants: Timber trees, wild sugar cane.

Other values: Distinct fauna.

Threats: Potential mining.

Conservation: Cagar Alam Pulau Waigeo Barat (West Waigeo Island Nature Reserve) covers 1530 km² (IUCN Management Category I: Strict Nature Reserve). Raja Ampat Marine Nature Reserve (proposed) encompasses scattered islets and reefs to the south.

Geography

Pulau Waigeo (meaning "Water Island") is the largest of the Raja Ampat (Four Kings) island group off the north-west coast of the Vogelkop Peninsula, between latitudes 0°00'–0°28'S and longitudes 130°10'–131°20'E. South of Waigeo are the other islands of the Raja Ampat group (Batanta, Salawati and Misool). There are also numerous scattered islets and reefs.

Waigeo is approximately 130 km long and 50 km broad, and is almost divided into two by Majalibit Bay. It is separated from mainland New Guinea by the Selat Dampir (Dampir Strait). Along with the other islands in the Raja Ampat group, Waigeo is part of the Sahul Shelf and has had recent intermittent land connections with New Guinea (Petocz 1984). The topography is generally rugged, comprising dissected karst limestone forming ridges in the central part of the island and steep, inaccessible coastal cliffs, alternating with low-lying muddy areas (van Royen 1960). Ultramafic peridotites and serpentine rocks outcrop in the north of the island. A ridge of c. 400 m (the Go Isthmus) in the north connects the two parts of the island.

The highest points are the summit of Mount Samlor (999 m) and Mount Buffelhoorn (Mt Nok) (c. 980 m) in the eastern part of the island; the highest point in the western part is 815 m.

Vegetation

Van Royen (1960) provides an account of the vegetation of various parts of the island and a useful summary. There are three main types of lowland rain forest. Forest on muddy, clayey soils is dominated by *Pometia pinnata*, *Alstonia spectabilis*, *Tabernaemontana aurantiaca*, *Vitex* and *Teysmanniodendron*. On lateritic loamy soils derived from limestone and ultramafic rocks, the forest includes the dipterocarp *Vatica rassak*, along with *Intsia bijuga*, *Pertusadina multifolia* and *Dillenia* spp. There are extensive stands of *Agathis labillardieri*. On coastal limestone cliffs the forest is dominated by *Intsia bijuga* and *Pinanga*. Some limestone cliffs are very steep and devoid of vegetation.

Riverine forest is best developed in the east, and includes *Myristica*, *Ficus*, *Syzygium* and *Pometia pinnata*; *Octomeles sumatrana* is locally dominant, and there are also large stands of herbaceous vegetation, including wild *Saccharum spontaneum*.

Xeromorphic vegetation is found on ultramafic rocks and on limestone in the north. On limestone, the vegetation is a rather open scrub, with Myrtaceae and a few scattered trees, the tallest of which are *Buchanania papuana* and *Vitex*. This grades into closed lowland rain forest on limestone and low-lying muddy areas. On the ultramafic outcrops in the north, the vegetation is similar to that found on the limestone. Gnarled and stunted Myrtaceae occur, together with *Exocarpus latifolius*, *Alphitonia moluccana*, *Dillenia* and *Ilex*. Grass-sedge vegetation occurs along with *Dicranopteris* fern scrub.

Serpentine vegetation (as at Mount Buffelhoorn) below 500 m includes many of the same forest components as those found on limestone, but above 500 m the forest is richer in ferns, mosses and orchids. The summit area of Mt Buffelhoorn includes numerous rhododendrons, *Drimys piperata* and *Elaeocarpus* (van Royen 1960).

Coastal forest includes *Thespesia populnea*, *Barringtonia asiatica*, *Intsia bijuga*, *Calophyllum inophyllum* and *Hibiscus tiliaceus*. There are also patches of coastal scrub of *Dicranopteris*, *Ficus* and *Spathoglottis*. Mangroves occur in parts of Majalibit Bay, particularly at the mouth of the Siam River, but are not extensive elsewhere.

Flora

Van Royen (1960) lists 322 vascular plant species (280 flowering plant species and 42 ferns), collected during an expedition in 1955 lasting just over a month. The list includes many local endemics, but also some cultivated plants found in and around villages. This is clearly an incomplete list of the total flora, which remains very poorly known (W. Vink 1992, *in litt.*). *Dimorphanthera ovatifolia*, a species of *Drimys*, *Rhododendron cornu-bovis* and *Vaccinium steinii* are apparently restricted to the island. Extreme rarities include *Calophyllum microphyllum*, not collected on the island for 150 years and known only from one other locality. It is likely that distinctive plants like *Ploiarium sessile*, known from the nearby island of Gebeh, will also be found on Waigeo.

Useful plants

The main food plants of the local inhabitants are manioc (*Manihot esculenta*) and sweet potatoes (*Ipomoea batatas*). These, together with pineapple (*Ananas comosus*), are introductions to the island. Bananas (*Musa* spp.), coconuts (*Cocos nucifera*) and *Citrus maxima* are also cultivated.

Van Royen (1960) records that houses on Waigeo are typically built over water using *Pertusadina* wood as the frame and split leaves of *Metroxylon sagu* as walls and roofs. Planks made from the palm trunk are used as flooring.

Social and environmental values

On the basis of faunal distinctiveness, Petocz (1984) ranks Waigeo second in importance of 8 islands belonging to the Indonesian province of Irian Jaya. Some 55 mammals are expected to occur on Pulau Waigeo Barat (West Waigeo) (McCarthy 1991). Waigeo forms part of the West Papuan Islands and Vogelkop Lowlands Endemic Bird Area (which also includes Batanta, Salawati, Kofiau and Misool, and the lowland forests, mangroves and swamps of the Vogelkop and Bomberai peninsulas). A total of 20 restricted-range bird species occur in the region, of which 11 can be found on Waigeo. Of these, Bruijn's brush turkey (*Aepypodius bruijnii*) is endemic to Waigeo, and Wilson's bird-of-paradise (*Cicinnurus respublica*) and the red bird-of-paradise (*Paradisaea rubra*) are near-endemics, being shared with Batanta.

The island is inhabited; most people live in small settlements along the south coast. The main staple food is fish, and either manioc or sweet potatoes (van Royen 1960). Coconut palms, citrus fruits and pineapples are also cultivated.

Threats

A potential threat is mining. A mining company has undertaken exploratory drilling for nickel on the island of Gag to the west of Waigeo, and holds a concession lease on Waigeo which overlaps with Cagar Alam Pulau Waigeo Barat (West Waigeo Island Nature Reserve) (Petocz 1984). Prior to any contemplated expansion of mining activity to Waigeo, Petocz (1984) recommends that an environmental impact study should be made.

Conservation

The western half of the island was established as a Nature Reserve in 1981 – Cagar Alam Pulau Waigeo Barat (IUCN Management Category: I) – covering 1530 km^2 (McCarthy 1991). In addition, Raja Ampat Marine Nature Reserve (proposed) encompasses the scattered islets and reefs that lie to the south of Waigeo. A management plan for West Waigeo is proposed by WWF that will involve community participation in management of the reserve to mitigate against future mineral, timber and wildlife over-exploitation.

References

McCarthy, A.J. (comp.) (1991). *Conservation areas of Indonesia. Final draft*. World Conservation Monitoring Centre, Cambridge, U.K. in collaboration with Directorate General of Forest Protection and Nature Conservation (PHPA), Ministry of Forestry, Republic of Indonesia, and IUCN Commission on National Parks and Protected Areas, Gland, Switzerland.

Petocz, R.G. (1984). *Conservation and development in Irian Jaya: a strategy for rational resources utilisation*. WWF/ IUCN Conservation for Development Programme in Indonesia Report. PHPA, Bogor, Indonesia. 279 pp.

Royen, P. van (1960). *Sertulum Papuanum* 3. The vegetation of some parts of Waigeo Island. *Nova Guinea, Botany* 5: 25–62.

Acknowledgements

This Data Sheet was written by Stephen D. Davis and Dr Peter F. Stevens (Harvard University Herbaria, Cambridge, Massachusetts), with grateful thanks to Dr Wim Vink (Rijksherbarium, Leiden) for commenting on an earlier draft.

South East Asia (Malesia)

MOUNT GILUWE – TARI GAP – DOMA PEAKS
Papua New Guinea

Location: Southern Highlands Province; southern region of the Central Highlands, from the border of Western Highlands to Enga Province, centred on latitude 5°54'S and longitude 143°09'E.

Area: 3346 km².

Altitude: 1000–4368 m, including the most extensive contiguous subalpine area in Papua New Guinea.

Vegetation: The area includes a wide variety of vegetation types, including most types of montane and subalpine communities occurring above 1500 m in Papua New Guinea; extensive montane anthropogenic grasslands. Alpine communities are restricted to the summit of Mount Giluwe. A small area of *Dacrydium* swamp forest is unique.

Flora: Estimated >3000 vascular plant species.

Useful plants: Many species of fruits and vegetables, fibre sources, seed sources of potential timber species, ornamental plants.

Other values: Very rich fauna with a large number of species of birds-of-paradise; many tribal groups inhabit the area and depend on biological resources for their sustenance; potential ecotourism; high landscape quality; local village communities.

Threats: Logging, road building, agricultural plantations. Low population pressure, therefore subsistence agriculture poses no significant threat.

Conservation: Local reserves in Tari Gap area.

Geography

The region includes two proposed conservation areas: Mount Giluwe and the Tari-Doma Peaks area, which could be extended to include Sugarloaf. These areas are located in the Southern Highland Province and marginally in the Enga Province.

Mount Giluwe and the volcanic deposits of the Tari Gap-Doma Peak area are extinct, dome-shaped volcanoes with multiple vents and, surrounding Giluwe, several parasitic cones. The underlying rocks are thick, folded Miocene marine sediments (Perry, in C.S.I.R.O. Land Research Series 1965), covered by thick Pleistocene volcanic deposits, and forming part of the Papuan Geosyncline. The deposits were uplifted during the Pliocene. Most of the area is blanketed with volcanic ash, scoria and agglomerate. The volcanic peaks are steep-sided, conical strato-volcanoes with a series of lava flows (Mount Ambua and Mount Kerewa). Apart from volcanic landforms, the region includes steep-sided mountains and hills, associated with deeply incised rivers to the south.

During the last glaciation the summit area of Mt Giluwe was covered by an ice cap covering some 190 km², and this has resulted in well-preserved terminal moraines. Recessional moraines are evident in high-altitude valleys. Despite the absence of deep glacial lakes, Mount Giluwe is of particular interest because the succession of volcanic events has preserved evidence of glacial activity between lava flows. They indicate at least two previous glaciations at 340,000 years BP and 290,000 years BP.

The mountainous areas are uninhabited, apart from groups hunting in their traditional lands. The steepness of the terrain, and the altitudinal limits of traditional crop cultivation, impose limits on permanent settlement in the mountains. Permanent settlement is therefore restricted to the lower slopes of Mount Giluwe and the Doma Peaks, below the *Nothofagus* forest zone. The population density averages about 13 people/km².

Road access is via the Highlands Highway, which borders the southern slopes of Mount Giluwe to Mendi, and then reaches over 3000 m through the Tari Gap, also giving access to the Doma Peaks. A poorly maintained road circles Mount Giluwe to the north, from Tambul to Mendi. Some logging roads penetrate through the *Nothofagus* forests on the southern slopes of Mount Giluwe, to within a few kilometres of the subalpine grasslands.

Vegetation

The Tari Gap has mid-montane *Nothofagus* forest, upper montane forest, subalpine forest and subalpine grasslands. There are majestic *Nothofagus* stands on Mounts Ne and Ambua.

The vegetation of the Mount Giluwe area is dominated by several major formations: *Nothofagus* forest, coniferous upper montane forest, subalpine forests and extensive grasslands; the bog communities in the latter are particularly noteworthy. Alpine communities are restricted to the very summit of Mount Giluwe.

Castanopsis and *Lithocarpus* forest have been largely cleared for agricultural land. *Dacrydium nidulum* var. *araucaroides* dominates some small, but important, areas of swamp forest in the Mendi Valley and the Tari area (Johns 1980).

Flora

It is estimated that the flora of the region includes more than 3000 vascular plant species. However, the flora is relatively poorly known. Many endemic species occur at high altitudes. They include distinctive species of *Rhododendron, Schefflera, Eriocaulon* and *Isoetes*. The enigmatic species *Senecio gnoma*, known elsewhere only from Mount Wilhelm, occurs on the very highest parts of Mount Giluwe.

Rhododendron saxifragoides occurs on several peaks in the Western and Southern Highlands. This species is a significant component of bog vegetation. Cushion communities occur in the flat glaciated valleys of the summit area of Mount Giluwe.

Useful plants

Many species are used as sources of food, fibre and building materials. The forests represent an important seed source of potential timber species. Many of the high-altitude species, particularly *Rhododendron* spp., are of potential ornamental value.

Social and environmental values

The region has a very rich fauna. Mount Giluwe has 6 endemic species of bush rat, an unnamed giant water rat, wild dogs, cuscus, bandicoots, lizards, large beetles, frogs, crabs, snakes and fish. There are also many species of birds, including the Harpy eagle. The area falls within the Central New Guinean Mountain Endemic Bird Area (EBA) and some 30 restricted-range landbirds are likely to occur in the area, including three threatened species which have very restricted ranges: long-bearded melidectes (*Melidectes princeps*), Sanford's bowerbird (*Archboldia sanfordi*) and ribbon-tailed astrapia (*Astrapia mayeri*). 12 species of birds-of-paradise are present (out of a total of 43 species in New Guinea, 33 species of which are endemic to Papua New Guinea). *Astrapia mayeri* (ribbon-tailed bird-of-paradise) and *Astrapia stephanie* (Princess Stephanie bird-of-paradise) have been observed in both the Tari Gap and on Mount Giluwe where they occur at 2740 and 2590 m, respectively; both species have a restricted distribution in the Central Highlands of Papua New Guinea. *Chemophilus macgregorii* and *Paradisia rudolphi* have been sited in *Nothofagus* forest in the Tari Gap. Both species are rare. Dwarf cassowary (*Casuarius bennetti*) occurs up to 3000 m on Mount Giluwe and the Doma Peaks. It is a rare species although it is more common on Mount Giluwe than in other areas studied. Archbold's bower bird (*Archboldia papuensis*) has a patchy distribution along the Central Range. A distinctive race, *A. papuensis sanfordi*, is restricted to south-west Mount Hagen, Giluwe and Tari. Seasonal migratory birds, such as the shovel-billed kingfisher and the Australian pratincole (May to November), have been observed in the area.

The area is inhabited by a large number of tribal groups who depend on the biological resources of the region for their sustenance.

There is potential for developing ecotourism in the area, based on the extensive subalpine forests and grasslands of Mount Giluwe and the Doma Peaks. The primary *Nothofagus* and subalpine forests are of exceptional scenic interest.

Tourism is also developing at Tari, based on the local village communities.

Threats

Logging operations are common in the area. *Dacrydium nidulum* var. *araucaroides* swamp forests, in both the Mendi Valley and in the swamp areas along the Magarima River, were extensively logged soon after European contact. Present stands are limited in extent.

Recent photographs indicate that there are no restrictions on the diameter size of the trees being logged on the slopes of Mount Giluwe to supply the Wokabaut sawmills (which are promoted as "environmentally friendly").

Logging is a particular threat when it is followed by gardening and intensive hunting. Intensive hunting of birds-of-paradise for their plumes, which are used for ornamental purposes and for trade (the latter being illegal) is a major threat to populations of these species. The dwarf cassowary is valued for its meat and feathers, and living birds are also used as part of the bride price. Bower birds are also hunted for their ornamental plumage.

Extensive dieback in the *Nothofagus pullei* forest was noticed in the 1970s (Ash 1982).

Conservation

A few local reserves exist in Tari Gap area; otherwise no formal protection. The region was included among those of high biological importance in the Papua New Guinea conservation needs assessment (Johns 1992).

References

Ash, J.E. (1975). *The ecology of Nothofagus and mixed species forests on south-east Mt. Giluwe, Papua New Guinea.* Research School of Pacific Studies, Australian National University, Canberra. (Unpublished report.)

Ash, J.E. (1982). The *Nothofagus* Blume (Fagaceae) of New Guinea. In Gressitt, J.L. (ed.), *Biogeography and ecology of New Guinea.* Vol. 1. Junk, The Hague. Pp. 355–380.

Bowers, N. (1968). *The ascending grasslands: an anthropological study of ecological succession in a high mountain valley of New Guinea.* Ph.D. thesis, Columbia University.

Cartledge, E., Shaw, E. and Stamps, D. (1975). Studies in relation to dead patches of *Nothofagus* in Papua New Guinea. P.N.G. Department of Agriculture, Stock and Fisheries. *Research Bulletin* 13: 1–26.

Cavanaugh, L.G. (1957). *Resource survey, Western Highlands.* Department of Forests, File No. 90-14-5. (Unpublished report.)

Clunie, N.M.U. (1975). *Dead patches in Nothofagus forest Mt. Giluwe.* Ecol. Progress Rep. No. 1. Division of Botany, Department of Forests, Lae.

Costin, A.B., Hoogland, R.D. and Lendon, C. (1977). Vegetation changes in the Lake Mamsin area, Saruwaged Plateau, New Guinea. *Bull. Amer. Mus. Nat. Hist.* 1–9.

C.S.I.R.O. Land Research Series (1965). *Lands of the Wabag-Tari Area, Papua New Guinea.* C.S.I.R.O. Land Research Series 15.

C.S.I.R.O. Land Research Series (1970). *Lands of the Goroka-Mount Hagen Area, Papua New Guinea.* C.S.I.R.O. Land Research Series 27.

Gillison, A.N. (1969). Plant succession in an irregular fired grassland area – Doma Peak region, Papua. *J. Ecol.* 57: 415–427.

Gillison, A.N. (1970). Structure and floristics of a montane grassland/forest transition, Doma Peaks region, Papua. *Blumea* 18: 71–79.

Gillison, A.N. (1971). *Dynamics of biotically induced grassland/forest transitions in Papua New Guinea.* M.Sc. thesis, Australian National University, Canberra.

Holdsworth, D.K. and Longley, R.P. (1972). Some medicinal and poisonous plants from the Southern Highlands District of Papua. *Proc. Papua New Guinea Scient. Soc.* 24: 21–24.

Hope, G.S. (1980). New Guinea mountain vegetation communities. In Royen, P. van, *The alpine flora of New Guinea*, Vol. 1. Cramer, Vaduz. Pp. 153–222.

Hynes, R.A. (1970). *Nothofagus* forest in New Guinea – an ecological introduction. Paper presented to Botany Section, ANZAAC 42nd Congress, Port Moresby.

Hynes, R.A. (1974). Altitudinal zonation in New Guinea *Nothofagus* forest. In Flenley, J.R. (ed.), *An altitudinal zonation of forests in Malesia.* Department of Geography, University of Hull, U.K.

Johns, R.J. (1974). *Observations on the Nothofagus stands occurring at lower altitudes on Mt. Giluwe and Kaisenik.* P.N.G. Forestry College Library. (Unpublished report.)

Johns, R.J. (1976). A provisional classification of the montane vegetation of New Guinea. *S.I.N.G.* 4: 105–107.

Johns, R.J. (1980). Notes on the forest types of Papua New Guinea. The *Dacrydium* swamp forests of the Southern Highlands. *Klinkii* 1(4): 3–9.

Johns, R.J. (1986). The instability of the tropical ecosystem in Papuasia. *Blumea* 31: 341–371.

Johns, R.J. (1992). Biodiversity and conservation of the native flora of Papua New Guinea. In Beehler, B.M. (ed.), *Papua New Guinea conservation needs assessment. Volume 2: A biodiversity analysis for Papua New Guinea.* Government of Papua New Guinea, Department of Environment and Conservation, Papua New Guinea. Pp. 15–32.

Johns, R.J. and Burua, N. (1976). The *Castanopsis* forests of Papua New Guinea. Paper presented to the 4th meeting of the Botanical Society, P.N.G.

Kalkman, C. and Vink, W. (1970). Botanical exploration in the Doma Peaks Region, New Guinea. *Blumea* 18: 87–135.

Kalkman, C. and Vink, W. (1970). Botanical exploration of the Doma Peaks and adjacent mountains in the Southern Highlands District, Territory of Papua, Australian New Guinea. *WOTRO Report* (1966–1967): 50–52.

Paijmans, K. (ed.) (1976). *New Guinea vegetation.* Elsevier, Amsterdam. 213 pp.

Robbins, R.G. (1958). Montane formations in the Central Highlands of New Guinea. In *Proceedings UNESCO Symposium on Humid Tropics Vegetation.* Tijawi, Indonesia. Pp. 176–195.

Robbins, R.G. (1961). The montane vegetation of New Guinea. *Tuatara* 8: 121–134.

Robbins, R.G. (1970). Vegetation of the Goroka-Mount Hagen area. *C.S.I.R.O. Aust. Land. Res. Ser.* 27: 104–118.

Robbins, R.G. and Pullen, R. (1965). Vegetation of the Wabag-Tari area. *C.S.I.R.O. Aust. Land. Res. Ser.* 15: 100–115.

Smith, J.M.B. (1980). Ecology of the high mountains of New Guinea. In Royen, P. van, *The alpine flora of New Guinea*, Vol. 1. Cramer, Vaduz. Pp. 111–132.

Smith, J.M.B. (1980). Origins, affinities and distribution of the high altitude flora. In Royen, P. van, *The alpine flora of New Guinea*, Vol. 1. Cramer, Vaduz. Pp. 133–151.

Williams, P.W., McDougall, I. and Powell, J.M. (1972). Aspects of the Quaternary geology of the Tari-Koroba Area, Papua. *J. Geol. Soc. Austr.* 18: 333–347.

Acknowledgements

This Data Sheet was written by Professor Robert J. Johns (Royal Botanic Gardens, Kew), with grateful thanks to Dr Peter F. Stevens (Harvard University Herbaria, Cambridge, Massachusetts) and Dr W. Vink (Rijksherbarium, Leiden) for their valuable advice and information.

BISMARCK FALLS – MOUNT WILHELM – MOUNT OTTO – SCHRADER RANGE – MOUNT HELLWIG – GAHAVISUKA
Papua New Guinea

Location: Northern flanks of the Central Cordillera, extending along the Bismarck Ranges from Mount Otto to Mount Hellwig and the Schrader Range. In the administrative provinces of Madang, Simbu, Eastern and Western Highlands.

Area: 9754 km².

Altitude: 250–4499 m (summit of Mount Wilhelm, the highest mountain in Papua New Guinea).

Vegetation: The area includes a wide variety of vegetation types, from lowland rain forests and swamp forests to lower, mid- and upper montane forests, extensive areas of subalpine forests and grasslands, alpine communities on the summit ridge of Mount Wilhelm.

Flora: Estimated >5000–6000 vascular plant species; over 600 vascular plant species so far recorded from above 2743 m on Mount Wilhelm.

Useful plants: Many species at lower altitudes provide fruits, vegetables, fibres, building materials, timber. Some species used traditionally for adornment, e.g. *Papuapteris (Polystichum) linearis*; medicinal plants.

Other values: Very rich fauna, including several species of birds-of-paradise and a large number of mammals. A large number of tribal groups depend partly on the biological resources of the region for sustenance. Ecotourism has considerable potential.

Threats: High population pressure in the upper Chimbu Valley has caused extensive deforestation for subsistence gardens along the flanks of the mountains; expansion of coffee and cardamom plantations; logging; road building; potential mining.

Conservation: Mount Wilhelm was proposed as a National Park but has not been purchased. Gahavisuka is a small Provincial Park on the western flanks of Mount Otto. The whole region has been proposed as a World Heritage Site.

Geography

The area lies within the administrative provinces of Madang, Simbu, Eastern and Western Highlands. It stretches over 200 km along the north-eastern falls of the major alpine fault which bounds the Sepik, Ramu and Markham depressions in the Central Cordillera, and it includes a variety of prominent ranges, among which are Mount Wilhelm (the highest peak in Papua New Guinea), Mount Herbert, Mount Otto, the Schrader Range, Mount Hellwig and Gahavisuka, the last named being the only area gazetted as a conservation area (Provincial Park).

Mount Wilhelm is part of a granodiorite batholith uplifted during Plio-Pleistocene times. Extensive glaciation occurred on Mount Wilhelm during the Pleistocene. The mountain contains many classic glacial features, including deep cirques, over-deepened valleys that contain large lakes, and lateral and terminal moraines. At its widest extent the glacial cap covered only 21 km² of Mount Wilhelm with glacial moraines descending to about 3260 m, as shown by the terminal moraine at Kombugumambino. Only a small area on the summit of Mount Otto was affected by an ice-sheet of very limited extent. Associated with this glacial action are deep Pleistocene deposits in the Ramu Valley.

The summit of Mount Wilhelm (4499 m) is very near the level of permanent snowfields further west in Irian Jaya. There is growing evidence that more than one glaciation occurred on the New Guinea mountains but remnants of the earlier glaciations have been mostly removed by erosion. The boundaries of the grasslands during the last glaciation (30,000

to 12,000 years BP) were down to a lower limit of 2000 m, a greater degree of depression below the snow-line than presently observed. Mount Wilhelm has a small area of periglacial solifluction just below the main summit. Solifluction screes, stone stripes and rings occur above 4350 m altitude.

Much of the region has a wet tropical climate with very high humidity. Drier periods occur from June–July to October, when clear nights often result in heavy frosts at lower altitudes. References to the high-altitude climates of Mount Wilhelm can be found in McVean (1968), Wade and McVean (1969) and Hnatiuk, McVean and Smith (1974).

Access to the area is via the Highlands Highway, with road access to Gahavisuka Provincial Park from Goroka, and road and walking tracks to Mount Otto. Mount Wilhelm can also be reached by a well-used walking track from Keglsugl. Access to some parts of the region is difficult during the rainy season, but there are several airstrips catering for small aircraft.

Vegetation

The vegetation types included within the area proposed for World Heritage listing (Johns 1992) range from lowland swamp forest and rain forest at c. 200–300 m along the Ramu River to alpine communities at the summit of Mount Wilhelm. Included are freshwater lowland swamp forest dominated by *Campnosperma brevipetiolata*, mixed lowland rain forest, a range of montane forest and grassland types, including mixed forests, *Castanopsis* and *Lithocarpus* forests, and ridge top

Nothofagus forest at higher altitudes, subalpine forest, subalpine grasslands and alpine vegetation. Extensive areas of montane vegetation occur throughout the area but are virtually unstudied.

Some of the lowland forest is developed on ultramafic parent rocks. All three montane forest zones (lower, mid- and upper) are well-represented.

Lowland swamp forests dominate the southern regions of the Ramu Valley, with extensive stands dominated by *Campnosperma* occurring in the area under consideration. These distinctive forest types are often rich in bird populations. Lowland rain forests are typically diverse, with extensive stands dominated by species of *Pometia*, *Mangifera* and *Ficus* (and others). Dipterocarps have not been collected from the area.

A distinctive, but little-studied, type of vegetation grows on ultramafic soils along the Bismarck foothills. At 600–700 m, lowland rain forest grades into mixed montane forest. Stands of *Castanopsis* and *Lithocarpus* forest occur in the drier valley floors and slopes up to 1500–1600 m. Small areas of *Araucaria* forest occur locally. Above this zone, ridges are either dominated by mixed forest or by stands of *Nothofagus*.

Upper montane forest is dominated by podocarps. Those on Mount Kerigomna are described in Grubb and Stevens (1979). Subalpine forest is dominated by *Dacrycarpus compactus*, and includes locally a significant component of other high-altitude conifers, such as *Libocedrus papuanus* and *Phyllocladus hypophyllus*. Subalpine forests on Mount Wilhelm are described in detail by Wade (1968) and Wade and McVean (1969).

Subalpine grassland and shrubby communities extend as tongues down the glaciated valleys to c. 2745 m. Forest margins support a variety of species of predominantly red-flowered rhododendrons, *Dimorphanthera*, *Vaccinium*, *Drimys*, *Senecio* and *Olearia*. Tree ferns (*Cyathea*) are common, as are many terrestrial ferns, such as *Plagiogyria* and *Gleichenia*. This community is locally variable, decreasing in species diversity with increasing altitude. It grades into grassland communities rich in shrubs and tree ferns. Herbaceous plants, such as species of *Drosera*, *Ranunculus*, *Astelia* and *Gentiana*, are commonly associated with grasses, such as *Deschampsia klossii*. The dominant species of tree fern varies with altitude: *Cyathea atrox* and *C. aenefolia* at altitudes below 3400 m; *C. macgregorii* and *C. gleichenioides* amongst the many species at slightly higher altitudes. *Styphelia*, *Coprosma* and *Gaultheria* are commonly associated with tussock grasses and shrubs.

At higher altitudes alpine grasslands and herb fields occur, in which tall shrubs are absent. On Mount Wilhelm, clumps of the fern *Polystichum lineare* (*Papuapteris linearis*) form a distinctive community.

Short alpine grasslands are dominated by *Danthonia*, *Poa*, *Carpha*, *Carex* and *Astelia*. An alpine meadow community, dominated by *Astelia alpina*, occurs on moderate slopes above 4200 m. Bog and lichen communities are less extensive than on the higher mountains of Irian Jaya.

Flora

Plant diversity is estimated at more than 5000 species of vascular plants. Johns and Stevens (1972) list over 600 species from a restricted collecting area (the Pindaunde

Valley) on Mount Wilhelm, at an altitude above 2743 m. Several species have been added to that list following more recent fieldwork. Investigation of the subalpine communities on other parts of the Wilhelm massif would add significantly to the list of species.

There has been little collecting at lower altitudes within the region, in the zones where the greatest diversity of plant species and plant communities occurs. The regions along the eastern foothills of the Asaro Valley were collected during the Archbold Expeditions (Brass 1964). An intensive collecting programme was initiated by Rev. N. Cruttwell in the Gahavisuka Provincial Park and, with the exception of Mount Wilhelm and the Marafunga area (Grubb and Stevens 1979), this is the only area where the flora is reasonably known.

There are numerous endemics known from the subalpine and alpine flora, while the lowland ultramafic rocks are the only known locality of *Lauterbachia* (Monimiaceae).

Johns and Stevens (1972) include a detailed list of collections from Mount Wilhelm (up to 1971). The northern flanks of the Bismarck Ranges and the Ramu Valley were extensively collected by Schlechter and Lauterbach, among others, on a series of expeditions. The first detailed collections at higher altitudes in the Bismarck Ranges were made from Mount Wilhelm by Hoogland and Pullen in 1956–1957 and by Womersley in 1956. In 1959, L.J. Brass collected some 900 plant numbers.

Useful plants

There are a large number of wild relatives of fruit trees, including species of *Mangifera* and *Artocarpus*. *Ficus dammaropsis* is used as a vegetable. Many important timber trees occur throughout the region, but not in stands of sufficient size to make logging economical, except for local village sawmills. Many species are used locally for building village houses.

Pandanus (garuga) is extensively used for food and roofing. Many local plants are used as sources of greens and spices, including *Gnetum gnemon* and *G. costatum* (tulip), edible grasses, and *Cinnamomum* spp.

Palms in lowland and lower montane areas are used for flooring, roofing and for securing poles and walls for buildings (e.g. *Calamus* spp.). *Lygodium* is also used locally for tying.

The alpine fern *Polystichum* (*Papuapteris*) *papuanus* was traded extensively by villagers from the upper Chimbu Valley, throughout the highlands in exchange for pots.

Social and environmental values

The region has a very rich fauna and falls within the Central New Guinean Mountains Endemic Bird Area (EBA) which runs from the isthmus of the Vogelkop in Irian Jaya, Indonesia, to Milne Bay in Papua New Guinea. Some 30 restricted-range landbirds are likely to occur in the Bismarck Falls area of which three have very restricted ranges in this region: long-bearded melidectes (*Melidectes princeps*), Sanford's bowerbird (*Archboldia sanfordi*) and ribbon-tailed astrapia (*Astrapia mayeri*). All these three birds are considered threatened as a result of habitat destruction within their small ranges, and *A. mayeri* is also hunted for its plumes.

Several tribal groups live in the valleys. The largest group is the Simbu people of the upper Chimbu Valley. This valley is the most densely settled in Papua New Guinea, with an old traditional agriculture dependent upon *Casuarina oligodon*. This remarkable nitrogen-fixing tree is used also as a source of timber for building and firewood. The practice of using the tree as a means of increasing soil fertility is probably about 700 years old. The fertile volcanic ash soils of the valley were thus able to support a large population well before the arrival of the first missionaries.

Preservation of the remaining forest is essential to help protect and regulate the water supplies of this densely populated region. The forests also provide the local population with an important source of traditional foods, medicines and firewood. The wildlife has been extensively hunted and many species were already extinct from the upper Chimbu by the time of first European contact.

The region is important scientifically and historically. Some of the first extensive scientific expeditions in Papua New Guinea were conducted by the German New Guinea Company along the Ramu and the northern flanks of the Bismarck Ranges.

Spectacular glacial lakes and valleys, and shrubbery rich in species of *Rhododendron* and other mountain plants familiar to bush walkers from both Australasia and north temperate areas, could be the basis of increased ecotourism. Access is comparatively easy by car. Already Mount Wilhelm is regularly visited by scientists, and by climbers wishing to scale the highest mountain in Papua New Guinea. A research laboratory and huts are available for visitors to Mount Wilhelm.

Threats

Population pressure in the montane valleys is perhaps the major threat to the vegetation of the Bismarck Ranges. The population is rapidly increasing and, although large numbers of people are migrating to urban and coastal areas, without some form of population control the traditional practices will continue to disrupt and place strains on the natural resources.

The extension of agriculture is the greatest threat to the forests. The threat comes from the increased number of small village plantations of coffee and cardamom, and the introduction of vegetable crops which can withstand the colder climate above the traditional upper limits of cultivation imposed by sweet potato. Population growth also increases the demand for timber, and this could result in logging of forests on very steep slopes.

Mining does not present a threat at present, but there are large chromite deposits along the banks of the Ramu River.

Conservation

Mount Wilhelm was proposed as a National Park but has not been purchased. Gahavisuka is a small Provincial Park on the western flanks of Mount Otto. The whole region has been proposed as a World Heritage Site (World Bank 1990) and included among those areas of high biological importance in a Papua New Guinea conservation needs assessment (Johns 1992).

References

Brass, L.J. (1964). Results of the Archbold expeditions No. 86. Summary of the Sixth Archbold expedition to New Guinea 1959. *Bull. Amer. Mus. Nat. Hist.* 127: 145–216.

Brookfield, H.C. and Brown, P. (1963). *Struggle for land: agriculture and group territories among the Chimbu of the New Guinea Highlands.* Oxford University Press, Melbourne.

C.S.I.R.O. Land Research Series (1970). *Lands of the Goroka-Mount Hagen area, Papua New Guinea.* C.S.I.R.O. Land Research Series 27.

Grubb, P.J. and Stevens, P.F. (1979). *The forests of the Fatima and Mt. Kerigomna and a review of montane and subalpine forest elsewhere in Papua New Guinea.* Bio. Geo. Series. BG/5 Australian National University, Canberra.

Hnatiuk, R.J. (1975). *Aspects of the growth and climate of tussock grasslands in montane New Guinea and Sub-Antarctic Islands.* Ph.D. thesis, Australian National University, Canberra.

Hnatiuk, R.J., McVean, D.N. and Smith, J.M.B. (1974). *The climate of Mt. Wilhelm.* Mt. Wilhelm Studies 11. Bio. Geo. Series BG/4. Australian National University, Canberra.

Hoogland, R.D. (1958). The alpine flora of Mt. Wilhelm (New Guinea). *Blumea Suppl.* 4: 220–238.

Hope, G.S. (1973). *The vegetation history of Mount Wilhelm.* Ph.D. thesis, Canberra.

Hope, G.S. (1975). *Some notes on the non-forest vegetation and its environment, northern flank of Mt Albert Edward, Central District, Papua New Guinea.* Australian National University, Canberra. (Unpublished report.)

Hope, G.S. (1976). The vegetational history of Mt Wilhelm, Papua New Guinea. *J. Ecol.* 64: 627–664.

Hope, G.S. (1980). New Guinea mountain vegetation communities. In Royen, P. van, *The alpine flora of New Guinea*, Vol. 1. Cramer, Vaduz. Pp. 153–222.

Johns, R.J. (1992). Biodiversity and conservation of the native flora of Papua New Guinea. In Beehler, B.M. (ed.), *Papua New Guinea conservation needs assessment. Volume 2: A biodiversity analysis for Papua New Guinea.* Government of Papua New Guinea, Department of Environment and Conservation, Papua New Guinea. Pp. 15–32.

Johns, R.J. and Stevens, P.F. (1972). Mt Wilhelm flora: a check list of the species. *Botany Bulletin Department of Forests, Papua New Guinea* 6: 60 pp.

McVean, D.N. (1968). A year of weather records at 3,480 m. on Mt. Wilhelm, New Guinea. *Weather* 23: 377–381.

McVean, D.N. (1974). Mountain climates of the southwest Pacific. In Flenley, J.R. (ed.), *An altitudinal zonation of forests in Malesia.* Department of Geography, University of Hull, U.K.

Robbins, R.G. (1970). Vegetation of the Goroka-Mount Hagen area. *C.S.I.R.O. Aust. Land. Res. Ser.* 27: 104–118.

Smith, J.M.B. (1974). *Origins and ecology of the non-forest flora of Mt. Wilhelm, New Guinea.* Ph.D. thesis, Australian National University, Canberra.

Smith, J.M.B. (1974). Southern biogeography on the basis of continental drift: a review. *J. Austr. Mammal Soc.* 1: 213–230.

Smith, J.M.B. (1975). Living fragments of the flora of Gondwanaland. *Aust. Geogr. Studies* 13: 3–12.

Smith, J.M.B. (1975). Mountain grasslands of New Guinea. *J. Biogeogr.* 2: 27–44.

Smith, J.M.B. (1975). Notes on the distribution of herbaceous angiosperm species in the mountains of New Guinea. *J. Biogeogr.* 2: 87–101.

Smith, J.M.B. (1977). Man's impact upon some New Guinea mountain ecosystems. In Bayliss-Smith, T.P. and Feachem, R.G.A. (eds), *Subsistence and survival. Rural ecology in the Pacific.* Pp. 185–214.

Smith, J.M.B. (1977). Origins and ecology of the tropical alpine flora of Mt Wilhelm, New Guinea. *Biol. J. Linn. Soc.* 9: 87–131.

Smith, J.M.B. (1977). Vegetation and microclimate of east- and west-facing slopes in the grasslands of Mt. Wilhelm, Papua New Guinea. *J. Ecol.* 65: 39–53.

Smith, J.M.B. (1980). Ecology of the high mountains of New Guinea. In Royen, P. van, *The alpine flora of New Guinea*, Vol. 1. Cramer, Vaduz. Pp. 111–132.

Smith, J.M.B. (1980). Origins, affinities and distribution of the high altitude flora. In Royen, P. van, *The alpine flora of New Guinea*, Vol. 1. Cramer, Vaduz. Pp. 133–151.

Wade, L.K. (1968). *The alpine and subalpine vegetation of Mt. Wilhelm, New Guinea.* Ph.D. thesis, Australian National University, Canberra.

Wade, L.K. and McVean, D.N. (1969). *Mt. Wilhelm studies I. The alpine and subalpine vegetation.* Department of Biogeography and Geomorphology Publ. BG/1. Australian National University, Canberra.

Walker, D. (1968). A reconnaissance of the non-arboreal vegetation of the Pindaunde catchment, Mt. Wilhelm, New Guinea. *J. Ecol.* 56: 445–466.

World Bank (1990). *Papua New Guinea. The forestry sector: a tropical forestry action plan review.* (A report prepared under the auspices of the Tropical Forestry Action Plan.)

Acknowledgements

This Data Sheet was written by Professor Robert J. Johns (Royal Botanic Gardens, Kew), with grateful thanks to Dr Peter F. Stevens (Harvard University Herbaria, Cambridge, Massachusetts) and Dr W. Vink (Rijksherbarium, Leiden) for their valuable advice and information.

HUON PENINSULA
(MOUNT BANGETA – RAWLINSON RANGE; CROMWELL RANGES AND SIALUM TERRACES)
Papua New Guinea

Location: Includes three major areas of the Huon Peninsula: the Sialum Terraces, Cromwell Mountains and an area extending from the high-altitude grasslands of Mount Bangeta and the Rawlinson Range to the southern coast. All areas are located in the Morobe Province.

Area: 3415 km².

Altitude: 0–4120 m (summit of Mount Bangeta).

Vegetation: Wide variety of vegetation types: coastal vegetation (narrow fringe), lowland and hill rain forests; montane forests, subalpine forests and some subalpine grassland communities on Mount Bangeta. Many communities are developed on limestone.

Flora: Probably includes in excess of 4000–5000 vascular plant species; the flora is comparatively poorly known.

Useful plants: Species used for fruits, vegetables, fibre, building materials; gene pool of potential timber species.

Other values: Rich fauna. Tribal groups depend on the biological resources of the region for sustenance. Ecotourism potential; geological and archaeological sites.

Threats: Helicopter logging in parts of the Cromwell Mountains; proposed logging of *Dacrydium*; road building on steep slopes; subsistence agriculture could pose significant threats in local areas of high population.

Conservation: No formal protection; included in the list of sites of high biological diversity in the conservation needs assessment for Papua New Guinea (Johns 1992).

Geography

The Huon Peninsula is the eastern extension of the mountain blocks that border the northern side of the Mamberamo-Sepik-Ramu-Markham intermontane depression. The area includes the Sialum Terraces (uplifted coral limestones), the Cromwell Range, the summit regions of Mount Bangeta and a broad zone to the southern coast of the peninsula, covering the Rawlinson Range. Extensive karst areas also occur in the Cromwell Mountains and in the glaciated summit region of Mount Bangeta. All the mountain blocks are actively uplifting.

Population density is low, with people concentrated in the Finschhafen area and the larger montane valleys. Small villages are scattered along the northern and southern coast. Road access is limited. During the 1940s a road was built from Lae to Finschhafen but it rapidly became difficult to use due to severe flooding.

Vegetation

There is a narrow strip of coastal vegetation and mangroves. Lowland tropical rain forest occurs up to 300 m altitude. In the south-west, it is dominated by stands of *Anisoptera thurifera*, but these forests have been extensively logged for timber exports. Mixed forests dominate other lowland areas, with a canopy of some 30 m and occasional emergent trees up to 45 m; *Pometia pinnata* is a common component. Above 350 m *Palaquium supfianum* is dominant.

Lower montane forest is dominated by *Castanopsis* and *Lithocarpus*, and reaches up to some 1800–2000 m altitude. Isolated hills along the southern coast support *Lithocarpus*

forest, often mixed with *Anisoptera* as low as 300 m. Open ridge crests above 2000 m are dominated by *Xanthomyrtus-Vaccinium-Rhododendron* communities. *Elmerrillia tsiampaca* is co-dominant with *Lithocarpus* around 2300 m, particularly on poor soils where the trees are widely spaced and have a relatively dense undergrowth. Above 2400 m the *Lithocarpus-Elmerrillia* forest gives way to one dominated by *Elaeocarpus* and conifers, in particular *Phyllocladus*, *Podocarpus* (*Dacrycarpus*) and *Dacrydium*.

Subalpine communities occur above 3000 m. Grasses dominate in association with *Gentiana*, *Viola*, *Euphrasia* and *Cardamine*. Ericaceae increase above 3000 m and dominate the subalpine vegetation and forest communities at 3300 m. Tree ferns (*Cyathea tomentosissima*) are a feature of subalpine grasslands (Botany Division, Lae 1963). The extensive forest stands on limestone dominated by *Dacrydium* are unique in the Southern Hemisphere; almost pure dryland forests of *Dacrydium* occur only in the Cromwell Mountains.

The uplifted coral surfaces of the Sialum Terraces are dominated by a mixture of lowland grass communities.

Flora

The flora probably includes over 4000–5000 vascular plant species; but is still comparatively poorly known. Many local endemics in both herbaceous and woody genera occur at higher altitudes, but insufficient is known to be definite about any patterns of endemism. Even wide-ranging species of genera such as *Oreomyrrhis* and *Drimys* may be distinct from their relations on the main ranges.

Useful plants

Many species are used as fruits and vegetables, as well as for fibre and building materials. The forests are a gene pool of potential timber trees.

Social and environmental values

A large number of local tribal groups depend on the biological resources of the region for sustenance.

The rich fauna includes a number of species with restricted ranges. For example, the Huon tree kangaroo (*Dendrolagus matschiei foresteri*) is restricted to the Huon Peninsula and Umboi Island between 1600 and 3300 m altitude, and the black spotted cuscus from 1600 to 3300 m altitude. The latter is also common in the Northern Province. Alpine wallabies occur in the subalpine grasslands around Mount Bangeta. Ten restricted-range landbirds occur in the mountains, four of them endemic, including the Huon astrapia (*Astrapia rothschildi*) and emperor bird-of-paradise (*Paradisaea guilielmi*). This latter species may be threatened, being a forest bird which occurs at altitudes which are good for agriculture.

The Sialum Terraces are a base-line for Pleistocene sea-level changes. Stone axes more than 40,000 years old, have been found. Evidence suggests that a settled coastal population created small gaps in the rain forest to grow bananas, taro and other crops.

Ecotourism has considerable potential in the region, based on the rich flora and fauna.

Threats

Population density is very low. Spices, cocoa and coffee are grown around the villages on the margins of the region and traditional hunting is practised. These activities provide the major source of funds for villagers, the crops being marketed in Finschhafen or Lae. Subsistence agriculture could pose a significant threat in local areas of high population density.

Copper and gold occur in the Huon Peninsula, but the deposits appear to be too small to be economically viable.

Logging occurs in the southern coastal forests of the Huon Peninsula, helicopters extracting the timber; currently c. 90 km² are logged annually (Arentz 1992). Helicopter logging apparently has a relatively low environmental impact as access roads are not needed and the forest suffers less damage during extraction. Proposals exist to log the last substantial dry land stand of *Dacrydium* in New Guinea. Road building on steep slopes is also a potential threat.

Conservation

No formal protection exists. The region is included in the list of sites of high biological diversity in the conservation needs assessment for Papua New Guinea (Johns 1992).

References

Arentz, F. (1992). Low impact logging – helicopter logging in Papua New Guinea. *Trop. For. Management Update* 2(6): 6.

Botany Division, Lae (1963). *Report of Saruwaket trip. 20 February to 3 March 1963*. National Herbarium, Lae, Papua New Guinea. (Unpublished report.)

Clunie, N.M.U. and Croft, J.R. (1977). Lowland hill forest communities in the Moikisung area, Huon Peninsula. National Herbarium, Lae, Papua New Guinea. (Unpublished report.)

Costin, A.B., Hoogland, R.D. and Lendon, C. (1977). Vegetation changes in the Lake Mamsin area, Saruwaged Plateau, New Guinea. *Bull. Amer. Mus. Nat. Hist.* 1–9.

Diels, L. (1929). Bietrage zur Flora dis Saruwaged Gebirges. *Bot. Jahrb.* 62: 452–501.

Gillison, A.N. (1969). Plant succession in an irregular fired grassland area – Doma Peak region, Papua. *J. Ecol.* 57: 415–427.

Johns, R.J. (1975). *The role of historical factors in the vegetation pattern of the lowland tropics – the Anisoptera forests of Papua New Guinea*. P.N.G. Forestry College Library. (Unpublished report.)

Johns, R.J. (1976). A provisional classification of the montane vegetation of New Guinea. *S.I.N.G.* 4: 105–107.

Johns, R.J. (1986). The instability of the tropical ecosystem in Papuasia. *Blumea* 31: 341–371.

Johns, R.J. (1992). Biodiversity and conservation of the native flora of Papua New Guinea. In Beehler, B.M. (ed.), *Papua New Guinea conservation needs assessment. Volume 2: A biodiversity analysis for Papua New Guinea*. Government of Papua New Guinea, Department of Environment and Conservation, PNG. Pp. 15–32.

Paijmans, K. (ed.) (1976). *New Guinea vegetation*. Elsevier, Amsterdam. 213 pp.

Robbins, R.G. (1970). *Vegetation of the Goroka-Mount Hagen area*. C.S.I.R.O. Aust. Land. Res. Ser. 27: 104–118.

Royen, P. van (1964). *Sertulum Papuanum 12. Sketch of the alpine vegetation of Mt. Bangeta*. Trans. P.N.G. Sci. Soc. Pp. 14–18.

Smith, J.M.B. (1980). Ecology of the high mountains of New Guinea. In Royen, P. van, *The alpine flora of New Guinea*, Vol. 1. Cramer, Vaduz. Pp. 111–132.

Smith, J.M.B. (1980). Origins, affinities and distribution of the high altitude flora. In Royen, P. van, *The alpine flora of New Guinea*, Vol. 1. Cramer, Vaduz. Pp. 133–151.

Acknowledgements

This Data Sheet was written by Professor Robert J. Johns (Royal Botanic Gardens, Kew), with grateful thanks to Dr Peter F. Stevens (Harvard University Herbaria, Cambridge, Massachusetts) and Dr W. Vink (Rijksherbarium, Leiden).

SOUTHERN FLY PLATFORM (LAKE DAVIUMBU – ORIOMO – WASSI KUSSA – TONDA WILDLIFE MANAGEMENT AREA) Papua New Guinea

Location: South of the Fly River, in four areas extending from the border of Irian Jaya to Daru, in the Western Province of Papua New Guinea.

Area: 18,644 km².

Altitude: 0–30 m. (The most extensive area of low relief in Papua New Guinea.)

Vegetation: The region includes a wide variety of vegetation types, including most types of monsoon and savanna vegetation, as well as lowland swamp forests and herbaceous communities, with mangroves along the coast and tidal rivers.

Flora: Probably includes >2000 vascular plant species. Flora closely related to that of Australia.

Useful plants: Edible palms (e.g. *Licuala* sp.), traditional food and medicinal plants.

Other values: Very rich fauna with a large number of migratory birds. The region is inhabited by a large number of tribal groups who depend on the biological resources of the region for sustenance. Ecotourism based on hunting of rusa deer has considerable potential.

Threats: No major threats to region as a whole; low population pressure. Some species threatened by grazing pressure caused by rusa deer. Potential threat from Ok Tedi copper/gold mine which could cause silting up of lakes along the Fly River (e.g. Lake Daviumbu).

Conservation: Tonda Wildlife Management Area (IUCN Management Category: VIII) covers 5900 km² of the western border area of the Fly Platform. The areas considered here as a CPD site are included in the list of sites of high biological diversity in the conservation needs assessment for Papua New Guinea (Johns 1992).

This account covers four major areas in the Southern Fly Platform which are recognized for their high biodiversity in a conservation needs assessment for Papua New Guinea (Johns 1992). Three of them are located along the southern part of the platform, the other in the region of Lake Daviumbu.

Geography

The Southern Fly region is located in the Western Province of Papua New Guinea. The province has the lowest population density of any province in the country, mainly because the deeply weathered soils, developed on the geologically old northern extension of the Australian plate, are of low fertility. North of the Fly River, soils are more fertile and support diverse lowland rain forest communities. The Southern Fly region is subject to frequent flooding and malaria is prevalent. Access to all regions is poor.

The Wassi-Kussa area is bounded by a line from Mari village on the coast to Arufi, along the Mai Kussa, following the Tamaria Kussa back to the coast near Mari village. It covers an area of some 2300 km² of fluvial and poorly drained swamp environments restricted to the Fly Platform, with a maximum elevation of just 30 m above sea-level. The area is the most extensive lowland area in all of Papua New Guinea. The dominant vegetation types are savanna and swamp.

Tonda Wildlife Management Area borders Irian Jaya in the southern region of the Western Province and covers several thousand square kilometers. The area includes a series of woodland and grassland habitats unique in Papua New Guinea. Dominant tree species are *Melaleuca* and *Acacia*. There is a very high diversity of species, although intensive grazing by naturalized deer is a threat to some edible herbs (Brass 1938; CSIRO Land Research Series 1971).

The Oriomo area has a poorly known flora closely related to that occurring in Cape York Peninsula, Queensland, Australia. The climatic regime is different from other areas of the Fly Platform.

Lake Daviumbu includes an extensive lake system to the north of the Fly River. The area includes a variety of swamp, savanna and monsoon communities, with rain forest limited to better drained ridges and along river banks. Many areas are subject to seasonal inundation during the wet season, and become parched (and often burnt) during the 3–4 month dry season.

Access to inland villages is by river, or by light aircraft which use small airfields, like Morehead, located near to many villages.

Vegetation

The first extensive plant collections were made by Brass during the Archbold Expedition to Papua in 1936–1937. A general account of the expedition was published (Archbold and Rand 1935) together with a detailed description of the vegetation (Brass 1938).

Mangroves form a narrow fringe (often only a few metres wide) along the southern coast and along tidal river systems, such as the Wassi Kussa. Tidal rivers also have dense stands of nipa palm (*Nypa fruticans*) along their banks. Towards the east, the large quantities of fresh water discharged from the Fly River limit the development of mangrove communities.

There are areas of coastal woodland, scrub, mixed herbaceous vegetation and grassland on salt flats. Beach forest is dominated by *Pterocarpus indicus*, *Terminalia* spp., *Planchonia papuana*, *Nauclea coadunata*, *Acacia* spp., *Syzygium* and *Pongamia*. The climbing fern *Stenochlaena* is locally abundant.

The western region is essentially a dry area of low ridges and extensive flat lands supporting savanna and savanna forest. These communities extend into Irian Jaya (van Royen 1963). Rain forest occurs in isolated patches along the streams and in restricted ridge areas. These savanna formations are closely related to the open forests of the Australian continent. The dominant trees and grasses are the same species in both areas, and most of the flora is common to both (e.g. species of such genera as *Eriocaulon* and *Lomandra* are found on both sides of the Torres Strait).

The vegetation of tall savanna forest is composed of *Eucalyptus* (over 14 species of which are known to occur in the area), *Tristania* and several species of *Melaleuca*. Common grass species in the savanna forest are *Themeda triandra* and *Ophiurus exaltatus*. The dominance of savanna vegetation is probably due to the highly seasonal nature of the rainfall.

Swamp forests dominated by *Melaleuca* occur north of the Wassi Kussa river. These areas, drained during the dry season, support tall forest of 20–25 m. An exposed series of roots surround the tree trunks at c. 7–8 m up the bole; these are active during the wet season when the forest is inundated by 6–8 m of water (Johns and Moi 1977).

Lake Daviumbu supports a very diverse aquatic vegetation.

Useful plants

Many plants are traditionally used as sources of medicines. Edible palms (e.g. *Licuala* sp.) are among traditional food plants. The staple food source is sago (*Metroxylon sagu*).

Social and environmental values

The area is inhabited by a large number of tribal groups who depend on the biological resources of the region for sustenance.

The region has a very rich fauna. Lake Daviumbu and swamp areas along the Fly River are important for waders and migratory birds. Large populations of parrots and cockatoos have also been observed in the area.

Six restricted-range landbirds occur; three are entirely confined to the area and a further two are confined to the area and to the Aru Islands. The Fly River grassbird (*Megalurus albolimbatus*) is known only from Lake Daviumbu and from the Bensbach River, where its reedbed habitat is threatened through overgrazing by introduced rusa deer. The region is a famous haven for wintering Australian and Palearctic waders and waterfowl.

The region has potential for ecotourism based on hunting of rusa deer.

Threats

The low intensity of shifting agriculture and dependence upon sago palm as a staple food source has resulted in the region suffering little disturbance. Population density is very low.

Some edible palms (e.g. *Licuala*) are quite rare within collecting distances of the villages. The timber resource is of insufficient volume to support any substantial local timber industry or to result in extensive logging operations.

Populations of rusa deer provide a major threat to some species of edible plants. E.E. Henty (pers. comm.) has observed a marked decline of edible species in areas of the Western Province with a high density of rusa deer. Extinction of some species seems likely as a result of grazing pressure.

The Ok Tedi copper/gold mine could result in silting up of lakes along the Fly River (e.g. Lake Daviumbu).

Conservation

The areas considered here as a CPD site are included in the list of sites of high biological diversity in the conservation needs assessment for Papua New Guinea (Johns 1992). The only area under formal protection at present is the Tonda Wildlife Management Area (IUCN Management Category: VIII), which covers 5900 km² along the western border of the Fly Platform.

References

Archbold, R. and Rand, A.L. (1935). The results of the Archbold expeditions. No. 7. Summary of the 1933–1934 Papuan expedition. *Bull. Amer. Mus. Nat. Hist.* 68: 527–579.

Barlow, B.A. (1972). The significance of Torres Strait in the distribution of Australasian Loranthaceae. In Walker, D. (ed.), *Bridge and barrier: the natural and cultural history of Torres Strait*. Department of Biogeography and Geomorphology. BG/3. Australian National University Press, Canberra.

Brass, L.J. (1938). Notes on the vegetation of the Fly and Wassi Kussa rivers, British New Guinea. *J. Arn. Arb.* 19: 190, 221–223.

C.S.I.R.O. Land Research Series (1971). *Land resources of the Morehead-Kiunga area, Papua New Guinea*. C.S.I.R.O. Land Research Series 29.

Heyligers, P.C. (1966). Observations on *Themeda australis – Eucalyptus* savannah in Papua. *Pac. Sci.* 20: 477–489.

Hoogland, R.D. (1972). Plant distribution patterns across the Torres Strait. In Walker, D. (ed.), *Bridge and barrier: the natural and cultural history of Torres Strait*. Department of Biogeography and Geomorphology. BG/3. Australian National University Press, Canberra. Pp. 131–152.

Johns, R.J. (1992). Biodiversity and conservation of the native flora of Papua New Guinea. In Beehler, B.M. (ed.), *Papua New Guinea conservation needs assessment. Volume 2: A biodiversity analysis for Papua New Guinea.* Government of Papua New Guinea, Department of Environment and Conservation, Papua New Guinea. Pp. 15–32.

Johns, R.J. and Moi, W. (1977). The vegetation of the Western Province – an Australian outlier. (Paper presented to the 6th meeting of the Papua New Guinea.)

Paijmans, K. (1971). Vegetation, forest resources, and ecology of the Morehead-Kiunga area. *C.S.I.R.O. Aust. Land. Res. Ser.* 29: 89–113.

Paijmans, K. (ed.) (1976). *New Guinea vegetation.* Elsevier, Amsterdam. 213 pp.

Royen, P. van (1956). Notes on a vegetation of clay plains in southern New Guinea. *Nova Guinea* 7: 175–180.

Royen, P. van (1963). *Sertulum Papuanum* 7. Notes on the vegetation of south New Guinea. *Nova Guinea Botany Series* 13: 195–241.

Schodde, R. and Calaby, J.H. (1972). The biogeography of the Australo-Papuan bird and mammal faunas in relation to Torres Strait. In Walker, D. (ed.), *Bridge and barrier: the natural and cultural history of Torres Strait.* Department of Biogeography and Geomorphology. BG/3. Australian National University Press, Canberra.

Acknowledgements

This Data Sheet was written by Professor Robert J. Johns (Royal Botanic Gardens, Kew), with grateful thanks to Dr Peter F. Stevens (Harvard University Herbaria, Cambridge, Massachusetts) and Dr W. Vink (Rijksherbarium, Leiden) for their valuable advice and information.

MENYAMYA – ASEKI – AMUNGWIWA – BOWUTU MOUNTAINS – LASANGA ISLAND
Papua New Guinea

Location: Central Ranges, including Mount Amungwiwa, Mount Missim and the Bowutu Mountains to Lasanga Island. Located in Morobe Province. Mount Amungwiwa is centred on latitude 7°29'S and longitude 146°39'E.

Area: 6695 km².

Altitude: 0–3278 m (summit of Mount Amungwiwa).

Vegetation: The area includes most vegetation types occurring along altitudinal gradients in Papua New Guinea from lowland to subalpine zones, including lowland rain forest (with extensive dipterocarp forests along the foothills of the Bowutu Mountains), lowland swamp forests, extensive areas of ultramafic vegetation in Bowutu Mountains, lower to upper montane forests, extensive areas of subalpine forests.

Flora: Probably includes 1500–3000 vascular plant species; many local endemics.

Useful plants: Many species of fruits and vegetables, plants used for fibre and building materials, seed sources of potential timber species.

Other values: Very rich fauna with a large number of migratory birds and birds-of-paradise. The area is inhabited by a large number of tribal groups who depend on the biological resources of the region for sustenance. Potential for ecotourism.

Threats: Serious threats from logging in many areas, road building threatens McAdam National Park. Population pressure in Wau-Bulolo area threatens forest areas through hunting and subsistence agriculture.

Conservation: McAdam National Park (IUCN Management Category: II) covers 20.8 km²; McAdam Memorial Park. There is considerable local support for an area in the Bowutu Mountains to be treated as a conservation area for the development of ecotourism. The whole area considered here as a CPD site is included in the list of sites of high biological diversity in a conservation needs assessment for Papua New Guinea (Johns 1992). Several reserves need to be established throughout the region.

Geography

The region under consideration is located in Morobe Province, and includes part of the Central Ranges, including Mount Amungwiwa, Mount Missim and the Bowutu Mountains, extending to Lasanga Island. Mount Amungwiwa is centred on latitude 7°29'S and longitude 146°39'E. To the west, the area includes the Ekuti Dividing Range and the Angakumia Ranges. Altitudes in the Bowutu Ranges are from sea-level at Buso-Kui-Lasanga to the highest peaks of all the Ekuti Range (Amungwiwa, 3278 m; Bell, 2985 m; Kwamunga, 2800 m; and Leahy 2647 m).

Rocks date from Mesozoic to the Pliocene and include limestone (with sinkholes, submerged rivers and other karst scenery), granites, igneous and undifferentiated sedimentary rocks. The area is divided into a series of blocks by faults. The rugged hills and mountains are dissected by a dense pattern of streams and have very irregular slopes. The region is prone to severe erosion and massive landslips.

Access to the region is limited to a single road which links Bulolo and Wau to Aseki. The area is surrounded by settlements, the Watut Valley being the major centre, with the small industrial town of Bulolo and the administrative centre of Wau. To the east, the Bowutu Mountains are largely unpopulated except for a series of small coastal villages (Kui, Sipoma, Buso). The upper Watut Valley (Slate Creek) supports a series of small villages. Menyamya and Aseki occur to the west of the region. Other settlements include the Angiwanki and Pingamanga, Langimar and Olete villages.

At lower altitudes, rainfall is seasonal, varying from 3000 to 3500 mm, with temperature maxima between 23° and 27°C and minima between 12° and 16°C. No high-altitude records exist for the whole region.

Vegetation

The coastal vegetation includes forest dominated by *Casuarina equisetifolia*, mixed coastal forests with *Calophyllum*, *Terminalia* and *Anisoptera*, and coastal herbaceous communities. Swamp forests also occur in the lowlands.

Dipterocarp forests, dominated by *Anisoptera thurifera* var. *polyandra*, are common along the coast to the east of Buso. These have provided a major resource which has been extensively logged. Mixed lowland forest occurring up 1400 m is dominated by *Pometia*, *Terminalia*, *Myristica*, *Horsfieldia*, *Celtis* and *Ficus*.

Lower montane forests are found up to 1700 m altitude. They comprise a mixture of species of *Lithocarpus*, *Elaeocarpus*, Lauraceae and podocarps. Abandoned cultivation plots are usually dominated by *Castanopsis acuminatissima*. Small patches of forest can be dominated by *Eucalyptopsis*, which is also common on coastal ridges in the east of the Bowutu Mountains. Small stands of *Agathis* occur in the Watut Valley and some areas are still dominated by *Araucaria hunsteinii* and *A. cunninghamii*. Extensive natural stands of these two species provided the basis for the development of the plywood industry in Bulolo. In natural forests both species form emergents up to 70 m in height. Extensive plantations of the two species have been established in the vicinity of Bulolo and Wau.

The mid-montane forests are dominated by *Nothofagus grandis* on ridges, or have a very diverse mix of montane tree species. In places, the canopy can reach 35 m. Smaller stands of *Nothofagus pullei* can be dominant at higher altitudes (Johns 1974). *Dacrycarpus compactus* (dominant) and *Libocedrus papuanus* (rarer) form a dense forest at higher altitudes above 3400 m. The small crowns reach 7–15 m in height. Patches of subalpine grasslands occur in the forests on the summit ridge of Amungwiwa. In these high-altitude podocarp forests there is a significant component of Myrtaceae, *Drimys* and the ericaceous genera, *Rhododendron* and *Dimorphanthera*.

Extensive areas of ultramafic vegetation are developed in the Bowutu Mountains.

Flora

The flora probably includes between 1500–3000 vascular plant species. The area includes the only known sites for the parasitic genus *Langsdorffia* (Balanophoraceae) in Asia. The single species, *L. papuana*, occurs at three sites in the Watut Valley system. A small area in McAdam Memorial Park is one of the few sites known in Papuasia for *Mitrastemon yamamoti*. The monotypic genus *Piora* (Compositae) is known only from Mount Amungwiwa and Mount Piora. Local endemics include species of *Drimys*, *Agapetes*, *Schefflera* and *Dimorphanthera*, and a species of the endemic genus *Sericolea* (Elaeocarpaceae), all of which are known only from Mount Amungwiwa.

The flora of Mount Amungwiwa shows interesting links with the Main Range to the north-west and south-south-east, as well as to the Saruwaged and Finisterre Mountains to the north-north-east.

Polygonal karst landforms support a flora that has not been studied.

A network of reserves needs to be set up to protect areas of outstanding botanical importance (see Conservation section).

Useful plants

There are many species of fruits and vegetables, and plants used for fibre and building materials. The forests are a seed source of potential timber species.

Social and environmental values

The area includes a high diversity of mammal and bird species. The yellow-streaked honey-eater (*Ptilopropa meekiana*) is rare throughout its range from Mount Michael (Eastern Highlands Province) to Aseki. The Papuan parrot-finch (*Erythrura papuana*) has a patchy distribution from the Wissel Lakes in Irian Jaya to Aseki, while the white-rumped robin (*Reneothello bimaculatus*), has a similar patchy distribution from the Vogelkop to this region. Cassowaries are common in the coastal ranges of the Bowutu Mountains. No species of birds are strictly endemic to this CPD site, which falls within the Central New Guinean Mountain Endemic Bird Area (EBA). However, some 30 restricted-range landbirds are likely to occur here, including the threatened blue bird-of-paradise (*Paradisaea rudolphi*).

There is considerable potential for developing ecotourism based on the coastal areas of Kui, Buso and Lasanga and possible walking trails into the Lake Trist area.

There are a large number of tribal groups who depend on the biological resources of the region for their sustenance.

Threats

Logging is a major threat to the forests in the region. The resource base for the ply mill at Bulolo has been virtually exhausted and logs are now being obtained from a wider area. Plantations cannot yet provide sufficient resources to sustain the plywood industry in Bulolo.

Shifting cultivation is the major subsistence activity, with the staple food crops being yam and sweet potato. Introduced vegetables of considerable variety are grown for local consumption and marketing in Bulolo, Wau and Lae. Smallholder activity also includes cattle raising and fishing, and high quality coffee is produced in several areas. Larger coffee plantations are centred at Wau. Population pressure in Wau-Bulolo area threatens forest areas through hunting and subsistence agriculture.

The mining industry, based on alluvial gold, is centred in the Wau and Edie Creek areas. Most gold is now extracted using sluicing techniques on a small-scale, but historically the alluvial gold in the Wau and Bulolo valleys was extracted by dredging.

The steep mountain slopes are continuously subject to mass movement, landslides, and the threat of earthquake activity. Road building often creates unstable slopes, which results in landslips.

Local cyclonic winds can devastate ridge forests over several hectares, resulting in pure regenerating patches of *Castanopsis acuminatissima* (Johns 1986).

Conservation

McAdam National Park (IUCN Management Category: II) covers 20.8 km². There is considerable local support for an area in the Bowutu Mountains to be treated as a conservation area for the development of ecotourism.

The whole area considered here as a CPD site is included in the list of sites of high biological diversity in a conservation needs assessment for Papua New Guinea (Johns 1992). Several reserves need to be established throughout the region to protect the flora. Particularly important areas include: Menyamya-Aseki, Mount Lawson, Mount Amungwiwa and the Bowutu Mountains.

References

Blackwood, B. (1939). Life on the Upper Watut, New Guinea. *Geogr. J.* 94: 1: 11–28.

Blackwood, B. (1940). Use of plants among the Kukukuku of southeast central New Guinea. *Proc. 6th Pac. Sci. Congress* 4: 111–126.

Brass, L.J. (1956). Results of the Archbold expeditions No. 75. Summary of the fourth Archbold expedition to New Guinea 1953. *Bull. Amer. Mus. Nat. Hist.* 111: 77–152.

Enright, N.J. (1982). The araucaria forests of New Guinea. In Gressitt, J.L. (ed.), *Biogeography and ecology of New Guinea*, Vol. 1. Junk, The Hague. Pp. 381–400.

Johns, R.J. (1974). *Observations on the Nothofagus stands occurring at lower altitudes on Mt. Giluwe and Kaisenik.* P.N.G. Forestry College Library. (Unpublished report.)

Johns, R.J. (1976). A provisional classification of the montane vegetation of New Guinea. *S.I.N.G.* 4: 105–107.

Johns, R.J. (1986). The instability of the tropical ecosystem in Papuasia. *Blumea* 31: 341–371.

Johns, R.J. (1987). A provisional classification of the dipterocarp forests of P.N.G. In Kostermans, A.J.G.H. (ed.), *Proceedings of the 3rd Round Table Conference on Dipterocarps.* Samarinda, Indonesia.

Johns, R.J. (1992). Biodiversity and conservation of the native flora of Papua New Guinea. In Beehler, B.M. (ed.), *Papua New Guinea conservation needs assessment. Volume 2: A biodiversity analysis for Papua New Guinea.* Government of Papua New Guinea, Department of Environment and Conservation, Papua New Guinea. Pp. 15–32.

Johns, R.J. and Burua, N. (1976). The *Castanopsis* forests of Papua New Guinea. (Paper presented to the 4th meeting of the Botanical Society, P.N.G.)

Johns, R.J. and Simaga, J.M. (1987). The vegetation of the Watut catchments. In Johns, R.J. (ed.), *The Watut water catchment project. Final report.* South Pacific Regional Environmental Programme.

Paijmans, K. (ed.) (1976). *New Guinea vegetation.* Elsevier, Amsterdam. 213 pp.

Robbins, R.G. (1961). The montane vegetation of New Guinea. *Tuatara* 8: 121–134.

Streimann, H. (1983). *The plants of the Upper Watut watershed of Papua New Guinea.* National Botanic Gardens, Canberra.

Valkenburg, J.L.C.H. van (1987). *Floristic changes following human disturbance of mid-montane forest.* Wageningen Agricultural University, Wageningen, The Netherlands.

Acknowledgements

This Data Sheet was written by Professor Robert J. Johns (Royal Botanic Gardens, Kew), with grateful thanks to Dr Peter F. Stevens (Harvard University Herbaria, Cambridge, Massachusetts) and Dr W. Vink (Rijksherbarium, Leiden) for their valuable advice and information.

REGIONAL OVERVIEW: AUSTRALIA AND NEW ZEALAND

ROBERT BODEN (AUSTRALIA), DAVID GIVEN (NEW ZEALAND)

AUSTRALIA

Total land area: 7,682,428 km² (excluding External Territories).

Population (1990): 16,870,000[a].

Altitude: -15 m to 2228 m (summit of Mount Kosciusko).

Natural vegetation: Major types include closed forest, open forest and woodland dominated by *Eucalyptus* and *Acacia*, shrubland, scrub, heath, herbland.

Number of vascular plants: 15,638 species listed in most recent national census[b]. Estimated 3000–5000 taxa still to be named.

Number of country endemics: c. 14,260 species (c. 90% of those so far recorded).

Number of vascular plant families: 279.

Number of genera: c. 1700.

Number of endemic genera: c. 566.

Important plant families: Myrtaceae, Leguminosae, Orchidaceae, Proteaceae, Rutaceae.

NEW ZEALAND

Total land area: c. 269,000 km², including North Island (114,500 km²), South Island (150,700 km²) and Stewart Island (1750 km²), together with Chatham Islands, Kermadec Islands and Subantarctic Islands.

Population (1991): 3,430,000.

Altitude: 0–3764 m (summit of Aoraki or Mount Cook).

Natural vegetation: c. 60,000 km² of indigenous forests remaining, of which there are 4 main types: southern beech (*Nothofagus*) forests, lowland and montane conifer/broadleaved forests and coastal forests; extensive grasslands (now covering c. 60% of the land area), bushland, heath, scrub and fernland; wetland and alpine vegetation.

Number of vascular plants: c. 2400 species.

Number of country endemics: 1942 species (c. 81% endemism).

Number of endemic genera: c. 35.

Important plant families: Compositae, Gramineae, Cyperaceae, Scrophulariaceae, Orchidaceae, Umbelliferae.

Sources:
[a] United Nations Population Division (World Resources Institute 1992).
[b] Hnatiuk (1990).

Introduction

The Australia and New Zealand region, as here defined, includes Australia, New Zealand and surrounding islands, including Norfolk Island and Lord Howe (Australia), the Chatham and Kermadec Islands (New Zealand), together with subantarctic groups, such as the Antipodes Islands, Auckland Islands, Campbell Islands, Heard Island and Macquarie Island. Christmas Island (Indian Ocean), an External Territory of Australia, is included in the region for convenience, although its flora is related to that of South East Asia. The first part of this chapter deals with Australia.

AUSTRALIA

Australia is an island continent situated in the Southern Hemisphere approximately between latitudes 10°41'–43°39'S and longitudes 113°09'–154°39'E having a maximum width east-west of 4000 km and north-south of 3680 km and a coastline of 36,735 km. Of its land area of 7,682,428 km² (about 5.7% of the land surface of the Earth), 39% lies within the tropical zone and 61% in the temperate zone. It is bordered to the north and west by the Indian Ocean, to the south by the Great Southern Ocean, and to the east by the Pacific Ocean. Torres Strait, about 140 km wide, separates Australia from New Guinea to the north; Timor is 520 km to the north-west, while the nearest neighbour to the east is New Zealand, 1900 km away. The island of Tasmania is 225 km to the south of mainland Australia.

Geology

The geological history of Australia began early in the Archaean era around 3500 million years ago with the formation of rocks that now underlie much of the Pilbara region of Western Australia. Throughout the Proterozoic

TABLE 60. SITES IDENTIFIED AS CENTRES OF PLANT DIVERSITY AND ENDEMISM: AUSTRALIA AND NEW ZEALAND

Sites selected for Data Sheet treatment appear in bold.

Au1. **Australian Alps** (New South Wales, Victoria and Australian Capital Territory, Australia)

Au2. **Border Ranges** (Queensland and New South Wales, Australia)

Au3. **Central Australian Mountain Ranges** (Northern Territory, South Australia and Western Australia, Australia)

Au4. **Kakadu-Alligator Rivers Region** (Northern Territory, Australia)

Au5. **Norfolk and Lord Howe Islands** (Australia)

Au6. **North Kimberley Region** (Western Australia, Australia)

Au7. **South-west Botanical Province** (Western Australia, Australia)

Au8. **Sydney Sandstone Region** (New South Wales, Australia)

Au9. **Western Tasmanian Wilderness** (Tasmania, Australia)

Au10. **Wet Tropics of Queensland** (Queensland, Australia)

Au11. McIlwraith Range and Iron Range (Queensland, Australia)

Au12. Sclerophyll forests of Far South-east New South Wales (New South Wales, Australia)

Au13. Christmas Island (Australia)

Au14. **Northland** (North Island)

Au15. **North-west Nelson** (South Island)

Au16. **Chatham Islands** (New Zealand)

Au17. **Subantarctic Islands** (Australia and New Zealand)

MAP 15. CENTRES OF PLANT DIVERSITY AND ENDEMISM: AUSTRALIA AND NEW ZEALAND
The map shows the location of CPD Data Sheet sites for Australia and New Zealand

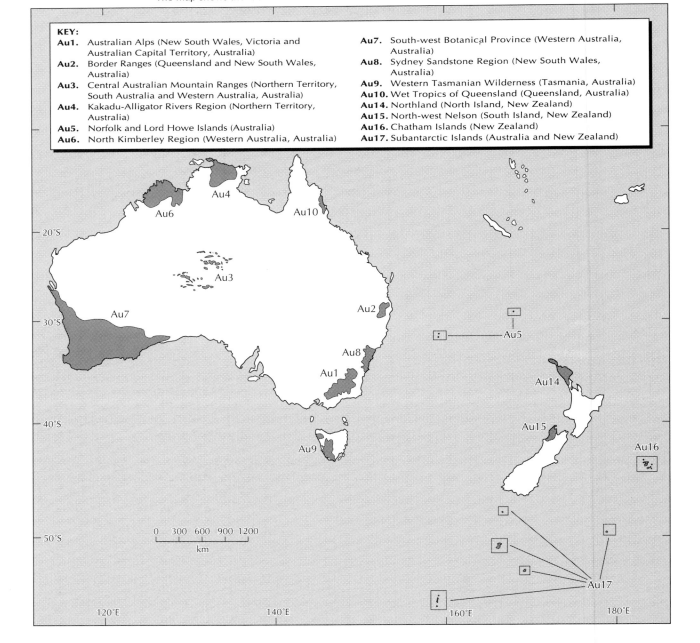

KEY:

Au1. Australian Alps (New South Wales, Victoria and Australian Capital Territory, Australia)

Au2. Border Ranges (Queensland and New South Wales, Australia)

Au3. Central Australian Mountain Ranges (Northern Territory, South Australia and Western Australia, Australia)

Au4. Kakadu-Alligator Rivers Region (Northern Territory, Australia)

Au5. Norfolk and Lord Howe Islands (Australia)

Au6. North Kimberley Region (Western Australia, Australia)

Au7. South-west Botanical Province (Western Australia, Australia)

Au8. Sydney Sandstone Region (New South Wales, Australia)

Au9. Western Tasmanian Wilderness (Tasmania, Australia)

Au10. Wet Tropics of Queensland (Queensland, Australia)

Au14. Northland (North Island, New Zealand)

Au15. North-west Nelson (South Island, New Zealand)

Au16. Chatham Islands (New Zealand)

Au17. Subantarctic Islands (Australia and New Zealand)

434

much of the continent was consolidated through mountain building and sedimentary deposition. Precambrian rocks comprise gneisses, schists, amphibolites and other strongly folded and more or less metamorphosed sedimentary and volcanic rocks. Granitic intrusions are the source of most of the important Precambrian ore deposits, including iron ore in the Hamersley Ranges in Western Australia, silver and lead at Broken Hill in New South Wales and Mt Isa in Queensland, and uranium in the Alligator Rivers Region of the Northern Territory. The latter part of the Palaeozoic Era was significant for the development of dense swamp forests which led to the formation of major coal deposits.

During the Mesozoic Era, the Triassic sandstones and shales which form much of the country around Sydney were laid down. Extensive coal deposits were formed in the Jurassic and Cretaceous periods.

The early part of the Caenozoic Era saw major formation of estuarine lakes and swamps; marine incursions led to the deposition of limestone. Thick lignite deposits were laid down in Victoria and auriferous and stanniferous deposits in all the eastern states. In the Oligocene there were vast outpourings of basalt in eastern Australia with some volcanoes remaining active in South Australia, Victoria and Queensland until early Recent times. During this period, rainfall was high; large freshwater lakes and abundant vegetation supported megafauna such as the giant wombat *Diprotodon* and giant emus. Central Australia, which is now arid, was well vegetated at this time.

Since the Tertiary the Australian continent has been mostly stable, the forces of erosion slowly levelling large areas of the continent to low-lying plains and plateaux with an average altitude of 300 m. Today there are only limited areas above 1200 m, the highest point being Mount Kosciusko (2228 m). The lowest point is Lake Eyre towards the centre of the continent.

Jennings and Mabbutt (1986) identified three distinct physiographic regions: the Western Plateau, the Interior Lowlands and the Eastern Uplands. The Western Plateau occupies about two-thirds of the continent with the landscape dominated by sand plains and low tablelands. The Interior Lowlands are flat, low-lying and generally deeply weathered, with the landscape featuring vast floodplains and landforms of low relief along the western and eastern margins. The younger Eastern Uplands occupy a narrow belt along the eastern side of the continent sloping gradually westward to the Interior Lowlands and sharply eastward to narrow coastal plains. They are more complex than the Western Plateau and Interior Lowlands, with elevated remnants of the Tasman Fold Belt exposed at various levels.

There were many glacial and interglacial periods during the Quaternary, the last glacial being about 20,000 years ago. During the last glaciation ice covered only a small area (c. 25 km^2) of mainland Australia in the vicinity of Mt Kosciusko.

Climate

The Australian climate is predominantly continental; however, the insular nature of the land mass results in some modification of the continental pattern. For example, absence of extensive mountain ranges and the expanse of the surrounding oceans mean that extreme minimum temperatures are not as low as those recorded in other continents.

Apart from Antarctica, Australia is the world's driest continent. Two-thirds of Australia's land surface receives an average annual rainfall of less than 500 mm. The driest area is in the central and western part of the country. For example, Lake Eyre in South Australia receives about 100 mm of rain annually. Areas receiving an annual average rainfall of more than 500 mm occupy a strip less than 500 km wide stretching around the north, east and south-east coasts, coastal areas of the extreme south-west of the mainland, and the island of Tasmania. The wettest place in Australia is Tully in northern Queensland, which receives 4058 mm. The mountainous region of western Tasmania also has a high annual rainfall, with Lake Margaret receiving 3559 mm. Over much of the country, rainfall is unreliable, varying widely from year to year. Droughts and floods occur so frequently in many areas they are considered part of the normal climatic pattern.

The climate of the western two-thirds of the country north from about latitude 20°S is of the monsoonal type and that to the south of latitude 32°S is of the Mediterranean type. The intermediate zone is largely desert. Climate in the eastern third of the continent is more complex due, in part, to the Great Dividing Range, extending almost continuously from north to south. North of the Tropic of Capricorn rain occurs in all seasons whenever the south-east tradewinds strike a mountainous coast. South of the Tropic, both the northern drought in winter and the southern drought in summer are modified by the proximity of the Pacific Ocean. Although most of New South Wales and Victoria have an even distribution of rain throughout the year, summer rainfall is so erratic and ineffective that the climate is better considered as a modified Mediterranean type.

Summers are warm to hot with maximum temperatures in inland Australia often exceeding 40°C. Winters are warm in the north but cool to cold in the south, with the July average less than 10°C. During the three winter months, conditions in the highlands of Victoria and New South Wales are too cold for plant growth; snow is recorded above 610 m altitude.

Soils

Stephens (1977) concluded there are both normal and unusual features about the Australian continental soil pattern. Some soils, such as podzols, red-brown earths and black earths have fairly clear counterparts in other continents while others, such as arid red earths, red and brown hardpan soils, and stony desert tableland soils appear to be unique. Saline and solonized soils are unduly extensive while others, like brown forest soils and prairie soils, commonly found elsewhere, are poorly represented. Desert sand-dunes show an extreme redness of colour although otherwise morphologically typical of desert dune formations elsewhere. Stephens (1977) considered the unusual features of the soil landscape could generally be attributed to three factors: "... first, the great prevalence of very old and moderately aged land surfaces bearing ancient soils only partly modified by the passage of time; second, relatively ineffectual continental drainage leading to the prevalence of saline and solonized soils; and third, the prevalence of limestones and, to a lesser degree, basic igneous rocks as parent materials which impose limitations on the types of weathering that can take place during soil formation".

Soils in Australia are generally low in phosphorus. Many plant species, particularly in the Proteaceae, are so well-adapted to this condition they will not thrive in phosphate-enriched soils in cultivation. The addition of superphosphate to large areas of the country has enabled widespread cultivation of cereals. Nitrogen levels in most soils are also low, but they have been increased by extensive use of legumes in pastures of exotic grasses. These have replaced native grasses over vast areas of southern Australia. Natural deficiencies in trace elements such as copper, zinc and molybdenum have been corrected as part of the development of land for grazing, crops and plantation forestry.

Large areas of soils are acid to highly acid, with pH values less than 6. The absence of suitable liming materials at reasonable cost, and acid tolerance of many introduced pasture species, have meant that no major effort has been put into attempting to reduce soil acidity.

High salt levels are typical of large areas. Salinity problems have been exacerbated by land management involving the removal of tree cover. This has led to a rise in the water-table in many areas. The problem of high salt levels has increased markedly in irrigated areas; 10,000 km² in the non-arid zone are now considered degraded.

Other distinctive features in Australian soils include laterization, duplex profiles and gilgai. The term laterite, as used in Australia, implies a peneplain with ironstone at the surface or subsurface overlying more than a metre of kaolinitic clay. The ironstone may be as gravel or as boulders. In large areas of Western Australia, sand overlies the gravel constituting "sand plain" (Leeper 1970). This laterite is a relic of a warm and wet environment in the Tertiary, during which the various parent rocks were deeply weathered and degraded leaving at best an extremely poor soil. Bauxite mining for aluminium smelting occurs in lateritic areas in south-west Western Australia and Cape York Peninsula.

Duplex soils are those showing a sharp textural change from a permeable loam or silty loam above to an impermeable clay below; the transition from clay to weathered parent material is more gradual. The clay horizon bars the roots of some plants and holds up water to form a perched water-table in wet seasons. The subsurface may become semi-fluid leading to "tunnel erosion".

Gilgai is an Aboriginal word describing a soil pattern in which hummocks alternate with depressions due to differentially swelling clays. This formation has been recorded in both temperate and tropical Australia. After levelling and cultivating, the original mosaic pattern of the surface may show for many years or even remain permanently in the form of a calcareous patch at the site of the former hummock.

Soil erosion following a combination of excessive tree clearing, extension of cropping into marginal lands, drought and overgrazing by feral animals, such as the European rabbit, is the major factor in soil degradation in Australia. A national survey in 1975 revealed that degradation had occurred on 55% of the arid zone due largely to deterioration of vegetation followed by wind erosion. In the non-arid zone, 68% of extensive cropping land, 63% of intensive cropping land and 36% of grazing land had deteriorated to the extent that remedial work was needed. In 1991 values, the cost of

construction works to treat land degradation is estimated to exceed A$2000 million (Roberts 1989).

Population

The population of Australia in 1990 was 16,870,000 (World Resources Institute 1992), having almost doubled since 1945. The growth rate between 1985 and 1990 averaged 1.37% per annum. Most of the population is of European origin; Asians now account for 3.4% of the population, while Aborigines and Torres Strait Islanders together account for 1.4%. The population density of 2 people/km² is low by world standards, but 70.6% of the population is concentrated in the eight state and territory capitals and five regional cities with populations of more than 100,000. Vast areas of central and western Australia are virtually unpopulated.

Aborigines

The first Australians were hunter-gatherers who migrated from South East Asia, arriving in the north of the country at least 40,000 years BP. The settling of Australia marked the first human expansion beyond the single land mass comprising Africa, Europe and Asia (Flood 1989). The Aborigines gradually spread southwards and, despite the extreme cold, occupied caves then above the tree-line in the extreme south-east of the country, 21,000 years BP. Even in Tasmania, which is further south than any other place in the Southern Hemisphere inhabited during the Ice Age, there has been a continual human presence over the last 30,000 years. Survival for over 10,000 years, before gradual warming occurred, is remarkable, given that the basic facilities for warmth, shelter and clothing were open fires, caves and animal skins.

Tasmania was isolated from the mainland between 8000 and 12,000 years ago by post-glacial rise in sea-levels. The Aborigines had no craft suitable to cross the rough waters of Bass Strait so they lived in isolation for over 8000 years until the first European convict settlement began in 1803. The small population of Tasmanian Aborigines, numbering about 3000–4000 people, was decimated by direct killing and disease. The last person of full Aboriginal blood in Tasmania died in 1876. Today, there are about 2000 people of recognized Aboriginal descent in Tasmania.

The Aboriginal people on the mainland numbered about 750,000 when European settlement commenced in 1788. They were divided into about 500 small groups speaking a variety of languages and dialects. The groups were further divided into small bands or clusters of family groups which formed self-sufficient units. There is archaeological evidence of some very limited cultivation, but they mostly lived nomadically, feeding on native plants and animals. Labour was divided between the sexes: men hunted, while women foraged for smaller animals and plant roots and seeds. For example, the seeds of *Araucaria bidwillii* (bunya pine), a native conifer which occurs in rain forest in northern New South Wales and Queensland, were harvested as a food source. Aborigines would forgo tribal boundaries and travel distances of up to 300 km to share in abundant harvests during years of heavy seed crops.

Aborigines used a wide range of plants for food, utensils and weapons such as spears and throwing sticks. Simple canoes were made from tree bark. Although there was no conventional agriculture, *Dioscorea transversa* (parsnip yam) was planted on offshore islands to ensure a reserve food supply. When yams were harvested the top of the tuber was left in the ground so that the yam would grow again (Flood 1989). Another semi-agricultural practice was the habit of deliberately spitting-out fruit tree seeds into the debris of fish remains in refuse heaps at the edge of a camp. Stands of native fruit trees are now accepted by archaeologists as indicators of former campsites. *Santalum acuminatum* (quandong), a desert tree yielding a nutritious fruit with high vitamin C content, was deliberately watered in a form of simple management. There is no evidence that Aborigines depleted any plant species. On the contrary, over-harvesting of some plants and animals was deliberately avoided by a system of taboos which made certain foods forbidden for particular members of a tribe.

"Fire-stick farming" is well documented for Tasmania, Bunya Mountains in southern Queensland, on the Atherton Plateau in northern Queensland and in south-west Western Australia. Jones (1969) cites evidence that fire-stick farming was carried out in the course of hunting, to clear paths through the rain forest, to regenerate plant food both for humans and their prey, for signalling hunters, and possibly to extend human habitat. Different fire regimes were used in different parts of the continent. In Arnhem Land in the north, fire management is designed to spare fire-sensitive jungle thickets which contain many edible plants that do not readily regenerate after burning. Wide firebreaks are burnt around these areas early after the wet season so that later burning in the dry period will not enter the protected areas. Aborigines had no capacity or incentive to put fires out and camp fires were left to smoulder and hunting fires to burn themselves out. Regular burning of tribal territory every three or four years prevented the accumulation of litter and disastrous wildfires.

Intentional burning of territory used by rival groups sometimes occurred. Indeed, it may well have been revenge (or frustration) that led to Aborigines setting fire to the grass around Captain James Cook's camp on the banks of the Endeavour River in north Queensland in 1770. Joseph Banks may well have been the first European to learn about fire in the hands of the Aborigines. He wrote in his diary for 19 July, 1770: "I had little Idea of the fury with which the grass burnt in this hot climate, nor of the difficulty of extinguishing it when once lighted: this accident will, however, be a sufficient warning for us if ever we should again pitch tents in such a climate to burn Every thing round us before we begin".

It has been demonstrated convincingly that the sedgeland of the west coast of Tasmania is the result of long use of fire which gradually changed the original rain forest, dominated by the fire-sensitive beech, *Nothofagus cunninghamii*, through a phase of mixed eucalypts and rain forest to scrub and, finally, to heath and sedgeland. With cessation of Aboriginal burning, rain forest is invading its former habitat in some places.

The open grassy woodlands maintained by the practice of mosaic burning were coveted by the European settlers for their stock. However, they failed to recognize that by driving the Aborigines off their land, conditions became ideal for scrubby vegetation to colonize rapidly, leading to massive accumulations of fuel and uncontrollable bushfires which destroyed their homes, fences and livestock. Ironically,

conservation managers are now trying to mimic Aboriginal burning practices to maintain open grassland in some parks and reserves. In Kakadu National Park, in the Alligator Rivers Region of the Northern Territory (CPD Site Au4, see Data Sheet), local Aborigines are engaged to carry out burning.

European discovery and settlement

The earliest records of European discovery date from the early part of the 17th century when the Dutch mariner Willem Jansz landed on the western side of Cape York Peninsula in 1606 and Dirk Hartog landed on the west coast in 1616. The eastern part of Australia was not discovered until 1770 when James Cook, accompanied by the botanists Joseph Banks and Daniel Solander, journeyed up the east coast claiming possession in the name of Great Britain. Eighteen years later the first European settlement was established at Sydney Cove under the British Captain Arthur Phillip. The first arrivals were convicts and mariners. Transportation continued to New South Wales until 1850 and to Tasmania until 1853.

Exploration of the continent began soon after arrival of the First Fleet in 1788, when it became clear that the poor soils of Sydney were unsuitable for agriculture. Powell (1991) discusses the sequence of white settlement. By 1830, the south-eastern coast and immediate hinterland and parts of Tasmania had been explored and settled. By 1860, settlement had extended throughout the south-eastern part of the country and the south-western part of Western Australia. This involved extensive clearing of vegetation and introduction of exotic plants and animals, some of which escaped into the wild and became pests. By 1900, settlement had extended north and inland, although the climate determined that occupation was sometimes tenuous and always sparse. The only additional settlement after 1900 has been inland in Western Australia; however, large parts of that state, South Australia and the Northern Territory remain unsettled due to arid conditions.

Population growth was initially slow. The first major growth occurred in the 1850s, with the discovery of gold. The population doubled to 1 million in less than 10 years at that stage, mainly as a result of immigration. The second major growth occurred between 1877–1889 as a result of economic diversification and pastoral expansion. By 1889, the population had reached 3 million. The third growth period occurred between 1918–1925, when the 6 million figure was reached. More recently, rapid growth in population occurred from 1945 as a result of an active migration programme and an increasing birth rate after the Second World War. By 1971, the population was 13 million, and by 1988 it had reached 16.5 million.

Vegetation

Similarities between the floras of Australia, South America, South Africa and New Zealand were observed early in the 18th century. In 1859, Charles Darwin remarked on the likeness "... between the flora of the south-western corner of Australia and the Cape of Good Hope". Fifty years later, the theory of plate tectonics and continental drift helped to explain the similarities. Briefly, Gondwanaland separated into Africa, South America, Australia, India, New Zealand, Madagascar and Antarctica. About 110 million years BP, Africa and South America separated. Africa then moved away from Antarctica followed by New Zealand and India. Australia, Antarctica and South America remained in contact until about 45 million years BP when Australia began to drift away. It has moved northwards some 15° of latitude and continues to do so at a rate of about 40–50 mm each year.

When Australia was still linked to Antarctica at the beginning of the Tertiary, the vegetation was more or less continuous, closed subtropical rain forest. The genus *Nothofagus* was widespread, as were plants similar to present-day *Araucaria*, *Podocarpus* and *Dacrydium* and members of the Myrtaceae and Proteaceae. As Australia became more isolated and drifted further north, the Gondwanan flora was subjected to climatic change resulting in the evolution of a large autochthonous element. An Asian element arrived from the north after the Australian and Sunda Plates collided in the Miocene.

Today, the Australian element occurs throughout the continent and contains a high level of endemism, particularly in south-western Western Australia. Here the level of strict species endemism is 68%, but if species are included whose main distribution is focused on the region but which also occur to some extent beyond the region, the level of endemism reaches 83% (see Data Sheet on the South-west Botanical Province, CPD Site Au7). A corollary of this high level of endemism is that many species have a very small geographical range and are, therefore, more easily placed at risk as a result of habitat loss. Indeed, Western Australia has 42% of Australia's rare or threatened plant taxa, and its flora is, therefore, the most endangered flora of any state in Australia (Leigh and Briggs 1991).

Scleromorphy is a recurring character in the Australian element of the flora. Many species are small in size and have relatively small, rigid leaves and short internodes. This is particularly evident in the families Myrtaceae, Proteaceae, Rutaceae, Epacridaceae, Leguminosae and Goodeniaceae. Barlow (1981) discussed the various interpretations placed on the evolutionary development of scleromorphy. He concluded that environmental conditions, such as low soil nutrient status and Mediterranean climate, favours scleromorphic vegetation "... resulting in an expression of scleromorphy not matched in other continental floras".

The Indomalayan element is most evident in northern Queensland, Northern Territory and, to a lesser extent, in the Kimberley Region of north-western Australia (see Data Sheets for Kakadu-Alligator Rivers Region, North Kimberley Region and the Wet Tropics of Queensland, CPD Sites Au4, Au6 and Au10, respectively). The level of generic endemism in the Indomalayan element is about 14% (Burbidge 1960). There are also a significant number of non-endemic Indomalayan genera in the tropical zone having only one, or a few, species in Australia. Burbidge (1960) identified about 360 non-endemic genera in the tropical zone being represented by a single species, and 320 genera by 2–5 species. She concluded that this is evidence for relatively recent immigration of the Indomalayan element into an already floristically rich area.

Major floristic elements tend to be more prominent in certain areas rather than in others. For example, the Antarctic or Gondwanan element, which has links with New Zealand, subantarctic islands and South America, is prominent in south-eastern Australia (especially Tasmania), but is less prominent in northern Australia. (See, for example, the Data Sheet on Western Tasmanian Wilderness, CPD Site Au9.) Specht (1981a), however, identified a significant integration of floristic units within each major plant formation. He distinguished 32 plant formations in Australia and, after analysing the distributions of 1285 genera represented in them, concluded that almost every formation contained a mixture of genera belonging to different floristic groups in terms of geographical distribution and relationships.

During the Quaternary glacial and inter-glacial periods, the area of rain forest would have expanded and contracted as a result of temperature and rainfall fluctuations. With contraction of rain forest, drier vegetation types including characteristic sclerophyll genera, such as *Eucalyptus*, *Casuarina*, *Callitris* and *Acacia* became prominent. About 15,000 years ago, much of south-eastern Australia was covered in grass and low shrub vegetation. Increased fire frequency following the arrival of Aborigines added to the effects of increasing aridity and favoured the development of vegetation dominated by *Eucalyptus*. Communities characterized by more fire-sensitive genera, such as *Callitris* and *Casuarina*, were severely depleted (Singh, Kershaw and Clark 1980). European settlement brought even greater rates of change to the vegetation.

Map 16 shows the original vegetation cover in Australia. Brief descriptions of the major vegetation types follow (based on Specht 1970). More detailed descriptions and alternative classifications can be found in Beard and Webb (1974), Beadle (1981), Groves (1981), Carnahan (1986) and AUSLIG (1990).

Closed forest

Closed forest, or rain forest, occurs in eastern Australia from Cape York to Tasmania with small outliers near the northern coasts of the Northern Territory and Western Australia. It is associated with mean annual rainfalls ranging from less than 1200 mm to more than 2400 mm and occurs on a wide range of soil types at altitudes ranging from sea-level to 1200 m. There are four main types: tropical, subtropical, warm temperate and cool temperate. These closely approximate the terms mesophyll vine forest, notophyll fern forest and nanophyll moss forest adopted by Webb (1959). Webb and Tracey (1981) in reviewing northern Australian rain forests concluded that latitude *per se* has little significance in differentiating between the various climatic types. Tropical and subtropical types extend as far south as the Illawarra district of New South Wales and outliers of temperate elements occur within the tropical zone of northern Queensland.

A major difference between the northern (tropical) and southern (temperate) closed forests is the number of tree species present in a given area. Northern closed forest contains a great diversity of species representing a wide range of families. For example, 164 different tree species were recorded in a plot of only 0.1 hectare of rain forest on the Atherton Tableland in north Queensland. By contrast, southern closed forest is dominated primarily by two species of *Nothofagus*, namely *N. cunninghamii* (myrtle beech) in Tasmania and Victoria, and *N. moorei* (niggerhead beech) in New South Wales and southern Queensland. There are also small areas of southern closed forest dominated by *Atherosperma moschatum* (black sassafras), *Ceratopetalum apetalum* (coachwood) and *Acacia melanoxylon* (blackwood). Another major difference between northern and southern closed forests is that lianas and plank buttress roots are common in northern closed forests but are absent from the cool temperate rain forests of Tasmania and Victoria.

Today, closed forests exist as scattered remnants of the original Gondwanaland rain forests which previously covered the entire land mass of Australia and provided the primitive stocks which gave rise to the bulk of the modern Australian flora (Barlow 1981). It has been estimated by Webb and Tracey (1981) that about 60,000 km² of Australian rain forest have been cleared, representing about 75% of the total area present in 1788. Some areas of closed forest in Australia have been retained as managed forests but most have been cleared for agricultural use, including intensive stock rearing on sown exotic pastures, or converted to sugarcane and banana plantations (in the north) or for crops such as potatoes (in temperate regions). Tourism and recreation pressures have resulted in further alienation of Crown Land containing rain forests. The establishment of *Araucaria cunninghamii* (hoop pine) plantations in southern Queensland has replaced about 400 km² of drier rain forest. Remaining areas of tropical rain forests in Australia have been recently mapped and described in Collins, Sayer and Whitmore (1991).

Open forest

Open forest occurs in areas with 500–1000 mm annual rainfall. Individual forests are usually dominated by a few species of *Eucalyptus*, although in drier areas species of *Acacia* and *Callitris* may assume dominance. Open forest is found in the wetter parts of south-west Western Australia, where it is dominated by *Eucalyptus diversicolor* (karri). It also occurs in the Kimberleys and across the Northern Territory to Cape York in Queensland. The best developed open forests are along the east coast of the continent, from Cape York to Tasmania. In the northern, higher rainfall areas *E. saligna* predominates, whilst *E. regnans* is the main species in the wetter regions of Victoria and Tasmania where it may reach a height of 100 m. In lower rainfall areas other eucalypts, such as *E. marginata* (jarrah), in Western Australia, *E. maculata*, in warmer parts of eastern Australia, and *E. obliqua*, in cooler parts of Victoria and Tasmania, become prominent. In drier areas, *Acacia* spp., such as *A. harpophylla* (brigalow) and *Callitris* spp., (e.g. *C. columellaris*, white cypress pine), dominate the forest.

The structure and composition of the understorey of open forest vary with rainfall, latitude and soil type. In tall wet open forest there is a dense understorey usually containing tree ferns, *Dicksonia* and *Cyathea* spp. and tall shrubs. In drier

MAP 16. MAJOR VEGETATION TYPES IN AUSTRALIA

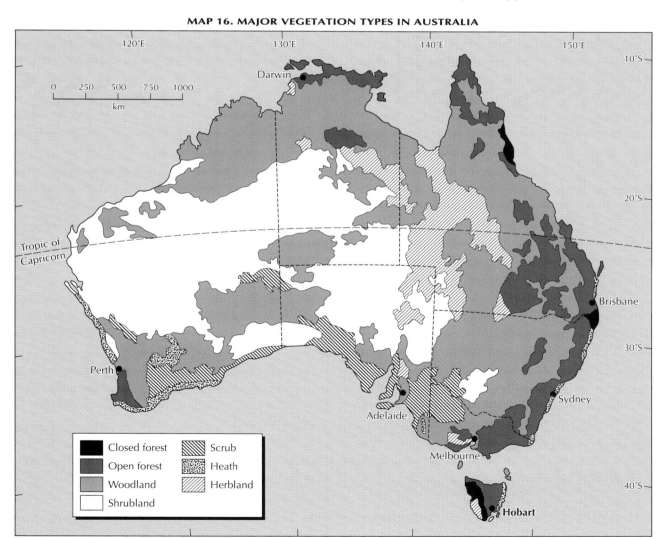

areas the understorey may be completely dominated by grasses and herbs.

Open forest is subject to periodic bush fires. Some of the dominant eucalypts in wetter open forest are fire-sensitive and are killed if severely burnt. Dense regeneration from seed usually follows burning. Provided fire does not recur until the trees have reached the age to produce flowers and seeds, the dominant tree species will persist. Many species of drier open forest are fire-resistant and may regenerate from epicormic buds or from underground lignotubers, or have seeds which are protected in woody fruits which open after burning. Some understorey species have seeds with protective fire-resistant coats. *Acacia harpophylla* (brigalow) has the ability to sucker vigorously, enabling it to recover from fire and making its eradication difficult in areas cleared for agriculture. However, about 50,000 km² of "brigalow country" have been cleared for grazing.

Extensive areas of open eucalypt forest are managed for forestry, either by selective logging or clear-felling, followed by natural or assisted regeneration with eucalypts. Large areas have been cleared to establish plantations of exotic species, such as *Pinus radiata*. Exotic plantations cover over 8920 km². Considerable areas of open forest in wetter regimes have been cleared for agriculture, including grazing. In lower rainfall areas, open forest has been thinned and domestic stock introduced to graze on native grasses, or else the forest has been cleared and pastures of exotic grasses and legumes established. *Callitris* open forest has been retained in many areas; about 15,000 km² are managed for timber production. Some of the southern open *Callitris* forest has been cleared for wheat or sown to pasture using exotic species of *Medicago*.

The area of native forest and woodland available for timber production is 335,000 km². In addition, 8918 km² have been allocated to softwood and 846 km² to hardwood plantations (Resource Assessment Commission 1991a).

Woodland

Woodland dominated mainly by species of *Eucalyptus*, *Callitris*, *Casuarina*, *Melaleuca* and *Acacia*, is widespread in Australia. It occurs in areas with about 200–300 mm annual rainfall and occupies large areas of inland Australia in a broad crescent from the Kimberleys in northern Western Australia to the inland side of the Great Dividing Range in Queensland, New South Wales and Victoria; it also occurs in small areas in South Australia. Restricted occurrences are found in south-west Western Australia and Tasmania.

Gillison and Walker (1981) stated that species richness of perennial flowering plants ranges from as low as three species per hectare in some low open woodlands to 80 species per hectare in sub-coastal woodlands. Approximately 80% of *Eucalyptus* taxa and most Australian *Acacia* species occur in woodland. The understorey in woodland and open woodland may vary in a manner similar to that of open forest, with which they intergrade. Eucalypt woodland, characterized by an understorey of tussock grasses, is prominent on heavier or more fertile soils in northern Australia as well as in eastern Australia. Some grassy woodland of monsoonal northern Australia contains deciduous species of *Eucalyptus* among the dominants. These deciduous eucalypts are unusual in an otherwise evergreen genus. The wide range of tussock grasses occurring as woodland understorey include *Aristida*, *Stipa*, *Themeda* and other genera. In lower rainfall areas, or on poorer soils, the understorey includes low trees or tall shrubs from a wide range of genera including *Acacia*, *Casuarina*, *Callitris*, *Grevillea*, *Eremophila* and *Melaleuca*. Low woodland occurs on poor sandy soils in various temperate coastal areas and includes a wide range of shrubby species on mountain soils above about 1500 m in south-eastern mainland Australia.

Most eucalypt woodland has been modified since European settlement. In temperate regions, woodland has been heavily cleared for grazing and agricultural crops. Woodlands which have a grassy understorey have been extensively grazed by sheep in the south and cattle in the north. Tree regeneration is restricted by grazing, cultivation and (in the north) by annual burning. Open woodland has increased in area since European settlement, the gains mainly occurring as a result of degradation of forest and woodland, while there has been some loss of open woodland to pasture. Presently, there are about 2,000,000 km² of open woodland in Australia and about 1,000,000 km² of other woodland.

Scrub

Scrub consists of tall shrubs 2–8 m high with a foliage cover of greater than 30%. The dominant genera are *Eucalyptus*, *Acacia* and *Casuarina*. The eucalypts have mainly a "mallee" form consisting of many stems emerging from a large lignotuber. Mallee scrub covers vast areas of Australia within the 250–500 mm rainfall belt. The understorey varies markedly with soil type and degree of aridity and may consist of tussock grasses, dense hard-leaved shrubs, annuals and ephemerals. Clearing for agriculture, mainly cereal cropping, has had the greatest impact on scrub and, while some clearing is still occurring, the most serious threat to remaining mallee vegetation is the destruction of seedlings by grazing rabbits.

Heath

Australian heath is a species-rich dense shrubby vegetation of less than 2.5 m high. There are about 3700 heath species in Australia, over 1850 of which occur on lateritic soils and sand plains in south-west Western Australia (see Data Sheet on South-west Botanical Province – CPD Au7). 750 heath species occur in the Sydney Sandstone Region (CPD Site Au8, see Data Sheet). The families Epacridaceae, Proteaceae, Restionaceae, Myrtaceae, Liliaceae, Leguminosae and Orchidaceae dominate heathland vegetation (Specht 1981b).

Distribution of heath is controlled primarily by soil nutrients such as phosphorus and nitrogen. If the levels of these are increased, other species will invade and assume dominance over heathland species. Fire is important in heathland ecology with some species having woody fruits which release seed only after heating, while others have hard coated seeds which are cracked by fire and stimulated to germinate. Lignotubers, rhizomes, tubers and bulbs are common adaptive characteristics which aid in regeneration of heath after burning.

Since the early days of European settlement, heath has been used to some extent for cattle grazing; however, the heathland soils are unsuitable for agriculture. Plant nutrition research has now established methods of increasing suitability of heathland soils for crops, pastures and plantation forestry. Large areas of heathland in Queensland, Victoria, South Australia, Western Australia and Tasmania have been drained, cleared and "improved", while much coastal heathland has been cleared for urban and recreational development or, in places, removed during mining operations to recover heavy minerals such as rutile and zircon. Fragmented patches of relict heath in agricultural areas are threatened by fertilizer drift from surrounding land. The raised soil-nutrient status favours invasion by exotic and non-heath native species.

Shrubland

Shrubland is dominated by multi-stemmed shrubs 2–8 m tall with a foliage cover of 10–30%. It occurs in semi-arid regions receiving 150–300 mm annual rainfall. *Acacia* spp. dominate tall shrubland, while mallee *Eucalyptus* spp. dominate open shrubland. Low shrubland, or chenopod shrubland (formerly called shrub steppe), is dominated by low saltbush and bluebush shrubs up to 2 m tall. Herbaceous understoreys of perennial and ephemeral grasses and other herbaceous species are common, although some shrubland has a well-developed understorey of shrubs, including *Eremophila* spp. Chenopod shrubland is extensive, occupying about 6% of mainland Australia (Leigh 1981). The community lies mainly south of the Tropic of Capricorn in areas receiving annual rainfall ranging from 120–270 mm per annum with about half falling in winter. The most common genera are *Sclerolaena*, *Maireana*, *Atriplex* and *Chenopodium*.

Leigh (1981) reported that physical and chemical soil properties and soil moisture status were largely responsible for the original distribution of individual species but that present-day occurrence reflects the introduction of domestic and feral animals. Chenopod shrubland is estimated to support about 2.75 m sheep and 84,000 cattle. Newman and Condon (1969) estimated that only 10% of this formation showed little or no deterioration since European settlement. Leigh (1981) stated that chenopod shrubland is well understood ecologically and can be managed conservatively provided economic pressures do not force owners or lessees to overstock.

Johnson and Burrows (1981) discussed *Acacia* shrublands of Central and Western Australia, which are dominated by *Acacia aneura* (mulga) and occupy about 20% of the total area of Australia. Mulga often has a low, but rarely continuous, shrub layer consisting of species of *Eremophila*, *Cassia*, *Dodonaea* and *Maireana*. A herbaceous layer of perennial or seasonal forbs and grasses is usually well-developed. *Acacia* shrubland is largely unoccupied and not used commercially due to aridity and lack of surface water. Where it is used for either sheep or cattle grazing, *Acacia aneura* is browsed and, during drought, trees and tall shrubs may be felled to provide stock fodder. Johnson and Burrows (1981) suggested that the potential for replacement of *Acacia* shrublands with more productive pasture species is low, but that during the next 30–50 years about 40,000 km² could be converted to pasture based on the introduced buffel grass, *Cenchrus ciliaris*. They also stated that *Acacia* shrublands other than *A. aneura* can be expected to be of little commercial importance and so should retain their floristic integrity for the foreseeable future.

Herbland

The term herbland embraces tussock and hummock grassland, sedgeland and herbfield. Tussock grassland or tussock sedgeland consist of discrete tussocks of perennial grasses, rushes or sedges which cover up to 70% of the surface. An herbaceous or ground layer is frequently conspicuous. Mitchell

grass plains dominated by *Astrebla* spp. cover vast areas of northern Australia, from the Kimberleys to the Barkly Tableland and south into northern New South Wales. Kangaroo grass grassland, dominated by *Themeda* spp. and occasionally by wallaby grass, *Danthonia* spp., occurs in southern Australia. Kangaroo grass grassland has been extensively altered by farming and only remnants now remain. Hummock grassland, which occurs over vast areas of arid Australia, is dominated by large, perennial evergreen tussocks of the grasses *Triodia* and *Plectrachne* (commonly called spinifex). The foliage of *Triodia* is sharply-pointed and unattractive as forage. Spaces between the hummocks are virtually bare except after rain when ephemerals may appear. Alpine herbland is restricted to treeless areas of high mountains where high rainfall and humus soils occur. *Celmisia*, *Neopaxia*, *Craspedia* and *Plantago* spp. form a continuous ground cover. Grasses such as *Poa* and *Chionochloa* are also present.

Vegetation change

An inquiry into the use of forests and timber by the Commonwealth Resource Assessment Commission (1991a), found that about 50% of forest had been cleared or severely modified since European settlement, and about 5% of woodlands had been cleared, with a further 19% being severely modified. These figures relate primarily to tree cover and do not reveal the impact of grazing by introduced animals on the understorey and tree regeneration. Also, some areas have been modified more than others. For example, southern temperate woodlands have been more severely affected than those in the north.

The mean annual deforestation rate for forest and woodland from 1788–1985 has been estimated at 3590 km² (0.09% per annum) (AUSLIG 1990). (Forest and woodland were defined as natural vegetation dominated by trees, excluding mallee and mangroves.) AUSLIG (1990) mapped the areas of present day vegetation and that which was believed to have occurred in 1788. The area now used for agriculture and forestry covers more than 5 million km² (nearly 70% of the continent). Table 61 provides statistics for the changes in area of vegetation types since European settlement. Clearly, the major increase has been in grassland and pasture which has increased from 547 km² to 1195 km² (15.6% of the land area).

TABLE 61. CHANGE IN AREA OF VEGETATION TYPES SINCE EUROPEAN SETTLEMENT

Vegetation type	Natural area (000 km²)	Natural area (% of land area)	Present area (000 km²)	Present area (% of land area)
Closed forest	46	0.5	36	0.4
Open forest	642	8.4	359	4.7
Woodland	3224	42.1	3051	39.7
Shrubland	2974	38.7	2822	36.7
Scrub	90	1.1	28	0.4
Heath	13	0.2	26	0.4
Grassland	547	7.1	759	10.0
Sparse open herbfield	59	0.8	59	0.8
Littoral complex	22	0.3	22	0.3
Sown pasture	-	-	436	5.6
Urban complex	-	-	7	0.1
Intensive cropping/ horticulture	-	-	11	0.1
No vegetation	65	0.8	66	0.8
Total	**7682**	**100.0**	**7682**	**100.0**

Source: Derived from AUSLIG (1990).

TABLE 62. CHANGES IN AREA OF VEGETATION TYPE (1780s–1980s)

Vegetation type	Area in 1780s (000 km²)	Losses to (000 km²)	Gains from (000 km²)	Area in 1980s (000 km²)
Forest	690	Woodland, 175 Grassland, 140	Woodland, 15	390
Woodland	3220	Forest, 15 Grassland, 370	Forest, 175 Grassland, 60	3070
Shrubland	3080	Grassland, 200	-	2880
Grassland/pasture	500	Woodland, 60	Forest, 140 Woodland, 370 Shrubland, 200	1150

Source: Derived from AUSLIG (1990). Figures used are approximations.

It is difficult to predict trends; however, if the present environmental awareness continues there are likely to be only minor losses in the area of forest and possibly some gains from plantation establishment. Grassland will probably increase at the expense of woodland unless major effort is made, at least in southern Australia, to encourage regeneration on a large scale. The concern expressed in the South-west Botanical Province (CPD Site Au7) at the expansion of *Phytophthora* root rot fungus, if realised, may result in losses of forest, heath and scrub (see Data Sheet). As human population grows there will be further losses in most vegetation types for urban and industrial development, and for the development of tourist facilities. The total area occupied by these and ancillary uses, such as railways and roads, is about 210,000 km² (2.7% of the land area).

Flora

The most recent national census of native vascular plants, completed in 1990, listed 15,638 species (Hnatiuk 1990). In addition, 787 subspecies, 1355 varieties and 81 forms were recorded. Court (pers. comm.) estimates there are 3000–5000 vascular plant taxa still to be named. There is no similar census of non-vascular plants available; however, estimates presented in Table 63 indicate there are 26,500 described species. Court (pers. comm.) suggests there are at least another 23,000 unnamed lower plant taxa. The number of both vascular and non-vascular species will undoubtedly increase as taxonomic revisions are carried out and further botanical exploration occurs.

Flora censuses for vascular plants have been produced for most states and territories during the last ten years. They include: New South Wales (Jacobs and Pickard 1981), South Australia (Jessop 1984), Western Australia (Green 1985), Northern Territory (Dunlop 1987), Victoria (Forbes and Ross 1988) and Australian Capital Territory. The *Flora of Australia* project was formally launched with Volume 1 in 1981. It is planned to comprise 50 volumes to be published over 20 years.

The Australian flowering plants are grouped in about 237 families, which include almost all the larger plant families of the world. Most of the families are widespread elsewhere. A different situation exists at the generic and specific levels. Burbidge (1960) identified 1700 genera of phanerogams in Australia (out of a world total of approximately 9800), with 566 (33.3%) endemic to Australia. These figures have not yet been revised on a national basis. Table 64 lists the most numerically important families in the Australian flora and the numbers of endemic genera they contain.

TABLE 63. AUSTRALIAN NATIVE PLANT FAMILIES, GENERA AND SPECIES

Plant group	Families	Genera	Species, sub-species, varieties, forms
Angiosperms	237		c. 17,850
Dicotyledons	187 [a]		
Monocotyledons	50 [a]		
Gymnosperms	7 [b]	15 [b]	62 [b]
Pteridophyta	35 [c]	121 [c]	386 [c]
Total vascular	**262** [d]	**2179** [d]	**c. 18,000**
Bryophyta: liverworts		800 [g]	
Bryophyta: mosses		1200 [g]	
Lichens	53 [e]	205 [e]	2500 [e]
Algae, non-marine		300 [f]	2000 [f]
Mycophyta			20,000 [d]
Total non-vascular			**c. 26,500**

Sources:

[a] *Flora of Australia* (1981).
[b] Morley and Toelken (1983).
[c] Clifford and Constantine (1980).
[d] Chapman pers. comm.
[e] McArthy (1991).
[f] Entwistle (unpublished).
[g] Leigh and Briggs (1991).

TABLE 64. IMPORTANT FAMILIES WITH ENDEMIC GENERA

Family	Number of genera	Number of endemic genera
Gramineae	135	32
Leguminosae	109	37
Compositae	104	55
Orchidaceae	75	17
Myrtaceae	47	33
Liliaceae	47	30
Euphorbiaceae	47	15
Cyperaceae	41	12
Proteaceae	37	28
Rubiaceae	36	5
Rutaceae	35	20
Chenopodiaceae	30	19

Source: Burbidge (1960).

Two significant genera within the Australian flora which give it a distinctive national character are *Eucalyptus* and *Acacia*. Eucalypts dominate most of the vegetation in all but the treeless arid and alpine areas and in true rain forest. There are only two eucalypt species which do not occur naturally in Australia. With over 500 species, the genus is exceeded numerically only by *Acacia*. Eucalypts vary in height from over 150 m (the tallest broadleaved tree in the world) to stunted mallees only 2 m high. The genus occurs on almost all soil types with some species growing in areas waterlogged for most of the year. *Eucalyptus* spp. are planted widely throughout the world as fast-growing trees for fuel and timber production, and as ornamentals. By contrast, although *Acacia* is well-represented in the floras of Africa and tropical America, only one section, Phyllodinae, is dominant in Australia. Members of this scleromorphic section occur as the dominant tree species in the arid zone. However, only 14% of Australia's *Acacia* species occur there, whereas the South-west Botanical Province contains 40% of the species, many of which are strict endemics.

The national census was based on approximately 6 million herbarium records, but many of these lack detailed collection site information and the distribution of many species is unclear. Areas that are particularly poorly known botanically are Western Australia, Northern Territory and the Cape York Peninsula of Queensland.

Naturalized taxa

A wide range of agricultural, horticultural, pastoral and ornamental plant species has been introduced to Australia in the last 200 years. Hnatiuk (1990) reported 1952 naturalized species, 74 subspecies, 107 varieties and 82 forms (about 11% of the flora). Ross (1976) calculated the rate of introduction of non-Australian species to the state of Victoria had averaged five to six species per year over the previous 100 years; there was no sign that the rate was diminishing.

Some species have become serious pests, competing with crops and contaminating wool and hides. The estimated total cost of weeds to Australia annually is A$4000 million (Anon. 1991). Well-documented weeds are *Opuntia* spp. (prickly pear) and *Rubus procerus* (blackberry). Prickly pear was introduced as a food source for the cochineal beetle used to produce red dye and to provide "living fences" to contain stock. The estimated annual losses due to blackberry in New South Wales, Victoria and Tasmania have risen from A$42 m in 1988 to at least A$77 m in 1990. A virulent strain of blackberry rust, *Phragmidium violaceum*, was released in 1991 in further attempts at biological control.

Other major weed species include *Acacia nilotica* (prickly acacia), which has colonized about 50,000 km² of former grassland in north-central Queensland, and *Mimosa pigra*, which is invading large areas in northern Australia, including the Kakadu-Alligator Rivers Region (CPD Site Au4 – see Data Sheet). Garden escapes include species of *Olea*, *Ligustrum*, *Lantana*, *Cinnamomum* and *Cortaderia*. They are a threat in the Sydney Sandstone Region (CPD Site Au8 – see Data Sheet), while *Chrysanthemoides monilifera* is a major problem in coastal vegetation. *Olea africana* and *Psidium littorale* are now naturalized in native vegetation on Norfolk Island (see Data Sheet on Norfolk and Lord Howe Islands, CPD Site Au5) and *Tamarix aphylla* is expanding in some of the dry river beds in the Central Australian Mountain Ranges (CPD Site Au3 – see Data Sheet).

Useful plants

Aborigines used a wide range of plants and either learnt to avoid those which were toxic or developed methods to remove the toxic properties.

Timber species

Many species, primarily in the genera *Eucalyptus*, *Acacia*, *Tristaniopsis*, *Callitris* and *Araucaria* are harvested from native forest for sawn timber, pulpwood and fuel. Timber harvesting of rain forest species is now limited to trees growing on private land. Softwood plantation forestry, covering 8920 km², is based on four introduced *Pinus* species from North America and southern Europe, and the native conifer, *Araucaria cunninghamii*, (hoop pine).

In 1988–1989, 17.6 million m³ of wood (65% hardwood, 35% softwood) were harvested from native and plantation forests managed for wood production (see Table 65). This does not include fuelwood obtained from logs. Fuelwood amounts to 2.5% of primary energy supplies in Australia with 6.1 million tonnes being used annually for domestic and industrial purposes. The value of forest wood products exported in 1989–1990 was A$510 million, of which 72% by value was woodchips sent mainly to Japan. By contrast, the value of timber imports was A$2343 million, 65% as pulp and paper and 21% as sawn timber mainly from South East Asia and North America.

There is an existing export market worth A$8 million for seed of native plants for afforestation programmes and ornamental planting. At present this is mainly from temperate species, but there is considerable potential for export of species from the wet and dry tropics and from arid areas.

Forest and forest processing industries directly employed 80,000 people in 1987–1988, 1% of the Australian paid workforce (Department of the Arts, Sport, the Environment and Territories 1991; Resource Assessment Commission 1991a).

TABLE 65. ESTIMATED REMOVALS FROM AUSTRALIAN FORESTS BY END USE (1988–1989)

Product	Broadleaved forest (000 m³)	Coniferous forest (000 m³)	Total (000 m³)
Saw and veneer logs	4523	3791	8314
Sleeper logs	377	-	377
Pulp logs	6222	2190	8412
Other, including fencing, poles, mine timbers	353	172	525
Grand total			**17,628**

Source: Resource Assessment Commission (1991a).

Essential oils

About 1500 native plants, mainly in the families Rutaceae and Myrtaceae, yield an essential oil. Twenty eucalypts are exploited to produce oils rich in cineole used in preparation of embrocations, soaps and ointments. Principal among these are *Eucalyptus polybractea*, *E. dives*, *E. leucoxylon* and *E. radiata*. Most of the oil is extracted from natural stands; however, plantations of *E. polybracteata* have been established in western New South Wales. Annual output of all types of eucalypt oil in Australia is about 150 tonnes.

Oil from *Melaleuca* spp. is distilled for use as a bactericide and flavouring agent. Current annual production from both natural stands and plantations is about 30,000–40,000 litres with a total value of between A$1.8–2.4 million. Other leaf products from native species include rutin used in haemorrhoidal preparations, coumarins used in anticoagulants and alkaloids used for treatment of stomach ulcers, travel sickness and in the production of atropine.

Ornamental plants

About 2500 native species are cultivated for ornamental purposes. Most are grown as wild species. The incentive for plant selection and breeding has been encouraged by recent Plant Variety Rights legislation. Many rain forest species have potential for indoor plant use both in Australia and for export. Management programmes have been developed to regulate harvesting of tree ferns, *Dicksonia antarctica* and *Cyathea australis*, from the wild. The production of palms for indoor use and landscaping is prodigious. The export of palm seeds is a major industry for Lord Howe Island (see Data Sheet on Norfolk and Lord Howe Islands, CPD Site Au5). Native cycads are also increasing in popularity as ornamentals.

Honey plants

Australia is the world's fourth largest exporter of honey, exporting 40% of total production. Much of this is derived from native plant species. It is estimated that the apiary industry has an additional value of about A$1000 million a year through the pollination of crops and native plants. Siting of beehives in conservation reserves is now either prohibited or being phased out because of adverse effects on native bees and pollination of some native plant species.

Social and environmental values

Vegetation and native plants have important social and environmental values in water catchment and erosion amelioration, fauna habitat, grazing, recreation, cultural tourism, scientific research and heritage.

Water catchment

Several Australian CPD sites are important catchments for water for domestic, industrial, irrigation and hydroelectricity purposes. For example, much of the Central Plateau of the Western Tasmanian World Heritage Site is catchment for hydroelectricity dams outside the area (see Data Sheet on Western Tasmanian Wilderness, CPD Site Au9) and the Australian Alps (CPD Site Au1) yields large quantities of water for domestic and agricultural purposes. The Australian Alps also produces electricity at about 60% of the cost of energy produced by thermal plants and is currently yielding electricity to the value of A$200 million annually (Brown and Milner 1990). The Sydney Sandstone Region (CPD Site Au8) supplies water for over 4 million people in Sydney and Wollongong, while the water for Perth is obtained in forested catchments of the South-west Botanical Province (CPD Site Au7). The Queensland Wet Tropics (CPD Site Au10) yield water for the expanding tourist industry and sugar mills in north Queensland. (See the Data Sheets on these areas for more details.)

There have been few attempts in Australia to quantify the benefits of forests in terms of water yield. However, it has been estimated that each hectare of *Eucalyptus regnans* forest in Victoria produces water worth A$1800 a year.

Fauna habitat

The Australian fauna includes 7 endemic mammal families, including that of the platypus and koala, and 4 endemic bird families. At the species level, 88% of the 700 species of reptiles, 70% of 850 species of birds and 94% of the 180 species of frogs are endemic. Australia and its islands have an estimated 146 of the world's 280 marsupials. There are 3600 species of fish and tens of thousands of species of molluscs. There are 65,000 known species of insects in Australia with at least as many more still to be identified.

Ten species of birds have become extinct since European settlement and 26 are classified as Endangered or Vulnerable. Sixteen mammals are presumed extinct and 24 are Endangered, while 9 reptiles and 6 amphibians are Endangered. Major threats to fauna are habitat loss and introduced animals.

Native fauna have evolved with native flora and, while some faunal species, such as the larger kangaroos, have adapted well to changed environments, the survival of many depends upon the maintenance of native vegetated habitats. At the same time, some plant species rely on native insects for effective pollination or seed dispersal.

Grazing

Large areas of forest are used for grazing sheep and cattle, particularly in northern parts of the country. Forests are particularly important as an additional feed source for grazing animals in times of drought. Some tree species, such as *Casuarina* spp. and *Brachychiton* spp., are used as emergency drought fodder.

Scrub and shrubland are also used extensively for sheep grazing in southern Australia, while vast areas of Mitchell grass plains (with *Astrebla* spp.) in northern Australia are used for cattle grazing. Summer cattle grazing in alpine regions occurred in the past, persisting in some areas even after they were declared National Parks. During droughts there is still pressure from some parts of the farming community to resume grazing in alpine areas. The long-term adverse effects of cattle grazing on conservation, recreation and water catchment values have been clearly demonstrated from research, assisting conservation managers to resist pressure to allow grazing to resume.

Recreation and cultural tourism

The Australian flora has significant values for recreation and cultural tourism. For example, the Australian Alps (CPD Site Au1, see Data Sheet) attracts 3–4 million visitors a year. While most of these are drawn by the prospect of winter snow sports, increasing numbers are being attracted by the beauty of summer flowering alpine plants. Large numbers of international and interstate tourists visit Western Australia each spring for the wildflower display there. Considerable tourism infrastructure has been established around this annual event. Heath vegetation in flower in National Parks in the Sydney Sandstone Region (CPD Site Au8) also draws large numbers of visitors each spring.

Several Australian CPD sites are within, or encompass, World Heritage Sites which are becoming significant components of Australia's tourist industry. The number of visitors to Kakadu National Park, which is within the Kakadu-Alligator Rivers Region (CPD Site Au4), increased from 45,800

TABLE 66. COINCIDENCE OF AUSTRALIAN CENTRES OF PLANT DIVERSITY AND WORLD HERITAGE SITES

CPD Site	Area (km²)	World Heritage Site	Area (km²)	Date listed
Border Ranges	600	East Coast Rain Forest Parks	2037	1986
Kakadu-Alligator Rivers Region	30,000	Kakadu National Park (Stages 1 and 2)	13,073	1981/1987
Norfolk and Lord Howe Islands	54	Lord Howe Island Group	1450 *	1982
Western Tasmanian Wilderness	14,050	Tasmanian Wilderness	10,813	1982/1989
Wet Tropics of Queensland	11,000	Wet Tropics	8990	1988

* Site includes surrounding ocean and Ball's Pyramid.

in 1982 to 230,000 in 1989 (Wood 1990). Expenditure actually incurred by visitors to Kakadu in 1990–1991 was estimated at approximately A\$34 million; this figure excludes spending outside park boundaries, but related to visits to Kakadu (Resource Assessment Commission 1991b).

National Parks and equivalent reserves contributed A\$61 million to the Tasmanian economy in 1986–1987, with a significant portion being generated by the Western Tasmanian Wilderness (CPD Site Au9). The wilderness concept is being promoted in Australia by a relatively small but articulate component of the population. Large natural areas undisturbed by intrusive human activities are essential to pursue the wilderness experience and, inevitably, there is conflict between management for forestry and other resource based activities and wilderness values.

Scientific research

Flora and vegetation are subject to a wide range of research in ecology, taxonomy, physiology, horticulture and forestry. Recently, more attention is being given to research in ecosystem functioning and conservation management.

Twelve parks and reserves are designated as Biosphere Reserves under the UNESCO Man and Biosphere Programme. Scientific research is a major function within Biosphere Reserves. The Kosciusko, Fitzgerald River and Southwest Tasmania Biosphere Reserves are within CPD Sites Au1, Au7 and Au9, respectively (see Data Sheets).

Defence

The Department of Defence controls relatively large areas in a variety of vegetation types. For example, 140 km² of rain forest between Tully and Innisfail in north Queensland are managed as a Tropical Trials Establishment and Field Force Battle School.

Heritage

The heritage value of flora and vegetation is considerable. Many forested areas are entered on the Register of the National Estate established under the Australian Heritage Commission Act 1975. The "National Estate" is defined in the legislation as those parts of the natural and cultural environment which: "have aesthetic, historic, scientific or social significance or other special value for future generations as well as for the present community". By 30 June 1990 there were 9146 sites on the Register of the National Estate, including most National Parks and declared conservation reserves. Inclusion on the Register has implications only for Federal Government actions. Listing a place on the Register does not provide any legal constraints or controls over actions of State/Territory or Local Government, or private owners. Most individual states and

territories have specific legislation covering the identification and protection of sites of heritage value; however, there are differing public opinions on the scope and effectiveness of the protection achieved.

Many vegetated places including forests are sacred to Aboriginal people and also provide spiritual enrichment to some Europeans (Frawley and Semple 1988).

Australia ratified the World Cultural and Natural Heritage Convention in August 1974. Eight areas in Australia have been inscribed as World Heritage Sites under the Convention. Five CPD sites coincide entirely, or in part, with World Heritage Sites (see Table 66).

Rare or threatened Australian plants

Lists of rare or threatened species for some Australian states and territories were published in Specht, Roe and Broughton (1974). These lists were prepared on a state or territory basis, but did not take into account species whose distributions crossed state boundaries. Subsequently, a national committee was established in 1975 to review the conservation of species throughout their Australian distribution. This has resulted in three status reports: Hartley and Leigh (1979); Leigh, Briggs and Hartley (1981); and Briggs and Leigh (1988), together with a review and presentation of case studies (Leigh and Briggs 1991). These reports have stimulated additional surveys and have encouraged more collaborators to contribute to a national programme.

Leigh and Briggs (1991) reveals that 3580 taxa (20%) of the described flora from mainland Australia and Tasmania are considered to be rare or threatened. It is important to note, however, that 32.8% of the rare or threatened species are classified as Rare and not believed to be under any foreseeable threat. A further 41.4% are believed to be rare or possibly threatened, but further surveys are needed to establish clearly their conservation status. There are 83 species presumed to have become extinct since European settlement, largely as a result of clearance of their habitat to make way for agriculture and grazing. A further 179 taxa are classified as Endangered and 661 as Vulnerable. Extinct, Endangered and Vulnerable species represent 5.2% of described taxa. Families in the 1988 report with large numbers of rare or threatened species are: Myrtaceae (441 species), Leguminosae (385), Proteaceae (300) and Orchidaceae (170). Genera with high numbers of rare or threatened species include: *Acacia* (164 species), *Eucalyptus* (152), *Grevillea* (109), *Daviesia* (51) and *Leucopogon* (46). Except for *Acacia*, these genera are endemic to Australia or have a very limited extension to eastern Asia with occasional outliers elsewhere.

42% of the species listed as rare or threatened are from Western Australia, the majority occurring in the South-west Botanical Province (CPD Site Au7, see Data Sheet). However, it must be noted that 46.7% of species recorded in the *Census of Australian Vascular Plants* (Hnatiuk 1990) occur in Western Australia. Other regions with high concentrations of rare or threatened plants are the Cape York Peninsula, the Wet Tropics of Queensland (CPD Site Au10, see Data Sheet), and the intensively developed east coast between Sydney and Brisbane.

Briggs and Leigh (1988) also revealed that 172 (5.2%) of rare or threatened species were known only from the type collection, while 1840 (55.2%) were species with a total range restricted to less than 100 km. The large number of species (1484) classified as Poorly Known, but suspected of being either rare or threatened, reflects the poor state of botanical knowledge for parts of Western Australia, the Northern Territory and Cape York Peninsula, Queensland. Further survey work is needed to establish the conservation status of these species.

Only 53.2% of Australia's rare or threatened species have at least some of their populations within a National Park or conservation reserve. For a range of reasons, including management strategies and population size, only 13.7% of the total of reserved species are considered to be adequately conserved (i.e. 1000 plants or more of that species are known to occur within conservation reserves); 43.4% are known to be inadequately reserved. For 43% of threatened taxa complete estimates of reserved population size are unavailable (Leigh and Briggs 1991). Five Endangered species and 43 Vulnerable species have their entire known populations confined to National Parks and reserves. Clearly their continued survival depends upon management strategies to maintain or increase their population sizes. These management strategies may involve *ex situ* propagation and reintroduction to areas of former occurrence.

In the period between the 1981 and 1988 reports, the percentage of rare or threatened species in declared parks or reserves rose by 13.2% to 53.2%. Briggs and Leigh (1988) considered the major reasons for the increases to be the creation of additional reserves and a substantial increase in botanical surveys within existing reserves, leading to discoveries of many new populations of rare species within the existing reserve system. The position remains, however, that half the species classified as rare or threatened are not in parks or reserves.

Briggs and Leigh (1988) also provided information on the number of reserved rare or threatened species in each plant collecting region to highlight those regions with the highest priority for establishment of reserves for protecting threatened species.

Conservation

The responsibility for nature conservation including National Parks and reserves and wildlife management rests with each of the six states and two mainland territories. Nature conservation agencies have been established in each, sometimes linked with forestry, fishery, and environment and planning agencies.

There is an Australian Nature Conservation Agency (formerly called the Australian National Parks and Wildlife Service) responsible to the Australian Government for monitoring and, in some cases implementing, international conservation agreements. The Agency also manages Kakadu and Uluru (Ayers Rock-Mount Olga) National Parks in the Northern Territory in association with the traditional Aboriginal

landowners, and National Parks on the offshore territories of Norfolk and Christmas Islands. A Council of Nature Conservation Ministers (CONCOM) consisting of ministers responsible for nature conservation in the State, Territory and Australian Governments was established in 1975 to foster national cooperation in nature conservation policy and administration. CONCOM is now part of ANZECC, the Australian and New Zealand Environment and Conservation Council.

The first National Park in Australia, Royal National Park south of Sydney, was established in 1879. Since then, National Parks and conservation reserves have been established in all states and territories. By 1991, there were 3429 terrestrial protected areas under the jurisdiction of the various Australian states and territories, covering 501,394 km^2 (Hooy and Shaughnessy 1992). This is approximately 6% of the total land surface. In addition, approximately 396,387 km^2 were reserved in 158 marine and estuarine protected areas. In some cases, these reserves are part of, or are contiguous with, terrestrial reserves.

TABLE 67. SUMMARY OF PROTECTED AREAS IN EACH JURISDICTION IN AUSTRALIA

Jurisdiction	Number of Protected Areas*	Area (km^2)	% State/ Territory
COMMONWEALTH			
Terrestrial	13	27,312	
Marine	18	366,045	
Total	**31**	**393,357**	
AUSTRALIAN CAPITAL TERRITORY			
Terrestrial	5	1015	41.7
Total	**5**	**1015**	
NEW SOUTH WALES			
Terrestrial	464	38,889	4.9
Marine	8	959	
Total	**472**	**39,848**	
NORTHERN TERRITORY			
Terrestrial	96	21,144	1.6
Marine	3	2292	
Total	**99**	**23,436**	
QUEENSLAND			
Terrestrial	649	41,416	2.4
Marine	88	14,932	
Total	**737**	**56,348**	
SOUTH AUSTRALIA			
Terrestrial	294	166,751	16.9
Marine	14	152	
Total	**308**	**166,903**	
TASMANIA			
Terrestrial	228	18,143	26.6
Marine	5	67	
Total	**233**	**18,210**	
VICTORIA			
Terrestrial	501	29,404	12.9
Marine	15	486	
Total	**516**	**29,890**	
WESTERN AUSTRALIA			
Terrestrial	1179	157,319	6.2
Marine	7	11,454	
Total	**1186**	**168,773**	
NATIONAL TOTALS			
Terrestrial	3429	501,394	c. 6
Marine	158	396,387	
Total	**3587**	**897,781**	

Source: Derived from Hooy and Shaughnessy (1992).

* It is important to note that the figures included under terrestrial protected areas cover all types of protected sites, including Historic Sites and Hunting Reserves, where the primary management aims may not be flora conservation.

The extent to which the proclaimed conservation reserves adequately cover the diversity of plants and animals is currently subject to investigation as part of a National Biodiversity Strategy, which includes a National Index of Ecosystems Program to identify nationally important ecosystems, assess their representation in existing parks and reserves, and examine their conservation status outside parks and reserves.

The Australian Network for Plant Conservation promotes plant conservation and organizes training workshops. It is establishing an Australia-wide endangered species collection at botanic gardens and other places, and is developing an integrated plant conservation strategy for Australia.

A review of the protected areas system and conservation legislation, together with a list of protected sites, is given in IUCN (1992).

Centres of plant diversity and endemism

Eleven major centres of plant diversity and endemism on mainland Australia are identified below as CPD sites. Nine have been selected by regional experts for Data Sheet treatment. In addition to the mainland sites, the oceanic island floras of Lord Howe and Norfolk Island are selected for treatment in Data Sheets on account of their high endemism. Christmas Island (Indian Ocean), however, does not have a sufficiently high number of endemics to warrant selection for Data Sheet treatment. Australia's subantarctic islands are not floristically rich, but taken with the New Zealand subantarctic islands they are considered to be worthy of treatment on the basis of their genetic distinctiveness.

In 1989 an Environmental Resources Information Network (ERIN) was established by the Australian Government "to draw together, upgrade and supplement information on the distribution of endangered species, vegetation types and heritage sites". In 1991, ERIN provided funds to capture and upgrade distributional data held on plant specimens and in databanks in herbaria throughout the country. Within the first year the programme established databases for over 200,000 records of *Eucalyptus*, representing about 70% of known collections of this significant genus in the Australian vegetation. ERIN databases now also include over 80,000 records of Gramineae and the majority of *Melaleuca, Callitris* and Casuarinaceae. In Australia, individual states and territories have responsibility for flora within their boundaries and the extent of knowledge varies with the size and diversity of each and the resources which have been made available to herbaria, botanic gardens and nature conservation agencies. Many plant species occur in more than one state or territory and the extent of knowledge of the distribution of the same species may vary considerably from state to state. An advantage of the ERIN project is that through cooperation with state and territory agencies and federal funding, plant distribution databases will be established to the same format for the whole country. The results of these efforts will greatly assist in projects to determine levels of species endemism, but will not be available for some years. Meanwhile, the task of selecting CPD sites for Australia for the present project has been based on the collective knowledge of members of the IUCN Australasian Plant Specialist Group and others with intimate knowledge of the Australian flora and vegetation, and

supplemented by reference to published and unpublished work. The selected sites cover a wide range of vegetation types and geographic regions and capture a significant percentage of the native plant diversity.

Australia

Au1. Australian Alps (New South Wales, Victoria and Australian Capital Territory)

– see Data Sheet.

Au2. Border Ranges (Queensland and New South Wales)

– see Data Sheet.

Au3. Central Australian Mountain Ranges (Northern Territory, South Australia and Western Australia)

– see Data Sheet.

Au4. Kakadu-Alligator Rivers Region (Northern Territory)

– see Data Sheet.

Au5. Norfolk and Lord Howe Islands

– see Data Sheet.

Au6. North Kimberley Region (Western Australia)

– see Data Sheet.

Au7. South-west Botanical Province (Western Australia)

– see Data Sheet.

Au8. Sydney Sandstone Region (New South Wales)

– see Data Sheet.

Au9. Western Tasmanian Wilderness (Tasmania)

– see Data Sheet.

Au10. Wet Tropics of Queensland (Queensland)

– see Data Sheet.

Au11. McIlwraith Range and Iron Range (Queensland)

Area: The McIlwraith Range covers c. 900 km² between latitudes 14–15°S in the Cape York Peninsula. The Iron Range covers c. 989 km² to the north of the McIlwraith Range and extends to latitude 12°30'S. The highest point is 823 m (in the McIlwraith Range).

❖ Vegetation: The largest single block of Cape York Peninsula rain forests which are at their southernmost limit. The two areas are distinct in that upland rain forests occur almost exclusively in the McIlwraith Range. 15 vegetation types have been identified, several of which do not occur elsewhere in significant amounts. These include extensive high granite plateau rain forests, tall semi-deciduous mesophyll vine forests, *Melaleuca viridiflora* forests, natural grassland communities dominated by *Imperata cylindrica*, tall deciduous monsoon vine forest and *Brachychiton*-dominated deciduous vine thicket.

❖ Flora: >900 vascular plant species in 153 families so far identified, many of which are East Gondwanan relicts. The remoteness and rugged nature of the area suggest that many species remain to be discovered. Rare endemics include *Croton stockeri* and *Syzygium argyropedicum*. *Acacia (Senegalia) albizioides* represents one of only two examples surviving in Australia of an early evolutionary line of the genus. The McIlwraith Range is particularly rich in orchids with about 16% of the entire Australian orchid flora occurring there. Of the 223 rare and threatened plant species recorded in the McIlwraith and Iron Ranges, 16 are restricted entirely to the McIlwraith Range, 35 to the Iron Range, whilst a further 37 are shared but occur nowhere else.

❖ Conservation: The Iron Range National Park (IUCN Management Category II) covers 346 km².

Au12. Sclerophyll forests of Far South-east New South Wales

❖ Vegetation: Sclerophyll forest with a rich representation of the genus *Eucalyptus*. Keith and Sanders (1990) listed a number of communities which are unique to the region.

❖ Flora: The flora includes 183 vascular plant species (including some rain forest taxa) at their southernmost limit of distribution; 38 species are at their northernmost limit. 53 *Eucalyptus* spp. are present, including 3 nationally Rare or Vulnerable species. A further 38 vascular plant species are on the national rare or threatened plant list.

❖ Threats: Logging.

❖ Conservation: Mosley and Costin (1992) propose that c. 11,600 km² of far south-east New South Wales temperate forest should be added to the proposed Alpine Region World Heritage Site.

Au13. Christmas Island (Indian Ocean)

An uplifted coral atoll located 360 km south of Java and 1400 km north-west of Port Hedland on mainland Australia. The island is the tip of an ancient volcanic cone which approached the surface of the ocean about 60 million years BP. A coral cap formed on top of the submerged cone and subsequent uplift and weathering have given the island its characteristic stepped appearance. Area: 135 km².

❖ Vegetation: Mixed closed forest above 180 m and occasionally extending down to the coastal terraces. Main canopy trees are species of *Tristiropsis*, *Dysoxylon*, *Cryptocarya* and *Barringtonia*, while species of *Eugenia*,

Planchonella and *Hernandia* are emergents. *Celtis*, *Terminalia* and *Pisonia* forest occurs on the coastal terraces.

❖ Flora: Estimated c. 200 flowering plant species of which between 12 and 21 are believed to be endemic. No known endemic genera. The flora has affinities with that of Sumatra and is essentially Malesian in character.

❖ Conservation: Phosphate mining has ceased. The expansion of the National Park in 1989 to 87 km² (64% of the island) has given added security.

(For Subantarctic Islands, see CPD Site Au17 under New Zealand.)

NEW ZEALAND

New Zealand (Aotearoa) is an isolated archipelago in the southern Pacific Ocean, over 2000 km east of Australia, the nearest large landmass. It consists of two principal islands (North Island and South Island) and Stewart Island (just south of South Island), together with the Chatham Islands (800 km to the east) and smaller offshore and outlying islands, including the Kermadec Islands and the Subantarctic Islands. In addition, New Zealand has jurisdiction over the territories of Tokelau in the Pacific Ocean and of the Ross Dependency of Antarctica.

The land area of New Zealand is 269,000 km². North and South Islands, together with Stewart Island, extend over 1600 km from north to south, between latitudes 34°20'–47°20'S. The whole of the New Zealand region, from the Kermadec Islands in the north to Campbell Island in the south, lies between latitudes 29°–55°S and longitudes 158°E–176°W. New Zealand is mostly hilly to mountainous, reaching a maximum altitude of 3764 m at the summit of Aoraki (Mount Cook). Over 50 peaks reach 2750 m, and about 75% of the land area is above 200 m altitude. In North Island the central volcanoes reach 2797 m.

The coastline of the main islands provides a great variety of habitats, from sandy, gravelly and rocky shores, salt marshes and brackish lagoons, to extensive sand dunes, high and exposed cliffs, storm-lashed promontories and sheltered inlets. Large rivers have formed lowland plains augmented in South Island by outwash gravels from glaciers. Wetland habitats are a major feature. There are many cold lakes, 12 of which each cover an area of over 65 km², and innumerable tarns.

Major geological events which influenced the floristic and faunistic history and evolutionary relationships include the separation of New Zealand from Australia around 80 million years BP, following the break-up of Gondwana; a period of mountain building during the Cretaceous; a period of relative quiescence during much of the Tertiary, resulting in New Zealand being reduced to small, low-lying islands; and renewed tectonic activity culminating in mountain building, vulcanism and glaciation in the Pliocene and Quaternary.

Although the oldest rocks found in New Zealand are Precambrian, and there are extensive areas of Mesozoic and some Palaeozoic rocks, geologically New Zealand is a young country. Rates of land uplift and erosion are amongst the highest in the world. Heavy rainfall, steep topography and erodible, shattered bedrock result in high natural erosion rates of over 5 mm per year.

In many regions extensive river terraces, glaciated U-shaped valleys and alluvial plains are evidence of the most recent period of glaciation. This reached its peak only 25,000 years ago and ended less than 15,000 years ago. Glaciers are still very evident along the Southern Alps, the largest being the Tasman Glacier which is some 29 km long.

New Zealand is a land of geological upheaval, laying astride two tectonic plates which have undergone several hundred kilometres of movement during and since the Tertiary Era. Minor earthquakes are relatively common and each year at least one severe earthquake can be expected, although few have caused widespread destruction. There is a long history of vulcanism, and volcanoes are a prime tourist attraction in the North Island. Volcanic activity has been a major force in shaping the New Zealand landscape. Some eruptions, such as that which formed Lake Taupo about AD 130, have been major by world standards. A number of North Island and offshore volcanoes are still active and have erupted in historic times.

Climate

New Zealand's climate is strongly influenced by its location in the Southern Hemisphere mid-latitudes, its north-south orientation and the presence of high mountain ranges. The mountains form a barrier to the prevailing westerly winds and cause precipitation that is often both heavy and prolonged in western and upland areas. Annual precipitation in such areas can exceed 10,000 mm per year, with very heavy snowfalls and prolonged snow cover above 1000 m altitude. In contrast, eastern parts of the country experience rain-shadow effects, which are particularly pronounced in some inland basins located between the main mountain ranges and outlier ranges. In Central Otago, in the southern part of New Zealand, conditions are semi-arid with rainfall as low as 300 mm annually.

Temperatures, generally, are sufficiently high to enable plant growth to occur throughout the year in most lowland areas. Permanent snow is absent from most parts of North Island, although occasional winter snowfalls can be experienced as far north as Auckland. In South Island the snow-line lies at about 2200 m; snow can lie for several months in winter above about 1500 m. Heavy frosts are experienced in many parts of South Island and inland North Island.

The Kermadec Islands have a subtropical climate, the Chatham Islands a cloudy, humid climate and the Subantarctic Islands have a windy cool temperate/montane climate. Throughout, maritime influences have a strong effect on climate.

Many parts of the country are occasionally affected by catastrophic events such as heavy rain and flooding, wind storms, prolonged dry spells, heavy snowfalls and unseasonal cold periods of weather. Occasionally, tropical cyclones are driven far enough south to affect New Zealand, bringing heavy rain and rarely, catastrophic hurricane-force winds.

Population

The population of New Zealand reached 3.43 million in 1991 and is expected to reach 4.04 million by 2021. The population growth rate between 1985 and 1990 averaged 0.87% per annum (World Resources Institute 1992).

New Zealand is a multiracial society with people of Maori, Polynesian, European and Asian origin. There is a high level of intermixing and considerable movement between New Zealand and adjacent south-western Pacific countries. The Maori proportion (loosely defined as those people with some Maori ancestry who wish to call themselves Maori) is projected to rise from 15% of total population to about 30% by 2021.

Vegetation

About 60% of the land retains substantially intact indigenous vegetation. The remainder is radically modified and used chiefly for intensive agriculture, grazing, exotic forestry or urban purposes. Table 68 provides recent estimates of plant cover.

TABLE 68. MAIN VEGETATION TYPES IN NEW ZEALAND

Type	% cover
Grassland (native)	40
Grassland (adventive pasture)	30
Forest (native)	24
Grass and scrub	19
Forest and scrub	5
Forest (exotic plantations)	4.5
Scrub	4
Bare ground	3
Cropland	1
Miscellaneous	1

Source: Newsome (1987).

Forest

Before people arrived in New Zealand, most of the country was covered in forest. Much of the vegetation and wildlife was unique, as the land mass had been isolated for some 80 million years. Ancient plants and wildlife were abundant, and included the kauri, flightless kiwi and moa, the tuatara (a lizard-like reptile) and large ground snails. The flora and fauna had evolved in the absence of mammalian herbivores. Very considerable changes took place in the distribution and composition of vegetation types as a result of Pleistocene glaciation. This resulted in such phenomena as the "beech gap" of central Westland in South Island, and relict distributions of vegetation types. To a large extent, vegetation cover is still adjusting to the effects of changes in climate following the cessation of extensive glaciation.

It is estimated that up until about 100 years ago, forests covered 70–80% of New Zealand. By 1990, forests remained on less than 40% of the land area. Indigenous forests covered just over 60,000 km² while exotic plantations covered 13,000 km².

Indigenous forests occur from sea-level to the subalpine tree limit, and on the main islands contain some 48 species of tall- and medium-sized trees, and over 70 tree species that do not normally exceed 10 m. Although forests in many parts of New Zealand have been fragmented, large tracts of unbroken forests still extend from the coast to subalpine areas on the western side of South Island. Indigenous forests can be divided into four main groups, namely southern beech (*Nothofagus*) forests, lowland conifer/

broadleaved forests (including warm temperate mixed forests), montane conifer/broadleaved forests and coastal forests.

Southern beech forests occur throughout much of New Zealand. Dominated by species of *Nothofagus*, these forests vary from almost monotypic stands to mixed forests with podocarp and/or broadleaved species. They occur from sea-level to the tree-line. In eastern South Island, mountain beech (*Nothofagus solandri* var. *cliffortioides*) forest forms an almost unbroken tree-line along many of the axial ranges and the Southern Alps. In some lowland regions beech forests may consist mostly of *N. truncata* (hard beech) with *N. fusca* (red beech) on colluvial slopes. In regions such as northern and north-western South Island, *N. menziesii* (silver beech) often dominates, but in eastern South Island mountain beech dominates. Further south, silver, mountain and red beech coexist in northern and eastern Fiordland (south-west South Island). Silver beech becomes overwhelmingly dominant in valleys in Fiordland which experience exceptionally high rainfall.

Lowland conifer/broadleaved forests vary considerably in their composition and stature depending on soil nutrient status, aspect, slope and altitude. The canopy of warm temperate mixed forests are usually two-tiered, with conifers forming the upper tier and broadleaved trees forming the lower tier. A layer of smaller trees may also be present in the understorey, while tall herbs and ferns occur in the ground layer. A lower ground layer (<10 cm high) is often dominated by cryptogams. Epiphytes are often abundant.

In the far north of New Zealand, *Agathis australis* (kauri) once dominated the canopy on infertile soils but is now mainly confined to ridges and high plateaux. Other North Island forests are dominated by podocarps such as *Dacrydium cupressinum* (rimu), *Dacrycarpus dacrydioides* (kahikatea), *Podocarpus totara* (totara) and *Prumnopitys taxifolia* (matai). *Metrosideros robusta* (northern rata), *Weinmannia racemosa* (kamahi), *Knightia excelsa* (rewarewa) and *Beilschmiedia tawa* (tawa) are other important elements in these forests.

The western part of South Island has the largest remaining areas of podocarp/broadleaved forests in New Zealand. The most widespread is rimu/kamahi forest which grades into other forest types, such as mixed podocarp forest, kahikatea swamp forest and southern rata (*Metrosideros umbellata*) hill forest.

Montane conifer/broadleaved forests are best developed on the western side of South Island where there is an extensive gap in beech distribution. These forests have many of the species of lowland forest but are floristically poorer. Conspicuous trees include *Metrosideros umbellata*, *Podocarpus hallii* (mountain totara), *P. totara*, *Quintinia acutifolia* and *Libocedrus bidwillii*, with *Pseudopanax* spp., *Pseudowintera colorata* and tree ferns in the understorey. Woody composite trees and shrubs in the genera *Olearia* and *Brachyglottis*, and smaller podocarps, become prominent with increasing altitude.

Coastal forests can be highly varied in floristic composition. They occur along sheltered estuaries and inlets, and the lower parts of coastal valleys where maritime influences dominate. In the far north of New Zealand *Metrosideros tomentosa* (pohutukawa) is often dominant, and in southern parts of New Zealand tree composites can be prominent.

Bushland, heath, scrub and fernland

Bushland vegetation is formed by small trees, shrubs or ferns, variable in stature and usually existing as patches among other vegetation, especially forest and grassland. Some patches represent sub-seral stages in succession, others result from degradation of forests by fire, wind-throw or logging, or as a result of environmental conditions. In sites which have suffered deforestation short-lived seral trees dominate, but these are generally succeeded by increasingly long-lived species. Forest lianas are also frequent in such sites. Coastal bushland in a variety of forms occurs throughout mainland New Zealand and on smaller islands. Several local endemics occur in such habitats.

In the western part of South Island and in uplands, shallow, leached soils are often dominated by heathlands, scrub and stunted bushland. Species of *Dracophyllum*, *Epacris* and *Cyathodes* (all in the Epacridaceae), together with smaller species of Podocarpaceae, are frequent on such sites, especially on the varied temperate heaths of lowland Westland. Some subalpine heaths include stunted *Nothofagus* spp. and are replaced by southern beech forest where conditions permit. A large proportion of temperate heaths has been burnt and replaced by secondary vegetation dominated by *Leptospermum scoparium* (manuka).

Primary heathlands are abundant on Stewart Island and in the south of New Zealand, in association with large areas of almost impenetrable *Olearia* "muttonbird" scrub.

Grassland and herbfield

Grasslands, and mosaics of grassland and scrub, cover nearly 60% of New Zealand at the present time. Inland, and at higher altitudes, they were originally dominated by tussock grasses (bunch grasses) especially in the genus *Chionochloa* (snowgrass). *Chionochloa* grasslands are still widespread in the mountains and descend towards sea-level in the southern part of South Island. Where undisturbed they can form dense stands.

Burning and grazing have reduced the abundance of tussock grasslands. As their range has contracted they have been replaced by smaller tussocks, such as *Poa cita*, *P. colensoi*, *Festuca novae-zelandiae* and other grasses, such as *Rhytidosperma* spp., and herbaceous Compositae. Prior to human arrival short tussock grasslands were probably only significant in drier intermontane basins of South Island, but became extensive following burning of forests by both Maori and European settlers.

Herbfields are extensive in alpine regions and contain a rich assortment of species from many families. Characteristic and prominent genera include *Aciphylla*, *Celmisia*, *Ranunculus*, *Senecio*, *Gentiana*, *Geum*, *Ourisia* and *Euphrasia*, and a wide range of grasses and sedges. Coastal herbfields occur locally and contain some notable rare species of very restricted distribution.

Wetlands

Wetlands were originally very widely distributed throughout New Zealand, but it has been estimated that in many lowland regions over 90% have now been destroyed or grossly modified. Saline coastal wetlands and salt marshes are, however, still extensive and in the north of New Zealand mangrove (*Avicennia resinifera*) communities occur south to 38°S. Inland saline communities occur in the dry central basins of Otago in the southern part of South Island, where they support a very distinctive flora and fauna including local endemics.

Lakes, ponds and streams are common throughout and support distinctive aquatic communities, some of which are now invaded by exotic species. Flushes, oligotrophic and eutrophic swamps and marshes are associated with areas of low-lying ground and watercourses. A notable variation is found in parts of North Island where geothermal activity results in hot water swamps and lakes. Among the distinctive flora which can be found near geothermal sites are species of subtropical ferns.

On infertile sites where there is little ground-water movement, extensive oligotrophic mires, wet heaths and peat deposits occur. Peat mires of the Waikato and Hauraki lowlands in North Island, and on the Chatham Islands, reach depths of many metres, and are dominated by genera such as *Baumea*, *Schoenus*, *Lepidosperma* and the endemic monotypic restiad *Sporodanthus traversii*. Red tussock (*Chionochloa rubra*) is an important component of infertile wetlands in upland and southern regions. At higher altitudes, and in western South Island, extensive *Sphagnum*-dominated bogs occur, and provide the basis for a moss peat industry. Montane cushion bogs are found throughout the mountains and become increasingly common towards the south.

Coastal and pioneer communities

Coastal, open communities are associated with sand-dune systems or gravel deposits. Woody shrubs, low-growing trees and spreading or short-lived herbs provide a variety of vegetation types in such areas. Invasive plants are often prominent, including *Lupinus arboreus* (tree lupin), *Glaucium flavum* (horned poppy), *Ammophila arenaria* (marram grass) and various pasture species.

Pioneer communities dominated by low-growing herbs and mat plants are found on flood plains of large rivers, such as those west of the Southern Alps, and the braided beds of eastern South Island rivers. Other types of open vegetation are found on cliffs, boulder fields eroded from mountain slopes, and on unconsolidated volcanic tephra in central North Island.

Alpine vegetation

Above the limits of continuous grassland, freeze-thaw cycles, rock-wasting, a short growing season and limited soil development, result in very patchy vegetation of cushion and mat-forming plants. An endemic-rich assemblage of plants of talus slopes include species of *Epilobium*, *Haastia*, *Stellaria* and the genera *Lignocarpa* and *Notothlaspi*. These exhibit features of convergent evolution, including short rootstocks with rhizomes elongated in a downhill direction, greyish wax or tomentum on leaves and stems, and low osmotic concentration in sap and high leaf-water contents. Cushion and mat plants are also characteristic, including the "vegetable sheep" growth form in species of *Raoulia* and *Haastia* which can grow into woody mounds up to 2 m in diameter. Other mat-forming plants include species of *Colobanthus*, *Hectorella* and *Phyllacne*. Bryophytes and lichens are an important element in the

vegetation at high altitudes, reaching their upper limit above 3000 m.

Flora

The indigenous flora contains about 2400 vascular plants, including c. 2160 species of flowering plants, 22 species of conifers and c. 200 species of pteridophytes; 1942 (81%) of these are endemic. In addition, there are estimated to be c. 1600 species of marine algae, c. 2700 species of freshwater algae, c. 1000 species of macro-lichens and c. 1000 species of liverworts and mosses.

The largest families of flowering plants in terms of species numbers (with estimated numbers of species in parentheses) are Compositae (340), Gramineae (200), Cyperaceae (180), Scrophulariaceae (130), Orchidaceae (100) and Umbelliferae (90). Several families are poorly represented, notably Leguminosae (27–50), Cruciferae (30), Solanaceae (2) and Labiatae (2). The small number of species in families such as Proteaceae, Myrtaceae and Rutaceae contrasts with neighbouring Australia. No families are endemic to New Zealand.

The largest genera (with estimated numbers of species in parentheses) are *Hebe* (100), *Celmisia* (60), *Coprosma* (50), *Aciphylla* (40), *Ranunculus* (40), *Poa* (35), *Olearia* (>30), *Myosotis* (>30) and *Carmichaelia* (between 15–38). About 35 genera are endemic and several more (for instance *Aciphylla* and *Hebe*) are near-endemic. Most of the endemic genera contain very few species, and most are closely related to larger genera. Among the most distinctive genera are those found on outlying islands, and include such genera as *Myosotidium* (Boraginaceae) and *Pleurophyllum* (Compositae).

Forest trees generally belong to genera represented by few species within New Zealand. Major genera are *Metrosideros*, *Nothofagus*, *Agathis*, *Podocarpus* and *Dacrydium* (including segregate genera), *Weinmannia*, *Laurelia* and *Beilschmiedia*. In contrast, some shrub genera contain numerous species, notably *Brachyglottis*, *Coprosma*, *Hebe* and *Olearia*.

Four main elements are recognized in the flora. The first comprises species which have their origins in Miocene (or earlier) New Zealand. This includes most lowland trees of forests and some abundant species of uplands. The assemblage also includes endemic monotypic genera confined mainly to warmer parts of New Zealand; examples are *Knightia*, *Ixerba*, *Entelea* on the mainland, *Elingamita* on the Three Kings Islands, and *Myosotidium* on the Chatham Islands.

The second assemblage contains cold-tolerant plants belonging to small, taxonomically-isolated and seemingly ancient genera which often occur on other fragments of Gondwana. These are plants of infertile, wet soils. Examples include *Lepidothamnus*, *Donatia*, *Tetrachondra*, *Oreostylidium* and *Carpha*. It is possible that this element, and the first, survived the mid-Tertiary warm period in habitats analogous to present-day lowland habitats in western South Island.

The third assemblage comprise species belonging to larger, more widely-distributed genera that may be later trans-oceanic immigrants. This includes genera among epacrids, ferns and orchids which also occur in Australia.

The fourth element includes the New Zealand shrubs and herbs which have evolved in response to the new environments of the Quaternary Era. It includes five groups:

1. Cosmopolitan genera with secondary centres of distribution in New Zealand: *Ranunculus*, *Epilobium*, *Euphrasia*, *Myosotis* and *Poa*;

2. Southern hemisphere genera with distinctive species clusters in New Zealand: *Helichrysum*, *Olearia*, *Parahebe* and *Ourisia*;

3. Genera with a large proportion of their species in the New Zealand lowlands, that can be reasonably assumed to have radiated into mountain environments: *Hebe*, *Astelia*, *Brachyglottis* and *Coprosma*;

4. Genera whose main development is in the mountains, but which also contain a few lowland species: *Celmisia*, *Aciphylla* and *Chionochloa*;

5. Small genera of higher altitudes or latitudes that are satellites of larger genera: *Pachycladon* and *Notothlaspi*, *Pleurophyllum*, *Damnamenia*, *Leucogenes* and *Corallospartium*.

Continuing evolutionary development is suggested by numerous clusters of closely related species and by the common occurrence of natural hybrids, sometimes involving morphologically very dissimilar parents.

Over 10% of the vascular flora is presently classified as rare or threatened according to IUCN Categories of Threat. Included are some notable Endangered species, such as *Tecomanthe speciosa* and *Pennantia baylisiana* (each represented by a single wild individual), *Clianthus puniceus* and a recently discovered single individual which is undescribed and probably belongs to the family Cunoniaceae. National threatened plant lists and priority assessments have been produced since 1976, and reassessments are now carried out by a committee established by the New Zealand Botanical Society and serviced by the Department of Conservation.

Useful plants

New Zealand is not recognized as a major centre of diversity for indigenous genetic resources. Despite this, many indigenous species of plants are of considerable importance to Maori, both as life-support species and for their cultural importance. Timber trees, pasture species and fibre plants continue to form the basis of major forestry, livestock and weaving industries.

Timber

A major indigenous plant resource for both Maori and European is timber. The Maori used native hardwood timber for general construction, but especially for making canoes. The Maori people preferred *Podocarpus totara* (totara) for large carvings, canoes and house frames, although in northern North Island they used *Agathis australis* (kauri). The latter tree was one of the earliest natural resources to be commercially harvested by Europeans, and by the 1830s formed the basis of a thriving trade, especially in the far north of New Zealand. Other timbers, such as *Beilshmiedia tawa* (tawa), *Olea cunninghamii* (maire) and *Dodonaea viscosa* (ake ake), had specialized uses, such as for house battens and weapons.

The traditional indigenous timber industry, which developed during the 19th century and was sustained until the middle of the 20th century, is rapidly giving way to an industry based on exotic plantation timbers. Thus, sawn timber production from indigenous forests has progressively declined to about 87,000 m³ in 1990, partly as a result of a policy to limit indigenous forestry to sustainable yields and partly to protect much of the remaining forests. Today, much of the timber industry is based on exotic hardwoods. Indeed, New Zealand has 13,000 km² of exotic forests managed for high-quality timber production, the largest such area in the world.

Agreements between government and industry will, in the future, greatly limit milling of indigenous hardwoods from New Zealand rain forests, centred on the West Coast of the South Island and central North Island. Kauri milling ceased as a major industry in the early part of this century, although there is interest in selection of superior genotypes for development of a sustainable industry based on this valuable timber species. A controversial issue is that concerning the use of indigenous *Nothofagus* spp. for the supply of wood chips for export.

Pasture species

New Zealand's temperate and oceanic climate has resulted in a largely agricultural economy based on pastoral and crop farming, as well as forestry. The overwhelming contribution to agriculture comes from imported exotic crop plants, as well as from improved pastures containing a high proportion of introduced plants, such as clover and European ryegrass. However, indigenous tussock (bunchgrass) grasslands with varying proportions of exotic species provide a fundamental resource for high country pastoral farming of sheep, cattle and deer. Management varies from minimal intervention to extensive over-sowing or burning.

Edible plants

Many species have been used traditionally by Maori as food sources. Examples include *Freycinetia banksii* (kiekie), *Corynocarpus laevigata* (karaka), *Sonchus oleraceus* (sowthistle) and *Alectryon grandis* (titoki).

Fibres

Phormium spp. (New Zealand flax or harakeke) and *Desmoschoenus spiralis* (pingao or golden sand sedge) are still major resources for weaving. New Zealand flax was the basis of a fibre industry during the early stages of European settlement and this continued up until the 1950s.

Medicinal plants

A very large number of species have long been exploited by Maori for their medicinal qualities, including *Hebe* spp. (koromiko), which was used during the Second World War by New Zealand troops.

Ornamental plants

New Zealand has contributed many species to the horticultural trade and several genera are commonly seen as amenity plants in temperate regions worldwide. These include *Hebe*, *Cordyline* (cabbage tree), *Phormium tenax* (New Zealand flax), *Leptospermum* spp. and *Clianthus puniceus*. Some smaller herbaceous native plants are in demand as rock garden plants, especially in Europe.

Tree ferns (principally *Dicksonia* spp.) are traded for tree fern fibre and as ornamental carved items in the tourist trade. A local, but lucrative, export industry is based on the harvesting of *Sphagnum* moss from the western South Island.

Factors causing loss of biodiversity

Habitat loss

One of the unique features about New Zealand is that it was the last significant landmass to be peopled. The first inhabitants were Polynesian, later called Maori, and they arrived only about 1000 years ago. European settlement commenced only in the early part of the 19th century. In a very short time, humans, along with domesticated and feral animals and introduced exotic plants, have had a great (and sometimes catastrophic) impact on many ecosystems which have evolved over tens of millions of years in the absence of grazing mammals and human interference.

During the period of Maori occupation and settlement there was significant modification of the natural environment, especially deforestation in regions such as eastern South Island. However, the rate and scale of modification accelerated markedly with European settlement. During the 19th and early 20th centuries the New Zealand landscape was transformed in many places. Indigenous forests and grasslands were replaced by exotic plantations and pastures on a large scale, and by urban developments, while marginal lands became dominated by introduced species, such as *Sarothamnus scoparius* (broom) and *Ulex europaeus* (gorse).

An important contributing factor to the loss of natural habitats was the Wakefield system of planned settlement which encouraged an orderly, but profound transition from indigenous "wilderness" to a "tamed" landscape dominated by British plants and land utilization systems. To this has been added a more recent overlay of exotic plantations and revegetation, with important elements provided by Australian *Eucalyptus* and *Acacia* spp., North American *Pinus radiata* (Monterey pine), *Cupressus macrocarpa* (Monterey cypress), and Eurasian *Salix* and *Populus* (willows and poplars).

Critical habitats are still being destroyed. Plants of wetlands, and other specialized habitats which are not able to survive once the dominant habitat determinants are removed, are particularly at risk. Many lowland plant species are threatened as a result.

Introduced animals

Along with introduced exotic food plants, such as taro and sweet potato, the Maori introduced animals, such as the Polynesian rat (*Rattus exulans*) and dog. The Polynesian rat probably had the greatest impact on New Zealand biota, especially on larger invertebrates, lizards and ground-nesting birds. Immense colonies of seabirds continue to survive on some smaller islands, but on the mainland seabird populations are now generally small and scattered, and occur in inaccessible locations.

European settlement unleashed a flood of immigrant plants and animals, some of which became uncontrollable pests and have had profound effects on natural and managed ecosystems. Wild populations of deer, sheep, goats, pigs, horses and cats have become established, along with rabbits, Norway rats, black rats and mice. European passerine birds were introduced and other birds introduced for game. Mustelids, introduced to control rabbits, have wreaked havoc on indigenous wildlife. The introduction of honey bees and bumble bees has probably affected floral evolution among native plants, and the arrival of the wasps *Vespa germanica* and *V. vulgaris* in the last few decades may correlate with population collapse in several species of native birds, with potential effects for some plant species.

Introduced Australian brush-tailed possums have had a profound effect on the native flora and vegetation. Possums were originally introduced for the fur trade. The wild population now numbers 80 million animals and occurs throughout New Zealand. The indigenous flora, especially important forest trees, such as *Metrosideros* spp., appear to lack mechanisms to combat the effects of browsing. As a result, dieback is common throughout large areas of forest. Possums have also devastated indigenous mistletoes, which are now locally extinct in many parts of New Zealand.

Invasive plants

A total of about 1500 plant species, hybrids and cultivars, in 617 genera and 132 families, are currently accepted as occurring in New Zealand in a naturalized state (non-cultivated and reproducing without human intervention). Naturalized plants have invaded all natural plant habitats, but are most obvious in lowland open habitats such as grasslands, riverbeds, cliffs and modified sites. Some, such as *Sarothamnus scoparius* (broom), *Ulex europaeus* (gorse), *Clematis vitalba* (traveller's joy), *Hieracium* spp. (hawkweeds) and *Pinus contorta* are major threats.

Conservation

Protected area coverage

National Parks, Nature Reserves, and other land protected for the purposes of biological conservation, amount to nearly 20% of the total land area. Included in this system of land protection are 12 National Parks, an equivalent number of Forest Parks, well over 1000 reserves administered by the Department of Conservation (or delegated to local authorities and other bodies), and extensive Stewardship lands with partial protection. The National Conservation Authority and regional Conservation Boards work cooperatively with the Department of Conservation to administer these protected areas. In addition, the Queen Elizabeth II Trust has negotiated several hundred covenants and other land agreements, chiefly on private land, to preserve open space and natural areas.

Protected area coverage is generally best in mountain lands and on offshore and outlying islands (many of which are Nature Reserves). In lowland regions with agriculturally rich soils, protected areas tend to be small and fragmentary. These lowlands were the regions to first feel the impacts of human occupation, they usually have the most fragmentary remnants of indigenous vegetation, and they are lands in high demand for alternative uses to nature conservation.

A workshop in 1981 proposed a consolidated division of New Zealand into a national system of 268 Ecological Districts grouped into 85 Ecological Regions. This has been designed to allow the systematic selection of protected areas, and has been the geographic basis for a Protected Natural Area (PNA) survey to identify Representative Areas for Protection (RAPs). Although a number of surveys have been completed for ecological districts, considerable debate has ensued, especially relating to the difficulty in effectively implementing recommendations of these surveys.

Significant protected areas are now established under a variety of other tenures. These include private trusts, local government reserves, management agreements involving private companies, and large regional protective regimes, such as the forest protection accord between the government, non-governmental organizations and the timber industry in central North Island.

Major gaps in the network

Probably the greatest gaps exist in lowland parts of New Zealand where significant ecosystems are still underprotected. The historical tendency to protect forests and mountainlands has also left gaps in the protection of grassland and scrub communities which are relatively underprotected. This particularly applies to mid-altitude grasslands of eastern South Island (the traditional pastoral lands), basin and range systems in Otago in the southern part of South Island, and central North Island grasslands where both rare plant species and tussock grasslands are within the range of protected feral horse herds.

Considerable gaps also exist in *ex situ* conservation. Although New Zealand has a number of botanic gardens and collections of native plants in both private and public tenure, it is only now that a national database and network of collections is being set up. Within the existing botanic garden system conspicuous gaps exist in the northern and western South Island, and the floristically rich far north of New Zealand. No comprehensive germplasm banks yet exist for long-term storage of wild species material, except for a small number of forest trees regarded as having commercial potential.

Opportunities for conservation

The natural environment is one of the most important parts of New Zealand's heritage, including a temperate climate, clean air, abundant water, a generally unpolluted coastline, and an extensive network of National Parks and other protected areas. For the Maori people this is an important *taonga* (treasure) which is the subject of Article II of the Treaty of Waitangi, signed by representatives of the English Crown and the Chiefs of the Confederation of the United Tribes of New Zealand. Article II guarantees "to protect the Chiefs, subtribes, and all the people of Aotearoa in the unqualified exercise of their chieftainship over their lands, villages, and all their treasures".

The Treaty provides a foundation for stewardship and use of New Zealand natural resources. A further foundation is provided by the Resource Management Act (1991). This Act, whose purpose is "to promote the sustainable management of natural and physical resources", recognizes both the concern for the social, economic and cultural well-being of communities, and the intrinsic value of biological diversity.

Maori, as *tangata whenua* (people of the land), have a special relationship with land. By the time Europeans arrived in New Zealand, the Maori had developed strategies to conserve their resources, particularly marine resources and timber trees. For example, *rahui* (closed seasons for harvesting) were established. An interdependence between people and the environment created a sense of belonging to nature rather than being ascendent to it. Part of the development of a multicultural society in New Zealand involves obligations to ensure that cultural and spiritual environmental values remain intact, while responding to the demands for social and economic development.

It is likely that in the future there will be an increasing emphasis on the role of private individuals, landowners, local trusts and the business community in active conservation. Four issues may well dominate as opportunities are considered. Firstly, although the rate of habitat loss is probably slowing, the formidable task remains of ensuring that what is currently preserved, and is likely to be protected in the future, is appropriately managed with long-term goals in mind. Secondly, there is need to systematically fill gaps in the existing system of protection. Thirdly, if sustainability is to become a predominant land-use ethic, there may need to be radical changes in some land management and associated legislation. Fourthly, vegetation and habitat restoration will be a necessary but expensive option especially in lowland sites.

Centres of plant diversity and endemism

Site selection has been determined by a process of enquiry and concensus among experts, recognizing that a larger number of important botanical sites of regional and national importance exist than those which are considered here as global priorities.

New Zealand

Au14. Northland

– see Data Sheet.

Au15. North-west Nelson

– see Data Sheet.

Au16. Chatham Islands

– see Data Sheet.

Australia and New Zealand

Au17. Subantarctic Islands

– see Data Sheet.

12

Other candidate centres of plant diversity which may qualify as regionally or globally important sites after further study are:

- Central North Island mountains including the north-west Ruahine Mountains and Moawhango Plateau;
- North-eastern South Island, especially the catchments of the Awatere and Clarence Rivers;
- Intermontane basins of Canterbury east of the Southern Alps;
- Central Otago dry basins and ranges;
- Fiordland (south-west South Island);
- Stewart Island.

References

Allan, H.H. (1961). *Flora of New Zealand. Volume I. Indigenous Tracheophyta. Psilopsida, Lycopsida, Filicopsida, Gymnospermae, Dicotyledones.* Government Printer, Wellington.

Anon. (1991). Beating the dreaded blackberry. *Australian Horticulture* 89(5): 66.

AUSLIG (1990). *Atlas of Australian resources, Third Series, Volume 6: Vegetation.* Australian Surveying and Land Information Group, Canberra. 64 pp.

Australian National Parks and Wildlife Service (1991). *Plant invasions – the incidence of environmental weeds in Australia.* Australian National Parks and Wildlife Service, Canberra. 188 pp.

Barlow, B.A. (1981). The Australian flora: its origins and evolution. In Bureau of Flora and Fauna, *Flora of Australia Vol. 1: Introduction.* Australian Government Publishing Service, Canberra.

Beadle, N.C.W. (1981). The vegetation of Australia. Cambridge University Press, Cambridge, U.K. 690 pp.

Beard, J. (1984). Endemism in Western Australian flora at the species level. *Journal of the Royal Society of Western Australia* 52: 18–20.

Beard, J.S. and Webb, M.J. (1974). *The vegetation survey of Western Australia: its aims, objects and methods. Part 1 of explanatory notes to sheet 2, Great Sandy Desert.* Vegetation Survey of Western Australia: 1:1,000,000 Vegetation Series. University of Western Australia Press, Perth.

Boyden, S., Dovers, S. and Shirlow, M. (1990). *Our biosphere under threat.* Oxford University Press, Melbourne. 347 pp.

Briggs, J.D. and Leigh, J.H. (1988). *Rare or threatened Australian plants.* Special Publication 14. Australian National Parks and Wildlife Service, Canberra. 278 pp.

Brown, J.A.H. and Milner, F.C. (1990). Aspects of the meteorology and hydrology of the Australian Alps. In Good, R. (ed.), *The scientific significance of the Australian Alps.* The Australian Alps National Parks Liaison Committee in association with the Australian Academy of Science, Canberra. 392 pp.

Buchanan, A.M., McGeary-Brown, A. and Orchard, A.E. (1989). *Census of vascular plants of Tasmania.* Tasmanian Herbarium, Hobart. 28 pp.

Burbidge, N.T. (1960). The phytogeography of the Australian region. *Australian Journal of Botany* 8(2): 75–212.

Bureau of Flora and Fauna (1981). *Flora of Australia Vol. 1: Introduction.* Australian Government Publishing Service, Canberra. 200 pp.

Carnahan, J. (1986). Vegetation. In Jeans, D.N. (ed.), *Australia – a geography. Vol. 1: The natural environment.* Sydney University Press, Sydney. Pp. 260–282.

Clifford, H.T. and Constantine, J. (1980). *Ferns and fern allies and conifers of Australia.* University of Queensland Press, St Lucia, Queensland. 150 pp.

Collins, N.M., Sayer, J.A. and Whitmore, T.C. (eds) (1991). *The conservation atlas of tropical forests: Asia and the Pacific.* Macmillan, London. 256 pp.

Costin, A.B. (1971). Vegetation. In Costin, A.B. and Frith, H.J. (eds), *Conservation.* Penguin Books Australia, Victoria.

Davis, B.W. and Drake, G.A. (1983). *Australia's Biosphere Reserves: conserving ecological diversity.* Australian Government Publishing Service, Canberra. 48 pp.

Department of the Arts, Sport, the Environment and Territories (1991). *Australian National Report to the United Nations Conference on Environment and Development.* Australian Government Publishing Service, Canberra. 276 pp.

Dunlop, C.R. (ed.) (1987). *Checklist of the vascular plants of Northern Territory.* Technical Report No. 26. Conservation Commission of the Northern Territory, Darwin. 87 pp.

Flood, J. (1989). *Archaeology of the dreamtime: the story of prehistoric Australia and its people.* Collins, Australia. 302 pp.

Forbes, S.J. and Ross, J.H. (1988). *Census of the vascular plants of Victoria.* 2nd Ed. National Herbarium of Victoria, Department of Conservation, Forests and Lands, Melbourne. 192 pp.

Frawley, K.J. and Semple, N. (eds) (1988). *Australia's ever changing forests.* Proceedings of the First National Conference on Australian Forest History Special Publication No. 1. Department of Geography and Oceanography, Australian Defence Force Academy, Campbell ACT. 529 pp.

George, A.S. (1981). The background to the Flora of Australia. In Bureau of Flora and Fauna, *Flora of Australia, Vol. 1: Introduction*. Australian Government Publishing Service, Canberra. Pp. 3–24.

Gillison, A.N. and Walker, J. (1981). Woodlands. In Groves, R.H. (ed.), *Australian vegetation*. Cambridge University Press, Cambridge, U.K. Pp. 177–197.

Given, D.R. (1981). *Rare and endangered plants of New Zealand*. Reed, Wellington.

Green, J.W. (1985). *Census of the vascular plants of Western Australia*. 2nd Ed. (plus supplements 1–6). Western Australian Herbarium, Western Australian Department of Agriculture, Perth.

Groves, R.H. (ed.) (1981). *Australian vegetation*. Cambridge University Press, Cambridge, U.K. 449 pp.

Hartley, W. and Leigh, J. (1979). *Plants at risk in Australia*. Occasional Paper No. 3. Australian National Parks and Wildlife Service, Canberra. 80 pp.

Healy, A.J. and Edgar, E. (1980). *Flora of New Zealand. Volume III. Adventive Cyperaceae, petalous and spathaceous monocotyledones*. Government Printer, Wellington.

Hnatiuk, R.J. (1990). *Census of Australian vascular plants*. Australian Flora and Fauna Series No. 11. Australian Government Publishing Service, Canberra. 650 pp.

Hooy, T. and Shaughnessy, G. (eds) (1992). *Terrestrial and marine protected areas in Australia (1991)*. Australian National Parks and Wildlife Service, Canberra. 86 pp.

IUCN (1992). *Protected areas of the world: a review of national systems. Volume 1: Indomalaya, Oceania, Australia and Antarctic*. IUCN, Gland, Switzerland and Cambridge, U.K. xx, 352 pp. (Prepared by the World Conservation Monitoring Centre.)

Jacobs, S.W.L. and Pickard, J. (1981). *Plants of New South Wales: a census of the cycads, conifers and angiosperms*. Royal Botanic Gardens, Sydney. 226 pp.

Jennings, J.W. and Mabbutt, J.A. (1986). Physiographic outlines and regions. In Jeans, D.N. (ed.), *Australia – a geography. Vol. 1: The natural environment*. Sydney University Press, Sydney. Pp. 80–96.

Jessop, J.P. (ed.) (1984). *A list of the vascular plants of South Australia*. 2nd Ed. Adelaide Botanic Gardens and State Herbarium, Department of Environment and Planning, Adelaide. 100 pp.

Johnson, R.W. and Burrows, W.H. (1981). *Acacia* open forests, woodland and shrublands. In Groves, R.H. (ed.), *Australian vegetation*. Cambridge University Press, Cambridge, U.K. Pp. 198–226.

Jones, R. (1969). Fire-stick farming. *Australian Natural History* 16: 224–228.

Keith, D.A. and Sanders, J.M. (1990). Vegetation of the Eden Region, south eastern Australia: species composition, diversity and structure. *Journal of Vegetation Science* 1: 203–232.

Kershaw, A.P. (1981). Quaternary vegetation and environments. In Keast, A. (ed.), *Ecological biogeography of Australia, Vol. 1*. Junk, The Hague. Pp. 81–102.

Keto, A. and Scott, K. (1989). *A proposal for a National Park in the McIlwraith Range area, Cape York Peninsula*. Rainforest Conservation Society Inc., Bordon, Queensland. 62 pp.

Laut, P. (1988). Changing patterns of land use in Australia. In *Year book Australia 1988*. Australian Bureau of Statistics, Canberra. Pp. 547–556.

Leeper, G.W. (1970). Soils. In Leeper, G.W. (ed.), *The Australian environment*. Melbourne University Press, Melbourne. Pp. 21–31.

Leigh, J., Boden, R. and Briggs, J. (1984). *Extinct and endangered plants of Australia*. Macmillan Australia, Melbourne. 369 pp.

Leigh, J.H. (1981). Chenopod shrublands. In Groves, R.H. (ed.), *Australian vegetation*. Cambridge University Press, Cambridge, U.K. Pp. 276–292.

Leigh, J.H. and Briggs, J.D. (eds) (1991). *Australian plants: overview and case studies*. Australian National Parks and Wildlife Service, Canberra. 120 pp.

Leigh, J.H, Briggs, J. and Hartley, W. (1981). *Rare or threatened Australian plants*. Special Publication No. 7. Australian National Parks and Wildlife Service, Canberra. 178 pp.

McCarthy, P.M. (1991). *Checklist of Australian lichens*. 4th Ed. National Herbarium of Victoria, Melbourne. 177 pp.

Ministry for the Environment (1992). *New Zealand's national report to the United Nations Conference on Environment and Development. Forging the links*. Ministry for the Environment, Wellington.

Moore, L.B. and Edgar, E. (1970). *Flora of New Zealand. Volume II. Indigenous Tracheophyta. Monocotyledones except Gramineae*. Government Printer, Wellington.

Morley, B.D. and Toelken, H.R. (eds) (1983). *Flowering plants in Australia*. Rigby, Adelaide. 416 pp.

Mosley, G. and Costin, A. (1992). *World heritage values and their protection in far south east New South Wales*. Earth Foundation Australia, Sydney. 98 pp.

Newman, J.C. and Condon, R.W. (1969). Land use and present condition. In Slatyer, R.O. and Penny, R.A. (eds), *Arid lands of Australia*. Australian National University Press, Canberra. Pp. 105–132.

Newsome, P. (1987). *The vegetation cover of New Zealand.* Ministry of Works and Development.

Norton, D.A. (1989). *Management of New Zealand's natural estate.* New Zealand Ecological Society Occasional Publication No. 1. Christchurch.

Parsons, R.F. (1981). *Eucalyptus* scrubs and shrublands. In Groves, R.H. (ed.), *Australian vegetation.* Cambridge University Press, Cambridge, U.K. Pp. 227–252.

Parsons, W.T. (1973). *Noxious weeds of Victoria.* Inkata Press, Melbourne. 300 pp.

Powell, J.M. (1991). *An historical geography of modern Australia.* Cambridge University Press, Cambridge, U.K. 400 pp.

Resource Assessment Commission (1991a). *Forest and timber inquiry draft report, Vol. 1.* Australian Government Publishing Service, Canberra. 656 pp.

Resource Assessment Commission (1991b). *Kakadu Conservation Zone, draft report, Vol. 1 and 2.* Australian Government Publishing Service, Canberra. (Vol. 1: 251 pp.; vol. 2: 302 pp.)

Roberts, R.W. (1989). *Land conservation in Australia – a 200 year stocktake.* Soil and Water Conservation Association of Australia, Sydney. 32 pp.

Ross, J.H. (1976). An analysis of the flora of Victoria. *Muelleria* 3(3): 169–176.

Singh, G., Kershaw, A.P. and Clark, R. (1980). Quaternary vegetation and fire history of Australia. In Gill, A.M., Groves, R.H. and Noble, I.R. (eds), *Fire and the Australian biota.* Australian Academy of Science, Canberra. Pp. 23–54.

Specht, R.L. (1970). Vegetation. In Leeper, G.W. (ed.), *The Australian environment.* Melbourne University Press, Melbourne. Pp. 44–67.

Specht, R.L. (1981a). Conservation of vegetation types. In Groves, R.H. (ed.), *Australian vegetation.* Cambridge University Press, Cambridge, U.K. Pp. 393–410.

Specht, R.L. (1981b). Heathlands. In Groves, R.H. (ed.), *Australian vegetation.* Cambridge University Press, Cambridge, U.K. Pp. 253–275.

Specht, R.L., Roe, E.M. and Boughton, V.H. (eds) (1974). *Conservation of major plant communities in Australia and Papua-New Guinea.* Australian Journal of Botany Supplement Series No. 7. CSIRO Melbourne. 667 pp.

Stephens, C.G. (1977). Soils. In Jeans, D.N. (ed.), *Australia – a geography. Vol. 1: The natural environment.* Sydney University Press, Sydney. Pp. 152–174.

Wardle, P. (1991). *Vegetation of New Zealand.* Cambridge University Press, Cambridge, U.K.

Webb, C.J., Sykes, W.R. and Garnock Jones, P.J. (1988). *Flora of New Zealand. Volume IV. Naturalised pteridophytes, gymnosperms, dicotyledons.* Botany Division, DSIR, Christchurch.

Webb, L.J. (1959). A physiognomic classification of Australian rainforests. *Journal of Ecology* 47: 551–570.

Webb, L.J. and Tracey, J.G. (1981). The rainforests of northern Australia. In Groves, R.H. (ed.), *Australian vegetation.* Cambridge University Press, Cambridge, U.K. Pp. 67–101.

Wilson, C.M. and Given, D.R. (1989). *Threatened plants of New Zealand.* DSIR, Wellington.

Wood, J. (1990). *The use of the Kakadu Conservation Zone for recreation and tourism.* Resource Assessment Commission Kakadu Conservation Zone Inquiry Consultancy Series. Australian Government Publishing Service, Canberra. 69 pp.

World Resources Institute (1992). *World resources 1992–93: a guide to the global environment.* Oxford University Press, New York. 385 pp. (Prepared in collaboration with UNEP and UNDP.)

Acknowledgements

Grateful thanks are extended to the following members of the IUCN Australasian Plant Specialist Group for advice on site selection: John Benson, Stephen Harris, Frank Ingwersen, Dr John Leigh, Dr Ian Lunt, Dr Bob Parsons and Neville Scarlett. Drs Garry Werren, Geoff Tracey, Stephen Goosem, Peter Stanton, Peter Williams, Peter de Lange, David Norton and Colin Meurk also provided help in CPD site selection.

AUSTRALIAN ALPS
New South Wales, Victoria and Australian Capital Territory, Australia

Location: South-eastern Australia, extending over 600 km in New South Wales, Victoria and the Australian Capital Territory, between latitudes 35°00'–38°00'S and longitudes 146°00'–150°00'E.

Area: c. 30,000 km², of which 370 km² are treeless alpine areas.

Altitude: c. 200–2228 m (summit of Mount Kosciusko).

Vegetation: Grasslands, shrublands, woodlands, forests, alpine herbfields, fen and bog communities.

Flora: c. 780 vascular plant species (>1000 species if lowland areas included), of which 230 species occur above the tree-line. Many endemic taxa and disjunct species having affinities with other Southern Hemisphere alpine and high-altitude floras.

Useful plants: Timber trees, ornamental plants.

Other values: Major water catchment of mainland Australia providing water for hydroelectricity and irrigation; tourism.

Threats: Tourist pressure and associated commercial developments; potential threats from extension of hydroelectric facilities, introduced plants.

Conservation: Approximately half of the total area is included within the Australian Alps National Parks (c. 15,000 km²) and several other State and National Parks (2000 km²).

Geography

The Australian Alps comprise the highest parts of the Great Dividing Range which runs parallel to the eastern coastline of Australia. The area extends southward from the Brindabella Ranges in the Australian Capital Territory (ACT), through the Snowy Mountains in New South Wales (NSW) to the high country in Victoria, covering some 30,000 km² (approximately 0.3% of Australia). The Alps include areas of semi-permanent snow above 1360 m altitude and descend to c. 200 m altitude near the coast.

In ACT and NSW the Australian Alps are an almost continuous high plateau bounded to the east and west by steep scarps and river valleys. In Victoria the Alps are more dissected, the high plateau being broken up into prominent peaks and high plains separated by deep valleys and undulating lowlands. However, none of the very steep and rugged landscapes evident in much younger mountain systems occur in the Australian Alps. Much of the plateau terrain and the high peaks (including the highest, Mount Kosciusko, at 2228 m) are rounded, a testament to the very long geological evolution of south-eastern Australia.

The only evidence of glaciation exists in the vicinity of Mount Kosciusko. Here, several cirques, moraines and other glacial features are evident. The absence of severe and extensive glaciation has allowed the development of deep alpine and subalpine humus soils in all but the most exposed sites. Bogs and fens occur in poorly drained areas, while podzolic soils are common at lower altitudes.

Annual precipitation ranges from 400 mm in south-eastern rain-shadow areas to over 3000 mm at the highest elevations. Snowfalls contribute in excess of 60% of total precipitation in the alpine zone, with snow cover lasting for 3–4 months each year. In the alpine zone, large semi-permanent snow patches form each winter and infrequently remain throughout the summer. Rainfall is evenly distributed throughout the summer in the alpine zone, but is increasingly variable in amount and distribution with descending altitude. Winters are mild in comparison with alpine areas elsewhere, temperatures seldom falling below -20°C.

Covering less than 0.3% of the continent but receiving 20–25% of the total precipitation, the Australian Alps are the most significant catchment area of mainland Australia. Rivers arising in the Alps provide water supplies to more than half of the population and to the largest hydroelectric scheme in Australia.

Vegetation

The vegetation is diverse and varies according to altitude, climate and latitude. These gradients provide for great ecological diversity which is effectively conserved over the complete geographical and altitudinal range, from sea-level to the highest peaks. Four floristic zones are recognized: tableland (up to 1100 m altitude and occupying 41% of the total area), montane (between 1100–1400 m and occupying about 32% of the total area), subalpine (between 1400–1850 m, about 25% of the total area) and alpine (which covers approximately 370 km², 1.2% of the total area). *Eucalyptus* spp. predominate in all but the treeless alpine zone. The adaptation of a single genus to all environments from sea-level to the treeline is unique in world floras.

Eucalypt forests cover 810 km² and have closed canopies reaching 60 m high. Eucalypt woodlands cover 19,200 km² and are open canopied communities to 20 m high. Forests and woodlands contain some 50 species of eucalypt (about one-tenth of all Australian eucalypt species), the most common of which is the snow gum, *Eucalyptus pauciflora*. Most of the eucalypt species are widespread within their altitudinal range but several species are restricted to only a few small or disjunct areas. *E. neglecta*, for example, is rare and limited to one area in Victoria, while *E. chapmaniana* occurs in one small site in New South Wales but is more common in Victoria.

In both eucalypt forests and woodlands there is a dense understorey of shrubs, including leguminous *Acacia, Bossiaea, Hovea* and *Oxylobium* species. Remnant rain forest communities survive in sheltered sites, or sites with suitable climatic and soil conditions, within eucalypt forests of southern latitudes. Other phytogeographically significant communities and species also survive in some atypical climatic conditions, such as the rain forest scrubs which occur on drier exposed sites at about 1000 m altitude in the New South Wales part of the Australian Alps.

While the almost ubiquitous eucalypt forests and woodlands dominate the landscapes of the Australian Alps, the most floristically and morphologically diverse vegetation occurs in the treeless alpine zone. Vegetation types here include tall and short alpine herbfields, feldmark communities, tussock grasslands, fens and bogs.

Tall alpine herbfields on well-developed alpine humus soils are dominated by species of Compositae, Cyperaceae, Gramineae, Juncaceae, Ranunculaceae and Umbelliferae.

A specialized form of tall alpine herbfield exists on shallow steeper and rocky soils in Victoria. This community has much in common physiognomically with the arctic/alpine rock-ledge vegetation of Europe. Short alpine herbfields, rich in flowering plants, occur in down-slope, outwash areas below large snow patches.

Two distinctly different feldmark communities exist on the windswept ridges and on the upper edges of large snow patches. The latter is restricted to the New South Wales part of the Alps in the vicinity of Mount Kosciusko, where *Coprosma* and *Colobanthus* species colonize feldmark sites. Cushion plants are almost absent from the Alps, but, of the 10 species present, 4 are endemic. Feldmark of high windswept ridges is the most restricted plant community in the Alps, covering less than 0.1% of the total area. *Epacris* and *Veronica* species in this community grow in a cycle of burial by windblown gravel, foliage destruction and regrowth.

Sod tussock grasslands replace tall herbfields in some flat valleys where high soil moisture levels exist. Similar communities occur in subalpine valleys where cold air drains into them at night. Sod tussock grasslands are more common in Victoria where humidity and cloudiness are greater than further north.

Raised bogs cover about 10% of the Alps in Victoria, but less than 5% in NSW and ACT. Valley bogs are often underlain by deep peat beds which are important in the

MAP 17. AUSTRALIAN ALPS (CPD SITE Au1)

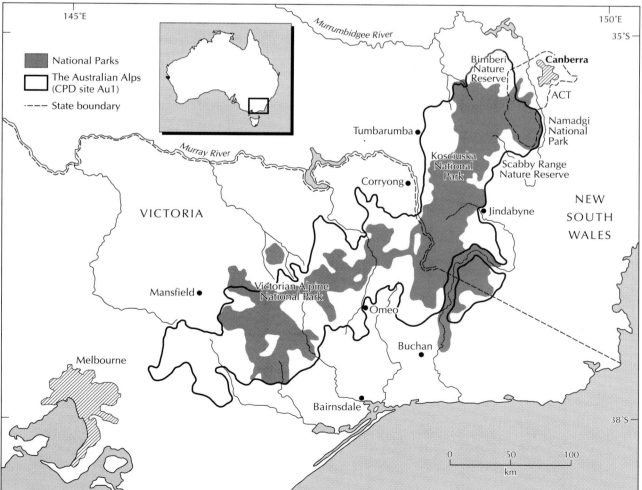

control and release of snow melt waters to streams and rivers. Extensive heaths of woody shrubs occur in areas of free-draining soils, boulderfields and glacial moraines. Shrub species of the Proteaceae, Myrtaceae, Rutaceae, Compositae, Leguminosae and Podocarpaceae dominate shrub communities; the last family being represented by the only alpine conifer in the Alps, *Podocarpus lawrencei*. Tall heath communities are replaced by short heaths in wet sites, where species of Epacridaceae and Myrtaceae are most common.

Flora

The flora of the alpine zone of the Australian Alps is diverse and includes elements from lower elevations and from more distant alpine areas. Millions of years of isolation has enabled speciation to give rise to many endemics, while affinities with South American alpines lend support to the concept that the Australian part of Gondwana was the origin of some alpine species.

The flora of the four floristic zones (described in the Vegetation section) contains approximately 780 vascular plant species. If the flora of the lowlands is also included, the total is well over 1000 species. This is approximately 5% of the total Australian vascular flora.

Some 230 species are herbaceous alpines, of which 66 species are the only representatives of their genus and 23 species are the only representatives of their family. With some 26 strict endemics in the alpine and upper subalpine flora, the degree of endemism (11%) is significant in comparison with alpine floras elsewhere. Interestingly, only 30 species of the total Australian Alps flora are obligate alpines, many of the alpine zone species occurring at lower elevations in Australia or elsewhere.

Several of the alpine endemics are very localized. For example, *Chionochloa frigida* occurs only in the vicinity of Mount Kosciusko. Other species are more widespread but their habitats are restricted to only a few localities. *Leucopogon pilifer*, for example, is only found in a few small boggy areas on the Nunniong and Bogong plateaux in Victoria. Approximately 30 species in the alpine zone are classified as Rare or Endangered (Leigh, Boden and Briggs 1984). A further 110 Rare or Endangered species occur in the other three floristic zones. The relatively large number of Rare and Endangered species reflects both the small area of the various plant communities and recent land use practices, particularly that of grazing domestic stock.

The non-vascular flora is poorly known, but representatives of some 50 lichen genera (more than 20% of the total number of Australian lichen genera) have so far been recorded. One endemic species (*Cetrara australiensis*) occurs at the tree-line. Some 80 species of macrofungi have been recorded, including the sole representative of the Australian endemic and monotypic genus *Flammulina*.

The significance of the Australian alpine flora lies not only in its diversity and high degree of endemism but also in its phytogeographical relationships and differences with other alpine Australasian and Southern Hemisphere continental and subantarctic island floras. The flora is, therefore, a major resource for further phytogeographical studies, particularly focusing on differences with New Guinea and subantarctic island alpine floras (Barlow 1986; Good 1989).

CPD Site Au1: Australian Alps, looking towards Mount Kosciusko showing the Upper Snowy River. Photo: C. Totterdell.

Useful plants

The alpine flora has been little studied in terms of useful plants; however, the high level of species diversity and endemism represents a genetic resource which possibly contains many useful biochemical properties.

Several genera and species have been studied as indicators of environmental stability. Species of Rosaceae have been used to identify and monitor the impact on native species of biological control vectors introduced for exotic weed control.

The eucalypt forests at lower altitudes support commercial forestry operations. The adaptation of eucalypts to nearly all edaphic and climatic conditions in the region, and the variation of populations over their ranges, is a potentially valuable genetic resource.

Many alpine species have potential as horticultural subjects.

Social and environmental values

The Australian Alps, although a very small area of the Australian continent, encompass the most important water catchment on the mainland. Rivers arising in the Australian Alps provide water supplies for about 50% of the population of Australia and very large quantities of water for hydroelecticity generation and agricultural production.

The landscapes of the Alps, being so markedly different to other Australian landscapes, are a major destination for tourists, both national and international, attracting 3–4 million visitors a year. The diversity of landscapes also provides for many recreational activities, most of which are undertaken in areas designated as National Parks.

Economic assessment

The Australian Alps make a significant contribution to regional and national economies. It has been estimated that about A$130 million is expended annually on tourism and recreational activities, particularly skiing. Skiing and other tourist infrastructure in the Australian Alps is estimated to be worth A$800–900 million.

Snow melt water provides for the generation of hydroelectricity worth about A$200 million annually. Water discharged from the hydroelectric schemes provides for irrigation and agricultural production valued at A$150–180 million annually.

Grazing of domestic stock is carried out in parts of the Alps and extensive commercial forestry is undertaken in non-park areas. Forestry operations produce about A$40–50 million annually. There are some mining and other extractive industries within the Alps, contributing to the economic value of the region.

Threats

There are no serious threats to the fragile alpine zone flora as it is well conserved and protected within National Parks. However, the increasing number of tourists and the continuing expansion of recreation infrastructure, particularly that for skiing, do pose threats to some plant communities and species. The associated problems of pollution and waste disposal are already evident in several vegetation communities, particularly the bog and fen communities. Water quality in alpine streams has deteriorated in recent years, but they remain the purest waters on the continent.

Introduced exotic plants do not pose a major threat to undisturbed native vegetation. However, at lower elevations (subalpine, montane and tableland zones), domestic stock grazing, feral and pest animals, inappropriate agricultural practices and some commercial forestry operations have had, and are having, an impact on native plant communities and account for many of the Rare and Endangered species of the region.

Mining and the possible extension of hydroelectric schemes are a minor threat to the integrity of the National Parks, but their impacts should be ameliorated through effective planning and management.

Conservation

The need to protect water catchments in the Australian Alps was recognized in the late 1800s and early 1900s when the first moves to limit, and eventually remove, domestic grazing from the Alps were made. In 1944, a State Park was established over approximately 5000 km² of the Australian Alps in New South Wales (Kosciusko State Park). This was made a National Park of some 6900 km² in 1967. In Victoria, 6 National and State Parks were established in the late 1970s and early 1980s. Additions to the protected areas system were made in 1989 and all the areas were gazetted together as the Victorian Alps National Park of almost 6300 km².

The Australian Alps National Parks are now a contiguous area and include Namadgi National Park (ACT), Kosciusko National Park (NSW) and the Victorian Alps National Park. This large area encompasses nearly 15,000 km² (almost half the total area of the Australian Alps) and, together with several other State and National Parks covering a further 2000 km², effectively conserves all the treeless alpine zone and a good representative sample of the subalpine, montane and tableland ecosystems.

References

Australian National Parks and Wildlife Service (1988). *A bibliography of information on the conservation and management of ecosystems*. Australian National Parks and Wildlife Service Report No. 13. 88 pp.

Barlow, B.A. (ed.) (1986). *Flora and fauna of alpine Australasia. Ages and origins*. CSIRO, Melbourne. 543 pp.

Good, R.B. (ed.) (1989). *The scientific significance of the Australian Alps*. Australian Alps Liaison Committee and the Australian Academy of Science, Canberra. 392 pp.

Leigh J., Boden, R. and Briggs J. (1984). *Extinct and endangered plants of Australia*. Macmillan Australia, Melbourne. 369 pp.

Acknowledgements

This Data Sheet was prepared by Dr R.B. Good (Australian National Parks and Wildlife Service, New South Wales).

AUSTRALIA: CPD SITE AU2

BORDER RANGES
New South Wales and Queensland, Australia

Location: Straddling the boundary between Queensland and New South Wales, centred on the McPherson Range and extending north to Mount Tamborine, south to the Nightcap Range and Richmond River and west to the Main Range (Great Dividing Range). Between latitudes 27°50'–28°40'S and longitudes 152°30'–153°30'E.

Area: c. 600 km².

Altitude: 0–1360 m (summit of Mount Barney).

Vegetation: A diverse array of rain forest communities, reflecting the wide range in altitude, rainfall and lithology. Rain forest types include: warm and cool subtropical rain forest (complex and mixed notophyll vine forest) (the largest area of subtropical rain forest in Australia), warm temperate rain forest (simple notophyll vine forest), montane cool temperate rain forest (microphyll mossy forest) and dry rain forest (araucarian notophyll and microphyll vine forest). Major areas of eucalypt tall open forests, open forests and woodlands, upland (montane) shrublands and heaths on acid volcanic substrates.

Flora: >1200 vascular plant species recorded so far. Lamington National Park alone has c. 850 vascular plant species. Many endemic species, notably in the lowland warm subtropical rain forests, warm temperate rain forests and montane shrublands and heaths. Many species at their limits of distribution.

Useful plants: Timber trees, including *Toona australis* (red cedar) and *Dysoxylum fraserianum* (rose mahogany). Many species of horticultural potential.

Other values: High landscape value, watershed protection, rich fauna.

Threats: Some small-scale logging, clearance for grazing, residential development, tourist pressure (especially on montane heaths), invasive introduced plant species.

Conservation: Most of area has National Park status. There are also some significant areas of State Forest. Major rain forest areas in the Border Ranges region are now included in the Central Eastern Rainforest Reserves (Australia) World Heritage Natural Property (3665 km²), listed in 1994.

Geography

The Border Ranges region is centred on the McPherson Range, which forms the state boundary between Queensland and New South Wales. This mountainous region covers 500–600 km², extending from Mount Tamborine south to the Nightcap Range, and from sea-level at Burleigh Heads to 1360 m at Mount Barney.

The region is formed from the eroded remnants of two large Tertiary shield volcanoes, active c. 23–20 million years BP, one centred on Mount Warning and the other originating c. 6 km north-west of present-day Mount Barney. The volcanic rocks are predominantly basalt lavas with interbedded rhyolite and other acid and intermediate lavas and pyroclastics. They were deposited in numerous sub-horizontal layers, and a number of distinct formations have been described (Stevens 1977; Ewart, Stevens and Ross 1987). The structure of the Mount Warning Shield Volcano is still recognizable, with a central core (Mount Warning) and outer shield remnants (the McPherson, Tweed and Nightcap Ranges). The Tweed River has produced an erosion caldera which is of major significance, notable for its size and age, for the presence of a prominent central mountain mass and for the erosion of the caldera floor down to basement Mesozoic and Palaeozoic rocks. Rhyolite is more resistant to erosion than basalt, leading to the formation of spectacular cliffs, although cliffs of basalt are also common. The Focal Peak Shield Volcano has been more extensively eroded and its remnants form the prominent Mount Barney peaks (including Mount Lindesay and Mount Glennie) and the basalt caps on the western McPherson Range and the Richmond, Tooloom and Koreelah Ranges, as well as the adjacent Main (Great Dividing) Range.

The two major rock types produced by the volcanoes (basalt and rhyolite) weather to give very different soil types. The basalts give rise to krasnozems and xanthozems on the plateaux and prairie soils on the slopes. Rhyolites weather to form yellow podzolic soils of much lower fertility than the basalt-derived soils.

The region has a moist subtropical climate dominated by high and low pressure systems moving from west to east across Australia. The usual summer climate is influenced by moist, unstable easterly air streams while in winter dry westerly winds tend to predominate. Average monthly summer temperatures range between 24.1°C maximum and 19.7°C minimum near the coast (Coolangatta) and 21.5°C and 17.7°C on the ranges (Mount Tamborine). Corresponding winter averages are 21.0°C and 14.4°C at Coolangatta and 17.8°C and 12.3°C at Mount Tamborine. Frosts are common in winter; light snowfalls have been recorded at higher altitudes.

Rainfall is seasonal, with 65–70% of the annual total falling in summer (October–March). The major component is orographic rainfall associated with south-easterly winds. The McPherson Range produces rain-shadows in the low country to the west. Additional irregular but high intensity falls of rain are associated with summer thunderstorms and with cyclones, generally during late summer and autumn. Cyclonic winds and landslips frequently cause severe local disturbance and are a major influence in the development of plant communities in the Border Ranges. Average annual rainfall ranges from c. 1500 mm on the coast to more than 3000 mm along the crest of the McPherson and Tweed Ranges, decreasing to less than 1000 mm at Beaudesert.

Vegetation

At the time of European settlement the Border Ranges region supported one of the largest expanses of rain forest in Australia. The "Big Scrub" (750 km²) was the largest stand of lowland subtropical rain forest in Australia and one of the largest in the world. Despite the reduction of the Big Scrub to a few fragments, the region still has extensive rain forests and is a major centre of diversity for rain forest flora and fauna (Adam 1987).

The two major rain forest formations are subtropical and dry rain forest, but there are also areas of warm and cool subtropical rain forest of great scientific and scenic importance, as well as a diversity of sclerophyll communities. The distribution of the various communities can be related to climatic gradients (temperature and rainfall) and variations in geology and soil type (McDonald and Whiteman 1979; Young and McDonald 1989; Floyd 1990a, b).

Subtropical rain forest is restricted to more fertile soils derived from basic igneous rocks, or enriched alluvial soils in sheltered areas. Below 700–800 m, there are species-rich lowland (warm) subtropical rain forests (complex notophyll vine forests) in which *Argyrodendron* spp. are prominent (e.g. *A. trifoliolatum* at lower altitudes and *A. actinophyllum* at higher altitudes). This structurally and floristically complex community is found most extensively in the eastern Border Ranges (Springbrook and Lamington National Parks, and Limpinwood and Numinbah Nature Reserves), on the lower slopes of Mount Warning and in the lower basins on the Nightcap Range. Other significant stands are found in the lower reaches of watercourses flowing west from the Tweed Range and in the headwaters of Long, Findon and Middle Creeks and on Levers Plateau in the western section of Border Ranges National Park. Further west there are limited stands on the lower slopes of Mount Lindesay, on Mount Glennie and in the Mount Nothofagus Flora Reserve, and major occurrences on the Richmond Range at Murray Scrub and Cambridge Plateau Flora Reserves. A floristically distinct gallery fringe, characterized by the presence of *Castanospermum australe* (black bean), occurs where the major rain forested creeks run into broader, drier valleys. Much of this forest type has been cleared for agriculture.

At 800–1100 m cool high-altitude subtropical rain forest is extensively developed in the eastern Border Ranges, occurring on the Springbrook and Lamington Plateaux, and on sheltered ridges and in the upper valleys on the west of the Tweed Range. Further west it is less extensive although it is the major rain forest type in Mount Barney National Park. The main canopy species in this forest type are *Sloanea woollsii*, *Geissois benthamii*, *Cryptocarya erythroxylon*, *Dysoxylum fraserianum* and *Caldcluvia paniculosa*.

Dry rain forest (araucarian notophyll/microphyll vine forest) is characterized by a discontinuous overstorey of *Araucaria cunninghamii*. Most of the dry rain forest in the Border Ranges occurs at lower altitudes although extending to more than 1000 m in the eastern part of Mount Barney National Park. Dry rain forest is found on fertile soils, particularly on drier northern and western aspects on sites where there is normally a marked dry season in spring and early summer. The most extensive unlogged area of dry rain forest is on the Darlington Range in Lamington National Park. Other important stands occur in Mount Chinghee National Park and in the western part of the Border Ranges National Park and in Mount Clunie Flora Reserve.

Cool temperate rain forest (microphyll mossy forest/thicket), dominated by *Nothofagus moorei*, reaches its northern limit in the Border Ranges. Most stands occur above 1000 m, often on high peaks frequently capped by persistent mist and rain clouds. In the most exposed locations along ridge crests the community is reduced to a dense thicket, but in more sheltered localities forest structure is well-developed. The largest single stand of *Nothofagus* in the Border Ranges, about 1.5 km² in extent, occurs partly in Mount Nothofagus Flora Reserve and partly in the adjacent Mount Barney National Park. The other stands are all smaller and confined to the eastern McPherson and Tweed Ranges. In some stands *Tristaniopsis collina* is an important canopy component with *Nothofagus moorei*.

Warm temperate rain forest (simple notophyll vine forest) approaches the northern limit of its distribution within the Border Ranges (although there are isolated outliers of *Ceratopetalum apetalum* on Kroombit Tops in central Queensland and structurally similar, but floristically different, communities in north-eastern Queensland). This rain forest type is found mainly on sites which cannot support subtropical rain forest because of infertile soils (i.e. on rhyolite rather than basic igneous rocks). It also occurs on windswept ridges where shallow soils and exposure to strong cold winds prevent the development of more complex rain forest communities. *Ceratopetalum apetalum*, the most widespread dominant of warm temperate rain forest further south, is localized in its distribution within the Border Ranges. The major occurrence is on soils derived from rhyolite on the Nightcap Range. There is also a well-developed stand on the mid-slopes of Mount Warning. In Lamington National Park *Ceratopetalum*-dominated rain forest is found associated with *Nothofagus moorei* on basalt on south-facing slopes along tributaries of the upper Coomera River and on the left branch of the Albert River above Lightning Falls. Areas of *Ceratopetalum* are found in both Springbrook and Lamington National Parks as an understorey to *Lophostemon confertus* on rhyolite soils enriched by alluvium, especially below clifflines. In the western McPherson Range (i.e. the Focal Peak volcano) warm temperate rain forest on less fertile soils is dominated by *Schizomeria ovata*.

Although rain forest covers large areas of the Border Ranges, there are also major stands of sclerophyll forests, woodlands and shrublands. The intergradations between rain forest and wet sclerophyll forest are spatially and ecologically complex. Wet sclerophyll forests (with an upper canopy of either *Lophostemon confertus* or *Eucalyptus* spp.) frequently have a well-developed rain forest understorey. On fertile soils maintenance of these communities appears to depend on disturbance (from agencies such as fire, landslip or storms). In the absence of disturbance they will eventually develop into rain forest. On less fertile soils (for example those derived from rhyolite) some examples of wet sclerophyll forest may be distinct self-perpetuating communities in their own right. *Lophostemon confertus* communities are widespread in the Border Ranges. At Terania Creek they include some of the oldest radiocarbon-dated trees on mainland Australia, the oldest sampled being about 1200 years old (Turner 1984).

Eucalyptus grandis stands also tend to have a well-developed rain forest understorey. They are widespread and are particularly prevalent on moist alluvial or detrital shelfs below rhyolite outcrops. *Eucalyptus microcorys* and *E. saligna* are other important wet sclerophyll canopy species at lower altitudes, while *E. pilularis* occurs on the Nightcap Range and Springbrook Plateau. The major wet sclerophyll canopy species at higher altitudes (above about 600 m) on soils derived from rhyolite is *E. campanulata*. At higher altitudes, *E. oreades* may be locally dominant.

While wet sclerophyll forest generally occurs at sites with at least 1200 mm annual rainfall, dry sclerophyll forests and woodlands are found on drier northern or western aspects, or on shallow soils on steep slopes. There are a number of shrub-dominated communities on exposed rock knolls and cliff lines. Montane heathlands with the endemic mallee eucalypt, *Eucalyptus microcodon*, occur on Mount Glennie, in the Mount Barney National Park (particularly on Mount Barney and Mount Maroon), the Daves Creek area of

Lamington National Park and limited areas of Springbrook National Park. Other areas of rhyolite carry a shrubby open forest or woodland of *Eucalyptus signata* and *E. gummifera*, e.g. Ship Stern Range and Minyon Falls area of Nightcap Range. On basalt, the major sclerophyll communities are grassy woodlands of *Eucalyptus tereticornis*, *E. melliodora*, *E. crebra* and *Angophora subvelutina*, while in wetter, less exposed areas, open forests of *Eucalyptus biturbinata*, *E. eugenioides*, *E. tereticornis*, *E. microcorys* and *Lophostemon confertus* occur with important disjunct populations of *Eucalyptus quadrangulata* and *E. dunnii*.

Flora

More than 1200 vascular plant species have been recorded from the rain forests and associated sclerophyll communities of the Border Ranges. They include species with tropical distributions (megatherms), subtropical distributions (mesotherms) and temperate distributions (microtherms) (Nix 1982). This floristic diversity reflects both the range of habitats and the probable continuity of environmental conditions for the rain forest flora over long periods of geological time, and especially during the onset of continental aridity in the late Tertiary and throughout the climatic oscillations of the Quaternary (Webb and Tracey 1981).

CPD Site Au2: Border Ranges, showing Pinnacle Hill (or the Tweed Pinnacle), part of the Tweed Range, which forms the western wall of the Mount Warning Caldera. In the foreground is subtropical rain forest. The photograph is taken in a south-easterly direction, with the Nightcap Range in the background. Photo: Peter Lahmann.

Of the dicotyledonous plants, c. 140 genera are of Gondwanan origin. These include rain forest genera such as *Nothofagus*, *Ceratopetalum*, *Akania*, *Corokia* and *Austrobuxus*, as well as non-rain forest genera such as *Cassinia*, *Bauera*, *Hibbertia*, *Leucopogon* and *Eriostemon*.

There are more than 70 strictly endemic species, i.e. confined to the Border Ranges region. They comprise three main groups:

1. species of the lowland subtropical rain forests – the Tweed and adjacent Currumbin and Tallebudgera valleys are a particular focus of endemism;

2. warm temperate and cool temperate rain forest species on rhyolite and other acid or intermediate volcanics associated with the Mount Warning volcano;

3. species of the montane shrublands on acid volcanics of both the Mount Warning and Focal Peak volcanoes.

Because of extensive clearing of lowland rain forests in the past, many species are now threatened. 35 species from the Border Ranges are listed as Endangered or Vulnerable (Briggs and Leigh 1988; Thomas and McDonald 1989).

Useful plants

There are many important timber species in the Border Ranges rain forests. They include *Toona australis*, *Araucaria cunninghamii*, *Gmelina leichhardtii*, *Dysoxylum fraserianum*, *Flindersia australis* and *Owenia cepiodora* (which is threatened). Logging of hardwood species continues in State Forests. The main species harvested are *Lophostemon confertus*, *Eucalyptus microcorys*, *E. saligna*, *E. grandis* and *E. pilularis*.

There are important populations of several species of economic importance. These include *Macadamia integrifolia* and *M. tetraphylla* (macadamia nuts), *Microcitrus australasica* (a source of genetic material for disease resistance in commercial citrus) and *Araucaria cunninghamii*, extensively planted in dry rain forest areas of south-eastern Queensland. *Eucalyptus dunnii* is one of the most valued eucalypts for afforestation in other countries; the demand for seed has placed pressure on the relatively limited natural stands. *Grevillea robusta* is also extensively planted overseas and there have been recent provenance studies. This species is also favoured for ornamental plantings, and is just one of several species of horticultural value. Others include *Brachychiton acerifolius*, *Cassia brewsteri* subsp. *marksiana*, *Harpullia pendula*, *Stenocarpus sinuatus* and *Archontophoenix cunninghamiana*.

A compound that is active against the AIDS virus has been isolated from *Castanospermum australe* which occurs in gallery forests in the region.

Social and environmental values

The landscapes of the Border Ranges are considered amongst the most dramatic on the Australian continent. The views both of and from the Tweed Caldera rim encompass some of the most extensive rain forest stands in subtropical Australia. Mount Warning is the dominant landscape feature from much of the Tweed Valley. Further west, Mount Lindesay also presents a memorable silhouette from many angles and the peaks of the Mount Barney National Park are popular with bushwalkers. The region has probably the highest concentration of precipitous waterfalls (associated with clifflines in the rhyolite flows) on the continent.

Management of the National Parks provides for a spectrum of activities, with some areas accommodating high visitor use (as in the northern part of Lamington National Park) and others where few facilities for visitors are provided – as in southern Lamington National Park and the contiguous areas of Border Ranges National Park.

The Border Ranges are of international significance because of the diversity of the fauna and the intermingling of different biogeographic elements (Archer and Fox 1984). The area is rich in species of mammals (Calaby 1966), reptiles, amphibians, birds and many invertebrates. Many birds are broadly confined to South-east Australia (a region which extends from the coast to the Great Dividing Range from southern Queensland, through New South Wales, to eastern Victoria); of these, 10 are restricted-range species. A few have very small ranges, for example, black-breasted buttonquail (*Turnix melanogaster*) and Albert's lyrebird (*Menura alberti*). Most species occur in forest, both rain forest and eucalypt forest, and a few are considered threatened. Amongst the herpetofauna, the Border Ranges are the main distribution centre for the pouched frog (*Assa darlingtoni*).

The Border Ranges are important water catchment areas. The Hinze Dam (165,000 megalitres) on the Nerang River is the main water supply for the city of Gold Coast. Several smaller dams store water for both irrigation and urban supply purposes. The protection afforded by natural forests to water catchments assures a reliable supply of water and reduces the risk of soil erosion and flooding downstream.

Threats

The major threat within the National Parks is increasing visitor pressure. Some of the more restricted plant communities, such as the montane heaths and the *Nothofagus* thickets on the edge of the McPherson and Tweed scarps, have been affected by track development and visitor impact. Damage is also apparent on the summits of Mount Barney and Mount Warning. Areas of the Springbrook plateau and foothills are under pressure from residential development.

Remarkably, the plant communities of the Border Ranges are free of the effects of feral animals, particularly wild pigs which have a major impact in rain forest areas elsewhere in Australia. There is some localized invasion by alien tree species, notably *Ligustrum* spp. (privet) and *Cinnamomum camphora* (camphor laurel). *Lantana camara* is a major weed at lower altitudes in (disturbed) subtropical and dry rain forests and in transitional communities. *Eupatorium* spp. are locally abundant in eucalypt communities on basalt and along watercourses and in light-gaps and other open areas (e.g. rock outcrops) within rain forest.

Conservation

Most of the Border Ranges rain forests and associated sclerophyll communities are now protected within National Parks or other nature conservation reserves. The balance of eucalypt forests and woodlands largely lies within State Forests which are subject to logging on a sustainable basis. Witches Falls on Mount Tamborine was proclaimed as the first National Park in Queensland in 1908, but the first major National Park in the Border Ranges region was Lamington (now 205 km^2 in extent), gazetted in 1915. Warrie and Gwongorella National Parks were established in 1937 and 1940 respectively; they now form part of Springbrook National Park (26.2 km^2). Mount Maroon and Mount Barney National Parks were established at about the same time and now comprise an expanded Mount Barney National Park (119 km^2). The most recent National Park to be established in the Queensland sector of the Border Ranges is Mount Chinghee (11.1 km^2).

After its establishment in 1920, Mount Warning National Park (23.8 km^2) remained the only significant reserve in the southern Border Ranges region until the gazettal of Limpinwood Nature Reserve (26.5 km^2) in 1963. In 1979 Border Ranges National Park was established adjacent to Lamington National Park.

After a review of rain forest management in New South Wales, which resulted in the Rainforest Policy of 1982, Border Ranges National Park was greatly extended to 315 km^2 in 1983, and Nightcap National Park (49.5 km^2) was established. Other major rain forest stands on the western McPherson and Richmond Ranges are protected in the Mount Nothofagus (6.5 km^2), Murray Scrub (7.4 km^2) and Cambridge Plateau (8.7 km^2) Flora Reserves.

In 1986 the major rain forest areas within New South Wales were inscribed as the Australian East Coast Temperate and Subtropical Rainforest Parks World Heritage Site covering 2035.6 km^2. A proposal is being prepared to include the Queensland section of the Border Ranges in the World Heritage Site.

References

Adam, P. (1987). *New South Wales rainforests – the nomination for the World Heritage List*. National Parks and Wildlife Service of New South Wales, Sydney. 160 pp.

Archer, M. and Fox, B. (1984). Background to vertebrate zoogeography in Australia. In Archer, M. and Clayton, G. (eds), *Vertebrate zoogeography and evolution in Australasia (animals in space and time)*. Hesperon Press, Carlisle. Pp. 1–15.

Briggs, J.D. and Leigh, J.H. (1988). *Rare or threatened Australian plants*. Special Publication 14. Australian National Parks and Wildlife Service, Canberra. 278 pp.

Calaby, J.H. (1966). *Mammals of the Upper Richmond and Clarence Rivers, New South Wales*. CSIRO Division of Wildlife Research Technical Paper 10. 55 pp.

Ewart, A., Stevens, N.C. and Ross, J.A. (1987). The Tweed and Focal Peak Shield Volcanoes, southeast Queensland and northeast New South Wales. *Papers of the Department of Geology, University of Queensland* 11(4): 1–82.

Floyd, A.G. (1990a). *Australian rainforests in New South Wales. Vol. 1*. Surrey Beatty, Chipping Norton. 135 pp.

Floyd, A.G. (1990b). *Australian rainforests in New South Wales. Vol. 2*. Surrey Beatty, Chipping Norton. 179 pp.

McDonald, W.J.F. and Whiteman, W.G. (1979). *Moreton region vegetation map series: Murwillumbah*. Botany Branch, Queensland Department of Primary Industries, Brisbane. 58 pp.

Nix, H.A. (1982). Environmental determinants of biogeography and evolution in *Terra Australis*. In Barker, W.R. and Greenslade, P.J.M. (eds), *Evolution of the flora and fauna of arid Australia*. Peacock Publications, Frewville. Pp. 47–66.

Stevens, N.C. (1977). Geology and landforms. In Monroe, R. and Stevens, N.C. (eds), *The Border Ranges. A land use conflict in regional perspective*. Royal Society of Queensland, Brisbane. Pp. 1–6.

Thomas, M.B. and McDonald, W.J.F. (1989). *Rare and threatened plants of Queensland*. Information Series QI88011. Queensland Department of Primary Industries, Brisbane. 76 pp.

Turner, J. (1984). Radiocarbon dating of wood and charcoal in an Australian forest ecosystem. *Australian Forestry* 47(2): 79–83.

Webb, L.J. and Tracey, J.G. (1981). Australian rainforests: patterns and change. In Keast, A. (ed.), *Ecological biogeography of Australia*. Junk, The Hague. Pp. 605–694.

Young, P.A.R. and McDonald, T.J. (1989). *Vegetation map and description, Warwick, south-eastern Queensland*. Queensland Botany Bulletin No. 8. Queensland Department of Primary Industries, Brisbane. 47 pp.

Acknowledgements

This Data Sheet was prepared by W.J.F. McDonald (Queensland Herbarium, Queensland Department of Environment and Heritage, Indooroopilly, Queensland) and Paul Adams.

CENTRAL AUSTRALIAN MOUNTAIN RANGES
Northern Territory, South Australia and Western Australia, Australia

Location: Southern Northern Territory, northern South Australia and eastern Western Australia between latitudes 23°00'–26°30'S and longitudes 128°00'–136°00'E.

Area: c. 168,000 km².

Altitude: c. 500–1531 m.

Vegetation: Hummock grasslands on hills, sandplains and dunes; shrub steppe in saline areas; tussock grasslands on clay plains; shrublands; woodlands on more fertile lowland soils and protected uplands; riparian vegetation in gorges and gullies; rock and cliff vegetation.

Flora: 1300 vascular plant species (65% of the known flora of Central Australia), of which 120 (9.2%) are strict endemics. Many disjunct species, with Gondwanan, tropical and southern temperate elements.

Useful plants: Many species have a long history of use by Aboriginal people for medicine and food.

Other values: Tourism, rare and threatened vertebrates, Aboriginal and European heritage.

Threats: Increasing tourist pressure, fire, introduced plant species, grazing impact of cattle, horses and rabbits, mining, seed collecting.

Conservation: 2.2% of the area is currently reserved in National Parks and other conservation areas.

Geography

The Central Australian Mountain Ranges are the major topographic feature in Australia's arid region and are located between latitudes 23°00'–26°30'S and longitudes 128°00'–136°00'E. Included are the MacDonnell Ranges in Northern Territory, the Petermann Ranges which straddle the border between Western Australia and Northern Territory, the Musgrave Ranges in South Australia, along with several other smaller mountain ranges, such as the Gardiner's Range, Waterhouse Range and George Gill's Range. The famous Uluru (Ayers Rock) (867 m) is situated east of the Petermann Ranges. The highest point is 1531 m in the north of the MacDonnell Ranges.

The central portion of the MacDonnell Ranges is made up of more or less parallel strike ridges of metamorphic rocks running east-west and attaining heights of up to 350 m above the surrounding plains. To the north these give way to more rounded gneissic or granitic hills rising to 1531 m above sea-level, while to the south are lower ranges composed predominantly of tabular sandstone. The southern part of the region is dominated by the Petermann and Musgrave Ranges which reach 1046 m and 1435 m respectively. The southern Petermanns and Musgraves are composed mainly of granite, gneiss and schists. Their rounded profile contrasts with the steep and angular quartzite ridges in the northern Petermanns.

Even though the grandeur of these stark desert hills is impressive, they occupy only a small proportion of the whole area; much of the surrounding land is flat. Although the rivers are large and impressive near the ranges, most of them only flow for short periods after rains and soon disappear into the desert sands. Salt lakes are found in the western half of the area. The largest is Lake Amadeus which extends for some 130 km. Only one of the larger lakes (Napperby Lake) is fed by a river of any significance. Gorges incised through the ranges are a spectacular feature, often with permanent or semi-permanent water.

Of particular note are the ancient rocks of the Arunta Block deposited approximately 2000 million years BP, and more recent rocks deposited in two periods of inundation by the sea, approximately 340 million years BP and 135–65 million years BP. The younger rocks are derived from erosion of the ancient hills and both are now exposed, often as adjacent hills. This juxtaposition adds to the spectacular nature of the ranges and results in stark contrasts in landforms, soils and vegetation.

Climatic ranges are extreme. Summers are hot, with maximum temperatures frequently exceeding 40°C. By contrast, winter nights are cold, with frosts occurring from late May to early September. Annual rainfall is low and shows extreme variability. The lowest annual rainfall measured at Alice Springs is 60 mm (in 1928); the highest on record is 782 mm (in 1974). The mean annual rainfall is 285 mm. A large proportion of the annual rainfall is derived from a few episodes of high rainfall. For example, at Alice Springs, 65% of the annual rainfall is received in falls of over 25 mm and 25% in falls of over 75mm (Roeger 1989). Most rain occurs in the summer; however, winter rainfall is more effective as less is evaporated. The average annual evaporation potential at Alice Springs is over ten times the mean annual rainfall. There is a definite rain-shadow effect with the ranges receiving more rainfall than the plains between them.

Vegetation

About half of the area is dominated by hummock grasslands and a further third is dominated by shrublands. The remaining area contains various communities, including low shrubland (chenopod scrub or shrub steppe), woodlands and tussock grasslands.

Hummock grasslands are mostly restricted to sandy or skeletal upland soils with *Triodia basedowii* and *Plectrachne schinzii* on sandplains and dune fields. *Triodia clelandii* mostly dominates the northern uplands and is replaced by *Triodia irritans* in the south. Associated species include members of *Acacia*, *Eucalyptus*, *Senna* and *Aristida*. Many of the smaller shrubs in the hummock grasslands form large colonies and may spread over an area of 250 m^2 or more. Their ability to shoot from dormant roots is an adaptation to frequent fires and severe frosts and droughts. *Astrebla* and *Iseilema* spp. are the main components of grasslands found on clay plains.

Low shrubland communities, mostly dominated by *Atriplex vesicaria* or *Maireana astrotricha* and other halophytes, occur in restricted areas in the south. Tall shrublands, dominated by *Acacia aneura* (mulga), are common throughout the area. They occur on a variety of soils but are most often found on neutral to acidic red earths. *Acacia kempeana* shrubland is often found on low hills while *A. georginae* dominates in eastern parts of the region. *A. macdonnelliensis* shrubland occurs on the upper parts of many of the larger ranges; along with rare *A. ammobia* and *A. undoolyana* communities, it is being reduced in extent by wildfires. *Acacia estrophiolata* and *Hakea divaricata* dominate woodlands which occur in the lowlands in areas of fertile soils.

Although only occupying a relatively small proportion of the region, gorges, watercourses and floodouts are the areas which conatin the highest species diversity. Deep spring-fed gorges shelter a variety of relictual ferns, such as *Cyclosorus interruptus* and *Doodia caudata*, the main population of the former being 800 km to the north and that of the latter 1150 km to the south. *Eucalyptus camaldulensis* is the dominant tree on relatively fertile soils along riversides. Rare endemics, such as *Hakea standleyensis*, *Macrozamia macdonnellii* and *Leucopogon sonderensis* (a relict Gondwanaland species), are found in the highest mountain areas and on protected cliff faces.

Flora

A Flora of Central Australia was produced in 1981 (Jessop 1981). With recent additions, over 2000 vascular plant species have been recorded from the region. Of these, 1300 species (65%) occur in the Central Australian Mountain Ranges. There are 120 strictly endemic species (9.2% of the total flora of the Central Australian Mountain Ranges). Of these, 20% are in the families Gramineae, Myrtaceae and Compositae, and over 25% are members of the genera *Acacia*, *Goodenia* and *Eucalyptus*. 61% of the endemics occur in the highlands and

CPD Site Au3: Central Australian Mountain Ranges, showing quartzite mountains and conglomerate plateaux of the West MacDonnell Ranges. Quartzite ridges are the habitat for such endemics as *Eucalyptus sessilis* and *Acacia macdonnelliensis*. Photo: B.G. Thomson.

mountains. 20 species are restricted to sheltered gorges or cliff faces. No genera or families are endemic to the Central Australian Ranges. Approximately 20 new species are discovered each year; the least accessible areas remain poorly known floristically.

The present flora is considered to be relatively young, developing after the last major period of severe aridity between 18,000 and 10,000 years BP. The lack of endemic genera and families is a reflection of this short history. The flora is derived from a number of sources: autochthonous, Gondwanan, southern and tropical regions. The deserts themselves seem rarely to have been centres of speciation in the past, but contain plants migrating from surrounding areas and relict species from previous periods of migration.

80 vascular plant species have been classified as Rare or Endangered (6% of the total flora) (Briggs and Leigh 1988). A further 60 species are considered to be relictual. They include species of palms, cycads and ferns in such families as Gleicheniaceae, Psilotaceae, Dennstaedtiaceae, Lindsaeaceae, Adiantaceae, Thelypteridaceae, Blechnaceae and Aspleniaceae, which would have been more common during wetter climatic periods in the Oligocene and early Miocene (40–22 million years BP). Many are now rare in Central Australia and are restricted to specific habitats, most notably the permanently wet, deep gorges in the quartzite hills, such as in the MacDonnell Ranges, Petermann Ranges, the George Gill Range, Palm Valley and the James Ranges. Relict Gondwanan species, mostly in Proteaceae, Epacridaceae, Goodeniaceae, Myoporaceae, Umbelliferae and Euphorbiaceae, are also found. Most of the relict species have larger populations elsewhere in Australia.

Useful plants

Aboriginal people have occupied the region for at least 22,000 years (Smith 1989). Today, Aborigines still retain a strong cultural link with the area. Native plants continue to be used by the Aborigines, although detailed ethnobotanical knowledge is now mostly held only by the most senior people. Historically, approximately 140 species were used as sources of food, 70 species for medicinal purposes, 6 species as chewing tobacco, 5 species for resinous cement and 4 species to poison game (Latz 1982). Other products derived from plants include timber, fibres, cultural artefacts and ornaments for ritual purposes, tanning agents and toys. Ceremonies to ensure a continued supply of plant produce are still sometimes performed today. Unfortunately, some Aboriginal ethnobotanical knowledge has been lost, but understanding of Aboriginal ethnobotany in the region is relatively high compared to other parts of Australia.

The specialized adaptations of plants to the arid environment, the large number of endemic species and the continuing discovery of new species make the flora of the Central Australian Mountain Ranges a particularly valuable potential genetic resource. Some species are already grown in other arid areas of the world as soil stabilizers, or for timber, as shade trees, for ornamental purposes or as sources of food. There is great potential for further utilization.

Social and environmental values

Tourism is a major contributor to the economy of the region and is projected to increase. The landscape, flora, fauna, geology and Aboriginal heritage all contribute to the attraction of the area. The geology of the region is of considerable interest for educational and research purposes, as are Aboriginal and European heritage sites.

A number of rare and threatened vertebrate animals occur in the region, including the Central Australian brushtail possum (*Trichosurus vulpecula*), black-footed rock wallaby (*Petrogale lateralis*), bilby (*Macrotis lagotis*) and malleefowl (*Leipoa ocellata*). The invertebrate fauna is almost completely unstudied. The potential for the discovery of new species, particularly among aquatic invertebrates, is high.

Economic assessment

Tourism is the largest industry in this region of Australia. The income generated from overseas and interstate visitors to the region amounted to A$47,700,000 in 1981–1982, and increased to A$158,420,000 by 1988–1989 (Northern Territory Tourism Commission 1991). It is not possible to separate income generated by ecotourism based on the native flora and fauna, from that generated by general tourism.

Aboriginal artefacts and visual art forms, many of which are dependent upon the regional flora, are increasingly sought. They are becoming the second most important trade item for the region. Placing a monetary value on the sale of Aboriginal art is difficult as there is no organized structure for collation of data. A conservative estimate is that income generated per annum is around A$5 million.

It is envisaged that the regional flora will become increasingly important as a genetic resource for drought-resistant ornamental plants, food and medicinal plants, and plants producing wood of exceptionally fine grain for specialized craftwork.

Threats

The vegetation is still relatively intact. However, wildfires, introduced animals and exotic plants (of which there are 110 species recorded in the region), combined with disturbances from tourism and mining, are all having an adverse effect. Many of the region's rare and relict plant species occur near permanent water courses; however, it is precisely these areas which have come under pressure from grazing during years of drought (Morton 1990). Since the last severe drought of 1963–1965, there has been a considerable increase in the number of watering points as a result of tapping underground water supplies. This has had the effect of allowing grazing to spread throughout the region. Today, the Petermann Ranges are the only significant area which has not been subject to grazing by domesticated animals.

Periodically, extremely high densities of rabbits have severely affected the vegetation throughout most of the region during this century. Recently, feral horses and camels have increased in numbers. All but the steepest hills and the least fertile sand deserts have escaped grazing pressure from feral animals.

Fire is an integral part of the ecology of hummock grass vegetation. If fire frequency is reduced, litter can build up to the extent that huge wildfires can be severely damaging and extend into shrublands and other fire sensitive communities (Griffin and Hodgkinson 1986).

Tourism is the region's biggest industry and considerable growth is expected in the future. So far, the impact of tourism on the native vegetation has been minor and is mostly concentrated in gorges and along watercourses. However, it is these areas which are the most important refuges for many rare and relict plant species. The increasing number of tourists to these areas is therefore a potential threat. Illegal seed collection, especially from rare and relict plants, may also increase in the future.

The spread of exotic plant species is perhaps the most serious threat to the native flora. As well as out-competing some native species, introduced grasses allow fires to spread more easily.

Mining has had an impact on a local scale.

Conservation

At present, only 2.2% of the area is included in 23 National Parks and reserves, including Uluru (Ayers Rock-Mount Olga) National Park (1326 km^2), Simpsons Gap National Park (520 km^2) and Finke Gorge National Park (458 km^2). However, none of the Petermann and Musgrave Ranges is set aside for nature conservation.

The Arunda people of the MacDonnell Ranges had a complex system of conservation reserves and techniques of managing natural resources. These were intimately linked to their religious beliefs (Latz and Johnson 1986). This system broke down soon after the settlement of the region by Europeans. Recently, however, Aboriginal land has been leased back to conservation agencies who are conducting joint management of the areas with traditional land owners (Young *et al.* 1991). Hopefully this trend will continue and enable the protection of representative samples of the flora in the Petermann and Musgrave Ranges, both of which are mostly Aboriginal Land.

The Northern Territory Government, in conjunction with CSIRO, is currently conducting research which will highlight key areas in the MacDonnell Ranges for conservation and tourism. It will suggest appropriate land tenure and management procedures for the area, especially in respect to feral animals, fire, weeds and other threats to the vegetation.

References

Barker, W.R. and Greenslade, P.J.M. (eds) (1982). *Evolution of the flora and fauna of arid Australia*. Peacock Publications, Adelaide. 392 pp.

Briggs, J.D. and Leigh, J.H. (1988). *Rare or threatened Australian plants*. Special Publication 14. Australian National Parks and Wildlife Service, Canberra. 278 pp.

Gibson, D.F., Cole, J.R., Thomson, B.G. and Latz, P.K. (1991). *A biological survey of the west MacDonnell Ranges, Northern Territory*. Conservation Commission of the Northern Territory, Alice Springs.

Griffin, C.E. and Hodgkinson, K.C. (1986). The use of fire for the management of the mulga land vegetation in Australia. In Sattler, P.S. (ed.), *The mulga lands*. Royal Society of Queensland, Brisbane. 160 pp.

Jessop, J.P. (ed.) (1981). *Flora of Central Australia*. The Australian Systematic Botany Society, Reed, Sydney. 537 pp.

Latz, P.K. (1982). Bushfires and bushtucker: Aborigines and plants in Central Australia. M.A. thesis, University of New England.

Latz, P.K. and Johnson, K. (1986). Nature conservation on Aboriginal land. In Foran, B. and Walker, B. (eds), *Science and technology for Aboriginal development*. CSIRO Press, Melbourne. 210 pp.

Morton, S.R. (1990). The impact of European settlement on the vertebrate animals of arid Australia: a conceptual model. *Proceedings of the Ecological Society of Australia* 16: 201–213.

Northern Territory Tourism Commission (1991). *NT selected tourism data*. Northern Territory Tourism Data, Darwin.

Roeger, L. (1989). *Climate and land use in the Alice Springs region*. Agnote 322, Department of Primary Industry and Fisheries, Alice Springs.

Smith, M.A. (1989). The case for a resident population in the Central Australian Ranges during full glacial aridity. *Archaeo. Oceania* 24: 93–105.

Young, E., Ross, H., Johnson, J. and Kesteven, J. (1991). *Caring for country: Aborigines and land management*. Australian National Parks and Wildlife Service, Canberra. 261 pp.

Acknowledgements

This Data Sheet was prepared by Peter K. Latz and Brenda Pitts (Conservation Commission of the Northern Territory, Alice Springs).

KAKADU-ALLIGATOR RIVERS REGION
Northern Territory, Australia

Location: North coast of Northern Territory, c. 150 km east of Darwin extending c. 150 km inland from the coast, between latitudes 12°05'–14°30'S and longitudes 131°50'–133°30'E.

Area: 30,000 km².

Altitude: Sea-level to c. 370 m.

Vegetation: Tropical sclerophyll forest, woodland, small areas of rain forest, swamp forest, mangroves, saltmarsh, sedgeland, grassland.

Flora: c. 1400 vascular plant species, including 1430 flowering plants, 3 gymnosperms, c. 53 pteridophytes. c. 40 endemic species; c. 58 species considered rare or threatened. c. 42 bryophyte species.

Useful plants: c. 275 species have been used in the past by Aborigines as sources of food, medicines and for cultural purposes; native pasture species are the basis of rangeland grazing.

Other values: "Wilderness" landscape and cultural values, tourism, scientific research.

Threats: Grazing pressure, invasive exotic plant species, visitor pressure in some localized areas, mining.

Conservation: Kakadu National Park, a World Heritage Property, covers 19,804 km² (c. 66% of the region).

Geography

The Kakadu-Alligator Rivers Region lies within the limits of latitudes 12°05'–14°30'S and longitudes 131°50'–133°30'E in Northern Territory. It encompasses Kakadu National Park and the eastern and upper parts of the East Alligator River catchment (beyond the eastern boundary of the park) and river catchments extending beyond the western boundary of the park. The southern part of the region is drained by streams flowing away from the park in the Mary River catchment. There are four major rivers: the Wildman, West, South and East Alligator. Catchments of major tributaries east of the park include Cooper Creek, Magela Creek (East Alligator) and Deaf Adder Creek (South Alligator).

The topography ranges from sandstone plateaux with sharp relief in the headwaters zone of the eastern and southern parts of the South and East Alligator Rivers, through rolling to undulating upland hills, to ridges and peneplains of low relief, and flat coastal plains dissected by meandering river channels and subject to heavy inundation in the tropical wet season (October–April). There are no highland areas, but occasional emergent hills rising to 370 m altitude are a feature of inland areas. The region includes spectacular escarpments and gorges, and mesa-like outliers in adjacent lowlands.

The region's lower ridges and plains are composed of Tertiary laterite overlaying dolomites, siltstones, sandstones, metamorphic rocks and granite. Weathering has produced shallow, gravelly soils and deeper, sandy soils. Flat coastal plains lie between the lowland ridge country and the Arafura Sea. They are covered by heavy clay soils which are often saline near river estuaries. Mudflats, lateritic cliffs and sand dunes occur along the coast.

Average annual rainfall varies from 971 mm at Katherine Experimental Farm (120 m altitude) to 1655 mm at Darwin Airport (31 m altitude). Average daily temperatures at Darwin Airport vary from 34.4°C to 15.9°C (Australian Bureau of Meteorology 1990).

Vegetation

The major regional vegetation types have been described by Story (1976) and Christian and Aldrick (1977). Detailed studies have identified many communities within the broad vegetation categories. For example, seven communities are described for the sandstone plateaux (Bowman, Wilson and Fensham 1990). 13 vegetation units have been proposed for the region at a mapping scale of 1:250,000 (Wilson *et al.* 1990). The main vegetation types are briefly described below.

Rain forest

Lowland rain forest (monsoon forest, semi-deciduous forest, mixed closed forest, to 25 m high) occurs as small patches associated with springs and moist areas on the margins of the coastal plain. They may include thickets ("jungles") of scrub and are often rich in vines, palms and lianes. Some species are deciduous. Dominants include *Acacia auriculiformis, Bombax ceiba, Canarium australianum, Carpentaria acuminata* (endemic), *Drypetes lasiogyna, Ficus virens, Sterculia quadrifida* and *Syzygium* spp.

Escarpment rain forest (closed forest and sandstone monsoon forest to 35 m high) occurs as small patches within gorges and close to sandstone escarpments, where runoff increases effective dry season groundwater reserves, and where fire may be reduced in frequency by local topography (Jones 1983). *Allosyncarpia ternata* (endemic) is usually dominant and there may also be *Calophyllum sil, Carpentaria acuminata, Gmelina schlecteri, Horsfieldia australianum* and *Ilex arnhemensis*. Understorey trees and shrubs include *Cryptocarya exfoliata*, *Glycosmis sapindoides*, *Rhodamnia australis* and *Xanthostemon* spp. Vines include *Desmos wardianus*, *Gynochtodes australiensis* and *Melodorum* sp.

Tall forest
Tall forest (mixed open forest to 20 m high) is widespread on deeper lateritic and sandy soils. Dominants include *Eucalyptus miniata* and *E. tetrodonta*; associated species may include *E. bleeseri* and *Erythrophleum chlorostachys*. Components of the understorey include the palm *Livistona humilis*. *Pandanus* thickets are common in low-lying areas. Annual flammable grasses appear seasonally. They include species of *Eriachne*, *Sorghum* and *Thaumastochloa*. Perennial grasses include *Chrysopogon* spp. and *Heteropogon* spp.

Woodland
Woodland (including eucalypt woodland, stunted woodland, sandstone woodland, savanna and open forest up to 13 m high) is extensive in drier areas on shallow soils and in upland areas on plateau sandstone with skeletal soils. A grassy understorey develops seasonally and is usually burnt in the dry season. There are various types of eucalypt woodlands, including *Eucalyptus tectifica-E. latifolia* woodland (the most widespread type), *E. tintinans* woodland (on sandstone, quartzite and granite in the south), mixed *Melaleuca viridiflora* and eucalypt woodland (often ecotonal between *Melaleuca* forest and woodland), *E. papuana-E. polycarpa* woodland (on clay flood plain margins), *E. tetrodonta-E. miniata-E. ferruginea* woodland (on the sandstone escarpment) and *E. dichromophloia-E. miniata* woodland (on sandstone escarpment, forming heath or shrubland on the poorest sites).

Swamp forest
Swamp forest (paperbark forest to 17 m tall) occurs in extensive patches on non-saline clay plains where inundation occurs for 6–8 months. The main species are *Melaleuca cajuputi*, *M. leucadendron* and *M. viridiflora* as dominants, with *Barringtonia*, *Pandanus* and *Bambusa* as minor associates along rivers. Rarely, species of *Nauclea*, *Syzygium*, Orchidaceae and *Eucalyptus papuana* occur as associates. The ground cover is strongly seasonal and includes aquatics such as species of *Eleocharis*, *Nymphoides* and *Utricularia*, and grasses in the genera *Echinochloa*, *Hymenachne*, *Oryza* and *Pseudoraphis*.

Mangal low closed forest
Mangroves are well-developed along muddy shores and river estuaries. There are usually five or more species of mangrove present, including *Avicennia marina*, *Sonneratia* spp., *Rhizophora stylosa*, *Bruguiera* spp., *Ceriops tagal* and *Lumnitzera racemosa*. Monospecific stands also occur. About 25 arborescent species have been recorded in mangrove scrub (Wightman 1989). Rarities include the vine *Finlaysonia obovata*.

CPD Site Au4: Kakadu-Alligator Rivers Region, near Mount Callahan, showing open eucalypt woodland.
Photo: David Whitfield.

Samphire shrubland (saltmarsh)

Saltmarsh forms a distinct zone on the inland side of mangroves on saline clay soils. *Halosarcia* is dominant with *Suaeda arbusculoides, Sesuvium portulacastrum* and *Tecticornia australasica*. Numerous salt-tolerant grasses also occur.

Mixed closed grassland-sedgeland

Sedgeland occurs in seasonally waterlogged, generally non-saline lowlands between the coastal estuaries and higher, inland areas. Dominant genera include *Caldesia, Cyperus, Eleocharis, Fimbristylis, Nymphaea, Nymphoides, Schoenoplectus* and *Sporobolus*, together with *Nelumbo nucifera, Oryza rufipogon* and *Pseudoraphis spinescens. Hymenachne acutigluma* and *Leersia hexandra* may form floating rafts of vegetation.

Flora

The native vascular flora includes 1430 flowering plant species (in 143 families and 539 genera), 3 species of gymnosperms (including one genus of cycads) and c. 53 species of pteridophytes. In addition, there are about 42 bryophyte species (Lazarides *et al.* 1988).

About 40 vascular plant species are endemic to the region, including 24 which are restricted entirely to Kakadu National Park and have ranges of less than 100 km (Briggs and Leigh 1988). A further 10 species occur only in the Northern Territory, mostly on the sandstone plateau (Taylor and Dunlop 1985). In addition, 20 species which may fall into these categories are the subject of ongoing assessment, and many undescribed species are also likely to be endemic. About 58 species are regarded as rare or threatened.

The flora of the Kakadu-Alligators Rivers Region is derived from the rain forests of the Australian tropics and has affinities with Asian and Australian sclerophyll floras. Both elements are of Gondwanic origin (Webb, Tracey and Jessup 1986). Subsequent changes in the flora may have been strongly influenced by the arrival of Aboriginal people some 50,000 years ago (Roberts, Jones and Smith 1990). Burning, combined with seasonal aridity, would have allowed sclerophyll species to become increasingly dominant. Today, about 50% of lowland woodland is still burnt annually (Press 1988).

Useful plants

About 275 plant species have been used by Aborigines for a variety of purposes, including as sources of food, medicines, and for making tools and weapons and cultural artefacts (Golson 1971; Jones 1980; Russell-Smith 1985). Today, however, the dependence upon native wild plants has declined among the Aboriginal population, as a result of the disruption of traditional lifestyles following European settlement and the establishment of large leasehold cattle and buffalo ranches in the region (Schrire 1982; Clarke 1985). Aboriginal groups who still gather wild plants for traditional purposes now live mainly in the east of the region. Plants known to have been used by the Aborigines have assumed cultural interest among biologists, anthropologists and other visitors to the National Park (Gabirrigi 1983; Gangale 1983).

For over a century, the rangeland grazing industry was largely based on native species. Grazing has now been withdrawn from the National Park, except for a small area where Aborigines continue to graze buffalo.

Social and environmental values

Kakadu National Park receives some 230,000 visitors annually (Mobbs 1989) and is highly regarded nationally and internationally as a "wilderness" area. Much of the native woody vegetation remains intact and adds to the aesthetic qualities of the landscape.

Aborigines view the National Park and World Heritage status of much of the region as a way of protecting natural resources for hunting, for spiritual and cultural reasons, and as a way of preserving their traditional lifestyles (Gabirrigi 1983; Gangale 1983).

Kakadu is an important refuge for wildlife now lost from other parts of the Australian continent (Braithwaite and Werner 1987).

Threats

Grazing has altered some drainage systems as well as disrupting the traditional lifestyles of the Aborigines, and has strongly influenced the timing and frequency of fire (Braithwaite and Estbergs 1985; Press 1988). Fire has led to the attrition of rain forests containing *Allosyncarpia* and also *Callitris* stands (Bowman, Wilson and Davis 1988). The effects of grazing can be long-term. For example, feral buffalo have created channels in coastal clay plains allowing salt water to encroach upon the freshwater zone (Stocker 1970; Braithwaite *et al.* 1984).

There are about 90 exotic plant species in the region. Wetlands in the region are particularly threatened by the invasion of *Hyptis suaveolens, Mimosa pigra, Salvinia molesta* and *Senna obtusifolia*. Some grasses introduced for improvement of rangeland pastures have become invasive. They include *Brachyaria mutica* and *Pennisetum polystachyon*.

Uranium mines at Ranger and Jabiluka could constitute a threat to the East Alligator River and surrounds if the current stringent controls are relaxed. Koongarra uranium mine is in a highly sensitive location, high in the catchment of the South Alligator River. Precious metals occur at Coronation Hill. Until recently, this area was excluded from the National Park; however, it is now to be incorporated into it and will not be mined.

An indirect effect of the mines and tourism is the increase in population pressure locally, creating demand for better roads and services. These effects are not widespread, although they may be locally intense and may lead to further weed introductions.

Conservation

Considerable legislative protection is afforded Kakadu and its environs. Kakadu National Park, a World Heritage Property, covers 19,804 km² (c. 66% of the region). It is leased, in part, from the traditional Aboriginal owners for the purpose of providing a National Park (Resource Assessment Commission 1991).

Nature conservation outside Kakadu is effected under the Conservation Commission Act and the Territory Parks and Wildlife Act, both of which are under Northern Territory Legislative control administered by the Northern Territory Conservation Commission (CCNT). Such legislation applies also to Kakadu except where there is conflict with Federal Legislation.

The Kakadu region has an abundant and diverse avifauna and other wildlife. The stability of wetlands and the availability of habitat are strongly linked to good vegetation management. Buffalo are being systematically removed and grazing leases in Kakadu have been terminated, except for one which is now under Aboriginal management. Fire management remains to be defined. *Mimosa pigra* is controlled throughout much of the National Park but remains a threat to wetlands.

It is especially important that Kakadu is conserved since many areas of dry tropical forest and woodland elsewhere in the world are under severe threat (Murphy and Lugo 1986).

References

AUSLIG (1987). *Kakadu National Park and surrounds.* (Map at scale 1:250 000.)

Australian Bureau of Meteorology (1990). "Tabs elements". Microfiche.

Australian National Parks and Wildlife Service (1986). *Kakadu National Park plan of management.* Australian Government Publishing Service, Canberra.

Bowman, D.M.J.S., Wilson, B. and Fensham, R.J. (1990). Sandstone vegetation pattern in the Jim Jim Falls region, Northern Territory, Australia. *Australian Journal of Ecology* 15: 163–174.

Bowman, D.M.J.S., Wilson, B.A. and Davis, G.W. (1988). Response of *Callitris intratropica* R.T. Baker & H.G. Smith to fire protection, Murgenella, Northern Australia. *Australian Journal of Ecology* 13: 147–159.

Braithwaite, R.W., Dudzinski, M.L., Ridpath, M.G. and Parker, B.S. (1984). The impact of water buffalo in the monsoon forest ecosystem in Kakadu National Park. *Australian Journal of Ecology* 9: 309–22.

Braithwate, R.W. and Estbergs, J.A. (1985). Fire patterns and woody vegetation trends in the Alligator Rivers region of Northern Australia. In Tothill, J.C. and Mott, J.J. (eds), *Ecology and management of the world's savannas.* Australian Academy of Science, Canberra. 384 pp.

Braithwaite, R.W. and Werner, P.A. (1987). The biological value of Kakadu National Park. *Search* 18(6): 296–301.

Briggs, J.D. and Leigh, J.H. (1988). *Rare or threatened Australian plants.* Special Publication 14. Australian National Parks and Wildlife Service, Canberra. 278 pp.

Christian, C.S. and Aldrick, J.M. (1977). *Alligator Rivers study – a review report.* Australian Government Publishing Service, Canberra.

Clarke, A. (1985). A preliminary archaeobotanical analysis of the Anbangbang site. In Jones, R. (ed.), *Archaeological research in Kakadu National Park.* Special Publication 13. Australian National Parks and Wildlife Service, Canberra. 317 pp.

Cowie, I.D. (1991). Alien plant species invasive in Kakadu National Park, tropical northern Australia. *Journal of Biogeography.*

Gabirrigi, N. (1983). Back to my country. In Sullivan, H. (ed.), *Visitors to Aboriginal sites: access, control and management.* Australian National Parks and Wildlife Service, Canberra. 123 pp.

Gangale, T. (1983). Still living on the land. In Sullivan, H. (ed.), *Visitors to Aboriginal sites: access, control and management.* Australian National Parks and Wildlife Service, Canberra. 123 pp.

Golson, J. (1971). Australian Aboriginal food plants: some ecological and culture-historical implications. In Mulvaney, D.J. and Golson, J. (eds), *Aboriginal man and environment in Australia.* Australian National University Press, Canberra. 389 pp.

Jones, R. (1980). Hunters in the Australian coastal savanna. In Harris, D. (ed.), *Human ecology in savanna environments.* Academic Press, London.

Jones, R. (1983). From Xanadu to Kakadu. In Sullivan, H. (ed.), *Visitors to Aboriginal sites: access, control and management.* Australian National Parks and Wildlife Service, Canberra. 123 pp.

Lazarides, M., Craven, L.A., Dunlop, C.R., Adams, L.G. and Byrnes, N. (1988). *A checklist of the flora of Kakadu National Park and environs, Northern Territory, Australia.* Occasional Paper No. 15. Australian National Parks and Wildlife Service, Canberra. 42 pp.

Mobbs, C.J. (1989). *Nature conservation reserves in Australia (1988).* Occasional Paper No. 19. Australian National Parks and Wildlife Service, Canberra. 70 pp.

Murphy, P.G. and Lugo, A.E. (1986). Ecology of tropical dry forest. *Annual Review of Ecology and Systematics* 17: 67–88.

Press, A.J. (1988). Comparison of the extent of fire in different land management systems in the Top End of the Northern Territory. *Proceedings of the Ecological Society of Australia* 15: 167–175.

Resource Assessment Commission (1991). Kakadu Conservation Zone, draft report. Australian Government Publishing Service, Canberra. Vol. 1: 251 pp.; vol. 2: 302 pp.

Roberts, G., Jones, R. and Smith, M.A. (1990). Thermoluminescence dating of a 50,000-year-old human occupation site in Northern Australia. *Nature* 345(6271): 153–156.

Russell-Smith, J. (1985). Studies in the jungle: people, fire and monsoon forest. In Jones, R. (ed.), *Archaeological research in Kakadu National Park*. Special Publication 13. Australian National Parks and Wildlife Service, Canberra. 317 pp.

Russell-Smith, J. (1986). The forest in motion. Ph.D. thesis, Australian National University, Canberra.

Schrire, C. (1982). *The Alligator Rivers – prehistory and ecology in Western Arnhem Land. Terra Australis* 7. Department of Prehistory, Research School of Pacific Studies, Australian National University, Canberra.

Specht, R.L. (1958). The climate, geology, soils and plant ecology of the northern portion of Arnhem Land. In Specht, R.L. and Mountford, C.P. (eds), *Records of the American-Australian expedition to Arnhem Land, volume 3. Botany and plant ecology.* Melbourne University Press, Melbourne. Pp. 313–413.

Stocker, G.C. (1970). The effect of water buffaloes in paper bark forests in the Northern Territory. *Australian Forest Research* 5(1): 29–34.

Story, R., (1976). *Lands of the Alligator Rivers region, Northern Territory.* Land Research Series No. 38. CSIRO, Melbourne.

Taylor, J.A. and Dunlop, C.R. (1985). Plant communities of the wet-dry tropics of Australia: the Alligator Rivers region, Northern Territory. *Proceedings of the Ecological Society of Australia* 13: 83–127.

Webb, L.J., Tracey, J.G. and Jessup, L.W. (1986). Recent evidence for autochthony of Australian tropical and sub-tropical rainforest floristic elements. *Telopea* 2(6): 575–590.

Wightman, G.M. (1989). *Mangroves in the Northern Territory.* Northern Territory Botanical Bulletin No. 7. Conservation Commission of the Northern Territory, Darwin. 130 pp.

Wilson, B.A., Brocklehurst, P.S., Clark, M.J. and Dickinson, K.J.M. (1990). *Vegetation survey of the Northern Territory.* Conservation Commission of the Northern Territory, Technical Report 49.

Acknowledgements

This Data Sheet was written by Mr F. Ingwersen (A.C.T. Parks and Conservation Service, Tuggeranong, Australia). The author thanks Dr J. Russell-Smith (Darwin) and Mr I. Cowie and Mr B. Wilson (Conservation Commission of the Northern Territory) for additional information.

NORFOLK AND LORD HOWE ISLANDS
Australia

Location: Norfolk Island is located in the South-west Pacific Ocean, 1450 km north-east of Sydney, 800 km north-west of New Zealand, centred on latitude 29°05'S and longitude 167°59'E; Lord Howe Island is located in the Tasman Sea, c. 600 km north-east of Sydney and 850 km south-west of Norfolk Island, at 31°28'S, 159°09'E.

Area: Norfolk Island – 36 km², Phillip Island – 2.5 km², Nepean and smaller islets – 0.5 km²; Lord Howe – 15.2 km².

Altitude: Norfolk Island – sea-level to 319 m (summit of Mount Bates). Lord Howe Island – sea-level to 875 m (summit of Mount Gower).

Vegetation: Norfolk Island – pine forest dominated by *Araucaria heterophylla*, mixed hardwood forest, palm/hardwood forest, palm/tree fern forest; Lord Howe Island – evergreen rain forest, palm forest, *Pandanus* forest, mossy forest, scrub vegetation, small areas of grassland, mangroves.

Flora: Combined flora of 392 native vascular plant species; c. 40% species endemic. Norfolk Island has 165 native vascular plant species, of which 50 species are island endemics. A further 7 subspecies are endemic to Norfolk Island. Lord Howe Island has 228 native vascular plant species, of which 93 are island endemics. A further 9 subspecies are endemic to Lord Howe Island, and an additional 2 taxa are endemic to Lord Howe and Norfolk islands.

Useful plants: *Araucaria heterophylla* (Norfolk Island pine), export of seeds and plants of *Howea forsteriana* and *H. belmoreana* (Kentia palms).

Other values: Tourism, threatened fauna; the most southerly coral reef in the world.

Threats: On Norfolk Island – tourist impact, cattle grazing, introduced weeds such as *Olea africana*, *Schinus terebinthifolius* and *Psidium littorale*. No major threats on Lord Howe.

Conservation: Norfolk Island National Park (4.6 km²) contains 57% of the native vascular plant flora. Lord Howe World Heritage Site (1450 km²) includes the adjacent coral reef, Ball's Pyramid, adjacent islets to the south and the Admiralty Islands to the north.

Although there are major differences between the vegetation of the two islands, there are sufficient similarities for them to be grouped as one centre of plant diversity.

Geography

Both Lord Howe Island, formed about 30 million years ago, and Norfolk Island, about 2–3 million years ago, are of volcanic origin. Norfolk Island is located at latitude 29°05'S and longitude 167°59'E, about 1450 km east of mainland Australia and 800 km north-west of New Zealand. It occupies an area of about 36 km², with Phillip Island (2.5 km²) and Nepean and smaller islets nearby. The highest point is the summit of Mount Bates (319 m above sea-level). Lord Howe Island (31°28'S, 159°09'E) is a small oceanic island of about 15.2 km², 600 km east of mainland Australia and 850 km south-west of Norfolk Island. It is broadly crescent-shaped, about 10 km long and 0.3 to 6 km wide. There are several small islets within about 3 km of the main island. The most southerly coral reef in the world occurs on the western side of Lord Howe. Mount Gower (875 m) and Mount Lidgbird (777 m) dominate the island. About 80% of the island is composed of basalt, the remainder being calcarenite derived from coral sand.

The climate of Norfolk Island is subtropical. Temperatures range from a minimum of about 7°C to a maximum of about 28°C, with an average diurnal range of only about 6°C. The mean annual rainfall is 1326 mm. The four wettest months are from May to August, with monthly averages of about 140–150 mm. The driest months are between November to January, with monthly averages of about 70–90 mm per month. Salt-laden windstorms damage vegetation; wind-pruned shrubs and trees are evident on many parts of the coast. Fog and persistent drizzle often occur. The climate and fertile soils enable plant growth throughout the year.

The climate of Lord Howe Island is similar to that of Norfolk Island, but the dramatic relief gives rise to local variability. The higher ground is often shrouded in cloud, as warm, moist sea breezes are suddenly forced hundreds of metres upwards into colder air surrounding Mount Gower and Mount Lidgbird.

Vegetation

The natural vegetation of Norfolk Island is mainly subtropical rain forest. However, much has been cleared or extensively modified for settlement and agriculture, and through the introduction of a wide range of exotic plant species, many of which have become invasive. The main area of semi-natural vegetation is in the Norfolk Island National Park, which occupies about 4.6 km² (c. 13%) of the island. There are four main communities in the park: pine forest, mixed hardwood forest, palm/hardwood forest and palm/tree fern forest (Australian National Parks and Wildlife Service 1984).

Pine forest is dominated by the endemic *Araucaria heterophylla* with various hardwood species in the understorey.

The ground flora consists of scattered patches of ferns, mainly *Arachnoides aristata*, and the trailing native grass, *Oplismenus* sp. The epiphytic fern *Pyrrosia confluens* is common on pines and the epiphytic orchid *Taeniophyllum muelleri* appears to be confined to pines.

Mixed hardwood forest is dominated by *Baloghia inophylla*, *Elaeodendron curtipendulum*, *Nestegis apetala* and *Rapanea crassifolia*. The understorey comprises smaller trees, scattered palms and tree ferns (*Cyathea* spp.), together with some shrubs. The ground layer includes ferns, such as *Arachnoides aristata*, while the epiphytic ferns *Pyrrosia confluens* and *Microsorum pustulatum* occur on older trees.

The palm *Rhopalostylis baueri* is visually dominant in mixed palm/hardwood forest. This also contains scattered native hardwood species which form an almost complete canopy.

Palm/tree fern forest is more or less confined to narrow strips along gullies. Although scattered hardwood trees often emerge above the palm and tree fern canopy, they rarely form a continuous canopy. Tall palms and the tree ferns *Cyathea brownii* and *C. australis* subsp. *norfolkensis* dominate the community.

The most recent detailed vegetation survey and analysis of Lord Howe Island (Pickard 1983) identifies 10 formations and physiographic units. They are: closed forest, closed scrub, dwarf scrub, broadleaved herb vegetation, tall grass, short grass, closed and open submerged meadow, coral sand/beaches and disturbed areas. 25 plant associations in 19 alliances have been identified and mapped. Major associations are *Drypetes australasica* (*D. deplandiei* ssp. *affinis*)-*Cryptocarya triplinervis* (355 ha), *Howea forsteriana* (170 ha), *Howea belmoreana* (75 ha), *Cleistocalyx fullagarii*

(126 ha), *Chionanthus quadristaminea* (93 ha) and lowland mixed forest (192 ha). Pickard (1983) concluded that about 57% of Lord Howe Island supports forest; scrub, grass and herbland covers the rest. Salt spray, driven by almost constant on-shore winds, appears to be a major determinant of vegetation distribution.

Flora

The most recent comprehensive survey of the floras of Norfolk and Lord Howe islands has been completed for the *Flora of Australia* project (Green 1994). The combined floras of the two islands include 392 native vascular plant species, of which about 40% are endemic to the islands.

Norfolk Island has 165 native vascular plant species. Included are 57 island endemic taxa, of which 7 are endemic subspecies. A further 2 taxa (*Solanum bauerianum*, now extinct, and *Lagunaria patersonia* subsp. *patersonia*) are endemic to Norfolk and Lord Howe islands (P.S. Green 1992, *in litt.*). Two tree ferns, *Cyathea australis* ssp. *norfolkensis* and *C. brownii*, are endemic; other local ferns have wide distributions, including New Zealand, the Australian mainland, Lord Howe Island and tropical islands to the north. Norfolk Island has 2 endemic genera, *Ungeria* and the presumed extinct *Streblorrhiza*.

Lord Howe Island has 228 native vascular plant species. 102 taxa are endemic to Lord Howe, including 9 endemic subspecies (P.S. Green 1992, *in litt.*). There are 5 endemic genera: *Hedyscepe*, *Howea*, *Lepidorrhachis*, *Lordhowea* and *Negria*. Ramsay (1984) recorded 105 species of mosses in 36 families on Lord Howe Island. The mosses bear a close

CPD Site Au5: Norfolk and Lord Howe Islands. A lagoon and mountains on Lord Howe Island. Photo: Peter Green.

relationship to those of the Australian mainland and those of New Zealand, but 21 (about 20%) are endemic.

There are strong floristic links between the Norfolk Island and New Zealand floras, mainly evident in the monocotyledons, excluding orchids. By contrast, the tree species have strong links with New Caledonia, Lord Howe Island and, to a lesser extent, the Australian mainland. For example, *Lagunaria patersonia* is common on Norfolk Island, also native to Lord Howe Island, and occurs in Queensland as a different subspecies. *Baloghia inophylla* and *Elaeodendron curtipendulum* are native to both New Caledonia and Norfolk Island.

Sykes and Atkinson (1988) recommend conservation management programmes for 14 of the rare and endangered plant species. Hicks (1989) lists 10 Endangered and 8 Vulnerable endemics, and 18 species either Endangered or Vulnerable on Norfolk Island (although not necessarily threatened elsewhere). These are included in a conservation programme being carried out by the Australian National Parks and Wildlife Service. In addition to one presumed extinct species, *Solanum bauerianum*, Briggs and Leigh (1988) record 18 species on Lord Howe Island which are nationally Vulnerable or Rare. The Vulnerable species *Asplenium pteridoides* (*A. howeanum*) and 12 of the 17 Rare species are endemic. Six of the Rare species are considered to be inadequately protected with populations of less than 1000 individuals.

There are 216 naturalized species on Lord Howe Island, including the Norfolk Island pine *Araucaria heterophylla*. Rodd and Pickard (1983) reported difficulty in determining

CPD Site Au5: Norfolk and Lord Howe Islands. Norfolk Islands pine (*Araucaria heterophylla*) on the summit of Mount Bates, Norfolk Island. Photo: Peter Green.

whether some species were native or naturalized, a difficulty enhanced by the occurrence of recent natural invasions by a number of species.

Useful plants

Export of seeds of the endemic palm *Howea forsteriana* (known commercially as Kentia palm), *H. belmoreana*, *Hedyscepe canterburyana* and *Lepidorrhachis mooreana* from Lord Howe Island began about 1890. Gross revenue was estimated at A$1,718,400 for 1990–1991 (Lord Howe Island Board 1990). *Howea forsteriana* is grown in plantations on Norfolk Island for seed production; exports in 1986–1987 yielded A$1,106,755. More than two-thirds of palm seeds went to Europe, the balance to Australia and New Zealand (Office of the Administrator, Norfolk Island 1987). According to Pickard (1983), the level of harvesting seed from wild plants on Lord Howe Island is not damaging the vegetation. He supports the establishment of plantations for seed production and propagation of other native plants for export.

Plantations of *Araucaria heterophylla* have been established on Norfolk Island to produce timber for local use. About 30 ha of exotic eucalypt plantations have also been established. A small plantation of the exotic conifer *Araucaria cunninghamii* was established but, following concerns that the genetic integrity of *A. heterophylla* could be prejudiced, a programme to remove all exotic species of *Araucaria* on the island has been implemented. Heavy crops of Norfolk Island pine seeds occur every three to five years. In 1986–1987 seed exports returned A$2052 (Office of the Administrator, Norfolk Island 1987).

Social and environmental values

Lord Howe and Norfolk Island are regarded as distinct Endemic Bird Areas. Seven and six restricted-range birds occur, or occurred, on Norfolk and Lord Howe Islands respectively. Today, three Norfolk Island species and four Lord Howe species are extinct. Only one of the extinct (none of the extant) species were shared. Two species on Norfolk Island are largely confined to forest, namely Norfolk parakeet (*Cyanoramphus cookii*) and white-chested white-eye (*Zosterops albogularis*), and are highly threatened. Lord Howe rail (*Gallirallus sylvestris*) was close to extinction in the 1970s but is now more secure following an intensive conservation effort.

Captain James Cook landed on Norfolk Island in 1774. Although unoccupied at that time, subsequent discoveries of artefacts and the presence of *Musa* spp. (bananas) suggest previous human occupation (Sykes 1980). The island was occupied as a penal colony between 1788–1814 and 1826–1856. Free settlers arrived in 1856 as refugees who had been forced to leave Pitcairn Island by order of the British Government. Many of these people were descendants of mutineers of the "Bounty", captained by William Bligh. At the population census of June 1986, about 46% of the permanent residents of Norfolk Island claimed direct descendancy from Pitcairn islanders. The present permanent population of Norfolk Island numbers about 2000. About 29,000 tourists visit the island each year. They are attracted by the equitable climate, cultural history and duty-free shopping. About two-thirds of tourists come from Australia and about one-third from New

Zealand. The number of tourists present at any one time varies seasonally from 400 to 900. Most tourists arrive by scheduled air services, some by yachts.

Lord Howe Island was discovered in 1788 by Lieutenant Henry Ball. Free settlers arrived in 1833. They engaged in subsistence farming and fishing, and traded with passing whalers. The permanent population of Lord Howe is now about 300; the number of tourists is restricted to 400 at any one time. About 4500 tourists visit the island each year. They are attracted by the spectacular scenery, mild climate, recreational fishing, general absence of motor vehicles, and the occurrence of rare fauna and flora. Most visitors arrive by air and some by yachts.

Threats

Major threats on both islands result from introduced plants and animals which have become naturalized. The spread of *Psidium cattleianum* (guava) poses a greater threat to native vegetation than any other exotic weed. On Norfolk Island, the only areas free of guava in the National Park are dense palm forests in valley bottoms. Other problem species are *Solanum mauritianum* (Mauritius tobacco) and, to a lesser degree, *Homalanthus populifolius* (bleeding heart). Both these quick-growing, soft-wooded trees occupy key habitats for rare species in some valley bottoms (Sykes and Atkinson 1988).

Uncontrolled cattle grazing on Norfolk Island, and to a lesser extent on Lord Howe Island, is a continuing threat. Cattle grazing is now excluded from the Norfolk Island National Park. Progressive dieback of vegetation adjacent to cleared areas is a major threat to lowland areas of Lord Howe Island.

Another serious threat is the impact of tourism, including waste disposal. There is no mining on either island and controls on the number of permanent residents and tourists should prevent urban and agricultural expansion. There is no logging of native forest, and timber harvesting on Norfolk Island is largely restricted to plantations and moribund Norfolk Island pines.

A root rot fungus, *Phellinus noxious*, is a threat to mature Norfolk Island pines. Management techniques are being implemented to modify those grazing and logging practices which spread the disease.

Conservation

Norfolk Island National Park and Botanic Garden were proclaimed under the Australian National Parks and Wildlife Conservation Act in January 1986 and under complementary Norfolk Island legislation. The park occupies approximately 4.6 km² (c. 13% of the island) and is managed according to a plan approved by the Australian Parliament and the Norfolk Island Legislative Assembly (Australian National Parks and Wildlife Service 1984).

The Botanic Garden occupies about 0.6 ha at present. There are proposals for its expansion. The objectives of the garden include cultivation of common native species, as well as those considered rare or endangered, and propagation of native plants for the garden, for re-introduction to Norfolk Island National Park, Phillip Island and other public reserves, and for sale to residents.

The Lord Howe Island Group was inscribed as a World Heritage Site (of area 15.4 km²) in 1982 for its unique landforms and biota, the diverse and largely intact ecosystems, the spectacular natural beauty, and for its rare and threatened species, which include the Endangered Lord Howe Island wood rail (*Tricholimas sylvestris*). The Lord Howe Island Permanent Park Reserve, which occupies 11.8 km² of Lord Howe Island, is protected under Lord Howe Island Act (1953).

References

Australian National Parks and Wildlife Service (1984). *Plan of management. Norfolk Island National Park and Norfolk Island Botanic Garden.* Australian National Parks and Wildlife Service, Canberra.

Briggs, J.D. and Leigh, J.H. (1988). *Rare or threatened Australian plants.* Special Publication 14. Australian National Parks and Wildlife Service, Canberra. 278 pp.

Green, P.S. (1994). Flora of Norfolk and Lord Howe islands. Bureau of Flora and Fauna, *Flora of Australia Vol. 49.* Australian Government Publishing Service, Canberra.

Hicks, J. (1989). Conservation of endangered and rare plants of Norfolk Island – work program. Australian National Parks and Wildlife Service, Working Paper.

Lord Howe Island Board (1990). *Report of the Lord Howe Island Board for the year ended 30th June 1990.* Lord Howe Island Board.

Office of the Administrator, Norfolk Island (1987). *Norfolk Island report, 1986–87.* Australian Government Printer, Canberra.

Pickard, J. (1983). Vegetation of Lord Howe Island. *Cunninghamia* 1(2): 133–265.

Ramsay, H. (1984). The mosses of Lord Howe Island. *Telopea* 2(5): 549–558.

Rodd, A.N. and Pickard, J. (1983). Census of vascular flora of Lord Howe Island. *Cunninghamia* 1(2): 267–280.

Sykes, W.R. (1980). The vegetation of Norfolk Island. *Royal New Zealand Institute of Horticulture Annual Journal* 8: 45–56.

Sykes, W.R. and Atkinson, I.A.E. (1988). Rare and endangered plants of Norfolk Island. Unpublished consultancy report undertaken by the Botany Division, New Zealand Department of Scientific and Industrial Research for the Australian National Parks and Wildlife Service.

Acknowledgements

This Data Sheet was prepared by Dr Robert Boden, with thanks to Peter S. Green, Helen Hewson and Bill Sykes for providing valuable comment and additional information.

AUSTRALIA: CPD SITE AU6

NORTH KIMBERLEY REGION
Western Australia, Australia

Location: The northernmost region of the Northern Botanical Province of Western Australia, also known as the Gardner Botanical District, north of latitude c. 17°00'S.

Area: 99,100 km².

Altitude: 0–854 m.

Vegetation: Mostly high-grass savanna, other savannas with short grasses, small areas of eucalypt woodland, mangroves, rain forest patches.

Flora: c. 1476 vascular plant species (c. 75% of the flora of the whole Kimberley region), of which 102 species are strict endemics; 453 vascular plant species recorded so far from rain forest patches.

Useful plants: >200 species used by Aborigines as sources of food; many species used in traditional medicine, also fish poisons, and for cultural uses.

Other values: Spectacular scenery, potential tourism (as yet undeveloped). Most of the area is uninhabited and remains as wilderness.

Threats: Overgrazing, fire.

Conservation: National Parks and Nature Reserves cover substantial areas and are currently being increased.

Geography

Kimberley is the general term for the northern portion of Western Australia. It forms a distinct administrative and ecological unit and is isolated by desert from the more populated parts of the state. The North Kimberley Region corresponds to the Gardner Botanical District of Beard and Sprenger (1984). It is the northernmost and most humid region of the Kimberley, its southern boundary coinciding roughly with the 700 mm isohyet, and contains the most luxuriant vegetation, the greatest number of species and the largest number of endemics in the whole of the Kimberley. It is also the most remote region of the Kimberley and is relatively unaffected by human activity. Most of the area is uninhabited.

The climate is tropical, semi-arid to arid and monsoonal. Rainfall is highly seasonal, almost all occurring between November and April. Mean temperatures are high throughout the year, always exceeding 18°C in the dry months and rising to 32°C in the wet season. Daily maxima are frequently over 40°C during the wet season. Light frosts can occur at nights in inland areas during the dry season.

The landscape of the Kimberley is primarily determined by the geological structure. A central core, the Kimberley Plateau, consists of a plateau 40–600 m above sea-level (854 m at the highest point) formed by flat-lying sandstones and volcanics of Proterozoic age. These give rise to a topography of sandstone-capped plateau and mesas bounded by impressive scarps, alternating with plains formed on less resistant basalt and dolerite of volcanic formations. Sandstone predominates in North Kimberley, the topography becoming more rugged towards the coast. Indeed, access to some areas can only be made from the sea or by helicopter. This factor has contributed markedly to the preservation of the wilderness character of the region. The Kimberley Plateau is bounded to the east by

a sedimentary basin, the Ord Basin, containing rocks of Palaeozoic and Mesozoic age which have been eroded into scarps and valleys (for example around Wyndham and Kununurra).

The Kimberley as a whole is drained by a number of substantial, mostly temporary, rivers. In North Kimberley, wet season flash-flood runoff soon dwindles away, leaving watercourses with little flow during dry months.

Vegetation

Closed canopy forests are of minimal extent in the Kimberley region and consist of scattered patches of rain forest and coastal mangroves. The Kimberley rain forests are of particular interest. They occur as small patches, some 1500 in all, covering in total an area of about 60 km². Almost all rain forest patches occur in the North Kimberley Region and most are within 10 km of the coast in areas receiving more than 1000 mm of annual rainfall. Some patches also occur further inland in sheltered sites in rugged terrain or in drier areas behind sand dunes. Structurally, the forests range from semi-evergreen mesophyll vine forest to deciduous vine thicket, using the classification of Webb (1959). No clear explanation for their presence has emerged from soil and landform surveys. It is possible that they develop in areas protected from fire where microclimates are favourable. For data on Western Australian rain forests, see McKenzie, Johnston and Kendrick (1991).

North Kimberley mangroves contain more species than similar habitats elsewhere in Western Australia (11 mangrove species having been recorded so far in the North Kimberley mangroves); however, all the mangrove species are abundant in South East Asia.

Woodlands are confined to some laterite-capped areas, such as the Mitchell Plateau. *Eucalyptus tetrodonta* and *E. miniata* are the main species present in woodlands, but *E. nesophila* and the palm *Livistona eastonii* can also be found.

The vast majority of the North Kimberley Region is covered by grassland of various types, of which high-grass savanna is the most widespread. High-grass savanna includes drought-evading grasses, such as *Sorghum* spp., which grow to 1–3 m in height during the rainy season. Associated shorter grasses include species of *Themeda*, *Sehima* and *Chrysopogon*, depending on the substrate. Scattered trees include *Eucalyptus* spp. (such as *E. tetrodonta*, *E. tectifera* and *E. grandiflora*) and *Terminalia*, depending on the type of savanna.

Gardner (1942) recognized two principal types of savanna depending on the underlying geology, namely sandstone savanna and basalt savanna. Basalt savanna consists typically of various grassland types with *Eucalyptus tectifera* as a component of the tree layer. It is much less extensive than other grassland types in the North Kimberley. Sandstone savanna includes *Sorghum-Plectrachne* communities in the ground layer. It covers 70% of the entire Kimberley region.

Drought-resisting spinifex communities, dominated by species of *Triodia* and *Plectrachne*, occur on very shallow substrates or in rocky areas. These communities, along with short bunch grass savanna, which include *Sporobolus* and *Xerochloa* spp., are treeless.

The vegetation of the Kimberley has been mapped as part of the Vegetation Survey of Western Australia and published at a scale of 1:1,000,000 (Beard 1979). Subsequently this was incorporated into a state-wide vegetation map at a scale of 1:3,000,000 (Beard 1981) in which 16 vegetation units were recognized in the North Kimberley Region.

Flora

There are an estimated 1476 vascular plant taxa in the North Kimberley Region, of which 102 (c. 7%) are strict endemics (data supplied in 1992 by the Census of Australian Vascular Plants [CAVP] Index). The North Kimberley Region therefore contains about 75% of the vascular plant flora of the whole of the Kimberley. North Kimberley possesses a significantly higher degree of species diversity than the rest of the Northern Botanical Province. A Flora of the Kimberley region has recently been published (Wheeler *et al.* 1992).

A total of 453 species is now known from the Kimberley rain forests. In spite of the very small aggregate area of the rain forests, they contain 30% of the regional flora. It is fair to note that 78 of the 453 recorded species are found at the margins of rain forest patches or in large glades within the patches, and are not considered to be "true" rain forest elements.

MAP 18. NORTH KIMBERLEY REGION (CPD SITE Au6), WESTERN AUSTRALIA

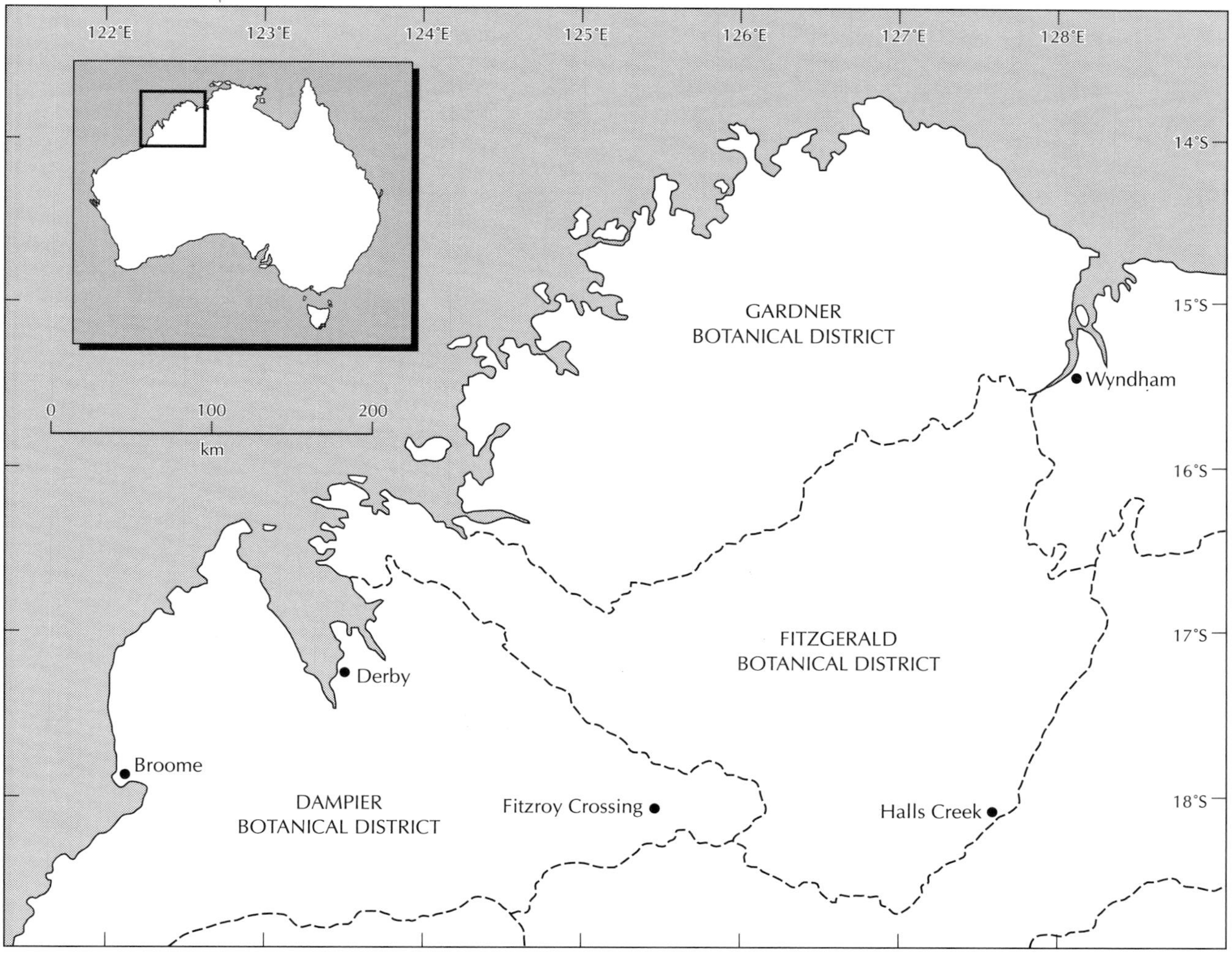

Nevertheless, the remaining 375 rain forest species represent 25% of the North Kimberley flora.

The Kimberley rain forests are known so far to include only one strictly endemic species. This low level of endemism is contrary to expectation but it has been shown by Russell-Smith (1986) that many rain forest species produce edible fruits and seeds which are dispersed widely by birds and bats. Furthermore, the flora of the Kimberley as a whole is rather immigrant in character, the original flora having been displaced by aridity during the last Ice Age. Thus, many species found in the North Kimberley Region extend widely across the north of the continent in the tropical zone.

Useful plants

More than 200 species of plants in the Kimberley are used by Aborigines as sources of food (M. Sands 1992, pers. comm.). These include many rain forest trees which have succulent edible fruits. Other species are used as sources of medicines, fish poisons and raw materials for implements and ornaments. Today, however, a decreasing number of Aborigines lead a tribal life dependent upon native plants and animals for food. Crawford (1983) and Smith and Kalotas (1985) provide some information on Aboriginal uses of plants.

Many species provide good stock feed. Petheram and Kok (1983) list 68 good pasture species among the grasses, while 11 species of shrubs are listed as good browsing material.

Many species of trees are used for posts and rails or for firewood, but most tree species in the Kimberley are of poor form for timber purposes or are otherwise unsuitable, e.g. *Eucalyptus tetrodonta* has a good straight bole but the heartwood is usually damaged by termites.

Social and environmental values

Many birds are broadly confined to the Kimberley and Top End region of Australia; of these, 14 are restricted-range species (two confined to Kimberley, six to the northern Northern Territory, and the remaining six shared between the two regions). Habitat requirements vary from mangroves, rain forest and eucalypt woodland to sandstone gorges and spinifex.

The Kimberley is a remote and thinly populated region. At the last census the population of the whole of the Kimberley was 25,000 (or 1 person/12 km²), of which most are dependent upon cattle ranching. Most of the population is concentrated in three coastal towns (Broome, Derby and Wyndham) and three inland settlements (Fitzroy Crossing, Hall's Creek and Kununura). The remainder are thinly spread over the 99 cattle ranches ("stations") which occupy about 224,000 km² (Petheram and Kok 1983). However, only about half of the area of North Kimberley is under pastoral use, the remaining being effectively wilderness.

The rugged nature of the terrain, spectacular scenery and its remoteness (much of the northern part of the region can only be approached by sea or from helicopter) offer great potential for "ecotourism". Deep inlets, estuaries, headlands and innumerable islands around the coast provide landscapes of exceedingly high scenic quality.

Reports by early travellers indicate that this area was occupied by Aborigines leading a traditional tribal life.

Following the establishment of the Catholic Mission at Kalumburu in the 19th century the Aboriginal population was decimated by disease. In recent years the Aboriginal population has become increasingly concentrated in the three settlements, formerly Missions, of Oombulgurri, Kalumburu and Kunmunya.

Economic assessment

Beef cattle production in Western Australia was valued at A$986,000 (Pink 1990), most of which would have been from the Kimberley region. However, cattle ranching in North Kimberley is relatively poorly developed due to the remoteness of the region and communication difficulties.

Ecotourism based on the native flora and fauna and spectacular scenery is a potential source of revenue.

Threats

The open-range system of grazing, introduced to the region by pioneer cattlemen, and which allows for little or no control over breeding or grazing, is easily adapted to local conditions and is still the prevailing method of cattle production on most properties. As high costs have limited the amount of fencing and the number of watering points, livestock have consistently overgrazed the more attractive and productive pastures along river fronts and on alluvial flats. Severe pasture degradation has occurred in these areas and erosion is widespread (Petherham and Kok 1983).

Fire is another factor which may lead to deterioration of the vegetation. Aborigines set fires annually and throughout the dry season to burn accumulated plant debris (Haynes 1985). The system ensured a mosaic of burnt and unburnt patches, since fires were not allowed to spread over the entire area. The introduction of commercial pastoral activities has resulted in large areas being burned every year to encourage new growth. It has been recommended by CSIRO (Stewart *et al.* 1970) that to get the best results burning should take place during dry spells of the wet season when there is sufficient moisture for effective regrowth to take place, but it is believed that many station managers prefer to burn off early in the dry season. Neither of these two regimes conform to previous Aboriginal practices. No long-term experiments on the effects of different fire regimes on the vegetation cover and floristic composition appear to have been conducted in Australia as they have in Africa (see, for example, Trapnell 1959).

The problems of overgrazing and trampling are exacerbated by the increasing number of uncontrolled feral grazing animals, particularly feral cattle and donkeys. McKenzie and Belbin (1991) report that feral cattle are spreading into remote areas of the North Kimberley wilderness and are beginning to damage rain forest patches. According to Kenneally (1989), there are 90 species of introduced plants in the Kimberley. So far, however, they do not constitute any significant threat to the flora of the region.

A dam has been built on the Ord River to impound water for irrigation, creating Lake Argyle (1700 km²). Technical problems and remoteness from markets have so far thwarted the development of irrigated agriculture below the dam.

The only mine of any consequence (the Argyle diamond mine) is operated on a fly-in/fly-out basis so that it supports little or no resident population.

Four taxa, *Eucalyptus ceracea*, *E. mooreana*, *Pandanus spiralis* var. *flammeus* and *Pittosporum moluccanum*, have been gazetted as rare flora.

Conservation

Substantial parts of the North Kimberley are protected in Nature Reserves and National Parks. These areas are Prince Regent Nature Reserve (6349.5 km²), Drysdale River National Park (4483 km²), Point Spring Nature Reserve (3 km²) and Hidden Valley National Park (20.7 km²). Walcott Inlet proposed National Park covers more than 3000 km².

A recent study (McKenzie and Belbin 1991) has recommended reservation of a network of areas to protect different rain forest communities. However, the rain forests are relatively safe anyway, since all occur in remote parts of the region.

Large parts of the Kimberley are reserved for traditional hunting and gathering by Aborigines, but they are rarely visited. Much unallocated Crown Land remains as wilderness.

References

Beard, J.S. (1965). *Descriptive catalogue of west Australian plants*. Society for Growing Australian Plants, Sydney.

Beard, J.S. (1979). *The vegetation of the Kimberley area. Vegetation Survey of Western Australia 1:1,000,000 series, sheet 1, Kimberley*. University of Western Australia Press.

Beard, J.S. (1980). A new phytogeographic map of Western Australia. *Res. Notes W.A. Herbarium* 3: 37–58.

Beard, J.S. (1981). *The vegetation of Western Australia at the 1:3,000,000 scale (with map)*. Forests Department, Western Australia.

Beard, J.S. and Sprenger, B.S. (1984). *Geographical data from the vegetation survey of Western Australia*. Vegetation Survey of Western Australia Occasional Paper No. 2. Vegmap Publications, Applecross, Western Australia.

Bolton, G.C. (1954). The Kimberley pastoral industry. *University Studies in History and Economics* 2(2): 7–53.

Burbidge, N.T. (1960). The phytogeography of the Australian region. *Australian Journal of Botany* 8: 75–211.

Crawford, I.M. (1983). Traditional Aboriginal plant resources in the Kalumburu area: aspects in ethno-economics. *Rec. W.A. Museum* Supplement 15.

Gardner, C.A. (1942). The vegetation of Western Australia with special reference to climate and soils. *J. Proc. Roy. Soc. West. Aust.* 28: 11–87.

Haynes, C.D. (1985). The pattern and ecology of *munwag*: traditional Aboriginal fire regimes in north central Arnhemland. In Ridpath, M.J. and Corbett, L.K. (eds), Ecology of the wet-dry tropics. *Proc. Ecol. Soc. Aust.* 13: 203–214.

Kenneally, K.F. (1989). *Checklist of vascular plants of the Kimberley, Western Australia*. Handbook 14. W.A. Naturalists Club, Perth.

Kenneally, K.F., Keighery, G.J. and Hyland, B.P.M. (1991). Floristics and phytogeography of Kimberley rainforests. In McKenzie, N.L., Johnston, R.B. and Kendrick, P.G. (eds), *Kimberley rainforests Australia*. Surrey Beatty, New South Wales.

McKenzie, N.L. and Belbin, L. (1991). Kimberley rainforest communities: reserve recommendations and management considerations. In McKenzie, N.L., Johnston, R.B. and Kendrick, P.G. (eds), *Kimberley rainforests Australia*. Surrey Beatty, New South Wales.

McKenzie, N.L., Johnston, R.B. and Kendrick, P.G. (eds) (1991). *Kimberley rainforests Australia*. Surrey Beatty, New South Wales.

Petheram, R.J. and Kok, B. (1983). *Plants of the Kimberley region of Western Australia*. Univ. West. Aust. Press, Nedlands.

Pink, B.N. (1990). *Western Australia yearbook 1990*. Bureau of Statistics, Government Printer, Perth.

Russell-Smith, J. (1986). The forest in motion. Ph.D. thesis, University of Sydney.

Smith, M. and Kalotas, A.C. (1985). Bardi plants: an annotated list of plants and their use by Bardi Aborigines of Dampierland, in north-western Australia. *Rec. W.A. Museum* 12: 317–359.

Stewart, G.A. *et al.* (1970). *Lands of the Ord-Victoria area, Western Australia and Northern Territory*. CSIRO Australia Land Research Series 9.

Trapnell, C.G. (1959). Ecological results of woodland burning experiments in Northern Rhodesia. *Journal of Ecology* 47: 129–168.

Van Leeuwen, S. (1984). Rare and geographically restricted plants of the Kimberley, Northern Botanical Province. Unpublished report No. 25. Department of Fisheries and Wildlife, Perth.

Webb, L.J. (1959). A physiognomic classification of Australian rainforests. *Journal of Ecology* 47: 551–570.

Wheeler, G.R., Bye, B.L., Koch, B.L. and Wilson, A.J.G. (eds) (1992). *Flora of the Kimberley region*. West. Aust. Herb., Perth.

Acknowledgements

This sheet was prepared by Dr J.S. Beard (Western Australia).

SOUTH-WEST BOTANICAL PROVINCE
Western Australia, Australia

Location: South-west Western Australia, between latitudes 26°00'–36°00'S and longitudes 114°00'–126°00'E.

Area: 309,840 km².

Altitude: 0–400 m.

Vegetation: Eucalypt forests and woodlands, mallee and sclerophyll scrub (kwongan).

Flora: c. 5500 vascular plant species, of which 2472 (68%) are strict endemics; c. 83% of the flora restricted to the western part of Australia.

Useful plants: Timber trees, sandalwood, ornamental plants.

Other values: Watershed protection for drinking and industrial water, tourism.

Threats: Fire, *Phytophthora cinnamomi* root disease. Clearance for agriculture has ceased.

Conservation: National Parks and Nature Reserves cover 25,969 km² (8.4% of the area); State Forest Parks cover 17,458.6 km² (c. 5.6% of the area). The distribution of protected areas is uneven and coverage is inadequate in the agricultural belt.

Geography

The South-west Botanical Province, as defined by Beard (1975–1981), has an area of 309,840 km² and comprises about 12% of Western Australia. The province lies between latitudes 26°00'–36°00'S and longitudes 114°00'–126°00'E.

A sedimentary basin forms a strip 20 to 100 km wide parallel to the west coast, consisting principally of arenaceous sediments of Jurassic and Cretaceous age. The topography is undulating, rarely exceeding 200 m above sea-level. Inland, the Yilgarn Plateau is underlain mainly by granite and gneiss of Archaean age dating consistently to within 2400 and 2700 million years BP. This country rock is traversed by belts of metamorphosed volcanics and sediments of similar age which are mineralized and yield gold, nickel and iron. The plateau is gently undulating, with occasional granite monadnocks. The land rises inland from the Darling Scarp at about 250 m to some 400 m above sea-level. The surface rocks have become weathered to as much as 50 m in depth and are capped in many places by ferruginous duricrusts and sands (the so-called sandplains). Agriculturally these are among the poorest soils in the world, highly leached and deficient in plant nutrients. For successful crop production, phosphate must be added to all soils, while those of the sandplains normally require zinc, copper, cobalt and molybdenum in addition. Native plants are adapted to tolerate these low levels of nutrition.

The climate is Mediterranean in character, with most rain falling in winter. The total average rainfall varies from over 1400 mm in the extreme south-west to 300 mm in the interior. The boundary of the province approximates to the 300 mm isohyet and the boundary of the "Extra-dry Mediterranean" zone (which has 7–8 dry months).

Vegetation

The vegetation of the South-west Botanical Province has been mapped as part of the Vegetation Survey of Western Australia project and published at two scales: 1:250,000 (Smith 1972–1974; Beard 1972–1980) and 1:1,000,000 (Beard 1975–1981). The vegetation is almost entirely woody, forming forest, woodland, shrubland and heath. There are no grasslands. The main vegetation types are in Table 69 below.

Mallee is defined as *Eucalyptus*-dominated shrubland. Kwongan is a term adapted from the Aboriginal Nyungar language to cover the various Western Australian types of Mediterranean shrubland, comparable with the maquis, chaparral and fynbos of other Mediterranean lands (Pate and Beard 1984). The principal structural types of kwongan are thicket, scrub heath and heath, which together comprised c. 30% of the original vegetation of the province. Clearing

TABLE 69. SOUTH-WEST BOTANICAL PROVINCE, MAIN VEGETATION TYPES

Vegetation	% area of Province
Tall forest and woodland (mainly *Eucalyptus diversicolor*)	1.3
Forest, *E. marginata*	10.3
Woodlands	25.9
Low forest	0.5
Low woodland, *Banksia* spp.	2.2
Low woodland, other spp.	0.7
Mallee	22.1
Kwongan: *Acacia-Casuarina-Melaleuca* thickets	11.5
Kwongan: other thickets and scrub	3.0
Kwongan: heath	18.8
Reed swamps	0.2
Halophytes	1.6
Bare areas	2.0

for agriculture has largely affected woodlands, thickets and heaths. Tall forest and forest now largely constitute State Forests. Large areas of mallee have escaped clearance for agriculture as a result of the soil being unsuitable for the cultivation of crops.

The only substantial remnant of cypress pine low forest occurs on Garden Island, a Commonwealth Naval Base. *Banksia* low woodland with scattered jarrah, was once the common vegetation on the sands of the coastal plain south of Perth; there are substantial remnants, but all are in private hands and at risk of being cleared. Other vegetation units which are over 90% cleared are: *Acacia rostellifera* low forest, thicket with scattered eucalypts, York gum and wandoo woodlands, tall woodland of tuart, marri-wandoo woodlands and open wandoo woodland.

Many of the vegetation units are of an endemic character. While eucalypt-dominated forests, woodlands and mallee occur in eastern Australia, the dominant species and a majority of the associated species in the west are endemic. Kwongan is a formation unique to Western Australia. Although analogous "heaths" occur in the east, certain structural forms of kwongan, such as the *Acacia-Casuarina-Melaleuca* thickets, are endemic. The majority of species in the kwongan flora are also endemic. The component botanical districts of the province differ widely in character, as described briefly below.

Darling Botanical District (South-west Forest Region)

The principal units are the jarrah (*E. marginata*) forest, which originally covered 46% of the district, the marri-wandoo (*E. calophylla-E. wandoo*) woodland (23%), the tall forest of karri (*E. diversicolor*), marri and jarrah (6%) and *Banksia* low woodland (9%). Forest originally covered 52% of the district, woodland 27%, low forest and low woodland 14%. The district contains all the province's tall forests, all the tuart woodlands, jarrah and cypress pine low forest, peppermint low woodland and scrub, and freshwater lakes. The district also contains virtually all the jarrah forest, marri-wandoo woodland and sedgeland. The Darling District is 60% cleared, varying from 31% in the karri forests of the south to 78% on the Swan Coastal Plain.

Irwin Botanical District (Northern Sandplains Region)

The Irwin District covers 39,656 km² (12.8% of the province) and contains 18 vegetation units. In complete contrast to the Darling District, woodlands originally covered only 2% of the total area, and shrublands 96%. The principal unit is scrub-heath, covering 56% of the district. *Acacia-Casuarina-Malaleuca* thickets cover 14% and *Acacia* scrub with scattered *E. loxophleba* cover 13%. The latter occupies bottomland soils which might elsewhere be expected to carry woodland. Tree heath, a unique formation, covers 3635 km² (9%) in the far north of the district. *Acacia rostellifera* low forest and *Eucalyptus dongarraensis* mallee are unique to the district.

MAP 19. SOUTH-WEST BOTANICAL PROVINCE (CPD SITE Au7), WESTERN AUSTRALIA

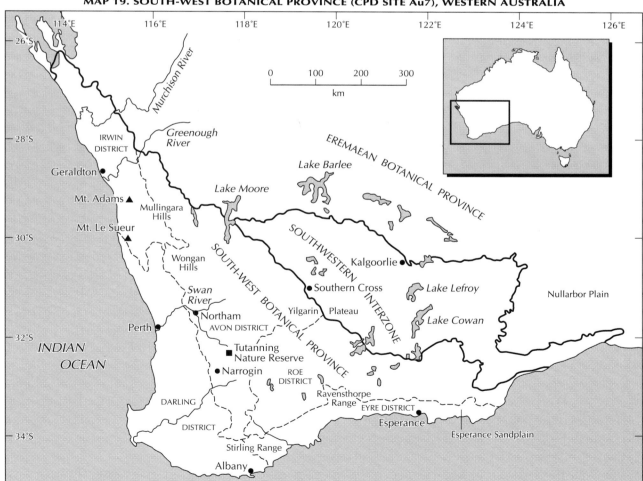

Avon Botanical District (Wheatbelt Region)

The Avon District is the largest of the south-west regions, covering 93,520 km² (30% of the province). It includes the principal area now under cereal cultivation (93% of the original vegetation in the district having been cleared). Small areas of jarrah forest and woodlands of marri-wandoo and mallet-powderbark are peripheral to the Darling District. Woodlands are typically formed of *Eucalyptus loxophleba*, *E. wandoo*, *E. salmonophloia*, *E. salubris* and, in the extreme south, *E. occidentalis*. Woodlands originally covered 54% of the district. The principal formation of the upland sandplains is *Acacia-Casuarina-Melaleuca* thicket, which once covered 31% of the district. Salt lakes cover 1367 km² and their associated halophyte communities cover 4013 km² (4.3% of the district).

Roe Botanical District (Mallee Region)

The Roe District covers 78,957 km² (25.5% of the province). Mallee makes up the overwhelming proportion of the plant cover, originally covering 76% of the district, either as mallee or mallee with patches of woodland. 44% of the original vegetation has been cleared; there are only small areas of woodland and low forest, while scrub-heath covers 6% of the district.

Eyre Botanical District (Esperance Plains Region)

The Eyre District stretches along the south-eastern coast and covers 28,702 km² (or 9.2% of the province). 52% of the original vegetation has been cleared. Mallee-heath and mallee are the two principal formations comprising 76% of the remaining native vegetation. Scrub-heath covers 13% and coastal dune scrub 3.8% of the district. Woodland is of very limited extent. Some *E. marginata*, *E. calophylla* and *E. wandoo* occurs in valleys of the Stirling Range, and some *E. loxophleba* and *E. occidentalis* elsewhere on bottomland soils. Low forest is confined to islands off the coast.

Flora

Beard (1969) listed 3611 vascular plant species for the South-west Botanical Province. This number has been considerably enlarged by subsequent taxonomic research (W.A. Herbarium, pers. comm.) and, on the basis of the national census of Australian vascular plants (Hnatiuk 1990), the number of known species approaches 5500.

There is a high rate of endemism at all taxonomic levels, comparable to many oceanic island floras which have evolved in isolation and from limited source material. It is abnormal to find this level of endemism on part of a continental landmass, suggesting that the south-west has functioned as an island for a considerable period, isolated by desert from the humid east of Australia. Burbidge (1960) listed 462 genera in 96 families in the South-west Botanical Province of which 111 genera (24%) and 5 families (5%) were endemic. Beard (1969) made a tentative analysis at the species level for the 3611 species recorded at that time for the province, finding that 2472 (68%) were restricted entirely to the province. The true rate of endemism for the south-west is about 83% (2991 species). This higher figure

CPD Site Au7: South-west Botanical Province. Stirling Range, Eyre Botanical District, showing *Eucalyptus* woodland and *Xanthorrhoea preissii* in the foreground. Photo: R.J. Whittaker.

includes species whose main distribution is in the South-west Botanical Province, but which extend beyond the province to some extent, but do not reach eastern Australia.

Available data suggest that species-richness is greater in kwongan than in woodlands and forests. The latter have a sclerophyll-shrub understorey which accounts for most of the floristic richness, but this appears to be reduced, relative to open shrublands, by the competition of the trees. Naveh and Whittaker (1979) showed that kwongan is generally richer than comparable Mediterranean shrublands in other countries (Lamont, Hopkins and Hnatiuk 1984).

The Mount Lesueur-Eneabba area in the northern sandplains and the Stirling Range-Fitzgerald River area in the south-east have unusually high topographic diversity, providing a diverse habitat range (George, Hopkins and Marchant 1979; Lamont, Hopkins and Hnatiuk 1984). Recent work by Brown (1989) shows that the floras of these areas are still imperfectly known and that previous indications of their diversity may have been based on inadequate collecting.

Many of the endemic species have restricted ranges and are considered Rare, Endangered or Threatened by Briggs and Leigh (1988). Western Australia has 1442 or 43% of Australia's total of 3329 rare or threatened species. In 1989, 238 taxa were legally declared "Endangered (Rare) Flora" under provisions of the Western Australian Wildlife Conservation Act. These have been listed and illustrated by Hopper *et al.* (1990): all of them occur only in the South-west Botanical Province. Approximately 190 plant species collected from Western Australia have been listed

Banksia coccinea, a member of the Proteaceae.
Photo: R.J. Whittaker.

as presumed extinct in various publications over the past 20 years, but Hopper *et al.* (1990); were able to list 72 as recently rediscovered and only 94 as believed extinct.

710 species have been legally listed as poorly known and 79 as requiring monitoring. Marchant and Keighery (1979), using different criteria, listed over 2000 species as poorly known or of restricted range, but only defined 124 as "Rare". Whatever criteria are adopted, however, it is evident that Western Australia has more threatened species than any other state in Australia, or indeed more than most countries in the world: and all these known species are limited to the South-west Botanical Province.

Useful plants

Dioscorea hastifolia (a wild yam) was semi-cultivated by Aborigines (Hallam 1975) but few plants in the south-west provide abundant sources of food. In European times, *Santalum spicatum* (sandalwood) has been the basis for an export trade, and the timber trees *Eucalyptus marginata* (jarrah) and *E. diversicolor* (karri) have been exploited from the forests. An export industry in wood chips has developed using mill waste and otherwise unusable species, such as *Eucalyptus calophylla*. More recently, native flowering plants have been in demand for both the local and export floristry trade. Both wild and cultivated stocks are used.

Social and environmental values

The heterogeneity of the vegetation provides habitats for a rich fauna, including 14 restricted-range species of birds, 13 of which are endemic. Many species are declining as a result of habitat loss and degradation, for example white-tailed black-cockatoo (*Calyptorhynchus baudinii* and *C. latirostris*).

The South-west Botanical Province contains Western Australia's capital city, Perth, and most of the other larger towns, all of the farming development, and all of the industry, except for mining, together with most of the state's population. This has resulted in pressure on the environment and large-scale clearance and modification of the natural vegetation. It is perhaps surprising that so much of it remains (see Conservation section), mostly as a result of large areas of land being unsuitable for agriculture.

State Forests are important producers of timber and play a vital role in protecting water catchments. All of the state's dams for water supplies are in forested areas.

The clearance of forests results in increased salinization. Urbanization has led to an appreciation of the amenity value of wilderness and natural vegetation. Tourism has been increasing, one of the greatest attractions being the display of wildflowers.

Economic assessment

The population of Western Australia in 1988 was 1,544,806, of which 925,000 (60%) lived in the Perth metropolitan area and 32% elsewhere in the South-west Botanical Province (Pink 1990). Most of the state's farming, forestry and manufacturing industries are in the south-west. The south-west also includes bauxite mines and the world's largest gold mine.

The Darling Botanical District contains all the State Forests and associated timber plantation areas which in 1989 produced the following (Pink 1990):

- ❖ Sawlogs
  - hardwood   862,749 m³
  - softwood   135,737 m³
- ❖ Other log production including pulpwood
  - hardwood   705,162 m³
  - softwood   239,759 m³
- ❖ Sawn timber
  - hardwood   287,257 m³
  - softwood   47,834 m³

The gross value of forest products for the year is estimated at A$650 million (Forest Products Association, pers. comm.).

Threats

65% of the South-west Botanical Province has been cleared for agriculture and other purposes (Beard and Sprenger 1984). Forests were logged and cleared for agriculture until the introduction of the Forests Act which conserved remaining forest stands as State Forests. Clearing of other vegetation continues. A land boom promoted by the State Government in the 1960s added several million hectares to the cultivated area. Further clearing is limited to land already in private ownership.

The long dry season results in frequent bush fires. However, this has been the case for a very long period, since Aborigines regularly burned areas when hunting, and fires are also regularly started by lightning. Native plants exhibit a high degree of adaptation to fire (e.g. Bell, Hopkins and Pate 1984), but ecosystems may come under stress if burning regimes are altered or intensified.

The most serious current threat is from the spread of root disease ("jarrah dieback") caused by *Phytophthora cinnamomi* and which was first noticed in the jarrah forests in about 1940. The pathogen responsible was not identified until 1965, by which time thousands of hectares of forest had died. By 1974, it was estimated that 2820 km² were affected and that the disease was spreading at the rate of 200 km² per year. In the event, this figure was an over-estimate. Although, the disease can be severe on certain sites where soil drainage is obstructed, elsewhere it normally affects isolated trees. *Phytophthora* has recently been found to attack other native plants in kwongan, causing mortality among susceptible plants such as grass trees (*Xanthorrhoea*) and many of the Proteaceae, such as *Banksia* spp.

Bauxite mining is a potential threat to some jarrah forests in the Darling Range; however, only 6% of the mining lease is likely to be mined.

Conservation

An assessment of the conservation status of various vegetation types has been made by Beard and Sprenger (1984). Vegetation is protected in State Forests, National Parks,

TABLE 70. AREAS OF CONSERVATION RESERVES (km²)

CALM Regions	State Forest Parks	National Parks	Nature Reserves	Other Reserves
South-west Forests	17,389	3280	1617	2213
South Coast	41	8610	8420	0.1
Wheatbelt	28.6	0	541.5	-
Greenough and Gascoyne	0	3300	200.5	-
Total	**17,458.6**	**15,190**	**10,779**	**2213.1**

Note: The three forest regions together roughly correspond to the Darling Botanical District of the South-west Botanical Province. The South Coast Region comprises the Eyre Botanical District and part of the Roe District but also includes a substantial area outside the province which contains some extensive areas of Nature Reserves. An adjustment has been made to exclude these from the figures.

TABLE 71. AREAS OF UNCLEARED LAND (km²)

CALM Regions	Area of uncleared land	Area of reserves (from Table 70)	Vacant Crown Land
South-west Forests	27,818	24,499	3319
South Coast	57,415	17,071	40,344
Wheatbelt	6026	5696	330
Greenough and Gascoyne	16,263	5305	10,958
Total	**107,522**	**52,571**	**54,951**

Note: Data for the Wheatbelt, Greenough and part of the Gascoyne CALM Regions (the latter up to Shark Bay) were computed from Land Administration records kept by local government units called Shires. An endeavour has been made to exclude reserves outside the South-west Botanical Province but there has been doubt as to boundaries both with the province and the above named CALM Regions. Owing to possible gaps or duplication, the figures must be considered a reasonable approximation only.

Source: Departments of Conservation and Land Management (CALM) and of Land Administration (DOLA).

Nature and Wildlife Reserves and vacant Crown Land. Tables 70 and 71 show the principal areas of the first three of these. Many of the Nature and Wildlife Reserves are very small. National Parks and Nature Reserves cover 25,969 km² (8.4% of the area); State Forest Parks cover 17,458.6 km² (c. 5.6% of the area). The distribution of protected areas is uneven and coverage is inadequate in the agricultural belt. In addition to actual reserves, there are substantial areas of vacant Crown Land within the province. This is land which has not been transferred to private ownership for farming or other purposes, and is not under pastoral lease. It may be assumed that any remaining vacant Crown Land within the province retains its natural plant cover and is unsuitable for either agricultural or pastoral use. It is therefore not under threat, but it enjoys no legal protection. Approximately half the uncleared area has been reserved.

It must also be taken into account that natural vegetation remains to a large extent on road verges and that, during the land boom of the 1960s, verges of increased width, up to 200 metres, were frequently laid down in kwongan country where the flora was considered of special interest. Road verges may play some useful role as corridors for wildlife, but are subject to progressive decline as they are invaded by agricultural weeds.

The steps taken to protect rare flora and to conduct research thereon are outlined by Hopper *et al.* (1990) and it is confidently asserted that "the State has the opportunity to conserve 99% of the native plant species with which it was endowed".

References

Beard, J.S. (1965). *Descriptive catalogue of West Australian plants.* Society for Growing Australian Plants, Sydney.

Beard, J.S. (1969). Endemism in the Western Australian flora at the species level. *J. Roy. Soc. West. Aust.* 52: 18–20.

Beard, J.S. (1972-1980). *Vegetation survey of Western Australia 1:250,000 Series.* Vegmap Publications, Applecross, Western Australia. (21 titles.)

Beard, J.S. (1975-1981). *Vegetation survey of Western Australia 1:1,000,000 Series.* (1975: Nullarbor; 1976: Murchison; 1981: Swan.) University of Western Australia Press, Nedlands.

Beard J.S. (1980). A new phytogeographic map of Western Australia. *Res. Notes W.A. Herbarium* 3: 37–58.

Beard, J.S. (1981). The vegetation of the Swan area. *Veg. Surv. W.A. 1:1,000,000 Series 7.* University of Western Australia Press, Nedlands.

Beard, J.S. (1984). The biogeography of kwongan. In Pate, J.S. and Beard, J.S. (eds), *Kwongan: the plant life of the sandplain.* University of Western Australia.

Beard, J.S. (1990). *The plant life of Western Australia.* Kangaroo Press, Sydney.

Beard, J.S. and Sprenger, B.S. (1984). Geographical data from the vegetation survey of Western Australia. *Veg. Surv. W.A. Occ. Paper No. 2.* Vegmap Publications, Applecross, Western Australia.

Bell, D.T., Hopkins, A.J.M. and Pate, J.S. (1984). Fire in the kwongan. In Pate, J.S. and Beard, J.S. (eds), *Kwongan: the plant life of the sandplain.* University of Western Australia Press, Nedlands.

Briggs, J.D. and Leigh, J.H. (1988). *Rare or threatened Australian plants.* Special Publication 14. Australian National Parks and Wildlife Service, Canberra. 278 pp.

Brown, J.M. (1989). Regional variation in kwongan in the central wheatbelt of south-western Australia. *Aust. J. Ecol.* 14: 345–356.

Burbidge, N.T. (1960). The phytogeography of the Australian region. *Aust. J. Bot.* 8: 75–211.

Diels, L. (1906). Die Pflanzenwelt von West-Australien südlich des Wendekreises. *Vegn. Erde* 7, Leipzig.

Gardner, C.A. (1942). The vegetation of Western Australia with special reference to climate and soils. *J. Roy. Soc. West. Aust.* 28: 11–87.

George, A.S., Hopkins, A.J.M. and Marchant, N.G. (1979). The heathlands of Western Australia. In Specht, R.L. (ed.), *Heathlands and related shrublands of the world.* Elsevier, Amsterdam.

Green, J.W. (1985). *Census of the vascular plants of Western Australia.* Department of Agriculture, South Perth.

Hallam, S.J. (1975). *Fire and hearth.* Aust. Inst. Abor. Stud. 58, Canberra.

Hnatiuk, R.J. (1990). *Census of Australian vascular plants.* Australian Flora and Fauna Series No. 11. Australian Government Publishing Service, Canberra. 650 pp.

Hopper, S.D. *et al.* (1990). *Western Australia's endangered flora.* Department of Conservation and Land Management, Wanneroo, Western Australia.

Lamont, B.B., Hopkins, A.J.M. and Hnatiuk, R.J. (1984). The flora – composition, diversity and origins. In Pate, J.S. and Beard, J.S. (eds), *Kwongan: the plant life of the sandplain.* University of Western Australia Press, Nedlands.

Marchant, N.G. and Keighery, G.J. (1979). Poorly collected and presumably rare vascular plants of Western Australia. *King's Park Research Notes 5.*

Marchant, N.G. *et al.* (1987). *Flora of the Perth region,* 2 vols. W.A. Herbarium, South Perth.

Naveh, Z. and Whittaker, R.H. (1979). Structural and floristic diversity of shrublands and woodlands in northern Israel and other Mediterranean lands. *Vegetatio* 41: 171–190.

Pate, J.S. and Beard, J.S. (1984). *Kwongan, the plant life of the sandplain.* University of Western Australia Press, Nedlands.

Pink, B.N. (1990). *Western Australian yearbook No. 27.* Australian Bureau of Statistics.

Smith, F.G. (1972-1974). *Vegetation survey of Western Australia 1:250,000 Series.* Department of Agriculture, South Perth. (3 titles.)

Acknowledgements

This Data Sheet was written by Dr J.S. Beard (Western Australia).

SYDNEY SANDSTONE REGION
New South Wales, Australia

Location: East coast of New South Wales from near Newcastle to Jervis Bay and inland to the Great Dividing Range, approximately between latitudes 33°00'–35°15'S and longitudes 150°00'–151°30'E.

Area: c. 24,000 km².

Altitude: Sea-level to c. 1300 m.

Vegetation: Evergreen sclerophyll forests, woodlands, shrublands, grasslands, coastal dunes and swamps, mangroves, small areas of rain forest.

Flora: c. 2200 vascular plant species, including c. 2000 species of flowering plants, 7 species of gymnosperms, c. 112 species of ferns. About 50 species are endemic to the region. Lower plants include c. 308 species of bryophytes.

Useful plants: Timber trees, ornamental plants.

Other values: Important water catchment, rich fauna, tourism.

Threats: Urban and industrial development.

Conservation: Extensive protected areas system covering 11,709 km² (c. 49% of the region), flora protection legislation.

Geography

The Sydney Sandstone Region is a botanical province encompassing the area covered by the *Flora of the Sydney Region* (Beadle, Carolin and Evans 1986) and the "Coastal Division" of New South Wales (Anderson 1961) with the addition of Jervis Bay and areas inland to the coastal escarpment. It covers the geologically defined Sydney Basin (Branagan and Packham 1970) and related sandstone areas of the Central and Southern Fold Belt. The main regions included are the Blue Mountains, Jamberoo and Robertson Plateaux, Budawang Range, Shoalhaven Valley, Bhewerre Peninsula, Beecroft Peninsula, Hornsby and Woronora Plateaux and the Cumberland Plain. In the west of the region are sandstone plateaux, abrupt cliffs and gorges at altitudes up to about 1300 m. Undulating country occurs below 600 m altitude, especially on softer sediments and depositional plains. To the east are narrow coastal plains, dunes and cliffs. The principal rivers in the region are the Hawkesbury, Nepean, Parramatta, Georges and Shoalhaven.

The predominant rock type is Triassic sandstone which is horizontally bedded without significant folding. In places, shales overlie part of the Triassic sandstone giving rise to gentle slopes with low ridges and plains. Permian sandstone occurs in the south. There are also small areas of Tertiary volcanics forming caps, sills and dykes. Weathering of the sandstone has produced podzolic soils and dunes of low nutrient status. In contrast, volcanics and shales have given rise to richer soils, particularly where weathered material has enriched alluvial soils in river valleys. Small areas of laterite also occur.

The climate is warm temperate, the hottest months being January and February, and the coldest months June and July. Variations in precipitation and temperatures occur as a result of topographic variations and distance from the coast. At Point Perpendicular (Jervis Bay) at 85 m altitude, the average annual rainfall is 1365 mm and average monthly temperatures range from 13.6°C to 19°C. Frosts are not known. By contrast, at Lithgow (950 m altitude) the average annual rainfall is 911 mm and average monthly temperatures range from 6.1°C to 18.1°C. Frosts are recorded on 56 days/year and snowfalls of short duration are known (Australian Bureau of Meteorology 1989).

Vegetation

There is wide range of vegetation types due to the variety of substrates and altitudinal gradients. Floristic composition is influenced by the latitudinal climatic gradient from north to south.

Rain forest (i.e. closed forest reaching 40 m high) occurs on basalt (Pidgeon 1937) and coastal podzols (e.g. at Beecroft Peninsula) (Helman 1979), and as admixtures of mesic species in moist sclerophyll forests developed on fertile valley soils which have been enriched by nutrient leaching from elsewhere in their catchments (Beadle 1962). The principal components of rain forests include families with northern or warm temperate rain forest affinities, such as Cunoniaceae (*Callicoma*, *Ceratopetalum* and *Schizomeria*), Urticaceae (*Dendrocnide*), Moraceae (*Ficus*), Meliaceae (*Toona*), Rutaceae and Cyatheaceae. Members of Myrtaceae with mesic affinities (*Acmena*, *Backhousia*, *Syzygium* and *Tristaniopsis*) and some members of Proteaceae (*Helicia*, *Lomatia* and *Stenocarpus*) may also be present. Southern or cool temperate elements include Eucryphiaceae, Escalloniaceae, Lauraceae (*Atherosperma*, *Doryphora*) and Winteraceae (*Tasmannia*). *Livistona australis*, previously more abundant on the whole east coast, survives in gullies and on coastal flats. *Archontophoenix cunninghamiana*, the only other species of palm in the Sydney Sandstone Region, occurs in the north, where many tropical species reach their southernmost limit.

Wet sclerophyll forest (i.e. tall open forest reaching 60 m high) occurs in high rainfall areas on lithosols and moderately deep soils of lower fertility, and also in valley bottoms. *Eucalyptus* spp. (such as *E. cypellocarpa*, *E. deanei*, *E. fastigata*, *E. oreades*, *E. pilularis* and *E. saligna*) dominate along with admixtures of rain forest species. *Syncarpia* spp. sometimes dominate or co-dominate. Species of *Acacia* and *Casuarina* are widespread elements of the understorey, which also includes ferns and cycads.

Dry sclerophyll forest and woodland (i.e. low open forest and woodland reaching 15 m high) occurs on shallow soils, bare rock and in exposed situations and contains the most diverse communities of any formation in the region. *Eucalyptus* spp. (such as *E. agglomerata*, *E. crebra*, *E. globoidea*, *E. gummifera*, *E. piperita* and *E. rossii*) dominate most communities, but *Angophora* and *Banksia* spp. may dominate in places. The understorey is usually a very diverse assemblage of sclerophyll species, often heath-like. Woodland with a grassy understorey occurs on clay soils. *Eucalyptus molluccana* and *E. tereticornis* occur on heavier soils, particularly in relict vegetation on the Cumberland Plain. *Themeda australis* and *Aristida* spp. form a grassy understorey or patches of grassland where woodland has been cleared. The shrub *Bursaria spinosa* may also be common.

Heath, or shrubland reaching 2.5 m high, is widespread on thin soils on sandstone and on deeper sandy soils where seasonal dryness or exposure to wind reduced tree dominance. Heath is particularly species-rich. Characteristic dominant genera include *Banksia*, *Casuarina*, *Hakea*, *Leptospermum* and *Xanthorrhoea* as dominants; Cyperaceae and Restionaceae occur in more open areas. Variations in the structure and floristic composition of heath result from differing soil moisture conditions and fire regimes. Grassland (to 0.75 m) is widespread, being mostly of secondary origin and often improved or replaced by exotic pasture.

Rain forest vine thicket, thicket, low woodland, tall shrubland, grassland, saltmarsh and mangroves occur along the coast.

Sandstone rock surfaces allow the development of cryptogamic communities (mosses and liverworts) where moisture conditions are favourable. Ferns and some orchids also favour such habitats.

River floodplains were among the earliest cleared lands after European settlement. Native vegetation on fertile soils has been cleared for cropland, cattle and sheep grazing, and for market gardens.

Vegetation maps at many scales cover parts of the region (Thomas and Dlugaj 1990); vegetation mapping continues under the auspices of the National Herbarium of New South Wales. Vegetation maps and descriptions for the southern part of the region include those of Hurrel (1971) and Helman (1979) for the Beecroft Peninsula, and that of Ingwersen (1976) for the Bherwerre Peninsula.

Flora

The flora of the Sydney Sandstone Region includes about 2200 native vascular plant species. There are an estimated 2000 angiosperm species, 7 gymnosperm species and 112 fern species, representing approximately 166 families and 890 genera (Beadle, Carolin and Evans 1986). Of the gymnosperms,

CPD Site Au8: Sydney Sandstone Region, showing eucalypt low forest along the Georges River.
Photo: Frank Ingwersen.

Microstrobus fitzgeraldii, a rare endemic, is present, along with three species of *Callitris* and two of *Podocarpus*. Thus, 36% of Australia's gymnosperm genera occur in the region. Endemic vascular plant species with a range of less than 100 km are estimated to number around 50; a further 23 species are near-endemics whose distribution extends beyond the limits of the region. Bryophytes number around 308 species, of which 5 are endemic (Ramsay 1984a, b). Lichens are less well known (Archer 1980); however, Stevens (1979) investigated lichens occurring in mangrove communities.

Climatic and edaphic variations allow a mixing of northern rain forest and cooler southern sclerophyll elements in the flora. However, the main area of conjunction between these floras occurs further north (Baur 1951; Howard 1981). Many subspecific taxa occur in the region, representing ecotypes of widespread species occupying separate altitudinal zones.

Rare or threatened species number around 150 (Briggs and Leigh 1988). More than 7 species are probably extinct.

Checklists are available for many areas within the Sydney Sandstone region (see Bryant and Benson 1981; Keith 1988).

Useful plants

Timber trees have been utilized on a large scale since European settlement. The species harvested have changed as resources were exhausted or as society's needs altered. *Toona australis* (Australian red cedar) was cut from rain forests for cabinet making. Sclerophyll forests provided *Eucalyptus paniculata* (grey iron bark) for railway sleepers, while *Syncarpia glomulifera* (turpentine) was selectively cut from wetter coastal lowland forests for wharf timbers. *Casuarina* spp. were among other timbers cut for various minor uses, such as fencing, roof shingles and firewood. Props were cut from various species for coal mines in the area. Hardwoods are still cut today from sclerophyll forests managed in State Forest Reserves. Other products derived from forest species have included eucalypt oil from *Eucalyptus* spp. and grass-tree resin from *Xanthorrhoea* spp.

Ornamental species of commercial importance include *Telopea speciosissima* (waratah), *Blandfordia nobilis*, *Ceratopetalum gummiferum* and species of *Acacia, Banksia, Callistemon, Dodonaea, Grevillea* and *Hakea*.

Social and environmental values

The landscape is aesthetically and culturally very important on account of its varied and rugged nature, spectacular seasonal wildflower displays and its historical association with the origins of European settlement in Australia (including Captain James Cook's initial exploration of 1770 which brought Joseph Banks and Daniel Solander to the region and, in 1801, Robert Brown who accompanied Matthew Flinders).

The natural vegetation protects large water catchments supplying Australia's largest city, Sydney, and also Wollongong, with a total population of around 4,000,000.

Many birds are broadly confined to south-east Australia (a region which extends from the coast to the Great Dividing Range from southern Queensland, through New South Wales, to eastern Victoria); of these, 10 are restricted-range species. A few have very small ranges, for example, origma (*Origma solitaria*). Most species occur in forest, both rain forest and eucalypt forest; a few species are considered threatened.

Tourism, local recreation and scientific research benefit from the richness of the flora, and an abundant and diverse avian, reptilian and mammalian fauna depend upon it.

Threats

The main threat is clearance for urban and industrial development in the more accessible parts of the region, together with associated road building, oil and chemical pollution and accidental fires. Along the coast, mangroves are particularly threatened by clearance, drainage schemes and landfill projects. Although part of the natural ecology of the region, fire may also be a threat when its intensity, seasonality and frequency differs from the fire regime of pre-settlement times. Rain forests are particularly sensitive to fire over long periods. There is much current research into fire management.

Some 700 exotic vascular plant species have been recorded in the region. Among the most serious are *Chrysanthemoides monilifera*, which competes with native *Leptospermum laevigatum* on dunes and also invades forest, and species of *Cinnamomum, Cortaderia, Lantana, Ligustrum* and *Olea*, which have invaded the understorey of forests and woodlands locally (Benson and Howell 1990a, b).

Conservation

Royal National Park, near Sydney, was established in 1879 as Australia's first National Park. Today there are 14 major National Parks or equivalent reserves covering c. 49% of the region (Table 72).

TABLE 72. NATIONAL PARKS IN THE SYDNEY SANDSTONE REGION	
National Park or equivalent	Area (km²)
Wollemi NP	4876.5
Blue Mountains NP	2470.2
Morton NP	1623.9
Yengo NP	1398.6
Kanangra Boyd NP	682.8
Royal NP	150.7
Dharug NP	148.3
Ku-Ring-Gai Chase NP	148.0
Marramarra NP	117.6
Jervis Bay NP	41.4
Heathcote NP	22.5
Barren Grounds NR	20.2
Botany Bay	4.4
Sydney Harbour	3.9
Total	11,709.0

Sources: Mobbs (1989); Hooy and Shaughnessy (1992).

National Parks and the conservation of flora beyond their boundaries are subject to provisions of the National Parks and Wildlife Act (1974). The Forestry Act (1916) provides specifically for Flora Reserves in State Forests. The Jervis Bay National Park in the Australian Capital Territory was declared under the National Parks and Wildlife Conservation Act ACT 1975.

Some Nature Reserves have strict rules of exclusion usually covering scientifically significant areas. Public and private lands in the region are subject to soil conservation legislation which can contribute to maintaining stream bank vegetation.

Community-based programmes currently focus on maintaining public awareness and community action in tree planting and removing exotic species from native bushland.

The Royal Botanic Gardens, Sydney, Australia's largest and oldest botanic garden, founded in 1816, and The National Herbarium of New South Wales, are based within the region. The Australian National Parks and Wildlife Service manages an annex of the Australian National Botanic Gardens, Canberra.

References

Anderson, R.H. (1961). Introduction. *Contributions from the New South Wales Herbarium, Flora Series* 1–18: 1–15.

Archer, A.W. (1980). List of lichens collected in New South Wales, 1977–1980 (unpub.). In Keith, D.A. (1988). Floristic lists of New South Wales (III). *Cunninghamia* 2(1): 39–73.

Australian Bureau of Meteorology (1989). "Tabs elements". Microfiche.

Baur, G.N. (1951). Nature and distribution of rainforests in New South Wales. *Australian Journal of Botany* 5(2): 190–234.

Beadle, N.C.W. (1962). Soil phosphate and the delimitation of plant communities in eastern Australia. *Ecology* 43: 281–288.

Beadle, N.C.W., Carolin, R.C. and Evans, O.D. (1986). *Flora of the Sydney Region.* Reed, Sydney. 724 pp.

Benson, D.H. and Howell, J. (1990a). Sydney's vegetation 1788–1988: utilization, degradation and rehabilitation. *Proceedings of the Ecological Society of Australia* 16: 115–127.

Benson, D.J. and Howell, J. (1990b). *Taken for granted, the bushland of Sydney and its suburbs.* Kangaroo Press, Sydney. 160 pp.

Branagan, D.F. and Packham, G.H. (1970). *Field geology of New South Wales.* The Science Press, Sydney. 191 pp.

Briggs, J.D. and Leigh, J.H. (1988). *Rare or threatened Australian plants.* Special Publication 14. Australian National Parks and Wildlife Service, Canberra. 278 pp.

Bryant, H.J. and Benson, D.H. (1981). Recent floristic lists of New South Wales. *Cunninghamia* 1(1): 59–77.

Clark, C.M.H. (1962). *A history of Australia*, Vol. 1. Melbourne University Press. 422 pp.

Clarke, L.D. (1967). The mangrove swamp and salt marsh communities of the Sydney district. I. Vegetation, soils and climate. *Journal of Ecology* 55: 753–771.

Hayden, E.J. (1971). *Map: natural vegetation of New South Wales.* Department of Decentralization and Development, New South Wales, Central Mapping Authority, Bathurst.

Helman, C. (1979). A study of the rainforest vegetation of Beecroft Peninsula, New South Wales. Thesis, University of New England, Armidale.

Hooy, T. and Shaughnessy, G. (eds) (1992). *Terrestrial and marine protected areas in Australia (1991).* Australian National Parks and Wildlife Service, Canberra. 86 pp.

Howard, T.M. (1981). Southern closed forests. In Groves, R.H. (ed.), *Australian vegetation.* Cambridge University Press, Cambridge, U.K. 449 pp.

Hurrel, F. (1971). Vegetation of the Beecroft Peninsula. B.Sc. thesis, Australian National University, Canberra.

Ingwersen, F. (1976). *Vegetation of the Jervis Bay Territory.* Conservation Series No. 3, Australian Government Publishing Service, Canberra. 80 pp.

Ingwersen, F. (1977). Vegetation development after fire in the Jervis Bay Territory. M.Sc. thesis, Australian National University.

Jacobs, S.W.L. and Pickard, J. (1981). *Plants of New South Wales.* Government Printer, Sydney. 226 pp.

Keith, D.A. (1988). Floristic lists of New South Wales (III). *Cunninghamia* 2(1): 39–73.

Keith, D.A. and Benson, D.H. (1988). The natural vegetation of the Katoomba 1: 100 000 map sheet. *Cunninghamia* 2(1): 107–144.

Mobbs, C.J. (1989). *Nature conservation reserves in Australia (1988).* Occasional Paper No. 19. Australian National Parks and Wildlife Service, Canberra. 70 pp.

Phillips, M.E. (1947). Vegetation of the Wianamatta Shale and associated soil types. M.Sc. thesis, University of Sydney.

Pickard, J. (1972). Annotated bibliography of floristic lists of New South Wales. *Contributions from the New South Wales National Herbarium* 4(5): 291–317.

Pidgeon, I.M. (1937). The ecology of the central coast area of New South Wales. I. The environment and general features of the vegetation. *Proc. Linn. Soc. New South Wales* 62: 315–340.

Pidgeon, I.M. (1938). The ecology of the central coastal area of New South Wales. II. Plant succession on the Hawkesbury Sandstone. *Proc. Linn. Soc. New South Wales* 63: 1–26.

Pidgeon, I.M. (1941a). The ecology of the central coastal area of New South Wales. III. Types of primary succession. *Proc. Linn. Soc. New South Wales* 65: 221–249.

Pidgeon, I.M. (1941b). The ecology of the central coastal area of New South Wales. IV. Forest types on soils from Hawkesbury Sandstone and Wianamatta Shale. *Proc. Linn. Soc. New South Wales* 66: 113–137.

Ramsay, H.P. (1984a). Census of New South Wales mosses. *Telopea* 2(5): 455–534.

Ramsay, H.P. (1984b). Phytogeography of the mosses of New South Wales. *Telopea* 2(5): 535–548.

Stevens, G.N. (1979). Distribution and related ecology of macrolichens on mangroves on the eastern Australian coast. *Lichenologist* 11: 293–305.

Thomas, J. and Dlugaj, H.H. (1990). Index to vegetation maps and related surveys of New South Wales and the Australian Capital Territory. *Cunninghamia* 2(2): 183–196.

Acknowledgements

This Data Sheet was written by Mr F. Ingwersen (A.C.T. Parks and Conservation Service, Tuggeranong, Australia). The author thanks Mr Doug Benson (Royal Botanic Gardens, Sydney) and Mr Bob Makinson Australian National Botanic Gardens).

WESTERN TASMANIAN WILDERNESS
Tasmania, Australia

Location: Includes the Tasmanian Wilderness World Heritage Site, located in south-western and central Tasmania, between latitudes 41°35'–43°40'S and longitudes 145°25'–146°55'E, and the north-western forests and moorlands located between latitudes 41°10'–41°45'S and longitudes 144°35'–145°40'E.

Area: c. 14,050 km², of which the Tasmanian Wilderness World Heritage Site covers 13,800 km² and the north-western forests cover c. 250 km².

Altitude: 0–1617 m.

Vegetation: Cool temperate rain forest, alpine vegetation, subalpine scrub, eucalypt woodlands and forests, wet eucalypt forests, buttongrass moorlands, myrtaceous scrub, grasslands, coastal vegetation.

Flora: Estimated 800 vascular plant species; many endemic genera and species in the alpine flora. The rain forest, alpine heath and buttongrass moorland are strongholds of Gondwanan species and genera.

Useful plants: Timber trees, ornamental plants, honey production from *Eucryphia lucida*.

Other values: Important archaeological and geological sites, wilderness and high landscape values, recreation and tourism.

Threats: Inappropriate fire frequency, increasing tourist pressure, plant diseases.

Conservation: The Tasmanian Wilderness World Heritage Site covers 13,800 km² (98% of the area under consideration). Parts of the north-western forests (excluded from the World Heritage Site) are proposed as Recommended Areas for Protection. Most of the World Heritage Site has National Park status and the portion of the area covered by the Southwest National Park is a Biosphere Reserve.

Geography

The area under consideration includes the Tasmanian Wilderness World Heritage Site, comprising 13,800 km² of almost uninhabited mountainous wilderness in south-west and central Tasmania between latitudes 41°35'–43°40'S and longitudes 145°25'–146°55'E, and the north-western forests and moorlands between latitudes 41°10'–41°45'S and longitudes 144°35'–145°40'E.

The eastern and north-eastern parts of the Tasmanian Wilderness World Heritage Site comprise infertile Permian and Triassic sediments and dolerite rocks which weather to give fertile soils. The south-western region is dominated by infertile, metamorphosed, pre-Carboniferous sediments (Burett and Martin 1989). A number of recent glaciations in Tasmania occurred during the Pleistocene, producing widespread glacial, erosional and depositional features (Kiernan 1985). Thousands of lakes and tarns occur, especially on the Central Plateau. Post-glacial sea-level rise flooded the lower valleys of rivers, producing a very convoluted coastline. Periglacial processes continue on higher mountain ranges resulting in distinctive landforms.

The wide variety of soil types (Pemberton 1986a, b) ranges from deep yellow-brown gradational profiles (typical of areas covered by forest) to shallow gravelly soils on exposed mountain ridges. Peat occurs in areas of high rainfall, low evaporation and relatively high humidity. Bogs have formed under oligotrophic and ombrotrophic conditions.

Western Tasmania is the coolest and wettest region on the Australian continent, having relatively mild winters and cool summers compared with other regions at similar latitude. The area lies within the path of westerly winds (Bosworth 1977) and has a temperate, maritime climate influenced by local topography. which creates some continental effects. Some sites receive up to 3600 mm annual rainfall. Snow, hail, fog and frost are frequent over much of the area, although there is no permanent snow-line in Tasmania.

Vegetation

The region is a stronghold of Australia's cool temperate rain forest and alpine flora. Other vegetation types in the region include subalpine vegetation, eucalypt forest, buttongrass (*Gymnoschoenus sphaerocephalus*) moorlands, blackwood (*Acacia melanoxylon*) swamps and myrtaceous scrub. The largest unbroken extent of cool temperate rain forest remaining in Australia is in the north-western area (outside of the Tasmanian Wilderness World Heritage Site).

Rain forest covers less than 25% of the Tasmanian Wilderness World Heritage Site, occurring in sites where fires are infrequent. Rain forest is more extensive in the north-west. Dominance by small-leaved Gondwanan tree species is a characteristic of Tasmanian rain forests (Hill 1990). The main dominants are species of *Nothofagus*, *Eucryphia*, *Atherosperma, Athrotaxis, Lagarostrobos* and *Diselma* (Jarman, Brown and Kantvilas 1984). *Nothofagus cunninghamii* and *Atherosperma moschatum* are the two most common dominants, but sites which have remained totally free of fire can be dominated by *Athrotaxis selaginoides, Lagarostrobos franklinii* and *Diselma archeri*. Although the forests have relatively low species diversity among vascular plants, the degree of endemism is high. There is a very rich cryptogamic flora. Nearly half of Tasmania's c. 600 species of lichens occur in rain forest, mostly as epiphytes (Kantvilas 1990). The Tasmanian temperate rain forest differs from tropical and subtropical rain forests in the low number of vascular plant species, the rarity of climbers, the lack of vascular epiphytes and the absence of typical rain forest morphological adaptations. There are some similarities with the temperate rain forests of New Zealand and South America.

Sclerophyll forests of the region include mixed forests (eucalypt forests with rain forest species in the understorey), wet eucalypt forests, dry eucalypt forests, swamp (*Acacia melanoxylon*) forests and tea tree (*Leptospermum scoparium*) forests. Large contiguous areas of *Eucalyptus obliqua* tall forest occur within the area (Askey-Doran, in press).

Much of the region is covered by moorland vegetation (Jarman, Brown and Kantvilas 1988) dominated by

Gymnoschoenus sphaerocephalus (buttongrass), often in association with other sedges, rushes, tea trees, paperbarks and heaths. There are also substantial areas of scrub and heath communities, dominated by *Leptospermum* spp. and *Melaleuca* spp. *Gahnia grandis* (cutting grass) and *Bauera rubioides* (bauera) are common components of scrub vegetation. Scrub communities have apparently increased in some areas at the expense of more fire-sensitive communities, such as rain forest.

Alpine vegetation occurs above the tree-line (which occurs at 800 m near the coast, but rises to 1400 m inland), corresponding to the altitude at which the mean summer temperature is 10°C (Kirkpatrick 1982). The vegetation comprises: deciduous heath dominated by *Nothofagus gunnii*; coniferous heath, dominated by *Podocarpus lawrencei*, *Microstrobos niphophilus*, *Microcachrys tetragona* and *Diselma archeri*; bolster heath, dominated by cushion plant species; alpine heath, comprising

MAP 20. WESTERN TASMANIAN WILDERNESS (CPD SITE Au9), TASMANIA

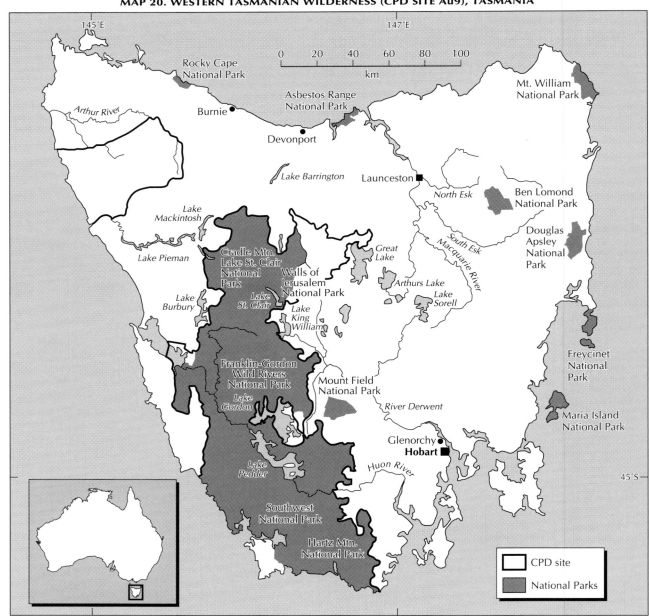

CPD Site Au9: Western Tasmanian Wilderness, showing rain forest on the Lower Gordon River. Photo: Stephen Harris.

shrub-dominated vegetation; fjaeldmark, dominated by prostrate shrubs; bogs, dominated by sphagnum moss (Whinam 1990); alpine herbfields and tussock grasslands. The alpine zone in the region is the most important habitat for the endemic Tasmanian vascular flora (Kirkpatrick and Brown 1984); about half of the 300 endemic plant species are found in this zone. Nearly 60% of the species in the alpine flora are endemic to Tasmania (Balmer and Whinam 1991).

Flora

The total vascular flora in the region under consideration is probably about 800 species, of which over 700 species occur within the World Heritage Site (Kirkpatrick *et al.* 1991). The World Heritage Site also contains approximately 240 (or two-thirds) of Tasmania's endemic higher plant taxa, of which about half have the large parts of their areas of distribution within the World Heritage Site. Of the 20 Tasmanian endemic genera, only two are not represented within the World Heritage Site, while all the species in genera with a Gondwanan distribution are present. The World Heritage Site contains populations of approximately 50 rare or threatened plant species.

Tasmania is thought to have retained an environment similar to that which prevailed in Gondwana prior to its fragmentation (Nelson 1981). The flora contains many Gondwanan genera, such as *Caltha*, *Coprosma*, *Gunnera*, *Lomatia*, *Nothofagus* and *Orites*. Cool temperate rain forest, buttongrass and alpine moorland are especially rich in plant groups with Gondwanan affinities

(Barlow 1981). Tasmania is the only remaining region in the Southern Hemisphere to have representatives of the family Taxodiaceae. *Lagarostrobos franklinii* was widespread across Australia in Gondwanan times but is now found only in western Tasmania. Other notable taxa descended from the Gondwanan flora include members of the families Cunoniaceae, Escalloniaceae and Winteraceae, together with three ancient and monotypic genera of Proteaceae – *Agastachys*, *Bellendena* and *Cenarrhenes*.

Useful plants

There are many tree species which yield excellent sawn timber for a number of purposes, although the timber industry is now sustained by forests outside the World Heritage Site. *Eucalyptus regnans* (mountain ash) and *Eucalyptus obliqua* (stringybark), and the native conifers *Lagarostrobos franklinii* (Huon pine) and *Athrotaxis selaginoides* (King Billy pine), are especially valuable.

Eucryphia lucida (leatherwood) is a nectar source for a distinctive and prized honey. Leatherwood honey is an important part of the Tasmanian apiary industry.

Some of the plants in the region, such as the endemic *Anopterus glandulosus* (native laurel) and the endemic *Telopea truncata* (waratah), have been brought into cultivation as ornamentals. There are many other plants of potential horticultural importance.

Phytochemical screening for anti-tumour properties and presence of alkaloids has been carried out on a small proportion of the flora.

Social and environmental values

Fifteen bird species are confined to Tasmania. Most of these are forest-dwelling species which are found throughout the island. One notable exception is the threatened orange-bellied parrot (*Neophema chrysogaster*) which breeds only in the south-west, where it is protected by the Tasmanian Wilderness World Heritage Site.

Much of the region is uninhabited wilderness. Access is difficult – consequently most of the area is only accessible to bushwalkers and mountaineers. The World Heritage Site is bisected by one major highway and intruded by a small number of other roads. However, tourism is mostly confined to specific corridors and nodes, such as Strathgordon, Lake St Clair, Cradle Mountain and Lower Gordon River. There are several special interpretation and visitor centres.

The World Heritage Site provides a strong inspirational source for photographic and other art, books and films. The region has important archaeological sites, and includes some of the oldest dated works of art in the world (Harris, Ranson and Brown 1988; Loy *et al.* 1990). The north-west area is now sometimes referred to as the Tarkine Wilderness Area.

There are numerous biological and geological features of interest in the region, including meromictic lakes, caves and glacial tarns, which are a focus of scientific study.

Economic assessment

The most significant economic asset of the region is its scenery. A large number of tourists visit the region for wilderness experiences, such as bushwalking, rafting and mountaineering, as well as for scenic cruises on the Gordon River, scenic flights, bus tours and fishing. Johnson (1987) calculated that tourism in the state's National Parks and equivalent reserves contributed A$61 million to the economy (representing 1.25% of Tasmanian Gross State Product). A significant portion of this figure is generated by the World Heritage Site. The value of the water catchments on the Central Plateau which feed hydroelectric dams outside the World Heritage Site has not been directly costed but must be very significant.

Threats

The most serious threat to the flora and vegetation of the region is fire. In the case of communities containing *Athrotaxis* spp., *Lagarostrobos franklinii* and *Nothofagus gunnii*, any fire event is likely to cause local extinction of these species. There has been a 32% loss of *Athrotaxis selaginoides* (King Billy pine) forest over the last 100 years (Brown 1988). Alpine vegetation is also highly susceptible to destruction by fire. Inappropriate fire frequency can eliminate rain forest, causing a shift to mixed forest, eucalypt forest, myrtaceous scrub and buttongrass or heath depending on the frequency of burning. The area of rain forests has decreased to the advantage of the latter vegetation types.

Phytophthora cinnamomi, a root-rotting fungus, attacks a wide range of native plant species. The main limiting factor for the fungus in the region is temperature. At soil temperatures below 15°C sporangial production is limited. As a result, the fungus occurs up to about 900 m altitude (Podger and Brown 1989). The fungus can be distributed in infected soil on the boots of walkers or even in fragments of soil clinging to animals. The fungus occurs near roads, tracks and settlements. Myrtle wilt is a native disease of *Nothofagus cunninghamii* caused by the infection of trees by the pathogenic fungus *Chalara australis* (Packham, Elliott and Brown 1990). The disease is more virulent in trees near disturbed areas.

A total of 135 exotic plant species has been recorded in the World Heritage Site (Ziegeler 1990), but few of these pose any real threat to the native vegetation. A programme to eliminate the exotic *Cortaderia richardii* is underway in some areas along the Lyell Highway.

Plans in the 1970s to construct large dams for hydroelectricity production have now been abandoned. However, the north-west region is threatened by logging, mining exploration, fires and off-road vehicle recreation.

There are 7 threatened vascular plant species in the Western Tasmanian Wilderness: *Crassula moschata*, *Centrolepis pedderensis* and *Helipterum albicans* are listed as Endangered at a national or state level (Briggs and Leigh 1988; Kirkpatrick *et al.* 1991); *Lomatia tasmanica*, *Milligania longifolia*, *M. johnstonii* and *Oreomyrrhis gunnii* are listed as Vulnerable. There are many more rare species which appear to have highly specialized habitats. These are not regarded as threatened but could become so if there are substantial changes in fire patterns or climate.

Conservation

The Tasmanian Wilderness World Heritage Site (13,800 km²) is one of nine Australian sites inscribed on the World Heritage List and is subject to the World Heritage Properties Conservation Act 1983 in Australia which empowers the Commonwealth to pass regulations to prevent activities that threaten World Heritage values. The Commonwealth and State Governments have recognized the importance of the World Heritage Area and have allocated many resources for the preparation of a comprehensive management plan for the region. 4032 km² of the Southwest National Park (of area 6052 km²) has been proclaimed a Biosphere Reserve under the Unesco Man and Biosphere Programme.

Under Tasmanian Legislature, several categories of land tenure apply within the World Heritage Area, the vast majority being proclaimed as State Reserve under the National Parks and Wildlife Act 1970. This status provides the highest level of protection under the Act, being exempt from the exercise of statutory powers under other State Acts and requiring both Houses of Parliament to agree to revocations and the exercise of other statutory powers not in accord with the Act. Other categories of land tenure within the World Heritage Area reserved under the National Parks and Wildlife Act 1970 are Game Reserves and Conservation Areas. The total area reserved under the Act is 13,792 km². Additionally, there are 3 Forest Reserves totalling 34 km² which are reserved under the Forestry Act 1920. Freehold land comprises about 3.3 km².

The north-west area is predominantly unallocated Crown Land, Protected Area (a category of Crown Land to which some controlling regulations apply) and State Forest. Within the area are 11 Recommended Areas for Protection which have been proposed by the Working Group for Forest Conservation. The largest of these has an area of 353 km². Although these Recommended Areas for Protection have not yet been formally proclaimed as reserves, there has been agreement that no logging is to occur within them.

References

Askey-Doran, M. (in press). Botanical values – far north west Tasmania. Report to Australian Heritage Commission.

Balmer, J. and Whinam, J. (1991). Vegetation within the World Heritage Area. *Tasforests* 3.

Barlow, B.A. (1981). The Australian flora: its origins and evolution. In Bureau of Flora and Fauna, *Flora of Australia Vol. 1: Introduction.* Australian Government Publishing Service, Canberra. 200 pp.

Bosworth, P.K. (1977). *A collation of meteorological information for south-west Tasmania.* Occasional Paper No. 2. National Parks and Wildlife Service, South West Tasmania Resources Survey.

Briggs, J.D. and Leigh, J.H. (1988). *Rare or threatened Australian plants.* Special Publication 14. Australian National Parks and Wildlife Service, Canberra. 278 pp.

Brown, M.J. (1988). *Distribution and conservation of King Billy pine.* Tasmanian Forestry Commission, Hobart.

Burett, C.F. and Martin E.L. (eds) (1989). *Geology and mineral resources of Tasmania.* Special Publication. Geological Society of Australia.

Department of Parks, Wildlife and Heritage, Tasmania (1991). Western Tasmanian Wilderness, World Heritage Area resources and issues. Unpublished draft. Hobart.

Harris, S., Ranson, D. and Brown, S. (1988). Maxwell River archaeological survey 1986. *Australian Archaeology* 14: 89–97.

Hill, R.S. (1990). Sixty million years of change in Tasmania's climate and vegetation. *Tasforests* 2(2): 89–98.

Jackson, W.D. (1968). Fire, air, water and earth: an elemental ecology of Tasmania. *Proc. Ecol. Soc. Australia* 3: 9–16.

Jarman, S.J., Brown, M.J. and Kantvilas, G. (1984). *Rainforest in Tasmania.* National Parks and Wildlife Service.

Jarman, S.J., Brown, M.J. and Kantvilas, G. (1988). *Buttongrass moorland in Tasmania.* Research Report No. 2. Tasmanian Forest Research Council Inc., Hobart.

Johnson, L.E. (1987). *The contribution of the National Parks and Wildlife Service to the Tasmanian economy in 1986–87.* Centre for Regional Economic Analysis, University of Tasmania.

Kantvilas, G. (1990). Succession in rainforest lichens. *Tasforests* 2(2): 167–171.

Kiernan, K. (1985). Late Cainozoic glaciation and mountain geomorphology in the Central Highlands of Tasmania. Unpublished Ph.D. thesis, University of Tasmania.

Kirkpatrick, J.B. (1982). Phytogeographical analysis of Tasmanian alpine floras. *Journal of Biogeography* 9: 255–271.

Kirkpatrick, J.B. (1983). Treeless plant communities of the Tasmanian high country. *Proc. Ecol. Soc. Australia* 12: 61–77.

Kirkpatrick, E.C. and Brown, M.J. (1984). A numerical analysis of Tasmanian higher plant endemism. *Bot. J. Linn. Soc.* 88: 165–183.

Kirkpatrick, J.B., Gilfedder, L., Hickie, J. and Harris, S. (1991). Reservation and conservation status of Tasmanian native higher plants. Wildlife Division Scientific Report No. 91/2. Department of Parks, Wildlife and Heritage, Tasmania.

Loy, T.H., Jones, R., Nelson, D.E., Meehan, B., Vogel, J., Southon, J. and Cosgrove, R. (1990). Accelerator radiocarbon dating of human blood proteins in pigments from late Pleistocene art sites in Australia. *Antiquity* 64: 110–116.

Nelson, E.C. (1981). Phytogeography of southern Australia. In Keast, A. (ed.), *Ecological biogeography of Australia.* Junk, The Hague.

Packham, J., Elliott, H. and Brown, M.J. (1990). Myrtle wilt. In Hickey, J.E., Brown, M.J., Rounsevell, D.E. and Jarman, S.J. (eds), *Tasmanian rainforest research.* Tasmanian NRCP Report No. 1.

Pemberton, M. (1986a). *Land systems of Tasmania – Region 5, Central Plateau.* Department of Agriculture, Tasmania.

Pemberton, M. (1986b). *Land systems of Tasmania – Region 7, South West.* Department of Primary Industry, Tasmania.

Podger, F.D. and Brown, M.J. (1989). Vegetation damage caused by *Phytophthora cinnamomi* on disturbed sites in temperate rainforest in western Tasmania. *Australian Journal of Botany* 37: 443–480.

Whinam, J. (1990). A study of the ecology of Tasmania Sphagnum peatlands. Unpublished Ph.D. thesis, University of Tasmania.

Ziegeler, D. (1990). *A survey of weed infestation within the Tasmanian Wilderness World Heritage Area and peripheral areas.* Department of Parks, Wildlife and Heritage, Tasmania.

Acknowledgements

This Data Sheet was prepared by Stephen Harris, Jayne Balmer and Dr Jennifer Whinam of the Tasmanian Department of Parks, Wildlife and Heritage.

WET TROPICS OF QUEENSLAND
Queensland, Australia

Location: North-east coastal region of Queensland, between latitudes 15°39'S and 19°17'S and longitudes 144°58'E and 146°27'E.

Area: The biogeographic province covers c. 11,000 km².

Altitude: 0–1622 m (summit of Mount Bartle Frere).

Vegetation: 13 major rain forest structural types, woodlands and open forests dominated by *Acacia, Eucalyptus* and *Melaleuca*, shrublands dominated by *Allocasuarina, Banksia* and *Acacia*, and tracts of mangrove forest.

Flora: >3400 vascular plant species recorded; total flora may exceed 3850. Within rain forests, a minimum of 1160 described species of vascular plants representing at least 523 genera and 119 families. 75 rain forest genera are endemic to Australia while 43 are entirely restricted to Australia's Wet Tropics. About 710 species are Australian endemics while c. 500 (43%) are restricted entirely to the Wet Tropics of Queensland. 13 of the 19 recognized primitive angiosperm families are represented in the area.

Useful plants: Timber tree provenances, ornamental plants (especially Orchidaceae, Araceae, Proteaceae, Cycadaceae and Myrtaceae), many plant taxa with considerable pharmacological and therapeutic value or potential; many species of Araucariaceae, Podocarpaceae, Myrtaceae and Sapindaceae are edible.

Other values: Watershed protection for water supply and hydroelectricity generation, scenic attraction, tourism, jungle defence training, restricted fauna habitat, important endemic vertebrate populations, evolutionary significance of biota, scientific values.

Threats: Clearance of lowland forests for agriculture and residential development, drainage schemes, visitor pressure at some sites, installation of telecommunication facilities in fragile summit habitats, stock grazing in certain areas, feral animals, some invasive exotic plants, mining, plant collecting, localized illegal logging, potential hydroelectricity schemes.

Conservation: World Heritage Site covers 8990 km² (c. 82%) of the biogeographic province with 2073 km² in c. 50 separate National Parks. 9919 km² is Crown Land (publically owned land) under a variety of land tenures, including State Forest/Timber Reserve, National Parks and special purpose, grazing and mining leasehold. The mix of different tenures is a challenge to World Heritage Area management. Legislation is urgently required to enable consistent management policies to apply to all types of tenure within the World Heritage Site.

Geography

The Wet Tropics biogeographical province occupies the north-east coastal region of Queensland, between latitudes 15°39'S and 19°17'S and longitudes 144°58'E and 146°27'E. The major rain forests lie astride three major geomorphic units:

❖ the uplands/tablelands of the Great Dividing Range
❖ the Great Eastern Escarpment
❖ the lowland coastal plain belt.

The tablelands consist of undulating country at an altitude of around 900 m, with rounded summits rising to more than 1200 m. The highest peak is Mt Bartle Frere (1622 m). To the east of the tablelands is the Eastern Escarpment, typified by rugged topography, rapid geomorphic processes and great environmental diversity. Below the escarpment are the coastal lowlands, comprising an alluvial plain of variable width interrupted by ridges of the Great Divide and several large rivers, such as the Herbert, North and South Johnstone, Tully, Russell-Mulgrave, Barron, Daintree and Bloomfield, which originate from the tablelands.

The main rocks of the region are slates and greywackes derived from marine sediments deposited during the Silurian,

Devonian and Carboniferous periods. Volcanics and granites occur at the southern margin of the Hodgkinson Basin. Much of the granite was probably exposed by the end of the Palaeozoic or beginning of the Mesozoic. The tablelands were uplifted between the Jurassic and Tertiary periods. Climatic change and geomorphic processes during the Quaternary led to sea-level changes until approximately 4500 years ago when present day sea-levels were attained.

The volcanics of the tablelands and adjacent basaltic/rhyolitic provinces, which formed from around 12 million years BP, are characterized by scoria cones, lava cones and maars. The tablelands and some portions of the coast were subject to basalt flows throughout the Pliocene-Pleistocene. Soils derived from basalt are nutrient-rich and may have helped the rain forest flora resist environmental stresses during periods of fluctuating climatic conditions associated with Pleistocene glacial cycles.

The mean annual rainfall ranges from about 1200 mm to over 8000 mm, and as much as 10,472 mm over an eight month period (during January to August 1979) on Mt Bellenden Ker (at an altitude of 1561 m). The same location has received 1140 mm of rain in a 24-hour period (Tracey 1982). Rainfall intensities at this station are among the highest recorded in the world. Rainfall in the region is distinctly seasonal, with over 60% falling in the summer months of December to March.

Intense tropical cyclones occur at an average rate of one severe cyclone every three years. This is the highest recorded incidence of tropical cyclones in the world, and is a major factor shaping the structural and floristic differentiation of the vegetation – particularly with respect to the mosaics of the coastal lowlands. Mean daily temperatures in the coastal belt range from a January maximum of 31°C to a minimum of 23°C. The uplands/tablelands are cooler with mean daily temperatures ranging from 28°C to 17°C in January and from 22°C to 9°C in winter.

Vegetation

The major vegetation formation represented in the region is closed canopy mesic forest (rain forest). Variations throughout the region in the amount of rainfall, soil type, drainage and altitude, together with a complex evolutionary history, have resulted in a wide variety of different rain forest communities which are floristically and structurally the most diverse of any in Australia. The region's rain forests have been classified into 13 major structural types (Tracey 1982) as follows:

❖ complex mesophyll vine forest (types 1a, 1b, 1c)
❖ mesophyll vine forest (types 2a, 2b)
❖ mesophyll vine forest with dominant palms (types 3a, 3b)
❖ semi-deciduous mesophyll vine forest (type 4)
❖ complex notophyll vine forest (types 5a, 5b)
❖ complex notophyll vine forest with emergent *Agathis robusta* (type 6)
❖ notophyll vine forest – rarely without *Acacia* spp. (types 7a, 7b)
❖ simple notophyll vine forest – often with *Agathis microstachya* (type 8)
❖ simple microphyll vine-fern forest – often with *A. atropurpurea* (type 9)
❖ simple microphyll vine-fern thicket (type 10)
❖ deciduous microphyll vine thicket (type 11)
❖ closed forest with wattle (*Acacia* spp.) emergents/co-dominants (types 12a, 12b, 12c, 12d)
❖ closed forest with sclerophyll (particularly *Eucalyptus* spp. and some wattles) emergents and co-dominants (types 13a, 13b, 13c, 13d, 13e, 13f).

Rain forests attain their peak development as complex mesophyll vine forests on the very wet and wet lowlands and foothills where parent materials range from basalts, basic volcanics, mixed colluvia and riverine alluvia. These communities have an uneven canopy, 20–40 m high, and are structurally complex with many emergents having large spreading crowns. These forests are the most complex of any terrestrial vegetation type on the continent. Plank buttressing is common, robust woody lianes, vascular epiphytes and palms are typical, and fleshy herbs with wide leaves (e.g. gingers and aroids) are prominent (Tracey 1982). Forests on exposed sites, such as foothill ridges and seaward-facing slopes, often exhibit cyclone-disturbed or broken canopies with "climber towers" and dense vine tangles. These are locally known as "cyclone scrubs" (Webb 1958). Palms may be locally abundant in areas of impeded drainage; gingers and aroids are particularly plentiful in gullies and along creek banks which are permanently saturated with water (Tracey 1982).

Notophyll vine forest includes a diverse group of communities (types 5, 6, 7 and 8 of Tracey 1982). These occur on small areas of basic volcanic parent materials on cool wet uplands and highlands (type 5a) and on a range of drier sites at various elevations (type 5b), the western and northern fringes of the main rain forest massif from Cardwell extending to Julatten, the Hann Tableland and to the north of Bloomfield (type 6), on sandy beach ridges in drier coastal zones and on exposed sites backed by the foothills north of Cairns (type 7), and, as one of the most extensive, an even-canopy mountain forest assemblage (type 8) on granitic ranges rising from 400–1000 m altitude between Ingham and Cooktown. These communities, while extraordinarily variable, are characterized by a canopy range of 12–45 m in height, and the occurrence of rattans, strangler figs and conspicuous epiphytes, ferns, walking stick palms (*Linospadix* spp.) and fleshy herbs. On the summits and upper slopes of the higher peaks, which are frequently enshrouded by cloud and often exposed to strong winds, simple microphyll fern forests (wet montane forests) or thickets dominate. These are rich in mosses and are sometimes referred to as "cloud" or "elfin" forests.

Many sites which experience significant water stress during the dry season support closed forest/thicket communities characterized by the occurrence of taxa which are semi-deciduous to deciduous. Semi-deciduous mesophyll vine forest (type 4) is restricted to minor occurrences to the north-west of the Whitfield Range, Cairns, and to the foothills between the Bloomfield River and Cooktown (Tracey 1982). The canopy is comparatively even, reaching a height of 25–32 m, with deciduous emergents reaching 36 m. Figs, including both cluster (cauliflorous) and strangler types, and lianes (rather than rattans) are relatively conspicuous, but epiphytes are less common. There are sporadic occurrences of deciduous microphyll vine thicket (type 11) on fire-free rocky sites and exposed headlands between Ingham and Cooktown. Constituents are mainly multi-stemmed and fully deciduous. The canopy is generally uneven and around 3–5 m tall with emergents rising to 10 m. Scramblers and shrubs, usually with thorns, are common, and epiphytic and lithophytic ferns and more xerophytic orchids occur low in the canopy. Vine forest with sclerophyll emergents (types 12, 13) are also encountered. These represent different stages of post-disturbance succession following, for example, fire, logging or cyclones, and vary considerably in floristic composition. Each sub-type is characterized by the dominance/co-dominance of certain sclerophyll species (eucalypts and wattles).

About one-third of the property listed as the Wet Tropics of Queensland World Heritage Area comprises non-rain forest communities. These include tall open forest (wet sclerophyll communities – types 14a, 14b – typified by the occurrence of *Eucalyptus grandis* and *E. resinifera* respectively, and a mesic understorey), medium open sclerophyll forest and woodland (types 14c, 14d, 15, 16, 17, 18, 19) dominated by a variety of eucalypts together with *Lophostemon suaveolens* and *Melaleuca quinquenervia*, heathy shrublands characterized by *Allocasuarina*, *Banksia* and *Acacia* on mountain rock pavements (type 21) and various species of wattle and *Melaleuca* spp., and swamp communities. Stunted paperbark (*M. viridiflora*) low forest/woodland (type 20) occurs on acid soils with impeded drainage adjacent to mangroves (type 22a) which, with around 31 species (Le Cussan pers. comm.), are amongst the richest in the world.

Salt-marshes, almost exclusively dominated by chenopods (type 22b), are also a feature of the coastal mosaics.

Flora

The Wet Tropics is the most floristically rich (at family and generic levels) of Australia's biogeographic provinces. A survey of plant records registered with the Queensland Herbarium (Guymer and McDonald pers. comm.) indicates that the region's total vascular flora exceeds 3400 species, and possibly exceeds 3850. At least 1160 species of vascular plant, representing 523 genera of 119 families are recorded from the region's rain forests; 75 of these genera are Australian endemics, with 43 of these entirely restricted to this region. Some 710 species are endemic to Australia, with 500 (or 43% of the total regional species complement) endemic to wet tropical closed forests. Thirteen of the 19 angiosperm families recognized to be primitive are represented in the Wet Tropics. These include Annonaceae, Austrobaileyaceae, Eupomatiaceae, Himantandraceae, Myristicaceae and Winteraceae (from the order Magnoliales) and Atherospermataceae, Gyrocarpaceae, Hernandiaceae, Idiospermaceae, Lauraceae, Monimiaceae and Trimeniaceae (of the Laurales). Of these, Austrobaileyaceae and Idiospermaceae are monotypic endemic families.

Some "primitive" taxa are very well-represented. For example, the Wet Tropics contains 38 of the world's 100 species of *Endiandra*. There are also many monotypic and oligotypic taxa at the generic level restricted to this region. This may be interpreted as indicative of the outcome of an enormous sifting process as climatic factors changed during continental drift. The level of endemicity in the Australian Wet Tropics is second only to New Caledonia in the number of endemic genera per unit area (Webb and Tracey 1981).

Many Gondwanic families are very well-represented in the Wet Tropics. For example, among the Proteaceae, 13 of the world's 76 genera occur in the Wet Tropics province and 40 species are endemic to it. Several of these are highly restricted, e.g. *Sphalmium racemosum* and *Stenocarpus davallioides* of the upland forest "islands", and/or are highly disjunct, e.g. *Athertonia diversifolia* and *Austromuellera trinervia* of complex notophyll vine forest on basalt. Other families which are well-represented in the flora of the region include Lauraceae, Cunoniaceae, Sapindaceae, Sterculiaceae, Rutaceae and Anacardiaceae.

Microphyll vine-fern forests of summit zones exhibit very high regional species endemism. Examples of species narrowly restricted to this habitat type are *Aceratium ferrugineum*, *Acronychia chooreechillum*, *Cinnamomum propinquum*, *Dracophyllum sayeri*, *Elaeocarpus thelmae*, *Flindersia oppositifolia*, *Hexaspora pubescens*, *Orites fragrans*, *Polyscias bellendenkerensis*, *Rhododendron lochiae*, *Uromyrtus metrosideros* and *Xanthostemon graniticus*. The flora of summit zones has affinities with that of other montane habitats at higher latitudes within Australia (i.e. the temperate rain forests of the Great Dividing Range to the south) and with those of New Zealand, Papua New Guinea and West Malesia.

Within notophyll vine forest on basalt are several narrowly restricted, disjunct species, including *Athertonia diversifolia*, *Austrobaileya scandens* and *Austromuellera trinerva*, the

CPD Site Au10: Wet Tropics of Queensland. Rain forest meets the sea at Cape Tribulation. Photo: Garry Werren.

cycads *Bowenia spectabilis* and *Lepidozamia hopei*, and club mosses of the genus *Lycopodium*. Narrowly restricted species in lowland forests include *Endiandra cooperana, Gardenia actinocarpa, Noabdendron nicholasii, Storkiella australiensis, Idiospermum australiense, Lindsayomyrtus brachyandrus, Ristantia pachysperma* and *Xanthostemon formosus* (all restricted to a very small area near Cape Tribulation). The primitive *Gymnostoma australiense*, related to casuarinas which are typical of more xeric environments elsewhere in Australia, occurs as two small populations (one at Noah Creek and the other at Roaring Meg). Similarly, taxa in the genera *Barongia, Mitrantia, Ristantia, Sphaerantia* and "*Stockwellia*", representing developmental stages in the evolution of more drought-adapted myrtaceous genera such as *Eucalyptus*, occur as refugial populations at various localities within the Wet Tropics.

Another significant aspect of the flora is the presence of archaic Australian endemic Araucariaceae (Kershaw 1980), including three species of *Agathis* – the Kauri pines – two of which are endemic to the Wet Tropics. *Araucaria bidwillii* (the Bunya pine) occurs as a disjunct in the Wet Tropics, the main population occurring in the Bunya Mountains-Gympie District, over 1200 km to the south-east.

Sclerophyll communities, dominated in the canopy layer by *Eucalyptus, Acacia* and *Melaleuca*, are found throughout Queensland's Wet Tropics on fire-prone ridges, swamps and wet acid soils in the lowlands, and in adjacent communities where moisture stress and/or fire precludes the survival of rain forest. Among the woody shrubs and trees are (for example) 21 species of *Eucalyptus*, 10 species of *Acacia*, 8 species of *Melaleuca*, 5 species of *Casuarina/Allocasuarina* and 4 species of *Banksia*. This comparative richness of sclerophyll genera suggests a long history of climate change, with attendant increases and decreases in the frequency and intensity of fires, and ongoing competition with the mesic rain forest flora around the fringes of refuge areas which have enabled rain forests to survive in this region for millenia (Webb and Tracey 1981).

Useful plants

The region contains many valuable timber species. Land within the Wet Tropics of Queensland World Heritage Area is now excluded from commercial logging by law; however, timber extraction still occurs in adjacent areas and in outlying patches of wet tropical forest. Among the species most prized for their high quality woods are *Agathis robusta* and *A. microstachya* (Kauri pines), *Flindersia brayleyana, F. bourjotiana* and *F. pimenteliana* (Queensland maples), *F. ifflaiana* (Cairns hickory), *Endiandra palmerstonii* and *Beilschmiedia bancroftii* (Queensland walnuts), *Toona ciliata* (red cedar) and many species of Proteaceae, such as *Cardwellia sublimis, Carnarvonia araliifolia, Opisthiolepis heterophylla* and *Grevillea baileyana*, collectively known as silky oaks. Species used for general purpose timbers and which continue to be harvested from areas beyond the designated conservation reserves include *Eucalyptus grandis, E. pellita, E. resinifera, E. tereticornis* and *Syncarpia glomulifera*.

Among the horticulturally important species are the proteads *Alloxylon* (syn. *Oreocallis*) *flammeum, Darlingia darlingiana, Stenocarpus sinuatus*, the spectacular flame

tree *Brachychiton acerifolium* (Sterculiaceae) and myrtles, such as *Syzygium canicortex, S. dansiei, S. wilsonii, Xanthostemon chrysanthus* and *X. whitei*. In addition, palms, cycads and ferns are used widely in landscaping and interior decorating. Many orchids, such as species of *Dendrobium* and *Phalaenopsis*, are of horticultural value.

Many species are used, or offer potential, in modern medicine (Collins *et al.* 1990). The families Annonaceae, Apocynaceae, Lauraceae and Monimiaceae contain a high proportion of genera containing alkaloids. Collins *et al.* (1990) report on the significance of the discovery of a large group of very complex alkaloids in *Galbulimima belgraveana*, endemic in Australia to the Wet Tropics. Pyrrolidine alkaloids have been isolated from *Darlingia darlingiana* and *D. ferruginea. Eupomatia laurina* has yielded two aporphinoids and three new alkaloids. Rain forest Liliaceae and Euphorbiaceae (particularly species of *Glochidion* and *Alchornea*), among many others, have also been found to be rich in alkaloids. *Tabernaemontana* (syn. *Ervatamia*) *pubescens, Excoecaria agallocha, Graptophyllum ilicifolium, Ochrosia elliptica, Tylophora crebriflora, Sarcomelicope simplicifolia* and *Bruguiera sexangula* have considerable potential in cancer study and treatment. *Castanospermum australe* has been found to boost the human immune system and contains a compound that is active against the AIDS virus. Many plants from the Wet Tropics also show promise in the treatment of cardio-vascular conditions and possess anti-spasm, diuretic, analgesic/anti-inflammatory and/or anti-convulsant properties (Collins *et al.* 1990).

Many plants of the Wet Tropics have been used as sources of food by Aboriginal people for millennia. There is an expanding interest in "bush tucker". For example, there is a growing market in Melbourne and Sydney for such products. Isaacs (1987) has assembled ethnobotanical information which features a number of Wet Tropics plants. Some notable examples include the roots of *Alocasia macrorrhiza* (cunjevoi), *Alpinia* spp. (wild ginger) and *Dioscorea* spp. (yams), and the fruits of *Antidesma bunius* (Herbert River cherry), *A. ghaesembilla* (blackcurrant tree), *Buchanania arborescens* (wild gooseberry), *Diospyros australis* (black plum), *Diploglottis* spp., *Elaeocarpus bancroftii* (Queensland almond), *Endiandra palmerstonii* (black walnut), *Eugenia reinwardtiana* (sweet cherry), *Ficus* spp. (figs), *Grewia* spp. (wild currants and emu bushes), *Macadamia* spp. (macadamia nuts), *Pandanus* spp., *Planchonella* spp., *Pleiogynium timorense* and *Syzygium* spp.

Many species are used to produce artefacts for sale which contribute to the income generated by the growing tourist industry.

Social and environmental values

The natural features of the area, including the vegetation, provide a landscape of high scenic quality, including spectacular forest-clad mountains, deeply incised gorges, plunging waterfalls and a sweeping tropical coastline. International and domestic visitors come to raft the wild rivers, trek through the rain forests, and experience the lushness and splendour of the region's vegetation.

Water is drawn from the forested catchments for both domestic and agricultural consumption, as well as for a limited amount of hydroelectric generation. The protection afforded to the water catchments by the natural forests is, therefore, vital.

The Wet Tropics province supports over 700 species of rare and/or threatened plants and animals and has more rain forest-dependent endemic vertebrates than any other area in Australia. Sixty species of vertebrates are endemic to the area. Most notable among them are antechinus, ring-tailed possums (4 species), rat kangaroo, tree kangaroos (2 species) and melomys (Winter 1991). The region also contains the known Australian distributions of two other species – *Cercartetus caudatus* (long-tailed pygmy-possum) and *Murina florium* (tube-nosed insectivorous bat) – found also in New Guinea and South East Asia, respectively.

The region is important for birds. A total of 17 restricted-range species occur, of which 13 are endemic. All the birds are rain forest species and a number are (now) confined to higher altitudes. Many of the species are taxonomically very distinct, for example chowchilla (*Orthonyx spaldingii*) and golden bowerbird (*Prionodura newtoniana*).

Some 24 species of rain forest-dependent reptiles occur in the Wet Tropics. The high rate of endemism (75%) appears to be without parallel in Australia. Of the more than 60 species of anurans occurring within the area, about 25 are found nowhere else. There are several species of Wet Tropics reptiles and frogs which await scientific description, as do many freshwater fish (Trenerry and Werren 1991). Despite the lack of knowledge it is established that this region contains a greater diversity of freshwater fishes (about 33% of the Australian total for this group) than any other in Australia.

The Wet Tropics contains numerous sites of significance to Aboriginal people (Rainforest Conservation Society of Queensland 1986). These include many of the Gugu-Yalanji clan-group, occurring along the coast between Cape Tribulation and the Bloomfield River (Anderson 1979). There remain relatively intact segments of a major Yidinyji communication trail traversing dense rain forest and tracts of open forest from the Mulgrave lowlands to the Atherton Tableland (Davis and Covacevich 1984). The now-extinct Bandjin clan-group of the Hinchinbrook Island area was responsible for some of the most complex prehistoric structures known to be associated with Aboriginal culture. These are in the form of tidal fish traps covering 200 km² (Rainforest Conservation Society of Queensland 1986).

Of significance is the association of the Wet Tropics with the survival of a long-standing non-literate oral tradition of the rain forest Aboriginal peoples dating back some 15,000 years (Rainforest Conservation Society 1986). Remnants of these cultures survive – in fact, the Bloomfield area represents a major centre of survival of rain forest Aboriginal people in north-east Queensland; these people maintain their strong attachment to the land, certain of their gather-hunter practices and use of bush medicines (Anderson 1979). The everyday use of potentially toxic food plants, which involves elaborate traditional preparation techniques, distinguishes the Aboriginal inhabitants of the Wet Tropics from those of others (Horsfall 1991).

Economic assessment

The economy of the region is fundamentally dependent on resource-based industries (including tourism). Sugar cane production was traditionally the major pursuit accounting for around 60% of the regional economic base in the 1950s. However, it now contributes around 20% of the value of the base industries, compared to tourism which contributes c. 25% to the regional economy with an estimated value in excess of A$400,000,000 (Cummings Economic Research Services 1990). The Wet Tropics of Queensland World Heritage Area, along with the Great Barrier Reef, are the major attractions for visitors.

While no figures are available, products taken from the forests of the Wet Tropics are fashioned into items which are sold as part of the tourist trade. Wood carving and turning produces souvenirs of local timber in the form of bowls, boxes, figurines and boomerangs. *Calamus* spp. (rattans) are woven into baskets and furniture. A range of fruit capsules and distinctive seeds are fashioned into decorative items and "jewelry".

Other industries in the region include some dairying, beef cattle grazing, vegetable, tropical fruit and tobacco cultivation, and fishing. A limited amount of small-scale mining extraction also occurs. This economic base supports a population of around 180,000 people of which about 50% live in Cairns City and its immediate surrounds. The population growth rate is unusually high at around 5% per annum.

Threats

Although logging ceased when the Wet Tropics was inscribed as a World Heritage Site, other threats continue and some – especially those associated with the region's expanding tourist industry and growing resident population – are intensifying.

The Tully-Millstream hydroelectric scheme proposal looms as one of the major threats to significant tracts of Wet Tropics forests and woodlands. It is proposed to increase impoundments to cover 56 km² on the south-east section of the Atherton Tableland. Tall open/wet sclerophyll forest communities (mostly type 14b) are particularly threatened if the scheme proceeds. In addition, almost 20 km² of low open forest/woodland would be cleared or inundated, together with 1.3 km² of simple notophyll vine forest (Queensland Electricity Commission 1988). A number of vertebrate species of special conservation concern are threatened by the scheme.

Increasing tourist pressure is affecting a number of areas in the Wet Tropics, particularly the Cape Tribulation area. To date there has been largely *ad hoc* development of tourist infrastructure. With increasing demands for more tourist accommodation, roads, walking tracks, interpretative facilities, the problems of trampling, waste disposal and local forest clearances, may directly threaten local endemics unless very careful planning is exercised. There is a need for an integrated approach to planning for tourism, and perhaps a requirement of limiting visitor numbers or access to some places.

Agricultural and residential expansion in the lowlands is a threat to remnant patches of lowland rain forest and associated communities, and the large concentration of Endangered and Vulnerable plant species which they contain. Concerns focus on the very poor representation of relatively undisturbed lowland forest in existing reserves and the fear that further fragmentation could preclude their viability. Drainage alteration associated with sugar cane production is also a significant problem. Water-tables are lowered with consequent impacts on entire communities, such as those dominated by the feather palm *Archontophoenix alexandrae* (type 3a) and the fan palm *Licuala ramsayi* (type 3b) which are dependent on almost perennially moist soils.

The construction of telecommunication facilities is a threat to montane summit zones throughout the area. These contain highly restricted and often disjunct populations of plants and animals, including local endemics. Telecommunication facilities now occupy significant proportions of this habitat and are often serviced by transport corridors which intrude on patches of upland rain forest and heath.

Grazing by domestic stock (almost exclusively beef cattle and largely confined to the western margins of the Wet Tropics) and feral animals, particularly pigs (*Sus scrofa*) and cattle, prevents the regeneration of forests and initiates erosion in some areas. Cattle are also responsible for the spread of certain weed species. Other feral species include, in some areas, horses (*Equus caballus*), dogs (*Canis familiaris*) and cats (*Felis cattus*), the latter two species affecting the region's fauna rather than directly impacting upon vegetation.

A variety of exotic weed species have proliferated in the Wet Tropics region. The most significant of these include the vines *Ipomoea tilacea*, *Thunbergia grandiflora* and *Turbina corymbosa*, and the shrubs *Coffea arabica* and *Cassia obtusifolia*. *Spathodea campanulata* (African tulip tree) and *Mangifera indica* (mango) are becoming widespread in certain areas, as is *Annona glabra* (pond apple) in lowland feather palm and mangrove forests. Disturbed areas can be colonized rapidly by exotic grasses, such as *Melinus minutiflorus* and *Panicum maximum*, increasing the potential for the spread of fires into rain forest, resulting in its further loss and fragmentation, while *Brachiaria mutica* is a problem in some waterways.

A limited amount of mining still occurs but it is no longer a major threat. However, there is a potential conflict between mining and conservation because some areas of high mineralization (including some sites in the Mossman district within the Wet Tropics) coincide with local plant refugia.

Plant collecting (particularly of orchids, cycads, tassel "ferns" and other plants of ornamental value) is assumed to be significant and increasing, particularly in areas traversed by roads, due to the growing demand for ornamental native plants.

In 1990, road works were responsible for the elimination of the only known population of the rain forest tree *Toechima pterocarpum* in the Julatten area. Subsequently, a second population was found to the south of Mossman. This example attests to the problems of conserving often highly restricted plant species and the need for ongoing information collection and vigilance on the part of conservation managers.

Conservation

In 1988, some 8990 km² of the Wet Tropics province was inscribed as a World Heritage Site (Werren and King 1991). This means that Australia has entered into an international agreement to "protect, conserve and present" the area's World Heritage values for present and future generations. The variety of land tenures embraced by the Wet Tropics of Queensland World Heritage Area has resulted in a mosaic of management practices. National Parks cover 29% of the World Heritage Area and are managed explicitly for conservation. State Forests and associated Timber Reserves cover 48% of the Area and were once primarily managed for timber production. They are now managed for public recreation and conservation. Other land in public ownership may be vacant (16%) or in the form of leaseholdings (15%) where activities which are not necessarily conducive to conservation of native plant communities and their attendant wildlife continue to be practised. About 2% of the Area remains in private ownership in the form of Aboriginal lands covered by Deeds of Grant in Trust and private freeholdings. While World Heritage listing does not necessarily require that primary land uses or the underlying tenure should change, a consistent approach to conservation management of the entire listed property is required so that Australia can meet its international obligations under the World Heritage Convention.

To this end a deed of agreement was struck between the Commonwealth and State governments in March 1990. This agreement enshrined the concept of an independent Management Authority, supported by scientific and community advisory committees, which is responsible for setting management policy directions; it also assigns dedicated State conservation management agencies to implement management policy on the ground. Legislation is currently being formulated to give this management structure some legal force.

There is an initiative to establish an Australian National Tropical Botanical Gardens complex at Mareeba to collect, display and research plants from the Wet Tropics and from other provinces of tropical Australia.

References

Anderson, D. (1979). Aboriginal economy and contact relations at Bloomfield River. *Australian Institute of Aboriginal Studies Newsletter* 12: 33–37.

Cassells, D.S., Bonell, M., Gilmour, D.A. and Valentine, P.S. (1988). Conservation and management of Australia's tropical rain forests: local realities and global responsibilities. *The Ecology of Australia's Wet Tropics: Proceedings of the Ecological Society of Australia* 15: 313–326.

Collins, D.J., Culvenor, C.C.J., Lamberton, J.A., Loder, J.W. and Price, J.R. (1990). *Plants for medicines: a chemical and pharmacological survey of plants in the Australian region.* CSIRO, Melbourne. 303 pp.

Covacevich, J. and McDonald, K. (1991). Reptiles. In Nix, H.A. and Switzer, M.A. (eds), *Kowari I – rainforest animals: atlas of vertebrates endemic to Australia's Wet Tropics.* Australian National Parks and Wildlife Service, Canberra.

Crome, F. and Nix, H. (1991). Birds. In Nix, H.A. and Switzer, M.A. (eds), *Kowari I – rainforest animals: atlas of vertebrates endemic to Australia's Wet Tropics.* Australian National Parks and Wildlife Service, Canberra.

Cummings Economic Research Services (1990). *Cairns and Far North Queensland economic development profile.* Far North Queensland Promotion Bureau, Cairns. 74 pp.

Davis, G. and Covacevich, J. (1984). Aboriginal walkway: mapping a communication trail of the Yidinyji rain forest people of north-eastern Australia. *Wildlife Australia* 21: 8–10.

Horsfall, N. (1991). The prehistoric occupation of Australian rainforests. In Werren, G.L. and Kershaw, A.P. (eds), *The rainforest legacy, Volume 3 – rainforest history, dynamics and management.* Australian Heritage Commission Special Australian Heritage Publication Series No. 7(3). AHC, Canberra. Pp. 77–84.

Isaacs, J. (1987). *Bush food: Aboriginal food and herbal medicine.* Weldon, Willoughby. 256 pp.

Kershaw, A.P. (1980). Long term changes in north-east Queensland rain forest. In Wright J., Mitchell, N. and Watling, P. (eds), *Reef, rain forest, mangroves, man.* WPSQ, Cairns. Pp. 32–38.

Queensland Electricity Commission (1988). *Tully-Millstream Hydro-electric Scheme environmental audit report.* Environment Science Services/QEC, Brisbane.

Rainforest Conservation Society of Queensland (1986). *Tropical rainforests of north Queensland: their conservation significance.* Australian Heritage Commission Special Australian Heritage Publication Series No. 3. AHC, Canberra. 195 pp.

Switzer, M.A. (1991). Introduction. In Nix, H.A. and Switzer, M.A. (eds), *Kowari I – rainforest animals: atlas of vertebrates endemic to Australia's Wet Tropics.* Australian National Parks and Wildlife Service, Canberra. Pp. 1–10.

Tracey, J.G. (1982). *The vegetation of the humid tropical region of north Queensland.* CSIRO, Melbourne. 124 pp.

Trenerry, M.P. and Werren, G.L. (1991). Fishes. In Nix, H.A. and Switzer, M.A. (eds), *Kowari I – rainforest animals: atlas of vertebrates endemic to Australia's Wet Tropics.* Australian National Parks and Wildlife Service, Canberra. Pp. 104.

Webb, L.J. (1958). Cyclones as an ecological factor in tropical lowland rain forest, North Queensland. *Australian Journal of Botany* 6: 220–228.

Webb, L.J. and Tracey, J.G. (1981). Australian rainforests: patterns and change. In Keast, A. (ed.), *Ecological biogeography of Australia.* Junk, The Hague. Pp. 605–694.

Werren, G.L. and King, D. (1991). Conservation and management. In Nix, H.A. and Switzer, M.A. (eds), *Kowari I – rainforest animals: atlas of vertebrates endemic to Australia's Wet Tropics.* Australian National Parks and Wildlife Service, Canberra. Pp. 41–42.

Whiffin, T. and Hyland, B.P.M. (1991). Current status of the taxonomic knowledge of the Australian rainforest flora. In Werren, G.L. and Kershaw, A.P. (eds), *The rainforest legacy, volume 2 – Flora and fauna of the rainforests.* Australian Heritage Commission Special Australian Heritage Publication Series No. 7(2). AHC, Canberra. Pp. 93–103.

Winter, J. (1991). Mammals. In Nix, H.A. and Switzer, M.A. (eds), *Kowari I – rainforest animals: atlas of vertebrates endemic to Australia's Wet Tropics.* Australian National Parks and Wildlife Service, Canberra. Pp. 43.

Acknowledgements

This Data Sheet was prepared by Garry L. Werren (former Conservation Officer, Wet Tropics, Department of Environment and Heritage, Cairns, Queensland), Dr Stephen Goosem (Department of Environment and Heritage, Far Northern Region, Cairns, Queensland), J. Geoff Tracey (former Senior Scientist, CSIRO Centre for Tropical Forest Research, Atherton, Queensland) and J. Peter Stanton (Department of Environment and Heritage, Far Northern Region, Cairns, Queensland). The material supplied and the interpretations offered are those of the authors entirely and should not be considered to reflect on institutions to which the authors are affiliated.

NEW ZEALAND: CPD SITE AU14

NORTHLAND
New Zealand

Location: Includes the North Island mainland of New Zealand south to the Kaipara Habour and Whangarei (approximately between latitudes 34°30' and 37°00'S), and the offshore and outlying islands bordering this area.

Area: c. 14,000 km².

Altitude: 0–766 m.

Vegetation: Evergreen warm-temperate to subtropical forest, scrub, wetland communities, including mangrove forest, coastal communities.

Flora: c. 620 vascular plant species; c. 60 endemic taxa. c. 40 taxa are nationally threatened.

Useful plants: Timber trees (especially kauri), many species used traditionally by Maoris, ornamental plants.

Other values: Tourism, high landscape value, soil and water conservation.

Threats: Clearance for agriculture and grazing, feral animals, invasive plant species, tourism, exotic timber plantations.

Conservation: >200 protected areas, State Forests and Sanctuaries, including Waipoua State Forest Sanctuary (91 km²), some Stewardship lands.

Geography

Northland includes the North Island mainland of New Zealand south to the Kaipara Habour and Whangarei (approximately between latitude 34°30' and 37°00'S), and the offshore and outlying islands bordering this area. It excludes Little Barrier and Great Barrier Islands, and the Hauraki Gulf islands. The region approximates the Northland Botanical Province, and includes the more recently defined Three Kings, Te Paki, Aupouri, Western Northland, Eastern Northland, Poor Knights and Kaipara ecological regions. The total area included is approximately 14,000 km².

The region as a whole is warm temperate, verging in some parts on subtropical, with humid summers and mild winters. Occasional snow may fall on the higher ranges. Much of the region is intricately dissected hill country and the coastline is indented by many bays and inlets. The following physiographic regions and island groups can be distinguished:

1. Three Kings Islands
Steep islands of eroded basaltic and acidic volcanics and indurated sediments at latitude 34°10'S, about 56 km north-west of Cape Reinga. Climate very mild, with annual rainfall of between 1000–1200 mm. No introduced mammals present.

2. Te Paki region
An area of low, dissected hills at the northern tip of North Island. The area has been periodically isolated from the rest of North Island by higher sea-levels. Climate is very mild, almost subtropical, with some laterization of soils. Annual rainfall is up to 1500 mm.

3. Aupouri region
A tombolo-like isthmus of mobile Holocene sands connecting Te Paki and the mainland. The climate is very mild, approaching subtropical, with annual rainfall up to 1500 mm. Seasonal droughts occur.

4. Western Northland
Rolling to rugged hill country up to 776 m altitude, and including an indented coastline. The region is composed mainly of mid-Tertiary basalts and sedimentary rocks. The climate is very mild and humid, with annual rainfall up to 2400 mm.

5. Eastern Northland and islands
Low, dissected hill country up to 440 m altitude, including an intricately embayed coastline with numerous islands close to the shore. The climate is warm and humid with annual rainfall of 1500–2400 mm. Some areas are drought-prone in summer.

6. Taranga
A group of rugged off-shore volcanic and sedimentary islands which were probably connected with the mainland during the last glacial period. The climate is oceanic, warm and humid. There are no introduced mammals, except the Polynesian rat.

7. Poor Knights Islands
A group of rugged volcanic off-shore islands with oceanic subtropical climate, irregular rainfall and periodic drought.

Vegetation

Most of Northland was covered by evergreen warm temperate forest before humans arrived, probably about 1000 years ago. The following major vegetation types occur:

Coastal broadleaved forest
This occurs along the mainland coast and on most off-shore islands. Dominants include *Metrosideros excelsa* (pohutukawa),

507

Dysoxylum spectabile (kohekohe), *Corynocarpus laevigatus* (karaka), *Beilschmiedia tarairi* (tarairi) and *B. tawa* (tawa). *Meryta sinclairii* (puka) is present locally on Taranga, and *Kunzea ericoides* (kanuka) and *Knightia excelsa* (rewarewa) are often present on recently disturbed sites.

Kauri forest

This is found from North Cape southwards, although highly fragmented in regions such as Te Paki. The dominant emergent tree is *Agathis australis* (kauri), accompanied by a diverse range of broadleaved tree species. The largest stands of gigantic kauri trees occur in western Northland.

Podocarp-broadleaved forest

Inland forests, in particular, often include varying proportions of podocarps. Higher altitude variants include patches of swamp mire and *Ascarina* spp. On wetter sites and valley floors kahikatea forest was formerly common.

Scrub

Secondary scrub is common, especially on soils with an impermeable iron pan. Common species include *Kunzea ericoides*, *Leptospermum scoparium*, *Pomaderris* spp. and regenerating kauri. Much of the hill scrubland shows subfossil evidence of former kauri forest. Coastal scrub may contain a high number of shrub species, including locally evolved species and genotypes on serpentine cliffs at North Cape.

Wetlands

Swamps and lakes are common, especially near the coast. Interdune lakes are frequent along the western coast of the mainland. Some of the lakes are the only known habitat for the threatened regional endemic *Hydatella inconspicua*. Fern and sedge dominated, species-rich wetlands occur on level to gently sloping sites with impeded drainage. Oligotrophic to mesotrophic bogs contain locally threatened species, including *Lycopodium serpentinum*, *Thelypteris confluens* and *Cryptostylis subulatus*. Highly specialized wetlands occur adjacent to geothermal warm springs, especially those at Ngawha which are almost the only extant sites for a sedge, *Baumea complanata*.

Coastal vegetation

Cliffs occur along much of the coastline, especially on the islands. They are colonized by a wide range of broadleaved shrubs and small trees. Coastal grasslands, dominated by cushion plants, are locally common. Extensive beaches and coastal sand-dunes, well-developed on Aupouri Peninsula and along the west coast of Northland, are extensively invaded by exotic species or have been planted with timber species.

Mangroves

Mangroves occur along estuaries of the mainland coast and cover several thousand hectares. The largest area is in the Kaipara Harbour. Mangrove forest is dominated by low-canopied *Avicennia resinifera*.

Flora

The region has a rich flora of c. 620 vascular plant species, including some of New Zealand's only subtropical species,

such as *Hibiscus diversifolius*, *Cassytha paniculata* and *Todea barbara*. Some species of ferns and orchids probably originated from Australia and are otherwise unknown in New Zealand.

About 60 vascular plant taxa are endemic to the region. Of these, about 12 taxa are endemic to the northernmost point on the mainland (North Cape) and are associated with ultramafic outcrops. 12 species are endemic to the Three Kings Islands, including the monotypic genus *Elingamita*, and two of the world's rarest species (*Pennantia baylisiana* and *Tecomanthe speciosa*) which are both known in the wild from single plants. The Poor Knights Islands has several species of endemic or near-endemic plants, including the spectacular *Xeronema callistemon*. A number of plant taxa differ from mainland relatives but have yet to be described. A significant number of the islands' species are very large-leaved.

About 40 vascular plant taxa are nationally threatened. The Te Paki area is the centre of distribution for several of these, most notably the recently discovered tree, *Metrosideros bartlettii*, of which less than 30 individuals exist in the wild. Sand-dune communities harbour several species which are under some degree of threat nationally, including some of New Zealand's largest populations of pingao, *Desmoschoenus spiralis*.

The region includes scattered and disjunct occurrences of species whose main distribution lies further south. These include such species as *Hoheria angustifolia*, *Metrosideros umbellata*, *Nothofagus truncata* and *Dacrydium colensoi*.

Useful plants

Prior to the arrival of Europeans, many plants of this region were used by the Polynesian Maori for food, fuel, implements, medicines and clothing. Some species, such as *Desmoschoenus spiralis*, *Metrosideros excelsa* and the giant forest tree *Agathis australis* (kauri), still have particular spiritual significance for the Maori.

The area has been long recognized for its important reserves of timber, especially kauri, which was the basis for an important milling industry that was a catalyst for European settlement. Collection of subfossil and fresh kauri gum was the basis of an industry which at one time employed many hundreds of "gum diggers".

A number of plant species from Northland, and the outlying and off-shore islands, are important horticultural subjects. Among them are *Tecomanthe speciosa* and *Plectomirtha baylisiana* from the Three Kings Islands, *Xeronema callistemon* from the Poor Knights and Hen and Chicken Islands (Taranga), *Pratia physaloides* and several species of *Hebe*. The near-endemic *Fuchsia procumbens* is widely cultivated, and the Northland population of threatened *Hebe speciosa* from Maunganui Bluff has contributed to the development of horticultural cultivars.

Social and environmental values

Native forests are particularly important in the protection they afford to soil and water resources in the region, as well as providing important wildlife habitats. Native plants are also a major contribution to tourism values in Northland.

TABLE 73. LIST OF TERRESTRIAL PROTECTED AREAS (>100 HA) NORTH OF LATITUDE 37°S IN THE NORTHLAND REGION

Name of area	Area (ha)	Name of area	Area (ha)
Curtis Island NR	306	Motukawanui ScR	355
Cuvier Islands NR	171	Moturua Island ScR	136
Double and Stanley Islands NR	120	Onekura SFEA	2351
Hen and Chickens Islands NR	842	Papakai SFEA	3366
Hugh W Crawford Memorial Bush SR	111	Poor Knights Islands NR	271
Kaukapakapa Estuary SciR	210	Pouto Point WRef	6789
Little Barrier Island NR	2817	Rangitoto Island ScR	2333
Mangamuka Gorge ScR	2832	Raoul Island and Kermadec Group NR	3089
Manganuiowae SFEA	1760	Tauhoa NR	301
Maungatautari ScR	2389	Three Kings NR	685
Mercury Island ScR	226	Waipoua FoS	9105
Moehau SFEA	3634	Waipoua Kauri Management Area	3747
Mokohinau Islands NR	108	Whangamumu ScR	2154

KEY:
FoS – Forest Sanctuary; NR – Nature Reserve; SciR – Scientific Reserve; ScR – Scenic Reserve; SFEA – State Forest Ecological Area; SR – State Reserve; WRef – Wildlife Refuge

For example, *Agathis australis* and *Metrosideros excelsa* are spectacular components of the landscape.

Threats

Much of Northland, including most islands, coastal areas adjacent to good fishing areas, and lowland sites with deep alluvial soils, was quite extensively modified by Maori before Europeans arrived. Following European settlement, accessible forests were extensively logged for timber and cleared for farming. Some of this land has reverted to secondary scrub, providing habitat for a number of rare herbs, shrubs and orchids.

Large areas are now modified for sheep and cattle farming, or have been planted with exotic timber tree species, such as *Pinus radiata* (Monterey pine). These include former sand-dunes which once supported communities of indigenous *Spinifex* and *Desmoschoenus spiralis*. Sand-dunes in the Aupouri region, in particular, have been stabilized using marram grass and exotic trees and converted to pasture and plantations, leaving only relics of original forest and dune vegetation.

In lowland areas with fertile soils and abundance of water, such as in the environs of Hokianga Harbour, only very small and scattered remnants of the indigenous vegetation remain.

Feral animals are an increasing problem, especially on the mainland, where goats are widespread. Australian possums have now reached practically all of Northland. Wild pigs are also common. Pigs were exterminated from the Poor Knights Islands in 1936 and goats from the Three Kings Islands in 1946.

Conservation

There are more than 200 protected areas, including Scenic Reserves, Scientific Reserves and Nature Reserves. The Waipoua Forest Sanctuary (91 km²) is the largest of these and protects one of New Zealand's largest areas of kauri (*Agathis australis*) forest. The Bay of Islands Maritime Park, as well as being a popular tourist destination, also gives protection to an important array of islands and adjacent coastline in eastern Northland. Some of New Zealand's most important Nature Reserves include several of the offshore islands of Northland.

Some of the more important protected areas are listed in Table 73 (note that this list is indicative only and that many more protected areas occur in the region).

References

Baylis, G.T.S. (1958). Botanical survey of the small islands of the Three Kings group. *Records of Auckland Institute and Museum* 5: 1–12.

Clunie, N.M. and Wardle, P. (1983). *Botany of the Ahipara gumlands and Tauroa Peninsula.* Report 435, Botany Division, DSIR, Christchurch, New Zealand.

Dodson, J.R., Enright, N.J. and McLean, R.F. (1988). A late Quaternary vegetation history for far northern New Zealand. *Journal of Biogeography* 15: 647–656.

Ecroyd, C.E. (1982). Biological flora of New Zealand. 8. *Agathis australis* (D.Don) Lindl. (Araucariaceae) kauri. *New Zealand Journal of Botany* 20: 63–75.

Enright, N.J. (1989). Heathland vegetation of the Spirits Bay area, far northern New Zealand. *New Zealand Journal of Ecology* 12: 63–75.

Oliver, W.R.B. (1948). Vegetation of the Three Kings Islands. *Records of Auckland Institute and Museum* 3: 211–238.

Wheeler, J.M. (1963). The vegetation of the North Cape area. *Tane* 9: 63–84.

Acknowledgements

This Data Sheet was prepared by Dr David R. Given (Christchurch, New Zealand).

NORTH-WEST NELSON
New Zealand

Location: North-western part of South Island, New Zealand, south to approximately 41°53'S between longitudes 171°38'–173°01'E.

Area: c. 9500 km².

Altitude: 0–1875 m (summit of Mount Owen).

Vegetation: Moist temperate to montane forest and scrub; wetlands and coastal communities; rock, cliff and scree vegetation; alpine herbfield and grassland.

Flora: c. 1200 flowering plant taxa.

Useful plants: Timber trees, ornamental plants, many species traditionally used by Maori.

Other values: Protection of soil and water resources, tourism.

Threats: Logging, mining, agriculture, invasive exotic plant species, introduced animals.

Conservation: Abel Tasman National Park (225.4 km²) (IUCN Management Category: II), Kahurangi National Park status for much of Crown-owned land in the region, more than 40 reserves, Stewardship lands.

Geography

North-west Nelson includes that part of South Island west of the Tasman Bay lowlands and Moutere Hills, and north of the Buller River, approximately between longitudes 171°38'–173°01'E and south to latitude 41°53'S. The total area is about 9500 km². Much of the region is very rugged and mountainous, the hinterland being mostly 900–1500 m above sea-level. The highest peak is Mount Owen at 1875 m. Many of the ranges are block-faulted, contrasting with rolling, or flat, plateaux and subalpine downland of the Gunner and Gouland Downs, Garibaldi Ridge, the Matiri Range, and Denniston and Stockton plateaux. Cirques, U-shaped valleys and moraines are evidence of glacial activity at higher altitudes.

The region is geologically complex, including Palaeozoic granite, schist, phyllite, marble and volcanic sequences, Tertiary quartz sandstones, mudstones, coal measures and limestones, and Recent sand dunes and gravels. It includes New Zealand's oldest rocks, and has been subjected to several periods of mountain building. In the early Tertiary period, the region was largely reduced to a low-lying peneplain, on which coal measures and limestones accumulated. The diversity of geological processes has produced a wide range of rock types and soils, from podzolized soils of low nutrient status to more fertile soils (especially those developed on marbles and limestones, and the fertile loams of lowland valleys and river flats). Rendzinas are locally developed on marble. Waterlogged soils with an impermeable iron-pan are a feature of some river terraces.

The climate is generally warm and wet in the lowlands, while at higher altitudes winters are cold, with heavy frosts and snowfalls. The annual rainfall ranges from 1200 to 6400 mm. Occasional tropical storms can bring exceptionally high rainfall, leading to flooding and landslips. Wind is a prominent feature of much of the region.

Vegetation

Much of the region is still forested. All the New Zealand species of *Nothofagus* (southern beech) occur here, and often dominate the forest, sometimes in association with *Podocarpus* spp. and *Metrosideros* spp. Forests at lower altitudes are very rich, with *Podocarpus* spp., *Nothofagus* spp. and many other broadleaved species, such as *Metrosideros robusta* (northern rata) and *Elaeocarpus dentatus* (hinau). At higher altitudes, extensive areas of low canopy forest and scrub occur, with *Nothofagus menziesii* (silver beech) or *Nothofagus solandri* var. *cliffortioides* (mountain beech) occurring at the tree-line.

Poorly drained sites are often occupied by scrubland (pakihi) on highly leached soils with an impermeable ironpan. Heath species, sedges and ferns are common components of pakihi. At higher altitudes, extensive alpine tussock (*Chionochloa*) grasslands, herbfields and fellfields are present. Large areas of flat to rolling moorland, often dominated by *Chionochloa rubra* (red tussock), occur on poorly drained sites, especially in the western margin of the mountains.

Flora

North-west Nelson is generally recognized as having the highest floristic diversity of any area in New Zealand. So far, 1226 vascular plant species are known to occur in the area (over half the New Zealand vascular plant flora). The flora along the north-western coast shows strong relationships with that of northern North Island, and may represent a remnant of a continuous pre-Pleistocene land mass. Many plants of northern New Zealand, including major tree species such as *Dysoxylum spectabile* (kohekohe), *Laurelia novae-zelandiae* (pukatea) and *Libocedrus plumosa* (northern cedar), reach their southern limits here.

The mountainous interior of North-west Nelson supports a rich alpine and subalpine flora developed on a wide range of geological substrates and soils. The area includes about 80% of the total New Zealand alpine flora. Within North-west Nelson are several local centres of plant endemism. One of the most notable of these is the Matiri Range, where a limestone karst plateau supports a rich and highly distinctive flora. In the western and south-western parts of the region, a few areas of low-alpine vegetation support species occurring significantly below their usual lower altitudinal limit. They occur mostly on nutrient-poor soils associated with plateaux, or in coastal gorges.

About 67, and perhaps as many as 80, vascular plant species are believed to be endemic or near-endemic to the region, of which about 50% are undescribed. Notable examples of regional endemics include *Celmisia gibbsii*, *Clematis marmoraria*, *Coprosma talbrockei* and *Pittosporum dallii*. Some of the endemics are associated with distinctive soil types, especially those developed on calcareous, serpentine or volcanic substrates.

More than 20 nationally threatened flowering plant species occur in North-west Nelson. A further 29 species have very restricted and localized distributions. Species with disjunct distributions also occur in parts of North-west Nelson, particularly at Mount Domett and West Whanganui Inlet. The region was probably a major refugia during ice ages.

Useful plants

Before the arrival of Europeans, Maoris traditionally used many native plant species as sources of medicines, craft and building materials, and some foods. Important useful plants include *Phormium tenax* (harakeke or New Zealand flax), *Freycinetia banksii* (kiekie) and many lowland tree species. Local commercial gathering of *Sphagnum* moss occurs under licence.

Following European settlement, *Phormium tenax* provided a commercial source of fibre for rope-making. Flax processing mills were established but this industry has now ceased. In lowland regions, indigenous hardwood trees formerly provided a valuable timber resource. Commercial logging commenced in the 1840s but had largely ceased by the 1980s. Nineteenth century goldrushes saw large areas of trees felled to provide timber for dams and water races.

Social and environmental values

Much of the indigenous vegetation of the region has high value as protection forest for conservation of soil and water resources. In addition, the high landscape value provided by native forests is a major factor in the increase in tourism in the region.

Threats

The impact of Polynesian settlement over a period of about 600–700 years prior to European colonization, was probably less than in many other parts of New Zealand because the population was mostly concentrated in coastal areas and depended largely on marine food resources. European settlement from the 1840s saw a dramatic impact on lowland regions and some inland areas. The discovery of coal (1836), gold (1856) and a millable timber resource, led to rapid settlement and the transformation of accessible coastal and lowland valleys.

Farming is now a major regional activity in lowland areas and has resulted in the conversion of extensive areas of forest to agricultural land or secondary vegetation. Grazing has now ceased in alpine areas. Many wetlands, such as the Kongahu Swamp near Karamea, have been drained and converted to farmland. Some logging and vegetation clearing continues, chiefly on private land.

One hydroelectric plant has been developed at the Cobb Valley, and other river systems have been assessed for their hydroelectric potential.

Mining continues in some areas, notably at Mount Stockton in the south-west of the region where high grade coal is extracted by opencast methods. Indeed, the region is still regarded as favourable for mineral prospecting because of the complex and rich mineralogy of the older rocks.

Tourism is an important and increasing industry and has both positive and negative effects in the region. The positive effects have been the increased level of protection for forests, mountain areas and wildlife habitats, but the negative effects have been the opening of wilderness areas for vehicle access, including a road connection between Collingwood and Karamea.

Feral animals are probably the greatest threat to the flora. Australian possum, goats, pigs, chamois, red deer and fallow deer are found throughout the region, sometimes in high numbers. Between 1964 and 1984 a culling programme using helicopters greatly reduced the numbers of deer; feral goats, however, are still a major problem.

Naturalized plants, including some invasive species, are common in the lowlands. Fortunately, few species have spread into the interior mountains.

Conservation

Abel Tasman National Park (225.4 km²) is an important conservation area in the north-east of the region. In addition, much of the Crown-owned land has been under investigation for National Park status by the Department of Conservation. The central mountain core (c. 3764 km²) has been classified as Forest Park, but the new Kahurangi National Park includes smaller outlying areas of land under a variety of protective tenures.

Farewell Spit Nature Reserve (113.9 km²) is designated as a Ramsar Site under the Convention on Wetlands of International Importance especially as Waterfowl Habitat.

Over 40 reserves administered by the Department of Conservation preserve sites of biological and landscape significance. These are supplemented by numerous private land covenants, chiefly administered by the Queen Elizabeth II Trust, protecting very valuable vegetation remnants.

Forest logging of indigenous species is highly restricted following establishment of the West Coast Forest Accord in 1986. Constraints on land use also result from the need to protect watersheds for water supply or as measures against erosion.

511

Most threatened plant species in the region have been surveyed and sites entered on a national database. However, small populations of threatened species are still being discovered and, for a significant number, there is inadequate monitoring or information on long-term management needs.

References

Burrows, C.J. (1965). Some discontinuous distributions of plants in New Zealand and their ecological significance. 2: Disjunctions between Otago-Southland and Nelson-Marlborough and related distribution patterns. *Tuatara* 13: 9–29.

Department of Conservation (1992). *North West South Island National Park investigation discussion document.* Nelson/ Marlborough Conservancy Occasional Publication No. 8.

Druce, A.P. and Simpson, R. (1974). Flora of Gouland Downs, Mount Gouland and Mount Perry, Northwest Nelson. *Wellington Botanical Society Bulletin 38*: 6–24.

Druce, A.P., Williams, P.A. and Heine, J.C. (1987). Vegetation and flora of Tertiary calcareous rocks in the mountains of western Nelson, New Zealand. *New Zealand Journal of Botany 25*: 41–78.

Williams, P.A. (1991). Subalpine and alpine vegetation of the granite ranges in western Nelson, New Zealand. *New Zealand Journal of Botany* 29: 317–330.

Acknowledgements

This Data Sheet was prepared by Dr David R. Given (Christchurch, New Zealand).

CHATHAM ISLANDS
New Zealand

Location: c. 800 km east of the New Zealand mainland at latitude 43°58'S and longitude 176°32'W.

Area: c. 965 km² (Chatham Island: 900.4 km²; Pitt Island: 63.3 km²; several smaller islands).

Altitude: Sea-level to c. 300 m.

Vegetation: Evergreen cool temperate forest, mixed broadleaved forest, scrub, rush/shrubland, grasslands, peatlands, wetland and coastal communities.

Flora: c. 320 vascular plant species; c. 40 endemic taxa.

Useful plants: *Olearia chathamica* used for fence posts, many species with traditional Maori uses, ornamental plants.

Other values: Tourism, peat deposits.

Threats: Land clearance for agriculture, invasive plant species, feral animals, fire, loss of biological obligates, potential mining of peat for fuel oil and wax.

Conservation: Network of small Scenic Reserves and Nature Reserves.

Geography

The Chatham Islands lie at the eastern end of the submerged Chatham Rise, approximately 800 km east of the New Zealand mainland. The group consists of Chatham Island (900.4 km²), Pitt Island (63.3 km²), several smaller islands, and numerous islets and stacks. The main island rises to just under 300 m altitude.

The islands are geologically diverse, and include Mesozoic schists overlain by Tertiary limestones, mudstones, tuffs and sands. Vulcanism has resulted in extensive areas of basic volcanics, especially on Pitt Island and in the southern part of Chatham Island. Beds of Tertiary and Quaternary peat, up to 9 m thick, blanket much of the main island's surface.

Land forms on the main island range from flat, bleak, peat dome topography to precipitous cliffs. Te Whanga Lagoon occupies a large area in the northern part of the island. The south is occupied by a tableland with numerous lakes and incised streams. Pitt Island and the smaller islets have generally steeper topography.

Vegetation

Endemic akeake forest, characterized by *Olearia chathamica*, once dominated coastal areas but is now greatly reduced in extent. Kopi (*Corynocarpus laevigatus*) forests were once more widespread on fertile lowland soils on Chatham and Pitt Islands. This species may be an early Polynesian introduction. On less fertile or poorly drained sites kopi gives way to mixed broadleaved forest with relatively few canopy species.

On Chatham, Pitt and South East Islands, sites with poor drainage and organic soils were formerly dominated by *Dracophyllum arboreum* forest. This is the only forest type of any extent left on Chatham Island itself, where it is particularly prominent on the Southern Tablelands.

Olearia chathamica scrub occurs on exposed cliffs of the southern shore of Chatham Island, and on Pitt and South East Islands. Other coastal cliffs support shrubland assemblages of mixed composition, often with prominent *Hebe* and *Corokia*.

With the demise of akeake forest along the coastline, there has been replacement by *Cyathodes/Pimelea* scrub and grassland, particularly at the rear of sand-dunes. On sandy organic soils on broad ridges and plateaux where *Dracophyllum* forest has been degraded, scrub dominated by *Cyathea robusta* is widespread, especially on the northern slopes of the Southern Tableland.

Of particular note are rush/shrubland communities characterized by *Sporodanthus traversii* and *Olearia semidentata*. Chatham Island, and especially the Southern Tablelands, is the last place where these species are seen growing over large areas. This vegetation type forms the "clears" of organic soils, which include large peat domes.

Sandy and bouldery shores were formerly characterized by a coastal herbaceous zone in which the endemic megaherbs *Myosotidium* and *Embergeria* were prominent. This vegetation type is much reduced in extent, often being replaced by extensive sheets of *Disphyma*. Sand-dune communities, including endemic plant species, such as *Desmoschoenus* spp. (pingao), have been largely replaced by introduced marram grass.

Wetland communities are extensive and include *Leptocarpus* rushland and turf herbfields around lakes. Other indigenous vegetation types are locally significant. They include ngaio (*Myoporum*) forest, *Leptinella-Carex* herbfield on highly fertile soils of "bird islands", kowhai (*Sophora*) woodland at Te Whanga Lagoon, and coastal *Dodonaea* forest.

In accessible lowland and coastal areas, much of the indigenous vegetation is highly modified, or replaced by pasture. Some introduced species, such as gorse and blackberry, are widespread. In the north of Chatham Island, Chilean guava (*Ugni molinae*) is an increasingly common element of scrub on organic soils. This latter species threatens to invade large areas of indigenous shrubland of high value as wildlife habitat.

Flora

The native vascular plant flora is estimated at about 320 indigenous species. In addition, there are about 200 naturalized plant species. About 40 taxa are endemic, including two monotypic endemic genera. Several taxa are not yet described or belong to species complexes which require further study. Despite considerable botanical exploration of the islands, new records, including possible new taxa, are still being found, and there is much pioneer work to be done, especially on non-vascular plants which are very poorly known.

The flora of the Chatham Islands has its closest affinities with that of mainland New Zealand. There are several distinct floristic elements. Some species are common to both the Chatham Islands and the mainland. Others are endemic to the Chatham Islands but belong to groups which are widespread on the mainland. Several endemic plants are related to species found in warm temperate, northern New Zealand, for example *Cortaderia turbaria* (toitoi) and some species of *Hebe*. Several Chatham Island endemics, such as the Chatham Island species of *Olearia*, have affinities with those of southern New Zealand and the Subantarctic Islands.

Some of the most distinctive plants of the Chatham Islands may belong to a much older element. Included here are the megaherbs of two endemic, monotypic genera, *Embergeria* (a giant sowthistle) and *Myosotidium* (a giant forget-me-not).

Like many islands, the flora has a biased range of life forms. Although forest was once widespread, there are only about a dozen indigenous tree species. Plant groups with light, windborn seeds, such as ferns and orchids, are well-represented on these islands.

Useful plants

Many indigenous species have considerable traditional value within Maori culture. Tree species were utilized by Polynesian and later European settlers on the islands. The wood of *Olearia chathamica* (akeake) is still valued for its durability and was used in the past for fence posts.

Social and environmental values

An indirect value of the vegetation lies in the extensive organic peats of Chatham Island. The peats have been investigated with a view to mining them for fuel oil and waxes.

The Chathams are well-known for their high degree of avian endemism. Today there are 5 extant species of land birds endemic to the islands. The Chatham robin (*Petroica traversi*) is one highly threatened species; it survives on the islands of Mangere and Rangatira (a total of 130 birds in 1992) following translocation from Little Mangere in 1976 (the entire remnant population of seven birds). The Chatham Islands are identified as an Endemic Bird Area (EBA) (ICBP 1992). Although nature tourism currently focuses on the endemic avifauna, there is growing awareness of the attractiveness of many Chatham Island plants.

Threats

The depletion of the native flora and vegetation is a disturbing feature of the islands. Even early this century, the botanist Leonard Cockayne noted on the main island that, "... without doubt in a year or two there will be no longer any virgin plant formations on the island, except those of inaccessible rocks or of the larger pieces of water". His comments have been repeated and amplified by most botanical visitors up to the present time.

The most serious threats are destruction of vegetation through land clearance for farming and development, grazing and trampling by feral animals, and the spread of introduced weeds. On the two largest islands, forest is now mostly confined to small remnants. The northern part of Chatham Island has been particularly affected by forest clearance and at some sites the loss of plant cover has resulted in soil erosion to the extent that the bedrock is exposed. Degradation of scrub and forest by cattle browsing and sheep grazing, accompanied by the removal of trees for firewood, construction and fence posts, has probably been the primary cause; local fires and wind-throw are also significant.

In some instances, especially with repeated burning, there has been reversion to almost impenetrable *Cyathodes* scrub and extensive thickets of bracken and *Dracophyllum paludosum*. This has particularly occurred on the northern approaches to the Southern Tablelands and on ridges in the northern part of Chatham Island. Fire plays a significant role in maintaining shrub/rushland "clears" on the Southern Tablelands of the main island.

Apart from domestic stock, feral animals are having a major impact on some parts of the Chatham Islands. Pigs, wild cattle and horses have been present for many decades. Recently, goats were introduced and there have been instances of goats browsing in protected reserves. Australian brush-tailed possums occur throughout the main island and have considerable effect on favoured palatable shrubs and trees.

Several of the many exotic plants now found on the Chatham Islands are an actual or potential threat to the indigenous flora. *Ammophila arenaria* (marram grass), introduced to stabilize sand blow-outs, has now displaced native vegetation from most foredunes. *Rubus* spp. (blackberries), brought in with the settlers in the mid-1800s, form extensive thickets in scrub and disturbed forest. *Ugni molinae* (Chilean guava) is rapidly spreading into scrub and rushland on organic soils in the northern part of Chatham Island, and *Ulex europaeus* (gorse) is widespread throughout Chatham and Pitt Islands.

A threat factor which has been overlooked until recently, but which may be highly significant, is the catastrophic reduction in the endemic avifauna. Studies indicate that some plant species, such as kowhai and the endemic form of nikau palm (*Rhopalostylis*), may be at risk as a result of the extinction or decline in numbers of particular bird species, such as the bellbird (Extinct), tui (Endangered) and pigeon (Endangered), which may act as pollinators and/or seed dispersers, or assist in seed germination by ingesting seeds.

Peat extraction for fuel oil and wax is a potential threat. The high wax content of Chatham peats have attracted considerable attention, although current world prices do not make peat mining a viable proposition at present. If peat mining takes place it will be extensive and will have profound effects on remaining areas of indigenous vegetation.

Conservation

The modern era of botanical exploration of the Chatham Islands began in 1840 with a visit by Ernest Dieffenbach. His account of the people and vegetation provides an important base-line against which to assess subsequent changes. Since then, many botanists have visited the islands, making extensive collections and commenting on the flora and vegetation. This has included visits by horticulturists to collect propagation material. As a result, much of the Chathams flora is grown in gardens worldwide, although only recently has there been acceptable documentation and systematic selection of more desirable forms for cultivation.

Much of the conservation initiative on the Chatham Islands has come from concern for the plight of the endemic avifauna. This has led to a high level of protection for several smaller islands in the Chathams group, notably Mangere and South East Islands. Revegetation is part of the management strategy for these islands.

The New Zealand Department of Conservation is adding to the network of protected areas on Chatham Island and Pitt Island. Although the majority of reserves tend to be small, several, such as Rangaika Scenic Reserve, Tuku Nature Reserve and the Big Glory Scenic Reserve, are of considerable size. Recent land acquisition at the north end of Chatham Island gives opportunity for protection of extensive peatlands and coastal forest restoration.

Recently, there has been a growing awareness of the need to protect the unique flora of the Chatham Islands. Recommendations have been made for protection of further areas, and recovery plans have been drafted for several species at risk.

Much of the Chatham Islands is privately owned and the land itself is an important traditional element in the life of indigenous people. It is vital that future protection and conservation of the flora takes account of such realities. This will require a focus on private protected land agreements,

and management practices which enhance natural values. As part of this, nature tourism and advocacy (both to local people and visitors) play an important role in long-term conservation strategies and the preservation of the flora of the Chatham Islands.

References

Cockayne, L. (1902). A short account of the plant covering of the Chatham Islands. *Transactions of the New Zealand Institute* 34: 243–324.

Devine, W.T. (1982). Nature conservation and land-use history of the Chatham Islands, New Zealand. *Biological Conservation* 23: 127–140.

Given, D.R. (1991). *Studies on threatened plants, part 2: autecological study of Chatham Island species*. N.Z. Department of Conservation Contract Report No 91/57 (part 2).

Given, D.R. and P.A. Williams (1985). *Conservation of Chatham Island flora and vegetation*. Botany Division, N.Z. DSIR.

ICBP (1992). *Putting biodiversity on the map: priority areas for global conservation*. International Council for Bird Preservation, Cambridge, U.K. 90 pp.

Kelly, G.C. (1971). *Reserves in the Chatham Islands*. Botany Division, DSIR Report to N.Z. Department of Lands and Survey.

Kelly, G.C. (1983). *Distribution and ranking of remaining areas of indigenous vegetation in the Chatham Islands, with site notes and introductory text*. N.Z. Department of Lands and Survey Resources. (Inventory map with extended legend.)

Wardle, P., Molloy, B.P.J., Brown, C.M., Manning, D., Given, D.R. and Atkinson, I.A.E. (1986). *Botany Division trip to the Chatham Islands, February–March 1985*. Botany Division, N.Z. DSIR, Vegetation Report 551a. (Report to the Liquid Fuels Trust Board.)

Acknowledgements

This Data Sheet was prepared by Dr David R. Given (Christchurch, New Zealand).

SUBANTARCTIC ISLANDS
Australia and New Zealand

Location: c. 200–800 km south-west of the New Zealand mainland and 500 km south-east of Tasmania in the southern Tasman Sea and Southern Ocean. The islands considered here are the Auckland Islands, Campbell Islands, Antipodes Islands and Macquarie Island.

Area: 949 km².

Altitude: 0–668 m (summit of Mount Dick, Adams Island in the Auckland group).

Vegetation: Grasslands, fellfields, herbaceous communities, wetlands, forests, coastal vegetation.

Flora: Transitional between temperate New Zealand flora to circum-polar Subantarctic flora, with a distinct "mega-herb" element; c. 250 vascular plant taxa, of which 35 are endemic.

Useful plants: *Stilbocarpa polaris* (Macquarie Island cabbage) used by early settlers to ward off scurvy; ornamental species.

Other values: Native vegetation stabilizes mineral and peat slopes; important bird colonies.

Threats: Introduced plants and animals.

Conservation: All the islands are Nature Reserves (IUCN Management Category: I). Macquarie Island is also a Biosphere Reserve.

Geography

The New Zealand and eastern-Australian Subantarctic Islands lie approximately 200–800 km south-west of the New Zealand mainland and 500 km south-east of Tasmania in the southern Tasman Sea and the Southern Ocean. The northern islands, consisting of Auckland Island (600 km²), Campbell Island (113 km²), Antipodes Island (118 km²) and Bounty Islands (small islets), are sometimes referred to collectively as the Campbell Botanic Province within the New Zealand Botanical Region. The southernmost island, Macquarie Island (118 km²) is referred botanically to the circum-polar Subantarctic Region which consist of islands generally near the Antarctic oceanic convergence zone, and possess a vascular flora without woody plants.

The maximum altitude is 668 m (the summit of Mount Dick, Adams Island, in the Auckland group). All but one of the islands consist, for the most part, of the rocky and generally precipitous eroded remnants of Pliocene volcanoes bedded on the relatively shallow Campbell Plateau. Campbell Island also has small areas of underlying limestone, mudstone and schist. Macquarie Island is the exception. It occurs on the Macquarie Ridge, separated from the Campbell Plateau by deep trenches. The island is a long narrow ridge of oceanic crust – one of the few aerial exposures not deformed by continental processes. It consists of basalt, diorite, gabbro and related rocks.

Thick peat overlies much of the rock on the larger islands. Auckland Islands and Campbell Island are steeply cliffed (especially in the west) but with long inlets and harbours on the eastern coasts. Macquarie Island is significantly further south than the other islands. Its upper portion, being above the zone of vascular plants, is covered by a tundra of sparse mosses. Peat clothes the slopes and coastal zone.

Rivers are short and generally little more than precipitous streams. The few lakes are generally shallow and small. Quaternary glaciers have left shallow cirques, moraines and fjords on some islands. Glaciation appears to have had little impact on Macquarie Island. Cool, equable temperatures, strong westerly winds, few hours of sunshine and high humidity prevail. Small amounts of snow fall in the winter, and although rain is frequent it is seldom torrential.

Vegetation

Subantarctic vegetation is characterized by the dominance of herbaceous plants. Some islands at the northern fringes of the Subantarctic also have shrub and tree dominated vegetation. Exposed coastal sites above 200 m on the Auckland Islands, at somewhat lower altitudes on Campbell Island, below about 300 m on Macquarie Island, and throughout Antipodes Island, are dominated by herbaceous or grassland communities characteristic of the Subantarctic zone. Coastal vegetation in localized areas has been profoundly affected by biotic influences associated with the breeding and resting sites of the large numbers of seals, penguins and many other sea birds which use the islands. Grassland communities dominated by large tussocks of *Poa litorosa*, *P. foliosa* and *Chionochloa*, and herbfields, occur throughout the islands. In herbfield communities, the "mega-herb" genera *Pleurophyllum* and *Stilbocarpa* are prominent.

On the mountaintops of Aucklands, Campbell Island and Antipodes Island, and above about 200 m on Macquarie Island, fellfield is the main vegetation type. Genera typical of fellfield are *Acaena, Azorella, Bulbinella, Damnamenia,*

516

Luzula, *Pleurophyllum* and *Ranunculus*. Cryptogams are prominent and widespread in fellfield and on rocks.

Wetland communities occur extensively on saturated peats throughout the islands. Characteristic genera of bogs include *Oreobolus*, *Phyllacne*, *Astelia*, *Centrolepis*, *Isolepis*, *Cyathodes*, *Gentiana* and *Luzula*. *Sphagnum* is generally rare, but other mosses are usually conspicuous. Distinctive rock outcrop and cliff vegetation occur widely, and provides the habitat for *Colobanthus* spp., *Puccinellia* spp. and *Crassula moschata*, along with a wide variety of lichens and mosses.

The Auckland Islands have the most diverse vegetation, ranging from forest to fellfield. Forest along sheltered shores and valleys is dominated by *Metrosideros umbellata* (southern rata). Small areas of forest near sea-level on Campbell Island comprise species of *Dracophyllum*, *Myrsine* and *Coprosma*. Ferns are prominent on the forest floor; tree ferns occur rarely. On the Auckland Islands, with increasing altitude and exposure, forest grades into scrub containing *Metrosideros*, *Cassinia*, *Dracophyllum*, *Myrsine* and *Coprosma*. On Campbell Island there is dense *Dracophyllum* scrub and tall heath, with *Myrsine* and *Coprosma* often present. Herbs and bryophytes play an important part in scrub especially at higher altitudes.

On Campbell Island and parts of the Auckland Islands, much of the indigenous vegetation has been modified through human intervention with some replacement of species. Campbell Island is the most altered, as this was subjected to sheep and cattle farming from the late 19th century until about 1930. As a result, much of the original *Chionochloa* tussock grassland was replaced by the less palatable *Poa* tussock grassland and some of the herbaceous elements became locally extinct. Settlements on both Campbell and Auckland Islands resulted in the introduction of weed species, although with cessation of occupation many are now eliminated or have only a tenuous hold. On Campbell Island, sheep grazing resulted in the spread of indigenous *Bulbinella rossii* into many upland communities where it previously did not occur.

The colonization by humans of Macquarie Island has had much less impact than on the more northerly islands. The perpetually cool temperatures and low light levels were not conducive to the growing of food or crop plants, though these were tried. The very steep or boggy terrain was equally inhospitable to the establishment of domestic livestock. The deliberate introduction of rabbits had a profound impact on the vegetation whilst the introduction of cats, now feral, has had a marked affect on populations of small- and medium-sized birds.

Flora

The flora includes c. 250 vascular plant taxa. Although not rich, the vascular flora is genetically very distinct, and includes 35 endemic taxa. The flora is transitional between the diverse, temperate New Zealand flora (represented by genera such as *Dracophyllum*, *Myrsine*, *Cyathodes* and *Phyllachne*) and the less diverse, circum-polar Subantarctic flora (represented by such genera as *Azorella* and *Stilbocarpa*).

The flora includes a highly distinctive "mega-herb" (large-leaved herb) element (*Pleurophyllum* and *Stilbocarpa*). Besides the endemic taxa, there are some more or less circum-Antarctic species which do not reach the New Zealand and Australian mainlands. Among the most prominent and notable plant genera are *Pleurophyllum* (Asteraceae), all 3 species of which are confined to the region, and *Stilbocarpa* (Araliaceae), of which *S. polaris* is endemic to the islands and 2 further species also occur in southern New Zealand. A second genus of the Asteraceae (*Damnamenia*) is endemic to the Subantarctic Islands. *Azorella macquariensis*, *Puccinellia macquariensis* and *Corybas dienemus* are endemic to Macquarie Island. The latter is the only orchid known in the Subantarctic Region.

Campbell Island holds almost the full complement of the endemics from this region. Prominent among the endemic species are the grasses *Chionochloa antarctica* and *Poa litorosa*, the brilliantly flowered *Myosotis capitata*, the herbaceous daisies noted above, and *Bulbinella rossii*, which is the largest species in this liliaceous genus. Despite its small size, Antipodes Island has 3 taxa endemic to it.

Numbers of plant species recorded from the islands are shown in Table 74.

TABLE 74. NUMBERS OF PLANT SPECIES RECORDED FROM THE SUBANTARCTIC ISLANDS

Island/island group	Vascular plant taxa	Mosses	Liverworts	Lichens
Antipodes Islands	64	15	?	?
Auckland Islands	228	?	?	?
Campbell Islands	218	119	?	?
Macquarie Island	40	50	30	55

Source: Clark and Dingwall (1985).

Useful plants

Prior to European exploration these islands were not settled by humans and, even since then, their occupation has been intermittent and (with the exception of Campbell Island) of very limited extent. As a result, there are no traditional uses of plants in the region, although *Stilbocarpa polaris* (Macquarie Island cabbage) was used by the early sealers to ward off scurvy.

The native vegetation is essential for the stabilization of mineral and peat slopes, and provides the habitat for important bird populations.

Social and environmental values

The islands support large colonies of birds, especially pelagic seabirds and penguins. Two-restricted range land bird species occur on the Auckland Islands, namely Auckland rail (*Lewinia muelleri*) and Subantarctic snipe (*Coenocorypha aucklandica*). The former was once thought to be extinct but persists on predator-free Adams and Disappointment islands. The islands are important for breeding seabirds and are amongst the major breeding grounds in the world for several species of albatross (*Diomedia*).

Until the arrival of humans, the islands supported immense colonies of fur seals, sea lions and elephant seals. These were hunted from the early 19th century until the industry collapsed several decades later.

There is continued scientific interest in these islands. Nature tourism is attracting an increasing number of tourists. The main tourism resource is wildlife, especially marine birds and seals, but there is a growing interest in the flora.

Although many attractive plant species occur on these islands, past attempts to cultivate them have not generally been successful. However, since 1989 the Australian National Botanic Gardens in Canberra has developed a specific programme to determine the horticultural requirements of Subantarctic plants. There has been considerable success in cultivating the spectacular *Stilbocarpa polaris*. Some taxa, however, such as *Epilobium* spp., are potentially serious weeds and their introduction into horticulture requires considerable caution.

Threats

Adams Island and Disappointment Island of the Auckland group, along with some smaller islets such as Dent Island of the Campbell group, remain in virtually pristine condition, being rat-free and rarely visited by humans. Macquarie Island and the Antipodes Islands have undergone minimal alteration, although sealing gangs were resident early last century; Macquarie has a permanently occupied scientific station. Campbell Island was occupied for some three decades as a sheep and cattle farm. After 1931 the sheep and cattle became feral, but they have since been totally removed since and the degraded vegetation has steadily recovered.

Introduced plants and animals continue to be a threat to the native flora. Strict quarantine regulations apply to all approved landings of people, equipment and goods on Macquarie Island and the New Zealand islands, and ongoing inspection and vigilance are needed to ensure early action is taken to eliminate introduced species where needed. Programmes to remove alien animals such as cats, rabbits and wekas from Macquarie Island require a carefully balanced approach which takes account of the interactions of the introduced animals with the native plants and animals.

Conservation

Extensive monitoring of vegetation is being undertaken on some islands (e.g. Macquarie and Campbell) and vegetation mapping of Campbell Island is fully digitized.

All the islands are Nature Reserves (IUCN Management Category: I). Macquarie Island is also a Biosphere Reserve. Permits are required for visits; landings are carefully monitored.

References

Clark, M.R. and Dingwall, P.R. (1985). *Conservation of islands in the Southern Ocean: a review of the protected areas of Insulantarctica*. IUCN, Gland, Switzerland and Cambridge, U.K. 188 pp.

Foggo, M.N. and Meurk, C.D. (1981). Notes on a visit to Jacquemart Island in the Campbell Island group. *New Zealand Journal of Ecology* 4: 29–32.

Godley, E.J. (1970). Botany of the southern zone. Exploration to 1843. *Tuatara* 13: 140–181.

Godley, E.J. (1975). Botany of the southern zone. Exploration, 1847–1891. *Tuatara* 18: 140–181.

Godley, E.J. (1989). The flora of Antipodes Island. *New Zealand Journal of Botany* 27: 531–563.

Johnson, P.N. and Campbell, D.J. (1975). Vascular plants of the Auckland Islands. *New Zealand Journal of Botany* 13: 665–720.

Meurk, C.D. (1975). Contributions to the flora and plant ecology of Campbell Island. *New Zealand Journal of Botany* 13: 721–742.

Meurk, C.D. (1977). Alien plants in Campbell Island's changing vegetation. *Mauri Ora* 5: 93–118.

Meurk, C.D. (1982). Regeneration of subantarctic plants on Campbell Island following exclusion of sheep. *New Zealand Journal of Ecology* 5: 51–58.

Meurk, C.D. and Given, D.R. (1990). *Vegetation map of Campbell Island*. DSIR Land Resources, Lower Hutt, New Zealand.

Sorensen, J.H. (1951). An annotated list of the vascular plants. *Bulletin New Zealand DSIR Cape Expedition Series* 7: 25–38.

Taylor, B.W. (1955). The flora, vegetation and soils of Macquarie Island. *Australian National Antarctic Research Expeditions Reports (Botany), Series B, 2*: 1–192.

Acknowledgements

This Data Sheet was written by Dr David R. Given (Christchurch, New Zealand) and Dr Roger Hnatiuk (National Forest Inventory, Canberra, Australia).

REGIONAL OVERVIEW: PACIFIC OCEAN ISLANDS

PIETER VAN ROYEN AND STEPHEN D. DAVIS

Total land area: c. 91,000 km².

Population: >3,300,000.

Altitude: 0–4205 m (summit of Mauna Kea, Hawai'i; from sea-level it is a further 9400 m to the ocean floor, making Mauna Kea the tallest volcano in the world). Most of the islands of the Pacific are low atolls and small islets.

Natural vegetation: Beach vegetation, coastal dunes, lowland rain forest, dry savanna and open scrubland, shrub vegetation, mid-montane rain forest and scrub, montane forest, mossy forest, subalpine and alpine vegetation.

Number of vascular plants: 11,000–12,000 species. Much of the flora is closely related to that of Malesia. Introduced species abound; in Hawai'i there are now more alien species growing in the wild than there are native species.

Number of island or island group endemics: 6375

Number of regional endemics: c. 7000 species. Species endemism is high on the larger islands (e.g. 83% in the Hawaiian Islands, 77% in New Caledonia and 50% in the Fijian Islands).

Number of endemic families: 7.

Number of genera: c. 1600.

Introduction

The Pacific Ocean is the Earth's largest geographical feature, covering one-third of the world's surface. The region, as defined here, includes about 1100 islets, atolls and islands. New Caledonia forms the south-western limit of the region; Micronesia forms the north-western limit. Micronesia comprises the Marshall Islands, the Mariana Islands and the Caroline Islands. The Bonin (Ogasawara) Islands, politically part of Japan, are to the north. Kiribati (Gilbert Islands) connects Micronesia with Polynesia, a broad swathe of islands from Fiji, in the west, to the Pitcairn group in the east. Towards the north-west, the Polynesian group continues into the Tokelau and Phoenix Islands and the long chains of volcanoes comprising the Line Islands. To the north and east, the Hawaiian Islands and Emperor Seamounts, chains of volcanoes and submerged guyots, extend north-westward to the Aleutian Trench. The Galápagos Islands (off the Ecuadorian coast) and Juan Fernández (off the Chilean coast) form the easternmost outliers of the Pacific region as defined here.

Table 75 provides summary data on the physical nature of some of the larger islands and groups, together with population statistics. For comprehensive lists of Pacific Islands, see Douglas (1969), IUCN (1986) (covers west and central Pacific) and Motteler (1986).

Geology

The islands of the Pacific can be grouped into the following categories:

1. younger volcanic islands that are shield-shaped and little eroded, such as the younger parts of the Big Island of Hawai'i;

2. older volcanic islands that have been eroded and are highly dissected, such as Kaua'i and Oahu in the Hawaiian archipelago;

3. atolls and volcanic remnants surrounded by coral reefs, such as Bora-Bora in the Society Islands which consists of a ring of such coral reefs and islands;

4. coral atolls in which the volcanic remnants of the former high islands are now completely submerged, such as the Tuamotus;

5. elevated atolls and limestone islands, such as Guam;

6. islands in which there is a mosaic of volcanic and limestone substrates; and

7. islands which are (at least in part) continental in origin, often containing a complex of volcanic and limestone substrates, such as New Caledonia, which is believed to have been originally part of the Queensland Plateau.

The oldest islands in the region are at least 60–80 million years old. The islands of the Central Pacific Basin are characterized by the predominance of basaltic rocks, with relatively minor amounts of andesite and oligoclase-andesite, trachyte and, in a few groups, with nepheline basalts, or their intrusive equivalents. In this group belong the Society, Marquesas, Galápagos, Samoan, Caroline and Hawaiian Islands.

Two types of islands can be distinguished based on their origins, namely the Benioff and Darwin types. The Benioff type arose as a result of volcanic activity near the subduction zones of colliding crustal plates. The Darwin type of volcanoes developed above a more or less stationary hotspot.

TABLE 75. PHYSICAL AND POPULATION STATISTICS OF SOME PACIFIC OCEANIC ISLANDS

	Area (km²)	Maximum altitude (m)	Number of islands	Population total	Population density [a] (km²)
American Samoa	197	931	26	46,800	238
Bonin Islands	73	462	30	1800	25
Cook Islands	230	643	15	16,900	73
Fed. Micronesia	1170	721	70	107,500	92
Fiji	18,270	1324	332	732,000	40
French Polynesia[b]	3583	2241	121	196,300	55
Galápagos Islands	7900	1707	13 [c]	10,000	1
Guam	450	152	1	133,400	296
Hawaiian Islands	16,641	4205	132	>1,000,000	>60
Juan Fernández	100	1319	3 [c]	500	5
Kiribati	684	81	33	71,800	105
Marquesas	1275	1260	12	5000	4
Marshall Islands	181	5	33	46,200	255
Nauru	21	71	1	9300	443
New Caledonia[d]	19,200	1628	30	167,600	9
Niue	259	61	1	2500	10
North Marianas	477	965	16	44,200	93
Palau	494	200	10	15,200	31
Pitcairn Islands	43	333	4	48	1
Tokelau Islands	10	5	3	1800	180
Tonga	699	1030	164	96,300	138
Tuvalu	26	10	9	10,200	392
Vanuatu	14,763	1889	82	146,400	10
Wallis and Futuna	250	500	2	13,700	55
Western Samoa	2940	1857	8	157,700	55
Totals (whole region)			**c. 1100**	**>3,300,000**	

Notes:

[a] Note that in many archipelagos, population density varies markedly from one island to another, and some islands are uninhabited.
[b] French Polynesia includes the Marquesas which are also given a separate entry.
[c] Figure refers to the main islands in the group.
[d] Includes the main island, Grande Terre, and associated islands.
Source: Given (1992) and information from CPD Data Sheets.

Biogeography

Plate movements since the break-up of Pangaea help to explain present day patterns of plant and animal distribution in the Pacific in which the dominant direction of plant migration has been from south-west to north-east.

In the true oceanic islands, indigenous large mammals are rare or absent. In Hawai'i, for example, there was only one species of bat and one species of seal. The absence of large mammals allowed the evolution of many species of large and flightless birds which took on the role of herbivores. The best example of this is in New Zealand (treated in the Regional Overview on Australia and New Zealand).

The earliest evidence of humans in New Guinea (see Regional Overview on South East Asia) dates from about 40,000 years ago. By 30,000 years ago, humans had reached the Solomon Islands. Melanesia was reached 4000 years ago followed by Micronesia about 2000 years ago (Dodson 1992). In the Polynesians, a culture had developed that allowed humans to colonize even the most remote islands of the Pacific, such as Easter Island and, for a time, Henderson. Such colonization depended upon the existence of trees large and sturdy enough to make the large outriggers necessary for long ocean voyages. However, after settling many of the islands, particularly the smaller ones, forests were cleared and destroyed, leaving the islanders stranded. Such a scenario occurred on Easter Island, for example.

There is no doubt that the native flora and fauna of islands colonized by the Polynesians was changed and depleted dramatically, at least on the smaller islands (Fosberg 1973, 1991). Whistler (1991), for example, identified 72 species of plants thought to have been introduced intentionally by Polynesians to central and eastern Pacific islands. The changes were to continue with the arrival of Europeans and accelerated in the latter part of the 18th century. Johnson and Stattersfield (1990) have shown that the Pacific has the highest number of known avian extinctions in the world. In Hawai'i alone, over 70% of the known bird life has become extinct since human colonization (Olson and James 1984). The Pacific has half the world's known Endangered species of birds, and well over 40% of those believed to be Endangered (Given 1992). The floras of some of the Pacific islands, such as those of the Hawaiian Islands and Juan Fernández, are among the most threatened in the world.

Vegetation

The environments in the region range from tropical rain forest to sand deserts. Lowland, mid-montane and montane zones occur mainly on the larger islands of Hawai'i, New Caledonia, Juan Fernández, the Galápagos Islands, Fiji, the Samoan Islands and, to some extent, on the Marquesas and Society Islands. Vegetation zonation is clearly evident in the Galápagos (CPD Site PO7, see Data Sheet) and in Juan Fernández (CPD Site PO8, see Data Sheet). In all zones, grassland or grassland/fernland often develops after forest clearance. At high altitudes the grasses tend to dominate the ferns. However, in Hawai'i landslides at high altitudes are often covered naturally by the fern *Dicranopteris linearis*. At all altitudes and in all types of ecosystems, swampy and riverine vegetation occur.

The vegetation of the region includes beach vegetation, coastal dunes, lowland rain forest, dry savanna, shrub vegetation, mid-montane rain forest and scrub, montane forest, mossy forest, dry open scrubland, subalpine and alpine vegetation. Over 100 vegetation facies are recognized in Hawai'i alone. The main formations in the region are described briefly below.

Lowland forest

Lowland forest occurs from sea-level to 1200 m. Lowland rain forest once covered most of the high islands. Apart from one or two exceptions, such as on New Caledonia and some of the islands in the Fijian and Samoan groups, lowland rain forests have mostly been logged or cleared for agriculture and other development, and survive today only as small fragments. The forests tend to be richer in the western part of the region. Dominant species differ from one floristic province to another. The main dominant trees are members of the Sapotaceae (*Burckella*, *Manilkara*), Rutaceae, Rubiaceae, Euphorbiaceae, Myrtaceae (*Metrosideros*) or Leguminosae. In the western islands, *Agathis*, *Araucaria* and *Podocarpus* frequently form large stands. From Samoa eastwards the genus *Pandanus* becomes more prominent and sometimes forms dense stands. Lowland forests are usually poorly developed or non-existent on the smaller atolls. In drier areas, a dry, shrubby, sclerophyllous vegetation occurs.

Special forest types, such as riverine forest, freshwater swamp forest and semi-deciduous forest, occur in localized areas. Their species composition is rather different from other forest types. Samples of these forests should be protected as part of any comprehensive conservation plan (IUCN 1986).

Limestone forest

Limestone forest is a distinct type of lowland rain forest with a distinct assemblage of species growing on raised coral substrates. Many such forests have been cleared. Limestone forests of particular conservation significance occur on Henderson (one of the least disturbed islands in the whole Pacific region) and in Fiji.

Montane and submontane forests

Montane forest is well-developed on the larger islands. The dominant species are, in many cases, members of the genus *Metrosideros*. Tree ferns sometimes form large monospecific stands in moist areas in the eastern islands; mixed stands of tree ferns and *Pandanus* occur in drier areas. On some islands, well-developed mossy vegetation is found in the montane belt. Dry montane forests, dominated by *Acacia*, *Metrosideros* and *Santalum*, are found on some of the larger islands. The steep slopes of many montane areas have provided some natural protection from disturbance; however, some areas have been logged or cleared for agriculture. The main threat to montane forests is uncontrolled burning, invasion by introduced plants and grazing pressure from feral animals.

Scrub

Various forms of scrub vegetation occur in the region. Frequently, they are of secondary origin but, nevertheless, provide suitable habitat for nesting birds. The scrub (maquis)

of New Caledonia (see Data Sheet on Grande Terre, CPD Site PO2) is developed on ultramafic substrates and is exceptionally rich in endemic plant species. It is, therefore, of great conservation significance.

Grasslands and savannas

The region's grasslands and savannas are mostly of secondary origin. Grasslands occur in all zones on many islands. In many cases, grasslands resulting from slash and burn cultivation are dominated by *Imperata* and *Miscanthus*. Natural grasslands include such genera as *Deschampsia* and *Eragrostis* and, in wet areas and bogs, *Rhynchospora*, *Oreobolus*, *Cyperus*, *Gahnia* and *Fimbristylis*.

Littoral vegetation

Atoll and beach forest has often been cleared for coconut plantations and tourist developments. Whilst mainly comprising relatively few species of plants which are mainly pan-Pacific or pantropical species, surviving remnants of atoll and beach forest are, nevertheless, important bird habitats and protect coastlines from erosion. In the Galápagos Islands, genera of American origin are found in the littoral zone. They include *Lycium*, *Grabowskya* and *Nolana*.

Mangroves are a common feature along muddy estuaries and shorelines, particularly in the western Pacific.

Flora

The boundaries of the region are artificial from a botanical point-of-view. Both van Balgooy (1971) and Takhtajan (1986) conclude that, for the most part, the flora of the Pacific is a derivative of the Malesian flora. There is a distinct decrease of genera from west to east. The eastern biological border of the region is the Engler Line, close to the Americas. The floras of the islands and island groups east of the Engler Line, such as the Galápagos Islands and Juan Fernández, have distinct American affinities with almost no Malesian representation.

Takhtajan (1986) recognizes several distinct floristic regions within the Pacific. The flora of New Caledonia (see Data Sheet on Grande Terre, the main island – CPD Site PO2) is so highly distinctive that it is placed within its own Floristic Region (the Neocaledonian Floristic Region). This alone forms a separate floristic unit, the Neocaledonian Subkingdom.

The flora of the Fijian Floristic Region belongs to the Indomalesian Subkingdom. Included are Fiji, Vanuatu, Tonga, the Rotuma Islands, Niue and the Samoan Islands. The flora has much in common with Malesia (see Regional Overview on South East Asia), and especially New Guinea and the Solomon Islands. The greatest concentration of endemic genera and species is found on Fiji (CPD Site PO3, see Data Sheet).

The Polynesian Subkingdom includes the Polynesian and Hawaiian Floristic Regions. The Polynesian Floristic Region includes the islands of Micronesia (e.g. Palau, the Caroline Islands, the Marianas and Marshall Islands) and those of Polynesia (e.g. the Society Islands, Easter Island and the Pitcairn group). There are relatively few endemic genera (see Table 76). The greatest number of endemic species occurs in French Polynesia (including the Society Islands and Marquesas – CPD Site PO5, see Data Sheet), the Federated States of

Micronesia, Palau, the North Marianas, Guam and the Cook Islands. Rapa and the Pitcairn group (particularly Henderson) also contain numerous endemics.

The flora of the Hawaiian Islands (CPD Site PO6, see Data Sheet) is exceedingly rich in endemic species and genera. The flora is so distinct that it is treated as a separate floristic region (the Hawaiian Floristic Region) by Takhtajan (1986) and others.

In the west of the Pacific Ocean are the Bonin (Ogasawara) Islands (CPD Site PO1, see Data Sheet). These islands form part of the Volcano-Bonin Floristic Province of the Eastern Asiatic Region. The flora includes a large number of endemic species whose closest affinities are mostly with species occurring in continental East Asia.

In the east of the region, the floras of the Galápagos Islands (CPD Site PO7, see Data Sheet) and Juan Fernández (CPD Site PO8, see Data Sheet) are relatively poor in species but have relatively high degrees of endemism (41.4% and 60.4%, respectively). The floras of these two island groups are most closely related to those of the American mainland.

TABLE 76. VASCULAR PLANT GENERA AND FAMILY STATISTICS FOR SOME PACIFIC ISLANDS

Islands	Number of genera	Endemic genera	Number of families	Endemic families
Bonin (Ogasawara) Islands	-	2	-	0
Caroline Islands	336	-	-	0
Fiji	1013	12	210	1
Galápagos Islands	292	7	90	0
Gambier Islands	200	0	70	0
Hawaiian Islands	216	32	87	0
Juan Fernández	693	12	16	1
Loyalty Islands	262	0	-	0
Mariana Islands	215	1	80	0
Marquesas	177	3	85	0
New Caledonia	863	110	191	5
Rapa	-	0	-	0
Samoan Islands	387	1	120	0
Society Islands	189	1	77	0
Tonga	295	0	75	0
Tubuai	88	0	-	0
Vanuatu	534	1	-	0

Notes:

Figures refer to native plants. Many of the genera occur on more than one island or island group; the total number of genera in the region is estimated at c. 1600.

- indicates figure not available.

TABLE 77. VASCULAR PLANT STATISTICS FOR SOME PACIFIC ISLANDS

	Vascular plant species[a]	Native vascular plant species	Endemic species[b]	Naturalized species	Native gymnosperm species	Native fern species[c]	Native flowering plant species
American Samoa	576	471	15	110	0	135	336
Bonin Islands	-	400	150	-	-	-	-
Cook Islands	557	284	33	273	0	100	184
Fed. Micronesia	1574	1194	293	380	1	201	992
Fiji	2628	1628	812	1000	11	310	1307
French Polynesia[d]	1519	959	560	560	-	269	690
Galápagos Islands	801	541	224	260	0	110	431
Guam	550	330	69	220	0	-	330
Hawaiian Islands	2200	1200	1000	1000	0	167	980
Juan Fernández	362	210	127	152	-	-	-
Kiribati	102	22	2	80	0	-	22
Marquesas	-	318	132	-	0	108	210
Marshall Islands	304	100	5	204	1	11	88
Nauru	108	54	1	54	0	4	50
New Caledonia	>4820	3322	2551	>1500	44	261	3017
Niue	423	178	1	245	0	28	150
North Marianas	471	221	81	250	1	64	156
Palau	629	175	-	454	-	-	-
Pitcairn Islands	-	76	14	-	0	20	56
Tokelau Islands	58	32	0	26	0	6	26
Tonga	837	463	25	374	1	102	360
Tuvalu	86	44	0	42	0	4	40
Vanuatu	1000	870	150	130	-	-	-
Wallis and Futuna	625	475	7	150	0	59	416
Western Samoa	894	737	134	157	0	223	514

Notes:
[a] Includes introduced species.
[b] Refers to species endemic to the island or island group concerned.
[c] Includes fern allies.
[d] Includes Marquesas which are also given a separate entry.
- Figure not available.

Sources: Given (1992) and World Conservation Monitoring Centre statistics and information from CPD Data Sheets.

Takhtajan (1986) places the Galápageian Floristic Province within the Caribbean Floristic Region (which also includes Florida, the Caribbean Islands, Central America, the coastal parts of Colombia, Ecuador and Venezuela, and the Cocos Islands), while the Juan Fernández (together with the Desventuradas Islands) form a distinct floristic region (the Fernandezian Region) containing only one floristic province (the Fernandezian Province).

Table 76 gives some data on the presently known or estimated number of genera and families for the main islands in the Pacific. It is estimated that the Pacific region contains approximately 22,000 vascular plant species (including about 10,000 introduced species). The total number of native vascular plant species is estimated at 11,000–12,000. Of these, about 7000 species are endemic to the region. There are 7 endemic families (5 in New Caledonia, 1 in Fiji and 1 in Juan Fernández). The oldest and most primitive families are found in Fiji (Degeneriaceae) and Juan Fernández (Lactoridaceae). Amborellaceae, Oncothecaceae, Paracryphiaceae, Phellinaceae and Strasburgeriaceae are restricted to New Caledonia.

The number of naturalized taxa has been growing rapidly over the past century, aided by the advent of air travel and the massive influx of tourists since the beginning of this century. In Hawai'i there are now more alien species growing in the wild than there are native species and, in terms of biomass, the alien introductions far outweigh the native species.

Useful plants

A wide range of native plant resources have been utilized, first by Polynesian settlers and then by other arriving cultures. Native plants have provided food, medicines, fibres, wood for house- and boat-building, tools, ornaments, and plants used in ceremonies. At least some traditional uses continue today.

Valuable timber trees include species of *Acacia* (e.g. *A. koa* in Hawai'i), *Araucaria*, *Agathis* (in New Caledonia) and *Metrosideros*. Formerly, sandalwood (*Santalum* spp.) was the most sought after timber for home and canoe construction, but over-exploitation reduced most species in number and size. Some species have come close to extinction.

The most important food staples are *Colocasia esculenta* (taro), *Cocos nucifera* (coconut), *Saccharum* (sugarcane), *Artocarpus* (breadfruit), *Dioscorea* (yam), *Canarium* (pili nut), *Metroxylon* (sago) and *Ipomoea batatas* (sweet potato). Many ornamental plants commonly cultivated in the region are introduced species. However, there are many native ornamental plants worthy of cultivation, in families such as Epacridaceae (e.g. *Styphelia* and *Epacris*), Theaceae (*Montrouziera*) and Myrtaceae.

For a comprehensive overview of the ethnobotany of the Polynesian islands, see Cox and Banack (1991). The Data Sheets which follow provide further examples of useful plants in the region.

Threats

Threats differ in their seriousness according to the type of island. The main threats on large high islands, such as New Caledonia (see Data Sheet on Grande Terre, CPD Site PO2),

Fiji (CPD Site PO3, see Data Sheet) and Vanuatu are logging, fire, mining, tourism and trade in endangered species. Slash and burn agriculture and rapidly expanding populations are additional threats on Fiji and Vanuatu. In New Caledonia, mining has resulted in the removal of the original vegetation over large areas and has resulted in increased run-off from areas with high concentrations of aluminium and iron. This has polluted water courses and damaged coral reefs.

The floras of remote oceanic islands, such as the Hawaiian Islands (CPD Site PO6, see Data Sheet), some of the Society Islands and some of the Micronesian Islands are threatened principally by clearance for agriculture, introduced plants and animals, logging, fire, and (in the case of the Hawaiian Islands) urban and tourist developments.

Population pressure, arising from the increase in tourism and indigenous population growth, has led to the wholesale clearance of native vegetation in the coastal and lowland areas of many islands in the region, for the construction of towns, hotels, recreation facilities, airports and roads. Urban developments and tourist facilities need to be carefully planned so as not to destroy fragile environments or areas of biological importance.

One of the most serious threats throughout the region is the effects of introduced plants and domestic and feral animals (see Data Sheets PO1–PO8 for details). Natural threats (depending on the island) include damage by hurricanes, destruction by volcanic activity and landslides.

Conservation

IUCN (1986) reviewed the conservation status of islands in Oceania, covering those islands of the western and central Pacific Ocean, as far east as the Pitcairn group, and including Norfolk and Lord Howe Islands (treated in this present study in the Regional Overview on Australia and New Zealand), Papua New Guinea and associated offshore islands, and the Solomon Islands (treated in the Regional Overview on South East Asia). The Bonin Islands, Hawaiian Islands and the islands in the eastern Pacific were not included within the review.

The review concluded that less than 20% of Oceania's ecosystems were included in protected areas at that time. Throughout the Pacific, many highly endangered atolls and low islands remain totally unprotected, while the protected area coverage of the botanically-richer higher islands remains inadequate. Within the central Pacific, only the Phoenix-Line-Cook Islands can be considered well covered by protected areas. Of the 50 islands with protected areas covered in IUCN (1986), only 19 have parks and reserves totalling more than 10 km², and only 5 have protected areas of more than 100 km². In the east, most of the Bonin (Ogasawara) Islands (CPD Site PO1, see Data Sheet) are included within a National Park and active programmes are underway to rescue and reintroduce threatened plants.

The majority of protected areas in the Pacific region, with the notable exception of New Caledonia, have not been designated primarily on the basis of their plant diversity. Many, for example, are bird sanctuaries. Land has also been set aside on some of the high islands as Forest Reserves, tourist areas and hydrological reserves, where nature conservation values are not the primary objective of management. Such botanically important islands and island groups as New Caledonia, Guam, Fiji and the Samoan Islands have between 3–9% of their area protected. However, in French Polynesia, the islands with the highest concentrations of endemics have very few (and, in some cases, no) protected areas, although there are some Forest Reserves. The present protected areas on Marquesas (CPD Site PO5) are inadequate (see Data Sheet), while Tahiti, Rapa and Moorea are all at risk from human activities. Of the last named, only Tahiti has a protected area – Vallée de Faaiti Park (IUCN Management Category: IV), notified in 1989, covering 7.5 km².

In the Hawaiian Islands, State Forest Reserves and the State Conservation District amount to over 8000 km² of lands that restrict agricultural or other development (c. 48% of the land area of the archipelago). Protected areas managed primarily for nature conservation cover 2029.4 km² (c. 12% of land area). However, while many examples of native Hawaiian vegetation occur on protected lands, there are still many botanically important sites and threatened species which are in jeopardy (see Data Sheet on the Hawaiian Islands, CPD Site PO6).

In the east of the region, the Galápagos National Park (IUCN Management Category: II) covers 7278 km² (96.7% of the land area of the Galápagos archipelago). In addition, the archipelago has been designated both a World Heritage Site and a Biosphere Reserve. Conservation programmes undertaken by the Charles Darwin Research Station (CDRS) and the Galápagos National Park Service (GNPS) during the last 30 years have successfully ensured the survival of many endemic animal and plant species on the islands. Despite problems from introduced plants and animals (particularly on the inhabited islands), zoning of land uses (and remoteness) has ensured that large parts of the archipelago are protected and remain in a relatively pristine condition (Anon. 1974). During recent years, the GNPS and the CDRS have started campaigns against some of the invasive plants and a comprehensive plant conservation programme has been developed following recommendations from a major international workshop (Lawesson, Hamann and Black 1990) (see Data Sheet on the Galápagos Islands, CPD Site PO7, for further details).

The Juan Fernández are a National Park and Biosphere Reserve; CONAF (Corporación Nacional Forestal) is working to save the endemic plants of the islands. A conservation development plan has been prepared by the Chilean Government (with support from WWF), although more funds are needed to implement its recommendations fully.

Not only is there is an urgent need to establish more protected areas throughout the region, particularly in the west and central parts of the Pacific, but better protection and management are necessary for those areas which are already established as protected areas. IUCN (1986) concluded that few, if any, protected areas in Oceania are well managed. There is also a great need for basic ecological studies and more botanical research throughout the region upon which to base conservation programmes. This is particularly the case in Fiji (CPD Site PO3, see Data Sheet) and many parts of French Polynesia, including the Society Islands.

Protected areas in the Pacific are described in detail in IUCN (1991); IUCN (1992) provides a review of conservation legislation and protected areas in the region.

It is important, of course, to designate land as protected, and to ensure that all the major habitat types are represented within the protected areas system. However, the options for doing this are rapidly disappearing in some parts of the region as a result of the continued loss and fragmentation of habitats. A further important factor is land ownership. Most land in the Pacific remains in customary ownership. In Melanesia, for example, 85–90% of all land is owned by local people rather than central governments (Lees 1992). In Western Samoa, 80% of land is communally owned by indigenous groups who are highly dependent upon subsistence agriculture. In many parts of Polynesia, cultural traditions have placed particular significance on some species and sites, and have played an important role in protecting some natural resources. However, these conservative traditions among local people are being lost or replaced as increasing populations and the pressures of global economics force more and more people to clear forests for subsistence agriculture or to grow cash crops. Conservation efforts, if they are to succeed, must operate within a framework of customary land ownership and traditional practices, and must pay particular attention to the needs of local people.

Centres of plant diversity and endemism

Data Sheet sites have been chosen to represent each of the major floristic regions described above (see Flora section). All the islands selected for Data Sheet treatment have more than 100 native vascular plant species, of which more than 25% are endemic to the island group.

EASTERN ASIATIC REGION

Japan

PO1. Bonin (Ogasawara) Islands

– see Data Sheet.

NEOCALEDONIAN REGION

New Caledonia

PO2. Grande Terre

– see Data Sheet.

FIJIAN REGION

PO3. Fiji

– see Data Sheet.

Western Samoa, American Samoa

PO4. Samoan Islands

– see Data Sheet.

POLYNESIAN REGION

French Polynesia

PO5. Marquesas

– see Data Sheet.

HAWAIIAN REGION

U.S.A.

PO6. Hawaiian Islands

– see Data Sheet.

GALAPAGEIAN FLORISTIC PROVINCE (CARIBBEAN REGION)

Ecuador

PO7. Galápagos Islands

– see Data Sheet.

FERNANDEZIAN REGION

Chile

PO8. Juan Fernández

– see Data Sheet.

Other candidates for selection as globally important CPD sites are: Palau, which has the richest and most diverse floras in Micronesia (F.R. Fosberg 1992, *in litt.*), Rapa and the Society Islands (all in the Polynesian Region). Insufficient information was available on the floras of these islands on which to base selection.

References

Anon. (1974). *Plan Maestro Parque Nacional Galápagos.* PNUD/FAO/ECU/71/022. Santiago, Chile. Pp. 1–91.

Balgooy, M.M.J. van (1971). Plant geography of the Pacific. *Blumea Suppl.* 6.

Balgooy, M.M.J. van (ed.) (1975). *Pacific plant areas, vol. 3.* Rijksherbarium, Leiden, The Netherlands. 386 pp.

Balgooy, M.M.J. van (ed.) (1984). *Pacific plant areas, vol. 4.* Rijksherbarium, Leiden, The Netherlands. 270 pp.

Banack, S.A. (1991). Plants and Polynesian voyaging. In Cox, P.A. and Banack, S.A. (eds), *Islands, plants and Polynesians. An introduction to Polynesian ethnobotany.* Dioscorides Press, Portland, U.S.A. Pp. 25–40.

Birnbaum, P. and Hammes, C. (1988). Study of the perturbations of a vegetal species, *Miconia calvescens,* in the Tahitian ecosystem and development of a method of biological control. 4 pp. (Unpublished draft report.)

Carlquist, S. (1970). *Hawai'i, a natural history.* Natural History Press, New York. 463 pp.

Carlquist, S. (1974). *Island biology.* Columbia University Press, New York. 660 pp.

Carlquist, S. (1980). *Hawai'i, a natural history, ed. 2. Geology, climate, native flora and fauna above the shoreline.* Pacific Tropical Botanic Garden, Honolulu, Hawai'i. 468 pp.

Chazeau, J. (1990). *Workshop on terrestrial biodiversity in New Caledonia, Noumea, 19–26 September 1990.* Report to ORSTOM, Noumea, New Caledonia. 24 pp.

Cox, P.A. and Banack, S.A. (eds) (1991). *Islands, plants and Polynesians. An introduction to Polynesian ethnobotany.* Dioscorides Press, Portland, U.S.A. 228 pp.

Dahl, A.L. (1980). *Regional ecosystems survey of the South Pacific area.* SPC Technical Paper 179, Noumea, New Caledonia.

Dodson, J.R. (ed.) (1992). *The native lands – prehistory and environmental change in the South Pacific.* Longman Cheshire, Melbourne, Australia.

Douglas, G. (1969). Draft check list of Pacific Ocean islands. *Micronesica* 5(2): 327–463.

Flannery, T. (1989). Plague in the Pacific. *Australian Natural History* 23: 20–28.

Fosberg, F.R. (1948). Derivation of the flora of the Hawaiian Islands. In Zimmerman, E.C. (ed.), *Insects of Hawai'i,* vol. 1. University Press of Hawaii, Honolulu, Hawai'i. Pp. 107–119.

Fosberg, F.R. (1973). On present condition and conservation of forests in Micronesia. In Pacific Science Association, *Symposium: planned utilization of the lowland tropical forests.* Bogor, Indonesia. Pp. 165–71.

Fosberg, F.R. (1991). Polynesian plant environments. In Cox, P.A. and Banack, S.A. (eds), *Islands, plants and Polynesians. An introduction to Polynesian ethnobotany.* Dioscorides Press, Portland, U.S.A. Pp. 11–23.

Given, D.R. (1992). *An overview of the terrestrial biodiversity of Pacific Islands.* South Pacific Regional Environment Program, Apia, Western Samoa. 36 pp.

Hay, R. (1986). *Bird conservation in the Pacific Islands.* International Council for Bird Preservation, Study Report 7. ICBP, Cambridge, U.K. 102 pp.

Huguenin, B. (1974). La vegetation des Iles Gambier. *Cahiers Pacifique* 18(1): 459–472.

IUCN (1986). *Review of the protected areas system in Oceania*. IUCN/UNEP, Gland, Switzerland and Cambridge, U.K. 239 pp.

IUCN (1991). *IUCN directory of protected areas in Oceania*. IUCN, Gland, Switzerland and Cambridge, U.K. xxiii, 447 pp. (Prepared by the World Conservation Monitoring Centre.)

IUCN (1992). *Protected areas of the world: a review of national systems. Volume 1: Indomalaya, Oceania, Australia and Antarctic*. IUCN, Gland, Switzerland and Cambridge, U.K. xx, 352 pp. (Prepared by the World Conservation Monitoring Centre.)

Johnson, T.H. and Stattersfield, A.J. (1990). A global review of island endemic birds. *Ibis* 132: 169–179.

Lawesson, J.E., Hamann, O. and Black, J. (1990). Combined recommendations from the Workshop: Botanical Research and Management in Galápagos. In Lawesson, J.E., Hamann, O., Rogers, G., Reck, G. and Ochoa, H. (eds), *Botanical research and management in Galápagos*. Missouri Botanical Garden, St Louis, Missouri. Pp. 291–295.

Lees, A. (1992). Lessons from the Pacific: linking traditional ownership, development needs and protected areas. Unpublished paper for the IV World Congress on National Parks and Protected Areas, Caracas, Venezuela, February 1992. 8 pp.

Morat, Ph., Jaffré, T., Veillon, J.M. and MacKee, H.S. (1981). *Végétation*. Carte et Pl. 15 in Atlas de la Nouvelle-Calédonie. ORSTOM, Paris.

Motteler, L.S. (1986). *Pacific island names*. Bishop Museum Press, Honolulu, Hawai'i. 91 pp.

Mueller-Dombois, D., Bridges, K.W. and Carson, H.L. (1981). *Island ecosystems. Biological organization in selected Hawaiian communities*. US/IBP Synthesis Series 15. Hutchinson Ross, Woods Hole, Massachusetts, U.S.A. 583 pp.

Olson, S.L. and James, H.F. (1984). The role of Polynesians in the extinction of the avifauna of the Hawaiian Islands. In Martin, P. S. and Klein, R.G. (eds), *Quaternary extinctions, a prehistoric revolution*. University of Arizona Press, Tucson, Arizona, U.S.A.

Savidge, J.A. (1984). Guam: paradise lost for wildlife. *Biological Conservation* 30: 305–317.

Skottsberg, C.J.F. (ed.) (1920-1956). *The natural history of Juan Fernández and Easter Island*, 3 vols. Almqvist and Wiksell, Uppsala, Sweden.

Smith, A.C. (1979-). *Flora Vitiensis Nova*. Pacific Tropical Botanical Garden, Kauai, Hawai'i.

Sohmer, S.H. (1990). Elements of Pacific biodiversity. In Baas, P., Kalkman, K. and Geesink, R. (eds), *The plant diversity of Malesia. Proceedings of the Flora Malesiana Symposium commemorating Professor Dr. C.G.G.J. van Steenis, Leiden, August 1989*. Kluwer Academic Press, Dordrecht. Pp. 293–304.

Steenis, C.G.G.J. van (ed.) (1963). Pacific plant areas, vol. 1. *Monogr. Natl Inst. Sci. Technol. (Manila)* 8(1): 1–297.

Steenis, C.G.G.J. van and Balgooy, M.M.J. van (eds) (1966). Pacific plant areas, vol. 2. *Blumea Suppl.* 5: 1–312.

Stone, B.C. (1970). Flora of Guam. *Micronesica* 6: 1–659.

Sykes, W.R. (1983). Conservation of South Pacific islands. In Given, D.R. (ed.), *Conservation of plant species and habitats*. Nature Conservation Council, Wellington, New Zealand. Pp. 37–42.

Takhtajan, A. (1986). *Floristic regions of the world*. University of California Press, Berkeley. 522 pp.

Wagner, W.L., Herbst, D.R. and Sohmer, S.H. (1990). *Manual of the flowering plants of Hawai'i*. University of Hawaii Press and Bishop Museum Press, Honolulu, Hawai'i.

Whistler, W.A. (1991). The ethnobotany of Tonga: the plants, their Tongan names and their uses. *Bishop Museum Bulletin in Botany* 2: 155 pp.

Whistler, W.A. (1992). The vegetation of Samoa and Tonga. *Pacific Science* 46(2): 159–178.

Wodzicki, K. (1981). Some nature conservation problems in the South Pacific. *Biological Conservation* 21: 5–18.

Acknowledgements

Dr David R. Given (Christchurch, New Zealand) kindly provided much useful information for the account, including flora statistics. The authors also gratefully acknowledge the help of Dr Sy Sohmer (Botanical Research Institute, Fort Worth, Texas) in preparing and co-ordinating comments on earlier versions of the text. Charles H. Lamourex commented on the manuscript and improved it greatly. Warren L. Wagner and the late Benjamin C. Stone reviewed drafts.

BONIN (OGASAWARA) ISLANDS
Japan

Location: 30 small islands in the western Pacific Ocean, c. 1000 km south of Honshu, between longitudes 20°00'–28°00'N and latitudes 135°00'–155°00'E.

Area: 73 km².

Altitude: 0–462 m (summit of Mount Chibusa-yama).

Vegetation: Subtropical evergreen broadleaved forests, but only little remains intact; scrub.

Flora: 400 native vascular plant species, of which 150 are endemic. >80 species are rare or threatened.

Useful plants: *Morus boninensis* provides valuable timber; ornamental plants.

Other values: Tourism.

Threats: Visitor pressure, infrastructure developments, invasive plants.

Conservation: National Park (IUCN Management Category: II) covers 61 km². Active programmes to propagate and reintroduce threatened plants.

Geography

The Bonin (Ogasawara) Islands are a group of about 30 oceanic islands situated some 1000 km south of Honshu in the western Pacific Ocean between latitudes 20°00'–28°00'N and longitudes 135°00'–155°00'E. The largest islands, Chichijima (Father Island) and Hahajima (Mother Island), are a little over 20 km² in area. The islands are volcanic and first appeared during the Eocene epoch. The present structure of the islands was formed some 3 million years BP. The highest point is Mount Chibusa-yama (462 m) on Hahajima.

The islands were uninhabited until 1830 when some 25 people settled and began agricultural activities, first on Chichijima and then on Hahajima. At that time the islands were covered with dense forests (Miyawaki 1989). Transmigration to the islands was recommended by the Japanese Government in the latter half of the 19th century. Thereafter, much of the forest was cleared to establish pastures on the larger islands. By 1984, the population had risen to 1798 people.

The climate is subtropical, the average temperature being about 23°C. Average annual precipitation has fluctuated on Chichijima from 1612 mm during 1907 and 1940 to 1240 mm between 1969 and 1980.

Vegetation

The islands were once covered by dense subtropical evergreen broadleaved forests. Most of the native forest has been cleared or seriously degraded over the last one hundred years and little remains intact. Some evergreen broadleaved forests remain at higher elevations on Hahajima and on some smaller islands, but all have been modified, directly or indirectly, by human activities.

Low dry scrub vegetation occurs mostly on Anijima. The main species are *Distylium racemosum* var. *lepidotum* and *Pouteria obovata*.

Flora

Although the flora of the Bonin Islands is not especially rich, it has a remarkably high degree of endemism. There are 400 native vascular plant species recorded from the islands, of which 150 (37.5%) are endemic (Toyoda 1981).

The flora contains Indomalesian, Polynesian, Micronesian and Japanese elements and belongs to the Volcano-Bonin Province of the Eastern Asiatic Region, according to Takhtajan (1986). Some authors place the Bonin Islands in the Micronesian Region. However, the flora is characterized by the predominance of endemics of Eastern Asiatic stock (van Balgooy 1971) and has rather more in common with the floras of the Ryukyu Islands, Taiwan and southern China than with the flora of the closer lying Mariana Islands.

Indomalesian elements, whose distribution extends into the Ryukyus, Taiwan, southern China and Indochina, include *Ardisia sieboldii*, *Distylium racemosum* var. *lepidotum*, *Fatsia oligocarpela*, *Planchonella obovata* var. *dubia*, *Schima mertensiana* and *Syzygium buxifolium*. Polynesian elements include *Crepidiastrum platyphyllum*, *Hedyotis mexicana*, *Lycium sandwicense* and *Santalum boninensis*. Micronesian elements include such species as *Gaultheria miqueliana*, while Japanese elements include *Circium toyoshimae* and *Miscanthus condensatus* var. *boninensis*.

It is inferred from the present flora that daily mists used to occur at higher altitudes on the larger islands. However, mist zones do not occur on the islands today. It is suspected that some species have declined in numbers as a result of the drier conditions.

527

Useful plants

Morus boninensis provides a valuable wood used in making a variety of handicrafts. Larger trees of this species have been cut down and the species is now Endangered. Most forest production is now derived from exotic plantations. Several ornamental species have potential in horticulture.

Social and environmental values

The subtropical landscape is of high scenic value and attracts many visitors. There is a frequent boat service from Tokyo, and the number of visitors is increasing.

Ten species of endemic land snail are now restricted to Anijima, having once occurred elsewhere in the Bonin Islands. Many of the endemic snails are confined to, or are associated with, the dry scrub vegetation.

One bird species is endemic to the Bonin Islands – the Bonin honeyeater (*Apalopteron familiare*); a further 3 endemics are extinct. All species inhabited forest. The honeyeater has survived the almost total clearance of its preferred habitat by adapting to secondary vegetation. Today, this bird persists only on Hahajima where it is considered threatened.

Threats

There is a proposal to construct an airport on Anijima (Kitayama 1991). While this will boost the local economy by allowing easier access to tourists, there is concern that the airport could result in further infrastructure developments and the destruction of the natural environment.

Forests on slopes and flat areas at lower altitudes are invaded by *Casuarina equisetifolia*, *Leucaena leucocephala* and *Pinus luchuensis*.

More than 80 vascular plant species from the islands are recorded in the Red Data Book of Japan. More than half of the endemic species are threatened. *Circium toyoshimae, Malaxis boninensis* and *Zeuxine boninensis* are Extinct; several other species are known only from a single or a few individuals in the wild.

Conservation

The vegetation was seriously damaged during the Second World War as a result of military activities. Following the war, only military personnel occupied the islands. Japanese inhabitants returned to the Ogasawaras after the islands returned to Japanese control in 1968. Since then, the Local Ogasawara Government, under the Tokyo Metropolitan Government, has had responsibility for development and conservation of the islands.

In 1972, 61 km² of the islands were designated a National Park (IUCN Management Category: II). An active conservation programme is underway involving close collaboration between the Botanical Gardens, University of Tokyo, the Ogasawara Local Government and local inhabitants. The programme includes propagation and reintroduction of threatened plants. Among them, *Melastoma tetramerum* (a seriously endangered species endemic to Chichijima Island) has been propagated in a botanic garden and reintroduction to the wild seems to be successful (Shimozono and Iwatsuki 1986). Reintroduction programmes are also underway for *Calanthe hoshii, Metrosideros boninensis, Morus boninensis* and *Rhododendron boninense* (Iwatsuki and Shimozono 1989). The local inhabitants, including primary school pupils, are involved in planting out young stock and monitoring endangered species on the islands. As a result, over-collection of plants from the wild is no longer a threat.

Biosystematic studies on the endemic species are underway as a contribution to research on speciation on oceanic islands. Further studies on endangered species are required.

The present initiatives underway to conserve the biodiversity of the islands are encouraging, although many problems remain to be solved.

References

Balgooy, M.M.J. van (1971). Plant-geography of the Pacific. *Blumea Suppl.* 6: 1–222.

Iwatsuki, K. and Shimozono, F. (1989). *A trial of reintroduction of endangered species*. Kensei-sha, Tokyo. (In Japanese.)

Kitayama, K. (1991). Threatened endemic species of the Bonin (Ogasawara) Islands. *Pacific Science Association Information Bulletin* 43(3–4): 9–10.

Miyawaki, A. (ed.) (1989). *Vegetation of Japan, vol. 10. Ryukyu and Ogasawara*. Shibundo, Tokyo. (In Japanese.)

Shimozono, F. and Iwatsuki, K. (1986). Botanical gardens and the conservation of an endangered species in the Bonin Islands. *Ambio* 15: 19–21.

Takhtajan, A. (1986). *Floristic regions of the world*. University of California Press, Berkeley. 522 pp.

Toyoda, T. (1981). *Flora of Bonin Islands*. Aboc-sha, Kamakura. 396 pp. (In Japanese.)

Acknowledgements

This Data Sheet was prepared by Professor K. Iwatsuki (Botanical Gardens, University of Tokyo, Japan).

GRANDE TERRE
New Caledonia, France

Location: The main island of the New Caledonian archipelago, which is situated in the South Pacific Ocean, to the north of the Tropic of Capricorn and approximately 1500 km from the east coast of Australia, between latitudes 18°00'–23°50'S and longitudes 154°45'–176°20'E.

Area: 16,890 km².

Altitude: 0–1628 m (summit of Mont Panié).

Vegetation: Lowland and montane tropical evergreen rain forests (covering c. 18% of Grande Terre), sclerophyllous forest, maquis (30% of Grande Terre), mangroves.

Flora: 3322 vascular plant species, of which 2551 (76.8%) are endemic. 5 endemic families; 110 endemic genera. Endemic-rich gymnosperm and palm flora.

Useful plants: c. 20 species used as sources of wood for construction, many ornamental and medicinal species.

Other values: Catchment protection; endemic-rich fauna; pioneer species that are resistant to heavy metals, of potential value for revegetating mine workings; flora and vegetation of particular scientific importance for understanding processes of evolution, island colonization and adaptive mechanisms.

Threats: Fire, clearance for agriculture, grazing pressure, over-exploitation of certain species, mining, urbanization.

Conservation: Protected areas on Grande Terre cover 1480 km² (9% of the land area), and include 13 designated Special Botanical Reserves. Protected area coverage is inadequate as some vegetation types and many localities of threatened endemic species are not currently protected.

The main island of Grande Terre is treated here as one CPD site; however, it is important to note that virtually every sizeable tract of native vegetation on the island contains at least some endemic plants. The account below includes summary information on some sites of outstanding botanical importance. It is hoped that further identification and documentation of important plant sites will be forthcoming in the future.

Geography

The New Caledonian archipelago is situated in the South Pacific Ocean, just to the north of the Tropic of Capricorn and approximately 1500 km from the east coast of Australia. It is located between latitudes 18°00'–23°50'S and longitudes 154°45'–176°20'E. It consists of Grande Terre (16,890 km², or 88% of the total land area of the archipelago), Iles Belep, d'Entrecasteaux Récifs, Ile des Pins, the Loyalty Islands (Iles Loyautés: Ouvéa, Lifou, Maré, Tiga), and a number of other scattered islands (the Chesterfields and Walpole) and active volcanoes (Matthew and Hunter). Grande Terre (the main island of New Caledonia) is floristically and ecologically the most diverse island in the group.

New Caledonia, which represents a fragment of Gondwanaland situated on the Norfolk Ridge, was separated from Australasia (Australia, New Guinea and New Zealand) in the early Cretaceous by the Rangitata Orogeny (Stevens 1977; Paris 1981). Grande Terre is mountainous, reaching 1628 m at the summit of Mont Panié, in the north, and

1618 m at Mont Humboldt, in the south. The eastern slopes of the island are more abrupt than those in the west. The oldest rocks date from the early Permian and comprise the main core of mountains running along the axis of New Caledonia (Paris 1981). At the beginning of the Tertiary (upper Eocene) a major geological event took place: the schist substrate then present was covered by a thick layer (of nearly 2000 m) of ultramafic rocks (peridotites and serpentinites). This very slow process, which first began some 39 million years ago, fundamentally modified the original flora and vegetation (Guillon 1975). Today, ultramafic substrates cover approximately 5500 km², principally located in the south (Massif du Sud) and also occurring as isolated massifs, primarily along the west coast (see Map 21).

The climate is tropical, but somewhat moderated by the surrounding ocean, and strongly affected by the trade winds. Windward (eastern) slopes often receive more than 4000 mm of rain per annum, while leeward (western) slopes receive less than 1000 mm annual rainfall.

European discovery occurred in 1774 (by Captain James Cook on his second voyage), but traces of human occupation date from 4000 years ago. The origin of the island's first occupants remains poorly understood (Frimigacci and Maitre 1981), although it is known that New Caledonia was a centre of dispersion and migration for the early inhabitants of Oceania (probably coming from Asia) in their migration eastwards. New Caledonia became an Overseas Territory of France in 1946. The current population is approximately 167,600, with approximately 146,000 living on Grande Terre.

MAP 21. NEW CALEDONIA: ULTRAMAFIC OUTCROPS

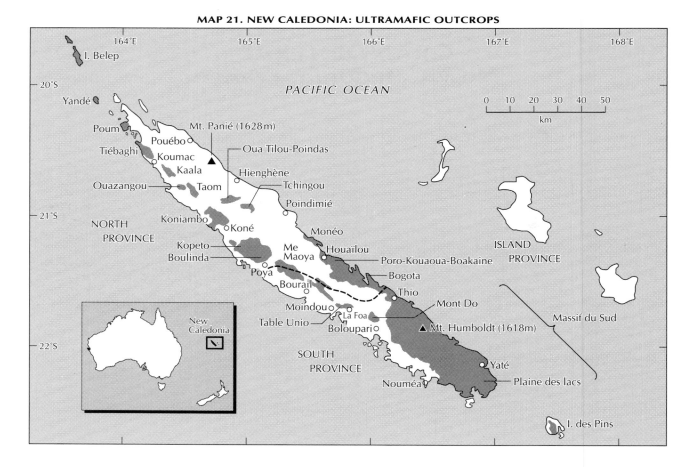

Vegetation

As a result of its geographic isolation, the variety of geological substrates, the fragmentation of habitats, and the climatic variation resulting from its relief, New Caledonia, despite its small size, has an exceptionally rich flora with high endemism at species, genus and family levels and a diversity of vegetation types. Each of the main primary vegetation types is described briefly below. See Morat, Veillon and MacKee (1984) for more detailed descriptions.

Evergreen rain forest

Evergreen rain forest (dense, humid evergreen forest) covers approximately 18% of Grande Terre and is scattered over the central mountain chain, and particularly well-represented in the east due to the higher rainfall. These forests occur on all types of substrate (including ultramafics) from 300 m elevation to the highest summits. Evergreen forest is poorly developed on the western slopes, where it occupies only the most favourable sites, in particular the slopes of certain isolated massifs (Koghis, Mont Mou, Mé Maoya) (Centre Technique Forestier Tropical 1974; Morat, Veillon and MacKee 1984). Evergreen forests comprise trees of moderate height (20 m on average), although in certain localities significantly taller emergents can be found (e.g. *Araucaria*, *Agathis*, *Cyathea*). Most of the important timber trees (see Useful Plants section) occur in this vegetation type.

Approximately 1500 species of flowering plants occur in evergreen forests, of which 90% are endemic; these represent 108 families, of which the most abundant are Rubiaceae, Myrtaceae, Leguminosae, Sapotaceae, Proteaceae,

Araucariaceae, Guttiferae and Araliaceae (Morat, Veillon and MacKee 1984). Of particular note is the presence of the parasitic gymnosperm *Parasitaxus ustus*. There are some gregarious species, such as *Araucaria* spp. and *Nothofagus* spp.

At higher elevations, the trees are lower in stature, and the flora is less rich, although some groups (e.g. pteridophytes, Palmae, Winteraceae, Trimeniaceae and Paracryphiaceae) are more abundant. The vegetation takes on a distinctive appearance on ultramafic rocks above 1000 m . The ground, as well as tree trunks, stems and leaves, is covered with lichens, filmy ferns and bryophytes.

Forests on calcareous substrates with highly developed karst formations (in the Koumac and Hienghène regions) are rich in Sapotaceae, Leguminosae and Euphorbiaceae. There is an abundance of *Microsorium punctatum* and *Asplenium nidus*, which colonize rock outcrops.

Monospecific stands of *Araucaria columnaris* (sometimes reaching over 40 m) occur in a few places near the coast, such as at Goro and Kuébeni. (On outlying islands, such as Loyautés and Ile des Pins, this vegetation is well-developed.)

Sclerophyllous forest

This formation was once widespread along the west coast of Grande Terre, from sea-level to 300 m altitude. It occurs in dry areas (rainfall <1000 mm and with a long dry season) and on various geological substrates (sandstone, calcareous substrates, chert), but has become very degraded to woody savanna, dominated by *Melaleuca quinquenervia* and woodlands of *Acacia spirorbis* and *Leucaena leucocephala*, or cleared for cultivation. Remnant stands are dominated by

530

species in the genera *Terminalia*, *Diospyros* and *Cupaniopsis*, accompanied by evergreen sclerophyllous species belonging to the genera *Psydrax*, *Codiaeum*, *Gardenia*, *Pittosporum*, *Austromyrtus* and *Eugenia*. The discontinuous herb layer comprises a mixture of Cyperaceae and Gramineae. Near the ocean shore, this forest type becomes a dense woodland rich in *Cycas* spp.

The flora comprising the sclerophyllous forests, while not as rich as that of the humid, evergreen forest or the maquis, nevertheless contains numerous endemic species, belonging to genera such as *Terminalia*, *Diospyros* and *Captaincookia*, as well as species that are more widely distributed but whose occurrence in New Caledonia is limited to this formation.

Maquis

Maquis is a specialized, edaphic formation covering more than 30% of the land area of Grande Terre. It forms a distinctive vegetation type associated mostly with ultramafic substrates. The soils on which maquis occurs are generally nutrient-poor and have high concentrations of magnesium, nickel, manganese and chromium (Jaffré 1976).

Maquis occurs from sea-level to the highest summits, and in areas with annual rainfall ranging between 900 mm to 4000 mm (Morat *et al.* 1986). It includes sclerophyllous, dwarf, evergreen formations, generally less than 2.5 m tall, but it is sometimes dominated by trees or shrubs, or it may comprise a mixture of woody and herbaceous species, with

CPD Site PO2: New Caledonia. Tree fern (*Cyathea novae-caledoniae*) in dense forest on Mont Koghi. Photo: P. Morat.

a dense layer of Cyperaceae. The vegetation is occasionally dominated by an open woody stratum comprising *Araucaria* spp. or *Agathis ovata*, and species with thick and often shiny leaves, arranged in rosettes at the tips of branches (e.g. *Dracophyllum*, *Styphelia*, *Hibbertia*, *Pancheria*, *Xanthostemon* and *Pittosporum*). The herbaceous layer includes species of Cyperaceae (*Costularia* spp.), Orchidaceae, Droseraceae and lichens.

Speciose families represented in maquis include Myrtaceae, Cunoniaceae, Dilleniaceae, Epacridaceae, Proteaceae and Casuarinaceae. Many of the species are endemic and restricted entirely to these formations, and many have spectacular flowers (e.g. *Xanthostemon*, *Bikkia*, *Hibbertia*). In some areas, single species may dominate (e.g. *Tristaniopsis guillainii*, *Gymnostoma deplancheanum*, *G. chamaecyparis*, *Dacrydium araucarioides*, *Neocallitropsis pancheri*).

Maquis occuring at higher altitudes is similar in structure to lowland maquis, but differs floristically. Noteworthy species at higher altitudes include *Metrosideros tetrasticha*, *Xeronema moorei*, *Hibbertia nana* and *Logania imbricata*. Maquis on siliceous schists and chert at low and mid-altitudes on northern New Caledonia also has a distinct floristic composition, although somewhat poorer in species than maquis on ultramafic substrates. Two woody species (a dwarf form of *Melaleuca quinquenervia* and *Codia montana*) and one herbaceous species (*Costularia arundinacea*) are dominant on schists and chert (Morat *et al.* 1981).

Mangroves

Mangroves cover approximately 200 km², mostly along the western coastline where the estuaries of the main rivers are wider and deeper than on the east coast. This vegetation comprises about 20 species, all of which occur throughout the Indo-Pacific region. However, *Rhizophora lamarckii* is only known from the east coast of New Caledonia and on the north-eastern coast of Australia.

Other vegetation types

Littoral vegetation comprises common Indo-Pacific species; open halophytic vegetation comprises species of *Suaeda* and *Salicornia*. Marsh vegetation is poorly represented in New Caledonia. The most interesting areas of marshland occur at the southern end of the main ultramafic massif, where there is a complex of small lakes linked by streams (the Plaine des Lacs). A large number of wetland species occurs here, all of which are New Caledonian endemics. They include *Lepidosperma perteres*, *Chorizandra cymbaria*, *Cloëzia aquarum*, *Baeckea leratii* and *Pancheria communis*. The endemic gymnosperms *Decussocarpus minor* and *Dacrydium guillauminii* are restricted entirely to this area. Marshy niaouli forest (*Melaleuca quinquenervia*) occurs in depressions along the west coast and in the north. This is the native habitat of this now widespread species.

Early human settlement resulted in changes to the vegetation long before the arrival of Europeans, as a result of the use of fire and the clearance of forest for agriculture. Plants were introduced for food, medicine, rituals and ornamental purposes. Among the early introductions were species of *Dioscorea*, *Alocasia*, *Colocasia*, *Artocarpus*, *Musa*, *Hibiscus*, *Codiaeum* and *Pueraria* (Barrau 1962; Bourret 1981). Today, over half of the primary vegetation has been cleared or severely degraded (see Threats section, below).

CPD Site PO2: New Caledonia. Maquis with _Araucaria rulei_ at Massif du Boulinda. Photo: P. Morat.

Flora

New Caledonia has more than 3320 native species of vascular plants (of which 77% are endemic). There are 863 genera of vascular plants, 110 of which (13%) are endemic (see Table 78). Five families (Amborellaceae, Oncothecaceae, Paracryphiaceae, Phellinaceae and Strasburgiaceae) are also endemic.

Evergreen rain forests of New Caledonia have an exceptional concentration of genera and species considering the restricted area they occupy. For example, 11 genera of Palmae have been found on the 25 km² area which comprises the eastern slope of Mont Panié, and 131 species of woody plants with a dbh >10 cm have been recorded were found in 1.25 ha of forest on a slope near the Rivière Bleue (as many as in some Amazonian forest plots of similar size) (Jaffré and Veillon 1990).

1200 species are strictly limited to ultramafic rocks, while 1300 species are restricted to a variety of substrates (Morat et al. 1986; Jaffré 1987; Lowry 1990). Species endemism on ultramafic substrates exceeds 98%. At the generic level, 38 of 108 endemic genera present in New Caledonia are found only on ultramafic rocks.

Seven families (including Myrtaceae and Xanthorrhoeaceae) and two endemic families of strictly forest species (Oncothecaceae and Strasburgiaceae) are restricted to ultramafics. The majority of species in other families, including the best represented (Sapotaceae, Proteaceae, Cunoniaceae and Rutaceae) are also restricted to ultramafic substrates (Jaffré et al. 1987).

Species-rich flowering plant families include Myrtaceae, Cunoniaceae, Cyperaceae, Pandanaceae and Palmae (which includes 32 species in 17 genera, of which 16 are endemic) (Laubenfels 1972; Moore and Uhl 1984; MacKee, Morat and Veillon 1985). For gymnosperms, 43 out of 44 native species are endemic (the exception being _Cycas circinalis_, which is found throughout the Old World tropics). Primitive

TABLE 78. NATIVE VASCULAR PLANTS OF NEW CALEDONIA

	Pteridophytes	Gymnosperms	Angiosperms	Total
Families	26	5	160	191
Total genera	75	15	773	863
Endemic genera	2	2	106	110
Total species	261	44	3017	3322
Endemic species	103 (39.5%)	43 (97.7%)	2405 (79.7%)	2551 (76.8%)

CPD Site PO2: New Caledonia. *Araucaria columnaris* on the Ile des Pins. Photo: P. Morat.

angiosperms with archaic or vessel-less wood are represented by several families (Amborellaceae, Annonaceae, Atherospermataceae, Chloranthaceae, Menispermaceae, Piperaceae and Trimeniaceae).

Floristic affinities are strongest with Australia and New Guinea, and then (in decreasing order) with Malesia, Fiji, Vanuatu, the Solomon Islands and New Zealand (Thorne 1965; Morat, Veillon and MacKee 1984; Morat *et al*. 1986).

The floristic richness and high level of plant endemism can be explained largely by the isolation of New Caledonia (a Gondwanan fragment) since the early Cretaceous. The relatively stable climate has enabled intense speciation of the primitive flora, which has been enriched by elements that reached the island by long-distance dispersal. In addition, at the beginning of the Tertiary, the slow overthrust of all (or part of) the island by ultramafic substrates was largely responsible for the evolution of New Caledonia's very distinctive flora (the flora of the "terrains miniers"), adapted to the specialized edaphic conditions. Pre-Eocene relicts which adapted to ultramafic substrates did not have to face competition from species arriving from outside of New Caledonia, as the new arrivals were unable to colonize these specialized substrates. Subsequent isolation of populations due to the fragmentation of ultramafic outcrops favoured the development of micro-endemism (i.e. the very localized occurrence of endemic species) and the phenomenon of vicariance.

Useful plants

Only a small proportion of the flora has been utilized to date. The main timber species, which occur in evergreen rain forest at low and mid-altitudes, include *Agathis* spp., *Kermadecia* spp., *Macadamia* spp., *Sleumerodendron* spp., *Hernandia cordigera, Calophyllum caledonicum, Montrouziera cauliflora, Archidendropsis granulosa, Neoguillauminia cleopatra, Santalum austrocaledonicum* and numerous species of Myrtaceae (Sarlin 1954). The wood of *Acacia spirorbis* and *Arillastrum gummiferum* is frequently used as fence posts, exterior carpentry and flooring (Centre Technique Forestier Tropical 1983). Native species supply 13% of New Caledonia's timber needs (21,000 m³ of timber from native species being produced in 1979, but only 7000 m³ produced in 1989) (Service Forêts et du Patrimoine National archives). This represents less than 5% of New Caledonia's total revenues.

Numerous distillates used in the production of scents and pharmaceuticals are extracted from aromatic species, such as *Melaleuca quinquenervia, Santalum austrocaledonicum* and *Neocallitropsis pancheri*; the latter, which has a very limited distribution in "maquis minier", deserves special protection. A number of species, including *Ochrosia elliptica* and *Duboisia myoporoidesare*, are used locally as medicines and for industrial purposes (Rageau 1973).

Some species of Araliaceae and of gymnosperms (*Araucaria* spp., in particular) are now widely grown outside New Caledonia as ornamental plants (Guillaumin 1952).

Social and environmental values

The native flora of New Caledonia is an important resource for scientific research in numerous fields, such as the study of evolution, adaptations to serpentine soils, and mechanisms of resistance to heavy metals, including the hyper-accumulation of nickel and manganese in species such as *Macadamia neurophylla* and *Sebertia acuminata* (Jaffré 1976).

New Caledonia's native forests and maquis provide habitats for many endemic animal species. There is a high degree of endemism in arthropods, reptiles and birds (Solem 1961; Holloway 1979; Sadlier 1986; Bauer and Vindum 1990; Raven 1991). New Caledonia and the Loyalty Islands are rich in restricted-range land bird species, with 30 species present, of which 20 are endemic. The majority of the endemics (13 species) are found only in New Caledonia. Most species occur in forest and several are (today) confined to higher altitudes. One species of particular note is the kagu (*Rhynochetus jubata*), the sole representative of its family. It is a wingless bird that is of special scientific interest and a tourist attraction (Hannecart and Letocart 1980, 1983), and is also the emblem of New Caledonia. A recent census shows that this bird has a patchy, mostly inland distribution in the less disturbed, mountainous areas. Its total population is estimated at 500–600 individuals.

Although international tourism is poorly developed (with approximately 75,000 overseas visitors in 1991), many New Caledonians visit the reserves near Nouméa. At the Parc provincial de Rivière Bleue, the number of visitors increased from 7800 in 1989 to 18,500 in 1991, while at the Parc Corbasson, the number of visitors increased from 45,000 to 55,000 over the same period. There is great potential for developing international ecotourism based on the remarkable scenery and vegetation.

Pioneer species that are able to colonize soils rich in heavy metals could be useful for revegetating mine spoil elsewhere.

A total area of 940 km² of natural vegetation has been set aside to protect catchments supplying drinking water.

Threats

The principal threats to the New Caledonian flora are fire, over-exploitation of certain species, mining activities and, with respect to sclerophyllous forest, agriculture and extensive livestock production.

Fires are sometimes set to regenerate grazing lands or during hunting, and can spread into "maquis miniers" and the edges of forests.

Some species are over-exploited. Among them are *Agathis lanceolata*, *Santalum austrocaledonicum*, *Arillastrum gummiferum*, *Neocallitropsis pancheri*, *Cyathea* spp. (used as a support for growing orchids), and ornamental species such as Orchidaceae.

About 3–5% of the area of evergreen rain forests has been cleared during the last 20 years. The few remnants of sclerophyllous forests are mostly located on private land and their future depends entirely on the goodwill of the land owners. Sclerophyllous forests are not represented in the existing reserve system, with the exception of a few hectares of very degraded forest in Nouméa and its immediate environs.

Opencast nickel mining, New Caledonia's primary economic activity, destroys the most luxuriant vegetation occurring in the upper parts of certain massifs, and results in bare slopes and spoil heaps which are vulnerable to erosion. Attempts to recolonize mine spoil with native species have had encouraging results (Jaffré, Latham and Schmid 1987). Until 1970 mining was practically unregulated, but today there are strict controls on prospecting, road building and the siting of spoil heaps. New Caledonia, according to recent estimates, still contains more than 50% of the world's nickel reserves. An increase in the world price of nickel could mean that more mining activity is allowed and environmental regulations slackened, especially if the economy is in recession.

There are more than 1500 introduced plant species, many of which have become naturalized and now form part of the botanical landscape (MacKee 1985). Most introduced species are unable to colonize ultramafic substrates, and thus far the majority of introductions do not constitute a major threat to intact or slightly disturbed vegetation. However, several species rapidly invade secondary vegetation types and impede the regeneration of native vegetation. Among the species concerned are *Lantana camara*, *Psidium guajava*, *Furcraea foetida*, *Mimosa invisa* and *Leucaena leucocephala*. *Graptophyllum pictum* has penetrated forested areas in some places, but is not a serious threat (MacKee 1985).

Introduced Java deer (*Cervus timorensis*) prevent the regeneration of native species in some places.

The vegetation of some frequently visited localities (e.g. Chutes de la Madeleine) is suffering localized damage from tourism.

Numerous species in the New Caledonian flora are only known from a single locality or even a single population (e.g. *Dacrydium guillauminii*). This considerably increases the risk of their extinction, either from man-made or natural causes.

Conservation

Since 1950, several Special Botanical Reserves (IUCN Management Category: IV) have been created. Today, there are 13 such reserves, including Mont Panié (50 km²), Mont Humboldt (32 km²), Pic du Pin (14 km²) and Forêt de Sailles (11 km²) and 9 smaller reserves. The statute creating the Massif des Lèvres reserve has never been enforced.

Montagne des Sources (58.7 km²) became New Caledonia's only terrestrial Strict Nature Reserve ("Réserve Naturelle intégrale") (IUCN Management Category: I) in 1950.

Eight Territorial Parks have been established, covering 113 km². Nearly 1000 km² are included in reserves established at 148 sites for the protection of certain watersheds that provide drinking water to inhabited areas. In addition, there are 5 Special Fauna Reserves protecting, in particular, the avifauna, and specifically the kagu, and 2 Special Fauna and Flora Reserves. Hunting and plant collecting is controlled within the reserves. With the exception of the Montagne des Sources Strict Nature Reserve, all protected areas have statutes that permit prospecting for minerals.

Altogether, about 9% of the land area of New Caledonia is currently included within protected areas. Although there are representative samples of dense forests on schist and ultramafic rocks, "maquis miniers" and several other distinct vegetation types, the reserve coverage is inadequate to protect the flora of New Caledonia. Mangroves, sclerophyllous forests and forests on calcareous substrates, as well as a large number of localities containing micro-endemic species, are not currently protected. The sites listed in Table 79, and shown on Map 22, which are protected are of particular note.

TABLE 79. EXAMPLES OF PROTECTED SITES WITH IMPORTANT VEGETATION TYPES AND NOTEWORTHY TAXA
The numbers in bracket refer to localities on Map 22

A. Water supply reserves (North and South Provinces)
148 separate areas.

B. Strict Nature Reserve (South Province)

Montagne des Sources (1).
Protected: evergreen rain forest; maquis: population of *Neocallitropsis pancheri*; mountain forest dominated by *Araucaria humboldtensis*.
Notable species: *Platyspermation crassifolium, Basselinia porphyrea, Canacomyrica monticola*.

C. Special Botanical Reserves (South Province)

Chutes de la Madeleine (2).
Protected: populations of *Neocallitropsis pancheri, Dacrydium guillauminii, Nageia minor*; swamp and riverine associations.

Plaine des Lacs (3), (7 separate areas).
Protected: evergreen rain forest, *Agathis lanceolata*; populations of *Arillastrum gummiferum*; shrub-herb maquis.
Notable species: *Nothofagus* spp., *Kermadecia pronyensis, Xanthostemon aurantiacum, Gymnostoma deplancheanum*.

Mont Mou (500–1200 m) (4).
Protected: montane forest and scrub; associations rich in bryophytes and filmy ferns.
Notable species: *Nothofagus baumanniae, Metrosideros porphyrea, Strasburgeria robusta*.

Mont Humboldt (1000–1618 m) (5).
Protected: evergreen rain forest; montane maquis.
Notable species: *Araucaria humboldtensis, Paracryphia alticola, Logania imbricata, Libocedrus chevalieri, Metrosideros tetrasticha, Greslania montana*.

Forêt de Saille (6), Mont Ninga (7), Mont Do (8).
Protected: evergreen rain forest with *Agathis lanceolata*; dense *Araucaria-Nothofagus* forest; *Greslania circinnata* association in shrub-herb maquis.
Notable species: *Pseudosciadium balansae, Oxera* spp., *Casearia coriifolia*.

Special Botanical Reserves (North Province)

Mont Panié (200–1630 m) (9).
Protected: dense forest rich in palms at mid- to high altitudes; montane scrub.
Notable species: *Araucaria schmidii, Agathis montana, Lavoixia macrocarpa*, various Cunoniaceae and Winteraceae.

D. Special Faunal Reserves

South Province: Upper Yaté (10), Le Prédour Island (11).
North Province: Mont Aoupinié (12), Pam Island (13).
Protected: birds only, particularly the kagu, in evergreen rain forest.

E. Territorial Parks

Mainly reserved for public recreation. Protected: evergreen rain forest: **Rivière Bleue (14), Thy (15)**; sclerophyll forest: **Parc Corbasson (16), Ouen-Toro (17)**.

F. Tourist Site (South Province)

Mont Koghi forest (100–1080 m) (18).
Protected: evergreen rain forest at middle altitudes, and montane scrub with *Araucaria* and *Nothofagus*.
Notable species: *Neisosperma thiollieri, Sloanea koghiensis, Acropogon megaphyllus*.

MAP 22. NEW CALEDONIA: PROTECTED AREAS
Numbers refer to localities mentioned in Table 79

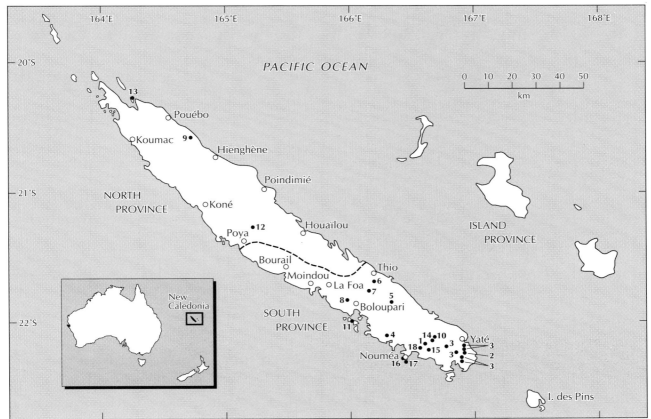

As a consequence of the massive degradation that resulted from mining exploitation, an Environmental Committee was set up in 1970 to develop measures to regulate mining activities in New Caledonia.

A number of rare or threatened species have been propagated successfully in *ex situ* collections. For example, the palm *Pritchardiopsis jeanneneyi*, which was thought to be extinct since the beginning of the century, was relocated in 1981 in two or three small populations. Only one fruiting adult individual is known in the wild (Morat 1986; Jaffré and Veillon 1989). Seeds have been distributed within New Caledonia, and to botanic gardens throughout the world, and have been found to germinate easily. The species is therefore no longer in danger of extinction. The survival of a second species of palm, *Lavoixia macrocarpa*, which is known from only four adult individuals, is more in question. There is no natural regeneration *in situ* and all attempts to germinate seeds of this species have so far failed. Fortunately, the remaining populations of these two species of palms are located in reserves.

References

Aubréville, A., Leroy, J.F., Morat, Ph. and MacKee, H.S. (eds) (1967-). *Flore de la Nouvelle-Calédonie et Dépendances*. Mus. Nat. Hist. Nat., Paris. 17 fascicles.

Barrau, J. (1962). Les plantes alimentaires de l'Océanie. Origine, distribution et usages. *Annales du Musée Colonial de Marseille* 3–9: 275 pp.

Bauer, A.M. and Vindum, J.V. (1990). A checklist and key to the herpetofauna of New Caledonia with remarks on biogeography. *Proc. Calif. Acad. Sci.* 47: 17–45.

Bourret, D. (1981). *Ethnobotanique*. Carte et Pl. 17 in Atlas de la Nouvelle-Calédonie. ORSTOM, Paris.

Centre Technique Forestier Tropical (1974). *Inventaires des ressources forestières de la Nouvelle-Calédonie*. Nouméa. Fasc. 1. 137 pp., 227 pp.

Centre Technique Forestier Tropical (1983). *Essences forestières exploitables en Nouvelle-Calédonie*. Nouméa, New Caledonia.

Frimigacci, D. and Maitre, J.C. (1981). *Archéologie et préhistoire*. Carte et Pl. 15 in Atlas de la Nouvelle-Calédonie. ORSTOM, Paris.

Guillaumin, A. (1952). L'acclimatation des plantes ornementales de la Nouvelle-Calédonie. *La Terre et la Vie* 1: 19–23.

Guillon, J.H. (1975). Les massifs péridotitiques de la Nouvelle-Calédonie. *Mémoires ORSTOM Paris* 76: 120 pp.

Hannecart, F. and Letocart, Y. (1980, 1983). *Oiseaux de Nouvelle-Calédonie et des Loyautés*, 2 vols. Editions Cardinalis, Nouméa, New Caledonia. (Vol. 1: 150 pp.; vol. 2: 135 pp.)

Holloway, J.D. (1979). A survey of the *Lepidoptera*, biogeography and ecology of New Caledonia. *Series Entomologica* 15. Junk, The Hague.

Jaffré, T. (1976). Accumulation du manganèse par les Protéacées de Nouvelle-Calédonie. *C.R. Acad. Sci. Paris, série D* 289: 425–428.

Jaffré, T. (1980). Etude écologique du peuplement végétal des sols dérivés de roches ultrabasiques en Nouvelle-Calédonie. T.D. no. 124, ORSTOM. 274 pp.

Jaffré, T. (1987). Composition chimique et conditions de l'alimentation des plantes sur roches ultrabasiques en Nouvelle-Calédonie. *Cah. ORSTOM, série Biologie* 11(1): 53–63.

Jaffré, T., Brooks, R.R., Lee, J. and Reeves, R.D. (1976). *Sebertia acuminata* a hyperaccumulator of nickel from New Caledonia. *Science* 193: 579–580.

Jaffré, T., Latham, M. and Schmid, M. (1987). Aspect de l'inflence de l'extraction du minerai de nickel sur la végétation et les sols de la Nouvelle-Calédonie. *Cah. ORSTOM, série Biologie* 12(4): 307–321.

Jaffré, T., Morat, Ph., Veillon, J.M. and MacKee, H.S. (1987). Changements dans la végétation de la Nouvelle-Calédonie au cours du Tertiaire: La végétation et la flore des roches ultrabasiques. *Bull. Mus. natn. Hist. nat., Paris*, 4e série, 9, section B, *Adansonia* 4: 365–391.

Jaffré, T. and Veillon, J.M. (1989). Morphology, distribution and ecology of palms in New Caledonia. In Dowe, J.L. (ed.), *Palms of the South West Pacific. Their origin, distribution and description*. Publication Fund, Palm and Cycad Societies of Australia.

Jaffré, T. and Veillon, J.M. (1990). Etude floristique et structurale de deux forêts denses humides sur roches ultrabasiques en Nouvelle-Calédonie. *Bull. Mus. natn. Hist. nat., Paris*, 4e série, 12 (publ. 1991), section B, *Adansonia* 3–4: 243–273.

Laubenfels, D.J. de (1972). Gymnospermes. In *Flore de la Nouvelle-Calédonie et Dépendances*, No. 4. Paris. 168 pp.

Lowry, P.P., II (1990). Evolutionary patterns in the flora and vegetation of New Caledonia. In Dudley, E.C. (ed.), *The unity of evolutionary biology*. Dioscorides Press, Portland, Oregon, U.S.A.. Vol. 1: 373–379.

MacKee, H.S. (1985). Les plantes introduites et cultivées en Nouvelle-Calédonie. In *Flore de la Nouvelle-Calédonie et Dépendances*, vol. hors série. 159 pp.

MacKee, H.S., Morat, Ph. and Veillon, J.M. (1985). Palms in New Caledonia. *Principes* 29(4): 166–169.

Moore, H.E. and Uhl, N.W. (1984). The indigenous palms of New Caledonia. *Allertonia* 5(5): 313–402.

Morat, Ph. (1986). Le palmier que l'on croyait perdu. In *L'Univers du Vivant* 7: 44.

Morat, Ph., Jaffré, T., Veillon, J.M. and MacKee, H.S. (1981). *Végétation.* Carte et Pl. 15 in Atlas de la Nouvelle-Calédonie. ORSTOM, Paris.

Morat, Ph., Jaffré, T., Veillon J.M. and MacKee, H.S. (1986). Affinités floristiques et considérations sur l'origine des maquis miniers de la Nouvelle-Calédonie. *Bull. Mus. natn. Hist. nat., Paris,* 4e série, 8, section B, *Adansonia* 2: 133–182.

Morat, Ph., Veillon, J.M. and MacKee, H.S. (1984). Floristic relationships of New Caledonian rain forest phanerogams. In Radovsky, F.J., Raven, P.H. and Sohmer, S.H. (eds), *Biogeography of the tropical Pacific.* Association of Systematics Collections and Bernice P. Bishop Museum. Pp. 71–128.

ORSTOM (1981). *Atlas de la Nouvelle-Calédonie.* Paris.

ORSTOM (1989). *Atlas de la Nouvelle-Calédonie.* Editions du Cagou. Nouméa, New Caledonia.

Paris, J.P. (1981). *Géologie de la Nouvelle-Calédonie. Un essai de synthèse.* B.R.G.M. Orléans. 278 pp.

Rageau, J. (1973). *Les plantes médicinales de la Nouvelle-Calédonie.* T.D. no. 23, ORSTOM, Paris. 139 pp.

Raven, R.J. (1991). A revision of the mygalomorph spider family *Anapidae* (Araneae). *Zoologia Neocaledonia,* vol. 2. *Mém. Mus. natn. Hist. nat.* (A) 149: 87–117.

Sadlier, R.A. (1986). A review of the scincid lizards of New Caledonia. *Rec. Aust. Mus.* 39: 1–66.

Sarlin, P. (1954). *Bois et Forêts de la Nouvelle-Calédonie.* Centre Technique Forestier Tropical, Nogent-sur-Marne. 303 pp.

Solem, A. (1961). New Caledonian land and fresh water snails, an annotated check-list. *Fieldiana, Zool.* 41: 417–501.

Stevens, G.R. (1977). Mesozoic biogeography of the South West Pacific and its relationship to plate tectonics. *Int. Symp. Geodyn. South West Pacific. Nouméa 1976.* Technic. Ed. Pp. 309–326.

Thorne, R.F. (1965). Floristic relationships of New Caledonia. *Univ. Iowa Stud. Nat. Hist.* 20(7): 1–14.

Veillon, J.M. (1976). Architecture végétative de quelques arbres néocalédoniens. Thesis, Université de Montpellier. 300 pp.

Virot, R. (1956). La végétation canaque. *Mém. Mus. natn. Hist. nat.,* série B, vol. 7, Bot.: 398 pp.

Acknowledgements

This Data Sheet was prepared by Professor Philippe Morat (Laboratoire de Phanérogamie, Muséum National d'Histoire Naturelle, Paris), and Drs Tanguy Jaffré and Jean-Marie Veillon (Centre ORSTOM, Nouméa, New Caledonia).

FIJIAN REGION: CPD SITE PO3

FIJI

Location: Two main islands (Viti Levu and Vanua Levu) and over 300 small islands, between latitudes 10°00'–25°00'S and longitudes 173°00'E–176°00'W in the south-west Pacific Ocean.

Area: 18,270 km². Vitu Levu (10,386 km²) and Vanua Levu (5534 km²) comprise 87% of the land area.

Altitude: 0–1324 m (summit of Mount Tomaniivi).

Vegetation: Rain forest on south and east sides of main islands, montane forest, dry forest and open woodland in areas with marked dry season, shrub and grassland, mangroves. Rain forests of all types (including selectively logged forests) cover 33% of the land area.

Flora: 1628 native vascular plant species, of which 812 species (50%) endemic; 1 endemic family; 12 endemic genera.

Useful plants: Timber trees; many plants used in traditional lifestyles for craft materials, medicines; ornamental plants.

Other values: Cultural attachment to certain species of trees (totem species), high landscape value, watershed protection.

Threats: Logging, clearance for agriculture, feral animals, invasive plant species, tourism, population pressure, breakdown of traditional lifestyles and taboos.

Conservation: 16 protected areas covering 65.9 km² (0.36% of the land area), including Sigatoka Sand Dunes National Park. Protection Forests, taboo sites, protection of totem species.

Geography

The Fijian archipelago consists of two main islands (Viti Levu and Vanua Levu) which comprise 87% of the land area, along with over 300 small islands between latitudes 10°00'–25°00'S and longitudes 173°00'E–176°00'W in the south-west of the Pacific Ocean. The complex includes high islands of volcanic origin, along with atolls, raised coral, limestone islands and extensive reef systems. Viti Levu and Vanua Levu may be remnants of Gondwanaland. The oldest volcanic eruptions date from 50 million years ago. Volcanic activity on Taveuni occurred as recently as 2000 years ago.

The interior of Viti Levu and Vanua Levu is rugged and reaches 1324 m above sea-level, Taveuni rises to 1241 m, while most of the other islands are below 1000 m. Many islands have spectacular coastal formations and cliffs, while the interior of the large islands include eroded plateaux, large rivers, basins and gorges.

The climate is hot and humid, especially in summer, and is influenced by the south-east trade winds which blow for most of the year. Rainfall is unevenly distributed owing to rain-shadow effects. The wettest areas are on the eastern sides of the most easterly high islands. For example, Taveuni receives up to 7600 mm rainfall annually, while the wet zones of Viti Levu and Vanua Levu receive an annual average of 3050–3450 mm. Dry leeward zones have 1650–2290 mm annual rainfall and can suffer droughts of several months duration. The coolest and driest months are April–October. Tropical cyclones occur during December–March.

The population of Fiji in 1988 was 732,000; the annual growth rate is 2% (World Bank 1990). 80% of the population live on the main island of Viti Levu, mostly concentrated in villages and urban centres near the coast. Between 25–35% of the population is urban or lives in the vicinity of towns.

Land held in customary ownership (about 83% of the land area, involving about 6000 land owners) is administered by the Native Lands Trust Board. 7% of the land area of Fiji is crown land and the remaining 10% is freehold land.

Vegetation

Rain forests occur on the south and east sides of the main islands. Lowland rain forests are comparatively rich in tree species, with no single species dominating the forest. Montane rain forests occur in wet areas on the high islands. Cloud forest occurs at the highest altitudes. The trees are stunted and there is a rich epiphytic flora, including many species of orchids, ferns and mosses. Rain forests of all types (including selectively logged forests) cover 6090 km² (33% of the land area) (Collins, Sayer and Whitmore 1991).

Dry forest and open woodland originally covered most of the coastal areas of the main islands and areas with a marked dry season. The dry zone has been considerably modified by repeated burning. As a result, the original vegetation has been largely replaced by grasslands (talasiga) and is now mostly confined to steep slopes and ravines and more remote parts of the coast.

Smith (1979–) recognizes an intermediate zone of vegetation between the wet and dry forest zones. Intermediate zone vegetation occurs in areas where the rainfall is more evenly distributed than in the dry zone but is less consistent than in the wet zone. The vegetation includes open forest on windward slopes, and a mixture of shrubs and grasslands on leeward slopes. Mount Evans (1195 m), western Viti Levu, contains a remnant of open forest rich in endemics (Lear 1991).

There are 520 km^2 of mangroves, bringing the total area covered by native forests of all types (including selectively logged forests) to 6610 km^2 (36% of the land area). In addition, exotic plantations (mostly of *Pinus caribaea*) cover 900 km^2 (Collins, Sayer and Whitmore 1991).

Beach vegetation, and that of many of the small, low islands is typical of that found in similar environments throughout the Pacific.

Flora

Fiji has a total of 2628 vascular plant species, of which 1628 species are indigenous. The native flora comprises 1307 species of angiosperms, 11 species of gymnosperms and 310 species of ferns. Of these, 812 species (50%) are endemic. There are 1013 families and 210 genera represented in the flora, including 12 endemic genera (figures based on Smith 1979– ; Brownlie 1977; Lear 1991; Given 1992).

The flora of Fiji has affinities with those of Papua New Guinea, the Solomon Islands and Vanuatu. There are also affinities with the floras of the Samoan Archipelago and western Polynesia to the east. The most species-rich islands are the high islands of Viti Levu, Vanua Levu and Taveuni, which also contain the most endemics. The floras of the lower and younger islands are poorer and include many pan-Pacific species.

The high level of endemism is a reflection of the geographical isolation of Fiji, although it is believed that some elements of the flora have evolved from species present in Gondwanaland at a time when there was a connection with the Austro-Indian Plate. The family Degeneriaceae (consisting of two species: *Degeneria vitiensis* and the recently discovered *D. rosiflora*) is endemic, and considered to be one of the most primitive flowering plant families.

27 of the 28 native species of palms are endemic to Fiji. Of these, 22 are considered to be rare or threatened according to IUCN Red Data Book criteria (Lear 1991). (Of the threatened species, only 6 occur in existing protected areas.)

Useful plants

Many indigenous plant species are used as sources of medicines, building and craft materials. The forests are an essential part of rural village life, and there is a strong relationship between the land owning clans (mataqali) and their environment. Thaman and Clarke (1987) recognize up to 70 cultural uses of trees. Clans may attach great spiritual importance to a particular species of tree, some of which are adopted as totems. As a result, sacred groves of particular tree species may be found near villages. Totem trees are also used to demarcate land boundaries.

About 40 timber tree species are recognized as having commercial value. The main native timber tree species (accounting for 90% of native timber production) are *Endospermum macrophyllum* (kauvalu), *Myristica* sp. (kaudamu), *Calophyllum vitiense* (damanu), *Syzygium* and *Cleistocalyx* sp. (yasiyasi), *Agathis vitiensis* (dakua makadre) and *Podocarpus vitiensis*. *Swietenia macrophylla* (mahogany)

and *Pinus caribaea* (Caribbean pine) are the main exotic plantation species.

Social and environmental values

The majority of the Fijian terrestrial fauna depends on native forests (see, for example, Watling 1982). All of Fiji's species of birds occur in primary forest, but many have adapted to secondary and man-made habitats, possibly as a result of the frequency of secondary forest in this cyclone-prone environment. However, it is likely that even these species are dependent on undisturbed forest patches for breeding and ultimate survival. Fiji is an important Endemic Bird Area, with 37 restricted-range land bird species, of which 25 are endemic.

Fiji has 27 species of reptiles and amphibians, of which 8 are endemic, including the crested iguana (*Brachylophus vitiensis*). There are estimated to be more than 3500 invertebrate species, including some of the world's largest beetles (Ryan 1988). There are no large mammals, the only native mammals being 6 species of fruit bat, of which 2 are endemic.

The wide variety of coastal and mountainous landscapes makes Fiji a popular tourist destination. Ecotourism, if carefully planned, could contribute greatly to the national and local economy.

Threats

Traditional cultural values are still strong in isolated villages and islands. However, tourism, urbanization and increased accessibility to markets, as a result of road building, are leading to an increase in western values and dependency upon the cash economy. More land is being cleared to grow cash crops to supply the urban market. As the native forests are cleared, the products which they once supplied freely must now be purchased, resulting in rural communities becoming increasingly dependent upon the cash economy.

The demand for wood for craft materials has increased as a result of the tourist trade. Certain timber species, such as *Intsia bijuga*, are particularly sought after and are possibly becoming locally scarce (Lear 1991).

The palm *Balaka pauciflora* was traditionally used for making dancing spears. It is possible that such use was not sustainable, as the species has not been refound since its discovery in 1860 (Lear 1991).

Feral animals include pigs and goats. The hunting of feral pigs (an aboriginal introduction to the islands) is an important cultural activity in Fiji and may, paradoxically, encourage the retention of some forested areas. Goats, however, are particularly damaging to native vegetation and have caused severe damage on some islands.

Currently, the annual deforestation rate is approximately 1% (Collins, Sayer and Whitmore 1991). Forest clearance for small-scale plantations and gardens is a traditional activity around villages. As a result, coastal and dry zones have been greatly modified, or cleared for agriculture and settlements. Increasing tourism (c. 200,000 tourists visit Fiji annually) is placing more pressure on the remaining lowland and coastal forests.

Although virtually all commercial logging is selective, the extraction rate in Fiji can be up to 30 trees per hectare. As far as is known no sustainable silvicultural systems have been implemented. Some logging has even taken place inside protected areas. On Vanua Levu, at least 50% of the forests have already been logged and 90% are destined for logging. Taveuni remains the only island with extensive forests which have not yet been logged. Most accessible forests on Viti Levu and Vanua Levu are likely to have been selectively logged by the year 2010. Once cut, the areas are either left to re-establish secondary forest, or further cut over and planted with exotic timber species.

There are about 1000 introduced species. Invasive species are a particular problem in disturbed areas (e.g. in logged forest, where they can spread into surrounding native forests). The most serious weed species are *Psidium guajava, Lantana camara, Mikania micrantha, Merremia peltata, Citharaexylum spinosum* and *Schefflera digitata.*

Mining for gold, copper and iron causes local damage. In some cases, areas rich in endemic species are threatened (e.g. Mount Kasi).

The forests of Fiji are subject to cyclone damage. Species which have restricted distributions are particularly at risk from such catastrophes. Research is needed to establish the response of vegetation to such natural threats.

Lear (1991) made a pilot survey of threatened plant species in which he identified a number of sites where clusters of endemic and threatened species occur (see Conservation section). For example, Mount Kasi (Vanua Levu) has 32 Fijian endemic species, including 8 species which are wholly restricted to the mountain. (Mount Kasi is not currently protected and has not been included in previously published proposals, see Conservation section, below.) Of 116 threatened taxa in the pilot survey, only 4 species occur in existing reserves and 12 in proposed reserves, indicating the present inadequacy of the existing and proposed protected areas system for the conservation of the flora (see Conservation section, below). By extrapolation, Lear concludes that only 20% of rare and threatened species would be protected if the proposed protected areas system was implemented.

Conservation

Cultural traditions, which place particular significance on some species of tree, give rise to a form of species conservation (as has been noted above in connection with totem species; see Useful Plants section). Fijian culture also protects certain taboo sites (the word taboo originates from the Fijian "tabu").

A summary and review of the protected areas system in Fiji is given in IUCN (1991). Currently, Fiji has 16 legally designated protected areas covering 65.9 km² (0.36% of the land area), varying in size from 1 ha to 40.2 km². In 1988, the first National Park was approved at Sigatoka Sand Dunes, Viti Levu. The majority of protected areas are administered by the Ministry of Forests; The National Trust for Fiji administers 7 protected areas.

There are 9 designated Nature Reserves, in which all customary rights of hunting, fishing, cultivation, grazing, collecting of fruits and forest products are denied (except under licence). They include Ravilevu (Taveuni) (40.2 km²), Naqaabuluti (Viti Levu) and Tomaniivi (Viti Levu) (13.2 km²), the two largest reserves.

About 313 km² of forest are protected in 19 Forest Reserves under the Forest Act. The J.H. Garrick Lowland Tropical Moist Forest Reserve, which is managed by The National Trust, covers 4.3 km². It was severely damaged by logging in 1988–1989 (Lear 1991). Protection Forests (covering 2288 km²) are administered by the Ministry of Forests. There is no legal restriction on logging, but the forests are often on land which is too steep for safe logging. A further 2250 km² is classed as Non-Commercial Forest by the Ministry.

Several reviews have noted the inadequacies of the present protected areas system (e.g. Ash and Vodonaivalu 1989; SPREP 1989). Recognizing the shortcomings of the protected areas system, an ecological survey of Fiji's forests was carried out by the Maruia Society and the Royal Forest and Bird Protection Society (two New Zealand NGOs) at the invitation of the Native Land Trust Board of Fiji. The recommendations (Lees 1989) include the following proposals:

❖ 5 major National Parks to protect the finest representative examples of unmodified Fijian forests, comprising:
  Mount Tomaniivi Nature Reserve with proposed extension into Wabu Creek Catchment (Viti Levu) (last large remaining stands of *Agathis vitiensis* forest, montane and cloud forests);
  Nadrau Plateau (western sector) (Viti Levu)
  Sovi Basin (Viti Levu) (Wet zone forests)
  Taveuni (forest area to be determined)
  Vunivia (Vanua Levu) (dry to wet zone forest, and from coastal mangroves to high inland ridge forest)
❖ 3 Forest Parks:
  Waikatakata (Viti Levu)
  Mount Evans (Viti Levu)
  Waisali (Vanua Levu)
❖ 8 Special Feature Forest Reserves to protect particularly rare habitats or species:
  Rokosalase (Vanua Levu) (dry zone *Fagraea gracilipes* forest)
  Sandalwood Reserve (to protect the last remaining stands of sandalwood)
  Vatu Vara (beach forest)
  Vanua Balavu lagoon (beach forest)
  Kadavu (forest site to be determined)
  Naqali (Viti Levu) (*Neoveitchia storckii* palm reserve)
  Selala Mangrove Reserve (River Samabula, to protect an endemic *Rhizophora* hybrid)
  Navua Swamp (Viti Levu) (sago palm community)
❖ 19 sites as Special Purpose Fauna Reserves, two of which would also protect threatened plant species, namely:
  Tunuloa Peninsula Silktail Reserve (*Weinmannia exigua*)
  Sovu Islands Redfooted Booby (*Pritchardia thurstonii*).

Of these, Sovi Basin is considered to be of World Heritage quality.

Attention is now being focused on the best way of achieving the conservation of these areas within the framework of customary land ownership.

Whilst protection of these areas is very important, Lear (1991) suggests that an additional network of small reserves needs to be established to protect clusters of threatened plant species, many of which occur OUTSIDE the existing and proposed protected areas. In particular, the following "endemic hot-spots" were identified in a pilot survey:

- ❖ Vanua Levu
  Mount Kasi
  Mount Mariko
  Mount Numbuiloa
  Mount Soro Levu
- ❖ Viti Levu
  Mount Nakorombamba
  Mount Voma-Korobasambasanga
  Nasouri Highlands

Clearly, there is an urgent need for further botanical surveys of these and other areas to establish priorities for plant conservation.

References

Ash, J. and Vodonaivalu, S. (1989). Fiji. In Campbell, D.G. and Hammond, H.D. (eds), *Floristic inventory in tropical countries: the status of plant systematics, collections, and vegetation, plus recommendations for the future*. The New York Botanical Garden, New York. Pp. 166–176.

Brownlie, C. (1977). *The pteridophyte flora of Fiji*. Cramer, Vaduz, Liechtenstein. 397 pp.

Collins, N.M., Sayer, J.A. and Whitmore, T.C. (eds) (1991). *The conservation atlas of tropical forests: Asia and the Pacific*. Macmillan, London. 256 pp.

Given, D.R. (1992). An overview of the terrestrial biodiversity of Pacific islands including those islands covered by the Biodiversity Programme of SPREP. 29 pp. (Unpublished report prepared for SPREP, Apia, Western Samoa.)

IUCN (1991). *IUCN directory of protected areas in Oceania*. IUCN Gland, Switzerland and Cambridge, U.K. xxiii, 447 pp. (Prepared by the World Conservation Monitoring Centre.)

Lear, M. (1991). *Plant conservation in Fiji. WWF 3334 – Small grants for plant conservation on islands (6) Fiji*. WWF, Gland, Switzerland. 26 pp., appendices.

Lees, A. (1989). *Representative national parks and reserves system for Fiji's tropical forests*. Maruia Society and Royal Forest and Bird Protection Society of New Zealand.

Ryan, P. (1988). *Fiji's natural heritage*. Southwestern, Auckland, New Zealand.

Smith, A.C. (1979-). *Flora Vitiensis Nova*. Pacific Tropical Botanical Garden, Kauai, Hawaii.

SPREP (1989). *Action Strategy for Nature Conservation in the South Pacific*. SPREP/IUCN, Noumea, New Caledonia.

Thaman, R. and Clarke, W.C. (1987). Pacific island agrosilvicultural systems for cultural and ecological stability. *Canopy International* 13(1): 6–7.

Watling, D. (1982). *Birds of Fiji, Tonga and Samoa*. Millwood Press, Wellington, New Zealand.

World Bank (1990). *World tables 1989–1990 edition*. John Hopkins University Press, Baltimore. 646 pp.

Acknowledgements

This Data Sheet was written by Stephen D. Davis, based on the report to WWF by Michael Lear in 1991, together with supplementary information.

SAMOAN ISLANDS
Western Samoa, American Samoa

Location: South Pacific Ocean, east of Fiji and north of Tonga, between latitudes 11°00'–15°00'S and longitudes 168°00'–173°00'W.

Area: 3114 km². (2940 km² for Western Samoa; 174 km² for American Samoa. Western Samoa comprises 93% of the total area of the archipelago.)

Altitude: 0–1857 m for Western Samoa (Savai'i); 0–931 m for American Samoa (Ta'u).

Vegetation: Littoral communities, wetlands (marshes, mangroves and freshwater swamp forests), rain forests (coastal, lowland, montane and cloud forests), upland scrub (summit scrub and montane scrub) and upland and lowland volcanic vegetation.

Flora: 775 native vascular plant species, including 550 native angiosperm species and 225 ferns and fern allies. About 32% of the angiosperms and 18% of the pteridophytes are endemic to the archipelago.

Useful plants: Timber trees; probably over 100 plant species are used in local medicine.

Other values: Watershed protection, rich fauna, ecotourism potential.

Threats: Population pressure, breakdown of traditional lifestyles, development projects, recent rapid spread of alien plant and animal species, devastating hurricanes.

Conservation: Traditional conservation practices. Legally designated protected areas in Western Samoa include O Le Pupu Pu'e National Park (28.5 km²) and 5 small reserves, covering c. 1% of the land area; American Samoa National Park (IUCN Management Category: II) covers 37 km²; Rose Atoll National Wildlife Refuge (IUCN Management Category: I) covers 6.5 km². Recently established NGOs in both Western and American Samoa.

Geography

Samoa is a volcanic archipelago situated in the South Pacific Ocean between latitudes 11°00'–15°00'S and longitudes 168°00'–173°00'W. Its nine inhabited and several uninhabited islands have a total area of about 3114 km². The archipelago is divided politically into Western Samoa, which is an independent country, and American Samoa, which is an unincorporated territory of the United States; the two are separated by a strait 64 km wide.

The main islands of Western Samoa (2940 km²) are Savai'i (area: 1820 km²; highest point: 1857 m) and 'Upolu (area: 1110 km²; highest point: 1100 m), and those of American Samoa (174 km²) are Tutuila (area: 124 km²; highest point: 650 m) and Ta'u (area: 39 km²; highest point: 931 m).

The archipelago extends in a west/north-west direction, with the most recent island (Savai'i, where the last volcanic eruptions occurred between 1903 and 1911) at the western end, and the oldest island (Rose Atoll) at the eastern end. Much of Tutuila and the eastern portion of 'Upolu comprise highly eroded clay soils, whereas parts of Savai'i are covered with recent lava flows. Savai'i, the third largest island (after Hawai'i and Maui) and fourth highest (after Hawai'i, Maui and Tahiti) in tropical Polynesia, has a largely undissected surface with few permanent streams or rivers. The other large islands have more rugged topography and more permanent water sources.

Samoa has a tropical, maritime climate. Typical temperatures at sea-level are 24–29° C, and the average difference between winter and summer temperatures is only about 2°C. The relative humidity is high, averaging about 80%. There is no real dry season, but rainfall is concentrated from December to March when the usual south-east trade-winds wane. The mean minimum annual precipitation is at least 2000 mm per year in all parts of the island, even in the lowlands of the western and northern sides of the larger islands, which are in a mild rain-shadow. Occasional droughts do occur. Hurricanes periodically hit the islands.

Vegetation

Most of the archipelago was originally covered with dense rain forest; also present were littoral vegetation, scrubby vegetation on recent lava flows (probably two series of eruptions have occurred since the islands were first colonized c. 3000 years ago), scrubby upland vegetation on peaks and summits, and disturbed forests resulting from hurricanes.

The present vegetation can be divided into 21 plant communities that are grouped into several larger categories – littoral strand, wetlands, rain forests, upland scrub and volcanic vegetation. Littoral vegetation can be subdivided into herbaceous strand, littoral shrubland, *Pandanus* scrub and littoral forest. Nearly all of the littoral vegetation has been removed from the islands by human activities over the last three millenia, with only scattered patches remaining on isolated coasts and offshore islets.

Several wetland communities occur in Samoa. Mangrove forest and mangrove scrub occur on Savai'i, 'Upolu, Tutuila and Aunu'u (a small island adjacent to Tutuila). Species that dominate this type of vegetation (Rhizophoraceae) extend no farther east in the Pacific. Mangroves are particularly well-developed on the south coast of 'Upolu.

Swamp forests occur in coastal and inland areas of the major islands. A unique type of inland swamp forest occurred in two basins at 300 m altitude on 'Upolu, but one was destroyed by development in 1991 and the other one, damaged by recent hurricanes, is threatened. Coastal marshes dominated by ferns and sedges occur in scattered localities along the coast, especially at the western end of 'Upolu and in 'Aunu'u Crater. Montane marshes occur in a number of mountain craters on 'Upolu.

Rain forest can be divided into coastal, lowland, montane and cloud forest. Coastal forest, which is shorter in stature and restricted mostly to tuffcone soil, is dominated by two species of *Syzygium* and two of *Diospyros*. Lowland forest can be divided into associations based on dominant species, such as *Pometia pinnata, Syzygium inophylloides, Planchonella torricellensis, Intsia bijuga, Inocarpus fagifer* and *Dysoxylum* spp. Montane forest is mostly dominated by *Dysoxylum huntii*. Cloud forest occurs mostly above 1000 m and is dominated by *Reynoldsia pleiosperma*.

Upland scrub vegetation can be divided into two communities – montane scrub, which occurs on the trachyte soil of several summits on Tutuila, and summit scrub, which occurs in the waterlogged soil at the summit of Ta'u Island. The volcanic vegetation can be divided into lowland volcanic scrub and upland volcanic scrub, but there is no distinct boundary between the two types.

Today, nearly all lowland forest has been cleared for agriculture and settlements, or logged for timber. The few remaining areas, mostly on Savai'i, have been damaged by the two recent hurricanes (1990 and 1991). Most lowlands are devoted to the cultivation of subsistence crops (mainly taro) and cash crops (mainly coconut). Shifting agriculture is spreading into the interior of both Savai'i and 'Upolu, leaving a wasteland of scrubby secondary vegetation. Fernlands dominated by *Dicranopteris linearis* occur in two areas of 'Upolu and are probably a result of long-term degradation of nutrient-poor soil.

Flora

The Samoan flora has been fairly well collected except for the montane and cloud forests of Savai'i. The vascular flora of Samoa consists of 536 native species of angiosperms and 228 native pteridophytes and fern allies. This makes it the most diverse flora in Polynesia, except for Hawai'i, which has more species but fewer genera. Table 80 gives a breakdown of flora statistics for the archipelago (as at July 1992).

The rate of species endemism in the whole archipelago for flowering plants, ferns and fern allies is approximately 28%. Only one genus, *Sacropygme* (Rubiaceae, 2 spp.), is endemic to the archipelago. Most of the indigenous Samoan species are also found in Fiji and, to a lesser extent, in Tonga.

The largest families are Orchidaceae (c. 100 native species), Rubiaceae (45), Urticaeae (24), Fabaceae (20), Myrtaceae (20), Gesneriaceae (20) and Euphorbiaceae (19). The largest genera are *Psychotria* (20 species, 17 endemic), *Cyrtandra* (20 species, 19 endemic), *Syzygium* (16 species, 9 endemic), *Elatostema* (12–14 species, all endemic), *Dendrobium* (12 species, 2 endemic) and *Bulbophyllum* (11 species, 1 endemic).

TABLE 80. SPECIES RICHNESS AND ENDEMISM IN THE SAMOAN ARCHIPELAGO

	Samoa[a]	Western Samoa	American Samoa
Fern allies[b]			
Families	3	3	3
Genera	4	4	3
Species	15	15	8
Endemic species	2	0	0
Species endemism (%)	13.3	0	0
Ferns			
Families	21	21	20
Genera	77	77	59
Species	213	208	127
Endemic species	38	18	4
Species endemism (%)	17.8	8.7	3.1
Angiosperms			
Families	96	95	80
Genera	306	302	238
Species	536	514	336
Endemic species	174	116	11
Species endemism (%)	32.4	22.6	3.3

Notes:
[a] refers to the whole archipelago.
[b] includes *Lycopodium, Psilotum, Selaginella* and *Tmesipteris*.

The most diverse and interesting groups of plants are the orchids and the ferns, many of which are restricted to the montane region of Savai'i and 'Upolu. The genera *Psychotria, Elatostema* and *Cyrtandra* are rich in endemic species.

There are a number of potentially rare and/or endangered species in Samoa. Several species have been collected only once, or only in the last century; the lowland species among these are the most likely to be extinct. Many other species thought to be rare or threatened are inconspicuous or are restricted to the montane area of Savai'i. Their populations may have been overlooked; further botanical exploration may remove them from the list of threatened species.

Areas of botanical importance

Within the archipelago, several localities and vegetation types are of outstanding importance for conservation. These are listed below with summary data.

Lowland forests of 'Upolu and Savai'i

Perhaps only five tracts of lowland forest remain in Samoa. Two of them, at Tafua and Falealupo on Savai'i, are village-controlled Nature Reserves established by donations and direction from overseas. The third is a National Park on 'Upolu. The remaining two are currently unprotected. One is between Sasina and A'opo on Savai'i; the other is a unique forest on the north-east 'Upolu coast, dominated in places by *Intsia bijuga*, the most valued timber tree in Samoa. The three protected forests were damaged in recent hurricanes, but will eventually recover if allowed to do so. The other two have not been evaluated since the last hurricane.

Lava flows of Savai'i

There are two lava flows on Savai'i: one extends from sea-level to 600 m (formed 1903–1911), the other from sea-level to 1500 m (formed c. 1750). They are high in scenic value and support an interesting flora. The areas are relatively safe from human exploitation as a result of the rocky substrate.

Montane and cloud forests of Savai'i and 'Upolu

These forests, above 600 m altitude, are rich in orchids, ferns and endemic species. The Savai'i upland forests are still intact, but those on 'Upolu are rapidly being reduced by logging, swidden agriculture and cattle-raising projects. The forests have been damaged by hurricanes, but since they are adapted to these perturbations they will naturally regenerate if allowed to do so.

Crater lakes of 'Upolu

There are a number of crater lakes on 'Upolu and some on Savai'i. Some are accessible and very scenic, but most of the forest around them has been cleared, leaving impenetrable thickets of scrubby secondary vegetation dominated by weedy species. Three lakes are found in the mountains behind Apia (the capital of Western Samoa), the largest of them being Lanoto'o which is about 400 m across. Three others are found in eastern 'Upolu, but are relatively inaccessible.

Montane swamp forest of 'Upolu

Two areas of this unique vegetation are found on 'Upolu. Both occur in montane basins in eastern 'Upolu. The better of the two, Punataemo'o, was completely destroyed by a hydroelectric project now under construction. The other major area, Vaipu, is threatened by a planned hydroelectric facility. Pockets of similar vegetation are found in a number of montane craters on the island.

Montane scrub of Tutuila

This is a unique plant community that occurs on several trachyte plugs from 300 to 650 m. The scrubby vegetation is dominated by low trees, ferns and a tangle of vines. Some Samoan species are recorded only from these areas, especially orchids. The area is safe from human activities, since the steep slopes and poor soil are entirely unsuitable for agriculture.

Summit scrub of Ta'u

The summit of Ta'u (American Samoa) is covered with a low scrubby vegetation unlike any other recorded from Samoa. It may owe its existence to hurricanes and heavy rainfall. Ta'u is a small island (31 km²), yet about 50 orchid species and 100 fern species have been collected there. Half of the island is currently being considered for inclusion in a National Park.

Aleipata Islands

The four uninhabited islands found off the east coast of 'Upolu are important nesting sites for many species of seabirds, and the two largest and most isolated islands, Nu'utele and Nu'ulua, have unique vegetation types (e.g. coastal forest). A number of plant species found on these islands are not recorded from the main islands.

Mangrove forests

The best remaining mangroves are at Sa'anapu-Sataoa (south-west 'Upolu) and at Pala Lagoon (Tutuila).

Coastal marshes

The best remaining examples are at the western end of 'Upolu, especially at Apolimafou.

Useful plants

A number of native species are utilized for timber but forest has been drastically reduced over the last 25 years and little remains. Many species are still utilized to make posts in native houses.

More than 100 plant species are likely to be used regularly or occasionally for native remedies, but many of these are increasingly hard to find. Some species are currently being studied overseas for possible value in the treatment of cancer. One rare endemic species, *Trichosanthes reineckeana* (Cucurbitaceae), is related to a Chinese species that has shown some promise in the treatment of AIDS.

Few native plants are edible, but many aboriginal varieties of breadfruit and taro still exist. The most useful plant in Samoa is the coconut, which is grown commercially as well as a source of food, timber, fuelwood, utensils and fibre.

Social and environmental values

The Samoan islands have 20 species of land birds with restricted ranges. Of these, 10 are endemic to the archipelago, 8 being restricted entirely to Western Samoa. All 20 species occur in forest but many are also found in plantations and gardens. Given the severe loss of native habitat on the islands, the exploitation of man-modified habitats is vital for the long-term survival of some of indigenous species. The species of most conservation concern is the tooth-billed pigeon (*Didunculus strigirostris*) which is avidly hunted (as are all the other columbids) and is also threatened by commercial deforestation.

The forests of Samoa have traditionally served as a source of timber and medicine. With a small population, absence of commercial crops, and lack of metal and mechanical tools, traditional swidden agriculture allowed the forest to regenerate while supplying Samoans with their food needs. This system also minimized the effects of erosion, as the forests protected watersheds. During the 20th century much of the lowland vegetation has been cleared (see Threats section).

The islands are very scenic, with waterfalls, crater lakes, panoramic lava flows, uncrowded beaches and a tropical climate. The islands have major potential for ecotourism.

Threats

The major threat to the natural areas of Samoa result from population growth and rising economic expectations. With few natural resources other than the land, there is increasing pressure on Samoans to clear forests for short-term economic gain by growing cash crops. This has gone hand in hand with an unregulated timber industry that in 25 years has nearly eliminated the lowland forests of the archipelago, particularly in Western Samoa, and is currently encroaching inland to the montane forest. Following clearance, the forest land is often cultivated. One or a few successive crops are grown before the land is abandoned, resulting in heavy erosion and formation of dense secondary scrub vegetation dominated by weedy species.

A major contributor to the loss of forest is the traditional land tenure system. Land is claimed by members of the adjacent village by clearing it; it is difficult to maintain ownership of land that is not being utilized. Deforestation has occurred on steep slopes, which increases the chances of erosion, low stream flow during the dry season, and floods during the rainy season.

The commercial timber industry has replanted large areas with alien species, such as *Eucalyptus deglupta*. These have proven susceptible to wind damage and are not suitable for native bird species.

Introduced species, particularly weeds such as *Mikania micrantha*, *Solanum torvum* and *Hyptis capitata*, and an invasive African rubber tree, *Funtumia elastica* (on 'Upolu), are a major threat. Introduced animal species are also a problem. The African snail is established in American Samoa, as is its predator *Euglandina*, which has proven to be devastating to native Polynesian snails. The marine toad *Bufa marinus* is also established in American Samoa. Fortunately, feral goats and cattle are not currently a problem.

Poorly planned development has been harmful to native vegetation and species. Several recent projects, financed from overseas, have been started or completed without any proper environmental impact studies. The worst case is the hydroelectric dam currently being built on 'Upolu that has destroyed one of the two areas of poorly understood montane swamp forest and threatens the other.

Conservation

Although there has been a long tradition of conservation practices in Samoa, most of these are concerned with food sources. However, the villages of Tafua and Falealupo on Savai'i have managed to preserve at least some of their native forests. Protests by local villages at Sala'ilua recently stopped felling operations there. The forest of Tafua-Salelaloga was also saved after direct action by local people.

Selling timber rights has seemed to many to be an economic necessity. This, coupled with a basic lack of education on ecological issues, has hindered any conservation progress. However, there are now local conservation groups established in both Western and American Samoa – the "Si' osi'omaga" and the "O le Vaomatua" respectively.

Legally designated protected areas in Western Samoa include O Le Pupu Pu'e National Park (28.5 km²) and 5 small reserves, covering c. 1% of the land area. In American Samoa, American Samoa National Park (IUCN Management Category: II) covers 37 km²; Rose Atoll National Wildlife Refuge (IUCN Management Category: I) covers 6.5 km².

References

Amerson, A.B., jr, Whistler, W.A. and Schwaner, T.D. (1982). *Wildlife and wildlife habitat of American Samoa. I. Environment and ecology; II. Accounts of flora and fauna.* U.S. Department of the Interior, Washington, D.C.

Christensen, C. (1943). A revision of the pteridophyta of Samoa. *Bull. Bernice P. Bishop Mus.* 177: 1–138.

Christophersen, E. (1935). Flowering plants of Samoa. *Bull. Bernice P. Bishop Mus.* 128: 1–221.

Christophersen, E. (1938). Flowering plants of Samoa – II. *Bull. Bernice P. Bishop Mus.* 154: 1–77.

Holloway, C.W. (1975). A national parks system for Western Samoa. U.N. Develop. Advisory Team for the South Pacific, Suva, Fiji. 71 pp. (Mimeo.)

Ollier, C., Whistler, W.A., Amerson, A.B., jr (1979). *'O le Pupu-Pu'e National Park.* U.N. Develop. Advisory Team for the South Pacific, Suva, Fiji. (Vol. 1 – Main report, 79 pp.; vol. 2 – Interpretive material, 83 pp.)

Park, G. *et al.* (1992). *Western Samoa national ecological survey.* New Zealand Conservation Service.

Pearsall, S.H. and Whistler, W.A. (1991). *Terrestrial ecosystem mapping for Western Samoa.* South Pacific Regional Environment Programme and the East-West Centre, Environment and Policy Institute, Honolulu, Hawai'i. (I – Summary, project report, and proposed national parks and reserves plan, 72 pp.; II – Technical report and appendices, 213 pp.)

Reinecke, F. (1896-1898). Die Flora der Samoa-Inseln. *Bot. Jahrb.* 23: 237–368 (1896); 25: 578–708 (1898).

Setchell, W.A. (1924). American Samoa. Part I. Vegetation of Tutila Island; Part II. Ethnobotany of the Samoans; Part III. Vegetation of Rose Atoll. *Publ. Carnegie Inst. Wash.* 341: (Dept Marine Biol. 20): 1–175.

Whistler, W.A. (1978). The vegetation of the montane region of Savai'i, Western Samoa. *Pacific Science* 32(1): 79–94.

Whistler, W.A. (1980). The vegetation of eastern Samoa. *Allertonia* 2(2): 45–190.

Whistler, W.A. (1984a). The vegetation and flora of the Aleipata Islands, Western Samoa. *Pacific Science* 37(3): 227–249.

Whistler, W.A. (1984b). Annotated list of Samoan plant names. *Economic Botany* 38(4): 464–489.

Whistler, W.A. (1992a). The vegetation of Samoa and Tonga. *Pacific Science* 46(2): 159–178.

Whistler, W.A. (1992b). *Botanical survey of the proposed Ta'u unit of the National Park of American Samoa.* U.S. Fish and Wildlife Service, Honolulu, Hawai'i.

Whistler, W.A. (1992c). The green world of Samoa. National University of Samoa. (Unpublished manuscript.)

Yuncker, T.G. (1945). Plants of the Manua Islands. *Bull. Bernice P. Bishop Mus.* 184: 1–73.

Acknowledgements

This Data Sheet was prepared by Dr W.A. Whistler (University of Hawai'i at Manoa, Honolulu, Hawai'i, U.S.A.). The flora statistics were subsequently updated by information provided by the author to the World Conservation Monitoring Centre.

MARQUESAS
French Polynesia

Location: An isolated group of 12 volcanic islands in the central Pacific Ocean, between latitudes 7°50'–10°35'S and longitudes 138°35'–141°30'W.

Area: 1275 km².

Altitude: 0–1260 m (Hiva Oa).

Vegetation: Lowland rain forest above 600 m, remnants of dry forest, intermediate (mesophytic) forest, grasslands, xerophytic scrub. The vegetation of all the islands has been devastated by overgrazing.

Flora: 318 vascular plant species, of which 132 species (42%) endemic; 2 endemic monotypic genera.

Useful plants: *Pandanus tectorius* (fibre), *Artocarpus utilis* (edible fruit), *Hibiscus tiliaceus* (ornamental).

Other values: Scientific value, endemic-rich fauna.

Threats: Overgrazing by introduced feral and domestic animals, competition from introduced invasive plants, fire, many species reduced to small relict populations. Severely threatened.

Conservation: 4 reserves, including Eiao Island Nature Reserve (40 km²), but inadequate coverage. Rescue plan needed for threatened plants.

Geography

The Marquesas (Iles Marquises) are an isolated group of 13 volcanic islands (Motteler 1986) in the central Pacific Ocean between latitudes 7°50'–10°35'S and longitudes 138°35'–141°30'W. They are one of the five distinctive island archipelagos of French Polynesia (the others being the Society Islands, the Tuamotus, Gambier Islands and Tubuai, or the Austral Islands). The Marquesas are further from any continent (4800 km from Mexico) than any other archipelago. Their nearest neighbours are the atolls of the Tuamotu Archipelago, 483 km to the south; the closest high islands are the Society Islands, 1370 km to the south-west.

Apart from Ua Pou (Ua Pu), each island appears to consist of half an original volcanic peak. There are three peaks over 1220 m high; the highest point is 1260 m, on Hiva Oa. Radiometric dating reveals the islands to range in age from 1.3 to over 6 million years old. Fatu Hiva is the youngest island; Eiao is the oldest. The islands fit the general Pacific pattern in which age progresses toward the north-west within an archipelago. The islands are not currently volcanically active.

The terrain is very rugged. There are virtually no coastal plains. Apart from Hiva Oa and Nuku Hiva, which have elevated plateaux, most of the islands have a central ridge. Ua Pou has spectacular, towering peaks. The ridge of Fatu Hiva has cavities several hundred metres deep. The rugged topography has produced a variety of habitats on the larger islands, ranging from dry on the leeward sides to mesic valleys and cloud covered summits.

The annual rainfall generally ranges from 1000 mm to over 2800 mm (based on very few records) (Wagner 1991). However, there may be prolonged droughts of 3–5 years.

The population of the islands is approximately 5000 (4800 in 1962), being mostly engaged in subsistence gardening, fishing, hunting feral goats, cattle and sheep, and copra production. Most of the population lives on Tahuata and Fatu Hiva.

Vegetation

Dry tropical vegetation, dominated by low grasses and suffruticose herbs, covers extensive areas of the lowlands on most islands, including coastal cliffs. A number of dry tropical species of trees and shrubs occur on less disturbed slopes and sheltered ravines inland. On some islands, the lowland vegetation is very sparse as a result of overgrazing by feral animals and fire. This is particularly the case on the windward slopes of Fatu Hiva, southern Tahuata, north-western and eastern Hivaoa, and most of the entire islands of Eiao and Mohotane (Decker 1992).

Dry forest, with *Hibiscus*, *Pandanus*, *Thespesia* and *Cordia*, originally covered the lower slopes below the cloud line, including most of Eiao and Fatu Huku (Melville 1970). Secondary vegetation, containing pantropical species, some of which have been introduced since human arrival, occupies most habitats below 800–900 m today (Decker 1992). *Indigofera suffruticosa*, for example, covers a large area of north-western Hiva Oa (Hivaoa). In north-eastern Hiva Oa, the grass *Tricholaena rosea* has colonized xeric slopes, while dense thickets of *Leucaena leucocephala* cover much of southern coastal Nuku Hiva.

Lowland rain forest, now much degraded and reduced in extent, occurs above 600 m in northern and western Nuku Hiva, Fatu Hiva, Ua Huka and Ua Pou, and above 1000 m on Hiva Oa. Genera represented include *Metrosideros* and *Weinmannia*. Tree ferns are also present. Mesophytic forest, with *Hibiscus*, *Macropiper* and *Freycinetia*, formerly covered the plateaux to the west and east of Mount Ootua and Hiva Oa, as well as most of central Nuku Hiva (Adamson 1936).

All the islands have been devastated by overgrazing by feral and domestic animals. Much of the original dry forest on the lower slopes below 1000 m has been totally destroyed, and replaced by the fern *Dicranopteris* and tussock grassland. On some islands, little vegetation remains.

Flora

The Marquesan flora consists of 318 vascular plant species, of which 132 (42%) are endemic. The relatively small size of the flora is a reflection of the small area of the islands, together with the relatively short-lived nature of the islands – erosion and subsidence of individual islands reduces islands to the low atoll stage within 7–8 million years, leaving little trace of the former flora. Although the flora is small, the level of species endemism is high. Table 81, below, summarizes statistics on the vascular plant flora.

TABLE 81. VASCULAR PLANT SPECIES RICHNESS AND ENDEMISM IN THE MARQUESAS

	Families	Genera	Species	Endemic species	% species endemism
Pteridophytes	26	53	108	17	16
Dicotyledons	53	101	174	96	55
Monocotyledons	6	23	36	19	53
Angiosperms	59	124	210	115	55
Vascular plants	85	177	318	132	41.5

As with other Pacific oceanic islands, the fern flora of the Marquesas is rich, resulting from the high dispersal ability of spores from distant land masses (Tryon 1970). At the generic level, 14% of the world's fern genera are represented in the Marquesan flora. The largest flowering plant family represented in the flora is Rubiaceae (26 native species). The largest genus is *Psychotria* (Rubiaceae), of which all 11 Marquesan species are endemic. The monocot flora is relatively poor.

The flora has affinities with that of the Society Islands (Sohmer 1990). There are two monotypic endemic genera: *Lebronnecia* (Malvaceae) (Fosberg and Sachet 1966) and *Pelagodoxa* (Palmae). IUCN (1986) gives details of the islands and endemic plant species on each.

Useful plants

Useful plants include *Pandanus tectorius* (fibre), *Artocarpus utilis* (edible fruit) and *Hibiscus tiliaceus* (ornamental).

Social and environmental values

As with other oceanic islands, the Marquesas are of outstanding interest to biologists for evolutionary studies and on account of their distinctive, endemic-rich flora and fauna.

The Marquesas are rich in restricted-range species of land bird, 11 of which are endemic. All species occur in forest and most are very restricted in their distribution. The majority are considered threatened. The red-moustached fruit-dove (*Ptilinopus mercierii*) was last reported in 1980 on Hiva Oa, while the total population of the Marquesan imperial-pigeon (*Ducula galeata*) numbered 100 birds on Nuku Hiva in 1990.

Threats

There has been a long history of modification of the flora and vegetation, beginning with the arrival of the Polynesians. The lowlands, and especially the leeward sides of the islands, have been greatly altered by overgrazing and disturbance by feral animals (goats, sheep, cattle, pigs and horses).

There are many introduced plants on the islands. Some introduced species form the main vegetation cover, particularly in the dry lowlands. Naturalized and aggressive aliens include *Coffea arabica* (coffee), *Psidium guajava* (guava), *Syzygium cumini*, *Leucaena leucocephala* and *Melinis minutiflora*.

Fire is a threat to dry tropical vegetation.

Most of the native plant species survive only in relict patches of dry forests and upland rain forests. Some are reduced to critically low numbers. For example, *Lebronnecia kokioides* is reduced to a single tree on Tahuata and also occurs on Mohotani (IUCN 1986). It has so far proved to be difficult to cultivate.

Conservation

Eiao Island Nature Reserve covers 40 km². It is a low island (reaching 557 m altitude) and lacks the rain forests found on other islands in the archipelago. The flora includes 70 vascular plant species, including introduced species (IUCN 1991). The vegetation consists of *Pisonia grandis* forest with a shrub layer of *Cordia lutea*, and a herb layer dominated by *Eragrostis xerophila* and *Portulaca* spp.

There are three other reserves in the Marquesas, but they are inadequate to protect the flora (IUCN 1991). A rescue plan is needed to conserve the endangered flora. Elements of this would include a network of reserves throughout the archipelago, research on regeneration of vegetation after removal of grazing pressure, and *ex situ* cultivation of the most endangered species.

References

Adamson, A.M. (1936). Marquesan insects: environment. *Bull. Bernice P. Bishop Mus.* 139: 73 pp.

Decker, B.G. (1992). Secondary plant cover on upland slopes. Marquesas Islands, French Polynesia. *Atoll Research Bulletin* 363: 1–36.

Fosberg, F.R. and Sachet, M.-H. (1966). Plants of southeastern Polynesia. *Micronesica* 2: 157–158.

ICBP (1992). *Putting biodiversity on the map: priority areas for global conservation*. International Council for Bird Preservation, Cambridge, U.K. 90 pp.

IUCN (1986). *Review of the protected areas system in Oceania*. IUCN, Gland, Switzerland and Cambridge, U.K. 239 pp. (Prepared in collaboration with UNEP.)

IUCN (1991). *IUCN directory of protected areas in Oceania*. IUCN, Gland, Switzerland and Cambridge, U.K. xxiii, 447 pp. (Prepared by the World Conservation Monitoring Centre.)

Melville, R. (1970). *The endemic plants of the Marquesas Islands and their conservation status*. Unpublished Red Data Bulletin material, Royal Botanic Gardens, Kew.

Motteler, L.S. (1986). *Pacific island names. A map and name guide to the new Pacific*. Bishop Museum Miscellaneous Publ. 34. Bishop Museum Press, Honolulu, Hawai'i. 91 pp.

Sohmer, S.H. (1990). Elements of Pacific phytodiversity. In Baas, P., Kalkman, K. and Geesink, R. (eds), *The plant diversity of Malesia. Proceedings of the Flora Malesiana Symposium commemorating Professor Dr. C.G.G.J. van Steenis, Leiden, August 1989*. Kluwer Academic Press, Dordrecht. Pp. 293–304.

Tryon, R. (1970). Development and evolution of fern floras of oceanic islands. *Biotropica* 2: 76–84.

Warren, W.L. (1991). Evolution of waif floras: a comparison of the Hawaiian and Marquesan archipelagoes. In *The unity of evolutionary biology. Evolution on island archipelagoes: the emerging picture – symposium*. 2 vols. Dioscorides Press. Pp. 267–284.

Acknowledgements

This Data Sheet was written by Stephen D. Davis, with grateful thanks to Dr Warren L. Wagner (Smithsonian Institution, Washington, D.C.) for providing comments on an earlier draft.

HAWAIIAN ISLANDS
Hawai'i, U.S.A.

Location: North-central Pacific Ocean, between latitudes 18°54'–28°15'N and longitudes 154°40'–178°75'W.

Area: 16,641 km².

Altitude: 0–4205 m (summit of Mauna Kea).

Vegetation: 38 major physiognomic formations, including herblands, grasslands, shrublands and forests. Dominant species of the native plant communities almost entirely endemic. Seral sequences from barren lava and cinder deserts to climax forest. About 50% of the native vegetation has been cleared.

Flora: Estimated 1200 native vascular plant species (c. 980 native flowering plant species), extremely high species endemism (89% for flowering plants); 32 endemic genera (15% generic endemism).

Useful plants: Medicinal plants, fibres, hardwood timbers, edible species, ornamental plants; rich in genetic resources. Plants utilized from Polynesian colonization to present.

Other values: Watershed protection for drinking and irrigation supplies, tourism, cultural and religious values.

Threats: Increasing development pressure; conversion of native vegetation to alien pasture, agriculture, or recreational landscapes; naturalized alien plants and animals; fire.

Conservation: 2029.4 km² (c. 12% of land area) protected, including 2 National Parks of area >10 km² (Haleakala NP: 117.3 km²; Hawai'i Volcanoes NP: 919.6 km²), National Wildlife Refuges, 20 State Natural Area Reserves, Wilderness Preserves, State Wildlife Sanctuaries, State Forest Reserves, State Conservation District, private preserve system, including preserves of The Nature Conservancy. The Hawai'i Volcanoes World Heritage Site covers 929.6 km²; the Hawaiian Islands Biosphere Reserve (comprising parts of Haleakala and Hawai'i Volcanoes National Parks) covers 995.5 km². Federal and State endangered species laws.

Geography

The Hawaiian archipelago is located between latitudes 18°50'–28°15'N and longitudes 154°40'–178°75'W and includes volcanic islands, offshore islets, shoals and atolls. The total land area is 16,641 km². Altitude ranges from sea-level to 4205 m (Armstrong 1983). The youngest island, Hawai'i, situated in the south-east of the archipelago, is volcanically active. The older islands are situated mostly in the north-west of the archipelago. They are greatly eroded; basaltic portions of the north-westernmost islands are entirely submerged, and coralline atolls and shoals are all that remain above sea-level.

The physiography of the Hawaiian Islands is characterized by diversity. On the youngest islands, gently sloping unweathered shield volcanoes with very poor soil development can be juxtaposed with older, heavily weathered valley systems with steep walls, well-developed alluvial and colluvial deposits overlain with humic soils and gently sloped floodplains. On a typical older island, sea cliffs and large amphitheatre-headed valleys on windward aspects contrast with erosionally younger dissected slopes on leeward aspects. Soils types are diverse; histosols and inceptisols (organic soils on lava and volcanic ash, respectively) are prominent, but all of the 10 orders of soils recognized by the U.S. Soil Conservation Service are represented in the Hawaiian region (Hawai'i being the only state in the U.S. with all 10 orders) (Foote *et al.* 1972; Sato *et al.* 1973).

The Hawaiian region has a tropical climate which is buffered by the surrounding ocean (Blumenstock and Price

1967). The strength of the prevailing north-east trade winds fluctuates seasonally. Storms, and even hurricanes, occur in winter. The maximum recorded temperature is 37.7°C, measured at 265 m elevation, and the minimum is -12.7°C at 4205 m. Mean monthly temperatures vary little over the year (on average by only of 5°C or less), with diurnal variation usually exceeding seasonal variation. Annual rainfall varies greatly according to location, with marked windward-leeward gradients over short distances. The minimum average annual rainfall is <250 mm and the maximum is well in excess of 11,000 mm. Precipitation peaks during the months of October–April. Leeward slopes experience a dry season, and receive most of their rainfall in winter. Windward slopes receive trade wind-driven orographic rainfall throughout the year, in addition to winter storm precipitation.

Vegetation

The natural vegetation of the islands varies according to altitude, prevailing moisture and substrate. The most recent classification of Hawaiian natural communities recognizes nearly 100 native Hawaiian vegetation types categorized in a hierarchy of elevation, moisture and physiognomy (Hawai'i Heritage Program, The Nature Conservancy of Hawai'i 1991). Within these types are numerous island-specific or region-specific associations, an extremely rich array of vegetation types within a very limited geographic area. Major vegetation formations include forests and woodlands, shrublands, grasslands (including savannas, tussock grasslands and sedge-dominated associations), herblands, and pioneer associations on lava and cinder substrates.

Forest formations include subalpine, montane and lowland forest types, ranging from sea-level to over 3000 m. There are 48 recognized forest types (Hawai'i Heritage Program, The Nature Conservancy of Hawai'i 1991). Coastal and lowland forests are generally dry or mesic, and open or closed canopied, with one summer-deciduous type and several sclerophyllous types. Coastal forests occur on an offshore islet near Moloka'i, and on the main islands of Kaua'i, O'ahu, Moloka'i, Maui and Hawai'i. Lowland forests are generally under 10 m high. Typical dominant trees of lowland forests include taxa in the genera *Acacia, Colubrina, Diospyros, Erythrina, Metrosideros, Nestegis, Pandanus, Pisonia, Pleomele, Pouteria, Pritchardia* and *Sapindus*. Lowland forests occur below 1000 m altitude on the islands of Kaua'i, O'ahu, Moloka'i, Maui, Lāna'i and Hawai'i. Historically such forests were present on the islands of Ni'ihau and Kaho'olawe, but these have been cleared or displaced by alien vegetation.

Montane forests occur between 1000 and 2000 m. They are dry to mesic on the leeward slopes of the islands, and mesic to wet on the windward slopes. The dry and mesic forests may be open to closed-canopied, and may exceed 20 m in stature. On some islands, there is a well-developed cloud forest in the montane zone, usually of low stature and densely canopied. Montane dry and mesic forests are dominated by trees in the genera *Acacia, Chamaesyce, Metrosideros,*

Sapindus, Sophora and *Santalum*. Montane wet forests and cloud forests are usually dominated by species of *Metrosideros, Cheirodendron* and tree ferns (*Cibotium* spp.). Montane forests are well-developed on the islands of Kaua'i, Moloka'i, Maui and Hawai'i. On the islands of Lāna'i and O'ahu, the highest occurring forests are similar to montane wet forests of the higher islands, but they occupy a limited area and include lowland forest elements. Lowland and montane mesic forests probably contain the most diverse tree flora.

In high montane and subalpine zones (at and above 3000 m altitude), the dominant trees include species of *Acacia, Metrosideros, Sophora* and *Myoporum*. Subalpine forests only occur on the islands of Maui and Hawai'i, geologically the youngest islands in the Hawaiian archipelago. The forests are usually open-canopied, and form mosaics with grasslands and shrublands.

Hawaiian shrubland formations are found from the coast to the subalpine zone. The majority of the 32 recognized Hawaiian shrubland types (Hawai'i Heritage Program, The Nature Conservancy of Hawai'i 1991) are in dry and mesic environments (that limit forest formation), or on cliffs and slopes too steep to support trees. Dominant genera along the coast include *Chenopodium, Ipomoea, Heliotropium, Lipochaeta, Myoporum, Santalum, Scaevola* and *Sida*. Species of *Bidens, Dicranopteris, Dodonaea, Metrosideros, Sesbania* and *Wikstroemia* are among the dominants in the lowlands and in the montane zone. *Metrosideros*-dominated wet

CPD Site PO6: Hawaiian Islands. Waimea Canyon, Kaua'i, with *Wilkesia gymnoxiphium* (Asteraceae) in the foreground. Photo: Peter Green.

shrublands and bogs are best developed at montane elevations on Kaua'i, Moloka'i, Maui and Hawai'i. Floristically diverse vegetation, dominated by a variety of shrubs and large ferns, especially *Sadleria, Athyrium, Dicranopteris, Sticherus* and *Diplopterygium*, is especially well-developed on the steep montane slopes of Kaua'i, Moloka'i, Maui and Hawai'i. Species-poor mat-fern (*Dicranopteris*) vegetation occurs on windward wet lowland and montane slopes of Kaua'i, O'ahu, Moloka'i, Maui, Lāna'i and Hawai'i. At subalpine elevations, shrubland dominants include species of *Argyroxiphium, Chenopodium, Dubautia, Styphelia* and *Vaccinium*.

Eleven native Hawaiian grassland types (including sedge-dominated associations) are found in coastal, lowland, montane and subalpine zones (Hawai'i Heritage Program, The Nature Conservancy of Hawai'i 1991). Coastal and lowland grasslands are dominated by members of the genera *Bulboschoenus, Cyperus, Fimbristylis, Eragrostis* and *Sporobolus*, among others, and are known from the Northwestern Hawaiian Islands, Kaua'i, O'ahu, Moloka'i, Lāna'i, Maui and Hawai'i. Montane grasslands are actually sedge formations associated with bogs and wet ground, and are best developed on Kaua'i, Maui and Hawai'i. The dominant genera here are *Rhynchospora, Oreobolus* and *Carex*. At high montane and subalpine zones, on the islands of Maui and Hawai'i, tussock grasslands of *Deschampsia* or *Eragrostis* occur.

Hawaiian herblands occur from the coast to subalpine zones. In coastal areas, and in the lowlands, the dominant species are in genera such as *Marsilea, Nama* and *Sesuvium*; *Rhacomitrium* moss occurs in montane bogs and subalpine deserts. There are only four Hawaiian herbland types currently recognized.

Pioneer vegetation is well-developed in areas of recent and active volcanism on the islands of Maui and Hawai'i. A variety of lichens, hepatics and mosses occur on lava flows and cinder beds, and are replaced by seres dominated by species of ferns in such genera as *Polypodium, Dicranopteris, Nephrolepis* and *Sadleria*, as well as shrubs, such as *Styphelia* spp. and *Vaccinium* spp., and ultimately trees (especially *Metrosideros* spp.).

Flora

According to the latest treatment (Wagner, Herbst and Sohmer 1990), the flora of the Hawaiian Islands includes approximately 980 species of native flowering plants, 89% of which are endemic. With additional field surveys and systematic work on the Hawaiian flora, it is possible that the number may be increased to about 1000 taxa. The native flora includes 216 genera in 87 families. There are 32 endemic and 5 near-endemic genera. The overall level of generic endemism is nearly 15%, one of the highest levels of generic endemism in the world.

Patterns of island endemism are an important consideration, since some taxa are restricted to islands of a certain age (e.g. Kaua'i-O'ahu endemics) or proximity (e.g. the "Maui Nui" taxa that contribute to the similarity of the Maui, Moloka'i and Lāna'i island flora).

The native flora is disharmonic relative to other tropical floristic regions, with few orchids, a single genus of palms, and with gymnosperms as well as primitive flowering plant families conspicuously absent. The largest eight families, the Campanulaceae, Asteraceae, Rutaceae, Rubiaceae, Lamiaceae,

Gesneriaceae, Poaceae and Cyperaceae, together constitute over half of the native species. It is believed that the present number of Hawaiian native flowering plant species has been derived from about 280 successful colonists, the majority from South East Asia (Malesia). The American element is relatively small, and there are affinities with the floras of Australia, New Zealand and southern South America. There are also pantropical and a few boreal taxa.

A recent study statistically demonstrated the relationship between the largest families and genera of several Pacific island groups and those of the Hawaiian archipelago (Sohmer 1990). The same families were represented on most of the island groups included in the survey. The Hawaiian flora is notable for many examples of adaptive radiation. Nearly 50% of the native flowering plant species of Hawai'i are derived from fewer than 12% of the 280 successful original colonization events (Wagner, Herbst and Sohmer 1990). Most of the rest of the colonists are represented in the present flora by single species. The combination of disharmonic founding taxa and adaptive proliferation of species has resulted in a flora so distinctive that it is assigned to its own floristic region by most phytogeographers (Udvardy 1975; Takhtajan 1986; Wagner, Herbst and Sohmer 1990).

Kipukas, islands of vegetation left when lava flows decimate areas around them, seem to be less important to plant evolution in the Hawaiian Islands than to animal

CPD Site PO6: Hawaiian Islands. *Wilkesia gymnoxiphium* **(Asteraceae), a monotypic endemic genus. Waimea Canyon, Kaua'i.** Photo: Peter Green.

evolution. They are more important as refugia from which propagules can colonize surrounding fresh lava. They are, therefore, important in community cycling and succession on volcanically-active islands.

Areas of botanical importance

Within the Hawaiian Islands, there are several subregions and localities that represent significant concentrations of floristic diversity. These are usually areas with relatively intact plant communities and where there is a high potential for long-term preservation of the habitat. Outstanding sites are listed, below (Table 82), with annotations, by island, in a roughly north-west to south-east sequence, and an indication is given as to whether the area is protected (P), incompletely protected (I) or not yet protected (N). It is important to note that Table 82 summarizes information on only the larger subregions and floristic areas within the Hawaiian archipelago. It should not be considered an

exhaustive treatment. Indeed, because of the high level of endemism in the Hawaiian flora, virtually all tracts of native vegetation will harbour endemics. Table 82 indicates the high degree of local diversity of plant habitats and natural areas of the Hawaiian Islands.

Useful plants

The Hawaiian Islands have been inhabited since about 600 AD. Native plant resources have been utilized, first by the Polynesian settlers who developed the ancient Hawaiian culture, then in post-contact (1778 to the present) times by a growing number of arriving cultures. Native plants provided materials for ancient Hawaiian clothing, textiles, foraging and agricultural tools, ornaments, recreational, ceremonial and religious objects, ocean-going vessels, shelter, food and medicine (Buck 1957; Krauss 1974). At least some of those

TABLE 82. AREAS OF OUTSTANDING BOTANICAL IMPORTANCE IN THE HAWAIIAN ISLANDS

Subregion/Locality		Significance
Northwestern Hawaiian Islands	(I)	Intact coastal plant communities, including 1 rare forest type restricted to the subregion; representative and rare coastal taxa.
Kōke'e-Alaka'i-Hanapēpē (Kaua'i)	(I)	Large expanse of intact plant communities in dry-mesic to very wet settings, extremely diverse topography; rich mesic forests, rain forest and bogs; high concentration of rare plants, many island endemics.
Nā Pali Coast (Kaua'i)	(I)	Topographically diverse coastal cliff and valley system in dry to mesic setting; intact plant communities; high diversity of rare plants.
Wai'anae Mountains (O'ahu)	(I)	Mesic to wet plant communities in very diverse topographic setting, very high concentration of rare plants, >10% of all Hawaiian rare plant taxa known from this region.
Ko'olau Mountains (O'ahu)	(N)	Mostly wet communities; topographically diverse; some unique plant communities, many rare plants.
Mo'omomi-Ho'olehua Coast (Moloka'i)	(I)	Intact coastal dune and sea cliff ecosystems, including representative and rare coastal strand flora.
East Moloka'i Mountains	(I)	Intact wet summit forests and bogs, topographically diverse setting, including windward sea cliffs, large valleys and leeward mesic-dry slopes. Major native plant concentration for the island, many rare plants.
West Maui Mountains	(I)	Topographically diverse, extremely rugged setting with strong windward-leeward moisture gradients and remote, largely intact native plant communities, including rain forest, bogs, mesic and dry formations; very large concentration of rare plants.
Windward East Maui	(I)	Large tracts of montane rain forest, bogs and other plant communities; significant watershed, habitat for endangered birds, many rare plants.
Leeward East Maui	(N)	Remnants of mesic and dry plant communities, from subalpine to coastal elevations, including extremely rare forest types, some restricted to the subregion; very high concentration of rare plants.
Haleakalā Summit (Maui)	(P)	Subalpine and alpine plant communities in a unique topographic and climatic setting; includes very rare plant communities, many rare plants.
Lāna'ihale-Kānepu'u (Lāna'i)	(I)	Rain forest summit, undergoing a transition through mesic and dry forests and shrublands downslope; extreme topographic diversity; rare plant communities, some restricted to the subregion, and rare plants.
Kohala Mountains (Hawai'i)	(I)	Rain forest summit, with bogs and wetlands, geologically oldest portion of the island, distinct flora. A few rare plant communities.
Hāmākua-Hilo Subregion (Hawai'i)	(I)	Wet, windward slopes supporting large tracts of rain forest and wetlands, subalpine transition to rare forest types; many rare plants.
Puna-Ka'ū Subregion (Hawai'i)	(I)	Transition to mesic slopes interrupted by active volcanic flows and cinder desert; many plant communities, including some restricted to the subregion; many rare plants.
Kona Subregion (Hawai'i)	I)	Dry to wet forest types; distinct flora due to unusual convectional climatic conditions on the lee of the island. Includes rare forest types, rare plants and endangered bird habitat; important for watershed protection.
Alpine summits (Hawai'i)	(I)	Includes subalpine and alpine plant communities in the summit regions of 3 massive volcanoes: Mauna Kea, Mauna Loa and Hualalai. Distinctive floristics, rare plant communities and rare plants.
Pōhakuloa-Saddle Area (Hawai'i)	(N)	Unique subalpine leeward saddle with distinctive floristics, rare plant communities and high density of rare plants.

TABLE 83. SOME COMMON AND IMPORTANT NATIVE PLANTS USED BY NATIVE HAWAIIANS

Taxon	Hawaiian name	Primary uses
Acacia koa	koa	canoe hulls, bowls, woodwork, paddles, etc.
Alyxia oliviformis	maile	ornaments (wreaths), sacred to hula patroness
Bidens spp.	ko'oko'olau	medicine
Bobea elatior	'ahakea	canoe gunwales, house posts and sills
Caesalpinia kavaiensis	uhiuhi	weapons, fishing implement
Cheirodendron trigynum	'olapa	dark blue dye
Cibotium spp.	hapu'u	starch source, preparing bodies for burial
Colubrina oppositifolia	kauila	digging sticks, weapons, trolling sticks, musical instruments, poles for royal feather standards
Cyperus laevigatus	makaloa	baskets, mats
Diospyros sandwicensis	lama	altar piece, infrequent food (fruit), medicine, fences
Freycinetia arborea	'ie'ie	baskets, helmets, mats, religious significance
Gossypium tomentosum	ma'o	green dye
Heteropogon contortus	pili	house thatching in dry areas
Hibiscus tiliaceus	hau	cordage, canoe outriggers, fire-making
Ipomoea indica	koali 'awa	medicine
Marine and freshwater algae	limu	food (near-daily intake)
Mariscus javanicus	'ahu'awa	cordage
Metrosideros polymorpha	'ohi'a lehua	canoes, food preparation boards, weapons, temple images, ornaments (wreaths), religious significance
Myoporum sandwicense	naio	thatching poles, posts
Pandanus tectorius	hala	baskets, mats, house thatching in wet areas
Pipturus albidus	mamaki	tapa for clothing
Solanum americanum	popolo	medicine
Sophora chrysophylla	mamane	sleds, thatching posts
Touchardia latifolia	olona	extremely strong cordage
Waltheria indica	'uhaloa	medicine
Wikstroemia spp.	akia	fish poison, medicine

Sources: Buck (1957); Krauss (1974); Wagner, Herbst and Sohmer (1990).

traditional ethnobotanical values have survived to the present. Table 83 summarizes a few of the better known examples of useful plants.

Currently utilized native plants of the Hawaiian region include a variety of hardwood trees, native taxa used as ornamentals, or hybridized with ornamentals, native plants hybridized with agricultural species, and certain taxa utilized in scientific research, especially in the fields of evolution and ecology. The genetic resource represented by the native Hawaiian biota, including its flora, is extremely significant, irreplaceable and largely unexplored.

Social and environmental values

The Hawaiian archipelago can be divided into three separate Endemic Bird Areas. The tiny north-western islands of Laysan and Nihoa are remarkable in having 4 restricted-range land bird species confined to them, and a further 2 which have become extinct. The island of Hawai'i has 17 restricted-range land bird species; a further 9 species have become extinct and 11 species are shared with the other Hawaiian Islands. These latter islands have a total of 26 restricted-range land bird species and a further 4 species which have become extinct. The demise of the avifauna on all the Hawaiian Islands has been due to a combination of factors, including hunting by early settlers, forest clearance, diseases, and introduced predators, browsers, birds and plants.

The montane wet forests of the main islands protect important watersheds which supply drinking and irrigation water. Native vegetation has been shown to buffer climate, ameliorate evapotranspiration, and intercept moisture that otherwise would not be captured by the land (Juvik and Perreira 1973).

The forested uplands of the main islands provide strikingly beautiful landscapes. This scenic richness attracts international and national tourists. There is an increasing interest in ecotourism, focusing on the Hawaiian biota, including its rich native flora.

A portion of the population in Hawai'i, including some of the indigenous Hawaiian population, places high value on the native biota (including plants) for the religious and cultural significance it had in indigenous culture. Ancient Hawaiian culture was inseparable from the native biological environment; the maintenance of the natural environment is fundamental to the maintenance of Hawaiian culture.

Threats

There has been a long history of degradation of the native plants and plant communities of the Hawaiian Islands (Cuddihy and Stone 1990). There are probably no sites left that have not experienced direct or indirect effects of human activities in the Hawaiian region. Introductions of alien plants and animals have increased logarithmically from first European contact to the present, so that, at this point, the number of naturalized alien plants in the Hawaiian Islands is rapidly approaching the number of native species. By 1992, there were 870 alien flowering plant taxa (including

553

varieties and subspecies) in the Hawaiian Islands (Anon. 1992). The biomass of alien plant species already exceeds that of native species.

Hawaiian native vegetation is easily disrupted by introduced species, especially large mammals and aggressive weeds (Hawai'i Heritage Program, The Nature Conservancy of Hawai'i 1987). Having evolved without large mammals, most native Hawaiian plants cannot withstand the effects of pig, goats, sheep, cattle and deer. All of these animals have established feral populations at various locations in the main island chain. These feral animals have spread into native ecosystems so readily that only two inaccessible plateaux are still free from them. Feral animals disturb native vegetation, exacerbating soil loss and permitting alien weeds to establish. Several weeds have shown the ability to invade native vegetation and displace it entirely. Many of these are recognized as noxious weeds by state and federal agencies. Other weeds are only a problem in areas subjected to continual disturbance of native vegetation. Some of the more important alien weeds, arranged by habitat, are given in Table 84.

TABLE 84. SOME IMPORTANT ALIEN WEEDS ESTABLISHED ON THE HAWAIIAN ISLANDS

Habitat	Taxa
Coastal and dry habitats	*Prosopis pallida, Leucaena leucocephala, Lantana camara, Opuntia ficus-indica, Cenchrus ciliaris, Cynodon dactylon, Pennisetum setaceum, Panicum maximum,* other grasses.
Mesic to wet lowlands	*Schinus terebinthifolius, Syzygium cumini, Myrica faya, Psidium* spp., *Clidemia hirta, Adenophora* spp., *Hedychium* spp., *Setaria palmifolia, Melinis minutiflora, Andropogon virginicus,* other grasses.
Mesic to wet montane	*Rubus* spp., *Tibouchina* spp., *Passiflora mollissima, Pennisetum clandestinum,* other grasses.

Human activities have destroyed native vegetation and continue to degrade native ecosystems (Hawai'i Heritage Program, The Nature Conservancy of Hawai'i 1987; Hawai'i Heritage Program, The Nature Conservancy of Hawai'i, and Division of Forestry and Wildlife, State Department of Land and Natural Resources 1989; Cuddihy and Stone 1990). There is no doubt that a significant portion of the native flora became extinct after humans colonized the archipelago. By the time of European contact in 1778, most of the lowland plant communities had been displaced by Polynesian agricultural practices which heavily utilized fire. Extinction and disturbance trends of the native flora have increased since.

Human population in the Hawaiian Islands has been growing at an accelerated pace since the late 1800s, exceeding 150,000 permanent residents at the turn of the century, at 500,000 by 1950, and exceeding 1,000,000 by the end of the 1980s (Armstrong 1983). The nearly ten-fold increase in population in 100 years contributed to the loss of coastal and lowland habitat for native plants, as these were converted to agriculture and residential areas for the growing population. The annual visitor population has expanded even more rapidly since World War II, barely exceeding 50,000 in 1950, but breaking 1,000,000 in 1966, 4,000,000 in 1980, and approaching 7,000,000 in 1990 (Armstrong 1983). The construction of tourism-related

infrastructure in the islands, and the direct and indirect impacts of the visitor load on water and other natural resources, have been proportional to this extraordinary growth.

Land conversion to agriculture, ranching, residential, recreational and other uses have permanently displaced native vegetation in about half of the Hawaiian region. Coastal and lowland communities have been particularly affected, but large tracts in montane and subalpine zones have been seriously affected on the islands of Maui and Hawai'i as well. Taking of native plants for wood or other products continues apace. Disturbance of native forest for illicit marijuana cultivation is a serious problem on several of the main islands. Wildfire, intensified by the spread of alien grasses, continues to be very damaging to Hawaiian lowland dry vegetation.

Conservation

A total land area of 2029.4 km² (c. 12% of land area of the archipelago) is actively managed for conservation. Conservation efforts have occurred at private, state and federal levels (Hawai'i Heritage Program, The Nature Conservancy of Hawai'i 1987). The majority of such efforts began in the early 1900s, when local foresters realized that unchecked cattle and goat populations on the main islands were seriously degrading forested watersheds and threatening the water supply of the islands' population. A system of watershed forest reserves was established on both government and private lands. Today, State Forest Reserves and the State Conservation District together amount to over 8000 km² of lands that restrict agricultural or other development. This is c. 48% of the land area of the region.

Certain protected lands receive active management, in addition to laws restricting development, that counteract threats to native resources. These include two National Parks of area over 10 km² (Haleakala NP: 117.3 km²; and Hawai'i Volcanoes NP: 919.6 km²), National Wildlife Refuges, State Natural Area Reserves, Wilderness Preserves and Sanctuaries, and private preserves. The U.S. National Park Service began setting up National Parks in the early 1900s, protecting a portion of the native flora along with areas of geological interest. More parks and National Wildlife Refuges have been established since then, amounting to a federal protected land system of over 1103.5 km².

Twenty State Natural Area Reserves have been established since 1976; the total reserve system currently amounts to over 414 km² on five of the main islands. Other State Wilderness Preserves and Sanctuaries for plants and animals cover about 374.8 km². Private preserves are maintained by The Nature Conservancy in cooperation with several private land owners. This private preserve system covers 112.9 km². A summary and review of the protected areas system is given in IUCN (1991).

State and federal laws recognize endangered plant species in the Hawaiian region, but there is a large backlog of plant taxa that are candidates for Endangered status. Only two of 23 listed Hawaiian plant taxa have recovery plans, and there are over 450 candidate taxa. There has been a recent commitment to accelerate the federal Endangered status listing process for Hawaiian taxa, over 150 of which are on the list for receiving Endangered status over the next few years. While many examples of native vegetation and plants occur on protected lands, there are still many cases in which rare plant taxa are in jeopardy. The latest statistics from the Hawaiian Endangered Species Task Force are given in Table 85.

TABLE 85. STATUS OF PLANT TAXA ON THE HAWAIIAN ISLANDS

	Number of flowering plant taxa*	% of flowering plant taxa
Native	1102	-
Endemic	1020	93
Extinct	97	9
Endangered	267	24
◆ 1 plant remaining	12	1
◆ 2–10 plants remaining	50	5
◆ 11–100 plants remaining	95	9

Note: *includes varieties and subspecies.
Source: Anon. 1992.

References

Anon. (1992). Hawaiian Endangered Species Task Force defines its priorities. *Herbarium Pacificum News* 9(2): 10.

Armstrong, R.W. (ed.) (1983). *Atlas of Hawaii*, 2nd Ed. Geography Department, University of Hawaii, University of Hawaii Press, Honolulu, Hawai'i.

Blumenstock, D.I. and Price, S. (1967). *Climates of the States: Hawaii*. U.S. Environmental Data Service, Climatography of the U.S., No. 60–51.

Buck, P. (1957). *Arts and crafts of Hawaii*. Bishop Museum Press, Honolulu, Hawai'i.

Cuddihy, L.W. and Stone, C.P. (1990). *Alteration of native Hawaiian vegetation: affects of humans, their activities and introductions*. University of Hawaii Press, Honolulu, Hawai'i.

Foote, D.E., Hill, E.L., Nakamura, S. and Stephens, F. (1972). *Soil survey of the islands of Kauai, Oahu, Maui, Molokai and Lanai, State of Hawaii*. U.S. Soil Conservation Service, Soil Survey Series.

Hawai'i Heritage Program, The Nature Conservancy of Hawai'i (1987). *Biological overview of Hawaii's Natural Area Reserves system*. Hawaii State Department of Land and Natural Resources, Honolulu, Hawai'i.

Hawai'i Heritage Program, The Nature Conservancy of Hawai'i (1991). Rare Element Database, Managed Area Database, and Hawaiian Natural Community Database.

Hawai'i Heritage Program, The Nature Conservancy of Hawai'i, and Division of Forestry and Wildlife, State Department of Land and Natural Resources (1989). *State of Hawaii Natural Area Reserves system: biological resources and management priorities summary report*. Hawaii State Department of Land and Natural Resources, Honolulu, Hawai'i.

IUCN (1991). *IUCN directory of protected areas in Oceania*. IUCN, Gland, Switzerland and Cambridge, U.K. xxiii, 447 pp. (Prepared by the World Conservation Monitoring Centre.)

Juvik, O. and Perreira, D.J. (1973). *The interception of fog and cloud water on windward Mauna Loa, Hawaii*. Island Systems IRP, U.S. International Biological Program, Technical Report No. 32.

Krauss, B.H. (1974). *Ethnobotany of Hawaii*. University of Hawaii Press, Honolulu, Hawai'i.

Sato, H., Ikeda, W., Paeth, R., Smythe, R. and Takehiro, M., jr (1973). *Soil survey of the island of Hawaii*. U.S. Soil Conservation Service, Soil Survey Series.

Sohmer, S. (1990). Elements of Pacific phytodiversity. In Baas, P., Kalkman, K. and Geesink, R. (eds), *The plant diversity of Malesia. Proceedings of the Flora Malesiana Symposium commemorating Professor Dr. C.G.G.J. van Steenis, Leiden, August 1989*. Kluwer Academic Press, Dordrecht. Pp. 293–304.

Takhtajan, A. (1986). *Floristic regions of the world*. University of California Press, Berkeley. 522 pp.

Udvardy, M.D.F. (1975). *A classification of the biogeographical provinces of the world*. IUCN Occasional Paper 18. IUCN, Gland, Switzerland.

Wagner, W.L., Herbst, D.R. and Sohmer, S.H. (1990). *Manual of the flowering plants of Hawai'i*. University of Hawaii Press and Bishop Museum Press, Honolulu, Hawai'i.

Acknowledgements

This Data Sheet was prepared by Dr Sy Sohmer (Botanical Research Institute, Fort Worth, Texas) and Dr Sam M. Gan III (The Nature Conservancy, Honolulu, Hawai'i).

GALAPAGOS ISLANDS
Ecuador

Location: Straddling the Equator, c. 1000 km west of continental Ecuador, between latitudes 1°25'S–1°40'N and longitudes 89°14'–92°01'W.

Area: 13 major islands and numerous smaller islets and rocks, in total about 7900 km², spread over 45,000 km² of ocean.

Altitude: 0–1707 m.

Vegetation: Seven vegetation zones recognized: littoral, arid, transition, *Scalesia*, *Miconia*, brown, and fern-sedge zone, relating in particular to increasing rainfall along altitudinal gradients, and to depth of soil; the vegetation types include desert scrub, shrub steppe savanna, steppe scrub, steppe forest (woodland), scrub, closed scrub with scattered trees, forest (dry season deciduous and evergreen), broadleaved herbaceous vegetation, and closed bryoid vegetation (*Sphagnum* bogs).

Flora: 596 indigenous taxa (including subspecific taxa), of which 229 (38%) are endemic; at the species level, c. 224 endemics (41.4%) out of a total of 541 vascular plant species. 7 endemic genera of flowering plants. The flora has affinities with that of adjacent South America. About 260 introduced species, of which c. 17 are considered to be aggressive invaders.

Useful plants: Timber trees for construction, fences, firewood (e.g. *Piscidia carthagenensis*, *Hippomane mancinella*, *Psidium galapageium*). Actual and potential genetic resources (e.g. *Lycopersicon cheesmannii*, *Gossypium* spp., respectively).

Other values: Scientific resource, particularly for evolutionary studies; native vegetation of fundamental importance for endemic and indigenous wildlife, such as reptiles (e.g. giant tortoises and land iguanas), birds (e.g. Darwin's finches); watershed protection; tourist attraction.

Threats: Introduced mammals and aggressive alien plants, habitat fragmentation, agricultural encroachment, over-exploitation of native woody species; increasing pressure from resident human population due to sharp increase in immigration to the islands; increasing tourist pressure; man-made fires.

Conservation: National Park (7278 km²), 96.7 % of the total land area of the archipelago; World Heritage Site and Biosphere Reserve (7665 km²).

Geography

The Galápagos Islands (Archipiélago de Colón) are true oceanic islands. The oldest islands are those in the east of the archipelago, comprising uplifted lava flows about 4.5 million years old. They include Española, Santa Fé, Plazas, Baltra, Seymour, and a narrow strip along the north-east coast of Santa Cruz. All the other islands are formed by great volcanoes and are much younger; no rocks older than 0.7 million years have been found on Fernandina, Isabela, Santiago, Pinta, Genovesa, Marchena or Darwin (Simkin 1984; Geist, McBirney and Duncan 1985). The islands consist typically of one or several shield volcanoes culminating in craters or large calderas. Eruptions are frequent, particularly in the westernmost islands Isabela and Fernandina, and the landscape displays a variety of craters, barren lava fields, ash or scoria, and vegetated areas.

The archipelago is situated at the point of convergence of the principal ocean currents of the eastern Pacific. The southern equatorial currents, with cool waters, and the south-east trade winds, cause a cool season from June to November, during which a low-level inversion creates overcast conditions and drizzle, called garúa. During the months of December to May, the weakening of the trade winds and the influence of warmer waters from the north, cause the occurrence of a hot season, which brings a tropical range of

temperatures and rain showers over the higher parts of the islands. The lowlands are arid while the highlands are comparatively moist; the mean annual precipitation ranges from about 0 to 100 mm at the coast (particularly low on north-exposed sides of small islands) to about 2000 mm or more at high elevations on the south-exposed slopes of the larger islands (Hamann 1979a).

The Galápagos were first discovered in 1535; there is no evidence of prehistoric settlements. The biological isolation of the islands ended with the arrival of English buccaneers in the 17th century. In 1832 the archipelago was annexed by Ecuador and a small, permanent colony established (Perry 1984), but until 1950 the resident population remained below one thousand.

Today, the archipelago is an Ecuadorian province, which has undergone great changes during the last three decades. Previously the local economy was based on subsistence fishing and farming, but the main economic activities are now centred around tourism. More than 40,000 tourists visit the National Park of Galápagos each year and contribute significantly to the local and national foreign currency income. Following the growth in tourism the number of resident inhabitants increased from 4000 in 1974 to over 10,000 in 1988, mainly because of an influx of immigrants from mainland Ecuador (Servicio Parque Nacional Galápagos [SPNG] 1990, pers. comm.).

Vegetation

The vegetation zones described from Santa Cruz island (Bowman 1961; Wiggins and Porter 1971) are: littoral, dry, transition, *Scalesia*, *Miconia*, brown and fern-sedge zones. However, many different vegetation types and plant communities have since been described using different approaches to vegetation classification. Below are outlined some characteristic vegetation types within the general framework of the vegetation zones. The local climatic conditions and the volcanic nature of the islands contribute to the formation of unique and characteristic ecological conditions and habitats, so, in addition to the mainly climatically determined zones, several azonal vegetation types are recognized (Bowman 1961; Wiggins and Porter 1971; Reeder and Riechert 1975; Werff 1978, 1979, 1990; Hamann 1979a, 1981, 1984; Eliasson 1984; Atkinson 1990; Itow 1990).

The littoral vegetation is, in fact, not zonal, but consists of structurally and floristically very different azonal vegetation types, such as mangrove forest and scrub (including *Rhizophora mangle*, *Avicennia germinans*, *Laguncularia racemosa* and *Conocarpus erecta*), xeromorphic evergreen scrub (including *Cryptocarpus pyriformis*, *Scutia pauciflora*, *Lycium minimum* and *Maytenus octogona*), and sand-dune and salt-flat vegetation (e.g. *Nolana galapagensis*, *Ipomoea pes-caprae*, *Sesuvium* spp., *Portulaca howellii*, *Heliotropium curassavicum*, *Polygala* spp., *Batis maritima* and *Salicornia fruticosa*).

The arid zone predominates at low elevations and comprises dry season deciduous forest, steppe forest (woodland), steppe scrub and various desert-like vegetation types. The zone is in most places characterized by *Bursera graveolens*, together with endemic cacti belonging to the genera *Opuntia* and *Jasminocereus* (an endemic genus). Other characteristic woody species are *Erythrina velutina*, *Croton scouleri*, *Acacia* spp., *Prosopis juliflora*, *Tournefortia psilostachya*, *Cordia lutea*, *Lantana peduncularis*, *Alternanthera echinocephala* and *A. filifolia*.

The transition zone is typically found on larger islands, above the arid zone, and includes a mixture of species, some of which also occur in the arid and *Scalesia* zones. However, the typical vegetation is dry season deciduous to semi-evergreen forest dominated by *Pisonia floribunda*, *Piscidia carthagenensis* and *Psidium galapageium*. In addition, such species as *Bursera graveolens* and *Opuntia* spp. are common. There is often a discernible shrub layer comprising *Tournefortia* spp., *Cordia* spp., *Croton scouleri*, *Chiococca alba* and *Zanthoxylum fagara*. Vines such as *Ipomoea triloba* are common, and the ground layer is often dominated by *Salvia occidentalis* and *Alternanthera halimifolia*.

The main vegetation of the *Scalesia* zone, found at intermediate elevations on the larger islands, is an evergreen forest with well-developed shrub and ground layers and many vines and epiphytes. On the central and eastern islands (San Cristóbal, Floreana, Santa Cruz and Santiago) the forest is dominated by *Scalesia pedunculata*, while *S. microcephala* dominates on Fernandina and northern Isabela, and *S. cordata* on southern Isabela. Other prominent woody species are *Psychotria rufipes*, *Zanthoxylum fagara*, *Psidium galapageium*, *Tournefortia rufo-sericea* and *Chiococca alba*. Vines such as *Stictocardia tiliifolia* and *Passiflora colinvauxii* are quite common in places, as are epiphytic orchids, peperomias and pteridophytes. The ground layer is often dominated by *Justicia galapagana*, *Alternanthera halimifolia*, *Borreria laevis*, and a number of ferns (*Thelypteris*, *Ctenitis* and *Asplenium* spp.).

In former times, a brown zone was found above the *Scalesia* zone on Santa Cruz and San Cristóbal (Bowman 1961). It received its name from the many epiphytic hepatics that covered the shrubs and low trees (mainly *Psidium galapageium* and *Zanthoxylum fagara*). Today, most has been cleared for agriculture and only small, scattered remnants survive.

The *Miconia* zone is found only at higher elevations on Santa Cruz and San Cristóbal and comprises an evergreen scrub dominated by *Miconia robinsoniana*. On other large islands, comparable scrubby vegetation types are found, but without *Miconia*. Only a few other woody species occur together with *Miconia*. The most conspicuous of these are *Acnistus ellipticus*, *Darwiniothamnus tenuifolius*, *Psychotria rufipes* and the tree fern *Cyathea weatherbyana*. The *Miconia* zone is rich in pteridophytes, both in the ground layer and as epiphytes; in addition, there is a rich epiphytic flora of mosses and hepatics.

The fern-sedge zone covers, to varying degrees, the tops of the higher islands. The vegetation types include various forms of broadleaved herb vegetation, heath-like vegetation and *Sphagnum* bogs (including vertical bogs). As the name implies, ferns (e.g. *Pteridium aquilinum*, *Blechnum occidentale*, *Pityrogramma* spp.), and sedges (e.g. *Scleria pterota*, *Eleocharis*, *Cyperus*, *Rhyncospora* spp.) dominate. Many grasses (e.g. *Paspalum*) and herbs (e.g. *Jaegeria gracilis*, *Lobelia xalapensis*, *Polygonum opelousanum*) are also common, as well as the dwarf shrub *Pernettya howellii*. In sheltered places *Cyathea weatherbyana* is conspicuous.

Flora

The isolation of the archipelago, its volcanic origin, and the constant presence of open pioneer habitats have resulted in a high number of endemic taxa in the flora. There are 596 native vascular plant taxa (including subspecific taxa), of which 229 (c. 38%) are endemic (Lawesson 1990a). Another estimate gives a total of 604 taxa as indigenous (Adsersen 1989). At the species level, there are about 224 endemics among a total of 541 vascular plant species, i.e. 41.4% endemism. Endemism among the flowering plants is 51%, while among the pteridophytes it is not more than 7% (Loope, Hamann and Stone 1988).

There are 7 endemic genera of flowering plants (*Darwiniothamnus*, *Lecocarpus*, *Macraea* and *Scalesia* in the Asteraceae, *Brachycereus* and *Jasminocereus* in the Cactaceae, and *Sicyocaulis* in the Cucurbitaceae). The genus *Scalesia* presents an outstanding example of adaptive radiation (Eliasson 1984; Hamann and Wium-Andersen 1986; Adsersen 1990), but many other genera, such as *Lecocarpus* (Adsersen 1980), *Acalypha* (Seberg 1984) and *Chamaesyce* (Huft and Werff 1985), display a similar pattern. The flora has affinities to that of adjacent South America (Porter 1976, 1979, 1983, 1984a, b).

About 260 introduced, non-native plants are now recorded from the archipelago and the number is steadily increasing (Hamann 1984; Lawesson 1990b). Many introduced plant species have become naturalized and about 17 of these are considered to be aggressive invaders (Hamann 1984, 1991; Lawesson 1990b).

An evaluation of the Galápagos flora in strict accordance with the IUCN Red Data Book categories (IUCN Threatened Plants Committee Secretariat 1980) gives 2 endemic species as Extinct (*Blutaparon rigidum* and *Sicyos villosa*), 20 endemic or indigenous taxa as Endangered, and 16 endemic or indigenous taxa as Vulnerable (Lawesson 1990a). In addition, 33 native taxa are listed as Rare, while 370 taxa are not threatened. As pointed out by Lawesson (1990a), many endemic taxa in Galápagos are rare because they are by definition restricted geographically and because many endemics have very small populations. Many Galápagos endemics occur in such numbers and over such areas that they probably never will become threatened, e.g. *Pisonia floribunda*, *Psidium galapageium*, *Scalesia affinis* and *Castela galapageia*.

Useful plants

There are only few species of indigenous hardwood trees in the Galápagos. The main usable ones are *Piscidia carthagenensis*, *Hippomane mancinella* and *Psidium galapageium*. *Piscidia* has been exploited for its excellent wood qualities, which makes it extremely useful for construction purposes (e.g. for houses, boats and furniture) and for durable fence posts. Some 20 years ago, only *Piscidia* and *Hippomane* were used to any extent, and the

extraction from the Special Use Zones of the National Park (see below) was fairly limited. Occasionally, some other woody species with much lighter wood, such as *Scalesia pedunculata*, were also used, e.g. for construction. However, recent studies indicate that the rate of exploitation of *Piscidia* today is far greater than the natural regeneration rate in the National Park (Ramirez 1988); the diminishing quantities of usable specimens of *Piscidia* and *Hippomane* have recently led to an increasing exploitation of *Psidium galapageium*.

The Galápagos flora includes a number of actual and potential genetic resources which have been insufficiently investigated, except for *Lycopersicon*. The endemic Galápagos tomato, *Lycopersicon cheesmanii*, has proved to be a valuable genetic resource: two genetic traits from this species (change in the pedicel stalk of the fruit and unusually thick skin) have contributed adaptations to the cultivated tomato that allow machine harvesting and improve the ability to withstand the rigours of transportation, respectively (Prescott-Allen and Prescott-Allen 1983). Furthermore, *L. cheesmanii* may also be able to contribute increased salt-tolerance to the cultivated tomato (Oldfield 1984).

Among potential genetic resources are *Gossypium barbadense* var. *darwinii* (an endemic variety) and *G. klotzschianum* (an endemic species); *G. barbadense* is one of the most important cotton species of the world, to which other wild populations of the species have

CPD Site PO7: Galápagos Islands. View of Santa Fé island with open vegetation dominated by *Opuntia echios* var. *barringtonensis*. Photo: O. Hamann.

contributed pest-resistance and other traits (Prescott-Allen and Prescott-Allen 1981).

The genus *Prosopis* is one of several prime candidates for wood production in the arid tropics, along with other woody legumes (Anon. 1980). The Galápagos species, *P. juliflora*, displays a marked morphological variability (Wiggins and Porter 1971), which may be paralleled by variability in other traits as well.

Social and environmental values

Because of the evolutionary history of the biota in the islands, the long biological isolation, and the relatively pristine state of the ecosystems, the flora and vegetation of the Galápagos represent an invaluable scientific resource.

The outstanding attractions for visitors to the Galápagos are the unique wildlife and volcanic landscapes. Among the extraordinary organisms that visitors come to see, and scientists come to study, are the giant *Opuntia* spp., sunflower trees (*Scalesia* spp.) and other endemic plants (as well as the giant tortoises, marine and land iguanas, sea lions, fur seals, penguins, flightless cormorants and Darwin's finches).

Fresh water is a very scarce resource in the Galápagos. The inhabited San Cristóbal is the only island having permanent streams and a small, permanent freshwater lake. In the highlands of the larger islands, a major part of the precipitation

CPD Site PO7: Galápagos Islands. Remnants of *Scalesia pendunculata* forest on Santiago Island. Photo: O. Hamann.

comes in the form of fog-drip condensation (Hamann 1979a). Over large areas of the San Cristóbal highlands not included in the National Park, *Scalesia* forests have been cut down, and *Miconia* shrub and *Cyathea* thickets have been destroyed by extensive grazing of cattle and goats. As a result of the removal of dense vegetation, there is less fog-drip condensation, and the water flow of small streams supplying human settlements has decreased (Lawesson and Estupinan 1987).

Economic assessment

The local economy has been based for a long period of time on subsistence farming and fishing. During the last few decades, however, there have been increasing economic relations with continental Ecuador, increasing tourism and increasing immigration. The transition from a subsistence economy to one depending on the continent is resulting in profound social and cultural changes, as well as incipient changes in Galápagos ecosystems.

The ecological services provided by plants and vegetation have not been quantified in economic terms, but they are of fundamental importance to both tourism and to the local settlements. No estimate has been made of the value of local timber resources in comparison with imported wood, but construction of boats and houses is of great importance to the growing human population in the islands. The economic value of the genetic resources has not been estimated, but, for example, the dollar-value of the genetic traits provided to the cultivated tomato from wild Galápagos tomatoes is undoubtedly immense.

The Galápagos Islands now receive about 48,000 tourists a year, of which some 50% are non-Ecuadorians (SPNG 1990, pers. comm.). Each visitor to the National Park pays an entrance fee of US$40, half of which goes to the SPNG and half to National Parks in continental Ecuador. Additional revenue is generated from payments for tours, boats, hotels, transportation and other services, local handicrafts and some limited agricultural production. However, it is estimated that, of the income made by the tourist companies operating in the Galápagos, only 5% remains in the islands, while the rest goes to mainland Ecuador. In total, Ecuador earns some US$150 million in direct income per year from tourism, of which probably 50% is generated by tourism in the Galápagos. Thus, the Galápagos are a driving force for the whole National Park and tourist trade in Ecuador (SPNG 1990, pers. comm.).

Threats

The main threats to the flora are introduced animals, introduced plants, and agricultural encroachment (Hamann 1984, 1991; Hoeck 1984; Brockie *et al.* 1988; Loope, Hamann and Stone 1988; Adsersen 1989; Macdonald *et al.* 1989; Schofield 1989; Lawesson 1990a; Lawesson and Ortiz 1990).

All the inhabited islands have large populations of introduced mammals, which have spread into the National Park. Even on uninhabited islands like Santiago, Pinta and Pinzón, introduced mammals are (or were) causing grave problems. Goats and pigs alter the composition and structure of native vegetation, as on Santiago (Calvopina and Vries 1975; Vries and Calvopina 1977) and Pinta (Hamann 1979b, 1984), as examples. The extent of alteration on Santiago, where perhaps as many as 100,000 feral goats and several thousand feral pigs are found, is so profound that erosion has started in places. The *Scalesia* zone vegetation, originally dominated by *Scalesia pedunculata*, is almost completely gone, and *S. stewartii* and the two varieties of *S. atractyloides* (*S. atractyloides* var. *atractyloides* and *S. atractyloides* var. *darwinii*) are now listed as Vulnerable and Endangered, respectively (Lawesson 1990a).

Introduced plants are recorded from most islands (Lawesson 1990b), but so far invasive species are mainly restricted to inhabited islands. However, many introduced species are spreading into uninhabited National Park areas on these islands, and one or two invasive taxa have also become established on uninhabited islands. The most dangerous threats to the native vegetation are *Psidium guajava*, *Cinchona succirubra*, *Lantana camara*, *Rubus* sp., *Pennisetum purpureum*, and perhaps *Passiflora edulis* and *P. ligularis* (Hamann 1984, 1991).

During the last 40 years or so, *Psidium guajava* (guava) has spread on the four inhabited islands in both colonized zones and outside. In south Isabela alone, guava is estimated to cover some 200 km² and on San Cristóbal some 120 km² (Lawesson 1990b). The species has been able to invade native vegetation, often helped by the activities of domestic or feral mammals, which open up the native vegetation and disperse the seeds. Guava presents a number of conservation problems: it alters the composition and structure of native vegetation types, prevents recruitment of native plant species, interacts with native and introduced animal species in a way that may favour further establishment and spread of introduced species, and it probably changes the fire regime (as witnessed during the great fire in south Isabela in 1985 which affected 200 km²) (Nowak *et al.* 1990).

Another major problem is presented by *Cinchona succirubra* (quinine) on Santa Cruz island. By 1986, it covered about 43 km² in the highlands (Ortiz and Lawesson 1987; Macdonald *et al.* 1988), and was out-competing native species in *Miconia* and fern-sedge vegetation. Considering that the highlands of Santa Cruz were probably originally treeless (Hamann 1984), the whole aspect of this part of the island is being altered.

The recent spread of *Lantana camara* and *Rubus* sp. shows that certain species are particularly aggressive and may take over large areas within a short span of time. *Lantana* was introduced as an ornamental to the island of Floreana in 1938 (Lawesson and Ortiz 1990), but during the last decade it has spread explosively in the remnants of the *Scalesia* zone vegetation on this island. Today, it covers some 20 km² and, in addition to displacing native plants and vegetation, its vigorous growth prevents the endangered Hawaiian petrel from easy access to its nesting area. Thus, *Lantana camara* may contribute to the global extinction of an endangered bird.

The spread of *Rubus* sp. has been even more rapid than that of *Lantana* and *Cinchona*. It was introduced to San Cristóbal in 1983 for its fruits, but already by 1989 it covered more than 2 km² in the highlands (SPNG 1990, pers. comm.). Two more introduced species, *Passiflora edulis* and *P. ligularis*, may turn out to be very troublesome in a few years (Lawesson and Ortiz 1990). Species of *Passiflora* are recorded as aggressive invaders in other parts of the world, e.g. on Hawai'i, and the recent spread of the two species on Santa Cruz island in the Galápagos is alarming.

Some land-use practices present a threat to the plants and vegetation types of the humid highlands on the southern slopes of the larger islands (Hamann 1984; Adsersen 1989). These humid areas are relatively small and are the only land appropriate for agricultural use in the islands; consequently, they were to a large extent taken over for agriculture early in colonization and were, therefore, not included in the National Park at its creation in 1959. However, the remaining areas of humid vegetation types and habitats within the National Park are under increasing threat because introduced animals and plants are able to spread into the National Park from the colonized zones, and because the growing human population is exerting increasing pressure for opening these parts of the park to agriculture.

Oceanic island ecosystems are vulnerable to biological invasions caused by human activities. In the Galápagos, giant tortoises and land iguanas are the largest indigenous herbivores, so the introduction and spread of herbivorous mammals completely altered the ecosystems and placed tremendous pressure on native plant species. At the same time, many of the introduced plant species evolved under high grazing and browsing pressure from herbivorous mammals and are, therefore, well-adapted to such pressure. Consequently, the combined effect of introducing into the Galápagos both herbivorous mammals and non-indigenous plants adapted to grazing are disastrous for the native plants. Furthermore, not only are endemic and native species and plant communities threatened with extinction, but the combined effects of land-use practices and invasive species may alter the biogeochemical cycles, change the fire regimen, prevent recruitment of native plants, and further the spread of introduced species.

The danger of introduced species causing genetic contamination of native species through hybridization is also present, e.g. when *Lantana camara* spreads into areas occupied by the endemic *L. peduncularis*.

Sometimes it is possible to predict which plants will be invasive, while others suddenly become invasive some years after their introduction. For example, *Cedrela odorata* gave no cause for concern for 25–30 years; but during the last 5 years an unexpected and sudden spread of the species into native vegetation has taken place (Lawesson and Ortiz 1990).

TABLE 86. DISTRIBUTION OF INTRODUCED MAMMALS IN THE GALÁPAGOS

Islands and areas

	1	2	3	4	5	6	7	8	9	10	11	12	13	14	15	16	17
Goats	*	*	*	*	*	*			*			×	×	×	×	×	
Pigs	*	*	*	*	*				*								
Donkeys	*	*	*	*	*	*			*								
Cattle	×	×	×	*	*												
Horses				*													
Sheep				*													
Cats	*	*	*	*	*	*	*	*									
Dogs	*	*	*	*	*												
Black rats	*	*	*	*	*	*	*	*	*	*	*						
Brown rats	*	*															
House mice	*	*	*	*	*	?	?	?									

KEY:

* = present; ? = maybe present; × = exterminated by the GNPS.

Islands and areas:
1 = Santa Cruz; 2 = San Cristóbal; 3 = Floreana; 4 = Isabela (Volcán Sierra Negra); 5 = Isabela (Volcán Cerro Azul); 6 = Isabela (Volcán Alcedo); 7 = Isabela (Volcán Darwin); 8 = Isabela (Volcán Wolf); 9 = San Salvador; 10 = Pinzón; 11 = Pinta; 12 = Marchena; 13 = Española; 14 = Santa Fé; 15 = Rabida; 16 = Genovesa; 17 = Fernandina.

TABLE 87. MAIN INVASIVE ALIEN PLANTS IN THE GALÁPAGOS

Species	Island
Agavaceae	
Furcraea cubensis	Santa Cruz; San Cristóbal; Floreana; Isabela (Volcán Sierra Negra)
Boraginaceae	
Cordia alliodora	Santa Cruz
Crassulaceae	
Kalanchoe pinnata	Santa Cruz; San Cristóbal; Floreana; Isabela (Volcán Sierra Negra)
Lauraceae	
Persea americana	Santa Cruz; San Cristóbal; Floreana; Isabela (Volcán Sierra Negra); San Salvador
Meliaceae	
Cedrela odorata	Santa Cruz; San Cristóbal; Floreana
Myrtaceae	
Eugenia jambos	Santa Cruz; San Cristóbal; Floreana; Isabela (Volcán Sierra Negra)
Psidium guajava	Santa Cruz; San Cristóbal; Floreana; Isabela (Volcán Sierra Negra, Volcán Cerro Azul)
Passifloraceae	
Passiflora edulis	Santa Cruz; Floreana
Passiflora ligularis	Santa Cruz
Passiflora quadrangularis	Santa Cruz; San Cristóbal; Floreana; Isabela (Volcán Sierra Negra)
Poaceae	
Axonopus compressus	San Cristóbal; Floreana; Isabela (Volcán Sierra Negra, Volcán Cerro Azul)
Digitaria decumbens	Santa Cruz; Isabela (Volcán Sierra Negra)
Pennisetum purpureum	Santa Cruz; San Cristóbal; Floreana; Isabela (Volcán Sierra Negra)
Rosaceae	
Rubus sp.	Santa Cruz; San Cristóbal
Rubiaceae	
Cinchona succirubra	Santa Cruz
Rutaceae	
Citrus limetta	Santa Cruz; San Cristóbal; Floreana
Solanaceae	
Solanum sp.	Santa Cruz
Verbenaceae	
Lantana camara	Santa Cruz; San Cristóbal; Floreana

Sources: Hamann (1984); Lawesson, Adsersen and Bentley (1987); Macdonald *et al.* (1988); Schofield (1989); Lawesson and Ortiz (1990); and from personal observations.

Conservation

The Galápagos National Park (IUCN Management Category: II), notified in 1959, covers 7278 km² (96.7% of the land area of the archipelago). In addition, the archipelago has been designated both a World Heritage Site (IUCN Management Category: X) (notified in 1978) and a Biosphere Reserve (IUCN Management Category: IX) (notified in 1984).

The management of the park aims to preserve the various unique island ecosystems and other features of scenic, scientific and/or cultural interest. The Master Plan for the Galápagos National Park (Anon. 1974) divided the archipelago into zones according to the intended land-use: Primitive-Scientific, Primitive, Extensive Use, Intensive Use, Special Use, and Colonized Zones, respectively.

The Primitive-Scientific Zone includes those areas that are essentially free of introduced species (e.g. Fernandina, and Volcán Darwin and Volcán Wolf on northern Isabela) and which require the highest order of protection to ensure their continued ecological integrity. Access is restricted and generally only given for scientific purposes.

The Primitive, Extensive Use, and Intensive Use Zones are managed according to their estimated carrying capacity with respect to visitors. The Primitive Zone is by far the largest in the park and includes, for example, Santiago and Volcán Alcedo on Isabela. Although somewhat ecologically altered by introduced species, these areas are managed so as to retain their primitive character. Access is regulated so that the zone serves as a buffer between the Primitive-Scientific Zone and more accessible zones.

The Extensive and Intensive Use Zones contain areas of outstanding features of visitor interest, and are predicted to be able to take a certain visitor load. The Special Use Zone includes substantially altered lands near settlements (e.g. on the south slope of Sierra Negra, Isabela, and on Santa Cruz and San Cristóbal). Although in need of careful management, this zone is not of the same quality as the rest of the park. Residents may collect firewood and timber, and extract wood on a limited basis, and collect introduced fruits from the Special Use Zone.

Conservation programmes undertaken by the Charles Darwin Research Station (CDRS) and the GNPS during the last 30 years have successfully ensured the survival of many unique and endemic animal species, such as the giant tortoises and land iguanas. Furthermore, the zoning system ensures that large parts of the archipelago are protected and remain relatively pristine (Anon. 1974).

Introduced mammals present the most immediate threat to the Galápagos ecosystems, and eradication or control of introduced mammals is a major priority for the GNPS and the CDRS. The goat eradication programme has been of great importance for the survival of plants and vegetation types in the archipelago. The complete elimination of feral goats has been achieved on a number of small and medium-sized islands, which has resulted in notable or even spectacular recovery of vegetation on such islands as Santa Fé and Pinta (Hamann 1979b, 1985; Whelan and Hamann 1989). However, on the large island of Santiago the destruction caused by goats and pigs is so profound that it is very doubtful whether the vegetation will ever be able to recover to its original state, even if the feral mammals can be completely eliminated. Very small remnants of the various native vegetation types on Santiago have been fenced to keep out feral mammals, and such fenced plots are at present serving as small, living seed banks. At the same time, they clearly demonstrate the devastating effect that goats and pigs have had on the native vegetation (Calvopina and Vries 1975; Vries and Calvopina 1977).

During recent years, the GNPS and the CDRS have started campaigns against some of the invasive plants, e.g. *Cinchona succirubra* and *Psidium guajava*. Some 10 km² of *Cinchona*-infested highland on Santa Cruz have been weeded annually by the GNPS. Several trials have been conducted on eradication of *Psidium guajava* with the help of arboricides and other means, but so far no efficient method has been devised (Utreras 1987).

In order to meet the demand for good quality wood and timber and to diminish the pressure on the native trees, the GNPS and the CDRS are carrying out a pilot project on the cultivation of indigenous and introduced, non-invasive hardwood trees. A small nursery has been established on Santa Cruz, and local farmers have provided land for more extensive plantation trials. A number of species are being investigated with respect to germination, growth and survival under Galápagos conditions. Introduced *Tectona grandis* seems to be the most promising species so far. Indigenous *Hippomane mancinella* and *Piscidia carthagenensis* may be possible candidates for future plantations on the islands.

A programme to rehabilitate small watersheds on San Cristóbal has been initiated by local authorities and the CDRS. It includes reforestation aimed at restoring ecological conditions around creeks in order to guarantee adequate supplies of fresh water (Lawesson and Estupinan 1987). The endemics *Scalesia pedunculata* and *Miconia robinsoniana*, and the introduced (but presumably non-invasive) *Juglans neotropica* are being investigated for their potential as reforestation subjects.

In 1987, a major plant conservation initiative was undertaken when the Charles Darwin Foundation (CDF), the CDRS and the GNPS organized an international workshop on botanical research and management in the Galápagos. Based on the recommendations of the workshop (Lawesson, Hamann and Black 1990), the CDF/CDRS formulated a comprehensive plant conservation programme for the Galápagos Islands consisting of an initial 3-year phase to halt the present negative trends, and a long-term phase focusing on changing the current agricultural practices into more rational agroforestry schemes.

The main short-term objectives and expected results are:

1. to protect threatened native plants and vegetation types by fencing against feral mammals, and thereby preserving selected areas of native ecosystems as living seed-banks;

2. to identify the most aggressive alien plants and their distribution in the National Park and cultivated farmland;

3. to develop safe, effective methods of control and eradication of introduced plants and to provide advice and help to farmers to control pest plants inside agricultural areas; and

4. to assess the natural timber resources and develop and promote alternative native and non-native timber sources, thereby providing sustainable sources of timber and wood and reducing pressure on National Park resources.

An important element of the long-term plant conservation efforts is an *ex situ* programme for threatened plants, to complement the ongoing and planned *in situ* activities in the archipelago. Target species are to be conserved in the seed- and genebanks of the Botanic Garden, University of Copenhagen. Micropropagation techniques will be employed to increase stocks of plants available for reintroduction in the future.

References

Adsersen, H. (1980). Revision of the Galápagos endemic genus *Lecocarpus* (Asteraceae). *Botanisk Tidsskrift* 75: 63–76.

Adsersen, H. (1989). The rare plants of the Galápagos Islands and their conservation. *Biological Conservation* 47: 49–77.

Adsersen, H. (1990). Intra-archipelago distribution patterns of vascular plants in Galápagos. In Lawesson, J.E., Hamann, O., Rogers, G., Reck, G. and Ochoa, H. (eds), *Botanical research and management in Galápagos*. Missouri Botanical Garden, St Louis, Missouri. Pp. 67–78.

Anon. (1974). *Plan Maestro Parque Nacional Galápagos*. PNUD/FAO/ECU/71/022. Santiago, Chile. Pp. 1–91.

Anon. (1980). *Genetic resources of tree species in arid and semi-arid areas. A survey for the improvement of rural living in Latin America, Africa, India and Southwest Asia*. FAO, Rome.

Atkinson, I.A.E. (1990). Mapping and classifying vegetation in the Galápagos Islands, some considerations. In Lawesson, J.E., Hamann, O., Rogers, G., Reck, G. and Ochoa, H. (eds), *Botanical research and management in Galápagos*. Missouri Botanical Garden, St Louis, Missouri. Pp. 101–115.

Bowman, R.I. (1961). *Morphological differentiation and adaptation in the Galápagos finches*. Palais des Académies, Brusells.

Brockie, R.E., Loope, L.L., Usher, M.B. and Hamann, O. (1988). Biological invasions of island nature reserves. *Biological Conservation* 44: 9–36.

Calvopina, L.H. and Vries, T. de (1975). Estructura de la población de cabras salvajes (*Capras hircus* L.) y los danos causados en la vegetación de la isla San Salvador, Galápagos. *Revista Univ. Católica, Quito*, Ano 3(8): 219–214.

Eliasson, U. (1984). Native climax forests. In Perry, R. (ed.), *Key environments. Galápagos*. Pergamon Press, Oxford. Pp. 101–114.

Geist, D.J., McBirney, A.R. and Duncan, R.A. (1985). Geology of Santa Fé Island: the oldest Galápagos volcano. *Journal of Volcanology and Geothermal Research* 26: 203–212.

Hamann, O. (1979a). On climatic conditions, vegetation types, and leaf size in the Galápagos Islands. *Biotropica* 11(2): 101–122.

Hamann, O. (1979b). Regeneration of vegetation on Santa Fé and Pinta islands, Galápagos, after the eradication of goats. *Biological Conservation* 15: 215–236.

Hamann, O. (1981). Plant communities of the Galápagos Islands. *Dansk Botanisk Arkiv* 34(2): 1–163.

Hamann, O. (1984). Changes and threats to the vegetation. In Perry, R. (ed.), *Key environments. Galápagos.* Pergamon Press, Oxford. Pp. 115–131.

Hamann, O. (1985). The El Niño influence on the Galápagos vegetation. In Robinson, G. and Pino, E.M. del (eds), *El Niño en las Islas Galápagos. El evento de 1982–1983.* Charles Darwin Foundation, Quito. Pp. 299–330.

Hamann, O. (1991). Indigenous and alien plants in the Galápagos Islands: problems of conservation and development. In Heywood, V.H. and Wyse Jackson, P.S. (eds), *Tropical botanic gardens: their role in conservation and development.* Academic Press, London. Pp. 169–192.

Hamann, O. and Wium-Andersen, S. (1986). *Scalesia gordilloi sp. nov.* (Asteraceae) from the Galápagos Islands, Ecuador. *Nordic Journal of Botany* 6(1): 35–38.

Hoeck, H.N. (1984). Introduced fauna. In Perry, R. (ed.), *Key environments. Galápagos.* Pergamon Press, Oxford. Pp. 233–245.

Huft, M.J. and Werff, H. van der (1985). Observations on *Chamaesyce* (Euphorbiaceae) in the Galápagos Islands. *Madrono* 32: 143–147.

Itow, S. (1990). Herbaceous and ericaceous communities in the highlands of Santa Cruz, the Galápagos Islands. In Lawesson, J.E., Hamann, O., Rogers, G., Reck, G. and Ochoa, H. (eds), *Botanical research and management in Galápagos.* Missouri Botanical Garden, St Louis, Missouri. Pp. 47–58.

IUCN Threatened Plants Committee Secretariat (1980). *How to use the IUCN Red Data Book categories.* IUCN Threatened Plants Committee Secretariat, Kew, U.K. 9 pp.

Lawesson, J.E. (1990a). Threatened plant species and the priority plant conservation sites in the Galápagos Islands. In Lawesson, J.E., Hamann, O., Rogers, G., Reck, G. and Ochoa, H. (eds), *Botanical research and management in Galápagos.* Missouri Botanical Garden, St Louis, Missouri. Pp. 153–167.

Lawesson, J.E. (1990b). Alien plants in the Galápagos, a summary. In Lawesson, J.E., Hamann, O., Rogers, G., Reck, G. and Ochoa, H. (eds), *Botanical research and management in Galápagos.* Missouri Botanical Garden, St Louis, Missouri. Pp. 15–20.

Lawesson, J.E., Adsersen, H. and Bentley, P. (1987). An updated and annotated check list of the vascular plants of the Galápagos Islands. *Reports from the Botanical Institute, University of Aarhus* 16: 1–74.

Lawesson, J.E. and Estupinan, I. (1987). The reforestation project on San Cristóbal Island. *Noticias de Galápagos* 45: 23.

Lawesson, J.E., Hamann, O. and Black, J. (1990). Combined recommendations from the Workshop: Botanical Research and Management in Galápagos. In Lawesson, J.E., Hamann, O., Rogers, G., Reck, G. and Ochoa, H. (eds), *Botanical research and management in Galápagos.* Missouri Botanical Garden, St Louis, Missouri. Pp. 291–295.

Lawesson, J.E. and Ortiz, L. (1990). Plantas introducidas en las Islas Galápagos. In Lawesson, J.E., Hamann, O., Rogers, G., Reck, G. and Ochoa, H. (eds), *Botanical research and management in Galápagos.* Missouri Botanical Garden, St Louis, Missouri. Pp. 201–210.

Loope, L.L., Hamann, O. and Stone, C.P. (1988). Comparative conservation biology of oceanic archipelagoes. Hawaii and the Galápagos. *BioScience* 38(4): 272–282.

Macdonald, I.A.W., Loope, L.L., Usher, M.B. and Hamann, O. (1989). Wildlife conservation and the invasion of nature reserves by introduced species: a global perspective. In Drake, J.A., Mooney, H.A., Castri, F. di, Groves, R.H., Kruger, F.J., Rejmánek, M. and Williamson, M. (eds), *Biological invasions. A global perspective.* Wiley, U.K. Pp. 215–255.

Macdonald, I.A.W., Ortiz, L., Lawesson, J.E. and Nowak, J.B. (1988). The invasion of highlands in Galápagos by the red quinine-tree *Cinchona succirubra. Environmental Conservation* 15(3): 215–220.

Nowak, J.B., Lawesson, J.E., Adsersen, H. and Vries, T. de (1990). A two-year study of post-fire vegetation dynamics on southern Isabela, Galápagos Islands, Ecuador. In Lawesson, J.E., Hamann, O., Rogers, G., Reck, G. and Ochoa, H. (eds), *Botanical research and management in Galápagos.* Missouri Botanical Garden, St Louis, Missouri. Pp. 123–136.

Oldfield, M.L. (1984). *The value of conserving genetic resources.* U.S. Department of the Interior, National Park Service, Washington, D.C.

Ortiz, L. and Lawesson, J.E. (1987). *Informe sobre los ensayos de control de Cinchona succirubra en la parte alta de Santa Cruz.* Charles Darwin Research Station, Isla Santa Cruz, Galápagos, Ecuador. Pp. 1–10.

Perry, R. (1984). The islands and their history. In Perry, R. (ed.), *Key environments. Galápagos.* Pergamon Press, Oxford. Pp. 1–14.

Porter, D.M. (1976). Geography and dispersal of Galápagos Islands vascular plants. *Nature* 264: 745–746.

Porter, D.M. (1979). Endemism and evolution in Galápagos Islands vascular plants. In Bramwell, D. (ed.), *Plants and islands.* Academic Press, London. Pp. 225–256.

Porter, D.M. (1983). Vascular plants of the Galápagos: origins and dispersal. In Bowman, R.I., Berson, M. and Leviton, A.I. (eds), *Patterns of evolution in Galápagos organisms.* AAAS, Pacific Division, San Francisco, California. Pp. 33–96.

Porter, D.M. (1984a). Endemism and evolution in terrestrial plants. In Perry, R. (ed.), *Key environments. Galápagos.* Pergamon Press, Oxford. Pp. 85–99.

Porter, D.M. (1984b). Relationships of the Galápagos flora. *Biological Journal of the Linnean Society* 21: 243–251.

Prescott-Allen, R. and Prescott-Allen, C. (1981). *In situ conservation of crop genetic resources. A report to the International Board for Plant Genetic Resources (IBPGR).* IUCN, Gland, Switzerland.

Prescott-Allen, R. and Prescott-Allen, C. (1983). *Genes from the wild.* Earthscan, London.

Ramirez, G. (1988). Preliminary study of matazarno (*Piscidia carthagenensis*) on Santa Cruz. In Charles Darwin Research Station *Annual Report 1984–1985.* Charles Darwin Research Station, Isla Santa Cruz, Galápagos, Ecuador. Pp. 32–34.

Reeder, W.G. and Riechert, S.E. (1975). Vegetation change along an altitudinal gradient, Santa Cruz Island, Galápagos. *Biotropica* 7(3): 162–175.

Schofield, E.K. (1989). Effects of introduced plants and animals on island vegetation: examples from the Galápagos archipelago. *Conservation Biology* 3(3): 227–238.

Seberg, O. (1984). Taxonomy and phylogeny of the genus *Acalypha* (Euphorbiaceae) in the Galápagos archipelago. *Nordic Journal of Botany* 4: 159–190.

Simkin, T. (1984). Geology of Galápagos Islands. In Perry R. (ed.), *Key environments. Galápagos.* Pergamon Press, Oxford. Pp. 15–41.

Utreras, M. (1987). Distribution of guayaba (*Psidium guajava*) and application of herbicides for its control on Santa Cruz Island. In Charles Darwin Research Station *Annual Report 1983.* Charles Darwin Research Station, Isla Santa Cruz, Galápagos, Ecuador. Pp. 16–17.

Vries, T. de and Calvopina, L.H. (1977). Papel de los chivos en los cambios de la vegetación de la Isla San Salvador, Galápagos. *Revista Univ. Católica, Quito,* Ano 5(16): 145–169.

Werff, H. van der (1978). *The vegetation of the Galápagos Islands.* Lakenman and Ochtman, Zierikzee.

Werff, H. van der (1979). Conservation and vegetation of the Galápagos Islands. In Bramwell, D. (ed.), *Plants and islands.* Academic Press, London. Pp. 391–404.

Werff, H. van der (1990). Ferns as indicators of vegetation types in the Galápagos archipelago. In Lawesson, J.E., Hamann, O., Rogers, G., Reck, G. and Ochoa, H. (eds), *Botanical research and management in Galápagos.* Missouri Botanical Garden, St Louis, Missouri. Pp. 79–92.

Whelan, P.M. and Hamann, O. (1989). Vegetation regrowth on Isla Pinta: a success story. *Noticias de Galápagos* 48: 11–13.

Wiggins, I.R. and Porter, D.M. (1971). *Flora of the Galápagos Islands.* Stanford University Press, California. 998 pp.

Acknowledgements

This Data Sheet was prepared by Professor Ole Hamann (Botanic Garden, University of Copenhagen).

JUAN FERNANDEZ ISLANDS
Chile

Location: South-eastern Pacific Ocean. Masatierra (Isla Robinson Crusoe) and Santa Clara are situated 600 km west of mainland Chile, at latitude 33°37'S and longitude 78°50'W; Masafuera (Isla Alejandro Selkirk) is 150 km further west at latitude 33°45'S and longitude 80°46'W.

Area: 100.2 km², comprising Masafuera (50 km²), Masatierra (48 km²) and Santa Clara (2.2 km²).

Altitude: 0–1319 m (Masafuera).

Vegetation: Tall dry forests, tree fern forests, ridge and cliff communities, "alpine zone" (on Masafuera only).

Flora: 210 native vascular plant species, of which 127 species (60.4%) are endemic. 1 endemic family (Lactoridaceae), 12 endemic genera.

Useful plants: Ornamental species with horticultural potential (e.g. *Wahlenbergia fernandeziana*), some of great scientific value (e.g. *Lactoris fernandeziana*).

Other values: Scientific value, tourist attraction, cultural interest.

Threats: Feral animals, especially goats and rabbits; introduced invasive weeds.

Conservation: National Park (IUCN Management Category: II) covers 91 km²; Biosphere Reserve covers 92.9 km².

Geography

The Juan Fernández (Robinson Crusoe) archipelago lies 580 km off the coast of continental Chile in the south-eastern part of the Pacific Ocean. There are three principal islands: Masatierra (Isla Robinson Crusoe) (33°37'S, 78°50'W), the closest to the mainland; Santa Clara, 1 km to the south-west of Masatierra; and Masafuera (Isla Alejandro Selkirk) (33°45'S, 80°46'W), 150 km further west.

All three islands are of volcanic origin. The rocks are lavas, basalts and volcanic ash (Hagerman 1924; Quensel 1952). Radiometric dating (Stuessy *et al.* 1984) reveals the following ages for each island: Santa Clara, 5.8 million years old; Masatierra, 3.8–4.2 million years old; and Masafuera, 1.0–2.4 million years old. Geomorphology reflects the relative age of the islands – Masatierra and Santa Clara are highly eroded, whereas Masafuera still retains a rounded shape and deep amphitheatre-headed valleys ("quebradas"). Such data are consistent with a "hot spot" hypothesis for the origin of the islands, which suggests that the islands were formed over a "hot spot" in the Earth's crust and then subsequently moved eastwards as the Nazca Plate has been subducted beneath the South American continent (Stuessy *et al.* 1984).

The total area of the islands is 100.2 km², based on recent measurements and aerial photographs (Ortiz 1982; and personal observations by T.F. Stuessy, H. Brecker and S. Benkowski), comprising Masafuera (50 km²), Masatierra (48 km²) and Santa Clara (2.2 km²). The highest point (1319 m) is on Masafuera. Masatierra reaches 916 m, while Santa Clara attains 350 m. The topography includes spectacular vertical cliffs and deeply cut ravines. It is in these less disturbed and more remote localities where the endemic flora has survived.

The climate is subtropical, with temperatures ranging throughout the year from 3–34°C, and with an annual mean of 15.4°C (Skottsberg 1952). Frost occasionally occurs on Masafuera, and local people claim that snow has been observed in the higher regions. Average annual rainfall is 1081 mm, varying yearly from 318 to 1698 mm (Skottsberg 1952). The rainy season lasts from March to December. As with many oceanic islands, the climate varies according to aspect and altitude. The lower, western side of Masatierra, and that of Santa Clara, are very dry, receiving rain only during tropical storms. In the higher regions of Masatierra and Masafuera (over 500 m), rainfall is often daily, but usually of short duration. Some areas are wet enough to support forests of tree ferns.

Vegetation

Each island has its own somewhat distinct types of vegetation. On Masatierra the zones are: grasslands (0–100 m altitude), introduced shrubs (100–300 m), tall forests (300–500 m), lower montane forests (500–700 m), tree fern forests (700–750 m) and high brushwood on exposed cliffs (500–850) m. Santa Clara has been denuded of shrubby vegetation and consists largely of grassy slopes throughout.

On Masafuera the zones are: grassland slopes (0–400 m) and deep ravines ("quebradas", 0–500 m), lower montane forests (400–600 m), upper montane forests (600–950 m), high brushwood (950–1100 m) and an "alpine zone" (1100–1300 m).

Grassy slopes, containing native and introduced species of grasses and other herbaceous weeds, cover much of the lower altitudes of both major islands, as well as nearly all of Santa Clara. Abundant here are *Danthonia collina, Stipa laevissima* and *Piptochaetium bicolor*. On Masafuera, *Anthoxanthum odoratum* is the most common grass species.

Acaena ovalifolia, with its barbed fruits, has become a widely dispersed weed on Masatierra, together with the two most noxious pests in the islands (especially on Masatierra), namely *Aristotelia chilensis* (maqui) and *Rubus ulmifolius* (zarzamora). These two cover many hectares and form impenetrable thickets almost to the total exclusion of other species.

Tall (lowland) forest is dominated by the largest trees in the archipelago: *Drimys confertifolia* (which occurs on both Masatierra and Masafuera), *Myrceugenia fernandeziana* (on Masatierra) and *M. schulzei* (on Masafuera). In moist areas there is a luxuriant ground cover of ferns.

Lower montane forest contains *Drimys confertifolia* and *Myrceugenia fernandeziana*, together with *Boehmeria excelsa*, *Coprosma oliveri*, *C. pyrifolia* and *Fagara mayu* (*F. externa* on Masafuera). Tree ferns begin to appear here too. A good example of this forest type occurs at Quebrada Villagra, close to a popular tourist spot, Mirador Selkirk (Selkirk's Lookout). The tree fern forest zone consists of dense stands of *Thyrsopteris elegans* and *Dicksonia berteriana*, with a dark, moist forest floor. On Masafuera, *D. berteriana* is replaced by the endemic *D. externa*, whose fronds form the canopy at about 4–5 m above the ground. Upper montane forest contains *Azara serrata* var. *fernandeziana*, *Blechnum cycadifolium*, *Cuminia eriantha*, *C. fernandezia*, *Lactoris fernandeziana* and *Rhaphithamnus venustus*.

Brushwood forest occurs on the highest slopes at about 850 m altitude, or on exposed escarpments and ridges (to 550 m). Species in this zone include *Berberis corymbosa*, *Colletia spartioides*, *Dendroseris marginata*, *Eryngium bupleuroides*, *Ochagavia elegans*, *Pernettya rigida* and *Robinsonia gayana*.

Flora

The Juan Fernández, together with the Islas Desventuradas to the north, are treated as a separate floristic region (the Fernándezian Region) by Takhtajan (1986).

The native flora of Juan Fernández includes 210 vascular plant species, of which 127 species (60.4%) are endemic. For angiosperms, the level of species endemism is 65%. There are 12 endemic genera (11% generic endemism) and one endemic family (Lactoridaceae). The endemic genera are: *Centaurodendron* (Compositae, 2 spp.), *Cuminia* (Labiatae, 2 spp.), *Dendroseris* (Compositae, 11 spp.), *Juania* (Palmae, 1 sp.), *Lactoris* (Lactoridaceae, 2 spp.), *Megalachne* (Gramineae, 2 spp.), *Ochagavia* (Bromeliaceae, 1 sp.), *Podophorus* (Gramineae, 2 spp.), *Robinsonia* (Compositae, 7 spp.), *Selkirkia* (Boraginaceae, 1 sp.), *Thyrsopteris* (Dicksoniaceae, 1 sp.) and *Yunquea* (Compositae, 1 sp.). These genera contain 33 species, or 26% of the endemic species of the islands. The most speciose family is Compositae. The occurrence of palms on Masatierra emphasizes the subtropical nature of the flora.

There are 152 introduced plant species. The total flora (native and introduced species) includes 51 species of ferns, 66 of monocots and 245 of dicots, representing 77 families and 213 genera (Stuessy *et al.*, in press). A new Flora is in preparation (Stuessy, Rodríguez and Marticorena, in prep.).

Useful plants

In the past, native species were cut to provide timber for sailing ships which refitted in Bahia Cumberland (Masatierra) to prepare for the continuation of their voyages westward into the Pacific (Stuessy, Rodríguez and Marticorena, in prep.). Many individuals of *Myrceugenia fernandeziana* and *Drimys confertifolia* were cut for lumber.

The endemic palm, *Juania australis*, was cut for its edible "palm cabbage" and for its ornamental stems. *Santalum fernandezianum* (sandalwood) was cut to extinction (by the beginning of this century) for its aromatic wood.

Some ornamental species have potential horticultural value (e.g. *Peperomia* spp. and *Wahlenbergia* spp.). *Lactoris fernandeziana* is of great scientific interest, representing an early stage of flowering plant evolution and perhaps providing a link between the monocots and dicots.

Among the introduced species, the branches of *Aristotelia chilensis* are used to make lobster traps, while the fruits of *Rubus ulmifolius* are used in jam-making. *Ugni molinae* also has an edible fruit.

Social and environmental values

The permanent population of approximately 500 people live in the only village, San Juan Bautista, surrounding Cumberland Bay on Masatierra. The necessity of maintaining good living conditions for the inhabitants, while at the same time protecting the natural heritage of the islands (which are a National Park; see Conservation section), has inevitably resulted in conflicting interests over the past 15 years (Hernandez and Monleon 1975). However, efforts are being made to explain the importance of conservation to the local population and to provide visitors with more natural history information.

The economy of Juan Fernández depends on lobster fishing and tourism. Lobster harvests are declining dramatically, and a total ban on lobster fishing for five years could be imminent. As a result, tourism could become even more important. At present, tourist infrastructure is poorly developed, and focussed on Selkirk's Lookout, the Caves of the Patriots and Selkirk's Cave (where the famous castaway supposedly lived from 1704 to 1709). There are no sandy beaches accessible to tourists; Masafuera can be reached only by boat, but there are no permanent settlements. Approximately 40 people travel to Masafuera for the eight months of the lobster season (October–May). The Chilean Government is hoping to develop tourism as a means of improving the economy of the islands. Careful planning is needed so as not to destroy the unique character of the islands and its rare plant life.

Threats

Many species of vascular plants in the Juan Fernández archipelago are in danger of extinction. More than 75% of the endemic species are regarded as rare or threatened, or occur only occasionally. The monotypic endemic family, represented by *Lactoris fernandeziana*, was once thought to be on the verge of extinction with only about six individuals remaining (Sanders, Stuessy and Marticorena 1981), but recent expeditions in 1990 and 1991 by personnel of the Universidad de Concepción and the Ohio State University have revealed at least 50 individuals in areas of difficult access. *Dendroseris* spp. are in much greater danger; most species in the genus are reduced to only a few individuals (e.g. *D. neriifolia*). A few species, such as *D. litoralis*, have been successfully cultivated and thrive in the village as well as on the mainland (e.g. at Viña del Mar).

Feral animals are the greatest threat to the flora, especially on Masafuera where there are several thousand goats (Mann 1975). Rabbits are the main threat on Masatierra, where several thousand occur in the drier zones (Saiz and Ojeda 1988). Coati mundi are less of a threat. Wild dogs and pigs have been eradicated from the islands (Wester 1991). Domesticated grazing animals used to roam the entire island of Masatierra, with devastating effects, but they are now restricted to Puerto Ingles, to the north of the village.

Invasive introduced plants are the main threat on Masatierra. *Rubus ulmifolius* and *Aristotelia chilensis* cover large areas (a clump may cover several hectares) in which no other species can compete. Both species regenerate from cut stumps, which makes control difficult. Studies have been made on fungal control of *Rubus ulmifolius* (Oehrens and Garrido 1986), but more research is needed. On upper ridges, the introduced *Ugni molinae* dominates some areas, replacing the endemic *U. selkirkii*.

Logging of native trees has now stopped, and all native plants are protected.

Conservation

The archipelago has been designated a National Park and Biosphere Reserve. Parque Nacional Archipiélago de Juan Fernández (IUCN Management Category: II) covers 91 km²; the Biosphere Reserve covers 92.9 km².

CONAF is working to save the endemic plants of Juan Fernández. With support from WWF and the Chilean Government, a plan for conservation development has been prepared (Anon. 1976). However, more funds are needed to implement its recommendations fully.

Priority should be given to conserving the richest areas, such as Quebrada Villagra, which receive most of the tourist pressure. Exclusion studies on Masafuera should be carried out to determine the impact of eliminating the goats. With nearly half of the flora consisting of introduced weeds, it is uncertain which direction the vegetation will take if all goats and rabbits are removed. Fences need to be constructed in certain areas to monitor the patterns of recovery in the absence of introduced herbivores.

There is a great need for basic ecological studies and more botanical research in the islands.

References

Anon. (1976). *Plan de manejo Parque Nacional Juan Fernández*. Docum. Tecn. de Trabajo No. 22 (CONAF).

Christensen, C. and Skottsberg, C. (1920). The pteridophyta of the Juan Fernández Islands. In Skottsberg, C. (ed.), *The natural history of the Juan Fernández and Easter Island, vol. 2, 1920-1953*. Almqvist and Wiksells, Uppsala. Pp. 763-792.

Hagerman, T.H. (1924). Beiträge zur Geologie der Juan Fernández-Inseln. In Skottsberg, C. (ed.), *The natural history of the Juan Fernández and Easter Island, vol. 2, 1920-1953*. Almqvist and Wiksells, Uppsala. Pp. 21-36.

Herman, T.H. (1924). Beiträge zur Geologie der Juan Fernández-Inseln. In Skottsberg, C. (ed.), *The natural history of the Juan Fernández and Easter Island, vol. 1, 1920-1956*. Almqvist and Wiksells, Uppsala. Pp. 21-36.

Hernandez, R. and Monleon, J. (1975). La comunidad de pescadores de Juan Fernández. In Orellana P., M. (ed.), *Las Islas de Juan Fernández: historia, arqueología y antropología de la Isla Robinson Crusoe*. Univ. de Chile, Santiago.

Hoffmann, A.J. and Marticorena, C. (1987). La vegetación de las islas oceánicas Chilensas. In Castilla, J.C. (ed.), *Islas oceánicas Chilenas: conocimiento científico y necesidades de investigaciones*. Univ. Católica de Chile, Santiago. Pp. 127-165.

Mann, W.G.W. (1975). Observaciones sobre el estado actual de algunos representantes de fauna y flora en el Parque Nacional Juan Fernández. *Bol. Mus. Nac. Hist. Nat. (Chile)* 34: 207-216.

Muñoz, P., C. (1974). *El Archipiélago de Juan Fernández y la conservación de sus recursos naturales renovables*. Ser. Educativa No. 9, Mus. Hist. Nat., Santiago.

Oehrens, E. and Garrido, N. (1986). Posibilidad del control biológico de la zarzamora en el Archipiélago de Juan Fernández. *Bol. Soc. Biol. Concepción, Chile* 57: 205-206.

Ortiz, R., A. (1982). *Estudios recursos físicos Archipiélago Juan Fernández*. Instit. Nac. Investigac. Recursos Nat., Santiago.

Quensel, P. (1952). Additional comments on the geology of the Juan Fernández Islands. In Skottsberg, C., (ed.), *The natural history of the Juan Fernández and Easter Island, vol. 1, 1920-1956*. Almqvist and Wiksells, Uppsala. Pp. 37-87.

Saiz, F. and Ojeda, P. (1988). *Oryctolagus cuniculus* L. en Juan Fernández. Problema y control. *An. Mus. Hist. Nat. Valparaiso* 19: 91-98.

Sanders, R.W., Stuessy, T.F. and Marticorena, C. (1981). Recent changes in the flora of the Juan Fernández Islands, Chile. *Taxon* 31: 284-289.

Skottsberg, C. (1922). The phanerograms of the Juan Fernández Islands. In Skottsberg, C. (ed.), *The natural history of the Juan Fernández and Easter Island, vol. 2, 1920-1953*. Almqvist and Wiksells, Uppsala. Pp. 95-240.

Skottsberg, C. (1951). A supplement to the pteridophytes and phanerogams of the Juan Fernández Islands. In Skottsberg, C. (ed.), *The natural history of the Juan Fernández and Easter Island, vol. 2, 1920-1953*. Almqvist and Wiksells, Uppsala. Pp. 763-792.

Skottsberg, C. (1952). The vegetation of the Juan Fernández Islands. In Skottsberg, C. (ed.), *The natural history of Juan Fernández and Easter Island, vol., 2, 1920–1953.* Almqvist and Wiksells, Uppsala. Pp. 793–960.

Stuessy, T.F., Foland, K.A., Sutter, J.F., Sanders, R.W. and Silva, O., M. (1984). Botanical and geological significance of potassium-argon dates from the Juan Fernández Islands. *Science* 225: 49–51.

Stuessy, T.F., Marticorena, C., Rodriguez, R., Crawford, D.J. and Silva, O., M. (in press). Endemism in the vascular flora of the Juan Fernández Islands. Aliso.

Stuessy, T.F., Rodríguez, R. and Marticorena, C. (in prep.). Phytogeography and evolution of the vascular flora of the Robinson Crusoe Islands.

Takhtajan, A. (1986). *Floristic regions of the world.* University of California Press, Berkeley. 522 pp.

Wester, L. (1991). Invasions and extinctions on Masatierra (Juan Fernández Islands): a review of early historical evidence. *J. Historical Geogr.* 17: 18–34.

Woodward, R.L. (1969). *Robinson Crusoe's Island.* Univ. North Carolina, Chapel Hill.

Acknowledgements

This Data Sheet was prepared by Professor Tod F. Stuessy (The Ohio State University, Columbus, Ohio, U.S.A.).

APPENDIX 1
DEFINITIONS OF SOME TERMS AND CATEGORIES

1. IUCN Conservation (Red Data Book) Categories

Conservation categories are given in the text for some threatened species where this information was readily available. The IUCN categories are given a capital letter to distinguish them from general usage of the terms.

A. Threatened Categories

Extinct (Ex)
Taxa which are no longer known to exist in the wild after repeated searches of their type localities and other known or likely places.

Endangered (E)
Taxa in danger of extinction and whose survival is unlikely if the causal factors continue operating.

Included are taxa whose numbers have been reduced to a critical level or whose habitats have been so drastically reduced that they are deemed to be in immediate danger of extinction.

Vulnerable (V)
Taxa believed likely to move into the Endangered category in the near future if the causal factors continue operating.

Included are taxa of which most or all the populations are *decreasing* because of over-exploitation, extensive habitat or other environmental disturbance; taxa with populations that have been seriously *depleted* and whose ultimate security is not yet assured; and taxa with populations that are still abundant but are *under threat* from serious adverse factors throughout their range.

Rare (R)
Taxa with small world populations that are not at present Endangered or Vulnerable, but are at risk.

These taxa are usually localized within restricted geographical areas or habitats or are thinly scattered over a more extensive range.

Indeterminate (I)
Taxa *known* to be Extinct, Endangered, Vulnerable, or Rare but there is not enough information to say which of the four categories is appropriate.

B. Unknown Categories

Status Unknown (?)
No information is available with which to assign a conservation category. [Note that this category was not used in CPD, but is included here for completeness.]

Insufficiently Known (K)
Taxa that are suspected but not definitely known to belong to any of the above categories, following assessment, because of lack of information.

C. Not Threatened Category

Safe (nt)
Neither rare nor threatened.

2. Categories and Management Objectives of Protected Areas

IUCN Management Categories for protected areas are given in the text where this information was readily available. In some cases, nationally designated areas (such as some National Parks) do not meet the criteria required to be assigned an IUCN Management Category. However, the omission of an IUCN category in the CPD text does not imply that the area concerned has not been assigned a management category.

Category I: Scientific Reserve/Strict Nature Reserve

To protect nature and maintain natural processes in an undisturbed state in order to have ecologically representative examples of the natural environment available for scientific study, environmental monitoring, education, and for the maintenance of genetic resources in a dynamic and evolutionary state.

Category II: National Park

To protect natural and scenic areas of national or international significance for scientific, educational and recreational use.

Category III: Natural Monument/ Natural Landmark

To protect and preserve nationally significant natural features because of their special interest or unique characteristics.

Category IV: Managed Nature Reserve/Wildlife Sanctuary

To assure the natural conditions necessary to protect nationally significant species, groups of species, biotic communities, or physical features of the environment where these require specific human manipulation for their perpetuation.

Category V: Protected Landscape or Seascape

To maintain nationally significant natural landscapes which are characteristic of the harmonious interaction of man and land while providing opportunities for public enjoyment through recreation and tourism within normal life style and economic activity of these areas.

Category VI: Resource Reserve

To protect resources of the area for future use and prevent or contain development activities that could affect the resource pending the establishment of objectives which are based upon appropriate knowledge and planning.

Category VII: Natural Biotic Area/ Anthropological Reserve

To allow the way of life of societies living in harmony with the environment to continue undisturbed by modern technology.

Category VIII: Multiple-Use Management Area/Managed Resource Area

To provide for the sustained production of water, timber, wildlife, pasture, and outdoor recreation, with the conservation of nature primarily oriented to the support of economic activities (although specific zones may also be designed within these areas to achieve specific conservation objectives).

Category IX: Biosphere Reserve

These are part of an international scientific programme, the UNESCO Man and the Biosphere (MAB) Programme, which is aimed at developing a reserve network representative of the world's ecosystems to fulfil a range of objectives, including research, monitoring, training and demonstration, as well as conservation roles. In most cases the human component is vital to the functioning of the Biosphere Reserve.

Category X: World Heritage Site

The *Convention Concerning the Protection of the World Cultural and Natural Heritage* (which was adopted in Paris in 1972 and came into force in December 1975) provides for the designation of areas of "outstanding universal value" as World Heritage Sites, with the principal aim of fostering international cooperation in safeguarding these important sites. Sites, which must be nominated by the signatory nation responsible, are evaluated for their world heritage quality before being declared by the World Heritage Committee. Article 2 of the Convention considers as natural heritage: natural features consisting of physical and biological formations or groups of such formations, which are of outstanding universal value from the aesthetic or scientific point of view; geological or physiographical formations and precisely delineated areas which constitute habitat of threatened species of animals or plants of outstanding universal value; and natural sites or precisely delineated areas of outstanding universal value from the point of view of science, conservation or natural beauty. Criteria for inclusion in the list are published by UNESCO.

The definitions above are abridged from:

IUCN (1990). *1990 United Nations list of national parks and protected areas.* IUCN, Gland, Switzerland and Cambridge, U.K. 284 pp.

McNeely, J.A. and Miller, K.R. (eds) (1984). *National parks, conservation, and development. The role of protected areas in sustaining society.* Smithsonian Institution Press, Washington, D.C. Pp. 47–53.

3. Endemic Bird Areas (EBAs)

Analysis of the patterns of bird distribution by BirdLife International shows that species of birds with restricted ranges tend to occur together in places which are often islands or isolated patches of a particular habitat, especially montane and other tropical forests. Boundaries of these natural groupings have been identified and the areas thus defined have been called Endemic Bird Areas (EBAs). They number 221 and embrace 2484 bird species, which is the vast majority (95%) of all restricted-range birds (which are those species with known breeding ranges below 50,000 km^2). The presence of restricted-range bird species in CPD sites is noted in the Data Sheets.

For more information and a full list of EBAs, the reader is referred to the following:

ICBP (1992). *Putting biodiversity on the map: priority areas for global conservation.* International Council for Bird Preservation, Cambridge, U.K. 90 pp.

Stattersfield, A.J., Crosby, M.J., Long, A.J. and Wege, D.C. (in prep.). *Global directory of Endemic Bird Areas.* BirdLife International, Cambridge, U.K.

APPENDIX 2
LIST OF ACRONYMS AND ABBREVIATIONS

ACT – Australian Capital Territory

AETFAT – Association pour l'Etude Taxonomique de la Flore d'Afrique Tropicale

ANCON – Asociación Nacional para la Conservación de la Naturaleza (Panama)

ASBOZA – Association des Botanistes du Zaïre

BIOTROP – Southeast Asian Regional Centre for Tropical Biology

BP – Before present (years)

CDF – Charles Darwin Foundation

CECON – Centro de Estudios Conservacionistas, Universidad de San Carlos (Guatemala)

CENARGEN – Centro Nacional de Pesquisas de Recursos Genéticos e Biotecnologia (Brazil)

CEPEC – Centro de Pesquisas do Cacau (Brazil)

CIPRA – International Commission for the Protection of the Alps

CITES – Convention on International Trade in Endangered Species of Wild Fauna and Flora

CMC – IUCN Conservation Monitoring Centre (now WCMC)

CNPPA – Commission on National Parks and Protected Areas (IUCN)

COA – Corporación Colombiana para la Amazonia (Colombia)

CODEFF – Comité Nacional Pro Defensa de la Fauna y Flora (Chile)

CONAF – Corporación Nacional Forestal (Chile)

CPD – Centres of Plant Diversity

CSIRO – Commonwealth Scientific Industrial Research Organisation, Australia

CTFT – Centre Technique Forestier Tropical (Paris)

CUMAT – Centro de Investigaciones de la Capacidad de Uso Mayor de la Tierra (Bolivia)

DANIDA – Ministry of Foreign Affairs, Department of International Development

dbh – Diameter at breast height

DoT – Department of Transmigration (Indonesia)

EBA – Endemic Bird Area

ECAN – Environmentally Critical Areas Network (Philippines)

ECE – Economic Commission for Europe (UN)

ECOCIENCIA – Fundación Ecuatoriana de Estudios Ecológicos (Ecuador)

EEC – European Economic Community

EIA – Environmental impact statement

ELC – Environment Liaison Centre

EMBRAPA – Empresa Brasileira de Pesquisa Agropecuária

ESCAP – Economic and Social Commission for Asia and the Pacific (UN)

FAO – Food and Agriculture Organization of the United Nations

FELDA – Federal Land Development Authority (Malaysia)

FINNIDA – Finnish International Development Agency

FRIM – Forest Research Institute, Malaysia

GEMS – Global Environment Monitoring System (UNEP)

GNPS – Galápagos National Park Service

GRID – Global Resources Information Database (UNEP/GEMS)

GTZ – Deutsche Gesellschaft für Technische Zusammenarbeit

HIID – Harvard Institute for International Development

IBGE – Instituto Brasileiro de Geografia Estatistica (Brazil)

IBP – International Biological Programme

IBPGR – International Board for Plant Genetic Resources (now IPGRI)

ICBP – International Council for Bird Preservation (now BirdLife International)

IIED – International Institute for Environment and Development

INBio – Instituto Nacional de Biodiversidad de Costa Rica

INDERENA – Instituto Nacional de los Recursos Naturales Renovables y del Ambiente (Colombia)

INPA – Instituto Nacional de Pesquisas da Amazônica (Brazil)

IPGRI – International Plant Genetic Resources Institute

IPT – Asian Wetland Bureau

ITTA – International Tropical Timber Agreement

ITTO – International Tropical Timber Organisation

IUCN – International Union for Conservation of Nature and Natural Resources – The World Conservation Union

IUFRO – International Union of Forestry Research Organisations

MAB – Man and the Biosphere Programme (UNESCO)

MOPAWI – Mosquitia Pawisa (Honduras)

NCS – National Conservation Strategy

NGO – Non-governmental organization

ODA – Overseas Development Administration (UK)

ORSTOM – Institut Français de Recherche Scientifique pour le Developpement en Cooperation

POSSCEF – Project on Study Survey and Conservation of Endangered Species of Flora (India)

Ramsar Convention – Convention on Wetlands of International Importance Especially as Waterfowl Habitat

RePPProt – Regional Physical Planning Programme for Transmigration (Indonesia)

SEDUE – Subsecretaría de Ecología, Dirección de Flora y Fauna Silvestres (Mexico)

SIDA – Swedish International Development Authority

SPREP – South Pacific Regional Environment Programme

SSC – Species Survival Commission (IUCN)

TFAP – Tropical Forestry Action Plan

TPU – Threatened Plants Unit (formerly of IUCN, now of WCMC)

UN – United Nations

UNCTAD – United Nations Conference on Trade and Development

UNDP – United National Development Programme

UNEP – United Nations Environment Programme

UNESCO – United Nations Educational, Scientific and Cultural Organisation

UNIDO – United Nations Industrial Development Organisation

UNSO – United Nations Sudano-Sahelian Office

US-AID – US Agency for International Development

USDA – United States Department of Agriculture

WCED – World Commission on Environment and Development

WCMC – World Conservation Monitoring Centre

WCS – World Conservation Strategy

WRI – World Resources Institute

WWF – World Wide Fund for Nature

INDEX

572